NEW ZEALAND CRICKET

2005 Cricket Almanack

58th Edition

Edited by
Francis Payne
&
Ian Smith

Hodder Moa

SKY SPORT

The Editors welcome contributions from readers for inclusion in the *2006 Almanack*

Please correspond directly with the editors:

Francis Payne,
97 Bond Crescent,
Forrest Hill,
AUCKLAND.
Phone/Fax: (09) 410-5259
E-mail: francisp@xtra.co.nz

Ian Smith,
91 Kamahi Street,
Stokes Valley,
WELLINGTON.
Phone: (04) 9766-477
E-mail: ianelizabeth@paradise.net.nz

Front cover: Daniel Vettori — Fotopress

Back cover: Hamish Marshall — Fotopress

ISBN 1-86971-028-2

A Hodder Moa Book

Published in 2005 by Hachette Livre NZ Ltd
4 Whetu Place, Mairangi Bay, Auckland 9, New Zealand
Printed by PrintLink, Wellington, New Zealand

CONTENTS

Office Bearers

2004/05

Patron
Her Excellency The Hon. Dame Silvia Cartwright P.C.N.Z.M., D.B.E.
Governor-General of New Zealand

President
J.R. Reid, O.B.E.

Vice-Presidents
The Presidents of Major Associations

Board
Sir John Anderson, K.B.E. *(chairman),* D.S. Currie Q.S.O, S.L. Boock,
A. Urlwin, A.R. Isaac, T.W. Jarvis, P.A. Sharp, D. Radford

Chief Executive
M.C. Snedden

Auditors
Ernst and Young, Chartered Accountants

Solicitor
L.M.C. Robinson, Saunders Robinson

Bankers
The National Bank of New Zealand

Life Members
M. Brito, C.F. Collins, O.B.E., W.A. Hadlee, C.B.E.,
J.H. Heslop C.B.E., J.L. Kerr, O.B.E., J. Lamason, T. Macdonald, Q.S.M.,
P. McKelvey, M.B.E., D.O. Neely, M.B.E.,
Hon. Justice B.J. Paterson, O.B.E. Q.C.,
K.L. Sandford, C.M.G.,Y. Taylor, Sir Allan Wright, K.B.E.

Honorary Cricket Members
J.C. Alabaster, F.J. Cameron, M.B.E., R.O. Collinge, B.E. Congdon, O.B.E.,
R.S. Cunis, A.E. Dick, G.T. Dowling, O.B.E., J.W. Guy, D.R. Hadlee,
B.F. Hastings, J.A. Hayes, H.J. Howarth, A.R. MacGibbon,
R.C. Motz, V. Pollard, G.O. Rabone, J.R. Reid, O.B.E.,
B.W. Sinclair, J.T. Sparling, E.W.T. Tindill, O.B.E.,
W.M. Wallace.

Honorary Members
I.A. Colquhoun *(deceased)*, H.H. Whiting.

National Selectors
Senior: J.G. Bracewell *(convenor),* Sir Richard Hadlee *(manager),*
B.J. McKechnie, R.A. Dykes.
Age Group: D.R. Hadlee *(convenor)*, B.D. Morrison.
Women: M.J.F. Shrimpton *(convenor),* J.E. Harris, D.A. Hockley.

Honorary Medical Advisors
Dr R.M. Edmond, Dr H. Fuard, Dr P. Borrie, Dr R. Campbell,
Mr G. Nuttridge, Dr M. Chitgopeker, Dr D. Thomson, Dr D.S. Velvin.

National Code of Conduct Commissioner
N.R.W. Davidson Q.C.

Statistician
F. Payne.

FROM THE EDITORS

The 58th edition of the *New Zealand Cricket Almanack* covers another eventful twelve months of cricket with everything from abandoned tours and dangerous pitches to test cricket in mid-April.

The year began with the ICC Champions Trophy, which was held in England in September, and was followed by New Zealand's first tour of Bangladesh. The Black Caps then went straight to Australia for two tests and the inaugural Chappell-Hadlee Trophy one-day series.

New Zealand hosted Sri Lanka and Australia as well as the FICA World XI while the White Ferns took part in the Rose Bowl series against Australia en route to defending their World Cup title in South Africa,

New Zealand are scheduled to tour Zimbabwe in August, return home and then go to South Africa, while Australia (Chappell-Hadlee Trophy), Sri Lanka (balance of one-dayers from their uncompleted tour), Zimbabwe and West Indies are all pencilled in for the summer at home although, just as we went to print, doubts arose over the two Zimbabwe series.

At Home

Sri Lanka's visit was thrown into turmoil as a result of the Boxing Day tsunami. After New Zealand had comfortably won the first one-day international of The National Bank Series the tour was called off, the ICC confirming Sri Lanka would suffer no financial penalty for returning home. The two test matches were rescheduled for April, the first time test matches had begun so late in New Zealand's summer.

A World XI was assembled to play three one-day games against New Zealand, who won the series 2-1. The series will be remembered for Stephen Fleming's 54-ball hundred at Christchurch and the debacle at Hamilton, where the wicket proved so difficult that Australia's scheduled one-day international at the ground was transferred to the Basin Reserve in Wellington.

The number-one ranked Australian side came in February and March, winning the one-day series 5-0 and the test series 2-0, with the other game affected by rain with the visitors well in control. New Zealand had a golden opportunity to win the first one-dayer but from there on it was mostly one-way traffic.

The Black Caps gained some recompense when they beat Sri Lanka 1-0 in the rescheduled test series, the win at the Basin Reserve being New Zealand's twelfth on that ground.

On Tour

The season started with the Champions Trophy in England where a record win over minnows USA was followed by a disappointing performance against Australia. A month later New Zealand made their first tour of Bangladesh, playing two tests and three one-day internationals.

The Black Caps won all the games, with Fleming getting his second test double century and James Franklin becoming only the second New Zealander to take a test hat-trick. Fleming was rested for the one-day series and Daniel Vettori captained New Zealand for the first time.

New Zealand then went to Australia for two tests and the new Chappell-Hadlee Trophy. New Zealand did well on the first three days of the first test but, as in the previous season, struggled on day four and eventually lost by an innings. Australia won the second test comfortably.

There was some comfort for the Black Caps when they won the first one-day game at the Telstra Dome in Melbourne but they lost the second at Sydney and the third game at Brisbane was abandoned without any play.

The White Ferns

The Rose Bowl series was played prior to the World Cup with Australia winning 3-0. New Zealand finished in third place in pool play in the World Cup, behind Australia and India (who they had beaten), and played India again in the semi-final.

It was unfortunate that New Zealand produced their worst performance of the tournament in this match, which marked the end for coach Mike Shrimpton, who confirmed he would be leaving New Zealand Cricket at the end of June, and for captain Maia Lewis, who announced her retirement from the game.

The Domestic Scene

Auckland won the State Championship after setting the pace throughout the season. In the final they convincingly beat the previous season's winners, Wellington. Northern Districts took the State Shield, also beating the defending champions, Central Districts, who had topped the round robin section. Both winning sides will be without their most experienced players in 2005/06 with Aaron Barnes and Matthew Hart having retired.

Michael Sharpe *(Canterbury)* and Glenn Turner *(Otago)* stepped down from their coaching roles with Turner later gaining a spot on the national selection panel. Canterbury retained their State League title, defeating Auckland by ten wickets in the final. State Shield matches and the State of Origin game again featured live on Sky Televison.

Injuries

The past season was notable for the amount of injuries suffered by international players. With Shane Bond already unavailable, Michael Papps was injured two days after being selected for the tour to Bangladesh and subsequently Chris Harris, Daryl Tuffey, Jacob Oram, Scott Styris, Ian Butler, Andre Adams and Daniel Vettori were all forced out with injuries for varying lengths of time.

The injury problem was not confined to the Black Caps with experienced White Fern Emily Drumm injured during the Women's World Cup and ruled out of most of the tournament.

Successful Rescheduling

After the Sri Lankan team returned home, New Zealand Cricket did extremely well to organise the World XI tour at short notice and the public responded most enthusiastically. Another plus which emerged from the rescheduling of the tour was the successful staging of test cricket in early to mid-April, definitely an option for future seasons.

The fading light at that time of the year can be countered by playing matches as far north as possible, another reason why Hamilton's unavailability was most disappointing.

NZC stood to lose around $3.5 million in projected income following the cancellation of the Sri Lankan tour, mostly from lost broadcast revenues. By rescheduling the test matches for April NZC was able to recoup a significant portion of the broadcasting revenues and sponsorship which were at risk.

With Sri Lanka coming back to complete the one-day series in 2005/06, NZC will have covered most of the financial position. The Australian tour helped return a profit of around $250,000 from ticket sales. Gate sales for the season were about $240,000 above budget. The gates for the FICA series allowed NZC to break even on costs of $1 million.

Obituaries

Some of New Zealand's oldest first-class cricketers passed away during the past twelve months including Norm Stokes, who was the oldest. Their obituaries appear in this edition.

This section is particularly difficult to keep up to date and we are most grateful for the assistance of Warwick Larkins, Warren Shirley, Brian Adams, John Heikell, Don Neely, Blair Furlong, Lindsay Knight, Evan Watkin, Pat Malcon and Adrian Hill.

This *Almanack* contains 22 obituaries, including New Zealand's first women's test captain, two test wicketkeepers, a player who became a first-class cricketer at the age of 64, another who was a graduate of Duntroon Military College, a champion sheep dog trialist, a New Zealand soccer representative, an Olympic hockey player, a player who took a double hat-trick in Zambia, two players who played in Ranfurly Shield winning teams, another who was wounded and taken prisoner in North Africa during the war and one who was an ordained Catholic priest.

Acknowledgments

We also wish to thank the associations, scorers and officials throughout the country who supplied information to us. In particular we would like to acknowledge the help of Catherine Campbell *(Women's Cricket)* and the rest of the staff at New Zealand Cricket and Chris McQuaid for his help with women's cricket.

Francis Payne & Ian Smith
June 2005

DIARY OF THE SEASON

September

1 Northern Districts reports a deficit of $280,000 for the year. Chairman Jeff Freeman says marketing and funding fell by $100,000, redundancies, retirement and recruitment added another $80,000 with $100,000 of depreciation on buildings. Life membership was given to Gerald Bailey and Alan Whimp.

3 Wellington turns a predicted deficit of $30,000 for the year into an operating surplus of $41,000. Chief executive Ervin McSweeney says a reduction in the first-class programme and savings in operational costs had helped create the surplus.

4 New Zealand Cricket posts a net deficit of $3.6 million for the year after grants to major associations and districts of $6.75m. NZC recorded a surplus of $3.135m for the period before the grants to the associations which are reliant on NZC for their financial survival. The forecast net surplus had been $4.5m but lower than expected match receipts and unbudgeted costs associated with the rescheduling of the tour to Pakistan impacted upon it despite increases in TV rights and sponsorship and investment income.

5 Central Districts achieves a $66,174 turnaround for the year to end with a surplus of $5942 after a deficit of $60,232 the previous year. Dermot Payton, former captain, selector, coach and president, was given life membership.

9 New Zealand manager Lindsay Crocker returns home from England because of ill health. New Zealand A manager Ross Dykes travels from South Africa to replace Crocker and he is replaced by Auckland manager Fred Thomas.

12 Arthur Ibbotson dies aged 93. Otago Patron and Life Member, he was New Zealand Cricket Council president from 1975 to 1977.

13 Harold Whitcombe, coach and administrator with the Cornwall club in Auckland, dies aged 82. He was regarded as an outstanding batting coach and analyst and among his pupils were Jeff and Martin Crowe.

22 New Zealand Cricket and Sky Television confirm a new five-year deal, giving the network exclusive rights for all televised cricket in New Zealand until the end of 2008/09.

24 Otago Cricket announce their move to University Oval will be marked with an official opening on 9 January when Otago plays Northern Districts in a State Shield match. Otago Cricket's offices will be housed at the ground and the Long Room at the ground will be at the heart of a new membership scheme.

Otago also reports an improved financial performance, reducing its net deficit from $106,858 to $35,825. The main reason for the continuing deficit was a drop in sponsorship from $214,824 to $69,023 this year.

30 Ross Dykes is confirmed as manager for the tour of Bangladesh while Lindsay Crocker continues his recovery from illness. Crocker eventually returns for the home series.

30 Stephen Fleming signs for Nottinghamshire for the 2005 season. Fleming will also captain the side.

October

1 Northern Districts name two captains for the season to replace Robbie Hart who had retired. James Marshall is appointed for the first part of the season with Daniel Vettori taking over on his return from international duties.

7 Mathew Sinclair is selected as the replacement for Michael Papps in the New Zealand test team to tour Bangladesh. Papps dislocated a shoulder in practice earlier in the week. Daniel Vettori is named captain of the one-day squad with Stephen Fleming returning home in an effort to rest an abdominal injury.

8 New Zealand Cricket announce that the New Zealand team will wear the beige one-day uniform of the 1980s for the opening match of Australia's tour. The world's first men's international Twenty20 match at Auckland's Eden Park is to be celebrated by creating a retro atmosphere for the game. 23,500 attend the match.

9 Chris Cairns marries Carin van den Berg in Blenheim. A number of past and present New Zealand players are amongst the 200 guests.

10 Chris Harris is appointed Canterbury captain for 2004/05, However, he is injured playing for New Zealand in Australia and misses Canterbury's entire campaign.

14 Matthew Walker parts company with Wellington, citing dissatisfaction with coach Vaughn Johnson. Neal Parlane takes his place on the list of contracted players.

15 Former New Zealand test cricket offspinner Grant Bradburn is named coach of Northern Districts A for the competition in Christchurch in January. He will continue as development manager for the Waikato Valley District Association while also managing his sports store at Hamilton's Westpac Park.

Craig Spearman signs a new four-year contract with Gloucestershire. Spearman will be available to play for England in 2005.

20 Scott Styris signs with Middlesex for the 2005 county season.

November

4 Canterbury selector and former coach Bob Carter is appointed as assistant to John Bracewell for the tour to Australia. Carter, who is general manager of the Canterbury United soccer team, also coached Wellington and Northamptonshire.

December

2 New Zealand Cricket announces that John Bracewell's initial two-year contract as national coach will continue to July 2007 to give him time to plan for the next World Cup. The contract had been extended earlier in the year but details had not previously been made public.

7 Former Northern Districts left-arm spinner Cliff Dickeson is named assistant coach of the New Zealand women's team for the Rose Bowl series against Australia and the World Cup in South Africa in March and April. Dickeson is the coach of Northern Districts in the State League competition.

10 Mark Richardson announces his retirement from all forms of the game. His last match will be the State Championship match between Auckland and Canterbury beginning on 13 December. Richardson played 38 tests, scoring 2776 runs at 44.77 and 9994 runs in 157 first-class games at 42.89.

29 Sri Lanka's tour is cut short following the tsunami disaster on Boxing Day. The tour was put on hold for a week but after the players made it known they wanted to return home and the ICC said there would not be any financial penalties if the two boards were in agreement, the decision to abandon the tour was made.

January

11 New Zealand Cricket announces that Sri Lanka will return to New Zealand and play two tests in April. The new dates for the four one-day internationals are still to be confirmed.

18 Andre Adams signs a one-year contract with Essex for the 2005 season.

Jacob Oram signs for Bacup in the Lancashire League but is unable to take up the position after a back injury rules him out of all cricket for the remainder of the season.

28 New Zealand Cricket decides to transfer the fourth one-day international against Australia from Hamilton following criticism of the pitch there during New Zealand's match against the FICA World XI. The match is moved to the Basin Reserve.

February

11 Sir Richard Hadlee is named as a selector for the ICC World XI to play Australia in October. He will be joined on the selection panel by Sunil Gavaskar, Michael Atherton, Jonty Rhodes, Aravinda de Silva and Clive Lloyd.

March

13 The New Zealand Cricket Players' Association announces the setting up of a player welfare and hardship fund. The aim of the fund is to provide assistance to cricketers who need support in times of difficulty. Fund distribution will remain confidential.

15 Scott Styris undergoes arthroscopic surgery on his left knee which he injured in February in a State Shield match. He subsequently misses the remainder of the season.

16 Daryl Tuffey is fined $1000 for off-field misconduct. Tuffey had earlier admitted that, during a brief involvement with a woman that included conduct of a sexual nature, he allowed himself to be video-taped, and did nothing to recover the recording, or prevent it from being shown.

19 Andrew Schwass announces his retirement from first-class cricket because of persistent ankle problems. He made his debut for Central Districts in 1998/99 and in 29 first-class games captured 109 wickets at 23.42. In 42 domestic one-day games he took 64 wickets at 23.48. He represented South Island in the State of Origin match in 2003/04.

25 Emily Drumm is ruled out of the remainder of the World Cup with a hamstring injury sustained during the match against Australia. She is replaced by Aimee Mason.

31 Daniel Vettori is named the National Bank New Zealand Player of the Year at New Zealand Cricket's awards night. Vettori also wins the Winsor Cup and Walter Hadlee Trophy for bowling while Hamish Marshall is awarded the Redpath Cup and Walter Hadlee Trophy for batting. Haidee Tiffen and Rebecca Steele win the Ruth Martin Cup and Phyl Blackler Cup, awarded for outstanding batting and bowling, while the State Medal and State Plate, for outstanding performances in domestic cricket, go to Craig Cumming and Nicola Browne. Merv Wallace is awarded the Sutcliffe Medal for outstanding services to cricket.

April

1 The 2007 World Cup groupings are announced. The 16 teams will be split into four groups of four for a round robin first stage. The top two teams will progress to the Super Eights stage, a round which has been expanded from what was the Super Sixes. New Zealand are in Group 3 in St Lucia with England, Kenya and an ICC Trophy qualifier.

7 Aaron Barnes confirms his retirement from first-class cricket after Auckland win the State Championship final. In 78 first-class games since 1993/94 Barnes scored 3006 runs at 27.08 and took 89 wickets at 31.87.

Brendon Bracewell's Cricket Academy in Masterton receives a grant of $10,000 from the Eastern and Central Community Trust. The Academy is based at Rathkeale College.

10 New Zealand women's captain Maia Lewis announces her retirement from all cricket. She played nine tests and 78 one-day internationals. Women's coach Mike Shrimpton also confirms he will step down from his position at the end of June.

19 Former New Zealand cricket captain John Wright steps down as coach of India and plans to return home to spend more time with his family. He had been away from New Zealand since 1997, spending four years coaching Kent before his stint in India.

May

3 New Zealand Cricket names nine players in the Academy intake for 2005. They are Todd Astle *(Canterbury)*, Hamish Bennett *(Canterbury)*, Carl Cachopa *(Auckland)*, Derek De Boorder *(Auckland)*, Jason Donnelly *(Auckland)*, Sean Eathorne *(Otago)*, Martin Guptill *(Auckland)*, Mathew Harvie *(Otago)*, Will Somerville *(Otago)*.

A Junior Academy squad is also selected to attend three camps during the off season. It is Marc Ellison *(Auckland)*, Ashley Newdick *(Wellington)*, Sam McLeod *(Northern Districts)*, Nick Fitzgerald *(Northern Districts)*, Charles Gallagher *(Wellington)*, Tim Southee *(Northern Districts)*, Dean Bartlett *(Auckland)*, Kurt Richards *(Central Districts)*, Doneel Hira *(Auckland)*, Colin Munro *(Auckland)*, Ronald Karaitiana *(Wellington)*, Shaun Fitzgibbon *(Otago)*.

4 Cricket Wellington elite player manager Christie van Dyk is appointed to monitor Pakistan coach Bob Woolmer during the team's tour of West Indies. Van Dyk was the recipient of a Prime Minister's scholarship designed to expose New Zealand coaches to best practice methods worldwide. He will present his findings to New Zealand Cricket, Sport and Recreation New Zealand (who funded the scholarship) and Cricket Wellington.

9 Vaughn Johnson is reappointed Wellington coach, agreeing to a new one-year term. He has coached Wellington since 1998/99.

10 New Zealand Cricket's high performance manager. John Reid, announces his resignation to take up a senior position with Sport and Recreation New Zealand. Reid joined New Zealand Cricket in 1996 as its operations manager and was caretaker national coach during the 1994/95 season.

Craig McMillan signs a short-term contract with Hampshire as cover for Simon Katich who will join the Australian team for the Ashes series. Nathan Astle accepts a similar contract with Durham as cover for Mike Hussey.

12 Billy Bowden is named on an unchanged elite panel of umpires for the next twelve months. and Jeff Crowe retains his place on the panel of match referees. Doug Cowie, Tony Hill and Evan Watkin (third umpire) remain on the international panel. Bowden is subsequently appointed to stand in three of the Ashes tests in England in 2005.

13 New Zealand Cricket names an Academy team to play in Cricket Australia's Emerging Players Tournament in early July. Two teams from the Australian Institute of Sport and an Indian Academy will play the Academy side in Twenty20 and one-day matches before each team plays a three-day match. The team is: Jacob Oram *(captain)*, Graham Aldridge, Todd Astle, Shane Bond, Te Ahu Davis, Derek De Boorder, Peter Fulton, Bruce Martin, Michael Papps, Jeetan Patel, Jesse Ryder, Hayden Shaw, Ross Taylor.

14 Brian McKechnie steps down as a national selector after five years in the position. He also spent five seasons as a Canterbury selector.

19 Ross Dykes also resigns as a national selector to take up the chief executive role with Otago Cricket. Dykes began as an Auckland selector in 1978/79 before moving to the national panel in 1991/92. He was also New Zealand team manager on several occasions.

31 New Zealand Cricket confirms it will bid with Australia to host the World Cup in 2011. NZC chief executive Martin Snedden says that a formal proposal is still a long way off but initial talks had been held between the boards.

June

3 Craig Cumming and James Marshall are awarded New Zealand Cricket contracts for the first time. From the previous year's list, Mathew Sinclair and Ian Butler are omitted while Mark Richardson, who retired in December, is replaced by James Franklin. The payment scale ranges from $125,000, for the number one ranked player, dropping in $5000 increments to $45,000 for those ranked 17-20. Rankings are not made public. Stephen Fleming also negotiates a captain's fee while match fees are $6000 per test and $2500 per one-day international. The full list is: Nathan Astle, Shane Bond, Chris Cairns, Craig Cumming, Stephen Fleming, James Franklin, Chris Harris, Brendon McCullum, Craig McMillan, Hamish Marshall, James Marshall, Chris Martin, Kyle Mills, Jacob Oram, Michael Papps, Scott Styris, Daryl Tuffey, Lou Vincent, Daniel Vettori, Paul Wiseman.

The ICC names Tony Hill as one of six umpires from the Emirates International Panel who will stand in the ICC Trophy in Ireland from 1 to 13 July.

4 Chris Martin announces that he is moving to Auckland before the 2005/06 season. Martin cites a change of lifestyle as the reason for the move.

6 Chris Cairns is made an Officer of the New Zealand Order of Merit in the Queen's Birthday Honours. Former New Zealand women's captain Pat McKelvey MBE is made Companion of the New Zealand Order of Merit for services to education and former New Zealand Cricket Council board member and New Zealand team manager Barry Paterson OBE, QC receives the same award for services to the judiciary.

7 Matthew Hart announces his retirement from first-class cricket. Since making his debut as an 18-year-old in 1990/91 Hart played 135 first-class matches, scoring 4418 runs at 25.68 and taking 212 wickets at 35.01. He played 14 tests, taking 5-77 in New Zealand's win at Johannesburg in 1994/95. He also played 13 one-day internationals. In recognition of his long service for Northern Districts, he is granted a testimonial year which will include a Twenty20 match at Westpac Park in December.

13 New Zealand Cricket names Glenn Turner and Dion Nash as national selectors, joining selection manager Sir Richard Hadlee and coach John Bracewell on the panel which is appointed until May 2007.

14 Scott Styris announces he will play for Auckland from 2005/06. Styris, who lives close to Eden Park, says with the amount of time he spends away from home on international duties, he did not want to do the same with his domestic cricket.

15 Auckland captain Brooke Walker announces his retirement from all cricket at the age of 28. In 84 first-class matches, since his debut in 1997/98, he scored 1769 runs at 21.57 and took 164 wickets at 32.46. He played five tests and 11 one-day internationals.

Jeff Wilson confirms he is applying for a training licence for the new harness racing season and will train in partnership with Ray Jenkins, of West Melton, near Christchurch. He has been assisting Jenkins since moving to Canterbury three years ago.

16 Bob Carter is reappointed New Zealand assistant coach and computer analyst. His first assignment is with the Academy team in Australia. Carter had resigned as executive director of Canterbury United soccer club after juggling both jobs the previous summer.

18 Tim McIntosh decides to return to Auckland after one season with Canterbury. He is playing and coaching in Holland during the off-season.

19 New Zealand Cricket launches a recruiting drive designed to attract recently retired first-class players to umpiring. If selected, the umpires will be on a retainer of $20,000 with a chance to earn up to another $10,000 a season through match fees. The scheme will be limited to one or two former players at first but, if successful, will be repeated annually.

22 The New Zealand squads to tour Zimbabwe in August are announced. The test lineup is Stephen Fleming *(captain)*, Daniel Vettori *(vice-captain)*, Nathan Astle, Shane Bond, Craig Cumming, James Franklin, Hamish Marshall, James Marshall, Chris Martin, Brendon McCullum, Kyle Mills, Jacob Oram, Scott Styris, Lou Vincent and Paul Wiseman. For the one-dayers Cumming, Franklin, James Marshall, Martin and Wiseman will be replaced by Andre Adams, Chris Cairns, Craig McMillan and Jeetan Patel, who is the only uncapped player.

The selectors also announce that Daryl Tuffey will join Vettori, Martin and Mills as extra players in the Academy team to play in Australia in July.

27 Foreign Affairs Minister Phil Goff says Zimbabwe's proposed tour of New Zealand, scheduled for December and January, will not proceed. He says the Government will refuse to supply visas to the players in protest at the regime of Robert Mugabe.

PLAYERS OF THE YEAR

Hamish Marshall started the season slowly. He played his second test in Bangladesh and scored 69 to go with his unbeaten 40 in his only other test in South Africa three seasons earlier. He missed out on playing in the tests in Australia but played a vital hand of 50 not out in securing a win for New Zealand in the first Chappell-Hadlee Trophy game.

In the State Championship Marshall finally scored his elusive maiden first-class hundred, getting 128 in Northern's successful fourth innings of 400-9. He scored 179 runs in the State Shield.

Marshall really came to the fore against Australia. In the one-day games he was New Zealand's most consistent batsman with scores of 76, 16, 55, 23 and 28, passing 1000 runs in one-day internationals. In the first test at Christchurch he scored his maiden test century, getting 146 plus 22 in the second innings. He scored 76 in the first innings of the third test at Auckland.

He continued in this vein against Sri Lanka, getting a career best 160 in the first test at Napier. In addition, he once again saved many runs in the field.

Marshall won both the Redpath Cup and the Walter Hadlee Trophy for Batting for his efforts during the past season.

Daniel Vettori came back into form with a vengeance during the past twelve months. He took 20 wickets in two tests against Bangladesh, getting six wickets in three successive innings. In the one-day series he was given the New Zealand captaincy when Stephen Fleming returned to New Zealand, and New Zealand won all three games.

On the tour to Australia Vettori took 4-154 and 5-152 in the two tests and had 3-31 in the first Chappell-Hadlee Trophy game.

Returning to New Zealand he captained Northern Districts when available and led from the front in the State Shield scoring 109 against Auckland and 138 versus Canterbury in the next game.

When Australia came to New Zealand Vettori again bowled well, being the only New Zealand bowler to concede less than four runs per over. He also scored his maiden one-day fifty, getting 83 at Christchurch. He took 5-106 in the first test giving him twelve five wicket bags in tests.

Vettori was unavailable for the games against Sri Lanka due to a recurrence of his back injury. He has now taken 196 test wickets, only four short of becoming the third New Zealand bowler to reach 200. In January he was one of three New Zealand players to play for the World XI in the tsunami appeal match.

Vettori was awarded the Winsor Cup and the Walter Hadlee Bowling Trophy and was also named Cricketer of the Year.

PROMISING PLAYERS

Graeme Aldridge shot into prominence with a magnificent State Shield campaign. His efforts for Northern Districts were a significant factor in them winning the competition.

After getting a wicket in each of his first two games, he never took less than two wickets in an innings in the remaining matches. He had a career best 5-34 against Canterbury and took four wickets in an innings on three further occasions, 4-46 in the Canterbury return, 4-43 against Auckland and 4-38 in the final against Central Districts. In all he took 30 wickets, a record for the one-day domestic competition. He also took two wickets for the North Island in the inter-island match.

Aldridge also had a successful State Championship season. He took 24 wickets in seven games, twice taking four wickets in an innings, 4-60 against Otago and 4-33 against eventual champions Auckland. With him coming of age this past season, more of the same will be expected of Aldridge in the future. New Zealand have had bowling problems in the one-day game so Aldridge has every opportunity to get himself on to the short list for national honours.

Mark Gillespie had ended the 2003/04 season playing for New Zealand A against Sri Lanka A. This summer he repeated the good work by again being Wellington's leading bowler, taking 32 wickets in the State Championship.

Gillespie showed increased maturity this past season, having to lead the Wellington attack when Franklin and O'Brien were called in to the New Zealand side. In the State Championship final he took his 100th wicket in the course of taking a career best 6-81, putting Wellington back in the match after a poor first innings. A capable batsman, he scored a useful 52 in the first game against Auckland.

In the one-day competition Gillespie took 13 wickets but, at times, was a trifle expensive. Gillespie has now shown consistent form at first-class level in successive seasons and it will be interesting to see if he can make it to the next level up.

Jamie How went on the New Zealand A tour to South Africa but scored only 72 runs in five innings. On his return to New Zealand, however, he had a dream start to the season. He scored 105 and 108 not out in the opening game against Otago and followed this with 121 and 72 versus Northern Districts. He then had some low scores but registered another fifty against Canterbury and finished with 573 runs at 47.75 in the State Championship.

He also had some useful spells at the bowling crease and excelled in the field. He was substitute fieldsman for New Zealand against Sri Lanka, taking one catch. How had a useful season in the State Shield scoring three fifties and a 45. He totalled 254 runs in 10 innings.

He has shown that he has the temperament to make big scores and a repeat of this season's form next summer could see him close to national selection.

Since this section was introduced in 1983, the following have been chosen as Promising Players of the Year: **1983**, P.S. Briasco, M.D. Crowe, T.J. Franklin, **1984**, K.R. Rutherford, D.A. Stirling, P.J. Visser, **1985**, T.E. Blain, T.D. Ritchie, W. Watson, **1986**, S.W. Duff, D.G. Scott, C.J.P. Smith, **1987**, M.J. Greatbatch, D.K. Morrison, B.A. Young, **1988**, J.P. Millmow, M.R. Pringle, S.A. Thomson, **1989**, F. Beyeler, C.L. Cairns, M.W. Douglas, **1990**, C.Z. Harris, C. Pringle, K.A. Wealleans, **1991**, P.W. Dobbs, P.W. O'Rourke, A.C. Parore, **1992**, M.N. Hart, L.G. Howell, J.W. Wilson, **1993**, S.P. Fleming, D.J. Nash, M.B. Owens, **1994**, R.L. Hayes, B.A. Pocock, A.T. Reinholds, **1995**, M.D. Bell, G.R. Jonas, C.D. McMillan, **1996**, C.J. Nevin, M.H. Richardson, P.J. Wiseman, **1997**, M.J. Horne, M.S. Sinclair, D.L. Vettori, **1998**, C.E. Bulfin, C.D. Cumming, S.B. O'Connor, **1999**, J.I. Englefield, C.S. Martin, L. Vincent, **2000**, T.K. Canning, B.P. Martin, J.D.P. Oram, **2001**, J.E.C. Franklin, K.D. Mills, D.R. Tuffey, **2002**, I.G. Butler, W.A. Cornelius, R.J. Nicol, **2003**, T.G. McIntosh, I.E. O'Brien, J.D. Ryder, **2004,** P.G. Fulton, B.B. McCullum, M.H.W. Papps.

HAPPENINGS

New Zealand's oldest surviving first-class cricketer, Norm Stokes, died in October at the age of 94. His obituary is included in this issue of the *Almanack.*

Former Auckland captain Herb Pearson is now the oldest living first-class player while Eric Tindill is New Zealand's oldest surviving test cricketer and the oldest from any country. Jack Kerr is now Canterbury's oldest player. Just before going to print we were advised that Peter Howden (21.10.1911) had died, meaning Jack Scandrett is now Otago's oldest player.

During the year we made contact with Jimmy Ell, who played 26 matches for Wellington between 1933/34 and 1945/46 and represented North Island. He now features on our list for the first time. As far as can be ascertained, the oldest New Zealand first-class cricketers are:

		Born
H.T. Pearson	*Auckland*	5. 8.1910
E.W.T. Tindill	*Wellington*	18.12.1910
J.L. Kerr	*Canterbury*	28.12.1910
L.A. Mahoney	*Canterbury*	13. 9.1911
C.L.W. Randall	*Wellington*	8. 8.1913
J.C. Scandrett	*Otago*	22. 2.1915
W.A. Hadlee	*Canterbury, Otago*	4. 6.1915
G.S. Botting	*Otago, Central Districts*	27. 6.1915
V. James	*Canterbury*	24. 8.1915
J.A. Ell	*Wellington*	15. 9.1915
N.A. McMahon	*Auckland*	24. 5.1916
W.M. Wallace	*Auckland*	19.12.1916
R.H. Scott	*Canterbury*	6. 3.1917
T.L. Pritchard	*Wellington*	10. 3.1917
C.A. Snedden	*Auckland*	7. 1.1918
S.A. McVicar	*Wellington*	15. 7.1918
J.L. Wyatt	*Northern Districts*	7. 3.1919

• • •

A right-hand top-order batsman, Pearson played in 30 first-class matches (28 for Auckland) from 1932/33 to 1947/48 scoring 1392 runs at 30.26. He represented North Island against South Island in 1944/45. Eric Tindill, Jack Kerr, Walter Hadlee, Merv Wallace, Roy Scott and Colin Snedden are New Zealand's oldest surviving test cricketers.

Laurie Mahoney is the stepfather of international umpire David Quested.

• • •

A number of New Zealand players have a high ratio of catches per match over their first-class careers. Stephen Fleming has taken 247 catches in 189 first-class games while James Marshall, who has taken 77 (one as a wicketkeeper) in 71 matches, and Jamie How, 43 in 40, also average more than one per game.

Other players high on the list are Craig Spearman 140 in 149, Matthew Hart 110 in 135, Chris Gaffaney 73 in 83, Richard Jones 70 in 80 and Neal Parlane 41 in 42.

• • •

When he took over as Wellington captain for the State Shield match against Canterbury at Timaru, it was the first time that Stephen Fleming had ever led a New Zealand provincial team. By that stage Fleming had captained New Zealand in 65 tests and 169 one-day internationals.

Fleming's first decision at domestic level was to send Canterbury in to bat but Michael Papps and Nathan Astle put on 168 for the first wicket on the way to a final total of 307-3 and Wellington went down by 92 runs.

For the second season in a row, Brooke Walker captained Auckland in every match, the only ever-present captain in the 2004/05 season. Canterbury's original appointment as captain was Chris Harris but he was injured in Australia and did not play at all.

Northern Districts named both James Marshall and Daniel Vettori as captains at the start of the season, with Vettori taking over once his international commitments permitted. Peter McGlashan captained a side at first-class level for the first time when James Marshall was withdrawn from the State Championship match against Canterbury at Gisborne to join the New Zealand team.

The sides were led by:

	Official captain	*Replacement*
Auckland	Brooke Walker	–
Canterbury	Chris Harris	Craig McMillan, Peter Fulton
Central Districts	Jacob Oram	Glen Sulzberger
Northern Districts	James Marshall	Daniel Vettori, Matthew Hart, Peter McGlashan
Otago	Craig Cumming	Chris Gaffaney
Wellington	Matthew Bell	Stephen Fleming

• • •

By the end of the series against Australia, Stephen Fleming had led New Zealand in 174 one-day internationals. Only eleven players have captained their side in as many as 100 one-day internationals and they are:

	P	*W*	*L*	*T*	*NR*	*Win%*
A. Ranatunga *(SL)*	193	89	95	1	8	46
A.R. Border *(A)*	178	107	67	1	3	62
S.P. Fleming *(NZ)*	174	75	87	1	11	43
M. Azharuddin *(I)*	173	89	76	2	6	51
S.C. Ganguly *(I)*	142	73	64	–	5	51
Imran Khan *(P)*	139	75	59	1	4	53
W.J. Cronje *(SA)*	138	99	35	1	3	71
S.T. Jayasuriya *(SL)*	118	66	47	2	3	55
Wasim Akram *(P)*	109	66	41	2	–	60
S.R. Waugh *(A)*	106	67	35	3	1	63
I.V.A. Richards *(WI)*	105	67	36	–	2	63

Fleming and Ganguly are the only currently active captains on the list. New Zealand's next highest is Geoff Howarth who had 60 games as captain (31 wins).

• • •

Only Allan Border and Clive Lloyd have captained their country in test cricket more often than Fleming. At the end of the summer the list of most games as captain read:

	P	*W*	*L*	*D*	*Win%*
A.R. Border *(A)*	93	32	22	39*	34
C.H. Lloyd *(WI)*	74	36	12	26	48
S.P. Fleming *(NZ)*	70	23	24	23	32
S.R. Waugh *(A)*	57	41	9	7	72
A. Ranatunga *(SL)*	56	12	19	25	21
M.A. Atherton *(E)*	54	13	21	20	24
W.J. Cronje *(SA)*	53	27	11	15	50
M.A. Taylor *(A)*	50	26	13	11	52
I.V.A. Richards *(WI)*	50	27	8	15	54

** includes a tie*

Fleming has had 55 consecutive tests as captain, second only to Border (93).

When Australia won the third test at Eden Park it was the 24th defeat for Stephen Fleming as New Zealand's test captain, taking him past Brian Lara as the captain with the most losses in test cricket. Fleming, however, had been captain in 70 matches while Lara had led West Indies on only 40 occasions.

• • •

New Zealand played nine test matches during the past twelve months, winning three and losing four. Stephen Fleming (577) scored the most runs while Daniel Vettori (38) captured the most wickets. New Zealand batsmen scored seven centuries, two to Hamish Marshall.

Over the 13 one-day internationals played in the same period (six wins, seven losses) Nathan Astle was the leading scorer with 465 runs while Chris Cairns (17) took the most wickets. Astle's century against USA was the only three figure score, the next highest being Daniel Vettori's 83 against Australia at Christchurch.

• • •

A total of 23 players took part in the 13 one-day internationals for New Zealand with Hamish Marshall, Chris Cairns and Brendon McCullum playing in every game. Peter Fulton, James Marshall and Lance Hamilton made their debuts with Fulton, Andre Adams, Ian Butler, Tama Canning and Michael Papps all making a solitary appearance.

In the nine test matches, 19 players were involved with only Stephen Fleming, Nathan Astle and Brendon McCullum playing in every game. Craig Cumming, James Marshall and Iain O'Brien made their debuts.

• • •

The highest run scorer in first-class cricket over the past twelve months was Lou Vincent who totalled 1125. Mathew Sinclair (1113) and Peter Fulton (1078) also scored more than one thousand runs. The most first-class wickets were taken by James Franklin (60) while Paul Wiseman captured 53.

• • •

New Zealand's most economical bowler in their 13 one-day internationals over the past twelve months was Daniel Vettori, who played in all but one of the games. He also bowled the most overs (108.5).

The most economical bowlers were:

	M	*O*	*M*	*R*	*W*	*Ave*	*Best*	*R/O*
D.L. Vettori	12	108.5	5	356	16	22.25	3-8	3.27
S.B. Styris	9	59.4	6	199	12	16.58	4-40	3.33
C.Z. Harris	6	36	7	123	3	41.00	1-21	3.42

• • •

During the season Matthew Hart and Michael Parlane both notched up 100 domestic one-day appearances while Llorne Howell became the first player to appear for four different sides. The most games in domestic one-day cricket have now been played by:

matches		*matches*	
122	R.G Hart *ND*	103	C.Z. Harris *C*
121	G.E. Bradburn *ND*	102	M.N. Hart *ND*
114	A.C. Barnes *A*	101	M.W. Douglas *CD, W*
105	L.G. Howell *CD, C, A, ND*	100	R.G. Petrie *C, W*
103	M.D. Bailey *ND*	100	M.E. Parlane *ND, W*

A total of 79 players have made 50 or more appearances.

Waikanae Park was again the only non-first-class venue to host a State Shield game during the season. The details of the nine grounds where domestic one-day matches have taken place but where no first-class games have been played are:

Venue	*Matches*	*Seasons*
Ashburton Domain	4	1980/81-1988/89
Knottingley Park, Waimate	1	1984/85
Blake Park, Mt Maunganui	24	1987/88-2001/02
Memorial Park, Motueka	1	1987/88
Mandeville Sports Ground, Ohoka	1	1990/91
Dannevirke Domain	1	1992/93
Waikanae Park	6	1993/94-2004/05
Yarrow Stadium, New Plymouth	3	1998/99-2002/03
WestpacTrust Stadium, Wellington	2	1999/00-2000/01

• • •

The Champions Trophy in England was the 41st one-day tournament which New Zealand had taken part in. A summary of the tournaments is:

	Series	*Seasons*
World Cup	8	1975-2002/03
World Series/Carlton & United/VB Series	8	1980/81-2001/02
World Championship of Cricket	1	1984/85
Sri Lankan Tournaments	3	1985/86-2002/03
Sharjah Tournaments	8	1987/88-2001/02
Rothmans Cup	1	1989/90
Wills World Series	1	1994/95
Mandela Trophy	1	1994/95
Bank of New Zealand Centenary Series	1	1994/95
Independence Cup Tournaments	2	1996/97-1997/98
ICC Tournaments	4	1998/99-2004
Singapore Tournament	1	2000/01
TVS Cup	1	2003/04
NatWest Series	1	2004

• • •

The Cornwall Cricket Club in Auckland again organised the limited-overs national club competition which was played from 5 to 10 April 2005. Teams involved were St Albans *(Canterbury)*, Green Island *(Otago)*, Fraser-Technical *(Northern Districts)*, Palmerston North United *(Central Districts)*, North City *(Wellington)* and Howick-Pakuranga *(Auckland)*.

Players with first-class experience who took part were Jordan Sheed, Bradley Scott and Shane Robinson *(Green Island)*, Grant Robinson and Jaden Hatwell *(Fraser-Technical)* Ewen Thompson and Bevan Griggs *(Palmerston North)*, James Ward *(St Albans)*, Andy McKay and Tafadzwa Madondo *(Howick-Pakuranga)* and Stu Mills, Sam Fairley and Mark Gillespie *(North City)*.

In the final **St Albans** 167-9 (A. Denford 36, D. Lobb 3-44) **lost to Green Island** 173-6 (S.A. Robinson 52, A. Kennedy 42, B.E. Scott 38*) by four wickets.

Tournament awards were: Batting – Jordan Sheed *(Green Island)*, Bowling – Dean Wedlake *(Howick-Pakuranga)*, Player of the Tournament – Bradley Scott *(Green Island)*.

• • •

Madondo is the younger brother of former Zimbabwe test player Trevor Madondo who died in June 2001 aged 24, just six months after playing against New Zealand at the Basin Reserve. Tafadzwa Madondo played one first-class game for Manicaland against Matabeleland in the Logan Cup in 2000/01. He emigrated to New Zealand in 2002 and played for Howick-Pakuranga in 2004/05 after having earlier been unavailable for cricket due to studies and work commitments.

Former Otago, Wellington and Auckland batsman Ian Billcliff further extended his first-class career when he played for Canada against United Arab Emirates and Scotland in the Inter-Continental Cup semi-final and final played in Sharjah in November.

Billcliff, who was born in Canada and represented them in the last World Cup, was captaining the side in the absence of World Cup star John Davison who was playing for South Australia. Billcliff scored 44 and 63 against UAE and 31 and 6 in the final which Scotland won by an innings.

• • •

New Zealand extended its run of one-day internationals without defeat to 12 before going down to Australia in the Champions Trophy at The Oval. This surpassed their previous best of seven matches unbeaten in 1983 and 1992.

The longest unbroken sequences by all teams are: 21 Australia, 14 Australia, South Africa, 12 England, New Zealand, 11 West Indies, Australia, South Africa.

• • •

Former Canterbury and Otago all-rounder Darron Reekers appeared for the Netherlands against Pakistan in August, 2004. The match, played at the VRA Ground at Amstelveen, was abandoned because of rain after 22.4 overs of the Pakistan innings. Reekers took 2-19 from four overs, dismissing Imran Farhat and Shahid Afridi.

Reekers also played in an Inter-Continental Cup match (first-class) against Ireland in July scoring 26 and 4 and taking 1-55. He also took part in the ICC Six Nations Challenge held in the United Arab Emirates in March 2004, along with UAE, Namibia, USA, Canada and Scotland. Opening the batting, he scored 67 off 73 balls against USA and 85 off 69 balls against UAE.

Reekers has also appeared for the Netherlands in county cricket's Cheltenham & Gloucester Trophy since 2002. His last match in New Zealand was for Canterbury in the State Shield final against Wellington in 2001/02.

• • •

The fifteenth Gillette Cup limited-overs competition for secondary school boys was played in Palmerston North from 3 to 5 December, 2004. A total of 172 teams entered the competition which was divided into eight zones and, after the qualifying rounds, King's College *(Auckland)*, Palmerston North Boys' High School, St Paul's Collegiate *(Hamilton)* and Christchurch Boys' High School played off for the title. Results were:

Round 1
Christchurch Boys' High School 228-7 lost to **King's College** 232-8 by 2 wickets
St Paul's Collegiate 113 lost to **Palmerston North Boys' High School** 114-0 by 10 wickets

Round 2
St Paul's Collegiate 235-9 lost to **King's College** 237-6 by 4 wickets
Christchurch Boys' High School 203 lost to **Palmerston North Boys' High School** 205-7 by 3 wickets

Round 3
No play possible

Final placings: Palmerston North Boys' High School and King's College 1st equal, Christchurch Boys' High School and St Paul's Collegiate 3rd equal.

The eleventh national secondary schools girls competition, sponsored by New Zealand Community Trust, was played in Palmerston North from 7 to 10 December, 2004. A total of 103 schools entered the competition and for the first time in its history, eight teams were represented at the finals. These were the winners from each major association plus the runners-up of the two associations with the most entries. Results were:

GROUP A

Round 1
Epsom Girls' Grammar School 58 lost to **Christchurch Girls' High School** 58-2 by 8 wickets
Taupo Nui-a-tia College 133 lost to **New Plymouth Girls' High School** 134-2 by 8 wickets

Round 2
Christchurch Girls' High School 211 defeated **Taupo Nui-a-tia College** 119-9 by 92 runs
New Plymouth Girls' High School 137 defeated **Epsom Girls' Grammar School** 61 by 76 runs

Round 3
New Plymouth Girls' High School 142-8 defeated **Christchurch Girls' High School** 110 by 32 runs
Epsom Girls' Grammar School 216-5 defeated **Taupo Nui-a-tia College** 103 by 113 runs

GROUP B

Round 1
Otago Girls' High School 219-9 defeated **Gisborne Girls' High School** 47 by 172 runs
Onslow College 98 lost to **Napier Girls' High School** 99-4 by 6 wickets

Round 2
Gisborne Girls' High School 65 lost to **Onslow College** 65-3 by 7 wickets
Otago Girls' High School 59 lost to **Napier Girls' High School** 60-2 by 8 wickets

Round 3
Gisborne Girls' High School 61 lost to **Napier Girls' High School** 62-3 by 7 wickets
Otago Girls' High School 181-9 defeated **Onslow College** 130 by 51 runs

Finals
New Plymouth Girls' High School 110 defeated **Napier Girls' High School** 88 by 22 runs
Otago Girls' High School 93 defeated **Christchurch Girls' High School** 68 by 25 runs
Epsom Girls' Grammar School 116 lost to **Onslow College** 119-7 by 3 wickets
Taupo Nui-a-tia College defeated **Gisborne Girls' High School**

Final placings: New Plymouth Girls' High School 1st, Napier Girls' High School 2nd, Otago Girls' High School 3rd, Christchurch Girls' High School 4th, Onslow College 5th, Epsom Girls' Grammar School 6th, Taupo Nui-a-tia College 7th, Gisborne Girls' High School 8th.

• • •

Former New Zealand representative Paul Hitchcock was the most expensive bowler in the 2004/05 State Shield competition, his 67 overs conceding 5.92 runs apiece. The most expensive bowlers in domestic one-day cricket (minimum 100 overs) have been:

		Overs	*Mdns*	*Runs*	*Wkts*	*Ave*	*RPO*
C.R. Pryor	*(A, O)*	157.4	3	863	23	37.52	5.47
J.A.F. Yovich	*(ND)*	334.5	20	1755	72	24.37	5.24
C.D. McMillan	*(C)*	167.5	8	833	34	24.50	4.96
M.R. Gillespie	*(W)*	252.2	12	1250	42	29.76	4.95
M.Y. Pasupati	*(W)*	322.3	14	1565	50	31.30	4.85

During the season Craig McMillan equalled the highest score by a number four batsman in domestic one-day cricket and Peter McGlashan set a new record for someone batting at number eight. The highest scores for each batting position are now:

1/2	161	B.R. Hartland	C v ND	Timaru	1993/94
3	149	C.J. Nevin	W v CD	Wellington	1997/98
4	124*	R.G. Twose	W v O	Wellington	2000/01
	124	C.D. McMillan	C v ND	Auckland	2004/05
5	125	J.D.P. Oram	CD v A	Auckland	2003/04
6	143	C.L. Cairns	C v A	Christchurch	1994/95
7	100	M.N. Hart	ND v CD	Napier	1996/97
8	65	P.D. McGlashan	ND v CD	Masterton	2004/05
9	68*	L.J. Doull	W v O	Alexandra	1993/94
10	63	A.J. Penn	CD v C	Napier	1996/97
11	40*	I.G. Butler	ND v C	Hamilton	2003/04

• • •

During the season Brendon McCullum and Jacob Oram registered test centuries while batting at number seven. It was Oram's second hundred from that position while McCullum later scored 99 against Sri Lanka at number seven.

Test centuries scored for New Zealand by a batsman coming in at number seven are:

C.L. Cairns	158	v South Africa	Auckland	2003/04
W.K. Lees	152	v Pakistan	Karachi	1976/77
R.J. Hadlee	151*	v Sri Lanka	Colombo	1986/87
B.B. McCullum	143	v Bangladesh	Dhaka	2004/05
J.D.P. Oram	126*	v Australia	Brisbane	2004/05
C.L. Cairns	126	v India	Hamilton	1998/99
C.L. Cairns	124	v Zimbabwe	Harare	2000/01
J.D.P. Oram	119*	v South Africa	Hamilton	2003/04
C.L. Cairns	109	v Australia	Wellington	1999/00
V. Pollard	105*	v England	Lord's	1973
J.V. Coney	101*	v Australia	Wellington	1985/86
A.C. Parore	100*	v West Indies	Christchurch	1994/95

Adam Gilchrist has hit eleven hundreds at number seven, Ian Botham six, Alan Knott and Kapil Dev five each. The highest score by a batsman at number seven is 270 by Don Bradman for Australia against England at Melbourne in 1936/37 while Gilchrist scored 204 not out for Australia against South Africa at Johannesburg in 2001/02

• • •

Nathan Astle hit six sixes in his innings of 145 not out against USA during the Champions Trophy in September. The most sixes in a one-day international for New Zealand is:

7	C.L. Cairns (115)	v India	Christchurch	1998/99
6	B.L. Cairns (52)	v Australia	Melbourne	1982/83
6	C.L. Cairns (75)	v West Indies	Auckland	1999/00
6	S.B. Styris (141)	v Sri Lanka	Bloemfontein	2002/03
6	C.L. Cairns (84)	v Pakistan	Lahore	2003/04
6	N.J. Astle (145*)	v USA	The Oval	2004
5†	C.D. McMillan (66)	v Zimbabwe	Harare	1997/98
5	C.D. McMillan (104*)	v Pakistan	Christchurch	2000/01
5	N.J. Astle (122*)	v Pakistan	Dunedin	2001/02

† *no fours*

Astle's score was the highest ever for New Zealand in a 50-over one-day international, surpassing Scott Styris' 141 against Sri Lanka at Bloemfontein in the last World Cup. The only higher innings for New Zealand is 171 not out by Glenn Turner against East Africa at Birmingham in the 1975 World Cup when the matches were 60 overs per side.

• • •

The British Combined Services team played three matches against the New Zealand Defence Force at Horton Park, Blenheim, in February. Scores were:

NZDF 123(D. Grant 58, R. Parker 4-21, S. Cooper 2-9) **lost to UKCS** 124-2 (G. Lumb 22, J. Fulton 34*, M. Heynes 38*) by 8 wickets.

UKCS 303-8 (P. Carlin 80, M. Heynes 46, A. Senneck 84, M. Beaven 3-49) **defeated NZDF** 205-9 (D. Grant 80, T. Beilby 30*, R. Parker 3-28, S. Cooper 2-43, M. Heynes 2-14) by 98 runs.

UKCS 311 (J. Fulton 127, N. Palmer 54, R. Parker 23 A. Senneck 23, J. Broderson 4-79, T. Beilby 2-30, A. McQuillan 2-62) **defeated NZDF** 218 (K. Bevins 51, D. Grant 48, G. Whitley 46, R. Parker 4-29, S. Cooper 2-46, I. Giles 2-39) by 93 runs.

NZDF player of the series: Darren Grant (RNZAF)

• • •

The Royal New Zealand Air Force won the inter-services tournament played at Fitzherbert Park, Palmerston North in March, for the fifth consecutive year. Scores were:

RNZN 212-9 (G. Simpkins 39, R. Jackson 30, R Bartholomew 27, J. Smilie 24*, S. MacGibbon 3-51, D. Stewart 2-16) **defeated NZ Army** 195 (J. Broderson 40, R. Fraser 40, D. Robinson 29, H. Moon 3-36, C. McKeich 3-46).

RNZN 58 (A. Julian 3-14, D. Grant 3-16, M. Whiteside 2-7) **lost to RNZAF** 60-2 (M. Beaven 32*, G. Burnnand 21*, G. Simpkins 2-22)

NZ Army 152 (M. Beaven 4-35, D. Croucher 3-36) **defeated RNZAF** 133 (D. Grant 45, A. McQuillan 3-4, J. Broderson 3-36)

Player of the tournament: Sgt Matt Beaven (RNZAF))

• • •

Auckland won the men's RNZAF Inter Base Tournament, claiming the Wilson Memorial Cup, defeating the previous winners, Ohakea, in the final. Scores were:

Auckland 262 for 7 (M. Chadwick 101, D. Croucher 35, K. Bevins 33, J. Reedy 28, G. Schofield 3-32, B. Cunningham 2-32) **defeated Ohakea** 218 (G. Burnnand 117, H. Overton 34*, D. Croucher 3-34, K. Mawston 2-42, K. Davison 2-50) by 44 runs.

• • •

James and Hamish Marshall became the sixth set of brothers to share a hundred partnership in a test with 107 for the second wicket against Sri Lanka at Napier. The highest partnership between brothers is 269 by Grant and Andy Flower for Zimbabwe against Pakistan at Harare in 1994/95. The highest by twins is 231 by Mark and Steve Waugh for Australia against West Indies at Kingston in 1994/95.

Brothers to have shared century partnerships in tests are: Steve and Mark Waugh (9), Ian and Greg Chappell (6), Grant and Andy Flower (3), Jeff and Martin Crowe (2), Hanif and Wazir Mohammad (2), James and Hamish Marshall (1).

New Zealand umpire Brent "Billy" Bowden officiated in ten tests and 25 one-day internationals during the past 12 months.

He stood in the second test between Sri Lanka and South Africa in Colombo, the first test between India and Australia at Bangalore and both tests between Pakistan and Sri Lanka at Faisalabad and Karachi.

He then went to Perth and Sydney for the first and third tests between Australia and Pakistan, to Cape Town for the first match between South Africa and Zimbabwe and then to Bangalore for the third test between India and Pakistan. He then officiated in the third and fourth tests between West Indies and South Africa at Bridgetown and St John's.

He also officiated in all five matches between Sri Lanka and South Africa, three matches in the Champions Trophy in England, the Tsunami Appeal match at Melbourne and five matches (including the first final) in the VB Series. He stood in the first three games between India and Pakistan and also in three one-day internationals in New Zealand.

Bowden then went to England where he umpired five matches (including the final) of the NatWest Series involving England, Australia and Bangladesh and was also due to stand in the third, fourth and fifth tests of the Ashes series.

• • •

Tony Hill, who is on the Emirates International Panel of umpires (backups to the Elite Panel), stood in the test between England and Bangladesh at Chester-le-Street, Durham in June. His only previous test appointment had been in December 2001 when Bangladesh met New Zealand at Hamilton. Hill has stood in 16 one-day internationals, all in New Zealand.

• • •

Former New Zealand captain Jeff Crowe was the ICC Match Referee in eight tests and 21 one-day internationals over the last 12 months. He was involved in Sri Lanka's tour to Pakistan and South Africa's series in India and West Indies and also officiated in the Paktel Cup one-day tournament in Pakistan.

Crowe was also the match referee for the NatWest Series which featured England, Australia and Bangladesh.

• • •

Steve Croft achieved the extremely rare feat of taking all ten wickets in an innings for his Caledonian Experience team in a Christchurch Suburban match during the season. Croft came on as first change with his medium pacers upwind at Nunweek Park and soon had the Glenbyre batsmen in the fourth grade C match bamboozled.

With the ball swinging, seven of Croft's victims fell to catches behind the wicket. Two were bowled and his tenth victim was leg before, the ball after a hat-trick delivery had been kept out. His captain had dropped a straightforward slips catch before Croft came on to bowl his last over.

• • •

The day before, also in Christchurch, Ben Enoka had achieved the even rarer feat of two hat-tricks in an innings, in a Gillette Cup secondary schoolboys qualifying match for St Bede's College against Cashmere High. In his fourth over he took wickets with the second, third and fourth deliveries, two bowled and one caught and bowled.

He repeated the dose at the start of his sixth over with two leg before wicket decisions and then a bowled, leaving him with the final figures of seven for 26 from 5.3 overs. St Bede's, which made 293 for seven, crushed Cashmere, who were dismissed for 52.

It was not Enoka's first hat-trick, as he had performed the feat for the school against Mount Hutt College in 2003/04. Enoka is the son of former New Zealand volleyballer and sports psychologist Gilbert.

Canterbury 18-year-olds Keryn Ambler and Todd Astle put togther an unbroken first wicket partnership of 374 against Auckland in the National Under 19 Tournament at Lincoln. Ambler was unbeaten on 200 from 305 balls, 21 fours and two sixes, while vice-captain Astle made 157 off 375 balls with 16 fours. The pair batted for 430 minutes.

On the first day they went to lunch at 85-0, at tea they were 200-0 and had reached 324-0 by stumps, Astle 129, Ambler 178. The innings was declared closed at 11.11 am next morning. The hundred partnership took 136 minutes, the two hundred came after 257 minutes and three hundred arrived just 99 minutes later.

Auckland were 286 for nine at stumps, the last pair holding out for 23 minutes, and the match ended in a draw. Astle is the son of national coaching and development manager Alec Astle, a former Central Districts representative, but is not related to Nathan Astle.

• • •

The partnership between Astle and Ambler was the highest unbroken first wicket stand in the history of New Zealand cricket at any level. The highest first wicket partnerships in all New Zealand cricket are now:

441	J.E. Mills & H.D. Gillespie	Eden v University	Auckland	1924/25
394	R.S. Scragg & J.V. Hill	Central Districts A v Otago A	Palmerston North	2001/02
393	M.E.L. Lane & J. Lane	Marlborough v Buller	Blenheim	1992/93
387	G.M. Turner & T.W. Jarvis	NZ v West Indies	Georgetown	1971/72
374*	T.D. Astle & K.R. Ambler	Canterbury U19 v Auckland U19	Lincoln	2004/05
373	B. Sutcliffe & L. Watt	Otago v Auckland	Auckland	1950/51
360	G. Marshall & H.C. Wilson	Napier United A v Napier United B	Napier	1898/99
360	B. Sutcliffe & F.J. Craig	Takapuna Grammar v Mt Albert Grammar	Devonport	1942/43

• • •

New Zealand players were also involved in some tenth wicket records during the season. In the second test at Chittagong, Enamul Haque helped Tapash Baisya add 45 for the last wicket without scoring a single run himself. This bettered the previous record set by Australia's Alan Hurst who remained scoreless while assisting Peter Toohey to put on 34 against India at Brisbane in 1977/78.

Three weeks later at Brisbane, Chris Martin made a 29 minute duck but helped Jacob Oram add 36 for the last wicket against Australia. In 1998/99 number eleven Geoff Allott batted for 101 minutes without scoring when he and Chris Harris put on 32 for the last wicket against South Africa at Auckland and Martin also helped Daniel Vettori put on 32 for the last wicket against Australia at Wellington without making any of the runs himself.

At Lord's in 2004, Martin contributed a single in a 48 run last wicket stand with Chris Cairns. This effort has only been bettered by Glenn McGrath who scored one run while he and Adam Gilchrist added 63 for Australia's last wicket against England at Birmingham in 2001.

• • •

Jamie How came within 28 runs of scoring four centuries in two consecutive games, a feat only two batsmen in the history of first-class cricket have ever achieved. In the first two State Championship matches How made 105 and 108 not out for Central Districts against Otago and 121 and 72 against Northern Districts.

Only Tom Hayward, for Surrey in June 1906, and David Hookes, for South Australia in February 1977, have achieved the feat of scoring two hundreds in consecutive matches. How did, however, join Bert Sutcliffe (who did it twice), John Reid, Martin Crowe, Andrew Jones, Mark Greatbatch and Jason Wells as the only New Zealanders to score three consecutive centuries in first class cricket.

This edition of the *Almanack* includes an obituary for Mark Beban, who played four times for Wellington in 1969/70. He is believed to be the only Catholic priest to have played first-class cricket in New Zealand and one of very few anywhere.

One such player was William Ignatius Rice who was headmaster of Douai School (a Catholic public school near Reading) from 1915 to 1952. He appeared twice for Warwickshire in 1920.

One of Beban's team mates in the St Patrick's College Old Boys side was Father Michael Donnelly, the nephew of Sir Arthur Donnelly, a former president of the New Zealand Cricket Council and manager of the 1931 New Zealand team to England.

When Beban played for Wellington against Auckland one of the umpires was Reverend (now Canon) David Bindon.

• • •

Clerics from other churches are not quite so uncommon and at least two have played for New Zealand. Reverend Ernest Blamires, an itinerant parson, played for Wellington and Otago as well as North Otago, Taranaki and Wairarapa.

In 1923/24, at the age of 42, he was selected to play for New Zealand against the powerful New South Wales side but bagged a pair. He did not retire until 1933 and the 6ft 2in clergyman was still good enough, at the age of 51, to thrash the Manawatu attack for 94 while playing for Wairarapa.

Archdeacon Harold Monaghan, of Wellington, played for New Zealand against the Melbourne Cricket Club in 1905/06, although he was not ordained until 1912. As late as 1924/25, when Vicar of Hawera, he appeared in the South Taranaki XI.

Monaghan was one of the very first New Zealanders to perceive and understand the mechanics of moving the ball in the air – "a forerunner to Maurice Tate" as he was once described.

• • •

Three South African-born players made their debuts in first-class cricket during the season. Ryan Shutte, who made his debut for Northern Districts against Auckland, was born in Queenstown, Cape Province and had played for Border B in the UCB Bowl (not first-class) in 2002/03.

Bradley-John (BJ) Watling came to New Zealand in 1996 aged ten, having started playing cricket at Durban Prep High School at the age of seven and was a member of the New Zealand team in the Under 19 World Cup in Bangladesh in 2004. He made his debut for Northern Districts in the same match as Shutte.

Carl Cachopa, who was born in Bloemfontein, made his first-class debut after having scored a double century in the National Under 19 Tournament. He had represented Free State at under 11, under 13 and under 15 levels. His brother, Bradley, was a member of the Auckland Under 17 team.

The only other South African-born players to appear in New Zealand first-class cricket are Matthew Cairns, who played one match for Auckland in 2001/02, Michael Austen, who played for Wellington and Otago from 1989/90 to 1996/97, and Wellington off-spinner Morrie Browne, who appeared from 1937/38 to 1951/52.

• • •

Craig Smith, whose debut was for Otago against Auckland, became just the tenth first-class cricketer to be born in Oamaru.

The others are A.M. "Joe" Ongley, who played for Hawke's Bay in 1901/02, fast bowler Don Cleverley, who played for New Zealand, Auckland and Central Districts between 1930/31 and 1952/53, Ken Uttley, Otago, Canterbury and Wellington batsman between 1933/34 and 1951/52, and Ross Nicholson, Canterbury and Otago left-arm pace bowler between 1959/60 and 1963/64.

In addition, recent players Mark Jefferson, Andrew Hore, Marcel McKenzie, Duncan Drew and Neil Rushton were all born in Oamaru.

Daniel Flynn, who made his debut for Northern Districts against Otago, is only the third first-class cricketer to be born in Rotorua. He follows Ray Hunter, Auckland off-spinner between 1975/76 and 1984/85, and left-arm pace bowler Kingsley Smith, who played for Northern Districts in 1993/94.

• • •

Will Somerville, the Otago off-spinner who his made his debut in the final round of the State Championship, moved to Sydney with his family in 1994 aged nine. He studied Health and Sports Science at the University of New South Wales and returned to New Zealand in July, 2004, to study commerce at Otago University and play cricket.

Somerville said he had hopes of playing first-class cricket in New Zealand and always wanted to come back and try to do so. He played junior cricket for Eastern Suburbs and first-grade in 2002/03, when he was in the New South Wales Under 19 squad.

The next season he played mainly second grade behind state representative Adrian Tucker. He also represented New South Wales secondary schools for two years. Somerville was one of the 2005 New Zealand Academy intake.

• • •

When Daniel Vettori and Craig McMillan scored centuries in the State Shield semi-final at Eden Park, it was the first time both captains had reached three figures in the same domestic one-day game. Vettori's innings was also the highest by a captain as the following table shows.

D.L. Vettori	138	Northern Dstricts v Canterbury	Auckland	2004/05
M.D. Crowe	125	Central Districts v Otago	Alexandra	1988/89
J.D.P. Oram	125	Central Districts v Auckland	Auckland	2003/04
C.D. McMillan	124	Canterbury v Northern Districts	Auckland	2004/05
R.G. Twose	121*	Wellington v Northern Districts	Wellington	1996/97

• • •

Lou Vincent went from 93 to 194 during the 160 minute session from lunch to tea on the third day of the test against Sri Lanka at the Basin Reserve. This was only the fourth time that a New Zealand batsman had registered one hundred runs in a single session of a test match and the first time in other than the final session. This short list is:

runs				
140	I.D.S. Smith (173)	v India	Auckland	1989/90
139	N.J. Astle (222)	v England	Christchurch	2001/02
105	C.L. Cairns (158)	v South Africa	Auckland	2003/04
101	L. Vincent (224)	v Sri Lanka	Wellington	2004/05

The record for all teams is 173 between lunch and tea by Denis Compton during his innings of 278 against Pakistan at Nottingham in 1954.

Vincent was run out going for what would have been his 1000th first-class run of the season. It was only the second time that the score of 224 had been made in test cricket. Vinod Kambli scored 224 for India against England at Bombay in 1993/94.

• • •

Stephen Fleming had a day to remember on the first day of the second test against Bangladesh at Chittagong. It was his 87th test, surpassing Richard Hadlee's New Zealand record, and when he lofted Mohammad Rafique over mid-off for four to move to 81 he went past Martin Crowe's record of 5444 runs in tests for New Zealand.

Fleming is now 88 runs short of becoming the first New Zealand batsman to score 6000 runs in test cricket.

Shane Warne reached his fifty from just 37 balls in the second test at Wellington, the fastest known fifty for Australia in terms of balls faced. He heads the following list:

balls				
37	S.K. Warne	v New Zealand	Wellington	2004/05
42	J.L. Langer	v New Zealand	Hamilton	1999/00
43	J.M. Gregory	v South Africa	Johannesburg	1921/22
43	D.R. Martyn	v England	The Oval	2001
45	W.J. O'Reilly	v South Africa	Johannesburg	1935/36

The fastest in terms of time for Australia (and for all countries) is by Victor Trumper who took only 22 minutes against South Africa at Johannesburg in 1902/03. O'Reilly's fifty (above) took 31 minutes.

• • •

When he bowled Hamish Marshall in the second innjngs of the first test at Christchurch, Warne became the eleventh Australian bowler to capture 1000 wickets in first-class cricket. He was the first Australian to achieve the feat since Graham McKenzie did so in 1972. The previous ten to reach 1000 wickets were:

	wkts	*ave*		*wkts*	*ave*
Albert Trott	1674	21.09	Graham McKenzie	1219	26.96
Frank Tarrant	1512	17.49	Jack Walsh	1190	24.55
Clarrie Grimmett	1424	22.28	Sammy Woods	1040	20.81
Ted McDonald	1395	20.76	George Giffen	1022	21.31
George Tribe	1378	20.55	Bruce Dooland	1016	21.98

• • •

There was some extraordinary scoring in the State Shield match between Northern Districts and Wellington at Taupo, as both teams fought to stay in contention for a semi-final spot.

Northern sent Wellington in but saw Chris Nevin and Stephen Fleming reach fifty at the end of four overs and bring up their century partnership after only 9.3 overs. After 15 overs, Wellington were 142-1. Fleming had needed just 29 balls for his fifty and 30 came off one Graeme Aldridge over (6, 6, 4, 3w, 4, 0, w, 6).

Rain ended the innings with the score 267-8 after 32 overs and also interrupted Northern's chase. They finally needed 163 off 20 overs and despite losing both openers for ducks had reached 158-5 with one ball to be bowled. Peter McGlashan, who had yet to face a ball, hit James Franklin over square leg for six to secure a remarkable win.

• • •

Jacob Oram set an unusual record in the first test against Australia at Brisbane when he became the first player in test history to score a century but also go wicketless while conceding one hundred runs in an innings with the ball in the same match. The following New Zealand players both scored and conceded a century in the same test:

R.J. Hadlee	v Sri Lanka	Colombo	1986/87	4-102 & 151*
C.L. Cairns	v India	Hamilton	1998/99	4-107 & 126
C.L. Cairns	v Australia	Wellington	1999/00	109 & 3-110
D.L. Vettori	v Pakistan	Hamilton	2003/04	137* & 1-117
J.D.P. Oram	v Australia	Brisbane	2004/05	126* & 0-116

• • •

There was an unusual incident in the Provincial A match between Wellington and Northern Districts at Lincoln Green. Umpires David Quested and Glenn Holdem awarded Wellington five penalty runs when a Northern player came back on the field and did not notify the umpires. Several warnings had been given beforehand.

Jeff Wilson's comeback to international cricket set two records. Since his last appearance, against Australia at Auckland in March 1993, he had missed 271 of New Zealand's one-day internationals. This put him well ahead of South Africa's Errol Stewart who missed 218 games between 1993/94 and 2002/03.

In terms of time, the gap of 11 years and 331 days was also well ahead of England's Wayne Larkins who had a break of nine years and 266 days between 1979/80 and 1989/90.

• • •

Daryl Tuffey's opening over of the third one-day international at Auckland cost 16 runs and took 14 balls to complete. The first six balls were either no-balls or wides. Bowling to Adam Gilchrist, the sequence was: 4 off a no-ball, nb, nb, nb, w, w, 4, w, 0, w, 0, 0, 0, 0.

In the Champions Trophy in September Zimbabwe's Tinashe Panyangara began the match with a 13-ball over to Marcus Trescothick which included seven wides. None of the legitimate balls were scored from. Under the old ruling, this would have been a maiden over.

• • •

Chris Martin was again in the news with his batting achievements during the season. By the end of the series against Sri Lanka, Martin had batted 32 times in tests without reaching double figures. This placed him well ahead of Zimbabwe's Pommie Mbangwa (25) and South Africa's Cuan McCarthy (24) who also never reached ten at any stage of their careers.

Martin also equalled the all-time test record of most consecutive single figure scores, being unbeaten on 4 when Stephen Fleming declared in the second test against Sri Lanka. This drew him level with India's B.S. Chandrasekhar and one ahead of Bruce Reid of Australia. Chandra also had another sequence of 27 innings without a double figure score.

Martin already held the record of nine consecutive scoreless innings in test cricket.

• • •

In the first test against Australia at Christchurch, New Zealand gained a first innings lead of one run yet still lost by nine wickets. Here is a list of matches which one side won by a large margin after the first innings scores had been within five runs of each other.

			margin
Pakistan (408 & 318) lost to West Indies (410 & 317-2)	Georgetown	1957/58	8 wkts
West Indies (222 & 443-7d) defeated India (222 & 240)	Kanpur	1958/59	203 runs
England (169 & 360) defeated Australia (164 & 160)	Adelaide	1978/79	205 runs
West Indies (224 & 94) lost to England (226 & 93-2)	Bridgetown	2003/04	8 wkts
New Zealand (433 & 131) lost to Australia (432 & 135-1)	Christchurch	2004/05	9 wkts

• • •

The last time that Australia had won a test after the opposition had begun the match with a score as high as New Zealand's 433 was as long ago as 1948. This was the famous occasion at Headingley when Australia became the first team to successfully chase a target of 400 or more in the fourth innings.

England made 496 and declared on the last day at 365-8. Australia replied with 458 and 404-3, Arthur Morris 182 and Don Bradman 173 not out.

• • •

When Marvan Atapattu scored 127 in the first test at Napier he completed his set of centuries against all nine other test playing countries. He joined Rahul Dravid, Gary Kirsten, Sachin Tendulkar and Steve Waugh as the only players to do so.

Atapattu has scored six test double centuries, behind only Don Bradman (12) and Walter Hammond and Brian Lara (7). He also has four pairs to his name, equalling the record held by tailenders B.S. Chandrasekhar, Courtney Walsh and Mervyn Dillon and one more than Chris Martin.

In the second test between New Zealand and Sri Lanka at the Basin Reserve, Chris Martin captured the first six Sri Lankan wickets to fall and when New Zealand batted Chaminda Vaas also took the first six wickets of the innings.

This was the first time in test history (1748 matches) that a bowler from each side had taken the first five opposition wickets to fall (let alone the first six).

• • •

The rescheduling of the Sri Lankan tour meant that the first test at Napier began on 4 April, the first time that any test in New Zealand had begun in that month.

When the second test began on 11 April, it was the latest date that first-class cricket had been played in the capital for 127 years, since Wellington met Nelson (then a first-class side) at the Basin Reserve on 15 and 16 April, 1878.

It was also the latest that first-class cricket had been played anywhere in New Zealand since Auckland and Wellington met at the Auckland Domain on 14 and 16 April, 1900. Auckland scored 84 and 89 but were too good for Wellington who managed just 59 and 62.

A report of the match stated that "the wicket was exceedingly difficult." Scottish-born leg-spinner Robert Neill took eleven wickets in the match. His brother, Tom, a former Auckland player, was one of the umpires.

• • •

The latest that first-class cricket has ever been played in New Zealand was the match between Taranaki and Hawke's Bay at King Edward Park, Hawera in 1892. It began on Saturday 16 April, there was no play, as usual, on the Sunday and the match was completed on the 18th.

Hawke's Bay had the prolific New Zealand batsman Hugh Lusk in their side while Taranaki were captained by George Bayly, who was president of the New Zealand Rugby Union in 1898. Two of his brothers were All Blacks and six brothers played rugby for Taranaki. Four of them played first-class cricket for the province.

• • •

At Brisbane, New Zealand became just the fourth side in test history to make 350 or more batting first and then lose the match by an innings. This short list reads:

England (405 & 251) v Australia (695)	The Oval	1930
West Indies (357 & 319) v Australia (758-8d)	Kingston	1954/55
India (395 & 218) v West Indies (631-8d)	Kingston	1961/62
New Zealand (353 & 76) v Australia (585)	Brisbane	2004/05

• • •

By sending Sri Lanka in to bat in the second test at the Basin Reserve, Stephen Flemimg now trails by just one Clive Lloyd's record as the captain who has inserted the opposition most often in test cricket. It was the 15th time that Fleming had chosen to field first and his record when doing so is six wins, three losses and six draws. Lloyd's record was 10 wins, five draws and just one loss.

• • •

Apart from being the first identical twins to play international cricket, James (the oldest) and Hamish are the only twins of any sort in New Zealand first-class history. Steve and Mark Waugh are the only other twins in international cricket.

Another notable pair of identical twins are Eric and Alec Bedser. Alec was one of England's greatest bowlers and took 236 wickets in 51 tests. Eric played in 457 first-class games over 24 years, mostly for Surrey, scored 14,716 runs and took 833 wickets, but never got to play for England.

During their century partnership in the first test at Napier, James Marshall scored 52 while Hamish went on to a century. The only other occasion when brothers have each reached fifty in the same test innings for New Zealand was when Jeff Crowe (55) and Martin Crowe (83) put on 156 for the third wicket against West Indies at Christchurch in 1986/87.

• • •

This was the first time the Marshall twins had been associated in a century stand in first-class cricket, their previous best being 80 for the first wicket against Wellington in 1998/99. They do, however, have two three-figure partnerships in one-day matches – 112 for the fourth wicket against Otago in 2001/02 and 107 for the second against Auckland in the State Shield Final in 2002/03.

• • •

Brendon McCullum became the eighth New Zealand player to be dismissed for 99 in a test when he was trapped by Sri Lanka's Lasith Malinga at Napier. He was the tenth from any country to be out lbw for 99, the only other New Zealander to suffer the fate being Mark Richardson against Zimbabwe at Harare in 2000/01.

• • •

When the third match against the World XI finished early (a day/night game completed in less than four hours) a 10-overs-per-side exhibition match was arranged for the benefit of the large crowd who had gathered at Hamilton's Westpac Park.

With the bowlers, who were allowed just one over each, generally operating from short run ups, there were some unusual incidents. Daryl Tuffey did a Daniel Vettori impersonation and bowled one ball left-arm while Shane Warne mimicked Merv Hughes.

Craig McMillan hit 63 off 18 balls, with nine sixes, five off Heath Streak's over, while Streak replied with 32 off just 11 balls in the World XI's innings. The match ended in a tie when Kumar Sangakkara was run out by a direct hit from Nathan Astle going for the winning run off the last ball of the game, bowled by Stephen Fleming.

• • •

Because of the problems encountered with the pitch in this game, the one-day international scheduled for Hamilton during the Australian tour was transferred to the Basin Reserve and Northern Districts' remaining home games were moved to Gisborne and Taupo. Northern also relinquished any home games during the second phase of the State Championship.

When Northern qualifed to host the State Shield semi-final against Canterbury, Gisborne and Taupo were ruled out, mainly due to lack of suitable facilities for television coverage, so they opted to play at Eden Park. An offer to play the match in Christchurch was declined.

If that was not enough, when Central won the right to host the final their preferred venue of McLean Park could not be used, as there was no available accommodation in Napier because of a Rod Stewart concert, so the game (and State of Origin the following day) was played at Pukekura Park, New Plymouth.

• • •

The State Shield semi-final was the first time a domestic one-day match had been played at a neutral venue but it was not the first time that a side had been unable to host a game they had won the right to.

During the 1993/94 Shell Cup competition Lancaster Park had been unfit to use because of problems with the outfield. Canterbury had played the semi-final at Hagley Park but wanted to use Lancaster Park for the final.

New Zealand Cricket, however, decided the ground was not ready and the match would be played at McLean Park, the other finalist's ground. Canterbury won the match, notable for Chris Cairns being run out for 99.

Ross Taylor became the fourth player to be dismissed for 99 in a domestic one-day game when he was caught behind off Northern Districts' Graeme Aldridge at Masterton. Four other players have been left on 99 not out. The full list is:

K.R. Rutherford	Otago v Canterbury	Christchurch	1984/85
J.F. Reid*	Auckland v Otago	Alexandra	1985/86
B.A. Edgar*	Wellington v Canterbury	Wellington	1987/88
R.H. Vance*	Wellington v Auckland	Wellington	1988/89
J.W. Wilson	Otago v Central Districts	Dannevirke	1992/93
C.L. Cairns	Canterbury v Central Districts	Napier	1993/94
J.A.H. Marshall*	Northern Districts v Canterbury	Timaru	2001/02
R.L. Taylor	Central Districts v Northern Districts	Masterton	2004/05

** not out*

• • •

When Stephen Fleming declared New Zealand's innings closed on the third day of the second test against Sri Lanka at Wellington, it left seven overs to be bowled for the day. Chris Martin and Kyle Mills opened the bowling but Fleming sprang a surprise when he threw the ball to Lou Vincent (who had just scored a double century) to bowl the fourth over.

Vincent was then replaced by Nathan Astle and then Paul Wiseman took over from Martin to bowl the last over. Next morning James Franklin (who had opened the bowling in the first innings) bowled the first over of the day, meaning six bowlers had been used in the first eight overs of the innings.

• • •

Hamish Marshall began the 2004/05 season without a first-class hundred to his name but by the time he scored a century in the test at Napier he had registered three in six games.

Marshall's maiden century (128) came during Northern Districts run chase when they scored 400-9 to beat Central Districts at Napier. It was Marshall's 50th first-class match and 81st innings. The drought broken, he then scored 146 against Australia at Christchurch and 160 against Sri Lanka.

His innings against Australia was the highest by a New Zealand batsman playing his first test against Australia, equalling Mark Greatbatch's epic unbeaten 146 at Perth in 1989/90.

• • •

Joseph Yovich had played 64 first-class matches, all for Northern Districts, when selected for the Major Association XI which met Sri Lanka at Christchurch. Unfortunately for Yovich, he made a duck on the first day and never got to bowl when rain washed out the rest of the match.

Yovich has now scored 2078 runs for Northern without ever reaching three figures, the most for any province without the aid of a century (his highest score is 99). Richard Hadlee is the only other player to score more than 2000 runs for a province without making a hundred, amassing 2012 runs in 62 games for Canterbury, with a highest score of 93.

• • •

Although Yovich's sequence has been broken, Northern Districts players are still prominent in the list of players who have played most first-class games in their career, all games being for just one team. They are:

90	C.W. Dickeson	*ND*	62	C.J.P. Smith	*CD*	52	B.W. Cederwall	*W*
75	S.J. McCullum	*O*	62	B.G. Cooper	*ND*	52	R.A. Young	*A*
69	D.J. Boyle	*C*	54	L.M. Crocker	*ND*	51	A.R. Knight	*O*
65	M.J.E. Wright	*ND*	53	R.A. Pierce	*CD*			
63	L.W. Stott	*A*	53	R.M. Schofield	*CD*			

Paul Wiseman returned the second best figures in the history of New Zealand first-class cricket when he took 9-13 for Canterbury against Central Districts at Christchurch in January. Only Albert Moss, who took 10-28 (on debut) for Canterbury against Wellington at Hagley Park in 1889/90, has a better analysis.

Chasing an unlikely 466 for victory, Central were 52-2 at the close of the third day, having lost Jamie How to Chris Martin and Peter Ingram to Wiseman, who had 1-1 off five overs.

Next morning Central were bowled out for 122, Wiseman capturing the eight remaining wickets for just 12 runs in 70 balls to finish with figures of 16.4-9-13-9. He took wickets in his 2nd, 7th, 9th, 11th, 13th (2), 15th, 16th and 17th overs, conceding 11 singles and a two.

Canterbury won by 343 runs, their biggest ever victory in terms of a runs margin.

• • •

In the first match against the FICA World XI at Lancaster Park, Stephen Fleming reached his century from just 54 deliveries. This was the fastest one-day century scored in New Zealand at domestic or international level. The fastest are:

balls				
54	S.P. Fleming	New Zealand v FICA World XI	Christchurch	2004/05
65	P.A. de Silva	Auckland v Canterbury	Auckland	1996/97
72	L.G. Howell	Central Districts v Otago	New Plymouth	1996/97
75	C.L. Cairns	New Zealand v India	Christchurch	1998/99
75	C.D. McMillan	New Zealand v Pakistan	Christchurch	2000/01

• • •

Nathan McCullum took four catches in the innings and five in the match for Otago against Auckland at Dunedin, equalling the Otago first-class records for a fielder. Amongst those who had previously performed the feat were McCullum's father, Stu, who did so in 1987/88, also against Auckland.

Otago wicketkeeper Gareth Hopkins was also amongst the records. He took seven catches in an innings for New Zealand A against South Africa A at Centurion and ten in the match for Otago against Canterbury at Dunedin, equalling New Zealand first-class records both times. He later accepted nine catches in the match against Wellington at Queenstown. The previous Otago record for dismissals in an innings had been seven, achieved on ten occasions.

• • •

When Daryl Tuffey dismissed Sri Lanka's Saman Jayantha with the third ball of the Boxing Day match at Eden Park, it was the 19th time he had taken a wicket in his first over in a test or one-day international, eleven times in the first over of a game. He has twice taken two wickets in the first over of a match.

He has performed the feat seven times in tests and on 12 occasions in one-dayers. Full details are on page 44 of the 2003 *Almanack*.

• • •

Rebecca Rolls became the first player from any country to make 100 dismissals in women's one-day internationals when she caught Sri Lanka's Dedunu Silva off Anna Corbin in the World Cup match at Pretoria. Six days later England's Jane Smit also reached the century mark when she caught Haidee Tiffen.

By the end of the tournament Rolls had extended her tally to 107 – 71 catches and 36 stumpings.

• • •

Adam Gilchrist caught the first five batsmen to be dismissed in New Zealand's innings at Christchurch. This was the first time in 2228 one-day internationals that the first five batsmen out had been caught by the same player.

Ricky Ponting recorded the highest individual score in a one-day international in New Zealand when he made an unbeaten 141 at Napier, just going past Glenn Turner's record. The highest innings played in New Zealand are:

141*	R.T. Ponting	Australia v New Zealand	Napier	2004/05
140	G.M. Turner	New Zealand v Sri Lanka	Auckland	1982/83
133*	C.G. Greenidge	West Indies v New Zealand	Christchurch	1986/87
128	A.C. Gilchrist	Australia v New Zealand	Christchurch	1999/00
126*	Shoaib Mohammad	Pakistan v New Zealand	Wellington	1988/89

• • •

Andre Adams produced some spectacular performances for Essex in the county championship in the 2005 season. He blasted the second fastest century of the season after his side had followed on 399 runs behind against Durham. He put on 169 for the eighth wicket with James Foster but could not prevent a Durham victory.

Adams reached three figures off just 76 deliveries with 11 fours and five sixes. He was dismissed two balls later for 103. Shane Warne had taken 72 balls for his maiden first-class century for Hampshire earlier in the season. On his debut for Essex in 2004, Adams recorded his maiden first-class hundred from just 80 balls against Leicestershire.

Adams also achieved the first hat-trick of his career, against Somerset at Taunton. He had Michael Burns caught behind and trapped Sanath Jayasuriya and James Hildreth lbw.

• • •

Azhar Abbas, who played in three State Championship matches for Wellington during the season, had previously appeared in 37 matches in Pakistan domestic cricket since his debut in 1995/96.

He has turned out for Pakistan Railways, Bahawalpur, Multan, Agriculture Development Bank of Pakistan and Sui Northern Gas Pipelines Limited and in 2001/02 represented Rest of Punjab in three games in the Quaid-e-Azam Trophy. His best effort with the ball was 6-38 (and 4-50) for Sui Northern Gas Pipelines Limited against Pakistan Customs at Gaddafi Stadium in 2001/02.

• • •

When Shivnarine Chanderpaul scored 203 not out for West Indies against South Africa at Georgetown, he became just the second player to register a double century in his first test as captain. The only other player to do so is Graham Dowling, who made 239 (then New Zealand's highest individual test innings) against India at Christchurch in 1967/68.

A total of 22 players have scored a century in their first test as captain. The four New Zealand players who have done so are:

107 & 68	G.O. Rabone	v South Africa	Durban	1953/54
239 & 5	G.T. Dowling	v India	Christchurch	1967/68
126	B.E. Congdon	v West Indies	Bridgetown	1971/72
120*	J.J. Crowe	v Sri Lanka	Colombo	1986/87

• • •

Graeme Aldridge established a New Zealand domestic one-day record by capturing 30 wickets in the 2004/05 State Shield. The most wickets in one season are:

	wkts	*ave*	
G.W. Aldridge	30	14.60	2004/05
A.R. Adams	28	13.50	1999/00
J.T.C. Vaughan	25	13.40	1995/96
G.R. Jonas	24	21.12	1995/96
P.A. Hitchcock	24	14.00	1999/00

The 2004/05 season was an eventful one for lower order batsmen. Central Districts' Ewen Thompson scored the first two centuries of his first-class career, both when batting at number eight. He made 102 off 89 balls against Auckland at Eden Park's Outer Oval, coming in at 146-6, and 126 off 96 balls against Canterbury at New Plymouth. He also hit 77 off 80 balls, against Canterbury at Christchurch, coming to the crease at 80-5.

Warren McSkimming came in at 116-7 against Auckland and scored 111, his maiden century, while number ten Bradley Scott, whose previous highest score was just 33, went on to make 96. Shane Bond also registered his maiden first-class hundred batting at number nine, scoring 100 against Northern Districts at Christchurch, coming in with the score 192-7.

• • •

There were also several very large partnerships recorded during the season. McSkimming and Scott put on 208, the third highest for the ninth wicket in New Zealand first-class history. Bond helped Gary Stead add 210, the second highest eighth wicket partnership by two New Zealand batsmen, athough well behind the world record 433 set by Victor Trumper and Arthur Sims at Christchurch in 1913/14.

Jesse Ryder and Neal Parlane put on 310 for Wellington against Central Districts at Palmerston North, the third highest fourth wicket partnership in New Zealand, and in the same match Jarrod Englefield and Ross Taylor put on 301, the fourth highest for the fifth wicket.

Peter Fulton and Neil Broom, who came together at 81-5, put on 293 together for Canterbury against Otago at Dunedin, the highest sixth wicket partnership in the history of New Zealand first-class cricket. It was also the highest partnership for any wicket by either side in the 162 matches between the two provinces since the first in 1863/64.

• • •

Fulton ended with 221 not out and joined Bert Sutcliffe, Roger Blunt, Ken Rutherford, Mark Richardson and Glenn Turner as players who have both a double and triple century to their name.

Fulton's score was also the highest ever by a Canterbury batsman against Otago, surpassing the 204 made in 1925/26 by Arthur Cox in just his second innings for Canterbury. At that time Cox was the youngest player to score a double century in New Zealand first-class cricket.

Cox had made his debut at the end of the previous season and scored 82 against Victoria. He followed up his double century with 87 against Auckland but played only once more after that summer, however, eyesight problems bringing his career to an abrupt end.

• • •

Apart from county matches, New Zealand players in England appeared in a number of other games during the 2005 season. Stephen Fleming captained the PCA Masters XI against Australia at Arundel (and was dismissed by Brett Lee with the first ball of the tour) and also led the MCC against an International XI in a tsunami appeal match at Lord's (making 62 off 59 balls). Chris Cairns played for the International team.

Fleming, Cairns and Scott Styris (39 off 18 balls) all played for an International XI against an Asian XI in another tsunami appeal match at The Oval.

• • •

James and Hamish Marshall became the eighth set of brothers to play one-day international cricket for New Zealand when James made his debut against Australia at Auckland.

The full list is: Brendon and John Bracewell, Jeff and Martin Crowe*, Barry, Dayle and Richard Hadlee*, Matthew and Robbie Hart, Matt and Phil Horne, Geoff and Hedley Howarth*, Hamish and James Marshall*, John and Murray Parker*. *(* signifies played in the same match).*

Craig Spearman took 34 off an over from leg-spinner Stephen Moreton for Gloucestershire against Oxford UCCE at The Parks. Spearman hit 6, 6, 6, 6, 4 and 6, creating an unwanted record for Moreton of most runs off a player's first over in first-class cricket. It was Moreton's only over of the match which ended in a draw after the county set a target of 680 runs.

Spearman eventually retired out for 216 made off just 168 deliveries. Spearman is the only New Zealand player to have been recorded as "retired out" in first-class cricket, having also done so during New Zealand's tour to South Africa in 2000/01.

• • •

Jamie How caught Farveez Maharoof while fielding substitute in the second test against Sri Lanka at Wellington, and, at least for the time being, joins the small list of players who have made a catch in a test for New Zealand without ever actually gaining a test cap.

James Marshall took his first official test catch in the same innings but he had previously taken two as substitute against South Africa in 2003/04.

The other players who have taken a catch as substitute but never gained test selection are: Tim Ritchie (v West Indies 1986/87), Mark Hastings (v Pakistan 1993/94) and Marcel McKenzie (v England 2001/02).

• • •

All but one of the Australian batsmen reached fifty in the two tests against New Zealand prior to Christmas (Michael Kasprowicz being the odd man out). Ten batsmen achieving the feat was a record for a two-match test series, beating the New Zealand effort of eight against India in 1998/99.

• • •

Two Central Districts venues reached landmarks during the season. McLean Park in Napier became the first ground in the association's region to host 50 first-class games when Central met Northern Districts in December.

In March, Pukekura Park in New Plymouth reached the half-century with Canterbury's visit. By the end of the season, Fitzherbert Park in Palmerston North had staged 49 matches.

The most first-class games have taken place at the Basin Reserve in Wellington (372) and Jade Stadium in Christchurch (333).

• • •

Chris Harris batted at number eleven for the first time in a one-day international after being injured in the Chappell-Hadlee Series match at Sydney. Apart from number ten he has batted in all other positions from opener down.

Abdul Razzaq *(Pakistan)* and Paul Strang *(Zimbabwe)* are the only players to have opened and batted in the other nine positions. Adam Parore batted in all positions except ten and eleven.

• • •

Former New Zealand fast bowler Brendon Bracewell opened a cricket academy at the Rathkeale College grounds in Masterton during the season. He had recently returned to the Wairarapa after a stint in Tauranga with visions of lifting Wairarapa cricket back to the standard of the late 1970s when they were the Hawke Cup holders.

With all-weather practice nets, and a full 22-yard run-up for quick bowlers, plus the existing cricket oval, a strategy for coaching and the import of quality young overseas players, Bracewell aims to raise the level of Wairarapa cricket coaching to rival any in the country.

The $80,000 needed to build the practice facility was raised by the Wairarapa Sports Education Trust, Rathkeale College and members of the community.

Tama Canning made his highest score and also produced career best bowling figures in Auckland's opening State Championship match of the season. He became the first player since Grant Bradburn, in 2000/01, to score a century and take five wickets in an innings of the same game. The feat has been achieved only six times in all for Auckland:

A.E. Relf	157	6-64 & 2-48	v Canterbury	1907/08
A.N.C. Snedden	139	5-13 & 2-21	v Hawke's Bay	1920/21
J.T. Sparling	105 & 51	7-98 & 2-13	v Canterbury	1959/60
R.W. Morgan	102 & 52	5-42 & 3-48	v NZ Under 23 XI	1970/71
D.N. Patel	6 & 204	6-117 & 4-116	v Northern Districts	1991/92
T.K. Canning	115	6-44 & 2-28	v Northern Districts	2004/05

Patel's achievement of a double century and ten wickets in the same match is unique in New Zealand first-class cricket.

• • •

The first test betwen Australia and New Zealand at Brisbane provided a very rare instance of separate partnerships of 200 and 100 being achieved by the lower order (i.e. after five wickets were down) in the same innings of a test. Details are:

wkt					
6th	215	L. Hutton & J. Hardstaff, jr	E v A	The Oval	1938
7th	106	J. Hardstaff, jr & A. Wood			
8th	217	T.W. Graveney & J.T. Murray	E v WI	The Oval	1966
10th	128	K. Higgs & J.A. Snow			
6th	216	M.J. Clarke & A.C. Gilchrist	A v NZ	Brisbane	2004/05
10th	115	J.N. Gillespie & G.D. McGrath			

• • •

Richard Collinge's record for the highest score by a number eleven batsmen in test cricket came under threat during the century partnership between Jason Gillespie and Glenn McGrath at Brisbane and less than a month later it was finally overtaken when Sachin Tendulkar and Zaheer Khan put on 133 for the last wicket against Bangladesh.

The highest scores by number elevens in test cricket are now:

75	Z. Khan	India v Bangladesh	Dhaka	2004/05
68*	R.O. Collinge	New Zealand v Pakistan	Auckland	1972/73
62*	A.E.E. Vogler	South Africa v England	Cape Town	1905/06
61	G.D. McGrath	Australia v New Zealand	Brisbane	2004/05
60*	Wasim Bari	Pakistan v West Indies	Bridgetown	1976/77

• • •

Central Districts equalled the biggest winning margin in a domestic one-day match when they defeated Otago by 200 runs at Invercargill. The record is also held by Central and also against Otago, at Cornwall Park in Hastings in 1998/99.

• • •

Chris Gaffaney was dismissed for 99 in the State Championship match against Wellington at the Basin Reserve, the first Otago player to be dismissed twice for that score.

Other New Zealand batsmen to be out for 99 on more than one occasion are Bert Sutcliffe (3), John Wright (3 – all for New Zealand, twice in tests), Gordon Leggat (twice – run out both times), Graham Dowling (twice in one season), Glenn Turner and Roger Twose (2). Mathew Sinclair has been dismissed once for 99 and has also been left 99 not out.

Twelve-year-old Napier schoolboy Matt Nelson achieved the rare feat of capturing five wickets with successive deliveries in an under 13 match for Taradale against Central Hawke's Bay in December.

Nelson, who had recently attended a coaching course run by Dipak Patel, captured his wickets, all bowled, in his fifth over and finished with figures of 6-8. He also hit 54 not out.

• • •

Seven New Zealand batsmen were dismissed lbw in the second innings of the first test against Australia at Christchurch. This equalled the record for test cricket which had been set by England's bowlers against Zimbabwe at Chester-le-Street in 2003.

Eleven New Zealand batsmen were lbw in the game, a test record, surpassing the ten New Zealanders who were dismissed in that fashion at Lahore in 1996/97.

A total of 13 players from both sides were lbw in the test at Christchurch, the all-time record being 17 in the test between West Indies (8) and Pakistan (9) at Port-of-Spain in 1992/93.

• • •

The seven lbw dismissals in one innings was also a New Zealand first-class record, eight instances of six in an innings having been recorded previously (all since 1992/93).

The record for one game is 17 in the match between Canterbury and Auckland at Rangiora in 1993/94. In total, there are 11 instances of 13 or more lbws in one game, and all have occurred since 1991/92.

• • •

Auckland's Natalee Scripps became the first player to capture 100 wickets in the State League when she bowled Canterbury's Beth McNeill at Redwood Park on 17 January. She finished the season with 107 victims. McNeill (76) and Helen Watson (70) are the next highest wicket takers in the competition. Emily Drumm (2515) is by far the highest run scorer.

• • •

Mark Richardson announced his retirement during the season, concluding a career which took him from left-arm spinner and tail-end bat to successful test opener. After a spell in the middle-order, he moved up to open the batting in Otago's last match of the 1999/00 season.

From then until his retirement he scored 6464 runs in 88 first-class matches at an average of 48.31, with 12 centuries (including a triple and a double) and 36 fifties. He ended six runs short of 10,000 for his career.

• • •

Former Otago all-rounder Derek Walker made his first-class umpiring debut during the season, standing in two State Championship matches. Walker played 39 matches for Otago from 1980/81 to 1987/88 and also spent several years in England playing for the Worcestershire second eleven alongside the likes of Dipak Patel and the young Graeme Hick.

Umpires with first-class playing experience have been relatively uncommon over the years in New Zealand but a number of former players have gone on to stand in test matches. They are Eric Tindill and Jack Cowie (who both played test cricket for New Zealand), Steve Dunne, Doug Dumbleton, Dick Torrance, Thomas Cobcroft, Dave Kinsella and Barney Clark. Tindill has the unique record of also playing and refereeing international rugby.

Cobcroft led the New South Wales team in New Zealand in 1895/96 but later represented both Canterbury and Wellington and captained New Zealand in Australia in 1898/99.

OBITUARIES

Gregory Martyn AIM

Born: *Wellington, 4 September, 1933*

Died: *Wellington, 1 April, 2005*

Right-hand batsman, right-arm medium-pace bowler

Top-order batsman Greg Aim played nine matches for Otago and Wellington spread over a period of eight years. He was also very prominent in business and the arts.

Aim was educated at Nelson College and when his father became rector of Otago Boys' High School the family moved to Dunedin. Aim graduated with a Bachelor of Commerce from Otago University in 1955.

While at university, Aim joined Shell Oil New Zealand Ltd, the start of a 34-year career which was to take him to Holland, Zambia and London.

Aim played for Otago Colts (led by Bert Sutcliffe) while still at school and in 1951/52 for Otago in a two-day match against Southland. He also gained selection in the New Zealand Brabin Cup side which played Auckland Colts.

After scoring 105 and 133 in trial matches against North Otago and Southland early in the 1955/56 season, Aim was selected for the Otago Plunket Shield side, playing in all four matches. However, like most of his team mates, he found runs very hard to come by that summer.

He made his debut against Canterbury at Carisbrook the day before Christmas, making 17 and 1. He made his best score of 41 in the second innings against Central Districts at Palmerston North. Coming to the crease on a pair, Aim resisted for 100 minutes but it was not enough to prevent an innings defeat.

Aim returned to first-class cricket in 1960/61 as a member of the Wellington side which met Dennis Silk's MCC team at the Basin Reserve. The home team were routed for 68 in their first innings and fared little better in their second although Aim (31) helped Paul Barton add 68 for the third wicket.

He kept his place, as opening batsman, for the rest of the season which culminated in Wellington winning the Plunket Shield in dramatic fashion at Carisbrook. Otago, who had taken the first innings points, needed only 166 to win in ample time but were bowled out for just 78, giving Wellington the ten points needed to go to the top of the table.

Aim reappeared two years later against Auckland, batting at number eight. but had to withdraw from the next game when his father died. Aim, who batted in spectacles, was described as a stylist who stood tall and enjoyed driving off the front foot. At first-class level, however, he struggled against shorter, faster deliveries that forced him on to the back foot.

Aim played cricket in a number of diverse locations around the world including Lord's, Arundel Castle, village greens in England and grounds in Holland and Zambia. At Oxford, in 1980, he captured all ten wickets in the innings, for 58 runs, for the London New Zealand Club against the Ectopics, and took a double hat-trick while playing for Copperbelt against Livingstone in Zambia.

After his retirement, Aim became involved in many community activities. He was chairman of the Wellesley College board, became the first chief executive of the Hillary Commission for Recreation and Sport and executive chairman of the Wellington City Opera Company. He later played a major role in the formation of the New Zealand Opera Company.

He also served on the management committee of the Wellington Cricket Association and chaired the Wellington-Hutt Valley intercity cricket board, which saw the two associations amalgamate as Cricket Wellington in 1999. He was also patron of the Victoria University Cricket Club.

Aim's record in first-class cricket is:

M	*I*	*NO*	*HS*	*Runs*	*Ave*	*ct*	*Wkts*	*Runs*	*Ave*	*Best*
9	16	2	41	190	13.57	5	0	6	–	–

Mark Albert BEBAN

Born: *Greymouth, 3 February, 1940*

Died: *Wellington, 4 April, 2005*

Right-hand batsman, right-arm off-spin bowler

Mark Beban, thought to be the only Catholic priest to have played first-class cricket in New Zealand, appeared in four matches for Wellington in the 1969/70 season. He died while playing golf, having suffered from heart problems for several years.

He came from a well known West Coast sporting family and was educated at the Greymouth Marist Brothers High School. A good rugby league player and an above average cricketer, he was also a top student.

His father was Jack Beban, who played league for West Coast and the South Island and was known as Westland's "Mr Boxing". His grandfather, Artie Beban, virtually ran wrestling and boxing on the Coast after a notable career as an all-round sportsman.

Young Beban was so promising as an off-spin bowler that, even from the Coast, he made the Canterbury Brabin Cup side. He first represented West Coast in 1956/57, aged just 16, when he took 3-25 against a Canterbury XI whose batting lineup included first-class players Bruce Bolton, Ray Hunt and Dave Crowe. Two weeks later he scored 56 and took five wickets in a match against Buller and also took four wickets against South Canterbury when West Coast won the final of the Canterbury Minor Associations' Cup.

Next season he was named in the Canterbury Minor Associations team for the Plunket Shield trial and then for the South Island Minor Associations against Otago, capturing the prized wicket of Bert Sutcliffe. He took part in the national colts' trial match in December (Merv Wallace captained one side, Lankford Smith the other) and gained selection in the New Zealand Colts team which met Auckland in January. Beban took 5-45 in the second innings to bowl his side to victory with just three minutes remaining. For West Coast against Buller he scored 67 and took 6-33.

Moving to Canterbury University College, he played for West Christchurch-University for two seasons, taking 33 wickets at 11.51 in 1959/60. The club's annual report said "he was the mainstay of the bowling and established himself as the leading spinner in the province."

That summer Beban also gained selection in the New Zealand Colts team which toured New South Wales. He captured 19 wickets at 16.16 on tour including 7-33 against North Coast Colts at Grafton. He also made 86 not out against Far North East Colts at Lismore. Future test batsmen Brian Hastings and Bruce Murray were members of the Colts side. Late in the season, Beban played for New Zealand University against Wellington, scoring an unbeaten 59.

In 1960/61 he played three games for West Christchurch-University, taking twelve wickets, before heading off to the Greenmeadows Seminary in Hawke's Bay to study for the priesthood where his only cricket was to be friendly weekend matches.

The club's report said "Our best wishes go to Mark Beban in his new vocation and we trust that he fully enjoys his new responsibilities. His off spin bowling leaves our team unbalanced and his determined attitude leaves a gap which will be hard to replace."

As an ordained priest, he was a member of the Society of Mary (Marists). He moved to Wellington where he taught at St Patrick's College, Silverstream and, after an absence of nearly eight years from serious cricket, he turned out for St Patrick's College Old Boys in the Wellington senior competition in the 1968/69 season.

The tall, bespectacled Beban gained immediate results with his fast off-spinners, pushed through with little flight, and his 39 wickets saw him included in the Wellington Plunket Shield squad that summer.

Beban made his first-class debut against Otago at the Basin Reserve on Christmas Day 1969. Otago were bowled out for 187 with Beban taking 1-24 off seven overs, dismissing Jack Alabaster. In reply, Wellington were in trouble at 103-8 before Beban and Michael Coles added 42 for the ninth wicket. Otago eventually gained a lead of 35 but the game petered out into a draw on the last day.

Wellington went into their next game without a specialist spinner with the three Bruces – batsmen Bolton, Murray and Smith – being used instead. Beban came back in to the side for the remaining three games having by far his greatest success in the final match against Auckland.

He took 3-96 off 39 overs in the first innings, dismissing Rodney Redmond, John Sparling and John Kemp, and 2-31 in the second, getting Redmond and Kemp again. Reviewing Wellington's season the *Almanack* noted that "spin was given little opportunity."

In 1970/71 St Pat's amalgamated with Midland and won the senior championship in its first year. Beban captured 35 wickets at 14.80 and was twelfth man for Wellington in three games that season. Saturday morning teaching commitments saw him drop out of senior cricket the following year but he continued his involvment in the sport as a district grade schoolboys coach.

He moved to St John's College, Hastings, where he taught from 1976 to 1981, and in 1977 acted as rector for the final term and was vice-rector from 1978 to 1981. He appeared twice for Hawke's Bay in 1977/78.

He was the first principal of Roncalli College in Timaru, when the former St Patrick's High School and Mercy College amalgamated in 1982. In 1996 he returned to Wellington where he was involved in the church's Emmaus Retreat and Spirituality Centre. He was also chairman of the National Association of Principals of Catholic Secondary Schools.

Beban's record in first-class cricket is:

M	*I*	*NO*	*HS*	*Runs*	*Ave*	*ct*	*Wkts*	*Runs*	*Ave*	*Best*
4	5	0	17	28	5.60	3	7	261	37.28	3-96

Trevor William BLAKE

Born: *Whangarei, 13 March, 1937*

Died: *Whangarei, 23 August, 2004*

Right-hand batsman

Trevor Blake, a member of the New Zealand hockey team at the 1964 Tokyo Olympics, played one match for Northern Districts in the 1964/65 season.

He first represented Northland as a 20-year-old in 1957/58. In 1962/63 he made 87 and 33 against Auckland and in 1964/65 had 104 against Waikato, 65 against Poverty Bay and 54 and 42 against Franklin.

That season Blake was called in to the Northern Districts team for the final Plunket Shield match of the summer. Bert Sutcliffe had moved up to partner Wynne Bradburn as opening batsman and Blake took his place in the middle order.

Canterbury batted first and scored 413. In reply Northern were 117-4 when Blake came to the wicket but he lasted only two balls before being bowled by Dick Motz. Northern were dismissed for 226 and made to follow on. Blake came in at number three in the second innings, got off a pair with a single but was then caught by Bryan Andrews off Jack Kiddey's bowling.

The match ended in a draw but the first innings decision was enough to give Canterbury the Plunket Shield by one point from Central Districts.

Blake continued playing for Northland until 1968/69, usually opening the batting. In the 1965/66 season he made 76 against Auckland, whose attack included Bob Cunis and Hedley Howarth, 82 against Auckland B and 92 against E.L. Child's XI. Cunis also played for Child's team, finishing with 0-81.

Blake represented New Zealand at hockey from 1958 to 1964 and coached the New Zealand men's team from 1984 to 1988. He was also a New Zealand selector between 1975 and 1988. He was a life member of both the Northland and New Zealand Hockey Associations and a former Northland player and coach.

New Zealand Hockey chief executive Ramesh Patel described Blake as an "icon" and a "legend" of the sport who would be sadly missed. Patel said that Blake was special as a player himself and as a player who was under him when he coached the New Zealand team at the World Cup in 1988, Patel said that he only had respect for him. He described Blake as an innovative coach who was also a very hard taskmaster.

Northland Hockey chief executive Grant McLeod said Blake would be sorely missed. "He had done everything you could to as a player, selector and coach and was a huge part of Northland hockey," McLeod said.

Roger Dean BROUGHTON

Born: *Gisborne, 7 October, 1958*

Died: *Hiruharama, 25 August, 2004*

Right-hand batsman, right-arm off-spin bowler

Roger Broughton, who played 21 first-class games for Northern Districts as a top order batsman in the 1980s, was electrocuted while working with a crew of lineman on high voltage overhead lines on the East Coast.

Poverty Bay Cricket Association president John Heikell described Broughton as a stylish batsman who stroked the ball sweetly, appearing to caress the ball to the boundary. Broughton played for the High School Old Boys' club in Gisborne and was the backbone of the batting. He had a talented group of partners who assisted him to run up big tallies in the local club competition.

Broughton played some fine innings for Poverty Bay including 115 against Counties in 1981/82, 131 against Midlands in 1983/84 plus 107 versus Thames Valley and 139 against Northland in 1984/85.

He won the Frazer Shield, for the most runs in a club season, four times and was also part of seven Old Boys championship winning teams.

He was seen as an exciting prospect from an early age and, while a third former at Gisborne Boys' High School, he particularly impressed the national coach Martin Horton who was amazed at the ability of one so young. Broughton spent three years in the 1st XI, first making the side while in the fourth form.

The Poverty Bay selectors did not take long to recognise his talent and as a 17-year-old he was picked for Poverty Bay's clash with Hawke's Bay in February 1976 and kept his place in the representative side until 1990/91. The Northern Districts selectors also spotted the talented youngster and picked him for their Brabin Cup and Under 23 sides in 1978/79.

John Childs, who later played for England, was the Poverty Bay coach in 1979/80 and he took Broughton back to England to gain further cricketing experience.

Broughton made 97 against Southern Hawke's Bay in 1977/78 and three seasons later early season scores of 84 against Hawke's Bay and 82 (five sixes) in a one-day game against Midlands saw him introduced into the Northern Districts Shell Trophy side.

He made his debut at Seddon Park against a strong Auckland side who went on to win the competition that year. He made just 7 in his only innings but fared better against Central Districts with scores of 17 and 47. He ended the season with 70 at Lancaster Park, sharing a partnership of 150 with Andy Roberts, still Northern's third wicket record against Canterbury.

Broughton had to wait until part way through the 1982/83 season, however, to reclaim a place in the Northern team. After an uncertain start he blossomed with a memorable hundred against Central Districts at Fitzherbert Park.

Northern had been set 321 to win and shortly after Broughton came to the wicket they were 17-2. Broughton took 50 minutes to get off the mark but did not panic. From then on he scored freely, reaching his only first-class hundred after 204 minutes and hitting 18 fours in his final tally of 122. He put on 139 for the third wicket with John Parker and Northern finally won by four wickets with one over to spare.

Two weeks later, in the Shell Cup Final at Eden Park, Broughton opened the innings and scored 52 off 54 balls. At the end of the season the *Almanack* said "Very solid in defence and not afraid to bat out of a crisis, Broughton proved a hard-hitting batsman and attractive to watch when in stride."

The following season Broughton made just two appearances but returned as an opening batsman in 1984/85 and played in all eight of Northern's Shell Trophy games. However, after scoring 67 and 26 in the first game against Central Districts, he could manage only 318 runs at 21.20. He had as many as seven scores between 4 and 12. Two games in 1986/87 completed his career.

Broughton was a most accomplished soccer player and was a long serving member of the Thistle club. He also joined the Kahutia Bowling Club and in his short time in the game he showed plenty of potential.

Broughton's record in first-class cricket is: *(all games for Northern Districts)*

Season	*M*	*I*	*NO*	*HS*	*Runs*	*Ave*	*100*	*50*	*ct*	*Wkts*	*Runs*	*Ave*
1980/81	3	5	0	70	149	29.80	–	1	3			
1982/83	6	11	0	122	335	30.45	1	–	6	0	28	–
1983/84	2	4	0	39	56	14.00	–	–	1			
1984/85	8	15	0	67	318	21.20	–	2	2	0	4	–
1986/87	2	4	0	11	22	5.50	–	–	–			
TOTAL	**21**	**39**	**0**	**122**	**880**	**22.56**	**1**	**3**	**12**	**0**	**32**	**–**

Broughton's Shell Cup record is:

Season	*M*	*I*	*NO*	*HS*	*Runs*	*Ave*	*100*	*50*	*ct*
1982/83	4	3	0	52	79	26.33	–	1	–
1983/84	2	2	0	11	13	6.50	–	–	1
1984/85	5	5	0	34	72	14.40	–	–	–
1986/87	5	5	0	22	55	11.00	–	–	–
TOTAL	**16**	**15**	**0**	**52**	**219**	**14.60**	–	1	1

Stewart Bruce CATER

Born: *Nelson, 4 February, 1952*

Died: *Ohakune, 5 February, 2005*

Right-hand batsman, right-arm medium-pace bowler

Wellington cricket lost of one of its personalities of the 1970s and 80s when Stew Cater collapsed and died from a heart attack shortly after leaving a wedding in Ohakune. He had turned 53 the previous day and had played a round of golf two days earlier.

Cater played 30 first-class games for Wellington as a barrel-chested medium-fast bowler and big hitting lower order batsman, but for all that his deeds at club level, both on and off the park, earned him wider acclaim.

Bowling big off-cutters, Cater took 339 wickets at an average of 11.70 in 97 matches for Johnsonville, including 9-61 against Tawa in 1979/80. He once took 9-19 for Karori against Kilbirnie during six years for that club in the early 1970s and his overall total of 584 wickets is the eleventh highest in Wellington senior club play.

Cater was a popular personality and entertaining in all aspects of his life. He made lower grade cricketers feel important, gave newcomers confidence and he conducted legendary fielding sessions, which club members queued up to participate in rather than bat or bowl.

Former Johnsonville captain Alan Isaac said he was a delight to play with, managing to get the best out of those around him and always leading from the front. "If you were in his team he made you feel special, but if you were in the opposition you weren't up to much" said Isaac.

Cater was a prolific hitter of sixes in club cricket, prompting leading radio personality Lindsay Yeo to put a 2ZB sticker on the back of his bat. "Cater could hit a ball like Lance or Chris Cairns, as he could hit a golf ball," Isaac also recalled. Cater held forthright views on all manner of things. He was a staunch Labour Party man and he also loved the horses.

Cater played in the Rothmans Under 23 Tournament for three seasons, gaining selection in the eleven which met Wellington in a one-day game in 1973/74. He made his first-class debut the following season, playing in four of Wellington's five Plunket Shield games.

In his first match, against Northern Districts at the Basin Reserve, he took 2-45 and 3-40, dismissing John Parker, Andy Roberts, Rod Fulton and Brian Dunning. At the end of the season the *Almanack* noted that "Cater made a satisfactory debut."

The following season Cater recorded career best performances with both bat and ball. He took 6-32 from 10.6 overs against Canterbury at Lancaster Park as he and Ewen Chatfield (3-44) bowled unchanged and routed the home team for just 82. Barry Hadlee, David Stead, Brian Hastings and Ken Wadsworth were amongst Cater's victims. Earlier in the season, against the same opponents, he had made his highest score of 40.

Having played just once in the previous two seasons, Cater returned to the first-class arena in 1979/80, taking 15 wickets at 17.13 in eight games. His most memorable performance came against West Indies at the Hutt Recreation Ground when Wellington upset the most feared team in the world by six wickets.

Cater (4-35 and 3-54) and Chatfield (6-33 and 7-53) took all twenty West Indies wickets between them, dismissing their opponents for 102 and 143. Bruce Taylor, who went wicketlesss, was the only other bowler the home side used. Wellington were bowled out for 93 themselves in the first innings but an unbeaten 69 from Jeremy Coney guided them home on the third morning.

Cater took 21 wickets in seven games in 1980/81, at times opening the bowling in the absence of Chatfield who was in Australia with the New Zealand team. His best figures that season were 5-71 against Auckland and 4-73 against Northern Districts. Two further matches in 1982/83, when Wellington won the Shell Trophy, rounded off his career.

Cater played in seven Shell Cup matches in the early years of one-day cricket in New Zealand and showed glimpses of his hitting prowess with 37 in 33 minutes, with five fours and a six, against Auckland in 1980/81.

The Nelson-born Cater lived the best part of his last 15 years in Auckland where he owned a fruit and vegetable supermarket.

Cater's record in first-class cricket is: *(all games for Wellington)*

Season	*M*	*I*	*NO*	*HS*	*Runs*	*Ave*	*50*	*ct*	*Wkts*	*Runs*	*Ave*	*5W*	*10W*	*Best*
1974/75	4	5	1	19	26	6.50	–	1	8	191	23.87	–	–	3-40
1975/76	3	5	0	40	43	8.60	–	2	12	266	22.16	1	–	6-32
1976/77	5	7	1	16	35	5.83	–	3	8	340	42.50	–	–	3-16
1977/78	1	–	–	–	–	–	–	1	1	76	76.00	–	–	1-39
1979/80	8	6	1	13	32	6.40	–	2	15	257	17.13	–	–	4-35
1980/81	7	12	0	36	147	12.25	–	4	21	601	28.61	1	–	5-71
1982/83	2	3	1	20	35	17.50	–	–	3	60	20.00	–	–	3-44
TOTAL	**30**	**38**	**4**	**40**	**318**	**9.35**	**–**	**13**	**68**	**1791**	**26.33**	**2**	**–**	**6-32**

Cater's Shell Cup record is:

Season	*M*	*I*	*NO*	*HS*	*Runs*	*Ave*	*ct*	*O*	*M*	*R*	*W*	*Ave*	*Best*	*RPO*
1980/81	5	5	1	37	87	21.75	1	45.4	6	147	8	18.37	4-26	3.21
1982/83	2	2	1	1	1	1.00	–	7	0	66	0	-	-	9.42
TOTAL	**7**	**7**	**2**	**37**	**88**	**17.60**	**1**	**52.4**	**6**	**213**	**8**	**26.62**	**4-26**	**4.04**

Ellis Lynley CHILD

Born: *Whangarei, 23 December, 1925*

Died: *Auckland, 8 May, 2005*

Right-hand batsman, right-arm medium-pace bowler

Ellis Child was a member of a well known Northland sporting family. His son, Murray, represented Northern Districts from 1975/76 to 1986/87 and several other members of the family played for Northland.

Child's first-class career comprised eight matches, for two different sides, in two different seasons, five years apart. His first games were prior to Northern Districts being granted Plunket Shield status. At that time players from the "country" areas had to force their way into the Auckland team to play cricket at first-class level.

Child first played for Northland in 1947/48 and appeared in the annual Town versus Country Plunket Shield trial match for the first time that season,

In January 1949 he took part in the North Island Minor Associations trial match, one of several games organised by the New Zealand Cricket Council who made every effort to look at talent in every corner of the country before the team to tour England was chosen.

In 1952/53 Child impressed with 100 against Auckland Colts at Eden Park and 5-41 against Waikato in a Hawke Cup elimination match. At the end of that season, the New Zealand Cricket Council staged two trial matches prior to selecting the team to tour South Africa later in the year.

Selected for North Island Minor Associations against the South at the Basin Reserve, Child scored 62 not out and 35 and gained inclusion in the final trial at Lancaster Park. Rain ruined the match, however, and Child had little opportunity. Child was one of six players in the final trial without first-class experience. The others, Jack Alabaster, John Beck, John Guy, Noel Harford and Ian Sinclair, all went on to play for New Zealand.

The following season Child took eight wickets in a three-day game for Northern Districts against Auckland (not first-class) and gained selection in the Auckland Plunket Shield side, retaining his place throughout the summer.

He made his debut at Lancaster Park on Christmas Day, 1953 and went on to capture 5-71 from 39 overs in Canterbury's first innings. Gordon Leggat, Zin Harris and Sam Guillen were among his victims.

He also contributed valuable runs, coming to the crease in the first innings at 102-5 and adding 74 with Tom Hambrook. In the second innings Canterbury had Auckland 71-6 with 90 minutes remaining but Child (21) and Hambrook, again, saved the day.

Auckland travelled to Dunedin to play Otago and Child continued his fine form with the ball. He took 4-54 off 28 overs and 5-37 off 24 to bowl Auckland to a 32 run win after Otago had needed only 140 for victory. In Auckland's second innings he also shared a valuable 59 run partnership with Bryce Postles for the sixth wicket, Auckland being only 60 ahead when he came in to bat.

Child finished his first season with a satisfactory 18 wickets at 25.44 and 155 runs at 19.37 but had to wait five years before he received another chance at first-class level, this time for Northern Districts who had come in to the Plunket Shield competition in 1956/57.

In his three matches for Northern he was used sparingly while two spinners, Tom Puna and Allen Lissette, did most of the bowling. Child took only three wickets but was extremely economical, his 67 overs costing just 117 runs. At the end of the season he took 8-16 for Northland in a match against Waikato, having had match figures of 11-120 against the same side two years earlier in a Hawke Cup match.

Child continued to play for Northland until 1962/63, having scored 107 against King Country the previous season. He was captain on many occasions and later selector. In April 1966 he led his own eleven (which included Bob Cunis) against Northland at Whangarei's Kensington Oval.

Child's early years were spent on the family farm in Tangihua. Horses played a big part in his life not only on the farm but also for riding to school. Later, he also rode his horse to gymkhanas in which he competed, as there was no other form of transport.

He was an all-round sportsman and coached his four sons at rugby and cricket. He also coached and selected many Northland age-group teams. He won several Northland age-group tennis titles and it was while playing tennis in Dargaville that he first became involved in competitive cricket.

Mid Western was playing cricket on the adjacent field and Child was called on to fill in. He did so well that he decided to turn his focus to cricket. He played for several of the clubs in the Mid Western competition, often riding his horse to Three Mile Bush to play some matches.

Sheep dog trials also played a big part in his life from an early age when he skipped school to run his dog at the local Maungakaramea trials. He won numerous Northland titles and at national level he became president and life member and judged New Zealand and North Island events as well as test matches and the television programme *A Dog's Show*.

He came second in the Northland Centre championships in 2005 and gained placings at the Maungakaramea and Papakura trials just three weeks before his death. Child's son, Graham, was a New Zealand hockey representative.

Child's record in first-class cricket is:

M	*I*	*NO*	*HS*	*Runs*	*Ave*	*ct*	*Wkts*	*Runs*	*Ave*	*Best*	*5WI*
8	13	1	41	230	19.16	5	21	575	27.38	5-37	2

Douglas Stewart CLARKE

Born: *Kaponga, 30 July, 1932*

Died: *Morrinsville, 31 January, 2005*

Left-hand batsman, wicketkeeper

The second eldest of five famous brothers, wicketkeeper batsman Doug Clarke played six matches for Northern Districts in the late 1950s and early 60s. Although always in the shadow of Eric Petrie as far as the wicketkeeping role was concerned, Clarke was considered good enough to play as a specialist batsman in the 1958/59 season.

Clarke first appeared for Waikato as an 18-year-old in 1950/51. His best efforts over the years included 87 against RNZAF in 1954/55, 87 against King Country in 1956/57 and 69 against Nelson in a Hawke Cup Challenge in 1958/59. He also captained the side on occasions.

Clarke made his first-class debut against Auckland at Eden Park in January 1958, when Petrie was unavailable. He scored 3 and 16, dismissed each time by Johnny Hayes, who took eleven wickets in Auckland's innings victory.

The following season he appeared in four matches for Northern, playing as a batsman while Petrie kept wicket. His best effort was 28 in the opening match against Central Districts at Palmerston North, putting on 72 for the fifth wicket in 122 minutes with Doug Gray. Omitted for the second game, he returned for the remaining three fixtures but could accumulate only 33 further runs.

One more match against Canterbury at the end of the 1960/61 season, when Petrie was playing for New Zealand, completed Clarke's first-class career. On this occasion Clarke made a valuable 27 in Northern's second innings, putting on 55 for the eighth wicket with Stuart Veitch. Northern eventually won by just ten runs.

Clarke appeared in 43 games for the Waikato rugby team from 1953 to 1962. Unlike his brothers, Don and Ian, Doug never played for the All Blacks although, according to former teammate Colin Meads, it was not because of lack of ability. "He was one of the unlucky ones who never got the big break at the top level but having two brothers there already made it awkward," Meads said.

When he retired from rugby in 1968, Clarke took up the whistle for the next fifteen years, rising to provincial level and eventually becoming president of the Waikato Rugby Referees' Association.

After becoming a Morrinsville sub-union delegate, Clarke quickly rose in the ranks of the Waikato Rugby Union, becoming president in 1995. After his time as union president, Clarke became the chairman of a sub-committee that was in charge of planning changes for Hamilton's Rugby Park.

Former mayor David Braithwaite said Clarke was instrumental in revamping the ground, heading the Waikato Regional Stadium Trust through the initial stages. "He was the catalyst in the 1990s in beginning the process which culminated with Waikato Stadium. Doug Clarke was a good man and I'll remember him for his decency, his courtesy and his integrity," Braithwaite said.

Doug and Don Clarke played together for Northern Districts against Auckland in 1957/58. With their three brothers, Brian, Graeme and Ian, they grew up on the family farm near Morrinsville. They all played rugby for Waikato during the 1950s and, on one occasion, against Thames Valley at Te Aroha in 1961, all five played together in the same game.

Clarke's record in first-class cricket is:

M	*I*	*NO*	*HS*	*Runs*	*Ave*	*ct*
6	11	3	28	107	13.37	3

Ian Alexander COLQUHOUN

Born: *Wellington, 8 June, 1924*

Died: *Paraparaumu Beach, 26 February, 2005*

Right-hand batsman, wicketkeeper

Ian Colquhoun kept wicket for Central Districts in 53 matches over a period of eleven years and played in two tests against England in the 1954/55 season. He died at his home while indulging in one of his favourite pastimes, watching cricket on television.

Colquhoun was a Manawatu sporting legend in cricket and rugby, as a player, coach and selector and not least as a formidable Palmerston North Boys' High School teacher. He taught at Boys' High for 36 years and rose to be deputy head and acting rector.

Colquhoun and wife Betty looked after thousands of boys who passed through the school's boarding establishment, College House. They were the house manager and matron from 1955 to 1984. "Coke" Colquhoun simultaneously ran College House, was deputy rector and coached the First XV, with which he undertook tours to Australia, Taiwan, Europe and the United States. He became a world authority on schoolboy rugby, visiting England and South Africa to give speeches on the subject.

He was educated at Rongotai College, where he was deputy head prefect and was in the First XI for all five years. He went on to teacher's college and soon found himself in the Wellington rugby team that caused a shock by upsetting Charlie Saxton's all-conquering Kiwis side in 1946.

Colquhoun studied at Otago University where he represented the Otago rugby team in 1947 under famous coach (and former first-class cricketer) Vic Cavanagh. A first five-eighth, Colquhoun played in Otago's Ranfurly Shield win against Southland and went on to play 13 games for Manawatu from the High School Old Boys' club.

He did home service in the army, moving to Boys' High as a physed teacher in 1948. He earned a feared reputation as a strict disciplinarian but mellowed and saw corporal punishment at the school almost phased out. He was one of the most successful secondary schools coaches, conducting coaching clinics in Britain in 1967 while following the All Black tour.

Above all, however, Colquhoun will be remembered as a stalwart member of the Central Districts team, captaining the side from 1960/61. He was tall for a keeper, but was slick, as he showed when standing up to sharpish bowlers like Harry Cave and Don Beard.

In December 1948 he played for West against East in the Wellington Minor Associations game, one of several trial matches arranged prior to the selection of the New Zealand team to England in 1949. By the early 1950s he was Manawatu's regular keeper and had registered scores of 91 versus Ian Cromb's XI, 72 against Nelson and 60 against Fiji.

Colquhoun was almost thirty years old when he entered first-class cricket, taking over from regular keeper Graham Botting who had moved to Otago. His first game was against Wellington at the Basin Reserve and started on Christmas Day, 1953. Dave Crowe was his first victim. Central went on to win the Plunket Shield for the first time that season.

The following summer Colquhoun's consistent form for Central saw him succeed Frank Mooney as New Zealand wicketkeeper. It was the first time in New Zealand's 25-year test history that someone other than a Wellington player had been behind the stumps. Ken James (11 tests), Eric Tindill (5), Mooney (14) and John Reid (1) had done the honours until then.

Colquhoun's debut was at Carisbrook against Len Hutton's side which had just triumphed in Australia. England won by eight wickets with Colquhoun catching Hutton in both innings and registering 0 and 1 (both unbeaten) batting at number eleven.

The second test at Eden Park appeared to be evenly balanced when England were 201-8 and then 246 all out in reply to the home team's 200. However, New Zealand were routed for just 26 in 104 minutes on the third afternoon with Frank Tyson, Brian Statham, Bob Appleyard and Johnny Wardle proving almost unplayable. Colquhoun caught Trevor Bailey and Appleyard but registered a pair, one of three New Zealand batsmen to do so.

Colquhoun did not gain national honours again but did play in one of the two trial matches at the end of the 1957/58 season prior to the selection of the team to tour England. The experienced Eric Petrie was chosen along with John Ward who had not even gained Canterbury selection that season and, in fact, made his first-class debut in one of the trials.

Although Colquhoun's batting record was modest, he did come to light on several occasions. He put on 76 for the ninth wicket against Canterbury with Ron Brown in 1953/54 and 79 against Otago in 1956/57, again for the ninth wicket and again with Brown, registering his career best 44 not out. He also made 44, in 33 minutes, against Northern in 1962/63.

His most notable effort with the bat, however, was at Eden Park in 1959/60. Auckland had led by four runs on the first innings and Central were 154-9 when Colquhoun came to the wicket to join Gary Bartlett. The pair added 51 by stumps and on the third morning extended their partnership to 133 in just 99 minutes before Colquhoun was run out for 32. Bartlett (who never did score a first-class hundred) was left stranded on 99.

Auckland now unexpectedly required 284 to win but were bowled out for 204 with Don Beard taking six wickets. Colquhoun was injured while batting and did not keep in the innings and missed the next match.

His place was taken by left-arm pace bowler Robin Schofield while Trevor Barber kept wicket. Ironically, when Colquhoun retired at the end of the 1963/64 season, he was succeeded by Schofield who by now had turned himself into a wicketkeeper.

Colquhoun was a leading light in establishing the Central Districts Trust, was Central's executive officer from 1984 to 1988, a selector for 13 seasons, president in its 50th season, a life member and was patron when he died. He was also a national selector and later New Zealand Cricket Council president from 1989 to 1991.

He settled at Paraparaumu Beach after his retirement in 1984, becoming a pennants selector and president of the Paraparaumu Beach Golf Club and was involved in bringing Tiger Woods to the 2002 New Zealand Open which was played at the course. He was awarded the Queen's Service Medal. He was one of the *Almanack's* Players of the Year in 1963.

Colquhoun's record in first-class cricket is:

Season	*M*	*I*	*NO*	*HS*	*Runs*	*Ave*	*ct*	*st*
1953/54	4	7	2	37	55	11.00	6	2
1954/55	7	12	3	35	76	8.44	15	2
1955/56	3	5	3	10*	20	10.00	6	3
1956/57	6	7	2	44*	144	28.80	5	5
1957/58	6	8	4	17*	49	12.25	15	2
1958/59	5	9	3	35	69	11.50	8	3
1959/60	5	8	4	32	71	17.75	10	3
1960/61	6	9	6	25*	86	28.66	11	2
1961/62	3	5	2	22	31	10.33	10	–
1962/63	6	8	3	44	127	25.40	8	3
1963/64	6	7	1	27	40	6.66	14	3
TOTAL	**57**	**85**	**33**	**44***	**768**	**14.76**	**108**	**28**

For	*M*	*I*	*NO*	*HS*	*Runs*	*Ave*	*ct*	*st*
NZ (Tests)	2	4	2	1*	1	0.50	4	–
CD	53	79	31	44*	730	15.20	102	28
NZ XI	1	1	0	2	2	2.00	2	–
North Island	1	1	0	35	35	35.00	–	–
TOTAL	**57**	**85**	**33**	**44***	**768**	**14.76**	**108**	**28**

Gordon Graeme COULL

Born: *Christchurch, 15 March, 1928*

Died: *Christchurch, 1 October, 2004*

Right-hand batsman, slow left-arm bowler

Graeme Coull played eight matches for Canterbury spread over a period of eight seasons, being recalled for two final matches six years after his previous outings.

After attending Medbury School he went on to Christ's College. He was in the First XI for three years, the last two as captain, the First XV in 1946 and was also in the shooting team, gaining third place in the Imperial Challenge Shield. He was Head Prefect in 1946 and was awarded the Ormsby Medal. He graduated with an Agricultural Science degree from Lincoln University in 1951.

Coull gained selection in the Canterbury Brabin Cup side after leaving school and in April 1949 was a member of the New Zealand University side, batting at number three, which played Wellington at Kelburn Park. The following season he captained the Varsity side (which included Murray Chapple and Zin Harris) against Canterbury.

In 1952 he left for England where he travelled, worked on farms and played cricket for the London New Zealand Club. On his return he gained selection in the Canterbury Plunket Shield team, making his debut at the Basin Reserve.

Coull was lbw to John Reid for a duck in his first innings and in the second came to the wicket with the score 15-4, following a devastating opening spell from Bob Blair. Coull helped Murray Chapple add 38 before he was out for 13. Two single figure scores against Auckland followed.

Canterbury won the Plunket Shield under Ray Dowker in 1955/56 and Coull played in three of the matches which were all won outright. He made 31 in the second innings total of 122-4 in a six wicket win against Auckland and 45 against Wellington, putting on 90 for the second wicket with Jack D'Arcy.

In the last match of the season, against Central Districts at Napier, Coull came to light with the ball. Having previously bowled just six overs in first-class cricket he took 3-26 in the first innings and 4-58 in the second. He captured Central's last three wickets to give Canterbury victory by 16 runs with just seven minutes remaining.

With a number of leading players absent with the New Zealand team in South Africa in 1961/62, Canterbury recalled several past representatives. Coull was one who was tried, as opening batsman, but he managed just 32 runs in four innings.

Coull's interest in cricket continued as a member of the St Albans Club and also with the Valley of Peace Cricket Club. He and his friends Orm Hutchinson and John Waters were the organising committee of the club leading up to and after its incorporation in 1955 until 1996.

Valley of Peace is a private cricket club in Hoon Hay valley, just out of Christchurch. It was founded in 1928 by Harry Waters, who owned cinemas in the city, for his staff who were unable to play sport on Saturdays and who were not able to use council parks for sport on Sundays. It is situated on a very small ground described by many as being more English than the English village greens.

The club plays every Sunday after mid-January and on occasional Sundays before Christmas. Former New Zealand captain Graham Dowling is the current secretary while other players such as Zin Harris and Bruce Irving have also been involved.

Coull was employed by Dalgety & Co before moving to a farm at West Melton in 1966, where he remained until retiring to the city. In 1977 he was elected a Fellow of Christ's College, representing the Old Boys' Association, and held this position for 18 years until his retirement in 1995.

He served on the school committee during his time on the board and in 1979 was also appointed to the building and planning committee where he was involved with the construction of the administration building, the extension to the art department and library, and the new swimming pool complex.

Coull's record in first-class cricket is:

M	*I*	*NO*	*HS*	*Runs*	*Ave*	*ct*	*Wkts*	*Runs*	*Ave*	*Best*
8	15	0	45	162	10.80	4	7	148	21.14	4-58

Raymond Thomas DOWKER

Born: *Christchurch, 6 July, 1919*

Died: *Christchurch, 17 December, 2004*

Right-hand batsman

Ray Dowker, who did not enter first-class cricket until he was aged 30, played 24 games for Canterbury. He captained the side against West Indies and Australia, led Canterbury to a Plunket Shield title and was one of the few non-internationals to be recognised by the *Almanack* in its Players of ther Year awards.

Having played senior cricket since 1943/44, Dowker finally got the chance for higher honours when Walter Hadlee was unavailable for the final Plunket Shield match of the 1949/50 season, against Otago at Carisbrook. Dowker scored 32 in his only innings, dominating a first wicket partnership of 49 with Gordon Leggat.

When Hadlee returned for the next game, against Bill Brown's Australian team, Dowker retained his spot with the New Zealand captain dropping down to number three.

Next season Dowker made 56 and 71 against Auckland at Eden Park in a dramatic match won by the home side with one wicket and one over to spare. An injured Merv Wallace, at number eleven, scored the winning run after the ninth wicket had fallen with the scores level.

Dowker, however, was not so successful at other times and after two matches in 1951/52 did not gain selection in the Plunket Shield side for two years, missing eleven games and only returning for the last match of 1953/54 against Fiji.

Undeterred by his non-selection, Dowker finally established himself in the Canterbury side in the 1954/55 season, by then aged 35, scoring 366 runs at 45.75 in the four Plunket Shield matches. Now batting in the middle order, he began the season with 74 and 47 against Otago, top scoring in both innings. His second knock included 22 off one over from test leg-spinner Alex Moir.

Scores of 8 and 30 against Central Districts and 35 and 0 versus Wellington followed before Dowker once again showed his liking for Eden Park, scoring 122 and 50 against Auckland. In the first innings he came to the wicket at 69-3 and was out at 246-9, having batted for 203 minutes with 18 fours. In the second innings he was forced to bat with a runner but reached 50 before being run out.

The *Almanack* named him as its Batsman of the Year for what it described as "his consistency and prominent position in the season's batting figures". His 386 runs were headed only by two of New Zealand's finest players, Bert Sutcliffe and John Reid. The *Almanack* described Dowker as "a sound and attractive right-hand batsman who can generally be depended upon for some runs in a crisis".

Next season Dowker was appointed Canterbury captain, taking over from Zin Harris who was with the New Zealand team in Pakistan and India. Canterbury romped to victory in the Plunket Shield competition, winning all four games outright, while Dowker showed consistency with the bat.

He scored half-centuries against Auckland and Central Districts but saved his best for the match against West Indies, top scoring with 74 against an attack which included Sonny Ramadhin and Gary Sobers. Canterbury made 227 and were 25-0 facing a deficit of 130 when rain washed out the last day's play.

Dowker played one more season, again as captain, before announcing his retirement during the last game of the summer against the touring Australian side led by Ian Craig. Dowker scored 26 (bowled by Richie Benaud) and was unbeaten on 42 in the second innings which ended leaving the Australians to score 222 in 160 minutes. They got the runs with ten minutes to spare, Benaud hitting 75 not out in just 70 minutes.

The *Press* described Dowker as "a neat batsman, a safe one, and one more gifted than most at finding and exploiting gaps in the field." Of his captaincy they said "His field placing is of a particularly high order and he is a cheerful personality which means much to a team."

During the match against Auckland in the 1955/56 season, Dowker persuaded Murray Chapple to put his usual slow spinners to one side and try something different. Chapple responded with some pacy and deceptive left-hand swerves. The plan worked with Auckland collapsing from 33-0 to be all out for 115 and Canterbury gained an unexpectedly comfortable victory after being behind on the first innings.

A stalwart of the Lancaster Park club, Dowker's senior career extended to 1968/69. By then he was nearing his fiftieth birthday but was still able to record a top score of 65 not out. He totalled almost 10,000 runs and averaged 35 in 223 first grade matches, hitting 16 centuries and 46 half-centuries. He also captured 38 wickets at reasonable cost.

Shortly after his retirement the *Press* wrote that Dowker had never been a player to thrill onlookers with huge sixes or a flurry of brilliant strokes but his worth as a batsman was reflected in his records,

However, there were exceptions. In 1950 Sydenham batted all of the first day and for 90 minutes into the second to score 360 in what became a first innings contest. Lancaster Park knocked the runs off just after tea, with Dowker making his highest score of 208.

When he retired in 1969 Dowker had scored more runs than any other player in post-war club cricket with the most centuries and most appearances.

He had first played senior cricket for Christchurch High School Old Boys but this team was so well supplied with batsmen that he often failed to get a bat, so at Ian Cromb's invitation he joined Lancaster Park.

A versatile sportsman, Dowker was also a junior provincial golf champion, represented Canterbury at tennis in 1949 and 1950, played on the wing for Canterbury soccer sides from 1945 to 1950 and was three times selected for South Island. He was also a skilled table tennis player, a semi-finalist in Canterbury snooker championships and got himself down to a single figure golf handicap within twelve months of taking up the sport.

Dowker's record in first-class cricket is: *(all games for Canterbury)*

Season	*M*	*I*	*NO*	*HS*	*Runs*	*Ave*	*100*	*50*	*ct*	*Wkts*	*Runs*	*Ave*	*Best*
1949/50	2	3	0	32	52	17.33	–	–	–				
1950/51	3	6	0	71	155	25.83	–	2	4				
1951/52	2	4	1	24*	41	13.66	–	–	–				
1953/54	1	2	0	35	61	30.50	–	–	1				
1954/55	5	10	0	122	386	38.60	1	2	4				
1955/56	5	9	2	74	271	38.71	–	3	5				
1956/57	6	9	2	42*	181	25.85	–	–	2	3	47	15.66	2-25
TOTAL	**24**	**43**	**5**	**122**	**1147**	**30.18**	**1**	**7**	**16**	**3**	**47**	**15.66**	**2-25**

Douglas Philip DUMBLETON

Born: *Wellington, 27 April, 1918*

Died: *Mt Maunganui, 4 March, 2005*

Right-hand batsman, right-arm medium-pace bowler

Medium-pace bowler Doug Dumbleton played in one match for Wellington in 1947/48 but is best known as a first-class umpire who stood in two test matches during the 1960s.

Dumbleton's only appearance in first-class cricket came in Wellington's final Plunket Shield match of the 1947/48 season against Auckland at Eden Park. A Verdun Scott century helped Auckland to reach 299 with Dumbleton, who opened the bowling, taking 2-86 from 32 overs.

His victims were opening batsman Ivan Wyatt and Don Taylor, who was caught by 44-year-old Stewie Dempster, playing the last match of his illustrious 26-year career. In the second innings Dumbleton had 0-47 off 18 overs and caught Merv Wallace. He made 1 not out batting at number eleven.

Dumbleton stood in 17 first-class matches, all but one at the Basin Reserve. His first appointment was the Plunket Shield match between Wellington and Otago at the Basin Reserve in 1953/54 and in 1957/58 he officiated in the North Island versus South Island match, a trial for the 1958 tour of England.

In 1962/63 he stood in the second test between New Zealand and England and the following season in the first test against South Africa. Trevor Martin was his fellow umpire on each occasion. His final match was the Plunket Shield game between Wellington and Auckland in January 1969.

He was a life member of the Hutt Valley Umpires' Association and when Wellington and Hutt Valley umpires combined he was made a life member of the Wellington Association. He was also a vice-president of Cricket Wellington.

Dumbleton played club cricket for Kilbirnie and was an old boy of Rongotai College. A professional soldier, he graduated from Duntroon Military College and during the war served with the artillery in the Middle East where he rose to the rank of major. He took part in many of the divisional matches which were played during the hostilities.

He opened the bowling for the New Zealand Services team in England in 1945 playing with and against the likes of Martin Donnelly, Ken James, Ted Badcock, Len Hutton, Cyril Washbrook, Bill Edrich and Walter Hammond.

Dumbleton stood in the following first-class matches:

1953/54 Wellington v Otago
1953/54 Wellington v Fiji
1957/58 North Island XI v South Island XI
1958/59 Wellington v Northern Districts
1958/59 Central Districts v Otago*
1959/60 Wellington v Otago
1960/61 Wellington v Auckland
1961/62 Wellington v Otago
1962/63 Wellington v Central Districts
1962/63 New Zealand v England *(2nd Test)*
1963/64 Wellington v Canterbury
1963/64 New Zealand v South Africa *(1st Test)*
1964/65 Wellington v Auckland
1964/65 Wellington v Northern Districts
1965/66 Wellington v Canterbury
1966/67 Wellington v Northern Districts
1968/69 Wellington v Auckland

** At Trafalgar Park, Nelson. Others at the Basin Reserve.*

Douglas John GRAY

Born: *Auckland, 22 March, 1936*

Died: *Matamata, 6 September, 2004*

Left-hand batsman, right-arm medium-pace bowler

Doug Gray was a member of the very first Northern Districts team in 1956/57, gained North Island selection and gave many years of service as coach to junior cricketers in the area.

He was just 16 when he first represented Waikato, in a Hawke Cup elimination match against Northland in the 1952/53 season, and became a regular in the side in the seasons leading up to Northern Districts' inclusion in the Plunket Shield.

In 1954/55 18-year-old Gray appeared in two matches for Northern who played three-day games (not first-class) against Auckland, Canterbury and Central Districts as part of their efforts to gain first-class status. Their bid for inclusion for the 1955/56 season was rejected but the following year their application was granted. Northern met Auckland and Wellington that season with Gray appearing in both games.

Northern's first Plunket Shield match began on Christmas Day, 1956 at Seddon Park. Eric Petrie won the toss and the home side batted, putting up a fair display. Jim Everest registered Northern's first fifty and he was followed by Gray who made 58 in 223 minutes. Northern finished with 258 and bowled Auckland out for 144 but rain ruined the game.

After this promising start, Gray's form fell away although late in the season he made 38 (run out), top score in Waikato's dismal 93 against Ian Craig's Australian team. The visitors' attack was made up of Ian Meckiff, Ron Gaunt, Johnny Martin and Richie Benaud.

Gray reappeared for Northern two years later, again showing glimpses of potential but, apart from one occasion, unable to register a score of note. He began the season well enough with an unbeaten 74 in 225 minutes against Central Districts at Palmerston North. The last five Northern batsmen scored just six runs between them, denying Gray the chance of a century.

Although he had scored only 143 runs at 20.42 in four Plunket Shield games, the New Zealand selectors, Giff Vivian, Jack Newman and John Reid, included Gray in the North Island side to meet the South at the Basin Reserve. The match was staged prior to the arrival of the MCC team from Australia who were coming to play two test matches. Gray scored 18, helping Northern team mate Dave Donald add 51 for the third wicket, and 6, falling to test spinners Ian Leggat and Alex Moir.

Gray played in all five of Northern's matches the following season but could total only 137 runs, with a highest of 33 against Canterbury. He continued to play for Waikato until the 1963/64 season.

He was convenor of selectors of the Northern Districts junior secondary school team from 1977/78 to 1985/86 and then for the under 16s from 1986/87 to 1992/93. He also coached most of these teams at their North Island tournaments.

Players in his teams who went on to International honours included Grant Bradburn, Bryan Young, Murphy Su'a, Shane Thomson, Brendon Julian, Mark Bailey, Matthew Hart, Robbie Hart, Matthew Bell, Gareth Hopkins and Daniel Vettori. He also served on the Northern Districts Junior Control Board for many years.

Despite being in the shadow of Northern Districts team mate Don Clarke, Gray still managed five matches for the Waikato rugby team as fullback and goalkicker between 1956 and 1959, also playing in two All Black trial games.

Gray's record in first-class cricket is:

Season	*M*	*I*	*NO*	*HS*	*Runs*	*Ave*	*100*	*50*	*ct*
1956/57	5	9	2	58	123	17.57	–	1	3
1958/59	6	11	1	74*	181	18.10	–	1	4
1959/60	5	9	1	33	137	17.12	–	–	2
TOTAL	**16**	**29**	**4**	**74***	**441**	**17.64**	–	2	9

For	*M*	*I*	*NO*	*HS*	*Runs*	*Ave*	*100*	*50*	*ct*
ND	14	26	4	74*	403	18.31	–	2	7
ND/CD	1	1	0	14	14	14.00	–	–	2
North Island	1	2	0	18	24	12.00	–	–	–
TOTAL	**16**	**29**	**4**	**74***	**441**	**17.64**	–	2	9

Julian Hugh Playfair HOUGHTON

Born: *Christchurch, 16 February, 1931*

Died: *Masterton, 6 October, 2004*

Right-hand batsman, wicketkeeper

Although his cricket career at first-class level was brief, Jules Houghton does have the distinction of playing in both a Plunket Shield winning side and a team which won the Ranfurly Shield.

Houghton attended Nelson College where he was in the First XI from 1947 to 1949 and the First XV in the last two years. He made his debut for Marlborough in 1952/53, scoring 70 in 77 minutes against Nelson in the Newman Shield match. Playing for Spring Creek (made famous years later by Lance Cairns and earlier the home of Fen Cresswell), Houghton gained selection for Central Districts the following season.

Central's opening Plunket Shield match began at the Basin Reserve on Christmas Day. Wellington were bundled out for just 133 and Central replied with 293-9 before Harry Cave declared. Houghton made just one run and was not used in the second innings when Central made 132-7, chasing 152 in 81 minutes.

In their next game Central defeated Auckland by 141 runs at Eden Park but Houghton could manage only a single in each innings. Otago were edged out by just five runs at Pukekura Park, Houghton this time scoring 2 and 0, dismissed both times by Alex Moir, who took fifteen wickets in the match.

For the last game of the season, against Canterbury. Houghton was replaced by Bruce Hamilton, who was making his debut. Central won by five wickets, giving them the Plunket Shield for the first time.

Houghton appeared in the Central Districts trial at Blenheim the following November but scored only 2 and 3. A week later at the same venue, though, he made 106 against Nelson in a Hawke Cup elimination fixture.

He continued to play for Marlborough until 1957/58 and, after a short spell in New Plymouth, moved to Masterton, where he turned out for Wairarapa from 1960/61 until 1967/68. At various times he was captain and selector of the Wairarapa team and later took up umpiring. A stock agent, he became manager of the Masterton branch of Wrightson NMA.

A five-eighth, Houghton played rugby for Canterbury from 1950 to 1952 and, as a 19-year-old in his first season, was a member of the team which defeated Otago 8-0 at Carisbrook to lift the Ranfurly Shield. Unfortunately for him, he was also in the side that lost the Shield 3-0 to Wairarapa in their first defence shortly afterwards.

He was forced to return to the family farm near Blenheim, after an accident to his father. and represented Marlborough from 1953 to 1956, sometimes captaining the side. In his last season he played for the combined Marlborough-Nelson-Golden Bay-Motueka team against the Springboks. He also took part in two New Zealand trial matches in 1953.

Houghton's record in first-class cricket is:

M	*I*	*NO*	*HS*	*Runs*	*Ave*	*ct*
3	5	0	2	5	1.00	–

Ruth Evelyn MARTIN

Born: *Christchurch, 3 October, 1913*

Died: *Christchurch, 11 September, 2004*

Right-hand batsman, right-arm medium-pace bowler

Ruth Martin (nee Symons) captained the first New Zealand women's team in their one-off test against England at Lancaster Park in February 1935 and was a member of the side that toured New South Wales in 1938.

The test at Christchurch was a tough introduction to international cricket for the New Zealanders who were dismissed for just 44 in their first innings. England then scored 503 for five wickets before declaring and dismissed New Zealand in their second innings for 122, to win by an innings and 337 runs.

In the test Martin was run out for five in the first innings but could not bat in the second because of injury. She took two for 71 from 20 overs, including the prize wicket of Betty Snowball for 189. This stood as the women's test record score for more than fifty years. It was to be Martin's only test appearance as New Zealand did not play another test match until the 1947/48 season.

She was selected in the team that toured New South Wales in 1938 although this team was captained by Ina Lamason. This was a five-match tour that was timed to coincide with the Empire Games in Sydney and the 150th anniversary of British settlement in Australia.

New Zealand Cricket's trophy for the most meritorious batting in women's cricket, presented at the annual awards dinner, is the Ruth Martin Cup.

Arthur Stewart MILLS

Born: *Invercargill, 20 December, 1923*

Died: *Auckland, 28 December, 2001*

Right-hand batsman, wicketkeeper

Dick Mills became a first-class cricketer at the age of 64 when the International Cricket Council ruled that matches played by Fiji against the major associations in New Zealand in 1947/48 should be ranked as first-class. This was despite the original and subsequent rulings of the New Zealand Cricket Council that the matches were not to be regarded as such.

The match in question began at Carisbrook on 13 March, 1948. Seven members of the Otago side had first-class experience but Mills, Noel McGregor, Vernon McArley and Eric Watson (future All Black coach) had not played before. Three of the newcomers appeared for Otago again, but for Mills it was to be his only match.

The retrospective reclassification of the match also meant that McGregor (who went on to play 25 tests for New Zealand) is now Otago's youngest ever player at 16 years and 86 days.

Otago made 217 and 251 (McGregor 71) while Fiji replied with 226 and 196, going down by 46 runs. Mills scored 1 and 15, took one catch and made as many as five stumpings. His four stumpings in the first innings, all off leg-spinner Les Groves, equalled the New Zealand first-class record of Charlie Jackman, Eric Tindill and Len Kent. Only Erv McSweeney (in 1984/85) has managed the feat since.

Mills' five stumpings in the match has only been surpassed by Jackman (7) and Kent (6). Mills is now deemed to be the first Otago keeper to make five dismissals in an innings, a record which stood until Martyn Croy took seven catches against Auckland in 2001/02.

Moving to Palmerston North, Mills played for Manawatu when they challenged Hutt Valley for the Hawke Cup in December 1949. Manawatu were well beaten by an innings but Mills came to light with the bat, scoring 50 in the second innings, putting on 96 for the eighth wicket with Joe Ongley. He also appeared for the Possibles against the Probables in the Wellington Plunket Shield trial in November.

Mills, who had been a fighter pilot in the Pacific during the war, flew for the National Airways Corporation who transferred him to Auckland. Because of his work commitments he had to give up cricket until he left NAC in the mid-1950s.

He then joined the Blockhouse Bay club in the Auckland City and Suburban competition and continued playing until he was well into his fifties.

Eris Annie PATON

Born: *Wellington, 9 October, 1926*

Died: *Invercargill, 23 November, 2004*

Right-hand batsman, right-arm medium-pace bowler

Eris Paton was an aggresive all-rounder from Otago. She was a hard-hitting batsman and right-arm seamer who played four times for New Zealand between 1954 and 1961.

She made her debut on the 1954 tour to England, playing in the first two tests of the three-match series. In the first test, at Headingley, in which New Zealand was beaten by six wickets, she scored three and seven and had figures of none for 24 and two for 17, bowling the England captain, Molly Hide.

The second test of the series, at Worcester, was drawn. Paton scored 12 and six and took one for 47 in the second innings. New Zealand batted through 134 overs to draw the match, ending on 174-6 after being set a target of 338.

Her next appearance for New Zealand was in the second test against England at Eden Park in 1956/57. She achieved her career-best score of 77 not out in New Zealand's first innings of 130 while captain Rona McKenzie's 14 was the next highest score. Paton's score was a New Zealand test record at the time.

After trailing by 56 on the first innings, New Zealand were set a target of 228. Paton again top scored with 43 in the second innings but at the close New Zealand were 25 runs short of victory while England needed just one more wicket.

Paton's fourth and final test was in the one-off match against Australia at Carisbrook in March 1961. New Zealand came very close to winning the game and gaining their first ever test victory (it eventually came at Melbourne eleven years later).

Batting first New Zealand made 241 with Paton scoring 16. She then took four wickets for 35 runs from 27.2 overs as Australia were dismissed for 193. In their second innings, New Zealand declared at 138 for seven with Paton repeating her first innings 16.

Set a target of 187 to win, Australia were 78-8 when Paton bowled Miriam Knee, but held on to finish at 100-8. Paton ended with two for 20 from 15 overs. Paton finished with 180 runs at 25.71 and nine wickets at 17.77 from her four test appearances.

Eric Charlton PETRIE

Born: *Ngaruawahia, 22 May, 1927*

Died: *Omokoroa, 14 August, 2004*

Right-hand batsman, wicketkeeper

Eric Petrie was a highly respected wicketkeeper whose first-class career spanned 17 seasons. He played 57 times for Northern Districts and was their first captain when they were admitted to the Plunket Shield competition.

He made his debut for Waikato at the age of 18 in a Hawke Cup match against Bay of Plenty and played in Auckland's annual Town v Country Plunket Shield trial in 1947/48. The following season the New Zealand Cricket Council organised a number of trial matches leading up to the selection of the team to tour England and Petrie was given an opportunity.

He scored 138, opening the batting, in the Northern Minor Associations trial and then made 50 for North Island Minor Associations against the Major Associations. Two years later, he made his first-class debut against Central Districts at New Plymouth when Auckland's regular keeper, Len Kent, was unavailable.

Petrie gained a regular place in the Auckland side in 1952/53 and was made captain for the 1954/55 season, a rare honour for a "country" player to captain the city team. In 1953/54 he recorded his maiden century, coming in to bat facing a king pair.

Having batted at number six in the first innings against Wellington he opened in the second and put on 182 for the third wicket with John Morris in only 131 minutes. He was finally dismissed for 151 scored in 317 minutes. His innings included a six but only five fours.

When New Zealand toured Pakistan and India for the first time in 1955/56, two uncapped wicketkeepers, Petrie and Wellington's Trevor McMahon, were chosen. Petrie played in four of the eight tests, two in Pakistan and two in India. The *Almanack* reported that "generally both wicketkeepers performed creditably in sharing appearances, each took some brilliant catches."

The next summer saw Northern Districts' entry into first-class cricket and Petrie was named captain of the side. By this stage, however, ex-West Indies test player Sam Guillen was New Zealand's preferred keeper, having been a member of the side which had gained New Zealand's first test victory the season before.

New Zealand had no international cricket at home the next season but consistent form with bat and gloves saw Petrie selected for the 1958 tour to England. The other keeper chosen was Canterbury's John Ward who had not been selected for his province and, in fact, only made his first-class debut in one of the two trial matches staged at the end of the season.

Petrie played in 20 matches on tour, including all five tests. He secured 45 dismissals and his glovework was such as to prompt the New Zealand manager, Jack Phillipps, to suggest his form was at least the equal of England's Godfrey Evans.

Petrie took eight catches against Sussex at Hove to equal the then New Zealand first-class record for catches and dismissals in a match. His five catches in the first innings and five against MCC at Lord's also equalled the existing New Zealand record.

In the fourth test of a disastrous series, Petrie helped John Sparling add 61 for the seventh wicket. He made 45 before being hit on the head by a bouncer from Freddie Trueman. Petrie staggered away from the wicket and then collapsed and was taken to hospital. John Reid kept for the rest of the day (making a stumping) but Petrie resumed his duties next morning.

At the end of the tour Petrie was given the unprecedented honour of being chosen for the Gentlemen against the Players, at the Scarborough Festival. He took one catch and made three stumpings, all in the Players' second innings. Ted Dexter, Peter May, Trevor Bailey and Mike Smith were amongst Petrie's team mates on this occasion.

The following summer he played in both tests against England and captained a combined Northern and Central Districts team against the tourists. In 1959/60 he scored 136 against Wellington, batting for 407 minutes. Northern's total of 384 was their highest to date.

Petrie played in three of the four unofficial tests against Ian Craig's Australian team that season and the first two matches against Dennis Silk's MCC side the next year. He was replaced by John Ward in what the *Almanack* termed "a doubtful selection."

Ward was named as the keeper for the tour to South Africa in 1961/62 and, when he was injured, Artie Dick, with minimal wicketkeeping experience behind him, was called upon. As it happened, Dick had a successful tour and Petrie's international career seemed over.

There was some compensation the following season when Petrie was a member of the Northern Districts side which won the Plunket Shield for the first time. His wicketkeeping was still first-rate. In 1964 the *Almanack* stated that he "again rendered grand service behind the stumps" and in 1965 said that "behind the stumps he was his usual efficient self."

In 1965/66, now aged almost 39, Petrie's form was rewarded with a surprise recall for all three tests against England. The *Almanack* said that "the selection of Petrie as wicketkeeper, after a lapse of four seasons, was just reward to a most able and consistent wicketkeeper."

Petrie also came to New Zealand's rescue with the bat during the series. In the first test at Christchurch he scored 55, putting on 89 for the eighth wicket with Dick Motz, and in the second at Dunedin he made 28, as he and Motz took New Zealand from 100-7 to 179-8.

In the second innings he came to the wicket with New Zealand 79-6, a lead of just 17 with almost two hours remaining. At 112-9, with 36 minutes remaining, he was joined by Northern team mate Tom Puna and the pair batted through until stumps.

Petrie retired at the end of the 1966/67 season and the *Almanack* said he "was always the most competent of wicketkeepers." His last match was against Les Favell's Australian side at Seddon Park, appropriately ending his career without conceding any byes.

Petrie was also a Northern Districts selector and he was one of the *Almanack's* Players of the Year in 1963. Late in his first-class career he left Hamilton to take up the post of Chief House Manager at Rotorua Hospital.

Petrie's record in first-class cricket is:

Season	***M***	***I***	***NO***	***HS***	***Runs***	***Ave***	***100***	***50***	***ct***	***st***
1950/51	1	2	0	4	4	2.00	–	–	3	–
1952/53	4	8	0	44	119	14.87	–	–	10	2
1953/54	5	10	0	151	276	27.60	1	–	8	4
1954/55	4	8	1	41	94	13.42	–	–	8	2
1955/56 (I)	5	6	2	15*	53	13.25	–	–	6	–
1955/56 (P)	4	5	0	7	13	2.60	–	–	5	1
1956/57	5	9	0	55	131	14.55	–	1	7	4
1957/58	6	9	2	56	214	30.57	–	1	20	1
1958 (E)	21	31	9	45*	246	11.18	–	–	46	3
1958/59	9	14	3	29	174	15.81	–	–	9	7
1959/60	8	14	2	136	334	27.83	1	–	12	4
1960/61	7	13	3	57*	287	28.70	–	1	13	1
1961/62	5	10	2	59	190	23.75	–	1	7	1
1962/63	6	9	2	42	86	12.28	–	–	7	3
1963/64	5	7	3	26*	84	21.00	–	–	12	1
1964/65	6	10	1	53*	161	17.88	–	1	9	–
1965/66	8	14	4	55	264	26.40	–	1	7	2
1966/67	6	10	0	18	58	5.80	–	–	9	1
TOTAL	**115**	**189**	**34**	**151**	**2788**	**17.98**	**2**	**6**	**198**	**37**

For	***M***	***I***	***NO***	***HS***	***Runs***	***Ave***	***100***	***50***	***ct***	***st***
NZ (Tests)	14	25	5	55	258	12.90	–	1	25	–
NZ (Other)	25	33	8	37	257	10.28	–	–	45	2
Auckland	13	26	1	151	486	19.44	1	–	26	8
ND	57	95	17	136	1625	20.83	1	4	90	22
ND/CD	1	1	0	8	8	8.00	–	–	–	1
Auckland XI	1	1	0	56	56	56.00	–	1	4	1
NZ XI	1	2	0	4	7	3.50	–	–	3	–
North Island	1	2	1	16*	27	27.00	–	–	3	–
Rest	1	2	1	34	43	43.00	–	–	1	–
Gentlemen	1	2	1	11	21	21.00	–	–	1	3
TOTAL	**115**	**189**	**34**	**151**	**2788**	**17.98**	**2**	**6**	**198**	**37**

Petrie bowled on three occasions in first-class cricket, all for Northern Districts when the opposition had a small fourth innings target – 0.3-0-6-0 v Central Districts in 1961/62, 1-1-0-0 v Wellington in 1962/63 and 2-0-10-0 v Central Districts in 1966/67. He opened the bowling on the latter two occasions.

Alan Herbert PRESTON

Born: *Wellington, 29 October, 1932*

Died: *Wellington, 2 September, 2004*

Right-hand batsman, right-arm off-spin bowler

Alan Preston was a notable all-round sportsman who appeared in 40 first-class matches, including a New Zealand trial, and was also a New Zealand soccer representative. "Sarsp" (a nickname gained because of his penchant for sarsparilla) was an opening then later middle-order batsman, a specialist gully fieldsman and a handy off-spin bowler.

Don Neely recalls that "he had a short run up, very little spin, rather flat through the air, rarely did he float the ball up. Maybe because he didn't spin the ball much. He was a wonderful gully fieldsman and he took some great catches off Blair and Morrison. If I was to rate his skills, his gully fielding would be as good as I've seen."

Preston played in the Wellington Colts team against Hutt Valley Colts (whose attack included Bob Blair) in 1950/51 while still at Wellington College and graduated to senior club ranks at 18. He made an inauspicious first-class debut against Central Districts at the Basin Reserve on the last day of 1955 but had more success in his next game, against Canterbury, after being promoted to open the batting.

Wellington had followed on 280 runs behind and were 31-2 in their second innings when John Beck joined Preston. The pair proceeded to add 206, still Wellington's third wicket record against Canterbury. Beck (149) dominated, recording his maiden century, but Preston played a valuable hand, scoring 63 in 246 minutes. Canterbury finally won but less comfortably than had appeared likely at one stage. Another half-century followed against Auckland.

Wellington won the Plunket Shield the following season with Preston making the only hundred of his career against Northern Districts at the Basin Reserve. He made 122 in 280 minutes, surviving five chances, out of Wellington's total of 379. Although not always scoring heavily, he still formed a useful opening partnership with Lawrie Miller that season.

The following season he was back in the middle order and had more success with the ball. He also gained selection for the North Island against the South in a trial match prior to the selection of the New Zealand team to tour England.

In 1958/59 he played in all five Plunket Shield matches, scoring 42 and 65 against Canterbury when Wellington won by just 18 runs. He again played for the North Island in a match staged just before the arrival of Peter May's MCC team.

When MCC played Wellington, Peter Richardson and Willie Watson piled on 225 for the first wicket with New Zealand representatives Bob Blair, John Reid, Eric Dempster and Les Butler all failing to break through. Preston came on and bowled Richardson with his second ball and shortly afterwards caught and bowled Watson.

Wellington won the Plunket Shield in 1960/61 and again the following season. Preston was sparingly used as a bowler but still played some useful innings. His last match was against Otago at Carisbrook in January 1963. This match was notable for Bob Blair bowling two consecutive overs due to a misunderstanding following a rain interruption.

In addition, Otago's twelfth man, Peter Semple, fielded for Wellington on the last day and actually ended the match by taking a brilliant diving catch to dismiss his team mate Lance Pearson.

Prior to breaking in to first-class cricket, Preston had already established himself on the sporting scene. He was captain of Victoria University's soccer team and was chosen as centre forward for Wellington in 1953.

The following year he gained North Island honours and was selected in the New Zealand team which toured Australia, making nine appearances in all. He was later named in the New Zealand side to visit Southeast Asia but the tour did not go ahead.

An avowed book lover, Preston was also the founder and owner of Unity Books which began in 1967 as a tiny store in the Empire Building in Willis Street and within two decades had become something of a New Zealand institution.

Abandoning plans to be an accountant he moved first to publications distributor Gordon and Gotch and then to various booksellers, Whitcombe and Tombs, South's Book Depot in Willis Street and Ferguson and Osborne's on Lambton Quay.

Preston, however, wanted a shop where books were everything, no stationery, no greeting cards or other items of distraction. He knew there were many publications that the major retailers did not stock – serious books, art books, political books, New Zealand books – and, as he said later, he decided to fill "the holes that Whitcoulls left."

After five years business was just good enough to cover a higher rent and he moved to larger premises across the street. In 1986 the business moved again and in 1998 to its current site. A store had been opened in Auckland in 1989 and won a bookshop of the year award.

In later years Preston took a history degree at Victoria University, giving him further inspiration for his world of books.

Preston's record in first-class cricket is:

Season	*M*	*I*	*NO*	*HS*	*Runs*	*Ave*	*100*	*50*	*ct*	*Wkts*	*Runs*	*Ave*	*Best*
1955/56	5	10	0	63	206	20.60	–	2	4	6	350	58.33	1-1
1956/57	5	8	2	122	214	35.66	1	–	3	4	166	41.50	2-32
1957/58	6	11	3	75*	168	21.00	–	1	–	8	204	25.50	3-32
1958/59	7	13	0	71	343	26.38	–	2	7	5	109	21.80	2-19
1959/60	5	9	2	51	249	35.57	–	1	6	8	198	24.75	3-44
1960/61	3	5	1	62	122	30.50	–	1	–	0	12	–	–
1961/62	5	8	1	51	119	17.00	–	1	6	1	19	19.00	1-19
1962/63	4	5	1	24*	27	6.75	–	–	4	0	45	–	–
TOTAL	**40**	**69**	**10**	**122**	**1448**	**24.54**	**1**	**8**	**30**	**32**	**1103**	**34.46**	**3-32**

For	*M*	*I*	*NO*	*HS*	*Runs*	*Ave*	*100*	*50*	*ct*	*Wkts*	*Runs*	*Ave*	*Best*
Wellington	38	65	10	122	1384	25.16	1	8	29	31	1066	34.38	3-32
North Island	2	4	0	31	64	16.00	–	–	1	1	37	37.00	1-21
TOTAL	**40**	**69**	**10**	**122**	**1448**	**24.54**	**1**	**8**	**30**	**32**	**1103**	**34.46**	**3-32**

David Norman STOKES

Born: *Christchurch, 16 November, 1909*

Died: *Christchurch, 31 October, 2004*

Right-hand batsman, right-arm off-spin bowler

Norm Stokes, who died just prior to his 95th birthday, had been New Zealand's oldest living first-class cricketer. A middle-order batsman, he played four matches, with some success, for Canterbury in the late 1930s.

Stokes is one of the few players to have gained provincial selection having come through the Christchurch Suburban competition, often regarded as the more "social" association. He showed he was equal to the best, however, scoring 124 not out for a Suburban representative side against a strong Canterbury XI at Lancaster Park in a Show Day trial match in 1937.

Stokes did have to cross over to the district association to ensure selection and spent the 1937/38 season with Sydenham. Stokes played in all three of Canterbury's Plunket Shield fixtures that season and topped the side's batting averages with 200 runs at 33.33, including three half-centuries.

He made his debut against Otago at Lancaster Park on Christmas Day, 1937. Otago batted first and made 172. In reply Canterbury were 54-2 when Stokes came to the wicket to join Bob Menzies. The pair added 51 and Stokes carried on to make 56, top score in the total of 213. Otago responded with 271 but Canterbury could manage only 141, losing by 89 runs. Stokes was dismissed for a duck, one of Jack Dunning's eleven victims in the match.

In the next match, at the Basin Reserve, Canterbury were 56-3 before Stokes (58 in 89 minutes) and Ian Cromb put on 67 for the fourth wicket. Another second innings failure, however, (99 all out) saw Canterbury go down by six wickets.

Canterbury then travelled north to play the very powerful Auckland team who were in the middle of a run of four successive Plunket Shield titles. The Auckland top order was so strong (Whitelaw, Postles, Weir, Wallace, Carson and Pearson) that the redoubtable Verdun Scott had to bat as low as number seven.

The Auckland batting did not end there. New Zealand all-rounder Mal Matheson came in at number eight and he and Scott both scored centuries as the pair piled on 224 for the seventh wicket (still Auckland's all time record) and the total reached 590.

Canterbury had no answer, losing by an innings. Stokes scored 59 and 24 thus top scoring for Canterbury in every match. The first-class season for Stokes and Canterbury had lasted just 17 days.

The following season Stokes played in the opening fixture, against Auckland, scored 23 and 3 but was replaced by a new player, 19-year-old Mac Anderson, for the next game against Wellington. Anderson went on to play for New Zealand in their first ever test against Australia at the Basin Reserve in 1945/46.

By now Stokes had returned to his original suburban side Beckenham, which he had joined as an 18-year-old. He scored more than 8000 runs for Beckenham (now Southern districts) and proved a handy wicket taker with his off-breaks. His highest score was 168, all scored before lunch.

In 1948/49 he was the club's leading run scorer, topped the averages and also took the most wickets. He retired from playing at the end of the 1952/53 season but that was far from the end of his connection with the Suburban association. He turned to administration and, in all, his affiliation lasted 76 years from 1928.

He was the Suburban vice-president from 1939 to 1949, president from 1955 to 1962 and patron from 1962 until his death. He was elected a life member in 1963. Stokes also served as the Suburban delegate on the Canterbury association for twelve years. He remained very actively involved into his latter years, attending annual meetings and end-of-year functions.

He later became a Canterbury Plunket Shield selector from 1968/69 to 1971/72 and also managed the provincial team.

Stokes' record in first-class cricket is:

M	*I*	*NO*	*HS*	*Runs*	*Ave*	*50*	*ct*
4	8	0	59	226	28.25	3	–

Margaret Jean TAYLOR

Born: *Christchurch, 19 February, 1917*

Died: *Christchurch, 22 July, 2004*

Right-hand batsman, right-arm medium-pace bowler

Peggy Taylor (later Davies) made her debut for New Zealand in their first ever test match against England at Lancaster Park in February 1935.

It was to be a tough introduction to international cricket for the New Zealanders who won the toss and batted. Taylor came to the crease with scoreboard reading 13-6 and was bowled by namesake Mary Taylor for 3. New Zealand were eventually all out for 44 in 28.2 overs.

In reply England scored a mammoth 503-5 before declaring. Davies bowled 16 overs, including three maidens, and took 1-62, dismissing Betty Archdale, the fifth wicket to fall at 432. In the second innings New Zealand was all out for 122 with Taylor out for a duck, one of Joy Partridge's four victims. England won by an innings and 337 runs.

It was to be Taylor's only test appearance as New Zealand did not play another test match until the 1947/48 season.

Ivan Alexander WALSH

Born: *Dunedin, 29 December, 1924*

Died: *Dunedin, 12 May, 2005*

Right-hand batsman, right-arm medium-pace bowler

Medium-pace bowler Ivan Walsh, who played for the North East Valley club in Dunedin, appeared in three matches for Otago in the late 1940s and figured in one of the trial matches for the 1949 tour to England. He was also a New Zealand soccer representative.

He made his debut in Otago's final Plunket Shield match of the 1948/49 season against Wellington at Carisbrook. Walsh caused an early sensation by bowling Geoff Rabone, John Reid and Jim Kemp to have Wellington 35-3, his own figures being 3-13. The *Almanack* reported that "Walsh made the ball swing sharply in the air."

Wellington were eventually dismissed for 245, Walsh taking 5-76 off 32 overs. Otago made 233 in reply and then dismissed Wellington for 200 in their second innings. Walsh took two more wickets, those of Reid and Harry Cave, with six of his seven victims in the match being out bowled.

Otago needed 213 to win but when Walsh was bowled by Cave (to complete a pair) they had slumped to 178-9. Wellington needed just one more wicket to secure their first Plunket Shield title since 1935/36 but they were thwarted by the unlikely pairing of 17-year-old Noel McGregor and number eleven Guy Overton (137 runs at 4.15 over his first-class career).

The two batsmen hit off the required runs in better than even time and the enthusiasm of the crowd mounted with the score. There was a wild rush on to the field to congratulate McGregor when he hit Cave through the covers for four to seal victory.

Otago's win actually put them level on points with Canterbury at the top of the table but an inferior runs per wicket average cost them the title they had won the previous season.

Walsh's success saw him selected for the South Island XI which played the South Island Major Associations XI three days later at Lancaster Park. This was one of several trial matches arranged to give exposure to as many players as possible before the team to tour England was named. Walsh opened the bowling but failed to take a wicket.

Walsh played two more games the following season but captured only one more wicket in 60 overs. His last game was the match against Auckland when Bert Sutcliffe established a New Zealand record score of 355 (surpassed by Sutcliffe himself with 385 against Canterbury three years later).

Walsh was a prominent soccer player and appeared in three Chatham Cup finals with the Northern Club in 1949, 1951 and 1953, although he was never on the winning side. He played four times for New Zealand in 1951 on an end of season tour, scoring a hat trick in a 9-0 win against New Hebrides (now Vanuatu) and one goal in three games against New Caledonia.

He was a primary school teacher and spent 25 years at the North East Valley School. He was educated at the convent school at Port Chalmers and at Christian Brothers in Dunedin. His son, Stephen, won a bronze medal in the long jump at the Commonwealth Games in Brisbane in 1982 and also represented New Zealand at the 1984 Olympics in Los Angeles.

Walsh's record in first-class cricket is:

M	*I*	*NO*	*HS*	*Runs*	*Ave*	*ct*	*Wkts*	*Runs*	*Ave*	*Best*
3	4	2	2*	2	1.00	3	8	270	33.75	5-76

Robert Courtney WEBB

Born: *Christchurch, 13 September, 1917*

Died: *Christchurch, 8 May, 1989*

Right-hand batsman, wicketkeeper

Bob Webb, Canterbury wicketkeeper in the 1930s and 40s, died as long ago as 1989 but the fact had not previously been brought to our attention. He played in 12 matches spread over 13 seasons, his appearances for Canterbury being restricted by overseas service during the war. He was wounded and taken prisoner in North Africa in November 1941.

Webb came into the Canterbury team as a 20-year-old in 1937/38, after New Zealand representative keeper Charlie Jackman had moved to Auckland. He immediately became a regular in the side, appearing in every Plunket Shield match in that and the following season.

He made his debut against Otago at Lancaster Park on Christmas Day, 1937 but did not secure any dismissals. His first victim came a few days later at the Basin Reserve when Herbie Rice became the first of three catches he took off Ted Mulcock's bowling.

The following season he made his highest score in first-class cricket, a valuable 40 against Otago at Carisbrook. Replying to Otago's 266, Frank Bellamy and Jack Kerr put on 102 for the first wicket before Canterbury collapsed to 126-6 bringing Webb to the crease. He made 40, before being trapped lbw by Sonny Moloney, and helped his side reach 202. Canterbury eventually won the game by scoring 297-5 in the fourth innings.

Webb took part in the opening game of the 1939/40 season but that was to be his last appearance for Canterbury for nine years. He reappeared in 1948/49, when Canterbury won the Plunket Shield, playing in all three games.

Two matches the following season wrapped up Webb's career, his final victim being Eric Dempster, caught off fast bowler Jack Alderson, who was in the process of taking 5-66 on debut.

After making his senior debut with Lancaster Park in 1934/35, Webb began an association with the St Albans club which was to continue until his death. He took 57 catches and made 41 stumpings for St Albans until his retirement at the end of the 1949/50 season. His two stumpings for Lancaster Park left him with exactly 100 dismissals at club level.

In all he played 59 senior matches for St Albans, scoring 1670 runs at 22.88 with a top score of 98. Webb maintained a keen interest in the progress of the club. He was the St Albans' patron and vice-president at the time of his death.

Inaugurated in the 1988/89 season, the Bob Webb Memorial Cup is awarded to the St Albans player who effects the most wicket-keeping dismissals in one grade during a season.

Webb's record in first-class cricket is: *(all games for Canterbury)*

Season	*M*	*I*	*NO*	*HS*	*Runs*	*Ave*	*ct*	*st*
1937/38	3	6	0	15	30	5.00	4	–
1938/39	3	5	0	40	72	14.40	6	1
1939/40	1	1	0	12	12	12.00	1	1
1948/49	3	3	0	26	44	14.66	3	2
1949/50	2	3	0	2	3	1.00	3	–
TOTAL	**12**	**18**	**0**	**40**	**161**	**8.94**	**17**	**4**

NEW ZEALAND A IN SOUTH AFRICA

After having resounding success against Sri Lanka A at home the New Zealand A side struggled against a strong South African side which included five players who had toured New Zealand just six months earlier.

Sinclair had a great series, getting a century and a double century and scored 460 runs in the three first-class games. The bowlers struggled at times and had a mixed series. If they got early wickets the South African middle order and tail then got runs, if the batsmen got a good start there were collapses.

In the one-day games New Zealand A had opportunities to win the first and third games but fell short.

The touring party was: M.D. Bell *(Wellington, captain)*, T.K. Canning *(Auckland)*, P.G. Fulton *(Canterbury)*, J.E.C. Franklin *(Wellington)*, G.J. Hopkins *(Otago)*, J.M. How *(Central Districts)*, B.P. Martin *(Northern Districts)*, C.S. Martin *(Canterbury)*, M.J. Mason *(Central Districts)*, R.R. Sherlock *(Canterbury)*, M.S. Sinclair *(Central Districts)*, R.L. Taylor *(Central Districts)*, L. Vincent *(Auckland)*, K.P. Walmsley *(Auckland)*, P.J. Wiseman *(Canterbury)*. Coach, A. Ross; Assistant Coach, M.F. Sharpe; Manager, R.A. Dykes (replaced by F. Thomas); Physiotherapist, A. Peterson. J.S. Patel *(Wellington)* replaced B.P. Martin who was injured in the first game.

New Zealand A First-class Averages

BATTING	*M*	*I*	*NO*	*HS*	*Agg*	*Ave*	*100s*	*50s*	*Ct*	*St*
M.S. Sinclair	3	5	0	268	460	92.00	2	-	4	-
P.G. Fulton	3	5	0	62	228	45.60	-	2	-	-
M.J. Mason	2	2	1	25	29	29.00	-	-	-	-
L. Vincent	3	5	0	63	126	25.20	-	1	1	-
C.S. Martin	3	3	2	11*	25	25.00	-	-	-	-
P.J. Wiseman	2	3	0	52	70	23.33	-	1	-	-
G.J. Hopkins	3	4	0	39	87	21.75	-	-	11	-
K.P. Walmsley	2	3	1	28	43	21.50	-	-	-	-
J.E.C. Franklin	3	5	1	63	65	16.25	-	1	1	-
R.L. Taylor	1	2	1	15*	15	15.00	-	-	-	-
J.M. How	3	5	0	37	72	14.40	-	-	1	-
T.K. Canning	1	1	0	14	14	14.00	-	-	-	-
M.D. Bell	3	5	0	20	39	7.80	-	-	-	-
R.R. Sherlock	1	2	1	4	7	7.00	-	-	-	-

BOWLING	*O*	*M*	*R*	*W*	*Ave*	*Best*	*5w*	*10w*
M.S. Sinclair	4	2	4	1	4.00	1-4	-	-
T.K. Canning	28	9	52	3	17.33	3-52	-	-
J.E.C. Franklin	81	31	173	6	28.83	3-43	-	-
K.P. Walmsley	43.2	13	144	4	36.00	4-69	-	-
C.S. Martin	86	28	226	4	56.50	2-86	-	-
R.R. Sherlock	18.1	6	78	1	78.00	1-59	-	-
L. Vincent	26	4	80	1	80.00	1-43	-	-
P.J. Wiseman	73	12	200	2	100.00	2-70	-	-
J.M. How	51	3	212	2	106.00	1-89	-	-
M.J. Mason	58	21	134	1	134.00	1-85	-	-
M.D. Bell	3	0	12	0	-	-	-	-
P.G. Fulton	6	1	26	0	-	-	-	-

LIONS v NEW ZEALAND A — Not First-class

at Isak Steyl Stadium, Vanderbijlpark on 3, 4, 5 September, 2004
Toss : New Zealand A. Umpires : S. Wadvalla & J. Cloete
Close of play: 1st day: New Zealand A 289-6, Canning 60, Hopkins 16; 2nd day: New Zealand A 68-4 Fulton 5
Match drawn

This three-day game did not carry first-class status as each side played 12 men. After New Zealand A lost two early wickets How, Franklin and Canning all reached fifties before an overnight declaration.

The Lions side had a catastrophic start and were reeling at 29-6 and then 75-7 before Crookes scored a century to pull the innings together. Sherlock bowled well, snaring three wickets. With a 114 run lead New Zealand A opted for batting practice but only Fulton and Canning took advantage.

When the Lions batted again Sherlock got another two wickets and was assisted by How who also got two wickets as the match finished in a draw. Bruce Martin injured his shoulder during the second innings and returned to New Zealand. Jeetan Patel, who had been playing in England, replaced him.

NEW ZEALAND A

FIRST INNINGS	*Runs*	*Mins*	*Balls*	*6s*	*4s*	*SECOND INNINGS*	*Runs*	*Mins*	*Balls*	*6s*	*4s*
J.M.How b Roe	61	105	84	-	12	(2) lbw b Bhayat	4	6	5	-	1
M.D.Bell* c Harris b Roe	12	40	29	-	2	(1) lbw b Bhayat	14	79	56	-	2
M.S.Sinclair b Bhayat	3	7	6	-	-	c Coetsee b Bhayat	28	90	62	-	6
L.Vincent b Roe	26	71	54	-	5	lbw b Bhayat	15	27	19	-	3
P.G.Fulton c Roe b Crookes	39	120	106	-	6	c Ackerman b Ontong	94	147	122	1	12
J.E.C.Franklin lbw b Roe	54	200	162	1	7						
T.K.Canning not out	60	120	100	-	10	(6) lbw b Crookes	41	96	86	1	5
G.J.Hopkins† not out	16	33	20	-	3	(7) not out	15	41	41	-	-
P.J.Wiseman											
B.P.Martin											
C.S.Martin											
R.R.Sherlock											
Extras (b 1, lb 6, w 1, nb 10)	18					(b 1, lb 1, nb 5)	7				
TOTAL (92 overs) (6 wkts dec)	**289**	336				(64.2 overs) (6 wkts dec)	**218**	249			

LIONS

	Runs	*Mins*	*Balls*	*6s*	*4s*		*Runs*	*Mins*	*Balls*	*6s*	*4s*
S.C.Cook b Martin C.S.	0	3	5	-	-	(2) not out	76	171	147	3	7
A.M.Bacher lbw b Sherlock	1	14	7	-	-	(1) b Sherlock	1	26	25	-	-
J.L.Ontong c Sinclair b Sherlock	8	33	21	-	1	lbw b Sherlock	29	78	45	-	2
N.D.McKenzie c Vincent b Sherlock	7	18	12	-	1	c sub (K.P.Walmsley) b How	6	30	26	-	-
H.D.Ackerman* b Franklin	9	44	30	-	1	c Sinclair b How	35	34	38	1	3
M.J.Harris† lbw b Canning	1	11	9	-	-						
E.Nkwe c Sinclair b Wiseman	18	107	75	-	2						
D.N.Crookes not out	101	141	148	-	19						
W.L.Coetsee not out	26	93	71	-	1						
R.L.Groeneveld											
G.H.Bhayat											
G.A.Roe											
Extras (b 1, lb 1, nb 2)	4						0				
TOTAL (62.4 overs) (7 wkts dec)	**175**	228				(46.5 overs) (4 wkts)	**147**	171			

Bowling	*O*	*M*	*R*	*W*	*O*	*M*	*R*	*W*
LIONS								
Roe	21	9	43	4				
Nkwe	13	1	64	0	10	6	23	0
Bhayat	14	2	56	1	18	8	60	4
Groeneveld	9	2	42	0	12	4	38	0
Crookes	24	5	47	1	5	0	14	1
Ontong	8	1	28	0	3.2	1	12	1
Bacher	3	1	2	0	4	0	24	0
Coetsee					12	0	45	0
NEW ZEALAND A								
Martin C.S.	8	3	15	1				
Sherlock	8	2	20	3	8	4	7	2
Franklin	10	5	18	1				
Martin B.P.	15.4	3	62	0	5	0	13	0
Canning	12	5	20	1	5	1	14	0
Wiseman	9	1	38	1	14	2	56	0
Fulton					4	1	16	0
Vincent					4	1	10	0
How					6.5	0	31	2

Fall of Wickets

	NZA	***L***	***NZA***	***L***
	1st	*1st*	*2nd*	*2nd*
1st	26	0	4	10
2nd	29	2	48	82
3rd	109	16	59	96
4th	110	17	68	147
5th	188	21	165	-
6th	257	29	218	-
7th	-	75	-	-
8th	-	-	-	-
9th	-	-	-	-
10th	-	-	-	-

SOUTH AFRICA A v NEW ZEALAND A — First Unofficial Test

at SuperSport Park, Centurion on 8, 9, 10, 11 September, 2004
Toss : New Zealand A. Umpires : I.L. Howell & K.H. Hurter
Close of play: 1st day: New Zealand A 241-7, Canning 4, Hopkins 0; 2nd day: South Africa A 136-4, McKenzie 18, Adams 1
3rd day: South Africa A 364-6, de Bruyn 117, Amla 87
Match drawn

After he had won the toss and batted first, Bell went in the third over, bringing Sinclair to the crease. He proceeded to get fifty off 123 balls and his 15th first-class century from a further 101 deliveries. He and Fulton added 137 for the fourth wicket. Fulton got his fifty off 120 balls. When Sinclair went there was a slump from 229-3 to 268-8. With the last two wickets adding 60 the New Zealand A side reached 328. Thomas bowled well for 4-48.

The New Zealand bowlers started well having their hosts 156-6 before de Bruyn and Amla added 247 for the seventh wicket. De Bruyn reached his hundred off 211 balls compared with Amla needing 278. Hopkins equalled the New Zealand wicket-keeping record with seven catches in the innings.

New Zealand A had a deficit of 163 and had reached 153-5 when the game ended. Fulton got another fifty to ensure the draw.

NEW ZEALAND A

FIRST INNINGS	*Runs*	*Mins*	*Balls*	*6s*	*4s*	*SECOND INNINGS*	*Runs*	*Mins*	*Balls*	*6s*	*4s*
M.D.Bell* c Amla b Willoughby	0	9	8	-	-	(2) lbw b Willoughby	20	51	39	-	4
J.M.How lbw b Thomas	37	110	61	-	6	(1) c de Villiers b Morkel	4	9	8	-	1
M.S.Sinclair b Thomas	115	306	248	-	17	c de Bruyn b Willoughby	35	162	107	-	6
L.Vincent lbw b de Bruyn	10	36	21	-	2	b Adams	16	39	32	-	3
P.G.Fulton lbw b de Bruyn	62	221	165	-	12	lbw b Thomas	54	124	90	4	3
R.L.Taylor lbw b Thomas	0	1	1	-	-	not out	15	74	54	-	2
J.E.C.Franklin c Morkel b de Bruyn	2	29	20	-	-	not out	0	30	19	-	-
T.K.Canning run out	14	82	65	-	2						
G.J.Hopkins† c de Villiers b Morkel	39	100	66	-	8						
M.J.Mason lbw b Thomas	25	72	47	-	4						
C.S.Martin not out	11	34	29	-	1						
Extras (b 1, lb 7, w 2, nb 3)	13					(lb 2, w 7)	9				
TOTAL (121.2 overs)	**328**	463				(57 overs) (5 wkts)	**153**	232			

SOUTH AFRICA A

	Runs	Mins	Balls	6s	4s
A.G.Puttick c Hopkins b Canning	19	70	49	-	3
A.B.de Villiers† c Hopkins b Martin	30	36	25	-	4
H.H.Dippenaar c Hopkins b Canning	22	103	69	-	3
A.G.Prince* c Hopkins b Canning	43	150	109	-	4
N.D.McKenzie c Hopkins b Mason	30	134	98	-	6
P.R.Adams b Martin	9	40	25	-	1
Z.de Bruyn c Hopkins b How	155	458	330	-	15
H.M.Amla c Hopkins b Franklin	115	370	291	1	12
J.A.Morkel not out	58	73	53	4	3
A.C.Thomas not out	1	2	1	-	-
C.M.Willoughby					
Extras (lb 2, w 1, nb 6)	9				
TOTAL (174 overs) (8 wkts dec)	**491**	675			

Bowling	*O*	*M*	*R*	*W*	*O*	*M*	*R*	*W*
SOUTH AFRICA A								
Willoughby	27	9	63	1	15	7	26	2
Morkel	24	5	74	1	12	3	40	1
Thomas	31.2	14	48	4	11	4	27	1
de Bruyn	22	5	77	3	5	1	13	0
Adams	17	3	58	0	14	7	45	1
NEW ZEALAND A								
Martin	35	11	86	2				
Mason	30	9	85	1				
Canning	28	9	52	3				
Franklin	35	12	80	1				
Vincent	13	2	37	0				
Fulton	6	1	26	0				
How	27	0	123	1				

Fall of Wickets	***NZA***	***SAA***	***NZA***
	1st	*1st*	*2nd*
1st	6	43	11
2nd	70	59	34
3rd	92	90	53
4th	229	134	128
5th	229	155	142
6th	232	156	-
7th	241	403	-
8th	268	490	-
9th	295	-	-
10th	328	-	-

SOUTH AFRICA A v NEW ZEALAND A Second Unofficial Test

at Willowmoore Park, Benoni on 14, 15, 16 September, 2004
Toss : New Zealand A. Umpires : M. Erasmus & B.G. Jerling
Close of play: 1st day: South Africa A 2-0, de Villiers 2, Puttick 0; 2nd day: South Africa A 292-6, Amla 2, Morkel 8
South Africa A won by 10 wickets

The New Zealand batsmen were disappointing and were dismissed just before stumps on the first day. Only Wiseman and Fulton were able to play the innings needed to get a larger total. Kruger and Thomas bowled well getting four wickets each.

When South Africa A batted Puttick and Prince put on 152 for the third wicket in 207 minutes off 228 deliveries. Prince reached a century from 168 balls in 275 minutes. McKenzie chimed in with a well-compiled fifty to give South Africa A a 92 run lead.

New Zealand batted poorly in its second innings being 65-7 at one stage. No one was able to reach thirty as the side capitulated to be dismissed for 127. Morkel, de Bruyn and Kruger all bowled well as South Africa A grabbed a ten wicket win to take a 1-0 lead in the three match series.

NEW ZEALAND A

FIRST INNINGS	*Runs*	*Mins*	*Balls*	*6s*	*4s*	*SECOND INNINGS*	*Runs*	*Mins*	*Balls*	*6s*	*4s*
M.D.Bell* c & b Kruger	10	27	15	-	2	(2) c de Villiers b Kruger	5	20	11	-	1
J.M.How c Puttick b Thomas	27	112	70	-	6	(1) c de Bruyn b Morkel	3	32	21	-	-
M.S.Sinclair c Amla b de Bruyn	28	62	43	-	7	c de Villiers b Morkel	14	63	41	-	2
L.Vincent c Kruger b Thomas	36	127	103	-	7	lbw b Kruger	1	7	6	-	-
P.G.Fulton c Adams b Thomas	47	180	122	-	7	c & b de Bruyn	24	110	71	-	4
J.E.C.Franklin lbw b de Bruyn	0	6	3	-	-	c de Villiers b Morkel	0	9	3	-	-
G.J.Hopkins† c de Villiers b Kruger	2	21	14	-	-	lbw b de Bruyn	24	106	57	-	3
P.J.Wiseman c de Bruyn b Thomas	52	99	82	1	6	lbw b de Bruyn	0	2	1	-	-
K.P.Walmsley b Kruger	15	81	55	-	-	c Thomas b Kruger	28	59	43	-	5
R.R.Sherlock not out	3	24	12	-	-	c Puttick b Morkel	4	46	39	-	-
C.S.Martin c & b Kruger	4	2	2	-	1	not out	10	31	12	-	1
Extras (lb 2)	2					(b 4, lb 9, nb 1)	14				
TOTAL (86.5 overs)	**226**	371				(50.5 overs)	**127**	246			

SOUTH AFRICA A

	Runs	Mins	Balls	6s	4s		Runs	Mins	Balls	6s	4s
A.B.de Villiers† c Hopkins b Franklin	14	28	21	-	2	not out	32	23	20	-	5
A.G.Puttick lbw b Franklin	66	222	134	-	11	not out	3	23	11	-	-
J.L.Ontong c Hopkins b Walmsley	8	26	18	-	-						
A.G.Prince* c Sinclair b Wiseman	103	261	187	-	18						
N.D.McKenzie lbw b Wiseman	65	126	94	2	9						
Z.de Bruyn c Sinclair b Walmsley	2	48	40	-	-						
H.M.Amla c Sinclair b Walmsley	4	50	50	-	-						
J.A.Morkel c Franklin b Sherlock	19	35	25	-	4						
A.C.Thomas c Sinclair b Martin	4	28	16	-	1						
P.R.Adams not out	7	27	20	-	1						
G.J.P.Kruger c Hopkins b Walmsley	0	18	9	-	-						
Extras (b 2, lb 12, w 2, nb 10)	26					(b 4)	4				
TOTAL (101.2 overs)	**318**	448				(5.1 overs) (0 wkts)	**39**	23			

Bowling	*O*	*M*	*R*	*W*	*O*	*M*	*R*	*W*
SOUTH AFRICA A								
Kruger	22.5	8	54	4	18	7	42	3
Morkel	17	6	50	0	12.5	4	30	4
Thomas	22	9	50	4	7	3	9	0
de Bruyn	10	2	31	2	12	4	31	3
Adams	11	3	31	0	1	0	2	0
Ontong	4	0	8	0				
NEW ZEALAND A								
Sherlock	16	6	59	1	2.1	0	19	0
Franklin	18	6	50	2				
Martin	22	9	56	1	3	1	16	0
Walmsley	19.2	8	69	4				
Wiseman	26	7	70	2				

Fall of Wickets

	NZA *1st*	***SAA*** *1st*	***NZA*** *2nd*	***SAA*** *2nd*
1st	22	26	5	-
2nd	59	42	9	-
3rd	69	194	14	-
4th	120	260	32	-
5th	124	282	32	-
6th	129	284	65	-
7th	166	305	65	-
8th	212	307	111	-
9th	222	311	113	-
10th	226	318	127	-

SOUTH AFRICA A v NEW ZEALAND A Third Unofficial Test

at Sedgars Park, Potchefstroom on 20, 21, 22, 23 September, 2004
Toss : New Zealand A. Umpires : M.W. Brown & M.Z. Nanabhay
Close of play: 1st day: New Zealand A 281-4, Sinclair 149, Franklin 13; 2nd day: South Africa A 79-0, Puttick 41, Dippenaar 35
3rd day: South Africa A 325-4, McKenzie 36, Amla 42
Match drawn

After losing both openers early on New Zealand A were able to reach 502-8 thanks to three century stands and a magnificent innings from Sinclair. He and Vincent added 154, he put on 104 with Fulton and then Franklin assisted in a 152 run stand. Sinclair reached his 16th century after 244 minutes and 184 balls and went to his fourth double century off 358 balls in 512 minutes.

His 268 was his highest score and the highest score made by a New Zealand player in South Africa, eclipsing John Reid's 203 against Western Province in 1961/62.

The New Zealand bowlers also struggled with the South African openers putting on 149 for the first wicket. Dippenaar got a century off 217 deliveries. Amla was then involved in two century stands. He and McKenzie added 133 and then de Bruyn helped add 110. Amla reached his hundred off 234 balls in 299 minutes. Franklin was by far the most economical bowler and also got three wickets.

The match ended in a draw when stumps were drawn an hour early. South Africa A had won the series 1-0.

NEW ZEALAND A

FIRST INNINGS	*Runs*	*Mins*	*Balls*	*6s*	*4s*
M.D.Bell* lbw b Kruger	4	5	6	-	1
J.M.How lbw b Thomas	1	34	21	-	-
M.S.Sinclair b Thomas	268	591	417	2	35
L.Vincent lbw b de Bruyn	63	190	123	-	7
P.G.Fulton c Tsolekile b Prince	41	122	111	-	4
J.E.C.Franklin c Prince b Ontong	63	194	130	-	9
G.J.Hopkins† lbw b Thomas	22	44	33	-	3
P.J.Wiseman c Amla b Kruger	18	16	14	1	2
K.P.Walmsley not out	0	15	5	-	-
M.J.Mason not out	4	6	6	-	1
C.S.Martin					
Extras (b 2, lb 12, w 2, nb 2)	18				
TOTAL (144 overs) (8 wkts dec)	**502**	612			

SOUTH AFRICA A

	Runs	Mins	Balls	6s	4s
A.G.Puttick lbw b Franklin	70	236	163	-	12
H.H.Dippenaar c & b How	103	298	222	-	18
J.L.Ontong lbw b Franklin	48	139	111	1	3
A.G.Prince* lbw b Franklin	16	93	67	-	2
N.D.McKenzie c Hopkins b Martin	59	233	142	-	9
H.M.Amla c & b Vincent	141	376	298	-	22
Z.de Bruyn lbw b Sinclair	40	148	111	-	5
T.L.Tsolekile† not out	13	48	38	-	2
A.C.Thomas not out	15	36	38	-	3
P.R.Adams					
G.J.P.Kruger					
Extras (b 6, lb 4, w 2, nb 6)	18				
TOTAL (197 overs) (7 wkts)	**523**	773			

Bowling	*O*	*M*	*R*	*W*
SOUTH AFRICA A				
Kruger	32	10	92	2
Thomas	37	9	82	3
de Bruyn	22	3	83	1
Adams	16	0	79	0
Ontong	28	3	118	1
Prince	9	0	34	1
NEW ZEALAND A				
Martin	26	7	68	1
Franklin	28	13	43	3
Mason	28	12	49	0
Walmsley	24	5	75	0
How	24	3	89	1
Wiseman	47	5	130	0
Vincent	13	2	43	1
Sinclair	4	2	4	1
Bell	3	0	12	0

Fall of Wickets

	NZA	**SAA**
	1st	*1st*
1st	4	148
2nd	8	193
3rd	162	237
4th	266	246
5th	418	379
6th	477	489
7th	480	493
8th	498	-
9th	-	-
10th	-	-

PRETORIA HIGH SCHOOL OLD BOYS v NEW ZEALAND A

at Willowmoore Park, Benoni on 26 September, 2004
Toss : Pretoria High School Old Boys. Umpires : A.Crafford & D.Ntuu
New Zealand A won by 101 runs.

In the game against the MTN club champions, Patel, who had replaced the injured Bruce Martin, played his first match on tour. New Zealand A had a 57 run opening stand but then lost another wicket quickly. All batsmen had some good time in the middle, particularly Taylor, Vincent and Hopkins who got fifties, and the score reached 337-5.

The local side was soon in trouble at 45-4 before a century to van Woerkom gave the innings some respectability. Sherlock, though expensive, took five wickets as New Zealand A won by 101 runs.

NEW ZEALAND A

	Runs	Mins	Balls	6s	4s
J.M.How lbw b Pienaar	27	66	45	-	5
M.D.Bell* c Morgan b Pienaar	17	56	33	-	3
M.S.Sinclair b Hampson	12	39	18	-	2
R.L.Taylor run out	65	101	81	-	7
L.Vincent b Hampson	93	114	76	4	6
G.J.Hopkins† not out	56	51	40	-	9
T.K.Canning not out	25	9	10	3	-
J.E.C.Franklin					
M.J.Mason					
J.S.Patel					
R.R.Sherlock					
Extras (lb 11, w 28, nb 3)	42				
TOTAL (50 overs) (5 wkts)	**337**	220			

PRETORIA HSOB

	Runs	Mins	Balls	6s	4s
G.Morgan*† c How b Franklin	2	42	25	-	-
M.Charlton c How b Mason	6	36	33	-	1
C.Williams c Hopkins b Sherlock	6	11	7	-	1
C.Bloemink b Sherlock	18	28	26	-	3
N.van Woerkom c Franklin b Sherlock	101	160	104	1	12
R.van der Merwe c Franklin b Sherlock	33	59	45	3	1
K.Pienaar c Franklin b Sherlock	11	22	16	-	1
H.Kuhn c Patel b Canning	23	24	21	1	1
G.M.Hampson not out	15	33	24	-	2
L.Jonker not out	1	2	1	-	-
J.P.Lee					
Extras (b 2, lb 4, w 12, nb 2)	20				
TOTAL (50 overs) (8 wkts)	**236**	212			

Bowling	*O*	*M*	*R*	*W*
PRETORIA HSOB				
Lee	1.4	0	6	0
van Woerkom	10	0	77	0
Pienaar	9.2	0	49	2
Williams	5	0	33	0
Hampson	10	1	73	2
Jonker	8	0	46	0
van der Merwe	6	0	42	0
NEW ZEALAND A				
Mason	10	2	32	1
Franklin	10	3	33	1
Sherlock	10	0	59	5
Canning	10	1	47	1
Patel	10	0	59	0

Fall of Wickets	***NZA***	***P***
1st	57	15
2nd	66	15
3rd	102	21
4th	198	45
5th	302	119
6th	-	147
7th	-	191
8th	-	234
9th	-	-
10th	-	-

SOUTH AFRICA A v NEW ZEALAND A — First One-day

at Wanderers Stadium, Johannesburg on 29 September, 2004
Toss : South Africa A. Umpires : I.L. Howell & S. Wadvalla
South Africa A won by 15 runs.

The home side were in trouble at 86-5 after 24.2 overs but then reached 267-6 thanks to an unbeaten 73 from Ackerman and a hurricane 67, from just 23 balls, by Morkel. He reached his fifty off only 19 deliveries as the bowlers took heavy punishment in the latter stages of the innings. Canning had bowled superbly in the early stages conceding just 15 runs from his 10 overs and also taking two wickets.

New Zealand A had a poor start to their innings being 37-4. Bell got to fifty from 59 balls but he went at 80-6. Canning then held the innings together with stands of 75 with Wiseman and 81 with Walmsley. Canning got to fifty off 60 balls. There was a rain stoppage at 233-7 and on the resumption Canning went straight away and the tourists fell short, going down by 15 runs.

SOUTH AFRICA A

	Runs	Mins	Balls	6s	4s
M.N.van Wyk† lbw b Canning	40	96	58	-	6
A.J.Hall c Sinclair b Walmsley	23	53	37	-	4
N.D.McKenzie c sub (JS.Patel) b Walmsley	3	27	18	-	-
A.G.Prince* c Hopkins b Wiseman	10	25	20	-	1
H.H.Dippenaar c Hopkins b Canning	2	17	13	-	-
H.D.Ackerman not out	73	106	76	-	11
J.M.Kemp c & b Wiseman	41	72	57	-	3
J.A.Morkel not out	67	30	23	6	5
J.L.Ontong					
A.C.Thomas					
G.J.P.Kruger					
Extras (w 6, nb 2)	8				
TOTAL (50 overs) (6 wkts)	**267**	213			

NEW ZEALAND A

	Runs	Mins	Balls	6s	4s
M.D.Bell* lbw b Hall	52	95	66	1	9
J.M.How c & b Kruger	1	9	2	-	-
M.S.Sinclair b Kruger	2	15	9	-	-
R.L.Taylor c Dippenaar b Kruger	2	8	5	-	-
L.Vincent b Kruger	0	8	5	-	-
G.J.Hopkins† c Dippenaar b Hall	14	45	24	-	2
T.K.Canning c Ontong b Thomas	85	123	96	3	7
P.J.Wiseman c & b Ontong	31	53	32	-	4
K.P.Walmsley c McKenzie b Thomas	44	76	56	-	3
M.J.Mason run out	7	8	4	-	1
C.S.Martin not out	1	4	2	-	-
Extras (b 3, lb 2, w 6, nb 2)	13				
TOTAL (49.5 overs)	**252**	225			

Bowling	*O*	*M*	*R*	*W*
NEW ZEALAND A				
Mason	5.5	1	28	0
Martin	10	1	69	0
Vincent	2.1	0	18	0
Walmsley	10	0	73	2
Canning	10	4	15	2
Wiseman	10	0	58	2
How	2	0	6	0
SOUTH AFRICA A				
Kruger	8	1	42	4
Morkel	9	0	41	0
Thomas	9.5	0	52	2
Hall	10	0	49	2
Ontong	10	0	35	1
Kemp	3	0	28	0

Fall of Wickets	***SAA***	***NZA***
1st	53	10
2nd	63	24
3rd	78	29
4th	82	37
5th	86	78
6th	181	80
7th	-	155
8th	-	236
9th	-	247
10th	-	252

SOUTH AFRICA A v NEW ZEALAND A — Second One-day

at Sedgars Park, Potchefstroom on 1 October, 2004 (d/n)
Toss : South Africa A. Umpires : K.H. Hurter & B.G. Jerling
South Africa A won by 9 wickets.

The New Zealand batting was very disappointing with only three players able to reach 20. It was thanks to a last wicket stand of 32 (the highest of the innings) that they were able to reach 100. Willoughby and Kemp were the most successful bowlers with three wickets each.

Hall went to the last ball of the first over but that was the only success for the bowlers as van Wyk (fifty off 65 balls) and McKenzie (fifty off 70 balls) scored the required runs in 25.2 overs. This gave the home side an unbeatable 2-0 lead in the series.

NEW ZEALAND A

	Runs	Mins	Balls	6s	4s
M.D.Bell* c van Wyk b Willoughby	20	45	28	-	4
J.M.How lbw b Willoughby	0	7	1	-	-
M.S.Sinclair lbw b Kruger	5	12	13	-	1
R.L.Taylor c Kruger b Willoughby	22	41	32	-	4
L.Vincent lbw b Morkel	16	55	27	1	1
G.J.Hopkins† c van Wyk b Hall	0	13	8	-	-
J.E.C.Franklin not out	36	83	53	-	3
P.J.Wiseman c Prince b Kemp	0	7	6	-	-
K.P.Walmsley c & b Kemp	0	10	7	-	-
J.S.Patel lbw b Kemp	0	7	8	-	-
R.R.Sherlock lbw b Hall	15	31	26	-	1
Extras (lb 1, w 10)	11				
TOTAL (34.5 overs)	**125**	160			

SOUTH AFRICA A

	Runs	Mins	Balls	6s	4s
M.N.van Wyk† not out	59	110	72	-	10
A.J.Hall c Hopkins b Walmsley	4	5	4	-	1
N.D.McKenzie not out	57	104	77	1	9
A.G.Prince*					
H.H.Dippenaar					
H.D.Ackerman					
J.M.Kemp					
J.L.Ontong					
J.A.Morkel					
G.J.P.Kruger					
C.M.Willoughby					
Extras (b 1, w 4, nb 1)	6				
TOTAL (25.2 overs) (1 wkt)	**126**	110			

Bowling	*O*	*M*	*R*	*W*
SOUTH AFRICA A				
Kruger	5	0	24	1
Willoughby	10	0	35	3
Hall	6.5	2	21	2
Kemp	6	0	18	3
Morkel	6	1	22	1
Ontong	1	0	4	0
NEW ZEALAND A				
Walmsley	7	0	47	1
Franklin	7	2	18	0
Sherlock	6	0	37	0
Patel	5.2	0	23	0

Fall of Wickets

	NZA	*SAA*
1st	6	5
2nd	14	-
3rd	32	-
4th	55	-
5th	61	-
6th	83	-
7th	84	-
8th	91	-
9th	93	-
10th	125	-

SOUTH AFRICA A v NEW ZEALAND A — Third One-day

at SuperSport Park, Centurion on 3 October, 2004
Toss : New Zealand A. Umpires : I.L. Howell & B.G. Jerling
South Africa A won by 4 runs.

South Africa lost both openers for 15 before Dippenaar rescued the situation, getting fifty from 67 balls and his century from a further 59 deliveries. Kemp gave him great support, hitting a quick fifty off 33 balls.Walmsley was the best of the New Zealand bowlers.

New Zealand had a positive start to the innings despite losing early wickets. Bell got fifty at a run a ball before going at 85-3. Fulton and Vincent added 107 in 20 overs and then Fulton and Hopkins put on 91 off 73 balls. Fulton got fifty from 58 balls but his departure triggered a huge collapse.

New Zealand lost six wickets in ten balls for just nine runs as South Africa A took a four run win and a clean sweep of the series.

SOUTH AFRICA A

	Runs	Mins	Balls	6s	4s
M.N.van Wyk† c Hopkins b Martin	0	11	8	-	-
A.J.Hall b Martin	8	31	23	-	1
H.H.Dippenaar lbw b Walmsley	113	188	131	2	13
A.G.Prince* b Canning	37	80	50	-	2
N.D.McKenzie c How b Walmsley	35	46	39	-	3
J.M.Kemp not out	79	53	45	4	8
J.A.Morkel c Bell b Walmsley	10	10	7	-	1
H.D.Ackerman not out	1	4	1	-	-
A.C.Thomas					
G.J.P.Kruger					
C.M.Willoughby					
Extras (b 4, lb 1, w 4, nb 4)	13				
TOTAL (50 overs) (6 wkts)	**296**	205			

NEW ZEALAND A

	Runs	Mins	Balls	6s	4s
M.D.Bell* c Prince b Thomas	53	68	52	2	6
J.M.How lbw b Hall	4	28	16	-	-
M.S.Sinclair c McKenzie b Hall	19	25	20	-	3
P.G.Fulton b Thomas	98	150	102	-	10
L.Vincent c Dippenaar b Kemp	42	81	57	1	2
G.J.Hopkins† not out	49	72	45	-	4
R.L.Taylor lbw b Hall	1	4	2	-	-
T.K.Canning b Hall	0	2	1	-	-
K.P.Walmsley run out	5	3	3	-	-
J.S.Patel b Morkel	0	2	1	-	-
C.S.Martin run out	0	3	1		-
Extras (lb 12, w 5, nb 4)	21				
TOTAL (49.2 overs)	**292**	224			

Bowling	*O*	*M*	*R*	*W*
NEW ZEALAND A				
Martin	10	2	57	2
Walmsley	10	1	46	3
Canning	10	0	41	1
Patel	8	0	58	0
Vincent	4	0	24	0
How	8	0	65	0
SOUTH AFRICA A				
Kruger	6	0	38	0
Willoughby	10	1	56	0
Hall	10	0	62	4
Thomas	9.1	1	40	2
Morkel	6.1	0	43	1
Kemp	8	0	41	1

Fall of Wickets	***SAA***	***NZA***
1st	6	30
2nd	15	68
3rd	105	85
4th	175	192
5th	265	283
6th	283	284
7th	-	284
8th	-	290
9th	-	290
10th	-	292

ICC CHAMPIONS TROPHY

West Indies won their first major trophy since the 1979 World Cup when they beat the hosts, England, in a thrilling final. Chasing 218 to win they were 147-8 before an unbroken ninth wicket stand of 71 (a record for West Indies) took them to victory.

The tournament was played in four groups which were based on one-day rankings as at December 1, 2003. At that stage New Zealand were ranked eighth and so drew the same group as world champions Australia.

In the group stages the lower ranked "minnow" sides never threatened and it was only when the top two sides played each other that there appeared to be any chance of an upset. To this degree the two finalists surprised higher ranked opponents to win their group finals and semi-finals.

New Zealand had a record win against USA by 210 runs but then disappointed against Australia to be eliminated.

The team was: S.P. Fleming, *(captain, Wellington)*, N.J. Astle *(Canterbury)*, I.G. Butler *(Northern Districts)*, C.L. Cairns *(Canterbury)*, C.Z. Harris *(Canterbury)*, B.B. McCullum *(Canterbury)*, C.D. McMillan *(Canterbury)*, H.J.H Marshall *(Northern Districts)*, K.D. Mills *(Auckland)*, J.D.P. Oram*(Central Districts)*, M.H.W Papps*(Canterbury)*, S.B. Styris*(Northern Districts)*, D.R. Tuffey *(Northern Districts)*, D.L. Vettori *(Northern Districts)*. Coach, J.G. Bracewell; Manager, L.M. Crocker (replaced by R.A. Dykes); Fitness Trainer, W. Frost; Physiotherapist, D.F. Shackel; Video Analyst, Z. Hitchcock.

New Zealand Averages

BATTING	*M*	*I*	*NO*	*HS*	*Agg*	*Ave*	*100s*	*50s*	*Ct*	*St*	*SR*
N.J. Astle	2	2	1	145*	163	163.00	1	-	-	-	95
C.D. McMillan	2	2	1	64*	82	82.00	-	1	-	-	151
B.B. McCullum	2	1	0	47	47	47.00	-	-	2	-	69
S.B. Styris	2	2	0	75	75	37.50	-	1	2	-	64
C.Z. Harris	2	1	0	26	26	26.00	-	-	-	-	50
S.P. Fleming	2	2	0	29	44	22.00	-	-	-	-	60
J.D.P. Oram	2	1	0	15	15	15.00	-	-	-	-	55
H.J.H. Marshall	2	2	0	11	11	5.50	-	-	-	-	50
C.L. Cairns	2	2	0	3	3	1.50	-	-	3	-	50
D.L. Vettori	2	1	1	29*	29	-	-	-	-	-	69
K.D. Mills	1	1	1	3*	3	-	-	-	-	-	100
D.R. Tuffey	1	-	-	-	-	-	-	-	-	-	-

BOWLING	*O*	*M*	*R*	*W*	*Ave*	*Best*	*R/O*
S.B. Styris	2	0	9	1	9.00	1-9	4.50
J.D.P. Oram	18.4	3	70	6	11.66	5-36	3.75
D.L. Vettori	20	3	66	3	22.00	3-14	3.30
C.Z. Harris	17	3	65	2	32.50	1-29	3.82
C.L. Cairns	8	0	33	1	33.00	1-16	4.13
C.D. McMillan	1	0	16	0	-	-	16.00
K.D. Mills	5.2	0	34	0	-	-	6.37
D.R. Tuffey	8	0	39	0	-	-	4.88

NEW ZEALAND v USA — Champions Trophy

at The Oval on 10 September, 2004
Toss : United States of America. Umpires : B. Doctrove & D.R. Shepherd
***New Zealand won by 210 runs.** Points: New Zealand 2, USA 0*

In what was to become the norm for the tournament, New Zealand were asked to bat after losing the toss. Fleming and Marshall went, leaving New Zealand at 43-2 but a 163 run stand off 166 balls between Astle and Styris swung the pendulum in New Zealand's favour.

Astle got his fifty from 79 balls and went to his 14th one day century after another 58 deliveries. Styris needed 55 balls for his half century. A total of 136 runs were scored from the last 7.4 overs as McMillan plundered the hapless attack. He scored his fifty off just 21 balls as the Black Caps reached 347-4.

After a good start the Americans then lost four wickets in seven balls to be 55-4. Oram had career best figures and Vettori was economical as USA were bowled out for just 137 giving New Zealand its biggest one-day win.

NEW ZEALAND

	Runs	Mins	Balls	6s	4s
S.P.Fleming* c Romero b Reid	15	19	22	-	3
N.J.Astle not out	145	177	151	6	13
H.J.H.Marshall c Desai b Romero	11	23	20	-	1
S.B.Styris c Ali b Staple	75	90	78	-	8
C.L.Cairns c sub (D.L.Blake) b Staple	3	6	5	-	-
C.D.McMillan not out	64	30	27	7	2
J.D.P.Oram					
B.B.McCullum†					
C.Z.Harris					
D.L.Vettori					
D.R.Tuffey					
Extras (10, w 21, nb 3)	34				
TOTAL (50 overs) (4 wkts)	**347**	177			

USA

	Runs	Mins	Balls	6s	4s
R.P.Alexander lbw b Oram	26	64	47	-	3
M.R.Johnson† c McCullum b Oram	20	39	18	-	3
L.C.Romero c Styris b Oram	0	2	2	-	-
S.J.Massiah c McCullum b Oram	0	2	2	-	-
R.W.Staple* lbw b Cairns	0	3	1	-	-
C.B.Lambert c Cairns b Vettori	39	88	84	1	4
J.H.Desai lbw b Vettori	16	43	38	-	1
Aijaz Ali c Styris b Harris	4	8	5	-	1
Rashid Zia c Cairns b Oram	8	38	41	-	2
C.A.Reid b Vettori	6	12	12	-	1
H.R.Johnson not out	0	4	5	-	-
Extras (lb 3, w 15)	18				
TOTAL (42.4 overs)	**137**	161			

Bowling	*O*	*M*	*R*	*W*
USA				
Johnson H.R.	7	1	43	0
Reid	10	0	37	1
Romero	4	0	52	1
Lambert	10	0	66	0
Zia	9	1	63	0
Staple	10	0	76	2
NEW ZEALAND				
Tuffey	8	0	39	0
Oram	9.4	1	36	5
Cairns	5	0	16	1
Harris	10	2	29	1
Vettori	10	3	14	3

Fall of Wickets

	NZ	*USA*
1st	25	52
2nd	43	52
3rd	206	52
4th	211	55
5th	-	63
6th	-	99
7th	-	114
8th	-	122
9th	-	132
10th	-	137

NEW ZEALAND v AUSTRALIA — Champions Trophy

at The Oval on 16 September, 2004
Toss : Australia. Umpires : S.A. Bucknor & R.E. Koertzen
Australia won by 7 wickets. *Points: Australia 2, New Zealand 0*

Mills replaced Tuffey from the previous game for New Zealand. New Zealand got to 30-0 and McGrath was struggling. Then Astle was dismissed and New Zealand were soon 49-4. McGrath had three wickets and never looked back. In a timid batting display only a 68 run stand for the ninth wicket enabled New Zealand to reach 198. Kasprowicz and McGrath each took three wickets.

Gilchrist went in the first over and Ponting went at 49 but then two good stands enabled Australia to cruise to victory. Martyn and Symonds added 100 off just 83 balls to give Australia a win with 12.4 overs to spare. Martyn got fifty from 63 balls while Symonds needed just 40 for his half-century.

NEW ZEALAND

	Runs	Mins	Balls	6s	4s
S.P.Fleming* c Gillespie b Kasprowicz	29	60	51	-	5
N.J.Astle lbw b McGrath	18	27	19	-	4
H.J.H.Marshall lbw b McGrath	0	5	2	-	-
S.B.Styris c Clarke b McGrath	0	18	11	-	-
C.D.McMillan run out	18	48	27	-	2
J.D.P.Oram c & b Kasprowicz	15	32	27	-	2
C.L.Cairns lbw b Kasprowicz	0	1	1	-	-
C.Z.Harris c & b Lehmann	26	52	51	-	1
B.B.McCullum† c Kasprowicz b Gillespie	47	87	68	-	4
D.L.Vettori not out	29	46	42	-	1
K.D.Mills not out	3	3	3	-	-
Extras (lb 4, w 7, nb 2)	13				
TOTAL (50 overs) (9 wkts)	**198**	199			

AUSTRALIA

	Runs	Mins	Balls	6s	4s
A.C.Gilchrist† b Oram	4	2	5	-	1
M.L.Hayden c Cairns b Harris	47	98	73	1	7
R.T.Ponting* b Styris	14	45	29	-	2
D.R.Martyn not out	60	90	71	-	9
A.Symonds not out	71	42	47	4	7
D.S.Lehmann					
M.J.Clarke					
S.R.Watson					
M.S.Kasprowicz					
J.N.Gillespie					
G.D.McGrath					
Extras (lb 1, w 1, nb 1)	3				
TOTAL (37.2 overs) (3 wkts)	**199**	143			

Bowling	O	M	R	W
AUSTRALIA				
McGrath	10	0	39	3
Gillespie	9	1	46	1
Kasprowicz	10	1	32	3
Watson	6	0	32	0
Symonds	10	2	29	0
Lehmann	5	0	16	1
NEW ZEALAND				
Oram	9	2	34	1
Mills	5.2	0	34	0
Vettori	10	0	52	0
Styris	2	0	9	1
Cairns	3	0	17	0
Harris	7	1	36	1
McMillan	1	0	16	0

Fall of Wickets	***NZ***	***A***
1st	30	4
2nd	36	49
3rd	49	99
4th	49	-
5th	79	-
6th	79	-
7th	89	-
8th	124	-
9th	192	-
10th	-	-

10, 11 September, 2004
Birmingham: **England beat Zimbabwe by 152 runs**
England 299 for 7 (50 overs) (P.D.Collingwood 80*, V.S.Solanki 62, G.O.Jones 38);
Zimbabwe 147 (39 overs) (E.Chigumbura 42*, T.Taibu 40, A.Flintoff 3-11, S.J.Harmison 3-29)

11 September, 2004
Southampton: **India beat Kenya by 98 runs**
India 290 for 4 (50 overs) (S.C.Ganguly 90, V.V.S.Laxman 79, M.Kaif 49*, R.S.Dravid 30*);
Kenya 192 for 7 (50 overs) (M.A.Ouma 49, Brijal Patel 40*, R.D.Shah 33, Harbhajan Singh 3-33)

12 September, 2004
Birmingham: **South Africa beat Bangladesh by 9 wickets**
Bangladesh 93 (31.3 overs) (Nafis Iqbal 40, C.K.Langeveldt 3-17, M.Ntini 3-19, N.Boje 3-23);
South Africa 94 for 1 (17.5 overs) (G.C.Smith 42*, J.H.Kallis 40*)

13 September, 2004
Southampton: **Australia beat United States of America by 9 wickets**
United States of America 65 (24 overs) (M.S.Kasprowicz 4-14, J.N.Gillespie 4-15);
Australia 66 for 1 (7.5 overs)

14 September, 2004
The Oval: **Sri Lanka beat Zimbabwe by 4 wickets**
Zimbabwe 191 (49.1 overs) (E.Chigumbura 57, P.Utseya 31, D.N.T.Zoysa 3-19, M.F.Maharoof 3-38);
Sri Lanka 195 for 6 (43.5 overs) (M.S.Atapattu 43, W.S.Jayantha 36, E.Chigumbura 3-37)

15 September, 2004
Birmingham: **Pakistan beat Kenya by 7 wickets**
Kenya 94 (32 overs) (K.O.Otieno 33, Shahid Afridi 5-11, Shoaib Malik 3-15);
Pakistan 95 for 3 (18.4 overs) (Yasir Hameed 41, Imran Farhat 38*)

15 September, 2004
Southampton: **West Indies beat Bangladesh by 7 wickets**
West Indies 269 for 3 (50 overs) (C.H.Gayle 99, W.W.Hinds 82, R.R.Sarwan 30*);
Bangladesh 131 (39.3 overs) (Khaled Mahmud 34*, M.Dillon 5-29)

17, 18 September, 2004
Southampton: **England beat Sri Lanka by 49 runs (D/L)**
England 251 for 7 (50 overs) (A.Flintoff 104, M.E.Trescothick 66, P.D.Collingwood 39);
Sri Lanka 95 for 5 (24 overs)

18, 19 September, 2004
The Oval: **West Indies beat South Africa by 5 wickets**
South Africa 246 for 6 (50 overs) (H.H.Gibbs 101, J.A.Rudolph 46, G.C.Smith 45, C.H.Gayle 3-50);
West Indies 249 for 5 (48.5 overs) (R.R.Sarwan 75, S.Chanderpaul 51*, B.C.Lara 49)

19 September, 2004
Birmingham: **Pakistan beat India by 3 wickets**
India 200 (49.5 overs) (R.S.Dravid 67, A.B.Agarkar 47, Naved-ul-Hasan 4-25, Shoaib Akhtar 4-36);
Pakistan 201 for 7 (49.2 overs) (Yousuf Youhana 81*, Inzamam-ul-Haq 41, I.K.Pathan 3-34)

Points
Pool A – Australia 4, New Zealand 2, USA 0.
Pool B – West Indies 4, South Africa 2, Bangladesh 0.
Pool C – Pakistan 4, India 2, Kenya 0.
Pool D – England 4, Sri Lanka 2, Zimbabwe 0.

21 September, 2004 (semi-final)
Birmingham: **England beat Australia by 6 wickets**
Australia 259 for 9 (50 overs) (D.R.Martyn 65, M.J.Clarke 42, D.S.Lehmann 38, A.C.Gilchrist 37, D.Gough 3-48);
England 262 for 4 (46.3 overs) (M.P.Vaughan 86, M.E.Trescothick 81, A.J.Strauss 52*)

22 September, 2004 (semi-final)
Southampton: **West Indies beat Pakistan by 7 wickets**
Pakistan 131 (38.2 overs) (Yasir Hameed 39);
West Indies 132 for 3 (28.1 overs) (R.R.Sarwan 56*, B.C.Lara 31*)

25 September, 2004 (final)
The Oval: **West Indies beat England by 2 wickets**
England 217 (49.4 overs) (M.E.Trescothick 104, A.F.Giles 31, W.W.Hinds 3-24);
West Indies 218 for 8 (48.5 overs) (S.Chanderpaul 47, C.O.Browne 35*, I.D.R.Bradshaw 34*, A.Flintoff 3-38)

NEW ZEALAND IN BANGLADESH

New Zealand made a six game tour of Bangladesh made up of two tests, three one-day internationals and a warm up game. In the internationals they had a clean sweep, convincingly winning all games. Fleming set records in the tests becoming New Zealand's most capped test player and leading run scorer. McCullum joined his captain as the only players to score test centuries on tour. Sinclair, Styris and Marshall all got fifties.

On the bowling front Vettori was the star taking 20 wickets in the two tests, getting six wickets in three innings, but the highlight was Franklin's hat-trick. He became only the second New Zealander to achieve the feat.

Fleming and Oram were rested for the one-day series with the captaincy going to Vettori. In the 3-0 win Sinclair got two fifties, while Mills, Vettori and Styris were the leading wicket-takers.

The touring party was S.P. Fleming *(captain, Wellington)*, D.L. Vettori *(vice-captain, Northern Districts)*, A.R. Adams *(Auckland)*, N.J. Astle *(Canterbury)*, I.G. Butler *(Northern Districts)*, C.L. Cairns *(Canterbury)*, J.E.C. Franklin *(Wellington)*, P.G. Fulton *(Canterbury)*, C.Z. Harris *(Canterbury)*, B.B. McCullum *(Canterbury)*, C.D. McMillan *(Canterbury)*, H.J.H. Marshall *(Northern Districts)*, C.S. Martin *(Canterbury)*, K.D. Mills *(Auckland)*, J.D.P. Oram *(Central Districts)*, M.H. Richardson *(Auckland)*, M.S. Sinclair *(Central Districts)*, S.B. Styris *(Northern Districts)*, P.J. Wiseman *(Canterbury)*. Coach, J.G. Bracewell; Manager, R.A. Dykes; Fitness Trainer, G. Owen; Physiotherapist, D.F. Shackel; Video Analyst, P. Mayell.

Fleming, Martin, Oram, Richardson and Wiseman left after the test series and their places were taken by Adams, Fulton, Harris, Cairns and McMillan. M.H.W. Papps *(Canterbury)* was originally selected for the first-class tour but was injured and replaced by Sinclair who retained his place in the one-day squad which was announced later.

New Zealand Test Averages

BATTING	M	I	NO	HS	Agg	Ave	100s	50s	Ct	St
B.B. McCullum	2	2	1	143	160	160.00	1	-	7	1
S.P. Fleming	2	2	0	202	231	115.50	1	-	3	-
H.J.H. Marshall	1	1	0	69	69	69.00	-	1	-	-
J.D.P. Oram	2	2	1	38*	61	61.00	-	-	1	-
M.S. Sinclair	2	2	0	76	99	49.50	-	1	5	-
S.B. Styris	2	2	0	89	91	45.50	-	1	5	-
P.J. Wiseman	2	1	0	28	28	28.00	-	-	1	-
N.J. Astle	2	2	0	39	50	25.00	-	-	4	-
D.L. Vettori	2	1	0	23	23	23.00	-	-	1	-
J.E.C. Franklin	2	1	0	23	23	23.00	-	-	1	-
M.H. Richardson	2	2	0	28	43	21.50	-	-	1	-
I.G. Butler	1	1	1	15*	15	-	-	-	-	-

BOWLING	O	M	R	W	Ave	Best	5w	10w
J.E.C. Franklin	35	11	75	7	10.71	5-28	1	-
D.L. Vettori	111.4	49	224	20	11.20	6-28	3	1
J.D.P. Oram	44.5	17	95	4	23.75	3-36	-	-
P.J. Wiseman	83.5	15	280	8	35.00	3-64	-	-
N.J. Astle	2	1	1	0	-	-	-	-
S.B. Styris	2	1	4	0	-	-	-	-
I.G. Butler	16	4	42	0	-	-	-	-

Bangladesh Test Averages

BATTING	M	I	NO	HS	Agg	Ave	100s	50s	Ct	St
Khaled Masud	2	4	1	51	94	31.33	-	1	2	-
Aftab Ahmed	1	2	0	28	48	24.00	-	-	-	-
Mohammad Ashraful	2	4	0	67	93	23.25	-	1	-	-
Tapash Baisya	2	4	1	66	66	22.00	-	1	1	-
Mohammad Rafique	2	4	0	32	87	21.75	-	-	1	-
Rajin Saleh	2	4	0	41	78	19.50	-	-	2	-
Javed Omer	2	4	0	58	74	18.50	-	1	-	-
Nafis Iqbal	2	4	0	49	72	18.00	-	-	1	-
Mushfiqur Rahman	1	2	0	20	35	17.50	-	-	2	-
Alok Kapali	2	4	0	14	40	10.00	-	-	1	-
Manjural Islam Rana	1	2	0	16	17	8.50	-	-	2	-
Hannan Sarkar	1	2	0	1	1	0.50	-	-	-	-
Tareq Aziz	1	2	0	0	0	0.00	-	-	-	-
Enamul Haque jnr	1	2	2	0*	0	-	-	-	-	-

BOWLING	O	M	R	W	Ave	Best	5w	10w
Mohammad Rafique	114.1	30	252	9	28.00	6-122	1	-
Manjural Islam Rana	42	12	84	3	28.00	3-84	-	-
Enamul Haque jnr	42	4	142	2	71.00	2-142	-	-
Rajin Saleh	20	0	85	1	85.00	1-81	-	-
Tapash Baisya	45	4	194	1	194.00	1-112	-	-
Mohammad Ashraful	2	0	12	0	-	-	-	-
Alok Kapali	5	0	23	0	-	-	-	-
Tareq Aziz	12	1	59	0	-	-	-	-
Mushfiqur Rahman	15	1	68	0	-	-	-	-

New Zealand One-day International Averages

BATTING	*M*	*I*	*NO*	*HS*	*Agg*	*Ave*	*100s*	*50s*	*Ct*	*St*	*SR*
M.S. Sinclair	2	2	0	66	128	64.00	-	2	3	-	85
C.L. Cairns	3	3	1	74	125	62.50	-	1	-	-	83
S.B. Styris	3	3	0	51	106	35.33	-	1	3	-	69
D.L. Vettori	3	3	2	18*	33	33.00	-	-	-	-	75
N.J. Astle	3	3	0	29	83	27.66	-	-	-	-	53
C.D. McMillan	3	3	0	39	63	21.00	-	-	1	-	63
P.G. Fulton	1	1	0	9	9	9.00	-	-	1	-	90
C.Z. Harris	3	3	0	9	21	7.00	-	-	2	-	44
A.R. Adams	1	1	0	4	4	4.00	-	-	1	-	57
B.B. McCullum	3	2	0	8	8	4.00	-	-	3	1	28
H.J.H. Marshall	3	3	0	7	9	3.00	-	-	-	-	34
K.D. Mills	3	1	1	0*	0	-	-	-	-	-	0
J.E.C. Franklin	2	-	-	-	-	-	-	-	2	-	-

BOWLING	*O*	*M*	*R*	*W*	*Ave*	*Best*	*R/O*
D.L. Vettori	22.5	0	69	7	9.85	3-9	3.02
S.B. Styris	23.4	5	60	6	10.00	3-16	2.53
K.D. Mills	25	3	78	7	11.14	4-14	3.12
C.L. Cairns	16	3	41	3	13.66	2-15	2.56
J.E.C. Franklin	13	2	63	3	21.00	2-34	4.85
C.Z. Harris	19	4	58	1	58.00	1-21	3.05
A.R. Adams	6	1	24	0	-	-	4.00

Bangladesh One-day International Averages

BATTING	*M*	*I*	*NO*	*HS*	*Agg*	*Ave*	*100s*	*50s*	*Ct*	*St*	*SR*
Khaled Masud	3	3	1	41	83	41.50	-	-	1	2	68
Nafis Iqbal	2	2	0	40	40	20.00	-	-	-	-	44
Alok Kapali	1	1	0	17	17	17.00	-	-	1	-	48
Manjural Islam Rana	3	3	1	13	33	16.50	-	-	-	-	29
Khaled Mahmud	1	1	0	14	14	14.00	-	-	1	-	50
Mohammad Rafique	3	3	0	21	36	12.00	-	-	2	-	48
Habibul Bashar	2	2	0	22	22	11.00	-	-	-	-	41
Mohammad Ashraful	3	3	0	17	32	10.66	-	-	-	-	59
Rajin Saleh	3	3	0	28	32	10.66	-	-	3	-	31
Javed Omer	3	3	0	12	23	7.66	-	-	1	-	62
Aftab Ahmed	3	3	0	8	16	5.33	-	-	-	-	51
Tapash Baisya	3	2	0	7	9	4.50	-	-	-	-	47
Nazmul Hossain	2	2	2	4*	4	-	-	-	1	-	36
Mushfiqur Rahman	1	-	-	-	-	-	-	-	-	-	-

BOWLING	*O*	*M*	*R*	*W*	*Ave*	*Best*	*R/O*
Aftab Ahmed	20	0	67	6	11.16	5-31	3.35
Nazmul Hossain	14.2	2	70	4	17.50	4-40	4.88
Mohammad Rafique	30	3	117	6	19.50	4-63	3.90
Tapash Baisya	25	2	126	4	31.50	2-58	5.04
Manjural Islam Rana	27.4	2	105	2	52.50	2-35	3.79
Alok Kapali	4	0	21	0	-	-	5.25
Khaled Mahmud	5	0	28	0	-	-	5.60
Mushfiqur Rahman	8	2	28	0	-	-	3.50
Rajin Saleh	10	0	49	0	-	-	4.90

BANGLADESH BOARD XI v NEW ZEALAND — Not first-class

at BKSP Ground, Savar on 14, 15, 16 October, 2004
Toss : New Zealand. Umpires : Showkatur Rahman & Ziaul Islam
Close of play: 1st day: NZ 285-6, McCullum 18, Vettori 5; 2nd day: Board XI 200-7, Nadif 11, Jubair 5
Match drawn

Martin, who did not get to play on tour, and Mills were omitted from the New Zealand squad. As the match was played as 12-a-side, it did not carry first-class status.

After New Zealand had lost four wickets for 86 runs, Marshall joined Fleming to add 119. The New Zealand captain went on to 129 before retiring. McCullum and Vettori added an unbeaten 70 for the seventh wicket before Fleming declared on the second morning.

The Board XI lost wickets regularly with test batsmen Hannan Sarkar and Mohammad Ashraful top scoring with 44 each. Five New Zealand bowlers captured two wickets apiece. When New Zealand batted a second time, Richardson again went cheaply but Sinclair and Astle shared a century stand for the second wicket and then Oram and Franklin prospered later in the innings.

The Board XI had a token 11 overs to bat before the game ended.

NEW ZEALAND

FIRST INNINGS	*Runs*	*Mins*	*Balls*	*6s*	*4s*	*SECOND INNINGS*	*Runs*	*Mins*	*Balls*	*6s*	*4s*
M.H.Richardson lbw Shahadat	2	14	6	-	-	lbw b Shahadat	0	5	7	-	-
M.S.Sinclair b Kabir	16	45	26	-	3	retired hurt	71	148	91	1	7
S.P.Fleming* retired hurt	129	235	176	3	13						
S.B.Styris run out	5	14	7	-	-	st Dhiman b Nadif	26	51	34	1	2
N.J.Astle c Sarkar b Kabir	15	30	27	-	1	(3) retired hurt	113	224	156	1	17
H.J.H.Marshall b Kabir	51	113	74	-	6						
J.D.P.Oram c Dhiman b Shahadat	19	68	52	-	1	(5) c Kabir b Ashraful	47	87	70	1	3
B.B.McCullum† not out	52	115	73	1	2						
D.L.Vettori not out	26	81	65	-	1						
J.E.C.Franklin						(6) st Dhiman b Ashraful	62	76	67	4	2
P.J.Wiseman						(7) not out	4	26	22	-	1
I.G.Butler						(8) not out	12	10	14	1	1
Extras (b 1, lb 2, w 6, nb 20)	29					(b 2, lb 5, w 3, nb 6)	16				
TOTAL (81 overs) (6 wkts dec)	**344**	365				(75.5 overs) (4 wkts dec)	**351**	320			

BOARD XI

FIRST INNINGS	*Runs*	*Mins*	*Balls*	*6s*	*4s*	*SECOND INNINGS*	*Runs*	*Mins*	*Balls*	*6s*	*4s*
Hannan Sarkar c McCullum b Wiseman	44	85	76	-	5	c McCullum b Franklin	6	19	14	-	-
Nafis Iqbal c Sinclair b Oram	0	40	27	-	-	not out	14	50	32	-	-
Aftab Ahmed c McCullum b Butler	14	50	29	-	1						
Alok Kapali* c & b Vettori	17	64	44	-	1						
Mohammad Ashraful c McCullum b Vettori	44	153	128	-	3	(3) not out	4	30	21	-	-
Shamsur Rahman c McCullum b Butler	37	150	123	-	2						
Dhiman Ghosh† c Astle b Wiseman	1	9	5	-	-						
Nadif Chowdhury c McCullum b Oram	13	84	73	-	-						
Talha Jubair c & b Franklin	9	33	30	-	2						
Anwar Hossain c Sinclair b Franklin	0	9	4	-	-						
Alamgir Kabir not out	0	4	2	-	-						
Shahadat Hossain											
Extras (b 8, w 3, nb 18)	29					(b1, w1, nb 1)	3				
TOTAL (87.1 overs)	**208**	349				(11 overs) (1 wkt)	**27**	50			

Bowling	*O*	*M*	*R*	*W*	*O*	*M*	*R*	*W*
BOARD XI								
Shahadat	11	0	59	2	14	1	45	1
Jubair	10	2	39	0	8	1	34	0
Kabir	21	2	72	3	4	1	28	0
Anwar	13	2	47	0	6	0	33	0
Nadif	18	0	85	0	15	2	60	1
Ashraful	2	0	20	0	12.5	2	62	2
Kapali	6	0	19	0	5	0	22	0
Rahman					8	1	29	0
Sarkar					1	0	12	0
Ghosh					2	0	19	0
NEW ZEALAND								
Butler	13	1	29	2	4	1	12	0
Franklin	12.1	2	36	2	2	0	5	1
Oram	11	7	16	2	2	2	0	0
Vettori	24	3	57	2				
Wiseman	21	4	56	2				
Styris	4	3	5	0	3	1	9	0
Astle	1	0	1	0				
Sinclair	1	1	0	0				

Fall of Wickets

	NZ	***BXI***	***NZ***	***BXI***
	1st	*1st*	*2nd*	*2nd*
1st	14	24	1	13
2nd	50	76	175	-
3rd	58	78	310	-
4th	86	110	335	-
5th	205	167	-	-
6th	274	171	-	-
7th	-	191	-	-
8th	-	205	-	-
9th	-	208	-	-
10th	-	208	-	-

BANGLADESH v NEW ZEALAND — First Test

at National Stadium, Dhaka on 19, 20, 21, 22 October, 2004
Toss : Bangladesh. Umpires : M.R. Benson & D.J. Harper
Close of play: 1st day: Bangladesh 165-6, Masud,12 Rana16; 2nd day: NZ 207-5, Oram 18, McCullum 48
3rd day: Bangladesh 41-2, Nafis 24, Saleh 0
New Zealand won by an innings and 99 runs

Nafis Iqbal made his test debut and umpire Benson stood in his first test. Bangladesh got off to a horror start after winning the toss and were 5-3 in the seventh over. Saleh and Ashraful then put on 115 before another collapse saw Bangladesh go from 120-3 to 177 all out.

The second morning saw Franklin claim just the second hat-trick by a New Zealand bowler in a test match. He took the wickets of Rana and Rafique with the last two balls of his first over, and then bowled Baisya, who did not offer a stroke, with the first ball of his next over. His 5-28 was his first five wicket bag in tests.

New Zealand had a steady start with Sinclair relishing his opener's role but then there was a collapse from 97-1 to 139-5 before Oram and McCullum added a valuable 84. McCullum received good support from all the lower order batsmen and got his fifty from 81 balls and went to his maiden test century after 158 deliveries and 222 minutes. In all the last five wickets put on 263 to give the Black Caps a first innings lead of 225. Rafique, during a marathon spell of 59.1 overs, became the first Bangladesh bowler to take 50 test wickets.

After an opening stand of 27 the Bangladesh batsmen struggled against the spin attack of Vettori and Wiseman, only the fourth wicket stand of 46 showing any resistance. Vettori got his first five wicket haul in tests since 2000/01 while Wiseman got his 50th test wicket as the tourists won by an innings and 99 runs.

BANGLADESH

FIRST INNINGS	*Runs*	*Mins*	*Balls*	*6s*	*4s*	*SECOND INNINGS*	*Runs*	*Mins*	*Balls*	*6s*	*4s*
Hannan Sarkar c Fleming b Oram	0	2	3	-	-	(3) c & b Vettori	1	15	15	-	-
Javed Omer b Franklin	1	28	19	-	-	c McCullum b Vettori	14	63	39	-	2
Nafis Iqbal c McCullum b Oram	1	29	18	-	-	(1) run out	49	148	111	1	5
Rajin Saleh c Oram b Franklin	41	197	136	1	5	c McCullum b Vettori	0	14	15	-	-
Mohammad Ashraful c Astle b Vettori	67	225	189	3	8	c Styris b Vettori	26	122	96	1	1
Alok Kapali c McCullum b Vettori	14	62	51	-	2	c McCullum b Wiseman	0	6	4	-	-
Khaled Masud*† not out	23	148	91	-	2	c Styris b Wiseman	2	8	7	-	-
Manjural Islam Rana c McCullum b Franklin	16	80	67	-	1	c Richardson b Vettori	1	27	19	-	-
Mohammad Rafique c Styris b Franklin	0	5	1	-	-	c Fleming b Wiseman	24	25	18	-	5
Tapash Baisya b Franklin	0	5	1	-	-	(11) not out	0	7	7	-	-
Tareq Aziz c Astle b Oram	0	27	22	-	-	(10) lbw b Vettori	0	3	1	-	-
Extras (lb 7, w 1, nb 6)	14					(b 6, nb 3)	9				
TOTAL (98.5 overs)	**177**	413				(54.5 overs)	**126**	233			

NEW ZEALAND

	Runs	Mins	Balls	6s	4s
M.H.Richardson c Masud b Rafique	15	35	27	-	2
M.S.Sinclair lbw b Rafique	76	200	173	-	10
S.P.Fleming* c Masud b Rana	29	74	54	-	4
S.B.Styris c Saleh b Rana	2	6	7	-	-
N.J.Astle c Rana b Rafique	11	41	35	-	-
J.D.P.Oram c Rana b Rafique	23	162	121	-	1
B.B.McCullum† c Kapali b Rafique	143	340	243	2	10
D.L.Vettori c Nafis b Rana	23	111	75	-	2
J.E.C.Franklin c Saleh b Baisya	23	77	61	-	2
P.J.Wiseman b Rafique	28	61	51	-	5
I.G.Butler not out	15	35	26	1	1
Extras (b 3, lb 5, w 4, nb 2)	14				
TOTAL (145.1 overs)	**402**	580			

Bowling	*O*	*M*	*R*	*W*	*O*	*M*	*R*	*W*
NEW ZEALAND								
Oram	22.5	9	36	3	7	4	6	0
Franklin	17	7	28	5	5	1	14	0
Styris	2	1	4	0				
Butler	12	3	34	0	4	1	8	0
Vettori	29	15	26	2	22	13	28	6
Wiseman	16	5	42	0	16.5	1	64	3
BANGLADESH								
Baisya	28	4	112	1				
Aziz	12	1	59	0				
Rafique	59.1	18	122	6				
Rana	42	12	84	3				
Saleh	1	0	4	0				
Kapali	2	0	6	0				
Ashraful	1	0	7	0				

Fall of Wickets

	B 1st	*NZ 1st*	*B 2nd*
1st	0	34	27
2nd	5	97	33
3rd	5	99	41
4th	120	122	87
5th	124	139	88
6th	136	223	92
7th	165	294	101
8th	165	351	112
9th	165	371	122
10th	177	402	126

NZC

NEW ZEALAND v FICA WORLD XI — 1st Match

Back row: H.J.H. Marshall, D.R. Tuffey, J.D.P. Oram, K.D. Mills, M.S. Sinclair, J.W. Wilson, B.B. McCullum.
Front row: S.B. Styris, C.D. McMillan, S.P. Fleming *(captain)*, D.L. Vettori, C.L. Cairns, N.J. Astle.

NZC

NEW ZEALAND v AUSTRALIA — Twenty20 International

Back row: D.F. Shackel *(physiotherapist)*, L.M. Crocker *(manager)*, A.R. Adams, J.W. Wilson, D.R. Tuffey, K.D. Mills, M.S. Sinclair, S.B. Styris, D.L. Vettori, B.B. McCullum, L. Vincent, W. Frost *(medical co-ordinator)*, J.G. Bracewell *(coach)*.
Front row: C.D. McMillan, C.L. Cairns, H.J.H. Marshall, S.P. Fleming *(captain)*, N.J. Astle, A. Clearwater *(communications advisor)*.

NZC

NEW ZEALAND v SRI LANKA — 2nd Test

Back row: C.S. Martin, J.M. How, I.E. O'Brien, P.J. Wiseman, K.D. Mills, C.D. Cumming, J.E.C. Franklin.
Front row: J.A.H. Marshall, H.J.H. Marshall, N.J. Astle, S.P. Fleming *(captain)*, B.B. McCullum, L. Vincent.

NDCA

NORTHERN DISTRICTS — 2004/05

Back row: B.R. Blair *(coach)*, G. Billington *(manager)*, A.P. Devcich, T.T. Davis, I.G. Butler, D.R. Flynn, B-J. Watling, T.W. Andersson *(scorer)*.
Front row: N.K.W. Horsley, J.A.F. Yovich, S.B. Styris, D.L. Vettori *(captain)*, M.N. Hart, D.R. Tuffey, G.W. Aldridge, B.P. Martin.

ACA

AUCKLAND — 2004/05

Back row: P. Sail *(physiotherapist)*, F. Thomas *(manager)*, P.A. Hitchcock, K.W.M. Todd, G.S. Shaw, K.P. Walmsley, A.J. McKay, R.J. Nicol, M.R. O'Donnell *(coach)*.

Front row: A.R. Adams, T.K. Canning, M.J. Horne, B.G.K. Walker *(captain)*, R.A. Jones, A.C. Barnes, R.A. Young, C. Cachopa.

ACA

AUCKLAND WOMEN — 2004/05

Back row: W. Stamp *(coach)*, E.B. Komp, F.J. Mann, N. Scripps, M. McElroy *(manager)*.

Second row: R.J. Kember, I. Cronin-Knight, S. Coetzee, D.J. Ramsay.

Front row: V.J. Lind, H.M. Watson, R.J. Rolls *(captain)*, E.C. Drumm, S.M Bullen.

Photo.co.nz

CANTERBURY — 2004/05

Back row: B. Warman *(manager)*, T.J.T. Papps, S.L. Stewart, H.J. Shaw, A.M. Ellis, B.B. McCullum, M.F. Sharpe *(coach)*.

Front row: M.H.W. Papps, G.R. Stead, S.J. Cunis, C.M. McMillan *(captain)*, P.G. Fulton, N.J. Astle, C.S. Martin.

Insets: C.L. Cairns, T.G. McIntosh, P.J. Wiseman, N.T. Broom, B.P. Donkers.

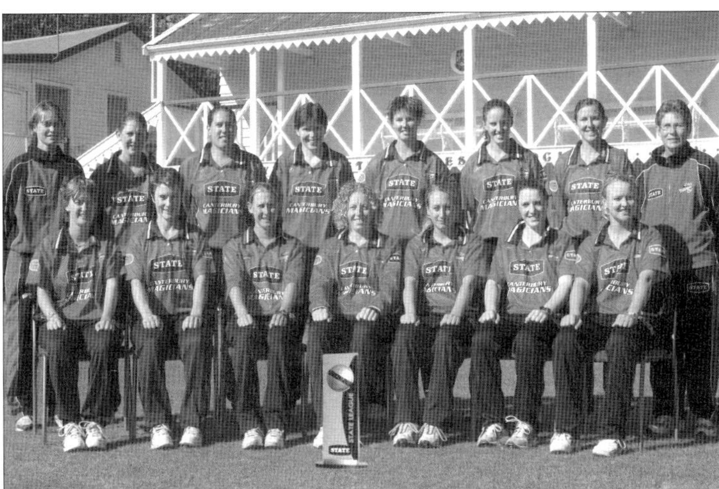

Photo.co.nz

CANTERBURY WOMEN — 2004/05

Back row: K.E. Flavell *(coach)*, M.F. Fahey, P.K. Gerrish, A.J. Wilkins, R.J. Steele, A.E. Satterthwaite, S.K. Burke, T.L. Anderson *(manager)*.

Front row: H.R. Daly, S.C. Taylor, R.C. Milburn, H.M. Tiffen (captain), H.J. Rae, S.E. Charteris, B.H. McNeill.

Photo.co.nz

OTAGO — 2004/05

Back row: A.J. Hore, C.M. Smith, M.J. Harvie, G.J. Todd, W.E.R. Somerville, D.G. Sewell.
Second row: M. Hesson *(manager)*, S.W. Eathorne, S.P. Beare, N.J. McCullum, M.N. McKenzie, G.M. Turner *(coach)*.
Front row: D.J. Drew *(physiotherapist)*, C.B. Gaffaney, G.J. Hopkins, W.C. McSkimming, J.W. Wilson, A.J. Redmond.

Photo.co.nz

OTAGO WOMEN — 2004/05

Back row: G. Rodden *(coach)*, J.A. Young, C.E. Taylor, P.B. Flannery, R.J. Pullar, S.W. Bates, R. McCambridge *(manager)*.
Front row: E.J. Scurr, M.J. Kane, T.J. Morrison, S.J. Tsukigawa *(captain)*, C.B. Winsloe, K.M. Spence, K.J. Martin.
Insets: A.L. Kane, A. Kitchin.

WCA

WELLINGTON — 2004/05

Back row: J. Tait *(fitness trainer)*, S.A. Fairley, S.M. Mills, J.D. Ryder, Azhar Abbas, M.E. Parlane, J.S. Patel, N.R. Parlane, G. Hooper *(selector)*.
Front row: V.F. Johnson *(coach)*, G.B. Murray, L.J. Woodcock, M.D. Bell *(captain)*, C.J. Nevin, M.R. Gillespie, D. Painter *(manager)*.

WCA

WELLINGTON WOMEN — 2004/05

Back row: S. Morrison *(manager)*, M.G. Wakefield, L.R.V.S. Harford, S.F.M. Devine, A.E. Cooper, M.A. Taylor, S.J. Hill, M.L. Tuapawa, R.J. Kerr *(coach)*.
Front row: A.J. Green, A.M. Little, A.M. Corbin, M.A.M. Lewis *(captain)*, M.L. Presland, M.C. Godliman, L.R. Doolan.

NZC

NEW ZEALAND WOMEN — 2004/05

Back row: A.M. Corbin, R.J. Steele, H.M. Tiffen, R.J. Rolls, N.J. Browne, M.F. Fahey.
Second Row: S.J. McGlashan, L.E. Milliken, R.J. Pullar, H.M. Watson, N. Scripps, S.K. Burke.
Front row: C.W. Dickeson *(assistant coach)*, C.A. Campbell *(manager)*, E.C. Drumm, M.A.M. Lewis *(captain)*, A. Cadogan *(physiotherapist)*, M.J.F. Shrimpton *(coach)*.

HCA

HAMILTON — 2004/05

Back row: N.K.W. Horsley, L.W. Martin, R.R. Shutte, C. Toombs, G.D. Steele, B.J. Winslade, G.G. Robinson, G.S.C. Hodgson *(player/selector)*, B.J. Hatwell.
Front row: C.J. Stevens *(selector)*, D.A. Holt, J.G. Hatwell, N.M. Daley *(captain)*, G.D. Irwin, T. Irwin *(selector/manager)*.

BANGLADESH v NEW ZEALAND — Second Test

at Chittagong Stadium on 26, 27, 28, 29 October, 2004
Toss : New Zealand. Umpires : M.R. Benson & D.J. Harper
Close of play: 1st day: NZ 338-3, Fleming 137, Astle 34; 2nd day: Bangladesh 82-3, Omer 45
3rd day: Bangladesh 210-8, Rafique 30, Baisya 15
New Zealand won by an innings and 101 runs

Aftab Ahmed made his test debut while Fleming became New Zealand's most capped player, appearing in his 87th test.

After the loss of Richardson and Astle, Fleming and Styris added 204 for the third wicket. Fleming got to fifty from 78 balls and when he hit a four to go to 82 he became the leading run scorer for New Zealand in tests, passing Martin Crowe's tally of 5444. The New Zealand captain went on to score his eighth test hundred from 154 balls in 206 minutes while Styris got his fifty off 151 balls in a circumspect display.

Fleming went to his second test double-century off 315 balls in 441 minutes before being fifth out. Marshall, playing in his first test since 2000/01, was lucky to survive his first ball but then went on to score his maiden test fifty off 126 balls. The innings was declared at tea on the second day.

Javed Omar got to fifty and became the second Bangladesh batsman to reach 1000 test runs, but wickets again fell regularly and the hosts were dismissed 363 behind the New Zealand total. It was New Zealand's third largest first innings lead in a test match. Vettori's 6-70 was his ninth haul of five wickets in tests.

In the Bangladesh second innings, the top order again failed and only a captain's knock from Masud and a cameo from Baisya (first test fifty and the fastest fifty by a Bangladesh batsman – 36 minutes and 35 balls) got the score to 262. Vettori, with another six wicket bag, took ten wickets in a test for the second time, only the second New Zealand bowler to do so. The win by an innings and 101 bettered the first test margin by two runs.

NEW ZEALAND

FIRST INNINGS	*Runs*	*Mins*	*Balls*	*6s*	*4s*	*SECOND INNINGS*	*Runs*	*Mins*	*Balls*	*6s*	*4s*
M.H.Richardson c Mushfiqur b Enamul	28	71	51	-	5						
M.S.Sinclair b Rafique	23	54	34	-	4						
S.P.Fleming* c Mushfiqur b Saleh	202	446	318	1	21						
S.B.Styris c & b Rafique	89	190	192	1	10						
N.J.Astle lbw b Rafique	39	123	95	-	6						
H.J.H.Marshall c Baisya b Enamul	69	191	145	-	6						
J.D.P.Oram not out	38	95	78	1	2						
B.B.McCullum† not out	17	18	17	-	3						
D.L.Vettori											
J.E.C.Franklin											
P.J.Wiseman											
Extras (b 9, lb 11, w 2, nb 18)	40										
TOTAL (152 overs) (6 wkts dec)	**545**	600									

BANGLADESH

	Runs	Mins	Balls	6s	4s		Runs	Mins	Balls	6s	4s
Nafis Iqbal c Styris b Vettori	13	42	33	-	3	b Wiseman	9	43	33	-	1
Javed Omer c Sinclair b Wiseman	58	198	151	-	5	c & b Franklin	1	14	12	-	-
Aftab Ahmed lbw b Vettori	20	39	39	-	3	b Vettori	28	54	42	-	5
Rajin Saleh c Sinclair b Wiseman	2	32	39	-	-	c Sinclair b Vettori	35	111	83	2	4
Mohammad Ashraful c Astle b Wiseman	0	1	2	-	-	c Styris b Vettori	0	5	4	-	-
Alok Kapali c Fleming b Vettori	13	46	48	-	2	c Astle b Wiseman	13	26	33	-	3
Khaled Masud*† lbw b Vettori	18	43	33	-	3	b Oram	51	111	87	-	9
Mushfiqur Rahman c McCullum b Franklin	15	56	43	-	3	b Vettori	20	38	33	-	3
Mohammad Rafique c Wiseman b Vettori	32	38	40	3	2	c Sinclair b Vettori	31	46	40	1	5
Tapash Baisya c Sinclair b Vettori	0	8	2	-	-	st McCullum b Vettori	66	45	47	2	10
Enamul Haque jnr not out	0	2	1	-	-	not out	0	8	8	-	-
Extras (b 4, lb 2, w 2, nb 3)	11					(b 4, lb 3, w 1)	8				
TOTAL (71.2 overs)	**182**	262				(70.2 overs)	**262**	260			

Bowling	*O*	*M*	*R*	*W*	*O*	*M*	*R*	*W*
BANGLADESH								
Baisya	17	0	82	0				
Mushfiqur	15	1	68	0				
Rafique	55	12	130	3				
Enamul	42	4	142	2				
Saleh	19	0	81	1				
Ashraful	1	0	5	0				
Kapali	3	0	17	0				
NEW ZEALAND								
Oram	5	0	20	0	10	4	33	1
Franklin	5	0	17	1	8	3	16	1
Vettori	32.2	12	70	6	28.2	9	100	6
Wiseman	27	5	68	3	24	4	106	2
Astle	2	1	1	0				

Fall of Wickets

	NZ *1st*	***B*** *1st*	***B*** *2nd*
1st	49	34	9
2nd	61	66	25
3rd	265	82	47
4th	364	82	51
5th	447	108	74
6th	517	128	123
7th	-	142	161
8th	-	181	183
9th	-	182	217
10th	-	182	262

BANGLADESH v NEW ZEALAND First One-day International

at Chittagong Stadium on 2 November, 2004
Toss : New Zealand. Umpires : A.F.M. Akhtaruddin & M.R. Benson
New Zealand won by 138 runs

Fulton made his debut for New Zealand, in place of Sinclair who was injured, and Vettori captained New Zealand for the first time. Fleming and Oram had returned home for a break.

Fulton scored a boundary off his first ball but went early. New Zealand were in some trouble at 94-5 but then a typical Cairns innings revived the innings. His fifty came off 76 balls and then he scored 24 off seven balls to get the score to 224. Hossain had his first wickets for the home side.

Mills struck in his first two overs and the home batsmen never recovered as they were dismissed for just 86. Mills had career best figures and was ably assisted by all the other bowlers. New Zealand thus cruised to an easy 138 run win. It was New Zealand's 100th win in a one-day international away from home.

NEW ZEALAND

	Runs	Mins	Balls	6s	4s
P.G.Fulton b Nazmul	9	7	10	-	2
N.J.Astle b Nazmul	27	45	37	-	5
H.J.H.Marshall st Masud b Rana	7	42	21	-	-
S.B.Styris run out	43	107	55	1	2
C.D.McMillan c Masud b Baisya	17	29	22	-	-
B.B.McCullum† b Rafique	8	26	26	-	-
C.L.Cairns b Nazmul	74	102	83	5	1
C.Z.Harris c Saleh b Rana	5	19	23	-	-
D.L.Vettori* b Baisya	12	20	15	-	1
A.R.Adams c Mahmud b Nazmul	4	12	7	-	-
K.D.Mills not out	0	1	0	-	-
Extras (lb 4, w 11, nb 3)	18				
TOTAL (49.2 overs)	**224**	214			

BANGLADESH

	Runs	Mins	Balls	6s	4s
Aftab Ahmed lbw b Mills	4	1	3	-	1
Javed Omer c Fulton b Mills	3	15	12	-	-
Rajin Saleh c McMillan b Mills	4	25	15	-	-
Habibul Bashar* lbw b Styris	22	59	41	-	3
Mohammad Ashraful c McCullum b Mills	2	11	9	-	-
Manjural Islam Rana c Styris b Vettori	13	64	47	-	2
Khaled Masud† lbw b Styris	2	7	6	-	-
Khaled Mahmud st McCullum b Vettori	14	37	28	-	3
Mohammad Rafique c Styris b Harris	11	11	16	-	2
Tapash Baisya c Adams b Vettori	2	16	8	-	-
Nazmul Hossain not out	0	11	7	-	-
Extras (lb1, w 7, nb 1)	9				
TOTAL (31.5 overs)	**86**	138			

Bowling	*O*	*M*	*R*	*W*
BANGLADESH				
Baisya	10	0	58	2
Nazmul	8.2	1	40	4
Rana	10	0	35	2
Mahmud	5	0	28	0
Rafique	10	2	28	1
Saleh	6	0	31	0
NEW ZEALAND				
Mills	7	2	14	4
Adams	6	1	24	0
Cairns	4	2	5	0
Styris	6	3	13	2
Harris	5	0	21	1
Vettori	3.5	0	8	3

Fall of Wickets	***NZ***	***B***
1st	11	4
2nd	49	10
3rd	50	23
4th	77	27
5th	94	45
6th	143	51
7th	168	68
8th	191	79
9th	224	83
10th	224	86

BANGLADESH v NEW ZEALAND Second One-day International

at National Stadium, Dhaka on 5 November, 2004
Toss : Bangladesh. Umpires : M.R. Benson & Mahbubur Rahman
New Zealand won by 3 wickets

Bangladesh won the toss and batted but lost two wickets in the first over of the game. Only a 57 run stand for the sixth wicket enabled them to get to 146. Styris and Harris were very economical while Masud was again a thorn in the bowlers' side.

New Zealand had a good start with a 74 run stand in 19 overs before Astle's departure triggered a collapse, New Zealand going to 133-7. Cairns and Vettori saw the Black Caps to safety but they batted for six balls more than the home side before reaching the target and taking a 2-0 lead. Aftab Ahmed, bowling for the first time in a one-day international, got a five wicket haul.

BANGLADESH

	Runs	Mins	Balls	6s	4s
Nafis Iqbal c Styris b Mills	0	2	2	-	-
Javed Omer b Franklin	12	37	18	-	2
Aftab Ahmed c McCullum b Mills	4	2	3	-	1
Habibul Bashar* b Franklin	0	22	12	-	-
Mohammad Ashraful c Franklin b Styris	17	30	15	-	3
Rajin Saleh c McCullum b Cairns	28	108	78	-	4
Khaled Masud† c Harris b Cairns	41	66	71	-	6
Manjural Islam Rana lbw b Styris	12	47	37	-	1
Mohammad Rafique c Franklin b Vettori	4	24	19	-	-
Tapash Baisya c Sinclair b Styris	7	12	11	-	-
Nazmul Hossain not out	4	7	4	-	-
Extras (lb 1, w 8, nb 8)	17				
TOTAL (43.4 overs)	**146**	188			

NEW ZEALAND

	Runs	Mins	Balls	6s	4s
M.S.Sinclair st Masud b Rafique	62	107	73	-	9
N.J.Astle c Omer b Aftab	29	82	57	1	2
H.J.H.Marshall lbw b Aftab	2	2	3	-	-
S.B.Styris b Aftab	12	35	30	-	-
C.D.McMillan lbw b Aftab	7	29	23	-	-
C.L.Cairns not out	17	67	51	1	1
B.B.McCullum† lbw b Aftab	0	2	2	-	-
C.Z.Harris c Nazmul b Baisya	7	18	11	-	1
D.L.Vettori* not out	3	28	19	-	-
K.D.Mills					
J.E.C.Franklin					
Extras (lb 4, w 4, nb 1)	9				
TOTAL (44.4 overs) (7 wkts)	**148**	192			

Bowling	*O*	*M*	*R*	*W*
NEW ZEALAND				
Mills	8	0	25	2
Franklin	4	0	34	2
Styris	7.4	1	16	3
Harris	10	4	19	0
Vettori	9	0	36	1
Cairns	5	1	15	2
BANGLADESH				
Nazmul	6	1	30	0
Baisya	10	2	33	1
Rana	8.4	2	24	0
Rafique	10	1	26	1
Aftab	10	0	31	5

Fall of Wickets	**B**	**NZ**
1st	1	74
2nd	5	76
3rd	22	102
4th	25	114
5th	52	125
6th	108	125
7th	125	133
8th	135	-
9th	139	-
10th	146	-

BANGLADESH v NEW ZEALAND Third One-day International

at National Stadium, Dhaka on 7 November, 2004
Toss : New Zealand. Umpires : A.F.M. Akhtaruddin & M.R. Benson
New Zealand won by 83 runs

New Zealand decided to bat after winning the toss and had a good start with 72 after 18.5 overs before Astle went. Sinclair got his second successive fifty from 59 balls before he was dismissed at 105. Styris and McMillan then added 86 for the fifth wicket with the former reaching his fifty off 65 deliveries. A quick 34 from Cairns got New Zealand to 250-7, the highest score of the series.

The Bangladesh batsmen were more disciplined in their innings as they batted the 50 overs out even though they were well short of the target. Masud again batted well with an unbeaten 40. The win gave New Zealand a clean sweep of the series 3-0.

NEW ZEALAND

	Runs	Mins	Balls	6s	4s
N.J.Astle run out	27	78	60	1	1
M.S.Sinclair c & b Rafique	66	110	77	-	7
C.Z.Harris lbw b Aftab	9	18	13	-	1
H.J.H.Marshall c Saleh b Rafique	0	4	2	-	-
S.B.Styris c Kapali b Rafique	51	86	68	1	1
C.D.McMillan c & b Rafique	39	66	54	1	-
C.L.Cairns c Saleh b Baisya	34	24	16	3	2
D.L.Vettori* not out	18	16	10	-	2
B.B.McCullum†					
J.E.C.Franklin					
K.D.Mills					
Extras (lb 3, w 3)	6				
TOTAL (50 overs) (7 wkts)	**250**	213			

BANGLADESH

	Runs	Mins	Balls	6s	4s
Javed Omer lbw b Franklin	8	9	7	-	2
Mohammad Rafique lbw b Mills	21	54	40	-	4
Nafis Iqbal c Sinclair b Vettori	40	98	87	1	3
Rajin Saleh lbw b Styris	0	15	9	-	-
Mohammad Ashraful c Sinclair b Vettori	13	49	30	-	-
Aftab Ahmed c Harris b Vettori	8	26	25	-	-
Khaled Masud*† not out	40	66	44	1	4
Alok Kapali b Cairns	17	31	35	-	-
Manjural Islam Rana not out	8	28	27	-	-
Tapash Baisya					
Mushfiqur Rahman					
Extras (lb 4, w 4, nb 4)	12				
TOTAL (50 overs) (7 wkts)	**167**	196			

Bowling	*O*	*M*	*R*	*W*
BANGLADESH				
Baisya	5	0	35	1
Mushfiqur	8	1	28	0
Rana	9	0	46	0
Aftab	10	0	36	1
Rafique	10	0	63	4
Saleh	4	0	18	0
Kapali	4	0	21	0
NEW ZEALAND				
Mills	10	1	39	1
Franklin	9	2	29	1
Styris	10	1	31	1
Cairns	7	0	21	1
Vettori	10	0	25	3
Harris	4	0	18	0

Fall of Wickets	***NZ***	***B***
1st	72	15
2nd	99	42
3rd	102	48
4th	105	86
5th	191	96
6th	207	109
7th	250	138
8th	-	
9th	-	-
10th	-	-

NEW ZEALAND IN AUSTRALIA

After leaving Bangladesh, New Zealand paid a short visit to Australia for two tests and three one-day internationals for the inaugural Chappell-Hadlee Trophy series.

New Zealand were on level terms for the first three days of the first test but were then outplayed for the rest of the series. The Black Caps drew first blood in the one-day series but the Australians levelled by winning the second game. The last match was washed out.

Jacob Oram scored a century at Brisbane and Mathew Sinclair got 88 and 79 against New South Wales and 69 in the first innings in the first test. The bowlers struggled to dismiss the opposition. Daniel Vettori continued his good form getting ten wickets, while Chris Martin got a five wicket bag in the first test. Chris Harris made his 250th one-day international appearance at Sydney but was injured while fielding and missed the rest of the season.

The touring party was: S.P. Fleming *(captain, Wellington)*, D.L. Vettori *(vice-captain, Northern Districts)*, A.R. Adams *(Auckland)*, N.J. Astle *(Canterbury)*, I.G. Butler *(Northern Districts)*, C.L. Cairns *(Canterbury)*, T.K. Canning *(Auckland)*, J.E.C. Franklin *(Wellington)*, C.Z. Harris*(Canterbury)*, G.J. Hopkins*(Otago)*, B.B. McCullum*(Canterbury)*, C.D. McMillan *(Canterbury)*, H.J.H. Marshall *(Northern Districts)*, C.S. Martin *(Canterbury)*, K.D. Mills *(Auckland)*, J.D.P. Oram *(Central Districts)*, M.H. Richardson *(Auckland)*, M.S. Sinclair *(Central Districts)*, S.B. Styris *(Northern Districts)*, P.J. Wiseman *(Canterbury)*. Coach, J.G. Bracewell; Manager: R.A. Dykes; Fitness Trainer, W. Frost/G. Owen; Physiotherapist, D.F. Shackel; Video Analyst, R.M. Carter.

Adams, Cairns and Harris replaced Franklin, Martin, Richardson and Wiseman for the one-day games. Canning later replaced Harris. Hopkins played the first game of the tour to rest McCullum and then returned home. McMillan was called into the team as cover for Fleming and Astle who were both carrying injuries.

New Zealand First-class Averages

BATTING	*M*	*I*	*NO*	*HS*	*Agg*	*Ave*	*100s*	*50s*	*Ct*	*St*
J.D.P. Oram	3	6	1	126*	213	42.60	1	-	1	-
M.S. Sinclair	3	6	0	88	238	39.66	-	3	1	-
K.D. Mills	1	2	1	29	33	33.00	-	-	1	-
N.J. Astle	2	4	0	52	126	31.50	-	1	2	-
P.J. Wiseman	2	4	2	21*	53	26.50	-	-	1	-
D.L. Vettori	2	4	0	59	102	25.50	-	1	1	-
S.P. Fleming	2	4	0	83	97	24.25	-	1	1	-
M.H. Richardson	3	6	0	50	112	18.66	-	1	1	-
S.B. Styris	3	6	0	28	98	16.33	-	-	3	-
B.B. McCullum	2	4	0	36	64	16.00	-	-	2	1
C.D. McMillan	2	4	0	23	63	15.75	-	-	2	-
H.J.H. Marshall	1	2	0	18	18	9.00	-	-	-	-
J.E.C. Franklin	2	4	0	13	26	6.50	-	-	-	-
G.J. Hopkins	1	2	0	4	5	2.50	-	-	2	-
C.S. Martin	3	6	2	3	8	2.00	-	-	-	-
I.G. Butler	1	2	0	0	0	0.00	-	-	-	-

BOWLING	*O*	*M*	*R*	*W*	*Ave*	*Best*	*5w*	*10w*
I.G. Butler	20	3	61	3	20.33	3-51	-	-
D.L. Vettori	123.2	21	341	10	34.10	5-152	1	-
P.J. Wiseman	81	15	289	6	48.16	3-140	-	-
C.S. Martin	102.5	22	354	5	70.80	5-152	1	-
J.E.C. Franklin	54.3	11	221	3	73.66	3-70	-	-
J.D.P. Oram	81	23	238	3	79.33	2-37	-	-
K.D. Mills	26	8	99	1	99.00	1-99	-	-
C.D. McMillan	9	4	25	0	-	-	-	-
S.B. Styris	19	4	53	0	-	-	-	-

New Zealand Test Averages

BATTING	M	I	NO	HS	Agg	Ave	100s	50s	Ct	St
J.D.P. Oram	2	4	1	126*	186	62.00	1	-	1	-
K.D. Mills	1	2	1	29	33	33.00	-	-	1	-
N.J. Astle	2	4	0	52	126	31.50	-	1	2	-
P.J. Wiseman	1	2	1	15*	26	26.00	-	-	1	-
D.L. Vettori	2	4	0	59	102	25.50	-	1	1	-
S.P. Fleming	2	4	0	83	97	24.25	-	1	1	-
M.S. Sinclair	2	4	0	69	71	17.75	-	1	-	-
S.B. Styris	2	4	0	28	70	17.50	-	-	1	-
C.D. McMillan	1	2	0	23	32	16.00	-	-	1	-
B.B. McCullum	2	4	0	36	64	16.00	-	-	2	1
M.H. Richardson	2	4	0	19	48	12.00	-	-	1	-
J.E.C. Franklin	1	2	0	13	20	10.00	-	-	-	-
C.S. Martin	2	4	1	2*	4	1.33	-	-	-	-

BOWLING	O	M	R	W	Ave	Best	5w	10w
D.L. Vettori	123.2	21	341	10	34.10	5-152	1	-
P.J. Wiseman	54	10	192	4	48.00	3-140	-	-
C.S. Martin	72.5	12	281	5	56.20	5-152	1	-
K.D. Mills	26	8	99	1	99.00	1-99	-	-
C.D. McMillan	5	1	23	0	-	-	-	-
S.B. Styris	8	1	33	0	-	-	-	-
J.E.C. Franklin	22	2	120	0	-	-	-	-
J.D.P. Oram	54	12	188	0	-	-	-	-

Australia Test Averages

BATTING	M	I	NO	HS	Agg	Ave	100s	50s	Ct	St
J.L. Langer	2	3	0	215	295	98.33	1	-	4	-
A.C. Gilchrist	2	2	0	126	176	88.00	1	1	8	1
M.J. Clarke	2	2	0	141	148	74.00	1	-	2	-
R.T. Ponting	2	3	1	68	145	72.50	-	2	4	-
J.N. Gillespie	2	2	1	54*	66	66.00	-	1	1	-
S.K. Warne	2	2	1	53*	63	63.00	-	1	4	-
G.D. McGrath	2	1	0	61	61	61.00	-	1	-	-
D.S. Lehmann	2	2	0	81	89	44.50	-	1	-	-
M.L. Hayden	2	3	0	70	132	44.00	-	2	3	-
D.R. Martyn	2	3	1	70	83	41.50	-	1	-	-
M.S. Kasprowicz	2	1	0	5	5	5.00	-	-	-	-

BOWLING	O	M	R	W	Ave	Best	5w	10w
G.D. McGrath	67.1	10	184	9	20.44	4-66	-	-
J.N. Gillespie	74	21	181	8	22.62	3-37	-	-
S.K. Warne	95.2	17	256	11	23.27	4-15	-	-
M.S. Kasprowicz	66	14	216	9	24.00	4-90	-	-
D.S. Lehmann	22	2	67	2	33.50	2-46	-	-

New Zealand One-day International Averages

BATTING	*M*	*I*	*NO*	*HS*	*Agg*	*Ave*	*100s*	*50s*	*Ct*	*St*	*SR*
H.J.H. Marshall	2	2	1	50*	59	59.00	-	1	-	-	77
B.B. McCullum	2	2	1	21	41	41.00	-	-	2	-	71
N.J. Astle	2	2	0	70	81	40.50	-	1	1	-	65
D.L. Vettori	2	1	0	33	33	33.00	-	-	-	-	91
M.S. Sinclair	2	2	0	48	65	32.50	-	-	1	-	56
C.L. Cairns	2	2	0	50	64	32.00	-	1	-	-	125
S.P. Fleming	2	2	0	34	34	17.00	-	-	1	-	73
J.D.P. Oram	2	2	0	24	26	13.00	-	-	-	-	86
S.B. Styris	2	2	0	5	10	5.00	-	-	-	-	62
C.Z. Harris	1	1	0	4	4	4.00	-	-	-	-	66
K.D. Mills	2	1	1	44*	44	-	-	-	1	-	169
I.G. Butler	1	-	-	-	-	-	-	-	1	-	

BOWLING	*O*	*M*	*R*	*W*	*Ave*	*Best*	*R/O*
D.L. Vettori	20	2	67	4	16.75	3-31	3.35
C.L. Cairns	20	0	99	4	24.75	3-39	4.95
K.D. Mills	14	0	77	2	38.50	2-49	5.50
I.G. Butler	8	0	58	1	58.00	1-58	7.25
J.D.P. Oram	19	0	128	2	64.00	2-51	6.74
S.B. Styris	19	0	72	1	72.00	1-37	3.79

Australia One-day International Averages

BATTING	*M*	*I*	*NO*	*HS*	*Agg*	*Ave*	*100s*	*50s*	*Ct*	*St*	*SR*
A.C. Gilchrist	2	2	0	68	128	64.00	-	2	2	-	125
D.S. Lehmann	2	2	0	52	102	51.00	-	2	-	-	68
R.T. Ponting	2	2	0	32	61	30.50	-	-	1	-	71
M.L. Hayden	2	2	0	43	56	28.00	-	-	1	-	65
M.J. Clarke	2	2	0	36	42	21.00	-	-	-	-	63
B. Lee	2	2	1	10*	18	18.00	-	-	1	-	112
D.R. Martyn	2	2	0	5	6	3.00	-	-	-	-	66
S.R. Watson	1	1	0	3	3	3.00	-	-	-	-	42
A. Symonds	2	2	0	0	0	0.00	-	-	-	-	0
G.B. Hogg	2	2	2	41*	61	-	-	-	-	-	80
M.S. Kasprowicz	1	1	1	9*	9	-	-	-	-	-	100
G.D. McGrath	1	-	-	-	-	-	-	-	1	-	-
J.N. Gillespie	1	-	-	-	-	-	-	-	-	-	-

BOWLING	*O*	*M*	*R*	*W*	*Ave*	*Best*	*R/O*
J.N. Gillespie	10	1	41	2	20.50	2-41	4.10
B. Lee	17	0	88	4	22.00	2-40	5.18
G.B. Hogg	15	0	78	3	26.00	3-45	5.20
G.D. McGrath	7.1	0	27	1	27.00	1-27	3.77
D.S. Lehmann	12	0	66	2	33.00	2-35	5.50
M.S. Kasprowicz	9	1	53	1	53.00	1-53	5.89
A. Symonds	18	1	82	1	82.00	1-47	4.56
S.R. Watson	8.4	0	42	0	-	-	4.84

NEW SOUTH WALES v NEW ZEALAND — First-class

at Sydney Cricket Ground on 11, 12, 13, 14 November, 2004
Toss : New Zealand. Umpires : N.S.D. Fowler & S.A. Reed
Close of play: 1st day: NSW 26-1, Mail 12, Phelps 5; 2nd day: NSW 278-8, Lee 28, Clark 0
3rd day: NSW 25-0, Mail 9, Jacques 16
New South Wales won by 9 wickets

Fleming, Vettori, Astle and McCullum were rested for this game, with Styris taking over the captaincy. Hopkins was to play in this game to rest McCullum and then return home.

After winning the toss and batting the tourists made a disappointing start and of the top eight batsmen, only Sinclair and Oram were able to reach twenty. Test players MacGill and Lee took seven wickets between them as New Zealand were bowled out for 213.

The New Zealand attack performed economically and Franklin and Butler took three wickets each as New South Wales got a lead of 73. Richardson and Sinclair knocked off the deficit with a 110 run opening stand but the last seven wickets fell for just 18 runs as 183-3 became 201 all out. MacGill got another four wicket haul leaving the home side to get 129. They achieved this losing only one wicket to have a comfortable win.

NEW ZEALAND

FIRST INNINGS	Runs	Mins	Balls	6s	4s	SECOND INNINGS	Runs	Mins	Balls	6s	4s
M.H.Richardson c Krejza b Nicholson	14	56	40	-	2	b MacGill	50	170	123	-	7
M.S.Sinclair c Krejza b Nicholson	88	252	180	-	12	b Nicholson	79	260	195	1	8
H.J.H.Marshall b Lee	18	51	41	-	1	c Thornley b MacGill	0	8	4	-	-
S.B.Styris* b Lee	10	23	21	-	-	lbw b Krejza	18	50	35	-	1
C.D.McMillan c Haddin b MacGill	14	16	13	-	3	b Nicholson	17	33	25	-	2
J.D.P.Oram c Mail b Krejza	26	81	58	1	2	lbw b Krejza	1	7	6	-	-
J.E.C.Franklin lbw b MacGill	0	25	17	-	-	b Lee	6	30	13	-	1
G.J.Hopkins† c Mail b MacGill	4	21	15	-	1	c Jaques b MacGill	1	19	11	-	-
P.J.Wiseman not out	21	49	39	-	2	lbw b MacGill	6	29	23	-	-
I.G.Butler lbw b MacGill	0	1	1	-	-	lbw b Lee	0	2	2	-	-
C.S.Martin c Phelps b Lee	3	29	16	-	-	not out	1	19	10	-	-
Extras (b 1, lb 8, w 1, nb 5)	15					(b 4, lb 10, w 1, nb 7)	22				
TOTAL (72.4 overs)	**213**	310				(73.3 overs)	**201**	318			

NEW SOUTH WALES

FIRST INNINGS	Runs	Mins	Balls	6s	4s	SECOND INNINGS	Runs	Mins	Balls	6s	4s
G.J.Mail c Styris b Wiseman	43	197	156	-	5	c McMillan b Oram	13	48	37	-	2
P.A.Jaques c Hopkins b Franklin	8	8	6	-	2	not out	70	188	133	-	8
M.J.Phelps b Butler	17	86	54	-	2	not out	39	139	92	-	3
D.J.Thornley c Sinclair b Franklin	59	194	136	-	8						
A.W.O'Brien c Hopkins b Butler	21	45	35	-	3						
B.J.Haddin*† b Wiseman	14	17	17	-	3						
J.J.Krejza c Styris b Franklin	54	162	123	-	7						
M.J.Nicholson b Butler	23	94	62	-	3						
B.Lee b Oram	33	65	48	1	5						
S.R.Clark not out	3	25	15	-	-						
S.C.G.MacGill b Oram	0	1	1	-	-						
Extras (b 2, lb 3, w 1, nb 5)	11					b 4, lb 2, nb 1)	7				
TOTAL (108 overs)	**286**	457				(43.3 overs) (1 wkt)	**129**	188			

Bowling	*O*	*M*	*R*	*W*	*O*	*M*	*R*	*W*
NEW SOUTH WALES								
Lee	16.4	4	52	3	16	3	37	2
Nicholson	17	6	41	2	14	3	31	2
Clark	12	4	29	0	9	3	19	0
MacGill	21	5	57	4	19.3	5	52	4
Krejza	6	2	25	1	13	4	48	2
Thornley					2	2	0	0
NEW ZEALAND								
Martin	20	7	40	0	10	3	33	0
Franklin	22	7	70	3	10.3	2	31	0
Oram	21	9	37	2	6	2	13	1
Butler	15	1	51	3	5	2	10	0
Wiseman	22	4	76	2	5	1	21	0
Styris	4	1	5	0	7	2	15	0

Fall of Wickets

	NZ 1st	*NSW 1st*	*NZ 2nd*	*NSW 2nd*
1st	39	8	110	29
2nd	68	42	110	-
3rd	83	112	145	-
4th	98	142	183	-
5th	176	156	184	-
6th	184	175	184	-
7th	184	229	192	-
8th	193	272	192	-
9th	193	286	192	-
10th	213	286	201	-

AUSTRALIA v NEW ZEALAND — First Test

at Woolloongabba, Brisbane on 18, 19, 20, 21 November, 2004
Toss : New Zealand. Umpires : Aleem Dar & S.A. Bucknor
Close of play: 1st day: NZ 250-7, Oram 63, Vettori 13; 2nd day: Australia 197-4, Martyn 59, Clarke 31
3rd day: Australia 534-9, Gillespie 44, McGrath 54
Australia won by an innings and 156 runs

Franklin suffered a groin strain after the team had been selected and was replaced by Mills and McMillan replaced Marshall from the side that had beaten Bangladesh.

After batting first New Zealand lost two wickets at 26 but Sinclair (fifty off 120 balls) stood firm before he and Astle were dismissed within four deliveries to leave the score at 138-5. Oram received valuable support from the tail enders and reached his second test century off 166 deliveries. Kasprowicz and Warne were the pick of the bowlers.

Australia lost an early wicket and at 222-5 Gilchrist was given the benefit of the doubt for a leg before decision. He then proceeded to add 216 for the sixth wicket with Clarke (hundred off 148 balls) who became just the third player to score a century on test debut home and away. Gilchrist scored his hundred from 130 balls. To add salt to New Zealand's wounds the last wicket pair of Gillespie and McGrath added 114 with both players getting maiden test fifties. Mc Grath needed 61 balls compared to Gillespie's 130 balls. Martin took his fifth five wicket haul.

Faced with a deficit of 232, New Zealand capitulated for just 76, its lowest score against Australia since the first game between the sides in 1945/46. Only Astle and Fleming were able to reach double figures and the innings lasted just 165 minutes, giving Australia a comprehensive win by an innings and 156 runs.

NEW ZEALAND

FIRST INNINGS	*Runs*	*Mins*	*Balls*	*6s*	*4s*	*SECOND INNINGS*	*Runs*	*Mins*	*Balls*	*6s*	*4s*
M.H.Richardson c Ponting b Kasprowicz	19	50	49	-	1	c Gilchrist b McGrath	4	4	5	-	1
M.S.Sinclair c Ponting b Gillespie	69	229	163	-	9	lbw b McGrath	0	15	10	-	-
S.P.Fleming* c Warne b Kasprowicz	0	2	3	-	-	c Langer b McGrath	11	33	18	-	2
S.B.Styris c Gilchrist b Kasprowicz	27	84	61	-	4	lbw b Warne	7	63	41	-	1
N.J.Astle run out	19	84	62	-	1	c Warne b Kasprowicz	17	43	39	-	2
C.D.McMillan c Gilchrist b Warne	23	73	56	1	2	lbw b Gillespie	9	73	48	-	1
J.D.P.Oram not out	126	258	178	3	12	c Hayden b Warne	8	28	23	-	1
B.B.McCullum† st Gilchrist b Warne	10	23	16	-	-	c Gilchrist b Gillespie	8	15	12	-	1
D.L.Vettori c Warne b Kasprowicz	21	62	46	-	3	c Hayden b Warne	2	26	10	-	-
K.D.Mills c Hayden b Warne	29	73	66	1	2	not out	4	12	7	-	1
C.S.Martin c Ponting b Warne	0	29	9	-	-	lbw b Warne	0	8	7	-	-
Extras (b 1, lb 2, w 3, nb 4)	10					(lb 2, nb 4)	6				
TOTAL (117.3 overs)	**353**	488				(36.2 overs)	**76**	165			

AUSTRALIA

	Runs	Mins	Balls	6s	4s
J.L.Langer lbw b Vettori	34	108	72	-	6
M.L.Hayden lbw b Mills	8	24	17	-	2
R.T.Ponting* c Astle b Martin	51	116	84	-	7
D.R.Martyn c McMillan b Martin	70	157	117	1	8
D.S.Lehmann c McCullum b Vettori	8	16	11	-	-
M.J.Clarke b Vettori	141	297	200	1	21
A.C.Gilchrist† c Styris b Martin	126	194	151	4	13
S.K.Warne lbw b Vettori	10	18	11	-	2
J.N.Gillespie not out	54	178	155	-	7
M.S.Kasprowicz c Mills b Martin	5	25	21	-	-
G.D.McGrath c Astle b Martin	61	139	92	1	5
Extras (b 1, lb 7, w 1, nb 8)	17				
TOTAL (153.5 overs)	**585**	641			

Bowling	*O*	*M*	*R*	*W*	*O*	*M*	*R*	*W*
AUSTRALIA								
McGrath	27	4	67	0	8	1	19	3
Gillespie	29	7	84	1	10	5	19	2
Kasprowicz	28	5	90	4	8	2	21	1
Warne	29.3	3	97	4	10.2	3	15	4
Lehmann	4	0	12	0				
NEW ZEALAND								
Martin	39.5	7	152	5				
Mills	26	8	99	1				
Styris	8	1	33	0				
Oram	25	4	116	0				
Vettori	50	9	154	4				
McMillan	5	1	23	0				

Fall of Wickets	***NZ***	***A***	***NZ***
	1st	*1st*	*2nd*
1st	26	16	6
2nd	26	85	7
3rd	77	109	19
4th	138	128	42
5th	138	222	44
6th	180	438	55
7th	206	450	69
8th	264	464	72
9th	317	471	72
10th	353	585	76

AUSTRALIA v NEW ZEALAND — Second Test

at Adelaide Oval on 26, 27, 28, 29, 30 November, 2004
Toss : Australia. Umpires : S.A. Bucknor & D.R. Shepherd
Close of play: 1st day: Australia 327-3, Langer 144, Lehmann 28; 2nd day: NZ 56-2, Fleming 38, Wiseman 4
3rd day: Australia 57-0, Langer 31, Hayden 21; 4th day: NZ 149-5, Oram 40, McCullum 34
Australia won by 213 runs

Wiseman and Franklin replaced McMillan and Mills for New Zealand while Australia were unchanged. Australia had century partnerships for three of its first four wickets while Langer scored his 21st test century from 212 balls and then his third double century from 343 balls. Five other batsmen scored fifties as Australia amassed 575-8 before declaring. Vettori's 5-152 was his eleventh bag of five wickets.

Sinclair went in the fourth over and the tourists were on the back foot again. Fleming and Astle both scored fifties (both from 82 deliveries) but the other batsmen struggled. Only Styris, batting at number ten because of an ear infection, looked happy. Australia decided not to enforce the follow on and batted circumspectly, taking 56 overs to reach 139 before leaving New Zealand 464 to win.

Four wickets were soon down for 34. One was Richardson who, as it turned out, was playing in his last test. The next four players all got starts but only Vettori (fifty from 64 balls) was able to get a half-century. Australia had another comfortable win and they took the series 2-0 with the 213 run margin.

AUSTRALIA

FIRST INNINGS	*Runs*	*Mins*	*Balls*	*6s*	*4s*	*SECOND INNINGS*	*Runs*	*Mins*	*Balls*	*6s*	*4s*
J.L.Langer c Oram b Vettori	215	499	368	3	25	lbw b Wiseman	46	137	111	-	3
M.L.Hayden c & b Wiseman	70	179	124	-	10	c McCullum b Vettori	54	181	131	-	4
R.T.Ponting* st McCullum b Vettori	68	96	79	-	11	not out	26	82	57	-	-
D.R.Martyn c Fleming b Wiseman	7	20	14	-	1	not out	6	39	38	-	-
D.S.Lehmann b Wiseman	81	242	172	-	10						
M.J.Clarke lbw b Vettori	7	16	16	-	1						
A.C.Gilchrist† c & b Vettori	50	97	80	-	6						
S.K.Warne not out	53	95	70	2	3						
J.N.Gillespie c Richardson b Vettori	12	21	13	-	3						
M.S.Kasprowicz											
G.D.McGrath											
Extras (b 4, lb 4, nb 4)	12					(lb 6, nb 1)	7				
TOTAL (155.2 overs) (8 wkts dec)	**575**	636				(56 overs) (2 wkts dec)	**139**	220			

NEW ZEALAND

	Runs	Mins	Balls	6s	4s		Runs	Mins	Balls	6s	4s
M.H.Richardson b Kasprowicz	9	75	59	-	-	c Langer b Kasprowicz	16	85	63	-	1
M.S.Sinclair c Warne b Gillespie	0	15	10	-	-	lbw b Gillespie	2	17	12	-	-
S.P.Fleming* c Gilchrist b McGrath	83	212	161	-	10	b McGrath	3	20	13	-	-
P.J.Wiseman lbw b Kasprowicz	11	46	33	-	1	(10) not out	15	43	37	-	2
N.J.Astle c Langer b McGrath	52	133	86	-	7	c Langer b Lehmann	38	92	71	-	6
J.D.P.Oram c Gilchrist b Gillespie	12	46	28	-	-	c Gilchrist b McGrath	40	135	97	-	3
B.B.McCullum† lbw b Gillespie	10	27	23	-	1	lbw b Gillespie	36	66	53	1	5
D.L.Vettori lbw b McGrath	20	89	60	-	1	c Gillespie b Lehmann	59	111	78	-	5
J.E.C.Franklin lbw b Warne	7	36	32	-	-	c Gilchrist b Kasprowicz	13	48	38	-	1
S.B.Styris c Clarke b McGrath	28	55	40	1	4	(4) c Clarke b Warne	8	48	34	-	2
C.S.Martin not out	2	11	6	-	-	c Ponting b Warne	2	2	4	-	-
Extras (b 3, lb 5, nb 9)	17					(b 1, lb 12, nb 5)	18				
TOTAL (88.1 overs)	**251**	377				(82.3 overs)	**250**	338			

Bowling	*O*	*M*	*R*	*W*	*O*	*M*	*R*	*W*
NEW ZEALAND								
Martin	27	4	118	0	6	1	11	0
Franklin	17	2	102	0	5	0	18	0
Oram	24	7	55	0	5	1	17	0
Vettori	55.2	10	152	5	18	2	35	1
Wiseman	32	7	140	3	22	3	52	1
AUSTRALIA								
McGrath	20.1	3	66	4	12	2	32	2
Gillespie	19	4	37	3	16	5	41	2
Warne	28	5	65	1	27.3	6	79	2
Kasprowicz	16	3	66	2	14	4	39	2
Lehmann	5	2	9	0	13	0	46	2

Fall of Wickets	***A***	***NZ***	***A***	***NZ***
	1st	*1st*	*2nd*	*2nd*
1st	137	2	93	11
2nd	240	44	119	18
3rd	261	80	-	34
4th	445	153	-	34
5th	457	178	-	97
6th	465	183	-	150
7th	543	190	-	160
8th	575	213	-	206
9th	-	242	-	243
10th	-	251	-	250

VICTORIA INVITATIONAL XI v NEW ZEALAND — One-day

at Albert Ground, Melbourne on 2 December, 2004
Toss not made. Umpires : J.D. Ward & G.T.D. Morrow
New Zealand won by 34 runs

New Zealand's three new players, Cairns, Adams and Harris, all played in this sole warm up match before the inaugural Chappell-Hadlee Series.

Fleming and Astle began with an opening stand of 112 in just 76 minutes. Astle retired at 161-3, allowing Styris and Sinclair to put on 67 in only 24 minutes. Sinclair and McMillan added another 23 in just 11 minutes and New Zealand ended with 277 off 40 overs.

The Invitational side were in deep trouble at 84-6 before Hewett joined Dart and the pair added 82 in only 49 minutes. Hewett and Lindsay added another 60 in 32 minutes and the home side finally reached a respectable 243.

NEW ZEALAND

	Runs	Mins	Balls	6s	4s
S.P.Fleming* b Hewett	67	76	59	-	9
N.J.Astle retired out	66	113	73	2	7
H.J.H.Marshall c Lindsay b Sandri	13	27	19	-	1
S.B.Styris retired out	39	33	26	2	2
M.S.Sinclair† retired out	44	36	28	2	3
C.D.McMillan c Cassell b Welsford	8	20	7	-	-
C.L.Cairns run out	3	4	8	-	-
C.Z.Harris not out	5	11	5	-	-
A.R.Adams not out	14	7	10	-	1
K.D.Mills					
I.G.Butler					
Extras (lb 5, w 8, nb 5)	18				
TOTAL (50 overs) (7 wkts)	**277**	167			

VICTORIA INVITATIONAL XI

	Runs	Mins	Balls	6s	4s
T.H.Welsford* c & b Adams	2	5	7	-	-
A.C.Blizzard c Cairns b Butler	43	73	47	-	7
L.G.L.Buchanan b Mills	5	4	5	-	-
A.J.Crosthwaite† c Styris b Mills	2	6	7	-	-
S.F.Hill run out	21	48	20	-	2
S.P.Dart c Astle b Mills	26	56	44	-	3
I.S.L.Hewett c Adams b Cairns	82	82	52	3	11
G.P.Lindsay c Astle b Butler	32	46	35	-	3
J.J.Taylor c Marshall b Cairns	2	2	3	-	-
C.S.Sandri b Butler	8	12	6	-	1
R.J.Cassell not out	1	1	1	-	-
C.S.Huckett					
Extras (b 3, lb 3, w 7, nb 6)	19				
TOTAL (47.1 overs)	**243**	172			

Bowling	*O*	*M*	*R*	*W*
VICTORIA INVITATIONAL XI				
Cassell	5	0	29	0
Huckett	7	0	46	0
Hewett	7	0	41	1
Taylor	6	0	56	0
Lindsay	5	0	40	0
Sandri	6	0	42	1
Welsford	4	0	18	1
NEW ZEALAND				
Mills	8	0	57	3
Adams	8	0	44	1
Butler	7.3	1	48	3
Cairns	6	1	20	2
Harris	5	0	36	0
Styris	4	0	32	0

Fall of Wickets	***NZ***	***V***
1st	112	3
2nd	137	8
3rd	161	10
4th	228	84
5th	251	84
6th	256	166
7th	260	226
8th	-	229
9th	-	242
10th	-	243

AUSTRALIA v NEW ZEALAND First One-day International

at Docklands Stadium, Melbourne (d/n) on 5 December, 2004
Toss : New Zealand. Umpires : S.J. Davis & R.E. Koertzen
New Zealand won by 4 wickets

With the Melbourne Cricket Ground undergoing renovations the game was played at Docklands Stadium (or Telstra Dome) with the roof closed.

Australia got off to a rollicking start courtesy of Gilchrist who got his fifty from just 39 balls. There was a mini collapse when Australia went from 113-1 to 123-5 and Vettori and Cairns bowled well and restricted Australia to 246.

Fleming went to the second ball of the New Zealand innings but then Astle and Sinclair added 128 from 185 balls. Astle (fifty off 75 balls) reached 6000 ODI runs. Marshall was playing well and when Cairns went 39 were needed from 23 balls. A total of 22 came from Kasprowicz's last over and New Zealand got home with two balls to spare to take the lead in the Chappell-Hadlee series.

AUSTRALIA

	Runs	Mins	Balls	6s	4s
A.C.Gilchrist† b Cairns	68	87	54	-	9
M.L.Hayden c Sinclair b Oram	13	34	21	-	-
R.T.Ponting* lbw b Vettori	29	53	49	-	4
D.S.Lehmann c Butler b Oram	50	109	73	-	2
D.R.Martyn lbw b Vettori	1	6	4	-	-
A.Symonds c Mills b Vettori	0	1	3	-	-
M.J.Clarke b Cairns	36	65	49	-	2
S.R.Watson c McCullum b Butler	3	9	7	-	-
G.B.Hogg not out	20	42	23	-	1
B.Lee b Cairns	8	14	11	-	-
M.S.Kasprowicz not out	9	7	9	-	1
Extras (b 2, lb 2, w 2, nb 3)	9				
TOTAL (50 overs) (9 wkts)	**246**	222			

NEW ZEALAND

	Runs	Mins	Balls	6s	4s
S.P.Fleming* lbw b Lee	0	1	2	-	-
N.J.Astle c Ponting b Lehmann	70	126	102	1	3
M.S.Sinclair run out	48	119	86	-	3
S.B.Styris c Lee b Lehmann	5	12	10	-	-
H.J.H.Marshall not out	50	83	52	-	1
J.D.P.Oram c Gilchrist b Kasprowicz	24	37	22	-	2
C.L.Cairns b Lee	14	12	11	-	1
B.B.McCullum† not out	20	22	13	-	3
D.L.Vettori					
K.D.Mills					
I.G.Butler					
Extras (lb 9, w 7)	16				
TOTAL (49.4 overs) (6 wkts)	**247**	209			

Bowling	*O*	*M*	*R*	*W*
NEW ZEALAND				
Mills	4	0	28	0
Butler	8	0	58	1
Oram	9	0	51	2
Cairns	10	0	39	3
Vettori	10	1	31	3
Styris	9	0	35	0
AUSTRALIA				
Lee	8	0	40	2
Kasprowicz	9	1	53	1
Watson	8.4	0	42	0
Hogg	7	0	33	0
Lehmann	9	0	35	2
Symonds	8	0	35	0

Fall of Wickets	*A*	*NZ*
1st	64	0
2nd	113	128
3rd	121	131
4th	123	140
5th	123	189
6th	194	208
7th	198	-
8th	220	-
9th	236	-
10th	-	-

AUSTRALIA v NEW ZEALAND — Second One-day International

at Sydney Cricket Ground (d/n) on 8 December, 2004
Toss : Australia. Umpires : R.E. Koertzen & P.D. Parker
Australia won by 17 runs

Harris became the first New Zealand player to make 250 appearances in one-day internationals, but he was unable to bowl after injuring his shoulder while fielding.

Australia again had a flying start as Gilchrist got another quick fifty, this time from 37 balls. When he went, at the end of the twelfth over, Australia were 86-1. After another middle order collapse, going from 140-1 to 161-6, Lehmann and Hogg added 74 off 103 balls to help Australia reach 261-7. Vettori and Styris bowled economically but Oram finished with the most expensive figures for a New Zealand bowler against Australia.

New Zealand lost wickets regularly being 86-6 before Cairns and McCullum put on 68. Vettori and Mills added 70 off 51 balls with both players reaching their highest scores in one-day internationals. Mills hit sixes off four successive balls. When Vettori went 26 were needed from 26 balls and the injured Harris strode to the crease as last man in. However, he was eventually bowled by McGrath to give Australia a 17 run win to level the series.

AUSTRALIA

	Runs	Mins	Balls	6s	4s
A.C.Gilchrist† c Astle b Styris	60	57	48	-	9
M.L.Hayden run out	43	116	65	-	2
R.T.Ponting* c Fleming b Mills	32	49	36	-	4
D.R.Martyn lbw b Mills	5	9	5	-	1
A.Symonds lbw b Vettori	0	4	2	-	-
D.S.Lehmann run out	52	97	77	-	5
M.J.Clarke c McCullum b Cairns	6	23	17	-	1
G.B.Hogg not out	41	86	53	-	2
B.Lee not out	10	11	5	-	1
J.N.Gillespie					
G.D.McGrath					
Extras (lb 2, w 2, nb 8)	12				
TOTAL (50 overs) (7 wkts)	**261**	229			

NEW ZEALAND

	Runs	Mins	Balls	6s	4s
S.P.Fleming* lbw b Hogg	34	92	44	-	3
N.J.Astle c Gilchrist b Lee	11	26	22	-	1
M.S.Sinclair c Hayden b Gillespie	17	38	30	-	2
S.B.Styris lbw b Symonds	5	6	6	-	1
H.J.H.Marshall b Lee	9	33	24	-	-
J.D.P.Oram lbw b Hogg	2	8	8	-	-
C.L.Cairns c McGrath b Gillespie	50	52	40	2	4
B.B.McCullum† lbw b Hogg	21	65	44	-	-
D.L.Vettori run out	33	32	36	-	2
K.D.Mills not out	44	46	26	4	1
C.Z.Harris b McGrath	4	11	6	-	-
Extras (lb 5, w 6, nb 3)	14				
TOTAL (47.1 overs)	**244**	219			

Bowling	O	M	R	W
NEW ZEALAND				
Mills	10	0	49	2
Oram	10	0	77	0
Cairns	10	0	60	1
Styris	10	0	37	1
Vettori	10	1	36	1
AUSTRALIA				
McGrath	7.1	0	27	1
Lee	9	0	48	2
Gillespie	10	1	41	2
Symonds	10	1	47	1
Hogg	8	0	45	3
Lehmann	3	0	31	0

Fall of Wickets	A	NZ
1st	86	27
2nd	140	63
3rd	147	68
4th	148	78
5th	148	84
6th	161	86
7th	235	154
8th	-	166
9th	-	236
10th	-	244

AUSTRALIA v NEW ZEALAND — Third One-day International

at Woolloongabba, Brisbane (d/n) on 10 December 2004
Abandoned without a ball being bowled.

SRI LANKA IN NEW ZEALAND

The Sri Lankan tour of New Zealand started in late December. The first one-day international was played at Auckland on Boxing Day before the balance of the tour was cancelled due to the Asian tsunami which devastated parts of Sri Lanka.

Sri Lanka returned at the end of March to play a three-day game and two tests, with the remaining one-day internationals to be played later in the year. In the tests Jayawardene, Atapattu, Samaraweera and Dilshan all showed form with the bat while Malinga and Vaas were the best bowlers.

The squad which came for the one-day internationals was: M.S. Atapattu *(captain)*, D.P.M.D. Jayawardene *(vice-captain)*, R.P. Arnold, U.D.U. Chandana, T.M. Dilshan, C.R.D. Fernando, H.M.R.K.B. Herath, W.S. Jayantha, S.T. Jayasuriya, K.M.D.N. Kulasekara, M.F. Maharoof, S.L. Malinga, K.C. Sangakkara, W.P.U.J.C. Vaas, D.N.T. Zoysa. Coach, J. Dyson; Manager, D.S.B.P. Kuruppu.

For the originally scheduled first-class section Chandana, Jayantha and Kulasekara were to be replaced by G.I. Daniel and T.T. Samaraweera. When the test series was rescheduled, however, Arnold, Fernando, Jayantha and Zoysa were replaced by S. Kalavitigoda, P.D.R.L. Perera and Samaraweera.

The original intinerary was December 21 – Central Districts at New Plymouth *(d/n)*, 23 – Northern Districts at Hamilton *(d/n)*, 26 – 1st ODI at Auckland, 29 – 2nd ODI at Napier, January 2 – 3rd ODI at Queenstown, 4 – 4th ODI at Christchurch *(d/n)*, 8 – 5th ODI at Wellington *(d/n)*, 10-12 – Auckland, 15-19 – 1st Test at Hamilton, 22-26 – 2nd Test at Wellington.

Before the decision to completely abandon the tour was made, the 2nd one-day international was postponed until 11 January with the three first-class games to be rescheduled.

Sri Lanka First-class Averages

BATTING	*M*	*I*	*NO*	*HS*	*Agg*	*Ave*	*100s*	*50s*	*Ct*	*St*
T.T. Samaraweera	2	3	0	88	178	59.33	-	2	2	-
D.P.M.D. Jayawardene	3	3	0	141	155	51.66	1	-	2	-
M.S. Atapattu	3	4	1	127	145	48.33	1	-	1	-
T.M. Dilshan	3	3	0	73	110	36.66	-	1	1	-
S.T. Jayasuriya	3	4	1	48	77	25.66	-	-	2	-
M.F. Maharoof	2	2	0	36	48	24.00	-	-	-	-
U.D.U. Chandana	3	3	0	41	68	22.66	-	-	-	-
K.C. Sangakkara	3	3	0	45	66	22.00	-	-	3	2
W.P.J.U.C. Vaas	2	3	0	38	60	20.00	-	-	2	-
S. Kalavitigoda	2	2	0	7	8	4.00	-	-	2	-
K.M.D.N. Kulasekara	1	1	0	0	0	0.00	-	-	1	-
H.M.R.K.B. Herath	2	1	0	0	0	0.00	-	-	-	-
S.L. Malinga	3	3	3	4*	4	-	-	-	1	-
P.D.R.L. Perera	1	-	-	-	-	-	-	-	-	-

BOWLING	*O*	*M*	*R*	*W*	*Ave*	*Best*	*5w*	*10w*
P.D.R.L. Perera	14.1	4	48	2	24.00	2-48	-	-
S.L. Malinga	111.4	14	391	14	27.92	5-80	1	-
W.P.J.U.C. Vaas	90	21	271	8	33.87	6-108	1	-
H.M.R.K.B. Herath	52.1	10	160	4	40.00	2-91	-	-
S.T. Jayasuriya	35	11	106	2	53.00	2-41	-	-
M.F. Maharoof	48	12	155	2	77.50	2-59	-	-
K.M.D.N. Kulasekara	36	9	89	1	89.00	1-70	-	-
U.D.U. Chandana	88	12	319	3	106.33	1-12	-	-
T.T. Samaraweera	1	0	6	0	-	-	-	-
D.P.M.D. Jayawardene	6	2	14	0	-	-	-	-
T.M. Dilshan	3	0	23	0	-	-	-	-

New Zealand Test Averages

BATTING	*M*	*I*	*NO*	*HS*	*Agg*	*Ave*	*100s*	*50s*	*Ct*	*St*
L. Vincent	2	3	0	224	276	92.00	1	1	4	-
H.J.H. Marshall	2	3	0	160	172	57.33	1	-	-	-
S.P. Fleming	2	3	0	88	145	48.33	-	1	5	-
N.J. Astle	2	3	0	114	133	44.33	1	-	3	-
J.A.H. Marshall	2	3	0	52	119	39.66	-	1	1	-
B.B. McCullum	2	3	0	99	106	35.33	-	1	4	-
P.J. Wiseman	2	3	1	32*	59	29.50	-	-	-	-
J.E.C. Franklin	2	3	0	55	77	25.66	-	1	-	-
C.D. Cumming	2	3	0	47	75	25.00	-	-	-	-
K.D. Mills	2	3	0	31	57	19.00	-	-	-	-
C.S. Martin	2	3	3	4*	9	-	-	-	1	-

BOWLING	*O*	*M*	*R*	*W*	*Ave*	*Best*	*5w*	*10w*
N.J. Astle	43.1	12	108	7	15.42	3-27	-	-
C.S. Martin	76	20	237	11	21.54	6-54	1	-
J.E.C. Franklin	67.3	13	254	9	28.22	4-71	-	-
K.D. Mills	54	16	143	2	71.50	2-34	-	-
P.J. Wiseman	66	14	215	1	215.00	1-128	-	-
L. Vincent	1	0	2	0	-	-	-	-

Sri Lanka Test Averages

BATTING	*M*	*I*	*NO*	*HS*	*Agg*	*Ave*	*100s*	*50s*	*Ct*	*St*
T.T. Samaraweera	2	3	0	88	178	59.33	-	2	2	-
D.P.M.D. Jayawardene	2	3	0	141	155	51.66	1	-	2	-
M.S. Atapattu	2	4	1	127	145	48.33	1	-	1	-
T.M. Dilshan	2	3	0	73	110	36.66	-	1	1	-
S.T. Jayasuriya	2	4	1	48	77	25.66	-	-	2	-
M.F. Maharoof	1	2	0	36	48	24.00	-	-	-	-
U.D.U. Chandana	2	3	0	41	68	22.66	-	-	-	-
K.C. Sangakkara	2	3	0	45	66	22.00	-	-	-	-
W.P.J.U.C. Vaas	2	3	0	38	60	20.00	-	-	2	-
S. Kalavitigoda	1	2	0	7	8	4.00	-	-	2	-
K.M.D.N. Kulasekara	1	1	0	0	0	0.00	-	-	1	-
H.M.R.K.B. Herath	1	1	0	0	0	0.00	-	-	-	-
S.L. Malinga	2	3	3	4*	4	-	-	-	1	-

BOWLING	*O*	*M*	*R*	*W*	*Ave*	*Best*	*5w*	*10w*
S.L. Malinga	92.4	11	334	11	30.36	5-80	1	-
W.P.J.U.C. Vaas	90	21	271	8	33.87	6-108	1	-
H.M.R.K.B. Herath	41.1	9	120	3	40.00	2-91	-	-
S.T. Jayasuriya	33	11	83	2	41.50	2-41	-	-
K.M.D.N. Kulasekara	36	9	89	1	89.00	1-70	-	-
U.D.U. Chandana	68	10	232	2	116.00	1-12	-	-
T.T. Samaraweera	1	0	6	0	-	-	-	-
D.P.M.D. Jayawardene	6	2	14	0	-	-	-	-
T.M. Dilshan	2	0	20	0	-	-	-	-
M.F. Maharoof	28	10	96	0	-	-	-	-

CENTRAL DISTRICTS v SRI LANKA — One-day

at Yarrow Stadium, New Plymouth (d/n) on 21 December, 2004
Toss : Sri Lanka. Umpires : G.A. Baxter & A.L. Hill
No result

The first game of the tour was played as a 12-a-side game but was abandoned after five overs of the Sri Lankan innings.

Central lost both openers early and then Sinclair followed at 43. Taylor and Oram came together and were going well before Taylor had to retire hurt. Oram got his fifty and added 90 with Sulzberger for the fourth wicket. Central got to 220-7. Jayantha and Sangakkara both fell to Hamilton at 14 before the rain came and the match was called off. Zoysa was injured while bowling and was ruled out of the first one-day international.

CENTRAL DISTRICTS

	Runs	Mins	Balls	6s	4s
J.M.How b Zoysa	2	29	22	-	-
C.M.Spearman b Zoysa	2	18	14	-	-
R.L.Taylor retired hurt	36	94	63	1	2
M.S.Sinclair c Zoysa b Maharoof	5	40	26	-	-
J.D.P.Oram st Sangakkara b Chandana	74	140	79	3	4
G.P.Sulzberger* c Maharoof b Chandana	39	61	54	-	2
J.I.Englefield b Herath	3	9	10	-	-
B.B.J.Griggs† b Kulasekara	2	5	6	-	-
E.P.Thompson not out	30	22	19	1	2
A.M.Schwass not out	9	18	6	-	1
M.J.Mason					
L.J.Hamilton					
Extras (b 4, lb 5, w 9)	18				
TOTAL (50 overs) (7 wkts)	**220**	213			

SRI LANKA

	Runs	Mins	Balls	6s	4s
W.S.Jayantha c Sinclair b Hamilton	5	16	16	-	-
M.S.Atapattu* not out	15	30	16	-	2
K.C.Sangakkara† c Griggs b Hamilton	0	1	2	-	-
D.P.M.D.Jayawardene not out	1	10	7	-	-
T.M.Dilshan					
R.P.Arnold					
U.D.U.Chandana					
W.P.J.U.C.Vaas					
M.F.Maharoof					
D.N.T.Zoysa					
K.M.D.N.Kulasekara					
H.M.R.K.B Herath					
Extras (w 3, nb 1)	4				
TOTAL (6.3 overs) (2 wkts)	**25**	30			

Bowling	O	M	R	W
SRI LANKA				
Zoysa	8.3	3	23	2
Kulasekara	10	1	27	1
Dilshan	1	0	8	0
Maharoof	10	1	41	1
Herath	6	0	29	1
Chandana	9	0	52	2
Arnold	5.3	0	31	0
CENTRAL DISTRICTS				
Hamilton	3.3	0	20	2
Mason	3	1	5	0

Taylor retired hurt at 76-3

Fall of Wickets	*CD*	*SL*
1st	3	14
2nd	10	14
3rd	43	
4th	166	-
5th	176	-
6th	176	-
7th	191	-
8th	-	-
9th	-	-
10th	-	-

NORTHERN DISTRICTS v SRI LANKA — One-day

at Westpac Park, Hamilton (d/n) on 23 December, 2004
Abandoned without a ball being bowled

NEW ZEALAND v SRI LANKA First One-day International

at Eden Park, Auckland on 26 December, 2004
Toss : New Zealand. Umpires : B.F. Bowden & P.D. Parker
New Zealand won by 7 wickets

Tuffey struck in the first over and three other wickets fell quickly. Jayasuriya and Dilshan both scored forties but could get no support and the visitors crumbled to be dismissed for 141 in 42 overs. Cairns had the best figures getting 4-33.

New Zealand were required to bat before the lunch break and Astle went at the end of the first over. Fleming and Sinclair then put on 57 off 94 balls with Fleming getting his fifty off 67 balls as New Zealand cruised to an easy win with 17 overs to spare

SRI LANKA

	Runs	Mins	Balls	6s	4s
W.S.Jayantha lbw b Tuffey	0	3	3	-	-
S.T.Jayasuriya c Marshall b Cairns	43	99	60	1	5
M.S.Atapattu* c McCullum b Tuffey	4	19	11	-	1
K.C.Sangakkara† c McCullum b Mills	1	5	5	-	-
D.P.M.D.Jayawardene c Sinclair b Oram	2	25	25	-	-
T.M.Dilshan c Fleming b Cairns	48	112	79	1	3
U.D.U.Chandana run out	20	48	36	-	1
W.P.U.J.C.Vaas b Cairns	0	5	6	-	-
M.F.Maharoof c Fleming b Cairns	2	6	8	-	-
K.M.D.N.Kulasekara not out	4	18	16	-	-
C.R.D.Fernando run out	3	9	4	-	-
Extras (lb 4, w 9, nb 1)	14				
TOTAL (42 overs)	**141**				

NEW ZEALAND

	Runs	Mins	Balls	6s	4s
S.P.Fleming* not out	77	136	92	2	8
N.J.Astle lbw b Vaas	6	5	5	-	1
M.S.Sinclair c & b Chandana	31	65	53	-	4
S.B.Styris run out	12	30	21	1	-
H.J.H.Marshall not out	14	33	28	-	1
J.D.P.Oram					
C.L.Cairns					
B.B.McCullum†					
D.L.Vettori					
K.D.Mills					
D.R.Tuffey					
Extras (b 2, lb 1, nb 1)	4				
TOTAL (33 overs) (3 wkts)	**144**	136			

Bowling	*O*	*M*	*R*	*W*
NEW ZEALAND				
Tuffey	8	1	17	2
Mills	8	3	24	1
Oram	7	0	23	1
Cairns	8	1	33	4
Vettori	6	0	22	0
Styris	5	0	18	0
SRI LANKA				
Vaas	8	1	31	1
Kulasekera	8	3	13	0
Maharoof	3	0	31	0
Fernando	5	0	22	0
Chandana	7	1	29	1
Jayasuriya	2	0	15	0

Fall of Wickets	***SL***	***NZ***
1st	1	7
2nd	17	64
3rd	18	101
4th	35	-
5th	70	-
6th	114	-
7th	116	-
8th	120	-
9th	134	-
10th	141	-

MAJOR ASSOCIATION XI v SRI LANKA — First-class

at Queen Elizabeth II Park, Christchurch on 28, 29, 30 March, 2005
Toss : Major Association XI. Umpires : A.L. Hill & E.A. Watkin
Close of play: 1st day: Major Association XI 321 all out; 2nd day: no play
3rd day: no play
Match drawn

The Major Association XI was selected from the four sides not involved in the State Championship final. The other two players in a 13-man-squad were Greg Todd, who was twelfth man, and Daryl Tuffey, who did not recover from injury in time to be considered.

All of the home team's main batsmen got starts, none more so than the captain, McMillan, who had just been omitted from the New Zealand team for the third test against Australia. Despite giving a chance in the seventies, he went on to reach his 13th first-class century after 175 minutes from 128 balls. Malinga looked the best of the Sri Lankan attack.

Rain and wet conditions prevented any play on the second and third days meaning Sri Lanka went in to the first test without any of their batsmen having had any time at the crease.

MAJOR ASSOCIATION XI

FIRST INNINGS	*Runs*	*Mins*	*Balls*	*6s*	*4s*
P.G.Fulton run out	22	74	56	-	3
J.M.How lbw b Maharoof	19	71	45	-	3
M.S.Sinclair st Sangakkara b Chandana	38	66	43	-	4
C.D.McMillan* c Sangakkara b Malinga	121	232	164	5	9
R.L.Taylor lbw b Maharoof	10	36	28	-	1
A.J.Redmond st Sangakkara b Herath	15	57	36	-	1
G.J.Hopkins† c Sangakkara b Malinga	50	119	106	-	4
J.A.F.Yovich c Sangakkara b Malinga	0	8	3	-	-
B.P.Martin b Perera	18	41	26	1	2
W.C.McSkimming not out	4	19	10	-	-
G.W.Aldridge b Perera	8	14	13	-	-
Extras (b 1, lb 3, w 5, nb 7)	16				
TOTAL (87.1 overs)	**321**	373			

SRI LANKA

M.S.Atapattu *
S.T.Jayasuriya
K.C.Sangakkara †
D.P.M.D.Jayawardene
T.M.Dilshan
S.Kalavitigoda
U.D.U.Chandana
M.F.Maharoof
H.M.R.K.B.Herath
P.D.R.L.Perera
S.L.Malinga

Bowling	*O*	*M*	*R*	*W*
SRI LANKA				
Perera	14.1	4	48	2
Malinga	19	3	57	3
Maharoof	20	2	59	2
Chandana	20	2	87	1
Herath	11	1	40	1
Dilshan	1	0	3	0
Jayasuriya	2	0	23	0

Fall of Wickets	***MA***
	1st
1st	46
2nd	46
3rd	111
4th	132
5th	206
6th	264
7th	268
8th	309
9th	309
10th	321

NEW ZEALAND v SRI LANKA — First Test

at McLean Park, Napier on 4, 5, 6, 7, 8 April, 2005
Toss : New Zealand. Umpires : S.A. Bucknor & D.B. Hair
Close of play: 1st day: NZ 267-3, H.J.H.Marshall 133, Astle 37; 2nd day: SL 48-0, Atapattu 14, Jayasuriya 31
3rd day: SL 351-3, Jayawardene 118, Samaraweera 34; 4th day: NZ 64-2, J.A.H.Marshall 33, Wiseman 0
Match drawn

Vettori was ruled out of the first test due to his back injury and was replaced by Mills. Kulasekera became Sri Lanka's 100th test player in the first test at Napier for ten years.

After the loss of Cumming, the Marshall twins added 107 for the second wicket in 139 minutes. James went to his maiden test fifty off 144 balls. Hamish continued his run of form and reached his second test century after 171 balls. His 160 was his highest first-class score. Astle was associated in two century stands, 125 with Hamish Marshall in 130 minutes off 197 balls and 129 with McCullum from 216 balls. Astle got his 10th test hundred after 181 balls.

McCullum got fifty from 97 balls but was out for 99. Franklin scored his maiden test fifty from 77 balls while Malinga, with his unusual action, troubled the New Zealand batsmen,

The Sri Lankan batsmen were also able to score runs with little difficulty. Atapattu scored his 16th hundred off 196 balls. Jayawardene also scored a hundred (his 13th) off 157 balls. However, there was a collapse and Sri Lanka went from 407-3 to 498 all out as Franklin and Martin each took four wickets.

New Zealand again had its second innings jitters. Fleming had to retire hurt, suffering from a bruised finger, and New Zealand were in a difficult position at 148-7 before a half-century from Vincent and Fleming's return saw them through to safety. Malinga got his first five wicket haul.

NEW ZEALAND

FIRST INNINGS	*Runs*	*Mins*	*Balls*	*6s*	*4s*	*SECOND INNINGS*	*Runs*	*Mins*	*Balls*	*6s*	*4s*
C.D.Cumming lbw b Vaas	12	60	45	-	2	lbw b Malinga	16	105	73	-	-
J.A.H.Marshall c Samaraweera b Chandana	52	200	148	-	5	lbw b Jayasuriya	39	173	122	-	6
H.J.H.Marshall c Vaas b Malinga	160	323	249	2	22	lbw b Malinga	6	21	17	-	-
S.P.Fleming* b Malinga	16	50	36	-	3	(5) c Kulasekara b Malinga	41	157	121	1	4
N.J.Astle c Jayasuriya b Vaas	114	279	203	-	17	(6) run out	19	66	51	-	1
L.Vincent c Dilshan b Kulasekara	0	3	2	-	-	(7) b Chandana	52	168	112	-	6
B.B.McCullum† lbw b Malinga	99	190	156	2	10	(8) c Samaraweera b Jayasuriya	7	15	12	-	1
J.E.C.Franklin c Malinga b Herath	55	118	84	1	4	(9) b Malinga	7	22	14	-	-
K.D.Mills b Malinga	4	6	3	-	1	(10) c Jayasuriya b Herath	22	36	31	-	4
P.J.Wiseman c Atapattu b Herath	27	45	35	1	2	(4) b Malinga	0	7	5	-	-
C.S.Martin not out	1	16	4	-	-	not out	4	19	8	-	1
Extras (b 5, lb 4, w 2, nb 10)	21					(b 6, lb 7, w 2, nb 10)	25				
TOTAL (159.1 overs)	**561**	653				(92.4 overs)	**238**	401			

SRI LANKA

	Runs	*Mins*	*Balls*	*6s*	*4s*		*Runs*	*Mins*	*Balls*	*6s*	*4s*
M.S.Atapattu* c Fleming b Astle	127	304	244	-	22	not out	2	9	7	-	-
S.T.Jayasuriya lbw b Martin	48	104	67	-	9	not out	5	9	2	-	1
K.C.Sangakkara† b Martin	5	9	5	-	1						
D.P.M.D.Jayawardene c McCullum b Franklin	141	338	243	1	19						
T.T.Samaraweera c Fleming b Martin	88	238	166	-	14						
T.M.Dilshan c Vincent b Martin	28	60	49	-	5						
W.P.J.U.C.Vaas c Astle b Wiseman	17	74	50	-	2						
U.D.U.Chandana c Martin b Franklin	19	77	55	-	2						
H.M.R.K.B.Herath b Franklin	0	6	7	-	-						
K.M.D.N.Kulasekara c Fleming b Franklin	0	7	5	-	-						
S.L.Malinga not out	0	10	10	-	-						
Extras (b 1, lb 6, w 6, nb 12)	25										
TOTAL (148.1 overs)	**498**	624				(1.3 overs) (0 wkts)	**7**	9			

Bowling	*O*	*M*	*R*	*W*	*O*	*M*	*R*	*W*
SRI LANKA								
Vaas	33	5	125	2	17	4	38	0
Malinga	34	5	130	4	24.4	4	80	5
Kulasekara	25	7	70	1	11	2	19	0
Herath	30.1	5	91	2	11	4	29	1
Chandana	33	4	123	1	7	2	12	1
Jayasuriya	3	1	8	0	21	8	41	2
Dilshan	1	0	5	0				
Samaraweera					1	0	6	0
NEW ZEALAND								
Martin	37	9	132	4	1	0	1	0
Franklin	32.1	8	126	4	0.3	0	6	0
Wiseman	38	7	128	1				
Mills	23	6	59	0				
Astle	18	6	46	1				

Fall of Wickets	***NZ***	***SL***	***NZ***	***SL***
	1st	*1st*	*2nd*	*2nd*
1st	35	95	51	-
2nd	142	101	64	-
3rd	187	285	69	-
4th	312	407	8	-
5th	317	452	115	-
6th	446	463	128	-
7th	487	488	148	-
8th	497	491	181	-
9th	540	497	222	-
10th	561	498	238	-

In New Zealand's 2nd innings Fleming retired hurt on 6 at 77-3 and returned at 148-7*

NEW ZEALAND v SRI LANKA — Second Test

at Basin Reserve, Wellington on 11, 12, 13, 14 April, 2005
Toss : New Zealand. Umpires : D.B. Hair & S.A. Bucknor
Close of play: 1st day: NZ 52-0, Cumming 14, J.A.H.Marshall 24; 2nd day: NZ 253-4, Vincent 80, Fleming 60
3rd day: Sri Lanka 10-1, Atapattu 5, Maharoof 1
New Zealand won by an innings and 38 runs

New Zealand had the same team but Sri Lanka made two changes. Kulasekara and Herath made way for Maharoof and debutant Kalavitigoda.

Martin captured five wickets before lunch on the first day and finished with his sixth five wicket bag. He took the first six wickets to fall. Samaraweera and Chandana more than doubled the score from 87-7 to 175-8 before Sri Lanka were dismissed for 211. Martin and Astle had career best figures.

New Zealand had a solid start with a fifty opening partnership.Vincent came in at number four for Fleming who had injured a knee while attempting to take a catch. He got fifty from 95 balls and his third test century off 223 deliveries.

His first double century needed 339 balls as he demolished the attack before being run out going for a second run. Fleming had got fifty from 98 balls. There were records against Sri Lanka for the seventh, eighth and ninth wickets, Vaas also took the first six wickets to fall.

Jayasuriya went early in the innings but nightwatchman Maharoof and Sangakkara looked in no trouble until New Zealand finally broke through. The loss of regular wickets had the visitors in trouble at 177-7 but Dilshan (fifty off 71 balls) and Vaas put on 78 off 118 balls before the end came. Franklin bowled well and for the second time in the match Astle had career best bowling. This win was New Zealand's 57th and the 12th at the Basin Reserve.

SRI LANKA

FIRST INNINGS	*Runs*	*Mins*	*Balls*	*6s*	*4s*	*SECOND INNINGS*	*Runs*	*Mins*	*Balls*	*6s*	*4s*
M.S.Atapattu* c Vincent b Martin	0	2	3	-	-	(2) c Fleming b Franklin	16	88	56	-	1
S.T.Jayasuriya c Astle b Martin	22	44	22	-	3	(1) c Vincent b Martin	2	10	9	-	-
K.C.Sangakkara† c Marshall J.A.H. b Martin	16	28	23	-	3	(4) b Franklin	45	147	114	-	7
D.P.M.D.Jayawardene lbw b Martin	1	4	4	-	-	(5) c McCullum b Franklin	13	37	30	-	1
T.T.Samaraweera lbw b Astle	73	250	163	-	8	(6) c Fleming b Astle	17	57	37	-	1
T.M.Dilshan c McCullum b Martin	9	52	33	-	2	(7) b Astle	73	121	99	1	10
S.Kalavitigoda c Vincent b Martin	7	45	36	-	1	(8) c McCullum b Mills	1	24	19	-	-
W.P.J.U.C.Vaas b Franklin	5	7	9	-	1	(9) b Franklin	38	94	72	1	4
U.D.U.Chandana lbw b Astle	41	98	82	-	6	(10) b Astle	8	16	13	-	2
M.F.Maharoof c sub (J.M.How) b Astle	12	28	25	-	2	(3) c Astle b Mills	36	153	115	-	3
S.L.Malinga not out	4	7	3	-	1	not out	0	4	1	-	-
Extras (b 4, lb 5, w 1, nb 11)	21					(b 4, lb 10, w 2, nb 8)	24				
TOTAL (65.1 overs)	**211**	287				(92.5 overs)	**273**	380			

NEW ZEALAND

	Runs	Mins	Balls	6s	4s
C.D.Cumming lbw b Vaas	47	217	157	-	5
J.A.H.Marshall lbw b Vaas	28	60	45	-	4
H.J.H.Marshall c Jayawardene b Vaas	6	25	6	-	-
L.Vincent run out	224	529	348	4	25
N.J.Astle c Kalavitigoda b Vaas	0	1	1	-	-
S.P.Fleming* c Kalavitigoda b Vaas	88	207	176	1	11
B.B.McCullum† c & b Vaas	0	2	1	-	-
J.E.C.Franklin lbw b Malinga	15	53	45	-	2
K.D.Mills c Jayawardene b Malinga	31	90	89	1	5
P.J.Wiseman not out	32	61	40	-	4
C.S.Martin not out	4	20	9	-	1
Extras (b 11, lb 23, w 1, nb 12)	47				
TOTAL (146 overs) (9 wkts dec)	**522**	637			

Bowling	*O*	*M*	*R*	*W*	*O*	*M*	*R*	*W*
NEW ZEALAND								
Martin	20	7	54	6	18	4	50	1
Franklin	11	1	51	1	23.5	4	71	4
Mills	20	6	50	0	11	4	34	2
Astle	12.1	2	35	3	13	4	27	3
Wiseman	2	0	12	0	26	7	75	0
Vincent					1	0	2	0
SRI LANKA								
Vaas	40	12	108	6				
Malinga	34	2	124	2				
Maharoof	28	10	96	0				
Jayawardene	6	2	14	0				
Chandana	28	4	97	0				
Jayasuriya	9	2	34	0				
Dilshan	1	0	15	0				

Fall of Wickets

	SL *1st*	***NZ*** *1st*	***SL*** *2nd*
1st	0	61	6
2nd	34	70	47
3rd	36	153	95
4th	41	153	117
5th	60	294	137
6th	80	294	164
7th	86	342	177
8th	175	440	255
9th	200	499	267
10th	211	-	273

FICA WORLD XI IN NEW ZEALAND

When the Sri Lankan tour of New Zealand was called off due to the tsunami disaster on Boxing Day, New Zealand Cricket and the Players' Association arranged a three-match series against a World XI. Fifteen players took part for the FICA team. The series was won by New Zealand 2-1.

The highlight of the games was the magnificent innings played by Stephen Fleming at Christchurch where he hit a century off just 54 balls, with ten sixes. The low point was the state of the ground at Hamilton where, after criticism of the pitch, it was decided to completely re-lay the wicket. The scheduled game against Australia was transferred to Wellington.

The World XI side was S.K. Warne *(captain)*, A.J. Bichel, G.S. Blewett, M.T.G. Elliott, I.J. Harvey *(Australia)*, G.A. Hick, N.V. Knight *(England)*, S.T. Jayasuriya, M. Muralitharan, K.C. Sangakkara, W.P.U.J.C Vaas *(Sri Lanka)*, L. Klusener, J.N. Rhodes *(South Africa)*, H.H. Streak *(Zimbabwe)*, C.M. Spearman *(New Zealand)*. Coach, J.N. Rhodes; Manager, J. Souter.

New Zealand Averages

BATTING	*M*	*I*	*NO*	*HS*	*Agg*	*Ave*	*100s*	*50s*	*Ct*	*St*	*SR*
N.J. Astle	3	3	1	109	168	84.00	1	-	2	-	88
S.P. Fleming	3	3	0	106	136	45.33	1	-	1	-	163
H.J.H. Marshall	3	2	1	16*	22	22.00	-	-	2	-	75
M.S. Sinclair	3	2	0	30	34	17.00	-	-	1	-	54
C.D. McMillan	2	2	0	33	33	16.50	-	-	-	-	89
S.B. Styris	2	1	0	16	16	16.00	-	-	-	-	100
J.W. Wilson	3	1	0	11	11	11.00	-	-	3	-	122
C.L. Cairns	3	3	1	9	18	9.00	-	-	2	-	66
K.D. Mills	3	1	0	8	8	8.00	-	-	-	-	80
B.B. McCullum	3	2	1	2*	2	2.00	-	-	8	-	25
D.L. Vettori	2	1	1	26*	26	-	-	-	-	-	123
D.R. Tuffey	3	1	1	0*	0	-	-	-	-	-	0

BOWLING	*O*	*M*	*R*	*W*	*Ave*	*Best*	*R/O*
C.L. Cairns	20.5	1	83	8	10.37	6-12	4.08
J.W. Wilson	19	1	59	5	11.80	3-6	3.11
D.L. Vettori	19.3	1	78	4	19.50	3-33	4.00
N.J. Astle	5	0	24	1	24.00	1-24	4.80
K.D. Mills	21	2	102	4	25.50	2-30	4.86
D.R. Tuffey	21.5	0	124	3	41.33	2-25	5.68
C.D. McMillan	1	0	10	0	-	-	10.00

FICA World XI Averages

BATTING	*M*	*I*	*NO*	*HS*	*Agg*	*Ave*	*100s*	*50s*	*Ct*	*St*	*SR*
A.J. Bichel	2	2	1	37*	42	42.00	-	-	-	-	82
N.V. Knight	2	2	0	43	72	36.00	-	-	-	-	84
M.T.G. Elliott	2	2	0	57	67	33.50	-	1	-	-	75
G.A. Hick	3	3	0	44	68	22.66	-	-	-	-	72
J.N. Rhodes	3	3	0	36	55	18.33	-	-	1	-	52
K.C. Sangakkara	3	3	0	51	51	17.00	-	1	3	-	82
C.M. Spearman	1	1	0	14	14	14.00	-	-	1	-	73
S.K. Warne	3	2	0	26	26	13.00	-	-	1	-	65
S.T. Jayasuriya	3	3	0	13	22	7.33	-	-	2	-	84
L. Klusener	2	2	0	4	8	4.00	-	-	1	-	40
H.H. Streak	2	2	1	2*	2	2.00	-	-	-	-	33
M. Muralitharan	2	1	0	0	0	0.00	-	-	-	-	0
G.S. Blewett	1	1	0	0	0	0.00	-	-	-	-	0
I.J. Harvey	2	2	0	0	0	0.00	-	-	-	-	0
W.P.J.U.C. Vaas	2	2	2	22*	42	-	-	-	2	-	102

BOWLING	*O*	*M*	*R*	*W*	*Ave*	*Best*	*R/O*
G.S. Blewett	2	0	7	1	7.00	1-7	3.50
I.J. Harvey	7.2	1	40	4	10.00	4-17	5.45
L. Klusener	7	1	35	2	17.50	2-35	5.00
A.J. Bichel	15	1	90	4	22.50	3-56	6.00
S.T. Jayasuriya	10	0	38	1	38.00	1-38	3.80
W.P.J.U.C. Vaas	10	0	66	1	66.00	1-35	6.60
S.K. Warne	13	0	70	1	70.00	1-26	5.38
M. Muralitharan	11.1	0	103	1	103.00	1-46	9.22
H.H. Streak	7	0	43	0	-	-	6.14

NEW ZEALAND v FICA World XI — First One-day

at Jade Stadium, Christchurch on 22 January, 2005
Toss : FICA World XI. Umpires : A.L. Hill & E.A. Watkin
New Zealand won by 9 wickets

After winning the toss the FICA side lost four wickets in ten balls to be reeling at 20-4. Only a 79 run stand off 102 balls for the fifth wicket by Hick and Rhodes gave the innings some substance. Vaas and Warne put on 45 for the ninth wicket to get the total to 158 off 39.3 overs.

The New Zealand openers demolished the FICA bowlers. They put on 148 off just 94 balls. Fleming got his first fifty from 35 balls and then went to a hundred from a further 19 deliveries as he hit ten sixes and nine fours. New Zealand reached 160-1 from just 16.1 overs

FICA WORLD XI

	Runs	Mins	Balls	6s	4s
S.T.Jayasuriya c Cairns b Tuffey	5	17	10	-	-
C.M.Spearman c Wilson b Tuffey	14	21	19	-	3
I.J.Harvey lbw b Mills	0	10	4	-	-
K.C.Sangakkara† c Cairns b Mills	0	2	1	-	-
G.A.Hick c McCullum b Wilson	44	88	59	-	6
J.N.Rhodes c Astle b Cairns	36	67	56	2	3
L.Klusener c McCullum b Vettori	4	20	16	-	-
H.H.Streak c Fleming b Vettori	0	10	3	-	-
W.P.J.U.C.Vaas not out	20	46	29	-	3
S.K.Warne* run out	26	37	38	-	3
M.Muralitharan b Vettori	0	1	2	-	-
Extras (lb 5, w 4)	9				
TOTAL (39.3 overs)	**158**	164			

NEW ZEALAND

	Runs	Mins	Balls	6s	4s
S.P.Fleming* c Spearman b Warne	106	65	57	9	10
N.J.Astle not out	36	69	38	-	4
C.L.Cairns not out	8	3	2	-	2
H.J.H.Marshall					
S.B.Styris					
M.S.Sinclair					
B.B.McCullum†					
J.W.Wilson					
D.L.Vettori					
K.D.Mills					
D.R.Tuffey					
Extras (lb 3, w 7)	10				
TOTAL (16.1 overs) (1 wkt)	**160**	69			

Bowling	*O*	*M*	*R*	*W*
NEW ZEALAND				
Tuffey	8	0	25	2
Mills	7	1	30	2
Cairns	8	1	38	1
Wilson	7	1	27	1
Vettori	9.3	1	33	3
FICA WORLD XI				
Vaas	5	0	31	0
Streak	3	0	20	0
Harvey	2	0	23	0
Muralitharan	3.1	0	57	0
Warne	3	0	26	1

Fall of Wickets	***FIC***	***NZ***
1st	16	148
2nd	20	-
3rd	20	-
4th	20	-
5th	99	-
6th	112	-
7th	112	-
8th	113	-
9th	158	-
10th	158	-

NEW ZEALAND v FICA World XI — Second One-day

at Westpac Stadium, Wellington (d/n) on 24 January, 2005
Toss : FICA World XI. Umpires : D.B. Cowie & E.A. Watkin
FICA World XI won by 3 wickets

Fleming went early after Warne had won the toss but Astle held the innings together with a century from 113 balls. His fifty had taken 43 deliveries. He received support from Sinclair and McMillan as New Zealand reached 256-9.

The World side had a positive start with an opening stand of 65 from 74 deliveries. Elliott got fifty from just 47 balls. Sangakkara then scored a fifty off 60 balls and he and Bichel added 50 for the seventh wicket. FICA World XI won with 13 balls to spare and levelled the series.

NEW ZEALAND

	Runs	Mins	Balls	6s	4s
S.P.Fleming* c & b Vaas	14	13	13	-	3
N.J.Astle c Rhodes b Bichel	109	179	124	1	9
M.S.Sinclair c Sangakkara b Klusener	30	67	51	1	1
C.L.Cairns c Warne b Klusener	9	24	23	-	1
H.J.H.Marshall c Vaas b Muralitharan	6	15	13	-	1
C.D.McMillan c & b Jayasuriya	33	42	35	3	-
B.B.McCullum† c Sangakkara b Bichel	0	4	2	-	-
D.L.Vettori not out	26	38	27	1	2
J.W.Wilson c Klusener b Bichel	11	13	9	1	1
K.D.Mills run out	8	14	10	-	-
D.R.Tuffey not out	0	1	0	-	-
Extras (lb 2, w 7, nb 1)	10				
TOTAL (50 overs) (9 wkts)	**256**	208			

FICA WORLD XI

	Runs	Mins	Balls	6s	4s
M.T.G.Elliott c Sinclair b Astle	57	52	40	1	3
N.V.Knight c McCullum b Cairns	29	94	61	3	3
S.T.Jayasuriya c Marshall b Mills	4	4	3	-	1
G.A.Hick lbw b Vettori	24	46	33	1	1
K.C.Sangakkara† c Marshall b Tuffey	51	85	63	2	3
J.N.Rhodes run out	16	38	31	-	1
L.Klusener c & b Wilson	4	4	5	-	-
A.J.Bichel not out	37	50	38	2	2
W.P.J.U.C.Vaas not out	22	17	12	1	3
S.K.Warne*					
M.Muralitharan					
Extras (lb 9, w 3, nb 1)	13				
TOTAL (47.5 overs) (7 wkts)	**257**	198			

Bowling	*O*	*M*	*R*	*W*
FICA WORLD XI				
Bichel	10	1	56	3
Vaas	5	0	35	1
Klusener	7	1	35	2
Jayasuriya	10	0	38	1
Warne	10	0	44	0
Muralitharan	8	0	46	1
NEW ZEALAND				
Tuffey	8.5	0	63	1
Mills	8	1	47	1
Cairns	7	0	33	1
Vettori	10	0	45	1
Astle	5	0	24	1
Wilson	8	0	26	1
McMillan	1	0	10	0

Fall of Wickets

	NZ	*FIC*
1st	25	65
2nd	107	74
3rd	134	111
4th	148	122
5th	202	167
6th	205	172
7th	214	222
8th	233	-
9th	252	-
10th	-	-

NEW ZEALAND v FICA World XI — Third One-day

at Westpac Park, Hamilton (d/n) on 26 January, 2005
Toss : FICA World XI. Umpires : A.L. Hill & D.B. Cowie
New Zealand won by 4 wickets

After winning the toss and batting and reaching 37 without loss, the FICA side were dismissed in just 20.5 overs. Cairns took 6-12 and Wilson 3-6 as the World team collapsed on a sub-standard pitch. Only Knight, with 43, got past 13 and nine wickets fell for 22 runs.

New Zealand also struggled with the bat losing six wickets before reaching the target. Harvey took 4-17 and New Zealand won the series 2-1.

A ten overs per side exhibition match was played after the early finish.

FICA WORLD XI

	Runs	Mins	Balls	6s	4s
N.V.Knight b Cairns	43	70	45	-	6
M.T.G.Elliott c McCullum b Mills	10	31	22	-	1
S.T.Jayasuriya c Wilson b Cairns	13	15	13	1	-
I.J.Harvey c McCullum b Cairns	0	9	6	-	-
G.S.Blewett c McCullum b Wilson	0	4	2	-	-
G.A.Hick c McCullum b Wilson	0	2	2	-	-
K.C.Sangakkara† c McCullum b Wilson	0	8	1	-	-
J.N.Rhodes lbw b Cairns	3	29	18	-	-
A.J.Bichel c Astle b Cairns	5	15	13	-	-
H.H.Streak not out	2	11	3	--	
S.K.Warne* b Cairns	0	1	2	-	-
Extras (lb 2, w 1, nb 2)	5				
TOTAL (20.5 overs)	**81**	102			

NEW ZEALAND

	Runs	Mins	Balls	6s	4s
S.P.Fleming* c Sangakkara b Bichel	16	19	13	-	3
N.J.Astle b Harvey	23	46	27	-	4
M.S.Sinclair b Harvey	4	15	11	-	-
S.B.Styris lbw b Harvey	16	22	16	-	4
H.J.H.Marshall not out	16	34	16	-	2
C.D.McMillan b Harvey	0	2	2	-	-
C.L.Cairns c Jayasuriya b Blewett	1	5	2	-	-
B.B.McCullum† not out	2	13	6	-	-
J.W.Wilson					
K.D.Mills					
D.R.Tuffey					
Extras (b 1, lb 1, w 2, nb 1)	5				
TOTAL (16.2 overs) (6 wkts)	**83**	81			

Bowling	*O*	*M*	*R*	*W*
NEW ZEALAND				
Tuffey	5	0	36	0
Mills	6	0	25	1
Cairns	5.5	0	12	6
Wilson	4	0	6	3
FICA WORLD XI				
Bichel	5	0	34	1
Streak	4	0	23	0
Harvey	5.2	1	17	4
Blewett	2	0	7	1

Fall of Wickets

	FIC	***NZ***
1st	37	29
2nd	59	44
3rd	67	55
4th	69	64
5th	69	64
6th	71	65
7th	71	-
8th	78	-
9th	81	-
10th	81	-

Exhibition Match (10 overs per side)
New Zealand 178-3 (C.D. McMillan 63 [18], S.B. Styris 44 [18], K.D. Mills 38 [14]) **tied with FICA World XI** 178-7 (A.J. Bichel 47 [14], H.H. Streak 32 [11]).

AUSTRALIA IN NEW ZEALAND

The Australian side, ranked number one in both tests and one-day internationals, made a nine match tour of New Zealand in February and March. They won every match except the second test at Wellington which was disrupted by the weather.

Apart from the first one-day international, when New Zealand threw away a golden opportunity to take an early lead in the series, the Australians were completely dominant. While the visitors were at full strength for the tour, from the New Zealand side which had played in Australia, Styris and Oram were injured and Richardson had retired from all cricket.

In the one-day series all the Australian batsmen made runs. If one player failed others came to the rescue. Hayden scored a century in the second game before injuring his shoulder while fielding and didn't play in the other three games. Ponting scored a blistering unbeaten 141 from just 127 balls in the final game when Australia scored a massive 347-5. Lee caused all the New Zealand batsmen problems with his pace and bounce and he had able allies in McGrath, Gillespie and Kasprowicz.

Hamish Marshall was New Zealand's most consistent batsman while Vettori, despite taking only two wickets, was the only bowler who conceded less than 3.5 runs per over.

In the test series Gilchrist scored centuries in the first two matches and an unbeaten fifty in the last game. Katich, Martyn and Ponting also scored centuries. McGrath took 18 wickets in the series and finished on 499 test wickets. World record holder Warne had 17 victims.

Hamish Marshall scored a century in his first test against Australia while Vettori and Franklin both had five wicket hauls.

The Australian touring party was R.T. Ponting *(captain)*, A.C. Gilchrist *(vice-captain)*, M.J. Clarke, J.R. Gillespie, M.L. Hayden, B.J. Hodge, G.B. Hogg, J.R. Hopes, M.E.K. Hussey, S.M. Katich, M.S. Kasprowicz, J.L. Langer, B. Lee, G.D. McGrath, D.R. Martyn, A. Symonds, S.K. Warne. Coach, J.M. Buchanan; Manager, S.R. Bernard.

Hogg, Hopes, Hussey and Symonds played only in the one-day games and were replaced by Hodge, Langer and Warne.

New Zealand Test Averages

BATTING	*M*	*I*	*NO*	*HS*	*Agg*	*Ave*	*100s*	*50s*	*Ct*	*St*
D.L. Vettori	3	5	2	65	198	66.00	-	1	-	-
H.J.H. Marshall	3	6	0	146	269	44.83	1	1	-	-
N.J. Astle	3	6	1	74	196	39.20	-	2	2	-
L. Vincent	3	6	0	63	160	26.66	-	1	2	-
C.D. Cumming	3	6	1	74	133	26.60	-	1	2	-
S.P. Fleming	3	6	0	65	104	17.33	-	1	2	-
B.B. McCullum	3	5	0	29	81	16.20	-	-	8	-
J.A.H. Marshall	1	2	0	29	32	16.00	-	-	-	-
P.J. Wiseman	1	2	0	23	31	15.50	-	-	1	-
J.E.C. Franklin	3	5	1	26	57	14.25	-	-	1	-
C.D. McMillan	2	3	0	20	38	12.66	-	-	-	-
I.E. O'Brien	2	3	0	5	10	3.33	-	-	1	-
C.S. Martin	3	5	2	4*	5	1.66	-	-	-	-

BOWLING	*O*	*M*	*R*	*W*	*Ave*	*Best*	*5w*	*10w*
J.E.C. Franklin	92.1	13	415	12	34.58	6-119	1	-
D.L. Vettori	123.5	22	397	8	49.62	5-106	1	-
N.J. Astle	55	15	155	3	51.66	1-32	-	-
P.J. Wiseman	34.3	7	77	1	77.00	1-64	-	-
I.E. O'Brien	43	7	197	2	98.50	1-73	-	-
C.S. Martin	94	17	397	2	198.50	1-92	-	-

Australia Test Averages

BATTING	*M*	*I*	*NO*	*HS*	*Agg*	*Ave*	*100s*	*50s*	*Ct*	*St*
A.C. Gilchrist	3	3	1	162	343	171.50	2	1	7	-
R.T. Ponting	3	5	2	105	293	97.66	1	1	2	-
D.R. Martyn	3	3	0	165	235	78.33	1	-	1	-
J.L. Langer	3	5	2	72*	206	68.66	-	2	3	-
S.M. Katich	3	3	0	118	188	62.66	1	-	3	-
M.S. Kasprowicz	3	3	2	23	38	38.00	-	-	-	-
M.L. Hayden	3	5	0	61	158	31.60	-	1	1	-
S.K. Warne	3	3	1	50*	53	26.50	-	1	1	-
J.N. Gillespie	3	3	0	35	49	16.33	-	-	4	-
M.J. Clarke	3	3	0	22	38	12.66	-	-	2	-
G.D. McGrath	3	2	0	0	0	0.00	-	-	1	-

BOWLING	*O*	*M*	*R*	*W*	*Ave*	*Best*	*5w*	*10w*
M.J. Clarke	8	1	24	2	12.00	1-8	-	-
G.D. McGrath	126.2	47	283	18	15.72	6-115	1	-
S.K. Warne	131.3	25	374	17	22.00	5-39	1	-
M.S. Kasprowicz	98.2	20	319	8	39.87	3-42	-	-
J.N. Gillespie	107	25	320	7	45.71	3-38	-	-
R.T. Ponting	4	1	10	0	-	-	-	-

New Zealand One-day International Averages

BATTING	*M*	*I*	*NO*	*HS*	*Agg*	*Ave*	*100s*	*50s*	*Ct*	*St*	*SR*
H.J.H. Marshall	5	5	0	76	198	39.60	-	2	1	-	76
C.D. McMillan	5	5	0	63	173	34.60	-	1	1	-	86
N.J. Astle	4	4	0	65	132	33.00	-	1	1	-	59
D.L. Vettori	4	4	1	83	99	33.00	-	1	1	-	101
B.B. McCullum	5	5	0	36	104	20.80	-	-	5	-	65
C.L. Cairns	5	4	0	36	70	17.50	-	-	-	-	94
T.K. Canning	1	1	0	16	16	16.00	-	-	-	-	59
S.P. Fleming	5	5	0	37	79	15.80	-	-	1	-	66
S.B. Styris	1	1	0	14	14	14.00	-	-	-	-	29
J.W. Wilson	2	2	0	22	23	11.50	-	-	3	-	79
C.D. Cumming	2	2	0	13	23	11.50	-	-	2	-	50
J.A.H. Marshall	3	3	0	14	23	7.66	-	-	-	-	60
M.S. Sinclair	2	2	0	15	15	7.50	-	-	1	-	42
K.D. Mills	5	5	1	10	20	5.00	-	-	-	-	58
D.R. Tuffey	3	3	2	1	1	1.00	-	-	-	-	50
M.H.W. Papps	1	1	1	3*	3	-	-	-	1	-	30
L.J.Hamilton	2	2	2	2*	3	-	-	-	-	-	50

BOWLING	*O*	*M*	*R*	*W*	*Ave*	*Best*	*R/O*
S.B. Styris	10	1	40	4	10.00	4-40	4.00
C.L. Cairns	36	1	203	5	40.60	2-56	5.64
K.D. Mills	45	3	271	5	54.20	2-62	6.02
D.L. Vettori	40	0	132	2	66.00	2-31	3.30
C.D. McMillan	21.2	0	141	2	70.50	1-31	6.61
T.K. Canning	10	0	80	1	80.00	1-80	8.00
J.W. Wilson	15	0	125	1	125.00	1-68	8.33
L.J. Hamilton	18	0	143	1	143.00	1-76	7.94
D.R. Tuffey	18	1	145	1	145.00	1-73	8.06
C.D. Cumming	3	0	17	0	-	-	5.67
N.J. Astle	18	0	85	0	-	-	4.72

Australia One-day International Averages

BATTING	M	I	NO	HS	Agg	Ave	100s	50s	Ct	St	SR
M.L. Hayden	2	2	0	114	185	92.50	1	1	2	-	79
R.T. Ponting	4	4	1	141*	266	88.66	1	2	1	-	93
M.J. Clarke	5	5	2	71*	147	49.00	-	1	2	-	100
D.R. Martyn	5	5	1	65*	171	42.75	-	2	1	-	80
A.C. Gilchrist	5	5	0	91	167	33.40	-	2	11	1	118
A. Symonds	5	5	0	53	152	30.40	-	1	1	-	113
S.M. Katich	4	4	0	58	106	26.50	-	1	2	-	76
M.E.K. Hussey	4	3	3	65*	97	-	-	1	3	-	104
G.B. Hogg	4	2	2	25*	34	-	-	-	1	-	80
B. Lee	5	1	1	4*	4	-	-	-	1	-	133
G.D. McGrath	4	-	-	-	-	-	-	-	1	-	-
M.S. Kasprowicz	4	-	-	-	-	-	-	-	2	-	-
J.N. Gillespie	3	-	-	-	-	-	-	-	-	-	-
J.R. Hopes	1	-	-	-	-	-	-	-	-	-	-

BOWLING	O	M	R	W	Ave	Best	R/O
G.D. McGrath	36.3	4	151	9	16.77	4-16	3.86
B. Lee	43	4	169	10	16.90	3-41	3.93
A. Symonds	31	1	154	7	22.00	3-41	4.97
J.N. Gillespie	25.4	1	105	4	26.25	2-45	4.09
M.S. Kasprowicz	36	6	160	5	32.00	3-36	4.44
J.R. Hopes	10	1	38	1	38.00	1-38	3.80
G.B. Hogg	36.5	0	191	4	47.75	3-45	5.18
M.J. Clarke	9	0	48	1	48.00	1-13	5.33
M.E.K. Hussey	3	0	22	0	-	-	7.33

NEW ZEALAND v AUSTRALIA — Twenty20 International

at Eden Park, Auckland (d/n) on 17 February, 2005
Toss : Australia. Umpires : B.F. Bowden & A.L. Hill
Australia won by 44 runs

New Zealand and Australia played the first 20/20 international. After Australia had lost two quick wickets, Ponting rescued the innings getting 98 off just 55 balls. Ponting and Hussey added an unbeaten 77 off 31 balls to see Australia reach 214-5.

New Zealand started well but only Fleming and Styris were able to reach 20. Styris got 66 off 39 balls but Australia won by 44 runs. The attendance was 23,500.

AUSTRALIA

	Runs	Mins	Balls	6s	4s
A.C.Gilchrist† c McMillan b Mills	1	7	3	-	-
M.J.Clarke c McMillan b Tuffey	7	4	4	1	-
A.Symonds c McCullum b Mills	32	12	13	2	4
R.T.Ponting* not out	98	63	55	5	7
D.R.Martyn b Mills	3	4	5	-	-
S.M.Katich b Cairns	30	19	25	1	2
M.E.K.Hussey not out	31	18	15	3	1
J.R.Hopes					
B.Lee					
M.S.Kasprowicz					
G.D.McGrath					
Extras (lb 9, w 3)	12				
TOTAL (20 overs) (5 wkts)	**214**	71			

NEW ZEALAND

	Runs	Mins	Balls	6s	4s
B.B.McCullum† c Ponting b Kasprowicz	36	29	24	1	5
S.P.Fleming* b Kasprowicz	18	19	13	-	3
M.S.Sinclair c Katich b Kasprowicz	0	1	1	-	-
S.B.Styris b Lee	66	46	39	3	4
C.D.McMillan c Hussey b Hopes	9	10	8	1	-
C.L.Cairns c McGrath b Kasprowicz	1	2	4	-	-
H.J.H.Marshall b Symonds	8	5	7	-	-
A.R.Adams run out	7	4	7	-	1
J.W.Wilson b McGrath	18	15	14	-	2
K.D.Mills c Kasprowicz b McGrath	0	5	1	-	-
D.R.Tuffey not out	5	2	2	-	1
Extras (nb 2)	2				
TOTAL (20 overs)	**170**	73			

Bowling	*O*	*M*	*R*	*W*
NEW ZEALAND				
Tuffey	4	0	50	1
Mills	4	0	44	3
Cairns	4	0	28	1
Wilson	4	0	43	0
Adams	4	0	40	0
AUSTRALIA				
Lee	4	0	26	1
McGrath	4	0	48	2
Kasprowicz	4	0	29	4
Hopes	3	0	23	1
Symonds	3	0	33	1
Clarke	2	0	11	0

Fall of Wickets	***A***	***NZ***
1st	10	49
2nd	21	49
3rd	46	67
4th	54	93
5th	137	95
6th	-	105
7th	-	121
8th	-	165
9th	-	165
10th	-	170

NEW ZEALAND v AUSTRALIA — First One-day International

at Westpac Stadium,Wellington (d/n) on 19 February, 2005
Toss : Australia. Umpires : B.F. Bowden & Aleem Dar
Australia won by 10 runs

Gilchrist went to the first ball of the second over, but then Hayden and Ponting added 133 runs off 180 balls. Hayden needed 82 balls for his fifty, 12 more than his captain. Five wickets fell for just 20 runs before Symonds and Hogg put on an unbeaten 76. Symonds got fifty from 43 deliveries. Styris and Vettori bowled tightly, with the former getting four wickets.

New Zealand lost two early wickets before Styris and Astle added 56. Styris aggravated a knee injury which sidelined him for the rest of the season. Astle got fifty from 94 balls. Marshall and McMillan put on 66 from 57 balls, including a six from McMillan which went out of the ground. Marshall got fifty off 78 balls. After being 218-6 New Zealand lost four wickets for a mere eight runs and Australia had a 10 run win.

AUSTRALIA

	Runs	Mins	Balls	6s	4s
A.C.Gilchrist† c Sinclair b Mills	4	5	5	-	-
M.L.Hayden b Styris	71	119	109	-	7
R.T.Ponting* c Vettori b Styris	61	128	85	-	3
D.R.Martyn b Styris	7	23	16	-	-
A.Symonds b Cairns	53	58	44	2	1
M.J.Clarke c Marshall b Styris	0	3	5	-	-
S.M.Katich c McCullum b Cairns	0	6	5	-	-
G.B.Hogg not out	25	42	33	-	-
B.Lee not out	4	2	3	-	-
M.S.Kasprowicz					
G.D.McGrath					
Extras (b 1, lb 1, w 4, nb 5)	11				
TOTAL (50 overs) (7 wkts)	**236**	197			

NEW ZEALAND

	Runs	Mins	Balls	6s	4s
S.P.Fleming* lbw b Lee	5	17	10	-	-
N.J.Astle b Hogg	65	128	112	-	3
M.S.Sinclair c Gilchrist b McGrath	0	12	8	-	-
S.B.Styris c Hayden b Symonds	14	64	47	-	-
C.L.Cairns run out	0	4	3	-	-
H.J.H.Marshall b McGrath	76	109	69	-	7
C.D.McMillan st Gilchrist b McGrath	37	44	30	1	3
B.B.McCullum† c Katich b Lee	8	27	13	-	-
D.L.Vettori b Lee	0	4	1	-	-
K.D.Mills not out	1	5	1	-	-
D.R.Tuffey b McGrath	1	4	2	-	-
Extras (lb 6, w 8, nb 5)	19				
TOTAL (48.4 overs)	**226**	213			

Bowling	*O*	*M*	*R*	*W*
NEW ZEALAND				
Tuffey	8	0	47	0
Mills	9	1	48	1
Cairns	10	0	56	2
Styris	10	1	40	4
Vettori	10	0	33	0
Astle	3	0	10	0
AUSTRALIA				
Lee	9	1	41	3
McGrath	9.4	3	16	4
Kasprowicz	10	1	62	0
Symonds	10	0	52	1
Hogg	9	0	44	1
Clarke	1	0	5	0

Fall of Wickets	***A***	***NZ***
1st	7	13
2nd	140	16
3rd	153	72
4th	158	73
5th	158	113
6th	160	179
7th	229	218
8th	-	224
9th	-	224
10th	-	226

NEW ZEALAND v AUSTRALIA Second One-day International

at Jade Stadium, Christchurch (d/n) on 22 February, 2005
Toss : New Zealand. Umpires : B.F. Bowden & Aleem Dar
Australia won by 106 runs

Australia made two changes with Hussey and Gillespie replacing Katich and Kasprowicz, while Wilson, who had last played for New Zealand in 1993, made a return for the injured Styris. Cairns was playing his 200th game for New Zealand.

Gilchrist again went early but Hayden dominated the innings. He was associated in stands of 99 and 133 for the next two wickets. He scored his fifty from 55 balls and got his fifth century off 110 deliveries. Ponting and Martyn got fifties from 51 and 65 balls respectively. Apart from Vettori all the bowlers suffered.

Chasing the target of 315, New Zealand started disastrously losing Fleming in the first over. Gilchrist caught the first five batsmen to be dismissed, the first time that this had happened in a one-day international. Coming in at 73-6, Vettori showed plenty of fight sharing two stands of 62. He got his maiden fifty off 49 balls but Australia won easily by 106 runs.

AUSTRALIA

	Runs	Mins	Balls	6s	4s
A.C.Gilchrist† c McCullum b Tuffey	0	1	2	-	-
M.L.Hayden c Wilson b Mills	114	164	124	2	12
R.T.Ponting* run out	53	68	57	2	6
D.R.Martyn run out	58	87	70	-	5
A.Symonds c Wilson b Mills	13	15	10	-	1
M.J.Clarke c McCullum b Cairns	23	22	13	-	4
M.E.K.Hussey not out	32	32	20	1	3
G.B.Hogg not out	9	19	9	-	-
B.Lee					
J.N.Gillespie					
G.D.McGrath					
Extras (lb 1, w 6, nb 5)	12				
TOTAL (50 overs) (6 wkts)	**314**	201			

NEW ZEALAND

	Runs	Mins	Balls	6s	4s
S.P.Fleming* c Gilchrist b Lee	1	5	4	-	-
N.J.Astle c Gilchrist b McGrath	3	23	8	-	-
M.S.Sinclair c Gilchrist b Lee	15	30	27	-	3
H.J.H.Marshall c Gilchrist b McGrath	16	27	20	1	1
C.D.McMillan c Gilchrist b Symonds	12	32	20	-	2
C.L.Cairns c Hayden b Symonds	22	20	16	1	4
B.B.McCullum† c & b Symonds	20	51	41	-	1
D.L.Vettori c sub (S.M.Katich) b Gillespie	83	91	77	-	10
J.W.Wilson c Ponting b Gillespie	22	33	27	-	2
K.D.Mills run out	4	10	7	-	-
D.R.Tuffey not out	0	1	0	-	-
Extras (lb 3, w 4, nb 3)	10				
TOTAL (40.4 overs)	**208**	166			

Bowling	*O*	*M*	*R*	*W*
NEW ZEALAND				
Tuffey	8	1	73	1
Mills	10	0	62	2
Cairns	10	0	62	1
Vettori	10	0	31	0
Wilson	6	0	57	0
Astle	6	0	28	0
AUSTRALIA				
Lee	8	2	28	2
McGrath	7	0	42	2
Gillespie	9.4	1	45	2
Symonds	6	0	41	3
Hogg	10	0	49	0

Fall of Wickets	***A***	***NZ***
1st	0	4
2nd	99	12
3rd	232	28
4th	237	49
5th	254	72
6th	283	73
7th	-	135
8th	-	197
9th	-	208
10th	-	208

NEW ZEALAND v AUSTRALIA Third One-day International

at Eden Park, Auckland (d/n) on 26 February, 2005
Toss : Australia. Umpires : D.B. Cowie & Aleem Dar
Australia won by 86 runs

Papps and James Marshall (making his debut) replaced Sinclair and Wilson. The Marshalls became the first identical twins to play international cricket.

The match started sensationally with Tuffey's first over lasting 14 balls. Katich, replacing the injured Hayden, opened the innings and got to fifty from 55 balls. After being 68-0, Australia lost five wickets for 60, but then Clarke and Hussey added an unbroken 136 off 134 balls in just 82 minutes. Clarke got fifty from 61 balls, three fewer than Hussey. who hit his highest score. Vettori and McMillan were the pick of the bowlers.

An early wicket followed by Papps retiring hurt, after twice being hit on the helmet by Lee, had the Black Caps in trouble again. Hamish Marshall and McMillan provided the only partnership of substance (69 off 90 balls). Marshall got fifty from 80 balls but New Zealand finished 86 runs short, Australia taking an unbeatable 3-0 lead in the series.

AUSTRALIA

	Runs	Mins	Balls	6s	4s
A.C.Gilchrist† c Astle b Cairns	18	47	36	-	3
S.M.Katich lbw b Vettori	58	114	78	-	9
R.T.Ponting* run out	11	18	18	-	2
D.R.Martyn lbw b Vettori	1	4	3	-	-
A.Symonds c Papps b Mills	21	25	27	-	3
M.J.Clarke not out	71	99	75	-	6
M.E.K.Hussey not out	65	82	73	1	3
G.B.Hogg					
B.Lee					
J.N.Gillespie					
M.S.Kasprowicz					
Extras (lb 2, w 7, nb 10)	19				
TOTAL (50 overs) (5 wkts)	**264**	197			

NEW ZEALAND

	Runs	Mins	Balls	6s	4s
S.P.Fleming* b Lee	1	10	6	-	-
N.J.Astle c Gilchrist b Kasprowicz	27	65	43	-	3
M.H.W.Papps retired hurt	3	16	10	-	-
H.J.H.Marshall run out	55	115	87	-	5
C.D.McMillan c Hussey b Symonds	26	53	43	-	2
J.A.H.Marshall run out	14	16	16	-	1
C.L.Cairns c Hussey b Lee	12	27	20	-	2
B.B.McCullum† c Hussey b Hogg	23	38	22	1	1
D.L.Vettori c Gilchrist b Hogg	0	3	1	-	-
K.D.Mills c Kasprowicz b Hogg	1	10	6	-	-
D.R.Tuffey not out	0	2	0	-	-
Extras (lb 8, w 4, nb 4)	16				
TOTAL (41.5 overs)	**178**	182			

Bowling	*O*	*M*	*R*	*W*
NEW ZEALAND				
Tuffey	2	0	25	0
Mills	9	0	57	1
Cairns	10	1	55	1
Astle	9	0	47	0
Vettori	10	0	31	2
McMillan	10	0	47	0
AUSTRALIA				
Lee	7	0	25	2
Gillespie	6	0	14	0
Kasprowicz	8	1	28	1
Symonds	10	1	36	1
Hussey	3	0	22	0
Hogg	7.5	0	45	3

Fall of Wickets	*A*	*NZ*
1st	68	7
2nd	85	45
3rd	90	114
4th	117	135
5th	128	136
6th	-	161
7th	-	162
8th	-	172
9th	-	178
10th	-	-

Papps retired hurt at 17-1

NEW ZEALAND v AUSTRALIA Fourth One-day International

at Basin Reserve, Wellington on 1 March, 2005
Toss : Australia. Umpires : A.L. Hill & Aleem Dar
Australia won by 7 wickets

The Basin Reserve hosted its first one-day international since 1998/99. The game was transferred from Hamilton because of the problems with the wicket at Westpac Park. Both sides had a player making their debut, Hamilton for New Zealand and Hopes for Australia.

Gilchrist, deputising for Ponting, asked New Zealand to bat first for the first time in the series. The New Zealand openers had their best start to the series with 84 off 106 balls but despite four players getting to thirty no one was able to push on.

In contrast, all of the Australian players dismissed managed to pass forty. Gilchrist blasted fifty from just 33 balls while Martyn was more circumspect, requiring 61 balls. Australia cantered to a win with more than 15 overs to spare.

NEW ZEALAND

	Runs	Mins	Balls	6s	4s
S.P.Fleming* c Lee b Gillespie	37	72	53	1	3
N.J.Astle c Gilchrist b Kasprowicz	37	85	60	-	6
C.D.Cumming c Clarke b McGrath	10	34	22	-	1
H.J.H.Marshall c & b Clarke	23	52	42	-	-
C.D.McMillan lbw b Hopes	35	46	36	-	4
J.A.H.Marshall c Gilchrist b Gillespie	9	28	21	-	1
C.L.Cairns c Martyn b Lee	36	38	35	2	2
B.B.McCullum† c Katich b Lee	17	39	21	-	1
J.W.Wilson lbw b McGrath	1	5	2	-	-
K.D.Mills run out	4	16	7	-	-
L.J.Hamilton not out	2	5	4	-	-
Extras (b 1, lb 12, w 5, nb 4)	22				
TOTAL (49.5 overs)	**233**	211			

AUSTRALIA

	Runs	Mins	Balls	6s	4s
A.C.Gilchrist*† c McMillan b Wilson	54	64	37	1	8
S.M.Katich c McCullum b Cairns	43	44	41	-	9
D.R.Martyn not out	65	97	78	-	8
A.Symonds c Wilson b McMillan	48	59	37	3	4
M.J.Clarke not out	10	19	17	-	1
M.E.K.Hussey					
J.R.Hopes					
B.Lee					
J.N.Gillespie					
M.S.Kasprowicz					
G.D.McGrath					
Extras (lb 3, w 8, nb 5)	16				
TOTAL (34.2 overs) (3 wkts)	**236**	144			

Bowling	*O*	*M*	*R*	*W*
AUSTRALIA				
Lee	9	1	41	2
McGrath	9.5	1	48	2
Gillespie	10	0	46	2
Kasprowicz	8	2	34	1
Hopes	10	1	38	1
Clarke	3	0	13	1
NEW ZEALAND				
Mills	7	1	37	0
Hamilton	8	0	67	0
Wilson	9	0	68	1
Cairns	6	0	30	1
McMillan	4.2	0	31	1

Fall of Wickets	***NZ***	***A***
1st	84	78
2nd	90	113
3rd	104	212
4th	145	-
5th	163	-
6th	173	-
7th	214	-
8th	220	-
9th	226	-
10th	233	-

NEW ZEALAND v AUSTRALIA Fifth One-day International

at McLean Park, Napier on 5 March, 2005
Toss : New Zealand. Umpires : D.R. Shepherd & A.L. Hill
Australia won by 122 runs

Katich went early but then Gilchrist and Ponting added 92 off 76 balls.Gilchrist again got a quick fifty, this time needing 37 balls. Ponting got fifty from 60 balls and his century from 110 deliveries. He added 94 with Clarke off 59 balls. The New Zealand attack was hampered with Cairns having to leave the field with an injury while Wilson suffered an injury just prior to the match and was replaced by Hamilton.

Chasing a mammoth 348 New Zealand always struggled. McMillan got his fifty from 57 balls to top score but the home team fell short by 122 to give Australia a clean sweep of the series.

AUSTRALIA

	Runs	Mins	Balls	6s	4s
A.C.Gilchrist† c Cumming b Canning	91	82	61	4	9
S.M.Katich c McCullum b Hamilton	5	25	15	-	-
R.T.Ponting* not out	141	170	127	5	10
D.R.Martyn c Fleming b Mills	40	46	46	1	3
A.Symonds run out	17	23	16	-	2
M.J.Clarke c Cumming b McMillan	43	40	36	-	5
M.E.K.Hussey not out	0	1	0	-	-
G.B.Hogg					
B.Lee					
M.S.Kasprowicz					
G.D.McGrath					
Extras (lb 7, w 2, nb 1)	10				
TOTAL (50 overs) (5 wkts)	**347**	197			

NEW ZEALAND

	Runs	Mins	Balls	6s	4s
C.D.Cumming lbw b Lee	13	38	24	-	1
S.P.Fleming* c Gilchrist b Kasprowicz	35	60	46	-	4
H.J.H.Marshall run out	28	45	41	1	1
J.A.H.Marshall b Kasprowicz	0	1	1	-	-
C.D.McMillan c Hogg b Symonds	63	73	69	1	7
B.B.McCullum† c McGrath b Symonds	36	67	60	2	2
T.K.Canning b Kasprowicz	16	31	27	1	-
D.L.Vettori not out	16	26	19	-	1
K.D.Mills c Kasprowicz b McGrath	10	18	13	-	-
L.J.Hamilton not out	1	2	2	-	-
C.L.Cairns absent hurt					
Extras (b 1, lb 1, w 3, nb 2)	7				
TOTAL (50 overs) (8 wkts)	**225**	190			

Bowling	*O*	*M*	*R*	*W*
NEW ZEALAND				
Mills	10	1	67	1
Hamilton	10	0	76	1
Canning	10	0	80	1
Vettori	10	0	37	0
McMillan	7	0	63	1
Cumming	3	0	17	0
AUSTRALIA				
Lee	10	0	34	1
McGrath	10	0	45	1
Kasprowicz	10	2	36	3
Hogg	10	0	53	0
Clarke	5	0	30	0
Symonds	5	0	25	2

Fall of Wickets	***A***	***NZ***
1st	37	39
2nd	129	60
3rd	204	60
4th	241	103
5th	335	167
6th	-	196
7th	-	199
8th	-	223
9th	-	-
10th	-	-

NEW ZEALAND v AUSTRALIA — First Test

at Jade Stadium, Christchurch on 10, 11, 12, 13 March, 2005
Toss : Australia. Umpires : Aleem Dar & D.R. Shepherd
Close of play: 1st day: NZ 265-3, Marshall 103, Astle 29; 2nd day: Australia 141-3, Ponting 41, Gillespie 0
3rd day: NZ 9-0, Cumming 2, Fleming 7
Australia won by 9 wickets

New Zealand had two debutants in Cumming and O'Brien while there were recalls for Vincent and Marshall to the test team.

Ponting sent the opposition in for the first time in his captaincy reign and it seemed to backfire as New Zealand had a good first day. Cumming joined the group of players who scored a fifty on test debut requiring 165 minutes and 152 balls. Marshall got fifty from 100 balls and then scored his maiden test century from 195 balls. Astle, who added 131 with Marshall for the fourth wicket, needed 114 balls for fifty.

On the second day McGrath struck getting his 26th five wicket haul as NewZealand slumped to 433 all out. Australia were in some trouble at 201-6 but then Gilchrist turned the game around as he and Katich put on 212 for the seventh wicket. Katich got his second century from 172 balls while Gilchrist's 14th century needed only 105 balls. New Zealand gained a one run lead as the last four wickets fell for 19. Vettori took his 12th five wicket bag.

New Zealand struggled throughout its second innings as Warne created havoc. The world record holder got his 29th five wicket haul and in the process took his 1000th first-class wicket. The seven lbw decision in the innings equalled the world record. Despite losing Hayden early, Langer and Ponting added an unbroken 110 to win the game late on the fourth day.

NEW ZEALAND

FIRST INNINGS	*Runs*	*Mins*	*Balls*	*6s*	*4s*	*SECOND INNINGS*	*Runs*	*Mins*	*Balls*	*6s*	*4s*
C.D.Cumming c Gillespie b Kasprowicz	74	232	206	-	10	lbw b Gillespie	7	66	38	-	1
S.P.Fleming* lbw b Warne	18	96	60	-	1	lbw b McGrath	17	44	41	-	3
H.J.H.Marshall b Warne	146	338	256	1	23	b Warne	22	115	77	-	2
L.Vincent lbw b Clarke	27	57	50	1	5	lbw b Gillespie	4	11	9	-	1
N.J.Astle lbw b McGrath	74	216	148	-	10	b Kasprowicz	21	54	34	-	4
C.D.McMillan c Gilchrist b McGrath	13	41	38	-	2	c Katich b Warne	5	8	7	-	1
B.B.McCullum† c Langer b McGrath	29	45	35	-	6	lbw b Gillespie	24	53	37	-	4
D.L.Vettori not out	24	52	32	-	4	lbw b Warne	23	51	34	-	3
J.E.C.Franklin lbw b McGrath	0	2	3	-	-	not out	5	28	16	-	1
I.E.O'Brien c Gilchrist b McGrath	5	15	13	-	1	lbw b Warne	0	9	7	-	-
C.S.Martin c Gilchrist b McGrath	1	17	7	-	-	lbw b Warne	0	1	1	-	-
Extras (b 4, lb 14, w 2, nb 2)	22					(b 1, lb 1, nb 1)	3				
TOTAL (141 overs)	**433**	561				(50 overs)	**131**	225			

AUSTRALIA

	Runs	*Mins*	*Balls*	*6s*	*4s*		*Runs*	*Mins*	*Balls*	*6s*	*4s*
J.L.Langer b Franklin	23	53	28	-	4	not out	72	126	85	1	12
M.L.Hayden c Astle b O'Brien	35	94	74	-	6	c Cumming b Vettori	15	31	30	-	2
R.T.Ponting* c McCullum b Martin	46	121	104	1	6	not out	47	93	75	1	7
D.R.Martyn lbw b Vettori	32	69	62	-	4						
J.N.Gillespie c Cumming b Vettori	12	108	73	-	2						
M.J.Clarke c McCullum b Franklin	8	11	8	-	2						
S.M.Katich c Vincent b Astle	118	273	229	1	20						
A.C.Gilchrist† c O'Brien b Vettori	121	183	126	6	12						
S.K.Warne c Astle b Vettori	2	32	20	-	-						
M.S.Kasprowicz not out	13	15	16	-	2						
G.D.McGrath lbw b Vettori	0	6	4	-	-						
Extras (b 2, lb 13, w 3, nb 4)	22					(nb 1)	1				
TOTAL (123.2 overs)	**432**	486				(31.3 overs) (1 wkt)	**135**	126			

Bowling	*O*	*M*	*R*	*W*	*O*	*M*	*R*	*W*
AUSTRALIA								
McGrath	42	9	115	6	14	7	19	1
Gillespie	29	5	87	0	12	2	38	3
Kasprowicz	25	6	85	1	10	3	33	1
Warne	40	6	112	2	14	3	39	5
Clarke	5	0	16	1				
NEW ZEALAND								
Martin	29	6	104	1	8	0	27	0
Franklin	26	5	102	2	5	1	26	0
O'Brien	14	3	73	1	5	0	27	0
Vettori	40.2	13	106	5	13.3	0	55	1
Astle	14	6	32	1				

Fall of Wickets

	NZ *1st*	**A** *1st*	**NZ** *2nd*	**A** *2nd*
1st	56	48	20	25
2nd	153	75	30	-
3rd	199	140	34	-
4th	330	147	71	-
5th	355	160	78	-
6th	388	201	87	-
7th	403	413	121	-
8th	403	418	127	-
9th	415	426	131	-
10th	433	432	131	-

NEW ZEALAND v AUSTRALIA — Second Test

at Basin Reserve, Wellington on 18, 19, 20, 21, 22 March, 2005
Toss : New Zealand. Umpires : R.E. Koertzen & D.R. Shepherd
Close of play: 1st day: no play; 2nd day: Australia 337-5, Martyn 106, Gillespie 45
3rd day: NZ 122-4, Vincent 38, Franklin 6; 4th day: NZ 244 all out
Match drawn

Both sides were unchanged. Rain caused play to be abandoned on the first day without a ball being bowled. Australia had got to 247-5 when Gilchrist again took control of the game. He and Martyn shared a record sixth wicket stand for Australia against New Zealand, putting on 256. Martyn got his century off 173 balls while the Australian wicket-keeper needed just 86. One of his sixes broke a window in the R.A. Vance Stand. When Warne reached fifty Ponting declared. Franklin had been the best of the bowlers.

New Zealand got to 122-4 by close on the third day. Play could not resume until after lunch on the fourth day and Marshall and Franklin took their stand to 58. Vettori and Martin added a valuable 32 for the last wicket but New Zealand were asked to follow on 326 behind.

Conditions were poor on the final day and after New Zealand had lost three quick wickets the game was called off as the weather had the last say.

AUSTRALIA

FIRST INNINGS	*Runs*	*Mins*	*Balls*	*6s*	*4s*
J.L.Langer c McCullum b Vettori	46	120	100	-	6
M.L.Hayden c Vincent b Franklin	61	210	147	-	6
R.T.Ponting* lbw b Vettori	9	37	30	-	-
D.R.Martyn c McCullum b O'Brien	165	349	287	-	24
M.J.Clarke c Fleming b Astle	8	39	32	-	-
S.M.Katich c McCullum b Franklin	35	73	63	-	6
A.C.Gilchrist† c & b Franklin	162	220	146	5	22
S.K.Warne not out	50	52	37	2	5
J.N.Gillespie b Franklin	2	6	8	-	-
M.S.Kasprowicz not out	2	8	6	-	-
G.D.McGrath					
Extras (b 4, lb 8, w 2, nb 16)	30				
TOTAL (140 overs) (8 wkts dec)	**570**	561			

NEW ZEALAND

	Runs	Mins	Balls	6s	4s		Runs	Mins	Balls	6s	4s
C.D.Cumming b Kasprowicz	37	93	69	-	5	not out	10	74	53	-	2
S.P.Fleming* lbw b McGrath	0	4	1	-	-	lbw b McGrath	1	10	7	-	-
H.J.H.Marshall c Gillespie b McGrath	18	47	29	-	4	lbw b McGrath	0	2	2	-	-
L.Vincent c Gilchrist b Kasprowicz	63	199	164	-	6	b Kasprowicz	24	48	3	-	2
N.J.Astle c Warne b Clarke	9	51	34	-	-	not out	4	11	10	-	-
J.E.C.Franklin c Gilchrist b Kasprowicz	26	87	71	-	3						
C.D.McMillan b Warne	20	50	34	1	2						
B.B.McCullum† c Clarke b Warne	3	5	3	-	-						
D.L.Vettori c Martyn b Warne	45	71	63	-	8						
I.E.O'Brien b Gillespie	5	11	8	-	1						
C.S.Martin not out	0	33	16	-	-						
Extras (b 4, lb 8, w 1, nb 5)	18					(b 3, lb 5, nb 1)	9				
TOTAL (81.1 overs)	**244**	330				(17.2 overs) (3 wkts)	**48**	74			

Bowling	*O*	*M*	*R*	*W*	*O*	*M*	*R*	*W*
NEW ZEALAND								
Martin	28	6	123	0				
Franklin	28	4	128	4				
O'Brien	24	4	97	1				
Vettori	47	5	170	2				
Astle	13	2	40	1				
AUSTRALIA								
McGrath	14	3	50	2	6	3	10	2
Gillespie	20	4	63	1	5	2	5	0
Kasprowicz	16	2	42	3	3	0	11	1
Warne	28.1	7	69	3	3.2	0	14	0
Clarke	3	1	8	1				

Fall of Wickets	**A** *1st*	**NZ** *1st*	**NZ** *2nd*
1st	82	9	3
2nd	100	55	3
3rd	146	78	37
4th	163	108	-
5th	247	166	-
6th	503	180	-
7th	557	184	-
8th	559	201	-
9th	-	212	-
10th	-	244	-

NEW ZEALAND v AUSTRALIA — Third Test

at Eden Park, Auckland on 26, 27, 28, 29 March, 2005
Toss : New Zealand. Umpires : R.E. Koertzen & J.W. Lloyds
Close of play: 1st day: NZ 199-5, Astle 7, McCullum 1; 2nd day: Australia 219-4, Clarke 18, Gillespie 1
3rd day: NZ 11-2, H.J.H.Marshall 3, Fleming 1
Australia won by 9 wickets

James Marshall made his debut and Wiseman came in to the side replacing McMillan and O'Brien. Hamish Marshall and Fleming (who had dropped down to number four) put on 126 for the third wicket. Marshall got fifty off 135 balls, 11 fewer than Fleming but then New Zealamd lost eight wickets for 113 to finish at 292.

Langer went early but Ponting got fifty off 58 balls and reached his 21st century off a further 46 balls. Gilchrist chimed in with 50 off 47 balls as Australia got a 91 run lead. Franklin had his best test bowling figures.

McGrath got a wicket with his second ball and New Zealand were soon 23-4 and then 83-6. Astle and Vettori put on 81 off 112 balls. Astle got fifty from 79 balls while Vettori got fifty from 84 deliveries. Warne finished off the innings while McGrath ended on 499 test wickets.

Needing 164 for victory Australia lost Hayden at 18 but then Langer and Ponting added 148 off 146 to win the game in with a day to spare, after taking the extra half hour. Langer got fifty from 67 balls, two balls less than Ponting. Australia won the series 2-0.

NEW ZEALAND

FIRST INNINGS	*Runs*	*Mins*	*Balls*	*6s*	*4s*	*SECOND INNINGS*	*Runs*	*Mins*	*Balls*	*6s*	*4s*
C.D.Cumming lbw b Gillespie	5	29	31	-	-	lbw b McGrath	0	1	2	-	-
J.A.H.Marshall c Hayden b McGrath	29	89	56	-	3	c Langer b McGrath	3	18	7	-	-
H.J.H.Marshall c Ponting b Warne	76	264	208	-	9	c Gilchrist b McGrath	7	62	50	-	-
S.P.Fleming* b Kasprowicz	65	218	169	1	8	c & b Gillespie	3	18	13	-	-
N.J.Astle c Langer b McGrath	19	104	60	-	2	c Katich b Warne	69	164	107	-	12
L.Vincent b Gillespie	2	40	30	-	-	run out	40	55	33	2	4
B.B.McCullum† c Gilchrist b McGrath	25	84	63	-	5	lbw b Warne	0	3	4	-	-
D.L.Vettori not out	41	80	50	-	8	c McGrath b Warne	65	153	108	-	8
J.E.C.Franklin c Katich b Warne	3	16	11	-	-	c Ponting b Warne	23	66	59	1	1
P.J.Wiseman c Gillespie b Warne	8	23	20	-	1	b McGrath	23	30	23	1	3
C.S.Martin c Clarke b Kasprowicz	0	4	2	-	-	not out	4	20	12	-	1
Extras (b 4, lb 13, nb 2)	19					(b 1, lb 14, nb 2)	17				
TOTAL (116.2 overs)	**292**	480				(69.2 overs)	**254**	301			

AUSTRALIA

	Runs	*Mins*	*Balls*	*6s*	*4s*		*Runs*	*Mins*	*Balls*	*6s*	*4s*
J.L.Langer b Franklin	6	9	11	-	1	not out	59	137	76	-	10
M.L.Hayden lbw b Franklin	38	70	49	-	7	run out	9	23	18	-	1
R.T.Ponting* c McCullum b Astle	105	154	110	4	13	not out	86	113	84	2	11
D.R.Martyn b Wiseman	38	149	137	-	4						
M.J.Clarke run out	22	97	71	-	1						
J.N.Gillespie c McCullum b Martin	35	150	145	-	6						
S.M.Katich c Wiseman b Franklin	35	113	81	-	4						
A.C.Gilchrist† not out	60	91	62	1	10						
S.K.Warne c Fleming b Franklin	1	10	10	-	-						
M.S.Kasprowicz b Franklin	23	68	40	-	3						
G.D.McGrath c McCullum b Franklin	0	6	2	-	-						
Extras (b 4, lb 7, nb 9)	20					(lb 10, nb 2)	12				
TOTAL (118.1 overs)	**383**	463				(29.3 overs) (1 wkt)	**166**	137			

Bowling	*O*	*M*	*R*	*W*	*O*	*M*	*R*	*W*
AUSTRALIA								
McGrath	34	20	49	3	16.2	5	40	4
Gillespie	25	8	64	2	16	4	63	1
Kasprowicz	30.2	7	89	2	14	2	59	0
Warne	23	4	63	3	23	5	77	4
Ponting	4	1	10	0				
NEW ZEALAND								
Martin	21	4	92	1	8	1	51	0
Franklin	26.1	3	119	6	7	0	40	0
Astle	21	7	50	1	7	0	33	0
Vettori	19	4	47	0	4	0	19	0
Wiseman	31	7	64	1	3.3	0	13	0

Fall of Wickets	***NZ*** *1st*	***A*** *1st*	***NZ*** *2nd*	***A*** *2nd*
1st	15	8	0	18
2nd	53	84	9	-
3rd	179	187	15	-
4th	183	215	23	-
5th	194	226	93	-
6th	228	297	93	-
7th	247	297	174	-
8th	262	303	220	-
9th	288	377	227	-
10th	292	383	254	-

INTERNATIONAL SUMMARY

2004/05

Test Matches

	Played	Won	Lost	Drawn
Bangladesh	2	2	–	–
Australia	5	–	4	1
Sri Lanka	2	1	–	1
TOTAL	**9**	**3**	**4**	**2**

New Zealand Test Averages

BATTING	*M*	*I*	*NO*	*HS*	*Agg*	*Ave*	*100s*	*50s*	*Ct*	*St*
J.D.P. Oram	4	6	2	126*	247	61.75	1	-	2	-
H.J.H. Marshall	6	10	0	160	510	51.00	2	2	-	-
L. Vincent	5	9	0	224	436	48.44	1	2	6	-
D.L. Vettori	7	10	2	65	323	40.37	-	2	2	-
S.P. Fleming	9	15	0	202	577	38.46	1	3	11	-
N.J. Astle	9	15	1	114	505	36.07	1	3	11	-
B.B. McCullum	9	14	1	143	411	31.61	1	1	21	2
J.A.H. Marshall	3	5	0	52	151	30.20	-	1	1	-
M.S. Sinclair	4	6	0	76	170	28.33	-	2	5	-
S.B. Styris	4	6	0	89	161	26.83	-	1	6	-
C.D. Cumming	5	9	1	74	208	26.00	-	1	2	-
P.J. Wiseman	6	8	2	32*	144	24.00	-	-	3	-
K.D. Mills	3	5	1	31	90	22.50	-	-	1	-
J.E.C. Franklin	8	11	1	55	177	17.70	-	1	2	-
M.H. Richardson	4	6	0	28	91	15.16	-	-	2	-
C.D. McMillan	3	5	0	23	70	14.00	-	-	1	-
I.E. O'Brien	2	3	0	5	10	3.33	-	-	1	-
C.S. Martin	7	12	6	4*	18	3.00	-	-	1	-
I.G. Butler	1	1	1	15*	15	-	-	-	-	-

BOWLING	*O*	*M*	*R*	*W*	*Ave*	*Best*	*5w*	*10w*
D.L. Vettori	358.5	92	962	38	25.31	6-28	5	1
N.J. Astle	100.1	28	264	10	26.40	3-27	-	-
J.E.C. Franklin	216.4	39	864	28	30.85	6-119	2	-
C.S. Martin	242.5	49	915	18	50.83	6-54	2	-
P.J. Wiseman	238.2	46	764	14	54.57	3-64	-	-
J.D.P. Oram	98.5	29	283	4	70.75	3-36	-	-
K.D. Mills	80	24	242	3	80.66	2-34	-	-
I.E. O'Brien	43	7	197	2	98.50	1-73	-	-
L. Vincent	1	0	2	0	-	-	-	-
C.D. McMillan	5	1	23	0	-	-	-	-
S.B. Styris	10	2	37	0	-	-	-	-
I.G. Butler	16	4	42	0	-	-	-	-

One-day Internationals

	Played	Won	Lost	Tied	NR
Australia	8	1	7	–	–
Bangladesh	3	3	–	–	–
USA	1	1	–	–	–
Sri Lanka	1	1	–	–	–
TOTAL	**13**	**6**	**7**	**–**	**–**

New Zealand One-day International Averages

BATTING	M	I	NO	HS	Agg	Ave	100s	50s	Ct	St	SR
N.J. Astle	12	12	1	145*	465	42.27	1	2	2	-	68
D.L. Vettori	12	9	4	83	194	38.80	-	1	1	-	88
C.D. McMillan	10	10	1	64*	318	35.33	-	2	2	-	90
M.S. Sinclair	7	7	0	66	239	34.14	-	2	6	-	67
H.J.H. Marshall	13	13	2	76	291	26.45	-	3	2	-	70
C.L. Cairns	13	11	1	74	262	26.20	-	2	3	-	93
S.P. Fleming	10	10	1	77*	234	26.00	-	1	4	-	70
S.B. Styris	9	9	0	75	217	24.11	-	2	5	-	66
B.B. McCullum	13	10	1	47	200	22.22	-	-	14	1	64
K.D. Mills	12	8	4	44*	67	16.75	-	-	1	-	106
T.K. Canning	1	1	0	16	16	16.00	-	-	-	-	59
J.D.P. Oram	5	3	0	24	41	13.66	-	-	-	-	71
J.W. Wilson	2	2	0	22	23	11.50	-	-	3	-	79
C.D. Cumming	2	2	0	13	23	11.50	-	-	2	-	50
C.Z. Harris	6	5	0	26	51	10.20	-	-	2	-	49
P.G. Fulton	1	1	0	9	9	9.00	-	-	1	-	90
J.A.H. Marshall	3	3	0	14	23	7.66	-	-	-	-	60
A.R. Adams	1	1	0	4	4	4.00	-	-	1	-	57
D.R. Tuffey	5	3	2	1	1	1.00	-	-	-	-	50
M.H.W. Papps	1	1	1	3*	3	-	-	-	1	-	30
L.J. Hamilton	2	2	2	2*	3	-	-	-	-	-	50
J.E.C. Franklin	2	-	-	-	-	-	-	-	2	-	-
I.G. Butler	1	-	-	-	-	-	-	-	1	-	-

BOWLING	O	M	R	W	Ave	Best	R/O
S.B. Styris	59.4	6	199	12	16.58	4-40	3.33
J.E.C. Franklin	13	2	63	3	21.00	2-34	4.85
D.L. Vettori	108.5	5	356	16	22.25	3-8	3.27
C.L. Cairns	88	5	409	17	24.05	4-33	4.65
J.D.P. Oram	44.4	3	221	9	24.55	5-36	4.94
K.D. Mills	97.2	9	484	15	32.26	4-14	4.97
C.Z. Harris	36	7	123	3	41.00	1-21	3.42
I.G. Butler	8	0	58	1	58.00	1-58	7.25
D.R. Tuffey	34	2	201	3	67.00	2-17	5.91
C.D. McMillan	22.2	0	157	2	78.50	1-31	7.03
T.K. Canning	10	0	80	1	80.00	1-80	8.00
J.W. Wilson	15	0	125	1	125.00	1-68	8.33
L.J. Hamilton	18	0	143	1	143.00	1-76	7.94
C.D. Cumming	3	0	17	0	-	-	5.67
A.R. Adams	6	1	24	0	-	-	4.00
N.J. Astle	18	0	85	0	-	-	4.72

PROVINCIAL SUMMARIES

AUCKLAND CRICKET ASSOCIATION

Formed 1883, affiliated 1894/95.

Selectors: M.R. O'Donnell, R.M.J. Armour and D.N. Patel

After outright wins in their first four State Championship games Auckland were never headed for the top qualifier berth and home final. Once the State Shield started, however, the batsmen struggled and this carried through to the later rounds of the Championship before they redeemed themselves in the final. The win was a boost from fourth the previous season.

Lou Vincent made 563 runs in five games, while Matt Horne (540) and Richard Jones (440), after four years with Wellington, were the other leading run scorers. Kerry Walmsley (38) was the leading wicket-taker in the competition and was assisted by Andre Adams (29) and Tama Canning (27). Reece Young, with 30 wicket-keeping victims, became Auckland's most successful gloveman.

In the State Shield Auckland had only one win and finished last. Kyle Mills (191) scored most runs and Paul Hitchcock (11) took most wickets. The team was again coached by Mark O'Donnell. Contracted players were: Andre Adams, Aaron Barnes, Tama Canning, Paul Hitchcock, Matt Horne, Richard Jones, Rob Nicol, Gareth Shaw, Brooke Walker, Kerry Walmsley, Reece Young.

CANTERBURY CRICKET ASSOCIATION

Formed 1877, affiliated 1894/95.

Selectors: C.H. Thiele, M.F. Sharpe and R.M. Carter

Canterbury finished third in both competitions after being beaten finalists in both the previous season. Peter Fulton was the leading scorer for all sides in the Championship with 828 runs and he had assistance from Shanan Stewart (424) and Gary Stead (401).

Six players received call-ups to the New Zealand side including their leading bowler, Paul Wiseman. He took 35 wickets, including 9-13 against Central Districts, while Chris Martin got 25 and Stephen Cunis 21. Michael Papps kept wicket for most of the season and had 19 catches and two stumpings.

In the State Shield Canterbury had three of the top four run scorers. Nathan Astle got 502 and became the second player to score 3000 runs at one-day domestic level. Papps scored 423 and Craig McMillan 354. The top wicket takers were Astle and Cunis with 12. Michael Sharpe coached the side before stepping down at the end of the season. Contracted players were: Neil Broom, Steve Cunis, Brendon Donkers, Andrew Ellis, Peter Fulton, Tim McIntosh, Hayden Shaw, Richard Sherlock, Gary Stead, Shanan Stewart, James Ward.

CENTRAL DISTRICTS CRICKET ASSOCIATION

Formed 1950, affiliated 1954/55.

Selectors: G.D. Barlow and P.S. Briasco

Central Districts surrendered their State Shield title after being top qualifier but losing the final to Northern Districts. In the State Championship they were not able to improve on their previous year's fifth placing.

Mathew Sinclair got 353 runs in the one-day format followed by Jarrod Englefield (295) and Craig Spearman (287), who played as an overseas player. Lance Hamilton was the leading wicket-taker with 18 while Andrew Schwass took 16 and Brent Hefford 13.

In the State Championship Jamie How began with three successive centuries and finished with 573 runs. Englefield scored 533 and all-rounder Ewen Thompson, who scored two hundreds, got 426. Captain Glen Sulzberger took 20 wickets and was followed by Thompson 19 and Hamilton 18. Bevan Griggs kept wicket and secured 24 victims. The team was coached for the first time by former England player Graham Barlow.

Contracted players were: Jarrod Englefield, Bevan Griggs, Lance Hamilton, Brent Hefford, Jamie How, Michael Mason, Andrew Schwass, Craig Spearman (overseas player), Glen Sulzberger, Ross Taylor, Ewen Thompson, Regan West.

NORTHERN DISTRICTS CRICKET ASSOCIATION

Formed 1953, granted Plunket Shield status 1956/57

Selectors: P.J. Malcon, B.R. Blair and C.J. Stevens

Northern Districts finished second in the round-robin stages of the State Shield and then went on to win the final – an excellent result after bottom placing in both competitions in 2003/04. Daniel Vettori captained the side when available and showed the way in the Shield competition. He scored 303 runs in five games including the highest score by a Northern Districts batsman. James Marshall (286) and Scott Styris (245) were the other leading run scorers. Graeme Aldridge set a record for wickets in a one-day season with 30. Daryl Tuffey took 15.

In the Championship the team finished in fourth place after making changes in team personnel after round three. All-rounder Joseph Yovich was the leading run scorer with 359 runs and also leading wicket taker with 31 victims. Mark Orchard got 336 runs and newcomer B-J Watling scored 320. Aldridge took 24 wickets and Tuffey 21. Paul McGlashan, who had previously played for Central Districts and Otago, kept wicket after the first two games and had 22 catches and 2 stumpings. Bruce Blair was again coach.

Contracted players were: Robbie Hart (announced his retirement and replaced by Nathan Daley), Graeme Aldridge, Te Ahu Davis, Matthew Hart, Nick Horsley, Llorne Howell, James Marshall, Bruce Martin, Mark Orchard, Grant Robinson, Joseph Yovich.

OTAGO CRICKET ASSOCIATION

Formed 1876, affiliated 1894/95.

Selectors: G.M. Turner, R.N. Hoskin and M. Hesson

Otago finished last in the Championship and fourth in the Shield. Captain Craig Cumming scored 380 runs in the Shield and was followed by Chris Gaffaney 299. Jeff Wilson was the leading wicket-taker with 14 and was recalled to the New Zealand one-day side.

In the Championship the batting went well with Gaffaney being leading run scorer with 554 ahead of two new recruits, Greg Todd (552) and Aaron Redmond (522). Cumming scored 452 in five games before his call up to the one-day and test side. McSkimming was the most effective bowler and took 25 wickets. Bradley Scott got 19 and David Sewell took 15 in three games. Gareth Hopkins set an Otago record for a wicket-keeper with 37 catches and a stumping. Coach Glenn Turner stepped down at the end of the season.

Contracted players were: Craig Cumming, Chris Gaffaney, Gareth Hopkins, Robert Lawson, Nathan McCullum, Marcel McKenzie, Warren McSkimming, Aaron Redmond, Bradley Scott, Greg Todd, Mohammad Wasim, Jeff Wilson.

WELLINGTON CRICKET ASSOCIATION

Formed 1875, affiliated 1894/95.

Selectors: V.F. Johnson and G.M. Hooper

Wellington relinquished their State Championship title, going down to Auckland in the final, and dropped one place in the Shield coming fifth. In the Championship Michael Parlane scored 646 runs, ahead of new signing Jesse Ryder (625) who also took 17 wickets. Neal Parlane scored 571 runs. Mark Gillespie took 32 wickets and Jeetan Patel 26. James Franklin got 23 wickets in four games and Iain O'Brien 20 in five matches.

Chris Nevin suffered a finger injury and the wicket-keeping duties were shared with Stuart Mills in the four-day games and Neal Parlane in the one-day matches. Nevin was the leading Shield run scorer with 337 runs, ahead of Stephen Fleming's 249. Gillespie was also the leading one day wicket taker with 13. Vaughn Johnson was again the coach.

Contracted players were: Matthew Bell, James Franklin, Mark Gillespie, Stu Mills, Chris Nevin, Iain O'Brien, Jeetan Patel, Jesse Ryder, Ashley Turner, Matthew Walker (withdrew and replaced by Neal Parlane), Luke Woodcock.

STATE CHAMPIONSHIP REVIEW 2004/05

Each side again played eight matches with the two top qualifiers meeting in the final. The top qualifier hosted the final while the second placed team had to win outright to take the title. The final (extended to five days) was scheduled for April so that it did not clash with the international calendar and to enable New Zealand team members to take part.

As it happened, the Sri Lankan tour had to be rescheduled and the final took place at the same time as the first test, meaning several leading players were unavailable for the match. Even so, the game turned out to be an absorbing affair which went into the fifth day. Auckland took the title after setting the pace throughout the season while defending champions Wellington had finished ten points clear of the third placed side to finish in second position.

The competition began on 6 December and two rounds took place prior to the commencement of the State Shield later in the month. At the half-way stage of the State Shield two more rounds of State Championship games were played and then the competition resumed again on 21 February. After each team had played each other once, the remaining three rounds saw the teams placed 1, 2, and 3 at that stage drawn against the sides placed 4, 5, and 6. Points were carried through from the first five rounds.

Nineteen of the 25 matches ended in an outright decision compared with only nine the season before. Prior to the final Auckland had five outright wins, Wellington four, Canterbury and Northern Districts three, Central Districts two and Otago one. Auckland and Wellington each lost only one match outright.

Auckland moved up from fourth place in 2003/04 while Canterbury went from second to third. Northern Districts, who failed to win any games the previous season, improved to fourth, Central Districts remained in fifth spot while Otago went from third to last.

Playing time was again six and a half hours per day, although this was extended if the number of overs to be bowled in the day had not been completed. Teams were required to bowl 100 overs a day with no reduction for change of innings. The only penalties for slow over rates were financial and these were calculated round by round instead of over the whole season.

Points were awarded as follows:

a) six points for an outright win
b) two points for a first innings win
c) three points for a tie
d) one point each for a first innings tie (providing the team did not win outright)
e) one point each for a no result on the first innings

Final points and placings were:

	P	*OW*	*OL*	*1st Inns W*	*1st Inns L*	*NR*	*Total*
Auckland	8	5	1	1	—	1	39
Wellington	8	4	1	2	1	—	36
Canterbury	8	3	3	1	1	—	26
Northern Districts	8	3	4	—	1	—	22
Central Districts	8	2	4	—	1	1	19
Otago	8	1	5	1	1	—	14

NB: *The following teams took first innings points in matches they lost outright: Central Districts (v Northern Districts), Otago (v Auckland and Wellington) and Wellington (v Auckland).*

NORTHERN DISTRICTS v AUCKLAND State Championship

at Westpac Park, Hamilton on 6, 7, 8 December, 2004
Toss : Auckland. Umpires : R.D. Anderson & D.B. Cowie
Close of play: ND 185-7, Watling 7, Shutte 6; 2nd day: Auckland 300-8, Canning 52, Walker 9
Auckland won by an innings and 89 runs. *Points: Auckland 8, Northern Districts 0*

Shutte made his first-class debut while Howell played his first game for his fourth province. Play began after lunch and Northern made a useful start before Howell was out at 58. Thereafter, wickets fell at regular intervals and Northern were dismissed for 237 on the second morning. Canning picked up his best first-class bowling figures.

Auckland began with a rush. Jones reached fifty off 40 balls and the opening stand of 90 took just 59 minutes. Auckland batted into the third day with Canning making his highest first-class score. His century took 168 minutes and 133 balls and the partnership with Walker was an Auckland seventh wicket record against Northern.

Facing a deficit of 181, and with their captain injured, Northern collapsed and were all out in under two hours. Walmsley finished with his best figures, his first ten wicket haul and the best analysis by an Auckland bowler against Northern.

NORTHERN DISTRICTS

FIRST INNINGS	*Runs*	*Mins*	*Balls*	*6s*	*4s*	*SECOND INNINGS*	*Runs*	*Mins*	*Balls*	*6s*	*4s*
J.A.H.Marshall* c Jones b Canning	25	63	49	-	4	absent hurt					
N.K.W.Horsley c Young b Walmsley	38	98	67	-	7	(1) c Vincent b Walmsley	0	1	2	-	-
M.G.Orchard c Young b Canning	53	200	128	-	10	c Vincent b Canning	0	5	7	-	-
M.N.Hart c Jones b Canning	16	39	32		2	c Vincent b Walmsley	1	29	15	-	-
L.G.Howell b Walmsley	10	49	45	-	2	(6) c Young b Walmsley	24	59	37	-	4
G.G.Robinson lbw b Canning	2	15	11	-	-	(5) lbw b Canning	8	3	5	-	2
J.A.F.Yovich lbw b Barnes	6	56	45	-	-	lbw b Walmsley	14	30	27	-	3
B-J.Watling† c Jones b Canning	37	119	87	-	8	(2) c Canning b Walmsley	1	12	4	-	-
R.R.Shutte c Nicol b Walmsley	8	69	52	-	1	(8) lbw b Walmsley	12	40	26	-	2
D.R.Tuffey c Nicol b Canning	18	33	23	1	2	(9) not out	24	35	24	1	4
G.W.Aldridge not out	1	10	4	-	-	(10) lbw b Walmsley	0	3	4	-	-
Extras (b 1, lb 15, w 2, nb 5)	23					(b 1, lb 5, nb 2)	8				
TOTAL (89.4 overs)	**237**	378				(24.5 overs)	**92**	115			

AUCKLAND

	Runs	Mins	Balls	6s	4s
M.H.Richardson c Hart b Yovich	46	136	95	-	8
R.A.Jones c Watling b Tuffey	58	59	48	1	10
M.J.Horne lbw b Tuffey	38	93	72	-	7
L.Vincent c Orchard b Aldridge	49	107	76	1	8
R.J.Nicol c Watling b Tuffey	9	41	25	-	1
A.C.Barnes lbw b Hart	29	75	59	-	4
T.K.Canning lbw b Shutte	115	216	166	6	12
B.G.K.Walker* c Aldridge b Tuffey	32	156	126	-	5
R.A.Young† c Watling b Shutte	14	41	33	1	1
K.P.Walmsley c Watling b Yovich	0	14	8	-	-
G.S.Shaw not out	0	5	4	-	-
Extras (b 8, lb 6, w 1, nb 13)	28				
TOTAL (116.3 overs)	**418**	476			

Bowling	*O*	*M*	*R*	*W*	*O*	*M*	*R*	*W*
AUCKLAND								
Walmsley	20	2	65	3	10.5	3	28	7
Shaw	18	2	72	0	2	0	18	0
Canning	28.4	11	44	6	8	2	28	2
Barnes	21	12	35	1	4	1	12	0
Walker	2	0	5	0				
NORTHERN DISTRICTS								
Tuffey	30	8	74	4				
Yovich	22.3	3	100	2				
Aldridge	22	4	89	1				
Shutte	14	3	39	2				
Orchard	16	2	62	0				
Hart	12	3	40	1				

Fall of Wickets	***ND***	***A***	***ND***
	1st	*1st*	*2nd*
1st	58	90	0
2nd	74	139	1
3rd	103	153	1
4th	118	175	10
5th	148	227	20
6th	170	249	51
7th	170	385	52
8th	205	412	92
9th	232	414	92
10th	237	418	-

CANTERBURY v WELLINGTON — State Championship

at Hagley Park, Christchurch on 7, 8, 9, 10 December, 2004
Toss : Canterbury. Umpires : D.J. Ellwood & E.A. Watkin
Close of play: 1st day: Wellington 184-2, Woodcock 31, N.R.Parlane 20; 2nd day: Canterbury 71-2, Fulton 40, Stewart 17
3rd day: Wellington 103-6, N.R.Parlane 41, Murray 4
First innings win to Wellington. *Points: Wellington 2, Canterbury 0*

Murray made his first-class debut while Ryder and McIntosh made their debuts for new provinces. Bell dominated the rain shortened first day and Woodcock reached his fifty next morning. Wellington's total was aided by a last wicket stand of 49 between Fairley and O'Brien who both made their highest scores.

Canterbury were in trouble at 98-6 before Stewart (highest score) and Cunis (fifty off 47 balls) came together. Shaw added a vigorous unbeaten 47 before Canterbury declared 86 runs behind.

Martin and Cunis then reduced Wellington to 34-5 before Fairley helped Neal Parlane add 50. Another fifty runs were added on the last day before the rain came and play was finally abandoned at 3.30 pm with Wellington 239 ahead.

WELLINGTON

FIRST INNINGS	Runs	Mins	Balls	6s	4s	*SECOND INNINGS*	Runs	Mins	Balls	6s	4s
M.D.Bell* lbw b Wiseman	86	224	141	-	9	lbw b Cunis	4	8	10	-	1
M.E.Parlane c Papps M.H.W. b Martin	29	131	95	-	4	c Papps T.J.T. b Martin	0	30	16	-	-
L.J.Woodcock c Fulton b Martin	64	223	180	-	4	lbw b Martin	17	43	37	-	2
N.R.Parlane c Papps T.J.T. b Wiseman	23	60	53	-	3	not out	50	237	150	-	8
J.D.Ryder b Shaw	13	45	34	-	1	c Fulton b Martin	0	2	3	-	-
C.J.Nevin† lbw b Cunis	41	91	71	-	4	c Papps M.H.W. b Cunis	8	35	23	-	2
S.A.Fairley not out	47	220	152	-	3	c Stewart b Wiseman	21	73	65	-	1
G.B.Murray b Martin	6	39	29	-	-	c Papps T.J.T. b Martin	4	36	31	-	-
M.R.Gillespie c Cornelius b Cunis	9	24	16	-	1	not out	37	64	57	-	6
A.D.Turner c Cunis b Wiseman	9	31	21	-	-						
I.E.O'Brien c Papps M.H.W. b Martin	28	55	48	-	4						
Extras (lb 13, w 1, nb 15)	29					(b 4, lb 5, w 1, nb 2)	12				
TOTAL (137.3 overs)	**384**	576				(65 overs) (7 wkts)	**153**	267			

CANTERBURY

	Runs	Mins	Balls	6s	4s
T.G.McIntosh lbw b Turner	0	7	10	-	-
M.H.W.Papps lbw b Turner	5	46	29	-	-
P.G.Fulton* c Bell b Gillespie	48	116	83	-	6
S.L.Stewart c Turner b O'Brien	82	248	170	-	8
G.R.Stead lbw b O'Brien	5	34	18	-	1
T.J.T.Papps† lbw b O'Brien	0	2	1	-	-
P.J.Wiseman c Bell b Gillespie	1	6	7	-	-
S.J.Cunis b O'Brien	59	76	58	-	11
H.J.Shaw not out	47	82	55	1	7
W.A.Cornelius not out	14	33	20	-	2
C.S.Martin					
Extras (b 10, lb 15, w 10, nb 2)	37				
TOTAL (74.5 overs) (8 wkts dec)	**298**	329			

Bowling	*O*	*M*	*R*	*W*	*O*	*M*	*R*	*W*
CANTERBURY								
Martin	28.3	6	63	4	16	4	44	4
Cornelius	25	5	82	0	10	2	31	0
Cunis	30	12	62	2	17	10	29	2
Shaw	24	2	98	1	8	2	27	0
Wiseman	29	7	63	3	10	4	9	1
Stewart	1	0	3	0				
Stead					4	2	4	0
WELLINGTON								
Gillespie	24	8	102	2				
Turner	16.5	5	60	2				
O'Brien	25	2	91	4				
Murray	9	3	20	0				

Fall of Wickets

	W *1st*	***C*** *1st*	***W*** *2nd*
1st	76	5	5
2nd	150	32	13
3rd	194	83	24
4th	235	97	25
5th	252	97	34
6th	289	98	84
7th	305	190	103
8th	320	251	-
9th	335	-	-
10th	384	-	-

OTAGO v CENTRAL DISTRICTS — State Championship

at Queenstown Events Centre on 7, 8, 9, 10 December, 2004
Toss : Central Districts. Umpires : G.A. Baxter & B.G. Frost
Close of play: 1st day: CD 103-2, How 63, Sulzberger 16; 2nd day: Otago 90-2, Cumming 34, Redmond 12
3rd day: CD 61-1, How 28, Barnett 27
***Central Districts won by 7 wickets.** Points: Central Districts 8, Otago 0*

Barnett made his first-class debut and Redmond and Todd played their first games for Otago. Cumming went to the first ball of the match and Otago never recovered. Otago's new pair added 81 for the sixth wicket while all the Central bowlers had success.

How was the mainstay of the Central innings, reaching his hundred from 160 balls in 229 minutes while Thompson chimed in with 49. Otago wiped off the 98 run deficit with only two wickets down but once Redmond went at 131 wickets began to fall regularly. Cumming reached his hundred after 365 minutes from 282 balls before being last man out.

Central needed 181 to win and were 61-1 at stumps. Next morning How carried on to another hundred, from 149 balls in 185 minutes. He became only the second batsman, after Martin Crowe, to score a century in each innings for Central. The match ended at 1.08 pm. Each team had now won 23 games of the 73 first-class matches between the two sides.

OTAGO

FIRST INNINGS	*Runs*	*Mins*	*Balls*	*6s*	*4s*	*SECOND INNINGS*	*Runs*	*Mins*	*Balls*	*6s*	*4s*
C.D.Cumming* c How b Mason	0	1	1	-	-	lbw b Thompson	125	423	324	1	17
Mohammad Wasim c Taylor b Schwass	14	53	38	-	1	c How b Mason	8	20	21	-	1
C.B.Gaffaney c Griggs b Schwass	17	66	52	-	2	c Griggs b Schwass	29	83	61	-	5
A.J.Redmond b Sulzberger	69	167	126	-	8	c Taylor b Sulzberger	30	86	63	-	2
G.J.Hopkins† c Englefield b Hamilton	16	45	34	-	2	c Griggs b Sulzberger	5	34	29	-	1
J.W.Sheed lbw b Schwass	1	20	17	-	-	c Ingram b Sulzberger	22	66	70	-	3
G.R.Todd lbw b Sulzberger	30	137	94	-	4	c Griggs b How	9	35	38	-	1
N.L.McCullum c Taylor b Sulzberger	0	33	28	-	-	c Hamilton b How	4	7	5	-	1
J.W.Wilson c Barnett b Thompson	9	11	9	-	2	b Schwass	34	72	47	-	3
W.C.McSkimming c Taylor b Mason	18	22	18	-	3	lbw b Schwass	0	7	6	-	-
J.M.McMillan not out	2	16	17	-	-	not out	0	4	0	-	-
Extras (b 3, lb 7, nb 7)	17					(b 1, lb 4, nb 7)	12				
TOTAL (71.1 overs)	**193**	290				(109.3 overs)	**278**	422			

CENTRAL DISTRICTS

	Runs	*Mins*	*Balls*	*6s*	*4s*		*Runs*	*Mins*	*Balls*	*6s*	*4s*
J.M.How c McSkimming b Wilson	105	240	166	1	13	(2) not out	108	199	162	2	14
P.J.Ingram b McMillan	17	34	26	-	2	(1) c Sheed b McMillan	0	10	7	-	-
G.E.F.Barnett c McCullum b McMillan	0	8	6	-	-	c Sheed b Redmond	36	104	101	-	4
G.P.Sulzberger* c Hopkins b Wilson	29	97	75	-	4	c McSkimming b McCullum	7	10	13	-	1
J.I.Englefield c Gaffaney b McCullum	39	177	134	-	5	not out	22	72	51	-	4
R.L.Taylor c Todd b Redmond	7	21	21	-	1						
B.B.J.Griggs† lbw b McSkimming	8	24	21	-	1						
E.P.Thompson lbw b McCullum	49	94	59	-	6						
A.M.Schwass c McSkimming b Wilson	14	65	51	-	2						
M.J.Mason b McMillan	5	18	20	-	-						
L.J.Hamilton not out	0	13	8	-	-						
Extras (b 1, lb 9, nb 8)	18					(b 1, lb 4, nb 3)	8				
TOTAL (96.3 overs)	**291**	401				(55.1 overs) (3 wkts)	**181**	199			

Bowling	*O*	*M*	*R*	*W*	*O*	*M*	*R*	*W*
CENTRAL DISTRICTS								
Mason	14.1	2	38	2	16	5	38	1
Hamilton	14	2	35	1	17	3	56	0
Schwass	15	2	50	3	18	9	33	3
Thompson	16	4	46	1	15.3	5	51	1
Sulzberger	12	5	14	3	28	8	67	3
How					15	6	28	2
OTAGO								
McMillan	21.3	6	74	3	5	1	15	1
McSkimming	24	6	64	1	5	0	12	0
Wilson	21	7	48	3	7	3	21	0
Todd	7	2	24	0				
Redmond	16	3	54	1	16.1	3	66	1
McCullum	7	0	17	2	18	7	47	1
Cumming					4	1	15	0

Fall of Wickets	*O 1st*	*CD 1st*	*O 2nd*	*CD 2nd*
1st	0	41	12	5
2nd	26	50	74	95
3rd	37	126	131	104
4th	60	181	146	-
5th	68	197	176	-
6th	149	206	195	-
7th	154	240	207	-
8th	167	286	268	-
9th	179	286	274	-
10th	193	291	278	-

CANTERBURY v AUCKLAND — State Championship

at Hagley Park, Christchurch on 13, 14 December, 2004
Toss : Canterbury. Umpires : A.L. Hill & T.J. Parlane
Close of play: 1st day: Auckland 156-6, Vincent 48, Walker 8;
***Auckland won by an innings and 60 runs.** Points: Auckland 8, Canterbury 0*

Sixteen wickets fell on the first day of the match which saw Auckland with a lead of 45 by the close. Mills and Adams wrecked the Canterbury innings which went from 24-4 to 52-7 before number nine Shaw came in and hit 39 off 41 balls.

Auckland began with a 64 run stand between Richardson (who had announced this was to be his last game) and Jones. However, six wickets fell for a further 54 runs and Canterbury were back in the game. On the second morning Adams swung the game back Auckland's way reaching fifty off just 46 balls and extended the lead to 185.

This proved far too much for Canterbury who again succumbed meekly. The openers were both out before a run had been scored and, apart from brief resistance from Ellis and Shaw, there was little else of note. Mills, who surpassed his previous best figures in each innings, recorded his first ten wicket haul in first-class cricket.

CANTERBURY

FIRST INNINGS	*Runs*	*Mins*	*Balls*	*6s*	*4s*	*SECOND INNINGS*	*Runs*	*Mins*	*Balls*	*6s*	*4s*
M.H.W.Papps c Jones b Mills	4	31	20	-	1	(2) c Adams b Mills	0	7	2	-	-
T.G.McIntosh lbw b Mills	3	40	31	-	-	(1) c Young b Walmsley	0	1	2	-	-
P.G.Fulton* c & b Adams	4	28	20	-	1	lbw b Adams	17	65	49	-	3
S.L.Stewart c Jones b Walmsley	15	77	57	-	-	c Vincent b Mills	17	73	52	-	2
C.D.McMillan c Mills b Adams	7	12	14	-	1	b Adams	0	1	1	-	-
T.J.T.Papps† lbw b Mills	11	38	27	-	2	b Mills	13	28	21	-	2
P.J.Wiseman c Canning b Mills	4	12	7	-	1	c Adams b Mills	0	6	3	-	-
A.M.Ellis lbw b Adams	12	38	27	-	1	c Adams b Walmsley	35	65	47	-	4
H.J.Shaw c Young b Adams	39	51	41	-	8	c Adams b Mills	31	21	19	-	7
W.A.Cornelius lbw b Mills	2	13	7	-	-	c Richardson b Canning	7	9	8	-	-
C.S.Martin not out	4	5	4	-	1	not out	1	23	11	-	-
Extras (lb 5, nb 1)	6					(b 4)	4				
TOTAL (42.3 overs)	**111**	177				(36 overs)	**125**	154			

AUCKLAND

	Runs	*Mins*	*Balls*	*6s*	*4s*
M.H.Richardson c Cornelius b Ellis	35	116	77	-	2
R.A.Jones c McMillan b Shaw	35	58	43	-	3
M.J.Horne c McIntosh b Ellis	4	38	37	-	-
L.Vincent c McIntosh b Martin	90	250	200	1	7
A.C.Barnes c Papps M.H.W. b Martin	0	4	4	-	-
T.K.Canning c Papps T.J.T. b Ellis	0	10	4	-	-
K.D.Mills c McIntosh b Cornelius	11	40	30	-	1
B.G.K.Walker* c Papps M.H.W. b Martin	31	149	124	-	2
R.A.Young† c Papps T.J.T. b Shaw	7	67	36	-	-
A.R.Adams b Shaw	56	57	49	2	6
K.P.Walmsley not out	0	14	8	-	-
Extras (lb 17, w 5, nb 5)	27				
TOTAL (101.1 overs)	**296**	406			

Bowling	*O*	*M*	*R*	*W*				
AUCKLAND								
Walmsley	11	4	13	1	8	3	25	2
Mills	14	5	33	5	12	4	49	5
Adams	10.3	3	45	4	9	2	19	2
Canning	7	1	15	0	7	0	28	1
CANTERBURY								
Martin	23	5	67	3				
Cornelius	20	3	65	1				
Ellis	28	9	81	3				
Shaw	13.1	2	37	3				
McMillan	11	3	23	0				
Wiseman	6	2	6	0				

Fall of Wickets	***C***	***A***	***C***
	1st	*1st*	*2nd*
1st	7	64	0
2nd	8	80	0
3rd	16	89	30
4th	24	90	30
5th	47	91	38
6th	48	118	42
7th	52	205	53
8th	78	225	89
9th	103	277	103
10th	111	296	125

CENTRAL DISTRICTS v NORTHERN DISTRICTS

at McLean Park, Napier on 13, 14, 15, 16 December, 2004
Toss : Northern Districts. Umpires : D.B. Cowie & D.M. Quested
Close of play: 1st day: CD 433-8, Schwass 1, Mason 13; 2nd day: ND 254-8, Watling 27, Aldridge 7
3rd day: ND 58-3, Styris 16, Aldridge 5
***Northern Districts won by 1 wicket.** Points: Northern Districts 6, Central Districts 2*

Central batted all the first day on their way to their highest ever total against Northern. The highlight was a record first wicket stand for Central against Northern. Sinclair reached his century with a six after 196 minutes (and was out next ball) and How's third consecutive hundred took 137 minutes and 110 balls. Central were 182-0 at lunch on the first day with How already having reached his hundred.

Northern were dismissed on the third morning still 206 behind but Sulzberger chose not to enforce the follow-on. Central batted again, with How once more amongst the runs, and led by 399 when their last wicket fell.

Northern lost three wickets before the close and, at 85-5 the next day, an early finish seemed likely. However, Hamish Marshall joined Hart and the pair proceded to add 216, a Northern sixth wicket record against all sides and their highest for any wicket against Central. Hart reached three figures after 192 minutes from 160 balls and Marshall's maiden first-class century arrived after 202 minutes and 154 balls.

Marshall went at 338-7 and when Watling and Tuffey fell to successive deliveries Northern still needed 48 with one wicket left. Butler proved an able partner for Yovich and in the rain and gloom the pair took Northern to a remarkable victory with the winning runs coming at 6.40 pm. It was only the fourth time in New Zealand first-class cricket that a team had won chasing 400 or more.

CENTRAL DISTRICTS

FIRST INNINGS	*Runs*	*Mins*	*Balls*	*6s*	*4s*	*SECOND INNINGS*	*Runs*	*Mins*	*Balls*	*6s*	*4s*
J.M.How c Butler b Hart	121	166	125	2	23	(2) c sub (R.R.Shutte) b Orchard	72	159	117	2	9
M.S.Sinclair c Howell b Hart	104	198	141	1	15	(1) b Tuffey	0	1	1	-	-
P.J.Ingram c & b Hart	36	105	91	-	6	c Watling b Butler	1	41	28	-	-
G.P.Sulzberger* b Aldridge	46	104	73	-	8	c Watling b Aldridge	15	62	42	-	1
J.I.Englefield c Styris b Tuffey	23	133	90	-	2	c Watling b Aldridge	52	142	98	-	8
R.L.Taylor lbw b Tuffey	46	63	42	-	9	c Watling b Tuffey	14	23	19	-	2
B.B.J.Griggs† c Styris b Tuffey	1	8	5	-	-	c Watling b Aldridge	13	54	44	-	1
E.P.Thompson c Orchard b Aldridge	11	30	25	-	1	c Howell b Tuffey	10	33	27	-	1
A.M.Schwass not out	34	67	46	1	4	c Aldridge b Tuffey	1	37	29	-	-
M.J.Mason b Aldridge	16	55	34	-	2	not out	4	25	13	-	1
L.J.Hamilton lbw b Styris	0	6	7	-	-	run out	1	11	10	-	-
Extras (b 2, lb 11, w 6, nb 22)	41					(lb 1, nb 9)	10				
TOTAL (109.3 overs)	**479**	473				(69.5 overs)	**193**	301			

NORTHERN DISTRICTS

	Runs	Mins	Balls	6s	4s		Runs	Mins	Balls	6s	4s
J.A.H.Marshall* c Ingram b Mason	1	5	5	-	-	lbw b Thompson	28	68	62	-	4
L.G.Howell c Schwass b Mason	35	100	75	-	5	lbw b Hamilton	1	16	10	-	-
M.G.Orchard lbw b Thompson	48	187	140	-	7	c Griggs b Hamilton	4	1	2	-	1
S.B.Styris st Griggs b Sulzberger	22	61	56	-	3	c Taylor b Sulzberger	36	125	78	-	5
M.N.Hart c Griggs b Hamilton	48	110	82	-	7	(6) c Schwass b Hamilton	107	209	172	1	14
H.J.H.Marshall c Griggs b Thompson	10	51	37	-	2	(7) c Sulzberger b Mason	128	239	184	-	21
J.A.F.Yovich c Ingram b Hamilton	24	42	33	-	5	(8) not out	54	122	77	-	9
B-J.Watling† b Hamilton	29	109	84	-	5	(9) c How b Mason	4	22	16	-	-
D.R.Tuffey c Englefield b Schwass	17	41	40	-	1	(10) c Sinclair b Mason	0	1	1	-	-
G.W.Aldridge c How b Mason	21	62	46	-	1	(5) b Thompson	10	70	56	-	1
I.G.Butler not out	0	11	4	-	-	not out	14	64	42	-	2
Extras (b 1, lb 4, nb 13)	18					(lb 6, w 2, nb 6)	14				
TOTAL (98.1 overs)	**273**	393				(115.5 overs) (9 wkts)	**400**	478			

Bowling	*O*	*M*	*R*	*W*	*O*	*M*	*R*	*W*
NORTHERN DISTRICTS								
Tuffey	27	3	125	3	20.5	9	38	4
Butler	19	4	102	0	8	1	39	1
Aldridge	18	7	48	3	12	5	22	3
Orchard	16	5	53	0	11	4	24	1
Yovich	6	0	51	0	4	0	28	0
Hart	16	2	67	3	1	0	11	0
Styris	7.3	3	20	1	13	4	30	0
CENTRAL DISTRICTS								
Hamilton	23	4	49	3	24.5	4	88	3
Mason	23.1	8	45	3	23	5	62	3
Schwass	19	3	70	1	20	4	79	0
Thompson	14	3	62	2	23	5	74	2
Sulzberger	19	5	42	1	21	6	77	1
How					4	0	14	0

Fall of Wickets	***CD 1st***	***ND 1st***	***CD 2nd***	***ND 2nd***
1st	215	1	0	7
2nd	255	72	25	11
3rd	299	113	69	46
4th	333	127	124	85
5th	396	171	139	85
6th	402	200	173	301
7th	415	207	178	338
8th	415	238	187	352
9th	478	266	192	352
10th	479	273	193	-

WELLINGTON v OTAGO

State Championship

at Basin Reserve, Wellington on 13, 14, 15, 16 December, 2004
Toss : Wellington. Umpires : I.W. Shine & E.A. Watkin
Close of play: 1st day: Otago 306-9, McCullum 26, McMillan 2; 2nd day: Otago 14-1, Cumming 10, Todd 4
3rd day: Wellington 85-2, Bell 4
***First innings win to Otago.** Points: Otago 2, Wellington 0*

Otago batted throughout the first day, the highlight being a partnership of 150 for the fourth wicket in even time between Gaffaney and Hopkins. The stand was broken when Gaffaney was trapped in front by Gillespie, becoming the first Otago batsman to be dismissed twice for 99. McCullum added some valuable runs later in the order.

Wellington were 49-4 in their reply before Ryder and Franklin combined to add 130 in only 118 minutes. Fairley, Gillespie and Patel all played useful hands but Wellington finally fell 36 runs short.

Otago lost Wasim before the close of the second day and continued to lose wickets at regular intervals throughout their innings. With all the Wellington bowlers having success, Otago were dismissed for 214, a lead of 250.

The home team began their chase with 77 for the first wicket before both openers went. Rain, however, prevented any play at all on the last day and the prospect of an interesting finish was ruined.

OTAGO

FIRST INNINGS	Runs	Mins	Balls	6s	4s	*SECOND INNINGS*	Runs	Mins	Balls	6s	4s
C.D.Cumming* lbw b O'Brien	11	55	31	-	1	b Ryder	57	171	108	-	9
Mohammad Wasim c Bell b Franklin	11	61	60	-	1	c Fairley b Franklin	0	8	9	-	-
C.B.Gaffaney lbw b Gillespie	99	192	138	-	12	(4) b Gillespie	11	36	26	-	2
A.J.Redmond c Patel b Gillespie	8	36	34	-	1	(5) b Gillespie	44	184	127	-	4
G.J.Hopkins† lbw b Franklin	86	218	170	-	12	(6) c Nevin b Ryder	4	2	3	-	1
G.R.Todd b Franklin	37	96	88	-	4	(3) c Nevin b O'Brien	14	38	45	-	2
J.W.Sheed c Ryder b Franklin	0	5	1	-	-	c Patel b Franklin	4	19	11	-	-
N.L.McCullum not out	46	90	73	1	5	b Ryder	23	46	36	-	3
J.W.Wilson run out	3	13	6	-	-	not out	38	79	60	-	5
W.C.McSkimming c Nevin b Ryder	6	22	13	-	-	c Parlane N.R. b Gillespie	1	12	8	-	-
J.M.McMillan c Nevin b Gillespie	2	31	17	-	-	c Franklin b Patel	8	35	29	-	-
Extras (lb 9, w 1, nb 8)	18					(b 4, lb 3, w 1, nb 2)	10				
TOTAL (103.5 overs)	**327**	413				(76.4 overs)	**214**	306			

WELLINGTON

FIRST INNINGS	Runs	Mins	Balls	6s	4s	*SECOND INNINGS*	Runs	Mins	Balls	6s	4s
M.D.Bell* b McMillan	13	43	41	-	1	(3) not out	4	19	21	-	-
M.E.Parlane c Hopkins b Wilson	2	21	10	-	-	(1) run out	42	86	52	1	6
L.J.Woodcock b McMillan	11	26	22	-	1	(2) b Cumming	31	106	89	-	5
N.R.Parlane c Hopkins b McSkimming	10	31	19	-	1						
J.D.Ryder lbw b Todd	72	143	121	1	11						
J.E.C.Franklin c Cumming b McCullum	79	196	153	-	10						
C.J.Nevin† c Hopkins b McMillan	16	36	33	-	1						
S.A.Fairley c Hopkins b Cumming	23	61	55	-	3						
M.R.Gillespie c Hopkins b McSkimming	26	59	47	2	2						
J.S.Patel not out	21	55	38	-	3						
I.E.O'Brien c & b McMillan	3	15	12	-	-						
Extras (b 4, lb 11)	15					(b 4, lb 3, nb 1)	8				
TOTAL (92 overs)	**291**	345				(26.5 overs) (2 wkts)	**85**	106			

Bowling	*O*	*M*	*R*	*W*	*O*	*M*	*R*	*W*
WELLINGTON								
Gillespie	25.5	7	96	3	23	6	58	3
Franklin	26	6	67	4	15	3	41	2
O'Brien	26	7	92	1	18	5	57	1
Ryder	7	1	18	1	12	1	31	3
Patel	19	4	45	0	8.4	2	20	1
OTAGO								
McMillan	20	9	36	4	6	1	35	0
Wilson	19	5	63	1	6	0	26	0
McSkimming	19	5	63	2	6	3	8	0
Todd	9	0	42	1				
McCullum	21	5	47	1	4	2	2	0
Redmond	3	0	25	0				
Cumming	1	1	0	1	4.5	1	7	1

Fall of Wickets

	O *1st*	*W* *1st*	*O* *2nd*	*W* *2nd*
1st	26	10	2	77
2nd	26	22	29	85
3rd	49	29	50	-
4th	199	49	101	-
5th	254	179	105	-
6th	254	203	109	-
7th	269	239	150	-
8th	281	260	174	-
9th	294	280	180	-
10th	327	291	214	-

WELLINGTON v NORTHERN DISTRICTS State Championship

at Basin Reserve, Wellington on 13, 14, 15 January, 2005
Toss : Wellington. Umpires : R.D. Anderson & A.L. Hill
Close of play: 1st day: Wellington 65-1, Woodcock 25, Fleming 38; 2nd day: ND 142-7, Yovich 30, McGlashan 23
***Wellington won by 8 wickets.** Points: Wellington 8, Northern Districts 0*

McGlashan made his debut for his third province while Vettori captained a side in first-class cricket for the first time. Marshall was the only Northern player to register a significant score as the visitors were bowled out for 184 with Franklin doing the early damage and ending with five wickets.

The Wellington batsmen also found runs hard to come by. Fleming top scored with 56 while Tuffey and Yovich claimed nine wckets between them. Trailing by 36, Northern lost two wickets before the deficit was erased and at 90-7 the match looked as though it might end in two days.

Yovich and McGlashan put on 56 for the eighth wicket and Aldridge helped add another 48 before he was last man out. Franklin claimed ten wickets in a match for the frst time.

Wellington needed 160 to win and scored the runs in better than even time. Fleming remained unbeaten on 80 off just 66 balls as the game was wrapped up by 3.16 pm.

NORTHERN DISTRICTS

FIRST INNINGS	*Runs*	*Mins*	*Balls*	*6s*	*4s*	*SECOND INNINGS*	*Runs*	*Mins*	*Balls*	*6s*	*4s*
L.G.Howell c Mills b Franklin	5	31	23	-	-	lbw b Franklin	17	26	21	-	2
B-J.Watling lbw b Franklin	14	55	43	-	3	c Mills b Franklin	0	14	4	-	-
M.G.Orchard c Fleming b Patel	27	137	98	-	4	c Mills b Franklin	13	29	25	-	2
S.B.Styris c Bell b Franklin	31	85	70	1	4	c Franklin b Gillespie	15	51	36	-	2
M.N.Hart c Mills b Franklin	0	1	1	-	-	c Ryder b Gillespie	4	17	9	-	-
H.J.H.Marshall c Ryder b O'Brien	51	119	90	-	7	b O'Brien	13	30	18	-	2
J.A.F.Yovich b Patel	9	24	22	-	1	not out	57	197	119	-	6
D.L.Vettori* run out	5	22	10	-	-	c Ryder b Franklin	7	16	16	-	1
P.D.McGlashan† lbw b Franklin	17	65	52	-	1	lbw b Franklin	25	81	78	-	3
D.R.Tuffey not out	10	24	23	1	-	lbw b O'Brien	0	11	7	-	-
G.W.Aldridge c Parlane b Patel	1	3	4	-	-	c Ryder b Patel	22	72	68	-	-
Extras (b 2, lb 11, nb 1)	14					(b 8, lb 14)	22				
TOTAL (72.3 overs)	**184**	288				(66.4 overs)	**195**	276			

WELLINGTON

	Runs	*Mins*	*Balls*	*6s*	*4s*		*Runs*	*Mins*	*Balls*	*6s*	*4s*
M.D.Bell* c McGlashan b Tuffey	0	12	12	-	-	lbw b Vettori	18	66	46	-	3
L.J.Woodcock c McGlashan b Tuffey	32	117	95	-	3	c Hart b Yovich	27	108	80	-	3
S.P.Fleming c McGlashan b Tuffey	56	119	96	-	11	not out	80	76	66	3	10
N.R.Parlane lbw b Yovich	25	100	66	-	4	not out	20	34	30	-	3
J.D.Ryder c Watling b Yovich	20	61	63	-	2						
J.E.C.Franklin c Styris b Yovich	8	25	18	-	2						
C.J.Nevin c McGlashan b Yovich	31	63	53	-	4						
S.M.Mills† not out	25	88	72	1	2						
M.R.Gillespie c McGlashan b Yovich	0	1	1	-	-						
J.S.Patel b Vettori	8	12	13	-	1						
I.E.O'Brien c Vettori b Tuffey	5	11	6	-	1						
Extras (lb 8, nb 2)	10					(lb 11, nb 4)	15				
TOTAL (82.1 overs)	**220**	309				(36.2 overs) (2 wkts)	**160**	143			

Bowling	*O*	*M*	*R*	*W*	*O*	*M*	*R*	*W*
WELLINGTON								
Gillespie	14	2	44	0	15	4	36	2
Franklin	17	8	23	5	16	2	48	5
O'Brien	15	2	48	1	18	2	53	2
Ryder	2	0	7	0				
Patel	24.3	5	49	3	17.4	5	36	1
NORTHERN DISTRICTS								
Tuffey	21.1	8	49	4	11	2	23	0
Aldridge	17	4	51	0	7	2	20	0
Orchard	9	5	21	0				
Vettori	26	7	52	1	11	3	38	1
Yovich	9	1	39	5	5	0	43	1
Styris					2.2	0	25	0

Fall of Wickets	***ND*** *1st*	***W*** *1st*	***ND*** *2nd*	***W*** *2nd*
1st	7	2	12	46
2nd	26	81	31	83
3rd	76	90	40	-
4th	76	126	56	-
5th	86	144	65	-
6th	111	145	75	-
7th	126	198	90	-
8th	164	198	146	-
9th	183	215	147	-
10th	184	220	195	-

AUCKLAND v CENTRAL DISTRICTS State Championship

at Eden Park Outer Oval, Auckland on 15, 16, 17, 18 January, 2005
Toss : Auckland. Umpires : T.J. Parlane & I.W. Shine
Close of play: 1st day: Auckland 20-1, Horne 12, Nicol 3; 2nd day: Auckland 345-8, Vincent 146, Adams 0
3rd day: CD 274-8, Griggs 76, Schwass 4
***Auckland won by 7 wickets.** Points: Auckland 8, Central Districts 0*

Central were in trouble on the first day when Thompson joined Englefield at the crease with the score at 146-6. The pair proceded to add 159 in just 117 minutes before Thompson was run out. His remarkable maiden century had come from only 82 balls in 99 minutes. Englefield carried on before he was ninth out and when Auckland lost Jones before stumps, it had been Central's day.

Auckland batted through the second day with Horne and Nicol adding 113 for the second wicket and Vincent and Young putting on 111 in only 83 minutes for an Auckland eighth wicket record against Central. Vincent remained unbeaten when the innings ended the next morning. It was his highest score and the highest by an Auckland batsman against Central. His hundred took 184 minutes and 162 balls.

Sinclair held Central's second innings together before he was out at 170-6. Griggs batted through the rest of the innings and when it ended early on the last day, Auckland needed 222 to win.

Jones and Horne looked as though they would achieve victory themselves as they compiled a first wicket record for Auckland against Central. Jones reached his hundred after 189 minutes from 168 balls and the game was over by 4.35 pm.

CENTRAL DISTRICTS

FIRST INNINGS	*Runs*	*Mins*	*Balls*	*6s*	*4s*	*SECOND INNINGS*	*Runs*	*Mins*	*Balls*	*6s*	*4s*
J.M.How c Nicol b Walmsley	4	26	11	-	-	(2) c Young b Adams	13	35	22	-	2
P.J.Ingram c Vincent b Mills	7	29	26	-	-	(1) lbw b Mills	15	69	48	-	2
M.S.Sinclair c Young b Canning	17	33	25	-	2	c Young b Canning	95	182	134	-	18
G.P.Sulzberger* lbw b Adams	16	37	28	-	2	b Walmsley	13	28	27	-	2
J.I.Englefield lbw b Canning	95	268	184	-	17	c Young b Canning	4	22	18	-	1
R.L.Taylor c Horne b Mills	42	53	39	2	5	run out	0	9	3	-	-
B.B.J.Griggs† c Nicol b Mills	22	62	46	-	3	not out	77	232	181	-	13
E.P.Thompson run out	102	117	89	4	14	c Vincent b Mills	24	30	31	-	3
R.M.West lbw b Canning	0	4	5	-	-	c Barnes b Canning	16	46	30	-	3
A.M.Schwass not out	25	56	46	-	4	b Canning	4	57	35	-	-
L.J.Hamilton b Walmsley	11	33	16	-	2	c Vincent b Adams	0	9	8	-	-
Extras (b 4, lb 2, nb 3)	9					(b 1, lb 8, w 3, nb 2)	14				
TOTAL (85.2 overs)	**350**	364				(89.1 overs)	**275**	363			

AUCKLAND

	Runs	*Mins*	*Balls*	*6s*	*4s*		*Runs*	*Mins*	*Balls*	*6s*	*4s*
R.A.Jones lbw b Hamilton	1	17	9	-	-	c Englefield b How	110	211	180	-	16
M.J.Horne c Ingram b Sulzberger	76	201	154	-	12	c Schwass b How	72	174	129	1	11
R.J.Nicol lbw b Schwass	35	242	180	-	5	not out	14	35	36	-	2
L.Vincent not out	185	308	253	4	29	c Englefield b West	8	6	5	-	2
A.C.Barnes c Hamilton b Sulzberger	16	31	19	-	4	not out	5	4	7	-	1
T.K.Canning c Griggs b Hamilton	12	37	37	-	1						
K.D.Mills lbw b Hamilton	0	3	3	-	-						
B.G.K.Walker* c Griggs b Hamilton	0	26	20	-	-						
R.A.Young† b Hamilton	35	83	60	-	8						
A.R.Adams lbw b Hamilton	14	29	22	1	1						
K.P.Walmsley lbw b Schwass	4	34	23	-	1						
Extras (lb 11, w 2, nb 13)	26					(lb 7, w 4, nb 3)	14				
TOTAL (127.5 overs)	**404**	510				(59 overs) (3 wkts)	**223**	222			

Bowling	*O*	*M*	*R*	*W*	*O*	*M*	*R*	*W*
AUCKLAND								
Mills	20	2	74	3	21	6	80	2
Walmsley	20.2	4	81	2	18	4	44	1
Canning	19	6	84	3	24	8	65	4
Adams	18	5	58	1	9.1	2	34	2
Walker	5	0	33	0	11	2	32	0
Barnes	3	0	14	0	5	1	10	0
Vincent					1	0	1	0
CENTRAL DISTRICTS								
Hamilton	33	14	80	6	8	2	22	0
Thompson	27	7	80	0	9	2	38	0
Schwass	24.5	2	118	2	6	1	27	0
Sulzberger	27	9	61	2	5	0	32	0
West	12	3	46	0	21	6	60	1
How	4	3	8	0	9	1	33	2
Sinclair					1	0	4	0

Fall of Wickets

	CD	**A**	**CD**	**A**
	1st	*1st*	*2nd*	*2nd*
1st	15	2	24	172
2nd	15	115	42	208
3rd	49	163	77	218
4th	49	190	89	-
5th	93	221	94	-
6th	146	221	170	-
7th	305	234	198	-
8th	305	345	234	-
9th	320	373	274	-
10th	350	404	275	-

OTAGO v CANTERBURY — State Championship

at University Oval, Dunedin on 15, 16, 17, 18 January, 2005
Toss : Canterbury. Umpires : G.A. Baxter & E.A. Watkin
Close of play: 1st day: Canterbury 18-1, McIntosh 3, Ellis 4; 2nd day: Otago 145-5, Sheed 77, Todd 4
3rd day: Otago 164-5, Sheed 83, Todd 13
***Otago won by 114 runs.** Points: Otago 8, Canterbury 0*

Otago batted for most of the first day after a shaky start. They were indebted to Todd whose maiden first-class hundred came from 144 balls in 187 minutes. He added 110 for the ninth wicket with McSkimming plus 27 for the last with McMillan who did not score. Todd was on 98 when the ninth wicket fell and reached his hundred with his fifteenth four.

Astle and McMillan added 87 for Canterbury's fifth wicket but both fell in the fifties and the visitors ended 110 in arrears. Otago scored at almost a run a minute in their second innings with Sheed registering his highest score and Todd adding an unbeaten fifty to his century.

Canterbury needed 353 to win but were soon in trouble at 26-3. McMillan made 82 but he was out at 173-7 and at 6.36 pm Wilson bowled Martin to complete the Otago victory.

Hopkins equalled the New Zealand first-class record for dismissals and catches in a match. His ten catches in the match easily surpassed the previous Otago record of seven.

OTAGO

FIRST INNINGS	Runs	Mins	Balls	6s	4s	SECOND INNINGS	Runs	Mins	Balls	6s	4s
C.D.Cumming* c McCullum b McMillan	43	102	88	1	7	(2) lbw b Cunis	1	16	7	-	-
C.B.Gaffaney c Fulton b Martin	5	45	24	-	-	(1) lbw b Astle	32	56	41	-	3
J.W.Sheed lbw b Cunis	2	30	20	-	-	c Papps b Martin	89	189	144	-	12
A.J.Redmond lbw b Cunis	55	135	108	-	10	lbw b Astle	12	9	10	-	2
Mohammad Wasim lbw b McMillan	0	7	2	-	-	run out	2	11	9	-	-
G.J.Hopkins† b Astle	20	79	74	-	2	c McCullum b Martin	15	69	53	-	2
G.R.Todd not out	123	196	157	2	18	not out	59	104	89	-	8
J.W.Wilson c Papps b Cunis	4	14	6	-	1	c McCullum b Wiseman	10	28	21	-	2
B.E.Scott lbw b Cunis	0	9	5	-	-	not out	11	17	17	1	-
W.C.McSkimming c McIntosh b Cunis	30	127	96	-	3						
J.M.McMillan c McCullum b McMillan	0	19	10	-	-						
Extras (b 9, lb 5, nb 12)	26					(lb 7, w 2, nb 2)	11				
TOTAL (96.3 overs)	**308**	387				(64.5 overs) (7 wkts dec)	**242**	253			

CANTERBURY

FIRST INNINGS	Runs	Mins	Balls	6s	4s	SECOND INNINGS	Runs	Mins	Balls	6s	4s
M.H.W.Papps lbw b McSkimming	3	6	6	-	-	c Hopkins b Wilson	13	33	27	-	2
T.G.McIntosh lbw b Scott	21	121	88	-	3	c Hopkins b McMillan	4	23	20	-	-
A.M.Ellis c Wasim b Wilson	7	24	19	-	1	(8) c Hopkins b Wilson	14	51	30	-	2
P.G.Fulton c Hopkins b McMillan	18	49	32	-	3	(3) c Hopkins b Redmond	23	93	62	-	3
N.J.Astle c Sheed b Wilson	53	124	92	-	9	(4) b Wilson	3	7	7	-	-
C.D.McMillan* c Gaffaney b Cumming	51	96	76	-	8	(5) c Wilson b Scott	82	172	137	3	6
G.R.Stead c Hopkins b Scott	5	31	18	-	1	(6) c Hopkins b McMillan	16	47	42	-	2
B.B.McCullum† lbw b Cumming	0	2	1	-	-	(7) c sub (D.G.Sewell) b Redmond	25	42	34	1	3
P.J.Wiseman c Hopkins b Scott	21	33	27	1	3	not out	41	78	65	-	9
S.J.Cunis c Hopkins b Scott	4	8	10	-	1	c Hopkins b Scott	0	4	3	-	-
C.S.Martin not out	0	7	4	-	-	b Wilson	9	27	20	-	2
Extras (b 5, lb 8, w 1, nb 1)	15					(lb 3, w 3, nb 2)	8				
TOTAL (62 overs)	**198**	257				(74.1 overs)	**238**	293			

Bowling	O	M	R	W	O	M	R	W
CANTERBURY								
Martin	25	5	61	1	17	2	46	2
Cunis	26	9	78	5	7	0	32	1
Ellis	14	2	53	0	11	3	35	0
McMillan	15.3	3	37	3	5	1	26	0
Astle	9	1	31	1	9	1	29	2
Wiseman	7	0	34	0	15.5	2	67	1
OTAGO								
McMillan	17	3	63	1	17	2	45	2
McSkimming	1	1	0	1				
Wilson	16	7	41	2	18.1	5	46	4
Scott	19	9	47	4	18	5	45	2
Todd	3	0	14	0	8	1	34	0
Cumming	6	2	20	2	2	0	9	0
Redmond					11	1	56	2

Fall of Wickets	O 1st	C 1st	O 2nd	C 2nd
1st	30	3	4	16
2nd	37	11	58	22
3rd	62	42	69	26
4th	64	72	79	79
5th	136	159	140	127
6th	143	171	187	171
7th	163	171	222	173
8th	171	179	-	216
9th	281	187	-	219
10th	308	198	-	238

CANTERBURY v CENTRAL DISTRICTS State Championship

at Queen Elizabeth II Park, Christchurch on 21, 22, 23, 24 January, 2005
Toss : Central Districts. Umpires : R.D. Anderson & D.J. Walker
Close of play: 1st day: Canterbury 342-8, Cunis 2, Shaw 0; 2nd day: Canterbury 46-1, Papps 30, Fulton 7
3rd day: CD 52-2, Barnett 5, Sulzberger 6
***Canterbury won by 343 runs.** Points: Canterbury 8, Central Districts 0*

Fulton dominated the first day's play coming in after Canterbury had lost their first wicket with just one run on the board. He reached his hundred off only 99 balls in 117 minutes and was finally dismissed at 226-5, having scored 126 runs in boundaries alone. Canterbury had been 144-2 at lunch with Fulton 105 not out.

Central wrapped up the innings quickly on day two but were soon in trouble. Barnett went without scoring and the visitors were 80-5 before Griggs and Thompson (fifty off 46 balls) combined in a record sixth wicket stand for Central against Canterbury.

Canterbury capitalised on their 65 run advantage with more runs from Fulton and a maiden hundred from Stewart in 214 minutes from 171 balls. When Canterbury declared they led by 465 and by the close of play had already captured two Central wickets.

The last day belonged to Wiseman who took the last eight wickets at a cost of ten runs to finish with 9-13, the second best analysis in New Zealand first-class history. It was both the best innings and match figures for Canterbury against Central. Cederman made his first-class debut in this match.

CANTERBURY

FIRST INNINGS	*Runs*	*Mins*	*Balls*	*6s*	*4s*	*SECOND INNINGS*	*Runs*	*Mins*	*Balls*	*6s*	*4s*
M.H.W.Papps† c Barnett b Hefford	0	7	11	-	-	(2) lbw b Hamilton	33	82	57	-	5
T.G.McIntosh c Ingram b Schwass	14	102	60	-	2	(1) lbw b Hefford	0	18	17	-	-
P.G.Fulton* c Hefford b Hamilton	154	225	195	1	30	c Thompson b Hefford	86	172	141	1	15
S.L.Stewart run out	35	57	50	1	5	c How b Schwass	149	264	213	2	17
G.R.Stead lbw b Hefford	12	51	31	-	1	st Griggs b Sulzberger	55	112	89	-	8
N.T.Broom c Barnett b How	22	54	43	-	5	st Griggs b Sulzberger	37	64	49	1	6
A.M.Ellis b Thompson	43	148	120	1	5	not out	17	26	13	1	2
P.J.Wiseman lbw b Schwass	46	82	62	1	6	not out	0	4	2	-	-
S.J.Cunis not out	3	58	43	-	-						
H.J.Shaw c Griggs b Hamilton	3	24	22	-	-						
C.S.Martin b Hamilton	0	1	2	-	-						
Extras (b 1, lb 4, nb 9)	14					(b 8, lb 9, w 1, nb 5)	23				
TOTAL (105 overs)	**346**	409				(96 overs) (6 wkts dec)	**400**	374			

CENTRAL DISTRICTS

	Runs	*Mins*	*Balls*	*6s*	*4s*		*Runs*	*Mins*	*Balls*	*6s*	*4s*
G.E.F.Barnett c Papps b Martin	0	2	3	-	-	(3) c & b Wiseman	30	94	71	-	5
P.J.Ingram c Papps b Shaw	21	117	70	-	3	b Wiseman	13	55	34	-	1
G.P.Sulzberger* lbw b Martin	37	108	88	-	4	(4) c McIntosh b Wiseman	30	92	80	-	4
J.I.Englefield lbw b Shaw	13	34	26	-	3	(5) c Stead b Wiseman	8	50	40	-	-
D.R.Cederman c Ellis b Martin	4	12	11	-	1	(6) c Stead b Wiseman	1	15	11	-	-
B.B.J.Griggs† c Ellis b Wiseman	75	161	117	-	13	(7) b Wiseman	2	34	25	-	-
E.P.Thompson b Martin	77	112	80	2	11	(8) c Fulton b Wiseman	0	1	2	-	-
J.M.How lbw b Wiseman	8	14	9	-	1	(1) c Shaw b Martin	23	36	28	-	4
A.M.Schwass not out	31	50	39	-	3	not out	5	31	25	-	-
B.E.Hefford c Shaw b Ellis	2	28	25	-	-	(11) c Papps b Wiseman	1	7	3	-	-
L.J.Hamilton c Broom b Wiseman	0	3	3	-	-	(10) lbw b Wiseman	0	8	5	-	-
Extras (b 5, lb 5, nb 3)	13					(b 1, lb 6, nb 2)	9				
TOTAL (78 overs)	**281**	325				(53.4 overs)	**122**	216			

Bowling	*O*	*M*	*R*	*W*	*O*	*M*	*R*	*W*
CENTRAL DISTRICTS								
Hamilton	22	10	42	3	19	6	67	1
Hefford	18	7	56	2	20	10	46	2
Thompson	20	0	109	1	10	1	59	0
Schwass	22	7	65	2	16.4	3	71	1
Sulzberger	17	7	40	0	27.2	4	122	2
How	6	1	29	1				
Barnett					3	0	18	0
CANTERBURY								
Martin	20	8	42	4	12	3	45	1
Cunis	13	3	56	0	9	1	37	0
Shaw	16	3	60	2	11	5	17	0
Ellis	10	2	40	1	5	3	3	0
Wiseman	19	2	73	3	16.4	9	13	9

Fall of Wickets

	C *1st*	***CD*** *1st*	***C*** *2nd*	***CD*** *2nd*
1st	1	0	10	34
2nd	98	61	50	44
3rd	173	61	176	98
4th	216	66	297	105
5th	226	80	355	109
6th	248	221	399	114
7th	326	236	-	114
8th	341	261	-	117
9th	346	278	-	118
10th	346	281	-	122

NORTHERN DISTRICTS v OTAGO — State Championship

at Harry Barker Reserve, Gisborne on 21, 22, 23, 24 January, 2005
Toss : Northern Districts. Umpires : B.G. Frost & D.M. Quested
Close of play: 1st day: Otago 320-7, Hopkins 60, Scott 19; 2nd day: ND 281-8, Devcich 43, Aldridge 5
3rd day: Otago 187-5, Cumming 99, Todd 5
***Northern Districts won by 8 wickets.** Points: Northern Districts 8, Otago 0*

Northern fielded five new players. Teenagers Wilson, Flynn, Devcich and Davis were all making their first-class debuts while Evans had previously played for Glamorgan.

Otago opened with 97 for the first wicket and by the close were 320-7. Next morning Northern wrapped the innings up for the addition of just a single but were soon in trouble themselves at 53-4. Wilson then found good partners in the middle order before he was bowled at 204-7, just four runs short of a century on debut.

This brought Devcich to the crease for his first innings. He was on 18 when Aldridge joined him and the pair added 96, equalling the ninth wicket record for Northern against Otago. Davis stayed while Devcich got to 94 before the number eleven was caught and bowled by Redmond.

Otago lost two wickets before the deficit was cleared but were in good shape at 176-4. The loss of Hopkins, however, saw the remaining wickets go quickly. Cumming reached his hundred off 227 balls in 281 minutes before he was out at 219-6. The innings ended at 231 leaving Northern 185 to win.

The home team had little trouble with the target. Watling registered a maiden fifty before the winning runs came at 4.43 pm.

OTAGO

FIRST INNINGS	Runs	Mins	Balls	6s	4s	*SECOND INNINGS*	Runs	Mins	Balls	6s	4s
C.D.Cumming* c Davis b Yovich	44	126	105	-	8	(2) c Devcich b Yovich	106	331	270	-	13
C.B.Gaffaney lbw b Orchard	37	137	97	-	6	(1) c Devcich b Yovich	17	44	44	-	2
J.W.Sheed lbw b Aldridge	7	29	21	-	1	lbw b Yovich	0	18	10	-	-
A.J.Redmond c McGlashan b Aldridge	70	133	114	-	11	c McGlashan b Davis	8	39	28	-	1
Mohammad Wasim lbw b Davis	8	72	41	-	1	lbw b Davis	0	1	1	-	-
G.J.Hopkins† lbw b Aldridge	61	192	144	-	9	b Aldridge	42	147	97	-	4
G.R.Todd c McGlashan b Yovich	22	69	53	-	2	b Aldridge	18	105	68	-	2
S.P.Beare c Evans b Orchard	17	43	32	-	2	c Davis b Aldridge	6	35	21	-	-
B.E.Scott c McGlashan b Yovich	19	30	23	-	4	run out	0	1	1	-	-
J.M.McMillan not out	0	6	5	-	-	(11) not out	0	2	0	-	-
D.G.Sewell b Aldridge	0	1	2	-	-	(10) b Yovich	0	3	6	-	-
Extras (b 11, lb 9, nb 16)	36					(b 11, lb 12, w 2, nb 9)	34				
TOTAL (103.3 overs)	**321**	424				(89.3 overs)	**231**	367			

NORTHERN DISTRICTS

FIRST INNINGS	Runs	Mins	Balls	6s	4s	*SECOND INNINGS*	Runs	Mins	Balls	6s	4s
B-J.Watling c Hopkins b McMillan	11	17	19	-	2	c Cumming b Sewell	64	172	165	-	13
B.S.Wilson b Cumming	96	264	229	-	11	run out	35	113	86	-	4
A.W.Evans b Scott	4	8	3	-	1	not out	35	105	82	-	5
M.N.Hart* c Sewell b Todd	5	38	33	-	-	not out	43	46	40	-	8
D.R.Flynn c Hopkins b Sewell	2	18	10	-	-						
M.G.Orchard lbw b Redmond	21	86	76	-	3						
J.A.F.Yovich c Sheed b Beare	41	67	55	-	6						
P.D.McGlashan† c Hopkins b Scott	33	76	63	-	5						
A.P.Devcich not out	94	213	164	-	15						
G.W.Aldridge lbw b Sewell	29	138	100	-	4						
T.T.Davis c & b Redmond	8	19	15	-	1						
Extras (b 9, lb 8, w 3, nb 4)	24					(lb 6, w 1, nb 3)	10				
TOTAL (127.1 overs)	**368**	478				(61.4 overs) (2 wkts)	**187**	219			

Bowling	*O*	*M*	*R*	*W*	*O*	*M*	*R*	*W*
NORTHERN DISTRICTS								
Yovich	24	8	62	3	21	3	42	4
Aldridge	28.5	12	60	4	18.3	5	55	3
Davis	13	2	61	1	18	3	52	2
Orchard	22.4	8	42	2	20	10	28	0
Devcich	10	0	64	0	7	1	24	0
Evans	5	1	12	0	5	2	7	0
OTAGO								
McMillan	3	0	15	1				
Sewell	30	8	94	2	15	3	44	1
Scott	33	17	49	2	17.1	5	46	0
Todd	20	5	51	1	4.5	3	6	0
Cumming	20	6	45	1	11	6	21	0
Redmond	16.1	2	72	2	12	1	51	0
Beare	3	1	13	1	1.4	0	13	0
Wasim	2	0	12	0				

Fall of Wickets	*O*	*ND*	*O*	*ND*
	1st	*1st*	*2nd*	*2nd*
1st	97	16	30	78
2nd	101	24	38	121
3rd	116	42	62	-
4th	157	53	62	-
5th	201	106	176	-
6th	248	178	219	-
7th	294	204	227	-
8th	321	251	227	-
9th	321	347	229	-
10th	321	368	231	-

AUCKLAND v WELLINGTON — State Championship

at Eden Park, Auckland on 22, 23, 24, 25 January, 2005
Toss : Auckland. Umpires : G.A. Baxter & P.D. Jones
Close of play: 1st day: Wellington 361-7, M.E.Parlane 181, Gillespie 21; 2nd day: Auckland 235-4, Barnes 36, Canning 4
3rd day: Wellington 97-6, Nevin 4, Mills 5
***Auckland won by 6 wickets.** Points: Auckland 6, Wellington 2*

Eighteen-year-old Cachopa made his debut for Auckland who sent Wellington in after winning the toss. Michael Parlane, who had come into the team in Stephen Fleming's absence, came to the crease after the early loss of Woodcock. He stayed for the rest of the day and was finally eighth man out at 399. His hundred came from 186 balls in 245 minutes and his first double century took 304 balls and 407 minutes.

Auckland had good contributions from Horne and Barnes but were still 99 runs in arrears when they were dismissed on the third day. They struck back quickly, however, with Walmsley trapping Woodcock with the first ball of the innings and by the close Wellington had slumped to 97-6.

Next morning Adams quickly captured the remaining four wickets to finish with career best figures and his first ten wicket haul. Auckland needed 207 to win and solid innings from all the batsmen saw victory achieved at 4.56 pm.

WELLINGTON

FIRST INNINGS	*Runs*	*Mins*	*Balls*	*6s*	*4s*	*SECOND INNINGS*	*Runs*	*Mins*	*Balls*	*6s*	*4s*
M.D.Bell* c Young b Adams	16	77	61	-	2	(2) c Walker b Barnes	17	108	91	-	2
L.J.Woodcock c Young b Walmsley	8	27	15	-	1	(1) lbw b Walmsley	0	1	1	-	-
M.E.Parlane lbw b Adams	203	416	313	5	31	c Vincent b Walmsley	9	41	34	-	2
N.R.Parlane lbw b Walker	21	70	54	-	4	c Young b Adams	41	132	88	1	5
C.J.Nevin c Jones b Walker	0	4	3	-	-	(7) lbw b Adams	7	46	36	-	-
J.E.C.Franklin c Jones b Adams	11	20	20	-	2	b Adams	10	48	36	-	1
J.D.Ryder lbw b Vincent	66	132	118	1	9	(5) c Walker b Walmsley	4	27	18	-	-
S.M.Mills† c Young b Walker	15	67	46	-	2	lbw b Adams	6	27	24	-	-
M.R.Gillespie c Young b Adams	52	98	89	-	7	c Nicol b Adams	0	1	2	-	-
J.S.Patel c Walker b Walmsley	12	31	22	-	1	not out	6	17	11	-	1
I.E.O'Brien not out	0	2	0	-	-	c Horne b Adams	0	9	9	-	-
Extras (b 1, lb 10, nb 12)	23					(lb 3, w 1, nb 3)	7				
TOTAL (122.1 overs)	**427**	481				(57.5 overs)	**107**	238			

AUCKLAND

	Runs	*Mins*	*Balls*	*6s*	*4s*		*Runs*	*Mins*	*Balls*	*6s*	*4s*
R.A.Jones b O'Brien	17	65	42	-	2	lbw b Patel	25	89	65	-	3
M.J.Horne lbw b O'Brien	88	194	148	-	12	c Mills b O'Brien	75	211	141	1	9
R.J.Nicol c Bell b Woodcock	49	227	172	-	6	lbw b Patel	16	48	46	-	2
L.Vincent c Ryder b Franklin	26	32	33	-	3	not out	53	144	123	-	4
A.C.Barnes c Bell b Ryder	75	183	130	-	14	b Patel	28	52	37	-	5
T.K.Canning b Franklin	4	29	27	-	-	not out	8	16	12	1	-
C.Cachopa b O'Brien	17	152	123	-	1						
B.G.K.Walker* c Woodcock b Franklin	11	78	65	-	-						
R.A.Young† not out	8	26	13	-	2						
A.R.Adams c Ryder b O'Brien	1	5	6	-	-						
K.P.Walmsley c Bell b Franklin	9	6	6	-	2						
Extras (b 1, lb 9, w 2, nb 11)	23					(b 1, lb 1, nb 3)	5				
TOTAL (125.5 overs)	**328**	458				(70.1 overs) (4 wkts)	**210**	284			

Bowling	*O*	*M*	*R*	*W*	*O*	*M*	*R*	*W*
AUCKLAND								
Walmsley	24.1	3	107	2	15	4	32	3
Adams	36	12	93	4	21.5	12	25	6
Canning	10	5	14	0				
Barnes	12	1	51	0	7	2	15	1
Walker	28	2	108	3	7	0	20	0
Vincent	12	3	43	1	7	3	12	0
WELLINGTON								
Gillespie	14	2	63	0	3	1	16	0
Franklin	28.5	8	64	4	7	2	32	0
O'Brien	36	14	76	4	19	4	44	1
Patel	16	1	53	0	21.1	4	65	3
Woodcock	26	9	46	1	20	4	51	0
Ryder	5	0	16	1				

Fall of Wickets

	W *1st*	***A*** *1st*	***W*** *2nd*	***A*** *2nd*
1st	19	37	0	60
2nd	42	137	24	95
3rd	102	170	62	149
4th	104	223	69	188
5th	133	239	87	-
6th	253	287	90	-
7th	331	310	100	-
8th	399	314	100	-
9th	427	315	101	-
10th	427	328	107	-

NORTHERN DISTRICTS v CANTERBURY State Championship

at Harry Barker Reserve, Gisborne on 21, 22 February, 2005
Toss : Canterbury. Umpires : G.A. Baxter & T.J. Parlane
Close of play: 1st day: Canterbury 265-8, Ellis 68, Shaw 0
***Canterbury won by an innings and 55 runs.** Points: Canterbury 8, Northern Districts 0*

The Papps brothers gave Canterbury a good start with 103 for the first wicket and by the time bad light ended the day's play the score had advanced to 265-8. Canterbury ended with 310 the next morning with Ellis posting his career best score.

Northern were soon in trouble at 8-3 and never recovered. They were eventually all out for just 90 and were asked to follow on. Wickets continued to fall. Northern were 4-2 and then 30-4 before Yovich helped Orchard to add 81 in even time.

Once the partnership was broken, however, the result was inevitable and Canterbury secured an innings victory at 6.53 pm with two days to spare. Michael Papps made six dismissals in the second innings, equalling the Canterbury record.

James Marshall was called into the New Zealand team on the first day and replaced by Robinson. McGlashan, who had not previously led a team at first-class level, took over as captain.

CANTERBURY

FIRST INNINGS	*Runs*	*Mins*	*Balls*	*6s*	*4s*	*SECOND INNINGS*	*Runs*	*Mins*	*Balls*	*6s*	*4s*
T.J.T.Papps c McGlashan b Davis	33	126	83	-	4						
M.H.W.Papps† b Davis	74	136	113	-	13						
T.G.McIntosh c Watling b Martin	1	26	20	-	-						
P.G.Fulton* c Aldridge b Davis	31	99	74	-	5						
S.L.Stewart c Davis b Martin	1	15	20	-	-						
G.R.Stead c Devcich b Yovich	4	6	5	-	1						
A.M.Ellis c Watling b Aldridge	78	170	137	-	14						
P.J.Wiseman lbw b Martin	13	29	22	-	3						
S.J.Cunis c Watling b Aldridge	14	54	56	-	2						
H.J.Shaw not out	23	41	28	1	2						
C.S.Martin c Orchard b Yovich	6	16	8	-	-						
Extras (lb 7, w 3, nb 22)	32										
TOTAL (90.4 overs)	**310**	364									

NORTHERN DISTRICTS

	Runs	Mins	Balls	6s	4s		Runs	Mins	Balls	6s	4s
B.S.Wilson c Papps T.J.T. b Martin	7	27	18	-	1	c McIntosh b Martin	0	11	11	-	-
B-J.Watling b Cunis	1	33	27	-	-	c Papps M.H.W. b Cunis	4	13	7	-	1
M.G.Orchard b Martin	0	8	3	-	-	c Papps M.H.W. b Martin	37	139	117	-	5
G.G.Robinson c McIntosh b Wiseman	17	48	34	-	3	c Papps M.H.W. b Cunis	13	35	28	-	2
D.R.Flynn b Shaw	9	52	38	-	1	c McIntosh b Shaw	1	14	10	-	-
J.A.F.Yovich c Fulton b Wiseman	9	19	12	-	1	st Papps M.H.W. b Cunis	59	107	77	-	10
A.P.Devcich c Fulton b Shaw	26	53	48	-	5	c Papps M.H.W. b Martin	4	16	11	-	1
P.D.McGlashan*† c Papps M.H.W. b Wiseman	0	9	6	-	-	c Papps M.H.W. b Shaw	24	33	30	-	4
B.P.Martin c Stead b Martin	0	17	13	-	-	not out	16	44	26	-	3
G.W.Aldridge not out	1	17	10	-	-	c Fulton b Wiseman	0	9	7	-	-
T.T.Davis c Papps M.H.W. b Shaw	1	5	6	-	-	lbw b Shaw	1	3	5	-	-
J.A.H.Marshall*											
Extras (b 4, lb 4, nb 11)	19					(lb 1, w 2, nb 3)	6				
TOTAL (34.4 overs)	**90**	148				(54.2 overs)	**165**	217			

Bowling	*O*	*M*	*R*	*W*	*O*	*M*	*R*	*W*
NORTHERN DISTRICTS								
Yovich	19.4	1	89	2				
Aldridge	18	3	72	2				
Orchard	17	5	48	0				
Davis	13	3	61	3				
Martin	23	9	33	3				
CANTERBURY								
Martin	12	4	27	3	11	3	18	3
Cunis	8	4	12	1	12	3	41	3
Shaw	5.4	0	27	3	10.2	2	41	3
Wiseman	9	2	16	3	15	5	54	1
Ellis					6	4	10	0

Fall of Wickets	***C***	***ND***	***ND***
	1st	*1st*	*2nd*
1st	103	8	4
2nd	117	8	4
3rd	126	8	20
4th	131	38	30
5th	135	41	111
6th	182	64	122
7th	219	70	122
8th	265	83	153
9th	287	88	160
10th	310	90	165

CENTRAL DISTRICTS v WELLINGTON State Championship

at McLean Park, Napier on 21, 22, 23 February, 2005
Toss : Wellington. Umpires : D.B. Cowie & B.G. Frost
Close of play: 1st day: Wellington 321-3, Bell 114, Patel 0; 2nd day: CD 106-8, Diamanti 3, Schwass 0
Wellington won by an innings and 33 runs. *Points: Wellington 8, Central Districts 0*

Bell and Michael Parlane dominated the first day with a partnership of 215, a second wicket record by any side against Central. The Wellington captain reached his century off 248 balls in 350 minutes while Parlane needed only 177 balls in 202 minutes.

Next morning Central did well to restrict Wellington to 402 but then spent the rest of the day crawling to 106-8 from 65 overs. Only an obdurate innings of 45 from Ingram, who was out at 103-7, prevented complete disaster.

Central were asked to follow on. Barnett registered his maiden fifty and Englefield scored 61. Diamanti and Schwass hit thirties towards the end of the innings but could not prevent Wellington from sealing an innings victory at 5.46 pm with a day to spare.

WELLINGTON

FIRST INNINGS	*Runs*	*Mins*	*Balls*	*6s*	*4s*	*SECOND INNINGS*	*Runs*	*Mins*	*Balls*	*6s*	*4s*
M.D.Bell* c Griggs b Thompson	118	418	292	1	16						
L.J.Woodcock b Hamilton	15	35	30	-	1						
M.E.Parlane c Englefield b Sulzberger	132	248	220	3	16						
J.D.Ryder c Barnett b Sulzberger	38	91	75	-	5						
J.S.Patel b Sulzberger	30	117	91	-	3						
N.R.Parlane lbw b Thompson	0	1	1	-	-						
J.E.C.Franklin c How b Thompson	0	17	12	-	-						
C.J.Nevin c Ingram b Diamanti	19	51	36	-	3						
S.M.Mills† c Griggs b Thompson	0	8	5	-	-						
M.R.Gillespie c Ingram b Sulzberger	16	36	31	-	1						
I.E.O'Brien not out	7	32	32	-	1						
Extras (b 2, lb 5, w 4, nb 16)	27										
TOTAL (135 overs)	**402**	533									

CENTRAL DISTRICTS

	Runs	Mins	Balls	6s	4s		Runs	Mins	Balls	6s	4s
P.J.Ingram b Gillespie	45	252	209	-	4	c & b O'Brien	8	74	51	-	1
J.M.How c Mills b Franklin	12	47	37	-	1	c Parlane N.R. b Franklin	22	48	37	-	3
G.E.F.Barnett c Mills b O'Brien	3	30	15	-	-	c Parlane M.E. b O'Brien	56	158	120	-	8
G.P.Sulzberger* c Patel b Gillespie	10	24	18	-	1	c O'Brien b Gillespie	7	24	20	-	-
J.I.Englefield run out	0	10	8	-	-	c Ryder b Woodcock	61	182	144	-	6
R.L.Taylor c Parlane N.R. b Patel	8	39	30	-	1	c Mills b Gillespie	1	4	4	-	-
B.B.J.Griggs† b Woodcock	9	49	48	-	1	b O'Brien	18	31	31	1	1
E.P.Thompson c Mills b Gillespie	5	31	17	-	1	c Patel b O'Brien	2	8	6	-	-
B.J.Diamanti not out	4	32	17	-	-	run out	33	55	43	-	5
A.M.Schwass c Parlane N.R. b Woodcock	0	4	4	-	-	not out	35	64	58	-	4
L.J.Hamilton lbw b O'Brien	0	11	20	-	-	lbw b Franklin	2	34	24	-	-
Extras (lb 2, nb 9)	11					(b 1, lb 7, nb 9)	17				
TOTAL (69 overs)	**107**	272				(88.1 overs)	**262**	350			

Bowling	*O*	*M*	*R*	*W*				
CENTRAL DISTRICTS								
Hamilton	25	6	75	1				
Thompson	33	11	81	4				
Schwass	14	2	41	0				
Diamanti	21	9	56	1				
Sulzberger	30	6	89	4				
How	12	0	53	0				
WELLINGTON								
Gillespie	12	3	16	3	16	3	65	2
Franklin	13	2	27	1	11.1	3	23	2
O'Brien	17	8	23	2	23	9	47	4
Patel	18	7	28	1	24	6	76	0
Woodcock	9	5	11	2	8	1	28	1
Ryder					6	1	15	0

Fall of Wickets	***W***	***CD***	***CD***
	1st	*1st*	*2nd*
1st	22	18	30
2nd	237	32	32
3rd	312	51	53
4th	333	55	139
5th	333	75	140
6th	335	95	161
7th	378	103	168
8th	378	104	199
9th	380	106	232
10th	402	107	262

AUCKLAND v OTAGO — State Championship

at Eden Park Outer Oval, Auckland on 21, 22, 23, 24 February, 2005
Toss : Otago. Umpires : I.W. Shine & E.A. Watkin
Close of play: 1st day: Otago 348-9, Scott 96, Smith 2; 2nd day: Auckland 318-4, Barnes 3, Canning 0
3rd day: Otago 33-0, Gaffaney 19, Cumming 12
First innings win to Auckland. *Points: Auckland 2, Otago 0*

After they had won the toss and batted Otago struggled and only Gaffaney, out at 137-8 for 78, showed any resistance. At this point, however, Scott (previous best 33) joined McSkimming (one first-class fifty) and the pair proceeded to add 208 in just 196 minutes.

This was a ninth wicket record for Otago against all teams and all teams against Auckland and the third highest for the wicket in New Zealand first-class cricket. Otago's previous best for the ninth wicket against Auckland was just 64 set back in 1936/37. McSkimming reached his century after 218 minutes from 164 balls while Scott just failed to register his maiden hundred.

Auckland's reply was built round a third wicket partnership of 244 between Nicol and Vincent. Nicol went to his hundred after 242 minutes and 231 balls while Vincent needed 172 balls in 195 minutes. Auckland finally declared late on the second day with a lead of 180.

Otago had no trouble in saving the match. Gaffaney reached his century after 294 minutes from 253 balls and Cumming and Redmond weighed in with half-centuries. Smith made his first-class debut in this game.

OTAGO

FIRST INNINGS	*Runs*	*Mins*	*Balls*	*6s*	*4s*	*SECOND INNINGS*	*Runs*	*Mins*	*Balls*	*6s*	*4s*
C.D.Cumming* b Walmsley	13	25	27	-	2	(2) lbw b Walmsley	52	213	180	-	11
C.B.Gaffaney lbw b Canning	78	190	133	-	14	(1) b Canning	103	316	272	1	12
A.J.Redmond c Young b Walmsley	6	32	26	-	1	not out	71	196	131	-	13
G.R.Todd c Cachopa b Barnes	12	23	18	-	3	lbw b Adams	4	9	5	-	1
G.J.Hopkins† c Adams b Canning	1	22	18	-	-	not out	20	83	69	-	1
J.W.Sheed c Young b Canning	5	10	9	-	1						
Mohammad Wasim c Young b Walmsley	3	22	20	-	-						
N.L.McCullum c Walker b Walmsley	10	23	13	-	2						
W.C.McSkimming b Barnes	111	223	170	2	16						
B.E.Scott b Walmsley	96	209	163	1	17						
C.M.Smith not out	2	14	10	-	-						
Extras (lb 6, w 1, nb 4)	11					(b 17, lb 7, w 5, nb 3)	32				
TOTAL (100.3 overs)	**348**	398				(109 overs) (3 wkts)	**282**	410			

AUCKLAND

	Runs	Mins	Balls	6s	4s
R.A.Jones lbw b Scott	17	38	30	-	3
M.J.Horne b Scott	35	75	53	-	5
R.J.Nicol c Sheed b McSkimming	100	302	239	1	13
L.Vincent c McSkimming b Todd	152	285	241	2	22
A.C.Barnes c Hopkins b McSkimming	43	155	126	-	4
T.K.Canning b McCullum	38	172	150	2	3
C.Cachopa st Hopkins b McCullum	40	158	115	-	6
A.R.Adams b Smith	53	68	58	1	8
B.G.K.Walker* not out	29	66	54	-	3
R.A.Young† not out	3	14	12	-	-
K.P.Walmsley					
Extras (b 1, lb 11, w 2, nb 4)	18				
TOTAL (179 overs) (8 wkts dec)	**528**	670			

Bowling	*O*	*M*	*R*	*W*	*O*	*M*	*R*	*W*
AUCKLAND								
Walmsley	23.3	6	73	5	20	6	65	1
Adams	27	6	90	0	25	9	53	1
Canning	30	7	100	3	27	13	45	1
Barnes	10	1	35	2	15	7	23	0
Walker	8	3	34	0	12	1	37	0
Vincent	2	0	10	0	2	0	2	0
Nicol					5	0	28	0
Cachopa					3	0	5	0
OTAGO								
McSkimming	39	14	85	2				
Scott	32	5	106	2				
Smith	28	6	87	1				
Todd	21	6	65	1				
McCullum	41	8	124	2				
Cumming	15	6	29	0				
Redmond	3	0	20	0				

Fall of Wickets	*O*	*A*	*O*
	1st	*1st*	*2nd*
1st	22	33	129
2nd	40	63	202
3rd	63	307	215
4th	71	317	-
5th	83	388	-
6th	95	405	-
7th	116	479	-
8th	137	519	-
9th	345	-	-
10th	348	-	-

OTAGO v AUCKLAND — State Championship

at University Oval, Dunedin on 4, 5, 6, 7 March, 2005
Toss : Auckland. Umpires : C.J. Morris & E.A. Watkin
Close of play: 1st day: Auckland 46-4, Barnes 16, Young 5; 2nd day: Auckland 161-7, Cachopa 6, Todd 0
3rd day: Otago 93-9, Scott 0
***Auckland won by 3 runs.** Points: Auckland 6, Otago 2*

Otago registered a solid first innings with half-centuries from Redmond and Todd plus more late runs from McSkimming. By the close they were well on top having captured four Auckland wickets and the visitors fared no better on the second day being dismisssed for just 101.

Auckland were required to follow on and lost seven wickets before the deficit was wiped off. On the third morning Cachopa (playing his third game) and Todd (on debut) put on 88 for the eighth wicket in 91 minutes. Shaw and McKay resisted while Todd added some more valuable runs.

Even so, Otago required just 112 to win but Barnes (who opened the bowling with Hitchcock), Shaw and McKay captured three wickets apiece to have Otago 93-9 at stumps. On the last morning Smith joined Scott and the pair had added 15 runs in 35 minutes before Barnes trapped the number eleven in front. It was just the fifth time in New Zealand first-class cricket that a team had won after following on.

Eighteen-year-old Eathorne made his first-class debut in this match while Gaffaney captained a side at first-class level for the first time. McCullum equalled the Otago fielding record for catches in an innings and match.

OTAGO

FIRST INNINGS	*Runs*	*Mins*	*Balls*	*6s*	*4s*	*SECOND INNINGS*	*Runs*	*Mins*	*Balls*	*6s*	*4s*
C.B.Gaffaney* b Shaw	8	31	22	-	2	b Barnes	10	12	13	-	1
A.J.Redmond c Jones b Horne	52	127	87	-	1	c Nicol b McKay	4	16	6	-	1
J.W.Sheed lbw b McKay	0	5	2	-	-	c Young b Barnes	0	11	4	-	-
G.R.Todd b Barnes	73	259	182	-	10	(5) b Shaw	25	122	86	-	1
M.N.McKenzie c Young b Shaw	1	15	9	-	-	(4) c Nicol b Barnes	3	23	10	-	-
G.J.Hopkins† lbw b Shaw	0	1	1	-	-	b McKay	9	60	36	-	1
S.W.Eathorne c Cachopa b Hitchcock	10	25	22	-	2	c Nicol b Shaw	13	34	31	-	1
N.L.McCullum c Young b McKay	22	54	35	-	3	lbw b Shaw	16	19	16	1	1
W.C.McSkimming c Young b Hitchcock	46	65	57	-	8	c & b McKay	5	26	13	-	1
B.E.Scott not out	10	31	18	-	1	not out	13	51	35	-	2
C.M.Smith c Young b Barnes	6	26	23	-	1	lbw b Barnes	2	34	23	-	-
Extras (b 4, lb 16, w 15, nb 5)	40					(lb 4, nb 4)	8				
TOTAL (75.3 overs)	**268**	322				(44.5 overs)	**108**	215			

AUCKLAND

FIRST INNINGS	*Runs*	*Mins*	*Balls*	*6s*	*4s*	*SECOND INNINGS*	*Runs*	*Mins*	*Balls*	*6s*	*4s*
R.A.Jones run out	17	58	43	-	3	b McSkimming	20	86	64	-	2
M.J.Horne c Hopkins b Scott	4	6	6	-	1	b Todd	45	154	125	-	8
R.J.Nicol c Hopkins b McSkimming	1	12	11	-	-	c Hopkins b McSkimming	0	1	1	-	-
C.Cachopa c Hopkins b McSkimming	0	7	4	-	-	(6) c McCullum b McSkimming	32	149	114	-	7
A.C.Barnes c Gaffaney b McSkimming	16	67	54	-	2	c McCullum b Scott	34	66	67	1	5
R.A.Young† run out	5	41	28	-	1	(7) lbw b McSkimming	6	16	13	-	1
K.W.M.Todd b McSkimming	5	36	26	-	1	(9) c McCullum b Scott	84	130	92	1	15
P.A.Hitchcock not out	31	125	97	-	3	b Scott	1	11	6	-	-
B.G.K.Walker* c McCullum b McSkimming	1	28	20	-	-	(4) c Todd b Smith	27	103	77	-	3
G.S.Shaw lbw b Scott	4	33	26	-	-	c McCullum b Smith	2	20	19	-	-
A.J.McKay c Sheed b Smith	1	31	25	-	-	not out	3	17	23	-	-
Extras (b 1, lb 11, w 2, nb 2)	16					(b 1, lb 19, w 1, nb 3)	24				
TOTAL (56.2 overs)	**101**	231				(99.4 overs)	**278**	386			

Bowling	*O*	*M*	*R*	*W*				
AUCKLAND								
Shaw	14	1	67	3	8	4	19	3
McKay	14	0	49	2	13	4	34	3
Barnes	19.3	6	50	2	16.5	2	41	4
Hitchcock	23	6	52	2	7	2	10	0
Horne	5	2	30	1				
OTAGO								
McSkimming	20	12	29	5	31	9	104	4
Scott	20	9	26	2	25.4	10	49	3
Smith	10.2	2	20	1	23	6	59	2
Todd	6	3	14	0	14	1	45	1
McCullum					6	5	1	0

Fall of Wickets	*O*	*A*	*A*	*O*
	1st	*1st*	*2nd*	*2nd*
1st	28	6	42	15
2nd	33	8	42	15
3rd	92	12	98	17
4th	95	31	110	22
5th	95	46	148	53
6th	121	50	160	70
7th	163	61	161	77
8th	241	69	249	88
9th	243	90	268	93
10th	268	101	278	108

CENTRAL DISTRICTS v CANTERBURY State Championship

at Pukekura Park, New Plymouth on 4, 5, 6, 7 March, 2005
Toss : Canterbury. Umpires : P.D. Jones & D.M. Quested
Close of play: 1st day: CD 439-7, Thompson 98, Diamanti 35; 2nd day: Canterbury 87-3, Fulton 37, Stead 7
3rd day: Canterbury 158-4, Stead 47, Broom 3
***Central Districts won by an innings and 19 runs.** Points: Central Districts 8, Canterbury 0*

Central took advantage of being sent in and ran up 439 on the first day. How, Englefield and Taylor (highest score) all made fifties but the star was Thompson, batting at number eight. He completed his second century of the season the next morning, requiring only 72 balls in 99 minutes. Extras also topped the half century.

Canterbury lost Papps in the first over and were 87-3 when rain curtailed play for the day. Fulton and Ellis registered fifties the next day but it was nowhere near enough for Canterbury to avert the follow-on.

Canterbury were 28-3 in their second innings before Stead helped Fulton add 111. The Canterbury captain dominated the scoring but went just before the close.

Stead went without adding a run the next day and Central worked their way through the rest of the batting to register an innings win just after midday. Hegglun made his first-class debut in this game.

CENTRAL DISTRICTS

FIRST INNINGS	*Runs*	*Mins*	*Balls*	*6s*	*4s*	*SECOND INNINGS*	*Runs*	*Mins*	*Balls*	*6s*	*4s*
P.J.Ingram b Ellis	18	128	95	-	3						
J.M.How c & b Ellis	50	56	53	1	7						
M.S.Sinclair c Papps b Ellis	0	5	2	-	-						
G.P.Sulzberger* c Ellis b Bond	10	31	23	-	2						
J.I.Englefield b Stewart	81	208	166	2	10						
R.L.Taylor b Stewart	78	142	110	1	12						
B.B.J.Griggs† lbw b Shaw	25	78	61	-	4						
E.P.Thompson c Broom b Shaw	126	133	96	3	19						
B.J.Diamanti b Shaw	44	70	64	-	10						
R.M.West not out	7	35	24	-	-						
G.J.T.Hegglun c McIntosh b Ellis	8	19	13	-	-						
Extras (b 7, lb 9, w 8, nb 28)	52										
TOTAL (113.1 overs)	**499**	460									

CANTERBURY

	Runs	Mins	Balls	6s	4s		Runs	Mins	Balls	6s	4s
T.J.T.Papps† c Taylor b Thompson	0	3	5	-	-	(2) lbw b Hegglun	9	47	33	-	-
T.G.McIntosh c Griggs b Thompson	5	50	36	-	-	(1) c & b Diamanti	1	21	19	-	-
P.G.Fulton* c Griggs b Diamanti	60	176	138	-	10	c How b West	91	142	115	1	17
S.L.Stewart lbw b Diamanti	25	72	62	-	5	lbw b Thompson	0	5	3	-	-
G.R.Stead c Griggs b Sulzberger	43	124	94	-	6	c How b Hegglun	47	166	130	-	7
N.T.Broom c Thompson b Diamanti	4	9	8	-	1	b Sulzberger	20	99	79	-	4
A.M.Ellis b Thompson	76	111	95	5	7	c Ingram b West	10	38	35	-	2
S.E.Bond c Englefield b West	15	38	41	-	2	b West	21	36	28	1	2
H.J.Shaw b West	0	8	3	-	-	c Sinclair b Sulzberger	22	19	14	3	1
J.S.Ward not out	0	10	5	-	-	not out	5	21	20	-	-
C.J.Cornelius c Griggs b Hegglun	0	3	4	-	-	c Thompson b Sulzberger	2	10	11	-	-
Extras (b 1, lb 12, w 3, nb 1)	17					(lb 3, w 1, nb 3)	7				
TOTAL (81.3 overs)	**245**	307				(80.4 overs)	**235**	309			

Bowling	*O*	*M*	*R*	*W*	*O*	*M*	*R*	*W*
CANTERBURY								
Bond	19	5	85	1				
Shaw	27	4	127	3				
Cornelius	13	3	76	0				
Ellis	35.1	9	103	4				
Ward	3	0	29	0				
Stewart	14	4	52	2				
Broom	2	0	11	0				
CENTRAL DISTRICTS								
Thompson	17	4	57	3	15	1	50	1
Hegglun	16.3	6	29	1	15	6	49	2
Diamanti	18	6	42	3	22	11	42	1
West	19	6	54	2	21	6	58	3
Sulzberger	11	3	50	1	7.4	2	33	3

Fall of Wickets	***CD***	***C***	***C***
	1st	*1st*	*2nd*
1st	62	0	4
2nd	62	22	27
3rd	84	72	28
4th	102	126	139
5th	261	132	158
6th	288	195	184
7th	347	232	186
8th	458	244	226
9th	482	244	230
10th	499	245	235

WELLINGTON v NORTHERN DISTRICTS State Championship

at Basin Reserve, Wellington on 4, 5, 6, 7 March, 2005
Toss : Wellington. Umpires : G.A. Baxter & M. Erasmus
Close of play: 1st day: ND 46-2, Evans 17, Hart 15; 2nd day: Wellington 22-1, Woodcock 1, M.E.Parlane 19
3rd day: ND 4-0, Watling 0, Wilson 3
***Wellington won by 37 runs.** Points: Wellington 8, Northern Districts 0*

Wellington made a disastrous start to the game being 54-6 before Murray joined Neal Parlane and took the score to 120. Gillespie and Patel also batted sensibly to ensure that Wellington finished with a respectable total.

Northern lost two wickets before the close and the following day, despite a maiden fifty from Flynn, just failed to reach the home team's total. The next day Mills recorded his first fifty as Wellington were bowled out just before stumps, leaving Northern 264 to win.

On the last day Northern made a good start to their chase and were 86-1 but then lost wickets regularly to be 128-5. Flynn and McGlashan added 48 for the seventh wicket but once the partnership was broken the remaining wickets soon fell, Wellington winning by 37 runs. Gilhooly made his first-class debut in this match.

WELLINGTON

FIRST INNINGS	Runs	Mins	Balls	6s	4s	SECOND INNINGS	Runs	Mins	Balls	6s	4s
M.D.Bell* lbw b Tuffey	5	20	21	-	1	lbw b Tuffey	0	8	11	-	-
L.J.Woodcock c Devcich b Yovich	6	24	12	-	-	lbw b Martin	25	141	96	-	2
M.E.Parlane c McGlashan b Yovich	10	54	32	-	1	c McGlashan b Tuffey	27	66	51	-	4
J.D.Ryder c & b Tuffey	19	30	28	1	-	(5) c Watling b Martin	23	87	65	1	4
N.R.Parlane c McGlashan b Tuffey	83	260	199	1	9	(4) lbw b Martin	11	33	26	-	-
C.J.Nevin c & b Martin	3	11	11	-	-	lbw b Tuffey	5	17	20	-	1
S.M.Mills† lbw b Martin	0	4	1	-	-	b Martin	64	218	176	-	10
G.B.Murray c McGlashan b Yovich	33	87	73	-	5	b Yovich	33	137	86	1	2
M.R.Gillespie b Orchard	28	62	57	-	5	c Devcich b Yovich	4	12	16	-	1
J.S.Patel lbw b Orchard	33	74	65	-	6	not out	35	46	41	1	4
R.J.Gilhooly not out	4	2	1	-	1	c Evans b Orchard	13	22	11	-	2
Extras (b 4, lb 9, w 1, nb 12)	26					(b 2, lb 3, w 1, nb 9)	15				
TOTAL (81.1 overs)	**250**	319				(98.2 overs)	**255**	397			

NORTHERN DISTRICTS

FIRST INNINGS	Runs	Mins	Balls	6s	4s	SECOND INNINGS	Runs	Mins	Balls	6s	4s
B-J.Watling c Mills b Gillespie	3	13	10	-	-	c Mills b Gillespie	7	82	63	-	1
B.S.Wilson lbw b Gillespie	4	32	24	-	-	b Ryder	48	250	184	-	5
A.W.Evans c Parlane N.R. b Gilhooly	27	109	85	-	5	c Parlane N.R. b Gillespie	37	118	102	-	2
M.N.Hart* b Ryder	36	130	91	-	6	c Parlane N.R. b Ryder	15	57	37	-	2
D.R.Flynn lbw b Patel	62	181	131	-	10	run out	26	117	96	-	2
J.A.F.Yovich b Patel	0	5	8	-	-	c & b Woodcock	9	13	15	-	2
A.P.Devcich lbw b Gillespie	21	101	77	-	4	lbw b Patel	19	38	36	-	4
M.G.Orchard c Bell b Patel	20	39	36	-	2	(10) not out	3	25	10	-	-
P.D.McGlashan† not out	24	60	54	-	3	(8) lbw b Patel	24	74	43	-	3
D.R.Tuffey c Parlane N.R. b Ryder	12	46	26	-	2	(9) lbw b Patel	19	26	19	-	3
B.P.Martin c Woodcock b Ryder	0	7	6	-	-	lbw b Gillespie	2	16	13	-	-
Extras (b 1, lb 12, w 8, nb 12)	33					(b 4, lb 7, nb 6)	17				
TOTAL (89.2 overs)	**242**	356				(102 overs)	**226**	392			

Bowling	*O*	*M*	*R*	*W*	*O*	*M*	*R*	*W*
NORTHERN DISTRICTS								
Tuffey	22	6	65	3	22.3	6	52	3
Yovich	19	2	62	3	20	3	63	2
Orchard	10.1	3	34	2	14.5	2	40	1
Martin	30	4	76	2	37	11	91	4
Evans					4	1	4	0
WELLINGTON								
Gillespie	25	5	53	3	30	11	47	3
Gilhooly	12	2	46	1	3	0	9	0
Ryder	12.2	6	32	3	16	4	39	2
Patel	20	8	48	3	32	9	81	3
Murray	13	5	33	0	4	1	11	0
Woodcock	7	0	17	0	17	5	28	1

Fall of Wickets

	W *1st*	***ND*** *1st*	***W*** *2nd*	***ND*** *2nd*
1st	11	4	1	26
2nd	13	10	38	86
3rd	41	71	65	114
4th	47	94	80	115
5th	54	95	93	128
6th	54	181	106	152
7th	120	203	192	200
8th	174	206	199	216
9th	226	242	226	221
10th	250	242	255	226

OTAGO v CANTERBURY — State Championship

at University Oval, Dunedin on 11, 12, 13, 14 March, 2005
Toss : Canterbury. Umpires : M. Erasmus & D.M. Quested
Close of play: 1st day: Canterbury 163-4, Stead 20, Broom 40; 2nd day: Canterbury 23-2, Fulton 2, Wiseman 10
3rd day: Canterbury 374-5, Fulton 221, Broom 109
***Canterbury won by 168 runs.** Points: Canterbury 8, Otago 0*

Canterbury finished a shortened first day at 163-4 but next morning Sewell claimed five wickets in seven overs to hasten the end of the innings. Otago were 133-2 in reply but faltered and were bowled out 16 runs short of Canterbury's score.

Otago responded by taking two Canterbury wickets before stumps and on the third morning had reduced the visitors to 81-5, a lead of just 97. At this stage Broom joined Fulton and the pair batted throughout the rest of the day, putting on 293 in even time. Their partnership was the highest for the sixth wicket in all New Zealand first-class cricket and the highest by either side for any wicket in 162 games between the two teams stretching back to 1863/64.

Fulton reached three figures after 230 minutes and 180 balls and his double century after 370 minutes and 298 balls. Broom's maiden hundred came after 285 minutes and 214 balls. Fulton's score was the highest for Canterbury against Otago and the highest at University Oval.

Fulton declared overnight, leaving Otago all day to score 391 to win. Gaffaney went second ball and Redmond soon followed. Todd resisted for over three hours but the end came at 4.38 pm when Scott became Wiseman's eleventh victim of the match.

CANTERBURY

FIRST INNINGS	*Runs*	*Mins*	*Balls*	*6s*	*4s*	*SECOND INNINGS*	*Runs*	*Mins*	*Balls*	*6s*	*4s*
T.J.T.Papps c Wasim b McSkimming	13	35	28	-	2	lbw b McSkimming	6	21	21	-	1
M.H.W.Papps† c Hopkins b McSkimming	1	7	5	-	-	lbw b McSkimming	4	26	18	-	-
P.G.Fulton* c McCullum b McSkimming	44	152	123	-	7	not out	221	416	332	4	28
S.L.Stewart lbw b Redmond	44	118	103	1	4	(5) lbw b Sewell	10	54	49	-	2
G.R.Stead b Sewell	20	98	69	-	2	(6) c Todd b McSkimming	4	33	20	-	-
N.T.Broom lbw b Sewell	40	81	83	-	7	(7) not out	109	295	222	1	18
A.M.Ellis b McSkimming	4	6	4	-	-						
P.J.Wiseman c McCullum b Sewell	13	59	42	-	2	(4) c Hopkins b McSkimming	12	26	28	-	1
S.J.Cunis c Hopkins b Sewell	22	45	42	-	4						
S.E.Bond not out	10	20	10	-	2						
H.J.Shaw c Hopkins b Sewell	6	11	7	-	1						
Extras (lb 1, nb 1)	2					(b 2, lb 6)	8				
TOTAL (85.5 overs)	**219**	325				(115 overs) (5 wkts dec)	**374**	438			

OTAGO

Batsman	*Runs*	*Mins*	*Balls*	*6s*	*4s*	Second innings	*Runs*	*Mins*	*Balls*	*6s*	*4s*
C.B.Gaffaney* st Papps M.H.W. b Wiseman	42	151	114	-	6	b Bond	0	1	2	-	-
Mohammad Wasim c Fulton b Cunis	23	96	69	-	2	c Cunis b Bond	45	166	114	-	4
A.J.Redmond b Wiseman	51	99	79	1	8	lbw b Cunis	7	15	15	-	1
G.R.Todd c Stead b Shaw	20	28	25	-	3	lbw b Wiseman	65	193	156	2	7
M.N.McKenzie b Wiseman	5	25	14	-	-	lbw b Wiseman	1	6	9	-	-
G.J.Hopkins† run out	3	14	12	-	-	b Wiseman	2	27	19	-	-
S.W.Eathorne b Wiseman	3	23	21	-	-	c Broom b Wiseman	28	68	54	-	4
N.L.McCullum c Shaw b Bond	35	67	43	-	5	c & b Stead	33	47	40	1	3
W.C.McSkimming c Papps T.J.T. b Wiseman	0	2	5	-	-	c Broom b Wiseman	11	32	29	-	2
B.E.Scott c Papps M.H.W. b Cunis	10	23	12	-	2	c Broom b Wiseman	18	36	29	-	3
D.G.Sewell not out	1	22	13	-	-	not out	0	15	10	-	-
Extras (lb 5, nb 5)	10					(b 6, lb 1, nb 5)	12				
TOTAL (67 overs)	**203**	284				(78.4 overs)	**222**	313			

Bowling	*O*	*M*	*R*	*W*	*O*	*M*	*R*	*W*
OTAGO								
Sewell	19.5	5	51	5	25	4	81	1
McSkimming	20	5	33	4	30	10	79	4
Scott	17	4	42	0	20	4	68	0
McCullum	10	1	37	0	22	3	63	0
Todd	7	3	18	0	15	4	49	0
Redmond	12	1	37	1	3	0	26	0
CANTERBURY								
Bond	11	1	42	1	20	5	51	2
Cunis	18	4	45	2	11	0	40	1
Shaw	15	2	44	1	10	1	52	0
Ellis	7	2	19	0	4	0	10	0
Wiseman	16	5	48	5	31.4	12	57	6
Stead					2	0	5	1

Fall of Wickets	*C* *1st*	*O* *1st*	*C* *2nd*	*O* *2nd*
1st	2	52	9	0
2nd	15	104	10	9
3rd	101	133	25	107
4th	105	146	53	108
5th	163	148	81	122
6th	168	151	-	133
7th	168	163	-	180
8th	198	163	-	193
9th	203	179	-	206
10th	219	203	-	222

CENTRAL DISTRICTS v WELLINGTON State Championship

at Fitzherbert Park, Palmerston North on 11, 12, 13, 14 March, 2005
Toss : Wellington. Umpires : I.W. Shine & D.J. Walker
Close of play: 1st day: Wellington 198-2, M.E.Parlane 52, Ryder 55; 2nd day: Wellington 587-8, Mills 6, Patel 0
3rd day: CD 360-4, Englefield 108, Taylor 131
***First innings win to Wellington.** Points: Wellington 2, Central Districts 0*

After a late start, Wellington took advantage of winning the toss and had reached 198-2 at the close. Michael Parlane went early next day making way for his brother who proceeded to put on 310 in 272 minutes with Ryder, the highest fourth wicket partnership in the history of New Zealand inter-provincial cricket and the third highest overall.

Ryder took 281 balls and 324 minutes to reach his century and went on to his first double century. It was the highest innings for Wellington against Central and the highest by any player at Fitzherbert Park. Parlane required 210 balls and 233 minutes for his hundred. Wellington's total was the highest by any side against Central and the best by any team at the ground.

Central began their innings on the third day and their reply was also built around a major partnership. Englefield, who reached his century after 218 minutes from 157 balls, and Taylor, whose maiden hundred arrived after 195 minutes and 169 balls, put on 301 together. This was a record fifth wicket stand for Central against all teams and for all teams against Wellington and the highest for any wicket for Central against Wellington. It was the fourth highest for the wicket in all New Zealand first-class cricket.

After looking likely to overhaul Wellington's total Central lost wickets rapidly and the game petered out. Central's total was their highest ever against Wellington. Pakistan player Azhar Abbas made his debut for Wellington in this match.

WELLINGTON

FIRST INNINGS	Runs	Mins	Balls	6s	4s	SECOND INNINGS	Runs	Mins	Balls	6s	4s
M.D.Bell* c Sinclair b Thompson	32	89	67	-	7	c Sinclair b Diamanti	7	29	29	-	-
L.J.Woodcock c Sinclair b West	34	114	96	-	3	not out	17	67	64	-	1
M.E.Parlane c Griggs b Thompson	58	227	177	1	6	b West	5	11	9	-	1
J.D.Ryder c Diamanti b Hegglun	236	475	397	1	32	not out	7	25	15	-	1
N.R.Parlane c Griggs b Hegglun	136	275	253	4	16						
C.J.Nevin† c Ingram b Diamanti	26	55	40	-	5						
S.A.Fairley c Griggs b Hegglun	20	57	37	-	4						
S.M.Mills not out	7	28	19	-	1						
M.R.Gillespie c Griggs b Sinclair	10	19	16	-	1						
J.S.Patel not out	2	4	3	-	-						
Azhar Abbas											
Extras (b 4, lb 18, nb 7)	29					(lb 1, nb 1)	2				
TOTAL (183 overs) (8 wkts dec)	**590**	679				(19 overs) (2 wkts)	**38**	67			

CENTRAL DISTRICTS

	Runs	Mins	Balls	6s	4s
P.J.Ingram c Ryder b Gillespie	17	44	35	-	4
J.M.How lbw b Woodcock	25	103	72	-	3
M.S.Sinclair b Azhar	47	108	90	-	6
G.P.Sulzberger* c Parlane M.E. b Woodcock	17	61	45	-	2
J.I.Englefield c Bell b Woodcock	127	292	213	4	17
R.L.Taylor c Nevin b Azhar	184	359	291	4	22
B.B.J.Griggs† b Patel	38	115	84	-	4
E.P.Thompson c & b Patel	12	11	7	-	3
B.J.Diamanti c Bell b Azhar	11	22	23	-	1
R.M.West not out	0	6	0	-	-
G.J.T.Hegglun b Patel	0	2	4	-	-
Extras (b 4, lb 9, w 1, nb 5)	19				
TOTAL (144 overs)	**497**	577			

Bowling	O	M	R	W	O	M	R	W
CENTRAL DISTRICTS								
Thompson	36	10	116	2	4	2	7	0
Hegglun	31	10	60	3	4	2	3	0
Diamanti	28	8	70	1	4	1	6	1
West	42	9	155	1	5	1	13	1
Sulzberger	36	5	116	0				
How	9	0	45	0	2	0	8	0
Sinclair	1	0	6	1				
WELLINGTON								
Gillespie	28	5	123	1				
Azhar	32	6	135	3				
Patel	42	8	144	3				
Woodcock	40	15	75	3				
Ryder	2	0	7	0				

Fall of Wickets

	W 1st	*CD 1st*	*W 2nd*
1st	59	27	11
2nd	72	81	16
3rd	215	110	-
4th	525	120	-
5th	525	421	-
6th	571	465	-
7th	571	482	-
8th	587	497	-
9th	-	497	-
10th	-	497	-

AUCKLAND v NORTHERN DISTRICTS State Championship

at Eden Park Outer Oval, Auckland on 11, 12, 13, 14 March, 2005
Toss : Northern Districts. Umpires : R.D. Anderson & T.J. Parlane
Close of play: 1st day: Auckland 12-1, Jones 4, Nicol 0; 2nd day: ND 48-1, Watling 25, Orchard 2
3rd day: Auckland 71-4, Barnes 21, Cachopa 0
***Northern Districts won by 240 runs.** Points: Northern Districts 8, Auckland 0*

After rain had delayed the start Northern batted and were indebted to Evans and Marshall who put on 83 in 66 minutes for the fourth wicket. Aldridge removed Horne before the close and next morning Auckland struggled. Cachopa top scored with 23 in almost two hours, after coming in at 32-4, and Auckland's final total of 153 was scored at less than two runs an over.

Northern led by 109 and extended this to 387 on the third day. Consistent batting, including Flynn's highest score, allowed Marshall to declare and Northern captured four Auckland wickets before the close. Barnes was the only batsman to offer much resistance the next day and Northern had completed a resounding win over the competition leaders by 12.46 pm.

NORTHERN DISTRICTS

FIRST INNINGS	*Runs*	*Mins*	*Balls*	*6s*	*4s*	*SECOND INNINGS*	*Runs*	*Mins*	*Balls*	*6s*	*4s*
B.S.Wilson c Cachopa b Canning	16	60	49	-	2	lbw b Barnes	16	95	80	-	1
B-J.Watling c Nicol b Walmsley	0	45	36	-	-	c Young b Walmsley	48	232	169	-	6
A.W.Evans lbw b Walker	91	137	100	1	15	(4) lbw b Canning	30	90	62	-	5
M.N.Hart c Walmsley b Barnes	26	56	44	-	5	(5) lbw b Canning	3	13	8	-	-
J.A.H.Marshall* run out	71	200	126	-	9	(6) c Young b Walmsley	51	108	75	-	8
D.R.Flynn c & b Walker	6	31	24	-	1	(7) not out	69	177	138	-	11
J.A.F.Yovich c Jones b Walker	0	1	1	-	-	(8) not out	31	78	53	-	2
M.G.Orchard c Canning b Shaw	20	66	42	-	4	(3) lbw b Barnes	13	68	58	-	2
P.D.McGlashan† lbw b Barnes	8	15	16	-	1						
B.P.Martin c Young b Shaw	4	3	2	-	1						
G.W.Aldridge not out	7	12	11	-	1						
Extras (lb 4, w 1, nb 8)	13					(b 2, lb 13, w 1, nb 1)	17				
TOTAL (74 overs)	**262**	317				(107 overs) (6 wkts dec)	**278**	433			

AUCKLAND

FIRST INNINGS	*Runs*	*Mins*	*Balls*	*6s*	*4s*	*SECOND INNINGS*	*Runs*	*Mins*	*Balls*	*6s*	*4s*
R.A.Jones b Yovich	9	55	40	-	2	c McGlashan b Aldridge	0	6	8	-	-
M.J.Horne c Wilson b Aldridge	5	21	14	-	1	b Yovich	4	21	13	-	1
R.J.Nicol c McGlashan b Aldridge	4	26	22	-	1	c Evans b Aldridge	0	9	8	-	-
T.K.Canning c Evans b Yovich	17	97	68	-	2	c Orchard b Martin	42	52	36	-	9
A.C.Barnes lbw b Yovich	4	11	9	-	1	c Martin b Yovich	57	161	116	-	9
C.Cachopa c Marshall b Martin	23	114	84	-	4	c McGlashan b Aldridge	9	73	68	-	1
K.W.M.Todd lbw b Martin	8	45	40	-	1	c McGlashan b Aldridge	1	9	4	-	-
B.G.K.Walker* b Orchard	17	106	89	-	2	lbw b Martin	4	25	21	-	1
R.A.Young† c McGlashan b Orchard	22	54	39	-	2	st McGlashan b Martin	8	20	11	-	2
K.P.Walmsley not out	5	71	48	-	-	c sub (A.P.Devcich) b Martin	7	25	18	-	-
G.S.Shaw c McGlashan b Orchard	14	28	32	-	3	not out	0	8	6	-	-
Extras (lb 12, w 1, nb 12)	25					(b 6, lb 5, nb 4)	15				
TOTAL (78.5 overs)	**153**	319				(50.4 overs)	**147**	209			

Bowling	*O*	*M*	*R*	*W*	*O*	*M*	*R*	*W*
AUCKLAND								
Walmsley	18	5	78	1	26	7	70	2
Canning	21	8	43	1	31	13	58	2
Shaw	7	1	50	2				
Barnes	15	5	36	2	30	8	63	2
Walker	13	0	51	3	18	0	62	0
Nicol					2	0	10	0
NORTHERN DISTRICTS								
Yovich	21	5	42	3	18	5	71	2
Aldridge	20	9	40	2	15	6	33	4
Orchard	18.5	11	33	3	2	0	13	0
Martin	19	8	26	2	15.4	8	19	4

Fall of Wickets	***ND*** *1st*	***A*** *1st*	***ND*** *2nd*	***A*** *2nd*
1st	18	12	37	1
2nd	28	23	66	1
3rd	82	23	113	5
4th	165	32	116	71
5th	189	74	127	101
6th	189	84	206	107
7th	239	85	-	126
8th	248	120	-	130
9th	253	135	-	143
10th	262	153	-	147

CANTERBURY v NORTHERN DISTRICTS State Championship

at Queen Elizabeth II Park, Christchurch on 19, 20, 21, 22 March, 2005
Toss : Canterbury. Umpires : A.L. Hill & P.D. Jones
Close of play: 1st day: Canterbury 291-7, Stead 112, Bond 52; 2nd day: ND 149-2, Watling 65, Flynn 2
3rd day: ND 218-4, Yovich 26, Orchard 13
***First innings win to Canterbury.** Points: Canterbury 2, Northern Districts 0*

Canterbury lost their first wicket without a run on the board and were 192-7 when Bond joined Stead. The pair were not parted until they had added 210, the highest eighth wicket partnership in inter-provincial cricket in New Zealand. Stead reached his hundred after 272 minutes from 205 balls and went on to record his highest score. Bond's maiden century came from 123 balls in 177 minutes.

Bond was soon back in the action when Northern batted. He trapped Wilson lbw and forced Evans to retire hurt with a broken hand. Watling (highest score) and Marshall added 134 for the second wicket before the Northern captain was out just before the close.

Only 29.4 overs were possible on the third day and play was delayed on the fourth. Northern were forced to follow on but had little trouble in saving the game.

CANTERBURY

FIRST INNINGS	*Runs*	*Mins*	*Balls*	*6s*	*4s*	*SECOND INNINGS*	*Runs*	*Mins*	*Balls*	*6s*	*4s*
M.H.W.Papps† c McGlashan b Yovich	0	9	9	-	-						
T.J.T.Papps b Aldridge	10	30	25	-	1						
P.G.Fulton* c Marshall b Yovich	31	89	56	-	6						
S.L.Stewart c Orchard b Martin	46	156	132	-	6						
G.R.Stead b Aldridge	190	399	315	1	27						
N.T.Broom c Aldridge b Orchard	9	45	42	-	1						
A.M.Ellis c Orchard b Yovich	14	62	60	-	1						
S.J.Cunis b Yovich	0	1	2	-	-						
S.E.Bond c McGlashan b Orchard	100	180	125	3	12						
P.J.Wiseman not out	32	47	37	1	4						
H.J.Shaw st McGlashan b Martin	10	27	15	-	1						
Extras (b 4, lb 6, w 5, nb 4)	19										
TOTAL (135.4 overs)	**461**	527									

NORTHERN DISTRICTS

	Runs	Mins	Balls	6s	4s		Runs	Mins	Balls	6s	4s
B-J.Watling lbw b Bond	77	259	214	-	10	c Fulton b Cunis	20	40	25	-	2
B.S.Wilson lbw b Bond	2	8	4	-	-	lbw b Bond	0	3	5	-	-
A.W.Evans retired hurt	4	11	7	-	1						
J.A.H.Marshall* c Papps M.H.W. b Cunis	62	168	113	-	11	b Wiseman	37	72	65	-	6
D.R.Flynn c Stewart b Wiseman	19	84	74	-	1	not out	23	113	102	-	2
J.A.F.Yovich c Fulton b Bond	30	78	53	-	4	not out	16	35	32	-	2
M.G.Orchard b Shaw	17	69	48	-	2	(3) c sub (I.A.Robertson) b Wiseman	60	187	151	-	7
A.P.Devcich c & b Cunis	10	54	37	-	1						
P.D.McGlashan† lbw b Bond	18	51	30	-	3						
G.W.Aldridge c Stead b Cunis	0	6	1	-	-						
B.P.Martin not out	0	2	3	-	-						
Extras (b 7, lb 7, w 2, nb 1)	17					(b 3, lb 8, w 1, nb 4)	16				
TOTAL (97.1 overs)	**256**	399				(62.4 overs) (4 wkts)	**172**	230			

Bowling	*O*	*M*	*R*	*W*				
NORTHERN DISTRICTS								
Yovich	28	10	93	4				
Aldridge	32	9	108	2				
Orchard	35	11	91	2				
Martin	38.4	7	148	2				
Evans	2	0	11	0				
CANTERBURY								
Bond	23	8	60	4	10	1	22	1
Cunis	20.1	9	28	3	7	1	27	1
Shaw	12	2	45	1	14	4	41	0
Ellis	16	1	54	0	5	1	19	0
Wiseman	26	3	55	1	24	7	34	2
Stead					2	0	16	0
Broom					0.4	0	2	0

Fall of Wickets	***C***	***ND***	***ND***
	1st	*1st*	*2nd*
1st	0	7	2
2nd	10	145	33
3rd	65	176	101
4th	109	182	144
5th	140	227	-
6th	192	227	-
7th	192	252	-
8th	402	256	-
9th	425	256	-
10th	461	-	-

Evans retired hurt at 11-1

During Northern Districts 2nd innings T.J.T.Papps took over as wicketkeeper after M.H.W.Papps was injured

CENTRAL DISTRICTS v AUCKLAND — State Championship

at McLean Park, Napier on 19, 20, 21, 22 March, 2005
Toss : Central Districts. Umpires : D.B. Cowie & I.W. Shine
Close of play: 1st day: Auckland 12-0, Jones 4, Horne 8; 2nd day: Auckland 29-0, Jones 8, Horne 21
3rd day: Auckland 140-3, Walker 10, Barnes 2
***No result.** Points: Central Districts 1, Auckland 1*

The five-man Auckland pace attack restricted Central to 214 after they had won the toss and batted. Ingram resisted for more than three hours before he was out at 118-5 while Taylor and Griggs each contributed thirties.

Rain allowed only nine overs on the second day and interrupted play on the third day when Auckland were very slow, scoring 111 at less than two runs an over. No play at all was possible on the last day, meaning each side took one point apiece.

CENTRAL DISTRICTS

FIRST INNINGS	*Runs*	*Mins*	*Balls*	*6s*	*4s*
J.M.How c Young b Adams	10	30	28	-	1
P.J.Ingram lbw b Adams	45	181	129	-	6
M.S.Sinclair lbw b Canning	15	36	33	-	1
G.P.Sulzberger* c Canning b Adams	12	25	23	-	1
J.I.Englefield b Mills	8	60	53	-	-
R.L.Taylor lbw b Barnes	33	73	65	-	2
B.B.J.Griggs† b Mills	36	142	97	-	5
E.P.Thompson c Young b Mills	8	16	13	-	-
R.M.West lbw b Canning	7	39	33	-	1
B.E.Hefford not out	18	53	42	-	1
L.J.Hamilton c Jones b Mills	5	17	16	-	-
Extras (b 6, lb 6, w 1, nb 4)	17				
TOTAL (87.5 overs)	**214**	347			

AUCKLAND

	Runs	*Mins*	*Balls*	*6s*	*4s*
R.A.Jones c Griggs b Thompson	10	64	53		1
M.J.Horne lbw b West	69	204	159	-	8
R.J.Nicol c Taylor b Thompson	43	193	164	-	3
B.G.K.Walker* not out	10	71	51	-	1
A.C.Barnes not out	2	16	16	-	-
C.Cachopa					
T.K.Canning					
K.D.Mills					
A.R.Adams					
P.A.Hitchcock					
R.A.Young†					
Extras (b 2, lb 3, nb 1)	6				
TOTAL (73.4 overs) (3 wkts)	**140**	280			

Bowling	*O*	*M*	*R*	*W*
AUCKLAND				
Mills	22.5	5	54	4
Adams	26	8	55	3
Canning	21	8	39	2
Hitchcock	8	1	24	0
Barnes	10	2	30	1
CENTRAL DISTRICTS				
Hamilton	4	1	7	0
Hefford	20	5	45	0
Thompson	21	11	32	2
Sulzberger	11	2	24	0
West	17.4	2	27	1

Fall of Wickets

	CD	***A***
	1st	*1st*
1st	17	31
2nd	41	115
3rd	58	133
4th	94	-
5th	118	-
6th	136	-
7th	150	-
8th	175	-
9th	202	-
10th	214	-

OTAGO v WELLINGTON — State Championship

at Queenstown Events Centre on 20, 21, 22, 23 March, 2005
Toss : Otago. Umpires : G.A.Baxter & D.M. Quested
Close of play: 1st day: Otago 9-0, Gaffaney 4, Wasim 4; 2nd day: Wellington 1-0, Woodcock 0, M.E.Parlane 0
3rd day: Wellington 268-9, Bell 32, Azhar Abbas 12
***Wellington won by 51 runs.** Points: Wellington 6, Otago 2*

This match had been postponed by a day after fog had closed Wellington airport and delayed the arrival of the Wellington team. Mike George was supposed to stand in this game but was stranded in Wellington and was replaced by Gary Baxter. When play did get underway, after further delays, Bell went lbw to the first ball of the game and apart from Ryder, all the batsmen struggled.

Otago batted carefully on the second day, amassing a lead of 76. No one reached fifty but Gaffaney (49) and Scott (43 at number nine) ensured a reasonable score. Bell's unhappy game continued when he was forced to retire hurt after three balls of Wellington's second innings.

He returned next day, however, and helped Wellington to a healthy lead. Neal Parlane and Fairley put on 107 for the fourth wicket to give the innings most of its substance.

Otago needed 198 to win on the last day, with ample time remaining, but fell short. Hopkins came in at 73-3 and was unbeaten on 44 when the innings ended. Patel returned career best bowling and the best in the short history of Queenstown as a first-class venue. Somerville made his first-class debut in this game.

WELLINGTON

FIRST INNINGS	*Runs*	*Mins*	*Balls*	*6s*	*4s*	*SECOND INNINGS*	*Runs*	*Mins*	*Balls*	*6s*	*4s*
M.D.Bell* lbw b Sewell	0	1	1	-	-	c Todd b Sewell	35	129	87	-	4
L.J.Woodcock c Somerville b Todd	18	65	40	-	2	c Hopkins b Scott	33	104	84	-	2
M.E.Parlane c Hopkins b Scott	23	67	57	-	2	c Hopkins b McSkimming	34	112	81	-	5
S.A.Fairley c Hopkins b Scott	13	86	74	-	-	c Eathorne b Redmond	47	190	151	-	2
J.D.Ryder c Hopkins b Somerville	81	151	111	-	12	c Hopkins b McSkimming	4	24	25	-	-
N.R.Parlane c Wasim b Somerville	5	49	37	-	1	c Hopkins b Redmond	65	140	121	-	9
C.J.Nevin† c Hopkins b Sewell	1	5	6	-	-	c Gaffaney b Redmond	1	5	6	-	-
G.B.Murray c Eathorne b Somerville	0	4	4	-	-	c McCullum b Somerville	0	5	6	-	-
M.R.Gillespie not out	10	24	18	-	1	lbw b Sewell	8	15	16	1	-
J.S.Patel lbw b Sewell	1	14	11	-	-	c Hopkins b Scott	16	42	33	-	1
Azhar Abbas c Eathorne b Sewell	0	1	1	-	-	not out	14	41	36	-	1
Extras (b 3, lb 5, w 2, nb 6)	16					(b 7, lb 5, w 1, nb 4)	17				
TOTAL (59 overs)	**168**	238				(107 overs)	**274**	408			

OTAGO

FIRST INNINGS	*Runs*	*Mins*	*Balls*	*6s*	*4s*	*SECOND INNINGS*	*Runs*	*Mins*	*Balls*	*6s*	*4s*
C.B.Gaffaney* c Nevin b Gillespie	49	159	104	1	6	b Patel	17	59	49	-	3
Mohammad Wasim c Woodcock b Azhar	16	64	44	-	1	c Nevin b Ryder	37	48	30	-	7
A.J.Redmond lbw b Gillespie	28	86	62	-	4	c Bell b Patel	8	38	33	-	-
G.R.Todd c Nevin b Woodcock	32	124	84	-	4	c & b Patel	9	47	31	-	2
G.J.Hopkins† c Nevin b Gillespie	7	62	43	-	1	not out	44	135	128	-	3
S.W.Eathorne lbw b Ryder	9	50	38	-	-	lbw b Ryder	4	6	10	-	-
N.L.McCullum lbw b Woodcock	0	12	9	-	-	c Woodcock b Patel	4	8	7	-	1
W.C.McSkimming c Ryder b Patel	25	62	62	-	3	lbw b Ryder	2	16	12	-	-
B.E.Scott c Parlane N.R. b Azhar	43	127	87	-	7	c Gillespie b Patel	11	29	28	-	1
W.E.R.Somerville b Azhar	16	60	43	-	1	c Bell b Patel	0	10	7	-	-
D.G.Sewell not out	3	14	14	-	-	c Bell b Ryder	2	42	36	-	-
Extras (lb 10, nb 6)	16					(b 2, lb 4, nb 3)	9				
TOTAL (97.2 overs)	**244**	414				(61.2 overs)	**147**	224			

Bowling	*O*	*M*	*R*	*W*	*O*	*M*	*R*	*W*
OTAGO								
Sewell	19	5	42	4	20	4	48	2
McSkimming	13	3	30	0	30	7	65	2
Scott	12	3	33	2	15	4	49	2
Todd	5	2	29	1	2	0	6	0
Somerville	10	2	26	3	25	5	59	1
McCullum					4	0	11	0
Redmond					11	4	24	3
WELLINGTON								
Gillespie	29	10	77	3	6	0	35	0
Azhar	28.2	7	60	3	4	1	14	0
Patel	11	2	38	1	18	4	32	6
Murray	5	3	5	0	7	1	19	0
Woodcock	15	3	33	2	12	6	18	0
Ryder	9	3	21	1	14.2	4	23	4

Fall of Wickets

	W	*O*	*W*	*O*
	1st	*1st*	*2nd*	*2nd*
1st	0	35	67	52
2nd	42	93	78	59
3rd	42	95	89	73
4th	115	125	196	80
5th	150	149	203	84
6th	151	149	205	88
7th	152	150	206	102
8th	157	193	221	120
9th	168	237	249	126
10th	168	244	274	147

In Wellington's 2nd innings Bell retired hurt on 1 at 1-0 and resumed at 196-4*

AUCKLAND v WELLINGTON — State Championship Final

at Eden Park Outer Oval, Auckland on 3, 4, 5, 6, 7 April, 2005
Toss : Wellington. Umpires : A.L. Hill & D.M. Quested
Close of play: 1st day: Wellington 222-8, N.R.Parlane 70, Patel 10; 2nd day: Auckland 208-5, Canning 55, Cachopa 19
3rd day: Wellington 111-4, Woodcock 41, N.R. Parlane 5; 4th day: Auckland 52-1, Jones 24, Nicol 7
Auckland won by 7 wickets

The five-day State Championship Final proved to be a worthy finale to the season with fortunes fluctuating throughout and the match going into the last day.

Wellington began badly and were 15-3 and then 80-5. Neal Parlane top scored with 74 before being ninth man out at 235 early on the second morning. Auckland had their share of problems and were 87-4 before Cachopa helped Canning to put on 86. On the third day Cachopa reached his maiden fifty and Canning went on to a hundred off 223 balls in 265 minutes. Gillespie returned career best figures.

By stumps on the third day Wellington had wiped off the deficit but had also lost four wickets and were only 21 runs ahead. A dedicated innings from Woodcock, however, gave Wellington hope. He put on 101 for the fifth wicket with Nevin and reached his maiden century after 421 minutes from 291 balls. He reached his century with last man Azhar at the crease and the pair had added 43 valuable runs before Woodcock was run out.

Auckland needed 208 to win and were guided home by Jones whose century came from 173 balls in 221 minutes. Barnes hit the winning four at 1.41 pm on the fifth day.

WELLINGTON

FIRST INNINGS	*Runs*	*Mins*	*Balls*	*6s*	*4s*	*SECOND INNINGS*	*Runs*	*Mins*	*Balls*	*6s*	*4s*
M.D.Bell* lbw b Adams	10	24	10	-	2	c Jones b Walmsley	1	3	4	-	-
L.J.Woodcock c Horne b Walmsley	2	21	17	-	-	run out	106	446	308	-	12
M.E.Parlane c Young b Adams	35	120	91	-	6	lbw b Canning	37	85	74	-	5
S.A.Fairley b Adams	0	8	5	-	-	c Young b Canning	5	13	17	-	1
J.D.Ryder lbw b Walmsley	30	115	89	-	6	c Young b Walker	12	47	42	-	2
N.R.Parlane b Adams	74	228	176	-	11	c Barnes b Walmsley	7	32	28	-	-
C.J.Nevin† lbw b Walmsley	35	70	54	-	8	lbw b Adams	68	121	106	-	7
S.M.Mills b Walker	10	43	42	-	2	c Young b Walmsley	1	13	9	-	-
M.R.Gillespie b Adams	10	60	46	-	1	lbw b Walmsley	14	40	23	-	-
J.S.Patel not out	18	50	37	-	3	c Nicol b Walmsley	5	18	16	-	1
Azhar Abbas run out	0	4	1	-	-	not out	22	65	50	-	2
Extras (b 3, lb 3, nb 5)	11					(b 5, lb 11, nb 3)	19				
TOTAL (94.3 overs)	**235**	376				(112.2 overs)	**297**	446			

AUCKLAND

	Runs	*Mins*	*Balls*	*6s*	*4s*		*Runs*	*Mins*	*Balls*	*6s*	*4s*
R.A.Jones b Gillespie	7	58	46	-	1	not out	114	241	192	-	18
M.J.Horne c Gillespie b Azhar	5	30	19	-	-	c Bell b Ryder	20	33	26	-	3
R.J.Nicol lbw b Woodcock	75	261	188	1	11	c Bell b Gillespie	36	138	105	1	4
B.G.K.Walker* lbw b Ryder	9	63	46	-	2	c Ryder b Patel	2	31	20	-	-
A.C.Barnes c Parlane N.R. b Gillespie	21	59	53	1	2	not out	21	36	19	-	4
T.K.Canning lbw b Gillespie	106	274	232	1	14						
C.Cachopa b Gillespie	69	207	145	1	10						
R.A.Young† b Gillespie	8	25	23	-	1						
P.A.Hitchcock not out	7	24	19	-	1						
A.R.Adams c Fairley b Gillespie	0	1	2	-	-						
K.P.Walmsley st Nevin b Woodcock	0	5	5	-	-						
Extras (b 1, lb 10, w 1, nb 6)	18					(b 10, nb 6)	16				
TOTAL (128.5 overs)	**325**	508				(59.3 overs) (3 wkts)	**209**	241			

Bowling	*O*	*M*	*R*	*W*	*O*	*M*	*R*	*W*
AUCKLAND								
Walmsley	24.3	5	85	3	26	3	94	5
Adams	23	10	39	5	39	12	75	1
Barnes	14	6	30	0	9	2	19	0
Canning	20	10	33	0	19	6	48	2
Walker	9	1	29	1	11.2	3	31	1
Hitchcock	4	0	13	0	8	2	14	0
WELLINGTON								
Gillespie	33	8	81	6	18	4	65	1
Azhar	24	13	34	1	6.3	0	32	0
Patel	31	5	82	0	17	3	57	1
Ryder	23	7	64	1	9	1	25	1
Woodcock	17.5	4	53	2	9	3	20	0

Fall of Wickets

	W *1st*	***A*** *1st*	***W*** *2nd*	***A*** *2nd*
1st	15	10	2	22
2nd	15	15	70	139
3rd	15	43	76	157
4th	80	87	100	-
5th	80	173	114	-
6th	134	298	215	-
7th	156	314	224	-
8th	206	325	246	-
9th	235	325	254	-
10th	235	325	297	-

2004/05 FIRST-CLASS STATISTICS

REGISTER OF PLAYERS

The following players appeared in first-class cricket for New Zealand teams during the 2004/05 season.

		Born	*At*	*Type*			*First-class debut*	
Adams Andre Ryan	A	17. 7.75	Auckland	RHB	RFM		A v O	97/98
Aldridge Graeme William	ND	15.11.77	Christchurch	RHB	RFM		ND v W	98/99
Astle Nathan John	C, NZ	15. 9.71	Christchurch	RHB	RM		C v CD	91/92
Azhar Abbas	W	1. 4.75	Khanewal, Pakistan	RHB	RM		PIA v Railways	95/96
Barnes Aaron Craig	A	21.12.71	Turangi	RHB	RM		A v CD	93/94
Barnett Geoffrey Edward Fulton	CD	3. 2.84	Nelson	LHB			CD v O	04/05
Beare Simon Peter	O	2. 7.79	Hamilton	RHB	RM		O v CD	01/02
Bell Matthew David	W	25. 2.77	Dunedin	RHB	ROB	WK	ND v NZA	93/94
Bond Shane Edward	C	7. 6.75	Christchurch	RHB	RF		C v CD	96/97
Broom Neil Trevor	C	20.11.83	Christchurch	RHB	RM		C v W	02/03
Butler Ian Gareth	ND, NZ	24.11.81	Auckland	RHB	RFM		ND v O	01/02
Cachopa Carl	A	17. 5.86	Bloemfontein, S.Africa	RHB	RM		A v W	04/05
Canning Tamahau Karangatukituki	A	7. 4.77	Adelaide, Australia	RHB	RFM		AA v Mat Inv	98/99
Cederman Duncan Robert	CD	18.10.78	Nelson	RHB	ROB		CD v C	04/05
Cornelius Cleighten James	C	2. 6.76	Christchurch	RHB	RFM		C v A	01/02
Cornelius Wade Alfred	C	5. 3.78	Christchurch	RHB	RFM		C v Z	00/01
Cumming Craig Derek	O, NZ	31. 8.75	Timaru	RHB	RM		C v CD	95/96
Cunis Stephen John	C	17. 1.78	Whakatane	RHB	RFM		C v CD	98/99
Davis Te Ahu Trevor	ND	9.12.85	Auckland	RHB	RFM		ND v O	04/05
Devcich Anton Paul	ND	28. 9.85	Hamilton	LHB	SLA		ND v O	04/05
Diamanti Brendon John	CD	30. 4.81	Blenheim	RHB	RM		CD v W	03/04
Eathorne Sean William	O	5. 5.86	Dunedin	RHB	ROB		O v A	04/05
Ellis Andrew Malcolm	C	24. 3.82	Christchurch	RHB	RFM		C v A	02/03
Englefield Jarrod Ian	CD	18.12.79	Blenheim	RHB			NZA v Pak A	98/99
Evans Alun Wyn	ND	20. 8.75	Glanamman, Wales	RHB	RM		Glam v OU	96
Fairley Samuel Anthony	W	19. 9.80	Whakatane	LHB	RM		W v O	01/02
Fleming Stephen Paul	W, NZ	1. 4.73	Christchurch	LHB	RSM		C v ND	91/92
Flynn Daniel Raymond	ND	16. 4.85	Rotorua	LHB	SLA		ND v O	04/05
Franklin James Edward Charles	W, NZ	7.11.80	Wellington	LHB	LFM		W v I	98/99
Fulton Peter Gordon	C	1. 2.79	Christchurch	RHB	RM		C v A	00/01
Gaffaney Christopher Blair	O	30.11.75	Dunedin	RHB			O v A	95/96
Gilhooly Richard John	W	26. 3.79	Hastings	LHB	RFM		W v ND	04/05
Gillespie Mark Raymond	W	17.10.79	Wanganui	RHB	RFM		W v O	99/00
Griggs Bevan Barry John	CD	29. 3.78	Palmerston North	RHB		WK	CD v O	00/01
Hamilton Lance John	CD	5. 4.73	Papakura	RHB	LFM		CD v W	96/97
Hart Matthew Norman	ND	16. 5.72	Hamilton	LHB	SLA		ND v A	90/91
Hefford Brent Edward	CD	8. 5.78	Blenheim	LHB	RM		CD v C	99/00
Hegglun Gregory James Tristran	CD	7. 8.84	Blenheim	RHB	RM		CD v C	04/05
Hitchcock Paul Anthony	A	23. 1.75	Wellington	RHB	RM		W v ND	99/00
Hopkins Gareth James	O, NZ	24.11.76	Lower Hutt	RHB	WK		NC v CC	97/98
Horne Matthew Jeffery	A	5.12.70	Auckland	RHB	RM		A v O	92/93
Horsley Nicholas Keith Woodward	ND	22. 9.80	Hamilton	LHB	ROB		A v CD	01/02
How Jamie Michael	CD	19. 5.81	New Plymouth	LHB	RM		CD v W	00/01
Howell Llorne Gregory	ND	8. 7.72	Napier	RHB	RM		C v O	90/91
Ingram Peter John	CD	25.10.78	Hawera	RHB	ROB		CD v O	01/02
Jones Richard Andrew	A	22.10.73	Auckland	RHB			A v C	93/94
Marshall Hamish John Hamilton	ND, NZ	15. 2.79	Warkworth	RHB	RM		ND v W	98/99
Marshall James Andrew Hamilton	ND, NZ	15. 2.79	Warkworth	RHB	RM		ND v W	97/98
Martin Bruce Philip	ND	25. 4.80	Whangarei	RHB	SLA		ND v CD	99/00
Martin Christopher Stewart	C, NZ	10.12.74	Christchurch	RHB	RFM		C v W	97/98
Mason Michael James	CD	27. 8.74	Carterton	RHB	RFM		CD v ND	97/98
McCullum Brendon Barrie	C, NZ	27. 9.81	Dunedin	RHB		WK	O v CD	99/00
McCullum Nathan Leslie	O	1. 9.80	Dunedin	RHB	ROB		O v W	99/00
McGlashan Peter Donald	ND	22. 6.79	Napier	RHB		WK	CD v O	00/01
McIntosh Timothy Gavin	C	4.12.79	Auckland	LHB			A v ND	98/99
McKay Andrew John	A	17. 4.80	Auckland	RHB	LFM		A v CD	02/03
McKenzie Marcel Norman	O	13. 5.78	Oamaru	RHB	RLB		C v O	98/99
McMillan Craig Douglas	C, NZ	13. 9.76	Christchurch	RHB	RM		C v O	94/95
McMillan James Michael	O	14. 6.78	Christchurch	RHB	RFM		O v CD	00/01
McSkimming Warren Charles	O	21. 6.79	Ranfurly	RHB	RM		O v C	99/00

		Born	At	Type			First-class debut	
Mills Kyle David	A, NZ	15. 3.79	Auckland	RHB	RFM		A v O	98/99
Mills Stuart Michael	W	22. 6.82	Wellington	RHB		WK	W v CD	03/04
Mohammad Wasim	O	8. 8.77	Rawalpindi, Pakistan	RHB	RLB		R'pindi B v Isl'bd	94/95
Murray Graham Bryan	W	3.10.76	Wellington	RHB	RM		W v C	04/05
Nevin Christopher John	W	3. 8.75	Dunedin	RHB		WK	W v ND	95/96
Nicol Robert James	A	28. 5.83	Auckland	RHB	ROB		A v CD	01/02
O'Brien Iain Edward	W, NZ	10. 7.76	Lower Hutt	RHB	RM		W v O	00/01
Oram Jacob David Philip	NZ	28. 7.78	Palmerston North	LHB	RM		NZA v B	97/98
Orchard Mark Geoffrey	ND	8.11.78	Hamilton	RHB	RM		ND v C	01/02
Papps Michael Hugh William	C	2. 7.79	Christchurch	RHB		WK	C v O	98/99
Papps Timothy James Terence	C	22. 4.81	Christchurch	LHB		WK	C v ND	03/04
Parlane Michael Edward	W	22. 7.72	Pukekohe	RHB		WK	ND v A	92/93
Parlane Neal Ronald	W	9. 8.78	Whangarei	RHB			ND v CD	96/97
Patel Jeetan Shashi	W	7. 5.80	Wellington	RHB	ROB		W v A	99/00
Redmond Aaron James	C	23. 9.79	Perth, Australia	RHB	RLB		SI v NI	99/00
Richardson Mark Hunter	A, NZ	11. 6.71	Hastings	LHB	LM		Pres v I	89/90
Robinson Grant Geoffrey	ND	24. 7.79	Gisborne	LHB	LM		ND v A	01/02
Ryder Jesse Daniel	W	6. 8.84	Masterton	LHB	RM		CD v ND	02/03
Schwass Andrew Mark	CD	11. 4.74	Nelson	RHB	RFM		CD v W	98/99
Scott Bradley Esmond	O	16. 9.79	Ashburton	LHB	LFM		O v A	00/01
Sewell David Graham	O	20.10.77	Christchurch	RHB	LFM		O v CD	95/96
Shaw Gareth Simon	A	14. 2.82	Auckland	RHB	RFM		A v C	01/02
Shaw Hayden Jonathan	C	31. 8.80	Christchurch	RHB	RFM		C v O	99/00
Sheed Jordan William	O	24. 9.82	Timaru	RHB	RLB		O v C	01/02
Sherlock Richard Roland	NZ A	15. 9.83	Palmerston North	RHB	RF		CD v W	03/04
Shutte Ryan Robert	ND	9. 7.82	Queenstown, S.Africa	LHB	RFM		ND v A	04/05
Sinclair Mathew Stuart	CD, NZ	9.11.75	Katherine, Australia	RHB	RM	WK	CD v C	95/96
Smith Craig Murray	O	9. 1.85	Oamaru	RHB	LM		O v A	04/05
Somerville William Edgar Richard	O	9. 8.84	Wellington	RHB	ROB		O v W	04/05
Stead Gary Raymond	C	9. 1.72	Christchurch	RHB	RLB		NZ XI v E	91/92
Stewart Shanan Luke	C	21. 6.82	Christchurch	RHB	RM		C v ND	01/02
Styris Scott Bernard	ND, NZ	10. 7.75	Brisbane, Australia	RHB	RM		ND v W	94/95
Sulzberger Glen Paul	CD	14. 3.73	Kaponga	LHB	ROB		CD v C	95/96
Taylor Ross Luteru	CD	8. 3.84	Lower Hutt	RHB	ROB		CD v C	02/03
Thompson Ewen Paul	CD	17.12.79	Warkworth	LHB	LFM		CD v O	00/01
Todd Gregory Rex	O	17. 6.82	Masterton	LHB	RM		CD v O	00/01
Todd Keeley William Martin	A	31. 7.82	Auckland	LHB	RM		A v O	04/05
Tuffey Daryl Raymond	ND, NZ	11. 6.78	Milton	RHB	RFM		ND v A	96/97
Turner Ashley Dean	W	13. 6.75	Lower Hutt	RHB	RFM		W v C	01/02
Vettori Daniel Luca	ND, NZ	27. 1.79	Auckland	RHB	SLA		ND v E	96/97
Vincent Lou	A, NZ	11.11.78	Warkworth	RHB	ROB	WK	A v O	97/98
Walker Brooke Graeme Keith	A	25. 3.77	Auckland	RHB	RLB		NZA v B	97/98
Walmsley Kerry Peter	A	23. 8.73	Dunedin	RHB	RFM		A v C	94/95
Ward James Sinclair	C	7. 6.74	Christchurch	LHB	SLA		C v A	00/01
Watling Bradley-John	ND	9. 7.85	Durban, S.Africa	RHB		WK	ND v A	04/05
West Regan Morris	CD	27. 4.79	New Plymouth	LHB	SLA		CD v ND	96/97
Wilson Bradley Svend	ND	10. 4.85	Auckland	RHB	ROB		ND v O	04/05
Wilson Jeffrey William	O	24.10.73	Invercargill	RHB	RFM		O v ND	91/92
Wiseman Paul John	C, NZ	4. 5.70	Auckland	RHB	ROB		A v CD	91/92
Woodcock Luke James	W	19. 3.82	Wellington	LHB	SLA	WK	W v O	01/02
Young Reece Alan	A	15. 9.79	Auckland	RHB		WK	A v C	98/99
Yovich Joseph Adam Frank	ND	15.12.76	Whangarei	LHB	RFM		ND v C	96/97

Key

RHB	right-hand batsman	*SLA*	slow left-arm	*RSM*	right slow-medium
LHB	left-hand batsman	*RLB*	right leg-break	*LFM*	left fast-medium
RM	right medium	*ROB*	right off-break	*LSM*	left slow-medium
LM	left medium	*RFM*	right fast-medium	*WK*	wicketkeeper
NC	Northern Conference	*CC*	Central Conference	*NZA*	New Zealand Academy
AA	Australian Academy				

FIRST-CLASS UMPIRES

2004/05

Eighteen local umpires stood in domestic cricket this season. Barry Frost went to South Africa on the annual exchange and stood in two games while Marais Erasmus officiated in two State Championship games. At international level Brent Bowden was again on the elite umpires panel, Tony Hill and Doug Cowie were on the second tier and Evan Watkin was on the third umpire panel.

Anderson, Robert Donald *(Manawatu).* Age 57. Debut in 1997/98. Has now officiated in 41first-class games and 28 one-day games.

Baxter, Gary Arthur *(Canterbury).* Age 52. Debut in 1998/99. Has now umpired 40 first-class games and 30 one-day matches.

Bowden, Brent Fraser *(Auckland).* Age 41. Debut in 1992/93 and has now stood in 82 first-class games including 27 tests. Has also officiated in 64 one-day matches and 79 one-day internationals. Member of ICC Elite Panel.

Busby, Jeremy Martin *(Canterbury).* Age 43. Made his debut in 1996/97 and has now stood in six first-class games and four one-day matches.

Cowie, Douglas Bruce *(Auckland).* Age 58. First umpired in 1985/86 and has now officiated in 112 first-class games including 22 tests. Has also umpired in 85 one-day games and 71 one-day internationals. Member of second level international panel.

Cross, Kathleen *(Wellington).* Age 46. Debut in 2003/04 and has now stood in two one-day games. Second woman umpire to officiate at major association level.

Ellwood, David John *(Wellington).* Age 40. Made his debut in 2002/03 and has now umpired in two first-class and four one-day matches.

Frost, Barry George *(Auckland).* Age 47. Debut in 1998/99 and has stood in 31 first-class games and 28 one-day matches. Includes two first-class games in South Africa.

George, Michael Peter *(Horowhenua-Kapiti).* Age 46. Made his debut in 1999/00 and has now officiated in 24 first-class games and 21 one-day games.

Hill, Anthony Lloyd *(Counties).* Age 54. Debut in 1993/94 and has now umpired 54 first-class games including two tests. Has also stood in 61 one-day matches and 16 one-day internationals. Member of second tier international panel.

Holdem, Glenn Clifford *(Canterbury).* Age 38. First stood in 2001/02 and has now umpired four first-class and six one-day matches.

Jones, Philip David *(Auckland).* Age 44. Debut in 2002/03 and has now stood in six first-class and two one-day matches.

Morris, Craig Justin *(Manawatu).* Debut in 2000/01 and has now officiated in six first-class and six one-day games.

Parlane, Tim James *(Northland).* Debut in 2001/02 and has now appeared in five first-class and seven one-day games.

Quested, David Murray *(Canterbury).* Age 58. Made his debut in 1990/91 and has now umpired 86 first-class matches including five tests. Has also officiated in 72 one-day games and 31 one-day internationals.

Shine, Ian William *(Counties).* Age 52. Debut in 1998/99 and has now umpired in 21 first-class games and 19 one-day matches.

Walker, Derek John *(Otago).* Age 45. Played for Otago from 1980/81 to 1988/89. Made umpiring debut this season standing in two first-class and two one-day games.

Watkin, Evan Allan *(Wellington).* Age 53. Debut in 1989/90 and has now umpired 87 first-class games including two tests. Has also officiated in 85 one-day matches including 21 one-day internationals. Member of second level international panel.

COMPLETE AVERAGES

Averages for Sri Lanka and Australia are on pages 94 and 106.

	M	In	NO	HS	Runs	Ave	100	50	Ct	St	O	M	R	W	Ave	5WI	10WM	Best
A.R.Adams	6	5	0	56	124	24.80	-	2	6	-	244.3	81	586	29	20.20	2	1	6-25
G.W.Aldridge	8	12	3	29	100	11.11	-	-	4	-	208.2	66	598	24	24.91	-	-	4-33
N.J.Astle	6	11	1	114	385	38.50	1	3	5	-	116.1	29	323	13	24.84	-	-	3-27
Azhar Abbas	3	4	2	22*	36	18.00	-	-	-	-	94.5	27	275	7	39.28	-	-	3-60
A.C.Barnes	9	14	3	75	351	31.90	-	2	2	-	191.2	56	464	15	30.93	-	-	4-41
G.E.F.Barnett	3	6	0	56	125	20.83	-	1	4	-	3	0	18	0	-	-	-	-
S.P.Beare	1	2	0	17	23	11.50	-	-	-	-	4.4	1	26	1	26.00	-	-	1-13
M.D.Bell	9	17	1	118	366	22.87	1	1	15	-								
S.E.Bond	3	4	1	100	146	48.66	1	-	-	-	83	20	260	9	28.88	-	-	4-60
N.T.Broom	4	7	1	109*	241	40.16	1	-	5	-	2.4	0	13	0	-	-	-	-
I.G.Butler	1	2	2	14*	14	-	-	-	1	-	27	5	141	1	141.00	-	-	1-39
C.Cachopa	6	7	0	69	190	27.14	-	1	3	-	3	0	5	0	-	-	-	-
T.K.Canning	8	9	1	115	342	42.75	2	-	4	-	272.4	98	644	27	23.85	1	-	6-44
D.R.Cederman	1	2	0	4	5	2.50	-	-	-	-								
C.J.Cornelius	1	2	0	2	2	1.00	-	-	-	-	13	3	76	0	-	-	-	-
W.A.Cornelius	2	3	1	14*	23	11.50	-	-	2	-	55	10	178	1	178.00	-	-	1-65
C.D.Cumming	10	19	1	125	660	36.66	2	3	4	-	63.5	23	146	5	29.20	-	-	2-20
S.J.Cunis	6	7	1	59	102	17.00	-	1	3	-	178.1	56	487	21	23.19	1	-	5-78
T.T.Davis	2	3	0	8	10	3.33	-	-	3	-	44	8	174	6	29.00	-	-	3-61
A.P.Devcich	4	6	1	94*	174	34.80	-	1	5	-	17	1	88	0	-	-	-	-
B.J.Diamanti	3	4	1	44	92	30.66	-	-	2	-	93	35	216	7	30.85	-	-	3-42
S.W.Eathorne	3	6	0	28	67	11.16	-	-	3	-								
A.M.Ellis	7	11	1	78	310	31.00	-	2	4	-	141.1	36	427	8	53.37	-	-	4-103
J.I.Englefield	8	13	1	127	533	44.41	1	4	6	-								
A.W.Evans	4	7	2	91	228	45.60	-	1	4	-	16	4	34	0	-	-	-	-
S.A.Fairley	5	8	1	47*	176	25.14	-	-	2	-								
S.P.Fleming	6	11	1	88	385	38.50	-	4	8	-								
D.R.Flynn	5	9	2	69*	217	31.00	-	2	-	-								
J.E.C.Franklin	9	13	1	79	242	20.16	-	2	3	-	293.4	60	994	44	22.59	3	1	6-119
P.G.Fulton	9	14	1	221*	850	65.38	2	3	10	-								
C.B.Gaffaney	8	16	0	103	554	34.62	1	2	4	-								
R.J.Gilhooly	1	2	1	13	17	17.00	-	-	-	-	15	2	55	1	55.00	-	-	1-46
M.R.Gillespie	9	14	2	52	224	18.66	-	1	2	-	315.5	79	977	32	30.53	1	-	6-81
B.B.J.Griggs	8	12	1	77*	324	29.45	-	2	21	3								
L.J.Hamilton	6	10	1	11	19	2.11	-	-	2	-	189.5	52	521	18	28.94	1	-	6-80
M.N.Hart	6	12	1	107	304	27.63	1	-	3	-	29	5	118	4	29.50	-	-	3-67
B.E.Hefford	2	3	1	18*	21	10.50	-	-	1	-	58	22	147	4	36.75	-	-	2-46
G.J.T.Hegglun	2	2	0	8	8	4.00	-	-	-	-	66.3	24	141	6	23.50	-	-	3-60
P.A.Hitchcock	3	3	2	31*	39	39.00	-	-	-	-	50	11	113	2	56.50	-	-	2-52
G.J.Hopkins	9	17	2	86	385	25.66	-	3	37	1								
M.J.Horne	9	14	0	88	540	38.57	-	5	3	-	5	2	30	1	30.00	-	-	1-30
N.K.W.Horsley	1	2	0	38	38	19.00	-	-	-	-								
J.M.How	9	14	1	121	592	45.53	3	2	8	-	61	11	218	5	43.60	-	-	2-28
L.G.Howell	3	6	0	35	92	15.33	-	-	2	-								
P.J.Ingram	8	13	0	45	243	18.69	-	-	9	-								
R.A.Jones	9	14	1	114*	440	33.84	2	1	11	-								
H.J.H.Marshall	7	13	0	160	643	49.46	3	2	-	-								
J.A.H.Marshall	8	12	0	71	426	35.50	-	4	3	-								
B.P.Martin	5	7	2	18	40	8.00	-	-	2	-	163.2	47	393	17	23.11	-	-	4-19
C.S.Martin	10	14	8	9	34	5.66	-	-	1	-	334.3	77	1047	38	27.55	1	-	6-54
M.J.Mason	2	3	1	16	25	12.50	-	-	-	-	76.2	20	183	9	20.33	-	-	3-45
B.B.McCullum	6	10	0	99	212	21.20	-	1	16	-								
N.L.McCullum	6	11	1	46*	193	19.30	-	-	9	-	133	31	349	6	58.16	-	-	2-17
P.D.McGlashan	6	9	1	33	173	21.62	-	-	22	2								
T.G.McIntosh	6	10	0	21	49	4.90	-	-	9	-								
A.J.McKay	1	2	1	3*	4	4.00	-	-	1	-	27	4	83	5	16.60	-	-	3-34
M.N.McKenzie	2	4	0	5	10	2.50	-	-	-	-								
C.D.McMillan	5	8	0	121	299	37.37	1	2	1	-	31.3	7	86	3	28.66	-	-	3-37
J.M.McMillan	4	7	4	8	12	4.00	-	-	1	-	89.3	22	283	12	23.58	-	-	4-36
W.C.McSkimming	8	13	1	111	259	21.58	1	-	4	-	238	75	572	25	22.88	1	-	5-29
K.D.Mills	5	5	0	31	68	13.60	-	-	1	-	143.5	38	433	21	20.61	2	1	5-33
S.M.Mills	6	9	2	64	128	18.28	-	1	11	-								

	M	In	NO	HS	Runs	Ave	100	50	Ct	St	O	M	R	W	Ave	5WI	10WM	Best
Mohammad Wasim	7	13	0	45	167	12.84	-	-	3	-	2	0	12	0	-	-	-	-
G.B.Murray	3	6	0	33	76	12.66	-	-	-	-	38	13	88	0	-	-	-	-
C.J.Nevin	9	14	0	68	261	18.64	-	1	9	1								
R.J.Nicol	8	13	1	100	382	31.83	1	1	10	-	7	0	38	0	-	-	-	-
I.E.O'Brien	7	9	2	28	53	7.57	-	-	3	-	240	60	728	22	33.09	-	-	4-47
M.G.Orchard	8	15	1	60	336	24.00	-	2	6	-	192.3	66	489	11	44.45	-	-	3-33
M.H.W.Papps	7	11	0	74	137	12.45	-	1	19	2								
T.J.T.Papps	6	9	0	33	95	10.55	-	-	8	-								
M.E.Parlane	8	15	0	203	646	43.06	2	1	2	-								
N.R.Parlane	9	15	2	136	571	43.92	1	4	11	-								
J.S.Patel	8	12	5	35*	187	26.71	-	-	6	-	320	73	854	26	32.84	1	-	6-32
A.J.Redmond	9	17	1	71*	538	33.62	-	6	1	-	103.2	15	431	10	43.10	-	-	3-24
M.H.Richardson	2	2	0	46	81	40.50	-	-	1	-								
G.G.Robinson	2	4	0	17	40	10.00	-	-	-	-								
J.D.Ryder	9	15	1	236	625	44.64	1	3	11	-	117.4	28	298	17	17.52	-	-	4-23
A.M.Schwass	5	9	5	35*	149	37.25	-	-	3	-	155.3	33	554	12	46.16	-	-	3-33
B.E.Scott	6	11	3	96	231	28.87	-	1	-	-	228.5	75	560	19	29.47	-	-	4-47
D.G.Sewell	3	6	3	3*	6	2.00	-	-	1	-	128.5	29	360	15	24.00	1	-	5-51
G.S.Shaw	3	5	2	14	20	6.66	-	-	-	-	49	8	226	8	28.25	-	-	3-19
H.J.Shaw	7	9	2	47*	181	25.85	-	-	3	-	166.1	29	616	17	36.23	-	-	3-27
J.W.Sheed	6	11	0	89	130	11.81	-	1	6	-								
R.R.Shutte	1	2	0	12	20	10.00	-	-	-	-	14	3	39	2	19.50	-	-	2-39
M.S.Sinclair	6	8	0	104	316	39.50	1	1	5	-	2	0	10	1	10.00	-	-	1-6
C.M.Smith	2	3	1	6	10	5.00	-	-	-	-	61.2	14	166	4	41.50	-	-	2-59
W.E.R.Somerville	1	2	0	16	16	8.00	-	-	1	-	35	7	85	4	21.25	-	-	3-26
G.R.Stead	7	11	0	190	401	36.45	1	1	6	-	8	2	25	1	25.00	-	-	1-5
S.L.Stewart	7	11	0	149	424	38.54	1	1	2	-	15	4	55	2	27.50	-	-	2-52
S.B.Styris	2	4	0	36	104	26.00	-	-	3	-	22.5	7	75	1	75.00	-	-	1-20
G.P.Sulzberger	8	13	0	46	249	19.15	-	-	1	-	252	62	767	20	38.35	-	-	4-89
R.L.Taylor	8	11	0	184	423	38.45	1	1	7	-								
E.P.Thompson	8	12	0	126	426	35.50	2	1	3	-	260.3	66	862	19	45.36	-	-	4-81
G.R.Todd	8	16	2	123*	552	39.42	1	3	4	-	121.5	30	397	5	79.40	-	-	1-29
K.W.M.Todd	2	4	0	84	98	24.50	-	1	-	-								
D.R.Tuffey	4	8	2	24*	100	16.66	-	-	1	-	154.3	42	426	21	20.28	-	-	4-38
A.D.Turner	1	1	0	9	9	9.00	-	-	1	-	16.5	5	60	2	30.00	-	-	2-60
D.L.Vettori	4	7	2	65	210	42.00	-	1	1	-	160.5	32	487	10	48.70	1	-	5-106
L.Vincent	10	16	2	224	999	71.35	3	4	14	-	25	6	70	1	70.00	-	-	1-43
B.G.K.Walker	9	12	2	32	173	17.30	-	-	5	-	124.2	12	442	8	55.25	-	-	3-51
K.P.Walmsley	7	7	2	9	25	5.00	-	-	1	-	265.2	59	860	38	22.63	3	1	7-28
J.S.Ward	1	2	2	5*	5	-	-	-	-	-	3	0	29	0	-	-	-	-
B-J.Watling	8	16	0	77	320	20.00	-	2	14	-								
R.M.West	4	5	2	16	30	10.00	-	-	-	-	137.4	33	413	9	45.88	-	-	3-58
B.S.Wilson	5	10	0	96	224	22.40	-	1	1	-								
J.W.Wilson	3	6	1	38*	98	19.60	-	-	1	-	87.1	27	245	10	24.50	-	-	4-46
P.J.Wiseman	10	16	4	46	273	22.75	-	-	2	-	325.4	81	821	37	22.18	3	2	9-13
L.J.Woodcock	9	17	1	106	446	27.87	1	1	5	-	180.5	55	380	12	31.66	-	-	3-75
R.A.Young	9	10	2	35	116	14.50	-	-	31	-								
J.A.F.Yovich	9	16	4	59	359	29.91	-	3	-	-	217.1	41	785	31	25.32	1	-	5-39

LEADING AVERAGES

BATTING *(top 20, qualification six innings)*

	M	I	NO	HS	Runs	Ave	100s	50s
L. Vincent	10	16	2	224	999	71.35	3	4
P.G. Fulton	9	14	1	221*	850	65.38	2	3
H.J.H. Marshall	7	13	0	160	643	49.46	3	2
A.W. Evans	4	7	2	91	228	45.60	-	1
J.M. How	9	14	1	121	592	45.53	3	2
J.D. Ryder	9	15	1	236	625	44.64	1	3
J.I. Englefield	8	13	1	127	533	44.41	1	4
N.R. Parlane	9	15	2	136	571	43.92	1	4
M.E. Parlane	8	15	0	203	646	43.06	2	1
T.K. Canning	8	9	1	115	342	42.75	2	-
D.L. Vettori	4	7	2	65	210	42.00	-	1
N.T. Broom	4	7	1	109*	241	40.16	1	-
M.S. Sinclair	6	8	0	104	316	39.50	1	1
G.R. Todd	8	16	2	123*	552	39.42	1	3
M.J. Horne	9	14	0	88	540	38.57	-	5
S.L. Stewart	7	11	0	149	424	38.54	1	1
N.J. Astle	6	11	1	114	385	38.50	1	3
S.P. Fleming	6	11	1	88	385	38.50	-	4
R.L. Taylor	8	11	0	184	423	38.45	1	1
C.D. McMillan	5	8	0	121	299	37.37	1	2

BOWLING *(top 20, qualification 10 wickets)*

	Overs	Mdns	Runs	Wkts	Ave	5WI	10WM	Best
G.D. McGrath	126.2	47	283	18	15.72	1	-	6-115
J.D. Ryder	117.4	28	298	17	17.52	-	-	4-23
A.R. Adams	244.3	81	586	29	20.20	2	1	6-25
D.R. Tuffey	154	42	426	21	20.28	-	-	4-38
K.D. Mills	143.5	38	433	21	20.61	2	1	5-33
S.K. Warne	131.3	25	374	17	22.00	1	-	5-39
P.J. Wiseman	325.4	81	821	37	22.18	3	2	9-13
J.E.C. Franklin	293.4	60	994	44	22.59	3	1	6-119
K.P. Walmsley	265.2	59	860	38	22.63	3	1	7-28
W.C. McSkimming	238	75	572	25	22.88	1	-	5-29
B.P. Martin	163.2	47	393	17	23.11	-	-	4-19
S.J. Cunis	178.1	56	487	21	23.19	1	-	5-78
J.M. McMillan	89.3	22	283	12	23.58	-	-	4-36
T.K. Canning	272.4	98	644	27	23.85	1	-	6-44
D.G. Sewell	128.5	29	360	15	24.00	1	-	5-51
J.W. Wilson	87.1	27	245	10	24.50	-	-	4-46
N.J. Astle	116.1	29	323	13	24.84	-	-	3-27
G.W. Aldridge	208.2	66	598	24	24.91	-	-	4-33
J.A.F. Yovich	217.1	41	785	31	25.32	1	-	5-39
C.S. Martin	334.3	77	1047	38	27.55	1	-	6-54

CENTURIES

There were 46 centuries in first-class cricket with 33 players reaching three figures this season. J.M. How, H.J.H. Marshall and L. Vincent each scored three while seven players scored two each. The fastest hundred of the season was scored by E.P. Thompson who took 72 balls to reach his century for Central Districts against Canterbury at Rangiora.

236	J.D. Ryder	Wellington v Central Districts	Palmerston North
224	L. Vincent	New Zealand v Sri Lanka *(Second Test)*	Wellington
221*	P.G. Fulton	Canterbury v Otago	Dunedin
203	M.E. Parlane	Wellington v Auckland	Auckland
190	G.R. Stead	Canterbury v Northern Districts	Christchurch
185*	L. Vincent	Auckland v Central Districts	Auckland
†184	R.L. Taylor	Central Districts v Wellington	Palmerston North
165	D.R. Martyn	Australia v New Zealand *(Second Test)*	Wellington
162	A.C. Gilchrist	Australia v New Zealand *(Second Test)*	Wellington
160	H.J.H. Marshall	New Zealand v Sri Lanka *(First Test)*	Napier
154	P.G. Fulton	Canterbury v Central Districts	Christchurch
152	L. Vincent	Auckland v Otago	Auckland
†149	S.L. Stewart	Canterbury v Central Districts	Christchurch
†146	H.J.H. Marshall	New Zealand v Australia *(First Test)*	Christchurch
141	D.P.M.D. Jayawardene	Sri Lanka v New Zealand *(First Test)*	Napier
136	N.R. Parlane	Wellington v Central Districts	Palmerston North
132	M.E. Parlane	Wellington v Central Districts	Napier
128	H.J.H. Marshall	Northern Districts v Central Districts	Napier
127	J.I. Englefield	Central Districts v Wellington	Palmerston North
127	M.S. Atapattu	Sri Lanka v New Zealand *(First Test)*	Napier
126	E.P. Thompson	Central Districts v Canterbury	New Plymouth
125	C.D. Cumming	Otago v Central Districts	Queenstown
†123*	G.R. Todd	Otago v Canterbury	Dunedin
121	J.M. How	Central Districts v Northern Districts	Napier
121	A.C. Gilchrist	Australia v New Zealand *(First Test)*	Christchurch
121	C.D. McMillan	Major Association XI v Sri Lanka	Christchurch
118	M.D. Bell	Wellington v Central Districts	Napier
118	S.M. Katich	Australia v New Zealand *(First Test)*	Christchurch
115	T.K. Canning	Auckland v Northern Districts	Hamilton
114	N.J. Astle	New Zealand v Sri Lanka *(First Test)*	Napier
114*	R.A. Jones	Auckland v Wellington	Auckland
†111	W.C. McSkimming	Otago v Auckland	Auckland
110	R.A. Jones	Auckland v Central Districts	Auckland
†109*	N.T. Broom	Canterbury v Otago	Dunedin
108*	J.M. How	Central Districts v Otago	Queenstown
107	M.N. Hart	Northern Districts v Central Districts	Napier
106	C.D. Cumming	Otago v Northern Districts	Gisborne
106	T.K. Canning	Auckland v Wellington	Auckland
†106	L.J. Woodcock	Wellington v Auckland	Auckland
105	J.M. How	Central Districts v Otago	Queenstown
105	R.T. Ponting	Australia v New Zealand *(Third Test)*	Auckland
104	M.S. Sinclair	Central Districts v Northern Districts	Napier
103	C.B. Gaffaney	Otago v Auckland	Auckland
†102	E.P. Thompson	Central Districts v Auckland	Auckland
100	R.J. Nicol	Auckland v Otago	Auckland
†100	S.E. Bond	Canterbury v Northern Districts	Christchurch

† *maiden first-class century*

CENTURY PARTNERSHIPS

There were 47 century partnerships in 2004/05.

FIRST WICKET

215	M.S.Sinclair & J.M.How	Central Districts v Northern Districts	Napier
172	R.A.Jones & M.J.Horne	Auckland v Central Districts	Auckland
129	C.D.Cumming & C.B.Gaffaney	Otago v Auckland	Auckland
103	T.J.T.Papps & M.H.W.Papps	Canterbury v Northern Districts	Gisborne

SECOND WICKET

215	M.D. Bell & M.E. Parlane	Wellington v Central Districts	Napier
148*	J.L.Langer & R.T.Ponting	Australia v New Zealand *(Third Test)*	Auckland
134	B-J.Watling & J.A.H.Marshall	Northern Districts v Canterbury	Christchurch
117	R.A.Jones & R.J.Nicol	Auckland v Wellington	Auckland
113	M.J.Horne & R.J.Nicol	Auckland v Central Districts	Auckland
110*	J.L.Langer & R.T.Ponting	Australia v New Zealand *(First Test)*	Christchurch
107	J.A.H.Marshall & H.J.H.Marshall	New Zealand v Sri Lanka *(First Test)*	Napier
100	M.J.Horne & R.J.Nicol	Auckland v Wellington	Auckland

THIRD WICKET

244	R.J.Nicol & L.Vincent	Auckland v Otago	Auckland
184	M.S.Atapattu & D.P.M.D.Jayawardene	Sri Lanka v New Zealand *(First Test)*	Napier
143	M.E.Parlane & J.D.Ryder	Wellington v Central Districts	Palmerston North
126	P.G.Fulton & S.L.Stewart	Canterbury v Central Districts	Christchurch
126	H.J.H.Marshall & S.P.Fleming	New Zealand v Australia *(Third Test)*	Auckland
103	R.T.Ponting & D.R.Martyn	Australia v New Zealand *(Third Test)*	Auckland

FOURTH WICKET

310	J.D.Ryder & N.R.Parlane	Wellington v Central Districts	Palmerston North
150	C.B.Gaffaney & G.J.Hopkins	Otago v Wellington	Wellington
131	H.J.H.Marshall & N.J.Astle	New Zealand v Australia *(First Test)*	Christchurch
125	H.J.H.Marshall & N.J.Astle	New Zealand v Sri Lanka *(First Test)*	Napier
122	D.P.M.D.Jayawardene & T.T.Samaraweera	Sri Lanka v New Zealand *(First Test)*	Napier
121	S.L.Stewart & G.R.Stead	Canterbury v Central Districts	Christchurch
111	P.G.Fulton & G.R.Stead	Canterbury v Central Districts	New Plymouth
107	S.A.Fairley & N.R.Parlane	Wellington v Otago	Queenstown

FIFTH WICKET

301	J.I.Englefield & R.L.Taylor	Central Districts v Wellington	Palmerston North
159	J.I.Englefield & R.L.Taylor	Central Districts v Canterbury	New Plymouth
141	L.Vincent & S.P.Fleming	New Zealand v Sri Lanka *(Second Test)*	Wellington
130	J.D.Ryder & J.E.C.Franklin	Wellington v Otago	Wellington
114	C.D.Cumming & G.J.Hopkins	Otago v Northern Districts	Gisborne

SIXTH WICKET

293*	P.G.Fulton & N.T.Broom	Canterbury v Otago	Dunedin
256	D.R.Martyn & A.C.Gilchrist	Australia v New Zealand *(Second Test)*	Wellington
216	M.N.Hart & H.J.H.Marshall	Northern Districts v Central Districts	Napier
141	B.B.J.Griggs & E.P.Thompson	Central Districts v Canterbury	Christchurch
129	N.J.Astle & B.B.McCullum	New Zealand v Sri Lanka *(First Test)*	Napier
125	T.K.Canning & C.Cachopa	Auckland v Wellington	Auckland
120	M.E.Parlane & J.D.Ryder	Wellington v Auckland	Auckland
101	L.J.Woodcock & C.J.Nevin	Wellington v Auckland	Auckland

SEVENTH WICKET

212	S.M.Katich & A.C.Gilchrist	Australia v New Zealand *(First Test)*	Christchurch
159	J.I.Englefield & E.P.Thompson	Central Districts v Auckland	Auckland
136	T.K.Canning & B.G.K.Walker	Auckland v Northern Districts	Hamilton

EIGHTH WICKET

210	G.R.Stead & S.E.Bond	Canterbury v Northern Districts	Christchurch
111	L.Vincent & R.A.Young	Auckland v Central Districts	Auckland
111	E.P.Thompson & B.J.Diamanti	Central Districts v Canterbury	New Plymouth

NINTH WICKET

208	W.C.McSkimming & B.E.Scott	Otago v Auckland	Auckland
110	G.R.Todd & W.C.McSkimming	Otago v Canterbury	Dunedin

WICKETKEEPING DISMISSALS

The following New Zealand players who appeared in 2004/05 have made at least one dismissal in first-class cricket while keeping wicket.

	ct	st	total
C.J.Nevin	202	7	209
G.J.Hopkins	184	12	196
R.A.Young *	162	3	165
B.B.McCullum	87	7	94
B.B.J.Griggs	89	3	92
P.D.McGlashan *	42	3	45
L.Vincent	25	–	25
M.H.W.Papps	19	3	22
S.M.Mills *	13	–	13
M.S.Sinclair	10	1	11
B-J.Watling	9	–	9
T.J.T.Papps	6	–	6
M.D.Bell	4	–	4
L.J.Woodcock	3	–	3
C.D.Cumming	1	–	1
J.A.H.Marshall	1	–	1

** no further catches taken as fielder*

NEW ZEALANDERS IN OVERSEAS CRICKET

Craig Spearman and James Franklin *(Gloucestershire)*, Ian Butler *(Kent)* and Andre Adams *(Essex)* all appeared in county cricket in 2004.

Spearman, Adams, Scott Styris *(Middlesex)*. Stephen Fleming *(Nottinghamshire)*, Craig McMillan *(Hampshire)* and Nathan Astle *(Durham)* appeared in 2005.

At the time of going to print we were not able to include the final figures for 2005 and the career records do not include performances in any of these matches.

The details for 2004 were:

	M	I	NO	HS	Runs	Ave	100	50	ct
A.R. Adams	7	8	0	124	196	24.50	1	–	4
I.G. Butler	5	8	2	68	185	30.83	–	1	2
J.E.C. Franklin	3	6	2	44	134	33.50	–	–	1
C.M. Spearman	17	28	2	341	1462	56.23	4	4	15

	O	M	R	W	Ave	5WI	10WM	Best
A.R. Adams	157.4	23	561	23	24.39	1	–	5-93
I.G. Butler	101.3	11	446	11	40.54	–	–	4-114
J.E.C. Franklin	83.1	27	252	12	21.00	1	–	7-60

BOWLING PERFORMANCES

There were 27 instances of a bowler taking five wickets or more in an innings. Nineteen bowlers took five wickets in an innings with J.E.C. Franklin, K.P. Walmsley and P.J. Wiseman performing the feat on three occasions each.

FIVE WICKETS IN AN INNINGS

9-13	P.J. Wiseman	Canterbury v Central Districts	Christchurch
7-28	K.P. Walmsley	Auckland v Northern Districts	Hamilton
6-25	A.R. Adams	Auckland v Wellington	Auckland
6-32	J.S. Patel	Wellington v Otago	Queenstown
6-44	T.K. Canning	Auckland v Northern Districts	Hamilton
6-54	C.S. Martin	New Zealand v Sri Lanka *(Second Test)*	Wellington
6-57	P.J. Wiseman	Canterbury v Otago	Dunedin
6-80	L.J. Hamilton	Central Districts v Auckland	Auckland
6-81	M.R. Gillespie	Wellington v Auckland	Auckland
6-108	W.P.J.U.C. Vaas	Sri Lanka v New Zealand *(Second Test)*	Wellington
6-115	G.D. McGrath	Australia v New Zealand *(First Test)*	Christchurch
6-119	J.E.C. Franklin	New Zealand v Australia *(Third Test)*	Auckland
5-23	J.E.C. Franklin	Wellington v Northern Districts	Wellington
5-29	W.C. McSkimming	Otago v Auckland	Dunedin
5-33	K.D. Mills	Auckland v Canterbury	Christchurch
5-39	A.R. Adams	Auckland v Wellington	Auckland
5-39	J.A.F. Yovich	Northern Districts v Wellington	Wellington
5-39	S.K. Warne	Australia v New Zealand *(First Test)*	Christchurch
5-48	J.E.C. Franklin	Wellington v Northern Districts	Wellington
5-48	P.J. Wiseman	Canterbury v Otago	Dunedin
5-49	K.D. Mills	Auckland v Canterbury	Christchurch
5-51	D.G. Sewell	Otago v Canterbury	Dunedin
5-73	K.P. Walmsley	Auckland v Otago	Auckland
5-78	S.J. Cunis	Canterbury v Otago	Dunedin
5-80	S.L. Malinga	Sri Lanka v New Zealand *(First Test)*	Napier
5-94	K.P. Walmsley	Auckland v Wellington	Auckland
5-106	D.L. Vettori	New Zealand v Australia *(First Test)*	Christchurch

TEN WICKETS IN A MATCH

12-86	P.J. Wiseman	Canterbury v Central Districts	Christchurch
11-105	P.J. Wiseman	Canterbury v Otago	Dunedin
10-71	J.E.C. Franklin	Wellington v Northern Districts	Wellington
10-82	K.D. Mills	Auckland v Canterbury	Christchurch
10-93	K.P. Walmsley	Auckland v Northern Districts	Hamilton
10-118	A.R. Adams	Auckland v Wellington	Auckland

CAREER AVERAGES

as at 15 April 2005 for players active during the 2004/05 season

	M	In	NO	HS	Runs	Ave	100	50	Ct	St	Wkts	Runs	Ave	5WI	10WM	Best
A.R.Adams	42	58	1	124	1197	21.00	1	8	23	-	165	3760	22.78	7	1	6-25
G.W.Aldridge	39	47	12	49	560	16.00	-	-	18	-	88	2701	30.69	1	-	5-50
N.J.Astle	144	230	22	223	8025	38.58	18	40	117	-	131	4272	32.61	2	-	6-22
Azhar Abbas	40	59	21	44*	288	7.57	-	-	10	-	142	3485	24.54	6	2	6-38
A.C.Barnes	78	121	10	134*	3006	27.08	4	12	39	-	89	2823	31.87	1	-	5-24
G.E.F.Barnett	3	6	0	56	125	20.83	-	1	4	-	0	18	-	-	-	-
S.P.Beare	6	11	0	60	137	12.45	-	1	9	-	8	106	13.25	-	-	2-5
M.D.Bell	125	215	13	219	6896	34.13	14	42	101	-	0	23	-	-	-	-
S.E.Bond	42	48	18	100	587	19.56	1	2	20	-	137	3731	27.23	6	-	5-37
N.T.Broom	16	26	2	109*	821	34.20	1	3	17	-	2	79	39.50	-	-	1-8
I.G.Butler	37	46	16	68	489	16.30	-	2	9	-	113	3505	31.01	2	-	6-46
C.Cachopa	6	7	0	69	190	27.14	-	1	3	-	0	5	-	-	-	-
T.K.Canning	50	70	8	115	1685	27.17	3	5	26	-	173	4068	23.51	6	-	6-44
D.R.Cederman	1	2	0	4	5	2.50	-	-	-	-						
C.J.Cornelius	3	6	1	19*	36	7.20	-	-	-	-	3	210	70.00	-	-	3-67
W.A.Cornelius	14	19	8	14*	58	5.27	-	-	6	-	40	1137	28.42	3	1	7-53
C.D.Cumming	83	153	14	187	4980	35.82	10	24	38	-	26	1121	43.11	-	-	3-31
S.J.Cunis	31	44	9	64*	553	15.80	-	2	8	-	78	2162	27.71	3	-	5-59
T.T.Davis	2	3	0	8	10	3.33	-	-	3	-	6	174	29.00	-	-	3-61
A.P.Devcich	4	6	1	94*	174	34.80	-	1	5	-	0	88	-	-	-	-
B.J.Diamanti	5	7	2	44	113	22.60	-	-	2	-	9	298	33.11	-	-	3-42
S.W.Eathorne	3	6	0	28	67	11.16	-	-	3	-						
A.M.Ellis	14	23	5	78	495	27.50	-	3	10	-	25	966	38.64	1	-	5-63
J.I.Englefield	46	82	5	172	2580	33.50	3	20	24	-	1	48	48.00	-	-	1-22
A.W.Evans	42	70	9	125	1731	28.37	1	7	28	-	0	39	-	-	-	-
S.A.Fairley	7	12	1	47*	214	19.45	-	-	3	-						
S.P.Fleming	189	316	28	274*	12,033	41.78	23	72	247	-	0	129	-	-	-	-
D.R.Flynn	5	9	2	69*	217	31.00	-	2	-	-						
J.E.C.Franklin	64	95	15	108*	2012	25.15	1	10	20	-	217	5195	23.94	8	1	7-60
P.G.Fulton	37	62	6	301*	2760	49.28	5	14	29	-	11	399	36.27	-	-	4-49
C.B.Gaffaney	83	152	11	194	4711	33.41	8	24	73	-	2	47	23.50	-	-	1-3
R.J.Gilhooly	1	2	1	13	17	17.00	-	-	-	-	1	55	55.00	-	-	1-46
M.R.Gillespie	31	41	7	81*	644	18.94	-	3	6	-	105	2705	25.76	4	-	6-81
B.B.J.Griggs	38	58	8	100*	1206	24.12	1	4	94	3						
L.J.Hamilton	50	69	22	23	232	4.93	-	-	16	-	182	4580	25.16	7	-	6-32
M.N.Hart	135	198	26	201*	4418	25.68	4	20	110	-	212	7424	35.01	7	-	6-73
B.E.Hefford	30	39	10	26	242	8.34	-	-	10	-	84	2089	24.86	1	-	5-50
G.J.T.Hegglun	2	2	0	8	8	4.00	-	-	-	-	6	141	23.50	-	-	3-60
P.A.Hitchcock	7	9	3	51	168	28.00	-	1	-	-	12	567	47.25	-	-	3-27
G.J.Hopkins	74	121	18	175*	2847	27.64	4	10	187	12	0	13	-	-	-	-
M.J.Horne	120	205	10	241	8199	42.04	24	30	75	-	7	531	75.85	-	-	2-58
N.K.W.Horsley	28	44	1	159	1450	33.72	3	7	12	-	1	24	24.00	-	-	1-15
J.M.How	40	67	4	169	2166	34.38	6	10	43	-	13	666	51.23	-	-	3-57
L.G.Howell	83	143	16	181	3586	28.23	3	20	48	-	0	110	-	-	-	-
P.J.Ingram	31	56	4	105*	1056	20.30	1	4	24	-						
R.A.Jones	80	140	8	188	4220	31.96	9	21	70	-	1	0	0.00	-	-	1-0
H.J.H.Marshall	56	92	5	160	2587	29.73	3	12	29	-	2	113	56.50	-	-	1-12
J.A.H.Marshall	71	121	2	235	3423	28.76	4	21	77	-	3	160	53.33	-	-	1-5
B.P.Martin	51	66	20	113*	950	20.65	1	2	26	-	134	3975	29.66	9	2	7-33
C.S.Martin	86	107	47	25	252	4.20	-	-	17	-	252	8212	32.58	10	1	6-54
M.J.Mason	50	65	19	44	743	16.15	-	-	15	-	158	4016	25.41	7	1	6-56
B.B.McCullum	41	71	4	143	1981	29.56	3	11	97	7						
N.L.McCullum	14	23	2	80	485	23.09	-	3	13	-	21	796	37.90	-	-	4-57
P.D.McGlashan	18	27	4	65	471	20.47	-	1	42	3						
T.G.McIntosh	50	82	7	182	2456	32.74	8	10	43	-	0	61	-	-	-	-
A.J.McKay	3	3	1	8	12	6.00	-	-	2	-	7	244	34.85	-	-	3-34
M.N.McKenzie	31	53	2	100	924	18.11	1	4	19	-						
C.D.McMillan	121	197	22	168*	6962	39.78	13	41	50	-	78	2744	35.17	1	-	6-71
J.M.McMillan	15	20	8	19	59	4.91	-	-	1	-	33	1143	34.63	-	-	4-36
W.C.McSkimming	34	50	10	111	756	18.90	1	1	17	-	123	2954	24.01	7	1	6-39
K.D.Mills	40	56	17	117*	1395	35.76	1	9	13	-	112	2987	26.66	3	1	5-33
S.M.Mills	7	10	2	64	136	17.00	-	1	13	-						
Mohammad Wasim	124	199	8	192	5857	30.66	14	26	123	5	5	342	68.40	-	-	2-12

	M	In	NO	HS	Runs	Ave	100	50	Ct	St	Wkts	Runs	Ave	5WI	10WM	Best
G.B.Murray	3	6	0	33	76	12.66	-	-	-	-	0	88	-	-	-	-
C.J.Nevin	74	115	17	143*	3259	33.25	3	15	205	7	0	0	-	-	-	-
R.J.Nicol	37	55	5	147*	1864	37.28	4	11	28	-	12	551	45.91	-	-	2-26
I.E.O'Brien	33	36	11	28	189	7.56	-	-	5	-	122	2828	23.18	5	-	6-55
J.D.P.Oram	53	82	13	155	2623	38.01	5	13	29	-	85	2510	29.52	1	-	5-30
M.G.Orchard	24	40	5	97	894	25.54	-	5	17	-	33	1170	35.45	1	-	5-10
M.H.W.Papps	60	108	9	192	3224	32.56	7	15	70	3	0	4	-	-	-	-
T.J.T.Papps	7	11	0	33	117	10.63	-	-	8	-						
M.E.Parlane	92	156	7	203	4426	29.70	9	15	51	-	1	17	17.00	-	-	1-14
N.R.Parlane	42	69	6	147	1971	31.28	2	13	41	-	0	21	-	-	-	-
J.S.Patel	46	54	21	58*	535	16.21	-	1	14	-	86	3488	40.55	3	-	6-32
A.J.Redmond	47	80	5	101	1961	26.13	1	12	25	-	68	2940	43.23	-	-	4-35
M.H.Richardson	157	264	31	306	9994	42.89	20	48	91	-	44	1911	43.43	1	-	5-77
G.G.Robinson	15	24	1	125*	551	23.95	1	2	4	-	0	16	-	-	-	-
J.D.Ryder	17	27	3	236	1071	44.62	2	4	14	-	18	349	19.38	-	-	4-23
A.M.Schwass	29	39	8	44	558	18.00	-	-	10	-	109	2554	23.42	6	-	7-36
B.E.Scott	19	24	7	96	319	18.76	-	1	7	-	61	1708	28.00	2	-	6-48
D.G.Sewell	61	82	40	24	266	6.33	-	-	15	-	199	5650	28.39	10	1	8-31
G.S.Shaw	11	13	7	14	43	7.16	-	-	2	-	40	964	24.10	1	-	5-73
H.J.Shaw	16	21	5	47*	275	17.18	-	-	6	-	36	1337	37.13	1	-	5-84
J.W.Sheed	23	39	3	89	508	14.11	-	3	17	-	1	56	56.00	-	-	1-30
R.R.Sherlock	3	5	2	14*	24	8.00	-	-	2	-	6	208	26.00	-	-	4-33
R.R.Shutte	1	2	0	12	20	10.00	-	-	-	-	2	39	19.50	-	-	2-39
M.S.Sinclair	110	186	20	268	7845	47.25	17	42	111	1	2	132	66.00	-	-	1-4
C.M.Smith	2	3	1	6	10	5.00	-	-	-	-	4	166	41.50	-	-	2-59
W.E.R.Somerville	1	2	0	16	16	8.00	-	-	1	-	4	85	21.25	-	-	3-26
C.M.Spearman	149	267	15	341	9654	38.30	21	46	140	-	1	55	55.00	-	-	1-37
G.R.Stead	94	153	10	190	4722	33.02	10	22	45	-	8	587	73.37	-	-	4-58
S.L.Stewart	26	47	1	149	1288	28.00	1	7	8	-	4	225	56.25	-	-	2-52
S.B.Styris	79	131	14	212*	3647	31.17	6	16	60	-	143	4334	30.30	6	-	6-32
G.P.Sulzberger	83	135	12	159	3836	31.18	8	17	56	-	147	5175	35.20	2	-	6-54
R.L.Taylor	23	33	2	184	1029	33.19	1	7	18	-						
E.P.Thompson	22	32	4	126	652	23.28	2	2	6	-	67	1964	29.31	2	1	7-55
G.R.Todd	18	34	7	123*	841	31.14	1	5	8	-	11	678	61.63	-	-	2-34
K.W.M.Todd	2	4	0	84	98	24.50	-	1	-	-						
D.R.Tuffey	69	85	20	89*	888	13.66	-	3	30	-	234	6062	25.94	9	1	7-12
A.D.Turner	8	7	1	16	42	7.00	-	-	1	-	17	635	37.35	1	-	5-66
D.L.Vettori	103	142	21	137*	2794	23.09	2	15	46	-	338	11012	32.57	22	2	7-87
L.Vincent	67	107	7	224	3715	37.15	8	24	87	-	4	334	83.50	-	-	2-37
B.G.K.Walker	84	109	27	107*	1769	21.57	1	4	38	-	164	5325	32.46	4	-	8-107
K.P.Walmsley	63	77	17	59	642	10.70	-	1	19	-	230	5861	25.48	8	1	7-28
J.S.Ward	2	4	3	8*	13	13.00	-	-	-	-	4	150	37.50	-	-	3-71
B-J.Watling	8	16	0	77	320	20.00	-	2	14	-						
R.M.West	15	19	4	44	250	16.66	-	-	8	-	25	1253	50.12	-	-	3-52
B.S.Wilson	5	10	0	96	224	22.40	-	1	1	-						
J.W.Wilson	39	64	7	78	1245	21.84	-	6	29	-	129	3113	24.13	7	-	5-34
P.J.Wiseman	144	197	40	107	3109	19.80	1	11	68	-	401	13264	33.07	17	4	9-13
L.J.Woodcock	28	47	2	106	1212	26.93	1	5	14	-	25	868	34.72	-	-	4-3
R.A.Young	52	61	10	101*	718	14.07	1	1	162	3						
J.A.F.Yovich	65	100	20	99	2078	25.97	-	13	16	-	185	5643	30.50	7	1	7-64

STATE SHIELD

2004/05

Northern Districts won the State Shield for the second time in three years when they defeated the previous season's winners, Central Districts, in the season final.

Central Districts won the round-robin section by three points from Northern Districts who had a comfortable ten point margin over Canterbury in third place. Otago, Wellington and Auckland failed to qualify for the semi-final stage. Otago and Wellington had chances but fell away at crucial times while Auckland, who had a commanding lead in the State Championship, failed completely in the one-day game.

The most exciting game of the season was in round nine when Welllington scored a massive 264-8 off 32 overs in a reduced innings match. When Northern Districts batted there were further interruptions but they won when Peter McGlashan hit a six off the last ball to reach the required 164-5 off the 20 overs which constituted a game.

The leading run scorers were: Nathan Astle (502), Michael Papps (423) and Craig Cumming (380) while the leading wicket takers were Graeme Aldridge, with a record breaking 30, followed by Lance Hamilton (18) and Andrew Schwass (15).

The same format as the previous season was in place with the top qualifier hosting the final and the second placed side hosting the semi-final. However, Northern's favoured home ground, Westpac Park in Hamilton, was not available because of problems with the pitch, so the semi-final was played at a neutral venue, Eden Park Outer Oval. Central's preferred venue of McLean Park could not be used as there was no available accommodation in Napier because of a Rod Stewart concert, so the game was played at Pukekura Park, New Plymouth.

Final points were:

	P	*W*	*L*	*NR*	*Bonus*	*Points*
Central Districts	10	7	2	1	5	35
Northern Districts	10	7	2	1	2	32
Canterbury	10	4	4	2	2	22
Otago	10	4	5	1	2	20
Wellington	10	3	6	1	–	14
Auckland	10	1	7	2	–	8

First Round

Barnett, Diamanti *(Central Districts)*, Flynn, Watling *(Northern Districts)* and Murray *(Wellington)* made their debuts. McIntosh made his debut for Canterbury, McGlashan and Howell made their Northern Districts debuts, Redmond and Todd made Otago debuts and Ryder made his Wellington debut.

Northern lost two early wickets but then Marshall, Hart and Yovich all reached fifty. Marshall needed 56 balls, Yovich 59 and Hart 73 as Northern got a competitive 262. Patel and Ryder had their best bowling figures. Wellington were soon in trouble but Bell was able to pass 2000 runs. Nevin and Woodcock both scored fifties, Nevin needing 45 balls and Woodcock 74 for his maiden fifty, but when a win looked likely Orchard produced his best bowling figures to give Northern a ten run win.

Auckland lost two wickets at 16 and struggled throughout against a tight Central attack. Only Canning and Adams got to thirty forAuckland. Mason, 4-23, and Sulzberger, 2-25, were the pick of the bowlers. Central were in a tight spot at 85-4 but then Sulzberger (50 off 55 balls) and Griggs had an unbroken stand of 89 to give Central a five wicket win and a bonus point.

Otago had an 87 run opening stand with Gaffaney getting 50 from 54 balls. Seven wickets fell for 60 before Scott got his highest score getting Otago to 247. McIntosh reached his highest score and supported McMillan in a 123 run stand for the third wicket, with McMillan getting his sixth century (from 92 balls) as Canterbury won with five deliveries to spare.

WELLINGTON v NORTHERN DISTRICTS — State Shield

at Basin Reserve, Wellington on 27 December, 2004
Toss : Wellington. Umpires : R.D. Anderson & M.P. George
Northern Districts won by 11 runs. *Points: Northern Districts 4, Wellington 0*

NORTHERN DISTRICTS

	Runs	Mins	Balls	6s	4s
L.G.Howell b Turner	4	28	12	-	-
B-J.Watling lbw b Turner	0	1	2	-	-
D.R.Flynn b Patel	27	68	52	-	3
J.A.H.Marshall* c Nevin b Patel	67	85	73	1	8
M.N.Hart b Ryder	67	112	85	-	7
J.A.F.Yovich run out	52	95	61	-	4
P.D.McGlashan† c Woodcock b Gillespie	12	12	10	-	2
I.G.Butler c & b Gillespie	1	1	2	-	-
M.G.Orchard not out	12	9	9	-	2
B.P.Martin					
G.W.Aldridge					
Extras (lb 4, w 11, nb 6)	21				
TOTAL (50 overs) (8 wkts)	**263**	213			

WELLINGTON

	Runs	Mins	Balls	6s	4s
C.J.Nevin† c Yovich b Butler	90	153	102	1	12
M.E.Parlane c McGlashan b Butler	2	12	9	-	-
J.D.Ryder c McGlashan b Butler	0	4	3	-	-
M.D.Bell* c Watling b Aldridge	11	28	21	1	-
N.R.Parlane c & b Martin	13	40	30	-	1
J.E.C.Franklin c McGlashan b Orchard	0	6	6	-	-
L.J.Woodcock c Howell b Orchard	71	109	91	1	8
G.B.Murray c Yovich b Marshall	15	18	15	-	2
M.R.Gillespie b Orchard	11	10	8	-	1
J.S.Patel b Orchard	10	23	12	-	1
A.D.Turner not out	0	3	0	-	-
Extras (lb 11, w 7, nb 11)	29				
TOTAL (47.5 overs)	**252**	212			

Bowling	*O*	*M*	*R*	*W*
WELLINGTON				
Turner	10	0	51	2
Franklin	10	0	44	0
Gillespie	10	0	68	2
Patel	10	1	37	2
Murray	7	0	37	0
Ryder	3	0	22	1
NORTHERN DISTRICTS				
Butler	9	0	42	3
Aldridge	8	0	39	1
Yovich	1	0	19	0
Orchard	8.5	0	47	4
Martin	10	0	35	1
Marshall	9	0	47	1
Hart	2	0	12	0

Fall of Wickets	***ND***	***W***
1st	1	10
2nd	24	10
3rd	84	35
4th	129	104
5th	225	106
6th	242	169
7th	245	196
8th	263	221
9th	-	252
10th	-	252

CENTRAL DISTRICTS v AUCKLAND — State Shield

at Fitzherbert Park, Palmerston North on 27 December, 2004
Toss : Central Districts. Umpires : G.A. Baxter & D.J. Ellwood
***Central Districts won by 6 wickets.** Points: Central Districts 5, Auckland 0*

AUCKLAND

	Runs	Mins	Balls	6s	4s
R.A.Jones c Griggs b Mason	12	16	11	-	1
M.J.Horne c Griggs b Schwass	18	69	47	-	2
L.Vincent c Griggs b Mason	0	1	2	-	-
R.J.Nicol run out	24	96	63	-	3
A.C.Barnes b Sulzberger	7	37	26	-	-
T.K.Canning c Englefield b Hamilton	34	88	90	-	3
P.A.Hitchcock c Thompson b Mason	0	8	7	-	-
A.R.Adams c Griggs b Sulzberger	34	40	20	1	4
R.A.Young† not out	18	39	27	-	1
K.P.Walmsley b Diamanti	3	9	6	-	-
B.G.K.Walker* c Schwass b Mason	1	3	3	-	-
Extras (lb 7, w 15)	22				
TOTAL (49.5 overs)	**173**	212			

CENTRAL DISTRICTS

	Runs	Mins	Balls	6s	4s
C.M.Spearman c Young b Walmsley	20	27	20	-	2
J.M.How lbw b Adams	14	15	12	-	3
G.E.F.Barnett c Horne b Hitchcock	22	49	44	-	3
J.I.Englefield c Vincent b Hitchcock	9	55	34	-	1
G.P.Sulzberger* not out	66	87	74	-	9
B.B.J.Griggs† not out	27	69	44	-	4
B.J.Diamanti					
E.P.Thompson					
A.M.Schwass					
M.J.Mason					
L.J.Hamilton					
Extras (lb 3, w 7, nb 6)	16				
TOTAL (37 overs) (4 wkts)	**174**	156			

Bowling	*O*	*M*	*R*	*W*
CENTRAL DISTRICTS				
Hamilton	10	0	56	1
Mason	9.5	2	23	4
Schwass	9	1	32	1
Thompson	4	0	14	0
Diamanti	9	2	16	1
Sulzberger	8	3	25	2
AUCKLAND				
Adams	10	3	35	1
Walmsley	7	0	42	1
Canning	6	0	24	0
Hitchcock	10	1	42	2
Walker	4	0	28	0

Fall of Wickets	***A***	***CD***
1st	16	27
2nd	16	37
3rd	46	72
4th	74	85
5th	76	-
6th	80	-
7th	125	-
8th	161	-
9th	168	-
10th	173	-

OTAGO v CANTERBURY — State Shield

at Molyneux Park, Alexandra on 27 December, 2004
Toss : Canterbury. Umpires : D.J. Walker & E.A. Watkin
***Canterbury won by 5 wickets.** Points: Canterbury 4, Otago 0*

OTAGO

	Runs	Mins	Balls	6s	4s
C.B.Gaffaney b McMillan	55	103	63	-	8
C.D.Cumming* c Fulton b Shaw	39	77	56	-	7
G.J.Hopkins† run out	25	26	23	-	4
Mohammad Wasim run out	4	10	8	-	-
J.W.Wilson c Shaw b McMillan	22	21	20	-	3
A.J.Redmond run out	14	40	30	-	-
N.L.McCullum run out	12	26	23	-	-
G.R.Todd not out	18	61	31	-	1
W.C.McSkimming lbw b Cunis	0	3	3	-	-
B.E.Scott c McMillan b Ellis	30	46	42	-	4
J.M.McMillan run out	2	7	4	-	-
Extras (lb 15, w 4, nb 7)	26				
TOTAL (49.2 overs)	**247**	212			

CANTERBURY

	Runs	Mins	Balls	6s	4s
M.H.W.Papps† c Gaffaney b McSkimming	29	60	49	-	4
T.G.McIntosh b Cumming	74	162	113	-	9
P.G.Fulton b Scott	1	2	2	-	-
C.D.McMillan* not out	113	147	100	3	10
G.R.Stead run out	11	31	18	-	1
S.L.Stewart c Hopkins b McMillan	1	4	5	-	-
P.J.Wiseman not out	14	10	9	-	2
A.M.Ellis					
S.J.Cunis					
H.J.Shaw					
C.S.Martin					
Extras (lb 2, w 2, nb 1)	5				
TOTAL (49.1 overs) (5 wkts)	**248**	213			

Bowling	*O*	*M*	*R*	*W*
CANTERBURY				
Martin	10	2	60	0
Cunis	9	1	36	1
Shaw	8.2	0	46	1
Ellis	5	0	28	1
Wiseman	10	1	42	0
McMillan	7	0	20	2
OTAGO				
McMillan	9.1	0	44	1
Wilson	9	0	43	0
McSkimming	10	0	41	1
Scott	7	0	34	1
McCullum	3	0	17	0
Cumming	9	0	48	1
Todd	2	0	19	0

Fall of Wickets	***O***	***C***
1st	87	59
2nd	130	60
3rd	137	183
4th	139	227
5th	166	229
6th	188	-
7th	190	-
8th	190	-
9th	235	-
10th	247	-

Second Round

The games between Auckland and Northern Districts, and Canterbury and Central Districts were both abandoned without a ball being bowled.

Play was possible between Otago and Wellington but rain stopped play after 46.2 overs with Wellington in a good position restricting Otago to 127-9. Only Todd (highest score) looked comfortable. Patel (best bowling) and Franklin were very economical.

OTAGO v WELLINGTON — State Shield

at Molyneux Park, Alexandra on 30 December, 2004
Toss : Otago. Umpires : D.B. Cowie & E.A. Watkin
***No result.** Points: Otago 2, Wellington 2*

OTAGO

	Runs	Mins	Balls	6s	4s
C.D.Cumming* b Franklin	10	35	27	-	-
C.B.Gaffaney c Nevin b Turner	2	9	13	-	-
A.J.Redmond b Gillespie	20	66	47	-	3
G.J.Hopkins† lbw b Turner	3	9	10	-	-
Mohammad Wasim c & b Patel	5	41	31	-	-
G.R.Todd not out	46	111	82	-	4
J.W.Wilson b Patel	0	1	2	-	-
N.L.McCullum c Parlane b Patel	3	24	14	-	-
W.C.McSkimming b Murray	14	44	36	-	1
B.E.Scott b Ryder	2	9	4	-	-
J.M.McMillan not out	9	15	13	-	-
Extras (b 4, lb 1, w 7, nb 1)	13				
TOTAL (46.2 overs) (9 wkts)	**127**	191			

WELLINGTON

	Runs	Mins	Balls	6s	4s
C.J.Nevin †					
S.P.Fleming					
J.D.Ryder					
M.D.Bell *					
N.R.Parlane					
J.E.C.Franklin					
L.J.Woodcock					
G.B.Murray					
M.R.Gillespie					
J.S.Patel					
A.D.Turner					

Bowling WELLINGTON	O	M	R	W
Turner	8.2	0	19	2
Franklin	10	1	23	1
Ryder	5	0	29	1
Gillespie	8	2	20	1
Patel	10	1	19	3
Murray	5	0	12	1

Fall of Wickets	O
1st	5
2nd	22
3rd	25
4th	42
5th	48
6th	48
7th	64
8th	99
9th	106
10th	-

CENTRAL DISTRICTS v CANTERBURY — State Shield

at Trafalgar Park, Nelson on 30 December, 2004
***Abandoned without a ball being bowled.** Points: Central Districts 2, Canterbury 2*

NORTHERN DISTRICTS v AUCKLAND — State Shield

at Owen Delany Park, Taupo on 30 December, 2004
***Abandoned without a ball being bowled.** Points: Northern Districts 2, Auckland 2*

Third Round

Otago had an opening stand of 145 against Auckland and this set them up to record their highest one-day score. Gaffaney reached his first century from 131 balls and Cumming passed 1000 runs. A cameo from Wilson, 50 off 32 balls, ensured a good total. Auckland lost two early wickets and never recovered. Wilson and Todd recorded best bowling figures and McSkimming reached 50 wickets as Otago won by a massive 152 runs.

Fleming captained a New Zealand provincial side for the first time and sent Canterbury in. This back-fired, however, as Papps and Astle broke the Canterbury first wicket record. Papps got 50 from 78 balls and his second hundred from 132. He also reached 1000 runs. Astle got his fifty from 57 balls as Canterbury reached 307-3. Wellington were always struggling and never threatened their target. Astle made a welcome return to the bowling crease as Canterbury gained a bonus point for its 92 run win.

Northern were sent in at Taupo and struggled throughout with no one able to score 20. Schwass had his best bowling figures and also reached 50 wickets. The Duckworth/Lewis system came into play twice and Central's target was revised to 98. However, they too struggled being 47-7 at one stage. Aldridge got his 50th wicket and Hart his 50th catch but Central were able to win with one wicket left.

AUCKLAND v OTAGO — State Shield

at Eden Park Outer Oval, Auckland on 1 January, 2005
Toss : Auckland. Umpires : A.L. Hill & I.W. Shine
Otago won by 152 runs. *Points: Otago 5, Auckland 0*

OTAGO	Runs	Mins	Balls	6s	4s
C.B.Gaffaney not out	101	208	132	1	9
C.D.Cumming* b Canning	73	101	79	1	6
G.J.Hopkins† lbw b Canning	0	1	1	-	-
A.J.Redmond run out	1	5	2	-	-
Mohammad Wasim lbw b Canning	4	10	15	-	-
G.R.Todd c Young b Hitchcock	23	43	35	-	2
J.W.Wilson b Mills	50	35	33	2	5
N.L.McCullum lbw b Adams	9	14	6	-	1
W.C.McSkimming					
B.E.Scott					
J.M.McMillan					
Extras (lb 18, w 13, nb 3)	34				
TOTAL (50 overs) (7 wkts)	**295**	208			

AUCKLAND	Runs	Mins	Balls	6s	4s
R.A.Jones c Redmond b McMillan	4	11	18	-	1
M.J.Horne b McMillan	1	2	2	-	-
L.Vincent b McMillan	28	26	24	1	4
A.C.Barnes c Redmond b Wilson	10	61	37	-	-
T.K.Canning lbw b McSkimming	4	10	10	-	1
K.D.Mills c Wilson b Todd	35	86	67	-	5
P.A.Hitchcock b Wilson	0	3	3	-	-
A.R.Adams b Wilson	0	1	1	-	-
R.A.Young† b McSkimming	35	73	61	-	4
K.P.Walmsley not out	11	39	27	-	1
B.G.K.Walker* c Scott b Todd	3	5	7	-	-
Extras (b 1, lb 4, w 7)	12				
TOTAL (41.4 overs)	**143**	168			

Bowling	O	M	R	W
AUCKLAND				
Mills	10	1	62	1
Walmsley	4	0	32	0
Adams	10	1	48	1
Canning	10	0	40	3
Walker	3	0	20	0
Hitchcock	10	0	62	1
Barnes	3	0	13	0
OTAGO				
McMillan	8	1	34	3
McSkimming	8	0	25	2
Scott	8	2	24	0
Wilson	8	2	23	3
Cumming	4	0	9	0
Todd	5.4	1	23	2

Fall of Wickets	O	A
1st	145	5
2nd	145	20
3rd	148	40
4th	165	45
5th	211	67
6th	280	67
7th	295	67
8th	-	105
9th	-	140
10th	-	143

CANTERBURY v WELLINGTON — State Shield

at Aorangi Park, Timaru on 1 January, 2005
Toss : Wellington. Umpires : G.C. Holdem & D.M. Quested
***Canterbury won by 92 runs.** Points: Canterbury 5, Wellington 0*

CANTERBURY

	Runs	Mins	Balls	6s	4s
M.H.W.Papps not out	129	203	153	1	13
N.J.Astle c Gillespie b O'Brien	88	129	100	2	11
C.D.McMillan* b Turner	30	39	24	2	2
C.L.Cairns c Parlane b Turner	0	1	1	-	-
B.B.McCullum† not out	43	31	24	2	5
P.G.Fulton					
G.R.Stead					
P.J.Wiseman					
H.J.Shaw					
S.J.Cunis					
C.S.Martin					
Extras (b 5, lb 5, w 5, nb 2)	17				
TOTAL (50 overs) (3 wkts)	**307**	203			

WELLINGTON

	Runs	Mins	Balls	6s	4s
C.J.Nevin† c Fulton b Cunis	45	83	51	-	7
S.P.Fleming* c McMillan b Shaw	5	17	12	-	1
J.D.Ryder c McCullum b Shaw	12	31	24	-	1
M.D.Bell lbw b Wiseman	26	60	47	-	3
N.R.Parlane lbw b Cunis	23	61	47	-	1
J.E.C.Franklin b Astle	46	61	51	1	4
M.R.Gillespie lbw b Astle	5	17	14	-	-
L.J.Woodcock b McMillan	1	5	6	-	-
J.S.Patel c Stead b Shaw	5	21	16	-	-
A.D.Turner b Martin	18	22	26	-	2
I.E.O'Brien not out	1	3	1	-	-
Extras (b 4, lb 12, w 9, nb 3)	28				
TOTAL (49 overs)	**215**	195			

Bowling	O	M	R	W
WELLINGTON				
Turner	9	0	53	2
Franklin	10	0	56	0
Gillespie	8	0	63	0
O'Brien	10	0	59	1
Patel	10	0	48	0
Ryder	3	0	18	0
CANTERBURY				
Martin	10	2	41	1
Shaw	8	0	31	3
Cairns	7	0	34	0
Cunis	10	0	44	2
Wiseman	6	1	28	1
Astle	5	1	13	2
McMillan	3	0	8	1

Fall of Wickets	***C***	***W***
1st	168	14
2nd	234	46
3rd	234	92
4th	-	115
5th	-	165
6th	-	184
7th	-	187
8th	-	187
9th	-	207
10th	-	215

NORTHERN DISTRICTS v CENTRAL DISTRICTS — State Shield

at Owen Delany Park, Taupo on 1 January, 2005
Toss : Central Districts. Umpires : R.D. Anderson & T.J. Parlane
***Central Districts won by 1 wicket (D/L).** Points: Central Districts 4, Northern Districts 0*

NORTHERN DISTRICTS

	Runs	Mins	Balls	6s	4s
L.G.Howell c Spearman b Hamilton	4	15	18	-	-
D.L.Vettori* c Sulzberger b Oram	19	59	27	-	2
M.N.Hart b Oram	12	34	31	-	1
J.A.H.Marshall lbw b Schwass	5	48	35	-	-
S.B.Styris c Griggs b Thompson	0	6	5	--	
H.J.H.Marshall c Griggs b Thompson	0	7	5	-	-
J.A.F.Yovich c Sinclair b Schwass	8	37	21	-	-
P.D.McGlashan† not out	19	40	32	-	1
D.R.Tuffey c Sulzberger b Schwass	17	16	19	-	2
I.G.Butler c How b Schwass	0	9	2	-	-
G.W.Aldridge lbw b Schwass	0	1	1	-	-
Extras (lb 5, w 5, nb 6)	16				
TOTAL (31.4 overs)	**100**	142			

CENTRAL DISTRICTS

	Runs	Mins	Balls	6s	4s
J.M.How c Styris b Tuffey	0	2	3	-	-
C.M.Spearman c Marshall J.A.H. b Butler	4	10	5	-	1
M.S.Sinclair b Tuffey	8	31	17	-	1
J.I.Englefield lbw b Butler	0	1	1	-	-
J.D.P.Oram* b Aldridge	7	52	35	-	1
G.P.Sulzberger c Aldridge b Butler	29	114	63	-	2
B.B.J.Griggs† c Hart b Styris	9	18	16	-	1
A.M.Schwass c Hart b Styris	0	2	4	-	-
E.P.Thompson c Marshall H.J.H. b Styris	15	27	19	-	2
M.J.Mason not out	18	37	32	-	2
L.J.Hamilton not out	1	1	2	-	-
Extras (w 7)	7				
TOTAL (32.5 overs) (9 wkts)	**98**	154			

Bowling	O	M	R	W
CENTRAL DISTRICTS				
Mason	8	1	22	0
Hamilton	5	0	23	1
Thompson	5.1	0	7	2
Oram	5	2	10	2
Sulzberger	2.5	0	11	0
Schwass	5.4	0	22	5
NORTHERN DISTRICTS				
Tuffey	7	0	11	2
Butler	6.5	1	26	3
Styris	7	4	15	3
Aldridge	6	0	30	1
Vettori	6	0	16	0

Fall of Wickets	***ND***	***CD***
1st	9	1
2nd	36	6
3rd	42	6
4th	45	20
5th	45	30
6th	58	47
7th	71	47
8th	89	66
9th	100	97
10th	100	-

Fourth Round

Otago again gave a good batting display and for the second time in as many matches reached its highest one-day score. Seven of the batsmen got past 20 including McCullum who got his highest score. Central struggled against a tight attack and only How and Englefield were able to get 25 as Otago cruised to a 95 run win and a bonus point.

Auckland had a breezy start but then were 75-4 before Nicol anchored the innings. He got 50 from 89 balls as Auckland reached 183, their highest score of the season to date. Wellington were going well until Canning came to the crease. He got three wickets in his first two overs and finished with his best bowling figures. Wellington needed 15 off the last two overs and scored 18 off the 49th over to have its first win of the season.

Northern got off to a reasonable start with 41 for the first wicket but then collapsed to be 148 all out. Howell became the first person to score 3000 runs in domestic one-day cricket. Canterbury were in total command at 86-0 but then lost all ten wickets for just 56. Aldridge had career best figures as Northern got an unlikely six run win.

CENTRAL DISTRICTS v OTAGO — State Shield

at Pukekura Park, New Plymouth on 3 January, 2005
Toss : Central Districts. Umpires : M.P. George & T.J. Parlane
Otago won by 95 runs. *Points: Otago 5, Central Districts 0*

OTAGO

	Runs	Mins	Balls	6s	4s
C.B.Gaffaney c Spearman b Oram	23	46	37	-	3
C.D.Cumming* c How b Schwass	57	95	62	1	8
A.J.Redmond c Sulzberger b Schwass	23	41	30	-	4
G.J.Hopkins† c Englefield b Hamilton	55	89	63	-	6
Mohammad Wasim c Mason b Sulzberger	23	53	41	-	2
J.W.Wilson c Griggs b Hamilton	9	19	12	-	1
N.L.McCullum b Schwass	34	38	24	-	3
G.R.Todd c Sulzberger b Diamanti	3	9	10	-	-
W.C.McSkimming c Englefield b Mason	5	11	5	-	1
B.E.Scott not out	29	15	16	2	2
J.M.McMillan not out	4	9	5	-	-
Extras (b 1, lb 16, w 12, nb 5)	34				
TOTAL (50 overs) (9 wkts)	**299**	222			

CENTRAL DISTRICTS

	Runs	Mins	Balls	6s	4s
C.M.Spearman c Wasim b McSkimming	1	6	4	-	-
J.M.How c McCullum b Wilson	55	103	78	1	7
M.S.Sinclair c Wasim b McMillan	23	54	42	-	3
J.I.Englefield st Hopkins b McCullum	34	68	54	-	4
J.D.P.Oram* c Cumming b Scott	17	42	32	-	2
G.P.Sulzberger c McMillan b Todd	12	27	13	-	1
B.B.J.Griggs† b McMillan	11	36	17	-	1
B.J.Diamanti run out	0	1	0	-	-
A.M.Schwass b Wilson	5	3	5	-	1
M.J.Mason b Wilson	8	8	9	-	1
L.J.Hamilton not out	1	8	4	-	-
Extras (b 1, lb 12, w 23, nb 1)	37				
TOTAL (42.5 overs)	**204**	183			

Bowling	*O*	*M*	*R*	*W*
CENTRAL DISTRICTS				
Mason	10	1	60	1
Hamilton	10	1	40	2
Oram	9	1	49	1
Schwass	10	0	66	3
Sulzberger	6	0	24	1
Diamanti	5	0	43	1
OTAGO				
McMillan	8.5	1	44	2
McSkimming	8	1	20	1
Wilson	9	0	39	3
Scott	8	0	30	1
McCullum	7	0	46	1
Todd	2	0	12	1

Fall of Wickets	*O*	*CD*
1st	61	12
2nd	119	56
3rd	124	104
4th	188	146
5th	215	163
6th	221	176
7th	226	176
8th	254	181
9th	270	197
10th	-	204

WELLINGTON v AUCKLAND — State Shield

at Basin Reserve, Wellington on 3 January, 2005
Toss : Auckland. Umpires : C.J. Morris & I.W. Shine
Wellington won by 3 wickets. *Points: Wellington 4, Auckland 0*

AUCKLAND

	Runs	Mins	Balls	6s	4s
R.A.Jones c Nevin b Franklin	23	57	42	-	3
M.J.Horne c Woodcock b Franklin	23	34	26	-	4
R.J.Nicol b Pasupati	52	144	91	-	4
L.Vincent c Fleming b O'Brien	0	8	7	-	
R.A.Young† c Nevin b Gillespie	6	32	24	-	-
A.C.Barnes c Bell b Pasupati	25	41	42	-	2
A.R.Adams c Franklin b Pasupati	9	27	23	-	1
T.K.Canning c Patel b Franklin	9	22	12	-	-
K.D.Mills c Bell b Pasupati	12	16	16	-	1
P.A.Hitchcock not out	10	17	9	-	1
B.G.K.Walker* run out	3	13	9	-	-
Extras (lb 2, w 5, nb 4)	11				
TOTAL (49.3 overs)	**183**	210			

WELLINGTON

	Runs	Mins	Balls	6s	4s
C.J.Nevin† b Canning	19	52	42	-	3
S.P.Fleming* c & b Mills	31	44	31	2	4
J.D.Ryder c Young b Canning	15	20	18	-	3
M.D.Bell c Walker b Canning	0	3	2	-	-
N.R.Parlane lbw b Adams	23	67	55	-	2
J.E.C.Franklin c Nicol b Canning	6	19	18	-	1
L.J.Woodcock c Canning b Mills	41	87	63	1	3
M.Y.Pasupati not out	38	75	49	1	4
M.R.Gillespie not out	8	26	17	-	1
J.S.Patel					
I.E.O'Brien					
Extras (w 5, nb 1)	6				
TOTAL (49 overs) (7 wkts)	**187**	200			

Bowling	O	M	R	W
WELLINGTON				
Gillespie	9.3	0	46	1
Franklin	10	2	35	3
O'Brien	9	0	31	1
Patel	10	0	27	0
Pasupati	10	0	37	4
Ryder	1	0	5	0
AUCKLAND				
Adams	10	1	34	1
Mills	9	2	32	2
Hitchcock	10	0	55	0
Canning	10	2	21	4
Walker	7	0	29	0
Barnes	3	0	16	0

Fall of Wickets	*A*	*W*
1st	37	51
2nd	55	56
3rd	56	56
4th	75	71
5th	118	82
6th	142	116
7th	152	153
8th	166	-
9th	170	-
10th	183	-

Parlane kept wicket from the 22nd over after Nevin was injured

CANTERBURY v NORTHERN DISTRICTS — State Shield

at Aorangi Park, Timaru on 3 January, 2005
Toss : Northern Districts. Umpires : G.C. Holdem & D.M. Quested
Northern Districts won by 6 runs. *Points: Northern Districts 4, Canterbury 0*

NORTHERN DISTRICTS

	Runs	Mins	Balls	6s	4s
L.G.Howell lbw b Astle	30	104	68	-	1
D.L.Vettori* c Papps b Cairns	28	31	26	-	4
M.N.Hart b Astle	10	27	25	-	1
S.B.Styris c McCullum b Astle	6	27	22	-	-
H.J.H.Marshall c McCullum b Wiseman	23	68	43	-	1
J.A.H.Marshall run out	3	9	8	-	-
J.A.F.Yovich lbw b Astle	2	5	4	-	-
P.D.McGlashan† b McMillan	25	58	55	1	2
D.R.Tuffey run out	0	3	1	-	-
G.W.Aldridge lbw b McMillan	0	5	4	-	-
I.G.Butler not out	2	12	14	-	-
Extras (b 1, lb 11, w 3, nb 4)	19				
TOTAL (44.2 overs)	**148**	179			

CANTERBURY

	Runs	Mins	Balls	6s	4s
M.H.W.Papps b Aldridge	41	120	85	-	5
N.J.Astle c Hart b Aldridge	45	87	72	-	6
T.G.McIntosh run out	0	9	8	-	-
P.G.Fulton b Aldridge	6	18	17	-	1
C.D.McMillan* c Vettori b Aldridge	0	7	4	-	-
C.L.Cairns c Vettori b Aldridge	3	11	4	-	-
B.B.McCullum† c McGlashan b Tuffey	17	26	21	-	3
P.J.Wiseman lbw b Styris	3	31	23	-	-
S.J.Cunis not out	13	35	30	-	2
H.J.Shaw b Styris	0	1	3	-	-
C.S.Martin run out	2	20	4	-	-
Extras (lb 6, w 5, nb 1)	12				
TOTAL (45 overs)	**142**	187			

Bowling	O	M	R	W
CANTERBURY				
Martin	7	1	16	0
Shaw	2	0	22	0
Cairns	6	1	23	1
Astle	10	3	19	4
Cunis	10	0	34	0
McMillan	5.2	2	5	2
Wiseman	4	0	17	1
NORTHERN DISTRICTS				
Tuffey	10	1	34	1
Butler	6	0	32	0
Styris	10	2	21	2
Vettori	10	2	15	0
Aldridge	9	0	34	5

Fall of Wickets	*ND*	*C*
1st	41	86
2nd	60	88
3rd	81	101
4th	98	102
5th	106	103
6th	112	112
7th	130	125
8th	130	129
9th	132	129
10th	148	142

Fifth Round

The Central versus Wellington game was reduced to 41 overs and Central won a vital toss as the ball seamed for the first ten overs. Wellington were indebted to Neal Parlane (50 off 62 balls) and some hitting from Gillespie and Pasupati to get to 166. Sulzberger and Hamilton both reached 50 wickets and the latter had his best bowling figures. Central lost two early wickets but then Spearman (50 off 71 balls) and Englefield (63 balls) added an unbeaten 148 from 155 balls to give Central an eight wicket win and a bonus point. Englefield got his highest score.

Otago reached 169 in its innings, rain having caused this game also to be reduced to 41 overs. No one was able to play the big innings that had been effective in their last two games. Northern in turn were made to work hard. Watling got his highest score and a cameo from McGlashan got them home with nine balls to spare.

Canterbury's game against Auckland was abandoned without any play.

AUCKLAND v CANTERBURY — State Shield

at Eden Park Outer Oval, Auckland on 7 January, 2005
Abandoned without a ball being bowled. *Points: Auckland 2, Canterbury 2*

CENTRAL DISTRICTS v WELLINGTON — State Shield

at Waikanae Park, Waikanae on 9 January, 2005
Toss : Central Districts. Umpires : P.D. Jones & C.J. Morris
Central Districts won by 8 wickets. *Points: Central Districts 5, Wellington 0*

WELLINGTON

	Runs	Mins	Balls	6s	4s
C.J.Nevin c Spearman b Hamilton	4	21	19	-	-
M.E.Parlane c & b Mason	1	32	24	-	-
J.D.Ryder c Griggs b Hamilton	1	26	15	-	-
M.D.Bell* c Griggs b Hefford	14	33	25	-	2
N.R.Parlane† b Hamilton	53	120	66	-	4
J.E.C.Franklin c Mason b Sulzberger	14	44	39	-	3
M.R.Gillespie c Spearman b Sulzberger	26	24	20	-	3
L.J.Woodcock st Griggs b Sulzberger	5	8	9	-	-
M.Y.Pasupati b Hamilton	27	16	17	2	1
G.B.Murray not out	3	12	6	-	-
J.S.Patel c Griggs b Mason	2	5	4	-	-
Extras (lb 2, w 11, nb 3)	16				
TOTAL (40.1 overs)	**166**	175			

CENTRAL DISTRICTS

	Runs	Mins	Balls	6s	4s
J.M.How b Gillespie	1	14	7	-	-
C.M.Spearman not out	68	130	86	1	6
M.S.Sinclair c Parlane M.E. b Gillespie	10	9	7	-	2
J.I.Englefield not out	80	105	86	2	10
J.D.P.Oram*					
G.P.Sulzberger					
B.B.J.Griggs†					
B.J.Diamanti					
B.E.Hefford					
M.J.Mason					
L.J.Hamilton					
Extras (lb 2, w 4, nb 2)	8				
TOTAL (30.4 overs) (2 wkts)	**167**	130			

Bowling	*O*	*M*	*R*	*W*
CENTRAL DISTRICTS				
Mason	8.1	2	28	2
Hamilton	8	4	13	4
Hefford	6	0	36	1
Oram	6	0	15	0
Diamanti	8	0	51	0
Sulzberger	4	0	21	3
WELLINGTON				
Gillespie	9	0	56	2
Franklin	6	0	21	0
Pasupati	4	0	24	0
Murray	2	0	9	0
Patel	7	0	33	0
Ryder	2	0	13	0
Woodcock	0.4	0	9	0

Fall of Wickets

	W	*CD*
1st	5	6
2nd	8	19
3rd	16	-
4th	33	-
5th	70	-
6th	108	-
7th	116	-
8th	155	-
9th	162	-
10th	166	-

OTAGO v NORTHERN DISTRICTS — State Shield

at University Oval, Dunedin on 9 January, 2005
Toss : Northern Districts. Umpires : R.D. Anderson & J.M. Busby
Northern Districts won by 2 wickets. *Points: Northern Districts 4, Otago 0*

OTAGO

	Runs	Mins	Balls	6s	4s
C.B.Gaffaney c Marshall H.J.H. b Tuffey	3	18	9	-	-
C.D.Cumming* c McGlashan b Aldridge	31	47	30	1	3
Mohammad Wasim c Marshall J.A.H. b Styris	27	39	33	1	3
G.J.Hopkins† c McGlashan b Yovich	27	68	48	-	3
A.J.Hore c McGlashan b Aldridge	9	25	16	-	1
J.W.Wilson c Marshall H.J.H. b Tuffey	1	9	7	-	-
G.R.Todd b Marshall H.J.H.	5	31	17	-	-
N.L.McCullum c Hart b Yovich	10	14	12	-	-
B.E.Scott b Tuffey	24	45	41	2	1
W.C.McSkimming b Styris	6	25	12	-	1
J.M.McMillan not out	2	14	8	-	-
Extras (lb 5, w 18, nb 1)	24				
TOTAL (38.4 overs)	**169**	172			

NORTHERN DISTRICTS

	Runs	Mins	Balls	6s	4s
L.G.Howell b McSkimming	6	19	16	-	-
B-J.Watling c Hopkins b Cumming	21	62	52	-	2
M.N.Hart b Scott	27	78	61	-	1
S.B.Styris c Hore b Cumming	0	8	4	-	-
H.J.H.Marshall c McMillan b McSkimming	21	59	40	-	1
J.A.F.Yovich b Todd	16	55	36	-	-
P.D.McGlashan† not out	41	40	20	3	3
D.R.Tuffey b Wilson	9	10	5	1	-
I.G.Butler c Todd b McMillan	1	4	3	-	-
J.A.H.Marshall* not out	1	1	1	-	-
G.W.Aldridge					
Extras (b 1, lb 13, w 12, nb 1)	27				
TOTAL (39.3 overs) (8 wkts)	**170**	172			

Bowling	*O*	*M*	*R*	*W*
NORTHERN DISTRICTS				
Tuffey	7.4	1	30	3
Butler	7	1	41	0
Styris	8	0	37	2
Aldridge	8	1	17	2
Marshall J.A.H.	2.2	0	7	0
Yovich	3.4	0	18	2
Marshall H.J.H.	2	0	14	1
OTAGO				
McMillan	6.3	0	28	1
McSkimming	8	1	39	2
Wilson	6	2	20	1
Scott	8	1	34	1
Cumming	8	0	18	2
Todd	3	0	17	1

Fall of Wickets

	O	*ND*
1st	20	17
2nd	66	55
3rd	70	65
4th	95	78
5th	98	104
6th	116	147
7th	130	167
8th	137	169
9th	153	-
10th	169	-

Sixth Round

Todd and McKay, both Auckland, made their debuts.

Central lost two wickets at 36 but thanks to Sinclair (fifty off 73 balls) they reached 229-8. He was assisted by Hamilton in an unbroken 42 run ninth wicket stand. Nicol had his best bowling figures. Auckland was in turmoil at 50-6 but highest scores to Mills and Hitchcock gave some respectability. Diamanti had his best bowling.

Otago had a good start courtesy of Gaffaney and Cumming. Gaffaney passed 2000 runs and then Hopkins reached 1000 runs as Otago got to a competitive 262. Wellington lost early wickets but Fleming reached fifty from 55 balls and then Franklin (fifty from 52 balls) registered his highest score and with good support got Wellington home with four balls to spare.

Northern had a 109 run stand for the third wicket between James Marshall and Styris, who both scored fifties from 72 balls which enabled Northern to get to 255-7. Canterbury had a 142 run opening stand between Papps and Astle but when the stand was broken Canterbury struggled and eventually fell 15 runs short. It was Astle's eighth century. McMillan reached 2000 domestic one-day runs.

AUCKLAND v CENTRAL DISTRICTS — State Shield

at Eden Park Outer Oval, Auckland on 28 January, 2005
Toss : Central Districts. Umpires : D.B. Cowie & A.L. Hill
Central Districts won by 55 runs. Points: Central Districts 5, Auckland 0

CENTRAL DISTRICTS

	Runs	Mins	Balls	6s	4s
C.M.Spearman c Canning b Mills	20	35	29	-	2
J.M.How lbw b Hitchcock	45	93	64	-	6
R.L.Taylor c Young b Mills	0	2	1	-	-
M.S.Sinclair not out	95	158	107	2	6
J.I.Englefield b Walker	11	12	13	1	-
G.P.Sulzberger* b Nicol	7	18	20	-	-
B.B.J.Griggs† c McKay b Nicol	0	6	9	-	-
B.J.Diamanti st Young b Nicol	18	29	33	-	1
A.M.Schwass b Hitchcock	10	14	13	1	-
L.J.Hamilton not out	12	14	13	-	-
B.E.Hefford					
Extras (b 1, lb 3, w 4, nb 3)	11				
TOTAL (50 overs) (8 wkts)	**229**	197			

AUCKLAND

	Runs	Mins	Balls	6s	4s
R.A.Jones c Griggs b Hamilton	6	26	24	-	1
A.C.Barnes c Taylor b Hefford	2	30	18	-	-
R.J.Nicol b Hefford	0	14	10	-	-
M.J.Horne lbw b Sulzberger	16	62	40	-	3
K.W.M.Todd c Spearman b Diamanti	4	45	22	-	1
T.K.Canning c Schwass b Sulzberger	0	20	13	-	-
K.D.Mills c How b Diamanti	47	75	66	2	3
P.A.Hitchcock b Diamanti	43	72	59	2	4
R.A.Young† not out	23	31	21	-	2
B.G.K.Walker* c Sinclair b Schwass	0	3	1	-	-
A.J.McKay b Hefford	7	16	14	-	1
Extras (lb 10, w 14, nb 2)	26				
TOTAL (47.4 overs)	**174**	202			

Bowling	*O*	*M*	*R*	*W*
AUCKLAND				
Mills	10	2	25	2
McKay	6	0	34	0
Barnes	5	0	29	0
Hitchcock	10	0	69	2
Walker	10	1	29	1
Nicol	9	0	39	3
CENTRAL DISTRICTS				
Hamilton	8	3	11	1
Hefford	8.4	3	29	3
Schwass	9	0	41	1
Diamanti	10	2	28	3
Sulzberger	8	1	37	2
How	4	0	18	0

Fall of Wickets	*CD*	*A*
1st	36	10
2nd	36	10
3rd	99	10
4th	115	39
5th	136	39
6th	138	50
7th	169	137
8th	187	147
9th	-	152
10th	-	174

WELLINGTON v OTAGO — State Shield

at Basin Reserve, Wellington on 28 January, 2005
Toss : Wellington. Umpires : G.A. Baxter & D.M. Quested
***Wellington won by 3 wickets.** Points: Wellington 4, Otago 0*

OTAGO

	Runs	Mins	Balls	6s	4s
C.B.Gaffaney c Franklin b Pasupati	84	119	86	-	12
C.D.Cumming* b Franklin	29	57	34	-	5
Mohammad Wasim c Parlane b Gillespie	4	23	17	-	-
A.J.Redmond run out	20	32	30	-	2
G.J.Hopkins† c Bell b Franklin	28	57	40	-	2
G.R.Todd c Nevin b Patel	27	36	21	-	5
J.W.Wilson c Parlane b Pasupati	21	28	28	-	1
A.J.Hore b Gillespie	15	31	16	-	1
N.L.McCullum b Turner	10	21	15	1	-
B.E.Scott b Turner	7	8	9	1	-
W.C.McSkimming not out	0	1	0	-	-
Extras (lb 9, w 6, nb 2)	17				
TOTAL (49.1 overs)	**262**	211			

WELLINGTON

	Runs	Mins	Balls	6s	4s
C.J.Nevin c Hore b McSkimming	18	26	26	-	3
S.P.Fleming* c Cumming b McCullum	64	73	58	2	7
J.D.Ryder c Hopkins b McSkimming	1	7	8	-	-
M.D.Bell c Gaffaney b Todd	13	63	38	-	1
N.R.Parlane† b Wilson	20	44	34	-	1
J.E.C.Franklin c Todd b Scott	76	102	65	4	3
L.J.Woodcock c Cumming b Todd	39	50	47	1	2
M.Y.Pasupati not out	30	25	26	2	1
M.R.Gillespie not out	0	4	1	-	-
J.S.Patel					
A.D.Turner					
Extras (b 1, lb 2, w 1, nb 1)	5				
TOTAL (49.2 overs) (7 wkts)	**266**	208			

Bowling	*O*	*M*	*R*	*W*
WELLINGTON				
Turner	9.1	1	52	2
Franklin	10	0	40	2
Patel	10	0	55	1
Gillespie	10	0	45	2
Pasupati	9	0	53	2
Woodcock	1	0	8	0
OTAGO				
Wilson	9.2	2	37	1
McSkimming	10	2	61	2
Scott	10	0	54	1
Todd	10	1	49	2
McCullum	8	0	47	1
Cumming	2	0	15	0

Fall of Wickets	***O***	***W***
1st	86	23
2nd	105	25
3rd	142	70
4th	146	103
5th	192	138
6th	227	216
7th	229	259
8th	254	-
9th	262	-
10th	262	-

NORTHERN DISTRICTS v CANTERBURY — State Shield

at Harry Barker Reserve, Gisborne on 28 January, 2005
Toss : Northern Districts. Umpires : B.G. Frost & E.A. Watkin
***Northern Districts won by 15 runs.** Points: Northern Districts 4, Canterbury 0*

NORTHERN DISTRICTS

	Runs	Mins	Balls	6s	4s
J.A.H.Marshall* c McCullum b Astle	85	154	109	-	11
N.K.W.Horsley c Stewart b Shaw	10	51	34	-	-
A.W.Evans b Cunis	0	16	10	-	-
S.B.Styris c McCullum b Martin	70	109	98	-	5
H.J.H.Marshall lbw b Astle	14	16	13	-	1
J.A.F.Yovich run out	24	25	21	-	2
P.D.McGlashan† not out	20	30	13	-	2
M.N.Hart c McMillan b Shaw	9	9	6	-	1
M.G.Orchard not out	0	1	0	-	-
D.R.Tuffey					
G.W.Aldridge					
Extras (lb 6, w 13, nb 4)	23				
TOTAL (50 overs) (7 wkts)	**255**	209			

CANTERBURY

	Runs	Mins	Balls	6s	4s
M.H.W.Papps c sub (T.T.Davis) b Yovich	51	130	91	-	6
N.J.Astle c McGlashan b Tuffey	123	205	146	2	14
P.G.Fulton b Yovich	0	10	5	-	-
C.D.McMillan* lbw b Aldridge	17	32	23	-	1
C.L.Cairns b Aldridge	3	9	8	-	-
B.B.McCullum† not out	18	37	19	-	-
P.J.Wiseman run out	3	12	8	-	-
S.J.Cunis b Aldridge	0	1	1	-	-
H.J.Shaw b Aldridge	0	1	1	-	-
S.L.Stewart not out	0	1	1	-	-
C.S.Martin					
Extras (b 1, lb 6, w 15, nb 3)	25				
TOTAL (50 overs) (8 wkts)	**240**	224			

Bowling	*O*	*M*	*R*	*W*
CANTERBURY				
Martin	8	0	36	1
Shaw	10	0	55	2
Cunis	8	1	32	1
Cairns	8	0	48	0
Wiseman	2	0	15	0
Astle	10	1	40	2
McMillan	4	0	23	0
NORTHERN DISTRICTS				
Tuffey	9	2	53	1
Aldridge	10	1	46	4
Orchard	9	0	52	0
Styris	10	2	30	0
Hart	5	0	21	0
Yovich	7	0	31	2

Fall of Wickets	***ND***	***C***
1st	48	142
2nd	57	152
3rd	166	183
4th	192	189
5th	197	225
6th	232	240
7th	251	240
8th	-	240
9th	-	-
10th	-	-

Seventh Round

Wellington got to 208 with most players getting a start but only Woodcock and Pasupati were able to pass 23. Auckland were again in trouble being 52-5 but a stout rearguard effort, with Mills getting a maiden fifty, saw them fall just seven runs short.

How (fifty off 90 balls) and Sinclair (fifty from 45 balls) had a stand of 80 after two wickets had fallen for 11. However some tight bowling restricted Central to 213. Astle and Fulton put on 117 for the second wicket. Astle's good form continued with fifty from 80 balls while Fulton required 56 balls for his half-century as Canterbury won with 10.1 overs to spare.

Otago struggled against a tight Northern attack and only an unbroken stand of 77 for the eighth wicket enabled them to get to 183-7. McCullum hit his maiden fifty off 37 balls. After James Marshall left early, Horsley and Evans added 98 for the second wicket. Northern won easily with 10.3 overs left.

AUCKLAND v WELLINGTON — State Shield

at Eden Park Outer Oval, Auckland on 30 January, 2005
Toss : Wellington. Umpires : I.W. Shine & T.J. Parlane
Wellington won by 7 runs. *Points: Wellington 4, Auckland 0*

WELLINGTON

	Runs	Mins	Balls	6s	4s
C.J.Nevin c Young b McKay	13	23	12	-	3
S.P.Fleming* c Horne b Barnes	23	66	46	-	4
M.E.Parlane c Jones b McKay	3	27	19	-	-
J.D.Ryder c Young b Walker	18	62	40	-	2
N.R.Parlane† st Young b Hitchcock	23	52	34	-	3
J.E.C.Franklin b Nicol	6	24	19	-	-
L.J.Woodcock lbw b Mills	42	88	71	-	3
M.Y.Pasupati run out	32	36	36	2	2
M.R.Gillespie b Hitchcock	10	17	13	-	-
J.S.Patel not out	12	16	11	-	2
A.D.Turner b Mills	2	2	3	-	-
Extras (lb 12, w 8, nb 4)	24				
TOTAL (50 overs)	**208**	211			

AUCKLAND

	Runs	Mins	Balls	6s	4s
R.A.Jones run out	1	17	11	-	-
A.C.Barnes lbw b Franklin	1	4	6	-	-
R.J.Nicol b Franklin	8	34	30	-	1
M.J.Horne b Turner	18	49	30	-	3
K.W.M.Todd c Parlane N.R. b Gillespie	6	32	21	-	1
T.K.Canning b Woodcock	31	66	53	-	3
K.D.Mills c Fleming b Patel	55	102	77	3	4
P.A.Hitchcock not out	38	65	55	1	2
R.A.Young† c Woodcock b Patel	5	14	13	-	-
B.G.K.Walker* not out	8	9	8	-	-
A.J.McKay					
Extras (b 5, lb 3, w 18, nb 4)	30				
TOTAL (50 overs) (8 wkts)	**201**	200			

Bowling	*O*	*M*	*R*	*W*
AUCKLAND				
Mills	10	1	34	2
McKay	10	2	37	2
Barnes	7	1	27	1
Hitchcock	6	0	39	2
Walker	10	1	33	1
Nicol	7	1	26	1
WELLINGTON				
Turner	10	1	34	1
Franklin	8	1	25	2
Gillespie	7	0	24	1
Patel	10	0	34	2
Pasupati	9	0	50	0
Woodcock	6	0	26	1

Fall of Wickets	*W*	*A*
1st	27	7
2nd	43	12
3rd	47	28
4th	93	51
5th	100	52
6th	119	123
7th	165	169
8th	185	183
9th	206	-
10th	208	-

CANTERBURY v CENTRAL DISTRICTS

State Shield

at Hagley Park, Christchurch on 30 January, 2005
Toss : Canterbury. Umpires : K. Cross & E.A. Watkin
***Canterbury won by 7 wickets.** Points: Canterbury 5, Central Districts 0*

CENTRAL DISTRICTS

	Runs	Mins	Balls	6s	4s
J.M.How c Cairns b Cunis	55	133	96	-	4
C.M.Spearman c McCullum b Martin	1	12	4	-	-
R.L.Taylor c Ellis b Cunis	6	6	8	-	1
M.S.Sinclair lbw b Astle	50	66	46	-	9
J.I.Englefield b Cunis	29	63	66	-	2
G.P.Sulzberger* c Cunis b McMillan	30	60	37	-	2
B.B.J.Griggs† b Cunis	3	11	8	-	-
B.J.Diamanti run out	5	11	9	-	-
A.M.Schwass b McMillan	19	22	14	-	3
L.J.Hamilton run out	1	6	2	-	-
B.E.Hefford not out	0	3	3	-	-
Extras (lb 10, w 2, nb 2)	14				
TOTAL (48.3 overs)	**213**	201			

CANTERBURY

	Runs	Mins	Balls	6s	4s
M.H.W.Papps c Taylor b Hefford	12	33	29	-	1
N.J.Astle c Englefield b Hamilton	65	132	100	-	8
P.G.Fulton not out	85	143	88	-	7
B.B.McCullum† b Hefford	34	40	20	2	3
C.L.Cairns not out	5	3	2	-	1
C.D.McMillan*					
S.L.Stewart					
P.J.Wiseman					
A.M.Ellis					
S.J.Cunis					
C.S.Martin					
Extras (b 1, lb 2, w 10)	13				
TOTAL (39.5 overs) (3 wkts)	**214**	177			

Bowling	*O*	*M*	*R*	*W*
CANTERBURY				
Martin	8	0	38	1
Cunis	10	0	38	4
Cairns	9.3	0	47	0
Astle	10	1	30	1
Wiseman	7	1	27	0
McMillan	3	0	12	2
Ellis	1	0	11	0
CENTRAL DISTRICTS				
Hamilton	10	3	41	1
Hefford	6.5	1	34	2
Schwass	10	0	54	0
Diamanti	8	0	61	0
Sulzberger	5	0	21	0

Fall of Wickets	***CD***	***C***
1st	2	30
2nd	11	147
3rd	91	208
4th	139	-
5th	153	-
6th	163	-
7th	173	-
8th	211	-
9th	212	-
10th	213	-

NORTHERN DISTRICTS v OTAGO

State Shield

at Harry Barker Reserve, Gisborne on 30 January, 2005
Toss : Otago. Umpires : D.B. Cowie & M.P. George
***Northern Districts won by 8 wickets.** Points: Northern Districts 5, Otago 0*

OTAGO

	Runs	Mins	Balls	6s	4s
C.B.Gaffaney b Aldridge	1	14	5	-	-
C.D.Cumming* c Horsley b Aldridge	16	34	32	-	2
G.J.Hopkins† c Styris b Tuffey	6	23	16	-	-
A.J.Redmond c Tuffey b Styris	12	51	33	-	1
A.J.Hore b Styris	11	57	38	-	1
G.R.Todd c Marshall J.A.H. b Orchard	13	29	26	-	2
J.W.Wilson c Styris b Hart	28	63	48	-	3
J.W.Sheed not out	32	85	64	-	3
N.L.McCullum not out	52	41	39	1	6
B.E.Scott					
W.C.McSkimming					
Extras (b 2, lb 5, w 4, nb 1)	12				
TOTAL (50 overs) (7 wkts)	**183**	202			

NORTHERN DISTRICTS

	Runs	Mins	Balls	6s	4s
J.A.H.Marshall* c Hore b Wilson	7	18	13	-	-
N.K.W.Horsley c Scott b McSkimming	77	109	90	2	12
A.W.Evans not out	58	134	103	-	5
S.B.Styris not out	30	43	31	-	4
M.N.Hart					
H.J.H.Marshall					
J.A.F.Yovich					
P.D.McGlashan †					
M.G.Orchard					
D.R.Tuffey					
G.W.Aldridge					
Extras (lb 4, w 11)	15				
TOTAL (39.3 overs) (2 wkts)	**187**	154			

Bowling	*O*	*M*	*R*	*W*
NORTHERN DISTRICTS				
Tuffey	8	1	32	1
Aldridge	8	0	26	2
Yovich	5	2	9	0
Styris	10	3	18	2
Orchard	10	0	44	1
Hart	9	0	47	1
OTAGO				
Wilson	8	1	38	1
McSkimming	10	1	28	1
Scott	8.3	2	45	0
Todd	3	0	15	0
Cumming	4	0	18	0
McCullum	4	1	23	0
Redmond	2	0	16	0

Fall of Wickets	***O***	***ND***
1st	11	24
2nd	26	122
3rd	26	-
4th	54	-
5th	57	-
6th	74	-
7th	106	-
8th	-	-
9th	-	-
10th	-	-

Eighth Round

Cachopa *(Auckland)* made his debut.

A 107 run stand between Papps and McMillan was the basis for Canterbury's 278. Papps had got his fifty off 54 balls and went to his second hundred of the season against Wellington after a further 84 deliveries. Nevin and Fleming gave Wellington a good start with Fleming getting fifty off 47 balls, 20 balls faster than Nevin. Wellington then struggled with only Neal Parlane able to score more than 25.

Auckland were 26-3 when Jones and debutant Cachopa put on 138. Cachopa got fifty from 87 balls, eight more than Jones who went on to record his highest score. Chasing 237 Otago started well and a 90 run second wicket stand between Cumming (fifty off 62 balls) and Hopkins (fifty off 65 balls) set them up and they won with 19 balls left.

Northern were struggling at 102-6 when McGlashan came to the wicket. He got his maiden fifty and Northern were able to get to 215-9. Diamanti's 4-39 were his best figures. How and Taylor added 172 for the second wicket as Central cantered to an easy win. Taylor was dismissed for 99.

WELLINGTON v CANTERBURY — State Shield

at Basin Reserve, Wellington on 1 February, 2005
Toss : Wellington. Umpires : D.M. Quested & E.A. Watkin
***Canterbury won by 15 runs.** Points: Canterbury 4, Wellington 0*

CANTERBURY

	Runs	Mins	Balls	6s	4s
M.H.W.Papps† c Patel b Pasupati	102	162	147	-	12
N.J.Astle c Ryder b Turner	8	24	13	-	1
P.G.Fulton c Nevin b Turner	20	38	30	-	3
C.D.McMillan* run out	49	81	43	1	5
S.L.Stewart b Franklin	22	38	25	-	2
C.L.Cairns c Patel b Pasupati	24	17	15	2	1
B.B.McCullum b Gillespie	15	14	11	-	1
A.M.Ellis b Patel	6	14	7	-	-
P.J.Wiseman c Turner b Gillespie	10	9	6	-	1
S.J.Cunis not out	8	9	6	1	-
C.S.Martin not out	0	3	1	-	-
Extras (b 1, lb 5, w 4, nb 4)	14				
TOTAL (50 overs) (9 wkts)	**278**	209			

WELLINGTON

	Runs	Mins	Balls	6s	4s
C.J.Nevin c Ellis b Wiseman	54	106	70	-	8
S.P.Fleming* c & b McMillan	54	80	52	1	6
M.E.Parlane run out	12	14	21	-	1
J.D.Ryder lbw b Astle	15	32	26	-	-
N.R.Parlane† c Papps b Cunis	36	53	49	-	2
J.E.C.Franklin c Papps b Wiseman	4	9	12	-	-
L.J.Woodcock b Cairns	8	27	14	-	-
M.Y.Pasupati c McMillan b Cairns	20	15	15	-	3
M.R.Gillespie not out	23	36	20	-	1
J.S.Patel c McMillan b Cunis	10	9	9	-	1
A.D.Turner not out	13	16	14	-	1
Extras (b 1, lb 6, w 5, nb 2)	14				
TOTAL (50 overs) (9 wkts)	**263**	203			

Bowling	*O*	*M*	*R*	*W*
WELLINGTON				
Turner	8	1	51	2
Franklin	10	0	61	1
Gillespie	10	1	53	2
Patel	10	0	50	1
Woodcock	1	0	7	0
Pasupati	9	0	43	2
Ryder	2	0	7	0
CANTERBURY				
Cunis	9	0	60	2
Martin	7	1	41	0
Astle	10	0	46	1
Cairns	10	0	41	2
McMillan	8	0	38	1
Wiseman	6	0	30	2

Fall of Wickets	*C*	*W*
1st	38	107
2nd	79	122
3rd	186	127
4th	201	160
5th	237	165
6th	241	190
7th	258	198
8th	262	220
9th	270	238
10th	-	-

OTAGO v AUCKLAND — State Shield

at Centennial Park, Oamaru on 1 February, 2005
Toss : Otago. Umpires : R.D. Anderson & D.J. Walker
***Otago won by 3 wickets.** Points: Otago 4, Auckland 0*

AUCKLAND

	Runs	Mins	Balls	6s	4s
M.J.Horne b Sewell	0	1	1	-	-
R.A.Jones c Redmond b Scott	92	176	113	1	11
R.J.Nicol lbw b Sewell	9	23	22	-	1
A.C.Barnes c Todd b Wilson	1	14	9	--	
C.Cachopa c Sewell b Todd	56	116	96	-	9
T.K.Canning run out	25	31	23	2	-
K.D.Mills c Wilson b Todd	7	9	10	-	-
P.A.Hitchcock not out	16	20	20	1	-
R.A.Young† not out	4	16	6	-	-
B.G.K.Walker*					
K.P.Walmsley					
Extras (lb 3, w 23)	26				
TOTAL (50 overs) (7 wkts)	**236**	207			

OTAGO

	Runs	Mins	Balls	6s	4s
C.B.Gaffaney c Young b Walmsley	28	55	36	-	4
C.D.Cumming* c Cachopa b Barnes	80	123	89	2	10
G.J.Hopkins† b Walker	54	93	72	-	6
A.J.Redmond lbw b Barnes	29	54	29	1	5
G.R.Todd c Hitchcock b Walker	8	16	20	-	1
J.W.Wilson c Canning b Barnes	2	4	6	-	-
N.L.McCullum not out	7	33	17	-	1
J.W.Sheed c Young b Barnes	0	1	2	-	-
B.E.Scott not out	8	25	13	-	-
W.C.McSkimming					
D.G.Sewell					
Extras (lb 12, w 6, nb 3)	21				
TOTAL (46.5 overs) (7 wkts)	**237**	206			

Bowling	*O*	*M*	*R*	*W*
OTAGO				
Sewell	7	0	34	2
McSkimming	10	2	35	0
Wilson	10	1	31	1
Scott	9	0	47	1
Cumming	3	0	19	0
Todd	8	0	55	2
McCullum	3	0	12	0
AUCKLAND				
Mills	9.5	1	54	0
Walmsley	10	0	53	1
Hitchcock	8	0	39	0
Walker	8	0	42	2
Barnes	10	1	30	4
Horne	1	0	7	0

Fall of Wickets	***A***	***O***
1st	0	74
2nd	21	164
3rd	26	179
4th	164	205
5th	194	207
6th	209	218
7th	216	218
8th	-	-
9th	-	-
10th	-	-

CENTRAL DISTRICTS v NORTHERN DISTRICTS — State Shield

at Queen Elizabeth Park, Masterton on 1 February, 2005
Toss : Central Districts. Umpires : G.A. Baxter & A.L. Hill
***Central Districts won by 5 wickets.** Points: Central Districts 4, Northern Districts 0*

NORTHERN DISTRICTS

	Runs	Mins	Balls	6s	4s
J.A.H.Marshall* c Spearman b Diamanti	17	45	40	-	3
N.K.W.Horsley c Griggs b Diamanti	22	50	28	-	3
A.W.Evans c Sulzberger b Diamanti	10	19	15	-	2
S.B.Styris b Hefford	43	141	85	-	1
H.J.H.Marshall b Diamanti	5	9	11	-	-
M.N.Hart c Diamanti b Sulzberger	2	20	15	-	-
J.A.F.Yovich lbw b Sulzberger	23	18	24	-	4
P.D.McGlashan† c Englefield b Hefford	65	72	68	1	6
D.R.Tuffey b Hefford	2	8	7	-	-
M.G.Orchard not out	6	9	5	-	1
G.W.Aldridge not out	1	2	2	-	-
Extras (b 6, lb 3, w 9, nb 1)	19				
TOTAL (50 overs) (9 wkts)	**215**	205			

CENTRAL DISTRICTS

	Runs	Mins	Balls	6s	4s
C.M.Spearman b Aldridge	6	20	11	-	-
J.M.How b Aldridge	60	152	97	-	9
R.L.Taylor c McGlashan b Aldridge	99	143	109	2	16
M.S.Sinclair c Hart b Tuffey	7	6	7	-	1
J.I.Englefield b Tuffey	0	1	1	-	-
G.P.Sulzberger* not out	18	25	13	-	3
B.B.J.Griggs† not out	8	24	18	-	1
A.M.Schwass					
B.J.Diamanti					
B.E.Hefford					
L.J.Hamilton					
Extras (lb 5, w 13, nb 2)	20				
TOTAL (42.3 overs) (5 wkts)	**218**	190			

Bowling	*O*	*M*	*R*	*W*
CENTRAL DISTRICTS				
Hamilton	10	1	48	0
Hefford	10	0	38	3
Diamanti	10	2	39	4
Sulzberger	10	0	34	2
Schwass	10	1	47	0
NORTHERN DISTRICTS				
Tuffey	10	2	39	2
Aldridge	10	0	37	3
Styris	7.3	0	30	0
Yovich	7	0	59	0
Orchard	3	0	17	0
Hart	3	0	17	0
Evans	2	0	14	0

Fall of Wickets	***ND***	***CD***
1st	46	11
2nd	48	183
3rd	57	192
4th	64	192
5th	73	192
6th	102	-
7th	198	-
8th	200	-
9th	208	-
10th	-	-

Ninth Round

Central, after being 51-2, got to 264-5 thanks to Spearman (highest score of the season) and Englefield. Central then completely demolished the Otago team who were routed for 64, equalling their lowest score and also equalling the biggest winning margin in New Zealand (also featuring the same two teams). Hamilton took his first five wicket bag.

Nicol and Canning added 84 for Auckland's fourth wicket. Nicol scored his fifty from 92 balls and Canning made his from 75 as Auckland reached 208-8. Astle was again the backbone of the Canterbury side getting fifty from 110 balls but he received little support and they fell short by eight runs to give Auckland its only win of the season.

The game between Northern and Wellington was full of drama. Wellington got off to a flying start and after rain interrupted the innings they had reached 267-8 off 32 overs. Fleming needed only 29 balls for fifty, Parlane required 48 and Nevin 50. Northern's innings was also interrupted and the target became 163. Six runs were required off the last ball of the 20th over and McGlashan duly despatched Franklin over the boundary to ensure Northern a home semi-final at least. Styris reached his fifty from 32 balls.

OTAGO v CENTRAL DISTRICTS — State Shield

at Queen's Park, Invercargill on 3 February, 2005
Toss : Central Districts. Umpires : D.M. Quested & E.A. Watkin
***Central Districts won by 200 runs**. Points: Central Districts 5, Otago 0*

CENTRAL DISTRICTS

	Runs	Mins	Balls	6s	4s
J.M.How c Hopkins b Wilson	12	37	22	-	2
C.M.Spearman c Hore b Wilson	94	170	128	-	8
R.L.Taylor c Todd b Wilson	3	14	18	-	-
M.S.Sinclair c Hore b Cumming	32	68	50	2	2
J.I.Englefield c Cumming b Scott	60	74	68	2	4
G.P.Sulzberger* not out	40	25	18	1	6
B.B.J.Griggs†					
B.J.Diamanti					
A.M.Schwass					
B.E.Hefford					
L.J.Hamilton					
Extras (lb 4, w 15, nb 4)	23				
TOTAL (50 overs) (5 wkts)	**264**	196			

OTAGO

	Runs	Mins	Balls	6s	4s
C.B.Gaffaney c Sulzberger b Hefford	2	6	6	-	-
C.D.Cumming* c Sulzberger b Hamilton	2	19	10	-	-
G.J.Hopkins† c & b Hefford	13	24	24	-	2
A.J.Redmond lbw b Hefford	0	26	11	-	-
A.J.Hore c Spearman b Hamilton	0	7	8	-	-
G.R.Todd b Hamilton	0	2	3	-	-
J.W.Wilson lbw b Hamilton	0	8	5	-	-
N.L.McCullum c Spearman b Hamilton	11	22	12	-	2
B.E.Scott not out	17	53	32	1	1
W.C.McSkimming c Griggs b Diamanti	2	17	14	-	-
D.G.Sewell c Spearman b Schwass	3	19	13	-	-
Extras (lb 3, w 6, nb 5)	14				
TOTAL (22.1 overs)	**64**	107			

Bowling	*O*	*M*	*R*	*W*
OTAGO				
Sewell	6	1	39	0
McSkimming	9	0	55	0
Wilson	10	0	47	3
Scott	6	0	36	1
McCullum	9	0	42	0
Cumming	10	0	41	1
CENTRAL DISTRICTS				
Hamilton	10	4	19	5
Hefford	6	2	21	3
Diamanti	5	1	15	1
Schwass	1.1	0	6	1

Fall of Wickets	***CD***	***O***
1st	43	6
2nd	51	14
3rd	134	20
4th	195	23
5th	264	23
6th	-	23
7th	-	23
8th	-	41
9th	-	49
10th	-	64

CANTERBURY v AUCKLAND — State Shield

at Hagley Park, Christchurch on 3 February, 2005
Toss : Auckland. Umpires : G.A. Baxter & I.W. Shine
Auckland won by 8 runs. *Points: Auckland 4, Canterbury 0*

AUCKLAND

	Runs	Mins	Balls	6s	4s
R.A.Jones c McMillan b Shaw	10	22	24	-	1
M.J.Horne b Shaw	6	33	17	-	-
R.J.Nicol c McMillan b Cairns	53	135	96	-	5
A.C.Barnes b Astle	16	59	41	-	1
T.K.Canning c Stead b McMillan	56	76	79	1	4
K.D.Mills c Fulton b Shaw	19	24	20	-	1
C.Cachopa lbw b Cunis	1	5	4	-	-
P.A.Hitchcock not out	24	22	14	1	2
R.A.Young† run out	2	3	1	-	-
K.P.Walmsley not out	7	11	7	-	-
B.G.K.Walker*					
Extras (lb 5, w 5, nb 4)	14				
TOTAL (50 overs) (8 wkts)	**208**	199			

CANTERBURY

	Runs	Mins	Balls	6s	4s
M.H.W.Papps† c Young b Walmsley	14	40	32	-	2
N.J.Astle c Horne b Hitchcock	93	208	145	1	5
P.G.Fulton b Barnes	8	36	20	-	-
P.J.Wiseman c Young b Barnes	2	4	5	-	-
C.D.McMillan* c Canning b Barnes	7	13	14	-	1
S.L.Stewart run out	29	54	40	-	4
C.L.Cairns c Horne b Canning	16	18	21	-	2
G.R.Stead lbw b Walker	2	8	2	-	-
A.M.Ellis not out	12	42	14	-	-
S.J.Cunis b Mills	4	8	6	-	-
H.J.Shaw not out	4	2	3	-	-
Extras (lb 4, w 3, nb 2)	9				
TOTAL (50 overs) (9 wkts)	**200**	220			

Bowling	O	M	R	W
CANTERBURY				
Cunis	10	2	36	1
Shaw	9	2	31	3
Cairns	10	1	47	1
Astle	10	0	38	1
McMillan	7	1	33	1
Ellis	2	0	12	0
Wiseman	2	0	6	0
AUCKLAND				
Mills	10	2	31	1
Walmsley	10	0	40	1
Canning	10	1	35	1
Barnes	10	1	22	3
Hitchcock	4	1	24	1
Walker	6	0	44	1

Fall of Wickets	A	C
1st	14	35
2nd	22	55
3rd	62	57
4th	146	71
5th	167	113
6th	169	138
7th	178	148
8th	180	190
9th	-	196
10th	-	-

NORTHERN DISTRICTS v WELLINGTON — State Shield

at Owen Delany Park, Taupo on 4 February, 2005
Toss : Northern Districts. Umpires : D.B. Cowie & T.J. Parlane
Northern Districts won by 5 wickets (D/L). *Points: Northern Districts 4, Wellington 0*

WELLINGTON

	Runs	Mins	Balls	6s	4s
C.J.Nevin c Yovich b Hart	70	127	74	-	8
S.P.Fleming* c Hart b Yovich	70	56	44	4	9
M.E.Parlane b Orchard	50	50	49	3	3
J.D.Ryder c Aldridge b Tuffey	17	14	11	-	2
N.R.Parlane† c Evans b Aldridge	5	21	10	-	-
J.E.C.Franklin c McGlashan b Aldridge	1	5	4	-	-
L.J.Woodcock st McGlashan b Hart	2	5	6	-	-
M.Y.Pasupati not out	13	30	15	-	1
M.R.Gillespie c Orchard b Tuffey	17	22	21	1	-
J.S.Patel not out	0	2	0	-	-
I.E.O'Brien					
Extras (lb 11, w 5, nb 6)	22				
TOTAL (38 overs) (8 wkts)	**267**	170			

NORTHERN DISTRICTS

	Runs	Mins	Balls	6s	4s
N.K.W.Horsley c Woodcock b Gillespie	0	2	3	-	-
A.W.Evans lbw b Franklin	0	9	2	-	-
J.A.F.Yovich c O'Brien b Gillespie	19	24	20	-	3
S.B.Styris c Nevin b Franklin	96	73	57	5	8
H.J.H.Marshall b Patel	11	23	16	-	-
M.N.Hart not out	18	33	22	-	1
P.D.McGlashan† not out	6	2	1	1	-
J.A.H.Marshall*					
M.G.Orchard					
D.R.Tuffey					
G.W.Aldridge					
Extras (lb 1, w 12, nb 1)	14				
TOTAL (20 overs) (5 wkts)	**164**	87			

Bowling	O	M	R	W
NORTHERN DISTRICTS				
Tuffey	8	0	49	2
Aldridge	7	0	71	2
Yovich	4	0	42	1
Styris	6	0	32	0
Hart	8	0	34	2
Orchard	5	0	28	1
WELLINGTON				
Gillespie	4	0	27	2
Franklin	4	0	31	2
O'Brien	3	0	30	0
Patel	5	0	43	1
Pasupati	4	0	32	0

Fall of Wickets	W	ND
1st	117	1
2nd	200	4
3rd	228	41
4th	229	98
5th	231	157
6th	236	-
7th	238	-
8th	265	-
9th	-	-
10th	-	-

Tenth Round

Eathorne and Smith *(Otago)* made their debuts. Hart and Michael Parlane were both playing their 100th game.

Canterbury had a century opening stand but then lost all ten wickets for 100 to finish on 202. Astle's 71 took him to 3000 runs, only the second player to achieve this. McCullum had his best bowling figures. Otago were in some bother at 136-6 but then Todd and debutant Eathorne saw them to a victory with 12 balls to spare. Todd reached his maiden fifty and Ellis had his best bowling figures.

Central Districts were looking good at 228-3 but then lost seven wickets for just 16 runs after Sinclair (fifty from 44 balls) was run out. He had passed 2000 runs. O'Brien took his first five wicket haul and Pasupati reached 50 wickets. Wellington struggled and only Franklin batted with any authority as they lost by 72 runs.

Vettori took to the Auckland attack getting fifty from 50 balls and then got his maiden century off 119 balls. He was ably assisted by Hamish Marshall (fifty off 62 balls). Auckland never threatened Northern's total and fell short by 112 runs. Canning finished the season with 999 one-day runs.

CANTERBURY v OTAGO — State Shield

at Hagley Park, Christchurch on 5 February, 2005
Toss : Canterbury. Umpires : A.L. Hill & G.A. Baxter
Otago won by 4 wickets. *Points: Otago 4, Canterbury 0*

CANTERBURY

	Runs	Mins	Balls	6s	4s
M.H.W.Papps c & b McCullum	43	85	68	1	5
N.J.Astle c Hopkins b Scott	71	123	84	1	7
B.B.McCullum† c Todd b McCullum	0	1	2	-	-
C.D.McMillan* c Smith b McCullum	14	30	37	-	1
C.L.Cairns run out	1	10	4	-	-
P.G.Fulton lbw b Wilson	4	22	20	-	-
S.L.Stewart c Smith b Scott	33	66	51	-	1
A.M.Ellis run out	14	34	21	-	-
P.J.Wiseman c Sheed b McSkimming	14	18	10	-	1
H.J.Shaw b McSkimming	0	5	1	-	-
C.S.Martin not out	0	1	0	-	-
Extras (lb 4, w 3, nb 1)	8				
TOTAL (49.3 overs)	**202**	202			

OTAGO

	Runs	Mins	Balls	6s	4s
C.D.Cumming* b McMillan	43	64	53	-	9
J.W.Sheed c Papps b Shaw	14	42	21	-	2
G.J.Hopkins† b Ellis	7	17	14	-	1
A.J.Redmond c McCullum b Martin	22	79	35	-	2
N.L.McCullum b Ellis	12	18	17	-	2
G.R.Todd not out	54	113	102	-	3
J.W.Wilson c McCullum b Martin	0	5	5	-	-
S.W.Eathorne not out	37	50	43	-	6
B.E.Scott					
W.C.McSkimming					
C.M.Smith					
Extras (lb 6, w 6, nb 2)	14				
TOTAL (48 overs) (6 wkts)	**203**	197			

Bowling	*O*	*M*	*R*	*W*
OTAGO				
Wilson	9	0	39	1
McSkimming	9.3	1	50	2
Scott	10	1	37	2
Smith	5	0	31	0
McCullum	10	2	23	3
Cumming	6	0	18	0
CANTERBURY				
Martin	9	3	28	2
Shaw	7	0	38	1
McMillan	10	1	41	1
Ellis	10	1	45	2
Wiseman	10	0	32	0
Astle	2	0	13	0

Fall of Wickets	***C***	***O***
1st	102	50
2nd	102	63
3rd	132	67
4th	134	82
5th	135	136
6th	142	136
7th	178	-
8th	195	-
9th	202	-
10th	202	-

WELLINGTON v CENTRAL DISTRICTS — State Shield

at Basin Reserve, Wellington on 6 February, 2005
Toss : Central Districts. Umpires : D.B. Cowie & I.W. Shine
***Central Districts won by 72 runs.** Points: Central Districts 5, Wellington 0*

CENTRAL DISTRICTS

	Runs	Mins	Balls	6s	4s
C.M.Spearman c Franklin b Pasupati	63	92	82	-	7
J.M.How c Gillespie b O'Brien	8	41	17	-	1
R.L.Taylor lbw b Pasupati	26	53	41	-	3
M.S.Sinclair run out	78	77	52	3	6
J.I.Englefield c Woodcock b O'Brien	54	81	70	1	2
G.P.Sulzberger* c Ryder b O'Brien	2	8	6	-	-
E.P.Thompson c Parlane N.R. b O'Brien	0	4	2	-	-
B.B.J.Griggs† run out	1	7	7	-	-
B.J.Diamanti lbw b O'Brien	0	7	6	-	-
A.M.Schwass not out	6	8	6	-	-
L.J.Hamilton b Patel	2	5	5	-	-
Extras (lb 2, w 1, nb 1)	4				
TOTAL (48.5 overs)	**244**	196			

WELLINGTON

	Runs	Mins	Balls	6s	4s
C.J.Nevin c Sinclair b Schwass	24	64	44	-	2
S.P.Fleming* c Taylor b Thompson	2	14	10	-	-
M.E.Parlane st Griggs b How	31	99	62	-	1
J.D.Ryder run out	5	10	11	-	1
N.R.Parlane† c Taylor b Schwass	8	21	14	-	1
J.E.C.Franklin run out	63	105	86	-	6
L.J.Woodcock c Spearman b Sulzberger	1	3	3	-	-
M.Y.Pasupati run out	3	8	6	-	-
M.R.Gillespie b Schwass	13	22	18	-	1
J.S.Patel lbw b Schwass	1	4	3	-	-
I.E.O'Brien not out	1	8	1	-	-
Extras (lb 5, w 11, nb 4)	20				
TOTAL (42.1 overs)	**172**	184			

Bowling	O	M	R	W
WELLINGTON				
Gillespie	6	0	34	0
Franklin	9	0	45	0
O'Brien	9	0	35	5
Pasupati	9	0	55	2
Patel	9.5	0	41	1
Woodcock	6	0	32	0
CENTRAL DISTRICTS				
Hamilton	7	1	21	0
Thompson	5	0	21	1
Schwass	8.1	1	27	4
Diamanti	8	1	30	0
Sulzberger	9	0	42	1
How	5	0	26	1

Fall of Wickets	*CD*	*W*
1st	52	9
2nd	99	19
3rd	104	37
4th	228	46
5th	234	141
6th	234	142
7th	234	153
8th	235	161
9th	237	163
10th	244	172

M.E.Parlane retired hurt on 1 at 11-1 and resumed at 37-3*

AUCKLAND v NORTHERN DISTRICTS — State Shield

at Eden Park Outer Oval, Auckland on 6 February, 2005
Toss : Auckland. Umpires : R.D. Anderson & B.G. Frost
***Northern Districts won by 112 runs.** Points: Northern Districts 5, Auckland 0*

NORTHERN DISTRICTS

	Runs	Mins	Balls	6s	4s
N.K.W.Horsley c Jones b Walmsley	6	43	28	-	1
D.L.Vettori* c Canning b Hitchcock	109	177	124	-	10
A.W.Evans lbw b Walker	21	49	33	-	2
H.J.H.Marshall b Hitchcock	69	102	80	-	8
J.A.F.Yovich not out	34	41	20	1	3
P.D.McGlashan† c Young b Hitchcock	32	15	15	2	4
M.N.Hart c Young b Walmsley	0	2	1	-	-
D.R.Flynn not out	1	3	1	-	-
M.G.Orchard					
D.R.Tuffey					
G.W.Aldridge					
Extras (b 2, lb 4, w 10, nb 2)	18				
TOTAL (50 overs) (6 wkts)	**290**	219			

AUCKLAND

	Runs	Mins	Balls	6s	4s
R.A.Jones c & b Aldridge	6	15	13	-	1
M.J.Horne b Aldridge	22	54	31	-	3
R.J.Nicol c Marshall b Tuffey	13	19	15	1	1
L.Vincent b Aldridge	8	9	9	-	2
A.C.Barnes c Orchard b Hart	48	87	65	-	5
T.K.Canning c McGlashan b Orchard	12	36	38	-	1
K.D.Mills c Evans b Orchard	16	10	11	1	2
P.A.Hitchcock b Hart	3	10	9	-	-
R.A.Young† run out	2	11	12	-	-
B.G.K.Walker* not out	12	25	22	-	1
K.P.Walmsley c Vettori b Aldridge	24	17	22	2	2
Extras (b 1, lb 6, w 5)	12				
TOTAL (41.1 overs)	**178**	151			

Bowling	O	M	R	W
AUCKLAND				
Mills	5	0	35	0
Walmsley	10	0	45	2
Canning	10	0	37	0
Barnes	8	0	55	0
Walker	5	0	29	1
Hitchcock	9	0	67	3
Nicol	3	0	16	0
NORTHERN DISTRICTS				
Tuffey	7	0	26	1
Aldridge	8.1	1	43	4
Hart	10	2	20	2
Vettori	8	0	33	0
Orchard	6	0	36	2
Evans	2	0	13	0

Fall of Wickets	*ND*	*A*
1st	41	10
2nd	100	39
3rd	206	49
4th	234	58
5th	283	96
6th	284	118
7th	-	126
8th	-	134
9th	-	144
10th	-	178

NORTHERN DISTRICTS v CANTERBURY — Semi-final

at Eden Park Outer Oval, Auckland on 9 February, 2005
Toss : Canterbury. Umpires : A.L. Hill & D.M. Quested
Northern Districts won by 7 wickets

McMillan was the dominant Canterbury batsman being the only one to pass 30 as he reached his sixth century from 94 balls, getting the Red and Blacks to 261-8.

When Northern batted Vettori again took control. He added 193 with James Marshall for the third wicket getting his second successive century from just 86 deliveries. This surpassed his previous highest score made in round ten. His fifty took 34 balls, while Marshall required 78. It was the first time opposing captains had scored centuries in New Zealand domestic one-day cricket. Northern won easily with 26 balls to spare.

CANTERBURY

	Runs	Mins	Balls	6s	4s
M.H.W.Papps c Orchard b Aldridge	2	13	14	-	-
N.J.Astle c Vettori b Tuffey	9	34	23	-	1
P.G.Fulton c McGlashan b Orchard	24	49	29	1	3
C.D.McMillan* b Aldridge	124	152	109	5	10
C.L.Cairns c Yovich b Vettori	23	34	36	-	3
S.L.Stewart c Evans b Marshall J.A.H.	21	43	43	-	1
B.B.McCullum† c Horsley b Hart	16	25	25	-	1
N.T.Broom not out	27	26	18	-	4
P.J.Wiseman c Marshall J.A.H. b Tuffey	4	4	4	-	-
S.J.Cunis not out	1	2	2	-	-
C.S.Martin					
Extras (lb 1, w 6, nb 3)	10				
TOTAL (50 overs) (8 wkts)	**261**	195			

NORTHERN DISTRICTS

	Runs	Mins	Balls	6s	4s
N.K.W.Horsley c McCullum b Martin	11	14	14	-	2
D.L.Vettori* c Martin b Astle	138	175	111	-	19
A.W.Evans lbw b Cunis	3	29	24	-	-
J.A.H.Marshall not out	95	142	119	-	12
H.J.H.Marshall not out	6	10	8	-	1
M.N.Hart					
J.A.F.Yovich					
P.D.McGlashan†					
M.G.Orchard					
D.R.Tuffey					
G.W.Aldridge					
Extras (lb 5, w 3, nb 2)	10				
TOTAL (45.4 overs) (3 wkts)	**263**	188			

Bowling	*O*	*M*	*R*	*W*
NORTHERN DISTRICTS				
Tuffey	10	1	42	2
Aldridge	10	0	57	2
Yovich	1	0	6	0
Orchard	6	0	34	1
Vettori	10	1	41	1
Hart	8	0	45	1
Marshall J.A.H.	5	0	35	1
CANTERBURY				
Cairns	8	1	42	0
Martin	6	1	39	1
Cunis	8	0	39	1
Astle	9	0	49	1
Wiseman	8.4	0	55	0
McMillan	6	0	34	0

Fall of Wickets	***C***	***ND***
1st	8	17
2nd	20	49
3rd	55	242
4th	94	-
5th	159	-
6th	207	-
7th	254	-
8th	259	-
9th	-	-
10th	-	-

CENTRAL DISTRICTS v NORTHERN DISTRICTS — Final

at Pukekura Park, New Plymouth on 12 February, 2005
Toss : Central Districts. Umpires : A.L. Hill & B.F. Bowden
Northern Districts won by 20 runs

The wicket was slower than had been expected and Northern scored just 190-9 after being put in to bat. Hamilton was again the best of the Central bowlers. Evans top scored wth 39 and Hamish Marshall reached 30 before being run out by How.

Central also struggled against some tight bowling and only Sinclair (fifty off 68 balls) and Sulzberger looked comfortable. Aldridge took his 30th wicket of the season, to set a new record, and Central were finally dismissed 20 runs short of Northern with 16 balls still remaining.

NORTHERN DISTRICTS

	Runs	Mins	Balls	6s	4s
N.K.W.Horsley c Griggs b Hefford	10	48	34	-	2
D.L.Vettori* c Hefford b Hamilton	9	17	13	-	2
A.W.Evans c Diamanti b Sulzberger	39	82	64	-	5
J.A.H.Marshall c Hamilton b Schwass	6	12	11	-	1
H.J.H.Marshall run out	30	67	47	-	2
M.N.Hart c Griggs b Hamilton	22	52	50	1	-
J.A.F.Yovich c Griggs b Hamilton	17	42	28	-	2
P.D.McGlashan† not out	19	53	34	-	1
M.G.Orchard run out	0	2	0	-	-
D.R.Tuffey c Sulzberger b Diamanti	13	25	18	-	1
G.W.Aldridge not out	1	3	1	-	-
Extras (b 5, lb 10, w 9)	24				
TOTAL (50 overs) (9 wkts)	**190**	210			

CENTRAL DISTRICTS

	Runs	Mins	Balls	6s	4s
J.M.How c McGlashan b Aldridge	14	33	30	-	2
C.M.Spearman lbw b Aldridge	10	42	28	-	-
R.L.Taylor b Aldridge	2	16	9	-	-
M.S.Sinclair c Evans b Yovich	50	105	71	1	5
J.I.Englefield c Aldridge b Vettori	18	48	30	-	1
G.P.Sulzberger* not out	40	110	76	-	3
B.B.J.Griggs† c Marshall J.A.H. b Yovich	0	3	2	-	-
B.J.Diamanti lbw b Vettori	11	30	29	-	1
A.M.Schwass c Marshall J.A.H. b Yovich	4	4	5	-	1
L.J.Hamilton b Aldridge	1	10	8	-	-
B.E.Hefford run out	1	3	2	-	-
Extras (lb 7, w 5, nb 7)	19				
TOTAL (47.2 overs)	**170**	209			

Bowling	*O*	*M*	*R*	*W*
CENTRAL DISTRICTS				
Hamilton	10	3	44	3
Hefford	9	1	28	1
Schwass	9	2	20	1
Diamanti	9	2	27	1
Sulzberger	8	0	34	1
How	5	0	22	0
NORTHERN DISTRICTS				
Tuffey	8.2	1	16	0
Aldridge	9	1	38	4
Yovich	10	0	42	3
Orchard	10	0	35	0
Vettori	10	0	32	2

Fall of Wickets	*ND*	*CD*
1st	11	29
2nd	49	31
3rd	60	32
4th	85	92
5th	117	128
6th	145	130
7th	154	157
8th	154	164
9th	185	169
10th	-	170

2004/05 STATE SHIELD AVERAGES

	M	In	NO	HS	Runs	Ave	100s	50s	Ct	St	O	M	R	W	Ave	R/O	Best
A.R.Adams	3	3	0	34	43	14.33	-	-	-	-	30	5	117	3	39.00	3.90	1-34
G.W.Aldridge	11	4	2	1*	2	1.00	-	-	4	-	93.1	4	438	30	14.60	4.70	5-34
N.J.Astle	8	8	0	123	502	62.75	1	4	-	-	66	6	248	12	20.66	3.76	4-19
A.C.Barnes	8	8	0	48	110	13.75	-	-	-	-	46	3	192	8	24.00	4.17	4-30
G.E.F.Barnett	1	1	0	22	22	22.00	-	-	-	-							
M.D.Bell	6	5	0	26	64	12.80	-	-	3	-							
N.T.Broom	1	1	1	27*	27	-	-	-	-	-							
I.G.Butler	4	4	1	2*	4	1.33	-	-	-	-	28.5	2	141	6	23.50	4.89	3-26
C.Cachopa	2	2	0	56	57	28.50	-	1	1	-							
C.L.Cairns	8	8	1	24	75	10.71	-	-	1	-	58.3	3	282	4	70.50	4.82	2-41
T.K.Canning	8	8	0	56	171	21.37	-	1	5	-	46	3	157	8	19.62	3.41	4-21
C.D.Cumming	10	10	0	80	380	38.00	-	3	4	-	46	0	186	4	46.50	4.04	2-18
S.J.Cunis	8	5	3	13*	26	13.00	-	-	1	-	74	4	319	12	26.58	4.31	4-38
B.J.Diamanti	9	5	0	18	34	6.80	-	-	2	-	72	10	310	11	28.18	4.31	4-39
S.W.Eathorne	1	1	1	37*	37	-	-	-	-	-							
A.M.Ellis	5	3	1	14	32	16.00	-	-	2	-	18	1	96	3	32.00	5.33	2-45
J.I.Englefield	10	10	1	80*	295	32.77	-	3	5	-							
A.W.Evans	7	7	1	58*	131	21.83	-	1	4	-	4	0	27	0	-	6.75	-
S.P.Fleming	8	7	0	70	249	35.57	-	3	2	-							
D.R.Flynn	2	2	1	27	28	28.00	-	-	-	-							
J.E.C.Franklin	10	9	0	76	216	24.00	-	2	3	-	87	4	381	11	34.63	4.38	3-35
P.G.Fulton	9	8	1	85*	148	21.14	-	1	3	-							
C.B.Gaffaney	9	9	1	101*	299	37.37	1	2	2	-							
M.R.Gillespie	10	9	3	26	113	18.83	-	-	3	-	81.3	3	436	13	33.53	5.34	2-27
B.B.J.Griggs	10	8	2	27*	59	9.83	-	-	16	2							
L.J.Hamilton	10	6	3	12*	18	6.00	-	-	1	-	88	20	316	18	17.55	3.59	5-19
M.N.Hart	11	9	1	67	167	20.87	-	1	6	-	45	2	196	6	32.66	4.36	2-20
B.E.Hefford	6	2	1	1	1	1.00	-	-	2	-	46.3	7	186	13	14.30	4.00	3-21
P.A.Hitchcock	8	8	4	43	134	33.50	-	-	1	-	67	2	397	11	36.09	5.93	3-67
G.J.Hopkins	10	10	0	55	218	21.80	-	2	5	1							
A.J.Hore	4	4	0	15	35	8.75	-	-	5	-							
M.J.Horne	8	8	0	23	104	13.00	-	-	4	-	1	0	7	0	-	7.00	-
N.K.W.Horsley	7	7	0	77	136	19.42	-	1	2	-							
J.M.How	10	10	0	60	264	26.40	-	3	3	-	14	0	66	1	66.00	4.71	1-26
L.G.Howell	4	4	0	30	44	11.00	-	-	1	-							
R.A.Jones	8	8	0	92	154	19.25	-	1	2	-							
H.J.H.Marshall	10	9	1	69	179	22.37	-	1	4	-	2	0	14	1	14.00	7.00	1-14
J.A.H.Marshall	10	9	2	95*	286	40.85	-	3	6	-	16.2	0	89	2	44.50	5.45	1-35
B.P.Martin	1	0	0	0	0	-	-	-	1	-	10	0	35	1	35.00	3.50	1-35
C.S.Martin	8	3	2	2	2	2.00	-	-	1	-	65	10	299	6	49.83	4.60	2-28
M.J.Mason	4	2	1	18*	26	26.00	-	-	3	-	36	6	133	7	19.00	3.69	4-23
B.B.McCullum	7	7	2	43*	143	28.60	-	-	9	-							
N.L.McCullum	10	10	2	52*	160	20.00	-	1	2	-	44	3	210	5	42.00	4.77	3-23
P.D.McGlashan	11	9	5	65	239	59.75	-	1	13	1							
T.G.McIntosh	2	2	0	74	74	37.00	-	1	-	-							
A.J.McKay	2	1	0	7	7	7.00	-	-	1	-	16	2	71	2	35.50	4.44	2-37
C.D.McMillan	9	8	1	124	354	50.57	2	-	8	-	53.2	4	214	10	21.40	4.01	2-5
J.M.McMillan	5	4	3	9*	17	17.00	-	-	2	-	32.3	2	150	7	21.42	4.61	3-34
W.C.McSkimming	10	6	1	14	27	5.40	-	-	-	-	82.3	8	354	11	32.18	4.29	2-25
K.D.Mills	7	7	0	55	191	27.28	-	1	1	-	63.5	9	273	8	34.12	4.27	2-25
Mohammad Wasim	6	6	0	27	67	11.16	-	-	2	-							
G.B.Murray	3	2	1	15	18	18.00	-	-	-	-	14	0	58	1	58.00	4.14	1-12
C.J.Nevin	10	9	0	90	337	37.44	-	3	7	-							
R.J.Nicol	7	7	0	53	159	22.71	-	2	1	-	19	1	81	4	20.25	4.26	3-39
I.E.O'Brien	4	2	2	1*	2	-	-	-	1	-	31	0	155	7	22.14	5.00	5-35
J.D.P.Oram	3	2	0	17	24	12.00	-	-	-	-	20	3	74	3	24.66	3.70	2-10
M.G.Orchard	8	4	3	12*	18	18.00	-	-	3	-	57.5	0	293	9	32.55	5.06	4-47
M.H.W.Papps	9	9	1	129*	423	52.87	2	1	4	-							
M.E.Parlane	6	6	0	50	99	16.50	-	1	1	-							
N.R.Parlane	10	9	0	53	204	22.66	-	1	6	-							
M.Y.Pasupati	7	7	3	38*	163	40.75	-	-	-	-	54	0	294	10	29.40	5.44	4-37
J.S.Patel	10	7	2	12*	40	8.00	-	-	4	-	91.5	2	387	11	35.18	4.21	3-19
A.J.Redmond	9	9	0	29	141	15.66	-	-	3	-	2	0	16	0	-	8.00	-
J.D.Ryder	10	9	0	18	84	9.33	-	-	2	-	16	0	94	2	47.00	5.88	1-22
A.M.Schwass	9	6	1	19	44	8.80	-	-	2	-	72	5	315	16	19.68	4.38	5-22
B.E.Scott	10	7	3	30	117	29.25	-	-	2	-	74.3	6	341	8	42.62	4.57	2-37

	M	In	NO	HS	Runs	Ave	100s	50s	Ct	St	O	M	R	W	Ave	R/O	Best
D.G.Sewell	2	1	0	3	3	3.00	-	-	1	-	13	1	73	2	36.50	5.62	2-34
H.J.Shaw	6	4	1	4*	4	1.33	-	-	1	-	44.2	2	223	10	22.30	5.03	3-31
J.W.Sheed	3	3	1	32*	46	23.00	-	-	1	-							
M.S.Sinclair	9	9	1	95*	353	44.12	-	4	3	-							
C.M.Smith	1	0	0	0	0	-	-	-	2	-	5	0	31	0	-	6.20	-
C.M.Spearman	10	10	1	94	287	31.88	-	3	10	-							
G.R.Stead	3	2	0	11	13	6.50	-	-	2	-							
S.L.Stewart	7	6	1	33	106	21.20	-	-	1	-							
S.B.Styris	7	7	1	96	245	40.83	-	2	3	-	58.3	11	183	9	20.33	3.12	3-15
G.P.Sulzberger	10	9	4	66*	244	48.80	-	1	8	-	60.5	4	249	12	20.75	4.09	3-21
R.L.Taylor	6	6	0	99	136	22.66	-	1	4	-							
E.P.Thompson	3	2	0	15	15	7.50	-	-	1	-	14.1	0	42	3	14.00	2.96	2-7
G.R.Todd	10	10	3	54*	197	28.14	-	1	5	-	33.4	2	190	8	23.75	5.64	2-23
K.W.M.Todd	2	2	0	6	10	5.00	-	-	-	-							
D.R.Tuffey	10	5	0	17	41	8.20	-	-	1	-	85	9	332	15	22.13	3.91	3-30
A.D.Turner	6	4	2	18	33	16.50	-	-	1	-	54.3	3	260	11	23.63	4.77	2-19
D.L.Vettori	5	5	0	138	303	60.60	2	-	4	-	44	3	137	3	45.66	3.11	2-32
L.Vincent	4	4	0	28	36	9.00	-	-	1	-							
B.G.K.Walker	8	6	2	12*	27	6.75	-	-	1	-	53	2	254	6	42.33	4.79	2-42
K.P.Walmsley	5	4	2	24	45	22.50	-	-	-	-	41	0	212	5	42.40	5.17	2-45
B-J.Watling	2	2	0	21	21	10.50	-	-	1	-							
J.W.Wilson	10	10	0	50	133	13.30	-	1	2	-	78.2	8	317	14	22.64	4.04	3-23
P.J.Wiseman	9	7	1	14*	50	8.33	-	-	-	-	55.4	3	252	4	63.00	4.52	2-30
L.J.Woodcock	10	9	0	71	210	23.33	-	1	5	-	14.4	0	82	1	82.00	5.59	1-26
R.A.Young	8	8	3	35	95	19.00	-	-	12	2							
J.A.F.Yovich	11	9	1	52	195	24.37	-	1	4	-	38.4	2	226	8	28.25	5.84	3-42

HIGHEST STRIKE RATES *(qualification 150 runs)*

		Runs	Balls	S/R
M.Y.Pasupati	*W*	163	158	103
D.L.Vettori	*ND*	303	301	100
C.D.McMillan	*W*	354	354	100
S.P.Fleming	*C*	249	252	98
P.D.McGlashan	*ND*	239	250	95
N.L.McCullum	*O*	160	180	88
M.S.Sinclair	*CD*	353	404	87
J.A.F.Yovich	*ND*	195	235	82
S.B.Styris	*ND*	245	302	81
C.D.Cumming	*O*	380	472	80

MOST ECONOMICAL BOWLING *(qualification 30 overs)*

		O	M	R	W	Ave	R/O
D.L.Vettori	*ND*	44	3	137	3	45.66	3.11
S.B.Styris	*ND*	58.3	11	183	9	20.33	3.12
T.K.Canning	*A*	46	3	157	8	19.62	3.41
L.J.Hamilton	*CD*	88	20	316	18	17.55	3.59
M.J.Mason	*CD*	36	6	133	7	19.00	3.69
N.J.Astle	*C*	66	6	248	12	20.66	3.76
A.R.Adams	*A*	30	5	117	3	39.00	3.90
D.R.Tuffey	*ND*	85	9	332	15	22.13	3.91
B.E.Hefford	*CD*	46.3	7	186	13	14.30	4.00
C.D.McMillan	*C*	53.2	4	214	10	21.40	4.01

CAREER RECORDS

	M	In	NO	HS	Runs	Ave	100s	50s	Ct	St	O	M	R	W	Ave	R/O	Best
A.R.Adams	40	33	8	47	375	15.00	-	-	9	-	339.5	26	1472	59	24.94	4.33	5-7
G.W.Aldridge	48	25	10	28	182	12.13	-	-	9	-	334.1	22	1483	78	19.01	4.43	5-34
N.J.Astle	91	82	12	131	3009	42.98	8	13	42	-	679.1	84	2278	98	23.24	3.35	4-14
A.C.Barnes	114	112	11	116	2866	28.37	2	20	30	-	439.3	28	1951	69	28.27	4.43	5-19
G.E.F.Barnett	1	1	0	22	22	22.00	-	-	-	-							
M.D.Bell	91	87	6	121*	2062	25.45	3	8	43	-	0.2	0	4	0	-	-	-
N.T.Broom	7	6	2	84*	138	34.50	-	1	1	-	6	0	32	0	-	5.33	-
I.G.Butler	20	12	5	40*	71	10.14	-	-	-	-	158	13	764	23	33.21	4.84	3-15
C.Cachopa	2	2	0	56	57	28.50	-	1	1	-							
C.L.Cairns	85	77	11	143	2145	32.50	3	10	17	-	538.2	39	2183	88	24.80	4.05	6-37
T.K.Canning	56	50	4	92*	999	21.71	-	5	13	-	387	27	1548	62	24.96	4.00	4-21
C.D.Cumming	64	60	0	80	1286	21.43	-	10	22	-	254	9	1128	22	51.27	4.44	2-18
S.J.Cunis	46	27	12	33	176	11.73	-	-	7	-	402	32	1570	62	25.32	3.91	4-37
B.J.Diamanti	9	5	0	18	34	6.80	-	-	2	-	72	10	310	11	28.18	4.31	4-39
S.W.Eathorne	1	1	1	37*	37	-	-	-	-	-							
A.M.Ellis	6	3	1	14	32	16.00	-	-	2	-	22	1	122	3	40.66	5.55	2-45
J.I.Englefield	26	26	6	80*	587	29.35	-	5	9	-							
A.W.Evans	7	7	1	58*	131	21.83	-	1	4	-	4	0	27	0	-	6.75	-
S.P.Fleming	69	64	10	131	2301	42.61	5	15	33	-							
D.R.Flynn	2	2	1	27	28	28.00	-	-	-	-							
J.E.C.Franklin	39	32	13	76	572	30.10	-	3	11	-	297.2	28	1275	42	30.35	4.28	4-30
P.G.Fulton	31	27	4	115*	784	34.08	1	6	12	-	3	0	24	0	-	8.00	-
C.B.Gaffaney	86	84	2	101*	2057	25.08	1	10	25	-	6	0	36	1	36.00	6.00	1-4
M.R.Gillespie	32	19	5	26	162	11.57	-	-	6	-	252.2	12	1250	42	29.76	4.95	4-31
B.B.J.Griggs	41	31	6	59	391	15.64	-	1	51	3							
L.J.Hamilton	48	24	10	12*	51	3.64	-	-	10	-	408.3	61	1659	60	27.65	4.06	5-19
M.N.Hart	102	92	11	100	1855	22.90	1	12	55	-	628.1	55	2442	89	27.43	3.88	4-7
B.E.Hefford	29	14	5	16*	49	5.44	-	-	4	-	232.3	27	925	49	18.87	3.97	3-13
P.A.Hitchcock	54	47	15	43	624	19.50	-	-	13	-	450.5	28	2052	90	22.80	4.55	5-10
G.J.Hopkins	72	57	8	82	1106	22.57	-	5	65	12							
A.J.Hore	45	43	1	102	860	20.47	1	3	24	-	11.4	0	78	1	78.00	6.68	1-35
M.J.Horne	70	69	1	96	1652	24.29	-	12	19	-	142.3	5	655	18	36.38	4.59	3-17
N.K.W.Horsley	26	26	2	89*	555	23.12	-	3	4	-							
J.M.How	31	30	0	94	657	21.90	-	5	9	-	19	0	91	2	45.50	4.79	1-17
L.G.Howell	105	105	14	134*	3022	33.20	5	22	25	-	15	0	98	2	49.00	6.53	2-35
R.A.Jones	79	78	6	92	1716	23.83	-	6	19	-							
H.J.H.Marshall	68	65	6	93	1309	22.18	-	8	30	-	3	0	18	1	18.00	6.00	1-14
J.A.H.Marshall	56	54	5	100*	1427	29.12	1	8	25	-	28.4	0	154	3	51.33	5.37	1-35
B.P.Martin	29	20	4	33	206	12.87	-	-	11	-	238.4	20	821	31	26.48	3.44	4-28
C.S.Martin	54	17	10	5*	31	4.42	-	-	8	-	452.1	46	2048	82	24.97	4.52	5-43
M.J.Mason	54	32	11	18*	166	7.90	-	-	10	-	413.2	50	1677	80	20.96	4.05	6-25
B.B.McCullum	19	18	2	55	336	21.00	-	2	13	1							
N.L.McCullum	32	30	9	52*	277	13.19	-	1	9	-	203	12	918	25	36.72	4.52	3-23
P.D.McGlashan	27	24	8	65	433	27.06	-	1	29	4							
T.G.McIntosh	15	15	0	74	292	19.46	-	2	9	-							
A.J.McKay	2	1	0	7	7	7.00	-	-	1	-	16	2	71	2	35.50	4.44	2-37
C.D.McMillan	75	71	10	125	2203	36.11	7	6	31	-	167.5	8	833	34	24.50	4.96	5-38
J.M.McMillan	19	13	8	9*	26	5.20	-	-	3	-	145	12	612	28	21.85	4.22	3-30
W.C.McSkimming	48	40	13	59*	423	15.66	-	1	11	-	379	31	1641	58	28.29	4.33	3-14
K.D.Mills	46	40	11	55	642	22.13	-	1	12	-	378.3	38	1530	68	22.50	4.04	4-40
Mohammad Wasim	26	25	0	70	594	23.76	-	6	6	-	20	1	91	1	91.00	4.55	1-34
G.B.Murray	3	2	1	15	18	18.00	-	-	-	-	14	0	58	1	58.00	4.14	1-12
C.J.Nevin	95	90	6	149	2429	28.91	4	13	132	12							
R.J.Nicol	26	26	1	78	530	21.20	-	4	10	-	26	1	118	4	29.50	4.54	3-39
I.E.O'Brien	6	3	3	1*	2	-	-	-	1	-	49	1	234	9	26.00	4.78	5-35
J.D.P.Oram	45	40	3	127	1069	28.89	2	4	13	-	179.3	16	682	25	27.28	3.79	3-44
M.G.Orchard	22	17	6	79	180	16.36	-	1	5	-	146.2	7	642	22	29.18	4.38	4-47
M.H.W.Papps	36	36	5	132	1296	41.80	3	7	26	2							
M.E.Parlane	100	100	3	122	2752	28.37	3	16	16	-	0.3	0	5	0	-	-	-
N.R.Parlane	62	58	3	96*	1274	23.16	-	7	26	-							
M.Y.Pasupati	51	38	10	40*	526	18.78	-	-	7	-	322.3	14	1565	50	31.30	4.85	4-33
J.S.Patel	14	8	2	12*	44	7.33	-	-	5	-	112.5	2	501	14	35.78	4.44	3-19
A.J.Redmond	30	29	4	43*	386	15.44	-	-	7	-	58	0	285	6	47.50	4.91	2-46
J.D.Ryder	21	20	0	63	351	17.55	-	2	5	-	31	1	175	2	87.50	5.65	1-22
A.M.Schwass	42	26	7	32*	194	10.21	-	-	17	-	336.5	23	1503	64	23.48	4.46	5-22
B.E.Scott	20	14	7	30	160	22.85	-	-	4	-	158.1	11	759	27	28.11	4.79	4-63

	M	In	NO	HS	Runs	Ave	100s	50s	Ct	St	O	M	R	W	Ave	R/O	Best
D.G.Sewell	18	10	5	11*	31	6.20	-	-	1	-	139	8	664	24	27.66	4.78	4-51
H.J.Shaw	11	6	1	24	37	7.40	-	-	2	-	71.3	5	333	18	18.50	4.65	5-14
J.W.Sheed	8	7	1	32*	112	18.66	-	-	3	-							
M.S.Sinclair	79	78	8	110	2073	29.61	1	16	39	1							
C.M.Smith	1	0	0	0	0	-	-	-	2	-	5	0	31	0	-	6.20	-
C.M.Spearman	90	90	2	126	2421	27.51	1	17	37	-	4	0	26	0	-	6.50	-
G.R.Stead	97	86	11	101*	2081	27.74	2	9	34	-	3	0	23	0	-	7.67	-
S.L.Stewart	35	34	1	102	935	28.33	1	3	9	-							
S.B.Styris	71	64	16	123	1693	35.27	1	11	30	-	525	44	2236	92	24.30	4.26	4-19
G.P.Sulzberger	81	71	12	71	1700	28.81	-	9	43	-	460.3	23	1932	56	34.50	4.19	3-18
R.L.Taylor	16	16	2	132*	658	47.00	1	6	8	-							
E.P.Thompson	16	7	1	16	47	7.83	-	-	5	-	112.2	8	481	20	24.05	4.28	4-41
G.R.Todd	14	14	3	54*	226	20.54	-	1	6	-	50.2	2	266	10	26.60	5.28	2-23
K.W.M.Todd	2	2	0	6	10	5.00	-	-	-	-							
D.R.Tuffey	61	30	19	23*	194	17.63	-	-	16	-	469.4	35	2009	69	29.11	4.27	3-11
A.D.Turner	26	13	9	18	69	17.25	-	-	3	-	231.5	29	921	46	20.02	3.97	5-12
D.L.Vettori	38	33	4	138	880	30.34	2	4	18	-	325.3	19	1226	37	33.13	3.76	3-24
L.Vincent	48	46	3	145	1299	30.20	2	7	53	3	4.4	0	19	1	19.00	4.32	1-8
B.G.K.Walker	63	39	10	33*	287	9.89	-	-	23	-	489.1	37	1901	62	30.66	3.88	4-39
K.P.Walmsley	52	30	17	26*	244	18.76	-	-	6	-	445.4	29	2014	66	30.51	4.51	4-24
B-J.Watling	2	2	0	21	21	10.50	-	-	1	-							
J.W.Wilson	41	38	3	99	719	20.54	-	4	23	-	277.3	26	1072	40	26.80	3.86	3-23
P.J.Wiseman	78	63	9	65*	824	15.25	-	2	20	-	557.4	48	2313	43	53.79	4.14	3-11
L.J.Woodcock	17	14	2	71	256	21.33	-	1	6	-	57.3	0	320	3	106.66	5.56	1-26
R.A.Young	31	25	9	36*	311	19.43	-	-	39	9							
J.A.F.Yovich	64	52	10	70	831	19.78	-	4	21	-	334.5	20	1755	72	24.37	5.24	4-50

STATE OF ORIGIN

NORTH ISLAND v SOUTH ISLAND — State of Origin

at Pukekura Park, New Plymouth on 13 February, 2005
Toss : North Island. Umpires : A.L. Hill & B.F. Bowden
North Island won by 58 runs

The players in the inter-island match were selected depending on which major association they had first played for. Fleming (originally Canterbury) captained the South and Hopkins (originally Northern Districts) led the North. The match was played before the New Zealand one-day team was announced.

Most of the North Island batsmen got starts but none was able to reach fifty. Canning top scored with 40 before being the second run out victim of the innings. His partnership of 57 with Vincent was the best of the innings while Hopkins and Franklin added 52 for the seventh wicket.

Fleming was bowled by Franklin with the score at 15 and South never really gained any momentum from then on. McMillan made 41 (top score of the match) but went at 139-7. McSkimming and Shaw hit out but the end came at 179, with 5.5 overs still remaining.

NORTH ISLAND

	Runs	Mins	Balls	6s	4s
J.M.How b McSkimming	31	76	48	-	6
M.S.Sinclair c Fleming b Martin	6	18	11	-	1
H.J.H.Marshall run out	25	41	28	-	4
L.Vincent c Papps b McMillan	24	87	48	-	3
R.L.Taylor c Papps b McMillan	2	25	18	-	-
T.K.Canning run out	40	60	61	-	6
G.J.Hopkins*† c Hefford b Shaw	23	48	45	1	1
J.E.C.Franklin not out	38	51	38	-	5
A.R.Adams not out	10	16	8	-	-
J.S.Patel					
G.W.Aldridge					
Extras (lb 4, w 29, nb 5)	38				
TOTAL (50 overs) (7 wkts)	**237**	215			

SOUTH ISLAND

	Runs	Mins	Balls	6s	4s
M.H.W.Papps† c Sinclair b Canning	28	91	52	-	5
S.P.Fleming* b Franklin	3	16	8	-	-
C.D.Cumming c & b Franklin	24	36	34	-	5
P.G.Fulton c Taylor b Franklin	0	2	2	-	-
C.D.McMillan c Vincent b Canning	41	78	61	-	6
J.I.Englefield b Patel	19	35	49	1	2
N.L.McCullum c How b Patel	3	9	8	-	-
W.C.McSkimming b Adams	25	39	26	1	3
H.J.Shaw b Aldridge	14	22	19	-	2
B.E.Hefford b Franklin	0	8	5	-	-
C.S.Martin not out	0	3	4	-	-
Extras (b 6, lb 6, w 7, nb 3)	22				
TOTAL (44.1 overs)	**179**	177			

Bowling	*O*	*M*	*R*	*W*
SOUTH ISLAND				
Martin	9	0	53	1
Hefford	5	1	35	0
McSkimming	10	0	47	1
Shaw	9	2	44	1
McMillan	10	2	32	2
McCullum	7	0	22	0
NORTH ISLAND				
Aldridge	8	0	40	1
Franklin	9	2	32	4
Adams	7.1	1	23	1
Canning	10	1	41	2
Patel	10	1	31	2

Fall of Wickets	*NI*	*SI*
1st	32	15
2nd	74	58
3rd	85	58
4th	96	95
5th	153	128
6th	163	138
7th	215	139
8th	-	173
9th	-	179
10th	-	179

PROVINCIAL A TEAM COMPETITION

The Provincial A competition was held at Lincoln from 2 to 15 January. Each team played five two-day games. Final placings were: Northern Districts, Otago, Wellington, Central Districts, Auckland, Canterbury.

CANTERBURY v OTAGO *First innings win to Otago*
At Bert Sutcliffe Oval, Lincoln 2, 3 January, 2005

Otago 366 (S.P. Beare 177, S. Wells 39, W.A. Cornelius 3-74) and 40-2

Canterbury 246 (T.J.T. Papps 77, I.A. Robertson 64, W.E.R. Somerville 4-44)

AUCKLAND v WELLINGTON *First innings win to Wellington*
At Lincoln No.3 2, 3 January, 2005

Auckland 203 (C. Cachopa 54, D.M. Wedlake 42, K.W.M. Todd 36, J. Stuart 3-34) and 45-0

Wellington 275 (R.E. Chatfield 98, M.V. Houghton 60*, J.R. Hill 49, T.I. Lythe 5-92)

NORTHERN DISTRICTS v CENTRAL DISTRICTS *First innings win to Northern*
At Lincoln Green 2, 3 January, 2005

Central Districts 162 (D.R. Cederman 31, T.V. Astill 31, P.J. Capstick 30, T.T. Davis 6-46, B.J. Winslade 3-53) and 150-5 (R.M. West 46*, G.R. Hay 43*, A.P. Devcich 5-47)

Northern Districts 259 (R.R. Shutte 78, T.T. Davis 41, G.G. Robinson 33, B.E. Hefford 4-44)

CENTRAL DISTRICTS v WELLINGTON *First innings win to Central Districts*
At Bert Sutcliffe Oval, Lincoln 4, 5 January, 2005

Central Districts 354 (P.J. Ingram 166, I.P. Sandbrook 41, T.V. Astill 37, G.J.T. Hegglun 33, M.V. Houghton 4-73, J. Stuart 3-61)

Wellington 266 (M.V. Houghton 47, L.M. Martin 42, J.R. Hill 37, R.E. Chatfield 36, S.A. Fairley 32, G.J.T. Hegglun 3-35, R.M. West 3-68)

OTAGO v AUCKLAND *First innings win to Otago*
At Lincoln Green 4, 5 January, 2005

Otago 345 (J.W. Sheed 111, M.N. McKenzie 65, S.P. Beare 45, J.D. Homer 30, M.J. Guptill 3-43, T.I. Lythe 3-75) and 25-0

Auckland 166 (H.M. Smith 53, T.I. Lythe 31, D.G. Sewell 5-34, M.J. Harvie 3-32)

NORTHERN DISTRICTS v CANTERBURY *First innings win to Northern Districts*
At Lincoln No.3 4, 5 January, 2005

Canterbury 169 (N.T. Broom 62, T.T. Davis 5-59) and 198-2

Northern Districts 172 (A.W. Evans 66, B.P. Donkers 4-39, L. Burtt 3-38)

OTAGO v WELLINGTON *No result*
At Lincoln No.3 7, 8 January, 2005

Wellington 212 (S.M. Mills 54, D.J. Bowden 42, D.G. Sewell 3-63)

Otago 140-6 (S.W. Eathorne 44)

CENTRAL DISTRICTS v CANTERBURY *No result*
At Lincoln Green 7, 8 January, 2005

Central Districts 289 (T.I. Weston 111, P.J. Ingram 42, G.D. Elliott 3-46)

Canterbury 111-6 (T.G. McIntosh 35, J.N. Kuru 3-20)

NORTHERN DISTRICTS v AUCKLAND *No result*
At Bert Sutcliffe Oval, Lincoln 7, 8 January, 2005

Northern Districts 405-6d (B.S. Wilson 181, A.W. Evans 141, G.S. Shaw 4-51)

Auckland 161-5 (A.K. Kitchen 82, M.J. Guptill 42, J.G. Hatwell 4-44)

NORTHERN DISTRICTS v WELLINGTON *First innings win to Northern Districts*
At Lincoln Green 9, 10 January, 2005

Welington 278-6d (S.J. Murdoch 100*, J.R. Hill 58, S.A. Fairley 39)

Northern Districts 338 (J.G. Hatwell 66*, N.K.W. Horsley 64, T.T. Davis 62, B.S. Wilson 39, G.G. Robinson 37, J. Stuart 3-58)

CENTRAL DISTRICTS v OTAGO *First innings win to Otago*
At Lincoln No.3 9, 10 January, 2005

Otago 387 (J.W. Sheed 159, M.N. McKenzie 86, S.P. Beare 31, R.M. West 7-124)

Central Districts 283 (D.R. Cederman 58, B.J. Diamanti 51, T.I. Weston 44, G.E.F. Barnett 41, R.M. West 32, D.G. Sewell 5-50)

CANTERBURY v AUCKLAND *No result*
At Bert Sutcliffe Oval, Lincoln 9, 10 January, 2005

Canterbury 429-9d (I.A. Robertson 126, T.H.T. Papps 72, N.T. Broom 68, A.M. Ellis 64, S.L. Stewart 50, G.S. Shaw 6-139)

Auckland 354-9 (M.G. Cairns 116*, P.A. Hitchcock 55, H.M. Smith 42, K.W.M. Todd 38, T.I. Lythe 32, L. Burtt 3-41)

NORTHERN DISTRICTS v OTAGO *First innings win to Northern Districts*
At Lincoln Green 12, 13 January, 2005

Otago 266 (J.W. Sheed 62, M.A. Joyce 53, S.W. Eathorne 52, J.D. Homer 40)

Northern Districts 351-7 (A.W. Evans 168, A.P. Devcich 104, C.M. Smith 3-37, D.G. Sewell 3-78)

AUCKLAND v CENTRAL DISTRICTS *First innings win to Auckland*
At Lincoln No.3 12, 13 January, 2005

Central Districts 210 (G.E.F. Barnett 47, P.J. Capstick 43, G.R. Hay 33, R.M. West 33, B.J. Leonard 4-40, T.I. Lythe 4-71)

Auckland 248 (G.S. Shaw 75, T.I. Lythe 54, B.J. Diamanti 3-36, P.J. Ingram 3-46)

CANTERBURY v WELLINGTON *First innings win to Wellington*
At Lincoln Green 14, 15 January, 2005

Canterbury 260 (B.P. Donkers 92, G.D. Elliott 66, J.S. Ward 32, R.J. Gilhooly 3-66)

Wellington 272-5 (R.E. Chatfield 101*, K.R. Lennon 52, S.J. Murdoch 45)

NEW ZEALAND ACADEMY

The New Zealand Academy team played eight games against major association teams in November 2004. The Academy side was bolstered by a number of New Zealand players at various times.

NEW ZEALAND ACADEMY XI v CANTERBURY
At Bert Sutcliffe Oval 3, 4 November, 2004

New Zealand Academy XI 306-5d (M.H. Richardson 74, B-J. Watling 66, P.W. Carey 56, B.R. Findlay 37*, D.R. Flynn 34) **drew with Canterbury** 335-8 (M.H.W. Papps 104, S.L. Stewart 100, G.D. Elliott 45, M.G. Orchard 4-62)

NEW ZEALAND ACADEMY XI v NORTHERN DISTRICTS
At Lincoln No.3 7, 8 November, 2004

Northern Districts 269-9d (J.A.F. Yovich 102, M.G. Orchard 45) **drew with New Zealand Academy XI** 293 (M.H. Richardson 62, D.R. Tuffey 52, A.P. Devcich 42, B.S. Wilson 40, B.J. Winslade 3-62)

NEW ZEALAND ACADEMY XI v NORTHERN DISTRICTS
At Lincoln No.3 12, 13 November, 2004

New Zealand Academy XI 304-7d (B-J. Watling 85, L.J. Woodcock 78, D.R. Flynn 48, B.S. Wilson 40, R.R. Shutte 3-30) **drew with Northern Districts** 255-8 (N.K.W. Horsley 67, L.G. Howell 34, M.N. Hart 31)

NEW ZEALAND ACADEMY XI v WELLINGTON
At Bert Sutcliffe Oval 15, 16 November, 2004

New Zealand Academy XI 231-9d (D.R. Flynn 66, B-J. Watling 65, L.J. Woodcock 33, A.D. Turner 5-60, I.E. O'Brien 3-28) **drew with Wellington** 241-4 (M.D. Bell 80, S.A. Fairley 54, N.R. Parlane 36*)

NEW ZEALAND ACADEMY XI v WELLINGTON
At Bert Sutcliffe Oval 19 November, 2004

New Zealand Academy XI 253-8 (C.L. Cairns 96, C.Z. Harris 50, M.R. Gillespie 3-47) **defeated Wellington** 231 (M.D. Bell 99, C.J. Nevin 39, T.T. Davis 3-34) by 22 runs

NEW ZEALAND ACADEMY XI v OTAGO
At Bert Sutcliffe Oval 21, 22 November, 2004

Otago 321-6d (J.W. Sheed 111*, A.J. Redmond 78, C.B. Gaffaney 35) and 19-0 **drew with New Zealand Academy XI** 225 (M.H.W. Papps 104*, D.R. Tuffey 35, J.M. McMillan 3-31)

NEW ZEALAND ACADEMY XI v AUCKLAND
At Bert Sutcliffe Oval 23, 24 November, 2004

New Zealand Academy XI 260-6d (C.Z. Harris 119*, B-J. Watling 56, B.R. Findlay 33) **drew with Auckland**

NEW ZEALAND ACADEMY XI v CENTRAL DISTRICTS
At Bert Sutcliffe Oval 26, 27 November, 2004

Central Districts 245 (G.E.F. Barnett 84, J.I. Englefield 40, P.J. Ingram 35, A.P. Devcich 4-57, M.J. Mason 3-26) **drew with New Zealand Academy XI** 263-9 (B-J. Watling 112, M.H.W. Papps 60, B. Findlay 36)

NATIONAL UNDER 19 TOURNAMENT

The 2004/05 Under 19 tournament was held at Lincoln from 11 to 22 December. Each team played four two-day games and three-one day matches with points from all matches being combined. Final placings were: Auckland, Canterbury, Wellington, Northern Districts, Central Districts, Otago.

TWO-DAY MATCHES

FIRST ROUND

AUCKLAND v NORTHERN DISTRICTS *First innings win to Auckland*

Northern Districts 271 (S. McLeod 135, C. Munro 5-60)

Auckland 486-9d (C. Cachopa 202*, M.J. Guptill 78, L.D. Webb 61, P.J. Cairns 54, K.V. Kurta 32, H. Evans 4-62)

OTAGO v WELLINGTON *First innings win to Wellington*

Otago 313 (W.G. Lawson 107, S.M. Fitzgibbon 65, S.W. Eathorne 34, K. Noema-Barnett 30) and 28-0

Wellington 342 (A.T. Newdick 127, J.A. Colson 83, A.T. Corliss 32*)

CANTERBURY v CENTRAL DISTRICTS *First innings win to Canterbury*

Central Districts 140 (T.C. Lance 39, K.J.B. Preston 35*, W.M. Lonsdale 3-47) and 122-3 (S.J. Cameron 50)

Canterbury 257 D.J. Broom 98, B.J. Rae 35, K.J.B. Preston 3-94)

SECOND ROUND

CANTERBURY v AUCKLAND *No result*

Canterbury 374-0d (K.R. Ambler 200*, T.D. Astle 157*)

Auckland 286-9 (C. Cachopa 73, P.J. Cairns 37, L.D. Webb 35, M.P. Ellison 31, J.P. Baxendale 3-80)

NORTHERN DISTRICTS v OTAGO *First innings win to Northern Districts*

Northern Districts 238-9d (N. Fitzgerald 106*, H. Chhagan 34) and 225-4 (S. McLeod 100*, H. Chhagan 43)

Otago 115 (S.W. Eathorne 48, A.P. Devcich 4-34, T. Te Moni 3-24)

CENTRAL DISTRICTS v WELLINGTON *First innings win to Wellington*

Central Districts 185 (J.C.M. Cunningham 38, M.R. Short 31, A.T. Corliss 4-33) and 107-2 (H.M.A. Cameron 50)

Wellington 333 (R.J. Kyne 93, A.M. McCash 64, J.D. Sole 52, J.W. Sewell 38, H.D. Templeton 30, B.S.M. McLennan 3-64)

THIRD ROUND

AUCKLAND v WELLINGTON *First innings win to Auckland*

Auckland 214 (D.C. De Boorder 47, M.J. Guptill 44, R.M. Hira 38) and 196-2 (M.J. Guptill 102*, L.D. Webb 63, A.T. Corliss 3-54, J.W. Sewell 3-54)

Wellington 162 (J.A. Colson 44, S.P. Devine 32*, C. Munro 5-43, J.P. Donnelly 3-39)

CENTRAL DISTRICTS v OTAGO *First innings win to Central Districts*

Otago 365 (R.L. Henaghan 110, M.D. Beer 91, H.A. Skelt 37, J.C.M. Cunningham 4-70, C. Turkington 3-67)

Central Districts 383-4 (B.R. Orton 114*, M.R. Short 71, G.J.A.D. Hodge 62, H.R. Beaumont 62, S.J. Cameron 31*)

NORTHERN DISTRICTS v CANTERBURY *First innings win to Canterbury*

Canterbury 394 (B. McCord 111, H.M.L. Fisher 56, A.C. Duncan 56, D.J. Broom 53, B.J. Rae 34, A.P. Devcich 5-102)

Northern Districts 278 (S. McLeod 79, J. Boult 49, A.P. Devcich 39, B. Parlane 36, W.M. Lonsdale 3-28)

FOURTH ROUND

CANTERBURY v OTAGO *Abandoned*

NORTHERN DISTRICTS v WELLINGTON *Abandoned*

CENTRAL DISTRICTS v AUCKLAND *Abandoned*

ONE-DAY MATCHES

FIRST ROUND

CENTRAL DISTRICTS v NORTHERN DISTRICTS *Northern won by 6 wickets*

Central Districts 186 (S.J. Cameron 38, B. Grant 33, G.J.A.D. Hodge 32, B. Wilcock 3-39)

Northern Districts 188-4 (N. Fitzgerald 54, S. McLeod 53*)

CANTERBURY v WELLINGTON *Canterbury won by 9 wickets*

Wellington 218-7 (A.T. Newdick 131, T.E. Johnston 3-47)

Canterbury 219-1 (T.D. Astle 81*, D.J. Broom 67*, K.R. Ambler 50)

AUCKLAND v OTAGO *Auckland won by 61 runs*

Auckland 213 (L.D. Webb 58, C. Frauenstein 30, W.G Lawson 5-30)

Otago 152 (K. Noema-Barnett 59, B.J. Stewart 4-23, C. Cachopa 3-19)

SECOND ROUND

AUCKLAND v NORTHERN DISTRICTS *Auckland won by 7 wickets*

Northern Districts 151 (A.P. Devcich 43, S. McLeod 36, R.M. Hira 4-12, M.J. Guptill 3-9)

Auckland 152-3 (C. Frauenstein 47, C. Cachopa 36*, L.D. Webb 33)

OTAGO v WELLINGTON *Wellington won by 7 wickets*

Otago 163 (S.M. Fitzgibbon 35, R.W. Barnett 33)

Wellington 164-3 (A.T. Newdick 62, A.M. McCash 41)

CENTRAL DISTRICTS v CANTERBURY *Central Districts won by 3 wickets*

Canterbury 257 (D.J. Broom 93, T.D. Astle 60, B. McCord 30, B.S.M. McLennan 3-39)

Central Districts 258-7 (M.R. Short 67, B.R. Orton 62, B. Grant 50, S.J. Cameron 33*)

THIRD ROUND

AUCKLAND v CANTERBURY *No result*

Canterbury 109-5 (B.R. Findlay 49)

Auckland

NORTHERN DISTRICTS v OTAGO *No result*

Northern Districts 132-2 (B. Wilcock 51)

Otago

CENTRAL DISTRICTS v WELLINGTON *No result*

Wellington 161-4 (A.M. McCash 71, A.T. Newdick 52)

Central Districts

At the conclusion of the tournament a team was named to play six matches against major association sides. It was: B.R. Findlay *(Canterbury, captain)*, T.D. Astle *(Canterbury)*, H.K. Bennett*(Canterbury)*, D.J. Broom*(Canterbury)*, C. Cachopa*(Auckland)*, D.C.De Boorder *(Auckland)*, J.P. Donnelly *(Auckland)*, C. Frauenstein *(Auckland)*, M.J. Guptill *(Auckland)*, W.M. Lonsdale *(Canterbury)*, S. McLeod *(Northern Districts)*, C. Munro *(Auckland)*, A.T. Newdick *(Wellington)*. Details of the matches are:

NEW ZEALAND UNDER 19 v WELLINGTON A *Match drawn*
At Bert Sutcliffe Oval, Lincoln 12, 13 January, 2005

Wellington A 236 (J.R. Hill 91, D.J. Bowden 45, S.A. Fairley 33, C. Munro 3-34) and 96-5 (K.R. Lennon 39)

New Zealand Under 19 244 (T.D. Astle 51, D.C. De Boorder 33)

NEW ZEALAND UNDER 19 v AUCKLAND A *Match drawn*
At Bert Sutcliffe Oval, Lincoln 14, 15 January, 2005

Auckland A 352 (A.K. Kitchen 145, B.J. Leonard 40*, R. Sharma 34, J.P. Donnelly 4-38)

New Zealand Under 19 349-9 (B.R. Findlay 83, D.C. De Boorder 83, C. Cachopa 42, A.T. Newdick 37, M.J. Guptill 30, P.A. Hitchcock 4-105)

NEW ZEALAND UNDER 19 v OTAGO A *Match drawn*
At Molyneux Park, Alexandra 18, 19 January, 2005

Otago A 398-8d (A.J. Hore 181, M.N. McKenzie 96, J.D. Homer 30, H.K. Bennett 3-40)

New Zealand Under 19 372 (T.D. Astle 162, A.T. Newdick 66, M.J. Guptill 32, W.E.R. Somerville 4-97, N. Turner 3-83)

NEW ZEALAND UNDER 19 v OTAGO A *New Zealand Under 19 won by 2 wickets*
At Molyneux Park, Alexandra 20 January, 2005

Otago A 249-9 (S.W. Eathorne 101*, S.M. Fitzgibbon 44, M.A. Joyce 34, C. Frauenstein 3-38)

New Zealand Under 19 250-8 (T.D. Astle 100, C. Frauenstein 58, N. Turner 3-31)

NEW ZEALAND UNDER 19 v CANTERBURY XI *NZ Under 19 won by 38 runs*
At Bert Sutcliffe Oval, Lincoln 23 January, 2005

New Zealand Under 19 250-9 (D.J. Broom 65, S. McLeod 55, T.E. Johnston 3-34)

Canterbury XI 212 (P.W. Carey 48, P.W. Borren 47, R.R. Sherlock 36, B.J. Rea 31, B.R. Findlay 3-23)

NEW ZEALAND UNDER 19 v CANTERBURY A *Match drawn*
At Bert Sutcliffe Oval, Lincoln 24, 25 January, 2005

Canterbury A 430 (G.D. Elliott 104, I.A. Robertson 86, L.J. Vivian 66, C. Romano 63, C. Frauenstein 4-46) and 175-6 (T.J.T. Papps 77, G.D. Elliott 39*)

New Zealand Under 19 227 (S. McLeod 71, A.T. Newdick 44, D.J. Broom 32, C. Romano 4-32, J.S. Ward 3-42)

NATIONAL UNDER 17 TOURNAMENT

The National Under 17 tournament was held in Napier from 30 December to 7 January. Canterbury won the title with 20 points followed by Northern Districts (14), Auckland (12), Wellington (10), Central Districts (8) and Otago (0).

A tournament team was selected at the completion of the fifth round. It was D. Bartlett, B. Cachopa *(Auckland)*, T. Muir, C. Bartholomeusz, B. Langrope *(Canterbury)*, K. Richards, B. Grant *(Central Districts)*, G. Bell, B. Simpson, T. Southee *(Northern Distrcts)*, R. Karaitiana, C. Gallagher *(Wellington)*.

FIRST ROUND

AUCKLAND v CENTRAL DISTRiCTS *First innings win to Auckland*

Auckland 196 (S. McCann 42, B. Cachopa 31, A. Mason 3-27) and 65 (J. Wheeler 3-6, K. Richards 3-18)

Central Districts 115 (B. Carmody 3-18) and 131-8 (B. Grant 34)

NORTHERN DISTRICTS v CANTERBURY *First innings win to Canterbury*

Northern Districts 152 (B. Simpson 51*, I. King 3-30) and 136 (G. Bell 44, I. King 4-21)

Canterbury 249 (B. Langrope 74*, T. Southee 4-48, S. Rae 3-11) and 13-2

OTAGO v WELLINGTON *Wellington won by 4 wickets*

Otago 114 (C. Rutherford 56*, C. Gallagher 4-17, R. Karaitiana 4-18) and 156 (G. Dawson 43, C. Gallagher 5-18)

Wellington 123 (R. Karaitiana 58*, C. Rutherford 3-25, P. Breen 3-29) and 148-6 (R. Karaitiana 47*, C. Gorrie 42*)

SECOND ROUND

WELLINGTON v AUCKLAND *First innings win to Auckland*

Wellington 138 (R. Candy 53, R. Karaitiana 31, D. Bartlett 3-19) and 108-3 (R. Karaitiana 42*, A. Russell 34*)

Auckland 153 (J. Raval 66, B. Turner 3-27, C. Gallagher 3-29)

CENTRAL DISTRICTS v CANTERBURY *First innings win to Canterbury*

Canterbury 254 (T. Muir 131, C. Bartholomeusz 31, D. Norman 4-23) and 26-2

Central Districts 143 (G. Worker 37, M. Taiaroa 36, B. Langrope 5-17)

NORTHERN DISTRICTS v OTAGO *Northern Districts won by an innings and 71*

Otago 106 (B. Hill 30, T. Southee 6-20) and 105 (J. Trembath 5-29, J. Standen 3-26)

Northern Districts 282-9d (G. Bell 87, A. Peacock 56, M. Dodunski 40, C. Rutherford 3-29, O. Newton 3-29)

THIRD ROUND

WELLINGTON v CANTERBURY *First innings win to Canterbury*

Canterbury 305-8d (C. Slade 81, C. Bartholomeusz 69, B. Langrope 43, H. Fisher 33, A. Pennell 4-56, C. Gallagher 3-51)

Wellington 174 (R. Karaitiana 83, M. Kain 3-30)

AUCKLAND v OTAGO *First innings win to Auckland*

Auckland 336-6d (B. Cachopa 70*, A. de Boorder 67, S. McCann 51, S. Badger 47, J. Abraham 43, M. Guptill-Bunce 39)

Otago 176 (D. Caldwell 72, D. Bartlett 3-21, T. Powell 3-30) and 60-2

CENTRAL DISTRICTS v NORTHERN DISTRICTS *First innings win to Northern*

Northern Districts 337-8d (S. Rae 66*, G. Bell 65, T. Jamieson 53, B. Simpson 42, D. Norman 3-35, J. Wheeler 3-63)

Central Districts 262 (R. Kennedy 75, R. O'Sullivan 47, M. Goodwin 42, T. Southee 4-32)

FOURTH ROUND

NORTHERN DISTRICTS v WELLINGTON *Wellington won by 50 runs*

Wellington 253-9 (R. Karaitiana 46, N. Gloag 43, R. Candy 34, M. Dodunski 3-56)

Northern Districts 203 (B. Simpson 55, G. Bell 36, C. Gallagher 3-29)

CANTERBURY v AUCKLAND *Canterbury won by 43 runs*

Canterbury 203-9 (A. Dixon 66, C. Bartholomeusz 43, T. Muir 35)

Auckland 160-9 (A. de Boorder 38, A. Dixon 3-30)

OTAGO v CENTRAL DISTRICTS *Central Districts won by 67 runs*

Central Districts 234 (M. Goodwin 37, M. Taiaroa 34, G. Frew 3-48, P. Breen 3-65)

Otago 167 (P. Breen 32, G. Dawson 31, K. Richards 3-17, R. O'Sullivan 3-23)

FIFTH ROUND

OTAGO v CANTERBURY *Canterbury won by 9 wickets*

Otago 120 (M. Kain 4-24)

Canterbury 122-1 (C. Slade 60*, H. Fisher 34)

WELLINGTON v CENTRAL DISTRICTS *Central Districts won by 64 runs*

Central Districts 209-6 (B. Grant 71*, G. Worker 37, R. Kennedy 35, R. Karaitiana 3-44)

Wellington 145 (D. Houghton 33, J. Wheeler 3-15, R. O'Sullivan 3-31)

NORTHERN DISTRICTS v AUCKLAND *Northern Districts won by 1 wicket*

Auckland 246 (J. Raval 64, A. de Boorder 40, S. Badger 38, B. Cachopa 34, S. Rae 3-27)

Northern Districts 247-9 (W. MacElrich 60, T. Goodin 44, M. Dodunski 43, S. Badger 3-23)

HAWKE CUP

The major competition for the District (formerly Minor) Associations reverted to the Hawke Cup from 1999/00. The Fuji Xerox Cup since 1995/96, it was renamed the National District Championship in 1998/99. The competition was for the U-Bix Cup from 1985/86 to 1994/95.

Apart from tournaments in 1910/11, 1912/13 and 2000/01, the competition has always been on a challenge basis. To reduce the number of challenges received by the holders it was decided to pair off all the Minor Associations. This scheme commenced in the 1924/25 season, when the first three elimination matches were played. Since then numerous elimination matches have been staged to determine the right to challenge the holders of the cup.

At the end of 1999/00 it was decided to exclude the teams from the four major centres who had taken part in the tournament in recent seasons. As Dunedin Metropolitan held the trophy at the time, a national zonal tournament was held to find a new holder and the challenge format resumed in 2001/02.

Holders

Southland, 1910/11; won the tournament of six matches.
Southland, March 14, 1911, to March 25, 1913; resisted one challenge.
South Auckland, 1912/13; won the tournament of four matches.

	Challenges resisted
Wanganui, December 26, 1913, to March 28, 1919	5
Poverty Bay, March 28, 1919, to February 15, 1921	4
Wairarapa, February 15, 1921, to December 26, 1921	1
Rangitikei, December 26, 1921, to January 3, 1922	—
Nelson, January 3, 1922, to April 1, 1922	2
Wanganui, April 1, 1922, to January 22, 1924	7
Nelson, January 22, 1924, to February 2, 1926	7
Wanganui, February 2, 1926, to December 6, 1926	2
Taranaki, December 6, 1926, to December 20, 1927	3
Wanganui, December 20, 1927, to February 23, 1928	2
Manawatu, February 23, 1928, to March 29, 1930	9
Rangitikei, March 29, 1930, to December 15, 1930	—
Waikato, December 15, 1930, to January 2, 1933	11
Nelson, January 2, 1933, to December 27, 1933	2
Taranaki, December 27, 1933, to December 27, 1934	3
Manawatu, December 27, 1934, to February 14, 1938	15
Waikato, February 14, 1938, to January 30, 1940	7
Manawatu, January 30, 1940, to April 7, 1947	9
Hawke's Bay, April 7, 1947, to February 14, 1948	1
Wanganui, February 14, 1948, to December 13, 1948	1
Hutt Valley, December 13, 1948, to April 11, 1950	7
Hawke's Bay, April 11, 1950, to January 3, 1951	2
Wairarapa, January 3, 1951, to March 12, 1951	1
Waikato, March 12, 1951, to December 10, 1951	—
Nelson, December 10, 1951, to December 30, 1952	6
Wanganui, December 30, 1952, to December 28, 1955	13
Hutt Valley, December 28, 1955, to January 2, 1956	—
Northland, January 2, 1956, to December 8, 1956	2
Waikato, December 8, 1956, to December 8, 1958	9
Nelson, December 8, 1958, to February 1, 1965	28
Manawatu, February 1, 1965, to January 24, 1967	9
North Canterbury, January 24, 1967, to February 27, 1967	—
Nelson, February 27, 1967, to December 17, 1967	—
Hutt Valley, December 17, 1967, to January 7, 1968	1
Marlborough, January 7, 1968, to March 3, 1968	1
Hawke's Bay, March 3, 1968, to February 23, 1969	4

	Challenges resisted
Waikato, February 23, 1969, to February 7, 1970	3
Southland, February 7, 1970, to December 29, 1970	1
Taranaki, December 29, 1970, to March 12, 1973	12
Southland, March 12, 1973, to February 27, 1977	14
Wairarapa, February 27, 1977, to February 5, 1979	6
Nelson, February 5, 1979, to February 21, 1983	14
Northland, February 21, 1983, to March 14, 1983	2
Hawke's Bay, March 14, 1983, to February 20, 1984	2
Northland, February 20, 1984, to February 27, 1984	—
Nelson, February 27, 1984, to February 24, 1986	8
Hawke's Bay, February 24, 1986, to March 18, 1986	1
Bay of Plenty, March 18, 1986, to February 23, 1987	2
Hawke's Bay, February 23, 1987, to March 16, 1987	—
Bay of Plenty, March 16, 1987, to March 23, 1987	—
Southland, March 23, 1987, to March 15, 1988	4
North Canterbury, March 15, 1988, to March 22, 1988	—
Taranaki, March 22, 1988, to February 13, 1989	—
Northland, February 13, 1989, to February 27, 1989	—
Southland, February 27, 1989, to February 24, 1992	15
Northland, February 24, 1992, to March 23, 1992	1
Nelson, March 23, 1992, to March 15, 1993	3
Canterbury Country, March 15, 1993, to March 29, 1993	—
Manawatu, March 29, 1993, to February 28, 1994	2
Marlborough, February 28, 1994 to March 14, 1994	—
Taranaki, March 14, 1994 to January 29, 1995	7
Central Otago, January 29, 1995 to February 12, 1996	—
Nelson, February 12, 1995 to February 26, 1996	—
Hutt Valley, February 26, 1996 to January 20, 1997	2
Nelson, January 20, 1997 to February 17, 1997	1
Auckland-Manukau, February 17, 1997 to March 3, 1997	—
Bay of Plenty, March 3, 1997 to January 26, 1998	1
Wellington City, January 26, 1998 to February 9, 1998	—
Manawatu, February 9, 1998 to February 23, 1998	—
Auckland-Waitakere, February 23, 1998 to March 9, 1998	—
Northland, March 9, 1998 to February 8, 1999	2
Wellington City, February 8, 1999 to February 22, 1999	—
Canterbury Country, February 22, 1999 to January 24, 2000	2
South Canterbury, January 24, 2000 to February 7, 2000	—
Dunedin Metropolitan, February 7, 2000 to March 26, 2001	3
Hamilton, March 26, 2001 to March 25, 2002	4
Manawatu, March 25, 2002 to February 17, 2003	—
Hawke's Bay, February 17, 2003 to 3 March, 2003	—
Northland, 3 March, 2003 to 16 February, 2004	2
Mid-Canterbury, 16 February, 2004 to 7 February, 2005	1
Canterbury Country, 7 February, 2005 to 7 March, 2005	1
Hamilton, 7 March, 2005	—

MID-CANTERBURY v CANTERBURY COUNTRY Hawke Cup

at Ashburton Domain on 5, 6, 7 February, 2005
Toss : Canterbury Country. Umpires : W.R. Knights & C.J. Morris
Close of play: 1st day: Canterbury Country 348-4, Donkers 23, Rugg 22;
2nd day: Canterbury Country 84-0, Edwards 39, Robertson 41
First innings win to Canterbury Country

CANTERBURY COUNTRY

FIRST INNINGS	Runs	Mins	Balls	6s	4s	SECOND INNINGS	Runs	Mins	Balls	6s	4s
S.J.Edwards c Overend b Harrison	7	19	18	-	1	lbw b Fine	55	142	109	-	6
A.W.Robertson† c Overend b Jemmett G.L.	13	46	38	-	-	b Blakely	42	95	80	-	3
R.M.Frew c Overend b Fine	131	288	204	-	12						
B.J.K.Doody c Overend b McCloy	138	243	218	2	19						
B.P.Donkers c Jemmett G.L. b Hastie	58	183	121	-	6						
P.J.Rugg* not out	72	201	135	1	9						
D.J.Bulman b Fine	15	22	17	-	2	(4) c Harrison b Jemmett L.G.	34	73	64	1	4
P.W.Borren c Moorhead b Blakely	20	6	9	1	1	(5) c Overend b Jemmett L.G.	1	8	3	-	-
C.J.Sowden not out	6	5	4	-	1	(3) b Hastie	41	126	115	-	3
M.Goldstein						(6) not out	0	2	3	-	-
D.J.Hay											
Extras (b 4, lb 8, w 10, nb 2)	24					(lb 11, w 1, nb 1)	13				
TOTAL (127 overs) (7 wkts dec)	**484**	510				(62.1 overs) (5 wkts)	**186**	225			

MID-CANTERBURY

	Runs	Mins	Balls	6s	4s
D.A.G.Jemmett b Donkers	9	56	47	-	1
L.G.Jemmett st Robertson b Sowden	17	49	31	-	2
S.W.Moorhead c Borren b Donkers	1	17	9	-	-
R.J.Madden* st Robertson b Sowden	2	13	8	-	-
J.S.Overend† c Robertson b Donkers	0	1	1	-	-
M.W.Fine lbw b Sowden	8	43	30	-	1
J.E.Blakely b Hay	6	16	17	-	1
G.L.Jemmett run out	25	76	56	-	4
C.J.Hastie not out	38	85	76	-	7
S.B.McCloy c Rugg b Borren	2	18	21	-	-
D.R.Harrison c Edwards b Goldstein	13	15	10	2	-
Extras (b 2, w 3, nb 8)	13				
TOTAL (49.4 overs)	**134**	199			

Bowling	O	M	R	W	O	M	R	W
MID-CANTERBURY								
Harrison	24	5	76	1	6	1	26	0
Jemmett G.L.	19	3	71	1	5	1	22	0
Fine	25	4	91	2	12.5	4	30	1
Hastie	22	1	97	1	11	3	26	1
Blakely	9	1	40	1	9	3	22	1
McCloy	17	1	62	1	2.1	1	3	0
Jemmett L.G.	11	1	35	0	14.1	1	37	2
Madden					2	0	9	0
CANTERBURY COUNTRY								
Donkers	13	4	32	3				
Hay	9	1	27	1				
Sowden	12	4	19	3				
Bulman	3	0	12	0				
Borren	9	3	21	1				
Goldstein	3.4	0	21	1				

Fall of Wickets	*CC*	*MC*	*CC*
	1st	*1st*	*2nd*
1st	10	27	89
2nd	28	31	123
3rd	286	34	179
4th	302	34	186
5th	418	34	186
6th	448	42	-
7th	468	51	-
8th	-	94	-
9th	-	107	-
10th	-	134	-

CANTERBURY COUNTRY v NELSON — Hawke Cup

at Rangiora Recreation Ground on 19, 20, 21 February, 2005
Toss : Canterbury Country. Umpires : G.C. Holdem & K.C. Manley
Close of play: 1st day: Canterbury Country 259-8, Sowden 8, Borren 1;
2nd day: Canterbury Country 6-0, Edwards 3, Robertson 2
First innings win to Canterbury Country

CANTERBURY COUNTRY

FIRST INNINGS	*Runs*	*Mins*	*Balls*	*6s*	*4s*	*SECOND INNINGS*	*Runs*	*Mins*	*Balls*	*6s*	*4s*
S.J.Edwards c Armstrong b Fraser	18	41	44	-	2	c Capstick b Scoble	14	53	54	-	1
A.W.Robertson† c Capstick b Armstrong	19	45	21	-	1	b Armstrong	9	64	40	-	-
D.H.Fulton c Cederman b Fraser	19	78	47	-	1	lbw b Leonard	25	54	50	-	2
R.M.Frew b Armstrong	2	3	5	-	-	not out	44	193	164	-	2
B.J.K.Doody c & b Scoble	77	164	137	1	8	c Hay b Scoble	21	47	43	-	2
B.P.Donkers c Armstrong b Fraser	70	222	194	1	3	not out	16	101	95	-	-
P.J.Rugg* c Cederman b Fraser	31	132	125	-	1						
D.J.Bulman c Greaney b Fraser	0	18	14	-	-						
C.J.Sowden not out	26	87	59	-	1						
P.W.Borren c Edwards b Armstrong	3	28	19	-	-						
L.C.Smith b Fraser	17	43	41	-	1						
Extras (b 2, lb 5, w 5, nb 4)	16					(b 3, lb 3, nb 2)	8				
TOTAL (117 overs)	**298**	450				(74 overs) (4 wkts)	**137**	258			

NELSON

	Runs	Mins	Balls	6s	4s
P.J.Capstick lbw b Smith	0	15	12	-	-
D.J.Leonard lbw b Smith	53	180	144	-	3
G.R.Hay c Robertson b Sowden	58	220	172	-	5
D.R.Cederman* c Robertson b Sowden	1	20	21	-	-
B.Krammer b Sowden	0	1	1	-	-
D.Greaney lbw b Sowden	0	14	11	-	-
R.Edwards† lbw b Donkers	1	5	5	-	-
M.Fraser lbw b Bulman	7	24	14	-	1
J.Boote lbw b Sowden	4	5	3	-	1
K.Scoble b Donkers	22	66	62	-	3
C.Armstrong not out	9	60	41	-	-
Extras (b 8, lb 6, w 2, nb 3)	19				
TOTAL (80.3 overs)	**174**	309			

Bowling	*O*	*M*	*R*	*W*	*O*	*M*	*R*	*W*
NELSON								
Fraser	35	14	87	6	6	4	8	0
Boote	20	3	63	0	6	0	15	0
Armstrong	23	6	57	3	12	4	24	1
Scoble	13	1	26	1	23	11	36	2
Leonard	14	5	29	0	6	1	12	1
Cederman	12	2	29	0	7	2	18	0
Greaney					7	3	11	0
Krammer					6	3	6	0
Capstick					1	0	1	0
CANTERBURY COUNTRY								
Donkers	14.3	8	28	2				
Smith	18	6	31	2				
Sowden	22	5	34	5				
Bulman	20	7	36	1				
Borren	6	0	31	0				

Fall of Wickets	***CC***	***N***	***CC***
	1st	*1st*	*2nd*
1st	40	2	26
2nd	40	110	34
3rd	42	112	59
4th	89	112	90
5th	157	116	-
6th	244	117	-
7th	248	127	-
8th	258	136	-
9th	263	138	-
10th	298	174	-

CANTERBURY COUNTRY v HAMILTON — Hawke Cup

at Rangiora Recreation Gound on 5, 6, 7 March, 2005
Toss : Canterbury Country. Umpires : K.C. Manley & W.R. Knights
Close of play: 1st day: Hamilton 103-3, Horsley 53, J.G.Hatwell 19; 2nd day: Hamilton 443 all out
First innings win to Hamilton

CANTERBURY COUNTRY

FIRST INNINGS	*Runs*	*Mins*	*Balls*	*6s*	*4s*
S.J.Edwards run out	30	107	81	-	2
A.W.Robertson† c Daley b Winslade	6	19	17	-	-
D.H.Fulton lbw b Winslade	2	7	5	-	-
R.M.Frew c Steele b Martin	15	32	22	-	-
B.J.K.Doody lbw b Hodgson	24	63	61	-	4
B.P.Donkers b Winslade	15	75	72	-	-
P.J.Rugg* lbw b Winslade	36	83	81	-	6
D.J.Bulman b Hatwell J.G.	1	4	6	-	-
C.J.Sowden b Irwin	28	80	72	-	3
P.W.Borren not out	45	68	64	1	7
D.J.Hay c Robinson b Winslade	0	7	2	-	-
Extras (b 1, lb 1, w 2, nb 2)	6				
TOTAL (80.1 overs)	**208**	277			

HAMILTON

	Runs	*Mins*	*Balls*	*6s*	*4s*
G.D.Steele lbw b Sowden	10	39	36	-	-
G.G.Robinson c Doody b Sowden	9	50	27	-	1
R.R.Shutte lbw b Sowden	0	1	3	-	-
N.K.W.Horsley lbw b Donkers	60	75	65	-	11
J.G.Hatwell c Edwards b Borren	167	345	263	-	31
B.J.Hatwell c Edwards b Bulman	110	305	256	-	14
L.W.Martin lbw b Fulton	21	29	25	-	4
G.D.Irwin b Borren	11	47	37	-	3
N.M.Daley*† not out	20	70	54	-	3
G.S.C.Hodgson b Borren	0	23	18	-	-
B.J.Winslade lbw b Borren	0	1	3	-	-
Extras (b 13, lb 8, w 5, nb 9)	35				
TOTAL (129.4 overs)	**443**	497			

Bowling	*O*	*M*	*R*	*W*
HAMILTON				
Winslade	20.1	3	74	5
Shutte	13	1	39	0
Martin	6	2	8	1
Hatwell J.G.	22	10	37	1
Hodgson	15	4	37	1
Irwin	4	1	11	1
CANTERBURY COUNTRY				
Donkers	27	8	51	1
Hay	15	2	74	0
Sowden	26	6	95	3
Bulman	30	10	90	1
Borren	23.4	6	85	4
Fulton	8	0	27	1

Fall of Wickets

	CC	***H***
	1st	*1st*
1st	16	27
2nd	22	27
3rd	51	36
4th	76	112
5th	84	371
6th	125	409
7th	126	409
8th	142	441
9th	196	443
10th	208	443

WOMEN'S CRICKET

Compiled by Catherine Campbell

The White Ferns played eleven one-day internationals during the 2004/05 season, including the annual Rose Bowl Series against Australia and the IWCC World Cup in South Africa. The Rose Bowl Series was played in Perth en route to the World Cup.

Australia convincingly won the first match and whilst New Zealand fought hard in the last two matches the series was lost 3-0. At the World Cup New Zealand reached the semi-finals where they lost to India. In round robin play they had matches rained out, against West Indies and South Africa, lost to Australia, easily beat Sri Lanka and Ireland and had two exciting victories against India and England.

In domestic cricket State Canterbury Magicians qualified top of the State League and played State Auckland Hearts in the final. In a one sided match in Christchurch Canterbury easily beat Auckland by ten wickets.

The National Development Tournament played at the Ilam Playing Fields, Christchurch, before Christmas was badly affected by wet weather and the title was shared by Auckland and Canterbury who were leading the points table going into the rained out final round of matches.

New Plymouth Girls' High School won the New Zealand Community Trust Cup and Havelock North Intermediate won the Milo Shield.

PLAYER OF THE YEAR

State Northern Spirit and White Ferns opening bowler **Louise Milliken** is the *Almanack's* Player of the Year.

In the State League she took 13 wickets at an average of 19.84 with an economy rate of 3.21. Her best return was 4-38 against Central Districts.

In the Rose Bowl Series in Perth she took two wickets with an economy rate of 4.00 but it was at the World Cup that 21-year-old Milliken performed at her best. She was New Zealand's leading wicket taker at the tournament with 11 wickets at an impressive average of 13.72 and an economy rate of 3.43.

Milliken bowls with genuine pace and her best performance of the season was against India in the round robin match at the World Cup where she returned career best bowling figures of 5-25. This was the best performance of any bowler at the tournament.

PROMISING PLAYER

Ros Kember is the 2004/05 Promising Player of the Year. A right-hand opening batsman from the State Auckland Hearts, Ros formed a consistent opening partnership with Victoria Lind at the top of the Auckland order.

In the State League she scored 381 runs at an average of 38.10 including two fifties. Her highest score was 94 in the match against State Otago Sparks at the Queenstown Events Centre when Auckland totalled 285-4 in their 50 overs.

Ros was a member of the New Zealand Cricket Academy in 2003 and was selected in the New Zealand A team in the 2003/04 season. She is an occasional leg-spin bowler

ROSE BOWL

The Rose Bowl Series was hosted by Cricket Australia in Perth while the New Zealand team were on their way to the World Cup in South Africa. Australia won the series 3-0. It was the first time New Zealand had played in Perth since the 1988 World Cup.

A warm up match was played against the Western Fury at Lilac Hill and the first match was played at the same venue with the last two matches played at the W.A.C.A. The third match was rescheduled as a day/nighter after water had leaked under the covers.

The highlights of the series were Haidee Tiffen's 91 in the second match, her highest one-day international score, and the bowling of Rebecca Steele who returned an economy rate of 2.37 in the series. Emily Drumm was injured in the warm up match and did not play in any of the Rose Bowl matches.

The team was Maia Lewis *(captain)*, Anna Corbin *(Wellington)*, Emily Drumm *(vice-captain)*, Rebecca Rolls, Natalee Scripps, Helen Watson *(Auckland)*, Nicola Browne, Louise Milliken *(Northern Districts)*, Sara McGlashan *(Central Districts)*, Sarah Burke, Maria Fahey, Rebecca Steele, Haidee Tiffen *(Canterbury)*, Rachel Pullar *(Otago)*. Coach, Mike Shrimpton; Assistant Coach, Cliff Dickeson; Manager, Catherine Campbell; Physiotherapist, Angela Cadogan.

New Zealand Averages

BATTING	*M*	*I*	*NO*	*HS*	*Agg*	*Ave*	*100s*	*50s*	*Ct*	*St*	*SR*
N.J. Browne	3	3	2	30	84	84.00	-	-	-	-	54
H.M. Tiffen	3	3	0	91	91	30.33	-	1	2	-	65
H.M. Watson	3	3	0	23	45	15.00	-	-	1	-	34
R.J. Pullar	2	2	0	14	26	13.00	-	-	-	-	57
R.J. Rolls	3	3	0	20	36	12.00	-	-	3	-	47
S.J. McGlashan	3	3	0	23	29	9.66	-	-	1	-	40
M.F. Fahey	3	3	0	21	28	9.33	-	-	1	-	24
R.J. Steele	3	2	1	5*	7	7.00	-	-	-	-	43
A.M. Corbin	2	2	0	7	12	6.00	-	-	1	-	31
L.E. Milliken	2	2	0	5	9	4.50	-	-	-	-	37
M.A.M. Lewis	3	3	0	11	12	4.00	-	-	2	-	22
S.K. Burke	1	1	0	0	0	0.00	-	-	-	-	0
N. Scripps	2	2	2	9*	9	-	-	-	-	-	47

BOWLING	*O*	*M*	*R*	*W*	*Ave*	*Best*	*R/O*
H.M. Watson	19	2	61	4	15.25	3-14	3.21
R.J. Steele	30	9	71	3	23.66	1-21	2.37
N.J. Browne	22	1	89	3	29.66	2-37	4.05
L.E. Milliken	16	3	64	2	32.00	1-28	4.00
N. Scripps	17.3	2	61	1	61.00	1-37	3.48
A.M. Corbin	15	2	64	1	64.00	1-24	4.27
S.K. Burke	6	1	34	0	-	-	5.67
R.J. Pullar	20	2	63	0	-	-	3.15

Australia Averages

BATTING	M	I	NO	HS	Agg	Ave	100s	50s	Ct	St	SR
B.J. Clark	3	3	0	86	127	42.33	-	1	-	-	65
K.L. Rolton	3	3	0	43	90	30.00	-	-	-	-	58
A.J. Blackwell	3	3	1	27	50	25.00	-	-	2	-	46
M. Jones	3	3	0	55	70	23.33	-	1	-	-	63
L.M. Keightley	3	3	0	29	47	15.66	-	-	1	-	32
C.L. Fitzpatrick	3	3	0	23	35	11.66	-	-	2	-	67
J.C. Price	3	3	1	9*	18	9.00	-	-	3	-	52
L.C. Sthalekar	2	2	0	9	12	6.00	-	-	1	-	22
L.C. Broadfoot	2	2	1	1	1	1.00	-	-	1	-	14
J. Hayes	3	2	2	9*	13	-	-	-	-	-	68
C.R. Smith	2	-	-	-	-	-	-	-	1	-	-
E. Liddell	2	-	-	-	-	-	-	-	-	-	-
S. Nitschke	1	-	-	-	-	-	-	-	-	-	-

BOWLING	O	M	R	W	Ave	Best	R/O
A.J. Blackwell	4	0	8	1	8.00	1-8	2.00
E. Liddell	19	2	58	5	11.60	4-17	3.05
K.L. Rolton	16	2	48	3	16.00	2-16	3.00
J. Hayes	28	7	64	4	16.00	2-24	2.29
S. Nitschke	9	0	16	1	16.00	1-16	1.78
C.R. Smith	18	5	51	3	17.00	2-29	2.83
C.L. Fitzpatrick	29	4	94	4	23.50	2-28	3.24
L.C. Sthalekar	11	4	29	1	29.00	1-27	2.64
L.C. Broadfoot	12	2	41	1	41.00	1-12	3.42

AUSTRALIA v NEW ZEALAND — Rose Bowl

at Lilac Hill Park, Perth on 10 March, 2005
Toss : Australia. Umpires : B. Bennett & A.R. Craig
Australia won by 87 runs.

Australia won the toss and chose to bat first. New Zealand had early success with Keightley being well caught by Lewis. Steele removed the dangerous Rolton before she was established and at 79-2 after 23 overs the game was evenly placed.

Clark and Jones then put on 97 for the third wicket before Clark was lbw to Browne for 86. New Zealand took four quick wickets and at the end of 50 overs Australia was 207-8. Milliken, Steele and Browne all took wickets for New Zealand.

New Zealand made a disastrous start to be 3-2 in the fifth over with both Lewis and Tiffen out bowled. Fahey and Rolls then consolidated but New Zealand lost regular wickets to be all out for 120 in 46 overs. Browne, batting at number eight, was left 29 not out off 42 balls including four fours. Australia won by 87 runs.

AUSTRALIA

	Runs	Mins	Balls	6s	4s
B.J.Clark* lbw b Browne	86	147	114	-	5
L.M.Keightley c Lewis b Browne	5	30	30	-	-
K.L.Rolton b Steele	16	45	40	-	2
M.Jones run out	55	83	78	-	7
A.J.Blackwell c Rolls b Milliken	6	9	11	-	-
L.C.Sthalekar run out	3	14	8	-	-
C.L.Fitzpatrick run out	11	15	14	-	-
J.C.Price† run out	4	7	5	-	-
L.C.Broadfoot not out	0	1	0	-	-
J.Hayes					
C.R.Smith					
Extras (lb 8, w 13)	21				
TOTAL (50 overs) (8 wkts)	**207**	190			

NEW ZEALAND

	Runs	Mins	Balls	6s	4s
M.A.M.Lewis* b Smith	1	5	4	-	-
M.F.Fahey run out	21	54	61	-	1
H.M.Tiffen b Fitzpatrick	0	8	6	-	-
R.J.Rolls†c Fitzpatrick b Broadfoot	20	68	46	-	2
S.J.McGlashan run out	5	19	25	-	-
R.J.Pullar c Sthalekar b Smith	12	20	20	-	1
H.M.Watson lbw b Blackwell	10	23	21	-	1
N.J.Browne not out	29	60	42	-	4
A.M.Corbin c Broadfoot b Hayes	7	18	23	-	-
L.E.Milliken c Price b Rolton	5	19	18	-	-
R.J.Steele b Rolton	2	6	10	-	-
Extras (lb 3, w 5)	8				
TOTAL (46 overs)	**120**	180			

Bowling	O	M	R	W
NEW ZEALAND				
Milliken	9	2	36	1
Pullar	10	0	42	0
Browne	8	0	37	2
Steele	10	2	24	1
Corbin	8	0	40	0
Watson	5	0	20	0
AUSTRALIA				
Fitzpatrick	9	0	26	1
Smith	10	2	29	2
Hayes	10	2	24	1
Rolton	6	1	16	2
Broadfoot	6	2	12	1
Blackwell	4	0	8	1
Sthalekar	1	0	2	0

Fall of Wickets	*A*	*NZ*
1st	28	1
2nd	79	3
3rd	176	36
4th	188	50
5th	189	55
6th	195	68
7th	206	82
8th	207	95
9th	-	112
10th	-	120

WESTERN AUSTRALIA v NEW ZEALAND

At Lilac Hill Park 8 March, 2005

New Zealand 220-6 (N.J. Browne 53*, M.A.M. Lewis 46) **defeated Western Australia** 128-9 (R. Chappell 36, N.J. Browne 3-11) by 92 runs

AUSTRALIA v NEW ZEALAND

Rose Bowl

at W.A.C.A. Ground, Perth on 12 March, 2005
Toss : Australia. Umpires : J.N. Brookes & A.R. Craig
Australia won by 12 runs.

Australia won the toss and batted and made a steady start putting on 67 for the first wicket. Wickets then fell regularly and after 50 overs Australia reached 202-7. Clark top scored with 38. Steele was the best of the New Zealand bowlers with 1-26 off her 10 overs.

Chasing 203 to win New Zealand made another poor start with both openers out cheaply. Tiffen held the innings together with 91 off 127 balls including five fours and had useful partnerships with McGlashan, who made 23 off 27 balls, and Browne, who made 25 off 28 balls. Tiffen was dismissed in the 48th over and New Zealand was unable to achieve victory with Australia winning by six runs to take the series.

AUSTRALIA

	Runs	Mins	Balls	6s	4s
L.M.Keightley c Rolls b Browne	29	67	59	-	5
B.J.Clark* c Rolls b Steele	38	89	70	-	2
K.L.Rolton c Lewis b Scripps	31	79	55	-	5
M.Jones c McGlashan b Milliken	11	17	20	-	2
L.C.Broadfoot b Watson	1	6	7	-	-
A.J.Blackwell run out	27	54	46	-	3
C.L.Fitzpatrick run out	23	28	19	-	2
J.C.Price† not out	9	16	16	-	-
J.Hayes not out	9	10	9	-	-
C.R.Smith					
E.Liddell					
Extras (lb 9, w 14, nb 1)	24				
TOTAL (50 overs) (7 wkts)	**202**	173			

NEW ZEALAND

	Runs	Mins	Balls	6s	4s
M.A.M.Lewis* c Price b Fitzpatrick	0	2	5	-	-
M.F.Fahey b Hayes	7	58	49	-	1
H.M.Tiffen c Fitzpatrick b Liddell	91	163	127	-	5
R.J.Rolls† c Smith b Hayes	16	25	26	-	3
S.J.McGlashan lbw b Smith	23	27	38	-	3
H.M.Watson b Rolton	12	23	21	-	-
N.J.Browne not out	25	38	28	-	3
L.E.Milliken run out	4	7	6	-	-
S.K.Burke run out	0	1	0	-	-
N.Scripps not out	0	1	1	-	-
R.J.Steele					
Extras (b 5, lb 6, w 5, nb 1)	17				
TOTAL (50 overs) (8 wkts)	**195**	170			

Bowling	*O*	*M*	*R*	*W*
NEW ZEALAND				
Milliken	7	1	28	1
Scripps	10	1	37	1
Browne	10	0	41	1
Burke	6	1	34	0
Steele	10	3	26	1
Watson	7	1	27	1
AUSTRALIA				
Fitzpatrick	10	2	40	1
Smith	8	3	22	1
Liddell	10	0	41	1
Hayes	10	3	24	2
Broadfoot	6	0	29	0
Rolton	6	0	28	1

Fall of Wickets	***A***	***NZ***
1st	67	0
2nd	81	42
3rd	105	66
4th	109	105
5th	137	136
6th	174	187
7th	180	194
8th	-	194
9th	-	-
10th	-	-

AUSTRALIA v NEW ZEALAND — Rose Bowl

at W.A.C.A. Ground, Perth (d/n) on 13 March, 2005
Toss : Australia. Umpires : J.K. Brookes & A.R. Craig
Australia won by 7 wickets.

Due to water leaking under the covers the third match in the series was rescheduled as a day/night game. Australia won the toss for the third time and decided to field on a damp wicket.

New Zealand was in serious trouble at 31-6 with Fahey, Tiffen and Rolls all failing to score. Pullar, Watson and Browne gave the total some respectability and New Zealand managed 114-9 after 50 overs. Browne top scored with 30 off 83 balls, including two fours.

Defending a meagre total New Zealand started well with left arm spinner Steele opening the bowing and removing Clark. Australia lost wickets regularly but the innings was held together by Rolton with 43 off 60 balls, including seven fours. Australia won in the 46th over achieving the target for the loss of seven wickets. Watson was the most successful of the New Zealand bowlers with 3-14 off seven overs and the spinners, Steele and Corbin, both took one wicket each.

NEW ZEALAND

	Runs	Mins	Balls	6s	4s
M.F.Fahey c Price b Fitzpatrick	0	2	5	-	-
M.A.M.Lewis* c Blackwell b Sthalekar	11	59	44	-	1
H.M.Tiffen b Liddell	0	4	5	-	-
R.J.Rolls† b Liddell	0	4	4	-	-
S.J.McGlashan c Blackwell b Fitzpatrick	1	16	8	-	-
R.J.Pullar c Keightley b Hayes	14	21	25	-	3
H.M.Watson b Nitschke	23	82	88	-	4
N.J.Browne b Liddell	30	103	83	-	2
A.M.Corbin b Liddell	5	15	15	-	-
N.Scripps not out	9	15	18	-	1
R.J.Steele not out	5	7	6	-	1
Extras (b 1, lb 5, w 9, nb 1)	16				
TOTAL (50 overs) (9 wkts)	**114**	167			

AUSTRALIA

	Runs	Mins	Balls	6s	4s
B.J.Clark* c Corbin b Steele	3	15	21	-	-
L.M.Keightley run out	13	47	44	-	1
K.L.Rolton c Tiffen b Watson	43	86	60	-	7
L.C.Sthalekar c Tiffen b Watson	9	43	45	-	-
A.J.Blackwell not out	17	72	50	-	3
C.L.Fitzpatrick c & b Watson	1	23	19	-	-
J.C.Price† c Fahey b Corbin	5	11	13	-	1
M.Jones run out	4	11	12	-	1
J.Hayes not out	4	14	10	-	1
S.Nitschke					
E.Liddell					
Extras (lb 3, w 15, nb 1)	19				
TOTAL (45.3 overs) (7 wkts)	**118**	185			

Bowling	O	M	R	W
AUSTRALIA				
Fitzpatrick	10	2	28	2
Liddell	9	2	17	4
Hayes	8	2	16	1
Sthalekar	10	4	27	1
Nitschke	9	0	16	1
Rolton	4	1	4	0
NEW ZEALAND				
Pullar	10	2	21	0
Steele	10	4	21	1
Scripps	7.3	1	24	0
Browne	4	1	11	0
Corbin	7	2	24	1
Watson	7	1	14	3

Fall of Wickets	*NZ*	*A*
1st	0	9
2nd	1	41
3rd	1	81
4th	11	82
5th	31	91
6th	31	101
7th	89	109
8th	98	-
9th	100	-
10th	-	-

WORLD CUP

In March and April 2005 the United Cricket Board of South Africa hosted the IWCC Women's World Cup in Pretoria. Eight countries, New Zealand, Australia, India, England, South Africa, Sri Lanka, Ireland and West Indies, participated in the tournament. The format was round robin with the top four teams progressing to the semi-finals at Potchefstroom and the top two teams contesting the final at SuperSport Park, Centurion.

In round robin play the first and last rounds were rained out and points were shared. The White Ferns lost to Australia but had exciting victories over both India and England to finish third on the points table. In a disappointing performance in the semi-final the White Ferns lost to India by 40 runs and in the final Australia convincingly beat India to win the World Cup.

During the World Cup Emily Drumm returned home due to injury and was replaced by all-rounder Aimee Mason. Captain Maia Lewis was the White Ferns leading run scorer at the tournament and Louise Milliken took the most wickets.

The team was Maia Lewis *(captain)*, Anna Corbin *(Wellington)*, Emily Drumm *(vice-captain)*, Rebecca Rolls, Natalee Scripps, Helen Watson *(Auckland)*, Nicola Browne, Louise Milliken *(Northern Districts)*, Sara McGlashan *(Central Districts)*, Sarah Burke, Maria Fahey, Rebecca Steele, Haidee Tiffen *(Canterbury)*, Rachel Pullar *(Otago)*.

Drumm was replaced by Aimee Mason *(Central Districts)*. Coach, Mike Shrimpton; Assistant Coach, Cliff Dickeson; Manager, Catherine Campbell; Physiotherapist, Angela Cadogan.

New Zealand Averages

BATTING	*M*	*I*	*NO*	*HS*	*Agg*	*Ave*	*100s*	*50s*	*Ct*	*St*	*SR*
M.F. Fahey	6	5	2	73*	114	38.00	-	1	-	-	62
M.A.M. Lewis	7	7	1	77	189	31.50	-	1	2	-	45
A.L. Mason	4	4	1	49*	93	31.00	-	-	2	-	77
S.J. McGlashan	6	5	1	57	120	30.00	-	1	2	-	53
E.C. Drumm	2	2	0	42	42	21.00	-	-	-	-	43
R.J. Rolls	7	6	0	60	121	20.16	-	1	13	1	72
H.M. Tiffen	7	6	1	43	89	17.80	-	-	1	-	43
H.M. Watson	6	4	1	21*	44	14.66	-	-	2	-	63
R.J. Pullar	6	5	0	16	51	10.20	-	-	-	-	68
N.J. Browne	7	4	0	25	31	7.75	-	-	3	-	43
A.M. Corbin	5	3	1	6*	14	7.00	-	-	-	-	58
R.J. Steele	4	2	1	5*	6	6.00	-	-	-	-	46
L.E. Milliken	6	3	1	3	7	3.50	-	-	4	-	38
S.K. Burke	1	-	-	-	-	-	-	-	-	-	-
N. Scripps	3	-	-	-	-	-	-	-	-	-	-

BOWLING	*O*	*M*	*R*	*W*	*Ave*	*Best*	*R/O*
N. Scripps	14.4	2	45	4	11.25	2-17	3.06
R.J. Pullar	56	17	133	10	13.30	4-39	2.38
L.E. Milliken	44	7	151	11	13.72	5-25	3.43
R.J. Steele	23	7	47	3	15.66	1-1	2.04
A.M. Corbin	28	3	72	3	24.00	2-15	2.57
H.M. Watson	49.3	6	173	6	28.83	3-19	3.49
N.J. Browne	50	6	161	4	40.25	2-33	3.22
S.K. Burke	6	1	12	0	-	-	2.00
A.L. Mason	16	2	63	0	-	-	3.94

NEW ZEALAND v WEST INDIES — World Cup

at Harlequins Oval, Pretoria on 22 March, 2005
Toss : West Indies. Umpires : S. George & D.J. Smith
***No result.** Points: New Zealand 3, West Indies 3*

West Indies won the toss and elected to field. Fahey and Lewis put on 50 for the first wicket before New Zealand lost three quick wickets, including Drumm who had returned to the team after injury. Lewis was the backbone of the innings with 77 off 148 balls including three fours. At the end of 50 overs New Zealand had scored 178-8.

Milliken and Scripps opened the bowling for New Zealand and both took an early wicket. When the rain came the West Indies were 18-2 off 3.4 overs. The players did not return to the field with the match being abandoned in mid-afternoon. The points were shared.

NEW ZEALAND

	Runs	Mins	Balls	6s	4s
M.F.Fahey b Williams E.	15	54	38	-	2
M.A.M.Lewis* c Nero b Thomas	77	177	148	-	3
E.C.Drumm run out	0	11	5	-	-
R.J.Rolls† c Power b Williams E.	1	6	5	-	-
H.M.Tiffen c Power b Felician	13	26	34	-	-
S.J.McGlashan c Power b Cummings	4	28	26	-	-
N.J.Browne b Thomas	25	41	35	-	2
A.M.Corbin b Lewis	6	7	6	-	-
L.E.Milliken not out	2	4	3	-	-
N.Scripps					
R.J.Steele					
Extras (b 6, lb 3, w 26)	35				
TOTAL (50 overs) (8 wkts)	**178**	182			

WEST INDIES

	Runs	Mins	Balls	6s	4s
N.George c Rolls b Milliken	0	14	12	-	-
N.Williams c Milliken b Scripps	10	17	9	-	2
J.Nero not out	0	7	1	-	-
P.Lavine not out	0	4	0	-	-
S.de Silva					
V.Felician					
S.Power*†					
E.Williams					
D.A.Lewis					
P.Thomas					
F.G.Cummings					
Extras (b 2, lb 1, w 5)	8				
TOTAL (3.4 overs) (2 wkts)	**18**	22			

Bowling	O	M	R	W
WEST INDIES				
Lewis	9	0	42	1
Thomas	7	2	19	2
Lavine	10	0	31	0
Williams E.	10	1	32	2
Cummings	4	1	11	1
Felician	10	1	34	1
NEW ZEALAND				
Milliken	2	0	4	1
Scripps	1.4	0	11	1

Fall of Wickets	WI	NZ
1st	50	16
2nd	60	16
3rd	66	-
4th	88	-
5th	104	-
6th	168	-
7th	171	-
8th	178	-
9th	-	-
10th	-	-

NEW ZEALAND v MPUMALANGA
At SACE Oval, Landau 18 March, 2005

New Zealand 305-5 (M.F. Fahey 89, R.J. Rolls 60, H.M. Waston 30*) **defeated Mpumalanga** 41 (N. Scripps 4-0, L.E. Milliken 3-0) by 264 runs

NEW ZEALAND v SOUTH AFRICA UNDER 19
At SACE Oval, Landau 20 March, 2005

New Zealand 305-5 (M.F. Fahey 78, R.J. Pullar 56, R.J. Rolls 51, H.M. Tiffen 50, S.J. McGlashan 37*) **defeated South Africa Under 19** 104 (A. Minnie 36, N. Scripps 4-3) by 201 runs

NEW ZEALAND v AUSTRALIA — World Cup

at L.C. de Villiers Oval, Pretoria on 24 March, 2005
Toss : Australia. Umpires : B.N. Harrison & G. Pienaar
Australia won by 32 runs. *Points: Australia 5. New Zealand 1*

Australia won the toss and elected to bat. New Zealand made a great start removing both openers when the score was 16. Steele had Rolton caught behind and at 50-5 New Zealand was in control. Blackwell and Fitzpatrick then came together in an 85 run sixth wicket partnership and with Price scoring 19 off 14 balls Australia recovered to reach 174-7 after 50 overs. Pullar and Browne both took two wickets and Steele had the impressive figures of 1-15 off her 10 overs.

New Zealand lost Fahey to the first ball of the run chase and then Lewis and Tiffen followed shortly after. Drumm and Rolls resurrected the innings with a partnership of 77 and New Zealand was well placed in their run chase when Rolls was caught at cover for 60 off 80 balls, including five fours. Their 50 run partnership had come from 69 balls.

Wickets then fell regularly with Drumm re-injuring her hamstring before she was run out for 42 off 92 balls, including two fours. New Zealand was all out in the last over for 142, falling 32 runs short.

AUSTRALIA

	Runs	Mins	Balls	6s	4s
L.M.Keightley lbw b Pullar	7	24	20	-	1
B.J.Clark* c Tiffen b Milliken	4	21	22	-	-
K.L.Rolton c Rolls b Steele	10	40	34	-	1
M.Jones c Watson b Browne	3	19	16	-	-
L.C.Sthalekar lbw b Watson	13	39	33	-	2
A.J.Blackwell lbw b Browne	53	109	95	-	6
C.L.Fitzpatrick c Rolls b Pullar	43	70	65	1	4
J.C.Price† not out	19	19	14	-	1
C.R.Smith not out	0	2	1	-	-
J.Hayes					
E.Liddell					
Extras (lb 6, w 16)	22				
TOTAL (50 overs) (7 wkts)	**174**	178			

NEW ZEALAND

	Runs	Mins	Balls	6s	4s
M.F.Fahey b Fitzpatrick	0	1	1	-	-
M.A.M.Lewis* c Keightley b Liddell	6	51	49	-	-
H.M.Tiffen c Price b Smith	3	13	11	-	-
R.J.Rolls† c Clark b Rolton	60	98	80	-	5
E.C.Drumm run out	42	130	92	-	2
H.M.Watson b Rolton	0	7	6	-	-
N.J.Browne run out	3	20	23	-	-
R.J.Pullar st Price b Hayes	8	5	4	-	2
A.M.Corbin run out	2	9	10	-	-
L.E.Milliken b Rolton	3	17	12	-	-
R.J.Steele not out	5	10	9	-	-
Extras (lb 7, w 3)	10				
TOTAL (49.3 overs)	**142**	184			

Bowling	*O*	*M*	*R*	*W*
NEW ZEALAND				
Milliken	10	1	44	1
Pullar	10	3	30	2
Browne	9	1	37	2
Steele	10	5	15	1
Watson	8	2	30	1
Corbin	3	0	12	0
AUSTRALIA				
Fitzpatrick	10	1	24	1
Smith	7	3	5	1
Liddell	6.3	0	20	1
Hayes	10	1	30	1
Sthalekar	4	0	23	0
Keightley	2	0	11	0
Rolton	10	2	22	3

Fall of Wickets	*A*	*NZ*
1st	16	1
2nd	16	6
3rd	30	23
4th	35	100
5th	50	102
6th	135	108
7th	167	118
8th	-	124
9th	-	132
10th	-	142

NEW ZEALAND v SRI LANKA — World Cup

at Harlequins Oval, Pretoria on 26 March, 2005
Toss : New Zealand. Umpires : S.W. Liebisch & J.E.P. Ostrom
***New Zealand won by 7 wickets.** Points: New Zealand 6, Sri Lanka 0*

New Zealand won the toss and chose to field bowling Sri Lanka out in the 35th over for just 58. Only one Sri Lankan player reached double figures. Pullar, Corbin and Watson each took two wickets with Scripps and Steele taking one each. A feature of the innings was Rolls' four wicketkeeping dismissals.

New Zealand promoted Pullar to open the batting with Lewis and New Zealand reached the target in the 19th over having lost three wickets but securing maximum points from the match.

SRI LANKA

	Runs	Mins	Balls	6s	4s
P.R.C.S.Kumarihami lbw b Pullar	0	9	7	-	-
P.M.Udawatte c Rolls b Pullar	2	30	23	-	-
W.H.D.Fernando c Rolls b Scripps	16	28	25	-	2
S.P.de Alwis c Watson b Corbin	8	64	42	-	1
L.E.Kaushalya run out	3	12	5	-	-
H.A.S.D.Siriwardene run out	4	8	7	-	1
S.K.Dolawatte* lbw b Watson	8	70	66	-	-
S.I.Galagedara c Rolls b Steele	0	5	6	-	-
L.D.V.V.Silva c Rolls b Corbin	2	12	11	-	-
A.D.Jakanthymala c McGlashan b Watson	1	9	10	-	-
E.M.T.P.Ekanayake† not out	0	5	6	-	-
Extras (lb 1, w 12, nb 1)	14				
TOTAL (34.3 overs)	**58**	130			

NEW ZEALAND

	Runs	Mins	Balls	6s	4s
M.A.M.Lewis* c Ekanayake b Udawatte	20	34	39	-	2
R.J.Pullar c & b Udawatte	10	22	22	-	1
R.J.Rolls† run out	15	31	20	-	-
H.M.Tiffen not out	11	25	27	-	-
S.J.McGlashan not out	1	6	4	-	-
H.M.Watson					
N.J.Browne					
A.M.Corbin					
S.K.Burke					
N.Scripps					
R.J.Steele					
Extras (w 2)	2				
TOTAL (18.4 overs) (3 wkts)	**59**	60			

Bowling	*O*	*M*	*R*	*W*
NEW ZEALAND				
Pullar	6	3	6	2
Scripps	5	1	17	1
Browne	3	0	6	0
Burke	6	1	12	0
Corbin	9	2	15	2
Steele	3	2	1	1
Watson	2.3	2	0	2
SRI LANKA				
Udawatte	7	0	27	2
Jakanthymala	8.4	1	24	0
Siriwardene	3	0	8	0

Fall of Wickets	***SL***	***NZ***
1st	4	29
2nd	17	32
3rd	21	55
4th	29	-
5th	34	-
6th	52	-
7th	53	-
8th	56	-
9th	57	-
10th	58	-

NEW ZEALAND v IRELAND — World Cup

at Harlequins Oval, Pretoria on 28 March, 2005
Toss : New Zealand. Umpires : G. Pienaar & S. Zoutendyk
***New Zealand won by 9 wickets.** Points: New Zealand 6, Ireland 0*

New Zealand won the toss and elected to field and dismissed Ireland in the 49th over for 91 with only Beggs reaching double figures. Watson took 3-19 and Milliken and Scripps each took two wickets. New Zealand bowled 15 wides.

New Zealand continued to open with both Lewis and Pullar although Pullar was out early. Lewis and Mason, who had replaced the injured Drumm, hit the winning runs in the 19th over. Lewis was 38 not out off 71 balls, including three fours, and the left handed Mason reached her highest one-day international score of 49 not out off 47 balls, including six fours. New Zealand took maximum points from the match.

IRELAND

	Runs	Mins	Balls	6s	4s
E.A.Beamish lbw b Scripps	4	31	27	-	-
J.L.W.Smythe run out	7	84	78	-	-
C.M.Beggs† c Rolls b Watson	30	130	102	-	3
M.E.Grealey c Rolls b Milliken	5	12	13	-	-
C.M.A.Shillington* run out	9	31	22	-	1
C.N.Joyce lbw b Scripps	0	2	2	-	1
N.J.Coffey st Rolls b Watson	0	10	11	-	-
U.G.Budd run out	0	10	8	-	-
H.Whelan not out	4	22	19	-	-
M.T.Herbert c Rolls b Watson	0	1	1	-	-
B.M.McDonald c & b Milliken	4	12	13	-	-
Extras (b 4, lb 7, w 15, nb 2)	28				
TOTAL (49 overs)	**91**	176			

NEW ZEALAND

	Runs	Mins	Balls	6s	4s
M.A.M.Lewis* not out	38	71	52	-	3
R.J.Pullar b Whelan	3	13	11	-	-
A.L.Mason not out	49	57	47	-	6
M.F.Fahey					
R.J.Rolls†					
H.M.Tiffen					
S.J.McGlashan					
H.M.Watson					
N.J.Browne					
L.E.Milliken					
N.Scripps					
Extras (w 5)	5				
TOTAL (18.2 overs) (1 wkt)	**95**	71			

Bowling	O	M	R	W
NEW ZEALAND				
Milliken	9	2	16	2
Pullar	10	4	12	0
Scripps	8	1	17	2
Browne	8	3	7	0
Watson	10	2	19	3
Mason	4	1	9	0
IRELAND				
Whelan	5	0	18	1
McDonald	7	0	33	0
Grealey	4	0	27	0
Herbert	2	0	12	0
Smythe	0.2	0	5	0

Fall of Wickets	I	NZ
1st	11	12
2nd	38	-
3rd	46	-
4th	67	-
5th	67	-
6th	72	-
7th	77	-
8th	81	
9th	81	-
10th	91	-

NEW ZEALAND v INDIA — World Cup

at Technikon Oval, Pretoria on 30 March, 2005
Toss : India. Umpires : Z. Ndamane & G. Pienaar
***New Zealand won by 16 runs.** Points: New Zealand 5, India 1*

In an important round robin match India won the toss and decided to field. Lewis was out early then Mason and Rolls put on 47 for the second wicket. McGlashan held the innings together with her highest one-day international score of 57 off 73 balls, including two fours and one six.

She featured in important partnerships with Fahey, batting at number six, and Pullar. New Zealand reached 184-9 at the end of 50 overs. Left-arm spinner Neetu David took 5-32 off her ten overs.

Milliken started impressively for New Zealand removing both openers to have India 10-2. Chopra and the captain, Raj, then put on 91 for the third wicket before Milliken returned to remove the left-handed Chopra. Pullar had Raj brilliantly caught by Milliken in the deep and India continued to lose wickets with Browne taking two wickets in her final spell.

India was 168-9 at the end of 50 overs to get a consolation bonus point while New Zealand won the match by 16 runs.

NEW ZEALAND

	Runs	Mins	Balls	6s	4s
M.A.M.Lewis* c Jain b Sharma A.	5	15	18	-	1
A.L.Mason lbw b David	36	84	57	-	2
R.J.Rolls† st Jain b Nooshin	23	44	31	-	3
H.M.Tiffen b David	8	45	36	-	-
S.J.McGlashan st Jain b David	57	99	73	1	2
M.F.Fahey b Nooshin	13	25	22	-	2
N.J.Browne c Jain b Nooshin	1	7	9	-	-
H.M.Watson c Jain b David	9	17	26	-	-
R.J.Pullar c & b David	16	19	23	-	2
A.M.Corbin not out	6	9	8	-	-
L.E.Milliken					
Extras (lb 2, w 5, nb 3)	10				
TOTAL (50 overs) (9 wkts)	**184**	184			

INDIA

	Runs	Mins	Balls	6s	4s
A.Jain† c Lewis b Milliken	1	31	18	-	-
J.Sharma c Mason b Milliken	0	9	9	-	-
A.Chopra lbw b Milliken	48	124	100	-	5
M.Raj* c Milliken b Pullar	52	140	102	-	3
R.Dhar lbw b Browne	17	29	28	-	1
H.Kala not out	17	40	24	-	-
A.Sharma run out	0	4	1	-	-
J.Goswami c Browne b Milliken	5	10	8	-	-
N.David b Browne	1	4	2	-	-
D.M.Marathe c Lewis b Milliken	1	5	4	-	-
A.K.Nooshin not out	3	7	5	-	-
Extras (b 1, lb 7, w 15)	23				
TOTAL (50 overs) (9 wkts)	**168**	203			

Bowling	O	M	R	W
INDIA				
Goswami	9	2	41	0
Sharma A.	6	1	30	1
Dhar	5	1	19	0
Nooshin	10	0	44	3
David	10	3	32	5
Marathe	10	0	16	0
NEW ZEALAND				
Milliken	10	4	25	5
Pullar	10	3	15	1
Browne	10	0	33	2
Watson	10	0	46	0
Corbin	6	0	21	0
Mason	4	0	20	0

Fall of Wickets	*NZ*	*I*
1st	12	1
2nd	59	10
3rd	75	101
4th	86	136
5th	113	143
6th	117	145
7th	135	156
8th	167	159
9th	184	162
10th	-	-

NEW ZEALAND v ENGLAND — World Cup

at L.C. de Villiers Oval, Pretoria on 1 April, 2005
Toss : England. Umpires : L.M. Englebrecht & Z. Ndamane
New Zealand won by 5 wickets. *Points: New Zealand 5, England 1*

England won the toss and elected to bat. Milliken removed promoted opener Shaw in her first over to have England 0-1. Newton and Taylor then put on 76 for the second wicket. Milliken injured herself in the field and did not return but the rest of the attack, already missing the injured Steele, responded well.

Combined with some excellent fielding they restricted England to 179-6 at the end of 50 overs. A highlight of the fielding was Tiffen's direct hit from the long on boundary to run out Birch at the bowler's end.

New Zealand put on 28 for the first wicket before Mason was run out. Some solid middle order batting from Tiffen and McGlashan put New Zealand into a match winning position with a 77 run fourth wicket partnership with Tiffen making 43 off 65 balls, including two fours, and McGlashan 35 off 76 balls.

Fahey and the experienced Watson then finished the match off with an unbroken 31 run sixth wicket partnership to achieve victory with seven balls to spare.

ENGLAND

	Runs	Mins	Balls	6s	4s
N.J.Shaw c Rolls b Milliken	0	2	5	-	-
L.K.Newton run out	30	80	71	-	2
S.C.Taylor run out	46	94	72	-	4
C.J.Connor* c Browne b Corbin	1	8	10	-	-
A.Brindle c sub (S.K.Burke) b Pullar	42	92	70	-	3
R.A.Birch run out	24	71	59	-	2
J.L.Gunn not out	11	16	12	-	-
J.Smit† not out	4	3	3	-	-
I.T.Guha					
L.C.Pearson					
K.H.Brunt					
Extras (w 20, nb 1)	21				
TOTAL (50 overs) (6 wkts)	**179**	184			

NEW ZEALAND

	Runs	Mins	Balls	6s	4s
M.A.M.Lewis* lbw b Connor	30	70	67	-	3
A.L.Mason run out	8	23	13	-	1
R.J.Rolls† c Taylor b Gunn	14	28	23	-	-
H.M.Tiffen c Smit b Shaw	43	90	65	-	2
S.J.McGlashan b Shaw	35	85	76	-	-
M.F.Fahey not out	13	38	27	-	1
H.M.Watson not out	21	22	21	-	1
N.J.Browne					
R.J.Pullar					
A.M.Corbin					
L.E.Milliken					
Extras (lb 3, w 13)	16				
TOTAL (48.5 overs) (5 wkts)	**180**	179			

Bowling	*O*	*M*	*R*	*W*
NEW ZEALAND				
Milliken	4	0	11	1
Pullar	10	2	31	1
Browne	10	1	42	0
Watson	10	0	47	0
Corbin	10	1	24	1
Mason	6	1	24	0
ENGLAND				
Pearson	1	0	4	0
Brunt	10	1	35	0
Gunn	10	1	33	1
Guha	7.5	1	30	0
Connor	9	1	31	1
Birch	6	0	22	0
Shaw	5	0	22	2

Fall of Wickets	*E*	*NZ*
1st	0	28
2nd	76	50
3rd	83	59
4th	91	136
5th	150	149
6th	173	-
7th	-	-
8th	-	-
9th	-	-
10th	-	-

NEW ZEALAND v SOUTH AFRICA — World Cup

at L.C. de Villiers Oval, Pretoria on 3 April, 2005
Abandoned without a ball being bowled. *Points: New Zealand 3, South Africa 3*

NEW ZEALAND v INDIA — World Cup Semi-final

at Sedgars Park, Potchefstroom on 7 April, 2005
Toss : New Zealand. Umpires : S. George & D.J. Smith
India won by 40 runs.

With rain forecast, New Zealand won the toss and fielded. A light shower forced the players from the field during the first over and when play resumed opener Sharma top edged Pullar to McGlashan and Jain was caught by Rolls off Milliken to have India 38-2. Chopra and Raj put on 66 for the third wicket with Raj batting through the innings to finish on 91 off 104 balls, including nine fours.

Pullar was the most successful of the bowlers with 4-39 but New Zealand conceded 16 wides, one no-ball and missed a number of chances in the field.

Chasing 205 to win, and a place in the final against Australia, New Zealand was in trouble at 37-4. McGlashan and Fahey fought hard in a 61 run fifth wicket partnership with McGlashan scoring 23 off 45 balls. Fahey batted impressively at number six to make 73 not out off 94 balls, including four fours, but New Zealand lost by 40 runs being all out in the 44th over.

Sharma and Nooshin each took three wickets for India and, in comparison to New Zealand, India bowled just two wides.

INDIA

	Runs	Mins	Balls	6s	4s
A.Jain† c Rolls b Milliken	11	60	38	-	2
J.Sharma c McGlashan b Pullar	0	8	4	-	-
A.Chopra c Browne b Steele	44	117	110	-	4
M.Raj* not out	91	134	104	-	9
R.Dhar c Rolls b Pullar	3	20	13	-	-
A.Sharma c Mason b Pullar	3	9	6	-	-
H.Kala c Milliken b Pullar	18	26	19	-	-
J.Goswami not out	11	11	7	-	1
D.M.Marathe					
N.David					
A.K.Nooshin					
Extras (lb 6, w 16, nb 1)	23				
TOTAL (50 overs) (6 wkts)	**204**	215			

NEW ZEALAND

	Runs	Mins	Balls	6s	4s
M.A.M.Lewis* st Jain b Nooshin	13	54	68	-	2
A.L.Mason run out	0	5	3	-	-
R.J.Rolls† b Sharma A.	8	15	9	-	1
H.M.Tiffen b Nooshin	11	36	31	-	2
S.J.McGlashan st Jain b David	23	56	45	-	1
M.F.Fahey not out	73	119	94	-	4
H.M.Watson c & b Nooshin	14	26	16	-	1
N.J.Browne lbw b Sharma A.	2	4	5	-	-
R.J.Pullar c & b Sharma A.	14	18	14	-	2
L.E.Milliken st Jain b David	2	7	3	-	-
R.J.Steele b Goswami	1	6	4	-	-
Extras (lb 1, w 2)	3				
TOTAL (43.4 overs)	**164**	177			

Bowling	*O*	*M*	*R*	*W*
NEW ZEALAND				
Milliken	9	0	51	1
Pullar	10	2	39	4
Browne	10	1	36	0
Steele	10	0	31	1
Watson	9	0	31	0
Mason	2	0	10	0
INDIA				
Goswami	6.4	3	18	1
Sharma A.	9	0	24	3
Dhar	8	0	34	0
Nooshin	10	0	39	3
David	7	1	28	2
Marathe	3	0	20	0

Fall of Wickets	*I*	*NZ*
1st	7	0
2nd	38	13
3rd	104	33
4th	127	37
5th	143	98
6th	182	126
7th	-	129
8th	-	153
9th	-	159
10th	-	164

22 March, 2005
Pretoria: **No result**
England 169 for 7 (50 overs) (J.L.Gunn 40*, L.K.Newton 31);
Australia

22 March, 2005
Pretoria: **No result**
Sri Lanka 116 (46.5 overs) (N.David 3-17);
India 4 for 0 (2 overs)

22 March, 2005
Centurion: **No result**
South Africa 204 for 7 (48 overs) (S.A.Fritz 48, C.S.Terblanche 41*, M.Terblanche 36);
Ireland

24 March, 2005
Pretoria: **England beat Sri Lanka by 214 runs**
England 284 for 4 (50 overs) (S.C.Taylor 136, C.M.Edwards 63, C.J.Connor 54, P.M.Udawatte 3-38);
Sri Lanka 70 (26 overs) (L.C.Pearson 3-23, J.L.Gunn 3-28)

24 March, 2005
Pretoria: **India beat Ireland by 9 wickets**
Ireland 65 (42.1 overs) (M.E.Grealey 38, A.Sharma 3-12);
India 68 for 1 (17.2 overs) (A.Jain 32*)

24 March, 2005
Pretoria: **South Africa beat West Indies by 1 run**
South Africa 169 (49 overs) (C.Z.Brits 72, P.Thomas 4-42);
West Indies 168 (49.4 overs) (J.Nero 41, C.Z.Brits 4-37)

26 March, 2005
Rustenburg: **Australia beat West Indies by 79 runs**
Australia 230 (49.2 overs) (K.L.Rolton 69, L.M.Keightley 56, E.Williams 3-38);
West Indies 151 (48.3 overs) (J.Nero 40)

26 March, 2005
Pretoria: **England beat Ireland by 128 runs**
England 221 for 6 (50 overs) (C.J.Connor 82*, A.Brindle 51);
Ireland 93 for 8 (50 overs)

26 March, 2005
Pretoria: **India beat South Africa by 4 wickets**
South Africa 80 (34.3 overs) (D.M.Marathe 4-1, A.Sharma 3-23);
India 81 for 6 (25.5 overs) (R.Dhar 33*, A.E.Smith 4-19)

28 March, 2005
Pretoria: **Australia beat South Africa by 97 runs**
Australia 256 for 5 (50 overs) (L.M.Keightley 103, K.L.Rolton 46);
South Africa 159 for 9 (49 overs) (C.Z.Brits 49)

28 March, 2005
Pretoria: **India beat England by 7 wickets**
England 139 (49.3 overs) (C.M.Edwards 58, A.Brindle 51*, J.Goswami 4-27, N.David 3-23);
India 141 for 3 (45.5 overs) (A.Chopra 64*, R.Dhar 42*)

28 March, 2005
Benoni: **West Indies beat Sri Lanka by 8 wickets**
Sri Lanka 152 (48.1 overs) (H.A.S.D.Siriwardene 52, S.P.de Alwis 32);
West Indies 156 for 2 (39.2 overs) (N.Williams 70*, J.Nero 44)

30 March, 2005
Pretoria: **Australia beat Sri Lanka by 8 wickets**
Sri Lanka 57 (38.2 overs) (S.Nitschke 3-5);
Australia 58 for 2 (16.4 overs)

30 March, 2005
Pretoria: **England beat South Africa by 8 wickets**
South Africa 174 for 6 (50 overs) (C.Z.Brits 46, A.E.Smith 31);
England 180 for 2 (39.5 overs) (C.M.Edwards 99, S.C.Taylor 55*)

30 March, 2005
Pretoria: **West Indies beat Ireland by 8 wickets**
Ireland 159 for 6 (50 overs) (C.N.Joyce 37, C.M.Beggs 31*);
West Indies 163 for 2 (36.3 overs) (J.Nero 71*, P.Lavine 66*)

1 April, 2005
Pretoria: **Australia beat Ireland by 10 wickets**
Ireland 66 for 8 (50 overs);
Australia 68 for 0 (14 overs) (B.J.Clark 35*)

1 April, 2005
Pretoria: **India beat West Indies by 8 wickets**
West Indies 135 (47.4 overs) (P.Lavine 43, N.George 33, J.Goswami 4-16, N.David 3-11);
India 139 for 2 (33 overs) (A.Jain 68*, J.Sharma 47)

1 April, 2005
Pretoria: **Sri Lanka beat South Africa by 32 runs**
Sri Lanka 158 (47.4 overs) (W.H.D.Fernando 78*, S.P.de Alwis 32);
South Africa 126 (43.4 overs) (J.Logtenburg 39, S.P.de Alwis 3-19)

3 April, 2005
Pretoria: **Australia v India – match abandoned**

3 April, 2005
Pretoria: **England v West Indies – match abandoned**

3 April, 2005
Pretoria: **Ireland v Sri Lanka – match abandoned**

Points: Australia 35, India 30, New Zealand 29, England 26, West Indies 19, Sri Lanka 12, South Africa 11, Ireland 6

5 April, 2005 (Semi-final)
Potchefstroom: **Australia beat England by 5 wickets**
England 158 (49.4 overs) (C.J.Connor 35, A.Brindle 32, C.L.Fitzpatrick 3-27);
Australia 159 for 5 (47 overs) (B.J.Clark 62)

10 April, 2005 (Final)
Centurion: **Australia beat India by 98 runs**
Australia 215 for 4 (50 overs) (K.L.Rolton 107*, L.C.Sthalekar 55);
India 117 (46 overs)

STATE LEAGUE

2004/05

Weather interfered significantly with the 2004/05 State League competition. One of the previous year's finalists, State Wellington Blaze, had four matches abandoned and State Otago Sparks lost three matches to bad weather.

A feature of the competition was the State Canterbury Magicians obtaining six bonus points and finishing as top qualifiers with the right to host State Auckland Hearts in the State League final at Redwood Park, Christchurch. Canterbury won in convincing style by ten wickets to regain the title they had not won since the 1998/99 season (they shared the title with Wellington in 2003/04 after the final was abandoned).

Leading run scorers in the competition were Rebecca Rolls *(Auckland),* who totalled 405 runs, and Maria Fahey *(Canterbury),* who scored 400. Three centuries were recorded during the season, one each by Rebecca Rolls, Otago opener Paula Flannery and State Northern Spirit opener Tamara Gould. Natalee Scripps *(Auckland)* took 22 wickets, the most in the competition.

Final points were:

	P	*W*	*L*	*T*	*NR*	*Bonus*	*Points*
Canterbury	10	8	1	–	1	6	40
Auckland	10	7	2	–	1	3	33
Wellington	10	3	3	–	4	2	22
Otago	10	3	4	–	3	2	20
Central Districts	10	3	6	–	1	1	15
Northern Districts	10	1	9	–	–	–	4

NORTHERN DISTRICTS v WELLINGTON — State League

at Wintec Oval, Hamilton on 27 December, 2004
Toss : Wellington. Umpires : B.G. Frost & I.W. Shine
***Wellington won by 49 runs.** Points: Wellington 5, Northern Districts 0*

WELLINGTON

	Runs	Mins	Balls	6s	4s
L.R.V.S.Harford c Hannay b Moore	28	85	66	-	3
M.C.Godliman c Ullyett b Moore	23	78	64	-	4
M.A.M.Lewis* c Brown b Hannay	6	31	31	-	-
M.G.Wakefield c & b Hannay ...	37	51	60	1	5
S.F.M.Devine b Browne	4	35	24	-	-
S.J.Hill† b Milliken	12	29	25	-	1
A.E.Cooper run out	8	28	11	-	-
A.M.Corbin lbw b Milliken	0	1	1	-	-
M.L.Presland run out	8	12	14	-	1
A.J.Green b Milliken	0	3	2	-	-
M.L.Tuapawa not out	0	2	0	-	-
A.M.Little					
Extras (b 3, lb 7, w 25, nb 1) ..	36				
TOTAL (49.3 overs)	**162**	182			

NORTHERN DISTRICTS

	Runs	Mins	Balls	6s	4s
N.J.Browne* c Harford b Corbin	8	88	69	-	-
J.M.Fraser b Presland	9	36	29	-	-
T.M.Gould run out	25	117	71	-	3
S.M.P.Sim c Hill b Cooper	11	50	47	-	1
M.P.Murphy lbw b Cooper	0	2	2	-	-
V.J.Brown b Cooper	20	50	41	-	-
M.J.Hannay lbw b Tuapawa	0	1	2	-	-
K.M.Goodson b Cooper	0	3	4	-	-
L.E.Milliken b Cooper	12	15	14	-	1
J.C.Ullyett† b Green	0	7	2	-	-
K.B.Moore not out	9	11	9	-	1
A.J.Lenssen					
Extras (b 3, lb 3, w 8, nb 5)	19				
TOTAL (46.3 overs)	**113**	183			

Bowling	O	M	R	W
NORTHERN DISTRICTS				
Milliken	8	2	18	3
Murphy	4	1	16	0
Browne	8.3	1	24	1
Goodson	9	0	36	0
Moore	10	1	29	2
Hannay	10	2	29	2
WELLINGTON				
Little	6	1	10	0
Presland	7	5	5	1
Devine	4	0	12	0
Corbin	10	3	18	1
Green	7	2	19	1
Cooper	8.3	2	21	5
Tuapawa	4	0	22	1

Fall of Wickets

	W	ND
1st	66	14
2nd	67	36
3rd	90	65
4th	122	65
5th	130	73
6th	149	73
7th	149	74
8th	153	98
9th	157	99
10th	162	113

CENTRAL DISTRICTS v CANTERBURY — State League

at Pukekura Park, New Plymouth on 27 December, 2004
Toss : Canterbury. Umpires : K.C. Manley & D.M. Quested
***Canterbury won by 9 wickets.** Points: Canterbury 5, Central Districts 0*

CENTRAL DISTRICTS

	Runs	Mins	Balls	6s	4s
S.L.Duffill c Steele b Daly	12	36	42	-	1
K.L.Pulford lbw b Daly	5	44	22	-	1
N.M.Thessman b Steele	7	23	19	-	1
C.J.Connor lbw b Charteris	26	81	75	-	-
A.L.Mason* c Taylor b Charteris	28	43	33	-	2
Z.A.McWilliams b Charteris	4	1	2	-	-
R.H.Priest† c Charteris b Burke	22	46	42	1	2
E.C.Perry c Charteris b Burke	5	12	11	-	1
C.Sim b Burke	0	23	18	-	-
D.M.Trow b Steele	4	4	8	-	1
K.M.Cocksedge not out	0	4	2	-	-
A.K.Burrows					
Extras (lb 2, w 10, nb 1)	13				
TOTAL (45 overs)	**126**	166			

CANTERBURY

	Runs	Mins	Balls	6s	4s
P.K.Gerrish c & b Burrows	1	9	12	-	-
M.F.Fahey not out	67	110	101	-	12
H.M.Tiffen* not out	47	99	84	-	5
S.C.Taylor					
H.J.Rae					
R.C.Milburn†					
B.H.McNeill					
A.E.Sattherthwaite					
S.K.Burke					
H.R.Daly					
R.J.Steele					
S.E.Charteris					
Extras (lb 5, w 7, nb 2)	14				
TOTAL (33 overs) (1 wkt) ...	**129**	110			

Bowling	O	M	R	W
CANTERBURY				
Burke	9	3	10	3
Daly	7	4	11	2
McNeill	6	1	15	0
Steele	10	2	44	2
Charteris	8	0	32	3
Sattherthwaite	5	0	12	0
CENTRAL DISTRICTS				
Burrows	4	0	16	1
Trow	8	3	22	0
Mason	5	1	21	0
Connor	6	1	21	0
Pulford	2	0	20	0
Sim	2	1	6	0
McWilliams	6	2	18	0

Fall of Wickets

	CD	C
1st	19	3
2nd	24	-
3rd	31	-
4th	75	-
5th	79	-
6th	92	-
7th	109	-
8th	121	-
9th	126	-
10th	126	-

NORTHERN DISTRICTS v WELLINGTON — State League

at Wintec Oval, Hamilton on 28 December, 2004
Toss : Northern Districts. Umpires : B.G. Frost & I.W. Shine
***Wellington won by 112 runs.** Points: Wellington 5, Northern Districts 0*

WELLINGTON

	Runs	Mins	Balls	6s	4s
L.R.V.S.Harford c Ullyett b Browne	35	107	73	-	2
M.C.Godliman c Gould b Browne	11	29	24	-	1
A.M.Corbin c Milliken b Murphy	15	36	27	-	1
M.A.M.Lewis* c Lenssen b Goodson	25	63	63	-	2
M.G.Wakefield b Browne	32	37	35	2	2
S.F.M.Devine c Murphy b Milliken	26	54	33	-	2
S.J.Hill† c Milliken b Murphy	27	25	29	-	3
A.E.Cooper c Lenssen b Murphy	0	2	2	-	-
M.L.Presland not out	11	14	14	-	-
M.A.Taylor c Moore b Murphy	0	3	1	-	-
A.M.Little					
A.J.Green					
Extras (lb 5, w 22, nb 1)	28				
TOTAL (50 overs) (9 wkts)	**210**	189			

NORTHERN DISTRICTS

	Runs	Mins	Balls	6s	4s
N.J.Browne* lbw b Devine	21	68	55	-	1
J.M.Fraser run out	12	28	23	-	2
T.M.Gould c & b Corbin	0	16	13	-	-
S.M.P.Sim run out	7	73	46	-	-
V.J.Brown lbw b Corbin	0	4	4	-	-
M.J.Hannay run out	0	6	5	-	-
L.E.Milliken c Cooper b Corbin	21	73	55	-	2
J.C.Ullyett† st Hill b Corbin	18	40	32	-	2
K.M.Goodson b Taylor	1	12	9	-	-
K.B.Moore not out	3	13	9	-	-
A.J.Lenssen b Cooper	2	8	9	-	-
M.P.Murphy					
Extras (lb 2, w 10, nb 1)	13				
TOTAL (43.1 overs)	**98**	176			

Bowling	O	M	R	W
NORTHERN DISTRICTS				
Milliken	10	1	35	1
Browne	9	3	22	3
Lenssen	7	0	45	0
Murphy	9	0	36	4
Moore	3	1	9	0
Hannay	9	0	48	0
Goodson	3	0	10	1
WELLINGTON				
Little	8	1	16	0
Presland	5	0	16	0
Corbin	10	1	22	4
Devine	6	2	11	1
Green	5	1	16	0
Cooper	5.1	1	7	1
Taylor	4	1	8	1

Fall of Wickets	W	ND
1st	20	22
2nd	58	27
3rd	95	41
4th	120	42
5th	142	42
6th	185	58
7th	186	85
8th	201	93
9th	210	93
10th	-	98

CENTRAL DISTRICTS v CANTERBURY — State League

at Pukekura Park, New Plymouth on 28 December, 2004
Toss : Central Districts. Umpires : K.C. Manley & D.M. Quested
***Canterbury won by 91 runs.** Points: Canterbury 5, Central Districts 0*

CANTERBURY

	Runs	Mins	Balls	6s	4s
P.K.Gerrish c Duffill b Connor	37	112	91	-	2
M.F.Fahey st Priest b Trow	6	39	36	-	-
H.M.Tiffen* c Perry b Mason	5	19	18	-	1
S.C.Taylor c Priest b McWilliams	80	102	90	2	4
H.J.Rae b McWilliams	4	4	5	-	1
R.C.Milburn† run out	6	22	18	-	-
B.H.McNeill not out	20	41	25	-	1
S.K.Burke run out	16	15	14	-	1
A.E.Satterthwaite not out	5	3	3	-	-
H.R.Daly					
R.J.Steele					
S.E.Charteris					
Extras (lb 1, w 19)	20				
TOTAL (50 overs) (7 wkts)	**199**	185			

CENTRAL DISTRICTS

	Runs	Mins	Balls	6s	4s
S.L.Duffill lbw b Daly	3	7	11	-	-
K.L.Pulford c Burke b McNeill	13	35	27	-	2
N.M.Thessman c Milburn b Satterthwaite	23	66	56	-	2
C.J.Connor run out	18	69	58	-	-
A.L.Mason* lbw b Charteris	31	64	52	-	3
Z.A.McWilliams c & b Steele	1	9	7	-	-
E.C.Perry c Satterthwaite b Charteris	6	19	8	-	1
S.J.McGlashan b McNeill	8	10	11	-	2
R.H.Priest† c Tiffen b Charteris	1	8	6	-	-
D.M.Trow not out	0	5	3	-	-
K.M.Cocksedge c Steele b Charteris	0	2	5	-	-
A.K.Burrows					
Extras (lb 1, w 3)	4				
TOTAL (41 overs)	**108**	150			

Bowling	O	M	R	W
CENTRAL DISTRICTS				
Burrows	10	0	36	0
Trow	10	1	37	1
McWilliams	10	1	58	2
Mason	10	2	39	1
Connor	10	0	28	1
CANTERBURY				
Burke	7	1	18	0
Daly	7	3	13	1
McNeill	8	0	31	2
Steele	10	3	17	1
Satterthwaite	5	0	15	1
Charteris	4	1	13	4

Fall of Wickets	C	CD
1st	24	3
2nd	41	23
3rd	103	49
4th	109	80
5th	131	83
6th	171	98
7th	193	99
8th	-	108
9th	-	108
10th	-	108

CENTRAL DISTRICTS v OTAGO — State League

at Fitzherbert Park, Palmerston North on 29 December, 2004
Toss : Central Districts. Umpires : M.P. George & D.M. Quested
***Central Districts won by 4 wickets.** Points: Central Districts 4, Otago 0*

OTAGO

	Runs	Mins	Balls	6s	4s
E.J.Scurr c Thessman b Burrows	0	13	13	-	-
P.B.Flannery c Connor b Mason	27	77	59	-	3
K.J.Martin† c Priest b Pulford	4	14	16	-	-
R.J.Pullar c Connor b Trow	0	5	7	-	-
S.J.Tsukigawa* c Priest b McWilliams	65	106	94	1	7
M.J.Kane c & b Mason	2	30	42	-	-
C.E.Taylor not out	40	67	45	-	3
S.W.Bates lbw b Burrows	11	18	11	-	1
C.B.Winsloe lbw b McWilliams	1	3	3	-	-
K.M.Spence run out	2	9	10	-	-
T.J.Morrison not out	0	1	0	-	-
J.A.Young					
Extras (lb 1, w 6)	7				
TOTAL (50 overs) (9 wkts)	**159**	176			

CENTRAL DISTRICTS

	Runs	Mins	Balls	6s	4s
K.L.Pulford not out	62	113	80	-	7
N.M.Thessman lbw b Spence	60	137	123	-	3
C.J.Connor lbw b Taylor	0	14	10	-	-
A.L.Mason* b Pullar	0	12	7	-	-
S.L.Duffill lbw b Pullar	0	8	6	-	-
Z.A.McWilliams b Morrison	5	30	25	-	-
R.H.Priest† run out	5	21	24	-	-
E.C.Perry not out	17	22	17	-	3
A.K.Burrows					
D.M.Trow					
K.M.Cocksedge					
R.H.Candy					
Extras (lb 2, w 7, nb 2)	11				
TOTAL (48.2 overs) (6 wkts)	**160**	182			

Bowling	*O*	*M*	*R*	*W*
CENTRAL DISTRICTS				
Burrows	7	1	23	2
Trow	10	5	8	1
Pulford	8	1	26	1
Connor	10	4	27	0
Mason	10	0	48	2
McWilliams	5	1	26	2
OTAGO				
Pullar	10	1	27	2
Morrison	10	4	31	1
Bates	9.2	1	37	0
Tsukigawa	4	0	23	0
Taylor	10	1	23	1
Scurr	1	0	9	0
Spence	4	2	8	1

Fall of Wickets	***O***	***CD***
1st	4	77
2nd	12	84
3rd	14	86
4th	37	103
5th	64	119
6th	121	130
7th	148	-
8th	149	-
9th	157	-
10th	-	-

Pulford retired hurt on 35 at 67-0 and returned at 103-4*

AUCKLAND v WELLINGTON — State League

at Melville Park, Auckland on 30 December, 2004
***Match abandoned without a ball being bowled.** Points: Auckland 2, Wellington 2*

CENTRAL DISTRICTS v OTAGO — State League

at Fitzherbert Park, Palmerston North on 30 December, 2004
Match abandoned without a ball being bowled. *Points: Central Districts 2, Otago 2*

AUCKLAND v WELLINGTON — State League

at Melville Park, Auckland on 31 December, 2004
Toss : Wellington. Umpires : P.D. Jones & W.R. Knights
Auckland won by 36 runs. *Points: Auckland 5, Wellington 0*

AUCKLAND

	Runs	Mins	Balls	6s	4s
R.J.Rolls*† c Lewis b Corbin	20	45	33	-	-
R.J.Kember b Cooper	42	125	115	-	3
E.C.Drumm b Tuapawa	13	52	36	-	-
I.Cronin-Knight run out	0	3	5	-	-
H.M.Watson b Little	14	55	36	-	-
V.J.Lind run out	6	15	15	-	-
E.B.Komp st Hill b Cooper	18	28	26	-	-
N.Scripps b Devine	8	27	17	-	-
D.J.Ramsay run out	5	7	5	-	1
F.J.Mann not out	3	9	5	-	-
S.Coetzee run out	0	1	1	-	-
S.M.Bullen					
Extras (lb 3, w 16)	19				
TOTAL (49 overs)	**148**	188			

WELLINGTON

	Runs	Mins	Balls	6s	4s
L.R.V.S.Harford b Scripps	0	2	4	-	-
M.C.Godliman c Rolls b Scripps	4	16	15	-	-
A.M.Corbin run out	24	47	38	-	1
M.L.Tuapawa st Rolls b Watson	3	42	30	-	-
M.A.M.Lewis* c Rolls b Watson	3	33	21	-	-
M.G.Wakefield c Kember b Scripps	22	64	63	-	2
S.F.M.Devine run out	2	14	9	-	-
S.J.Hill† lbw b Bullen	4	12	10	-	-
A.E.Cooper not out	15	62	52	-	-
A.M.Little c Cronin-Knight b Ramsay	2	18	15	-	-
M.A.Taylor run out	13	29	26	-	1
A.J.Green					
Extras (w 19, nb 1)	20				
TOTAL (46.4 overs)	**112**	175			

Bowling	*O*	*M*	*R*	*W*
WELLINGTON				
Little	10	1	30	1
Devine	10	2	35	1
Corbin	10	2	21	1
Cooper	9	0	27	2
Tuapawa	8	1	26	1
Harford	2	0	6	0
AUCKLAND				
Scripps	10	1	22	3
Ramsay	10	5	21	1
Coetzee	3	0	10	0
Watson	10	3	21	2
Mann	4.4	1	13	0
Bullen	7	1	15	1
Drumm	2	0	10	0

Fall of Wickets

	A	*W*
1st	35	0
2nd	76	8
3rd	76	36
4th	91	38
5th	105	50
6th	121	59
7th	134	75
8th	143	81
9th	148	91
10th	148	112

OTAGO v NORTHERN DISTRICTS — State League

at University Oval, Dunedin on 1 January, 2005
Toss : Northern Districts. Umpires : D.J. Ellwood & C.J. Morris
Otago won by 156 runs. *Points: Otago 5, Northern Districts 0*

OTAGO

	Runs	Mins	Balls	6s	4s
E.J.Scurr b Goodson	8	59	34	-	-
P.B.Flannery lbw b Browne	48	102	92	-	3
K.J.Martin† c Ullyett b Hannay	7	21	18	-	-
R.J.Pullar b Murphy	52	91	73	-	3
S.J.Tsukigawa* b Browne	1	6	7	-	-
S.W.Bates b Browne	24	45	39	-	4
C.E.Taylor not out	26	38	28	-	1
M.J.Kane b Milliken	0	2	2	-	-
C.B.Winsloe run out	14	11	8	-	2
T.J.Morrison not out	0	2	1	-	-
K.M.Spence					
J.A.Young					
Extras (b 5, lb 1, w 25, nb 2)	33				
TOTAL (50 overs) (8 wkts)	**213**	194			

NORTHERN DISTRICTS

	Runs	Mins	Balls	6s	4s
N.J.Browne* c Martin b Pullar	0	1	2	-	-
J.M.Fraser b Pullar	2	16	13	-	-
T.M.Gould c Spence b Tsukigawa	5	43	49	-	-
J.C.Ullyett† b Pullar	0	1	1	-	-
S.M.P.Sim st Martin b Bates	0	4	2	-	-
V.J.Brown b Bates	6	59	45	-	-
L.E.Milliken b Tsukigawa	3	6	10	-	-
M.J.Hannay b Taylor	4	48	42	-	-
K.M.Goodson b Pullar	0	3	4	-	-
M.P.Murphy lbw b Kane	6	32	34	-	1
K.B.Moore not out	4	13	15	-	-
A.J.Lenssen					
Extras (b 5, w 16)	21				
TOTAL (36.1 overs)	**51**	120			

Bowling	O	M	R	W
NORTHERN DISTRICTS				
Milliken	9	1	33	1
Murphy	9	0	50	1
Browne	10	2	39	3
Lenssen	2	0	19	0
Goodson	10	0	33	1
Hannay	6	0	21	1
Moore	4	0	12	0
OTAGO				
Pullar	8	3	6	4
Bates	8	2	14	2
Morrison	8	5	9	0
Tsukigawa	4	1	5	2
Young	1	0	6	0
Taylor	5	3	4	1
Kane	2.1	1	2	1

Fall of Wickets	O	ND
1st	51	0
2nd	74	5
3rd	83	5
4th	85	6
5th	148	14
6th	183	20
7th	184	31
8th	208	33
9th	-	43
10th	-	51

OTAGO v NORTHERN DISTRICTS — State League

at University Oval, Dunedin on 2 January, 2004
Toss : Northern Districts. Umpires : D.J. Ellwood & C.J. Morris
Otago won by 8 wickets. *Points: Otago 5, Northern Districts 0*

NORTHERN DISTRICTS

	Runs	Mins	Balls	6s	4s
N.J.Browne* b Bates	4	10	12	-	-
J.M.Fraser lbw b Bates	1	17	12	-	-
T.M.Gould c Martin b Spence	10	63	50	-	1
J.C.Ullyett† c Bates b Taylor	0	13	14	-	-
S.M.P.Sim run out	1	8	11	-	-
V.J.Brown run out	5	49	44	-	-
L.E.Milliken lbw b Pullar	4	28	26	-	-
M.J.Hannay c Scurr b Spence	14	56	56	-	2
M.P.Murphy not out	21	58	61	-	3
K.M.Goodson not out	6	14	15	-	1
K.B.Moore					
A.J.Lenssen					
Extras (b 1, lb 6, w 28, nb 1)	36				
TOTAL (50 overs) (8 wkts)	**102**	162			

OTAGO

	Runs	Mins	Balls	6s	4s
E.J.Scurr c Browne b Lenssen	6	29	25	-	-
P.B.Flannery not out	40	108	74	-	5
K.J.Martin† b Lenssen	11	15	17	-	2
R.J.Pullar not out	29	62	67	-	2
S.J.Tsukigawa*					
S.W.Bates					
C.E.Taylor					
M.J.Kane					
C.B.Winsloe					
T.J.Morrison					
K.M.Spence					
J.A.Young					
Extras (b 2, w 15)	17				
TOTAL (30.3 overs) (2 wkts)	**103**	108			

Bowling	O	M	R	W
OTAGO				
Pullar	10	3	11	1
Bates	10	2	28	2
Taylor	8	0	23	1
Morrison	10	4	11	0
Spence	9	2	18	2
Tsukigawa	3	1	4	0
NORTHERN DISTRICTS				
Milliken	7.3	0	14	0
Murphy	3	1	12	0
Lenssen	5	0	20	2
Browne	7	0	19	0
Hannay	6	1	27	0
Goodson	2	0	9	0

Fall of Wickets	ND	O
1st	6	23
2nd	8	41
3rd	17	-
4th	19	-
5th	39	-
6th	48	-
7th	52	-
8th	91	-
9th	-	-
10th	-	-

CANTERBURY v NORTHERN DISTRICTS — State League

at Redwood Park, Christchurch on 3 January, 2005
Toss : Northern Districts. Umpires : B.J. de Lore & D.J. Stuthridge
Canterbury won by 9 wickets. *Points: Canterbury 5, Northern Districts 0*

NORTHERN DISTRICTS

	Runs	Mins	Balls	6s	4s
N.J.Browne* b Daly	6	33	32	-	-
J.M.Fraser lbw b Daly	15	20	17	-	2
T.M.Gould run out	11	69	55	-	-
M.P.Murphy c Tiffen b Steele	6	19	28	-	1
S.M.P.Sim c Milburn b McNeill	12	56	47	-	-
V.J.Brown b Charteris	2	15	14	-	-
L.E.Milliken c Taylor b Charteris	0	8	7	-	-
M.J.Hannay c Charteris b McNeill	17	47	50	-	1
J.C.Ullyett† c Steele b McNeill	17	44	26	-	2
K.M.Goodson run out	0	7	6	-	-
K.B.Moore not out	1	5	1	-	-
A.J.Lenssen					
Extras (b 1, lb 3, w 11, nb 2)	17				
TOTAL (46.5 overs)	**104**	166			

CANTERBURY

	Runs	Mins	Balls	6s	4s
P.K.Gerrish not out	31	93	76	-	1
M.F.Fahey b Lenssen	26	60	48	-	3
H.M.Tiffen* not out	22	32	27	-	1
S.C.Taylor					
R.C.Milburn†					
H.J.Rae					
B.H.McNeill					
S.K.Burke					
A.E.Satterthwaite					
H.R.Daly					
R.J.Steele					
S.E.Charteris					
Extras (b 4, w 22)	26				
TOTAL (25.1 overs) (1 wkt)	**105**	93			

Bowling	O	M	R	W
CANTERBURY				
Burke	6.5	1	25	0
Daly	10	5	14	2
Steele	10	6	11	1
Charteris	10	4	20	2
McNeill	8	3	17	3
Satterthwaite	2	0	13	0
NORTHERN DISTRICTS				
Milliken	4	1	17	0
Goodson	2	0	10	0
Murphy	3	0	13	0
Browne	5	2	19	0
Lenssen	4	0	13	1
Hannay	4	0	7	0
Moore	3.1	0	22	0

Fall of Wickets	ND	C
1st	20	60
2nd	23	-
3rd	30	-
4th	44	-
5th	54	-
6th	56	-
7th	56	-
8th	102	-
9th	102	-
10th	104	-

AUCKLAND v CENTRAL DISTRICTS — State League

at Melville Park, Auckland on 4 January, 2005
Toss : Auckland. Umpires : A.L. Hill & P.D. Jones
Auckland won by 107 runs. *Points: Auckland 5, Central Districts 0*

AUCKLAND

	Runs	Mins	Balls	6s	4s
R.J.Rolls*† lbw b Pulford	23	42	32	-	3
R.J.Kember c Cocksedge b McWilliams	90	169	142	-	4
E.C.Drumm b Pulford	69	104	96	-	1
I.Cronin-Knight not out	20	31	25	-	-
H.M.Watson c Priest b Burrows	1	5	4	-	-
V.J.Lind not out	2	3	3	-	-
E.B.Komp					
N.Scripps					
D.J.Ramsay					
F.J.Mann					
S.Coetzee					
S.M.Bullen					
Extras (lb 5, w 7, nb 3)	15				
TOTAL (50 overs) (4 wkts)	**220**	179			

CENTRAL DISTRICTS

	Runs	Mins	Balls	6s	4s
K.L.Pulford c Rolls b Scripps	5	20	19	-	-
N.M.Thessman b Scripps	0	8	2	-	-
S.J.McGlashan c Rolls b Coetzee	8	40	39	-	-
C.J.Connor c & b Watson	21	59	50	--	
A.L.Mason* b Mann	20	68	46	-	2
A.C.Stockwell b Watson	3	17	8	-	-
Z.A.McWilliams c Kember b Watson	19	74	63	-	2
R.H.Priest† lbw b Mann	0	3	6	-	-
K.M.Cocksedge run out	2	7	6	-	-
D.M.Trow run out	8	31	32	-	-
A.K.Burrows not out	4	5	6	-	1
R.H.Candy					
Extras (lb 1, w 22)	23				
TOTAL (46.1 overs)	**113**	173			

Bowling	O	M	R	W
CENTRAL DISTRICTS				
Burrows	7	0	36	1
Trow	10	2	26	0
Pulford	7	0	36	2
Connor	10	1	27	0
Mason	10	0	45	0
Cocksedge	2	0	18	0
McWilliams	4	0	27	1
AUCKLAND				
Scripps	10	3	22	2
Ramsay	10	4	16	0
Coetzee	6	0	19	1
Mann	7	1	20	2
Watson	6.1	0	16	3
Bullen	7	2	19	0

Fall of Wickets	A	CD
1st	40	5
2nd	168	6
3rd	208	29
4th	215	47
5th	-	60
6th	-	79
7th	-	81
8th	-	84
9th	-	109
10th	-	113

CANTERBURY v NORTHERN DISTRICTS — State League

at Redwood Park, Christchurch on 4 January, 2005
Toss : Northern Districts. Umpires : B.J. de Lore & D.J. Stuthridge
***Canterbury won by 5 wickets.** Points: Canterbury 5, Northern Districts 0*

NORTHERN DISTRICTS

	Runs	Mins	Balls	6s	4s
T.M.Gould run out	18	69	52	-	1
J.M.Fraser c Milburn b Burke	16	34	19	-	2
S.M.P.Sim b Steele	18	42	35	-	1
M.P.Murphy c Milburn b Satterthwaite	9	35	41	-	1
N.J.Browne* c & b McNeill	19	58	43	-	1
V.J.Brown run out	14	52	43	-	-
L.E.Milliken run out	1	4	5	-	-
M.J.Hannay c Tiffen b McNeill	9	39	37	-	1
A.J.Lenssen c Tiffen b McNeill	7	15	13	-	-
J.C.Ullyett† c Charteris b Daly	1	3	3	-	-
K.B.Moore not out	0	2	1	-	-
K.M.Goodson					
Extras (b 1, lb 4, w 23, nb 3)	31				
TOTAL (48.3 overs)	**143**	181			

CANTERBURY

	Runs	Mins	Balls	6s	4s
R.C.Milburn† b Milliken	0	18	14	-	-
M.F.Fahey run out	32	77	54	-	3
H.J.Rae c Ullyett b Browne	24	81	74	-	1
S.C.Taylor c Ullyett b Browne	45	72	57	-	6
H.M.Tiffen* not out	24	54	42	-	3
A.E.Satterthwaite b Browne	0	2	1	-	-
B.H.McNeill not out	0	1	0	-	-
P.K.Gerrish					
S.K.Burke					
H.R.Daly					
R.J.Steele					
S.E.Charteris					
Extras (b 1, lb 1, w 19, nb 1)	22				
TOTAL (40.1 overs) (5 wkts)	**147**	155			

Bowling	*O*	*M*	*R*	*W*
CANTERBURY				
Burke	5	1	17	1
Daly	9	1	36	1
McNeill	9.3	0	27	3
Charteris	10	1	30	0
Steele	10	5	16	1
Satterthwaite	5	0	12	1
NORTHERN DISTRICTS				
Milliken	6.1	0	14	1
Murphy	7	3	9	0
Lenssen	7	0	36	0
Hannay	10	0	54	0
Browne	8	2	16	3
Moore	2	0	16	0

Fall of Wickets	***ND***	***C***
1st	36	6
2nd	60	59
3rd	67	82
4th	88	140
5th	107	143
6th	109	-
7th	123	-
8th	139	-
9th	142	-
10th	143	-

AUCKLAND v CENTRAL DISTRICTS — State League

at Melville Park, Auckland on 5 January, 2005
Toss : Auckland. Umpires : A.L. Hill & P.D. Jones
***Auckland won by 65 runs.** Points: Auckland 5, Central Districts 0*

AUCKLAND

	Runs	Mins	Balls	6s	4s
V.J.Lind c Priest b Burrows	2	17	15	-	-
R.J.Kember b Burrows	6	25	21	-	-
E.C.Drumm b Burrows	49	93	78	-	3
R.J.Rolls*† not out	75	157	118	-	-
I.Cronin-Knight c Priest b McWilliams	11	30	27	-	1
H.M.Watson not out	32	40	41	-	2
E.B.Komp					
K.A.Fraser					
N.Scripps					
D.J.Ramsay					
S.Coetzee					
S.M.Bullen					
Extras (lb 6, w 10)	16				
TOTAL (50 overs) (4 wkts)	**191**	183			

CENTRAL DISTRICTS

	Runs	Mins	Balls	6s	4s
K.L.Pulford c Drumm b Scripps	0	1	3	-	-
A.L.Mason* c Drumm b Ramsay	0	6	4	-	-
N.M.Thessman c Rolls b Coetzee	31	107	81	-	2
S.J.McGlashan c Rolls b Watson	19	60	60	-	2
C.J.Connor c Cronin-Knight b Ramsay	13	29	30	-	1
A.C.Stockwell not out	28	71	53	-	-
Z.A.McWilliams c Drumm b Scripps	16	26	24	-	1
R.H.Priest† c Drumm b Watson	2	16	14	-	-
K.M.Cocksedge c Komp b Watson	0	8	5	-	-
A.K.Burrows c Bullen b Scripps	3	3	3	-	-
R.H.Candy b Scripps	0	2	4	-	-
Extras (lb 1, w 13)	14				
TOTAL (46.5 overs)	**126**	169			

Bowling	*O*	*M*	*R*	*W*
CENTRAL DISTRICTS				
Burrows	7	3	10	3
Candy	7	1	22	0
Pulford	8	0	33	0
McWilliams	8	0	32	1
Mason	10	1	35	0
Connor	10	0	53	0
AUCKLAND				
Scripps	8.5	2	16	4
Ramsay	10	3	14	2
Coetzee	10	0	38	1
Watson	8	1	31	3
Bullen	10	2	26	0

Fall of Wickets	***A***	***CD***
1st	6	0
2nd	9	0
3rd	95	43
4th	125	67
5th	-	71
6th	-	100
7th	-	115
8th	-	122
9th	-	126
10th	-	126

WELLINGTON v OTAGO — State League

at Linden Park, Wellington on 5 January, 2005
Toss : Wellington. Umpires : D.M. Quested & I.W. Shine
***No result..** Points: Wellington 2, Otago 2*

OTAGO

	Runs	Mins	Balls	6s	4s
E.J.Scurr not out	15	75	72	-	-
P.B.Flannery not out	21	75	51	-	-
K.J.Martin†					
R.J.Pullar					
S.J.Tsukigawa*					
S.W.Bates					
C.E.Taylor					
M.J.Kane					
C.B.Winsloe					
T.J.Morrison					
K.M.Spence					
J.A.Young					
Extras (w 12, nb 1)	13				
TOTAL (20.2 overs) (0 wkts)	**49**	75			

WELLINGTON

	Runs	Mins	Balls	6s	4s
L.R.V.S.Harford					
M.C.Godliman					
A.M.Corbin					
M.A.M.Lewis *					
M.G.Wakefield					
S.F.M.Devine					
S.J.Hill†					
A.E.Cooper					
M.A.Taylor					
A.M.Little					
M.L.Presland					
A.J.Green					

Bowling **WELLINGTON**	*O*	*M*	*R*	*W*
Little	7	3	7	0
Presland	9	1	28	0
Devine	3.2	0	10	0
Corbin	1	0	4	0

Fall of Wickets	***O***
1st	-
2nd	-
3rd	-
4th	-
5th	-
6th	-
7th	-
8th	-
9th	-
10th	-

WELLINGTON v OTAGO — State League

at Linden Park, Wellington on 6 January, 2005.
***Match abandoned without a ball being bowled.** Points: Wellington 2, Otago 2*

WELLINGTON v CANTERBURY — State League

at Linden Park, Wellington on 8 January, 2005
Match abandoned without a ball being bowled. *Points: Wellington 2, Canterbury 2*

WELLINGTON v CANTERBURY — State League

at Linden Park, Wellington on 9 January, 2005
Toss : Wellington. Umpires : I.W. Shine & D.B. Cowie
Canterbury won by 67 runs. *Points: Canterbury 5, Wellington 0*

CANTERBURY

	Runs	Mins	Balls	6s	4s
P.K.Gerrish st Hill b Corbin	14	49	44	-	-
M.F.Fahey run out	36	93	70	-	3
H.M.Tiffen* c Lewis b Little	33	53	40	-	2
S.C.Taylor c Wakefield b Cooper	14	27	22	-	1
S.K.Burke run out	2	12	8	-	-
B.H.McNeill not out	4	10	6	-	-
H.J.Rae not out	4	4	4	-	-
R.C.Milburn†					
A.E.Satterthwaite					
H.R.Daly					
R.J.Steele					
S.E.Charteris					
Extras (b 6, lb 9, w 4, nb 2)	21				
TOTAL (32 overs) (5 wkts)	**128**	126			

WELLINGTON

	Runs	Mins	Balls	6s	4s
M.C.Godliman st Milburn b Steele	1	18	16	-	-
S.J.Hill† lbw b Daly	0	1	2	-	-
L.R.V.S.Harford c Daly b McNeill	9	36	30	-	-
M.A.M.Lewis* b Charteris	18	67	51	-	-
M.G.Wakefield c Taylor b McNeill	4	7	7	-	1
A.M.Corbin c McNeill b Burke	4	10	13	-	-
A.E.Cooper c Satterthwaite b Charteris	10	24	18	-	-
S.F.M.Devine c Taylor b Charteris	3	12	10	-	-
M.A.Taylor st Milburn b Steele	2	7	10	-	-
A.M.Little not out	4	10	10	-	1
A.J.Green lbw b Burke	2	7	9	-	-
M.L.Presland					
Extras (lb 1, w 2, nb 1)	4				
TOTAL (29.1 overs)	**61**	105			

Bowling	*O*	*M*	*R*	*W*
WELLINGTON				
Little	7	1	18	1
Presland	5	0	15	0
Green	6	1	25	0
Corbin	5	1	17	1
Devine	5	0	19	0
Cooper	4	1	19	1
CANTERBURY				
Daly	7	1	14	1
Steele	7	3	7	2
McNeill	6	0	17	2
Burke	5.1	1	14	2
Charteris	4	1	8	3

Fall of Wickets	*C*	*W*
1st	38	0
2nd	96	5
3rd	105	17
4th	116	22
5th	121	29
6th	-	48
7th	-	50
8th	-	55
9th	-	55
10th	-	61

OTAGO v AUCKLAND — State League

at Queenstown Events Centre on 15 January, 2005
Toss : Otago. Umpires : J.M. Busby & D.G. Paterson
Otago won by 7 wickets. *Points: Otago 4, Auckland 0*

AUCKLAND

	Runs	Mins	Balls	6s	4s
R.J.Kember c Martin b Morrison	18	26	24	-	4
V.J.Lind c Martin b Pullar	0	1	1	-	-
E.C.Drumm st Martin b Morrison	21	44	41	-	2
R.J.Rolls*† c Pullar b Taylor	118	142	125	-	13
I.Cronin-Knight run out	38	76	60	-	4
H.M.Watson not out	37	55	46	-	1
E.B.Komp not out	2	9	6	-	-
N.Scripps					
D.J.Ramsay					
S.Coetzee					
F.J.Mann					
S.M.Bullen					
Extras (lb 1, w 10, nb 3)	14				
TOTAL (50 overs) (5 wkts)	**248**	179			

OTAGO

	Runs	Mins	Balls	6s	4s
E.J.Scurr lbw b Drumm	71	155	119	-	6
P.B.Flannery c Komp b Bullen	110	161	139	-	11
S.W.Bates st Rolls b Watson	11	23	16	-	-
R.J.Pullar not out	18	26	11	-	3
S.J.Tsukigawa* not out	14	8	1	-	2
K.J.Martin†					
C.E.Taylor					
M.J.Kane					
C.B.Winsloe					
K.M.Spence					
T.J.Morrison					
J.A.Young					
Extras (b 2, lb 9, w 17)	28				
TOTAL (49.2 overs) (3 wkts)	**252**	188			

Bowling	O	M	R	W
OTAGO				
Pullar	10	0	46	1
Bates	10	0	57	0
Morrison	10	3	33	2
Tsukigawa	10	0	54	0
Taylor	10	0	57	1
AUCKLAND				
Scripps	10	1	45	0
Ramsay	10	0	39	0
Mann	4	0	15	0
Watson	8.2	0	50	1
Coetzee	6	0	20	0
Drumm	5	0	30	1
Bullen	6	0	42	1

Fall of Wickets	A	O
1st	1	199
2nd	34	207
3rd	47	236
4th	169	-
5th	237	-
6th	-	-
7th	-	-
8th	-	-
9th	-	-
10th	-	-

NORTHERN DISTRICTS v CENTRAL DISTRICTS State League

at Blake Park, Mt Maunganui on 15 January, 2005
Toss : Northern Districts. Umpires : K.C. Manley & D.M. Quested
Central Districts won by 7 wickets. *Points: Central Districts 5, Northern Districts 0*

NORTHERN DISTRICTS

	Runs	Mins	Balls	6s	4s
T.M.Gould c Thessman b Trow	7	43	43	-	1
J.M.Fraser c & b Connor	28	54	47	-	5
S.M.P.Sim c McGlashan b Connor	6	41	34	-	1
M.P.Murphy c Pulford b Connor	0	13	11	-	-
N.J.Browne* c Perry b Mason	53	79	68	-	3
V.J.Brown b Connor	2	16	15	-	-
L.E.Milliken not out	36	77	55	-	3
M.J.Hannay b Burrows	9	23	21	-	-
J.C.Ullyett† run out	6	5	6	-	1
K.M.Goodson					
K.M.Thompson					
A.J.Lenssen					
Extras (b 4, lb 5, w 7)	16				
TOTAL (50 overs) (8 wkts)	**163**	178			

CENTRAL DISTRICTS

	Runs	Mins	Balls	6s	4s
K.L.Pulford c & b Hannay	24	71	52	-	3
A.L.Mason* c Hannay b Milliken	2	11	5	-	-
N.M.Thessman not out	62	142	103	-	4
S.J.McGlashan c Brown b Milliken	35	71	66	-	6
C.J.Connor not out	10	10	12	-	1
A.C.Stockwell					
Z.A.McWilliams					
R.H.Priest †					
E.C.Perry					
D.M.Trow					
A.K.Burrows					
R.H.Candy					
Extras (b 1, lb 9, w 24)	34				
TOTAL (39.4 overs) (3 wkts)	**167**	154			

Bowling	O	M	R	W
CENTRAL DISTRICTS				
Candy	6	0	18	0
Trow	10	7	7	1
Burrows	9	0	35	1
Connor	10	4	11	4
Mason	9	0	41	1
McWilliams	6	0	42	0
NORTHERN DISTRICTS				
Milliken	8	0	20	2
Murphy	6	0	32	0
Lenssen	7	1	29	0
Browne	7	1	20	0
Hannay	9.4	3	43	1
Goodson	2	0	13	0

Fall of Wickets	ND	CD
1st	37	10
2nd	43	70
3rd	47	151
4th	56	-
5th	75	-
6th	126	-
7th	152	-
8th	163	-
9th	-	-
10th	-	-

OTAGO v AUCKLAND — State League

at Queenstown Events Centre on 16 January, 2005
Toss : Otago. Umpires : J.M. Busby & D.G. Paterson
***Auckland won by 28 runs.** Points: Auckland 4, Otago 0*

AUCKLAND

	Runs	Mins	Balls	6s	4s
R.J.Kember run out	94	156	140	-	8
V.J.Lind c Pullar b Taylor	48	100	71	-	5
E.C.Drumm c Tsukigawa b Bates	35	25	24	-	5
R.J.Rolls*† run out	39	43	34	-	4
I.Cronin-Knight not out	22	29	20	-	1
H.M.Watson not out	17	15	15	-	1
E.B.Komp					
N.Scripps					
D.J.Ramsay					
S.Coetzee					
F.J.Mann					
S.M.Bullen					
Extras (b 6, lb 8, w 12, nb 4)	30				
TOTAL (50 overs) (4 wkts)	**285**	200			

OTAGO

	Runs	Mins	Balls	6s	4s
E.J.Scurr c Rolls b Scripps	2	8	7	-	
P.B.Flannery run out	26	80	46	-	1
K.J.Martin† lbw b Scripps	0	1	1	-	-
R.J.Pullar c Rolls b Coetzee	61	39	40	1	12
S.J.Tsukigawa* run out	49	60	50	-	5
S.W.Bates run out	2	7	6	-	-
C.E.Taylor not out	54	110	65	-	3
M.J.Kane run out	3	28	24	-	-
C.B.Winsloe run out	25	28	28	-	4
K.M.Spence b Mann	16	28	24	-	1
T.J.Morrison run out	5	4	6	-	-
J.A.Young					
Extras (lb 8, w 6)	14				
TOTAL (48 overs)	**257**	206			

Bowling	O	M	R	W
OTAGO				
Pullar	10	0	57	0
Bates	8	1	50	1
Morrison	10	0	46	0
Tsukigawa	10	1	48	0
Spence	2	0	9	0
Taylor	10	0	61	1
AUCKLAND				
Scripps	10	0	48	2
Ramsay	10	1	67	0
Watson	9	0	52	0
Coetzee	7	2	31	1
Mann	7	0	27	1
Bullen	5	0	24	0

Fall of Wickets	A	O
1st	120	8
2nd	178	8
3rd	225	85
4th	251	124
5th	-	129
6th	-	164
7th	-	183
8th	-	222
9th	-	251
10th	-	257

NORTHERN DISTRICTS v CENTRAL DISTRICTS State League

at Blake Park, Mt Maunganui on 16 January, 2005
Toss : Northern Districts. Umpires : K.C. Manley & D.M. Quested
***Northern Districts won by 27 runs.** Points: Northern Districts 4, Central Districts 0*

NORTHERN DISTRICTS

	Runs	Mins	Balls	6s	4s
T.M.Gould not out	100	177	145	-	9
J.M.Fraser b Connor	40	65	53	-	5
S.M.P.Sim c Stockwell b Connor	0	2	3	-	-
M.P.Murphy not out	60	108	99	-	5
N.J.Browne*					
V.J.Brown					
L.E.Milliken					
M.J.Hannay					
J.C.Ullyett †					
K.M.Goodson					
K.M.Thompson					
A.P.Stowers					
Extras (lb 5, w 23)	28				
TOTAL (50 overs) (2 wkts)	**228**	177			

CENTRAL DISTRICTS

	Runs	Mins	Balls	6s	4s
N.M.Thessman b Milliken	40	104	77	-	4
A.L.Mason* c Brownx b Stowers	27	66	44	1	4
K.L.Pulford b Hannay	2	9	12	-	-
S.J.McGlashan lbw b Milliken	26	60	46	-	2
C.J.Connor lbw b Browne	30	45	37	-	3
A.C.Stockwell c Brown b Hannay	0	8	5	-	-
Z.A.McWilliams b Browne	2	13	8	-	-
R.H.Priest† c Fraser b Milliken	28	42	33	-	3
E.C.Perry b Murphy	16	26	26	-	1
A.K.Burrows b Milliken	1	3	4	-	-
D.M.Trow not out	1	1	1	-	-
R.H.Candy					
Extras (b 6, lb 5, w 17)	28				
TOTAL (49.4 overs)	**201**	193			

Bowling	O	M	R	W
CENTRAL DISTRICTS				
Burrows	9	1	53	0
Trow	10	2	33	0
Pulford	6	0	34	0
Connor	10	1	34	2
Mason	10	1	39	0
Candy	5	0	30	0
NORTHERN DISTRICTS				
Milliken	9.4	3	38	4
Murphy	8	1	22	1
Browne	9	1	39	2
Thompson	5	1	26	0
Hannay	10	1	27	2
Stowers	3	0	12	1
Goodson	5	0	26	0

Fall of Wickets	ND	CD
1st	71	62
2nd	71	68
3rd	-	99
4th	-	140
5th	-	146
6th	-	148
7th	-	157
8th	-	199
9th	-	200
10th	-	201

CANTERBURY v AUCKLAND — State League

at Redwood Park, Christchurch on 17 January, 2005
Toss : Canterbury. Umpires : P.J. Agent & R.D. Anderson
Auckland won by 1 wicket. *Points: Auckland 4, Canterbury 0*

CANTERBURY

	Runs	Mins	Balls	6s	4s
P.K.Gerrish run out	27	69	66	-	3
M.F.Fahey c Scripps b Ramsay	0	4	2	-	-
H.M.Tiffen* c Rolls b Scripps	37	108	87	-	2
S.C.Taylor not out	71	114	89	-	6
H.J.Rae b Scripps	0	2	1	-	-
R.C.Milburn† b Scripps	0	1	3	-	-
B.H.McNeill b Scripps	37	62	51	-	5
S.K.Burke not out	3	2	2	-	-
A.E.Satterthwaite					
S.E.Charteris					
R.J.Steele					
H.R.Daly					
Extras (lb 5, w 18, nb 1)	24				
TOTAL (50 overs) (6 wkts)	**199**	184			

AUCKLAND

	Runs	Mins	Balls	6s	4s
R.J.Kember run out	28	77	49	-	2
V.J.Lind c Milburn b Satterthwaite	31	84	66	-	4
E.C.Drumm lbw b Burke	24	74	60	-	1
R.J.Rolls*† c Burke b Steele	29	38	26	-	4
I.Cronin-Knight b Charteris	18	44	38	-	1
H.M.Watson not out	33	57	31	-	3
E.B.Komp c McNeill b Steele	3	5	7	-	-
N.Scripps c Fahey b Charteris	6	10	9	-	1
D.J.Ramsay c Burke b Daly	0	3	4	-	-
F.J.Mann run out	1	2	2	-	-
S.Coetzee not out	6	17	7	-	-
S.M.Bullen					
Extras (lb 9, w 12)	21				
TOTAL (49.5 overs) (9 wkts)	**200**	210			

Bowling	*O*	*M*	*R*	*W*
AUCKLAND				
Scripps	10	1	36	4
Ramsay	10	1	22	1
Coetzee	4	0	13	0
Watson	9	0	45	0
Bullen	7	2	26	0
Mann	4	0	19	0
Drumm	6	0	33	0
CANTERBURY				
Daly	10	1	30	1
Steele	10	3	37	2
Burke	8.5	0	37	1
McNeill	7	0	36	0
Satterthwaite	5	1	15	1
Charteris	9	1	36	2

Fall of Wickets	***C***	***A***
1st	1	71
2nd	59	72
3rd	108	122
4th	108	142
5th	108	159
6th	195	169
7th	-	180
8th	-	183
9th	-	186
10th-	-	-

CANTERBURY v AUCKLAND — State League

at Redwood Park, Christchurch on 18 January, 2005
Toss : Auckland. Umpires : P.J. Agent & R.D. Anderson
Canterbury won by 5 wickets. *Points: Canterbury 5, Auckland 0*

AUCKLAND

	Runs	Mins	Balls	6s	4s
R.J.Kember st Milburn b Charteris	37	95	74	-	2
V.J.Lind b Satterthwaite	40	91	85	-	3
E.C.Drumm c Tiffen b Burke	40	85	66	-	1
R.J.Rolls*† c Steele b Charteris	8	7	10	-	2
I.Cronin-Knight run out	1	3	3	-	-
H.M.Watson run out	11	43	37	-	-
E.B.Komp run out	2	9	5	-	-
N.Scripps b Burke	1	8	4	-	-
D.J.Ramsay not out	7	15	10	-	-
F.J.Mann not out	6	8	7	-	-
S.Coetzee					
S.M.Bullen					
Extras (b 2, lb 7, w 3, nb 1)	13				
TOTAL (50 overs) (8 wkts)	**166**	186			

CANTERBURY

	Runs	Mins	Balls	6s	4s
P.K.Gerrish c Rolls b Coetzee	35	58	61	-	6
M.F.Fahey not out	85	155	111	-	11
H.M.Tiffen* lbw b Drumm	9	52	34	-	-
S.C.Taylor c Komp b Watson	16	24	23	-	2
B.H.McNeill c Kember b Drumm	4	5	3	-	1
S.K.Burke b Scripps	1	8	4	-	-
A.E.Satterthwaite not out	2	3	4	-	-
R.C.Milburn†					
H.J.Rae					
S.E.Charteris					
R.J.Steele					
H.R.Daly					
Extras (b 1, lb 3, w 11)	15				
TOTAL (40 overs) (5 wkts)	**167**	155			

Bowling	*O*	*M*	*R*	*W*
CANTERBURY				
Burke	9	0	21	2
Steele	9	0	38	0
Daly	8	1	23	0
McNeill	4	0	16	0
Satterthwaite	10	3	29	1
Charteris	10	1	30	2
AUCKLAND				
Scripps	9	1	38	1
Ramsay	10	2	23	0
Coetzee	4	0	11	1
Bullen	3	0	20	0
Watson	6	1	27	1
Mann	3	0	15	0
Drumm	5	0	29	2

Fall of Wickets	***A***	***C***
1st	77	52
2nd	81	101
3rd	91	138
4th	92	148
5th	137	165
6th	146	-
7th	151	-
8th	156	-
9th	-	-
10th	-	-

NORTHERN DISTRICTS v AUCKLAND — State League

at Wintec Oval, Hamilton on 22 January, 2005
Toss : Auckland. Umpires : T.J. Parlane & I.W. Shine
***Auckland won by 47 runs.** Points: Auckland 4, Northern Districts 0*

AUCKLAND

	Runs	Mins	Balls	6s	4s
R.J.Kember c Browne b Hannay	29	55	47	-	4
V.J.Lind b Murphy	5	23	12	-	-
E.C.Drumm run out	90	160	137	-	8
R.J.Rolls*† c Ullyett b Hannay	68	99	83	-	9
I.Cronin-Knight not out	16	33	21	-	-
H.M.Watson not out	2	4	3	-	-
E.B.Komp					
K.A.Fraser					
N.Scripps					
D.J.Ramsay					
S.Coetzee					
S.M.Bullen					
Extras (lb 7, w 16, nb 3)	26				
TOTAL (50 overs) (4 wkts)	**236**	189			

NORTHERN DISTRICTS

	Runs	Mins	Balls	6s	4s
T.M.Gould run out	5	14	17	-	-
J.M.Fraser c Cronin-Knight b Drumm	53	110	64	-	8
V.J.Brown c Rolls b Scripps	7	16	19	-	1
M.P.Murphy c Ramsay b Bullen	18	43	46	-	2
N.J.Browne* c Cronin-Knight b Watson	51	74	67	-	6
S.M.P.Sim c Watson b Fraser	4	11	13	-	1
L.E.Milliken c Watson b Bullen	14	23	19	-	1
M.J.Hannay b Watson	2	11	6	-	-
J.C.Ullyett† b Scripps	10	11	10	-	2
K.B.Moore not out	4	19	14	-	-
K.M.Goodson b Scripps	7	15	15	-	1
A.P.Stowers					
Extras (lb 4, w 9, nb 1)	14				
TOTAL (48.1 overs)	**189**	178			

Bowling	*O*	*M*	*R*	*W*
NORTHERN DISTRICTS				
Milliken	10	1	40	0
Murphy	10	0	57	1
Browne	10	1	38	0
Goodson	10	2	48	0
Hannay	10	1	46	2
AUCKLAND				
Scripps	9.1	2	22	3
Ramsay	8	0	37	0
Coetzee	6	0	38	0
Watson	10	0	37	2
Bullen	7	1	16	2
Drumm	4	1	13	1
Fraser	4	0	22	1

Fall of Wickets	*A*	*ND*
1st	25	15
2nd	58	30
3rd	178	75
4th	229	111
5th	-	125
6th	-	160
7th	-	161
8th	-	173
9th	-	175
10th	-	189

WELLINGTON v CENTRAL DISTRICTS — State League

at Linden Park, Wellington on 22 January, 2005
Toss : Wellington. Umpires : K. Cross & R.S. Kinsey
***Central Districts won by 1 wicket.** Points: Central Districts 4, Wellington 0*

WELLINGTON

	Runs	Mins	Balls	6s	4s
L.R.V.S.Harford c Priest b Burrows	9	15	17	-	2
M.A.M.Lewis* c Cocksedge b Connor	27	88	81	-	3
M.C.Godliman c McGlashan b Connor	43	130	95	-	4
M.G.Wakefield b Burrows	18	45	42	-	2
S.J.Hill† b McWilliams	18	22	23	2	-
A.M.Corbin b Mason	7	18	10	-	-
S.F.M.Devine b McWilliams	0	1	2	-	-
M.L.Presland run out	13	19	20	-	-
M.A.Taylor b McWilliams	2	8	5	-	-
A.M.Little b Connor	3	2	4	-	-
M.L.Tuapawa not out	0	1	0	-	-
A.J.Green					
Extras (b 3, lb 6, w 14, nb 2)	25				
TOTAL (50 overs)	**165**	179			

CENTRAL DISTRICTS

	Runs	Mins	Balls	6s	4s
S.L.Duffill b Presland	3	6	6	-	-
A.L.Mason* lbw b Corbin	41	94	70	-	5
N.M.Thessman b Corbin	28	98	72	-	2
S.J.McGlashan lbw b Corbin	0	1	1	-	-
C.J.Connor c Wakefield b Green	34	87	66	-	4
R.H.Priest† c Hill b Little	14	51	39	-	1
Z.A.McWilliams not out	21	53	33	1	-
E.C.Perry b Green	4	9	7	-	-
A.K.Burrows run out	2	8	2	-	-
D.M.Trow run out	2	5	5	-	-
K.M.Cocksedge not out	0	1	0	-	-
R.H.Candy					
Extras (b 1, lb 2, w 14, nb 1)	18				
TOTAL (50 overs) (9 wkts)	**167**	211			

Bowling	*O*	*M*	*R*	*W*
CENTRAL DISTRICTS				
Burrows	10	1	24	2
Trow	10	1	19	0
Candy	5	2	10	0
Mason	10	1	42	1
Connor	10	1	44	3
McWilliams	5	0	17	3
WELLINGTON				
Little	10	2	27	1
Presland	6	1	22	1
Devine	9	0	38	0
Corbin	10	3	22	3
Green	10	1	37	2
Tuapawa	2	0	9	0
Harford	3	0	9	0

Fall of Wickets	*W*	*CD*
1st	15	3
2nd	71	81
3rd	112	81
4th	126	84
5th	144	124
6th	144	142
7th	150	149
8th	159	156
9th	162	161
10th	165	-

CANTERBURY v OTAGO — State League

at Redwood Park, Christchurch on 22 January, 2005
Toss : Canterbury. Umpires : J.M. Busby & G.C. Holdem
***Canterbury won by 5 wickets.** Points: Canterbury 4, Otago 0*

OTAGO

	Runs	Mins	Balls	6s	4s
E.J.Scurr c Rae b Burke	5	33	31	-	-
P.B.Flannery c Burke b Steele	13	12	10	-	3
C.B.Winsloe c McNeill b Charteris	48	131	122	-	4
R.J.Pullar run out	14	32	19	-	3
S.J.Tsukigawa* c Rae b Satterthwaite	12	25	17	-	-
K.J.Martin† c Taylor b Steele	28	56	39	-	2
C.E.Taylor c Taylor b Steele	5	17	14	-	-
S.W.Bates not out	43	35	36	-	5
M.J.Kane c Milburn b Burke	1	2	3	-	-
K.M.Spence run out	3	11	8	-	-
T.J.Morrison not out	7	9	5	-	1
J.A.Young					
Extras (b 1, lb 4, w 7, nb 4)	16				
TOTAL (50 overs) (9 wkts)	**195**	185			

CANTERBURY

	Runs	Mins	Balls	6s	4s
P.K.Gerrish run out	42	91	71	-	6
M.F.Fahey b Morrison	51	107	101	-	6
H.M.Tiffen* not out	43	89	52	-	4
S.C.Taylor b Spence	0	4	8	-	-
H.J.Rae b Morrison	6	24	27	-	-
B.H.McNeill c Taylor b Tsukigawa	30	39	29	-	3
S.K.Burke not out	1	3	2	-	-
R.C.Milburn†					
A.E.Satterthwaite					
S.E.Charteris					
R.J.Steele					
A.J.Wilkins					
Extras (b 3, lb 1, w 18, nb 1)	23				
TOTAL (48.2 overs) (5 wkts)	**196**	181			

Bowling	*O*	*M*	*R*	*W*
CANTERBURY				
Burke	10	2	37	2
Steele	10	2	19	3
Satterthwaite	10	1	52	1
McNeill	10	0	55	0
Charteris	10	0	27	1
OTAGO				
Morrison	10	1	32	2
Pullar	9.2	1	33	0
Tsukigawa	9	2	36	1
Bates	2	0	25	0
Taylor	8	0	41	0
Spence	10	0	25	1

	O	*C*
1st	14	96
2nd	19	110
3rd	59	111
4th	81	134
5th	134	194
6th	136	-
7th	146	-
8th	146	-
9th	173	-
10th	-	-

NORTHERN DISTRICTS v AUCKLAND — State League

at Wintec Oval, Hamilton on 23 January, 2005
Toss : Auckland. Umpires : T.J. Parlane & I.W. Shine
***Auckland won by 5 wickets.** Points: Auckland 4, Northern Districts 0*

NORTHERN DISTRICTS

	Runs	Mins	Balls	6s	4s
T.M.Gould lbw b Ramsay	12	32	28	-	1
J.M.Fraser st Rolls b Coetzee	15	36	22	-	2
V.J.Brown b Bullen	15	56	45	-	2
M.P.Murphy st Rolls b Bullen	24	62	50	-	3
N.J.Browne* c Scripps b Watson	41	59	46	-	6
S.M.P.Sim run out	5	28	19	-	-
L.E.Milliken b Drumm	18	41	38	-	1
M.J.Hannay b Scripps	9	25	21	-	1
J.C.Ullyett† b Scripps	4	11	6	-	-
K.B.Moore b Scripps	0	1	4	-	-
K.M.Goodson not out	2	4	3	-	-
A.P.Stowers					
Extras (lb 2, w 14, nb 3)	19				
TOTAL (48.1 overs)	**164**	182			

AUCKLAND

	Runs	Mins	Balls	6s	4s
R.J.Kember c Goodson b Browne	36	49	43	-	6
E.B.Komp c Murphy b Goodson	7	70	41	-	-
K.A.Fraser b Hannay	5	17	17	-	-
V.J.Lind b Milliken	34	41	40	-	7
R.J.Rolls*† b Hannay	4	12	10	-	-
I.Cronin-Knight not out	33	83	76	-	4
H.M.Watson not out	10	57	45	-	-
E.C.Drumm					
N.Scripps					
D.J.Ramsay					
S.Coetzee					
S.M.Bullen					
Extras (b 1, lb 2, w 33)	36				
TOTAL (45.2 overs) (5 wkts)	**165**	167			

Bowling	*O*	*M*	*R*	*W*
AUCKLAND				
Scripps	9.1	2	21	3
Ramsay	10	1	39	1
Coetzee	4	0	17	1
Watson	9	1	24	1
Bullen	8	1	19	2
Drumm	5	0	26	1
Fraser	3	0	16	0
NORTHERN DISTRICTS				
Milliken	8	0	29	1
Murphy	6.2	0	29	0
Stowers	6	0	29	0
Browne	10	0	29	1
Goodson	5	2	12	1
Hannay	10	2	34	2

Fall of Wickets

	ND	*A*
1st	28	54
2nd	29	63
3rd	71	63
4th	76	80
5th	99	115
6th	136	-
7th	153	-
8th	159	-
9th	159	-
10th	164	-

WELLINGTON v CENTRAL DISTRICTS — State League

at Linden Park, Wellington on 23 January, 2005
Toss : Central Districts. Umpires : K. Cross & R.S. Kinsey
***Wellington won by 4 wickets.** Points: Wellington 4, Central Districts 0*

CENTRAL DISTRICTS

	Runs	Mins	Balls	6s	4s
S.L.Duffill st Hill b Tuapawa	18	6	47	-	1
A.L.Mason* c & b Corbin	33	59	52	-	4
N.M.Thessman run out	3	22	21	-	-
S.J.McGlashan c & b Green	43	89	74	-	2
C.J.Connor run out	18	73	58	-	1
E.C.Perry b Green	3	13	9	-	-
R.H.Priest† run out	6	16	20	-	-
Z.A.McWilliams not out	14	12	18	-	1
A.K.Burrows not out	3	6	5	-	-
D.M.Trow					
K.M.Cocksedge					
R.H.Candy					
Extras (b 6, lb 4, w 22, nb 4)	36				
TOTAL (50 overs) (7 wkts)	**177**	183			

WELLINGTON

	Runs	Mins	Balls	6s	4s
M.A.M.Lewis* not out	75	182	144	1	4
S.J.Hill† c Perry b Trow	15	18	18	-	3
L.R.V.S.Harford b Candy	9	29	32	-	-
M.C.Godliman c Priest b Connor	32	60	40	-	2
M.G.Wakefield c McGlashan b Trow	25	38	38	-	3
S.F.M.Devine lbw b Mason	2	5	6	-	-
A.M.Corbin c Perry b McWilliams	4	20	12	-	-
M.L.Presland not out	5	6	5	-	1
A.M.Little					
M.L.Tuapawa					
A.J.Green					
L.R.Doolan					
Extras (b 1, lb 7, w 2, nb 1)	11				
TOTAL (49 overs) (6 wkts)	**178**	182			

Bowling	O	M	R	W
WELLINGTON				
Little	10	1	28	0
Presland	6	1	32	0
Devine	7	1	27	0
Corbin	10	3	31	1
Tuapawa	6	1	17	1
Green	10	0	27	2
Harford	1	0	5	0
CENTRAL DISTRICTS				
Trow	10	1	41	2
Burrows	8	2	24	0
Mason	8	0	33	1
Candy	8	2	20	1
McWilliams	7	0	23	1
Connor	8	0	29	1

Fall of Wickets	*CD*	*W*
1st	68	21
2nd	68	48
3rd	83	105
4th	146	143
5th	146	151
6th	156	171
7th	161	-
8th	-	-
9th	-	-
10th	-	-

CANTERBURY v OTAGO — State League

at Redwood Park, Christchurch on 23 January, 2005
Toss : Canterbury. Umpires : G.C. Holdem & J.M. Busby
***Canterbury won by 37 runs.** Points: Canterbury 4, Otago 0*

CANTERBURY

	Runs	Mins	Balls	6s	4s
P.K.Gerrish run out	6	22	23	-	-
M.F.Fahey run out	63	150	128	1	3
H.M.Tiffen* c sub b Taylor	37	58	45	-	5
S.C.Taylor c Tsukigawa b Taylor	3	13	8	-	-
H.J.Rae b Spence	21	45	43	-	1
R.C.Milburn† st Martin b Morrison	13	20	17	-	1
A.J.Wilkins c Tsukigawa b Morrison	13	15	13	-	2
B.H.McNeill c Taylor b Spence	15	18	10	-	-
S.K.Burke run out	1	8	4	-	-
A.E.Satterthwaite st Martin b Taylor	12	13	9	-	-
S.E.Charteris not out	4	7	3	-	-
R.J.Steele					
Extras (b 1, lb 3, w 8, nb 3)	15				
TOTAL (50 overs)	**203**	189			

OTAGO

	Runs	Mins	Balls	6s	4s
E.J.Scurr c Taylor b Burke	3	20	15	-	-
P.B.Flannery c Milburn b McNeill	27	74	69	-	3
C.B.Winsloe run out	4	8	8	-	-
R.J.Pullar c Tiffen b Steele	0	3	5	-	-
S.J.Tsukigawa* run out	40	90	68	-	3
K.J.Martin† c Tiffen b Rae	28	45	41	-	2
C.E.Taylor not out	18	54	38	-	1
S.W.Bates st Milburn b Charteris	17	15	16	-	2
M.J.Kane lbw b McNeill	2	9	10	-	-
K.M.Spence c Wilkins b Steele	1	8	7	-	-
T.J.Morrison c Steele b Burke	9	17	13	-	1
J.A.Young					
Extras (b 1, lb 3, w 13)	17				
TOTAL (49.2 overs)	**166**	177			

Bowling	O	M	R	W
OTAGO				
Pullar	10	2	29	0
Tsukigawa	10	2	34	0
Bates	2	0	15	0
Morrison	10	0	52	2
Taylor	9	0	34	3
Spence	9	1	35	2
CANTERBURY				
Burke	9.2	3	14	2
Steele	10	3	28	2
McNeill	9	1	24	2
Satterthwaite	6	0	34	0
Charteris	10	0	40	1
Rae	5	1	22	1

Fall of Wickets	*C*	*O*
1st	13	14
2nd	78	21
3rd	87	22
4th	141	51
5th	145	116
6th	161	116
7th	170	143
8th	178	148
9th	189	150
10th	203	166

CANTERBURY v AUCKLAND — State League Final

at Redwood Park, Christchurch on 29 January, 2005
Toss : Canterbury. Umpires : R.D. Anderson & K. Cross
Canterbury won by 10 wickets

Canterbury won the toss and elected to field. Auckland started disastrously with both openers out cheaply to be 3-2. The experienced Drumm and Rolls then put on 42 for the third wicket before another collapse occurred. Only Watson, with 34 not out off 87 balls including two fours, and Scripps with 19 not out off 26 balls, provided any resistance and at the end of 50 overs Auckland was 128-7.

All of the Canterbury bowlers bowled tightly with the two spinners Charteris and Steele conceding only 26 runs from their combined 18 overs.

Canterbury was not troubled in its run chase with the two left handers Gerrish and Fahey taking Canterbury to a ten wicket victory in the 35th over. Gerrish scored 65 not out off 116 balls, including nine fours, and Fahey 34 not out off 92 balls, including four fours.

AUCKLAND

	Runs	Mins	Balls	6s	4s
R.J.Kember b Daly	1	4	7	-	-
V.J.Lind b Burke	2	17	13	-	-
E.C.Drumm c Rae b McNeill	21	56	53	-	2
R.J.Rolls*† c Tiffen b Steele	21	68	48	-	1
I.Cronin-Knight st Milburn b Charteris	4	49	43	-	-
H.M.Watson not out	34	90	87	-	2
E.B.Komp run out	1	22	14	-	-
K.A.Fraser run out	1	13	9	-	-
N.Scripps not out	19	28	26	-	1
D.J.Ramsay					
S.Coetzee					
S.M.Bullen					
Extras (b 8, w 16)	24				
TOTAL (50 overs) (7 wkts)	**128**	177			

CANTERBURY

	Runs	Mins	Balls	6s	4s
P.K.Gerrish not out	65	124	116	-	9
M.F.Fahey not out	34	124	92	-	4
H.M.Tiffen*					
S.C.Taylor					
H.J.Rae					
R.C.Milburn†					
B.H.McNeill					
A.E.Satterthwaite					
S.K.Burke					
S.E.Charteris					
R.J.Steele					
H.R.Daly					
Extras (lb 1, w 29)	30				
TOTAL (34.4 overs) (0 wkts)	**129**	124			

Bowling	*O*	*M*	*R*	*W*
CANTERBURY				
Burke	8	1	26	1
Daly	10	3	22	1
McNeill	9	0	34	1
Steele	9	3	12	1
Satterthwaite	5	0	12	0
Charteris	9	1	14	1
AUCKLAND				
Scripps	10	1	29	0
Drumm	2	0	8	0
Coetzee	6	0	36	0
Watson	5	1	17	0
Ramsay	5.4	1	15	0
Bullen	4	2	7	0
Fraser	2	0	16	0

Fall of Wickets	***A***	***C***
1st	1	-
2nd	3	-
3rd	45	-
4th	59	-
5th	74	-
6th	83	-
7th	91	-
8th	-	-
9th	-	-
10th	-	-

REGISTER OF PLAYERS

		Born	At	Type	
Bates Suzannah Wilson	O	16. 9.87	Dunedin	RHB	RM
Brown Victoria Jayne	ND	30. 7.82	Hamilton	LHB	ROB
Browne Nicola Jane	ND, NZ	14. 9.83	Matamata	RHB	RM
Bullen Saskia Mary	A	20. 7.83	Auckland	RHB	SLA
Burke Sarah Kate	C, NZ	2. 1.82	Christchurch	RHB	RM
Burrows Abby Kirstyn	CD	29. 1.77	Kawerau	RHB	RM
Candy Rachel Helen	CD	23. 7.86	Palmerston North	RHB	RM
Charteris Selena Eloise	C	5. 6.81	Timaru	RHB	ROB
Cocksedge Kendra Margaret	CD	1. 7.88	New Plymouth	RHB	RM
Coetzee Shanna	A	11. 2.83	Cape Town, S.Africa	RHB	RM
Connor Clare Joanne	CD	1. 9.76	Brighton, England	RHB	SLA
Cooper Amanda Ellen	W	15. 5.83	Wellington	RHB	RM
Corbin Anna Maree	W, NZ	24.10.80	Foxton	RHB	ROB
Cronin-Knight Ingrid	A	6.10.77	Auckland	RHB	RM
Daly Helen Rachel	C	26. 5.76	Hamilton	RHB	LM
Devine Sophie Frances Monique	W	1. 9.89	Wellington	RHB	RM
Doolan Lucy Rose	W	11.12.87	Lower Hutt	LHB	ROB
Drumm Emily Cecilia	A, NZ	15. 9.74	Auckland	RHB	RLB
Duffill Sarah Luba	CD	17. 5.83	Wellington	RHB	RSM
Fahey Maria Frances	C, NZ	5. 3.84	Timaru	LHB	ROB
Flannery Paula Bernadette	O	27. 5.74	Clyde	RHB	ROB
Fraser Janice Mary	ND	3. 2.79	Tokoroa	RHB	RM
Fraser Kim Alice	A	31. 7.86	Invercargill	RHB	RLB
Gerrish Philippa Kathleen	C	4.10.82	Dannevirke	LHB	RLB
Godliman Mandie Claire	W	5. 4.73	Eton, England	RHB	WK
Goodson Kelly Maree	ND	11. 1.86	Rotorua	RHB	RM
Gould Tamara Michelle	ND	30. 6.86	Timaru	RHB	RLB
Green Amanda Jayne	W	19. 3.84	Turangi	RHB	RM
Hannay Maree Jennifer	ND	1. 3.84	Whakatane	RHB	ROB
Harford Losalini Ravucake Vuetibau Stephi	W	25. 3.73	Bridgetown, Barbados	RHB	ROB
Hill Sarah Joanne	W	31. 5.79	Feilding	RHB	WK
Kane Megan Joanna	O	1. 8.82	Tapanui	RHB	ROB
Kember Rosamond Jane	A	28. 1.85	Auckland	RHB	RLB
Komp Elfriede Berta	A	27.10.83	Pretoria, South Africa	RHB	LM
Lenssen Aimee Jane	ND	22. 3.85	Whangarei	RHB	RM
Lewis Maia Ann Mereana	W, NZ	20. 6.70	Christchurch	RHB	RSM
Lind Victoria Jayne	A	15. 5.85	Auckland	RHB	WK
Little Amber Margaret	W	22. 5.84	Lower Hutt	RHB	RM
Mann Fiona Jane	A	14. 9.75	Auckland	RHB	LM
Martin Katey Jane	O	7. 2.85	Dunedin	RHB	WK
Mason Aimee Louise	CD, NZ	11.10.82	New Plymouth	RHB	ROB
McGlashan Sara Jade	CD, NZ	28. 3.82	Napier	RHB	WK
McNeill Beth Hannah	C	10.11.82	Wellington	RHB	RM
McWilliams Zara Ann	CD	29.11.83	Hastings	RHB	RM
Milburn Rowan Claire	C	18. 6.77	Mosgiel	RHB	WK
Milliken Louise Elizabeth	ND, NZ	19. 9.83	Morrinsville	RHB	RFM
Moore Kirstin Blanche	ND	5. 3.80	Hamilton	RHB	ROB
Morrison Tanya Jeanette	O	1. 7.85	Gore	RHB	ROB
Murphy Megan Patricia	ND	22.11.87	Rotorua	RHB	RM
Perry Elizabeth Cecelia	CD	22.11.87	Taumarunui	RHB	RM
Presland Margaret Leona	W	28. 6.78	Suva, Fiji	LHB	RM
Priest Rachel Holly	CD	13. 6.85	New Plymouth	RHB	WK
Pulford Katherine Louise	CD	27. 8.80	Nelson	RHB	RM
Pullar Rachel Jane	O, NZ	3. 6.77	Balclutha	RHB	RFM
Rae Hannah Jane	C	13.10.81	Christchurch	LHB	LM
Ramsay Debbie Jayne	A	20. 3.80	Auckland	RHB	ROB
Rolls Rebecca Jane	A, NZ	22. 8.75	Napier	RHB	WK
Satterthwaite Amy Ella	C	7.10.86	Christchurch	LHB	RM
Scripps Natalee	A, NZ	9.12.78	Auckland	RHB	RM
Scurr Elizabeth Jessica	O	26. 7.83	Dunedin	RHB	ROB
Sim Courtney Jayne	CD	20. 2.87	New Plymouth	RHB	RM
Sim Sarah Monique Patricia	ND	24. 5.88	Whakatane	LHB	RM
Spence Kirsten Mary	O	21. 6.82	Dunedin	RHB	
Steele Rebecca Jayne	C, NZ	2. 1.85	Christchurch	RHB	SLA
Stockwell Andrea Catherine	CD	14.11.83	Palmerston North	LHB	WK
Stowers Aimie Patricia	ND	30. 9.85	Rotorua	RHB	RM

		Born	*At*	*Type*	
Taylor Clare Elizabeth	O	22. 5.65	Huddersfield, England	RHB	RM
Taylor Melissa Ann	W	13. 9.83	Hamilton	RHB	RM
Taylor Samantha Claire	C	25. 9.75	Amersham, England	RHB	WK
Thessman Nicole Maree	CD	12.11.76	Palmerston North	RHB	ROB
Thompson Kylie Marie	ND	17. 7.89	Hamilton	RHB	RM
Tiffen Haidee Maree	C, NZ	4. 9.79	Timaru	RHB	RM
Trow Donna Marie	CD	13. 7.77	Napier	RHB	RM
Tsukigawa Sarah Jane	O	16. 6.82	Balclutha	RHB	RM
Tuapawa Megan Louise	W	10. 9.82	Lower Hutt	RHB	RM
Ullyett Jeanette Christine	ND	2. 8.86	Standerton, S.Africa	RHB	WK
Wakefield Megan Gwenda	W	22. 9.82	Christchurch	RHB	RM
Watson Helen Maree	A, NZ	17. 2.72	Ashburton	RHB	RM
Wilkins Anna Jane	C	21. 5.80	Hamilton	RHB	WK
Winsloe Courtney Brooke	O	13.11.87	Gore	RHB	WK
Young Josie Anne	O	4.12.86	Queenstown	RHB	RM

2004/05 STATE LEAGUE AVERAGES

	M	In	NO	HS	Runs	Ave	100s	50s	Ct	St	O	M	R	W	Ave	R/O	Best
S.W.Bates	8	6	1	43*	108	21.60	-	-	1	-	49.2	6	226	5	45.20	4.58	2-14
V.J.Brown	10	9	0	20	71	7.88	-	-	4	-							
N.J.Browne	10	9	0	53	203	22.55	-	2	2	-	83.3	13	265	13	20.38	3.17	3-16
S.M.Bullen	10	-	-	-	-	-	-	-	1	-	64	11	214	6	35.66	3.34	2-16
S.K.Burke	10	6	2	16	24	6.00	-	-	4	-	78.1	13	219	14	15.64	2.80	3-10
A.K.Burrows	9	5	2	4*	13	4.33	-	-	-	-	71	8	257	10	25.70	3.61	3-10
R.H.Candy	7	1	0	0	0	0.00	-	-	-	-	31	5	100	1	100.00	3.22	1-20
S.E.Charteris	10	1	1	4*	4	-	-	-	4	-	84	10	250	19	13.15	2.97	4-13
K.M.Cocksedge	7	5	2	2	2	0.66	-	-	2	-	2	0	18	0	-	9.00	-
S.Coetzee	10	2	1	6*	6	6.00	-	-	-	-	56	2	233	5	46.60	4.16	1-11
C.J.Connor	9	9	1	34	170	21.25	-	-	3	-	84	12	274	11	24.90	3.26	4-11
A.E.Cooper	5	4	1	15*	33	11.00	-	-	1	-	26.4	4	74	9	8.22	2.77	5-21
A.M.Corbin	7	6	0	24	54	9.00	-	-	2	-	56	13	135	11	12.27	2.41	4-22
I.Cronin-Knight	10	10	4	38	163	27.16	-	-	4	-							
H.R.Daly	8	-	-	-	-	-	-	-	1	-	68	19	162	9	18.00	2.38	2-11
S.F.M.Devine	7	6	0	26	37	6.16	-	-	-	-	44.2	5	152	2	76.00	3.42	1-11
L.R.Doolan	1	-	-	-	-	-	-	-	-	-							
E.C.Drumm	10	9	0	90	362	40.22	-	2	4	-	29	1	149	5	29.80	5.14	2-29
S.L.Duffill	5	5	0	18	36	7.20	-	-	1	-							
M.F.Fahey	10	10	3	85*	400	57.14	-	4	1	-							
P.B.Flannery	8	8	2	110	312	52.00	1	-	-	-							
J.M.Fraser	10	10	0	53	191	19.10	-	1	1	-							
K.A.Fraser	4	2	0	5	6	3.00	-	-	-	-	9	0	54	1	54.00	6.00	1-22
P.K.Gerrish	10	9	2	65*	258	36.85	-	1	-	-							
M.C.Godliman	7	6	0	43	114	19.00	-	-	-	-							
K.M.Goodson	9	7	2	7	16	3.20	-	-	1	-	48	4	197	3	65.66	4.10	1-10
T.M.Gould	10	10	1	100*	193	21.44	1	-	1	-							
A.J.Green	7	2	0	2	2	1.00	-	-	1	-	38	5	124	6	20.66	3.26	3-27
M.J.Hannay	10	9	0	17	64	7.11	-	-	4	-	84.4	10	336	10	33.60	3.96	2-27
L.R.V.S.Harford	7	6	0	35	90	15.00	-	-	1	-	6	0	20	0	-	3.33	-
S.J.Hill	7	6	0	27	76	12.66	-	-	2	4	26	3	78	2	39.00	3.00	2-37
M.J.Kane	8	5	0	3	8	1.60	-	-	-	-	2.1	1	2	1	2.00	0.92	1-2
R.J.Kember	10	10	0	94	381	38.10	-	2	3	-							
E.B.Komp	10	6	1	18	33	6.60	-	-	3	-							
A.J.Lenssen	7	2	0	7	9	4.50	-	-	2	-	32	1	162	3	54.00	5.06	2-20
M.A.M.Lewis	7	6	1	75*	154	30.80	-	1	2	-							
V.J.Lind	10	10	1	48	170	18.88	-	-	-	-							
A.M.Little	7	3	1	4*	9	4.50	-	-	-	-	58	9	136	3	45.33	2.34	1-18
F.J.Mann	6	3	2	6*	10	10.00	-	-	-	-	29.4	2	109	3	36.33	3.67	2-20
K.J.Martin	8	6	0	28	78	13.00	-	-	4	4							
A.L.Mason	9	9	0	41	182	20.22	-	-	1	-	82	6	343	6	57.16	4.18	2-48
S.J.McGlashan	7	7	0	43	139	19.85	-	-	3	-							
B.H.McNeill	10	7	3	37	110	27.50	-	-	4	-	76.3	5	272	13	20.92	3.55	3-17
Z.A.McWilliams	9	8	2	21*	82	13.66	-	-	-	-	51	4	243	10	24.30	4.76	3-17
R.C.Milburn	10	4	0	13	19	4.75	-	-	7	5							
L.E.Milliken	10	9	1	36*	109	13.62	-	-	2	-	80.2	9	258	13	19.84	3.21	4-38
K.B.Moore	8	7	6	9*	21	21.00	-	-	1	-	22.1	2	88	2	44.00	3.97	2-29
T.J.Morrison	8	5	3	9	21	10.50	-	-	-	-	68	17	214	7	30.57	3.15	2-32
M.P.Murphy	10	9	2	60*	144	20.57	-	1	2	-	65.2	6	276	7	39.42	4.22	4-36
E.C.Perry	7	6	1	17*	51	10.20	-	-	4	-							
M.L.Presland	6	4	2	13	37	18.50	-	-	-	-	38	8	118	2	59.00	3.11	1-5
R.H.Priest	9	8	0	28	78	9.75	-	-	9	1							
K.L.Pulford	7	7	1	62*	111	18.50	-	1	1	-	31	1	149	3	49.66	4.81	2-36
R.J.Pullar	8	7	2	61	174	34.80	-	2	2	-	67.2	10	209	8	26.12	3.10	4-6
H.J.Rae	10	6	1	24	59	11.80	-	-	3	-	5	1	22	1	22.00	4.40	1-22
D.J.Ramsay	10	3	1	7*	12	6.00	-	-	1	-	93.4	18	293	5	58.60	3.12	2-14
R.J.Rolls	10	10	1	118	405	45.00	1	2	11	4							
A.E.Satterthwaite	10	4	2	12	19	9.50	-	-	2	-	53	5	194	5	38.80	3.66	1-12
N.Scripps	10	4	1	19*	34	11.33	-	-	2	-	96.1	14	299	22	13.59	3.10	4-16
E.J.Scurr	8	8	1	71	110	15.71	-	1	1	-	1	0	9	0	-	9.00	-
C.J.Sim	1	1	0	0	0	0.00	-	-	-	-	2	1	6	0	-	3.00	-
S.M.P.Sim	10	10	0	18	64	6.40	-	-	-	-							
K.M.Spence	8	4	0	16	22	5.50	-	-	1	-	34	5	95	6	15.83	2.79	2-18
R.J.Steele	10	-	-	-	-	-	-	-	6	-	95	30	230	15	15.33	2.42	3-19
A.C.Stockwell	4	3	1	28*	31	15.50	-	-	1	-							

	M	In	NO	HS	Runs	Ave	100s	50s	Ct	St	O	M	R	W	Ave	R/O	Best
A.P.Stowers	3	-	-	-	-	-	-	-	-	-	9	0	41	1	41.00	4.56	1-12
C.E.Taylor	8	5	4	54*	143	143.00	-	1	2	-	60	4	243	8	30.37	4.05	3-34
M.A.Taylor	5	4	0	13	17	4.25	-	-	-	-	4	1	8	1	8.00	2.00	1-8
S.C.Taylor	10	7	1	80	229	38.16	-	2	7	-							
N.M.Thessman	9	9	1	62*	254	31.75	-	2	2	-							
K.M.Thompson	2	-	-	-	-	-	-	-	-	-	5	1	26	0	-	5.20	-
H.M.Tiffen	10	9	4	47*	257	51.40	-	-	8	-							
D.M.Trow	8	5	2	8	15	5.00	-	-	-	-	78	22	193	5	38.60	2.47	2-41
S.J.Tsukigawa	8	6	1	65	181	36.20	-	1	3	-	50	7	204	3	68.00	4.08	2-5
M.L.Tuapawa	4	3	2	3	3	3.00	-	-	-	-	20	2	74	3	24.66	3.70	1-17
J.C.Ullyett	10	9	0	18	56	6.22	-	-	6	-							
M.G.Wakefield	7	6	0	37	138	23.00	-	-	2	-							
H.M.Watson	10	10	7	37*	191	63.66	-	-	3	-	80.3	7	320	13	24.61	3.97	3-16
A.J.Wilkins	2	1	0	13	13	13.00	-	-	1	-							
C.B.Winsloe	8	5	0	48	92	18.40	-	-	-	-							
J.A.Young	8	-	-	-	-	-	-	-	1	-	1	0	6	0	-	6.00	-

HIGHEST STRIKE RATES *(qualification 100 runs)*

		Runs	Balls	S/R
R.J.Pullar	*O*	174	184	94
B.H.McNeill	*C*	110	124	88
S.W.Bates	*O*	108	124	87
R.J.Rolls	*A*	405	519	78
S.C.Taylor	*C*	229	297	77
C.E.Taylor	*O*	143	190	75
S.J.Tsukigawa	*O*	181	248	72
J.M.Fraser	*ND*	191	299	63
E.C.Drumm	*A*	362	591	61
H.M.Tiffen	*C*	257	434	59

MOST ECONOMICAL BOWLING *(qualification 30 overs)*

		O	M	R	W	Ave	R/O
A.M.Little	*W*	58	9	136	3	45.33	2.34
H.R.Daly	*C*	68	19	162	9	18.00	2.38
A.M.Corbin	*W*	56	13	135	11	12.27	2.41
R.J.Steele	*C*	95	30	230	15	15.33	2.42
D.M.Trow	*CD*	78	22	193	5	38.60	2.47
K.M.Spence	*O*	34	5	95	6	15.83	2.79
S.K.Burke	*C*	78.1	13	219	14	15.64	2.80
S.E.Charteris	*C*	84	10	250	19	13.15	2.97
N.Scripps	*A*	96.1	14	299	22	13.59	3.10
R.J.Pullar	*O*	67.2	10	209	8	26.12	3.10

CAREER RECORDS

	M	*In*	*NO*	*HS*	*Runs*	*Ave*	*100s*	*50s*	*Ct*	*St*	*O*	*M*	*R*	*W*	*Ave*	*R/O*	*Best*
S.W.Bates	20	17	1	59	214	13.37	-	1	7	-	126.1	14	549	14	39.21	4.35	2-14
V.J.Brown	40	37	1	66	462	12.83	-	1	11	-	67	8	282	11	25.63	4.21	4-28
N.J.Browne	50	47	5	93	773	18.40	-	4	16	-	371	38	1466	54	27.14	3.95	3-16
S.M.Bullen	16	-	-	-	-	-	-	-	3	-	95	14	324	11	29.45	3.41	3-10
S.K.Burke	51	32	9	27	176	7.65	-	-	15	-	392.3	60	1320	61	21.63	3.36	3-10
A.K.Burrows	35	17	7	8*	35	3.50	-	-	7	-	252	28	888	34	26.11	3.52	3-10
R.H.Candy	14	1	0	0	0	0.00	-	-	1	-	48	7	170	5	34.00	3.54	3-33
S.E.Charteris	26	5	1	13	22	5.50	-	-	12	-	153	20	494	33	14.96	3.23	4-13
K.M.Cocksedge	7	5	2	2	2	0.66	-	-	2	-	2	0	18	0	-	9.00	-
S.Coetzee	11	2	1	6*	6	6.00	-	-	-	-	56	2	233	5	46.60	4.16	1-11
C.J.Connor	9	9	1	34	170	21.25	-	-	3	-	84	12	274	11	24.90	3.26	4-11
A.E.Cooper	46	33	7	30	415	15.96	-	-	10	-	230.5	34	808	44	18.36	3.50	5-21
A.M.Corbin	56	37	5	46	395	12.34	-	-	16	-	423	91	1221	54	22.61	2.89	4-11
I.Cronin-Knight	41	35	11	84	453	18.87	-	1	13	-							
H.R.Daly	33	10	5	11*	43	8.60	-	-	7	-	277.3	83	655	42	15.59	2.36	5-19
S.F.M.Devine	16	8	2	26	42	7.00	-	-	3	-	104.3	12	368	8	46.00	3.52	2-24
L.R.Doolan	1	-	-	-	-	-	-	-	-	-							
E.C.Drumm	70	68	15	118	2515	47.45	3	15	16	-	148.1	14	603	28	21.53	4.06	3-1
S.L.Duffill	21	21	2	62	288	15.15	-	1	3	-							
M.F.Fahey	50	45	6	85*	900	23.07	-	6	14	-	112.2	11	428	18	23.77	3.81	4-21
P.B.Flannery	57	56	7	110	1765	36.02	2	7	12	-	56	9	187	11	17.00	3.34	3-30
J.M.Fraser	56	55	0	53	890	16.18	-	1	18	-	69.2	8	295	6	49.16	4.25	1-12
K.A.Fraser	5	2	0	5	6	3.00	-	-	-	-	9	0	54	1	54.00	6.00	1-22
P.K.Gerrish	26	24	4	99*	509	25.45	-	3	4	-	8.3	0	33	3	11.00	3.88	2-8
M.C.Godliman	24	23	0	66	563	24.47	-	3	-	-	63	6	213	6	35.50	3.38	2-25
K.M.Goodson	22	20	3	29*	129	7.58	-	-	1	-	48	4	197	3	65.66	4.10	1-10
T.M.Gould	17	16	3	100*	245	18.84	1	-	1	-							
A.J.Green	45	19	6	15	81	6.23	-	-	2	-	278	53	867	38	22.81	3.12	4-24
M.J.Hannay	37	36	1	36	311	8.88	-	-	8	-	206.4	15	871	22	39.59	4.21	4-38
L.R.V.S.Harford	42	39	3	83	860	23.88	-	6	13	-	101.3	7	387	9	43.00	3.81	2-12
S.J.Hill	32	22	3	70*	325	17.10	-	1	24	14	26	3	78	2	39.00	3.00	2-37
M.J.Kane	59	51	3	65*	591	12.31	-	1	6	-	198.1	12	812	24	33.83	4.09	4-21
R.J.Kember	36	31	1	94	686	22.86	-	3	12	-							
E.B.Komp	42	26	6	25	194	9.70	-	-	5	-	103.3	10	393	16	24.56	3.79	2-13
A.J.Lenssen	19	14	3	29*	102	9.27	-	-	5	-	96	7	432	17	25.41	4.50	3-21
M.A.M.Lewis	52	48	10	100*	1578	41.52	1	10	24	-	9	0	45	0	-	5.00	-
V.J.Lind	16	16	1	56	316	21.06	-	1	1	-	7	0	24	0	-	3.43	-
A.M.Little	25	5	3	4*	10	5.00	-	-	5	-	207	27	644	19	33.89	3.11	5-27
F.J.Mann	6	3	2	6*	10	10.00	-	-	-	-	29.4	2	109	3	36.33	3.67	2-20
K.J.Martin	38	33	3	59*	389	12.96	-	2	15	12							
A.L.Mason	51	45	7	63	932	24.52	-	3	20	-	460.4	63	1540	64	24.06	3.34	5-25
S.J.McGlashan	41	36	3	58	610	18.48	-	2	18	6							
B.H.McNeill	56	43	14	51*	471	16.24	-	1	13	-	428.5	61	1534	76	20.18	3.57	6-31
Z.A.McWilliams	30	21	7	21*	155	11.07	-	-	5	-	165.4	16	756	20	37.80	4.56	3-17
R.C.Milburn	66	57	5	82	783	15.05	-	2	46	25							
L.E.Milliken	45	42	13	36*	333	11.48	-	-	9	-	333.4	22	1311	35	37.45	3.92	4-38
K.B.Moore	28	23	11	19	90	7.50	-	-	7	-	183.3	15	708	25	28.32	3.85	2-16
T.J.Morrison	18	10	5	9	39	7.80	-	-	-	-	147	32	461	13	35.46	3.14	2-17
M.P.Murphy	20	13	4	60*	149	16.55	-	1	4	-	121.3	9	556	12	46.33	4.57	4-36
E.C.Perry	21	14	4	17*	78	7.80	-	-	5	-	51	0	238	2	119.00	4.67	1-14
M.L.Presland	42	29	12	37	192	11.29	-	-	5	-	286.4	35	1059	40	26.47	3.69	4-34
R.H.Priest	19	16	3	28	141	10.84	-	-	20	3							
K.L.Pulford	55	53	8	153*	1401	31.13	2	8	15	-	337.1	28	1301	43	30.25	3.59	3-24
R.J.Pullar	47	44	7	78	961	25.97	-	7	13	-	382.4	57	1201	48	25.02	3.13	4-6
H.J.Rae	58	33	13	39	288	14.40	-	-	16	-	236.3	31	860	38	22.63	3.63	5-24
D.J.Ramsay	44	11	3	33	64	8.00	-	-	11	-	372.4	91	993	37	26.83	2.66	3-22
R.J.Rolls	70	69	6	118	1841	29.22	2	9	67	41							
A.E.Satterthwaite	20	9	6	12*	42	14.00	-	-	2	-	101	9	355	13	27.30	3.51	2-9
N.Scripps	58	26	9	30	164	9.64	-	-	6	-	486.1	68	1500	107	14.01	3.08	6-18
E.J.Scurr	37	35	6	71	393	13.55	-	2	4	-	84.5	10	317	6	52.83	3.73	3-22
C.J.Sim	1	1	0	0	0	0.00	-	-	-	-	2	1	6	0	-	3.00	-
S.M.P.Sim	10	10	0	18	64	6.40	-	-	-	-							
K.M.Spence	52	34	14	24	96	4.80	-	-	4	-	316.4	46	1107	41	27.00	3.49	4-35
R.J.Steele	40	11	4	11	38	5.42	-	-	15	-	331.2	79	879	49	17.93	2.65	4-20
A.C.Stockwell	4	3	1	28*	31	15.50	-	-	1	-							

	M	In	NO	HS	Runs	Ave	100s	50s	Ct	St	O	M	R	W	Ave	R/O	Best
A.P.Stowers	3	-	-	-	-	-	-	-	-	-	9	0	41	1	41.00	4.56	1-12
C.E.Taylor	36	31	7	65*	667	27.79	-	4	10	-	282.4	47	1020	32	31.87	3.60	3-14
M.A.Taylor	5	4	0	13	17	4.25	-	-	-	-	4	1	8	1	8.00	2.00	1-8
S.C.Taylor	27	23	2	80	882	42.00	-	8	13	-							
N.M.Thessman	50	48	8	85*	1117	27.92	-	6	13	-	2	0	12	0	-	6.00	-
K.M.Thompson	2	-	-	-	-	-	-	-	-	-	5	1	26	0	-	5.20	-
H.M.Tiffen	67	61	17	86	1410	32.04	-	5	34	-	251	29	889	55	16.16	3.54	5-51
D.M.Trow	52	29	13	30*	181	11.31	-	-	19	-	443.5	72	1291	59	21.88	2.90	6-20
S.J.Tsukigawa	53	46	7	65	515	13.20	-	1	15	-	205.3	19	843	30	28.10	4.09	3-19
M.L.Tuapawa	22	9	3	5	12	2.00	-	-	2	-	46.4	3	178	6	29.66	3.81	1-14
J.C.Ullyett	15	14	4	18	76	7.60	-	-	9	-							
M.G.Wakefield	35	30	5	74*	512	20.48	-	2	10	-	11	0	43	2	21.50	3.91	2-26
H.M.Watson	70	62	26	101	1355	37.63	1	5	15	-	490.3	77	1543	70	22.04	3.14	4-40
A.J.Wilkins	52	50	2	49	677	14.10	-	-	8	-	29.3	2	186	2	93.00	6.30	1-15
C.B.Winsloe	15	11	2	48	132	14.66	-	-	-	-							
J.A.Young	17	1	0	0	0	0.00	-	-	1	-	35	5	160	2	80.00	4.57	1-20

TEAM RECORDS

Highest Totals

302-5	Canterbury v Otago	Christchurch	1998/99
298-4	Canterbury v Wellington	Christchurch	1999/00
288-5	Auckland v Central Districts	Auckland	2000/01
285-4	Auckland v Otago	Queenstown	2004/05
270-4	Auckland v Northern Districts	Auckland	2001/02

Lowest Totals

43	Central Districts v Auckland	Wanganui	1999/00
46	Northern Districts v Wellington	Wellington	1999/00
51	Northern Districts v Otago	Dunedin	2004/05
59	Otago v Canterbury	Christchurch	2000/01
61	Otago v Auckland	Auckland	2001/02
61	Wellington v Canterbury	Wellington	2004/05

INDIVIDUAL RECORDS

Centuries

153*	K.L. Pulford	Central Districts v Canterbury	Christchurch	1999/00
141	D.A. Hockley	Canterbury v Auckland	Rangiora	1998/99
141	K.L. Pulford	Central Districts v Otago	Palmerston North	2000/01
128	D.A. Hockley	Canterbury v Wellington	Christchurch	1999/00
120	C.M. Edwards	Northern Districts v Wellington	Hamilton	2002/03
119*	C.M. Edwards	Northern Districts v Canterbury	Christchurch	2000/01
118	E.C. Drumm	Auckland v Central Districts	Auckland	2000/01
118	R.J. Rolls	Auckland v Otago	Queenstown	2004/05
117*	N. Payne	Canterbury v Wellington	Christchurch	1999/00
117	D.A. Hockley	Canterbury v Otago	Christchurch	1998/99
114*	E.C. Drumm	Auckland v Central Districts	Wanganui	1999/00
112*	E.C. Drumm	Auckland v Northern Districts	Auckland	2001/02
111*	R.J. Rolls	Auckland v Otago	Auckland	2003/04
110	P.B. Flannery	Otago v Auckland	Queenstown	2004/05
104*	P.B. Flannery	Canterbury v Otago	Christchurch	2000/01
104	M.K. Tyler	Auckland v Otago	Auckland	1999/00
102*	N.A. Pratt	Northern Districts v Otago	Hamilton	1999/00
101	D.A. Hockley	Canterbury v Central Districts	Palmerston North	1998/99
101	H.M. Watson	Auckland v Otago	Dunedin	2000/01
100*	M.A.M. Lewis	Wellington v Auckland	Wellington	2003/04
100*	T.M. Gould	Northern Districts v Central Districts	Mt Maunganui	2004/05

Five Wickets in an Innings

7.1-1-19-7	M.F. Tunupopo	Auckland v Central Districts	Wanganui	1999/00
10-3-18-6	N. Scripps	Auckland v Northern Districts	Auckland	2003/04
9.2-2-19-6	N. Scripps	Auckland v Wellington	Auckland	2002/03
9-1-20-6	D.M. Trow	Central Districts v Northern Districts	Wanganui	2003/04
9.5-1-31-6	B.H. McNeill	Canterbury v Auckland	Auckland	2001/02
5.5-1-12-5	C.A. Campbell	Canterbury v Northern Districts	Hamilton	1999/00
10-2-19-5	H.R. Daly	Canterbury v Northern Districts	Rangiora	2002/03
7-1-20-5	C.A. Campbell	Canterbury v Wellington	Wellington	1998/99
8.3-2-21-5	A.E. Cooper	Wellington v Northern Districts	Hamilton	2004/05
8-1-24-5	H.J. Rae	Canterbury v Wellington	Lower Hutt	2000/01
10-1-25-5	A.L. Mason	Central Districts v Wellington	Wanganui	1999/00
10-0-27-5	A.M. Little	Wellington v Otago	Wellington	2002/03

10-1-31-5	B.H. McNeill	Canterbury v Otago	Timaru	2002/03
10-1-34-5	H.J. Partridge	Northern Districts v Auckland	Auckland	1999/00
8.3-1-37-5	N. Scripps	Auckland v Canterbury	Christchurch	2000/01
10-1-51-5	H.M. Tiffen	Canterbury v Auckland	Christchurch	2000/01

Wicketkeeping

DISMISSALS IN AN INNINGS

	(ct/st)				
5	(2/3)	R.J. Rolls	Auckland v Canterbury	Christchurch	2000/01
5	(4/1)	R.C. Milburn	Canterbury v Auckland	Auckland	2003/04
4	(0/4)	R.J. Rolls	Auckland v Wellington	Auckland	1998/99
4	(1/3)	R.C. Milburn	Otago v Wellington	Dunedin	1999/00
4	(0/4)	J.L. Strachan	Canterbury v Northern Districts	Christchurch	2000/01
4	(4/0)	R.C. Milburn	Canterbury v Auckland	Christchurch	2002/03
4	(3/1)	S.J. McGlashan	Central Districts v Canterbury	Palmerston North	2002/03
4	(2/2)	K.J. Martin	Otago v Central Districts	Palmerston North	2002/03
4	(2/2)	S.J. McGlashan	Central Districts v Otago	Palmerston North	2002/03
4	(3/1)	R.J. Rolls	Auckland v Canterbury	Christchurch	2002/03
4	(3/1)	R.C. Milburn	Canterbury v Wellington	Christchurch	2003/04
4	(3/1)	S.J. Hill	Wellington v Otago	Dunedin	2003/04
4	(4/0)	R.H. Priest	Central Districts v Auckland	Napier	2003/04

Fielding

CATCHES IN AN INNINGS

4	M.M. Graham	Central Districts v Northern Districts	Wanganui	1999/00
4	S.J. Tsukigawa	Otago v Canterbury	Dunedin	2003/04
4	E.C. Drumm	Auckland v Central Distyricts	Auckland	2004/05

RECORD PARTNERSHIPS

AUCKLAND

1st	120	R.J. Kember & V.J. Lind	v Otago	Queenstown	2004/05
2nd	136	M.K. Fruin & E.C. Drumm	v Central Districts	Auckland	2000/01
3rd	134*	R.J. Rolls & R.J. Kember	v Otago	Auckland	2003/04
4th †	157	M.K. Fruin & H.M. Watson	v Otago	Dunedin	2000/01
5th †	115	H.M. Watson & K.D. Brown	v Central Districts	Waikanae	2001/02
6th	68	K.A. Ramel & A. Soma	v Canterbury	Christchurch	2000/01
7th	90	K.A. Ramel & A. Soma	v Wellington	Auckland	1998/99
8th	52	C.M. Nicholson & Z.A.A. Plummer	v Central Districts	Auckland	1998/99
9th	35	E.C. Drumm & S.E.M. Cowlrick	v Canterbury	Christchurch	1998/99
10th	16*	E.C. Drumm & M.F. Tunupopo	v Canterbury	Christchurch	1998/99

CANTERBURY

1st	163	D.A. Hockley & P.B. Flannery	v Central Districts	Christchurch	1999/00
2nd †	227	D.A. Hockley & N. Payne	v Wellington	Christchurch	1999/00
3rd	98	D.A. Hockley & N. Payne	v Otago	Christchurch	1998/99
4th	144	H.M. Tiffen & J.A. Lawler	v Central Districts	P. North	2000/01
5th	73	N. Payne & M.F. Fahey	v Northern Districts	Hamilton	2001/02
6th	87	S.C. Taylor & B.H. McNeill	v Auckland	Christchurch	2004/05
7th	57	S.K. Helmore & M.F. Fahey	v Central Districts	P. North	2000/01
8th	41	L.M. Astle & A.J.M.D. Marsh	v Northern Districts	Hamilton	1999/00
9th	23	S.K. Burke & H.J. Rae	v Central Districts	P. North	2002/03
10th	23	J. Maley & C.J. Moffat	v Auckland	Christchurch	1998/99
	23	R.J. Steele & H.J. Rae	v Central Districts	Christchurch	2001/02

CENTRAL DISTRICTS

1st	179*	P.K. Gerrish & C.L. Forsyth	v Wellington	Wellington	2000/01
2nd	94	S.L. Duffill & K.L. Pulford	v Otago	Dunedin	2003/04
3rd	118	K.L. Pulford & N.M. Thessman	v Wellington	Napier	2001/02
4th	91	K.L. Pulford & E.A. Travers	v Otago	P. North	2000/01
5th	102	S.J. McGlashan & H.J. Lloyd	v Auckland	Napier	2003/04
6th	83	M.M. Graham & S.J. McGlashan	v Otago	Dunedin	1998/99
7th	86	A.L. Mason & E.A. Travers	v Canterbury	P. North	2000/01
8th	42	R.H. Priest & E.C. Perry	v Northern Distrcts	Mt Maunganui	2004/05
9th †	67*	N.M. Thessman & K.M. Sutherland	v Otago	Dunedin	2001/02
10th	36*	D.M. Trow & A.K. Burrows	v Auckland	Auckland	2002/03

NORTHERN DISTRICTS

1st	88	V.J. Brown & N.J. Browne	v Otago	Hamilton	2003/04
2nd	69	N.J. Browne & A.J. Wilkins	v Wellington	Wellington	2003/04
3rd	157*	T.M. Gould & M.P. Murphy	v Central Districts	Mt Maunganui	2004/05
4th	64	J.M. Fraser & M.J. Hannay	v Wellington	Hamilton	2002/03
5th	49	S.A. Sandilands & K.B. Spence	v Auckland	Whangarei	2000/01
6th	62	S.A. Sandilands & J.M. Stafford	v Central Districts	Hamilton	2000/01
7th	66	A.J. Wilkins & K.J. Gibson	v Wellington	Wellington	1999/00
8th	46	M.J. Hannay & J.C. Ullyett	v Canterbury	Christchurch	2004/05
9th	51	K.B. Spence & L.E. Milliken	v Central Districts	Hamilton	2000/01
10th	24	N.H. Carruthers & J.A. Simpson	v Canterbury	Rangiora	2002/03

OTAGO

1st †	199	E.J. Scurr & P.B. Flannery	v Auckland	Queenstown	2004/05
2nd	94	R.J. Pullar & S.K Helmore	v Central Districts	Dunedin	2001/02
	94	R.C. Milburn & P.J. te Beest	v Canterbury	Oamaru	2001/02
3rd	139	R.C. Milburn & C.E. Taylor	v Central Districts	P. North	2000/01
4th	71	R.J. Pullar & N.A. Bannerman	v Northern Districts	Dunedin	2000/01
5th	66	S.K. Helmore & N.A. Bannerman	v Northern Districts	Hamilton	2001/02
	66	S.J. Tsukigawa & K.J. Martin	v Canterbury	Oamaru	2001/02
6th	57	S.J. Tsukigawa & C.E. Taylor	v Central Districts	P. North	2004/05
7th †	106	E.J. Scurr & S.W. Bates	v Auckland	Auckland	2003/04
8th †	62	R.J. Pullar & K.A. Craig	v Canterbury	Christchurch	2000/01
9th	56	S.K. Helmore & A.L. Kane	v Auckland	Auckland	2003/04
10th	25	K.J. Martin & T.J. Morrison	v Central Districts	Dunedin	2003/04

WELLINGTON

1st	118	L.R.V.S. Harford & M.C. Godliman	v Northern Districts	Wellington	2003/04
2nd	173*	L.R.V.S. Harford & M.A.M. Lewis	v Auckland	Wellington	2003/04
3rd †	159	L.R.V.S. Harford & M.A.M. Lewis	v Canterbury	Christchurch	1999/00
4th	98*	M.A.M. Lewis & F.S. King	v Otago	Lower Hutt	2000/01
5th	73	M.A.M. Lewis & A.M. Corbin	v Central Districts	Wellington	2002/03
6th †	144*	M.A.M. Lewis & M.G. Wakefield	v Auckland	Auckland	2002/03
7th	56	M.A.M. Lewis & A.M. Corbin	v Central Districts	Napier	2001/02
8th	36	M.G. Wakefield & A.E. Cooper	v Canterbury	Christchurch	2003/04
9th	38	S.J. Hill & E.T. McDonald	v Canterbury	Christchurch	2003/04
10th †	44	A.M. Corbin & A.J. Green	v Central Districts	Lower Hutt	2000/01

† *record for all teams*

CAREER RECORDS

BATTING	M	In	NO	HS	Runs	Ave	100s	50s
E.C. Drumm	70	68	15	118	2515	47.45	3	15
R.J. Rolls	70	69	6	118	1841	29.22	2	9
P.B. Flannery	57	56	7	110	1765	36.02	2	7
N. Payne	49	47	7	117*	1614	40.35	1	12
M.A.M. Lewis	52	48	10	100*	1578	41.52	1	10
H.M. Tiffen	67	61	17	86	1410	32.04	–	5
K.L. Pulford	55	53	8	153*	1401	31.13	2	8
H.M. Watson	70	62	26	101	1355	37.63	1	5
D.A. Hockley	19	17	1	141	1155	72.18	4	8
N.M. Thessman	50	48	8	85*	1117	27.92	–	6
M.K. Fruin	34	34	2	97	982	30.68	–	6
R.J. Pullar	47	44	7	78	961	25.97	–	7
A.L. Mason	51	45	7	63	932	24.52	–	3
A.M. O'Leary	36	34	5	84	909	31.34	–	5
M.F. Fahey	50	45	6	85*	900	23.07	–	6
J.M. Fraser	56	55	0	53	890	16.18	–	1
S.C. Taylor	27	23	2	80	882	42.00	–	8
L.R.V.S. Harford	42	39	3	83	860	23.88	–	6

BOWLING	M	O	M	R	W	Ave	R/O	Best
N. Scripps	58	486.1	68	1500	107	14.01	3.08	6-18
B.H. McNeill	56	428.5	61	1534	76	20.18	3.57	6-31
H.M. Watson	70	490.3	77	1543	70	22.04	3.14	4-40
A.L. Mason	51	460.4	63	1540	64	24.06	3.34	5-25
S.K. Burke	51	392.3	60	1320	61	21.63	3.36	3-10
D.M. Trow	52	443.5	72	1291	59	21.88	2.90	6-20
H.M. Tiffen	67	251	29	889	55	16.16	3.54	5-51
A.M. Corbin	56	423	91	1221	54	22.61	2.89	4-11
N.J. Browne	50	371	38	1466	54	27.14	3.95	3-16
R.J. Steele	40	331.2	79	879	49	17.93	2.65	4-20
E.T. McDonald	49	416.3	60	1378	48	28.70	3.30	4-30
R.J. Pullar	47	382.4	57	1201	48	25.02	3.13	4-6
P.A. Gruber	41	268.3	33	908	46	19.73	3.38	4-15
M.F. Tunupopo	30	224.2	24	772	44	17.54	3.44	7-19
A.E. Cooper	46	230.5	34	808	44	18.36	3.50	5-21
K.L. Pulford	55	337.1	28	1301	43	30.25	3.59	3-24
H.R. Daly	33	277.3	83	655	42	15.59	2.36	5-19
K.M. Spence	52	316.4	46	1107	41	27.00	3.49	4-35

WICKETKEEPING	ct	st	Total
R.J. Rolls	67	41	108
R.C. Milburn	46	25	71
E.A. Travers	29	19	48
S.J. Hill	24	14	38
K.J. Martin	15	12	27
K.B. Spence	13	10	23
J.L. Strachan	10	11	21

FIELDING	ct
H.M. Tiffen	34
M.A.M. Lewis	24
K.A. Ramel	21
A.L. Mason	20
M.M. Graham	19
D.M. Trow	19
J.M. Fraser	18

NATIONAL DEVELOPMENT TOURNAMENT

The National Development Tournament was played at the Ilam Playing Fields, Christchurch, from 13 to 19 December, 2004. Canterbury and Auckland were named winners as they were leading the tournament when the last round and finals day was rained out.

FIRST ROUND

Wellington 154 defeated **Otago** 153 by 1 run
Auckland 113 lost to **Canterbury** 117-8 by 2 wickets
Northern Districts 156 defeated **Central Districts** 132 by 24 runs

SECOND ROUND

Otago 144-7 lost to **Canterbury** 145-3
Northern Districts 158 defeated **Wellington** 151 by 7 runs
Central Districts 127 lost to **Auckland** 128-3 by 7 wickets

THIRD ROUND

Northern Districts 79 lost to **Auckland** 80-5 by 5 wickets
Central Districts 264-3 defeated **Otago** 102 by 162 runs
Canterbury 145 lost to **Wellington** 147-9 by 1 wicket

FOURTH ROUND

Central Districts 146-8 lost to **Canterbury** 147-7 by 3 wickets
Otago 131-8 lost to **Northern Districts** 132-3 by 7 wickets
Auckland 175-6 defeated **Wellington** 166 by 9 runs

FIFTH ROUND

Central Districts v Wellington
Northern Districts v Canterbury
Otago v Auckland

All matches abandoned without a ball being bowled

FINALS

First v Second
Canterbury v Auckland

Third v Fourth
Northern Districts v Central Districts

Fith v Sixth
Welington v Otago

All matches abandoned without a ball being bowled

Final placings: (based on points at the end of fourth round): Canterbury and Auckland 1, Northern Districts 3, Central Districts 4, Wellington 5, Otago 6.

TEST CAREER RECORDS

	M	In	NO	HS	Runs	Ave	100	50	Ct	St	Wkts	Runs	Ave	5WI	10WM	Best
E.P.Allan	4	6	4	29*	87	43.50	-	-	1	-	5	138	27.60	-	-	3-38
T.L.Anderson	2	3	0	63	108	36.00	-	1	-	-						
E.A.Badham	3	6	1	42	121	24.20	-	-	7	-	10	275	27.50	-	-	4-46
D.Bailey	1	2	0	5	6	3.00	-	-	-	-						
H.R.Bastion	1	-	-	-	-	-	-	-	-	-	0	59	-	-	-	-
K.E.Batty	4	7	1	24	67	11.16	-	-	6	-	2	78	39.00	-	-	1-18
L.I.Bayliss	1	-	-	-	-	-	-	-	-	-	5	70	14.00	1	-	5-28
B.L.Bevege	5	10	1	100*	400	44.44	1	2	3	-	0	70	-	-	-	-
M.C.Bishop	1	2	0	27	27	13.50	-	-	2	-	0	33	-	-	-	-
E.Blackie	1	2	1	13*	21	21.00	-	-	3	1						
P.Blackler	12	21	0	68	371	17.66	-	1	5	-	18	527	29.27	-	-	4-22
B.A.Brentnall	10	16	2	84*	301	21.50	-	1	16	12						
K.D.Brown	3	2	2	50*	52	-	-	1	4	-	7	160	22.85	-	-	3-47
S.H.Brown	6	9	3	19	59	9.83	-	-	1	-	9	432	48.00	-	-	3-64
N.Browne	1	2	2	5*	5	-	-	-	1	-	0	77	-	-	-	-
N.J.Browne	2	2	0	24	23	12.00	-	-	2	-	1	83	83.00	-	-	1-43
D.K.Brownlee	1	2	0	12	17	8.50	-	-	-	-						
H.Buck	1	2	0	16	16	8.00	-	-	-	-						
S.K.Burke	1	1	1	1*	1	-	-	-	-	-	1	57	57.00	-	-	1-57
J.A.Burley	6	9	0	46	110	12.22	-	-	3	-	21	553	26.33	1	-	7-41
V.E.Burt	3	5	0	15	40	8.00	-	-	-	-	0	28	-	-	-	-
V.L.Burtt	4	8	0	39	101	12.62	-	-	5	-						
C.A.Campbell	9	5	1	29	55	13.75	-	-	2	-	18	720	40.00	-	-	4-94
P.F.Carrick	7	11	3	21	63	7.87	-	-	4	-	21	489	23.28	1	-	6-29
J.Clark	11	18	0	79	482	26.77	-	2	7	-	0	5	-	-	-	-
A.L.Clough	1	1	0	0	0	0.00	-	-	-	-	1	70	70.00	-	-	1-70
W.J.Coe	3	5	1	34	83	20.75	-	-	-	-	6	222	37.00	-	-	2-30
M.C.Corby	1	2	0	12	13	6.50	-	-	-	-	0	36	-	-	-	-
D.A.Costello	1	1	0	0	0	0.00	-	-	-	-	2	104	52.00	-	-	2-77
J.M.Coulston	5	8	1	24	76	10.85	-	-	3	-	19	341	17.94	-	-	4-38
V.R.Coutts	6	11	0	41	136	12.36	-	-	1	-						
S.D.Cowles	7	14	0	46	324	23.14	-	-	6	-	0	13	-	-	-	-
J.Currie	3	5	2	3*	7	2.33	-	-	2	-	3	170	56.66	-	-	3-36
E.J.Dickson	2	4	0	65	114	28.50	-	1	-	-						
J.D.Doull	11	22	4	103	779	43.27	1	5	6	-	0	34	-	-	-	-
E.C.Drumm	5	6	3	161*	433	144.33	2	2	-	-	2	175	87.50	-	-	1-24
B.M.Duncan	2	3	3	1*	1	-	-	-	1	-	2	115	57.50	-	-	1-37
M.H.Dunlop	2	2	0	5	5	2.50	-	-	-	-	3	123	41.00	-	-	1-5
J.R.Dunning	6	12	2	71	320	32.00	-	2	5	-	6	170	28.33	-	-	2-16
A.E.Ell	1	2	0	1	2	1.00	-	-	-	-	0	55	-	-	-	-
M.F.Fahey	2	4	1	60*	125	41.66	-	1	1	-						
V.H.M.Farrell	3	4	0	5	12	3.00	-	-	5	3						
P.B.Flannery	1	2	0	46	64	32.00	-	-	-	-	0	5	-	-	-	-
K.E.Flavell	6	7	0	204	473	67.57	1	2	2	-						
J.W.Francis	5	7	1	19	46	7.66	-	-	2	-	14	362	25.85	-	-	4-72
L.M.Fraser	3	-	-	-	-	-	-	-	-	-	4	210	52.50	-	-	2-61
M.K.Fruin	6	8	0	80	188	23.50	-	2	3	1						
J.A.Fryer	3	1	1	7*	7	-	-	-	1	-	5	154	30.80	-	-	4-37
J.Fulford	1	2	0	10	12	6.00	-	-	-	-	2	46	23.00	-	-	2-46
S.M.Gilchrist	5	3	2	7*	12	12.00	-	-	5	-	14	384	27.42	-	-	3-42
G.P.Gooder	1	2	0	11	11	5.50	-	-	-	-	8	73	9.12	1	-	6-42
K.V.Gunn	9	12	0	49	194	16.16	-	-	6	1	11	429	39.00	-	-	3-40
J.E.Harris	10	7	3	9	26	6.50	-	-	1	-	15	691	46.06	-	-	4-119
J.C.Hatcher	4	7	0	23	79	11.28	-	-	-	-						
C.E.Henshilwood	1	2	0	41	48	24.00	-	-	-	-	0	14	-	-	-	-
D.A.Hockley	19	29	4	126*	1301	52.04	4	7	9	-	5	146	29.20	-	-	2-9
M.Hollis	1	2	0	24	26	13.00	-	-	-	-	1	81	81.00	-	-	1-81
S.L.Illingworth	6	7	3	40*	120	30.00	-	-	5	5						
I.C.P.Jagersma	9	13	5	52	271	33.87	-	1	10	2	4	38	9.50	-	-	4-38
Y.Kainuku	1	1	1	23*	23	-	-	-	-	-	1	50	50.00	-	-	1-50
K.M.Keenan	5	3	2	26*	32	32.00	-	-	4	-	15	348	23.20	1	-	6-73
P.D.Kinsella	6	8	0	53	131	16.37	-	1	3	-						
I.M.Lamason	4	6	2	37*	86	21.50	-	-	-	-	2	136	68.00	-	-	2-23
J.G.Lamason	4	8	0	24	87	10.87	-	-	-	-	8	264	33.00	-	-	4-51
B.J.Legg	3	4	1	26	30	10.00	-	-	-	-	4	149	37.25	-	-	2-57
M.A.M.Lewis	9	12	0	65	252	21.00	-	2	6	-						

	M	In	NO	HS	Runs	Ave	100	50	Ct	St	Wkts	Runs	Ave	5WI	10WM	Best
J.Lord	15	22	3	39*	258	13.57	-	-	5	-	55	1049	19.07	4	1	6-119
E.J.Maker	3	4	0	5	10	2.50	-	-	1	-	5	156	31.20	-	-	3-34
C.E.Marett	7	13	4	49	304	33.77	-	-	3	-	9	268	29.77	-	-	2-16
M.Marks	2	4	1	23	30	10.00	-	-	-	-						
K.J.Martin	1	2	0	46	49	24.50	-	-	-	-						
A.L.Mason	2	2	0	14	15	7.50	-	-	2	-	3	105	35.00	-	-	2-68
K.McDonald	1	1	0	1	1	1.00	-	-	-	-						
S.J.McGlashan	2	2	0	14	20	10.00	-	-	-	-						
P.F.McKelvey	15	26	2	155*	699	29.12	2	1	8	-						
A.McKenna	7	14	1	97*	465	35.76	-	3	7	-	0	6	-	-	-	-
R.U.McKenzie	7	13	0	61	295	22.69	-	2	3	-	8	214	26.75	-	-	4-18
S.McLauchlan	4	4	0	4	4	1.00	-	-	1	-	2	83	41.50	-	-	1-7
E.L.Miller	3	6	0	32	92	15.33	-	-	1	-						
H.Miller	1	2	0	11	11	5.50	-	-	-	-	1	77	77.00	-	-	1-77
L.E.Milliken	2	2	0	6	10	5.00	-	-	-	-	2	73	36.50	-	-	2-49
K.S.Molloy	2	1	1	1*	1	-	-	-	2	-	5	91	18.20	-	-	2-24
P.Moore	2	3	1	47*	80	40.00	-	-	3	-	0	31	-	-	-	-
L.J.Murdoch	6	10	0	72	253	25.30	-	1	1	-						
K.J.Musson	1	-	-	-	-	-	-	-	-	-						
C.M.Nicholson	4	5	0	46	140	28.00	-	-	1	-	5	170	34.00	-	-	2-25
A.M.O'Leary	1	1	0	27	27	27.00	-	-	1	-						
J.B.Olson	1	1	0	0	0	0.00	-	-	-	-	0	48	-	-	-	-
C.M.Oyler	5	8	2	67*	212	35.33	-	1	2	-						
E.A.Paton	4	8	1	77*	180	25.71	-	1	4	-	9	160	17.77	-	-	4-35
K.V.Plummer	4	6	0	13	28	4.66	-	-	2	-						
I.J.Powell	7	13	2	63	272	24.72	-	1	9	1						
L.Powell	4	7	0	66	145	20.71	-	1	1	-	0	8	-	-	-	-
L.M.Prichard	1	2	0	38	43	21.50	-	-	1	-						
K.L.Pulford	1	2	0	0	0	0.00	-	-	1	-	2	15	7.50	-	-	2-15
S.J.Rattray	9	17	2	59	412	27.46	-	4	1	-	19	461	24.26	1	-	5-76
D.Robinson	1	1	1	2*	2	-	-	-	-	-	1	16	16.00	-	-	1-16
R.J.Rolls	1	2	1	71	71	71.00	-	1	1	-						
E.F.Rouse	1	2	0	35	36	18.00	-	-	-	-						
M.T.Rouse	2	4	2	15*	18	9.00	-	-	-	-						
J.A.Russell	1	1	0	39	39	39.00	-	-	-	-	1	37	37.00	-	-	1-14
E.M.Ryan	5	8	4	10	38	9.50	-	-	3	11						
J.M.Saulbrey	11	16	4	62	198	16.50	-	1	6	-	35	951	27.17	1	-	5-32
P.Savin	1	2	0	15	18	9.00	-	-	-	-						
N.Scripps	1	1	1	10*	10	-	-	-	-	-	0	57	-	-	-	-
E.A.Signal	6	6	2	55*	82	20.50	-	1	3	-	8	325	40.62	-	-	2-34
R.J.Signal	1	2	1	8*	8	8.00	-	-	-	-	0	21	-	-	-	-
L.J.Simpson	1	2	0	4	6	3.00	-	-	-	-						
E.M.Sinclair	2	4	1	10	26	8.66	-	-	2	-						
C.Sinton	1	2	0	10	14	7.00	-	-	-	-						
J.E.Stead	9	18	2	95	433	27.06	-	3	3	-						
R.J.Steele	2	3	0	12	16	5.33	-	-	3	-	8	141	17.62	1	-	5-79
J.M.Stonell	4	8	0	47	127	15.87	-	-	2	-						
G.Sutherland	3	6	0	22	66	11.00	-	-	1	-	2	86	43.00	-	-	1-29
R.E.Symons	1	1	0	5	5	5.00	-	-	1	-	2	71	35.50	-	-	2-71
M.J.Taylor	1	2	0	3	3	1.50	-	-	-	-	1	62	62.00	-	-	1-62
H.M.Thompson	1	2	1	17*	17	17.00	-	-	1	-	0	18	-	-	-	-
B.I.Thorner	3	6	1	37	76	15.20	-	-	-	-	4	78	19.50	-	-	2-33
H.M.Tiffen	2	4	3	66*	124	124.00	-	1	1	-						
J.A.Turner	6	8	1	11*	30	4.28	-	-	2	-	19	469	24.68	-	-	3-42
N.J.Turner	6	9	2	65*	208	29.71	-	2	1	-						
F.M.Webb	4	8	0	42	110	13.75	-	-	-	-	6	66	11.00	-	-	3-32
E.White	3	5	0	17	33	6.60	-	-	-	-	2	85	42.50	-	-	1-5
U.Wickham	2	4	0	34	40	10.00	-	-	-	-	3	76	25.33	-	-	2-33
N.M.Williams	4	5	1	35*	70	17.50	-	-	1	-	3	158	52.66	-	-	2-19
T.Woodbury	2	3	3	7*	7	-	-	-	-	-	4	100	25.00	-	-	2-29

TEAM RECORDS

Highest Totals

517-8	v England	Scarborough	1996
403-8d	v India	Nelson	1994/95
362-5d	v England	Guildford	1996
359	v Australia	Wellington	1974/75
335	v Australia	Melbourne	1971/72

Lowest Totals

44	v England	Christchurch	1934/35
61	v England	Auckland	1948/49
63	v England	Worcester	1954
78	v Australia	Adelaide	1978/79
87	v Australia	Wellington	1947/48

INDIVIDUAL RECORDS

Centuries

204	K.E. Flavell v England at Scarborough	1996
161*	E.C. Drumm v Australia at Christchurch	1994/95
155*	P.F. McKelvey v England at Wellington	1968/69
126*	D.A. Hockley v Australia at Auckland	1989/90
117*	P.F. McKelvey v South Africa at Cape Town	1971/72
115	D.A. Hockley v England at Worcester	1996
112*	E.C. Drumm v England at Guildford	1996
107*	D.A. Hockley v England at Canterbury	1984
107	D.A. Hockley v India at Nelson	1994/95
103	J.D. Doull v England at Christchurch	1968/69
100*	B.L. Bevege v India at Dunedin	1976/77

Five Wickets in an Innings

7-41	J.A. Burley v England at The Oval	1966
6-29	P.F. Carrick v Australia at Melbourne	1971/72
6-42	G.P. Gooder v England at Auckland	1948/49
6-73	K.M. Keenan v England at Worcester	1996
6-119	J. Lord v Australia at Melbourne	1978/79
5-24	J. Lord v South Africa at Durban	1971/72
5-28	L.I. Bayliss v Australia at Dunedin	1960/61
5-32	J.M. Saulbrey v South Africa at Durban	1971/72
5-40	J. Lord v India at Dunedin	1976/77
5-76	S.J. Rattray v India at Cuttack	1984/85
5-78	J. Lord v Australia at Adelaide	1978/79
5-79	R.J. Steele v India at Vapi	2003/04

Ten Wickets in a Match

10-137	J. Lord v Australia at Melbourne	1978/79

Wicketkeeping

DISMISSALS IN AN INNINGS

	(ct/st)				
6	(2/4)	B.A. Brentnall	v South Africa	Johannesburg	1971/72
5	(3/2)	B.A. Brentnall	v England	Auckland	1968/69
4	(1/3)	V.H.M. Farrell	v England	Worcester	1954
4	(4/0)	V.H.M. Farrell	v England	The Oval	1954
4	(1/3)	E.M. Ryan	v Australia	Melbourne	1978/79

DISMISSALS IN A MATCH

	(ct/st)				
7	(3/4)	B.A. Brentnall	v South Africa	Johannesburg	1971/72
7	(2/5)	E.M. Ryan	v Australia	Melbourne	1978/79
6	(4/2)	B.A. Brentnall	v England	Auckland	1968/69
5	(3/2)	B.A. Brentnall	v South Africa	Durban	1971/72
5	(2/3)	S.L. Illingworth	v England	Guildford	1996

Fielding

CATCHES IN AN INNINGS

3	K.E. Batty	v England	Auckland	1948/49
3	P. Moore	v England	The Oval	1966
3	E.A. Badham	v Australia	Sydney	1978/79
3	M.A. M.Lewis	v England	Wanganui	1991/92
3	D.A. Hockley	v England	Scarborough	1996

CATCHES IN A MATCH

4	S.M. Gilchrist	v India	Ahmedabad	1984/85
4	M.A.M. Lewis	v England	Wanganui	1991/92

RECORD PARTNERSHIPS

1st	150	M.K. Fruin & D.A. Hockley	v England	Guildford	1996
2nd	146	M.K. Fruin & K.E. Flavell	v England	Scarborough	1996
3rd	106	K.E. Flavell & E.C. Drumm	v England	Guildford	1996
4th	94	I.J. Powell & R.U. McKenzie	v Australia	Dunedin	1960/61
5th	94*	E.C. Drumm & D.A. Hockley	v England	Guildford	1996
6th	83	D.A. Hockley & K.V. Gunn	v Australia	Christchurch	1989/90
7th	90	B.A. Brentnall & J.A. Burley	v England	Birmingham	1966
8th	87	C.E. Marett & J.M. Saulbrey	v Australia	Wellington	1974/75
9th	60*	K.E. Flavell & K.D. Brown	v England	Scarborough	1996
10th	55*	C.M. Oyler & J. Lord	v England	The Oval	1966

SUMMARY OF TEST CAREER RECORDS

Most Matches

D.A. Hockley	19	P. Blackler	12	J. Clark	11
P.F. McKelvey	15	J.D. Doull	11	J.E. Harris	10
J. Lord	15	J.M. Saulbrey	11	B.A. Brentnall	10

Most Runs

D.A. Hockley	1301	K.E. Flavell	473	J.E. Stead	433
J.D. Doull	779	A. McKenna	465	S.J. Rattray	412
P.F. McKelvey	699	E.C. Drumm	433	B.L. Bevege	400
J. Clark	482				

Most Wickets

J. Lord	55	J.M. Coulston	19	P. Blackler	18
J.M. Saulbrey	35	J.A. Turner	19	K.M. Keenan	15
J.A. Burley	21	S.J. Rattray	19	J.E. Harris	15
P.F. Carrick	21	C.A. Campbell	18		

Most Wicketkeeping Dismissals

	Ct	*St*	*Total*
B.A. Brentnall	15	12	27
E.M. Ryan	3	11	14
I.C.P. Jagersma	10	2	12
S.L. Illingworth	5	5	10

Most Catches

D.A. Hockley	9
P.F. McKelvey	8
E.A. Badham	7
A. McKenna	7
J. Clark	7

ONE-DAY INTERNATIONAL CAREER RECORDS

	M	In	NO	HS	Runs	Ave	100s	50s	Ct	St	O	M	R	W	Ave	R/O	Best
E.P.Allan	7	6	1	17	42	8.40	-	-	2	-	59	8	162	3	54.00	2.75	1-22
T.L.Anderson	26	25	0	85	440	17.60	-	2	9	-							
L.M.Astle	1	-	-	-	-	-	-	-	-	-							
E.A.Badham	13	10	1	30	86	9.55	-	-	5	-	135.3	33	290	12	24.16	2.14	2-14
H.R.Bastion	3	-	-	-	-	-	-	-	1	-	20	2	57	2	28.50	2.85	1-12
B.L.Bevege	16	16	1	101	488	32.53	1	3	3	-	22.2	7	48	3	16.00	2.16	3-17
B.A.Brentnall	5	3	0	18	40	13.33	-	-	3	3							
K.D.Brown	14	6	3	9*	19	6.33	-	-	4	-	86.4	14	252	10	25.20	2.90	2-8
S.H.Brown	18	9	4	17*	59	11.80	-	-	5	-	170	63	308	19	16.21	1.81	2-3
N.J.Browne	43	28	10	53	405	22.50	-	1	9	-	251.4	25	907	24	37.79	3.60	4-20
S.K.Burke	14	7	3	10	25	6.25	-	-	2	-	101	10	380	7	54.28	3.76	1-14
J.A.Burley	2	1	0	7	7	7.00	-	-	-	-	13	3	28	0	-	2.15	-
V.L.Burtt	9	8	0	46	168	21.00	-	-	4	-	6	0	31	2	15.50	5.17	2-31
D.Caird	4	4	1	45	72	24.00	-	-	-	-							
C.A.Campbell	85	30	15	12	69	4.60	-	-	15	-	753	150	2018	78	25.87	2.68	3-15
P.F.Carrick	3	2	1	6*	7	7.00	-	-	1	-	29	1	106	6	17.66	3.66	3-43
J.Clark	31	31	1	85	875	29.16	-	7	5	-							
A.M.Corbin	22	15	8	18*	110	15.71	-	-	5	-	140.1	16	503	21	23.95	3.58	3-13
D.A.Costello	7	2	1	1	1	1.00	-	-	1	-	56.4	8	139	2	69.50	2.45	2-37
S.D.Cowles	5	5	0	46	93	18.60	-	-	2	-	5	0	24	0	-	4.80	-
J.D.Doull	5	5	0	42	64	12.80	-	-	2	-							
E.C.Drumm	96	89	11	116	2570	32.94	2	16	21	-	257	53	778	37	21.02	3.03	4-31
J.R.Dunning	22	21	4	89	346	20.35	-	1	4	-	157	12	527	13	40.53	3.36	3-29
M.E.Fahey	24	23	2	91	640	30.47	-	6	5	-							
P.B.Flannery	17	17	2	49*	258	17.20	-	-	3	-							
K.E.Flavell	38	33	9	54	719	29.95	-	2	5	-	70	15	156	7	22.28	2.23	2-5
D.L.Ford	3	2	0	35	46	23.00	-	-	1	-	6	0	32	0	-	5.33	-
F.E.Fraser	5	3	2	54*	94	94.00	-	1	1	-							
L.M.Fraser	13	7	1	8	31	5.16	-	-	2	-	117	20	294	12	24.50	2.51	3-21
M.K.Fruin	23	23	4	51	385	20.26	-	1	4	1							
J.A.Fryer	7	1	1	1*	1	-	-	-	-	-	33	9	115	10	11.50	3.48	3-8
S.M.Gilchrist	8	5	1	12	19	4.75	-	-	4	-	77	21	202	7	28.85	2.62	3-20
A.J.Green	14	8	5	17*	23	7.66	-	-	3	-	108.3	17	392	12	32.66	3.61	5-15
P.A.Gruber	2	1	0	0	0	0.00	-	-	-	-	10	3	35	0	-	3.50	-
K.V.Gunn	45	34	9	52	461	18.44	-	1	14	-	458.5	110	1113	53	21.00	2.42	5-22
K.Hadlee	1	1	0	14	14	14.00	-	-	-	-							
L.R.V.S.Harford	3	3	0	9	20	6.66	-	-	-	-	7	0	30	0	-	4.29	-
J.E.Harris	45	24	12	19*	99	8.25	-	-	9	-	414.2	98	1124	61	18.42	2.71	4-8
S.A.Harris	2	1	1	1*	1	-	-	-	-	-	3	0	19	0	-	6.33	-
C.E.Henshilwood	2	1	1	15*	15	-	-	-	-	-							
D.A.Hockley	118	115	18	117	4064	41.89	4	34	41	-	253.4	41	853	20	42.65	3.36	3-49
S.L.Illingworth	37	29	7	51	342	15.54	-	1	27	21							
I.C.P.Jagersma	34	27	4	58*	453	19.69	-	2	24	9	22	5	48	4	12.00	2.18	2-14
Y.Kainuku	2	2	0	4	4	2.00	-	-	-	-	12	2	49	0	-	4.08	-
K.M.Keenan	55	36	9	57*	348	12.88	-	1	9	-	452	72	1253	70	17.90	2.77	4-5
F.S.King	15	10	3	31	81	11.57	-	-	2	-	108.1	14	404	21	19.23	3.73	4-24
P.D.Kinsella	20	20	3	57	443	26.05	-	2	-	-							
K.Le Comber	15	14	4	135*	442	44.20	1	2	2	-							
B.J.Legg	18	13	3	17	79	7.90	-	-	2	-	199.4	62	394	20	19.70	1.97	3-4
M.A.M.Lewis	78	73	12	105	1372	22.49	1	4	30	-	5	0	32	0	-	6.40	-
L.Lindsay	2	1	0	27	27	27.00	-	-	-	-	13	0	42	2	21.00	3.23	2-26
J.Lord	15	13	0	25	101	7.76	-	-	2	-	132.3	25	318	25	12.72	2.40	6-10
M.L.Lynch	6	6	0	29	105	17.50	-	-	-	-							
C.E.Marett	14	12	2	24	149	14.90	-	-	-	-	126.5	24	310	16	19.37	2.44	3-14
K.J.Martin	3	3	1	8*	18	9.00	-	-	1	1							
A.L.Mason	41	35	4	49*	570	18.38	-	-	15	-	324.1	42	1131	38	29.76	3.48	4-26
E.T.McDonald	3	-	-	-	-	-	-	-	1	-	24	4	50	5	10.00	2.08	2-17
K.McDonald	6	6	0	34	80	13.33	-	-	1	-							
S.J.McGlashan	34	30	7	57	460	20.00	-	1	6	-							
P.F.McKelvey	15	14	4	42	214	21.40	-	-	2	-							
A.McKenna	14	13	0	39	214	16.46	-	-	-	-							
S.McLauchlan	29	21	5	34*	137	8.56	-	-	6	-	227.5	47	665	19	35.00	2.91	2-6

	M	In	NO	HS	Runs	Ave	100s	50s	Ct	St	O	M	R	W	Ave	R/O	Best
B.H.McNeill	10	8	4	88*	157	39.25	-	1	3	-	74.1	9	306	10	30.60	4.12	2-42
L.E.Milliken	34	14	7	21	88	12.57	-	-	11	-	244.2	31	885	38	23.28	3.62	5-25
K.S.Molloy	5	2	1	0*	0	0.00	-	-	2	-	36	8	99	4	24.75	2.75	2-16
S.R.M.Morris	8	1	0	5	5	5.00	-	-	-	-	69	12	175	7	25.00	2.54	2-13
L.J.Murdoch	25	22	3	69	417	21.94	-	1	4	-							
K.J.Musson	13	10	2	31	86	10.75	-	-	3	-	87.2	12	253	10	25.30	2.89	3-22
C.M.Nicholson	35	22	10	73*	195	16.25	-	1	13	-	272.4	62	707	38	18.60	2.59	4-18
A.M.O'Leary	19	18	3	91*	497	33.13	-	3	3	-							
J.B.Olson	4	4	1	9*	17	5.66	-	-	-	-	27	9	52	4	13.00	1.93	3-16
G.L.Page	2	1	0	5	5	5.00	-	-	-	-	17.2	3	46	6	7.66	2.65	6-20
N.Payne	65	64	7	93	1178	20.66	-	4	17	-	158	48	407	20	20.35	2.57	3-20
M.H.Peters	16	12	5	24	79	11.28	-	-	3	-	155.5	63	291	19	15.31	1.86	2-3
K.V.Plummer	11	10	1	32	100	11.11	-	-	2	-	10	0	36	0	-	3.60	-
L.M.Powell	5	4	0	70	73	18.25	-	1	1	-							
K.L.Pulford	30	25	0	95	527	21.08	-	2	8	-	96.1	6	379	14	27.07	3.94	4-5
R.J.Pullar	51	32	11	27*	253	12.04	-	-	14	-	430.1	80	1215	74	16.41	2.82	5-7
K.A.Ramel	47	37	7	41	519	17.30	-	-	13	-	204.3	26	729	35	20.82	3.56	3-26
S.J.Rattray	15	15	7	60*	305	38.12	-	1	1	-	123.1	16	399	11	36.27	3.23	2-33
R.J.Rolls	88	75	2	114	1766	24.19	1	10	71	36							
E.F.Rouse	3	3	0	48	90	30.00	-	-	-	-							
J.A.Russell	5	4	1	8*	8	2.66	-	-	-	-	26	3	84	1	84.00	3.23	1-20
E.M.Ryan	15	5	1	6*	17	4.25	-	-	13	8							
J.M.Saulbrey	5	5	3	22*	75	37.50	-	-	-	-	43	12	100	4	25.00	2.33	2-32
N.Scripps	7	3	3	9*	12	-	-	-	-	-	50.2	6	206	6	34.33	4.09	2-17
V.S.Sexton	2	2	0	9	12	6.00	-	-	-	-							
E.A.Signal	19	12	5	28*	79	11.28	-	-	5	-	130.3	23	496	7	70.85	3.80	2-26
R.J.Signal	6	3	1	8	12	6.00	-	-	2	-	27	2	89	2	44.50	3.30	1-10
L.J.Simpson	12	11	1	23*	95	9.50	-	-	1	-							
R.J.Steele	32	12	6	8*	41	6.83	-	-	6	-	293	57	831	34	24.44	2.84	3-10
H.M.Tiffen	73	67	11	91	1690	30.17	-	10	20	-	258	43	842	47	17.91	3.26	4-43
E.A.Travers	3	-	-	-	-	-	-	-	-	-							
D.M.Trow	2	1	1	1*	1	-	-	-	1	-	12	3	18	4	4.50	1.50	3-8
M.F.Tunupopo	3	-	-	-	-	-	-	-	2	-	18	4	57	0	-	3.17	-
J.A.Turner	30	14	2	15	54	4.50	-	-	6	-	265.2	42	695	28	24.82	2.61	5-5
N.J.Turner	28	26	2	114	624	26.00	1	2	4	-							
H.M.Watson	37	28	6	115*	386	17.54	1	-	14	-	165.5	17	566	29	19.51	3.41	3-14
N.M.Williams	19	13	2	21*	80	7.27	-	-	1	-	110.5	19	374	15	24.93	3.37	3-37

TEAM RECORDS

Highest Totals

455-5	v Pakistan	Christchurch	1996/97
335-4	v Netherlands	Amstelveen	2002
297-5	v Netherlands	Sydney	1988/89
278-3	v Ireland	Dublin	2004
275-5	v England	Oamaru	2000/01

Lowest Totals

58	v Australia	Melbourne	1984/85
61	v Australia	Wellington	1998/99
73	v India	Indore	1984/85
80	v India	Auckland	1981/82
94	v Australia	Melbourne	1990/91

INDIVIDUAL RECORDS

Centuries

135*	K. LeComber v Ireland at Dublin	1996
117	D.A. Hockley v England at Chester-le-Street	1996
116	E.C. Drumm v England at Oamaru	2000/01
115*	H.M. Watson v Ireland at Dublin	2004
114	N.J. Turner v Netherlands at Sydney	1988/89
114	R.J. Rolls v Australia at Lincoln	2001/02
108*	E.C. Drumm v South Africa at Lincoln	2000/01
105	M.A.M. Lewis v Pakistan at Christchurch	1996/97
101	B.L. Bevege v International XI at Auckland	1981/82
100*	D.A. Hockley v Sri Lanka at Chandigarh	1997/98
100	D.A. Hockley v West Indies at Chandigarh	1997/98
100	D.A. Hockley v Australia at Melbourne	1999/00

Five Wickets in an Innings

6-10	J. Lord v India at Auckland	1981/82
6-20	G.L. Page v Trinidad & Tobago at St Albans	1973
5-5	J.A. Turner v Netherlands at Lindfield	1993
5-7	R.J. Pullar v South Africa at Hamilton	1998/99
5-10	R.J. Pullar v India at St Saviour	2002
5-15	A.J Green v Ireland at Dublin	2004
5-22	K.V. Gunn v Australia at Wellington	1989/90
5-25	L.E. Milliken v India, Pretoria	2004/05

Hat-tricks

7.1-1-18-3	J.E. Harris	v West Indies	Chiswick	1993
8-2-22-3	E.C. Drumm	v Australia	Adelaide	1995/96

Most Economical Bowling

10-7-3-0	C.A. Campbell	v Netherlands	Christchurch	2000/01
12-9-4-3	B.J. Legg	v Netherlands	Melbourne	1988/89
12-9-5-3	J.E. Harris	v Netherlands	Lindfield	1993
11.2-7-5-5	J.A. Turner	v Netherlands	Lindfield	1993
10-6-3-4	K.M. Keenan	v West Indies	Chandigarh	1997/98

Most Expensive Bowling

9-1-68-1	L.E. Milliken	v Australia	Auckland	2003/04
7-0-63-0	F.S. King	v Australia	Lincoln	2001/02
10-0-59-1	J.E. Harris	v Australia	Auckland	1996/97
10-0-58-1	H.M. Tiffen	v Australia	Lincoln	2001/02
9.4-0-57-0	D.A. Hockley	v Australia	Wellington	1996/97

Wicketkeeping

DISMISSALS IN AN INNINGS

	(ct/st)				
6	(4/2)	S.L. Illingworth	v Australia	Beckenham	1993
4	(2/2)	E.M. Ryan	v International XI	Auckland	1981/82
4	(2/2)	I.C.P. Jagersma	v Netherlands	Sydney	1988/89
4	(3/1)	S.L. Illingworth	v India	Ealing	1993
4	(3/1)	R.J. Rolls	v England	Oamaru	2000/01
4	(2/2)	R.J. Rolls	v England	Lincoln	2000/01
4	(4/0)	R.J. Rolls	v Australia	Lincoln	2001/02
4	(4/0)	R.J. Rolls	v India	Durham	2002
4	(4/0)	R.J. Rolls	v Sri Lanka	Pretoria	2004/05
4	(3/1)	R.J. Rolls	v Ireland	Pretoria	2004/05

Fielding

CATCHES IN AN INNINGS

3	S.H. Brown	v England	Hastings	1984
3	S.M. Gilchrist	v India	Indore	1984/85
3	D.A. Hockley	v Australia	Melbourne	1990/91
3	K.A. Ramel	v Netherlands	Ghaziabad	1997/98
3	D.A. Hockley	v Sri Lanka	Chandigarh	1997/98
3	H.M. Watson	v Netherlands	Christchurch	2000/01
3	H.M. Tiffen	v England	Lincoln	2002/03

RECORD PARTNERSHIPS

1st	180	B.L. Bevege & L.J. Murdoch	v International XI	Auckland	1981/82
2nd	170	R.J. Rolls & E.C. Drumm	v Australia	Lincoln	2001/02
3rd	138	D.A. Hockley & M.A.M. Lewis	v Australia	Wellington	1996/97
4th	116	D.A. Hockley & E.C. Drumm	v Australia	Sydney	1997/98
5th	102	D.A. Hockley & I.C.P. Jagersma	v Australia	Melbourne	1984/85
6th	82*	E.C. Drumm & H.M. Tiffen	v South Africa	Lincoln	2000/01
7th	73*	S.J. Rattray & D. Caird	v England	Bristol	1984
8th	43	N.J. Browne & L.E. Milliken	v England	Chelmsford	2004
9th	58	K.V. Gunn & S. McLauchlan	v Australia	Wellington	1991/92
10th	33	E.C. Drumm & C.A. Campbell	v Australia	Wellington	1996/97

SUMMARY OF ONE-DAY INTERNATIONAL CAREER RECORDS

Most Matches

D.A. Hockley	118	M.A.M. Lewis	78	K.A. Ramel	47
E.C. Drumm	96	H.M. Tiffen	73	K.V. Gunn	45
R.J. Rolls	88	K.M. Keenan	55	J.E. Harris	45
C.A. Campbell	85	R.J. Pullar	51	N.J. Browne	43

Most Runs

D.A. Hockley	4064	J. Clark	875	A.L. Mason	570
E.C. Drumm	2570	K.E. Flavell	719	N. Payne	547
R.J. Rolls	1766	M.F. Fahey	640	K.L. Pulford	527
H.M. Tiffen	1690	N.J. Turner	624	K.A. Ramel	519
M.A.M. Lewis	1372				

Most Wickets

C.A. Campbell	78	K.V. Gunn	53	L.E. Milliken	38
R.J. Pullar	74	H.M. Tiffen	47	E.C. Drumm	37
K.M. Keenan	70	C.M. Nicholson	38	K.A. Ramel	35
J.E. Harris	61	A.L. Mason	38	R.J. Steele	34

Most Wicketkeeping Dismissals

	Ct	*St*	*Total*
R.J. Rolls	71	36	107
S.L. Illingworth	26	21	47
I.C.P. Jagersma	24	9	33
E.M. Ryan	13	8	21

Most Catches

D.A. Hockley	41
M.A.M. Lewis	30
E.C. Drumm	21
H.M. Tiffen	20
C.A. Campbell	15

NEW ZEALAND FIRST-CLASS RECORDS

to 15 April, 2005

FIRST-CLASS MATCH DEFINED

The six countries represented at Imperial Cricket Conference on 19 May 1947, reached agreement in regard to definition of a first-class match. This did not have effect retrospectively.

A match of three or more days' duration between two sides of eleven players officially adjudged first-class shall be regarded as a first-class fixture. Matches in which either team has more than eleven players or which are scheduled for less than three days shall not be regarded as first-class. The governing body in each country shall decide the status of teams.

The records have been compiled on the following basis:

(1) Otago and Canterbury from 1863/64 to date
(2) Wellington and Auckland from 1873/74 to date
(3) Nelson from 1873/74 to 1891/92 inclusive
(4) West Coast (North Island) 1879/80
(5) Taranaki from 1882/83 to 1897/98 inclusive
(6) Hawke's Bay from 1883/84 to 1920/21 inclusive
(7) Southland from 1914/15 to 1920/21 inclusive
(8) Central Districts from 1950/51 to date
(9) Northern Districts from 1956/57 to date

Notes:

- Games played by the Melbourne Cricket Club teams of 1899/1900, 1905/1906 and 1926/27, are not treated as first-class in accordance with a decision of the New Zealand Cricket Council.
- Although set down for only two days each, the return matches played by A. Sims' Australian XI in 1913/14 against Canterbury and Wellington are included in these records; so is the match An Australian XI v Minor Associations, 1920/21, and MCC v Wellington, 1932/33.
- From 1933/34 season onwards, only games for which at least three days have been set down are treated as first-class.
- There have now been 1985 first-class matches in New Zealand.
- Unless otherwise stated, the first-class records relate to first-class matches in New Zealand and by New Zealand touring teams overseas. Apart from the games which have taken place in New Zealand, there are a further 555 played by New Zealand overseas as follows:

in Australia	1898/99 to 2004/05	83
in England	1927 to 2004	294
in South Africa	1953/54 to 2000/01	47
in Pakistan	1955/56 to 2001/02	33
in India	1955/56 to 2003/04	44
in West Indies	1971/72 to 2001/02	26
in Sri Lanka	1983/84 to 2002/03	16
in Zimbabwe	1992/93 to 2000/01	10
in Bangladesh	2004/05	2

plus four games by Young New Zealand in Zimbabwe in 1984/85, three games by New Zealand Young Internationals in Zimbabwe 1988/89, one match by Wellington in Australia 1990/91, one match by Canterbury in South Africa 1993/94, three matches by New Zealand Academy in South Africa 1997/98 and six games by New Zealand A in England 2000.

GROUNDS

	Ground	No of matches	First and most recent match		Highest and lowest team totals				Highest Innings / Best Bowling			
1	South Dunedin	9	O v C	1863/64	C	272	v O	1875/76	75	H.W. Moore	C v O	1877/78
	Recreation Ground		O v C	1877/78	MCC	34	v O	1863/64	8-28	W. Hendley	O v C	1869/70
2	Hagley Park *(old)*	1	C v O	1864/65	C	80	v O	1864/65	22	J. Fulton	O v C	1864/65
	Christchurch		only match		O	61	v C	1864/65	5-17	J.W. Stevens	C v O	1864/65
3	Hagley Park *(new)*	34	C v O	1866/67	SC	554	v Pk A	1998/99	301*	P.G. Fulton	C v A	2002/03
	Christchurch		C v W	2004/05	C	25	v O	1866/67	10-28	A.E. Moss	C v W	1889/90
4	Basin Reserve	372	W v A	1873/74	NZ	671-4	v SL	1990/91	299	M.D. Crowe	NZ v SL	1990/91
	Wellington		NZ v SL	2004/05	W	22	v C	1903/04	9-43	T. Eden	N v W	1875/76
5	Victory Square	7	N v W	1874/75	N	150	v A	1882/83	31	C.A. Knapp	W v N	1874/75
	Nelson		N v W	1887/88	W	19	v N	1885/86	8-26	F.H. Cooke	N v W	1887/88
6	Domain	33	A v C	1877/78	A	579	v O	1909/10	151*	Harold B. Lusk	C v A	1910/11
	Auckland		A v C	1912/13	A	13	v C	1877/78	9-75	R. Neill	A v C	1891/92
7	Caledonian Ground	4	O v C	1879/80	O	297	v W	1904/05	88	H.G. Seideberg	O v W	1904/05
	Dunedin		O v W	1904/05	A	48	v O	1889/90	8-36	A.W. Rees	A v O	1889/90
8	Lancaster Park §	333	C v A	1882/83	C	777	v O	1996/97	385	B. Sutcliffe	O v C	1952/53
	Christchurch		NZ v A	2004/05	O	35	v A	1884/85	9-72	F.H. Cooke	O v C	1884/85
9	Botanical Gardens	1	N v W	1883/84	N	56	v W	1883/84	17	L. Fowler	N v W	1883/84
	Nelson		only match		W	30	v N	1883/84	5-10	G. Fowler	N v W	1883/84
10	Carisbrook	250	O v Tas	1883/84	NSW	752-8d	v O	1923/24	355	B. Sutcliffe	O v A	1949/50
	Dunedin		O v W	2003/04	C	27	v O	1896/97	9-50	A.H. Fisher	O v Q'ld	1896/97
11	Recreation Ground	20½	HB v W	1884/85	MCC	394	v HB	1906/07	188	C.G. Wilson	O v HB	1908/09
	Napier		HB v A	1912/13	HB	42	v C	1897/98	9-47	T.H. Dent	HB v W	1900/01
12	Farndon Park	4½	HB v T	1891/92	Q'ld	492	v HB	1896/97	135	O.W. Cowley	Q'ld v HB	1896/97
	Napier		HB v Q'ld	1896/97	T	39	v HB	1891/92	8-14	S.W Austin	NSW v HB	1893/94
13	King Edward Park	2	T v HB	1891/92	T	135	v Fiji	1894/95	62	Hugh B. Lusk	HB v T	1891/92
	Hawera		T v Fiji	1894/95	T	29	v HB	1891/92	7-?	C.R. Smith	HB v T	1891/92
14	Bayly Park	2	T v HB	1896/97	C	260	v T	1897/98	106	W.J. Crawshaw	T v HB	1896/97
	Hawera		T v C	1897/98	HB	100	v T	1896/97	6-43	D. Reese	C v T	1897/98
15	Victoria Park	3	A v C	1908/09	A	470	v HB	1910/11	88	W. Carlton	C v A	1909/10
	Auckland		A v HB	1910/11	HB	28	v A	1910/11	7-42	A.E. Relf	A v C	1908/09
16	Nelson Cricket Ground	3	HB v W	1913/14	C	337	v HB	1914/15	111	V.S. Ransford	Aust v HB	1913/14
	Hastings		HB v C	1914/15	HB	89	v C	1914/15	8-51	A.A. Mailey	Aust v HB	1913/14
17	Eden Park	232	A v Aust	1913/14	A	693-9d	v C	1939/40	336*	W.R. Hammond	E v NZ	1932/33
	Auckland		NZ v A	2004/05	NZ	26	v E	1954/55	9-36	A.F. Wensley	A v O	1929/30
18	Rugby Park	5	S v O	1914/15	Aust	195	v S	1920/21	71	A. Galland	O v S	1919/20
	Invercargill		S v Aust	1920/21	C	37	v S	1920/21	8-84	D.J. McBeath	S v C	1920/21
19	Nelson Park	4	HB v W	1919/20	Aust	405-8d	v HB	1920/21	158	V.S. Ransford	Aust v HB	1920/21
	Napier		CD v C	1989/90	CD	153	v W	1985/86	5-51	F.S. Middleton	W v HB	1919/20
20	Wellington College	1	W v A	1923/24	W	569	v A	1923/24	163	J.S. Hiddleston	W v A	1923/24
	Ground		only match		A	280	v W	1923/24	6-172	S.G. Smith	A v W	1923/24
21	Sportsground †	49	CD v C	1950/51	W	590-8d	v CD	2004/05	236	J.D. Ryder	W v CD	2004/05
	Palmerston North		CD v W	2004/05	A	71	v CD	2001/02	7-31	H.B. Cave	CD v A	1952/53
22	Pukekura Park	50	CD v A	1950/51	O	543-8d	v CD	1978/79	242	M.D. Crowe	CD v O	1989/90
	New Plymouth		CD v C	2004/05	CD	59	v A	1958/59	9-100	B.W. Yuile	CD v C	1965/66
23	McLean Park	53	CD v O	1951/52	O	571-8	v CD	1995/96	200	R.A. Lawson	O v CD	1995/96
	Napier		NZ v SL	2004/05	CD	63	v W	2003/04	7-31	Abdul Qadir	P v Shell XI	1988/89
24	Trafalgar Park	28	N v W	1891/92	CD	448-3d	v O	1968/69	202*	B.E. Congdon	CD v O	1968/69
	Nelson		CD v ND	1996/97	CD	65	v W	1995/96	7-23	B.A. Bolton	C v CD	1961/62
25	Cook's Gardens	17	CD v WI	1955/56	MCC	376-7d	v CD	1960/61	138	M.G. Burgess	A v CD	1976/77
	Wanganui		CD v YNZ	1979/80	CD	71	v ND	1962/63	8-37	D.B. Clarke	ND v CD	1962/63
26	Seddon Park •	142	ND v A	1956/57	W	608-9d	v ND	1998/99	219	M.D. Bell	W v ND	1998/99
	Hamilton		ND v A	2004/05	ND	32	v A	1996/97	9-48	A.R. Tait	ND v A	1996/97

† now Fitzherbert Park *• now Westpac Park* *§ now Jade Stadium*

	Ground	No of matches	First and most recent match	Highest and lowest team totals	Highest Innings Best Bowling
27	Tauranga Domain Tauranga (Inner)	1	ND v CD 1965/66 only match	CD 232 v ND 1965/66 ND 163 v CD 1965/66	64 G.V. Giles ND v CD 1965/66 5-41 B.W. Yuile CD v ND 1965/66
28	Tauranga Domain Tauranga (Outer)	6	ND v C 1978/79 ND v A 1985/86	ND 370 v O 1982/83 O 90 v ND 1982/83	127 J.G. Gibson ND v C 1978/79 6-75 D.A. Stirling CD v ND 1981/82
29	Cobham Oval Whangarei	11	ND v A 1966/67 ND v C 2000/01	ND 363 v CD 1983/84 ND 127 v A 1966/67	195 J.M. Parker ND v C 1972/73 7-30 R.S. Cunis A v ND 1966/67
30	Queen Elizabeth Park Masterton	12	CD v A 1966/67 CD v W 2002/03	CD 414-7d v A 1998/99 CD 86 v A 1966/67	189 M.S. Sinclair CD v W 1996/97 6-33 A.J. Penn W v CD 2002/03
31	Smallbone Park Rotorua	17	ND v O 1968/69 ND v CD 1995/96	CD 456 v ND 1995/96 A 72 v ND 1991/92	237* R.T. Latham C v ND 1990/91 7-74 G.D. Alabaster O v ND 1968/69
32	Cornwall Park Auckland	3	A v U23 1970/71 A v W 2000/01	A 274-8d v U23 1970/71 A 274-9d v U23 1976/77 A 75 v W 2000/01	102 R.W. Morgan A v U23 1970/71 8-75 H.J. Howarth A v U23 1976/77
33	Horton Park Blenheim	10	CD v ND 1972/73 CD v A 2002/03	CD 538 v C 2000/01 ND 100 v CD 2001/02	212* D.P. Kelly CD v C 2000/01 7-36 A.M. Schwass CD v ND 2001/02
34	Harry Barker Reserve Gisborne	22	ND v O 1974/75 ND v C 2004/05	ND 474 v W 1996/97 O 77 v ND 1999/00	161* V.R. Brown C v ND 1986/87 6-32 S.B. Styris ND v O 1999/00
35	Eden Park No. 2 † Auckland	80	A v CD 1975/76 A v W 2004/05	CD 594-8d v A 1995/96 CD 61 v A 1996/97	241 M.J. Horne O v A 1997/98 7-27 N.A. Mallender O v A 1984/85
36	Queen's Park Invercargill	13	O v CD 1975/76 O v CD 2002/03	CD 348 v O 1996/97 O 68 v C 1977/78	162 B.A. Edgar W v O 1989/90 8-31 D.G. Sewell O v CD 1996/97
37	Bledisloe Park Pukekohe	2	ND v A 1976/77 ND v W 1989/90	W 297-5d v ND 1989/90 ND 152 v W 1989/90	123 R.H. Vance W v ND 1989/90 5-27 G.R. Larsen W v ND 1989/90
38	Hutt Recreation Ground Lower Hutt	14	W v ND 1976/77 W v C 1985/86	W 316 v O 1983/84 W 93 v WI 1979/80	145* J.G. Wright ND v W 1978/79 8-24 E.J. Chatfield W v ND 1979/80
39	Logan Park Dunedin	3	O v U23 1977/78 O v C 1979/80	O 313 v U23 1977/78 O 127 v C 1979/80	106 J.M. Parker ND v O 1978/79 6-44 P.J. Petherick O v U23 1977/78
40	Temuka Oval Temuka	1	YNZ v E 1977/78 only match	E 310 v YNZ 1977/78 YNZ 139 v E 1977/78	104 D.W. Randall E v YNZ 1977/78 6-71 G. Miller E v YNZ 1977/78
41	Molyneux Park Alexandra	28	O v CD 1978/79 O v SL A 2003/04	CD 444-8d v O 2001/02 O 81 v CD 2001/02	179 K.R. Rutherford O v CD 1988/89 8-27 J.T.C. Vaughan A v O 1996/97
42	University Oval Dunedin	9	O v Pak 1978/79 O v C 2004/05	O 396-6d v CD 1982/83 O 46 v Pak 1978/79	221* P.G. Fulton C v O 2004/05 6-20 R.J. Webb O v C 1983/84
43	Maidstone Park Upper Hutt	1	W v CD 1979/80 only match	W 216 v CD 1979/80 CD 50 v W 1979/80	63 B.R. Taylor W v CD 1979/80 6-17 J.V. Coney W v CD 1979/80
44	Dudley Park Rangiora	15	C v W 1984/85 C v W 2002/03	C 543-8d v CD 1996/97 C 62 v A 1998/99	251* C.Z. Harris C v CD 1996/97 7-17 S.J. Maguiness W v C 1984/85
45	Centennial Park Oamaru	9	O v CD 1984/85 O v W 1998/99	O 430 v CD 1984/85 C 94 v O 1994/95	182 K.R. Rutherford O v W 1987/88 6-36 S.W. Duff CD v O 1985/86
46	Levin Domain Levin	3	CD v C 1985/86 CD v W 1987/88	W 435-5d v CD 1987/88 C 68 v CD 1985/86	205* E.B. McSweeney W v CD 1987/88 6-28 P.J. Visser CD v C 1985/86
47	Recreational Ground Morrinsville	2	ND v CD 1986/87 ND v W 1988/89	CD 368-3d v ND 1986/87 ND 198 v CD 1986/87	151 M.D. Crowe CD v ND 1986/87 5-71 K.W. Martin CD v ND 1986/87
48	Albert Park Te Awamutu	1	ND v CD 1987/88 only match	ND 259 v CD 1987/88 CD 135 v ND 1987/88	94 B.A. Young ND v CD 1987/88 4-41 B.J. Barrett ND v CD 1987/88
49	Victoria Park Wanganui	11	CD v ND 1990/91 CD v O 2002/03	W 506-4d v CD 1993/94 CC 103 v SC 1997/98	203* M.S. Sinclair CD v ND 1998/99 6-20 B.C. Strang Z v NZ XI 1995/96
50	Burnside Park Christchurch	1	C v CD 1991/92 only match	C 189-7 v CD 1991/92 C 124 v CD 1991/92	63 T.E. Blain CD v C 1991/92 6-67 D.J. Leonard CD v C 1991/92
51	Petone Recreation Ground, Lower Hutt	2	W v O 1991/92 W v A 1998/99	O 300-8d v W 1991/92 W 142 v O 1991/92	107 E.B. McSweeney W v O 1991/92 5-37 N.A. Mallender O v W 1991/92
52	Sunnyvale Dunedin	1	O v A 1992/93 only match	O 193 v A 1992/93 A 105 v O 1992/93	51 I.S. Billcliff O v A 1992/93 4-21 N.A. Mallender O v A 1992/93
53	Lincoln Green Lincoln	5	NZA v B 1997/98 NZA v SA 1998/99	NZA 459-8d v PkA 1998/99 B 130 v NZA 1997/98	190 M.E. Parlane NZA v B 1997/98 6-69 Fazal-e-Akber Pk A v NZA 1998/99

† now Eden Park Outer Oval

	Ground	No of matches	First and most recent match		Highest and lowest team totals			Highest Innings Best Bowling			
54	Aorangi Park	4	C v Z	1997/98	Z	422-8d v C	1997/98	196	A.D.R. Campbell	Z v C	1997/98
	Timaru		C v O	2003/04	C	100 v Z	1997/98	6-56	M.J. Mason	CD v C	2002/03
55	Owen Delany Park	6	ND v O	1998/99	WI	450 v NZ A	1999/00	216*	S. Chanderpaul	WI v NZ 'A'	1999/00
	Taupo		ND v W	2002/03	A	131 v ND	1999/00	7-33	B.P. Martin	ND v A	1999/00
56	Colin Maiden Park	6	A v ND	1998/99	A	478 v ND	2002/03	175*	G.J. Hopkins	C v A	2002/03
	Auckland		A v CD	2002/03	A	182 v ND	1999/00	5-64	A.R. Adams	A v ND	1999/00
57	Queen Elizabeth II Park	15	C v O	1998/99	NZ A	537 v SL A	2003/04	235	J.A.H. Marshall	ND v C	2001/02
	Christchurch		MA v SL	2004/05	C	114 v O	1998/99	9-13	P.J. Wiseman	C v CD	2004/05
58	BIL Oval †	4	NI v E A	1999/00	NZ A	570 v SL A	2003/04	182	M.S. Sinclair	NI v E 'A'	1999/00
	Lincoln		NZ v SLA	2003/04	Pak	100 v NZ A	2000/01	6-70	A. Sheriyar	E 'A' v NZ'A'	1999/00
59	Queenstown Events	5	O v E	2001/02	NZ A	597-9d v SLA	2003/04	173	M.D. Bell	NZ A v SL A	2003/04
	Centre		O v W	2004/05	SL A	148 v NZ A	2003/04	6-32	J.S. Patel	W v O	2004/05
60	North Harbour Stadium	1	A v O	2002/03	A	289 v O	2002/03	157	T.G. McIntosh	A v O	2002/03
	Auckland		only match		O	185 v A	2002/03	4-34	S.B. O'Connor	O v A	2002/03
61	Rangiora Recreation	1	C v CD	2003/04	C	303 v CD	2003/04	78	C.Z. Harris	C v CD	2003/04
	Ground		only match		CD	178 v C	2003/04	5-35	W.A. Wisneski	C v CD	2003/04

† *now Bert Sutcliffe Oval*

PROVINCIAL CAREER RECORDS

Performances for the following teams are not included in the Provincial Career Records:

Team	*Opponent*	
D. Reese's Canterbury XI	Wellington	1913/14
Canterbury/Otago	MCC	1936/37
Auckland/Wellington	MCC	1936/37
Auckland XI	New Zealand	1957/58
ND/CD	MCC	1958/59
Otago Invitation XI	MCC	1962/63
Canterbury XI	New Zealand Touring Team	1967/68

Most Games for One Province

135 players have now represented their province on 50 or more occasions in first-class cricket.

120	Gray E.J.	W
119	Vance R.H.	W
115	Bradburn G.E.	ND
108	Lees W.K.	O
104	Roberts A.D.G.	ND
103	McEwan P.E.	C
102	McSweeney E.B.	W
101	Latham R.T.	C
99	White D.J.	ND
97	Shrimpton M.J.F.	CD
95	Hart M.N.	ND
93	Young B.A.	ND
90	Blair B.R.	O
90*	Dickeson C.W.	ND
90	Morgan R.W.	A
90	McGregor S.N.	O
90	O'Sullivan D.R.	CD
89	Morrison J.F.M.	W
88	Boock S.L.	O
88	Franklin T.J.	A
88	Priest M.W.	C
87	Edgar B.A.	W
86	Stead D.W.	C
85	Duff S.W.	CD
85	Hart R.G.	ND
84	Chatfield E.J.	W
83	Blain T.E.	CD
82	Dunning B.	ND
82	Hadlee B.G.	C
82	Kuggeleijn C.M.	ND
81	Blair W.L.	O
81	Briasco P.S.	CD
81	Stead G.R.	C
80	Howarth H.J.	A
80	Hoskin R.N.	O
79	Larsen G.R.	W
78	Mallender N.A.	O
78	Robertson G.K.	CD
78	Bailey M.D.	ND
77	McIntyre J.M.	A
76	Germon L.K.	C
76	Douglas M.W.	CD
75	Parker J.M.	ND
75*	McCullum S.J.	O
75	Gaffaney C.B.	O
74	Coney J.V.	W
74	Sulzberger G.P.	CD
73	Sparling J.T.	A
73	Barnes A.C.	A
72	Hastings B.F.	C
72	Troup G.B.	A
72	Wells J.D.	W
69	Alabaster G.D.	O
69	Reid J.F.	A
69*	Boyle D.J.	C
68	Burgess M.G.	A
68	Cameron F.J.	O
68	Sinclair B.W.	W
68	Rutherford K.R.	O
68	Nevin C.J.	W
67	Edwards G.N.	CD
67	Harris R.M.	A
67	Patel D.N.	A
66	Puna N.	ND
66	Lawson R.A.	O
65	Alabaster J.C.	O
65	Brown V.R.	C
65	Hunt A.J.	A
65	Webb P.N.	A
65*	Wright M.J.E.	ND
64	Parlane M.E.	ND
64	Murray B.A.G.	W
64	Harris C.Z.	C
64	Yovich J.A.F.	ND
63	Rutherford I.A.	O
63*	Stott L.W.	A
62	Cunis R.S.	A
62	Hadlee R.J.	C
62*	Smith C.J.P.	CD
62*	Cooper B.G.	ND
61	Yuile B.W.	CD
61	Campbell K.O.	O
61	Greatbatch M.J.	CD
61	Walker B.G.K.	A
60	Milburn B.D.	O
60	Newdick G.A.	W
60	Parsons A.E.W.	A
60	Sutcliffe B.	O
60	Roberts S.J.	C
60	Marshall J.A.H.	ND
59	Blair R.W.	W
59	Crowe J.J.	A
59	Smith I.D.S.	CD
59	Turner G.M.	O
59	Hartland B.R.	C
59	Smith L.D.	O
58	Dowling G.T.	C
58	Howarth G.P.	ND
58	Patrick W.R.	C
58	Reid J.R.	W
58	Ritchie T.D.	W
58	Thomson K.	C
58	Vivian G.E.	A
57	Bull C.L.	C
57	Burns K.J.	O
57	Petrie E.C.	ND
57	Bell M.D.	W
56	Brice A.W.S.	W
56	Motz R.C.	C
55	Bradburn W.P.	ND
55	Congdon B.E.	CD
55	Jordan A.B.	CD
55	Mills G.H.	O
55	Snedden M.C.	A
54	Bilby G.P.	W
54*	Crocker L.M.	ND
54	Cromb I.B.	C

54	McGirr H.M.	W
54	Moir A.M.	O
54	Sutton R.E.	A
54	Ward J.T.	C
54	Dobbs P.W.	O
54	Sinclair M.S.	CD
53	Colquhoun I.A.	CD
53*	Pierce R.A.	CD
53*	Schofield R.M.	CD
53	Toynbee M.H.	CD
53	Watson W.	A
52*	Cederwall B.W.	W
52*	Young R.A.	A
51*	Knight A.R.	O
51	Brown S.W.	A
51	Thomson S.A.	ND
50	Boxshall C.	C
50	Butler L.C.	W

** entire first-class career*

Longest Careers for One Province

Seasons			
34	Read R.J.	Canterbury	1904/05-1937/38
31	Reese T.W.	Canterbury	1887/88-1917/18
29	Luckie M.M.F.	Wellington	1891/92-1919/20
27	Fowke J.N.	Canterbury	1880/81-1906/07
27	Downes A.D.	Otago	1887/88-1913/14
27	Dempster C.S.	Wellington	1921/22-1947/48
26	Reese D.	Canterbury	1895/96-1920/21
26	Knight A.R.	Otago	1918/19-1943/44

Most Consecutive Games for One Province

74	White D.J.	Northern Districts	1985/86-1992/93
73	Hart R.G.	Northern Districts	1992/93-2002/03
70	O'Sullivan D.R.	Central Districts	1974/75-1982/83
64	Germon L.K.	Canterbury	1987/88-1993/94
63	Stead D.W.	Canterbury	1975/76-1983/84
60	Smith C.J.P.	Central Districts	1984/85-1990/91
59	Puna N.	Northern Districts	1957/58-1968/69
57	Edwards G.N.	Central Districts	1975/76-1981/82
56	Young B.A.	Northern Districts	1983/84-1989/90
54*	Cromb I.B.	Canterbury	1929/30-1946/47
54	Roberts A.D.G.	Northern Districts	1970/71-1978/79
54	Burns K.J.	Otago	1984/85-1990/91
53	Alabaster G.D.	Otago	1963/64-1972/73
52	Smith L.D.	Otago	1940/41-1955/56
52	Duff S.W.	Central Districts	1989/90-1994/95
51	Morrison J.F.M.	Wellington	1975/76-1982/83
51	Reid J.F.	Auckland	1976/77-1982/83
51	McEwan P.E.	Canterbury	1984/85-1990/91

** his complete career*

Highest Averages

2000 RUNS/45.00 AVE	*Province*	*M*	*In*	*NO*	*HS*	*Runs*	*Ave*	*100*
Hick G.A.	ND	17	30	4	211*	2055	79.03	10
Crowe M.D.	CD	32	55	7	242	3299	68.72	13
Harris C.Z.	C	64	95	25	251*	4444	63.48	10
Scott V.J.	A	44	74	15	204	3546	60.10	11
Sutcliffe B.	O	60	110	8	385	6028	59.09	17
Jones A.H.	W	39	67	11	181*	2978	53.17	7
Fulton P.G.	C	31	54	6	301*	2437	50.77	5
Wallace W.M.	A	47	73	5	211	3409	50.13	9
Crowe J.J.	A	59	95	9	156	4245	49.36	11
Reid J.R.	W	58	102	8	296	4538	48.27	13
Sinclair M.S.	CD	54	91	9	203*	3894	47.48	9
Turner G.M.	O	59	109	14	186*	4439	46.72	13
Hiddleston J.S.	W	41	75	1	212	3413	46.12	8
Horne M.J.	A	42	66	3	209*	2882	45.74	9

Most Centuries for One Province

	Province	100s		Province	100s		Province	100s
Sutcliffe B.	O	17	Crowe M.D.	CD	13	Bell M.D.	W	11
Edgar B.A.	W	15	Franklin T.J.	A	12	Hick G.A.	ND	10
Rutherford K.R.	O	14	Vance R.H.	W	12	Hadlee W.A.	C	10
Greatbatch M.J.	CD	14	Scott V.J.	A	11	Burgess M.G.	A	10
Reid J.R.	W	13	Crowe J.J.	A	11	Harris C.Z.	C	10
Turner G.M.	O	13	McEwan P.E.	C	11	Stead G.R.	C	10

Most Runs for One Province

	Province	M	In	NO	HS	Runs	Ave	100
Edgar B.A.	W	87	160	3	162	6494	44.17	15
Vance R.H.	W	119	205	18	254*	6440	34.43	12
Sutcliffe B.	O	60	110	8	385*	6028	59.09	17
McEwan P.E.	C	103	185	11	155	5940	34.13	11
Latham R.T.	C	101	176	17	237*	5919	37.22	8
Roberts A.D.G.	ND	104	192	35	128*	5533	35.24	7
Blair B.R.	O	90	154	5	143	5057	33.93	7
Franklin T.J.	A	88	157	14	181	5051	35.25	12
Rutherford K.R.	O	68	121	7	226*	5051	44.30	14
Morrison J.F.M.	W	89	160	22	180*	4694	34.01	6
White D.J.	ND	99	173	15	209	4656	29.46	7
Bradburn G.E.	ND	115	188	23	148*	4614	27.96	4
Parker J.M.	ND	75	139	19	195	4611	38.42	7
Shrimpton M.J.F.	CD	97	171	15	150	4551	29.17	5
Blain T.E.	CD	83	145	15	161	4547	34.97	7
Reid J.R.	W	58	102	8	296	4538	48.27	13
Harris C.Z.	C	64	95	25	251*	4444	63.48	10
Turner G.M.	O	59	109	14	186*	4439	46.72	13
Hadlee B.G.	C	82	151	11	163*	4429	31.63	6
Greatbatch M.J.	CD	61	107	8	202*	4363	44.07	14
Gaffaney C.B.	O	75	138	11	194	4326	34.06	7
Briasco P.S.	CD	81	146	16	157	4301	33.08	6
McSweeney E.B.	W	102	153	23	205*	4296	33.04	5
McGregor S.N.	O	90	167	13	114*	4259	27.65	3
Crowe J.J.	A	59	95	9	156	4245	49.36	11
Gray E.J.	W	120	181	38	128*	4228	29.56	5
Burgess M.G.	A	68	116	13	146	4228	41.04	10
Morgan R.W.	A	90	154	8	166	4162	28.50	7
Stead G.R.	C	81	134	10	190	4148	33.45	10

Most Wickets for One Province

	Province	M	Wkts	Runs	Ave	5WI	10WM	Best
Chatfield E.J.	W	84	403	7531	18.68	23	7	8-24
Boock S.L.	O	88	399	8235	20.63	28	5	8-57
O'Sullivan D.R.	CD	90	392	9560	24.38	21	3	6-40
Gray E.J.	W	120	357	9778	27.38	13	3	8-37
Howarth H.J.	A	80	332	7361	22.17	18	4	8-75
Blair R.W.	W	59	330	5004	15.16	30	10	9-72
Priest M.W.	C	88	290	8501	29.31	12	3	9-95
Downes A.D.	O	44	287	3902	13.59	33	13	8-35
Hadlee R.J.	C	62	285	4600	16.14	19	2	7-49
Moir A.M.	O	54	282	5926	21.01	20	5	8-37
Dickeson C.W.	ND	90	282	8242	29.22	9	2	7-79
Mallender N.A.	O	78	268	5433	20.27	14	3	7-27

Alabaster J.C.	O	65	264	5738	21.73	14	3	6-39
Cameron F.J.	O	68	258	5204	20.17	9	—	6-21

Most Dismissals for One Province

WICKETKEEPING	*Province*	*M*	*Caught*	*Stumped*	*Total*
McSweeney E.B.	W	102	289	39	328
Lees W.K.	O	108	208	36	244
Hart R.G.	ND	85	228	15	243
Germon L.K.	C	76	217	21	238
Nevin C.J.	W	68	190	7	197
Young B.A.	ND	93	179	11	190
Milburn B.D.	O	60	148	17	165
Young R.A.	A	52	162	3	165
Ward J.T.	C	54	136	17	153
Kelly P.J.	A	48	140	12	152
Blain T.E.	CD	83	124	19	143
Croy M.G.	O	42	127	4	131
Colquhoun I.A.	CD	53	102	28	130
Smith I.D.S.	CD	59	119	11	130
Sigley M.A.	CD	44	124	4	128
Schofield R.M.	CD	53	107	15	122
Robinson S.A.	O	45	117	5	122
Wright M.J.E.	ND	65	104	17	121
Petrie E.C.	ND	57	90	22	112
Mills G.H.	O	55	78	29	107
Boxshall C.	C	50	70	36	106
Hopkins G.J.	C	41	91	10	101
Therkleson I.J.	W	39	93	7	100

Represented Most Provinces

5	Guy J.W.	CD, C, O, W, ND
4	Anderson R.W.	C, ND, O, CD
	Congdon B.E.	CD, W, O, C
	Crawshaw W.J.	O, C, W, T
	Hounsell A.R.	C, W, A, ND
	Howell L.G.	C, CD, A, ND
	McGregor P.B.	A, ND, W, CD
	Worker R.V. de R.	A, C, O, W
3	Alabaster G.D.	O, C, ND
	Allcott C.F.W.	HB, A, O
	Alpe S.	A, C, W
	Andrews B.	C, CD, O
	Beard D.D.	W, CD, ND
	Billcliff I.S.	O, W, A
	Bracewell B.P.	CD, O, ND
	Cairns B.L.	CD, O, ND
	Clark L.A.	W, O, A
	Collinge R.O.	CD, W, ND
	Crowe M.D.	A, CD, W
	D'Arcy J.W.	C, O, W
	Frith W.	C, O, W
	Hastings B.F.	W, CD, C
	Holland P.J.	CD, ND, W
	Hopkins G.J.	ND, C, O
3	Hussey J.M.	HB, O, A
	Jones A.H.	CD, O, W
	King R.T.	O, A, CD
	Lane M.E.L.	W, CD, C
	Lusk Harold B.	A, C, W
	McBeath D.J.	O, C, S
	McGlashan P.D.	CD, O, ND
	Macleod D.N.	CD, W, C
	Mills G.	A, HB, O
	Moloney D.A.R.	O, W, C
	Neutze P.S.	O, A, ND
	Paterson J.L.	C, HB, A
	Riley J.D.	C, W, A
	Sampson H.C.	CD, O, C
	Salmon W.J.	W, HB, T
	Stephenson F.C.	O, W, C
	Sutcliffe B.	A, O, ND
	Tracy S.R.	A, C, O
	Twose R.G.	ND, CD, W
	Uttley K.F.M.	O, C, W
	Watson H.C.	O, C, W
	Wiseman P.J.	A, O, C
	Wright E.	A, W, C
	Wright J.G.	ND, C, A

T *Taranaki* S *Southland* HB *Hawke's Bay*

PROVINCIAL RECORDS

MOST WINS IN SUCCESSION

8	Canterbury	1873/74 to 1880/81
7	Canterbury	1912/13 to 1913/14
7	Wellington	1960/61 to 1961/62
6	Canterbury	1910/11 to 1911/12
6	Auckland	1939/40 to 1943/44
6	Wellington	1962/63 to 1963/64
6	Canterbury	1996/97

MOST LOSSES IN SUCCESSION

10	Otago	1961/62 to 1963/64
8	Otago	1929/30 to 1931/32
7	Otago	1874/75 to 1880/81
7	Otago	1920/21 to 1922/23
7	Otago	1926/27 to 1927/28
7	Auckland	1997/98 to 1998/99
7	Otago	2001/02

MOST DRAWS IN SUCCESSION

9	ND	1974/75 to 1975/76
8	Wellington	1974/75 to 1975/76
7	ND	1968/69 to 1969/70
7	CD	1991/92 to 1992/93
7	Wellington	1992/93

MOST GAMES WITHOUT A WIN

38	CD	1973/74 to 1978/79
36	Otago	1960/61 to 1965/66
24	ND	1972/73 to 1975/76
21	ND	1966/67 to 1970/71

MOST GAMES WITHOUT A LOSS

24	Wellington	1984/85 to 1986/87
23	Auckland	1978/79 to 1981/82
22	Auckland	1934/35 to 1943/44
18	Auckland	1961/62 to 1964/65
18	Canterbury	1966/67 to 1969/70

MOST GAMES WITHOUT A DRAW

42	Canterbury	1896/97 to 1909/10
30	Otago	1894/95 to 1907/08
22	Canterbury	1869/70 to 1883/84
20	Canterbury	1919/20 to 1924/25

Highest Individual Innings

for and against the major sides in NZ

	For		Against	
Auckland	290	W.N. Carson v Otago at Dunedin, 1936/37	355	B. Sutcliffe for Otago at Dunedin, 1949/50
Canterbury	301*	P.G. Fulton v Auckland at Christchurch, 2002/03	385	B. Sutcliffe for Otago at Christchurch, 1952/53
Central Dist.	242	M.D. Crowe v Otago at New Plymouth, 1989/90	264	B. Sutcliffe for Otago at Dunedin, 1959/60
Northern Dist.	235	J.A.H. Marshall v Canterbury at Chch, 2001/02	296	J.R. Reid for Wellington at Wellington, 1962/63
Otago	385	B. Sutcliffe v Canterbury at Christchurch, 1952/53	290	W.N. Carson for Auckland at Dunedin, 1936/37
Wellington	296	J.R. Reid v Northern Dist. at Wellington, 1962/63	207	R.T. Hart for Central Dist. at Wellington, 1985/86
MCC/England	336*	W.R. Hammond v NZ at Auckand, 1932/33	222	N.J. Astle for NZ at Christchurch, 2001/02
Australia	293	V.T. Trumper v Canterbury at Christchurch 1913/14	198	W.A. Hadlee for Otago at Dunedin, 1945/46
South Africa	275*	D.J. Cullinan v NZ at Auckland, 1998/99	170	S.B. Styris for NZ at Auckland, 2003/04
West Indies	258	S.M. Nurse v NZ at Christchurch, 1968/69	214	M.S. Sinclair for NZ at Wellington, 1999/00
Pakistan	271	Javed Miandad v NZ at Auckland, 1988/89	204	M.S. Sinclair for NZ at Christchurch, 2000/01
India	192	M. Azharuddin v NZ at Auckand, 1989/90	239	G.T. Dowling for NZ at Christchurch, 1967/68
Sri Lanka	267	P.A. de Silva v NZ at Wellington, 1990/91	299	M.D. Crowe for NZ at Wellington, 1990/91
New Zealand	299	M.D. Crowe v Sri Lanka at Wellington, 1990/91	336*	W.R. Hammond for England at Auckland, 1932/33
Zimbabwe	196	A.D.R. Campbell v Canterbury at Timaru, 1997/98	157	M.J. Horne for NZ at Auckland, 1997/98
Bangladesh	102	Al Sahariar v Southern at Dunedin, 1997/98	190	M.E. Parlane for NZ Academy at Lincoln, 1997/98

Best Bowling

for and against the major sides in NZ

	For		Against	
Auckland	9-36	A.F. Wensley v Otago at Auckland, 1929/30	9-48	A.R. Tait v Auckland at Hamilton, 1996/97
Canterbury	10-28	A.E. Moss v Wellington at Christchurch, 1889/90	9-72	F.H. Cooke for Otago at Christchurch, 1884/85
Central Dist.	9-100	B.W. Yuile v Canterbury at New Plymouth, 1965/66	9-13	P.J. Wiseman for Canterbury at Christchurch, 2004/05
Northern Dist.	9-48	A.R. Tait v Auckland at Hamilton, 1996/97	9-93	P.J. Petherick for Otago at Dunedin, 1975/76
Otago	9-50	A.H. Fisher v Queensland at Dunedin, 1896/97	9-36	A.E. Wensley for Auckland at Auckland, 1929/30
Wellington	9-67	A.W.S. Brice v Auckland at Wellington, 1918/19	10-28	A.E. Moss for Canterbury at Christchurch, 1889/90
MCC/England	8-45	F.S. Trueman v Otago at Dunedin, 1958/59	7-50	H.W. Monaghan for Wellington at Wellington, 1906/07
Australia	8-27	W.J. Whitty v Auckland at Auckland, 1909/10	8-66	G.O. Rabone for Auckland at Auckland, 1956/57
South Africa	6-47	P.M. Pollock v NZ at Wellington, 1963/64	7-75	C.F.W. Allcott for Auckland at Auckland, 1931/32
West Indies	7-37	C.A. Walsh v NZ at Wellington, 1994/95	7-27	C.L. Cairns for at Hamilton, 1999/00
Pakistan	7-16	Farooq Hamid v Wellington at Wellington, 1964/65	7-95	N.A. Huxford for Wellington at Wellington, 1964/65
India	8-76	E.A.S. Prasanna v NZ at Auckland, 1975/76	7-23	R.J. Hadlee for at Wellington, 1975/76
Sri Lanka	6-79	C.P.H. Ramanayake v Wellington at Wellington, 1990/91	6-45	C.H. Thiele for Canterbury at Christchurch, 1982/83
New Zealand	8-100	G.F. Cresswell v Australia B at Dunedin, 1949/50	8-33	H.S.T.L. Hendry for NSW at Wellington, 1923/24
Zimbabwe	6-20	B.C. Strang v NZ XI at Wanganui, 1995/96	5-16	A.R. Tait for NZ A at Dunedin, 1997/98
Bangladesh	6-143	Hasibul Hussain v Northern at Hamilton, 1997/98	7-53	C.L. Cairns for NZ at Hamilton, 2001/02

Highest Totals

for and against the major sides in NZ

	For		Against	
Auckland	693-9 dec	v Canterbury at Auckland, 1939/40	658	by Australians at Auckland, 1913/14
Canterbury	777	v Otago at Christchurch, 1996/97	693-9 dec	by Auckland at Auckland, 1939/40
Central Dist.	594-8 dec	v Auckland at Auckland, 1995/96	590-8	by Wellington at P. North, 2004/05
Northern Dist.	520-8 dec	v Otago at Hamilton, 1987/88	608-9 dec	by Wellington at Hamilton, 1998/99
Otago	602-8 dec	v Canterbury at Dunedin, 1928/29	777	by Canterbury at Christchurch, 1996/97
Wellington	608-9 dec	v Northern Districts at Hamilton, 1998/99	547-5 dec	by Canterbury at Christchurch, 1953/54
MCC/England	653-5 dec	v New Zealand at Dunedin, 1935/36	537	by New Zealand at Wellington, 1983/84
Australia	663	v New Zealand at Auckland, 1920/21	484	by New Zealand at Wellington, 1973/74
South Africa	621-5 dec	v New Zealand at Auckland, 1998/99	595	by New Zealand at Auckland, 2003/04
West Indies	660-5 dec	v New Zealand at Wellington, 1994/95	518-9d	by New Zealand at Wellington, 1999/00
Pakistan	616-5 dec	v New Zealand at Auckland, 1988/89	563	by New Zealand at Hamilton, 2003/04
India	512	v President's XI at New Plymouth, 1989/90	502	by New Zealand at Christchurch, 1967/68
Sri Lanka	498	v New Zealand at Napier, 2004/05	671-4	by New Zealand at Wellington, 1990/91
New Zealand	671-4	v Sri Lanka at Wellington, 1990/91	663	by Australia at Auckland, 1920/21
Zimbabwe	422-8 dec	v Canterbury at Timaru, 1997/98	487-7d	by New Zealand at Wellington, 2000/01
Bangladesh	286-9 dec	v Southern at Dunedin, 1997/98	495	by Auckland at Auckland, 2001/02

Lowest Totals

for and against the major sides in NZ

	For		Against	
Auckland	13	v Canterbury at Auckland, 1877/78	28	by Hawke's Bay at Auckland, 1910/11
Canterbury	25	v Otago at Christchurch, 1866/67	13	by Auckland at Auckland, 1877/78
Central Dist.	50	v Wellington at Upper Hutt, 1979/80	68	by Canterbury at Levin, 1985/86
Northern Dist.	32	v Auckland at Hamilton, 1996/97	51	by Central Dist. at Hamilton, 1957/58
Otago	34	v Wellington at Dunedin, 1956/57	25	by Canterbury at Christchurch, 1866/67
Wellington	19	v Nelson at Nelson, 1885/86	32	by Hawke's Bay at Wellington, 1883/84
MCC/England	64	v New Zealand at Wellington, 1977/78	26	by New Zealand at Auckland, 1954/55
Australia	103	v New Zealand at Auckland, 1985/86	42	by New Zealand at Wellington, 1945/46
South Africa	165	v NZ Academy XI at Nelson, 1994/95	73	by Canterbury at Christchurch, 1963/64
West Indies	77	v New Zealand at Auckland, 1955/56	74	by New Zealand at Dunedin, 1955/56
Pakistan	100	v New Zealand A at Lincoln, 2000/01	46	by Otago at Dunedin, 1978/79
India	81	v New Zealand at Wellington, 1975/76	94	by New Zealand at Hamilton, 2002/03
Sri Lanka	93	v New Zealand at Wellington, 1982/83	109	by New Zealand at Napier, 1994/95
New Zealand	26	v England at Auckland, 1954/55	64	by England at Wellington, 1977/78
Zimbabwe	67	v New Zealand A at Dunedin, 1997/98	100	by Canterbury at Timaru, 1997/98
Bangladesh	108	v New Zealand at Hamilton, 2001/02	311	by Central at Wellington, 1997/98

AUCKLAND

Highest Totals

693-9 dec	v Canterbury	Auckland	1939/40
643	v Canterbury	Auckland	1919/20
590	v Canterbury	Auckland	1937/38
579	v Otago	Auckland	1909/10
550-5 dec	v Otago	Auckland	1936/37
547-8 dec	v Northern Districts	Auckland	2000/01
539	v Otago	Dunedin	1926/27
539	v Canterbury	Christchurch	1907/08
537	v Hawke's Bay	Auckland	1920/21
537	v Canterbury	Christchurch	1930/31

Lowest Totals

13	v Canterbury	Auckland	1877/78
48	v Otago	Dunedin	1889/90
48	v Wellington	Wellington	1889/90
53	v Wellington	Wellington	1873/74
55	v Otago	Dunedin	1900/01
56	v Canterbury	Auckland	1931/32
69	v Northern Districts	Auckland	1963/64
71	v Central Districts	Palmerston North	2001/02
72	v Lord Hawke's XI	Auckland	1902/03
72	v Northern Districts	Rotorua	1991/92

Most Appearances

90	Morgan R.W.	68	Burgess M.G.	60	Parsons A.E.W.
88	Franklin T.J.	67	Harris R.M.	59	Crowe J.J.
80	Howarth H.J.	67	Patel D.N.	58	Vivian G.E.
77	McIntyre J.M.	65	Hunt A.J.	55	Snedden M.C.
73	Sparling J.T.	65	Webb P.N.	54	Sutton R.E.
73	Barnes A.C.	63	Stott L.W.	53	Watson W.
72	Troup G.B.	62	Cunis R.S.	52	Young R.A.
69	Reid J.F.	61	Walker B.G.K.	51	Brown S.W.

Longest Careers

Seasons			*Seasons*		
25	Garrard D.R.	1917/18-1941/42	21	Cleverley D.C.	1930/31-1950-51
24	Wallace W.M.	1933/34-1956/57	20	Stemson W.I.	1889/90-1908/09
22	Anthony A.	1909/10-1930/31	20	Horspool E.	1909/10-1928/29
22	McIntyre J.M.	1961/62-1982-83	20	Weir G.L.	1927/28-1946/47
21	Yates R.J.	1873/74-1893/94	20	Morgan R.W.	1957/58-1976/77

Benefits

Troup G.B.	1986/87	Watson W.	1994/95
Snedden M.C.	1989/90	Patel D.N.	1995/96
Crowe J.J.	1990/91	Morrison D.K.	1996/97
Franklin T.J.	1991/92	Pringle C.	1998/99
Hunt A.J.	1992/93	Barnes A.C.	2002/03

Batting

2000 RUNS	Career	M	In	NO	HS	Runs	Ave	100
Franklin T.J.	1980/81-1992/93	88	157	14	181	5051	35.25	12
Crowe J.J.	1982/83-1991/92	59	95	9	156	4245	49.36	11
Burgess M.G.	1966/67-1979/80	68	116	13	146	4228	41.04	10
Morgan R.W.	1957/58-1976/77	90	154	8	166	4162	28.50	7
Reid J.F.	1975/76-1987/88	69	117	17	173	3733	37.33	5
Patel D.N.	1985/86-1994/95	67	102	9	204	3648	39.22	8
Harris R.M.	1955/56-1973/74	67	119	4	157	3598	31.28	3
Scott V.J.	1937/38-1952/53	44	74	15	204	3546	60.10	11
Wallace W.M.	1933/34-1956/57	47	73	5	211	3409	50.13	9
Webb P.N.	1976/77-1986/87	65	114	18	136	3307	34.44	5
Sparling J.T.	1956/57-1970/71	73	123	17	105	2977	28.08	2
Barnes A.C.	1993/94-2004/05	73	113	10	134*	2893	28.08	4
Horne M.J.	1992/93-2004/05	42	66	3	209*	2882	45.74	9
Parsons A.E.W.	1973/74-1982/83	60	113	8	132	2820	26.85	3
Hemus L.G.	1904/05-1921/22	39	71	4	148	2701	40.31	8
Weir G.L.	1927/28-1946/47	42	67	6	191	2625	43.03	7
Whitelaw P.E.	1928/29-1946/47	42	68	4	195	2417	37.76	5
McIntosh T.G.	1998/99-2003/04	44	72	7	182	2407	37.03	8
Jarvis T.W.	1964/65-1976/77	46	80	3	118*	2403	31.20	2
Horne P.A.	1979/80-1990/91	40	67	6	209	2380	39.01	4
Vivian G.E.	1966/67-1978/79	58	98	16	111*	2327	28.37	2
Vaughan J.T.C.	1989/90-1996/97	48	81	14	127	2269	33.86	2
Gedye S.G.	1956/57-1964/65	40	73	4	104	2169	31.43	3
Mills J.E.	1925/26-1937/38	35	63	1	185	2126	34.29	3
Hunt A.J.	1981/82-1992/93	65	99	15	102*	2069	24.63	1
Redmond R.E.	1969/70-1975/76	29	55	4	141*	2004	39.29	4

CENTURY ON DEBUT FOR PROVINCE

† 112*	Brook-Smith W.	v Hawke's Bay	Auckland	1904/05
157	Relf A.E.	v Canterbury	Christchurch	1907/08
† 119	Snedden C.A.	v Hawke's Bay	Auckland	1920/21
† 122	Scott V.J.	v Canterbury	Auckland	1937/38
† 122	Kerr A.C.	v Wellington	Auckland	1941/42
174	Patel D.N.	v Canterbury	Christchurch	1985/86
† 106* & 1	Vaughan J.T.C.	v Wellington	Wellington	1989/90

† indicates player was making his first-class debut

MOST RUNS IN A SEASON

		Runs	Ave
Crowe J.J.	1991/92	1063	62.52
McIntosh T.G.	2002/03	820	58.57
Crowe M.D.	1982/83	736	52.57
Patel D.N.	1986/87	723	55.61
Horne M.J.	2001/02	696	69.60
Horne M.J.	2002/03	671	47.92
Horne P.A.	1986/87	670	67.00
Crowe J.J.	1990/91	667	44.46
Franklin T.J.	1982/83	664	51.07
Nicol R.J.	2002/03	664	47.42
Crowe J.J.	1988/89	644	71.55
Burgess M.G.	1977/78	643	46.00
Mills K.D.	2000/01	606	101.00
Crowe J.J.	1989/90	600	42.85

HIGHEST INDIVIDUAL INNINGS

290	Carson W.N.	v Otago	Dunedin	1936/37
256	Smith S.G.	v Canterbury	Auckland	1919/20
211	Wallace W.M.	v Canterbury	Auckland	1939/40
209*	Brown S.W.	v Canterbury	Christchurch	1990/91
209*	Horne M.J.	v Northern Districts	Auckland	2003/04
209	Horne P.A.	v Northern Districts	Auckland	1988/89

204	Scott V.J.	v Otago	Dunedin	1947/48
204	Patel D.N.	v Northern Districts	Auckland	1991/92
198	Scott V.J.	v Canterbury	Auckland	1939/40
195	Whitelaw P.E.	v Otago	Dunedin	1936/37

MOST CENTURIES IN A SEASON

4	Franklin T.J.	1987/88
4	Crowe J.J.	1991/92

TOTAL NUMBER OF CENTURIES		265
Most in one season	11	2001/02
1st	Mills G. 106* v Wellington	1895/96
100th	Playle W.R. 102* v Central Districts	1957/58
200th	Crowe J.J. 102 v Otago	1991/92

Bowling

150 WICKETS	*Career*	*M*	*Wkts*	*Runs*	*Ave*	*5WI*	*10WM*	*Best*
Howarth H.J.	1963/64-1978/79	80	332	7361	22.17	18	4	8-75
Sparling J.T.	1956/57-1970/71	73	248	5327	21.47	17	3	7-49
McIntyre J.M.	1961/62-1982/83	77	238	5447	22.88	8	1	6-84
Cunis R.S.	1960/61-1973/74	62	229	4603	20.10	14	2	7-29
Snedden M.C.	1977/78-1989/90	55	217	4631	21.34	10	2	7-49
Stott L.W.	1969/70-1983/84	63	214	5341	24.95	8	—	6-68
Troup G.B.	1974/75-1986/87	72	200	5213	26.06	4	—	6-48
Patel D.N.	1985/86-1994/95	67	184	4298	23.35	8	2	7-83
Watson W.	1984/85-1994/95	53	176	4110	23.35	7	—	7-60
Bracewell J.G.	1982/83-1989/90	42	168	4189	24.93	8	2	7-65
Morrison D.K.	1985/86-1996/97	49	168	4034	24.01	7	—	7-82
Canning T.K.	1999/00-2004/05	45	163	3848	23.60	6	—	6-44
Cowie J.	1932/33-1949/50	34	154	3379	21.94	6	—	6-44
Sutton R.E.	1958/59-1973/74	54	152	3364	22.13	6	—	7-64

MOST WICKETS IN A SEASON

		Wkts	*Ave*
Canning T.K.	2002/03	46	21.97
Bracewell J.G.	1986/87	43	20.90
Hayes J.A.	1957/58	42	11.38
Lankham W.	1882/83	41	6.31

BEST IN AN INNINGS

9-36	Wensley A.F.	v Otago	Auckland	1929/30
9-75	Neill R.	v Canterbury	Auckland	1891/92
9-86	Neill R.	v Canterbury	Auckland	1897/98
8-27	Vaughan J.T.C.	v Otago	Alexandra	1996/97
8-36	Rees A.W.	v Otago	Dunedin	1889/90
8-51	Neill R.	v Wellington	Auckland	1895/96
8-51	Garrard D.R.	v Canterbury	Auckland	1921/22
8-55	Smith S.G.	v Wellington	Auckland	1919/20
8-65	Smith S.G.	v Otago	Auckland	1923/24
8-66	Rabone G.O.	v Australia	Auckland	1956/57
8-75	Cleverley D.C.	v Wellington	Wellington	1945/46
8-75	Howarth H.J.	v NZ Under 23 XI	Auckland	1976/77

BEST IN A MATCH

14-63	Rees A.W.	v Otago	Dunedin	1889/90
14-65	Hayes J.A.	v Wellington	Auckland	1957/58
14-94	Howarth H.J.	v Otago	Dunedin	1973/74

14-119	Pringle C.	v Otago	Dunedin	1993/94
13-35	Lankham W.	v Taranaki	Auckland	1882/83
13-85	Cunis R.S.	v Canterbury	Christchurch	1963/64
13-104	Oliff C.	v Wellington	Auckland	1912/13
13-107	Smith S.G.	v Wellington	Auckland	1919/20

Wicketkeeping

100 DISMISSALS	*Career*	*M*	*Caught*	*Stumped*	*Total*
Young R.A.	1998/99-2004/05	52	162	3	165
Kelly P.J.	1981/82-1988/89	48	140	12	152

MOST DISMISSALS IN A SEASON

35	(33ct/2st)	Young R.A.	2001/02
35	(35ct)	Young R.A.	2002/03

MOST DISMISSALS IN A MATCH

8	(2ct/6st)	Kent L.A.W. v Wellington	Wellington	1944/45
8	(8ct)	Smith I.D.S. v Central Districts	Nelson	1988/89
8	(8ct)	Vincent L. v Central Districts	Palmerston North	2000/01

MOST DISMISSALS IN AN INNINGS

6	(6ct)	Young R.A.v Wellington	Wellington	2002/03

MOST CATCHES IN A MATCH

8	Smith I.D.S. v Central Districts	Nelson	1988/89
8	Vincent L. v Central Districts	Palmerston North	2000/01

MOST CATCHES IN AN INNINGS

6	Young R.A.v Wellington	Wellington	2002/03

Fielding

MOST CATCHES IN A MATCH

6	Williams N.T. v Hawke's Bay	Napier	1894/95
6	Jarvis T.W. v Northern Districts	Hamilton	1968/69

MOST CATCHES IN AN INNINGS

5	Williams N.T. v Hawkes Bay	Napier	1894/95
5	Crowe J.J. v Canterbury	Auckland	1988/89

Record Partnerships

FOR

Wicket	*Score*	*Batsmen*	*Against*	*At*	*Date*
1st	286	B. Sutcliffe & D.D. Taylor	Canterbury	Auckland	1948/49
2nd	241	T.J. Franklin & J.J. Crowe	Wellington	Wellington	1988/89
3rd	445	P.E. Whitelaw & W.N. Carson	Otago	Dunedin	1936/37
4th	280	J.J. Crowe & D.N. Patel	ND	Auckland	1991/92
5th	347*	M.J. Horne & A.C. Barnes	ND	Auckland	2003/04
6th	209*	A.C. Parore & A.P. O'Dowd	Otago	Dunedin	1991/92
7th	224	V.J. Scott & A.M. Matheson	Canterbury	Auckland	1937/38
8th	189	W.N. Carson & A.M. Matheson	Wellington	Auckland	1938/39
9th	122	R.S. Cunis & H.T. Schuster	Wellington	Wellington	1964/65
10th	119	W.N. Carson & J. Cowie	Otago	Auckland	1937/38

AGAINST

Wicket	*Score*	*Batsmen*	*For*	*At*	*Date*
1st	373	B. Sutcliffe & L. Watt	Otago	Auckland	1950/51
2nd	287	M.D. Bell & J.D. Wells	Wellington	Auckland	1997/98
3rd	261*	M.P. Maynard & S.A. Thomson	ND	Hamilton	1990/91
4th	252	S.A. Thomson & B.A. Young	ND	Auckland	1990/91
5th	266	B. Sutcliffe & W.S. Haig	Otago	Dunedin	1949/50
6th	220	M.H. Toynbee & I.D.S. Smith	CD	Napier	1982/83
7th	165	R.K. Brown & M.E.L. Lane	CD	Palmerston Nth	1993/94
8th	166	R.J. Hadlee & D.R. Hadlee	Canterbury	Christchurch	1983/84
9th	208	W.C. McSkimming & B.E. Scott	Otago	Auckland	2004/05
10th	133	G.A. Bartlett & I.A. Colquhoun	CD	Auckland	1959/60

CANTERBURY

Highest Totals

777	v Otago	Christchurch	1996/97
559	v Central Districts	Christchurch	1993/94
549	v Northern Districts	Christchurch	1996/97
547-5 dec	v Wellington	Christchurch	1953/54
543-8 dec	v Central Districts	Rangiora	1996/97
537	v Central Districts	Blenheim	1996/97
534	v Central Districts	Palmerston North	1994/95
526-8 dec	v Wellington	Wellington	1931/32
524	v Northern Districts	Rangiora	1997/98
523-7 dec	v Otago	Christchurch	1929/30

Lowest Totals

25	v Otago	Christchurch	1886/87
27	v Otago	Dunedin	1896/97
32	v Otago	Christchurch	1866/67
34	v Otago	Dunedin	1863/64
37	v Southland	Invercargill	1920/21
37	v Wellington	Wellington	1925/26
38	v Otago	Dunedin	1873/74
42	v Otago	Dunedin	1863/64
42	v Otago	Dunedin	1992/93
44	v Otago	Dunedin	1883/84
46	v Otago	Dunedin	1867/68
46	v Otago	Christchurch	1894/95
46	v Otago	Christchurch	1896/97
49	v Otago	Dunedin	1896/97

Most Appearances

103	McEwan P.E.	69	Boyle D.J.	58	Dowling G.T.
101	Latham R.T.	65	Brown V.R.	58	Thomson K.
88	Priest M.W.	64	Harris C.Z.	57	Bull C.L.
86	Stead D.W.	62	Hadlee R.J.	56	Motz R.C.
82	Hadlee B.G.	60	Roberts S.J.	54	Cromb I.B.
81	Stead G.R.	59	Hartland B.R.	54	Ward J.T.
76	Germon L.K.	58	Patrick W.R.	50	Boxshall C.
72	Hastings B.F.				

Longest Careers

Seasons			Seasons		
34	Read R.J.	1904/05-1937/38	22	Patrick W.R.	1905/06-1926/27
31	Reese T.W.	1887/88-1917/18	21	Stevens E.C.J.	1863/64-1883/84
27	Fowke J.N.	1880/81-1906/07	21	Wilding F.	1881/82-1901/02
26	Reese D.	1895/96-1920/21	21	Ridley A.E.	1889/90-1909/10
25	Moorhouse H.M.	1883/84-1907/08	20	Harman T.D.	1882/83-1901/02
22	Wheatley J.	1882/83-1903/04	20	Hadlee B.G.	1961/62-1980/81

Benefits

McEwan P.E.	1988/89	Germon L.K./Priest M.W.	1997/98
Hadlee R.J.	1989/90	Harris C.Z.	1998/99
Latham R.T.	1992/93	Cairns C.L.	1999/00

Batting

2000 RUNS	Career	M	In	NO	HS	Runs	Ave	100
McEwan P.E.	1977/78-1990/91	103	185	11	155	5940	34.13	11
Latham R.T.	1980/81-1994/95	101	176	17	237*	5919	37.22	8
Harris C.Z.	1989/90-2003/04	64	95	25	251*	4444	63.48	10
Hadlee B.G.	1961/62-1980/81	82	151	11	163*	4429	31.63	6
Stead G.R.	1993/94-2004/05	81	134	10	190	4148	33.45	10
Dowling G.T.	1958/59-1971/72	58	100	7	206	3690	39.67	8
Hastings B.F.	1961/62-1976/77	72	122	8	226	3540	31.05	7
Priest M.W.	1984/85-1998/99	88	130	21	119	3457	31.71	4
Boyle D.J.	1980/81-1994/95	69	121	12	149	3216	29.50	3
Hadlee W.A.	1933/34-1951/52	44	80	7	194	3183	43.60	10
Stead D.W.	1969/70-1985/86	77	133	11	193*	3169	25.97	1
Cromb I.B.	1929/30-1946/47	54	96	5	171	2986	32.81	3
Brown V.R.	1978/79-1986/87	65	111	11	161*	2872	28.72	5
Patrick W.R.	1905/06-1926/27	58	108	7	129*	2803	27.75	2
Hartland B.R.	1986/87-1996/97	59	103	8	150	2771	29.16	5
Papps M.H.W.	1998/99-2004/05	47	83	6	192	2677	34.76	6
Coman P.G.	1968/69-1977/78	44	78	4	104	2603	35.17	2
Thomson K.	1959/60-1973/74	58	103	11	136*	2543	27.64	4
Fulton P.G.	2000/01-2004/05	31	54	6	301*	2437	50.77	5
Page M.L.	1920/21-1936/37	41	75	2	206	2424	33.20	2
Leggat J.G.	1944/45-1955/56	35	66	6	166	2391	39.85	5
Chapple M.E.	1949/50-1960/61	44	79	9	165	2364	33.77	3
Germon L.K.	1987/88-1997/98	76	101	25	160*	2336	30.73	3
Kerr J.L.	1929/30-1939/40	32	61	3	196	2228	38.41	3
Guillen S.C.	1952/53-1960/61	42	73	5	197	2186	32.14	3
Reese D.	1895/96-1920/21	47	85	4	111	2066	25.50	2
Ryan M.L.	1965/66-1978/79	45	78	8	129	2041	29.15	2
Hadlee R.J.	1971/72-1988/89	62	100	22	93	2012	25.79	—
Roberts A.W.	1927/28-1940/41	35	60	8	181	2004	38.53	2

CENTURY ON DEBUT FOR PROVINCE

† 175	Watson G.	v Otago	Christchurch	1880/81
163	Williams A.B.	v Wellington	Christchurch	1896/97
† 108 & 18	Wood B.B.	v Wellington	Wellington	1907/08
† 105	Talbot R.O.	v Otago	Dunedin	1922/23
5 & 112*	Newman J.A.	v Otago	Christchurch	1927/28
149	Hastings B.F.	v Central Districts	Nelson	1961/62
8 & 135	Parker N.M.	v Wellington	Wellington	1973/74
115	Hopkins G.J.	v Central Districts	Christchurch	1998/99

† indicates player was making his first-class debut

HIGHEST INDIVIDUAL INNINGS

301*	Fulton P.G.	v Auckland	Christchurch	2002/03
251*	Harris C.Z.	v Central Districts	Rangiora	1996/97
237*	Latham R.T.	v Northern Districts	Rotorua	1990/91
226	Hastings B.F.	v NZ Under 23 XI	Christchurch	1964/65
221*	Fulton P.G.	v Otago	Dunedin	2004/05
206	Page M.L.	v Wellington	Wellington	1931/32
206	Dowling G.T.	v Wellington	Christchurch	1962/63
206	Harris C.Z.	v Central Districts	Blenheim	1996/97
204	Cox A.	v Otago	Christchurch	1925/26
198	Harris C.Z.	v Otago	Christchurch	1996/97

MOST RUNS IN A SEASON

		Runs	*Ave*
Stead G.R.	2000/01	852	50.11
Fulton P.G.	2004/05	828	69.00
McMillan C.D.	1996/97	809	73.54
Papps M.H.W.	2001/02	793	52.86
Wright J.G.	1986/87	780	60.00
McEwan P.E.	1988/89	758	44.58
Latham R.T.	1988/89	757	58.23
Harris C.Z.	1996/97	748	187.00
Englefield J.I.	2000/01	724	38.10
McEwan P.E.	1983/84	713	59.41
Harris C.Z.	2001/02	656	93.71
Fulton P.G.	2003/04	655	43.66
Papps M.H.W.	2003/04	633	57.54
Hastings B.F.	1964/65	629	62.90
Fulton P.G.	2002/03	628	52.33
Latham R.T.	1987/88	608	50.66

MOST CENTURIES IN A SEASON

3	Hadlee W.A.	1947/48
3	Harris C.Z.	1996/97
3	McMillan C.D.	1996/97
3	Stead G.R.	2000/01
3	Papps M.H.W.	2003/04

TOTAL NUMBER OF CENTURIES		**253**
Most in one season	9	1996/97
1st	Watson G. 175 v Otago	1880/81
100th	Hastings B.F. 136 v Auckland	1964/65
200th	Germon L.K. 114 v Central Districts	1993/94

Bowling

150 WICKETS	*Career*	*M*	*Wkts*	*Runs*	*Ave*	*5WI*	*10WM*	*Best*
Priest M.W.	1984/85-1998/99	88	290	8501	29.31	12	3	9-95
Hadlee R.J.	1971/72-1988/89	62	285	4600	16.14	19	2	7-49
Burtt T.B.	1943/44-1954/55	46	241	4991	20.70	16	3	8-35
Motz R.C.	1957/58-1968/69	56	239	4589	19.20	12	3	8-61
Bennett J.H.	1898/99-1919/20	40	205	3367	16.43	17	4	7-35
Hadlee D.R.	1969/70-1983/84	49	195	3918	20.09	10	3	7-55
Roberts S.J.	1985/86-1995/96	60	193	5738	29.73	6	–	5-56
Read R.J.	1904/05-1937/38	44	184	4704	25.56	11	1	7-24
Reese D.	1895/96-1920/21	48	168	3040	18.09	10	1	6-43
Stead D.W.	1969/70-1985/86	77	167	5009	29.99	6	—	7-99
Brown V.R.	1978/79-1986/87	65	159	4393	27.62	4	2	7-28
Merritt W.E.	1926/27-1935/36	24	154	3559	23.11	15	4	8-105
Wisneski W.A.	1996/97-2003/04	44	154	4092	26.57	7	—	7-151

BEST IN AN INNINGS

10-28	Moss A.E.	v Wellington	Christchurch	1889/90
9-13	Wiseman P.J.	v Central Districts	Christchurch	2004/05
9-56	McBeath D.J.	v Auckland	Christchurch	1918/19
9-95	Priest M.W.	v Otago	Dunedin	1989/90
9-98	Robertson W.	v Wellington	Christchurch	1894/95
8-18	Frith W.	v Otago	Christchurch	1880/81
8-33	Callaway S.T.	v Hawkes Bay	Napier	1903/04
8-35	Burtt T.B.	v Otago	Dunedin	1953/54
8-41	Callaway S.T.	v Otago	Dunedin	1900/01
8-59	Robertson W.	v Auckland	Christchurch	1893/94
8-61	Mulcock E.	v Otago	Christchurch	1937/38
8-61	Motz R.C.	v Wellington	Christchurch	1966/67
8-75	Edser H.	v Wellington	Wellington	1883/84
8-96	McBeath D.J.	v Auckland	Auckland	1921/22
8-99	Thomas A.W.	v Auckland	Auckland	1914/15
8-105	Merritt W.E.	v Auckland	Auckland	1931/32

BEST IN A MATCH

15-60	Callaway S.T.	v Hawkes Bay	Napier	1903/04
15-168	McBeath D.J.	v Auckland	Christchurch	1918/19
14-59	Read R.J.	v Southland	Invercargill	1920/21
14-107	Robertson W.	v Auckland	Christchurch	1893/94
13-72	Moss A.E.	v Wellington	Christchurch	1889/90
13-82	Howell W.B.	v Wellington	Christchurch	1902/03
13-90	Frankish F.S.	v Wellington	Wellington	1901/02
13-140	Edser H.	v Wellington	Wellington	1883/84
13-163	Robertson W.	v Wellington	Christchurch	1894/95
13-181	Merritt W.E.	v Otago	Wellington	1935/36

MOST WICKETS IN A SEASON

		Wkts	*Ave*
Boock S.L.	1977/78	56	15.66
Callaway S.T.	1903/04	47	8.49
Hadlee R.J.	1981/82	45	14.31
Hadlee R.J.	1986/87	45	12.91

Wicketkeeping

100 DISMISSALS	*Career*	*M*	*Caught*	*Stumped*	*Total*
Germon L.K.	1987/88-1997/98	76	217	21	238
Ward J.T.	1957/58-1970/71	54	136	17	153
Boxshall C.	1897/98-1914/15	50	70	36	106
Hopkins G.J.	1998/99-2002/03	41	91	10	101

MOST DISMISSALS IN A SEASON

34 (31ct/3st) Germon L.K. 1991/92

MOST DISMISSALS IN A MATCH

9	(9ct)	Germon L.K. v Northern Districts	Christchurch	1992/93

MOST DISMISSALS IN AN INNINGS

6	(6ct)	Germon L.K. v Northern Districts	Christchurch	1992/93
6	(5ct/1st)	Papps M.H.W. v Northern Districts	Gisborne	2004/05

MOST CATCHES IN A MATCH

9 Germon L.K. v Northern Districts Christchurch 1992/93

MOST CATCHES IN AN INNINGS

6	Germon L.K. v Northern Districts	Christchurch	1992/93

Fielding

MOST CATCHES IN A MATCH

6	Cromb I.B. v Otago	Christchurch	1937/38
6	MacDonald G.K. v Pakistan	Christchurch	1984/85
6	Latham R.T. v Otago	Oamaru	1994/95

MOST CATCHES IN AN INNINGS

5	MacDonald G.K. v Pakistan	Christchurch	1984/85
5	Harris C.Z. v England	Christchurch	2001/02

Record Partnerships

FOR

Wicket	*Score*	*Batsmen*	*Against*	*At*	*Date*
1st	306	L.A. Cuff & J.D. Lawrence	Auckland	Christchurch	1893/94
2nd	210	W.A. Hadlee & F.P. O'Brien	Otago	Christchurch	1940/41
3rd	394*	P.G. Kennedy & R.T. Latham	ND	Rotorua	1990/91
4th	278	M.L. Page & A.W. Roberts	Wellington	Wellington	1931/32
5th	290	G.R. Stead & C.Z. Harris	CD	Blenheim	1996/97
6th	293*	P.G. Fulton & N.T. Broom	Otago	Dunedin	2004/05
7th	265	J.L. Powell & N. Dorreen	Otago	Christchurch	1929/30
8th	210	G.R. Stead & S.E. Bond	ND	Christchurch	2004/05
9th	182*	L.K. Germon & R.M. Ford	Wellington	Christchurch	1989/90
10th	160	L.K. Germon & W.A. Wisneski	ND	Rangiora	1997/98

AGAINST

Wicket	*Score*	*Batsmen*	*For*	*At*	*Date*
1st	286	B. Sutcliffe & D.D. Taylor	Auckland	Auckland	1948/49
2nd	317	R.T. Hart & P.S. Briasco	CD	New Plymouth	1983/84
3rd	278	T.J. Franklin & D.N. Patel	Auckland	Christchurch	1985/86
4th	282	W.A.C. Wilkinson & A.P.F. Chapman	MCC	Christchurch	1922/23
5th	235*	G.P. Sulzberger & J.D. Ryder	CD	Napier	2002/03
6th	180	S.A. Thomson & M.N. Hart	ND	Hamilton	1992/93
7th	261	A.D.R. Campbell & P.A. Strang	Zimbabwe	Timaru	1997/98
8th	433	A. Sims & V.T. Trumper	Australia	Christchurch	1913/14
9th	134	J.W. Wilson & N.A. Mallender	Otago	Christchurch	1992/93
10th	184	R.C. Blunt & W. Hawksworth	Otago	Christchurch	1931/32

CENTRAL DISTRICTS

Highest Totals

594-8 dec	v Auckland	Auckland	1995/96
549-8 dec	v Canterbury	Christchurch	1998/99
542-4 dec	v Canterbury	Napier	2002/03
538	v Canterbury	Blenheim	2000/01
526	v Otago	Napier	1995/96
499	v Canterbury	New Plymouth	2004/05
497	v Wellington	Palmerston North	2004/05
485-7 dec	v Wellington	Wellington	1964/65
479	v Northern Districts	Napier	2004/05
475-9 dec	v Canterbury	Christchurch	1995/96

Lowest Totals

50	v Wellington	Upper Hutt	1979/80
51	v Northern Districts	Hamilton	1957/58
59	v Auckland	New Plymouth	1958/59
61	v Auckland	Auckland	1996/97
63	v Wellington	Napier	2003/04
65	v Wellington	Nelson	1995/96
71	v Northern Districts	Wanganui	1962/63
72	v Auckland	Palmerston North	2001/02
74	v Otago	Invercargill	1996/97
78	v Auckland	Auckland	1984/85

Most Appearances

97	Shrimpton M.J.F.
90	O'Sullivan D.R.
85	Duff S.W.
83	Blain T.E.
81	Briasco P.S.
78	Robertson G.K.
76	Douglas M.W
74	Sulzberger G.P.
67	Edwards G.N.
62	Smith C.J.P.
61	Greatbatch M.J.
61	Yuile B.W.
59	Smith I.D.S.
55	Congdon B.E.
55	Jordan A.B.
54	Sinclair M.S.
53	Colquhoun I.A.
53	Toynbee M.H.
53	Schofield R.M.
53	Pierce R.A.

Longest Careers

Seasons		
19	Shrimpton M.J.F.	1961/62-1979/80
17	Jones A.H.	1979/80-1995/96
16	Chapple M.E.	1950/51-1965/66
16	Schofield R.M.	1959/60-1974/75
16	Snook I.R.	1972/73-1987/88
15	Coutts P.J.C.	1958/59-1972/73

Benefits

O'Sullivan D.R.	1984/85
Robertson G.K.	1989/90
Briasco P.S.	1991/92
Blain T.E.	1994/95
Duff S.W.	1995/96
Greatbatch M.J.	1996/97
Douglas M.W.	2000/01

Batting

2000 RUNS	*Career*	*M*	*In*	*NO*	*HS*	*Runs*	*Ave*	*100*
Shrimpton M.J.F.	1961/62-1979/80	97	171	15	150	4551	29.17	5
Blain T.E.	1982/83-1994/95	83	145	15	161	4547	34.97	7
Greatbatch M.J.	1986/87-1999/00	61	107	8	202*	4363	44.07	14
Briasco P.S.	1982/83-1991/92	81	146	16	157	4301	33.08	6
Sinclair M.S.	1995/96-2004/05	54	91	9	203*	3894	47.48	9
Douglas M.W.	1987/88-2000/01	76	132	19	144	3838	33.96	7
Edwards G.N.	1973/74-1984/85	67	122	5	177*	3709	31.70	5
Sulzberger G.P.	1995/96-2004/05	74	120	12	159	3505	32.45	8
Smith C.J.P.	1983/84-1990/91	62	118	9	160*	3499	32.10	7
Crowe M.D.	1983/84-1989/90	32	55	7	242	3299	68.72	13
Duff S.W.	1985/86-1995/96	85	129	29	164*	3079	30.79	1
Spearman C.M.	1996/97-2003/04	44	76	3	144	2951	40.42	5
Congdon B.E.	1960/61-1970/71	55	93	8	202*	2807	33.02	3
Payton D.H.	1965/66-1976/77	49	92	4	145	2459	27.94	3
Pierce R.A.	1971/72-1984/85	53	98	5	100*	2296	24.68	1
Smith I.D.S.	1977/78-1986/87	59	95	12	145	2265	27.28	3
Hart R.T.	1982/83-1990/91	37	68	3	207	2222	34.18	5
Yuile B.W.	1959/60-1971/72	61	90	10	146	2190	27.37	1

CENTURY ON DEBUT FOR PROVINCE

† 117	MacLeod D.N.	v Wellington	Wanganui	1956/57
† 25 & 119	Sampson H.C.	v Wellington	Wellington	1970/71
119 & 0	Crowe M.D.	v Northern Districts	Whangarei	1983/84
112 & 21	Wilson S.W.J.	v Otago	Blenheim	1990/91
124 & 7*	Smith B.F.	v Otago	Wanganui	2000/01

† indicates player was making his first-class debut

HIGHEST INDIVIDUAL INNINGS

242	Crowe M.D.	v Otago	New Plymouth	1989/90
212*	Kelly D.P.	v Canterbury	Blenheim	2000/01
207	Hart R.T.	v Wellington	Wellington	1985/86
203*	Sinclair M.S.	v Northern Districts	Wanganui	1998/99
202*	Congdon B.E.	v Otago	Nelson	1968/69
202*	Greatbatch M.J.	v Otago	Palmerston North	1988/89
202	Greatbatch M.J.	v Northern Districts	Rotorua	1995/96
201*	Smith B.F.	v Canterbury	New Plymouth	2001/02
189	Sinclair M.S.	v Wellington	Masterton	1996/97
184	Taylor R.L.	v Central Districts	PalmerstonNorth	2004/05

MOST RUNS IN A SEASON

		Runs	*Ave*
Crowe M.D.	1986/87	1348	103.69
Smith B.F.	2000/01	939	58.68
Sinclair M.S.	1996/97	722	48.13
Douglas M.W.	1991/92	714	44.62
Briasco P.S.	1990/91	708	41.64
How J.M.	2002/03	704	44.00
Greatbatch M.J.	1986/87	680	48.57
Edwards G.N.	1980/81	679	56.59
Blain T.E.	1984/85	678	48.42
Smith C.J.P.	1985/86	674	39.64
Hart R.T.	1984/85	665	44.32
Twose R.G.	1991/92	653	36.27
Anderson R.W.	1977/78	646	40.37
Blain T.E.	1990/91	644	46.00
Sulzberger G.P.	1999/00	628	48.30
Greatbatch M.J.	1995/96	623	155.75
Spearman C.M.	2002/03	622	38.87
Kelly D.P.	2000/01	617	38.56
Spearman C.M.	2000/01	611	50.91
Smith C.J.P.	1989/90	610	38.12
Briasco P.S.	1988/89	605	46.53

MOST CENTURIES IN A SEASON

6 Crowe M.D. 1986/87

TOTAL NUMBER OF CENTURIES **168**

Most in one season	10	1986/87
1st	Hunter A.A. 108 v Otago	1951/52
100th	Blain T.E. 103* v Otago	1990/91

Bowling

150 WICKETS	*Career*	*M*	*Wkts*	*Runs*	*Ave*	*5WI*	*10WM*	*Best*
O'Sullivan D.R.	1972/73-1984/85	90	392	9560	24.38	21	3	6-40
Yuile B.W.	1959/60-1971/72	61	233	4485	19.24	11	2	9-100
Robertson G.K.	1979/80-1989/90	78	228	6573	28.78	8	1	6-47
Beard D.D.	1950/51-1960/61	49	213	4531	21.27	8	2	7-56
Duff S.W.	1985/86-1995/96	85	208	6856	32.96	4	2	6-36
Hamilton L.J.	1996/97-2004/05	47	168	4293	25.55	6	—	6-32
Jordan A.B.	1968/69-1979/80	55	157	4431	28.22	7	—	7-82
Cave H.B.	1950/51-1958/59	37	150	2962	19.74	7	1	7-31

BEST IN AN INNINGS

9-100	Yuile B.W.	v Canterbury	New Plymouth	1965/66
7-28	Yuile B.W.	v Northern Districts	Hamilton	1967/68
7-31	Cave H.B.	v Auckland	Palmerston North	1952/53
7-33	Cave H.B.	v Northern Districts	New Plymouth	1956/57
7-36	Yuile B.W.	v Otago	Nelson	1962/63
7-36	Schwass A.M.	v Northern Districts	Blenheim	2001/02

BEST IN A MATCH

13-64	Cave H.B.	v Auckland	Palmerston North	1952/53
11-99	Beard D.D.	v Otago	Dunedin	1956/57
11-115	Mason M.J.	v Canterbury	Timaru	2002/03
11-134	Robertson G.K.	v Northern Districts	Nelson	1986/87
11-138	Kay D.J.	v Canterbury	Palmerston North	1976/77

MOST WICKETS IN A SEASON

		Wkts	*Ave*
O'Sullivan D.R.	1978/79	52	19.01
Schwass A.M.	2001/02	45	14.73
O'Sullivan D.R.	1977/78	44	20.22
Blair R.W.	1955/56	42	17.28
Hamilton L.J.	2001/02	42	18.40
O'Sullivan D.R.	1980/81	40	22.00
Mason M.J.	2002/03	40	19.67

Wicketkeeping

100 DISMISSALS	*Career*	*M*	*Caught*	*Stumped*	*Total*
Blain T.E.	1982/83-1994/95	83	124	19	143
Colquhoun I.A.	1953/54-1963/64	53	102	28	130
Smith I.D.S.	1977/78-1986/87	59	119	11	130
Sigley M.A.	1994/95-2002/03	44	124	4	128
Schofield R.M.	1959/60-1974/75	53	107	15	122

MOST DISMISSALS IN A SEASON

31 (31ct) Griggs B.B.J. 2001/02

MOST DISMISSALS IN A MATCH

9 (9ct) Schofield R.M. v Wellington Wellington 1964/65

MOST DISMISSALS IN AN INNINGS

7 (7ct) Schofield R.M. v Wellington Wellington 1964/65

MOST CATCHES IN A MATCH

9 Schofield R.M. v Wellington Wellington 1964/65

MOST CATCHES IN AN INNINGS

7 Schofield R.M. v Wellington Wellington 1964/65

Fielding

MOST CATCHES IN A MATCH

5	Congdon B.E.v Wellington	Wellington	1964/65
5	Congdon B.E. v Otago	New Plymouth	1970/71
5	Smith I.D.S. v Auckland	New Plymouth	1978/79
5	Edwards G.N. v Otago	Palmerston North	1979/80
5	Briasco P.S. v Canterbury	Christchurch	1984/85
5	Douglas M.W. v Otago	Palmerston North	1988/89
5	How J.M. v Canterbury	Palmerston North	2003/04

MOST CATCHES IN AN INNINGS

4	Congdon B.E. v New Zealand XI	New Plymouth	1962/63
4	Neal D.W. v Auckland	Wanganui	1976/77
4	Unwin P.D. v Wellington	New Plymouth	1988/89

Record Partnerships

FOR

Wicket	*Score*	*Batsmen*	*Against*	*At*	*Date*
1st	250	R.T. Hart & C.J.P. Smith	Wellington	Wellington	1985/86
2nd	317	R.T. Hart & P.S. Briasco	Canterbury	New Plymouth	1983/84
3rd	224	M.S. Sinclair & C.M. Spearman	Auckland	Auckland	2003/04
4th	276*	M.D. Crowe & P.S. Briasco	Canterbury	Christchurch	1986/87
5th	301	J.I. Englefield & R.L. Taylor	Wellington	P. North	2004/05
6th	220	M.H. Toynbee & I.D.S. Smith	Auckland	Napier	1982/83
7th	219	B.W. Yuile & B.L. Hampton	Canterbury	Napier	1967/68
8th	173	I.D.S. Smith & G.K. Robertson	ND	Hamilton	1982/83
9th	239	H.B. Cave & I.B. Leggat	Otago	Dunedin	1952/53
10th	133	G.A. Bartlett & I.A. Colquhoun	Auckland	Auckland	1959/60

AGAINST

Wicket	*Score*	*Batsmen*	*For*	*At*	*Date*
1st	316	M.H. Austen & R.T. Hart	Wellington	Wanganui	1993/94
2nd	215	M.D. Bell & M.E. Parlane	Wellington	Napier	2004/05
3rd	227	K.R. Rutherford & B.R. Blair	Otago	Alexandra	1988/89
4th	310	J.D. Ryder & N.R. Parlane	Wellington	P. North	2004/05
5th	341	G.R. Larsen & E.B. McSweeney	Wellington	Levin	1987/88
6th	226	E.J. Gray & R.W. Ormiston	Wellington	Wellington	1981/82
7th	192	S.W. Brown & A.C. Parore	Auckland	Auckland	1990/91
8th	143	C.M. Presland & C.W. Dickeson	ND	Whangarei	1983/84
9th	113	G.J. Hopkins & S.J. Cunis	Canterbury	Christchurch	1998/99
10th	89	M.J.E. Wright & S.J. Scott	ND	Wanganui	1978/79

NORTHERN DISTRICTS

Highest Totals

520-8 dec	v Otago	Hamilton	1987/88
518-4 dec	v Canterbury	Christchurch	1996/97
498-6 dec	v Central Districts	Napier	1992/93
496-8 dec	v Canterbury	Christchurch	2001/02
492	v Auckland	Auckland	1990/91
474	v Wellington	Gisborne	1996/97
472	v Otago	Hamilton	1995/96
460-7 dec	v Otago	Hamilton	2001/02
453-8	v Wellington	Wellington	1995/96
445-9 dec	v Central Districts	Gisborne	2003/04

Lowest Totals

32	v Auckland	Hamilton	1996/97
52	v Canterbury	Hamilton	1966/67
57	v Wellington	Hamilton	1961/62
59	v Canterbury	Hamilton	1960/61
64	v Otago	Dunedin	1971/72
64	v Auckland	Auckland	1987/88
69	v Australia	Hamilton	1973/74
69	v England	Hamilton	1996/97
77	v Auckland	Auckland	2000/01
79	v Auckland	Auckland	1989/90

Most Appearances

115	Bradburn G.E.
104	Roberts A.D.G.
99	White D.J.
95	Hart M.N.
93	Young B.A.
90	Dickeson C.W.
85	Hart R.G.
82	Kuggeleijn C.M.
82	Dunning B.
78	Bailey M.D.
75	Parker J.M.
66	Puna N.
65	Wright M.J.E.
64	Parlane M.E.
64	Yovich J.A.F.
62	Cooper B.G.
60	Marshall J.A.H.
58	Howarth G.P.
57	Petrie E.C.
55	Bradburn W.P.
54	Crocker L.M.
51	Thomson S.A.

Longest Careers

Seasons		
17	Dunning B.	1961/62-1977/78
17	Roberts A.D.G.	1967/68-1983/84
17	Bradburn G.E.	1985/86-2001/02
16	Kuggeleijn C.M.	1975/76-1990/91
15	Giles G.V.	1961/62-1975/76
15	Cooper B.G.	1980/81-1994/95
15	Young B.A.	1983/84-1997/98
15	Hart M.N.	1990/91-2004/05
14	Dickeson C.W.	1973/74-1986/87
14	White D.J.	1979/80-1992/93

Benefits

Kuggeleijn C.M.	1990/91
White D.J.	1992/93
Cooper B.G.	1995/96
Young B.A.	1997/98

Batting

2000 RUNS	*Career*	*M*	*In*	*NO*	*HS*	*Runs*	*Ave*	*100*
Roberts A.D.G.	1967/68-1983/84	104	192	35	128*	5533	35.24	7
White D.J.	1979/80-1992/93	99	173	15	209	4656	29.46	7
Bradburn G.E.	1985/86-2001/02	115	188	23	148*	4614	27.96	4
Parker J.M.	1972/73-1983/84	75	139	19	195	4611	38.42	7
Dunning B.	1961/62-1977/78	82	148	10	142	3898	28.24	3
Young B.A.	1983/84-1997/98	93	148	36	138*	3853	34.40	5
Bailey M.D.	1989/90-2001/02	78	122	8	180*	3468	30.42	6
Kuggeleijn C.M.	1975/76-1990/91	82	138	12	116	3457	27.43	3
Hart M.N.	1990/91-2004/05	95	140	15	201*	3398	27.18	4
Wright J.G.	1975/76-1983/84	43	84	3	145*	3301	40.75	5
Howarth G.P.	1974/75-1985/86	58	105	6	151	3122	31.53	5
Cooper B.G.	1980/81-1994/95	62	110	4	116*	2982	28.13	4
Parlane M.E.	1992/93-2002/03	64	107	6	146	2958	29.28	6
Marshall J.A.H.	1997/98-2004/05	60	102	2	235	2856	28.56	3
Crocker L.M.	1982/83-1988/89	54	100	3	126	2663	27.45	2
Wright M.J.E.	1972/73-1983/84	65	114	10	115	2632	25.30	1
Gibson J.G.	1968/69-1980/81	49	92	5	128	2580	29.65	4

Thomson S.A.	1987/88-1996/97	51	80	20	167	2530	42.16	5
Hart R.G.	1992/93-2003/04	85	119	19	102*	2135	21.35	1
Yovich J.A.F.	1996/97-2004/05	64	99	20	99	2078	26.30	–
Hick G.A.	1987/88-1988/89	17	30	4	211*	2055	79.03	10
Wealleans K.A.	1988/89-1994/95	43	74	4	112*	2053	29.33	4
Bradburn W.P.	1957/58-1968/69	55	103	5	107	2015	20.56	1

CENTURY ON DEBUT FOR PROVINCE

118	McGregor P.B.	v Auckland	Hamilton	1962/63
† 127*	Mitchell W.J.	v Pakistan	Hamilton	1964/65
14 & 153*	Maynard M.P.	v Auckland	Hamilton	1990/91

† indicates player was making his first-class debut

HIGHEST INDIVIDUAL INNINGS

235	Marshall J.A.H.	v Canterbury	Christchurch	2001/02
212*	Styris S.B.	v Otago	Hamilton	2001/02
211*	Hick G.A.	v Auckland	Auckland	1988/89
209	White D.J.	v Central Districts	Hamilton	1985/86
201*	Hart M.N.	v Auckland	Auckland	2002/03
195	Parker J.M.	v Canterbury	Whangarei	1972/73
195	Maynard M.P.	v Auckland	Auckland	1991/92
194*	White D.J.	v Central Districts	Wanganui	1990/91
180*	Bailey M.D.	v Otago	Hamilton	1997/98
177*	Turner G.M.	v Central Districts	Napier	1976/77

MOST RUNS IN A SEASON

		Runs	*Ave*			*Runs*	*Ave*
Hick G.A.	1988/89	1228	94.46	Wright J.G.	1981/82	672	51.69
Maynard M.P.	1991/92	893	68.69	Styris S.B.	2001/02	662	44.13
Hick G.A.	1987/88	827	63.61	Parker J.M.	1979/80	640	49.23
Bradburn G.E.	1989/90	726	36.30	Parker J.M.	1981/82	618	103.00
Wealleans K.A.	1989/90	721	36.05	Wealleans K.A.	1990/91	613	40.86
Marshall J.A.H.	2001/02	706	39.22	Wright J.G.	1978/79	612	50.91
Wright J.G.	1979/80	694	43.43	White D.J.	1990/91	609	40.60
Turner G.M.	1976/77	672	67.20	Thomson S.A.	1990/91	602	60.20

MOST CENTURIES IN A SEASON

6 Hick G.A. 1988/89

TOTAL NUMBER OF CENTURIES		**128**
Most in one season	9	1988/89
1st	Everest J.K. 104 v Canterbury	1956/57
100th	Parlane M.E. 132* v Canterbury	1995/96

Bowling

150 WICKETS	*Career*	*M*	*Wkts*	*Runs*	*Ave*	*5WI*	*10WM*	*Best*
Dickeson C.W.	1973/74-1986/87	90	282	8242	29.22	9	2	7-79
Bradburn G.E.	1985/86-2001/02	115	231	7302	31.61	3	—	6-56
Puna N.	1956/57-1968/69	66	224	5314	23.72	11	—	6-25
Yovich J.A.F.	1996/97-2004/05	64	185	5643	30.50	7	1	7-64
de Groen R.P.	1990/91-1995/96	38	157	3320	21.14	8	2	7-50

BEST IN AN INNINGS

9-48	Tait A.R.	v Auckland	Hamilton	1996/97
8-21	Langdon M.C.	v Auckland	Auckland	1963/64
8-30	Alabaster G.D.	v NZ Under 23 XI	Hamilton	1962/63
8-37	Clarke D.B.	v Central Districts	Wanganui	1962/63
8-49	Kennedy K.D.	v Central Districts	Hamilton	1969/70

BEST IN A MATCH

16-130	Tait A.R.	v Auckland	Hamilton	1996/97
13-99	de Groen R.P.	v Otago	Alexandra	1992/93
12-55	Martin B.P.	v Auckland	Taupo	1999/00
12-109	Lissette A.F.	v Otago	Dunedin	1959/60
11-66	Tuffey D.R.	v Wellington	Hamilton	2000/01

MOST WICKETS IN A SEASON

		Wkts	*Ave*
Tait A.R.	1996/97	53	16.32
de Groen R.P.	1992/93	46	16.84
Yovich J.A.F.	2001/02	40	26.45

Wicketkeeping

100 DISMISSALS	*Career*	*M*	*Caught*	*Stumped*	*Total*
Hart R.G.	1992/93-2003/04	85	228	15	243
Young B.A.	1983/84-1997/98	93	179	11	190
Wright M.J.E.	1972/73-1983/84	65	104	17	121
Petrie E.C.	1956/57-1966/67	57	90	22	112

MOST DISMISSALS IN A SEASON

34 (33ct/1st) Hart R.G. 2001/02

MOST DISMISSALS IN A MATCH

9 (9ct) Young B.A. v Canterbury Christchurch 1986/87

MOST DISMISSALS IN AN INNINGS

7 (7ct) Young B.A. v Canterbury Christchurch 1986/87

MOST CATCHES IN A MATCH

9 Young B.A. v Canterbury Christchurch 1986/87

MOST CATCHES IN AN INNINGS

7 Young B.A. v Canterbury Christchurch 1986/87

Fielding

MOST CATCHES IN A MATCH

6 Young B.A. v Wellington Wellington 1995/96

MOST CATCHES IN AN INNINGS

4	Pairaudeau B.H. v Central Districts	Wanganui	1962/63
4	Harris S.J. (sub) v Otago	Dunedin	1965/66
4	Barton P.H. v Canterbury	Hamilton	1974/75
4	Young B.A. v Wellington	Wellington	1995/96
4	Bailey M.D. v Otago	Alexandra	1996/97

Record Partnerships

FOR

Wicket	Score	Batsmen	Against	At	Date
1st	165	J.G. Wright & G.M. Turner	Wellington	Lower Hutt	1976/77
2nd	237	J.G. Gibson & C.M. Kuggeleijn	Canterbury	Hamilton	1980/81
3rd	261*	M.P. Maynard & S.A. Thomson	Auckland	Hamilton	1990/91
4th	259	G.E. Bradburn & M.E. Parlane	Canterbury	Christchurch	1996/97
5th	149	K.A. Wealleans & B.A. Young	Wellington	Wellington	1991/92
6th	216	M.N. Hart & H.J.H. Marshall	CD	Napier	2004/05
7th	136	D.J. Nash & A.R. Tait	CD	Masterton	1997/98
8th	152	G.E. Bradburn & S.B. Doull	Canterbury	Christchurch	1991/92
9th	188	N.R. Parlane & D.R. Tuffey	Wellington	Wellington	1999/00
10th	97	R.G. Hart & G.L. West	Otago	Hamilton	2002/03

AGAINST

Wicket	Score	Batsmen	For	At	Date
1st	310	R.H. Vance & B.A. Edgar	Wellington	Wellington	1988/89
2nd	263	M.J. Greatbatch & M.D. Crowe	CD	Morrinsville	1986/87
3rd	394*	P.G. Kennedy & R.T. Latham	Canterbury	Rotorua	1990/91
4th	280	J.J. Crowe & D.N. Patel	Auckland	Auckland	1991/92
5th	347*	M.J. Horne & A.C. Barnes	Auckland	Auckland	2003/04
6th	175	S.P. Fleming & L.K. Germon	Canterbury	Hamilton	1993/94
7th	205	L.K. Germon & M.W. Priest	Canterbury	Christchurch	1991/92
8th	210	G.R. Stead & S.E. Bond	Canterbury	Christchurch	2004/05
9th	116	V. Pollard & R.O. Collinge	CD	Palmerston North	1964/65
10th	160	L.K. Germon & W.A. Wisneski	Canterbury	Rangiora	1997/98

OTAGO

Highest Totals

602-8 dec	v Canterbury	Dunedin	1928/29
589	v Canterbury	Christchurch	1931/32
571-8	v Central Districts	Napier	1995/96
558-8 dec	v Auckland	Dunedin	1949/50
548-7 dec	v Auckland	Dunedin	1996/97
543-8 dec	v Central Districts	New Plymouth	1978/79
521-7 dec	v Auckland	Auckland	1950/51
505	v Central Districts	Palmerston North	1999/00
500	v Canterbury	Christchurch	1952/53
495	v Wellington	Dunedin	1923/24

Lowest Totals

34	v Wellington	Dunedin	1956/57
35	v Auckland	Christchurch	1884/85
36	v New South Wales	Dunedin	1889/90
40	v Canterbury	Dunedin	1869/70
41	v Auckland	Dunedin	1873/74
42	v Canterbury	Dunedin	1871/72
43	v Canterbury	Christchurch	1872/73
44	v Canterbury	Dunedin	1904/05
46	v Pakistan	Dunedin	1978/79
47	v Canterbury	Christchurch	1888/89
49	v Canterbury	Christchurch	1870/71

Most Appearances

108	Lees W.K.	69	Alabaster G.D.	60	Milburn B.D.
90	Blair B.R.	68	Cameron F.J.	59	Smith L.D.
90	McGregor S.N.	68	Rutherford K.R.	59	Turner G.M.
88	Boock S.L.	66	Lawson R.A.	57	Burns K.J.
81	Blair W.L.	65	Alabaster J.C.	55	Mills G.H.
80	Hoskin R.N.	63	Rutherford I.A.	54	Moir A.M.
78	Mallender N.A.	61	Campbell K.O.	54	Dobbs P.W.
75	McCullum S.J.	60	Sutcliffe B.	51	Knight A.R.
75	Gaffaney C.B.				

Longest Careers

Seasons			*Seasons*		
27	Downes A.D.	1887/88-1913/14	22	McGregor S.N.	1947/48-1968/69
26	Knight A.R.	1918/19-1943/44	21	Groves L.J.	1929/30-1949/50
24	Siedeberg H.G.	1898/99-1921/22	21	Alabaster G.D.	1955/56-1975/76
24	Blair W.L.	1967/68-1990/91	20	Fisher A.H.	1890/91-1909/10
23	Torrance R.C.	1905/06-1927/28	20	Watt L.	1943/44-1962/63
23	Smith L.D.	1934/35-1956/57	20	Milburn B.D.	1963/64-1982/83
23	Mills G.H.	1935/36-1957/58			

Benefits

Lees W.K.	1987/88	Boock S.L.	1989/90	Mallender N.A.	1992/93

Batting

2000 RUNS	*Career*	*M*	*In*	*NO*	*HS*	*Runs*	*Ave*	*100*
Sutcliffe B.	1946/47-1961/62	60	110	8	385	6028	59.09	17
Blair B.R.	1977/78-1989/90	90	154	5	143	5057	33.93	7
Rutherford K.R.	1982/83-1994/95	68	121	7	226*	5051	44.30	14
Turner G.M.	1964/65-1982/83	59	109	14	186*	4439	46.72	13
Gaffaney C.B.	1995/96-2004/05	75	138	11	194	4326	34.06	7
McGregor S.N.	1947/48-1968/69	90	167	13	114*	4259	27.65	3
Lees W.K.	1972/73-1987/88	108	179	31	124	3754	25.36	4
Blair W.L.	1967/68-1990/91	81	149	9	140	3654	26.10	2
Hoskin R.N.	1980/81-1992/93	80	138	6	157	3573	27.06	6
McCullum S.J.	1976/77-1990/91	75	131	1	134	3174	24.41	2
Rutherford I.A.	1974/75-1983/84	63	115	3	222	3122	27.87	4
Richardson M.H.	1992/93-2000/01	49	89	10	166	3089	39.10	8
Lawson R.A.	1992/93-2003/04	66	120	5	200	2890	25.13	2
Cumming C.D.	2000/01-2004/05	42	79	9	128	2779	39.70	8
Burns K.J.	1980/81-1991/92	57	98	6	136	2699	29.33	3
Campbell K.O.	1963/64-1978/79	61	108	17	111	2613	28.71	3
Dobbs P.W.	1988/89-1994/95	54	99	6	144*	2606	28.02	3
Alabaster G.D.	1955/56-1975/76	69	108	16	108	2340	25.43	3
Smith L.D.	1934/35-1956/57	59	108	16	109	2277	24.75	1
Knight A.R.	1918/19-1943/44	51	97	3	152	2245	23.88	1

CENTURY ON DEBUT FOR PROVINCE

107 & 38	Patrick W.R.	v Canterbury	Christchurch	1917/18
† 157*	McMullan J.J.M.	v Southland	Dunedin	1917/18
172 & 16	Worker R.V.de R.	v Canterbury	Christchurch	1923/24
35 & 133	Blamires E.O.	v Canterbury	Christchurch	1923/24
† 15 & 105	Watt D.G.	v Canterbury	Christchurch	1943/44
157	Hadlee W.A.	v Auckland	Dunedin	1945/46

197 & 128	Sutcliffe B.	v MCC	Dunedin	1946/47
124 & 90	Horne M.J.	v Central Districts	Wanganui	1996/97

† indicates player was making his first-class debut

HIGHEST INDIVIDUAL INNINGS

385	Sutcliffe B.	v Canterbury	Christchurch	1952/53
355	Sutcliffe B.	v Auckland	Dunedin	1949/50
338*	Blunt R.C.	v Canterbury	Christchurch	1931/32
275	Sutcliffe B.	v Auckland	Auckland	1950/51
264	Sutcliffe B.	v Central Districts	Dunedin	1959/60
241	Horne M.J.	v Auckland	Auckland	1997/98
226*	Rutherford K.R.	v India	Dunedin	1989/90
222	Rutherford I.A.	v Central Districts	New Plymouth	1978/79
221	Blunt R.C.	v Canterbury	Dunedin	1928/29
201	Reid J.R.	v Canterbury	Dunedin	1957/58
201	Sutcliffe B.	v Northern Districts	Hamilton	1960/61
200	Lawson R.A.	v Central Districts	Napier	1995/96

MOST RUNS IN A SEASON

		Runs	*Ave*
Turner G.M.	1975/76	1027	85.58
Blair B.R.	1989/90	759	47.43
Cumming C.D.	2002/03	751	46.93
Rutherford K.R.	1989/90	747	67.90
Sutcliffe B.	1952/53	709	78.77
Turner G.M.	1974/75	703	78.11
Blair B.R.	1982/83	680	52.30
Richardson M.H.	2000/01	675	56.25
Rutherford K.R.	1991/92	655	50.38
Sutcliffe B.	1950/51	651	72.38
Mohammad Wasim	2002/03	651	40.68
Gaffaney C.B.	1996/97	642	40.12
Horne M.J.	2000/01	641	40.06
Rutherford K.R.	1985/86	638	53.16
Cumming C.D.	2000/01	626	44.71
Rutherford I.A.	1976/77	625	48.67
Blair B.R.	1986/87	621	47.76
Richardson M.H.	1995/96	615	68.33
Gaffaney C.B.	2001/02	609	30.45
Jones A.H.	1984/85	608	55.27
Dobbs P.W.	1990/91	603	50.25

MOST CENTURIES IN A SEASON

4	Turner G.M.	1974/75
4	Turner G.M.	1975/76

TOTAL NUMBER OF CENTURIES		**196**
Most in one season	9	2002/03
1st	Baker J.C. 103 v Hawke's Bay	1901/02
100th	Cairns B.L. 110 v Wellington	1979/80

Bowling

150 WICKETS	*Career*	*M*	*Wkts*	*Runs*	*Ave*	*5WI*	*10WM*	*Best*
Boock S.L.	1973/74-1989/90	88	399	8235	20.63	28	5	8-57
Downes A.D.	1887/88-1913/14	44	287	3902	13.59	33	13	8-35
Moir A.M.	1949/50-1961/62	54	282	5926	21.01	20	5	8-37
Mallender N.A.	1983/84-1992/93	78	268	5433	20.27	14	3	7-27
Alabaster J.C.	1956/57-1971/72	65	264	5738	21.73	14	3	6-39
Cameron F.J.	1953/54-1966/67	68	258	5204	20.17	9	—	6-21
Alabaster G.D.	1955/56-1975/76	69	205	4774	23.28	13	1	7-74
Fisher A.H.	1890/91-1909/10	40	176	2766	15.71	9	1	9-50
O'Connor S.B.	1994/95-2002/03	35	160	3321	20.75	11	2	6-31
Sewell D.G.	1995/96-2004/05	49	159	4588	28.85	7	1	8-31

BEST IN AN INNINGS

9-50	Fisher A.H.	v Queensland	Dunedin	1896/97
9-72	Cooke F.H.	v Canterbury	Christchurch	1884/85
9-93	Petherick P.J.	v Northern Districts	Dunedin	1975/76
8-28	Hendley W.	v Canterbury	Dunedin	1869/70
8-31	Sewell D.G.	v Central Districts	Invercargill	1996/97
8-35	Downes A.D.	v Canterbury	Dunedin	1891/92
8-37	Moir A.M.	v Northern Districts	Hamilton	1958/59
8-46	Cairns B.L.	v Wellington	Invercargill	1978/79
8-55	Moir A.M.	v Canterbury	Dunedin	1951/52
8-57	Boock S.L.	v Auckland	Dunedin	1989/90
8-59	Boock S.L.	v Wellington	Invercargill	1978/79
8-61	Cooke F.H.	v Canterbury	Christchurch	1882/83
8-66	Wiseman P.J.	v Wellington	Wellington	1996/97
8-70	Hay W.A.	v Southland	Dunedin	1917/18
8-99	Blunt R.C.	v Auckland	Dunedin	1930/31
8-119	Moir A.M.	v Central Districts	New Plymouth	1953/54
8-136	Shacklock F.J.	v Canterbury	Christchurch	1903/04

BEST IN A MATCH

15-94	Cooke F.H.	v Canterbury	Christchurch	1882/83
15-104	Boock S.L.	v Auckland	Dunedin	1989/90
15-203	Moir A.M.	v Central Districts	New Plymouth	1953/54
14-93	Torrance R.C.	v Hawke's Bay	Napier	1908/09
14-103	Downes A.D.	v Hawke's Bay	Dunedin	1893/94
14-126	Moir A.M.	v Canterbury	Dunedin	1951/52
13-111	Downes A.D.	v Hawke's Bay	Dunedin	1901/02
13-144	Boock S.L.	v Northern Districts	Whangarei	1980/81

MOST WICKETS IN A SEASON

		Wkts	*Ave*
Boock S.L.	1978/79	54	18.51
Mallender N.A.	1991/92	49	12.30
Boock S.L.	1986/87	48	15.48
Petherick P.J.	1977/78	45	17.15
Petherick P.J.	1975/76	42	20.16
O'Connor S.B.	2002/03	42	18.71
Moir A.M.	1953/54	41	17.58
Boock S.L.	1980/81	41	18.46
Boock S.L.	1987/88	41	21.82
Webb M.G.	1973/74	40	14.65
Cairns B.L.	1978/79	40	22.70

Wicketkeeping

100 DISMISSALS	*Career*	*M*	*Caught*	*Stumped*	*Total*
Lees W.K.	1972/73-1987/88	108	208	36	244
Milburn B.D.	1963/64-1982/83	60	148	17	165
Croy M.G.	1994/95-2001/02	42	127	4	131
Robinson S.A.	1984/85-1996/97	45	117	5	122
Mills G.H.	1935/36-1957/58	55	78	29	107

MOST DISMISSALS IN A SEASON

38 (37ct/1st) Hopkins G.J. 2004/05

MOST DISMISSALS IN A MATCH

10 (10ct) Hopkins G.J. v Canterbury Dunedin 2004/05

MOST DISMISSALS IN AN INNINGS

7 (7ct) Croy M.G. v Auckland Auckland 2001/02

MOST CATCHES IN A MATCH

10 Hopkins G.J. v Canterbury Dunedin 2004/05

MOST CATCHES IN AN INNINGS

7	Croy M.G. v Auckland	Auckland	2001/02

Fielding

MOST CATCHES IN A MATCH

5	Watson E.A. v Canterbury	Dunedin	1953/54
5	Lees W.K. v Wellington	Wellington	1973/74
5	McCullum S.J. v Auckland	Dunedin	1987/88
5	Burns K.J. v Northern Districts	Dunedin	1990/91
5	McCullum N.J. v Auckland	Dunedin	2004/05

MOST CATCHES IN AN INNINGS

4	Geddes A.E. v Canterbury	Christchurch	1903/04
4	Watson E.A. v Canterbury	Dunedin	1953/54
4	Campbell K.O. v Auckland	Dunedin	1969/70
4	Blair W.L. v Canterbury	Invercargill	1977/78
4	Blair W.L. v Northern Districts	Dunedin	1978/79
4	McCullum S.J. v Auckland	Dunedin	1987/88
4	Dobbs P.W. v India	Dunedin	1989/90
4	Burns K.J. v Northern Districts	Dunedin	1990/91
4	Gaffaney C.B. v Wellington	Wellington	1996/97
4	McCullum N.J. v Auckland	Dunedin	2004/05

Record Partnerships

FOR

Wicket	*Score*	*Batsmen*	*Against*	*At*	*Date*
1st	373	B. Sutcliffe & L. Watt	Auckland	Auckland	1950/51
2nd	254	K.J. Burns & K.R. Rutherford	Wellington	Oamaru	1987/88
3rd	227	K.R. Rutherford & B.R. Blair	CD	Alexandra	1988/89
4th	235	K.J. Burns & R.N. Hoskin	ND	Hamilton	1987/88
5th	266	B. Sutcliffe & W.S. Haig	Auckland	Dunedin	1949/50
6th	165	G.M. Turner & W.K. Lees	Wellington	Wellington	1975/76
7th	182	B. Sutcliffe & A.W. Gilbertson	Canterbury	Christchurch	1952/53
8th	165*	J.N. Crawford & A.G. Eckhold	Wellington	Wellington	1914/15
9th	208	W.C. McSkimming & B.E. Scott	Auckland	Auckland	2004/05
10th	184	R.C. Blunt & W. Hawksworth	Canterbury	Christchurch	1931/32

AGAINST

Wicket	*Score*	*Batsmen*	*For*	*At*	*Date*
1st	299	M.D. Bell & R.A. Jones	Wellington	Dunedin	2001/02
2nd	227	W.A. Baker & H.H.L. Kortlang	Wellington	Dunedin	1923/24
3rd	445	P.E. Whitelaw & W.N. Carson	Auckland	Dunedin	1936/37
4th	274	R.A. Jones & S.R. Mather	Wellington	Wellington	2000/01
5th	255	B.R. Taylor & J.V. Coney	Wellington	Dunedin	1972/73
6th	293*	P.G. Fulton & N.T. Broom	Canterbury	Dunedin	2004/05
7th	265	J.L. Powell & N. Dorreen	Canterbury	Christchurch	1929/30
8th	215	J.R. Murray & A.C. Cummins	West Indies	Dunedin	1994/95
9th	239	H.B. Cave & I.B. Leggat	CD	Dunedin	1952/53
10th	138	K.C. James & A.W.S. Brice	Wellington	Wellington	1926/27

WELLINGTON

Highest Totals

608-9 dec	v Northern Districts	Hamilton	1998/99
595	v Auckland	Wellington	1927/28
590-8 dec	v Central Districts	Palmerston North	2004/05
575-7 dec	v Otago	Wellington	1951/52
569	v Auckland	Wellington	1923/24
560	v Otago	Dunedin	1923/24
553	v Canterbury	Wellington	1931/32
544	v Canterbury	Christchurch	1997/98
508	v Northern Districts	Wellington	2000/01
506-4 dec	v Central Districts	Wanganui	1993/94

Lowest Totals

19	v Nelson	Nelson	1885/86
22	v Canterbury	Wellington	1903/04
29	v Nelson	Nelson	1879/80
30	v Nelson	Nelson	1883/84
31	v Nelson	Nelson	1887/88
34	v Canterbury	Wellington	1886/87
35	v Auckland	Wellington	1873/74
36	v Nelson	Nelson	1885/86
37	v Nelson	Nelson	1876/77
42	v New South Wales	Wellington	1895/96
42	v Otago	Wellington	1945/46
45	v Nelson	Wellington	1880/81
48	v Nelson	Nelson	1887/88

Most Appearances

120	Gray E.J.
119	Vance R.H.
102	McSweeney E.B.
89	Morrison J.F.M.
87	Edgar B.A.
84	Chatfield E.J.
79	Larsen G.R.
74	Coney J.V.
72	Wells J.D.
68	Sinclair B.W.
68	Nevin C.J.
64	Murray B.A.G.
60	Newdick G.A.
59	Blair R.W.
58	Reid J.R.
58	Ritchie T.D.
57	Bell M.D.
56	Brice A.W.S.
54	Bilby G.P.
54	McGirr H.M.
52	Cederwall B.W.
50	Butler L.C.

Longest Careers

Seasons		
29	Luckie M.M.F.	1891/92-1919/20
27	Dempster C.S.	1921/22-1947/48
25	Tucker K.H.	1895/96-1919/20
24	James K.C.	1923/24-1946/47
22	Hutchings J.H.	1903/04-1924/25
22	Collins D.C.	1905/06-1926/27
22	Reaney T.P.L.	1927/28-1948/49
20	McGirr H.M.	1913/14-1932/33
20	Lamason J.R.	1927/28-1946/47

Benefits

Morrison J.F.M.	1983/84
Chatfield E.J.	1985/86
Coney J.V.	1986/87
Edgar B.A.	1987/88
Gray E.J.	1989/90
Vance R.H.	1990/91
McSweeney E.B.	1991/92
Larsen G.R.	1996/97

Batting

2000 RUNS	Career	M	In	NO	HS	Runs	Ave	100
Edgar B.A.	1975/76-1989/90	87	160	13	162	6494	44.17	15
Vance R.H.	1976/77-1990/91	119	205	18	254*	6440	34.43	12
Morrison J.F.M.	1967/68-1983/84	89	160	22	180*	4694	34.01	6
Reid J.R.	1947/48-1964/65	58	102	8	296	4538	48.27	13
McSweeney E.B.	1981/82-1993/94	102	153	23	205*	4296	33.04	5
Gray E.J.	1975/76-1991/92	120	181	38	128*	4228	29.56	5
Murray B.A.G.	1958/59-1972/73	64	116	9	213	3753	35.07	3
Sinclair B.W.	1955/56-1970/71	68	116	14	148	3583	35.12	2
Bell M.D.	1997/98-2004/05	57	103	8	219	3873	40.76	11
Hiddleston J.S.	1913/14-1928/29	41	75	1	212	3413	46.12	8
Coney J.V.	1971/72-1986/87	74	126	21	120*	3251	30.96	4
Newdick G.A.	1970/71-1980/81	60	112	6	143	3236	30.52	4
Nevin C.J.	1995/96-2004/05	68	106	17	143*	3083	34.64	3
McGirr H.M.	1913/14-1932/33	54	97	4	141	3032	32.60	5
Wells J.D.	1989/90-2000/01	72	113	18	115	3016	31.74	5
Jones A.H.	1985/86-1993/94	39	67	11	181*	2978	53.17	7
Larsen G.R.	1984/85-1998/99	79	118	25	161	2938	31.59	2
Bilby G.P.	1962/63-1976/77	54	95	11	161	2852	33.95	3
Dempster C.S.	1921/22-1947/48	40	76	3	154	2602	35.64	4
Ritchie T.D.	1982/83-1990/91	58	92	14	106	2494	31.97	3
Tindill E.W.T.	1932/33-1949/50	39	73	5	149	2442	35.91	6
Jones R.A.	2000/01-2003/04	36	63	4	188	2343	39.71	7
Burnett G.P.	1987/88-1992/93	44	80	13	203*	2029	30.28	1

CENTURY ON DEBUT FOR PROVINCE

163	Williams A.B.	v Canterbury	Christchurch	1896/97
110 & 5*	Crawford J.N.	v Auckland	Auckland	1917/18
113 & 53	Kortlang H.H.L.	v Auckland	Wellington	1922/23
117 & 6	Bernau E.H.L.	v Auckland	Wellington	1922/23
† 106 & 0	Tindill E.W.T.	v Auckland	Auckland	1932/33
† 110	Ongley J.A.	v Otago	Wellington	1938/39
† 27 & 141*	Smith K.F.H.	v Central Districts	Wellington	1953/54
† 132 & 2*	Bilby G.P.	v Central Districts	Wellington	1962/63
† 39 & 156*	Aiken J.M.	v Canterbury	Christchurch	1989/90
115	Fleming S.P.	v Central Districts	Wellington	2001/02

† indicates player was making his first-class debut

HIGHEST INDIVIDUAL INNINGS

296	Reid J.R.	v Northern Districts	Wellington	1962/63
283	Reid J.R.	v Otago	Wellington	1952/53
254*	Vance R.H.	v Northern Districts	Wellington	1988/89
236	Ryder J.D.	v Central Districts	Palmerston North	2004/05
222*	Midlane F.A.	v Otago	Wellington	1914/15
219	Bell M.D.	v Northern Districts	Hamilton	1998/99
216	Bell M.D.	v Auckland	Auckland	1997/98
214*	Kortlang H.H.L.	v Auckland	Wellington	1921/26
213	Murray B.A.G.	v Otago	Dunedin	1968/69
212	Hiddleston J.S.	v Canterbury	Wellington	1925/26
205*	McSweeney E.B.	v Central Districts	Levin	1987/88
204	Hiddleston J.S.	v Auckland	Wellington	1925/26
203*	Burnett G.P.	v Northern Districts	Hamilton	1991/92
203	Parlane M.E.	v Auckland	Auckland	2004/05
202	Austen M.H.	v Central Districts	Wanganui	1993/94

MOST RUNS IN A SEASON

		Runs	Ave
Vance R.H.	1988/89	888	80.72
Jones R.A.	2000/01	849	47.16
Bell M.D.	2000/01	844	52.75
Edgar B.A.	1988/89	762	63.50
Edgar B.A.	1978/79	728	45.50
Jones R.A.	2002/03	726	45.37
Edgar B.A.	1989/90	720	40.00
Twose R.G.	1994/95	720	80.00
Jones A.H.	1988/89	701	87.62
Edgar B.A.	1987/88	676	52.00
Parlane M.E.	2004/05	646	43.06
Vance R.H.	1987/88	638	79.65
Jones A.H.	1986/87	627	62.70
Ryder J.D.	2004/05	625	44.64

MOST CENTURIES IN A SEASON

5 Bell M.D. 2000/01

TOTAL NUMBER OF CENTURIES		**244**
Most in one season	10	1988/89, 1994/95, 2000/01
1st	Heenan G.C. 146* v Hawke's Bay	1886/87
100th	Sinclair B.W. 102* v Northern Districts	1963/64
200th	Chandler P.J.B. 177 v Auckland	1996/97

Bowling

150 WICKETS	Career	M	Wkts	Runs	Ave	5WI	10WM	Best
Chatfield E.J.	1973/74-1989/90	84	403	7531	18.68	23	7	8-24
Gray E.J.	1975/76-1991/92	120	357	9778	27.38	13	3	8-37
Blair R.W.	1951/52-1964/65	59	330	5004	15.16	30	10	9-72
Brice A.W.S.	1902/03-1927/28	56	229	4684	20.45	17	7	9-67
Upham E.F.	1892/93-1909/10	40	227	3393	14.94	17	2	7-24
Reid J.R.	1947/48-1964/65	58	172	3115	18.11	10	—	7-29
McGirr H.M.	1913/14-1932/33	54	166	4326	26.06	7	1	7-45
Morrison B.D.	1953/54-1964/65	45	163	3858	23.66	7	2	7-42

BEST IN AN INNINGS

9-67	Brice A.W.S.	v Auckland	Wellington	1918/19
9-72	Blair R.W.	v Auckland	Wellington	1956/57
9-75	Blair R.W.	v Canterbury	Wellington	1956/57
8-13	Firth J.P.	v Hawke's Bay	Wellington	1883/84
8-21	Penn A.J.	v Canterbury	Wellington	2001/02
8-24	Chatfield E.J.	v Northern Districts	Lower Hutt	1979/80
8-34	Fisher F.E.	v Canterbury	Wellington	1952/53
8-36	Blair R.W.	v Otago	Dunedin	1952/53
8-37	Gray E.J.	v Canterbury	Lower Hutt	1985/86
8-50	Butler L.C.	v NZ Under 23 XI	Wellington	1965/66
8-58	Ashbolt F.L.	v Hawke's Bay	Napier	1897/98
8-59	Hiddleston J.S.	v Canterbury	Christchurch	1918/19
8-64	Collinge R.O.	v Auckland	Auckland	1967/68
8-78	Gray E.J.	v Auckland	Wellington	1989/90
8-83	Chatfield E.J.	v Otago	Dunedin	1986/87

BEST IN A MATCH

14-136	Blair R.W.	v Canterbury	Wellington	1956/57
14-151	Gray E.J.	v Canterbury	Lower Hutt	1985/86
13-58	Salmon I.J.	v Nelson	Wellington	1873/74
13-86	Chatfield E.J.	v West Indies	Lower Hutt	1979/80
13-91	Gore A.H.	v Hawke's Bay	Napier	1886/87
13-92	Middleton F.S.	v Hawke's Bay	Wellington	1919/20
13-97	Ashbolt F.L.	v Hawke's Bay	Napier	1897/98
13-157	Tucker K.H.	v Auckland	Wellington	1900/01
13-176	Brice A.W.S.	v Auckland	Wellington	1920/21

MOST WICKETS IN A SEASON

		Wkts	Ave
Chatfield E.J.	1979/80	49	10.51
Gray E.J.	1984/85	48	21.75
Chatfield E.J.	1981/82	47	16.87
Blair R.W.	1956/57	46	9.47
Walker M.D.J.	2002/03	45	18.00
Saunders J.V.	1913/14	41	17.58
Chatfield E.J.	1976/77	41	19.48
O'Brien I.E.	2000/01	41	19.68
Penn A.J.	2001/02	40	18.30

Wicketkeeping

100 DISMISSALS	*Career*	*M*	*Caught*	*Stumped*	*Total*
McSweeney E.B.	1981/82-1993/94	102	289	39	328
Nevin C.J.	1995/95-2004/05	68	190	7	197
Therkleson I.J.	1966/67-1973/74	39	93	7	100

MOST DISMISSALS IN A SEASON

46 (46ct) Nevin C.J. 2000/01

MOST DISMISSALS IN A MATCH

10	(10ct)	Nevin C.J. v Otago	Dunedin	1995/96

MOST DISMISSALS IN AN INNINGS

6	(6ct)	Vance R.H. v Otago	Wellington	1977/78
6	(5ct 1st)	Nevin C.J. v Central Districts	Nelson	1995/96

MOST CATCHES IN A MATCH

10	Nevin C.J. v Otago	Dunedin	1995/96

MOST CATCHES IN AN INNINGS

6	Vance R.H. v Otago	Wellington	1977/78

Fielding

MOST CATCHES IN A MATCH

7	Morrison J.F.M. v Northern Districts	Wellington	1980/81

MOST CATCHES IN AN INNINGS

5	Lamason J.R. v Otago	Dunedin	1937/38
5	Morrison J.F.M. v Northern Districts	Wellington	1980/81

Record Partnerships

FOR

Wicket	*Score*	*Batsmen*	*Against*	*At*	*Date*
1st	333	B.A. Edgar & A.H. Jones	Auckland	Wellington	1988/89
2nd	287	M.D. Bell & J.D. Wells	Auckland	Auckland	1997/98
3rd	346	G.P. Burnett & R.A. Verry	ND	Hamilton	1991/92
4th	310	J.D. Ryder & N.R. Parlane	CD	P. North	2004/05
5th	341	G.R. Larsen & E.B. McSweeney	CD	Levin	1987/88
6th	226	E.J. Gray & R.W. Ormiston	CD	Wellington	1981/82
7th	250	C.J. Nevin & M.D.J. Walker	Otago	Wellington	2003/04
8th	180	R.G. Twose & M.C. Goodson	Otago	Dunedin	1994/95
9th	127	F.L.H. Mooney & R.A. Buchan	Auckland	Wellington	1943/44
10th	138	K.C. James & A.W.S. Brice	Otago	Wellington	1926/27

AGAINST

Wicket	*Score*	*Batsmen*	*For*	*At*	*Date*
1st	287	B.R. Hartland & G.R. Stead	Canterbury	Christchurch	1994/95
2nd	254	K.J. Burns & K.R. Rutherford	Otago	Oamaru	1987/88
3rd	213	G.M. Turner & B.E. Congdon	Otago	Dunedin	1972/73
4th	278	A.W. Roberts & M.L. Page	Canterbury	Wellington	1931/32
5th	301	J.I. Englefield & R.L. Taylor	CD	P. North	2004/05
6th	209	C.Z. Harris & A.J. Redmond	Canterbury	Rangiora	2001/02
7th	241	N.J. Astle & M.W. Priest	Canterbury	Christchurch	1994/95
8th	189	W.N. Carson & A.M. Matheson	Auckland	Auckland	1938/39
9th	188	N.R. Parlane & D.R. Tuffey	ND	Wellington	1999/00
10th	97	A.C. Kerr & H.C. Nottman	Auckland	Auckland	1941/42

INTER-PROVINCIAL RECORDS

AUCKLAND v CANTERBURY

First match	*Played*	*Won by Auckland*	*Won by Canterbury*	*Drawn*
1873/74	121	45	39	37

Highest totals	**A**	693-9 dec	Auckland	1939/40
	C	514-6 dec	Christchurch	2002/03
Lowest totals	**A**	13	Auckland	1877/78
	C	62	Rangiora	1998/99
Highest innings	**A**	256 S.G. Smith	Auckland	1919/20
	C	301* P.G. Fulton	Christchurch	2002/03
Best bowling	**A**	9-75 R. Neill	Auckland	1891/92
(innings)	**C**	9-56 D.J. McBeath	Christchurch	1918/19
Best bowling	**A**	13-85 R.S. Cunis	Christchurch	1963/64
(match)	**C**	15-168 D.J. McBeath	Christchurch	1918/19

Record Partnerships

AUCKLAND

1st	286	B. Sutcliffe & D.D. Taylor	Auckland	1948/49
2nd	145	A.E.W. Parsons & J.F. Reid	Auckland	1978/79
3rd	278	T.J. Franklin & D.N. Patel	Christchurch	1985/86
4th	206	T.G. McIntosh & L. Vincent	Christchurch	2000/01
5th	161*	B. Sutcliffe & D.D. Taylor	Auckland	1946/47
6th	160	P.N. Webb & P.J. Kelly	Auckland	1985/86
7th	224	V.J. Scott & A.M. Matheson	Auckland	1937/38
8th	153	R.J. Nicol & R.A. Young	Auckland	2001/02
9th	96	C. Pringle & D.K. Morrison	Rangiora	1995/96
10th	83	S.W. Brown & C. Pringle	Christchurch	1990/91

CANTERBURY

1st	306	L.A. Cuff & J.D. Lawrence	Christchurch	1893/94
2nd	179	B.G. Hadlee & N.M. Parker	Auckland	1978/79
3rd	183	G.R. Stead & C.Z. Harris	Christchurch	2000/01
4th	147	M.L. Page & R.O. Talbot	Christchurch	1930/31
5th	158	P.G. Kennedy & M.W. Priest	Christchurch	1991/92
6th	172	L.A. Butterfield & R.C.S.A. Shand	Christchurch	1945/46
7th	142	G.J. Hopkins & P.J. Wiseman	Auckland	2002/03
8th	166	R.J. Hadlee & D.R. Hadlee	Christchurch	1983/84
9th	115	G.J. Hopkins & A.M. Ellis	Auckland	2002/03
10th	83	H.C. Wilson & H.W. Monaghan	Christchurch	1913/14
	83	M. Graham & A.P. Cobden	Auckland	1935/36

AUCKLAND v CENTRAL DISTRICTS

First match	*Played*	*Won by Auckland*	*Won by Central Districts*	*Drawn*
1950/51	71	26	18	27

Highest totals	**A**	526-4 dec		Auckland	1951/52
	CD	594-8 dec		Auckland	1995/96
Lowest totals	**A**	71		Palmerston North	2001/02
	CD	59		New Plymouth	1958/59
Highest innings	**A**	185*	L. Vincent	Auckland	2004/05
	CD	166	M.S. Sinclair	Masterton	1998/99
Best bowling *(innings)*	**A**	7-29	R.S. Cunis	Auckland	1961/62
	CD	7-31	H.B. Cave	Palmerston North	1952/53
Best bowling *(match)*	**A**	12-146	K.W. Hough	Auckland	1959/60
	CD	13-64	H.B. Cave	Palmerston North	1952/53

Record Partnerships

AUCKLAND

1st	172	R.A. Jones & M.J. Horne	Auckland	2004/05
2nd	167	G.O. Rabone & D.D. Coleman	Auckland	1951/52
3rd	151*	M.J. Horne & A.C. Barnes	Auckland	2001/02
4th	140	R.A. Jones & H.D. Barton	New Plymouth	1997/98
5th	234*	V.J. Scott & J.B. Morris	Auckland	1951/52
6th	165	J.J. Crowe & J.G. Bracewell	Auckland	1987/88
7th	192	S.W. Brown & A.C. Parore	Auckland	1990/91
8th	111	L. Vincent & R.A. Young	Auckland	2004/05
9th	104*	R.A. Young & C.J. Drum	Auckland	2000/01
10th	82	B.G.K. Walker & K.P. Walmsley	Auckland	2003/04

CENTRAL DISTRICTS

1st	172	C.J.P. Smith & P.S. Briasco	New Plymouth	1985/86
2nd	207*	R.G. Twose & M.W. Douglas	Auckland	1991/92
3rd	224	M.S. Sinclair & C.M. Spearman	Auckland	2003/04
4th	155	R.T. Hart & T.E. Blain	Masterton	1989/90
5th	127	M.W. Douglas & T.E. Blain	Nelson	1988/89
6th	220	M.H. Toynbee & I.D.S. Smith	Napier	1982/83
7th	165	R.K. Brown & M.E.L. Lane	Palmerston North	1993/94
8th	94	S.W. Duff & D.J. Leonard	Wanganui	1991/92
9th	68	I.R. Snook & A.B. Jordan	Nelson	1974/75
10th	133	G.A. Bartlett & I.A. Colquhoun	Auckland	1959/60

AUCKLAND v NORTHERN DISTRICTS

First match	Played	Won by Auckland	Won by Northern Districts	Drawn
1956/57	67	23	15	29

Highest totals	**A**	547-8 dec		Auckland	2000/01
	ND	492		Auckland	1990/91
Lowest totals	**A**	69		Auckland	1963/64
	ND	32		Hamilton	1996/97
Highest innings	**A**	209	P.A. Horne	Auckland	1988/89
		209*	M.J. Horne	Auckland	2003/04
	ND	211*	G.A. Hick	Auckland	1988/89
Best bowling	**A**	7-28	K.P. Walmsley	Hamilton	2004/05
(innings)	**ND**	9-48	A.R. Tait	Hamilton	1996/97
Best bowling	**A**	11-71	J.A. Hayes	Auckland	1957/58
(match)	**ND**	16-130	A.R. Tait	Hamilton	1996/97

Record Partnerships

AUCKLAND

1st	197	T.J. Franklin & P.A. Horne	Auckland	1985/86
2nd	175	B.A. Pocock & J.M. Aiken	Auckland	2000/01
3rd	152	T.J. Franklin & J.J. Crowe	Rotorua	1983/84
4th	280	J.J. Crowe & D.N. Patel	Auckland	1991/92
5th	347*	M.J. Horne & A.C. Barnes	Auckland	2003/04
6th	157	J.F. Reid & J.R. Wiltshire	Auckland	1977/78
7th	136	T.K. Canning & B.G.K. Walker	Hamilton	2004/05
8th	75*	H.T. Schuster & H.J. Howarth	Hamilton	1964/65
9th	91*	K.D. Mills & C.J. Drum	Auckland	2000/01
10th	103	P.J. Kelly & G.B. Troup	Auckland	1985/86

NORTHERN DISTRICTS

1st	156	J.A.H. Marshall & N.K.W. Horsley	Auckland	2003/04
2nd	167	M.D. Bell & G.E. Bradburn	Hamilton	1994/95
3rd	261*	M.P. Maynard & S.A. Thomson	Hamilton	1990/91
4th	252	S.A. Thomson & B.A. Young	Auckland	1990/91
5th	142	M.P. Maynard & B.A. Young	Auckland	1991/92
6th	146*	G.A. Hick & S.A. Thomson	Auckland	1988/89
7th	127	C.M. Kuggeleijn & S.A. Thomson	Auckland	1988/89
8th	90	R.G. Hart & M.E. Parlane	Hamilton	1994/95
9th	185	M.P. Maynard & S.B. Doull	Auckland	1991/92
10th	82	S.B. Doull & B.P. Martin	Taupo	1999/00

AUCKLAND v OTAGO

First match	*Played*	*Won by Auckland*	*Won by Otago*	*Drawn*
1873/74	109	57	23	29

Highest totals	**A**	579	Auckland	1909/10
	O	558-8 dec	Dunedin	1949/50
Lowest totals	**A**	48	Dunedin	1889/90
	O	35	Christchurch	1884/85
Highest innings	**A**	290 W.N. Carson	Dunedin	1936/37
	O	355 B. Sutcliffe	Dunedin	1949/50
Best bowling	**A**	9-36 A.F. Wensley	Auckland	1929/30
(innings)	**O**	8-57 S.L. Boock	Dunedin	1989/90
Best bowling	**A**	14-63 A.W. Rees	Dunedin	1889/90
(match)	**O**	15-104 S.L. Boock	Dunedin	1989/90

Record Partnerships

AUCKLAND

1st	240	T.G. McIntosh & M.J. Horne	Dunedin	2001/02
2nd	170	L.G. Hemus & A.E. Relf	Auckland	1909/10
3rd	445	P.E. Whitelaw & W.N. Carson	Dunedin	1936/37
4th	176	V.J. Scott & R.W.G. Emery	Dunedin	1945/46
5th	197	C.C.R. Dacre & C.F.W. Allcott	Dunedin	1926/27
6th	209*	A.C. Parore & A.P. O'Dowd	Dunedin	1991/92
7th	177*	A.C. Barnes & J.M. Mills	Alexandra	1995/96
8th	140	J.G. Kemp & J.M. McIntyre	Dunedin	1969/70
9th	75	R.S. Cunis & R.I. Harford	Auckland	1966/67
10th	119	W.N. Carson & J. Cowie	Auckland	1937/38

OTAGO

1st	373	B. Sutcliffe & L. Watt	Auckland	1950/51
2nd	227	P.W. Dobbs & M.J. Lamont	Dunedin	1990/91
3rd	199	W.S. Haig & B. Sutcliffe	Auckland	1954/55
4th	177	M.J. Lamont & M.H. Richardson	Alexandra	1995/96
5th	266	B. Sutcliffe & W.S. Haig	Dunedin	1949/50
6th	145	M.J. Horne & M.G. Croy	Auckland	1997/98
7th	164	A. Galland & A.R. Knight	Auckland	1925/26
8th	84	L.R. Pearson & J.C. Alabaster	Auckland	1964/65
9th	208	W.C. McSkimming & B.E. Scott	Auckland	2004/05
10th	60	L.D. Smith & G.W.F. Overton	Auckland	1946/47

AUCKLAND v WELLINGTON

First match	Played	Won by Auckland	Won by Wellington	Drawn
1873/74	128	56	30	42

Highest totals	**A**	522		Wellington	1918/19
	W	595		Wellington	1927/28
Lowest totals	**A**	48		Wellington	1889/90
	W	35		Wellington	1873/74
Highest innings	**A**	194	W.N. Carson	Auckland	1936/37
	W	216	M.D. Bell	Auckland	1997/98
Best bowling	**A**	8-51	R. Neill	Auckland	1895/96
(innings)	**W**	9-67	A.W.S. Brice	Wellington	1918/19
Best bowling	**A**	14-65	J.A. Hayes	Auckland	1957/58
(match)	**W**	13-157	K.H. Tucker	Wellington	1900/01

Record Partnerships

AUCKLAND

1st	201	A. Anthony & E. Horspool	Auckland	1924/25
2nd	241	T.J. Franklin & J.J. Crowe	Wellington	1988/89
3rd	203*	B.A. Pocock & A.C. Parore	Auckland	1997/98
4th	180	A.N.C. Snedden & C.C.R. Dacre	Wellington	1922/23
5th	174	R.W. Morgan & J.G. Kemp	Auckland	1967/68
6th	176	V.J. Scott & O.C. Cleal	Auckland	1940/41
7th	131	G.L. Weir & C.C.R. Dacre	Wellington	1927/28
8th	189	W.N. Carson & A.M. Matheson	Auckland	1938/39
9th	122	H.T. Schuster & R.S. Cunis	Wellington	1964/65
10th	97	A.C. Kerr & H.C. Nottman	Auckland	1941/42

WELLINGTON

1st	333	B.A. Edgar & A.H. Jones	Wellington	1988/89
2nd	287	M.D. Bell & J.D. Wells	Auckland	1997/98
3rd	201	E.G. McLeod & J.R. Lamason	Wellington	1935/36
4th	207	F.T. Badcock & T.C. Lowry	Wellington	1927/28
5th	192	W.A. Baker & J.N. Crawford	Auckland	1917/18
6th	134	K.C. James & H.M. McGirr	Wellington	1926/27
7th	144	J.R. Reid & P.T. Barton	Auckland	1959/60
8th	137	F.L.H. Mooney & F.E. Fisher	Wellington	1952/53
9th	127	F.L.H. Mooney & R.A. Buchan	Wellington	1943/44
10th	113	F.L.H. Mooney & E.C.V. Knapp	Wellington	1943/44

CANTERBURY v CENTRAL DISTRICTS

First match	Played	Won by Canterbury	Won by Central Districts	Drawn
1950/51	72	25	18	29

Highest totals	C	559	Christchurch	1993/94
	CD	549-8 dec	Christchurch	1998/99
Lowest totals	C	68	Levin	1985/86
	CD	91	Christchurch	1954/55
Highest innings	C	251* C.Z. Harris	Rangiora	1996/97
	CD	212* D.P. Kelly	Blenheim	2000/01
Best bowling (innings)	C	9-13 P.J. Wiseman	Christchurch	2004/05
	CD	11-115 M.J. Mason	Timaru	2002/03
Best bowling (match)	C	12-86 P.J. Wiseman	Christchurch	2004/05
	CD	11-138 D.J. Kay	Palmerston North	1976/77

Record Partnerships

CANTERBURY

1st	185	B.R. Hartland & D.J. Murray	Palmerston North	1994/95
2nd	166	G.T. Dowling & B.F. Hastings	Christchurch	1964/65
3rd	174	P.J. Rattray & P.E. McEwan	Palmerston North	1981/82
4th	204	T.W. Jarvis & K. Thomson	Wanganui	1969/70
5th	290	C.Z. Harris & G.R. Stead	Blenheim	1996/97
6th	149	M.W. Priest & L.K. Germon	Christchurch	1988/89
7th	184*	C.L. Bull & B.P. Isherwood	Nelson	1971/72
8th	136	G.R. Stead & C.J. Anderson	Christchurch	2000/01
9th	113	G.J. Hopkins & S.J. Cunis	Christchurch	1998/99
10th	85	G.T. Dowling & A.F. Rapley	Christchurch	1958/59

CENTRAL DISTRICTGS

1st	178	P.J. Ingram & J.M. How	Napier	2002/03
2nd	317	R.T. Hart & P.S. Briasco	New Plymouth	1983/84
3rd	197	M.J. Greatbatch & M.D. Crowe	New Plymouth	1986/87
4th	276*	M.D. Crowe & P.S. Briasco	Christchurch	1986/87
5th	235*	G.P. Sulzberger & J.D. Ryder	Napier	2002/03
6th	141	B.B.J. Griggs & E.P. Thompson	Christchurch	2004/05
7th	219	B.W. Yuile & B.L. Hampton	Napier	1967/68
8th	133*	B.L. Hampton & R.M. Schofield	Christchurch	1964/65
9th	89	S.W. Duff & D.J. Leonard	Christchurch	1993/94
10th	98	I.A. Rutherford & D.J. Kay	Napier	1977/78

CANTERBURY v NORTHERN DISTRICTS

First match	Played	Won by Canterbury	Won by Northern Districts	Drawn
1956/57	66	25	13	28

Highest totals	**C**	549		Christchurch	1996/97
	ND	518-4 dec		Christchurch	1996/97
Lowest totals	**C**	83		Christchurch	1961/62
	ND	52		Hamilton	1966/67
Highest innings	**C**	237*	R.T. Latham	Rotorua	1990/91
	ND	235	J.A.H. Marshall	Christchurch	2001/02
Best bowling	**C**	7-24	J.W. Kiddey	Hamilton	1960/61
(innings)	**ND**	7-58	R.P. de Groen	Hamilton	1995/96
Best bowling	**C**	12-81	R.J. Hadlee	Christchurch	1986/87
(match)	**ND**	11-129	R.P. de Groen	Hamilton	1995/96

Record Partnerships

CANTERBURY

1st	214	B.A. Bolton & G.T. Dowling	Christchurch	1959/60
2nd	190	M.H.W. Papps & P.G. Fulton	Christchurch	2003/04
3rd	394*	P.G. Kennedy & R.T. Latham	Rotorua	1990/91
4th	181	V.R. Brown & R.T. Latham	Gisborne	1986/87
5th	252*	R.T. Latham & M.W. Priest	Christchurch	1988/89
6th	175	S.P. Fleming & L.K. Germon	Hamilton	1993/94
7th	205	L.K. Germon & M.W. Priest	Christchurch	1991/92
8th	210	G.R. Stead & S.E. Bond	Christchurch	2004/05
9th	76	C.R.W. Dickel & K.I. Ferries	Hamilton	1974/75
10th	160	L.K. Germon & W.A. Wisneski	Rangiora	1997/98

NORTHERN DISTRICTS

1st	136	B.A. Pocock & M.D. Bell	Christchurch	1996/97
2nd	237	J.G. Gibson & C.M. Kuggeleijn	Hamilton	1980/81
3rd	150	R.D. Broughton & A.D.G. Roberts	Christchurch	1980/81
4th	259	G.E. Bradburn & M.E. Parlane	Christchurch	1996/97
5th	140	M.N. Hart & J.G. Hatwell	Gisborne	2003/04
6th	180	S.A. Thomson & M.N. Hart	Hamilton	1992/93
7th	111	J.A.F. Yovich & R.G. Hart	Gisborne	2003/04
8th	152	G.E. Bradburn & S.B. Doull	Christchurch	1991/92
9th	69	M.N. Hart & S.B. Doull	Rangiora	2000/01
10th	62	M.N. Hart & G.W. Aldridge	Rangiora	2000/01

CANTERBURY v OTAGO

First match	Played	Won by Canterbury	Won by Otago	Drawn
1863/64	162	76	59	27

Highest totals	C	777		Christchurch	1996/97
	O	602-8 dec		Dunedin	1928/29
Lowest totals	C	25		Christchurch	1866/67
	O	40		Dunedin	1869/70
Highest innings	C	221*	P.G. Fulton	Dunedin	2004/05
	O	385	B. Sutcliffe	Christchurch	1952/53
Best bowling *(innings)*	C	9-95	M.W. Priest	Dunedin	1989/90
	O	9-72	F.H. Cooke	Christchurch	1884/85
Best bowling *(match)*	C	13-181	W.E. Merritt	Christchurch	1935/36
	O	15-94	F.H. Cooke	Christchurch	1882/83

Record Partnerships

CANTERBURY

1st	226*	W.A. Hadlee & J.G. Leggat	Christchurch	1948/49
2nd	210	W.A. Hadlee & F.P. O'Brien	Christchurch	1940/41
3rd	178	R.M. Frew & M.H.W. Papps	Christchurch	2000/01
4th	166	G.T. Dowling & K. Thomson	Dunedin	1966/67
5th	236	C.Z. Harris & N.J. Astle	Christchurch	1996/97
6th	293*	P.G. Fulton & N.T. Broom	Dunedin	2004/05
7th	265	J.L. Powell & N. Dorreen	Christchurch	1929/30
8th	95	R.H. Scott & A.T. Burgess	Christchurch	1946/47
9th	109	J.H. Bennett & A.W. Thomas	Dunedin	1913/14
10th	98	S.A. Orchard & C. Boxshall	Dunedin	1908/09

OTAGO

1st	209	B. Sutcliffe & L. Watt	Dunedin	1947/48
2nd	170	C.C. Hopkins & G.G. Austin	Christchurch	1911/12
3rd	221	R.C. Blunt & J.J.M. McMullan	Dunedin	1928/29
4th	168	K.F.M. Uttley & V.J.T. Chettleburgh	Dunedin	1936/37
5th	147	K.J. Burns & D.J. Walker	Christchurch	1985/86
6th	118	P.C. Semple & G.D. Alabaster	Christchurch	1969/70
7th	182	B. Sutcliffe & A.W. Gilbertson	Christchurch	1952/53
8th	146	M.H. Austen & P.J. Wiseman	Christchurch	1996/97
9th	134	J.W. Wilson & N.A. Mallender	Christchurch	1992/93
10th	184	R.C. Blunt & W. Hawksworth	Christchurch	1931/32

CANTERBURY v WELLINGTON

First match	Played	Won by Canterbury	Won by Wellington	Drawn	Tied
1883/84	134	47	48	38	1

Highest totals	C	547-5 dec		Christchurch	1953/54
	W	553		Wellington	1931/32
Lowest totals	C	37		Wellington	1925/26
	W	22		Wellington	1903/04
Highest innings	C	206	M.L. Page	Wellington	1931/32
		206	G.T. Dowling	Christchurch	1962/63
	W	212	J.S. Hiddleston	Wellington	1925/26
Best bowling (innings)	C	10-28	A.E. Moss	Christchurch	1889/90
	W	9-75	R.W. Blair	Wellington	1956/57
Best bowling (match)	C	13-72	A.E. Moss	Christchurch	1889/90
	W	14-136	R.W. Blair	Wellington	1956/57

Record Partnerships

CANTERBURY

1st	287	B.R. Hartland & G.R. Stead	Christchurch	1994/95
2nd	174	G.T. Dowling & J.W. Burtt	Wellington	1967/68
3rd	187*	C.D. McMillan & R.T. Latham	Christchurch	1994/95
4th	278	M.L. Page & A.W. Roberts	Wellington	1931/32
5th	183	C.Z. Harris & C.D. McMillan	Christchurch	1996/97
6th	209	C.Z. Harris & A.J. Redmond	Rangiora	2001/02
7th	241	N.J. Astle & M.W. Priest	Christchurch	1994/95
8th	114	A.W. Thomas & H.B. Whitta	Christchurch	1919/20
9th	182*	L.K. Germon & R.M. Ford	Christchurch	1989/90
10th	85	A.W. Hart & C.H. Thiele	Rangiora	1984/85

WELLINGTON

1st	239	C.S. Dempster & W.H. Dustin	Wellington	1931/32
2nd	209*	A.H. Jones & M.D. Crowe	Christchurch	1992/93
3rd	206	A.H. Preston & J.E.F. Beck	Christchurch	1955/56
4th	187	H.M. McGirr & T.C. Lowry	Christchurch	1930/31
5th	134*	J.F.M. Morrison & R.W. Ormiston	Christchurch	1981/82
6th	140	J.E.F. Beck & E.W. Dempster	Wellington	1956/57
7th	168	H.M. McGirr & K.C. James	Wellington	1927/28
8th	154	K.C. James & F.T. Badcock	Christchurch	1926/27
9th	115	E.H.L. Bernau & K.C. James	Wellington	1923/24
10th	87	N.R. Hoar & R. Allen	Christchurch	1944/45

CENTRAL DISTRICTS v NORTHERN DISTRICTS

First match	*Played*	*Won by Central Districts*	*Won by Northern Districts*	*Drawn*
1956/57	64	20	17	27

Highest totals	**CD**	479		Napier	2004/05
	ND	498-6 dec		Napier	1992/93
Lowest totals	**CD**	51		Hamilton	1957/58
	ND	86		New Plymouth	1956/57
Highest innings	**CD**	203*	M.S. Sinclair	Wanganui	1998/99
	ND	209	D.J. White	Hamilton	1985/86
Best bowling *(innings)*	**CD**	7-28	B.W. Yuile	Hamilton	1967/68
	ND	8-37	D.B. Clarke	Wanganui	1962/63
Best bowling *(match)*	**CD**	11-134	G.K. Robertson	Nelson	1986/87
	ND	10-78	D.B. Clarke	Wanganui	1962/63

Record Partnerships

CENTRAL DISTRICTS

1st	215	J.M. How & M.S. Sinclair	Napier	2004/05
2nd	263	M.J. Greatbatch & M.D. Crowe	Morrinsville	1986/87
3rd	210	B.F. Smith & M.W. Douglas	Taupo	2000/01
4th	161	L.G. Howell & M.J. Greatbatch	Rotorua	1995/96
5th	199	M.D. Crowe & M.W. Douglas	Rotorua	1989/90
6th	132*	T.E. Blain & S.W. Duff	Wanganui	1990/91
7th	179	B.B.J. Griggs & C.J.M. Furlong	Hamilton	2001/02
8th	173	I.D.S. Smith & G.K. Robertson	Hamilton	1982/83
9th	116	V. Pollard & R.O. Collinge	Palmerston North	1964/65
10th	48	M.J. Mason & L.J. Hamilton	Blenheim	2001/02

NORTHERN DISTRICTS

1st	167	M.E. Parlane & M.D. Bell	New Plymouth	1994/95
2nd	199	R.E.W. Mawhinney & D.J. White	Hamilton	1985/86
3rd	142	D.J. White & G.W. McKenzie	Hamilton	1985/86
4th	169	D.J. White & B.S. Oxenham	Wanganui	1990/91
5th	128	D.J. White & B.G. Cooper	Nelson	1986/87
6th	216	M.N. Hart & H.J.H. Marshall	Napier	2004/05
7th	136	D.J. Nash & A.R. Tait	Masterton	1997/98
8th	143	C.M. Presland & C.W. Dickeson	Whangarei	1983/84
9th	107	R.G. Hart & A.R. Tait	Rotorua	1995/96
10th	89	M.J.E. Wright & S.J. Scott	Wanganui	1978/79

CENTRAL DISTRICTS v OTAGO

First match	Played	Won by Central Districts	Won by Otago	Drawn
1950/51	73	23	23	27

Highest totals	**CD**	526		Napier	1995/96
	O	571-8		Napier	1995/96
Lowest totals	**CD**	74		Invercargill	1996/97
	O	73		Dunedin	1986/87
Highest innings	**CD**	242	M.D. Crowe	New Plymouth	1989/90
	O	264	B. Sutcliffe	Dunedin	1959/60
Best bowling *(innings)*	**CD**	7-36	B.W. Yuile	Nelson	1962/63
	O	8-31	D.G. Sewell	Invercargill	1996/97
Best bowling *(match)*	**CD**	11-99	D.D. Beard	Dunedin	1956/57
	O	15-203	A.M. Moir	New Plymouth	1953/54

Record Partnerships

CENTRAL DISTRICTS

1st	137	T.E. Blain & R.T. Hart	Oamaru	1984/85
2nd	193	M.L. Ryan & B.E. Congdon	Nelson	1968/69
3rd	223	C.J.P. Smith & S.W.J. Wilson	Blenheim	1990/91
4th	207	G.P. Sulzberger & A.J. Penn	Napier	1995/96
5th	168	B.F. Smith & M.W. Douglas	Alexandra	2000/01
6th	144	T.E. Blain & S.W. Duff	Palmerston North	1991/92
7th	123	I.D.S. Smith & S.J. Gill	Napier	1981/82
8th	106	S.J. Gill & D.R. O'Sullivan	Dunedin	1982/83
9th	239	H.B. Cave & I.B. Leggat	Dunedin	1952/53
10th	60*	B.L. Cairns & A.B. Jordan	Wanganui	1975/76

OTAGO

1st	305	R.A. Lawson & M.G. Croy	Napier	1995/96
2nd	169	G.M. Turner & R.W. Anderson	Dunedin	1974/75
3rd	227	K.R. Rutherford & B.R. Blair	Alexandra	1988/89
4th	200	B.R. Blair & G.J. Dawson	Dunedin	1982/83
5th	192	M.H. Richardson & I.S. Billcliff	Napier	1994/95
6th	147	R.N. Hoskin & J.K. Lindsay	Oamaru	1985/86
7th	121*	W.K. Lees & B. Abernethy	Napier	1981/82
8th	96	M.H. Richardson & P.J. Wiseman	Napier	1995/96
9th	92	D.E.C. McKechnie & B.L. Cairns	Dunedin	1976/77
10th	78	C.B. Gaffaney & D.G. Sewell	Palmerston North	1999/00

CENTRAL DISTRICTS v WELLINGTON

First match	Played	Won by Central Districts	Won by Wellington	Drawn
1950/51	71	12	27	32

Highest totals	CD	497	Palmerston North	2004/05
	W	590-8 dec	Palmerston North	2004/05
Lowest totals	CD	50	Upper Hutt	1979/80
	W	88	Wellington	1991/92
Highest innings	CD	207 R.T. Hart	Wellington	1985/86
	W	236 J.D. Ryder	Palmerston North	2004/05
Best bowling (innings)	CD	7-55 E.P. Thompson	Napier	2003/04
	W	7-68 B.D. Morrison	Wellington	1955/56
Best bowling (match)	CD	11-149 E.P. Thompson	Napier	2003/04
	W	10-103 B.D. Morrison	Wellington	1955/56

Record Partnerships

CENTRAL DISTRICTS

1st	250	R.T. Hart & C.J.P. Smith	Wellington	1985/86
2nd	157	H.C. Sampson & B.E. Congdon	Wellington	1970/71
3rd	180	C.D. Ingham & M.J. Greatbatch	Napier	1994/95
4th	172*	P.S. Briasco & M.W. Douglas	Palmerston North	1990/91
5th	301	J.I. Englefield & R.L. Taylor	Palmerston North	2004/05
6th	92	M.J.F. Shrimpton & L.W. Downes	Masterton	1975/76
7th	134	M.W. Douglas & S.W. Duff	Napier	1991/92
8th	84	P.M. Blackbourn & G.K. Robertson	Palmerston North	1983/84
9th	70	D.W. Neal & J.H. Howell	Wellington	1972/73
10th	52	D.J. Leonard & A.J. Alcock	Wellington	1992/93

WELLINGTON

1st	316	M.H. Austen & R.T. Hart	Wanganui	1993/94
2nd	215	M.D. Bell & M.E. Parlane	Napier	2004/05
3rd	186	J.D. Wells & S.J. Blackmore	New Plymouth	1999/00
4th	310	J.D. Ryder & N.R. Parlane	Palmerston North	2004/05
5th	341	G.R. Larsen & E.B. McSweeney	Levin	1987/88
6th	226	E.J. Gray & R.W. Ormiston	Wellington	1981/82
7th	161	S.P. Fleming & M.D.J. Walker	Wellington	2001/02
8th	135	G.R. Larsen & J.E.C. Franklin	Wellington	1998/99
9th	83	T. Vaikvee & R.O. Collinge	New Plymouth	1973/74
10th	81	L.C. Butler & R.E. Reid	Wanganui	1959/60

NORTHERN DISTRICTS v OTAGO

First match	*Played*	*Won by Northern Districts*	*Won by Otago*	*Drawn*
1956/57	62	23	18	21

Highest totals	**ND**	520-8 dec		Hamilton	1987/88
	O	457		Hamilton	1987/88
Lowest totals	**ND**	64		Dunedin	1971/72
	O	77		Gisborne	1999/00
Highest innings	**ND**	212*	S.B. Styris	Hamilton	2001/02
	O	201	B. Sutcliffe	Hamilton	1960/61
Best bowling *(innings)*	**ND**	7-42	K. Treiber	Hamilton	1985/86
	O	9-93	P.J. Petherick	Dunedin	1975/76
Best bowling *(match)*	**ND**	13-99	R.P. de Groen	Alexandra	1992/93
	O	13-144	S.L. Boock	Whangarei	1980/81

Record Partnerships

NORTHERN DISTRICTS

1st	151	G.P. Howarth & R.W. Fulton	Gisborne	1974/75
2nd	222	L.M. Crocker & C.M. Kuggeleijn	Hamilton	1983/84
3rd	112	R.W. Fulton & J.M. Parker	Gisborne	1974/75
4th	203	S.A. Thomson & M.P. Maynard	Hamilton	1991/92
5th	117	W.J. Mitchell & P.D. Stone	Hamilton	1966/67
6th	191	S.B. Styris & R.G. Hart	Hamilton	2001/02
7th	130	M.D. Bailey & R.G. Hart	Invercargill	1994/95
8th	81	M.J.E. Wright & B.L. Cairns	Tauranga	1982/83
9th	96	R.G. Hart & B.P. Martin	Dunedin	2001/02
	96	A.P. Devcich & G.W. Aldridge	Gisborne	2004/05
10th	97	R.G. Hart & G.L. West	Hamilton	2002/03

OTAGO

1st	260	R.A. Lawson & Mohammad Wasim	Dunedin	2002/03
2nd	220	M.H. Richardson & C.D. Cumming	Hamilton	2000/01
3rd	150	K.B.K. Ibadulla & K.J. Burns	Gisborne	1989/90
4th	235	K.J. Burns & R.N. Hoskin	Hamilton	1987/88
5th	123	R. Hendry & L.R. Pearson	Dunedin	1961/62
6th	129	N.R. Thompson & A.M. Moir	Hamilton	1958/59
7th	134	W.K. Lees & R.E.W. Mawhinney	Hamilton	1983/84
8th	129	B. Sutcliffe & T. Flaws	Hamilton	1960/61
9th	39	P.W. Hills & S.L. Boock	Gisborne	1988/89
10th	59	P.W. Hills & V.F. Johnson	Gisborne	1988/89

NORTHERN DISTRICTS v WELLINGTON

First match	Played	Won by Northern Districts	Won by Wellington	Drawn
1956/57	66	12	30	24

Highest totals	ND	474		Gisborne	1996/97
	W	608-9 dec		Hamilton	1998/99
Lowest totals	ND	57		Hamilton	1961/62
	W	78		Hamilton	2000/01
Highest innings	ND	151	G.P. Howarth	Hamilton	1979/80
	W	296	J.R. Reid	Wellington	1962/63
Best bowling *(innings)*	ND	7-12	D.R. Tuffey	Hamilton	2000/01
	W	8-24	E.J. Chatfield	Lower Hutt	1979/80
Best bowling *(match)*	ND	11-66	D.R. Tuffey	Hamilton	2000/01
	W	12-39	E.J. Chatfield	Lower Hutt	1979/80

Record Partnerships

NORTHERN DISTRICTS

1st	165	G.M. Turner & J.G. Wright	Lower Hutt	1976/77
2nd	162*	J.G. Wright & J.G. Gibson	Lower Hutt	1978/79
3rd	169	J.M. Parker & A.D.G. Roberts	Wellington	1983/84
4th	208	S.A. Thomson & M.P. Maynard	Hamilton	1991/92
5th	149	K.A. Wealleans & B.A. Young	Wellington	1991/92
6th	170	E.C. Petrie & R.J. McPherson	Hamilton	1959/60
7th	87	E.C. Petrie & G.D. Alabaster	Wellington	1962/63
8th	136	G.A. Hick & S.A. Thomson	Wellington	1988/89
9th	188	N.R. Parlane & D.R. Tuffey	Wellington	1999/00
10th	83	J.A. Yovich & A.R. Tait	Hamilton	1996/97

WELLINGTON

1st	310	B.A. Edgar & R.H. Vance	Wellington	1988/89
2nd	215	M.D. Bell & J.D. Wells	Hamilton	1998/99
3rd	346	G.P. Burnett & R.A. Verry	Hamilton	1991/92
4th	179	P.T. Barton & J.R. Reid	Wellington	1964/65
5th	147*	J.V. Coney & G.P. Bilby	Lower Hutt	1976/77
6th	139	J.F.M. Morrison & R.W. Smith	Wellington	1972/73
7th	137	T.D. Ritchie & G.R. Larsen	Gisborne	1985/86
8th	80	M.D.J. Walker & L.J. Woodcock	Hamilton	2003/04
9th	87	I.J. Therkleson & R.O. Collinge	Whangarei	1973/74
10th	74	M.D.J. Walker & J.S. Patel	Hamilton	2003/04

OTAGO v WELLINGTON

First match	Played	Won by Otago	Won by Wellington	Drawn
1892/93	107	28	52	27

Highest totals	**O**	495		Dunedin	1923/24
	W	575-7 dec		Wellington	1951/52
Lowest totals	**O**	34		Dunedin	1956/57
	W	42		Wellington	1945/46
Highest innings	**O**	182	K.R. Rutherford	Oamaru	1987/88
	W	283	J.R. Reid	Wellington	1951/52
Best bowling *(innings)*	**O**	8-46	B.L. Cairns	Invercargill	1978/79
	W	8-36	R.W. Blair	Dunedin	1952/53
Best bowling *(match)*	**O**	12-277	A.W. Alloo	Dunedin	1923/24
	W	12-87	E.J. Chatfield	Wellington	1973/74

Record Partnerships

OTAGO

1st	193	M.H. Richardson & M.J. Horne	Wellington	2000/01
2nd	254	K.J. Burns & K.R. Rutherford	Oamaru	1987/88
3rd	213	G.M. Turner & B.E. Congdon	Dunedin	1972/73
4th	211*	K.J. Burns & A.H. Jones	Wellington	1984/85
5th	134	C.B. Gaffaney & G.J. Hopkins	Dunedin	2003/04
6th	165	G.M. Turner & W.K. Lees	Wellington	1975/76
7th	143	T.C. Fraser & C.D.G. Toomey	Dunedin	1939/40
8th	165*	J.N. Crawford & A.G. Eckhold	Wellington	1914/15
9th	80	G.H. Mills & L.J. Groves	Dunedin	1937/38
10th	90	B.L. Cairns & G.B. Thomson	Lower Hutt	1979/80

WELLINGTON

1st	299	M.D. Bell & R.A. Jones	Dunedin	2001/02
2nd	227	W.A. Baker & H.H.L. Kortlang	Dunedin	1923/24
3rd	246	B.A.G. Murray & J.F.M. Morrison	Dunedin	1968/69
4th	274	R.A. Jones & S.R. Mather	Wellington	2000/01
5th	255	B.R. Taylor & J.V. Coney	Dunedin	1972/73
6th	184	H.M. McGirr & D.C. Collins	Dunedin	1923/24
7th	250	C.J. Nevin & M.D.J. Walker	Wellington	2003/04
8th	180	R.G. Twose & M.C. Goodson	Dunedin	1994/95
9th	72	F.T. Badcock & K.C. James	Wellington	1926/27
10th	138	K.C. James & A.W.S. Brice	Wellington	1926/27

PROVINCIAL COMPETITION

Plunket Shield

1921/22 — 1974/75

Awarded by the Governor of New Zealand, Lord Plunket, the Shield was given to Canterbury as the association with the best record in the 1906/07 season. From 1907/08 to 1920/21 the trophy was competed for under a challenge system but thereafter on a competition basis.

HOLDERS	*Tenure*	*Challenges resisted*
Canterbury	17 December, 1907	—
Auckland	17 December, 1907 to 1 February, 1911	7
Canterbury	1 February, 1911 to 12 February, 1912	2
Auckland	12 February, 1912 to 31 January, 1913	1
Canterbury	31 January, 1913 to 27 December, 1918	9
Wellington	27 December, 1918 to 24 January, 1919	—
Canterbury	24 January, 1919 to 4 January, 1920	2
Auckland	4 January, 1920 to 10 January, 1921	3
Wellington	10 January, 1921	—

Shell Series

1975/76-2000/01

In 1975/76, a new competition, sponsored by Shell, was established. For the first four seasons this was played under a two-stage system — the first round of 15 games (all teams playing each other) was for the Shell Cup*, while the second round (on a knock-out basis culminating in a final) carried the season's major prize, the Shell Trophy.

From 1979/80, only the Shell Trophy was competed for. The Shell Cup was reallocated to the limited-over competition in 1980/81, while the Plunket Shield was reserved for matches between the North and South Islands.

WINNERS

1921/22	Auckland
1922/23	Canterbury
1923/24	Wellington
1924/25	Otago
1925/26	Wellington
1926/27	Auckland
1927/28	Wellington
1928/29	Auckland
1929/30	Wellington
1930/31	Canterbury
1931/32	Wellington
1932/33	Otago
1933/34	Auckland
1934/35	Canterbury
1935/36	Wellington
1936/37	Auckland
1937/38	Auckland
1938/39	Auckland
1939/40	Auckland
1945/46	Canterbury
1946/47	Auckland
1947/48	Otago
1948/49	Canterbury
1949/50	Wellington
1950/51	Otago
1951/52	Canterbury
1952/53	Otago
1953/54	Central Districts
1954/55	Wellington
1955/56	Canterbury
1956/57	Wellington
1957/58	Otago
1958/59	Auckland
1959/60	Canterbury
1960/61	Wellington
1961/62	Wellington
1962/63	Northern Districts
1963/64	Auckland
1964/65	Canterbury
1965/66	Wellington
1966/67	Central Districts
1967/68	Central Districts
1968/69	Auckland
1969/70	Otago
1970/71	Central Districts
1971/72	Otago
1972/73	Wellington
1973/74	Wellington
1974/75	Otago
1975/76	Canterbury *Canterbury**
1976/77	Otago *Northern Districts**
1977/78	Auckland *Canterbury**
1978/79	Otago *Otago**
1979/80	Northern Districts
1980/81	Auckland
1981/82	Wellington
1982/83	Wellington
1983/84	Canterbury
1984/85	Wellington
1985/86	Otago
1986/87	Central Districts
1987/88	Otago
1988/89	Auckland
1989/90	Wellington
1990/91	Auckland
1991/92	Central Districts & Northern Districts
1992/93	Northern Districts
1993/94	Canterbury
1994/95	Auckland
1995/96	Auckland
1996/97	Canterbury
1997/98	Canterbury
1998/99	Central Districts
1999/00	Northern Districts
2000/01	Wellington

State Championship

from 2001/02

State Insurance took over the sponsorship of the competition in 2001/02. The format remained unchanged.

WINNERS

2001/02	Auckland	2002/03	Auckland	2003/04	Wellington
2004/05	Auckland				

TEAM RECORDS

Playing Record of the First-class Sides in New Zealand

	P	*W*	*L*	*D*		*P*	*W*	*L*	*D*
Canterbury	608	226	207	175*	Victoria	6	1	1	4
Wellington	589	212	189	188†	NZ XI	6	—	3	3
Otago	570	164	257	149	Young New Zealand	5	—	2	3
Auckland	552	221	147	184	Queensland	5	3	1	1
Central Districts	378	95	125	158*	Pakistan A	5	—	1	4
Northern Districts	345	81	128	136	England A	5	3	—	2
New Zealand	218	44	73	101	Tasmania	4	—	3	1
England/MCC	128	61	9	58*	Sri Lanka A	4	—	3	1
Australia	109	59	7	43	Shell XI	3	1	1	1
Hawke's Bay	53	9	34	10	Emerging Players	3	—	1	2
Pakistan	51	20	6	25	Governor General's XI	2	1	1	—
West Indies	35	11	8	16	Commonwealth XI	2	2	—	—
India	33	10	8	15	D.H. Robins' XI	2	—	—	2
New South Wales	23	16	2	5	U-Bix XI	1	—	—	1
South Africa	22	9	1	12	West Coast (NI)	1	1	—	—
Sri Lanka	20	3	6	11	D. Reese's XI	1	—	1	—
Nelson	17	9	6	2*	Minor Associations	1	—	1	—
North Island	16	6	5	5	Sir Julien Cahn's XI	1	—	—	1
Fiji	15	5	8	2	South Island Army	1	1	—	—
South Island	15	4	8	3	North Island Army	1	—	1	—
New Zealand U23 XI	12	—	9	3	New Zealand Army	1	1	—	—
New Zealand A	11	7	1	3	New Zealand Air Force	1	—	1	—
Zimbabwe	10	2	3	5	New Zealand Services	1	—	—	1
President's XI	9	—	3	6	Canterbury/Otago	1	—	—	1
NZ Academy XI	9	3	3	3	Auckland/Wellington	1	—	1	—
Southland	8	1	5	2	ND/CD	1	—	—	1
Taranaki	8	1	6	1	Auckland XI	1	—	—	1
Southern	8	4	1	3	Otago Invitation XI	1	—	1	—
Northern	7	2	1	4	Canterbury XI	1	—	—	1
Central	7	2	3	2	Board XI	1	—	1	—
Bangladesh	7	—	7	—	Australian Academy XI	1	1	—	—
The Rest	6	1	3	2	NZ Major Association XI	1	—	—	1
					TOTALS	**3970**	**1303**	**1303**	**1364**

* *includes a tie* † *includes two ties*

Highest Match Aggregates

Runs-Wickets			
1945-18	Canterbury v Wellington	Christchurch	1994/95
1905-40	Otago v Wellington	Dunedin	1923/24
1567-37	Auckland v Wellington	Auckland	1936/37
1554-40	Wellington v Auckland	Wellington	1922/23
1531-39	Wellington v Auckland	Wellington	1923/24
1505-25	New Zealand v India	Auckland	1989/90
1501-37	Canterbury v Otago	Christchurch	1931/32

Highest Team Totals

by any first-class team in New Zealand

777	Canterbury v Otago at Christchurch	1996/97
752-8 dec	NSW v Otago at Dunedin	1923/24
693-9 dec	Auckland v Canterbury at Auckland	1939/40
671-4	New Zealand v Sri Lanka at Wellington	1990/91
663	Australia v New Zealand at Auckland	1920/21
660-5 dec	West Indies v New Zealand at Wellington	1994/95
658	Australians v Auckland at Auckland	1913/14
653-5 dec	MCC v New Zealand at Dunedin	1935/36
653	Australians v Canterbury at Christchurch	1913/14
643	Auckland v Canterbury at Auckland	1919/20
621-5 dec	South Africa v New Zealand at Auckland	1998/99
616-5 dec	Pakistan v New Zealand at Auckland	1988/89
610-6 dec	Australia v New Zealand at Auckland	1913/14
608-9 dec	Wellington v Northern Districts at Hamilton	1998/99
602-8 dec	Otago v Canterbury at Dunedin	1928/29

Most Runs in a Match by One Side

Runs-Wickets				
1025-20	560 & 465	Wellington v Otago	Dunedin	1923/24
973-6	498-2d & 475-4	Wellington v Canterbury	Christchurch	1994/95
972-12	496 & 476-2d	Canterbury v Wellington	Christchurch	1994/95
971-14	511-6d & 460-8	Australia v New Zealand	Wellington	1973/74
948-20	569 & 379	Wellington v Auckland	Wellington	1923/24
880-20	385 & 495	Otago v Wellington	Dunedin	1923/24
875-18	273 & 602-8d	Otago v Canterbury	Dunedin	1928/29
874-15	391 & 483-5d	New Zealand v India	Auckland	1989/90
855-20	595 & 260	Wellington v Auckland	Wellington	1927/28
851-18	280 & 571-8	Otago v Central Districts	Napier	1995/96
845-14	174 & 671-4d	New Zealand v Sri Lanka	Wellington	1990/91
832-17	401 & 431-7d	Auckland v Wellington	Auckland	1934/35
831-20	435 & 396	Wellington v Auckland	Wellington	1922/23
827-20	448 & 379	Wellington v Otago	Wellington	1926/27
821-20	447 & 374	Wellington v Auckland	Wellington	1925/26
808-13	476 & 332-3	NSW v Wellington	Wellington	1923/24
802-18	276 & 526-8d	Canterbury v Wellington	Wellington	1931/32

Lowest Match Aggregates

completed matches, i.e. not drawn

Runs-Wickets			
151-30	Canterbury v Otago	Christchurch	1866/67
153-31	Otago v Canterbury	Dunedin	1896/97
156-30	Nelson v Wellington	Nelson	1885/86
159-31	Nelson v Wellington	Nelson	1887/88
176-32	Otago v Tasmania	Dunedin	1883/84
183-40	Nelson v Wellington	Nelson	1883/84
192-30	Taranaki v Hawke's Bay	Hawera	1891/92

The lowest aggregates since 1900 are:

Runs-Wickets			
241-30	Otago v Southland	Dunedin	1919/20
278-40	Southland v Otago	Invercargill	1918/19
295-28	New Zealand v Australia	Wellington	1945/46

Lowest Match Aggregates by One Side

55	36 & 19	Wellington v Nelson	Nelson	1885/86
57	25 & 32	Canterbury v Otago	Christchurch	1866/67
64	35 & 29	Taranaki v Hawke's Bay	Hawera	1891/92
72	30 & 42	Wellington v Nelson	Nelson	1883/84
76	34 & 42	Canterbury v Otago	Dunedin	1863/64
76	27 & 49	Canterbury v Otago	Dunedin	1896/97
79	31 & 48	Wellington v Nelson	Nelson	1887/88
80	51 & 29	Wellington v Nelson	Nelson	1879/80
87	40 & 47	Tasmania v Otago	Dunedin	1883/84
95	43 & 52	Otago v Canterbury	Christchurch	1872/73
96	41 & 55	Southland v Otago	Invercargill	1918/19
96	42 & 54	New Zealand v Australia	Wellington	1945/46
97	37 & 60	Wellington v Nelson	Christchurch	1876/77
99	65 & 34	Wellington v Canterbury	Wellington	1886/87

Lowest Team Totals

by any first-class team in New Zealand

13	Auckland v Canterbury at Auckland (included 8 extras)	1877/78
19	Wellington v Nelson at Nelson	1885/86
22	Wellington v Canterbury at Wellington	1903/04
25	Canterbury v Otago at Christchurch	1866/67
26	NZ v England at Auckland	1954/55
27	Canterbury v Otago at Dunedin	1896/97
28	Hawke's Bay v Auckland at Auckland (included 13 extras)	1910/11
29	Wellington v Nelson at Nelson	1879/80
29	Taranaki v Hawke's Bay at Hawera	1891/92

Highest Second Innings Totals

671-4	New Zealand v Sri Lanka	Wellington	1990/91
602-8	Otago v Canterbury	Dunedin	1928/29
589	Otago v Canterbury	Christchurch	1931/32
575-7 dec	Wellington v Otago	Wellington	1951/52
571-8 dec	Otago v Central Districts	Napier	1995/96
539	Auckland v Otago	Dunedin	1926/27
537	Auckland v Canterbury	Christchurch	1930/31
537	New Zealand v England	Wellington	1983/84
526-8 dec	Canterbury v Wellington	Wellington	1931/32
519	Canterbury v Wellington	Christchurch	1930/31

Highest Fourth Innings Totals without Loss for Victory

226-0	Canterbury v Otago	Christchurch	1948/49
175-0	Otago v Central Districts	Masterton	1971/72
174-0	Otago v Northern Districts	Alexandra	1985/86
138-0	Auckland v Otago	Auckland	1937/38
130-0	Wellington v Otago	Wellington	1921/22
130-0	Canterbury v Auckland	Christchurch	1951/52

Highest Fourth Innings Totals

495	lost 145 runs	Otago v Wellington	Dunedin	1923/24
475-4	and won	Wellington v Canterbury	Christchurch	1994/95
473-6	and won	Canterbury v Auckland	Christchurch	1930/31
458	lost 276 runs	Auckland v Wellington	Wellington	1927/28
453-8	and won	Northern Districts v Wellington	Wellington	1995/96
451	lost 98 runs	New Zealand v England	Christchurch	2001/02
400-9	and won	Northern Districts v Central Districts	Napier	2004/05
388	lost 19 runs	Canterbury v Wellington	Wellington	1929/30
380-8	set 505 runs	Wellington v Auckland	Wellington	1929/30
375-5	and won	Central Districts v Canterbury	New Plymouth	1986/87
374-8	and won	North Island v South Island	Dunedin	1947/48
372	lost 38 runs	Canterbury v Wellington	Christchurch	2000/01
371-4	and won	Northern Districts v Wellington	Hamilton	1991/92
368-6	and won	Auckland v Central Districts	Auckland	2000/01
362-8	and won	Canterbury v Central Districts	Napier	2002/03
361-6	and won	Auckland v Canterbury	Christchurch	2002/03
357-6	and won	Canterbury v Otago	Christchurch	1927/28
353	lost 148 runs	Otago v Auckland	Alexandra	1995/96
353-2	and won	Wellington v Otago	Dunedin	2001/02
348-5	and won	West Indies v NZ	Auckland	1968/69
347-7	and won	Auckland v Wellington	Auckland	1936/37
345	lost 15 runs	Northern Districts v Central Districts	Nelson	1986/87
344-6	set 418 runs	Sri Lanka v New Zealand	Hamilton	1990/91
344	lost 163 runs	Otago v Wellington	Wellington	1927/28
342-6	and won	Otago v Central Districts	Oamaru	1985/86
341-5	and won	Central Districts v Northern Districts	New Plymouth	1984/85
340-5	and won	Wellington v Auckland	Wellington	1991/92
340	lost 16 runs	Auckland v Northern Districts	Auckland	2002/03
339-5	and won	Central Districts v Otago	Blenheim	1990/91
339	lost 96 runs	Canterbury v Otago	Christchurch	1933/34
339	lost 12 runs	Canterbury v Otago	Dunedin	1947/48
339-2§	and won	Central Districts v Northern Districts	Hamilton	2002/03
337	lost 108 runs	Auckland v Wellington	Wellington	1922/23
336	lost 105 runs	Auckland v Wellington	Wellington	1920/21
335-8	set 385 runs	Northern Districts v Auckland	Auckland	1991/92
335-5	and won	Canterbury v Otago	Christchurch	1995/96
335	lost 32 runs	South Island v North Island	Christchurch	1999/00
334-7	and won	Wellington v Northern Districts	Wellington	1958/59
334	lost 355 runs	Canterbury v Wellington	Christchurch	1926/27
333-8	set 577 runs	Otago v Wellington	Wellington	1951/52
331-6	set 417 runs	England A v New Zealand A	Lincoln	1999/00
328-6	and won	Otago v Canterbury	Christchurch	1974/75
324-5	and won	Canterbury v Auckland	Christchurch	1949/50
324-5	and won	Northern Districts v Auckland	Auckland	1988/89
324-5	and won	New Zealand v Pakistan	Christchurch	1993/94
324	lost 37 runs	Canterbury v Central Districts	Nelson	1982/83
324-7	and won	Wellington v Otago	Oamaru	1998/99
322-6	and won	Northern Districts v Central Districts	Palmerston North	1982/83
322	lost 57 runs	Wellington v Canterbury	Christchurch	1924/25
322-7	and won	Northern Districts v Wellington	Hamilton	1998/99
322	lost 55 runs	Canterbury v Otago	Christchurch	2000/01
320-4	and won	Central Districts v Northern Districts	Hamilton	1996/97
318	lost 36 runs	Fiji v Canterbury	Christchurch	1947/48

318	lost 23 runs	West Indies v Governor General's XI	Auckland	1968/69
318-3†	and won	Wellington v Central Districts	Wellington	1997/98
317-9	and won	Northern Districts v Central Districts	Gisborne	1979/80
317-7	and won	Otago v Central Districts	Dunedin	1997/98
316-8	and won	England XI v New Zealand XI	Nelson	1991/92
315-4	and won	South Island v North Island	Wellington	1934/35
313	lost 62 runs	Northern Districts v Canterbury	Christchurch	1988/89
313-7	and won	Central Districts v Northern Districts	Hamilton	1999/00
312-5	set 416 runs	Wellington v Canterbury	Christchurch	1917/18
311-7	and won	Otago v Wellington	Wellington	1996/97
310-4	and won	Otago v Central Districts	New Plymouth	1987/88
310-9	and won	Otago v Canterbury	Christchurch	1990/91
308-7	set 410 runs	Wellington v Canterbury	Rangiora	2001/02
307-8	set 341 runs	Australia v Canterbury	Christchurch	1909/10
307-9	set 348 runs	Wellington v Auckland	Wellington	1992/93
307-6	and won	England v New Zealand	Christchurch	1996/97
306-3	and won	Canterbury v Otago	Christchurch	1940/41
303-3	and won	Canterbury v Wellington	Wellington	1918/19
303	lost 365 runs	Auckland v Wellington	Wellington	1923/24
303	lost 197 runs	Wellington v Auckland	Auckland	1953/54
302	lost 69 runs	Canterbury v Wellington	Christchurch	1985/86
302-5	and won	Northern Districts v Wellington	Hamilton	1987/88
301	lost 6 runs	Central Districts v Northern Districts	Hamilton	1977/78
300-2	and won	Canterbury v Northern Districts	Christchurch	1984/85
300-8	set 320	Wellington v Northern Districts	Wellington	1991/92
300-9	set 351	Wellington v Otago	Dunedin	1990/91
300-9	set 303	Northern Districts v Central Districts	Nelson	1993/94
300	set 341	Auckland v Wellington	Auckland	1997/98

† after Central Districts had forfeited its second innings § after Northern Districts had forfeited its second innings

Large Victories

BY AN INNINGS AND

364 runs	Sims' Australian XI defeated Canterbury	Christchurch	1913/14
358 runs	Australia defeated New Zealand	Wellington	1904/05
356 runs	Australia defeated Otago	Dunedin	1949/50
354 runs	Auckland defeated Hawke's Bay	Auckland	1920/21
332 runs	Wellington defeated Canterbury	Wellington	1925/26
327 runs	NSW defeated Otago	Dunedin	1923/24
322 runs	Wellington defeated Hawkes Bay	Wellington	1905/06
322 runs	West Indies defeated New Zealand	Wellington	1994/95
277 runs	NSW defeated Canterbury	Christchurch	1923/24
275 runs	Auckland defeated Hawkes Bay	Auckland	1910/11
275 runs	Auckland defeated Northern Districts	Auckland	2000/01
258 runs	New Zealand A defeated Sri Lanka A	Christchurch	2003/04
256 runs	Wellington defeated Otago	Wellington	1899/00

BY A RUNS MARGIN

512 runs	Wellington defeated Auckland	Wellington	1925/26
446 runs	Wellington defeated Otago	Wellington	1926/27
438 runs	Auckland defeated Wellington	Auckland	1934/35
425 runs	Central Districts defeated Otago	Alexandra	2001/02
382 runs	Auckland defeated Canterbury	Christchurch	1920/21
365 runs	Wellington defeated Auckland	Wellington	1923/24
355 runs	Wellington defeated Canterbury	Christchurch	1926/27
343 runs	Auckland defeated Hawke's Bay	Napier	1912/13

343 runs	Canterbury defeated Central Districts	Christchurch	2004/05
342 runs	Canterbury defeated Auckland	Christchurch	1924/25
322 runs	Canterbury defeated Wellington	Christchurch	1910/11
318 runs	Canterbury defeated Auckland	Christchurch	1913/14
315 runs	Auckland defeated Otago	Auckland	1907/08
302 runs	Canterbury defeated Central Districts	Christchurch	1951/52
302 runs	Canterbury defeated Northern Districts	Hamilton	1998/99

Tied Matches

Wellington v Nelson	Wellington	1873/74
New Zealand v T.N. Pearce's XI	Scarborough	1958
Central Districts v England XI	New Plymouth	1977/78
Victoria v New Zealand	Melbourne	1982/83
Wellington v Canterbury	Wellington	1988/89

Close Finishes

VICTORY BY 1 WICKET

Canterbury defeated Tasmania	Christchurch	1883/84
Otago defeated Canterbury	Christchurch	1890/91
Wellington defeated Nelson	Nelson	1891/92
Auckland defeated Wellington	Wellington	1893/94
Canterbury defeated Wellington	Wellington	1899/00
Auckland defeated Wellington	Wellington	1911/12
Canterbury defeated Auckland	Auckland	1914/15
Wellington defeated Otago	Wellington	1924/25
Auckland defeated Otago	Auckland	1946/47
Fiji defeated Wellington	Wellington	1947/48
Otago defeated Wellington	Dunedin	1948/49
Auckland defeated Canterbury	Auckland	1950/51
Central Districts defeated Wellington	Wellington	1951/52
Otago defeated Wellington	Dunedin	1952/53
MCC defeated Canterbury	Christchurch	1960/61
Auckland defeated Canterbury	Christchurch	1963/64
Wellington defeated NZ Under-23 XI	Wellington	1965/66
Canterbury defeated Auckland	Auckland	1974/75
Northern Districts defeated Central Districts	Gisborne	1979/80
New Zealand defeated West Indies	Dunedin	1979/80
Otago defeated Wellington	Alexandra	1980/81
Otago defeated Canterbury	Christchurch	1990/91
Otago defeated Wellington	Dunedin	1991/92
Central Districts defeated Auckland	Auckland	1994/95
Canterbury defeated Northern Districts	Christchurch	1994/95
Southern defeated Central	Wanganui	1997/98
Wellington defeated Northern Districts	Hamilton	2001/02
Northern Districts defeated Central Districts	Napier	2004/05

VICTORY BY 10 RUNS OR LESS

1 run	Northern Districts defeated Central Districts	Rotorua	1989/90
2 runs	Auckland defeated Canterbury	Auckland	1903/04
	Wellington defeated Canterbury	Wellington	1935/36
3 runs	Otago defeated Wellington	Wellington	1953/54
	Central Districts defeated Wellington	Wellington	1970/71
	Central Districts defeated Otago	New Plymouth	1970/71
	Canterbury defeated Central Districts	Napier	1979/80

	Auckland defeated Otago	Dunedin	2004/05
4 runs	Auckland defeated Nelson	Nelson	1882/83
	Canterbury defeated Otago	Christchurch	1882/83
	Auckland defeated Wellington	Auckland	1977/78
5 runs	Central Districts defeated Otago	New Plymouth	1953/54
	Northern Districts defeated Central Districts	Napier	1976/77
6 runs	Canterbury defeated Tasmania	Christchurch	1883/84
	Auckland defeated Canterbury	Auckland	1952/53
	South Island XI defeated North Island XI	Wellington	1957/58
	Northern Districts defeated Central Districts	Hamilton	1977/78
	Northern Districts defeated Otago	Dunedin	1978/79
	Central Districts defeated Northern Districts	Napier	1988/89
7 runs	Auckland defeated Canterbury	Christchurch	1873/74
8 runs	Auckland defeated Wellington	Wellington	1945/46
	Auckland defeated Northern Districts	Auckland	1963/64
	Central Districts defeated Auckland	Napier	1982/83
	Auckland defeated Central Districts	Auckland	1999/00
9 runs	Central Districts defeated Auckland	Nelson	1983/84
10 runs	Northern Districts defeated Canterbury	Hamilton	1960/61
	Wellington defeated Central Districts	New Plymouth	1973/74
	Otago defeated Auckland	Dunedin	1975/76

Victory after Follow-on

Auckland (180 & 302)	beat Canterbury (392 & 84)	Auckland	1952/53
Northern Districts (165 & 275)	beat Otago (320-9d & 105)	Dunedin	1961/62
Auckland (69 & 303)	beat Northern Districts (224 & 140)	Auckland	1963/64
Canterbury (166 & 360)	beat Auckland (351-9d & 149)	Christchurch	1973/74
Auckland (101 & 278)	beat Otago (268 & 108)	Dunedin	2004/05

Matches Abandoned without a Ball Being Bowled

these matches are not included in any first-class records

Central Districts v Northern Districts	Napier	1970/71
†Wellington v Australia	Wellington	1973/74
Central Districts v Australia	Napier	1973/74
†New Zealand v Pakistan	Dunedin	1988/89
†New Zealand President's XI v Australia	Nelson	1992/93
New Zealand A v Sri Lanka	Gisborne	1996/97
Wellington v Canterbury	Wellington	1996/97
†Northern v Pakistan A	Auckland	1998/99
†New Zealand v India	Dunedin	1998/99

† replaced with a limited-overs match

Matches Completed in One Day

Otago v Canterbury	Dunedin	11. 2.1868
Wellington v Auckland	Wellington	29.11.1874
Nelson v Wellington	Nelson	26.12.1887
Otago v Auckland	Dunedin	27.12.1889
Hawke's Bay v Taranaki	Napier	9. 1.1892
Auckland v New South Wales*	Auckland	20. 1.1894
Ireland v New Zealand	Dublin	11. 9.1937
Auckland v Fiji†	Auckland	9. 3.1954

** no play on first day* *† after no play on first two days and three declarations on third*

Most Extras in an Innings

Extras	B	LB	NB	W				
† 66	2	9	54	1	NZ Academy XI (459-8d)	v Pakistan A	Lincoln	1998/99
62	25	21	13	3	England (562)	v New Zealand	Leeds	2004
† 60	18	17	20	5	Central Districts (460-4d)	v Wellington	Wellington	1997/98
58	41	14	3	—	Wellington (380-5)	v Auckland	Wellington	1929/30
†58	6	14	30	8	Auckland (322-4d)	v Wellington	Auckland	1993/94
58	4	12	33	9	New Zealand (563)	v Pakistan	Hamilton	2003/04
57	31	16	10	—	New Zealand (387)	v England	Auckland	1929/30
54	35	14	1	4	Auckland (200-8d)	v Wellington	Auckland	1973/74
54	5	16	33	—	New Zealand A (597-9d)	v Sri Lanka A	Queenstown	2003/04
53	26	10	17	—	Canterbury (473-6)	v Auckland	Christchurch	1930/31
†53	4	2	46	1	Wellington (498-2d)	v Canterbury	Christchurch	1994/95
52					Wellington (370)	v Canterbury	Christchurch	1922/23
52	12	7	33	—	New Zealand (468)	v Pakistan	Karachi	1976/77
52	1	27	33	1	Auckland (423-7d)	v Wellington	Wellington	1992/93
† 52	1	15	32	4	Canterbury (537)	v Central Districts	Blenheim	1996/97
52	21	28	3	1	New Zealand (630-6d)	v India	Mohali	2003/04
52	7	9	28	8	Central Districts (499)	v Canterbury	N.Plymouth	2004/05
51	10	11	30	—	Auckland (369)	v West Indies	Auckland	1999/00
50					Otago (602-8d)	v Canterbury	Dunedin	1928/29
50	13	24	11	2	Wellington (356)	v Canterbury	Wellington	1981/82
† 50	3	11	36	—	Southern (554)	v Pakistan A	Christchurch	1998/99

† no balls counted as two extras, regardless of whether runs were scored from the bat

Longest Matches in New Zealand

before 1900

FOUR DAYS

Otago v Canterbury	Dunedin	1875/76
Canterbury v Tasmania	Christchurch	1883/84
Otago v Canterbury	Dunedin	1884/85

Longest Matches in New Zealand

since 1900

SIX DAYS

New Zealand v England	Christchurch	1974/75
New Zealand v India	Christchurch	1975/76
*New Zealand v England	Auckland	1977/78
New Zealand v Pakistan	Napier	1978/79
New Zealand v West Indies	Auckland	1979/80
New Zealand v India	Christchurch	1980/81

** the only match where play took place on all six days.*
The other instances involved the rest day being used after a day's play was lost

FIVE DAYS

Canterbury v Otago	Christchurch	1911/12
Canterbury v Wellington	Christchurch	1922/23
Otago v Wellington	Dunedin	1923/24
Canterbury v Auckland	Christchurch	1924/25
Wellington v Otago	Wellington	1926/27
Northern Districts v Auckland	Taupo	1999/00
Auckland v Wellington	Auckland	2004/05

All other matches of five days duration since 1926/27 have been test matches. A complete list of these up to 1993/94 is on pages 288 and 289 of the 1994 Almanack. *The 1998/99 Shell Trophy final between Central Districts and Otago at Napier was scheduled for five days but completed in three.*

INDIVIDUAL RECORDS

BATTING

Highest Individual Scores

385	Sutcliffe B.	Otago v Canterbury	Christchurch	1952/53
355	Sutcliffe B.	Otago v Auckland	Dunedin	1949/50
338*	Blunt R.C.	Otago v Canterbury	Christchurch	1931/32
336*	Hammond W.R.	England v New Zealand	Auckland	1932/33
317	Rutherford K.R.	New Zealand v D.B. Close's XI	Scarborough	1986
306	Richardson M.H.	New Zealand v Zimbabwe A	Kwekwe	2000/01
301*	Fulton P.G.	Canterbury v Auckland	Christchurch	2002/03
299	Crowe M.D.	New Zealand v Sri Lanka	Wellington	1990/91
296	Reid J.R.	Wellington v Northern Districts	Wellington	1962/63
293	Trumper V.T.	Sims' Australian XI v Canterbury	Christchurch	1913/14
290	Carson W.N.	Auckland v Otago	Dunedin	1936/37
284	Woodfull W.M.	Australia v New Zealand	Auckland	1927/28
283	Reid J.R.	Wellington v Otago	Wellington	1951/52
275*	Cullinan D.J.	South Africa v New Zealand	Auckland	1998/99
275	Sutcliffe B.	Otago v Auckland	Auckland	1950/51
274*	Fleming S.P.	New Zealand v Sri Lanka	Colombo	2002/03
271	Javed Miandad	Pakistan v New Zealand	Auckland	1988/89
268	Sinclair M.S.	New Zealand A v South Africa A	Potchefstroom	2004/05
267*	Young B.A.	New Zealand v Sri Lanka	Dunedin	1996/97
267	de Silva P.A.	Sri Lanka v New Zealand	Wellington	1990/91
264	Sutcliffe B.	Otago v Central Districts	Dunedin	1959/60
259	Turner G.M.	New Zealand v Guyana	Georgetown	1971/72
259	Turner G.M.	New Zealand v West Indies	Georgetown	1971/72
258	Nurse S.M.	West Indies v New Zealand	Christchurch	1968/69
256	Smith S.G.	Auckland v Canterbury	Auckland	1919/20
255*	McGlew D.J.	South Africa v New Zealand	Wellington	1952/53
254*	Vance R.H.	Wellington v Northern Districts	Wellington	1988/89
251*	Harris C.Z.	Canterbury v Central Districts	Rangiora	1996/97
250	Walters K.D.	Australia v New Zealand	Christchurch	1976/77
247*	Chappell G.S.	Australia v New Zealand	Wellington	1973/74
243	Sutcliffe B.	New Zealand v Essex	Southend	1949
242*	Crowe M.D.	New Zealand v South Australia	Adelaide	1985/86
242	Crowe M.D.	Central Districts v Otago	New Plymouth	1989/90
241	Horne M.J.	Otago v Auckland	Auckland	1997/98
239	Dowling G.T.	New Zealand v India	Christchurch	1967/68
237*	Latham R.T.	Canterbury v Northern Districts	Rotorua	1990/91
236	Ryder J.D.	Wellington v Central Districts	Palmerston North	2004/05
235	Marshall J.A.H.	Northern Districts v Canterbury	Christchurch	2001/02
230*	Sutcliffe B.	New Zealand v India	New Delhi	1955/56
227	Hammond W.R.	England v New Zealand	Christchurch	1932/33
226*	Rutherford K.R.	Otago v India	Dunedin	1989/90
226	Hastings B.F.	Canterbury v NZ Under 23 XI	Christchurch	1964/65
225*	Blunt R.C.	New Zealand v Gentlemen	Eastbourne	1931
224	Vincent L.	New Zealand v Sri Lanka	Wellington	2004/05
223*	Turner G.M.	New Zealand v West Indies	Kingston	1971/72
223	Astle N.J.	New Zealand v Queensland	Brisbane	2001/02
222*	Midlane F.A.	Wellington v Otago	Wellington	1914/15
222	Rutherford I.A.	Otago v Central Districts	New Plymouth	1978/79
222	Astle N.J.	New Zealand v England	Christchurch	2001/02
221*	Fulton P.G.	Canterbury v Otago	Dunedin	2004/05

221	Macartney C.G.	NSW v Canterbury	Christchurch	1923/24
221	Blunt R.C.	Otago v Canterbury	Dunedin	1928/29
219	Bell M.D.	Wellington v Northern Districts	Hamilton	1998/99
216	Fletcher K.W.R.	England v New Zealand	Auckland	1974/75
216	Bell M.D.	Wellington v Auckland	Auckland	1997/98
216*	Chanderpaul S.	West Indies v New Zealand A	Taupo	1999/00
214*	Kortlang H.H.L.	Wellington v Auckland	Wellington	1925/26
214*	Booth B.C.	Australia B v Central Districts	Palmerston North	1966/67
214	Sinclair M.S.	New Zealand v West Indies	Wellington	1999/00
213	Murray B.A.G.	Wellington v Otago	Dunedin	1968/69
213	Trimble S.C.	Australia B v New Zealand	Wellington	1969/70
213	Greenidge C.G.	West Indies v New Zealand	Auckland	1986/87
212*	Woodfull W.M.	Victoria v Canterbury	Christchurch	1924/25
212*	Richardson M.H.	New Zealand A v Sussex	Hove	2000
212*	Kelly D.P.	Central Districts v Canterbury	Blenheim	2000/01
212*	Styris S.B.	Northern Districts v Otago	Hamilton	2001/02
212	Hiddleston J.S.	Wellington v Canterbury	Wellington	1925/26
212	Dempster C.S.	New Zealand v Essex	Leyton	1931
211*	Hick G.A.	Northern Districts v Auckland	Auckland	1988/89
211*	Gibbs H.H.	South Africa v New Zealand	Christchurch	1998/99
211	Warner P.F.	Lord Hawke's XI v Otago	Dunedin	1902/03
211	Wallace W.M.	Auckland v Canterbury	Auckland	1939/40
209*	Brown S.W.	Auckland v Canterbury	Christchurch	1990/91
209*	Horne M.J.	Auckland v Northern Districts	Auckland	2003/04
209	White D.J.	Northern Districts v Central Districts	Hamilton	1985/86
209	Horne P.A.	Auckland v Northern Districts	Auckland	1988/89
208*	Sutcliffe B.	North Island v South Island	Dunedin	1947/48
207	Hart R.T.	Central Districts v Wellington	Wellington	1985/86
206	Page M.L.	Canterbury v Wellington	Wellington	1931/32
206	Donnelly M.P.	New Zealand v England	Lord's	1949
206	Dowling G.T.	Canterbury v Wellington	Christchurch	1962/63
206	Harris C.Z	Canterbury v Central Districts	Blenheim	1996/97
205*	Lloyd C.H.	West Indies v South Island	Dunedin	1968/69
205*	McSweeney E.B.	Wellington v Central Districts	Levin	1987/88
204*	Sinclair M.S.	New Zealand v Pakistan	Christchurch	2000/01
204	Cox A.	Canterbury v Otago	Christchurch	1925/26
204	Hiddleston J.S.	Wellington v Auckland	Wellington	1925/26
204	Scott V.J.	Auckland v Otago	Dunedin	1947/48
204	Patel D.N.	Auckland v Northern Districts	Auckland	1991/92
203*	Burnett G.P.	Wellington v Northern Districts	Hamilton	1991/92
203*	Sinclair M.S.	Central Districts v Northern Districts	Wanganui	1998/99
203	Scott V.J.	New Zealand v Combined Services	Gillingham	1949
203	Reid J.R.	New Zealand v Western Province	Cape Town	1961/62
203	Edgar B.A.	Young New Zealand v Zimbabwe	Bulawayo	1984/85
203	Parlane M.E.	Wellington v Auckland	Auckland	2004/05
202*	Congdon B.E.	Central Districts v Otago	Nelson	1968/69
202*	Greatbatch M.J.	Central Districts v Otago	Palmerston North	1988/89
202	Turner G.M.	New Zealand v President's XI	Montego Bay	1971/72
202	Austen M.H.	Wellington v Central Districts	Wanganui	1993/94
202	Greatbatch M.J.	Central Districts v Northern Districts	Rotorua	1995/96
202	Fleming S.P.	New Zealand v Bangladesh	Chittagong	2004/05
201*	Hart M.N.	Northern Districts v Auckland	Auckland	2002/03
201*	Smith B.F.	Central Districts v Canterbury	New Plymouth	2001/02
201	Reid J.R.	Otago v Canterbury	Dunedin	1957/58
201	Sutcliffe B.	Otago v Northern Districts	Hamilton	1960/61
201	Mushtaq Mohammad	Pakistan v New Zealand	Dunedin	1972/73

200*	MacLaren A.C.	MCC v New Zealand	Wellington	1922/23
200*	Bardsley W.	NSW v Auckland	Auckland	1923/24
200*	Thorpe G.P.	England v New Zealand	Christchurch	2001/02
200	Lawson R.A.	Otago v Central Districts	Napier	1995/96

Most Runs in a Season in New Zealand

		M	I	NO	HS	Runs	Ave	100
Crowe M.D.	1986/87	11	21	3	175*	1676	93.11	8
Turner G.M.	1975/76	11	20	4	177*	1244	77.75	5
Hick G.A.	1988/89	8	16	3	211*	1228	94.46	6
Bell M.D.	2000/01	13	21	0	134	1092	52.00	6
Crowe J.J.	1991/92	10	19	2	142*	1063	62.52	4
Vance R.H.	1988/89	10	18	2	254*	1037	64.81	4
Richardson M.H.	2000/01	11	19	2	166	1035	60.88	2
Wright J.G.	1986/87	11	21	2	192	1019	53.63	3
Sinclair M.S.	1999/00	14	26	2	214	1004	41.83	3
Vincent L.	2004/05	10	16	2	224	999	71.35	3
Dowling G.T.	1967/68	10	18	1	239	968	56.94	4
Edgar B.A.	1978/79	12	23	0	134	944	41.04	2
Weekes E. de C.	1955/56	8	10	1	156	940	104.44	6
Rutherford K.R.	1989/90	13	19	2	226*	940	55.29	3
Smith B.F.	2000/01	10	17	1	168	939	58.68	2
Edgar B.A.	1981/82	11	19	1	161	934	51.88	3
Sutcliffe B.	1947/48	5	10	1	208*	911	101.22	4
Maynard M.P.	1991/92	10	13	0	195	893	68.69	4
Horne M.J.	1998/99	10	19	2	132	887	52.17	1
Jones A.H.	1988/89	8	15	2	181*	884	68.00	2
Stead G.R.	2000/01	12	20	2	121*	875	48.61	3
Hastings B.F.	1968/69	10	15	4	117*	872	79.27	4
Wright J.G.	1981/82	11	18	0	141	872	48.44	4
Dowling G.T.	1966/67	10	18	2	102*	871	54.43	1
Jones R.A.	2000/01	12	19	0	188	860	45.26	3
Sutcliffe B.	1952/53	7	13	0	385	859	66.07	1
Sinclair M.S.	2003/04	10	16	1	133	851	56.73	2
Fulton P.G.	2004/05	9	14	1	221*	850	65.38	2
Anderson R.W.	1977/78	11	22	0	123	849	38.59	2
Horne M.J.	1996/97	10	17	0	124	843	49.58	3
Bradburn G.E.	1989/90	12	23	1	96	842	38.27	—
Spearman C.M.	1998/99	11	17	1	137	842	52.62	2
Turner G.M.	1974/75	8	15	1	186*	838	59.85	4
Harris C.Z.	1996/97	5	7	1	251*	835	139.16	3
Hick G.A.	1987/88	9	14	1	146	827	63.61	4
Nurse S.M.	1968/69	5	9	0	258	826	91.77	3
Sinclair M.S.	1998/99	11	17	3	203*	823	58.78	2
McIntosh T.G.	2002/03	10	17	3	157	820	58.57	2
Wright J.G.	1989/90	9	12	2	185	818	81.80	3
Reid J.F.	1980/81	10	18	4	173	817	58.35	3
Edwards G.N.	1980/81	11	19	2	177*	812	47.76	2
McMillan C.D.	1996/97	8	12	1	159	809	73.54	3
Crowe M.D.	1992/93	7	14	1	163	803	61.76	3
Sutcliffe B.	1950/51	7	12	0	275	798	66.50	4
Edgar B.A.	1979/80	11	19	3	152*	798	49.87	3
Horne M.J.	2001/02	11	17	2	178	798	53.20	3
Crowe J.J.	1988/89	9	13	0	156	797	61.30	2
Patel D.N.	1986/87	11	21	2	170*	796	41.89	3

		M	I	NO	HS	Runs	Ave	100
Greatbatch M.J.	1987/88	10	19	1	149	795	44.16	2
Papps M.H.W.	2001/02	10	19	4	158*	793	52.86	2
Wright J.G.	1978/79	10	19	2	145*	790	46.47	1
Rutherford K.R.	1991/92	10	20	2	133	787	43.72	1
Bailey M.D.	1997/98	11	16	1	180*	786	52.40	3
Burgess M.G.	1977/78	13	24	3	132	785	37.38	1
Woodfull W.M.	1927/28	6	9	3	284	781	130.16	3
Latham R.T.	1988/89	10	19	4	142*	781	52.06	2
Richardson M.H.	2001/02	10	15	1	143	779	55.64	3
Wright J.G.	1979/80	11	21	0	97	777	37.00	—
Thomson S.A.	1990/91	11	18	5	166	774	59.53	2
Bell M.D.	2003/04	12	17	0	173	775	45.58	2
Horne P.A.	1986/87	9	17	2	150*	773	51.53	2
Douglas M.W.	1991/92	12	22	4	144	773	42.94	2
Harris C.Z.	2001/02	8	12	3	155*	770	85.55	2
Howarth G.P.	1979/80	12	22	2	151	767	38.35	2
Jones A.H.	1990/91	6	11	2	186	766	85.11	4
Edgar B.A.	1988/89	7	13	1	150	762	63.50	3
Blair B.R.	1989/90	11	16	0	131	759	47.43	1
McEwan P.E.	1988/89	9	17	0	137	758	44.58	2
Rutherford K.R.	1985/86	11	17	2	126	753	50.20	3
Cumming C.D.	2002/03	10	18	2	128	751	46.93	3
Turner G.M.	1976/77	9	16	2	177*	750	53.57	1

Most Runs in a Season for New Zealand

		M	I	NO	HS	Runs	Ave	100
Sutcliffe B.	1949	29	49	5	243	2627	59.70	7
Donnelly M.P.	1949	29	45	8	206	2287	61.81	5
Reid J.R.	*1961/62	20	36	2	203	2083	61.26	7

** includes South Africa & Australia*

Most Runs in Season of First-class Debut

			M	I	NO	HS	Runs	Ave
Cooper B.G.	ND	1980/81	7	13	0	105	520	40.00
Briasco P.S.	CD	1982/83	8	15	1	95	519	37.07
Carson W.N.	Auckland	1936/37	3	4	0	290	500	125.00

Highest Average in a Season in New Zealand

		M	I	NO	HS	Runs	Ave	100
Hammond W.R.	1932/33	3	3	1	336*	621	310.50	2
Woodfull W.M.	1924/25	6	9	5	212*	710	177.50	3
Greatbatch M.J.	1995/96	5	6	2	202	623	155.75	4
Javed Miandad	1988/89	4	5	1	271	597	149.25	3
Harris C.Z.	1996/97	5	7	1	251*	835	139.16	3
Woodfull W.M.	1927/28	6	9	3	284	781	130.16	3
Carson W.N.	1936/37	3	4	0	290	500	125.00	2
Bardsley W.	1923/24	6	7	2	200*	623	124.60	1
Cullinan D.J.	1998/99	5	7	2	275*	553	110.60	3
Hiddleston J.S.	1925/26	3	5	0	212	537	107.40	2
Weekes E. de C.	1955/56	8	10	1	156	940	104.44	6
Sutcliffe B.	1946/47	6	8	1	197	722	103.14	3
Parker J.M.	1981/82	7	13	7	117	618	103.00	2
Sutcliffe B.	1947/48	5	10	1	208*	911	101.22	4

minimum 500 runs

Centuries

George Watson registered the first century in New Zealand first-class cricket on 24 February, 1881 when he made 175 for Canterbury v Otago at Hagley Park, Christchurch.

To date, 1779 centuries have been scored in New Zealand with 51 in 1991/92 being the record for one season. A further 352 have been recorded for New Zealand teams overseas.

The following NZ players have made 15 or more centuries during their first-class careers:

Turner G.M.	103	Greatbatch M.J.	24	Hadlee W.A.	18
Crowe M.D.	71	Horne M.J.	24	Twose R.G.	18
Wright J.G.	59	Donnelly M.P.	23	Astle N.J.	18
Sutcliffe B.	44	Congdon B.E.	23	Wallace W.M.	17
Reid J.R.	39	Fleming S.P.	23	Sinclair M.S.	17
Dempster C.S.	35	Crowe J.J.	22	Scott V.J.	16
Rutherford K.R.	35	Parker J.M.	21	Dowling G.T.	16
Howarth G.P.	32	Spearman C.M.	21	Jones A.H.	16
Patel D.N.	26	Burgess M.G.	20	Hastings B.F.	15
Dacre C.C.R.	24	Richardson M.H.	20	Blunt R.C.	15
Edgar B.A.	24	Lowry T.C.	18	Franklin T.J.	15

Most Centuries in a Season in New Zealand

8	Crowe M.D.	1986/87	4	Turner G.M.	1974/75
6	Weekes E. de C.	1955/56	4	Wright J.G.	1981/82
6	Hick G.A.	1988/89	4	Franklin T.J.	1987/88
6	Bell M.D.	2000/01	4	Hick G.A.	1987/88
5	Turner G.M.	1975/76	4	Vance R.H.	1988/89
4	Sutcliffe B.	1947/48	4	Jones A.H.	1990/91
4	Hadlee W.A.	1947/48	4	Crowe J.J.	1991/92
4	Sutcliffe B.	1950/51	4	Maynard M.P.	1991/92
4	Dowling G.T.	1967/68	4	Greatbatch M.J.	1995/96
4	Hastings B.F.	1968/69			

Five Centuries in Consecutive Innings

Weekes E. de C.	156	West Indies v Auckland	Auckland	1955/56
	148	West Indies v Canterbury	Auckland	
	123	West Indies v New Zealand	Dunedin	
	119*	West Indies v Wellington	Wellington	
	103	West Indies v New Zealand	Christchurch	

Three Centuries in Consecutive Innings

Macartney C.G.	120	NSW v Wellington	Wellington	1923/24
	120	NSW v Otago	Dunedin	
	221	NSW v Canterbury	Christchurch	
Sutcliffe B.	103	Otago v Auckland	Auckland	1947/48
	118 125	Otago v Canterbury	Dunedin	
Sutcliffe B.	141 135	Auckland v Canterbury	Auckland	1948/49
	140	New Zealand XI v The Rest	Christchurch	
Reid J.R.	101 118*	New Zealand v Orange Free State	Bloemfontein	1961/62
	165	New Zealand v South African Colts XI	East London	

Chappell I.M.	128	Australia v Northern Districts	Hamilton	1973/74
	145 121	Australia v New Zealand	Wellington	
Crowe M.D.	151	Central Districts v Northern Districts	Morrinsville	1986/87
	144 151	Central Districts v Canterbury	New Plymouth	
Hick G.A.	211*	Northern Districts v Auckland	Auckland	1988/89
	144 132	Northern Districts v Wellington	Morrinsville	
Jones A.H.	186	New Zealand v Sri Lanka	Wellington	1990/91
	122 100*	New Zealand v Sri Lanka	Hamilton	
Maynard M.P.	142	Northern Districts v Otago	Hamilton	1991/92
	195 110	Northern Districts v Auckland	Auckland	
Greatbatch M.J.	115	Central Districts v Canterbury	Christchurch	1995/96
	202	Central Districts v Northern Districts	Rotorua	
	162*	Central Districts v Auckland	Auckland	
Campbell S.L.	112 109*	West Indies v Auckland	Auckland	1999/00
	170	West Indies v New Zealand	Hamilton	
Wells J.D.	143	Wellington v Canterbury	Wellington	1999/00
	107 132*	Wellington v Central Districts	New Plymouth	
How J.M.	105 108*	Central Districts v Otago	Queenstown	2004/05
	121	Central Districts v Northern Districts	Napier	

Century on First-class Debut

† Watson G.	175	Canterbury v Otago	Christchurch	1880/81
Brook-Smith W.	112*	Auckland v Hawke's Bay	Auckland	1904/05
† Wood B.B.	108 & 18	Canterbury v Wellington	Wellington	1907/08
McMullan J.J.M.	157*	Otago v Southland	Dunedin	1917/18
† Snedden C.A.	119	Auckland v Hawke's Bay	Auckland	1920/21
Talbot R.O.	105	Canterbury v Otago	Dunedin	1922/23
Tindill E.W.T.	106 & 0	Wellington v Auckland	Auckland	1932/33
Scott V.J.	122	Auckland v Canterbury	Auckland	1937/38
† Ongley J.A.	110	Wellington v Otago	Wellington	1938/39
† Kerr A.C.	122	Auckland v Wellington	Auckland	1941/42
† Watt D.G.	15 & 105	Otago v Canterbury	Christchurch	1943/44
Smith K.F.H.	27 & 141*	Wellington v Central Districts	Wellington	1953/54
MacLeod D.N.	117	Central Districts v Wellington	Wanganui	1956/57
Bilby G.P.	132 & 2*	Wellington v Central Districts	Wellington	1962/63
† Mitchell W.J.	127*	Northern Districts v Pakistan	Hamilton	1964/65
† Sampson H.C.	25 & 119	Central Districts v Wellington	Wellington	1970/71
Vaughan J.T.C.	106* & 1	Auckland v Wellington	Wellington	1989/90
Aiken J.M.	39 & 156*	Wellington v Canterbury	Christchurch	1989/90

† only century in first-class cricket

B.R. Williams scored 103 in his fourth first-class match, not having batted in his first three matches, for Wellington v Central Districts at Wellington, 1989/90.*

Century on First-class Debut in Other Countries

In ENGLAND

Dacre C.C.R.	107	New Zealand v MCC	Lord's	1927
Crowe M.D.	104	D.B. Close's XI v Pakistan	Scarborough	1982
Horne M.J.	133	New Zealand v British Universities	Oxford	1999
Spearman C.M.	111	Gloucestershire v Worcestershire	Worcester	2002
Adams A.R.	124	Essex v Leicestershire	Leicester	2004

J.D.P. Oram scored 103 for New Zealand v Worcestershire at Worcester in 2004 in his first innings in England after not batting in his first game*

In AUSTRALIA

Sutcliffe B.	142	New Zealand v Western Australia	Perth	1953/54
Miller L.S.M.	142	New Zealand v South Australia	Adelaide	1953/54
Patel D.N.	105	New Zealand v Western Australia	Perth	1987/88

In SOUTH AFRICA

Reid J.R.	111	New Zealand v Western Province	Cape Town	1953/54
Kasper R.J.	122*	Natal B v Transvaal B	Pietermaritzburg	1970/71
Harris C.Z.	118*	Canterbury v Eastern Province	Grahamstown	1993/94
Richardson M.H.	173*	New Zealand v Boland	Paarl	2000/01

In WEST INDIES

Hastings B.F.	100*	New Zealand v Jamaica	Kingston	1971/72
Crowe M.D.	118	New Zealand v Shell Award XI	Kingston	1984/85
Styris S.B.	107	New Zealand v West Indies	St George's	2001/02

In INDIA

Taylor B.R.	105	New Zealand v India	Calcutta	1964/65
Burgess M.G.	102	Prime Minister's XI v President's XI	Bombay	1967/68
Parker J.M.	104	New Zealand v India	Bombay	1976/77
Wright J.G.	104	New Zealand v West Zone	Rajkot	1988/89
Crowe M.D.	101*	New Zealand v President's XI	Rajkot	1995/96
Oram J.D.P.	101*	New Zealand v India A	Rajkot	2003/04

M.H. Richardson scored 128 for New Zealand v India at Rajkot in 2003/04 in his first innings in India after not batting in his first game.*

In PAKISTAN

Reid J.R.	105*	NZ v Chief Commissioner's XI	Karachi	1955/56
Anderson R.W.	103*	NZ v NWFP Chief Minister's XI	Peshawar	1976/77

In SRI LANKA

Dempster C.S.	112*	Sir Julien Cahn's XI v Ceylon	Colombo	1936/37
Rutherford K.R.	108	NZ v Board President's XI	Galle	1986/87

In ZIMBABWE

Franklin T.J.	153*	Young New Zealand v Zimbabwe	Harare	1984/85
Horne M.J.	181	New Zealand v Mashonaland	Harare	1997/98
Sinclair M.S.	100*	New Zealand v President's XI	Mutare	2000/01

In BANGLADESH

McCullum B.B.	143	New Zealand v Bangladesh	Dhaka	2004/05

Century in Last First-class Match

† Phillips J.	110*	Canterbury v Wellington	Christchurch	1898/99
Midlane F.A.	126 & 4	Auckland v Wellington	Wellington	1918/19
† Beechey E.M.	180 & 5	Wellington vAuckland	Wellington	1918/19
† Watt D.G.	15 & 105	Otago v Canterbury	Christchurch	1943/44
Redmond R.E.	103 & 22	Auckland v Otago	Auckland	1975/76
Wadsworth K.J.	117	Canterbury v Otago	Christchurch	1975/76
Parker J.M.	1* & 100	Northern Districts v Wellington	Wellington	1983/84
† Snook I.R.	100*	Central Dists v Northern Dists	Palmerston North	1987/88
Dempsey D.A.	121 & 44	Canterbury v Otago	Dunedin	1987/88
Reid J.F.	112	Auckland v Northern Districts	Hamilton	1987/88
Mawhinney R.E.W.	9* & 108	Otago v Canterbury	Christchurch	1990/91
Twose R.G.	108 & 6	Wellington v Auckland	Wellington	2000/01
Nash D.J.	118 & 11*	Auckland v Otago	Dunedin	2001/02

† only first-class century of career. (D.G. Watt was making his only appearance in first-class cricket. J. Phillips was playing his 124th first-class match and 203rd innings).
J.D. Riley scored 34, 121, 26 and 94 (run out) in his final two first-class matches, for Auckland in 1976/77.*

Century in Each Innings of a Match

Dacre C.C.R.	127* & 101*	Auckland v Victoria	Auckland	1924/25
† Whitelaw P.E.	115 & 155	Auckland v Wellington	Auckland	1934/35
Uttley K.F.M.	132 & 138	Otago v Auckland	Auckland	1937/38
Sutcliffe B.	197 & 128	Otago v MCC	Dunedin	1946/47
Sutcliffe B.	118 & 125	Otago v Canterbury	Dunedin	1947/48
Sutcliffe B.	141 & 135	Auckland v Canterbury	Auckland	1948/49
Sutcliffe B.	243 & 100*	New Zealand v Essex	Southend	1949
Reid J.R.	101 & 118*	New Zealand v Orange Free State	Bloemfontein	1961/62
† Gedye S.G.	104 & 101	Auckland v Central Districts	Auckland	1963/64
† Thomson K.	102 & 102*	Canterbury v Otago	Dunedin	1966/67
Chappell G.S.	247* & 133	Australia v New Zealand	Wellington	1973/74
Chappell I.M.	145 & 121	Australia v New Zealand	Wellington	1973/74
Turner G.M.	101 & 110*	New Zealand v Australia	Christchurch	1973/74
Turner G.M.	135 & 108	Otago v Northern Districts	Gisborne	1974/75
Turner G.M.	105 & 186*	Otago v Central Districts	Dunedin	1974/75
Howarth G.P.	122 & 102	New Zealand v England	Auckland	1977/78
Wright J.G.	113 & 105	Northern Districts v Auckland	Auckland	1981/82
Parker J.M.	117 & 102*	Northern Districts v Central Districts	Tauranga	1981/82
Rutherford K.R.	105 & 104*	Otago v Northern Districts	Alexandra	1985/86
Border A.R.	140 & 114*	Australia v New Zealand	Christchurch	1985/86
Cooper B.G.	105 & 100	Northern Districts v Canterbury	Gisborne	1986/87
Crowe M.D.	144 & 151	Central Districts v Canterbury	New Plymouth	1986/87
Vance R.H.	116* & 123	Wellington v Central Districts	New Plymouth	1988/89
Hick G.A.	144 & 132	Northern Districts v Wellington	Morrinsville	1988/89
Jones A.H.	122 & 100*	New Zealand v Sri Lanka	Hamilton	1990/91
Gurusinha A.P.	119 & 102	Sri Lanka v New Zealand	Hamilton	1990/91
Maynard M.P.	195 & 110	Northern Districts v Auckland	Auckland	1991/92
Crowe M.D.	152 & 137*	Wellington v Canterbury	Christchurch	1992/93
Dravid R.S.	190 & 103*	India v New Zealand	Hamilton	1998/99
Rhodes J.N.	101* & 106*	South Africa v New Zealand A	Lincoln	1998/99
Campbell S.L.	112 & 109*	West Indies v Auckland	Auckland	1999/00
Wells J.D.	107 & 132*	Wellington v Central Districts	New Plymouth	1999/00
Spearman C.M.	100 & 115	New Zealand v North West	Potchefstroom	2000/01
Hopkins G.J.	113 & 175*	Canterbury v Auckland	Auckland	2002/03
Horne M.J.	118 & 209*	Auckland v Northern Districts	Auckland	2003/04
How J.M.	105 & 108*	Central Districts v Otago	Queenstown	2004/05

† maiden first-class century

Highest Maiden Centuries

301*	Fulton P.G.	Canterbury v Auckland	Christchurch	2002/03
290	Carson W.N.	Auckland v Otago	Dunedin	1936/37
209	White D.J.	Northern Districts v Central Districts	Hamilton	1985/86
204	Cox A.	Canterbury v Otago	Christchurch	1925/26
203*	Burnett G.P.	Wellington v Northern Districts	Hamilton	1991/92
196	Kerr J.L.	Canterbury v Wellington	Christchurch	1932/33
194	Gaffaney C.B.	Otago v Auckland	Dunedin	1996/97
193*	Stead D.W.	Canterbury v Central Districts	Christchurch	1980/81
190	Moloney D.A.R.	Wellington v Auckland	Auckland	1936/37
189	Sinclair M.S.	Central Districts v Wellington	Masterton	1996/97
184	Taylor R.L.	Central Districts v Wellington	Palmerston North	2004/05
183	Gillespie H.D.	Auckland v Canterbury	Auckland	1929/30
182	McIntosh T.G.	Auckland v Canterbury	Christchurch	2000/01
180	Beechey E.M.	Wellington v Auckland	Wellington	1918/19
180	Dempster C.S.	New Zealand v Warwickshire	Birmingham	1927
180	Mooney F.L.H.	Wellington v Auckland	Wellington	1943/44
179	Ormiston R.W.	Wellington v Central Districts	New Plymouth	1982/83
177	Chandler P.J.B.	Wellington v Auckland	Wellington	1996/97
176	Cuff L.A.	Canterbury v Auckland	Christchurch	1893/94
175	Watson G.	Canterbury v Otago	Christchurch	1880/81
175	Astle N.J.	Canterbury v Northern Districts	Hamilton	1994/95
172	Worker R.V. de R.	Otago v Canterbury	Dunedin	1923/24
172	Englefield J.I.	Canterbury v Central Districts	Blenheim	2000/01
167*	Hart R.T.	Central Districts v Canterbury	New Plymouth	1983/84
167	Lawrence J.D.	Canterbury v Auckland	Christchurch	1893/94
165	Redgrave W.P.	Wellington v Hawkes Bay	Wellington	1905/06
165	Chapple M.E.	Canterbury v South Africans	Christchurch	1952/53
165	Truscott P.B.	NZ Under-23 v Auckland	Auckland	1963/64
164*	Duff S.W.	Central Districts v Auckland	Wanganui	1991/92
164	Powell J.L.	Canterbury v Otago	Christchurch	1929/30
163*	How J.M.	Central Districts v Northern Districts	Hamilton	2002/03
163	Menzies R.E.J.	Canterbury v Wellington	Christchurch	1938/39
163	Williams A.B.	Wellington v Canterbury	Christchurch	1896/97
163	Reade L.B.	Central Districts v Northern Districts	Palmerston North	1960/61
161	Larsen G.R.	Wellington v Central Districts	Levin	1987/88
159*	Kennedy P.G.	Canterbury v Northern Districts	Rotorua	1990/91
159	Vincent L.	Auckland v Northern Districts	Auckland	1998/99
158*	Papps M.H.W.	Canterbury v Otago	Christchurch	2001/02
158	Harford N.S.	New Zealand v Oxford University	Oxford	1958
157*	McMullan J.J.M.	Otago v Southland	Dunedin	1917/18
157	Briasco P.S.	Central Districts v Canterbury	New Plymouth	1983/84
156*	Aiken J.M.	Wellington v Canterbury	Christchurch	1989/90
155*	James V.	Canterbury v Otago	Dunedin	1940/41
155*	Parore A.C.	Auckland v Otago	Dunedin	1991/92
155	Badcock F.T.	Wellington v Canterbury	Christchurch	1926/27
155	Oram J.D.P.	Central Districts v Canterbury	Christchurch	1998/99
154	Meuli E.M.	Central Districts v Auckland	Palmerston North	1952/53
152	Knight A.R.	Otago v Canterbury	Dunedin	1940/41
152	Kemp R.J.	Wellington v Auckland	Auckland	1947/48
152	Coutts P.J.C.	Central Districts v Canterbury	Christchurch	1966/67
152	Lees W.K.	New Zealand v Pakistan	Karachi	1976/77
152	Brown S.W.	Auckland v Central Districts	Auckland	1990/91
151	Petrie E.C.	Auckland v Wellington	Auckland	1953/54
150	Crowe M.D.	Auckland v Central Districts	New Plymouth	1981/82

Watson, McMullan and Aiken scored their centuries on their debut in first-class cricket. Beechey was playing in his last first-class game. Carson (aged 20 years 168 days) and Cox (21 years 19 days) were both playing only their second first-class innings and remain the youngest players to score a double-century in New Zealand first-class cricket.

One Hundred Runs before Lunch

Runs	Mins					
*110	120		Smith S.G.	Auckland v Canterbury	Auckland	1919/20
112	113		Macartney C.G.	NSW v Wellington	Wellington	1923/24
*116	120	†	Punch A.T.E.	NSW v Otago	Dunedin	1923/24
*101	91		Macartney C.G.	NSW v Otago	Dunedin	1923/24
103	110		Hiddleston J.S.	Wellington v Canterbury	Wellington	1925/26
105	102		Dacre C.C.R.	Auckland v Otago	Dunedin	1926/27
103	103	†	Vorrath W.	Otago v Wellington	Dunedin	1927/28
*106	120		Blunt R.C.	Otago v Canterbury	Christchurch	1928/29
164	130	†	Powell J.L.	Canterbury v Otago	Christchurch	1929/30
105	105		Badcock F.T.	Otago v Canterbury	Christchurch	1931/32
*111	120		Hammond W.R.	England v New Zealand	Auckland	1932/33
102	120		Whitelaw P.E.	Auckland v Wellington	Auckland	1934/35
115	110		Wallace W.M.	New Zealand v Somerset	Taunton	1937
*110	120		Wallace W.M.	New Zealand v Sussex	Hove	1937
*103	120		Smith F.B.	Canterbury v Auckland	Auckland	1948/49
100	117		Sutcliffe B.	New Zealand v Essex	Southend	1949
*100	120		Reid J.R.	Wellington v Otago	Wellington	1951/52
*122	111		Guillen S.C.	Canterbury v Fiji	Christchurch	1953/54
*100	126		Smith K.F.H.	Central Districts v Wellington	Wanganui	1959/60
*108	131		Sutcliffe B.	Otago v Central Districts	Dunedin	1959/60
*100	140		Sutcliffe B.	Otago v Northern Districts	Wellington	1960/61
*174	140		Reid J.R.	Wellington v Northern Districts	Wellington	1962/63
120	125		Reid J.R.	Wellington v Northern Districts	Wellington	1964/65
103	120		Murray B.A.G.	New Zealand v President's XI	Rawalpindi	1969/70
*109	141		Dunning B.	Northern Dist. v Central Dist.	Blenheim	1972/73
111	150		Dempsey D.A.	Canterbury v Otago	Christchurch	1980/81
102	147	†	Crowe M.D.	Auckland v Central Districts	New Plymouth	1981/82
*100	107		Chappell G.S.	Australia v New Zealand	Christchurch	1981/82
*100	150		Crowe J.J.	Auckland v Northern Districts	Rotorua	1983/84
101	103		Rutherford K.R.	New Zealand v DB Close's XI	Scarborough	1986
*101	144		Jones A.H.	Wellington v Otago	Wellington	1986/87
*112	149		McSweeney E.B.	Wellington v Central Districts	Levin	1987/88
*122	150		Crowe J.J.	Auckland v Wellington	Wellington	1988/89
*117	160		Greatbatch M.J.	Central Districts v Otago	Palmerston North	1988/89
101	127		Blain T.E.	Central Districts v Wellington	New Plymouth	1988/89
107	136	†	Reid R.B.	Auckland v Central Districts	Masterton	1989/90
*116	136		Thomson S.A.	Northern Districts v Auckland	Auckland	1990/91
141	144		Maynard M.P.	Northern Districts v Auckland	Auckland	1991/92
*139	92		Patel D.N.	Auckland v Northern Districts	Auckland	1991/92
104	140		Spearman C.M.	Central Districts v Wellington	Wellington	1997/98
101	137		Cairns C.L.	Southern v Central	Wellington	1998/99
103	140		How J.M.	Central Districts v Northern Districts	Napier	2004/05
105	140		Fulton P.G.	Canterbury v Otago	Christchurch	2004/05

** batsman had been not out overnight*
† maiden first-class hundred. Punch, Vorrath, Powell and Reid did not score another century in first-class cricket

Scores of Ninety-nine

	Johnson P.R.	MCC v New Zealand	Christchurch	1906/07
†	Snedden A.N.C.	Auckland v Canterbury	Auckland	1921/22

§	Elmes C.J.	New Zealand v MCC	Auckland	1935/36
*	Whitelaw P.E.	Auckland/Wellington v MCC	Auckland	1936/37
	Sutcliffe B.	Otago v Auckland	Dunedin	1947/48
	Taylor D.D.	Auckland v Canterbury	Auckland	1948/49
†	Leggat J.G.	Canterbury v Auckland	Christchurch	1951/52
	Rae A.F.	West Indies v New Zealand	Auckland	1951/52
	O'Malley P.W.	Canterbury v Wellington	Christchurch	1953/54
†	Beck J.E.F.	New Zealand v South Africa	Cape Town	1953/54
	Hunter A.A.	Central Districts v Auckland	Auckland	1953/54
†	Leggat J.G.	Canterbury v MCC	Christchurch	1954/55
	Sutcliffe B.	Rest v New Zealand XI	Christchurch	1957/58
	Sutcliffe B.	New Zealand v Sussex	Hove	1958
§*	Bartlett G.A.	Central Districts v Auckland	Auckland	1959/60
	McGregor S.N.	Otago v Canterbury	Christchurch	1963/64
†	Cunis R.S.	Auckland v Wellington	Wellington	1966/67
	Surti R.F.	India v New Zealand	Auckland	1967/68
	Turner G.M.	New Zealand v Tasmania	Hobart	1969/70
	Burtt J.W.	Canterbury v Central Districts	Christchurch	1970/71
	Dowling G.T.	Canterbury v Northern Districts	Hamilton	1970/71
	Murray B.A.G.	Wellington v Northern Districts	Wellington	1970/71
	Dowling G.T.	New Zealand v Western Australia	Perth	1970/71
§*	O'Keeffe K.J.	Australia v Auckland	Auckland	1973/74
	Edwards G.N.	Central Districts v Australia	Nelson	1976/77
	Blair W.L.	Otago v Auckland	Auckland	1978/79
	Crowe M.D.	Auckland v Northern Districts	Auckland	1981/82
	Hadlee R.J.	New Zealand v England	Christchurch	1983/84
†	Lees W.K.	Otago v Northern Districts	Hamilton	1983/84
	Vance R.H.	Wellington v Canterbury	Wellington	1984/85
	Coney J.V.	New Zealand v President's XI	St Lucia	1984/85
	Jones A.H.	Wellington v Auckland	Auckland	1985/86
§*	Robertson G.K.	Central Districts v Otago	Oamaru	1985/86
	Wright J.G.	New Zealand v Australia	Melbourne	1987/88
	Crocker L.M.	Northern Districts v Wellington	Hamilton	1987/88
	Moxon M.D.	England v New Zealand	Auckland	1987/88
	McEwan P.E.	Canterbury v Wellington	Christchurch	1988/89
	Hart R.T.	Central Districts v Auckland	Masterton	1989/90
	Wright J.G.	New Zealand v Worcestershire	Worcester	1990
†	Patel D.N.	New Zealand v England	Christchurch	1991/92
+	Wright J.G.	New Zealand v England	Christchurch	1991/92
	Douglas M.W.	Central Districts v Auckland	Wanganui	1991/92
	McSweeney E.B.	Wellington v Canterbury	Wellington	1993/94
	Twose R.G.	Central Districts v Auckland	Palmerston North	1993/94
†	Jones R.A.	Auckland v Otago	Dunedin	1996/97
*	Sinclair M.S.	Central Districts v Northern Districts	Hamilton	1996/97
	Twose R.G.	Wellington v India	Wellington	1998/99
§	Yovich J.A.F.	Northern Districts v Auckland	Taupo	1999/00
	Richardson M.H.	New Zealand v Zimbabwe	Harare	2000/01
	Fleming S.P.	New Zealand v South Africa	Bloemfontein	2000/01
	Gaffaney C.B.	Otago v Auckland	Auckland	2000/01
	Nevin C.J.	Wellington v Otago	Wellington	2000/01
	Sinclair M.S.	Central Districts v South Africa	Napier	2003/04
	Gaffaney C.B.	Otago v Wellington	Wellington	2004/05
	McCullum B.B.	New Zealand v Sri Lanka	Napier	2004/05

** not out   † batsman was run out   + batsman was stumped   § highest score in first-class cricket*

Carried Bat Through a Complete Innings

	Score	Total			
Harris L.M.	41*	65	Otago v Tasmania	Dunedin	1883/84
Gatehouse G.H.	54*	146	Tasmania v Otago	Dunedin	1883/84
Mills I.	88*	156	Auckland v Otago	Dunedin	1893/94
† Collins J.C.	128*	187	Fiji v Hawke's Bay	Napier	1894/95
Cobcroft L.T.	85*	239	NSW v Wellington	Wellington	1895/96
Mills G.	106*	235	Auckland v Wellington	Auckland	1895/96
Collins D.C.	53*	131	Wellington v Canterbury	Christchurch	1906/07
§ Midlane F.A.	14*	60	Wellington§ v Canterbury	Christchurch	1910/11
Gibbes W.R.L.	75*	193	Wellington v Canterbury	Christchurch	1911/12
† Midlane F.A.	222*	498	Wellington v Otago	Wellington	1914/15
Blunt R.C.	137*	336	Canterbury v Wellington	Wellington	1919/20
† Bardsley W.	200*	352	NSW v Auckland	Auckland	1923/24
Blunt R.C.	131*	204	Otago v Canterbury	Dunedin	1926/27
Dempster C.S.	167*	345	New Zealand v Glamorgan	Cardiff	1927
Kerr J.L.	146*	243	Canterbury v MCC	Christchurch	1935/36
Whitelaw P.E.	99*	183	Auckland/Wellington v MCC	Auckland	1936/37
Tindill E.W.T.	47*	111	Wellington v Otago	Dunedin	1946/47
† Miller L.S.M.	81*	154	Wellington v Otago	Dunedin	1956/57
Playle W.R.	89*	139	Auckland v Northern Districts	Auckland	1959/60
Bradburn W.P.	45*	87	Northern Districts v Wellington	Wellington	1960/61
Bradburn W.P.	37*	57	Northern Districts v Wellington	Hamilton	1961/62
Holloway R.A.	61*	122	Otago v Central Districts	Nelson	1962/63
Turner G.M.	43*	131	New Zealand v England	Lord's	1969
Turner G.M.	223*	386	New Zealand v West Indies	Kingston	1971/72
Redpath I.R.	159*	346	Australia v New Zealand	Auckland	1973/74
Wettimuny S.	63*	144	Sri Lanka v New Zealand	Christchurch	1982/83
† Franklin T.J.	153*	311	Young NZ v Zimbabwe	Harare	1984/85
Rutherford K.R.	89*	241	Otago v Auckland	Dunedin	1984/85
Boon D.C.	58*	103	Australia v New Zealand	Auckland	1985/86
Wright J.G.	149*	307	Canterbury v Auckland	Auckland	1988/89
Smith C.J.P.	90*	154	Central Dists v Northern Dists	Rotorua	1989/90
Murray D.J.	106*	233	Canterbury v Northern Dists	Hamilton	1992/93
Dobbs P.W.	81*	177	Otago v Canterbury	Oamaru	1994/95
Atherton M.A.	94*	228	England v New Zealand	Christchurch	1996/97
Kelly D.P.	212*	538	Central Districts v Canterbury	Blenheim	2000/01
Ingram P.J.	105*	201	Central Districts v Auckland	Auckland	2003/04

† player was on the field for every ball of the match *§ one man absent*

Longest Individual Batting in a Match

Mins	Runs				
954	274* & 69*	Fleming S.P.	New Zealand v Sri Lanka	Colombo	2002/03
876	76 & 146*	Greatbatch M.J.	New Zealand v Australia	Perth	1989/90
835	122 & 102	Howarth G.P.	New Zealand v England	Auckland	1977/78
828	75 & 138	Wright J.G.	New Zealand v West Indies	Wellington	1986/87
813	93 & 101	Richardson M.H.	New Zealand v England	Lord's	2004
770	166* & 82	Congdon B.E.	New Zealand v West Indies	Port-of-Spain	1971/72

Longest Individual Innings

Mins	Runs				
741	306	Richardson M.H.	New Zealand v Zimbabwe A	Kwekwe	2000/01
720	163	Shoaib Mohammad	Pakistan v New Zealand	Wellington	1988/89
704	259	Turner G.M.	New Zealand v West Indies	Georgetown	1971/72
685	180	Reid J.F.	New Zealand v Sri Lanka	Colombo	1983/84
671	212*	Richardson M.H.	New Zealand A v Sussex	Hove	2000
659	211*	Gibbs H.H.	South Africa v New Zealand	Christchurch	1998/99
658	275*	Cullinan D.J.	South Africa v New Zealand	Auckland	1998/99
655	146*	Greatbatch M.J.	New Zealand v Australia	Perth	1989/90
655	274*	Fleming S.P.	New Zealand v Sri Lanka	Colombo	2002/03
648	158	Radley C.T.	England v New Zealand	Auckland	1977/78
647	251*	Harris C.Z.	Canterbury v Central Districts	Rangiora	1996/97
636	170*	Jones A.H.	New Zealand v India	Auckland	1989/90
625	222	Rutherford I.A.	Otago v Central Districts	New Plymouth	1978/79
610	299	Crowe M.D.	New Zealand v Sri Lanka	Wellington	1990/91
609	120*	Crowe J.J.	New Zealand v Sri Lanka	Colombo	1986/87
605	267*	Young B.A.	New Zealand v Sri Lanka	Dunedin	1996/97
603	259	Turner G.M.	New Zealand v Guyana	Georgetown	1971/72

Fastest Centuries

Mins	Balls				
52	45	Cairns B.L.	Otago v Wellington	Lower Hutt	1979/80
52	66	Cooper B.G.	Northern Districts v Canterbury	Gisborne	1986/87
53	63	Motz R.C.	Canterbury v Otago	Christchurch	1967/68

Slowest Centuries

Mins	Balls				
516	331	Crowe J.J.	New Zealand v Sri Lanka	Colombo	1986/87
487	397	Radley C.T.	England v New Zealand	Auckland	1977/78
464	390	Austen M.H.	Otago v Canterbury	Christchurch	1996/97
462	341	Greatbatch M.J.	New Zealand v Australia	Perth	1989/90
461	265	Crowe M.D.	New Zealand v Pakistan	Lahore	1990/91
458	341	Astle N.J.	New Zealand v Zimbabwe	Wellington	2000/01
455	307	Howarth G.P.	New Zealand v England	Auckland	1977/78
435	†	Guy J.W.	New Zealand v India	Hyderabad	1955/56
434	380	Reid J.F.	Auckland v Northern Districts	Hamilton	1987/88
434	309	Franklin T.J.	New Zealand v England	Lord's	1990
427	368	Burns K.J.	Otago v Northern Districts	Hamilton	1987/88
426	289	Saqlain Mushtaq	Pakistan v New Zealand	Christchurch	2000/01
422	349	Boyle D.J.	Canterbury v Otago	Rangiora	1993/94
421	291	Woodcock L.J.	Wellington v Auckland	Auckland	2004/05
420	332	Crowe M.D.	New Zealand v West Indies	Georgetown	1984/85
414	399	Wright J.G.	New Zealand v India	Auckland	1980/81
412	325	Wright J.G.	New Zealand v West Indies	Wellington	1986/87
404	311	Reid J.F.	New Zealand v Pakistan	Wellington	1984/85
402	289	Richardson M.H.	New Zealand v England	Lord's	2004

† details not available

Most Boundaries in an Innings

	6s	4s		Runs			
53	8	45	Rutherford K.R.	317	New Zealand v D.B. Close's XI	Scarborough	1986
50	15	35	Reid J.R.	296	Wellington v Northern Districts	Wellington	1962/63
49	3	46	Sutcliffe B.	385	Otago v Canterbury	Christchurch	1952/53
48	3	45	Fulton P.G.	301*	Canterbury v Auckland	Christchurch	2002/03
47	3	44	Trumper V.T.	293	Sims' Australian XI v Canterbury	Christchurch	1913/14
43	10	33	Hammond W.R.	336*	England v New Zealand	Auckland	1932/33
43	—	43	Richardson M.H.	306	New Zealand v Zimbabwe A	Kwekwe	2000/01
42	1	41	Reid J.R.	283	Wellington v Otago	Wellington	1951/52
42	1	41	Crowe M.D.	242*	New Zealand v South Australia	Adelaide	1985/86
42	3	39	Crowe M.D.	242	Central Districts v Otago	New Plymouth	1989/90
41	—	41	Blunt R.C.	338*	Otago v Canterbury	Christchurch	1931/32
40	—	40	de Silva P.A.	267	Sri Lanka v New Zealand	Wellington	1990/91

Most Sixes in an Innings

Sixes		Runs			
15	Reid J.R.	296	Wellington v Northern Districts	Wellington	1962/63
12	Patel D.N.	204	Auckland v Northern Districts	Auckland	1991/92
11	Astle N.J.	222	New Zealand v England	Christchurch	2001/02
11	Spearman C.M.	133	Central Districts v Auckland	Auckland	2003/04
10	Hammond W.R.	336*	England v New Zealand	Auckland	1932/33
10	Robinson R.T.	166	England XI v Northern Districts	Hamilton	1987/88
10	Styris S.B.	212*	Northern Districts v Otago	Hamilton	2001/02
9	Cairns B.L.	110	Otago v Wellington	Lower Hutt	1979/80
9	Botham I.T.	80	England XI v Central Districts	Palmerston North	1983/84
9	Cairns C.L.	120	New Zealand v Zimbabwe	Auckland	1995/96
8	Dacre C.C.R.	176	New Zealand v Derbyshire	Derby	1927
8	Bula I.L.	102	Fiji v Canterbury	Christchurch	1953/54
8	Rutherford K.R.	317	New Zealand v DB Close's XI	Scarborough	1986
8	Germon L.K.	160*	Canterbury v Wellington	Christchurch	1989/90
8	Parore A.C.	111*	Auckland v Wellington	Auckland	1997/98
8	Horne M.J.	209*	Auckland v Northern Districts	Auckland	2003/04
7	Tallon D.	116	Australia v New Zealand	Dunedin	1949/50
7	Sutcliffe B.	80*	New Zealand v South Africa	Johannesburg	1953/54
7	Cairns B.L.	68	New Zealand v New South Wales	Sydney	1980/81
7	Greenidge G.C.	213	West Indies v New Zealand	Auckland	1986/87
7	Hick G.A.	146	Northern Districts v England XI	Hamilton	1987/88
7	Maynard M.P.	195	Northern Districts v Auckland	Auckland	1991/92
7	Hick G.A.	115	England XI v Central Districts	New Plymouth	1991/92
7	Cairns C.L.	158	New Zealand v South Africa	Auckland	2003/04

Five Sixes off Consecutive Balls

Germon L.K.	off Vance R.H.	Canterbury v Wellington	Christchurch	1989/90

(Full tosses and deliberate no-balls were provided for him to hit).

Four Sixes off Consecutive Balls

Rutherford K.R.	off Doshi D.R.	New Zealand v DB Close's XI	Scarborough	1986

Three Sixes off Consecutive Balls

Hill C.	off Ollivier K.M.	Australia v New Zealand	Wellington	1904/05
Hammond W.R.	off Newman J.	England v New Zealand	Auckland	1932/33
McRae D.A.N.	off Burke C.	Canterbury v Auckland	Auckland	1937/38
Pritchard T.L.	off Groves L.J.	Wellington v Otago	Dunedin	1937/38

Edwards R.M.	off Carew M.C.	Governor General's XI v West Indies	Auckland	1968/69
Burgess M.G.	off Anderson R.W.	Auckland v Central Districts	Wanganui	1977/78
Stirling D.A.	off Brown V.R.	Central Districts v Canterbury	New Plymouth	1986/87
Thomson S.A.	off Bracewell J.G.	Northern Districts v Auckland	Auckland	1987/88
Hick G.A.	off Duff S.W.	England XI v Central Districts	New Plymouth	1991/92
Astle N.J.	off Wells J.D.	Canterbury v Wellington	Christchurch	1994/95
Vincent L.	off Vettori D.L.	Auckland v Northern Districts	Auckland	1998/99
Astle N.J.	off Caddick A.R.	New Zealand v England	Christchurch	2001/02
Spearman C.M.	off Nicol R.J.	Central Districts v Auckland	Auckland	2003/04

Most Ducks in Succession

5	Hayes J.A.	(C, NZ 1954/55)	17,0 / dnb / 0,0 / 0,0
5	Bateman S.N.	(C 1982/83)	5*,0 / 0,0 / 0,0
4	Silver R.C.D.	(O 1936/37-1937/38)	12,0 / 0,0 / 0,11
*4	Langdon M.C.	(ND 1957/58)	25,0 / 0,0 / 0,5
4	Hastings B.F.	(C 1963/64)	1,0 / 0,0 / 0,35
4	Bracewell B.P.	(NZ 1978)	0 / dnb / 0,0 / 0,0*
4	Bradburn G.E.	(ND 1987/88)	0 / 0,0 / 0
4	Steele H.K.C.	(A 1974/75)	0,0 / 0,0
4	Morrison D.K.	(NZ 1993/94)	0 / 0,0 / 0,20*
4	Davis H.T.	(NZ, W 1997/98)	7*,0 / 0,0 / 0,21
4	Young R.A.	(A 1999/00)	0,0 / 0,0
4	Martin C.S.	(C NZ 2000/01)	5,0 / 0,0 / 0
4	Gaffaney C.B.	(O 2001/02)	31,0 / 0,0 / 0,56
4	Hamilton L.J.	(CD 2004/05)	11,0/ 0,0/ 0,2

** first three games in first-class cricket*

Most Scoreless Innings in Succession

10	Visser P.J.	(CD 1984/85-1985/86)	0 / 0,0 / dnb / 0*,0 / dnb / 0*,0* 0,0 / dnb / 0
7	Hamilton L.J.	(CD 1999/00)	0,0* / 0 / 0*,0 / 0 / 0
6	Hayes J.A.	(C, NZ 1954/55-1955/56)	17,0 / dnb / 0,0 / 0,0 / 0*
6	de Groen R.P.	(A 1988/89-1989/90)	1,0* / dnb / 0,0 / 0* / 0*,0*
*5	Moss A.E.	(C 1889/90)	0,0* / 0,0 / 0*,4*
5	Burrows J.T.	(C 1932/33)	0*,0* / 0* / 0*,0*
5	Hill J.	(O 1961/62-1962/63)	0*,0* / 0* / 0*,0*
5	Unka H.	(ND 1968/69-1971/72)	0* / 0*,0* / dnb / 0*,0
5	Bracewell B.P.	(NZ 1978)	0 / dnb / 0,0 / 0,0*
5	Troup G.B.	(A, NZ 1980/81-1981/82)	0,0* / 0,0 / dnb / 0
5	Bateman S.N.	(C 1982/83)	5*,0 / 0,0 / 0,0

** first five innings in first-class cricket*

UNUSUAL DISMISSALS

HANDLED THE BALL

Benson E.T.	MCC v Auckland	Auckland	1929/30
Gilbertson A.W.	Otago v Auckland	Auckland	1952/53
Vaughan J.T.C.	NZ Emerging Players v England XI	Hamilton	1991/92

OBSTRUCTING THE FIELD

Hayes J.A.	Canterbury v Central Districts	Christchurch	1954/55

RUN OUT BY THE BOWLER *(while backing up before the ball had been bowled)*

Reese T.W. by Downes A.D.	Canterbury v Otago	Christchurch	1894/95
Smith J. by Allen R.	Canterbury v Wellington	Wellington	1943/44
Randall D.W. by Chatfield E.J.	England v New Zealand	Christchurch	1977/78

STUMPED BY A SUBSTITUTE

Pervez Sajjad by Congdon B.E.	Pakistan v New Zealand	Lahore	1964/65
Congdon B.E. by Burge P.J.P.	Central Districts v Australia	Palmerston North	1966/67

RETIRED (out)

Ransford V.S.	Australia v Hawke's Bay	Napier	1920/21
Chappell G.S.	Australia v Wellington	Wellington	1976/77
Saeed Anwar	Pakistan v New Zealand XI	Napier	1993/94
Basit Ali	Pakistan v New Zealand XI	Napier	1993/94
Inzamam-ul-Haq	Pakistan v New Zealand XI	Napier	1993/94
Spearman C.M.	New Zealand v North West	Potchefstroom	2000/01

REPLACEMENT PLAYERS

Substitute	*Player replaced*			
Lawrence —	Bell A.	Wellington v Nelson	Wellington	1873/74
Cotterill C.N.	White G.	Hawke's Bay v NSW	Napier	1893/94
unknown	Ratu Epeli	Fiji v Auckland	Auckland	1894/95
Kilgour W.A.	*Wilson C.G.	Otago v Auckland	Auckland	1907/08
Bryden J.S.	*Siedeberg H.G.	Otago v Canterbury	Dunedin	1913/14
Graham W.H.	Middleton F.S.	Auckland v Wellington	Wellington	1917/18
Whitta H.B.	*Foster P.S.	Canterbury v Wellington	Christchurch	1919/20
Samuels B.	*Brice A.W.S.	Wellington v Auckland	Auckland	1919/20
Wilson E.S.	Eastman L.C.	Otago v Wellington	Wellington	1927/28
Kubunavanua P.	Logavatu I.T.	Fiji v Canterbury	Christchurch	1947/48
Abernethy B.	Webb R.J.	Otago v Auckland	Dunedin	1982/83
Neutze P.S.	Brown V.R.	Auckland v Wellington	Auckland	1987/88
Brown R.K.	Greatbatch M.J.	CD v Otago	Palmerston North	1991/92
Lee C.D.	Larsen G.R.	Wellington v ND	Hamilton	1991/92
Fleming S.P.	Harris C.Z.	Canterbury v Auckland	Auckland	1991/92
Lee C.D.	*Patel D.N.	Auckland v Otago	Dunedin	1994/95
Garner C.D.	Spearman C.M.	CD v ND	Nelson	1996/97
Cooper D.M.	Howell L.G.	CD v ND	Nelson	1996/97
Lamont M.J.	Horne M.J.	Otago v Auckland	Dunedin	1996/97
Morland N.D.	Wiseman P.J.	Otago v Auckland	Dunedin	1996/97
Sewell D.G.	Kennedy R.J.	Otago v Auckland	Dunedin	1996/97
Irving R.J.R.	Mills J.M.	Auckland v Otago	Dunedin	1996/97
Weenink S.W.	Chandler P.J.B.	Wellington v Canterbury	Christchurch	1996/97
Jonas G.R.	Davis H.T.	Wellington v Canterbury	Christchurch	1996/97
Hartland B.R.	Murray D.J.	Canterbury v Wellington	Christchurch	1996/97
Frew R.M.	Harris C.Z.	Canterbury v Wellington	Christchurch	1996/97
Sharpe M.F.	Allott G.I.	Canterbury v Wellington	Christchurch	1996/97
Hotter S.J.	Davis H.T.	Wellington v CD	Masterton	1996/97
Muir G.A.	Priest M.W.	Canterbury v Zimbabwe	Timaru	1997/98
Pawson S.J.	Priest M.W.	Canterbury v Otago	Dunedin	1997/98
Dry L.R.	Bell M.D.	Wellington v ND	Hamilton	1998/99
Morland N.D.	*Wiseman P.J.	Otago v Auckland	Dunedin	1999/00
Spearman C.M.	Sinclair M.S.	CD v Otago	Palmerston North	1999/00
Todd G.R.	Oram J.D.P.	CD v Wellington	Napier	2000/01
McCullum N.L.	Wiseman P.J.	Otago v Canterbury	Alexandra	2000/01
Robinson G.G.	*Marshall J.A.H.	ND v Canterbury	Gisborne	2004/05

** indicates player did not bat or bowl before being replaced*

REPRESENTED TWO PROVINCES IN ONE SEASON

Sutcliffe B.	Auckland and Otago	1946/47
Sutcliffe B.	Otago and Auckland	1947/48
Clark L.A.	Otago and Auckland	1959/60
Andrews B.	Canterbury and Central Districts	1966/67

On each occasion, the second province was represented in a match against a non-provincial side. No player has played for two provinces in inter-provincial matches in the same season.

BOWLING

Ten Wickets in an Innings

	Overs	Maidens	Runs	Wickets			
* Moss A.E.	21.3	10	28	10	Canterbury v Wellington	Christchurch	1889/90

** on debut — the only instance in first-class cricket*

Nine Wickets in an Innings

	Overs	Maidens	Runs	Wickets			
Wiseman P.J.	16.4	9	13	9	Canterbury v CD	Christchurch	2004/05
Wensley A.F.	24	13	36	9	Auckland v Otago	Auckland	1929/30
Eden T.	15.2	0	43	9	Nelson v Wellington	Wellington	1875/76
Dent T.H.	28	11	47	9	Hawke's Bay v Wellington	Napier	1900/01
Tait A.R.	24.5	8	48	9	ND v Auckland	Hamilton	1996/97
Fisher A.H.	25.2	4	50	9	Otago v Queensland	Dunedin	1896/97
Hadlee R.J.	23.4	4	52	9	New Zealand v Australia	Brisbane	1985/86
Hadlee R.J.	24	5	55	9	New Zealand v West Zone	Rajkot	1988/89
McBeath D.J.	24	7	56	9	Canterbury v Auckland	Christchurch	1918/19
Brice A.W.S.	25.5	5	67	9	Wellington v Auckland	Wellington	1918/19
Cooke F.H.	56	24	73	9	Otago v Canterbury	Christchurch	1884/85
Blair R.W.	35	9	72	9	Wellington v Auckland	Wellington	1956/57
Neill R.	31	7	75	9	Auckland v Canterbury	Auckland	1891/92
Blair R.W.	29.5	9	75	9	Wellington v Canterbury	Wellington	1956/57
Neill R.	24.2	1	86	9	Auckland v Canterbury	Auckland	1897/98
Petherick P.J.	35	10	93	9	Otago v ND	Dunedin	1975/76
Priest M.W.	28.5	5	95	9	Canterbury v Otago	Dunedin	1989/90
Robertson W.	39.3	8	98	9	Canterbury v Wellington	Christchurch	1894/95
Yuile B.W.	45	19	100	9	CD v Canterbury	New Plymouth	1965/66

Sixteen Wickets in a Match

16-130	Tait A.R.	24.5-8-48-9/38.4-13-82-7	Northern Dists v Auckland, Hamilton	1996/97

Fifteen Wickets in a Match

15-60	Callaway S.T.	23.3-10-33-8/17-7-27-7	Canterbury v Hawke's Bay, Napier	1903/04
15-94	Cooke F.H.	40.3-16-61-8/33.3-14-33-7	Otago v Canterbury, Christchurch	1882/83
15-104	Boock S.L.	29.3-13-47-7/34.3-16-57-8	Otago v Auckland, Dunedin	1989/90
15-123	Hadlee R.J.	23.4-4-52-9/28.5-9-71-6	NZ v Australia, Brisbane	1985/86
15-168	McBeath D.J.	24-7-56-9/37-4-112-6	Canterbury v Auckland, Christchurch	1918/19
15-175	Callaway S.T.	35-14-77-7/43.4-11-98-8	NSW v New Zealand, Christchurch	1895/96
15-203	Moir A.M.	24.1-4-84-7/35.1-3-119-8	Otago v Central Dists, New Plymouth	1953/54

Fourteen Wickets in a Match

14-59	Read R.J.	13-3-35-7/14-5-24-7	Canterbury v Southland, Invercargill	1920/21
14-63	Eden T.	15.2-0-43-9/15.5-7-20-5	Nelson v Wellington, Wellington	1875/76
* 14-63	Rees A.W.	13-4-27-6/15.3-3-36-8	Auckland v Otago, Dunedin	1889/90
14-65	Callaway S.T.	36.3-18-47-7/18.2-7-18-7	NSW v Wellington, Wellington	1895/96
14-65	Hayes J.A.	18.2-6-28-7/12.1-3-37-7	Auckland v Wellington, Auckland	1957/58
14-93	Torrance R.C.	23-6-51-7/19-5-42-7	Otago v Hawke's Bay, Napier	1908/09
14-94	Howarth H.J.	22.1-5-42-7/23-6-52-7	Auckland v Otago, Dunedin	1973/74
14-103	Downes A.D.	30-12-32-7/30-8-71-7	Otago v Hawke's Bay, Dunedin	1893/94
* 14-107	Robertson W.	28.2-8-59-8/20.4-7-48-6	Canterbury v Auckland, Christchurch	1893/94
14-119	Pringle C.	27.4-10-63-7/23.5-5-56-7	Auckland v Otago, Dunedin	1993/94
14-126	Moir A.M.	18-1-55-8/25-6-71-6	Otago v Canterbury, Dunedin	1951/52
14-136	Blair R.W.	29.5-9-75-9/26-8-61-5	Wellington v Canterbury, Wellington	1956/57
14-151	Gray E.J.	50-19-114-6/26.1-12-37-8	Wellington v Canterbury, Lower Hutt	1985/86

** on debut*

Four Wickets with Consecutive Balls

Downes A.D.	Otago v Auckland	Dunedin	1893/94

Hat Tricks

Salmon I.J.	Wellington v Nelson	Wellington	1873/74
Lankham W.	Auckland v Taranaki	Auckland	1882/83
Frith C.	Otago v Canterbury	Dunedin	1884/85
Fannin H.A.	Hawkes Bay v Taranaki	Napier	1897/98
Barclay F.	Auckland v Canterbury	Auckland	1903/04
Orchard S.A.	Canterbury v Auckland	Auckland	1909/10
Bennett J.H.	Canterbury v Wellington	Wellington	1911/12
Olliff C.	Auckland v Wellington	Auckland	1912/13
Middleton F.S.	Wellington v Hawke's Bay	Wellington	1919/20
Allom M.J.C.*	England v New Zealand	Christchurch	1929/30
Mulcock E.	Canterbury v Otago	Christchurch	1937/38
Overton G.W.F.	Otago v Canterbury	Christchurch	1946/47
Murray R.M.	Wellington v Otago	Wellington	1949/50
Moir A.M.	Otago v Canterbury	Christchurch	1950/51
Jones J.F.	Wellington v Central Districts	Wellington	1953/54
Reid R.E.	Wellington v Otago	Dunedin	1958/59
Bartlett G.A.	Central Districts v Northern Districts	Hamilton	1959/60
Cameron F.J.	Otago v Northern Districts	Hamilton	1962/63
Blair R.W.	Wellington v Northern Districts	Wellington	1962/63
Alabaster G.D.	Northern Districts v Canterbury	Hamilton	1962/63
Furlong B.D.M.	NZ Under 23 XI v Canterbury	Christchurch	1964/65
Hadlee R.J.	Canterbury v Central Districts	Nelson	1971/72
Petherick P.J.	New Zealand v Pakistan	Lahore	1976/77
Toynbee M.H.	Central Districts v Northern Districts	Gisborne	1979/80
Visser P.J.	Central Districts v Auckland	Nelson	1983/84
Maguiness S.J.	Wellington v Northern Districts	Wellington	1983/84
Beard D.A.	Northern Districts v Central Districts	Nelson	1989/90
Gale A.J.	Otago v Canterbury	Dunedin	1992/93
Harris C.Z.	New Zealand v Orange Free State	Bloemfontein	1994/95
Hayes R.L.	Northern Districts v Central Districts	Rotorua	1995/96
Hotter S.J.	Wellington v Otago	Wellington	1996/97
Anderson T.R.	Central Districts v Auckland	Masterton	1998/99
Canning T.K.	Auckland v Central Districts	Auckland	1999/00
Orchard M.G.	Northern Districts v Canterbury	Gisborne	2003/04
Franklin J.E.C.	New Zealand v Bangladesh	Dhaka	2004/05

** Allom captured 4 wickets with 5 balls in the same over*

Most Wickets in a Single Day's Play in New Zealand

14	Rees A.W.	Auckland v Otago	Dunedin	1889/90
13	Lankham W.	Auckland v Taranaki	Auckland	1882/83
13	Smith C.R.	Hawke's Bay v Taranaki	Hawera	1891/92
13	Cave H.B.	Central Districts v Auckland	Palmerston North	1952/53

Outstanding Analyses

TEN WICKETS IN AN INNINGS

21.3	11	28	10	Moss A.E.	Canterbury v Wellington	Christchurch	1889/90

NINE WICKETS IN AN INNINGS

16.4	9	13	9	Wiseman P.J.	Canterbury v CD	Christchurch	2004/05
24	13	36	9	Wensley A.F.	Auckland v Otago	Auckland	1929/30
15.2	0	43	9	Eden T.	Nelson v Wellington	Wellington	1875/76
28	11	47	9	Dent T.H.	Hawke's Bay v Wellington	Napier	1900/01

EIGHT WICKETS IN AN INNINGS

13	6	13	8	Firth J.P.	Wellington v Hawke's Bay	Wellington	1883/84
19	12	14	8	Austin S.W.	NSW v Hawke's Bay	Napier	1893/94
29	21	18	8	Frith W.	Canterbury v Otago	Christchurch	1880/81
14.5	7	19	8	Fannin H.A.	Hawke's Bay v Auckland	Auckland	1897/98

SEVEN WICKETS IN AN INNINGS

10.1	6	9	7	Bracewell J.G.	Otago v Canterbury	Dunedin	1981/82
13	9	11	7	Fisher A.H.	Otago v Canterbury	Christchurch	1896/97
25.3	16	12	7	Downes A.D.	Otago v Canterbury	Dunedin	1896/97
16	8	12	7	Tuffey D.R.	Northern Districts v Wellington	Hamilton	2000/01
32.1	24	13	7	Lankham W.	Auckland v Taranaki	Auckland	1882/83
10.4	5	16	7	Farooq Hamid	Pakistan v Wellington	Wellington	1964/65
17	10	17	7	Armstrong W.W.	Australia v Wellington	Wellington	1913/14
14.2	7	17	7	Maguiness S.J.	Wellington v Canterbury	Rangiora	1984/85
18.2	7	18	7	Callaway S.T.	NSW v Wellington	Wellington	1895/96

SIX WICKETS IN AN INNINGS

8	5	3	6	Cowie J.	New Zealand v Ireland	Dublin	1937
8	5	4	6	Callaway S.T.	Canterbury v Wellington	Wellington	1903/04
9.2	3	5	6	Bennett A.P.	Nelson v Wellington	Nelson	1885/86
16	11	6	6	Haskell W.J.R.	Wellington v Otago	Wellington	1967/68
14	10	7	6	Dunlop D.	Canterbury v Wellington	Wellington	1886/87
18	14	7	6	Hampton B.L.	Central Districts v Otago	Dunedin	1963/64
15	10	8	6	Downes W.F.	Otago v Canterbury	Christchurch	1866/67
11.2	6	9	6	Fowler G.	Nelson v Wellington	Nelson	1887/88
9.3	6	10	6	Pearson F.A.	Auckland v Hawke's Bay	Auckland	1910/11

FIVE WICKETS IN AN INNINGS

15.2	13	2	5	Ashby D.A.	Canterbury v Auckland	Auckland	1877/78
5	3	3	5	Allcott C.F.W.	New Zealand v Somerset	Taunton	1927
10.3	6	5	5	Bright R.J.	Australia v Central Districts	Nelson	1976/77
9	6	6	5	Parker T.S.	Otago v Canterbury	Christchurch	1866/67
21	18	8	5	Frith C.	Otago v Tasmania	Dunedin	1883/84
4	2	8	5	Burnup C.J.	Lord Hawke's XI v NZ	Wellington	1902/03
8	4	8	5	McBeath D.J.	Southland v Canterbury	Invercargill	1920/21
9	3	9	5	Bennett J.H.	Canterbury v Wellington	Christchurch	1910/11
12	5	9	5	Butterfield L.A.	South Island v North Island	Auckland	1944/45
9.1	5	9	5	Boock S.L.	New Zealand v Middlesex	Lord's	1978

FOUR WICKETS IN AN INNINGS

3.2	2	1	4	Snedden C.A.	Auckland v Hawke's Bay	Auckland	1920/21
6.4	5	2	4	Puna N.	Northern Dists v Central Dists	Hamilton	1957/58
7	6	3	4	Carrington S.M.	Northern Districts v Otago	Tauranga	1982/83
6.5	5	3	4	Woodcock L.J.	Wellington v Otago	Wellington	2001/02

THREE WICKETS IN AN INNINGS

3	3	0	3	Smith K.F.H.	Central Districts v Canterbury	Nelson	1959/60
2.1	2	0	3	Barnes S.G.	Australia v Canterbury	Christchurch	1945/46
5	5	0	3	Gray E.J.	Wellington v Canterbury	Christchurch	1985/86
1.4	0	1	3	Bolton B.A.	Canterbury v Central Districts	Christchurch	1958/59
2	1	1	3	Thomson S.A.	Northern Districts v Canterbury	Christchurch	1992/93
1.4	0	2	3	Anthony A.	Canterbury v Wellington	Christchurch	1908/09
3.3	1	2	3	Thomas A.W.	Canterbury v Otago	Christchurch	1917/18
4	2	2	3	Sparling J.T.	Auckland v Wellington	Auckland	1957/58
5	2	3	3	Cowlishaw W.P.	Canterbury v Otago	Christchurch	1864/65
15	12	3	3	Frith W.	Canterbury v Auckland	Auckland	1877/78
2.3	1	3	3	Richardson G.	Nelson v Wellington	Wellington	1886/87
3	2	3	3	Dowson E.M.	Lord Hawke's XI v Otago	Dunedin	1902/03
5	2	3	3	Pollard V.	New Zealand v England	Auckland	1965/66

Seven Wickets in an Innings on First-class Debut

10-28	Moss A.E.	Canterbury v Wellington	Christchurch	1889/90
8-35	Wilson R.	Queensland v Auckland	Auckland	1896/97
† 8-36	Rees A.W.	Auckland v Otago	Dunedin	1889/90
8-37	Hole H.	Nelson v Wellington	Nelson	1874/75
8-48	O'Connell W.J.	Hawke's Bay v Wellington	Wellington	1919/20
8-59	Robertson W.	Canterbury v Auckland	Christchurch	1893/94
8-70	Hay W.A.	Otago v Southland	Dunedin	1917/18
7-31	Lynch D.	Auckland v Canterbury	Auckland	1877/78
7-36	Mills G.	Auckland v Wellington	Auckland	1886/87
7-39	Lankham W.	Auckland v Canterbury	Christchurch	1882/83
† 7-42	Morrison B.D.	Wellington v Otago	Wellington	1953/54
† 7-46	Stephens W.B.	Auckland v Otago	Auckland	1899/00
7-46	Doig J.A.	Southland v Otago	Invercargill	1914/15
† 7-50	Badcock F.T.	Wellington v Canterbury	Christchurch	1924/25
† 7-54	Turnbull J.A.	Auckland v Central Districts	Auckland	1955/56
7-61	Merrin R.C.	Canterbury XI v NZ Touring Team	Christchurch	1967/68
† 7-95	Noonan D.J.	New South Wales v Canterbury	Christchurch	1895/96
7-95	Huxford N.A.	Wellington v Pakistan	Wellington	1964/65

† 2nd innings

Ten Wickets in a Match on First-class Debut

14-63	Rees A.W.	Auckland v Otago	Dunedin	1889/90
14-107	Robertson W.	Canterbury v Auckland	Christchurch	1893/94
13-72	Moss A.E.	Canterbury v Wellington	Christchurch	1889/90
12-18	Bennett A.P.	Nelson v Wellington	Nelson	1885/86
12-90	Mills W.	Taranaki v Fiji	Hawera	1894/95
12-118	Hay W.A.	Otago v Southland	Dunedin	1917/18
11-43	Fuller E.T.A.	Canterbury v Otago	Christchurch	1872/73
11-97	Wilson R.	Queensland v Auckland	Auckland	1896/97
11-99	Lankham W.	Auckland v Canterbury	Christchurch	1882/83
11-112	Morrison B.D.	Wellington v Otago	Wellington	1953/54
11-126	Noonan D.J.	New South Wales v Canterbury	Christchurch	1895/96
10-30	Lawson H.	Wellington v Nelson	Nelson	1883/84
10-31	MacDonald F.	Otago v Canterbury	Dunedin	1863/64
10-39	Holderness H.V.A.	Otago v Southland	Invercargill	1918/19
10-61	Hole H.	Nelson v Wellington	Nelson	1874/75
10-70	Mills G.	Auckland v Wellington	Auckland	1886/87
10-71	Lawton J.C.	Otago v Canterbury	Christchurch	1890/91
10-90	Brown C.M.	Auckland v Canterbury	Rangiora	1993/94
10-105	Frame W.D.	Otago v Canterbury	Dunedin	1955/56
10-122	Badcock F.T.	Wellington v Canterbury	Christchurch	1924/25
10-133	Leonard D.J.	Central Districts v Northern Districts	Rotorua	1989/90

Ten Wickets in Last First-class Match

† 10-31	MacDonald F.	Otago v Canterbury	Dunedin	1863/64
† 10-61	Hole H.	Nelson v Wellington	Nelson	1874/75
10-91	Downes W.F.	Otago v Canterbury	Dunedin	1875/76
12-114	Lankham W.	Auckland v Canterbury	Auckland	1883/84
13-140	Edser H.	Canterbury v Wellington	Wellington	1883/84
11-25	Fowler G.	Nelson v Wellington	Nelson	1887/88
11-77	Carson W.	Otago v Canterbury	Dunedin	1887/88
† 10-39	Holderness H.V.A.	Otago v Southland	Invercargill	1918/19
10-108	Vivian H.G.	Auckland v Wellington	Auckland	1938/39
11-129	de Groen R.P.	Northern Districts v Canterbury	Hamilton	1995/96

† this was the player's only first-class appearance

Most Wickets in a Season

		Matches	Wkts	Runs	Ave	5WI	10WM	Best
Boock S.L.	1977/78	13	66	1088	16.48	6	—	7-57
Hadlee R.J.	1986/87	11	62	935	15.08	8	1	7-49
Hadlee R.J.	1981/82	10	59	867	14.69	7	—	6-26
Boock S.L.	1978/79	12	58	1238	21.34	4	1	8-59
Thompson G.J.	1902-03	7	57	668	11.71	6	3	8-124
Boock S.L.	1986/87	10	55	920	16.72	6	1	6-62
Callaway S.T.	1903/04	5	54	474	8.77	8	4	8-33
Blair R.W.	1956/57	8	53	784	14.79	6	4	9-72
Tait A.R.	1996/97	9	53	865	16.32	4	1	9-48
Drum C.J.	2001/02	9	53	827	15.60	3	2	6-34
Martin C.S.	2003/04	12	53	1144	21.58	6	1	6-76
Austin S.W.	1893/94	7	52	606	11.65	6	1	8-14
Armstrong W.W.	1913/14	8	52	789	15.17	7	1	7-17
O'Sullivan D.R.	1978/79	9	52	989	19.01	3	—	6-51
Chatfield E.J.	1981/82	10	51	868	17.01	2	—	5-29
Hadlee R.J.	1978/79	10	50	909	18.18	4	—	6-28
Douglas J.W.H.T.	1906/07	9	50	663	13.26	5	1	7-49

Most Wickets in a Season for New Zealand Overseas

		Matches	Wkts	Runs	Ave	5WI	10WM	Best
Burtt T.B.	1949	27	128	2929	22.28	11	2	7-102
Cowie J.	1937	24	114	2275	19.95	6	1	6-3
Merritt W.E.	1927	25	107	2530	23.64	5	1	6-38

Most Wickets in a Season of First-class Debut

			Overs	Mdns	Runs	Wkts	Ave
Robertson W.	Canterbury & NZ	1893/94	*1534	balls	570	47	12.12
Gillespie S.R.	Northern Districts	1979/80	384.5	98	998	45	22.17
Petherick P.J.	Otago	1975/76	286	57	847	42	20.16
Lankham W.	Auckland	1882/83	†1006	balls	259	41	6.31
O'Brien I.E.	Wellington	2000/01	319.1	81	807	41	19.68

** Robertson bowled 222.2 6-ball overs and 40 5-ball overs † Lankham bowled 96.2 5-ball overs and 131 4-ball overs*

Most Balls Bowled in an Innings

444	Howarth H.J.	74-24-138-2	NZ v West Indies	Bridgetown	1971/72
426	Tufnell P.C.R.	71-22-147-2	England v New Zealand	Wellington	1991/92
426	Vettori D.L.	71-24-171-2	New Zealand v India	Mohali	1999/00
420	Howarth H.J.	70-24-144-4	NZ v England	Lord's	1973
420	Boock S.L.	70-10-229-1	NZ v Pakistan	Auckland	1988/89
417	O'Sullivan D.R.	52.1-15-125-4	CD v Otago	New Plymouth	1978/79
414	Doshi D.R.	69-34-79-2	India v New Zealand	Auckland	1980/81
414	Tauseef Ahmed	69-28-106-1	Pakistan v New Zealand	Auckland	1988/89
414	Hick G.A.	69-27-126-4	England v New Zealand	Wellington	1991/92
408	Morgan H.A.	51-16-108-3	Wellington v Otago	Dunedin	1968/69
408	Wiseman P.J.	68-21-123-4	Otago v ND	Hamilton	1995/96
407	Boock S.L.	67.5-31-75-4	Otago v CD	Alexandra	1988/89
399	Cook N.G.B.	66.3-26-153-3	England v NZ	Wellington	1983/84
396	Puna N.	66-23-131-4	ND v Auckland	Hamilton	1964/65
396	Nadkarni R.G.	66-34-114-2	India v NZ	Christchurch	1967/68
390	Chatfield E.J.	65-14-158-1	NZ v Pakistan	Auckland	1988/89

Most Balls Bowled in a Match

629	Badcock F.T.	104.5-44-178-9	Otago v Canterbury	Christchurch	1933/34
624	Dickeson C.W.	104-45-142-11	ND v Wellington	Hamilton	1979/80
618	Gray E.J.	103-39-214-6	Wellington v Otago	Wellington	1984/85
600	Allcott C.F.W.	75-23-161-5	Auckland v Canterbury	Christchurch	1924/25
600	Butler L.C.	100-46-122-4	Wellington v Auckland	Auckland	1965/66

Most Runs Conceded in a Match

304	2-173, 0-131	Dickinson G.R.	Otago v Wellington	Dunedin	1923/24
300	6-172, 4-128	Smith S.G.	Auckland v Wellington	Wellington	1923/24
277	6-136, 6-141	Alloo A.W.	Otago v Wellington	Dunedin	1923/24
266	6-185, 2-81	Merritt W.E.	New Zealand v Kent	Canterbury	1927
243	6-128, 7-115	Grimmett C.V.	Australia v Canterbury	Christchurch	1927/28
241	2-99, 5-142	Brice A.W.S.	Wellington v Otago	Dunedin	1923/24
241	3-123, 1-118	Prabhakar M.	India v New Zealand	Auckland	1989/90
239	6-112, 3-127	McBeath D.J.	Otago v Auckland	Dunedin	1922/23
239	1-60, 4-179	Lambert H.N.	Wellington v Canterbury	Wellington	1931/32
237	0-99, 0-138	Bracewell J.G.	New Zealand v Sussex	Hove	1990
237	4-158, 0-79	Vettori D.L.	New Zealand v South Africa	Hamilton	2003/04
236	2-83, 2-153	Newman J.A.	Canterbury v Otago	Dunedin	1928/29
234	3-86, 4-148	Merritt W.E.	Canterbury v Otago	Dunedin	1928/29
234	4-165, 2-69	Vettori D.L.	New Zealand v Zimbabwe	Bulawayo	1997/98
233	6-117, 4-116	Patel D.N.	Auckland v ND	Auckland	1991/92

Most Runs Conceded in an Innings

70	10	229	1	Boock S.L.	New Zealand v Pakistan	Auckland	1988/89
23.2	0	218	5	Merritt W.E.	New Zealand v NSW	Sydney	1927/28
34	1	206	1	Alloo A.W.	Otago v NSW	Dunedin	1923/24
59	12	204	4	Furlong C.J.M.	CD v Canterbury	Palmerston Nth	1994/95
57	5	200	4	Vettori D.L.	New Zealand v India	Ahmedabad	1999/00
51.2	11	198	5	Pringle C.	Auckland v CD	Auckland	1995/96
41	3	194	3	Callaway S.T.	New Zealand v Australia	Wellington	1904/05
32	1	186	2	Torrance R.C.	Otago v NSW	Dunedin	1923/24
43.1	1	185	6	Merritt W.E.	New Zealand v Kent	Canterbury	1927
46	4	181	0	Hart M.N.	New Zealand v W. Indies	Wellington	1994/95
34	2	180	5	O'Connell W.J.	Hawke's Bay v Auckland	Auckland	1920/21
56	13	179	4	Bennett J.H.	Canterbury v Australia	Christchurch	1913/14
33	0	179	3	McBeath D.J.	Canterbury v NSW	Christchurch	1923/24
31	1	179	4	Lambert H.N.	Wellington v Canterbury	Wellington	1931/32
44	4	179	0	Su'a M.L.	New Zealand v W. Indies	Wellington	1994/95
38	2	178	4	Cunningham W.H.R.	Canterbury v NSW	Christchurch	1923/24
40	4	178	1	Vettori D.L.	New Zealand v Pakistan	Lahore	2001/02
24	1	177	4	Furlong C.J.M.	CD v India	Napier	1998/99

ALL ROUND CRICKET

500 Runs and 25 Wickets in the Same Season

		Runs	Ave	Wkts	Ave
Reid J.R.	1954/55	505	38.84	30	16.53
Sparling J.T.	1959/60	705	37.11	36	19.50
Reid J.R.	1960/61	549	34.31	37	14.78
Pollard V.	1967/68	537	31.58	31	24.74
Taylor B.R.	1968/69	518	39.84	30	28.06
Cairns B.L.	1975/76	538	41.38	27	25.66
Hadlee R.J.	1981/82	500	33.33	59	14.69
Brown V.R.	1984/85	540	38.57	31	31.35
Gray E.J.	1985/86	545	49.54	34	22.00
Priest M.W.	1988/89	603	43.07	28	40.14
Bradburn G.E.	1989/90	842	38.27	30	30.93
Patel D.N.	1990/91	679	52.23	41	28.09
Patel D.N.	1991/92	574	44.15	32	26.78
Duff S.W.	1991/92	559	46.58	28	27.64
Styris S.B.	2001/02	662	44.13	28	17.03
Wiseman P.J.	2003/04	535	38.21	31	31.00

A Century and Five Wickets in Each Innings of the Same Match

Armstrong W.W.	126*	5-27 & 5-25	Australia v New Zealand	Christchurch	1904/05
Crawford J.N.	110 & 4*	5-90 & 5-53	Wellington v Auckland	Auckland	1917/18

A Century and Ten Wickets in the Same Match

but not five in each innings

Woolley F.E.	132	6-50 & 4-38	MCC v Otago	Dunedin	1929/30
Patel D.N.	6 & 204	6-117 & 4-116	Auckland v ND	Auckland	1991/92

A Century and Five Wickets in One Innings of the Same Match

Wilding F.	104	6-55 & 0-4	Canterbury v Auckland	Christchurch	1884/85
Redgrave W.P.	165	5-37	Wellington v Hawke's Bay	Wellington	1905/06
Relf A.E.	157	6-64 & 2-48	Auckland v Canterbury	Christchurch	1907/08
Armstrong W.W.	110*	6-47 & 0-25	Australia v New Zealand	Auckland	1913/14
Crawford J.N.	6 & 178*	5-149	Otago v Wellington	Wellington	1914/15
Snedden A.N.C.	139	5-13 & 2-21	Auckland v Hawke's Bay	Auckland	1920/21
Andrews T.J.E.	111*	5-41	NSW v Canterbury	Christchurch	1923/24
McGirr H.M.	106	5-17 & 0-22	Wellington v Canterbury	Wellington	1925/26
Bellamy F.W.J.	113 & 22*	5-31 & 1-39	Canterbury v Wellington	Christchurch	1934/35
Cromb I.B.	171	5-66 & 0-56	Canterbury v Wellington	Wellington	1939/40
Reid J.R.	0 & 283	5-35 & 1-34	Wellington v Otago	Wellington	1951/52
Reid J.R.	150*	7-28 & 1-15	New Zealand v Chief Commissioner's XI	Karachi	1955/56
Sutcliffe B.	152*	5-102	Otago v ND	Hamilton	1956/57
Sparling J.T.	105 & 51	7-98 & 2-13	Auckland v Canterbury	Christchurch	1959/60
Reid J.R.	165	5-50 & 1-28	Wellington v Auckland	Auckland	1959/60
Butler L.C.	101*	5-34	Wellington v CD	New Plymouth	1961/62
Alabaster G.D.	108 & 35	1-34 & 5-49	Otago v CD	Wanganui	1964/65
Taylor B.R.	105 & 0*	5-86	New Zealand v India	Calcutta	1964/65
Pollard V.	146 & 16*	3-66 & 6-53	CD v Otago	Dunedin	1967/68
Motz R.C.	103*	3-41 & 6-57	Canterbury v Otago	Christchurch	1967/68
Yuile B.W.	146	6-68 & 1-13	CD v Canterbury	Napier	1967/68
Inverarity R.J.	108	5-28	Australia B v Otago	Dunedin	1969/70

Morgan R.W.	102 & 52	5-42 & 3-48	Auckland v NZ U 23 XI	Auckland	1970/71
Taylor B.R.	10 & 129*	5-37 & 2-34	Wellington v Canterbury	Wellington	1971/72
Mushtaq Mohammad	201	2-15 & 5-49	Pakistan v New Zealand	Dunedin	1972/73
Morrison J.F.M.	8 & 106	0-4 & 5-69	Wellington v Auckland	Auckland	1977/78
Botham I.T.	103 & 30*	5-73 & 3-38	England v New Zealand	Christchurch	1977/78
Hadlee R.J.	48 & 103	5-61 & 1-76	NZ v Queensland	Brisbane	1980/81
Stead D.W.	2 & 193*	6-79 & 1-67	Canterbury v CD	New Plymouth	1980/81
Crowe M.D.	17 & 151	0-20 & 5-18	CD v Auckland	Auckland	1983/84
Botham I.T.	138	5-59 & 1-137	England v New Zealand	Wellington	1983/84
Crowe M.D.	20 & 143	1-54 & 5-51	CD v ND	New Plymouth	1984/85
Gray E.J.	108	5-54 & 4-52	NZ v Minor Counties	Norwich	1986
Rutherford K.R.	11 & 146	5-72	Otago v Wellington	Wellington	1989/90
Astle N.J.	160	6-22 & 0-45	Canterbury v Otago	Christchurch	1996/97
Nash D.J.	135* & 62	7-39 & 0-22	NZ v Hampshire	Southampton	1999
Bradburn G.E.	35 & 104	5-114	ND v Wellington	Wellington	2000/01
Canning T.K.	115	6-44 & 2-28	Auckland v ND	Hamilton	2004/05

WICKETKEEPING

Most Dismissals in a Season

49	49/0	Nevin C.J.	2000/01
41	31/10	McSweeney E.B.	1984/85
41	35/6	McSweeney E.B.	1989/90
38	37/1	Hopkins G.J.	2004/05
36	32/4	Smith I.D.S.	1990/91
35	30/5	Smith I.D.S.	1979/80
35	33/2	Young R.A.	2001/02
35	35/0	Young R.A.	2002/03
34	29/5	Lees W.K.	1978/79
34	32/2	Smith I.D.S.	1986/87
34	31/3	Germon L.K.	1991/92
34	33/1	Nevin C.J.	1995/96
34	34/0	Hart R.G.	1997/98
34	33/1	Hart R.G.	2001/02
33	32/1	Wadsworth K.J.	1975/76
33	31/2	McCullum B.B.	2003/04
32	28/4	Smith I.D.S.	1983/84
32	28/4	McSweeney E.B.	1983/84
32	28/4	Robinson S.A.	1990/91
32	31/1	Nevin C.J.	2002/03
32	30/2	Hart R.G.	2003/04
31	30/1	Kelly P.J.	1983/84
31	28/3	Kelly P.J.	1986/87
31	31/0	McSweeney E.B.	1990/91
31	30/1	Young B.A.	1991/92
31	28/3	Blain T.E.	1991/92
31	30/1	Croy M.G.	1998/99
31	31/0	Griggs B.B.J.	2001/02
31	31/0	Young R.A.	2004/05
30	23/7	Murray J.T.	1960/61
30	28/2	Germon L.K.	1992/93
30	29/1	Baker G.R.	1994/95

Most Dismissals in a Match

10	10/0	Nevin C.J., Wellington v Otago	Wellington	1995/96
	10/0	Gilchrist A.C., Australia v New Zealand	Hamilton	1999/00
	10/0	Hopkins G.J., Otago v Canterbury	Dunedin	2004/05
9	9/0	Schofield R.M., Central Districts v Wellington	Wellington	1964/65
	9/0	Vance R.H., Wellington v Otago	Wellington	1977/78
	8/1	McSweeney E.B., Wellington v Otago	Lower Hutt	1983/84
	9/0	Young B.A., Northern Districts v Canterbury	Christchurch	1986/87
	9/0	Germon L.K., Canterbury v Northern Districts	Christchurch	1992/93
	9/0	Rashid Latif., Pakistan v New Zealand	Auckland	1993/94
	9/0	Hopkins G.J., Otago v Wellington	Queenstown	2004/05
8	3/5	James K.C., NZ v Derbyshire	Derby	1927
	1/7	Jackman C.K.Q., Canterbury v Wellington	Wellington	1935/36
	2/6	Kent L.A.W., Auckland v Wellington	Wellington	1944/45
	8/0	Curtis W.M., North Island XI v South Island XI	Wellington	1957/58
	8/0	Petrie E.C., NZ v Sussex	Hove	1958
	5/3	Dick A.E., NZ v Griqualand West	Kimberley	1961/62

	8/0	Parks J.M., England v NZ	Christchurch	1965/66
	7/1	Therkleson, I.J., Wellington v Northern Districts	Whangarei	1973/74
	8/0	Marsh R.W., Australia v NZ	Christchurch	1976/77
	8/0	Lees W.K., NZ v Sri Lanka	Wellington	1982/83
	4/4	McSweeney E.B., Wellington v Northern Districts	Wellington	1984/85
	8/0	Smith I.D.S., Auckland v Central Districts	Nelson	1988/89
	8/0	Smith I.D.S., NZ v Sri Lanka	Hamilton	1990/91
	7/1	Hart R.G., Northern Districts v Canterbury	Hamilton	1994/95
	7/1	Germon L.K., Canterbury v Central Districts	Palmerston North	1994/95
	7/1	Nevin C.J., Wellington v Central Districts	Nelson	1995/96
	8/0	Vincent L., Auckland v Central Districts	Palmerston North	2000/01
	8/0	Howell G.A., Wellington v Northern Districts	Hamilton	2001/02
	7/1	McCullum B.B., Canterbury v Northern Districts	Christchurch	2003/04
	7/1	Papps M.W.H., Canterbury v Northern Districts	Gisborne	2004/05

Most Dismissals in an Innings

7	7/0	Schofield R.M., Central Districts v Wellington	Wellington	1964/65
	7/0	Wasim Bari, Pakistan v NZ	Auckland	1978/79
	7/0	Young B.A., Northern Districts v Canterbury	Christchurch	1986/87
	7/0	Smith I.D.S., NZ v Sri Lanka	Hamilton	1990/91
	7/0	Croy M.G., Otago v Auckland	Auckland	2001/02
	7/0	Hopkins G.J., New Zealand A v South Africa A	Centurion	2004/05
6	4/2	Mooney F.L.H., NZ v Warwickshire	Birmingham	1949
	5/1	Wadsworth K.J., NZ v Surrey	The Oval	1973
	6/0	Downes L.W., Central Districts v Canterbury	Nelson	1975/76
	5/1	Kirmani S.M.H., India v NZ	Christchurch	1975/76
	6/0	Vance R.H., Wellington v Otago	Wellington	1977/78
	6/0	Downton P.R., England XI v Otago	Dunedin	1977/78
	6/0	Germon L.K., Canterbury v Northern Districts	Christchurch	1992/93
	5/1	Hart R.G., Northern Districts v Canterbury	Hamilton	1994/95
	5/1	Nevin C.J., Wellington v Central Districts	Nelson	1995/96
	6/0	Parore A.C., New Zealand A v Pakistan A	Hamilton	1998/99
	6/0	Young R.A., Auckland v Wellington	Wellington	2002/03
	6/0	Hopkins G.J., Otago v Canterbury	Dunedin	2004/05
	5/1	Papps M.H.W., Canterbury v Northern Districts	Gisborne	2004/05

Most Catches in a Season

49	Nevin C.J.	2000/01
37	Hopkins G.J.	2004/05
35	McSweeney E.B.	1989/90
35	Young R.A.	2002/03
34	Hart R.G.	1997/98
33	Nevin C.J.	1995/96
33	Hart R.G.	2001/02
33	Young R.A.	2001/02
32	Wadsworth K.J.	1975/76
32	Smith I.D.S.	1986/87
32	Smith I.D.S.	1990/91
31	McSweeney E.B.	1984/85
31	McSweeney E.B.	1990/91
31	Germon L.K.	1991/92
31	Griggs B.B.J.	2001/02
31	Nevin C.J.	2002/03
31	McCullum B.B.	2003/04
31	Young R.A.	2004/05
30	Smith I.D.S.	1979/80
30	Kelly P.J.	1983/84
30	Young B.A.	1991/92
30	Croy M.G.	1998/99
30	Hart R.G.	2003/04

Most Catches in a Match

10	Nevin C.J., Wellington v Otago	Wellington	1995/96
	Gilchrist A.C., Australia v New Zealand	Hamilton	1999/00
	Hopkins G.J., Otago v Canterbury	Dunedin	2004/05
9	Schofield R.M., Central Districts v Wellington	Wellington	1964/65
	Vance R.H., Wellington v Otago	Wellington	1977/78
	Young B.A., Northern Districts v Canterbury	Christchurch	1986/87
	Germon L.K., Canterbury v Northern Districts	Christchurch	1992/93
	Rashid Latif., Pakistan v New Zealand	Auckland	1993/94
	Hopkins G.J., Otago v Wellington	Queenstown	2004/05
8	Curtis W.M., North Island XI v South Island XI	Wellington	1957/58
	Petrie E.C., NZ v Sussex	Hove	1958
	Parks J.M., England v NZ	Christchurch	1965/66
	Marsh R.W., Australia v NZ	Christchurch	1976/77
	Lees W.K., NZ v Sri Lanka	Wellington	1982/83
	McSweeney E.B., Wellington v Otago	Lower Hutt	1983/84
	Smith I.D.S., Auckland v Central Districts	Nelson	1988/89
	Smith I.D.S., NZ v Sri Lanka	Hamilton	1990/91
	Vincent L., Auckland v Central Districts	Palmerston North	2000/01
	Howell G.A., Wellington v Northern Districts	Hamilton	2001/02

Most Catches in an Innings

7	Schofield R.M., Central Districts v Wellington	Wellington	1964/65
	Wasim Bari, Pakistan v NZ	Auckland	1978/79
	Young B.A., Northern Districts v Canterbury	Christchurch	1986/87
	Smith I.D.S., NZ v Sri Lanka	Hamilton	1990/91
	Croy M.G., Otago v Auckland	Auckland	2001/02
	Hopkins G.J., New Zealand A v South Africa A	Centurion	2004/05
6	Downes L.W., Central Districts v Canterbury	Nelson	1975/76
	Vance R.H., Wellington v Otago	Wellington	1977/78
	Downton P.R., England XI v Otago	Dunedin	1977/78
	Germon L.K., Canterbury v Northern Districts	Christchurch	1992/93
	Parore A.C., New Zealand A v Pakistan A	Hamilton	1998/99
	Young R.A., Auckland v Wellington	Wellington	2002/03
	Hopkins G.J., Otago v Canterbury	Dunedin	2004/05

Most Stumpings in a Season

13	Jackman C.K.Q.	1935/36	13	Kent L.A.W.	1944/45

Most Stumpings in a Match

7	Jackman C.K.Q., Canterbury v Wellington	Wellington	1935/36
6	Kent L.A.W., Auckand v Wellington	Wellington	1944/45
5	James K.C., NZ v Surrey	The Oval	1927
	James K.C., NZ v Derbyshire	Derby	1927
	Burns R.C., Canterbury v Otago	Dunedin	1928/29
	Mills A.S., Otago v Fiji	Dunedin	1947/48

Most Stumpings in an Innings

4	Jackman C.K.Q., Canterbury v Wellington	Wellington	1935/36
	Tindill E.W.T., NZ v Glamorgan	Cardiff	1937
	Kent L.A.W., Auckland v Wellington	Wellington	1944/45
	Mills A.S., Otago v Fiji	Dunedin	1947/48
	McSweeney E.B., Wellington v Northern Districts	Wellington	1984/85

FIELDING

Most Catches in a Season

23	Murray B.A.G.	1967/68	16	Fleming S.P.	1993/94
22	Coney J.V.	1977/78	15	Playle W.R.	1958/59
20	Howarth H.J.	1973/74	15	Bradburn W.P.	1963/64
18	Sinclair M.S.	2001/02	15	Turner G.M.	1975/76
17	Crowe M.D.	1986/87	15	Blair W.L.	1978/79
17	Boyle D.J.	1990/91	15	Crowe J.J.	1990/91
17	Parlane N.R.	2002/03	15	Knight N.V.	1996/97
16	Burgess M.G.	1977/78	15	Vincent L.	1999/00
16	Edgar B.A.	1978/79	15	Bradburn G.E.	2000/01
16	Crowe M.D.	1981/82	15	How J.M.	2003/04
16	Crowe M.D.	1983/84	15	Bell M.D.	2004/05

Most Catches in a Match

7	Morrison J.F.M., Wellington v Northern Districts	Wellington	1980/81
	Fleming S.P., New Zealand v Zimbabwe	Harare	1997/98
6	Marchant J.W.A., Wellington v Nelson	Wellington	1873/74
	Williams N.T., Auckland v Hawke's Bay	Napier	1894/95
	Cromb I.B., Canterbury v Otago	Christchurch	1937/38
	Ikin J.T., MCC v Auckland	Auckland	1946/47
	Reid J.R., NZ v South Zone	Bangalore	1955/56
	Jarvis T.W., Auckland v Northern Districts	Hamilton	1968/69
	Anderson R.W., Rest v NZ	New Plymouth	1974/75
	MacDonald G.K., Canterbury v Pakistan	Christchurch	1984/85
	Young B.A., New Zealand v Pakistan	Auckland	1993/94
	Latham R.T., Canterbury v Otago	Oamaru	1994/95
	Young B.A., Northern Districts v Wellington	Wellington	1995/96
	Chandler P.J.B., New Zealand A v England	Wanganui	1996/97
	McHardy D.S., Wellington v Northern Districts	Hamilton	1996/97
	Fleming S.P., New Zealand v Australia	Brisbane	1997/98
	Bell M.D., Wellington v Canterbury	Wellington	2003/04

Most Catches in an Innings

5	Williams N.T., Auckand v Hawke's Bay	Napier	1894/95
	Lamason J.R., Wellington v Otago	Dunedin	1937/38
	Lamason J.R., NI Army v SI Army	Wellington	1942/43
	Ikin J.T., MCC v Auckland	Auckland	1946/47
	Rabone G.O., NZ v Oxford University	Oxford	1949
	Reid J.R., NZ v South Zone	Bangalore	1955/56
	Morrison J.F.M., Wellington v Northern Districts	Wellington	1980/81
	MacDonald G.K., Canterbury v Pakistan	Christchurch	1984/85
	Crowe J.J., Auckland v Canterbury	Auckland	1988/89
	Fleming S.P., New Zealand v Zimbabwe	Harare	1997/98
	Harris C.Z., Canterbury v England	Christchurch	2001/02

OLDEST PLAYERS

AGE Years/days			
52/189	Boxshall C.	Canterbury v Wellington	1914/15
51/216	Read R.J.	Canterbury v Auckland	1937/38
51/203	Lyttelton C.J. †	Governor-General's XI v MCC	1960/61
51/87	Wilson C.G.	Wellington v Hawke's Bay	1919/20
51/32	MacLaren A.C.	MCC v New Zealand	1922/23
50/284	Wilson E.S.	Otago v Wellington	1927/28
50/269	Hay T.D.B.	New Zealand v Royal Navy	1927
50/184	Reese T.W.	Canterbury v Otago	1917/18
50/86	Dufaur F.E.	Auckland v Wellington	1882/83
49/88	Allcott C.F.W.	Otago v Auckland	1945/46
49/48	Wilding F.	Canterbury v Hawke's Bay	1901/02
48/96	Hartley J.C.	MCC v Auckland	1922/23
48/40	Hallamore R.G.	Southland v Otago	1918/19
48/26	Badcock F.T.	New Zealanders v H.D.G. Leveson-Gower's XI	1945
47/357	Board J.H.	Hawke's Bay v Wellington	1914/15
47/325	Rowntree R.W.	Auckland v South Africa	1931/32
47/177	Fox R.H.	New Zealand v Civil Service	1927
47/151	Jones S.P.	Auckland v Otago	1908/09
47/114	Hughes W.J.	Hawke's Bay v Wellington	1905/06
47/98	Brice A.W.S.	Wellington v Australia	1927/28
47/70	Fowke J.N.	Canterbury v MCC	1906/07
46/319	Kortlang H.H.L.	Wellington v Auckland	1926/27
46/149	Stevens E.C.J.	Canterbury v Otago	1883/84
46/125	Allen R.	Wellington v Fiji	1953/54
46/14	Downes A.D.	Otago v Canterbury	1913/14
45/364	Blackie D.D.	Australia v New Zealand	1927/28
45/292	Handford A.	Southland v Otago	1914/15
45/270	Wynyard E.G.	MCC v Wellington	1906/07
45/241	Blamires E.O.	Otago v Canterbury	1926/27
45/39	Smith S.G.	Auckland v Wellington	1925/26
45/6	Beard D.D.	Northern Districts v Wellington	1964/65
44/349	Levers W.C.S.	Hawke's Bay v Wellington	1908/09
44/338	Knight A.R.	Otago v Canterbury	1943/44
44/308	Chadwick C.S.	Otago v Auckland	1924/25
44/226	Tucker K.H.	Wellington v Hawke's Bay	1919/20
44/182	Anthony A.	Auckland v Wellington	1930/31
44/178	Siedeberg H.G.	Otago v Wellington	1921/22
44/126	Garrard D.R.	Auckland v Wellington	1941/42
44/105	Newman J.A.	Canterbury v Otago	1928/29
44/75	Cate W.A.	New Zealand v MCC	1922/23
44/70	Wallace W.M.	Governor General's XI v MCC	1960/61
44/59	Dempster C.S.	Wellington v Auckland	1947/48
44/7	Wheatley J.	Canterbury v Hawke's Bay	1903/04

† Lord Cobham

YOUNGEST PLAYERS

AGE Years/days			
15/224	Dacre C.C.R.	Auckland v Wellington	1914/15
15/272	Midlane F.A.	Wellington v Hawke's Bay	1898/99
15/319	Ollivier A.M.	Canterbury v Otago	1866/67
16/36	Hartland J.F.	Canterbury v Otago	1877/78

16/84	Broad C.H.	Nelson v Wellington	1888/89
16/86	McGregor S.N.	Otago v Fiji	1947/48
16/87	Dacre L.M.	Auckland v Wellington	1912/13
16/130	Coutts H.D.	Taranaki v Auckland	1882/83
16/147	Puna K.N.	New Zealand Under 23 XI v Otago	1971/72
16/173	Aaqib Javed	Pakistan v President's XI	1988/89
16/242	Collins J.U.	Nelson v Wellington	1884/85
16/250	Taylor L.G.	Auckland v Hawke's Bay	1910/11
16/273	Tendulkar S.R.	India v President's XI	1989/90
16/285	Reese D.	Canterbury v Wellington	1895/96
16/311	Hale H.	Tasmania v Otago	1883/84
16/325	Morgan R.W.	Auckland v Northern Districts	1957/58
16/330	Maunder P.A.	Central Districts v Auckland	1961/62
17/4	Wallace W.M.	Auckland v Wellington	1933/34
17/5	Frater R.E.	Auckland v Wellington	1918/19
17/12	Bell M.D.	Northern Districts v New Zealand Academy XI	1993/94
17/49	Williams A.B.	Otago v Canterbury	1886/87
17/52	Blunt R.C.	Canterbury v Otago	1917/18
17/65	Mitchell W.J.	Northern Districts v Pakistan	1964/65
17/66	Wilding A.F.	Canterbury v Auckland	1900/01
17/77	Clarke D.B.	Auckland v Central Districts	1950/51
17/93	Hay T.D.B.	Auckland v Wellington	1893/94
17/107	Rutherford K.R.	Otago v Auckland	1982/83
17/110	Cooke F.H.	Otago v Canterbury	1879/80
17/112	Barron J.R.	Otago v Canterbury	1917/18
17/119	Crowe M.D.	Auckland v Canterbury	1979/80
17/124	MacNeil H.	Otago v Canterbury	1877/78
17/152	Butler L.C.	Wellington v Auckland	1951/52
17/174	McIntyre J.M.	Auckland v Canterbury	1961/62
17/179	Rutherford I.A.	Otago v Canterbury	1974/75
17/182	Robin T.P.	Central Districts v Canterbury	1999/00
17/185	Robinson S.A.	Otago v Northern Districts	1984/85
17/213	Turner G.M.	Otago v Canterbury	1964/65
17/222	Hemi R.C.	Auckland v Wellington	1950/51
17/244	Ghulam Abbas	Pakistan v Auckland	1964/65
17/258	Rose G.A.	Central Districts v Northern Districts	1958/59
17/268	Snedden A.N.C.	Auckland v Wellington	1909/10
17/268	Beuth J.A.	Northern Districts v New Zealand Under 23 XI	1962/63
17/274	Ashbolt F.L.	Wellington v Auckland	1893/94
17/276	Collinge R.O.	Central Districts v Auckland	1963/64
17/278	Nicholls J.G.	Otago v Canterbury	1876/77
17/286	Hickmott R.G.	Canterbury v Wellington	1911/12
17/291	Bennett J.H.	Canterbury v Otago	1898/99
17/294	Cairns A.E.	Otago v Canterbury	1867/68
17/305	Gill M.F.	Central Districts v Wellington	1974/75
17/307	Currie E.W.	Otago v New South Wales	1893/94
17/307	Hastings B.F.	Wellington v Canterbury	1957/58
17/325	Bartlett G.A.	Central Districts v Northern Districts	1958/59
17/328	Cushen J.A.J.	Otago v Canterbury	1967/68
17/329	West R.M.	Central Districts v Northern Districts	1996/97
17/336	Lambert H.N.	Wellington v Canterbury	1917/18
17/352	Motz R.C.	Canterbury v Northern Districts	1957/58
17/355	Tarrant D.R.	Central Districts v Auckland	1954/55
17/362	Vettori D.L.	Northern Districts v England	1996/97

CAREER RECORDS

The following career records cover the complete first-class careers of New Zealand players. Matches for other than New Zealand teams e.g. county sides, are included.
To qualify for inclusion a player must have appeared in first-class cricket in New Zealand while a bona fide resident of the country — professional coaches and the like thus being excluded.

Batting

3000 RUNS	*Career*	*M*	*In*	*NO*	*HS*	*Runs*	*Ave*	*100*
Turner G.M.	1964/65-1982/83	455	792	101	311*	34,346	49.70	103
Wright J.G.	1975/76-1992/93	366	636	44	192	25,073	42.35	59
Crowe M.D.	1979/80-1995/96	247	412	62	299	19,608	56.02	71
Sutcliffe B.	1941/42-1965/66	233	407	39	385	17,447	47.41	44
Howarth G.P.	1968/69-1985/86	338	584	42	183	17,294	31.90	32
Reid J.R.	1947/48-1965	246	418	28	296	16,128	41.35	39
Patel D.N.	1976-1996/97	358	558	51	204	15,188	29.95	26
Rutherford K.R.	1982/83-1999/00	220	383	33	317	13,974	39.92	35
Congdon B.E.	1960/61-1978	241	416	40	202*	13,101	34.84	23
Hitchcock R.E.	1947/48-1964	323	519	71	153*	12,473	27.84	13
Dacre C.C.R.	1914/15-1936	269	439	20	223	12,230	29.18	24
Dempster C.S.	1921/22-1947/48	184	306	36	212	12,145	44.98	35
Hadlee R.J.	1971/72-1990	342	473	93	210*	12,052	31.71	14
Fleming S.P.	1991/92-2004/05	189	316	28	274*	12,033	41.78	23
Edgar B.A.	1975/76-1989/90	175	307	26	203	11,304	40.22	24
Parker J.M.	1971-1983/84	207	362	39	195	11,254	34.84	21
Smith S.G.	1899/00-1925/26	211	379	30	256	10,920	31.28	14
Cairns C.L.	1988-2004	216	340	38	158	10,680	35.36	13
Burgess M.G.	1963/64-1980/81	192	322	35	146	10,281	35.82	20
Crowe J.J.	1977/78-1991/92	180	304	34	159	10,233	37.90	22
Richardson M.H.	1989/90-2004/05	157	264	31	306	9994	42.89	20
Greatbatch M.J.	1982/83-1999/00	170	292	31	202*	9890	37.89	24
Twose R.G.	1989-2000/01	178	300	35	277*	9802	36.98	18
Spearman C.M.	1993/94-2004	149	267	15	341	9654	38.30	21
Lowry T.C.	1917/18-1937/38	198	322	20	181	9421	31.19	18
Dowling G.T.	1958/59-1971/72	158	282	13	239	9399	34.94	16
Donnelly M.P.	1936/37-1960/61	131	221	26	208*	9250	47.43	23
Jones A.H.	1979/80-1995/96	145	254	33	186	9180	41.53	16
Horne M.J.	1992/93-2004/05	120	205	10	241	8199	42.04	24
Astle N.J.	1991/92-2004/05	144	230	22	223	8025	38.58	18
Arnold P.A.	1953/54-1960	174	306	15	122	8013	27.53	7
Blunt R.C.	1917/18-1935	123	209	15	338*	7953	40.99	15
Coney J.V.	1970/71-1986/87	165	272	48	174*	7872	35.14	8
Sinclair M.S.	1995/96-2004/05	110	186	20	268	7845	47.25	17
Franklin T.J.	1980/81-1992/93	148	254	20	181	7794	33.30	15
Wallace W.M.	1933/34-1960/61	121	192	17	211	7757	44.32	17
Hastings B.F.	1957/58-1976/77	163	273	32	226	7685	31.89	15
Hadlee W.A.	1933/34-1951/52	117	203	17	198	7523	40.44	18
Young B.A.	1983/84-1998/99	163	276	43	267*	7489	32.14	10
McMillan C.D.	1994/95-2004/05	121	197	22	168*	6962	39.78	13
Vance R.H.	1976/77-1990/91	135	230	18	254*	6955	32.80	12
Bell M.D.	1993/94-2004/05	125	215	13	219	6896	34.13	14
Parore A.C.	1988/89-2001/02	163	252	43	155*	6826	32.66	10
McEwan P.E.	1976/77-1990/91	115	206	15	155	6677	34.95	12
McGregor S.N.	1947/48-1968/69	148	274	16	114*	6573	25.47	5
James K.C.	1923/24-1946/47	204	330	41	109*	6413	22.19	7

	Career	M	In	NO	HS	Runs	Ave	100
Latham R.T.	1980/81-1994/95	108	189	19	237*	6298	37.05	9
Murray B.A.G.	1958/59-1972/73	102	187	11	213	6257	35.55	6
Harris C.Z.	1989/90-2003/04	108	170	36	251*	6217	46.39	12
Morrison J.F.M.	1965/66-1983/84	126	225	25	180*	6142	30.71	7
Sinclair B.W.	1955/56-1970/71	118	204	18	148	6114	32.87	6
Blair B.R.	1977/78-1989/90	110	190	6	143	5995	32.58	7
Morgan R.W.	1957/58-1976/77	136	229	13	166	5940	27.50	8
Roberts A.D.G.	1967/68-1983/84	112	206	37	128*	5865	34.70	7
Page M.L.	1920/21-1942/43	132	213	17	206	5857	29.88	9
Shrimpton M.J.F.	1961/62-1979/80	122	218	23	150	5812	29.80	7
Blain T.E.	1982/83-1994/95	118	199	30	161	5749	34.02	8
Reid J.F.	1975/76-1987/88	101	170	22	180	5650	38.17	11
Scott V.J.	1937/38-1952/53	80	130	17	204	5620	49.73	16
Anderson R.W.	1967/68-1981/82	111	197	14	155	5609	30.65	8
Smith I.D.S.	1977/78-1991/92	178	250	42	173	5570	26.77	6
Gray E.J.	1975/76-1991/92	162	241	51	128*	5472	28.80	6
Chapple M.E.	1949/50-1971/72	119	201	16	165	5344	28.88	4
Pollard V.	1964/65-1974/75	130	207	33	146	5314	30.54	6
Mills J.E.	1925/26-1937/38	97	161	8	185	5025	32.84	11
Graham H.	1892/93-1906/07	113	200	9	124	5023	26.29	7
Weir G.L.	1927/28-1946/47	107	172	16	191	5022	32.19	10
Cumming C.D.	1995/96-2004/05	83	153	14	187	4980	35.82	10
Bradburn G.E.	1985/86-2001/02	127	206	27	148*	4978	27.81	4
McSweeney E.B.	1979/80-1993/94	121	177	30	205*	4947	33.65	6
Lees W.K.	1970/71-1987/88	146	243	43	152	4932	24.66	5
Pairaudeau B.H.	1946/47-1966/67	89	159	5	163	4930	32.01	11
White D.J.	1979/80-1993/94	106	187	17	209	4926	28.98	7
Kerr J.L.	1929/30-1942/43	89	157	7	196	4829	32.19	8
Douglas M.W.	1987/88-2000/01	94	160	23	144	4808	35.09	9
Miller L.S.M.	1950/51-1959/60	82	142	15	144	4777	37.61	5
Stead G.R.	1991/92-2004/05	94	153	10	190	4722	33.02	10
Grimmett C.V.	1911/12-1940/41	248	321	54	71*	4720	17.67	—
Gaffaney C.B.	1995/96-2004/05	83	152	11	194	4711	33.41	8
Pocock B.A.	1990/91-2000/01	100	176	16	167	4699	29.36	10
Jarvis T.W.	1964/65-1976/77	97	167	8	182	4666	29.34	6
Sparling J.T.	1956/57-1970/71	127	215	26	105	4606	24.11	2
Edwards G.N.	1973/74-1984/85	92	164	8	177*	4589	29.41	5
Taylor B.R.	1963/64-1979/80	141	210	25	173	4579	24.75	4
Hadlee B.G.	1961/62-1980/81	84	155	11	163*	4539	31.52	6
Vivian H.G.	1930/31-1938/39	85	143	15	165	4443	34.71	6
Parlane M.E.	1992/93-2004/05	92	156	7	203	4426	22.70	9
Hart M.N.	1990/91-2004/05	135	198	26	201*	4418	25.68	4
Briasco P.S.	1982/83-1991/92	83	148	16	157	4390	33.25	6
Bracewell J.G.	1978/79-1990	149	208	40	110*	4354	25.91	4
Jones R.A.	1993/94-2004/05	80	140	8	188	4220	31.96	9
Thomson S.A.	1987/88-1996/97	90	148	38	167	4209	38.26	6
Cairns B.L.	1971/72-1988	148	226	25	110	4165	20.72	1
McGirr H.M.	1913/14-1932/33	88	146	7	141	3992	28.71	5
Cromb I.B.	1929/30-1946/47	88	148	12	171	3950	29.04	3
Priest M.W.	1984/85-1998/99	109	154	25	119	3945	30.58	4
Dunning B.	1961/62-1977/78	83	150	10	142	3929	28.06	3
Guy J.W.	1953/54-1972/73	90	165	13	115	3923	25.80	3
Bailey M.D.	1989/90-2001/02	89	138	9	180*	3882	30.09	8
Harris R.M.	1955/56-1973/74	73	130	5	157	3863	30.90	3

	Career	M	In	NO	HS	Runs	Ave	100
Yuile B.W.	1959/60-1971/72	123	187	31	146	3850	24.67	1
Parsons A.E.W.	1971/72-1982/83	82	156	10	141	3847	26.34	4
Sulzberger G.P.	1995/96-2004/05	83	135	12	159	3836	31.18	8
Hiddleston J.S.	1909/10-1928/29	52	97	1	212	3818	39.77	8
Rutherford I.A.	1974/75-1983/84	79	144	4	222	3794	27.10	5
Taylor D.D.	1946/47-1960/61	95	168	6	143	3772	23.28	1
Hartland B.R.	1986/87-1996/97	83	150	8	150	3753	26.42	5
Kuggeleijn C.M.	1975/76-1990/91	89	151	15	116	3747	27.55	4
Vincent L.	1997/98-2004/05	67	107	7	224	3715	37.15	8
MacGibbon A.R.	1947/48-1961/62	124	206	20	94	3699	19.88	—
Blair W.L.	1967/68-1990/91	82	151	9	140	3698	26.04	2
Webb P.N.	1976/77-1986/87	75	130	19	136	3671	33.07	5
Wadsworth K.J.	1968/69-1975/76	118	164	23	117	3664	25.98	2
Styris S.B.	1994/95-2004/05	79	131	14	212*	3647	31.17	6
Roberts A.W.	1927/28-1950/51	84	135	17	181	3645	30.88	3
Leggat J.G.	1944/45-1955/56	57	106	9	166	3634	37.46	7
Austen M.H.	1982/83-1996/97	66	120	8	202*	3619	32.31	6
Howell L.G.	1990/91-2004/05	83	143	16	181	3586	28.23	3
Hoskin R.N.	1980/81-1992/93	81	140	7	157	3580	26.91	6
Nash D.J.	1990/91-2001/02	120	168	37	135*	3555	27.13	5
Patrick W.R.	1905/06-1926/27	74	138	8	143	3536	27.20	4
Smith C.J.P.	1983/84-1990/91	62	118	9	160*	3499	32.10	7
Motz R.C.	1957/58-1969	142	225	21	103*	3494	17.12	1
Larsen G.R.	1984/85-1998/99	103	157	35	161	3491	28.61	2
Brown V.R.	1978/79-1989/90	83	136	17	161*	3485	29.28	6
Rabone G.O.	1940/41-1960/61	82	135	14	125	3425	28.30	3
Marshall J.A.H.	1997/98-2004/05	71	121	2	235	3423	28.76	4
Pritchard T.L.	1937/38-1956	200	293	41	81	3363	13.34	—
Newdick G.A.	1970/71-1980/81	61	114	6	143	3292	30.48	4
Lawson R.A.	1992/93-2003/04	73	133	6	200	3278	25.81	3
Vivian G.E.	1964/65-1978/79	88	140	25	137*	3259	28.33	3
Nevin C.J.	1995/96-2004/05	74	115	17	143*	3259	33.25	3
Papps M.H.W.	1998/99-2004/05	60	108	9	192	3224	32.56	7
Moloney D.A.R.	1929/30-1940/41	64	119	7	190	3219	28.74	2
Boyle D.J.	1980/81-1994/95	69	121	12	149	3216	29.50	3
Stead D.W.	1968/69-1985/86	80	139	11	193*	3205	25.03	1
Alabaster G.D.	1955/56-1975/76	96	154	20	108	3200	23.88	3
Reese D.	1895/96-1920/21	72	134	8	148	3186	25.28	4
McCullum S.J.	1976/77-1990/91	75	131	1	134	3174	24.41	2
Duff S.W.	1985/86-1995/96	88	134	29	164*	3167	30.16	1
Vaughan J.T.C.	1989/90-1996/97	70	120	20	127	3159	31.59	2
Harford N.S.	1953/54-1966/67	74	122	8	158	3149	27.62	3
Merritt W.E.	1926/27-1946	125	191	33	87	3147	19.91	—
Mooney F.L.H.	1941/42-1954/55	91	150	14	180	3143	23.11	2
Redmond R.E.	1963/64-1975/76	53	100	7	141*	3134	33.69	5
Thomson K.	1959/60-1973/74	71	125	14	136*	3134	28.23	5
Tindill E.W.T.	1932/33-1949/50	69	116	13	149	3127	30.35	6
Harris P.G.Z.	1949/50-1964/65	69	120	9	118	3126	28.16	5
Germon L.K.	1987/88-2001/02	103	142	35	160*	3123	29.18	4
Wiseman P.J.	1991/92-2004/05	144	197	40	107	3109	19.80	1
Wells J.D.	1989/90-2000/01	73	115	18	143	3058	31.52	5
Ryan M.L.	1965/66-1978/79	66	113	9	129	3023	29.06	3
Barnes A.C.	1993/94-2004/05	78	121	10	134*	3006	27.08	4

Bowling

200 WICKETS	Career	M	Wkts	Runs	Ave
Hadlee R.J.	1971/72-1990	342	1490	26,998	18.11
Grimmett C.V.	1911/12-1940/41	248	1424	31,740	22.28
Smith S.G.	1899/00-1925/26	211	955	17,272	18.08
Pritchard T.L.	1937/38-1956	200	818	19,062	23.30
Patel D.N.	1976-1996/97	358	654	21,737	33.23
Cairns C.L.	1988-2004	216	643	18,278	28.42
Boock S.L.	1973/74-1989/90	164	640	14,314	22.36
Chatfield E.J.	1973/74-1989/90	157	587	13,429	22.87
Saunders J.V.	1899/00-1913/14	107	553	12,065	21.81
Howarth H.J.	1962/63-1978/79	145	541	13,674	25.27
Blair R.W.	1951/52-1964/65	119	537	9961	18.54
Merritt W.E.	1926/27-1946	125	536	13,669	25.50
Collinge R.O.	1963/64-1978	163	524	12,793	24.41
O'Sullivan D.R.	1971-1984/85	136	523	13,554	25.91
Bracewell J.G.	1978/79-1990	149	522	13,919	26.66
Motz R.C.	1957/58-1969	142	518	11,769	22.72
Alabaster J.C.	1955/56-1971/72	143	500	12,688	25.37
Cairns B.L.	1971/72-1988	148	473	12,544	26.52
Reid J.R.	1947/48-1965	246	466	10,535	22.60
Cameron F.J.	1952/53-1966/67	119	447	9658	21.60
Gray E.J.	1975/76-1991/92	162	444	12,522	28.20
Morrison D.K.	1985/86-1996/97	142	440	13,298	30.22
Taylor B.R.	1963/64-1979/80	141	422	10,605	25.13
Burtt T.B.	1943/44-1954/55	84	408	9054	22.19
Wiseman P.J.	1991/92-2004/05	144	401	13,264	33.07
Snedden M.C.	1977/78-1990	118	387	9918	25.62
Cunis R.S.	1960/61-1976/77	132	386	10,287	26.65
Yuile B.W.	1959/60-1971/72	123	375	8209	21.89
Moir A.M.	1949/50-1961/62	97	368	9040	24.56
Cave H.B.	1945/46-1958/59	117	362	8663	23.93
Cowie J.	1932/33-1949/50	86	359	8002	22.28
MacGibbon A.R.	1947/48-1961/62	124	356	9301	26.12
Hadlee D.R.	1966/67-1983/84	111	351	8853	25.22
Vettori D.L.	1996/97-2004/05	103	338	11,012	32.57
McIntyre J.M.	1961/62-1982/83	113	336	7917	23.56
Priest M.W.	1984/85-1998/99	109	329	10,478	31.84
Callaway S.T.	1888/89-1906/07	62	320	5460	17.06
Sparling J.T.	1956/57-1970/71	127	318	7226	22.72
Downes A.D.	1888/89-1913/14	51	311	4564	14.67
Hayes J.A.	1946/47-1960/61	78	292	6759	23.14
Dickeson C.W.	1973/74-1986/87	90	282	8242	29.22
Beard D.D.	1945/46-1964/65	66	278	6000	21.58
O'Connor S.B.	1994/95-2002/03	73	278	6582	23.67
Alabaster G.D.	1955/56-1975/76	96	275	6388	23.22
Troup G.B.	1974/75-1986/87	100	272	7541	27.72
Watson W.	1984/85-1994/95	93	272	7485	27.52
Upham E.F.	1892/93-1909/10	49	265	4414	16.65
Nash D.J.	1990/91-2001/02	120	255	7165	28.09
Robertson G.K.	1979/80-1989/90	88	252	7469	29.59
Penn A.J.	1994/95-2003/04	66	252	5806	23.03
Martin C.S.	1997/98-2004/05	86	252	8212	32.58
Bradburn G.E.	1985/86-2001/02	127	250	8174	32.69
Doull S.B.	1989/90-2001/02	99	250	7233	28.93

	Career	M	Wkts	Runs	Ave
Wisneski W.A.	1992/93-2003/04	71	248	6467	26.07
Brice A.W.S.	1902/03-1927/28	61	247	5260	21.29
Bennett J.H.	1898/99-1919/20	52	241	4476	18.58
McGirr H.M.	1913/14-1932/33	88	239	6571	27.49
Tuffey D.R.	1996/97-2004/05	69	234	6062	25.94
Walmsley K.P	1994/95-2004/05	63	230	5861	25.48
Puna N.	1956/57-1968/69	70	229	5597	24.44
Dunning J.A.	1923/24-1937/38	60	228	6290	27.58
Pollard V.	1964/65-1974/75	130	224	6931	30.94
Vivian H.G.	1930/31-1938/39	85	223	6160	27.62
Cromb I.B.	1929/30-1946/47	88	222	6152	27.71
Badcock F.T.	1924/25-1945	53	221	5211	23.57
Allcott C.F.W.	1920/21-1945/46	82	220	5882	26.73
Duff S.W.	1985/86-1995/96	88	217	7051	32.49
Franklin J.E.C.	1998/99-2004/05	64	217	5195	23.94
Davis H.T.	1991/92-2003/04	71	215	6693	31.13
Blunt R.C.	1917/18-1935	123	214	6638	31.01
Stott L.W.	1969/70-1983/84	63	214	5341	24.95
Hart M.N.	1990/91-2004/05	135	212	7424	35.01
de Groen R.P.	1987/88-1995/96	60	210	5266	25.07
Stirling D.A.	1981/82-1991/92	84	206	6948	33.72
Congdon B.E.	1960/61-1978	241	204	6125	30.02
Roberts S.J.	1985/86-1995/96	63	203	6001	29.56
Burke C.	1937/38-1953/54	60	200	5199	25.99

Wicketkeeping

100 DISMISSALS	Career	M	Caught	Stumped	Total
Smith I.D.S.	1977/78-1991/92	178	390	36	426
James K.C.	1923/24-1946/47	204	310	112	422
McSweeney E.B.	1979/80-1993/94	121	340	45	385
Parore A.C.	1988/89-2001/02	163	358	24	382
Lees W.K.	1970/71-1987/88	146	292	44	336
Hart R.G.	1992/93-2003/04	110	298	17	315
Wadsworth K.J.	1968/69-1975/76	118	256	26	282
Germon L.K.	1987/88-2001/02	103	256	26	282
Ward J.T.	1957/58-1970/71	95	227	27	254
Petrie E.C.	1950/51-1966/67	115	194	37	231
Mooney F.L.H.	1941/42-1954/55	91	164	54	218
Blain T.E.	1982/83-1994/95	118	190	26	216
Nevin C.J.	1995/96-2004/05	74	202	7	209
Croy M.G.	1994/95-2001/02	65	183	14	197
Young B.A.	1983/84-1997/98	163	185	11	196
Hopkins G.J.	1997/98-2004/05	74	184	12	196
Milburn B.D.	1963/64-1982/83	75	176	19	195
Young R.A.	1998/99-2004/05	52	162	3	165
Dick A.E.	1956/57-1968/69	78	133	21	154
Kelly P.J.	1980/81-1988/89	49	140	13	153
Colquhoun I.A.	1953/54-1963/64	57	108	28	136
Guillen S.C.	1947/48-1960/61	66	100	34	134
Sigley M.A.	1994/95-2002/03	44	124	4	128
Boxshall C.	1897/98-1914/15	65	81	43	124
Schofield R.M.	1964/65-1974/75	53	107	15	122

	Career	M	Caught	Stumped	Total
Robinson S.A.	1984/85-1996/97	45	117	5	122
Wright M.J.E.	1972/73-1983/84	65	104	17	121
Mills G.H.	1935/36-1957/58	59	85	34	119
Tindill E.W.T.	1932/33-1949/50	69	85	33	118
Edwards G.N.	1973/74-1984/85	92	88	16	104
Therkleson I.J.	1966/67-1973/74	39	93	7	100

Leading Career Averages

BATTING *(qualification 3000 runs)*	*M*	*In*	*NO*	*HS*	*Runs*	*Ave*
Crowe M.D.	247	412	62	299	19,608	56.02
Scott V.J.	80	130	17	204	5620	49.73
Turner G.M.	455	792	101	311*	34,346	49.70
Donnelly M.P.	131	221	26	208*	9250	47.43
Sutcliffe B.	233	407	39	385	17,447	47.41
Sinclair M.S.	110	186	20	268	7845	47.25
Harris C.Z.	108	170	36	251*	6217	46.39
Dempster C.S.	184	306	36	212	12,145	44.98
Wallace W.M.	121	192	17	211	7757	44.32
Richardson M.H.	157	264	31	306	9994	42.89
Wright J.G.	366	636	44	192	25,073	42.35
Horne M.J.	120	205	10	241	8199	42.04
Fleming S.P.	189	316	28	274*	12,033	41.78
Jones A.H.	145	254	33	186	9180	41.53
Reid J.R.	246	418	28	296	16,128	41.35
Blunt R.C.	123	209	15	338*	7953	40.99
Hadlee W.A.	117	203	17	198	7523	40.44
Edgar B.A.	175	307	26	203	11,304	40.22

BOWLING *(qualification 200 wickets)*	*M*	*Wkts*	*Runs*	*Ave*
Downes A.D.	51	311	4564	14.67
Upham E.F.	49	265	4414	16.65
Callaway S.T.	62	320	5460	17.06
Smith S.G.	211	955	17,272	18.08
Hadlee R.J.	342	1490	26,998	18.11
Blair R.W.	119	537	9961	18.54
Bennett J.H.	52	241	4476	18.58

(C.J. Drum took 199 wickets at 19.46)

HIGHEST PARTNERSHIPS

FIRST WICKET

387	Turner G.M.	Jarvis T.W.	NZ v West Indies	Georgetown	1971/72
373	Sutcliffe B.	Watt L.	Otago v Auckland	Auckland	1950/51
333	Edgar B.A.	Jones A.H.	Wellington v Auckland	Wellington	1988/89
316	Austen M.H.	Hart R.T.	Wellington v Central Districts	Wanganui	1993/94
310	Edgar B.A.	Vance R.H.	Wellington v Northern Districts	Wellington	1988/89
306	Cuff L.A.	Lawrence J.D.	Canterbury v Auckland	Christchurch	1893/94
305	Lawson R.A.	Croy M.G.	Otago v Central Districts	Napier	1995/96
299	Bell M.D.	Jones R.A.	Wellington v Otago	Dunedin	2001/02
287	Hartland B.R.	Stead G.R.	Canterbury v Wellington	Christchurch	1994/95
286	Sutcliffe B.	Taylor D.D.	Auckland v Canterbury	Auckland	1948/49
276	Dempster C.S.	Mills J.E.	NZ v England	Wellington	1929/30
276	Griffith A.F.G.	Campbell S.L.	West Indies v NZ	Hamilton	1999/00
268	Turner G.M.	Dowling G.T.	NZ v President's XI	Montego Bay	1971/72
260	Lawson R.A.	Mohammad Wasim	Otago v Northern Districts	Dunedin	2002/03
259	Austen M.H.	Aiken J.M.	Wellington v Otago	Wellington	1994/95
252	Sutcliffe B.	Scott V.J.	NZ v Rest	Christchurch	1948/49
250	Hart R.T.	Smith C.J.P.	Central Districts v Wellington	Wellington	1985/86
247	Sutcliffe B.	Scott V.J.	NZ v Combined Services	Gillingham	1949
244	Richardson M.H.	Papps M.H.W.	NZ v Kent	Canterbury	2004
240	McIntosh T.G.	Horne M.J.	Auckland v Otago	Dunedin	2001/02
239	Dempster C.S.	Dustin W.H.	Wellington v Canterbury	Wellington	1931/32
239	Smith D.	Parks J.H.	MCC v Otago	Dunedin	1935/36
235	Hadlee W.A.	Page M.L.	Canterbury v Wellington	Christchurch	1936/37
231	Richardson M.H.	Vincent L.	NZ v India	Mohali	2003/04
230	Murray B.A.G.	Turner G.M.	NZ v President's XI	Rawalpindi	1969/70
229	Sutcliffe B.	Scott V.J.	NZ v Surrey	Oval	1949
226*	Hadlee W.A.	Leggat J.G.	Canterbury v Otago	Christchurch	1948/49
225	Richardson P.E.	Watson W.	MCC v Wellington	Wellington	1958/59
225	Greenidge C.G.	Haynes D.L.	West Indies v NZ	Christchurch	1979/80
220	Sutcliffe B.	Taylor D.D.	Auckland v Canterbury	Auckland	1948/49
220	Bell M.D.	Jones R.A.	Wellington v Canterbury	Christchurch	2000/01
219*	Edgar B.A.	Vance R.H.	Wellington v Central Districts	Wellington	1987/88
218	Hadlee W.A.	Leggat J.G.	Canterbury v Wellington	Christchurch	1947/48
218	Dempsey D.A.	Hadlee B.G.	Canterbury v Otago	Christchurch	1980/81
215	Sinclair M.S.	How J.M.	Central Districts v Northern Districts	Napier	2004/05
214	Woodfull W.M.	Ponsford W.H.	Australia v Otago	Dunedin	1927/28
214	Bolton B.A.	Dowling G.T.	Canterbury v Northern Districts	Christchurch	1959/60
214	Spearman C.M.	Twose R.G.	NZ v Zimbabwe	Auckland	1995/96
213	Lawson R.A.	Bell M.D.	NZ Academy XI v Zimbabwe	Whangarei	1995/96
213	Gaffaney C.B.	Parlane M.E.	NZ Academy XI v Bangladesh	Christchurch	1997/98
211	Turner G.M.	Parker J.M.	NZ v MCC	Lord's	1973
211	Bell M.D.	Donaldson G.T.	Wellington v Central Districts	Wellington	2003/04
209	Sutcliffe B.	Watt L.	Otago v Canterbury	Dunedin	1947/48
209	Harris B.Z.	Boyle D.J.	Canterbury v Otago	Christchurch	1991/92
208	Blunt R.C.	Worker R.V. de R.	Canterbury v MCC	Christchurch	1922/23
208	Athey C.W.J.	Robinson R.T.	England XI v Northern Districts	Hamilton	1987/88
207	Sadiq Mohammad	Zaheer Abbas	Pakistan v Wellington	Wellington	1972/73
201	Anthony A.	Horspool E.	Auckland v Wellington	Auckland	1924/25

SECOND WICKET

317	Hart R.T.	Briasco P.S.	Central Districts v Canterbury	New Plymouth	1983/84
315*	Gibbs H.H.	Kallis J.H.	South Africa v NZ	Christchurch	1998/99
303	Dempster C.S.	Allcott C.F.W.	NZ v Warwickshire	Birmingham	1927
287	Bell M.D.	Wells J.D.	Wellington v Auckland	Auckland	1997/98
263	Greatbatch M.J.	Crowe M.D.	Central Districts v Northern Districts	Morrinsville	1986/87
256	Anderson R.W.	Edgar B.A.	NZ v Scotland	Dundee	1978
254	Burns K.J.	Rutherford K.R.	Otago v Wellington	Oamaru	1987/88
252	Baker W.A.	Beechey E.M.	Wellington v Auckland	Wellington	1918/19

250	Bell M.D.	Sinclair M.S.	New Zealand A v Sri Lanka A	Queenstown	2003/04
248	Horne M.J.	Fleming S.P.	Southern v Pakistan A	Christchurch	1998/99
245	Horne M.J.	Fleming S.P.	NZ v British Universities	Oxford	1999
244	Spearman C.M.	Sinclair M.S.	Central Districts v Northern Districts	Wanganui	1998/99
241	Franklin T.J.	Crowe J.J.	Auckland v Wellington	Wellington	1988/89
241	Wright J.G.	Jones A.H.	NZ v England	Wellington	1991/92
237	Gibson J.G.	Kuggeleijn C.M.	Northern Districts v Canterbury	Hamilton	1980/81
231	Carew M.C.	Nurse S.M.	West Indies v NZ	Christchurch	1968/69
229	Hemus L.G.	Midlane F.A.	Auckland v Wellington	Wellington	1918/19
227	Baker W.A.	Kortlang H.H.L.	Wellington v Otago	Dunedin	1923/24
227	Dobbs P.W.	Lamont M.J.	Otago v Auckland	Dunedin	1990/91
222	Warner P.F.	Fane F.L.	Lord Hawke's XI v Otago	Dunedin	1902/03
222	Crocker L.M.	Kuggeleijn C.M.	Northern Districts v Otago	Hamilton	1983/84
222	McCullum B.B.	Cumming C.D.	Otago v Auckland	Dunedin	2001/02
220	Macartney C.G.	Punch A.T.E.	NSW v Otago	Dunedin	1923/24
220	Richardson M.H.	Cumming C.D.	Otago v Northern Districts	Hamilton	2000/01
215	Bell M.D.	Wells J.D.	Wellington v Northern Districts	Hamilton	1998/99
215	Bell M.D.	Parlane M.E.	Wellington v Central Districts	Napier	2004/05
212	Horspool E.	Snedden A.N.C.	Auckland v Victoria	Auckland	1924/25
210	Hadlee W.A.	O'Brien F.P.	Canterbury v Otago	Christchurch	1940/41
210	Howarth G.P.	Crowe J.J.	NZ v West Indies	Kingston	1984/85
209*	Jones A.H.	Crowe M.D.	Wellington v Canterbury	Christchurch	1992/93
207*	Twose R.G.	Douglas M.W.	Central Districts v Auckland	Auckland	1991/92
207	Mills J.E.	Blunt R.C.	NZ v H.D.G. Leveson-Gower's XI	Scarborough	1927
207	Vaughan M.P.	Hussain N.	England v Canterbury	Christchurch	2001/02
206	Raman W.V.	Gursharan Singh	India v Otago	Dunedin	1989/90
204	Gavaskar S.M.	Amarnath S.	India v NZ	Auckland	1975/76
202	Naushad Ali	Saeed Ahmed	Pakistan v Canterbury	Christchurch	1964/65
200	Smith R.W.	Bilby G.P.	Wellington v Northern Districts	Whangarei	1973/74

THIRD WICKET

467†	Jones A.H.	Crowe M.D.	New Zealand v Sri Lanka	Wellington	1990/91
445	Whitelaw P.E.	Carson W.N.	Auckland v Otago	Dunedin	1936/37
394*	Kennedy P.G.	Latham R.T.	Canterbury v Northern Districts	Rotorua	1990/91
346	Burnett G.P.	Verry R.A.	Wellington v Northern Districts	Hamilton	1991/92
278	Franklin T.J.	Patel D.N.	Auckland v Canterbury	Christchurch	1985/86
265	Horne M.J.	Barnes A.C.	Auckland v Bangladesh	Auckland	2001/02
264	Chappell I.M.	Chappell G.S.	Australia v NZ	Wellington	1973/74
261*	Maynard M.P.	Thomson S.A.	Northern Districts v Auckland	Hamilton	1990/91
255	Lloyd C.H.	Davis C.A.	West Indies v South Island	Dunedin	1968/69
252*	Howarth G.P.	Roberts A.D.G.	Northern Districts v Pakistan	Gisborne	1978/79
248	Shoaib Mohammad	Javed Miandad	Pakistan v New Zealand	Auckland	1988/89
246	Rabone G.O.	Reid J.R.	NZ v Nottinghamshire	Nottingham	1949
246	Murray B.A.G.	Morrison J.F.M.	Wellington v Otago	Dunedin	1968/69
245	Crowe M.D.	Coney J.V.	NZ v South Australia	Adelaide	1985/86
244	Nicol R.J.	Vincent L.	Auckland v Otago	Auckland	2004/05
241	Wright J.G.	Crowe M.D.	New Zealand v West Indies	Wellington	1986/87
229	Miller L.S.M.	Sutcliffe B.	NZ v South Australia	Adelaide	1953/54
227	Rutherford K.R.	Blair B.R.	Otago v Central Districts	Alexandra	1988/89
226	Haynes D.L.	Richardson R.B.	West Indies v Shell XI	Napier	1986/87
224	Reid J.F.	Crowe M.D.	NZ v Australia	Brisbane	1985/86
224	Sinclair M.S.	Spearman C.M.	Central Districts v Auckland	Auckland	2003/04
223	Smith C.J.P.	Wilson S.W.J.	Central Districts v Otago	Blenheim	1990/91
222*	Sutcliffe B.	Reid J.R.	NZ v India	New Delhi	1955/56
222	Snedden A.N.C.	Smith S.G.	Auckland v Hawke's Bay	Auckland	1920/21
221	Blunt R.C.	McMullan J.J.M.	Otago v Canterbury	Dunedin	1928/29
221	Lara B.C.	Adams J.C.	West Indies v New Zealand	Wellington	1994/95
220	Shoaib Mohammad	Javed Miandad	Pakistan v New Zealand	Wellington	1988/89
218	Woodfull W.M.	Schneider K.J.	Australia v NZ	Auckland	1927/28
217	Dobbs P.W.	Rutherford K.R.	Otago v Central Districts	Blenheim	1990/91
216	Hemus L.G.	Smith S.G.	Auckland v Canterbury	Auckland	1919/20
214	Anthony A.	Gillespie H.D.	Auckland v Canterbury	Auckland	1929/30

213	Turner G.M.	Congdon B.E.	Otago v Wellington	Dunedin	1972/73
213	Jones A.H.	Crowe M.D.	NZ v Australia	Adelaide	1987/88
212	Booth B.C.	Burge P.J.P.	Australia B v NZ	Auckland	1966/67
210	Howarth G.P.	Crowe M.D.	NZ v Essex	Chelmsford	1983
210	Edgar G.A.	Crowe M.D.	NZ v England	Lord's	1986
210	Smith B.F.	Douglas M.W.	Central Districts v Northern Districts	Taupo	2000/01
209	McCosker R.G.	Chappell G.S.	Australia v Wellington	Wellington	1976/77
206	Preston A.H.	Beck J.E.F.	Wellington v Canterbury	Christchurch	1955/56
204	Harford N.S.	Reid J.R.	NZ v Oxford University	Oxford	1958
204	Twose R.G.	Crowe M.D.	NZ v Indian Colts XI	Hyderabad	1995/96
203*	Pocock B.A.	Parore A.C.	Auckland v Wellington	Auckland	1997/98
201	McLeod E.G.	Lamason J.R.	Wellington v Auckland	Wellington	1935/36

† *world record*

FOURTH WICKET

350	Mushtaq Mohammad	Asif Iqbal	Pakistan v NZ	Dunedin	1972/73
324	Reid J.R.	Wallace W.M.	NZ v Cambridge University	Cambridge	1949
310	Ryder J.D.	Parlane N.R.	Wellington v Central Districts	Palmerston North	2004/05
299	Wallace W.M.	Donnelly M.P.	NZ v Leicestershire	Leicester	1949
282	Wilkinson W.A.C.	Champman A.P.F.	MCC v Canterbury	Christchurch	1922/23
280	Crowe J.J.	Patel D.N.	Auckland v Northern Districts	Auckland	1991/92
278	Roberts A.W.	Page M.L.	Canterbury v Wellington	Wellington	1931/32
276*	Crowe M.D.	Briasco P.S.	Central Districts v Canterbury	Christchurch	1986/87
274	Jones R.A.	Mather S.R.	Wellington v Otago	Wellington	2000/01
266	Denness M.H.	Fletcher K.W.R.	England v NZ	Auckland	1974/75
259	Bradburn G.E.	Parlane M.E.	Northern Districts v Canterbury	Christchurch	1996/97
254	Reid J.R.	Miller L.S.M.	NZ v Natal	Durban	1953/54
252	Thomson S.A.	Young B.A.	Northern Districts v Auckland	Auckland	1990/91
243	Horne M.J.	Astle N.J.	New Zealand v Zimbabwe	Auckland	1997/98
240	Fleming S.P.	McMillan C.D.	New Zealand v Sri Lanka	Colombo	1997/98
235	Burns K.J.	Hoskin R.N.	Otago v Northern Districts	Hamilton	1987/88
229	Congdon B.E.	Hastings B.F.	NZ v Australia	Wellington	1973/74
219	Vivian H.G.	Page M.L.	NZ v Oxford University	Oxford	1931
218	Crowe J.J.	Coney J.V.	NZ v Glamorgan	Swansea	1986
214	Ransford V.S.	Lampard A.W.	Australia v NZ	Auckland	1920/21
211*	Jones A.H.	Burns K.J.	Otago v Wellington	Wellington	1984/85
211	White D.J.	Young B.A.	Northern Districts v Auckland	Auckland	1992/93
208	Thomson S.A.	Maynard M.P.	Northern Districts v Wellington	Hamilton	1991/92
207	Midlane F.A.	Richardson C.A.	Wellington v Otago	Wellington	1899/00
207	Badcock F.T.	Lowry T.C.	Wellington v Auckland	Wellington	1927/28
207	Sulzberger G.P.	Penn A.J.	Central Districts v Otago	Napier	1995/96
206	McCullum S.J.	Dawson G.J.	Otago v Northern Districts	Dunedin	1983/84
206	Stewart A.J.	Hussain N.	England v New Zealand XI	Palmerston North	1996/97
206	McIntosh T.G.	Vincent L.	Auckland v Canterbury	Christchurch	2000/01
204	Harvey R.N.	Simpson R.B.	Australia B v Otago	Dunedin	1956/57
204	Jarvis T.W.	Thomson K.	Canterbury v Central Districts	Wanganui	1969/70
203	Thomson S.A.	Maynard M.P.	Northern Districts v Otago	Hamilton	1991/92
200	Blair B.R.	Dawson G.J.	Otago v Central Districts	Dunedin	1982/83

FIFTH WICKET

347*	Horne M.J.	Barnes A.C.	Auckland v Northern Districts	Auckland	2003/04
341	Larsen G.R.	McSweeney E.B.	Wellington v Central Districts	Levin	1987/88
319	Rutherford K.R.	Gray E.J.	NZ v DB Close's XI	Scarborough	1986
301	Englefield J.I.	Taylor R.L.	Central Districts v Wellington	Palmerston North	2004/05
290	Harris C.Z.	Stead G.R.	Canterbury v Central Districts	Blenheim	1996/97
266	Sutcliffe B.	Haig W.S.	Otago v Auckland	Dunedin	1949/50
258	Salim Malik	Inzamam-ul-Haq	Pakistan v New Zealand	Wellington	1993/94
255	Taylor B.R.	Coney J.V.	Wellington v Otago	Dunedin	1972/73
252*	Latham R.T.	Priest M.W.	Canterbury v Northern Districts	Christchurch	1988/89
244	Reid J.R.	Chapple M.E.	NZ v Western Province	Cape Town	1962/63
242	Hammond W.R.	Ames L.E.G.	England v NZ	Christchurch	1932/33
236	Harris C.Z.	Astle N.J.	Canterbury v Otago	Christchurch	1996/97

235*	Woodfull W.M.	Ransford V.S.	Victoria v NZ	Christchurch	1924/25
235*	Sulzberger G.P.	Ryder J.D.	Central Districts v Canterbury	Napier	2002/03
234*	Scott V.J.	Morris J.B.	Auckland v Central Districts	Auckland	1951/52
233	Moloney D.A.R.	Kerr J.L.	NZ v England XI	Folkestone	1937
222	Astle N.J.	McMillan C.D.	New Zealand v Zimbabwe	Wellington	2000/01
213	Ritchie G.M.	Matthews G.R.J.	Australia v NZ	Wellington	1985/86
203	Booth B.C.	Davies G.R.	Australia B v Central Districts	Palmerston North	1966/67
201	Alexander W.C.	Richardson V.Y.	Australia v Auckland	Auckland	1927/28
201	Burgess M.G.	Jarvis T.W.	Auckland v Central Districts	Auckland	1971/72

SIXTH WICKET

293*	Fulton P.G.	Broom N.T.	Canterbury v Otago	Dunedin	2004/05
281	Thorpe G.P.	Flintoff A.	England v New Zealand	Christchurch	2001/02
269	Trumper V.T.	Hill C.	Australia v NZ	Wellington	1904/05
256	Martyn D.R.	Gilchrist A.C.	Australia v New Zealand	Wellington	2004/05
246*	Crowe J.J.	Hadlee R.J.	NZ v Sri Lanka	Colombo	1986/87
240	Parfitt P.H.	Knight B.R.	England v NZ	Auckland	1962/63
238	McDonald R.	Cowley O.W.	Queensland v Hawke's Bay	Napier	1896/97
233	Crawford J.N.	Armstrong W.W.	Australia v NZ	Auckland	1913/14
232	Botham I.T.	Randall D.W.	England v New Zealand	Wellington	1983/84
226	Gray E.J.	Ormiston R.W.	Wellington v Central Districts	Wellington	1981/82
220	Turner G.M.	Wadsworth K.J.	NZ v West Indies	Kingston	1971/72
220	Toynbee M.H.	Smith I.D.S.	Central Districts v Auckland	Napier	1982/83
216	Hart M.N.	Marshall H.J.H.	Northern Districts v Central Districts	Napier	2004/05
212*	McMillan C.D.	Parore A.C.	New Zealand v President's XI	Jodhpur	1999/00
209*	Parore A.C.	O'Dowd A.P.	Auckland v Otago	Dunedin	1991/92
209	Harris C.Z.	Redmond A.J.	Canterbury v Wellington	Rangiora	2001/02
203	Ormiston R.W.	Coney J.V.	Wellington v Central Districts	New Plymouth	1982/83
201	Harris C.Z.	Parore A.C	New Zealand v Orange Free State	Bloemfontein	1994/95
201	Tendulkar S.R.	Mongia N.R.	India v Central Districts	Napier	1998/99

SEVENTH WICKET

265	Powell J.L.	Dorreen N.	Canterbury v Otago	Christchurch	1929/30
261	Campbell A.D.R.	Strang P.A.	Zimbabwe v Canterbury	Timaru	1997/98
250	Nevin C.J.	Walker M.D.J.	Wellington v Otago	Wellington	2003/04
248	Yousuf Youhana	Saqlain Mushtaq	Pakistan v New Zealand	Christchurch	2000/01
246	McGlew D.J.	Murray A.R.A.	South Africa v NZ	Wellington	1952/53
244	Patrick W.R.	Allcott C.F.W.	NZ v NSW	Sydney	1925/26
241	Astle N.J.	Priest M.W.	Canterbury v Wellington	Christchurch	1994/95
229	Schneider K.J.	Oldfield W.A.S.	Australia v Canterbury	Christchurch	1927/28
225	Cairns C.L.	Oram J.D.P.	NZ v South Africa	Auckland	2003/04
224	Scott V.J.	Matheson A.M.	Auckland v Canterbury	Auckland	1937/38
219	Yuile B.W.	Hampton B.L.	Central Districts v Canterbury	Napier	1967/68
217	Walters K.D.	Gilmour G.J.	Australia v NZ	Christchurch	1976/77
212	Katich S.M.	Gilchrist A.C.	Australia v New Zealand	Christchurch	2004/05
205	Germon L.K.	Priest M.W.	Canterbury v Northern Districts	Christchurch	1991/92
192	Brown S.W.	Parore A.C.	Auckland v Central Districts	Auckland	1990/91
191	Wright J.G.	Smith I.D.S.	NZ v Western Australia	Perth	1989/90
186	Lees W.K.	Hadlee R.J.	NZ v Pakistan	Karachi	1976/77
186	Leggat R.I.	Hadlee D.R.	Canterbury v Sri Lanka	Christchurch	1982/83
184*	Bull C.L.	Isherwood B.P.	Canterbury v Central Districts	Nelson	1971/72
182	Sutcliffe B.	Gilbertson A.W.	Otago v Canterbury	Christchurch	1952/53
179	Griggs B.B.J.	Furlong C.J.M.	Central Districts v Northern Districts	Hamilton	2001/02
177*	Barnes A.C.	Mills J.M.	Auckland v Otago	Alexandra	1995/96
176	Rabone G.O.	Mooney F.L.H.	NZ v MCC	Lord's	1949

EIGHTH WICKET

433†	Trumper V.T.	Sims A.	Sims' Australian XI v Canterbury	Christchurch	1913/14
253	Astle N.J.	Parore A.C.	New Zealand v Australia	Perth	2001/02
215	Murray J.R.	Cummins A.C.	West Indies v Otago	Dunedin	1994/95
210	Stead G.R.	Bond S.E.	Canterbury v Northern Districts	Christchurch	2004/05

190*	Mills J.E.	Allcott C.F.W.	NZ v Civil Service	Chiswick	1927
189	Carson W.N.	Matheson A.M.	Auckland v Wellington	Auckland	1938/39
185	Nash D.J.	Mills K.D.	Auckland v Wellington	Wellington	2000/01
180	Twose R.G.	Goodson M.C.	Wellington v Otago	Dunedin	1994/95
173	Smith I.D.S.	Robertson G.K.	Central Districts v Northern Districts	Hamilton	1982/83
172*	Walker B.G.K.	Mills K.D.	Auckland v Wellington	Auckland	1999/00
166	Hadlee R.J.	Hadlee D.R.	Canterbury v Auckland	Christchurch	1983/84
165*	Eckhold A.G.	Crawford J.N.	Otago v Wellington	Wellington	1914/15
161	McSweeney E.B.	Snedden M.C.	Shell XI v West Indies	Napier	1986/87
157	McLaren A.C.	McLean J.F.	MCC v NZ	Wellington	1922/23
154	James K.C.	Badcock F.T.	Wellington v Canterbury	Christchurch	1926/27
153	Nicol R.J.	Young R.A.	Auckland v Canterbury	Auckland	2001/02
152	Bradburn G.E.	Doull S.B.	Northern Districts v Canterbury	Christchurch	1991/92

† *world record*

NINTH WICKET

239	Cave H.B.	Leggat I.B.	Central Districts v Otago	Dunedin	1952/53
209	Wiseman P.J.	Martin B.P.	New Zealand A v Sri Lanka A	Christchurch	2003/04
208	McSkimming W.C.	Scott B.E.	Otago v Auckland	Auckland	2004/05
188	Parlane N.R.	Tuffey D.R.	Northern Districts v Wellington	Wellington	1999/00
185	Maynard M.P.	Doull S.B.	Northern Districts v Auckland	Auckland	1991/92
182*	Germon L.K.	Ford R.M.	Canterbury v Wellington	Christchurch	1989/90
170*	Hart M.N.	Yovich J.A.F.	Northern Districts v South Africa	Hamilton	1998/99
163*	Cowdrey M.C.	Smith A.C.	England v NZ	Wellington	1962/63
139	Hart R.G.	Tait A.R.	Northern Districts v Wellington	Gisborne	1996/97
136	Smith I.D.S.	Snedden M.C.	NZ v India	Auckland	1989/90
135	Hart R.G.	Penn A.J.	Central v Northern	Rangiora	1998/99
134	Wilson J.W.	Mallender N.A.	Otago v Canterbury	Christchurch	1992/93
127	Mooney F.L.H.	Buchan R.A.	Wellington v Auckland	Wellington	1943/44
122	Schuster H.T.	Cunis R.S.	Auckland v Wellington	Wellington	1964/65
121	Cheetham J.E.	Murray A.R.A.	South Africa v Canterbury	Christchurch	1952/53
118	Coney J.V.	Cairns B.L.	NZ v England	Wellington	1983/84
116	Nevin C.J.	Davis H.T.	Wellington v Auckland	Auckland	1995/96
115	Robertson G.K.	Hart R.T.	Central Districts v Otago	Oamaru	1985/86
115	Hopkins G.J.	Ellis A.M.	Canterbury v Auckland	Auckland	2002/03

TENTH WICKET

184	Blunt R.C.	Hawksworth W.	Otago v Canterbury	Christchurch	1931/32
160	Germon L.K.	Wisneski W.A.	Canterbury v Northern Districts	Rangiora	1997/98
151	Hastings B.F.	Collinge R.O.	NZ v Pakistan	Auckland	1972/73
138	James K.C.	Brice A.W.S.	Wellington v Otago	Wellington	1926/27
133	Bartlett G.A.	Colquhoun I.A.	Central Districts v Auckland	Auckland	1959/60
124	Bracewell J.G.	Boock S.L.	NZ v Australia	Sydney	1985/86
123	Brice A.W.S.	Beard T.	Wellington v Otago	Wellington	1927/28
119	Carson W.N.	Cowie J.	Auckland v Otago	Auckland	1937/38
118	Astle N.J.	Cairns C.L.	New Zealand v England	Christchurch	2001/02
113	Mooney F.L.H.	Knapp E.C.V.	Wellington v Auckland	Wellington	1943/44
107	Motz R.C.	Cameron F.J.	NZ v Worcestershire	Worcester	1965
106*	Astle N.J.	Morrison D.K.	New Zealand v England	Auckland	1996/97
105	Cherry R.W.	Torrance R.C.	Otago v Canterbury	Christchurch	1925/26
104	James K.C.	Massey H.B.	Wellington v Australia	Wellington	1927/28
103	Kelly P.J.	Troup G.B.	Auckland v Northern Districts	Auckland	1985/86
101	Astle N.J.	Owens M.B.	Canterbury v Northern Districts	Hamilton	1994/95
100	Lee C.D.	Brown C.M.	Auckland v Otago	Dunedin	1994/95

Hundred Partnership for the First Wicket in Both Innings

154 & 155	Shepherd J.S.F.	Worker R.V. de.R.	Otago v Wellington	Dunedin	1923/24
220 & 286	Taylor D.D.	Sutcliffe B.	Auckland v Canterbury	Auckland	1948/49
102 & 155	Blair W.L.	Turner G.M.	Otago v Auckland	Auckland	1972/73
172 & 148	Briasco P.S.	Smith C.J.P.	Central Districts v Auckland	New Plymouth	1985/86
107	Broad B.C.	Moxon M.D.	England XI v Northern Districts	Hamilton	1987/88
208	Athey C.W.J.	Robinson R.T.			
109 & 111	Wealleans K.A.	White D.J.	Northern Districts v India	Hamilton	1989/90
116 & 102	Greatbatch M.J.	Latham R.T.	New Zealand v Zimbabwe	Bulawayo	1992/93
145 & 131	Lawson R.A.	Gaffaney C.B.	Otago v Wellington	Wellington	1996/97
118* & 179	Twose R.G.	Bell M.D.	Wellington v Central Districts	Wellington	1997/98
102 & 112	Spearman C.M.	Kelly D.P.	Central Districts v Wellington	New Plymouth	1999/00
220	Bell M.D.	Jones R.A.	Wellington v Canterbury	Christchurch	2000/01
127	Nevin C.J.	Jones R.A.			
141	Cumming C.D.	Mohammad Wasim	Otago v Wellington	Wellington	2002/03
147	Gaffaney C.B.	Cumming C.D.			
104 & 118	Richardson M.H.	McIntosh T.G.	Auckland v Northern Districts	Auckland	2002/03

FAMILIES IN FIRST-CLASS CRICKET

Great-grandfather and Great-grandson

Orchard S.A.	(C)	Orchard M.G.	(ND)

Three Generations

*Blair J.R.	(O)	Blair R.A.J.	(O)	Blair W.L. Blair B.R.	(O) (O, ND)
Burton H.G.E.L.	(W)	Burton H.E.L.	(W, A)	Burton J.E.L.	(W)
Snedden A.N.C.	(A)	Snedden W.N.	(A)	Snedden M.C.	(A)
Smith F.A.	(C)	Smith F.B.	(C)	Smith G.B.	(C)
*Carson W.	(O)	Carson W.N.	(A)	Carson J.R.	(A, ND)
Anderson W.M.	(C)	Anderson R.W.	(C, ND, O, CD)	Anderson T.R.	(CD)

* *J.R. Blair is the uncle of R.A.J. Blair. The Carsons are uncles and nephews.*

Grandfather and Grandson

Milnes L.A.	(O)	Milnes G.S.	(CD)

Father and Three Sons

Cotterill A.J.	(C)	Cotterill A.K.	(HB)	Cotterill B.W.	(HB)	Cotterill G.R.	(HB)
Hadlee W.A.	(C, O)	Hadlee B.G.	(C)	Hadlee D.R.	(C)	Hadlee R.J.	(C)

Father and Two Sons

Blacklock J.W.	(W)	Blacklock C.P.	(W)	Blacklock J.P.	(W)
Blair R.A.J.	(O)	Blair W.L.	(O)	Blair B.R.	(O, ND)
Crowe D.W.	(W,C)	Crowe M.D.	(A, CD, W)	Crowe J.J.	(A)
Garrard C.W.	(C)	Garrard W.R.	(A)	Garrard D.R.	(A)
Furlong B.D.M.	(CD)	Furlong J.B.M.	(CD)	Furlong C.J.M.	(CD)
Harris P.G.Z.	(C)	Harris B.Z.	(C, O)	Harris C.Z.	(C)
Howell J.H.	(CD)	Howell L.G.	(C, CD, A, ND)	Howell G.A.	(C, W)
McCullum S.J.	(O)	McCullum B.B.	(O, C)	McCullum N.L.	(O)
McVicar A.C.	(Minor Assocs)	McVicar S.A.	(W)	McVicar C.C.	(CD)
Puna N.	(ND)	Puna K.N.	(ND)	Puna A.	(ND)
Reaney P.S.	(HB)	Reaney H.E.I.	(W)	Reaney T.P.L.	(W, CD)

Father and One Son

Airey W.F.	(W)	Airey D.M.L.	(W)
Aldridge C.W.	(C)	Aldridge G.W.	(ND)
Allen R.	(W)	Allen G.S.	(W)
Andrews S.	(C)	Andrews B.	(C, CD, O)
Baker J.C.	(O)	Clark J.B.	(O)
Barclay W.S.	(W)	Barclay C.W.	(CD)
Barton P.H.	(ND, O)	Barton H.D.	(A, C)
Barry R.W.	(C)	Barry R.	(C)
Beard D.D.	(W, CD, ND)	Beard D.A.	(ND)
Blackmore J.H.	(ND)	Blackmore S.J.	(W)
Bradburn W.P.	(ND)	Bradburn G.E.	(ND)
Burgess G.C.	(A)	Burgess M.G.	(A)
Burtt N.V.	(C)	Burtt J.W.	(C, CD)
Cairns B.L.	(CD, O, ND)	Cairns C.L.	(ND, C)

Campbell K.O.	(O)	Campbell P.A.	(O)
Child E.L.	(A, ND)	Child M.J.	(ND)
Clark L.G.	(O)	Clark L.A.	(W, O, A)
Collins W.E.	(W)	Collins D.C.	(W)
Cuff L.A.	(C, A)	Cuff A.G.	(Tasmania)
Cunis R.S.	(A, ND)	Cunis S.J.	(C)
Douglas G.W.	(CD)	Douglas M.W.	(CD, W)
Edgar A.J.	(W)	Edgar B.A.	(W)
Freeman T.A.	(O)	Freeman B.T.	(O)
Fulton F.	(O, HB)	Fulton P.R.	(HB)
Gasson E.A. snr	(C)	Gasson E.A. jnr	(C)
Gearry G.N.	(C)	Gearry R.M.	(C, CD)
Gedye A.E.	(W)	Gedye S.G.	(A)
Gilbertson J.	(S)	Gilbertson A.W.	(O)
Hartland I.R.	(C)	Hartland B.R.	(C)
Hastings B.F.	(W, CD, C)	Hastings M.A.	(C)
Hay W.P.C.	(A)	Hay S.C.	(A)
Hill A.J.	(CD)	Hill J.V.	(CD)
Hill J.	(O)	Hill R.J.	(O)
Holden W.J.	(O)	Holden A.C.	(O)
Howden C.E.	(O)	Howden C.P.	(O)
Ibadulla K.	(O)	Ibadulla K.B.K.	(O)
Jefferson R.G.	(O, W)	Jefferson M.R.	(W)
Kelly J.W.H.	(W)	Kelly P.J.	(A)
Kerr A.	(A)	Kerr A.C.	(A)
Lankham G.	(A)	Lankham W.	(A)
Lowry T.H.	(HB)	Lowry T.C.	(A, W)
McGirr W.P.	(W)	McGirr H.M.	(W)
McKnight S.G.	(O)	McKnight K.J.	(O)
McKenzie N.M.	(O)	McKenzie M.N.	(C, O)
Mills G.	(A, HB, O)	Mills J.E.	(A)
Morgan H.A.	(W)	Morgan R.G.	(ND, A)
Murdoch D.H.	(O)	Murdoch G.H.	(O)
Newman A.	(W)	Newman P.A.	(CD)
O'Brien J.J.	(HB)	O'Brien M.A.	(W)
Oakley J.H.	(W)	Oakley D.F.	(W)
Ollivier A.M.	(C)	Ollivier K.M.	(C)
Ongley A.M.	(HB)	Ongley J.A.	(W, CD)
Parker N.M.	(O, C)	Parker M.M.	(O)
Postles A.J.	(A)	Postles B.J.	(A)
Redmond R.E.	(W, A)	Redmond A.J.	(C, O)
Rees W.L.	(A)	Rees A.W.	(A, HB)
Reese T.W.	(C)	Reese D.W.	(C)
Reid J.R.	(W, O)	Reid R.B.	(W, A)
Roberts A.	(W)	Roberts S.A.	(A)
Roberts H.	(W)	Roberts E.J.	(W)
Sale E.V.	(A)	Sale V.S.	(A)
Standidge J.A.	(W)	Standidge P.H.	(W)
Stead D.W.	(C)	Stead G.R.	(C)
Tindill E.W.T.	(W)	Tindill P.	(W)
Vance R.A.	(W)	Vance R.H.	(W)
Vivian H.G.	(A)	Vivian G.E.	(A)
Wallace W.M.	(A)	Wallace G.M.	(A)
Ward J.T.	(C)	Ward B.J.	(C)
Wilding F.	(C)	Wilding A.F.	(C)
Wright G.T.	(C)	Wright J.G.	(ND, C, A)

Father and Son in Same First-class Match

Reese T.W. & Reese D.W.	Canterbury v Otago	Dunedin	1917/18

Five Brothers

Cotterill A.J. (C) Cotterill C.N. (HB) Cotterill E.J. (C, A) Cotterill H. (C) Cotterill W.J. (C)

Four Brothers

Bayly A. (T)	Bayly F. (T)	Bayly G.T. (T)	Bayly H. (T)
Bracewell B.P. (CD, O, ND)	Bracewell D.W. (CD, C)	Bracewell J.G. (O, A)	Bracewell M.A. (O)
Mills E. (A)	Mills G. (A, HB, O)	Mills I. (A)	Mills W. (T, A)

Three Brothers

Alloo A.P.	(O)	Alloo A.W.	(O)	Alloo H.C.	(O)
Blacklock A.	(W)	Blacklock J.W.	(W)	Blacklock R.V.	(W)
Carlton W.	(A, C)	Carlton A.R.	(Vic)	Carlton J.	(Vic)
Cotterill A.K.	(HB)	Cotterill B.W.	(HB)	Cotterill G.R.	(HB)
Eden J.	(N)	Eden T.	(N)	Eden W.	(N)
Fowler G.	(N)	Fowler L.	(N)	Fowler S.	(N)
Gore A.H.	(W, HB)	Gore C.S.	(W)	Gore R.	(W)
Hadlee B.G.	(C)	Hadlee D.R.	(C)	Hadlee R.J.	(C)
Harman A.F.G.	(C)	Harman R.D.	(C)	Harman T.D.	(C)
Knapp C.	(N)	Knapp H.	(N)	Knapp K.	(N)
Lusk Hugh B.	(A, HB)	Lusk R.B.	(T)	Lusk W.N.B.	(A)
Mace C.	(O)	Mace H.	(W)	Mace J.	(O)
Meldrum A.L.	(A)	Meldrum D.	(A)	Meldrum W.	(A)
Newman A.	(W)	Newman J.	(C, W)	Newman S.	(W)
Parker K.J.	(A)	Parker J.M.	(ND)	Parker N.M.	(O, C)
Reese D.	(C)	Reese J.B.	(C)	Reese T.W.	(C)
Ridley A.E.	(C)	Ridley H.C.	(C)	Ridley R.	(C)
Salmon I.J.	(W)	Salmon J.A.N.	(W)	Salmon W.J.	(W, HB, T)

Two Brothers

Aberhart D.C.	(CD, C)	Aberhart W.M.	(W)
Alabaster G.D.	(O, C, ND)	Alabaster J.C.	(O)
Austin G.G.	(O)	Austin T.T.L.	(O)
Baker G.H.	(W)	Baker W.A.	(W)
Barton P.H.	(ND, O)	Barton R.H.	(ND)
Beal C.E.	(O, C)	Beal W.M.	(O)
Beuth D.	(CD)	Beuth A.J.	(ND)
Billcliff I.S.	(O, W, A)	Billcliff M.R.	(O)
Bishop H.A.	(HB, C)	Bishop R.E.	(HB)
Blacklock C.P.	(W)	Blacklock J.P.	(W)
Blair B.R.	(O, ND)	Blair W.L.	(O)
Blakely D.J.	(O)	Blakely J.W.	(O)
Blamires E.O.	(W, O)	Blamires H.L.	(HB)
Boddington E.R.	(N, W)	Boddington H.A.	(N, O)
Boyle D.J.	(C)	Boyle J.G.	(W, C)
Burtt N.V.	(C)	Burtt T.B.	(C)
Cairns A.E.	(O)	Cairns H.W.	(O)
Cameron D.S.	(O)	Cameron H.R.	(O)
Cederwall B.W.	(W)	Cederwall G.N.	(W)
Chadwick C.S.	(O)	Chadwick L.N.	(O)

Clarke D.B.	(A, ND)	Clarke D.S.	(ND)
Collins J.U.	(N, C)	Collins W.E.	(W)
Coney C.J.	(W)	Coney J.V.	(W)
Cornelius C.J.	(C)	Cornelius W.A.	(C)
Cresswell A.E.	(W, CD)	Cresswell G.F.	(W, CD)
Cross C.S.	(N, W)	Cross H.	(N)
Crowe J.J.	(A)	Crowe M.D.	(A, CD, W)
Dacre C.C.R.	(A)	Dacre L.M.	(A)
Doull L.J.	(W)	Doull S.B.	(ND)
Dryden C.H.	(W)	Dryden W.E.	(W)
Farrant A.J.	(C)	Farrant D.G.	(C)
Fisher A.H.	(O)	Fisher R.L.	(C)
Frankish E.H.	(C)	Frankish F.S.	(C)
Frith C.	(C, O)	Frith W.	(C, O, W)
Fulton F.	(O, HB)	Fulton J.C.	(O)
Furlong C.J.M.	(CD)	Furlong J.B.M.	(CD)
Garrard D.R.	(A)	Garrard W.R.	(A)
Gatenby D.J.	(C)	Gatenby P.R.	(Tasmania)
Gilbertson J.	(S)	Gilbertson J.H.	(S)
Graham A.C.	(O)	Graham C.G.	(O)
Hamilton A.J.	(S)	Hamilton D.C.	(S)
Hampton B.L.	(CD)	Hampton I.R.	(CD)
Harris B.Z.	(C, O)	Harris C.Z.	(C)
Hart M.N.	(ND)	Hart R.G.	(ND)
Hatch K.	(W)	Hatch R.J.	(W)
Hay T.D.B.	(A)	Hay W.P.C.	(A)
Hickson H.C.	(W)	Hickson W.R.S.	(W)
Holdship A.R.	(W)	Holdship W.E.	(Middlesex)
Horne M.J.	(A, O)	Horne P.A.	(A)
Howarth G.P.	(A, ND)	Howarth H.J.	(A)
Howell L.G.	(C, CD, A, ND)	Howell G.A.	(C, W)
Howden A.M.	(A)	Howden C.E.	(O)
Lynch D.	(A)	Lynch R.F.	(W)
Lynch R.K.	(A)	Lynch S.M.	(A)
McCullum B.B.	(O, C)	McCullum N.L.	(O)
McVicar S.A.	(W)	McVicar C.C.	(CD)
Marshall J.A.H.	(ND)	Marshall H.J.H.	(ND)
Martin J.H.	(HB)	Martin H.	(HB)
Matthias H.R.	(C)	Matthias R.B.	(C)
Morris J.B.	(A)	Morris P.P.W.	(A)
Naughton D.	(W)	Naughton M.P.	(W)
Neill R.	(A)	Neill T.	(A)
Nicholson C.R.	(C, O)	Nicholson K.A.	(O)
O'Rourke M.H.	(A)	O'Rourke P.W.	(W)
Ollivier A.M.	(C)	Ollivier F.M.	(C)
Ormiston I.W.	(W)	Ormiston R.W.	(CD, W)
Papps M.H.W.	(C)	Papps T.J.T.	(C)
Parlane M.E.	(ND, W)	Parlane N.R.	(ND, W)
Powell J.L.	(C)	Powell R.F.J.	(C)
Powys A.L.	(C)	Powys R.A.N.	(C)
Puna A.	(ND)	Puna K.N.	(ND)
Reaney H.E.I.	(W)	Reaney T.P.L.	(W, CD)
Richardson C.A.	(W)	Richardson W.A.	(NSW)
Ritchie A.W.	(A)	Ritchie D.C.	(A)
Robertson G.K.	(CD)	Robertson S.P.	(CD)
Rutherford I.A.	(O, CD)	Rutherford K.R.	(O)
Schofer J.W.J.	(W)	Schofer P.J.	(W)

Scott A.H.	(A)	Scott V.J.	(A)
Snedden A.N.C.	(A)	Snedden Cyril A.	(A)
Snedden Colin A.	(A)	Snedden W.N.	(A)
Sorenson B.J.	(A)	Sorenson R.G.	(A)
Toomey C.D.G.	(O)	Toomey F.J.	(O)
Thomson K.	(C)	Thomson W.A.	(C)
Tucker K.H.	(W)	Tucker S.G.	(W)
Turnbull A.J.	(O)	Turnbull P.J.	(O)
Wallace G.F.	(A)	Wallace W.M.	(A)
Watson E.A.	(O)	Watson L.F.	(O)
Watson H.C.	(O)	Watson L.C.	(O)
Webb M.G.	(O, C)	Webb R.J.	(O)
Weir A.F.	(A)	Weir G.L.	(A)
West G.L.	(CD, ND)	West R.M.	(CD, W)
Westbrook K.R.	(Tasmania)	Westbrook R.A.	(O)
White N.M.	(HB)	White P.C.	(HB)
Williams P.F.C.	(Gloucestershire)	Williams J.N.	(HB)
Wilson A.C.	(C)	Wilson W.C.	(C)
Wyatt I.E.	(A)	Wyatt J.L.	(ND)

Uncle and Nephew

instances not included in previous lists

Bailey J.F.	(ND)	Bailey M.D.	(ND)
CarltonW.	(A, C)	Carlton T.A.	(C, O)
Carson W.	(O)	Carson W.N.	(A)
Carson W.N.	(A)	Carson J.R.	(A, ND)
Crawford C.G.	(C)	Playle W.R.	(A)
Cunningham W.H.R.	(C)	Anderson G.F.	(C)
Dacre C.C.R. (A) & Dacre L.M.	(A)	Coleman D.D.	(A)
Fulton J.	(O)	Fulton F.	(O, HB)
		Fulton J.C.	(O)
Fulton R.W.	(C, ND)	Fulton P.G.	(C)
Griffiths B.G.	(W)	Maguiness S.J.	(W)
Pocock M.G.	(ND)	Pocock B.A.	(A, ND)
Roberts B.L.	(ND)	Cairns C.L.	(ND, C)
Westbrook N.R.	(Tasmania)	Westbrook R.A.	(O)
Wilson R.S.	(O)	Paul J.M.	(O)
Wilson T.J.	(O)	Wilson J.W.	(O)

Cousins

Bateman G.C.	(C)	Bateman S.N.	(C)
Hoskin R.N.	(O)	Lamont M.J.	(O)
Hotter S.J.	(W)	Verry R.A.	(W)
Leggat I.B.	(CD)	Leggat J.G.	(C)
Lusk Harold B.	(A, C, W)	Lusk Hugh B.	(A, HB)
		Lusk R.B.	(T)
		Lusk W.N.B.	(A)
McMillan C.D.	(C)	McMillan J.M.	(O)
Pringle M.R.	(A)	Webb P.N.	(A)
Reid B.A.	(WA)	Reid J.F.	(A)
Talbot G.L.	(C)	Talbot R.O.	(C, O)
Vettori D.L.	(ND)	Hill J.V.	(CD)

REDPATH CUP

Presented by Mr David Redpath

Awarded to the New Zealand batsman whose performances in first-class cricket have been, in the opinion of the Board of Control, the most meritorious since the award was last made.

HOLDERS

Season's first-class figures

		Team	In	NO	HS	Runs	Ave
1920/21	Anthony A.	Auckland	5	1	113	251	62.75
1921/22	Hiddleston J.S.	Wellington	8	1	118	396	56.57
1922/23	Blunt R.C.	Canterbury	12	1	174	583	53.00
1923/24	Hiddleston J.S.	Wellington	12	—	163	619	51.58
1924/25	Worker R.V. de R.	Otago	12	2	121*	491	49.10
1925/26	Allcott C.F.W.	Auckland	9 †	2	116	359	51.28
1926/27	Blunt R.C.	Otago	12 §	1	187	758	69.80
1927/28	Dempster C.S.	Wellington	12	1	145	616	56.00
1928/29	Weir G.L.	Auckland	4	2	106*	262	131.00
1929/30	Dempster C.S.	Wellington	10	4	141*	559	93.16
1930/31	Dempster C.S.	Wellington	42 †	6	212	1901	52.80
1931/32	Roberts A.W.	Canterbury	10	1	181	476	52.88
1932/33	Dempster C.S.	Wellington	9	2	83*	336	48.00
1933/34	Vivian H.G.	Auckland	5	—	64	263	52.60
1934/35	Whitelaw P.E.	Auckland	7	—	155	472	67.42
1935/36	Kerr J.L.	Canterbury	13 †	2	146	655	59.54
1936/37	Whitelaw P.E.	Auckland	6	1	195	410	82.00
1937/38	Uttley K.F.M.	Otago	6	—	138	420	70.00
1938/39	Wallace W.M.	Auckland	6	1	105	270	54.00
1939/40	Donnelly M.P.	Canterbury	5	1	104	302	75.50
1940-45	no award						
1945/46	Hadlee W.A.	Otago	7	—	198	449	66.14
1946/47	Sutcliffe B.	Auckland & Otago	8	1	197	722	103.14
1947/48	Sutcliffe B.	Otago	10	1	208*	911	101.22
1948/49	Sutcliffe B.	Auckland	6	—	141	511	85.16
1949/50	Sutcliffe B.	Otago	9	—	355	695	77.55
1950/51	Sutcliffe B.	Otago	12	—	275	798	66.50
1951/52	Scott V.J.	Auckland	10	2	151*	459	57.37
1952/53	Miller L.S.M.	Central Districts	9	3	128*	545	90.83
1953/54	Sutcliffe B.	Otago	34 †	2	196	1691	52.84
1954/55	Reid J.R.	Wellington	15	2	106	505	38.84
1955/56	Reid J.R.	New Zealand	33 †	6	150*	1227	45.44
1956/57	Miller L.S.M.	Wellington	13	3	83	559	55.90
1957/58	Miller L.S.M.	Wellington	14	1	95	549	42.23
1958/59	Pairaudeau B.H.	Northern Districts	11	1	80	456	45.60
1959/60	Reid J.R.	Wellington	16	1	165	724	48.26
1960/61	Harris P.G.Z.	Canterbury	14	2	108	597	49.75
1961/62	Reid J.R.	Wellington	40 †	2	203	2188	57.57
1962/63	Reid J.R.	Wellington	14	1	296	681	52.38
1963/64	Sinclair B.W.	Wellington	15	1	138	641	45.78
1964/65	Pollard V.	Central Districts	43 †	6	85	1081	29.21
1965/66	Sinclair B.W.	Wellington	17	2	114	700	56.66
1966/67	Dowling G.T.	Canterbury	18	2	102*	871	46.66
1967/68	Dowling G.T.	Canterbury	18	1	239	968	56.94
1968/69	Hastings B.F.	Canterbury	15	4	117*	872	79.27
1969/70	Murray B.A.G.	Wellington	51 †	3	157	2079	43.31

		Team	In	NO	HS	Runs	Ave
1970/71	Dowling G.T.	Canterbury	16	1	102	667	44.66
1971/72	Turner G.M.	Otago	27 †	5	259	1708	77.63
1972/73	Congdon B.E.	Otago	38 †	6	126	1728	54.00
1973/74	Turner G.M.	Otago	17 †	2	110*	714	47.60
1974/75	Turner G.M.	Otago	15	1	186*	838	59.85
1975/76	Turner G.M.	Otago	20	4	177*	1244	77.75
1976/77	Burgess M.G.	Auckland	28 †	1	138	1064	39.40
1977/78	Howarth G.P.	Northern Districts	22	1	122	685	32.61
1978/79	Howarth G.P.	Northern Districts	11	1	147*	505	50.50
1979/80	Howarth G.P.	Northern Districts	22	2	151	767	38.35
1980/81	Reid J.F.	Auckland	18	4	173	817	58.35
1981/82	Edgar B.A.	Wellington	19	1	161	934	51.88
1982/83	Edgar B.A.	Wellington	30 †	5	146	1116	44.64
1983/84	Coney J.V.	Wellington	19 †	4	174*	736	49.06
1984/85	Coney J.V.	Wellington	26 †	4	111*	877	39.86
1985/86	Crowe M.D.	Central Districts	31 †	9	242*	1667	75.77
1986/87	Crowe M.D.	Central Districts	22 †	3	175*	1703	89.63
1987/88	Crowe M.D.	Central Districts	16 †	2	144	1064	76.00
1988/89	Jones A.H.	Wellington	25 †	2	181*	1079	46.91
1989/90	Wright J.G.	Auckland	32 †	5	185	1641	60.77
1990/91	Crowe M.D.	Wellington	15 †	3	299	847	70.58
1991/92	Wright J.G.	Auckland	14	0	116	518	37.00
1992/93	Rutherford K.R.	Otago	26 †	3	105	907	39.43
1993/94	Jones A.H.	Wellington	20 †	0	143	934	46.70
1994/95	Parore A.C.	New Zealand	36 †	7	127*	1050	36.20
1995/96	Twose R.G.	New Zealand	10 †	2	119*	452	56.50
1996/97	Fleming S.P.	Canterbury	16 †	1	129	629	41.93
1997/98	Horne M.J.	Otago	22 †	1	241	1114	53.04
1998/99	Horne M.J.	Otago	19	2	132	887	52.17
1999/00	Cairns C.L.	New Zealand	26 †	3	109	903	39.26
2000/01	Richardson M.H.	Otago	45 †	5	306	2672	66.80
2001/02	Astle N.J.	Canterbury	15 †	3	223	899	74.91
2002/03	Richardson M.H.	Auckland	25 †	2	113	885	38.47
2003/04	Styris S.B.	Northern Districts	17 †	1	170	663	41.43
2004/05	Marshall H.J.H.	Northern Districts	16 †	0	160	730	45.62

† *including matches for New Zealand teams overseas*
§ *these figures include Blunt's scores for Otago and New Zealand against the Melbourne Cricket Club*

WINSOR CUP

Presented by Sir Arthur Donnelly to perpetuate the memory of Mr W.H. Winsor

Presented to the New Zealand bowler whose performances in first-class cricket have been, in the opinion of the Board of Control, the most meritorious since the award was last made.

HOLDERS

Season's first-class figures

		Team	Matches	O	M	R	W	Ave
1938/39	Cowie J.	Auckland	4	150	20	444	21	21.14
1939/40	Pritchard T.L.	Wellington	3	113.3	9	404	23	17.56
1940-45	no award							
1945/46	Cowie J.	Auckland	5	209	69	433	24	18.04
1946/47	Cowie J.	Auckland	5	257.4	61	578	26	22.23
1947/48	Burtt T.B.	Canterbury	4	256	57	666	26	25.61
1948/49	Cresswell A.E.	Wellington	4	152	27	343	22	15.59
1949/50	Cresswell G.F.	Wellington	4	235	111	304	20	15.20
1950/51	Burtt T.B.	Canterbury	6	363.2	151	673	44	15.29
1951/52	Burtt T.B.	Canterbury	6	317	120	643	37	17.37
1952/53	Rabone G.O.	Auckland	5	174	44	405	23	17.60
1953/54	MacGibbon A.R.	Canterbury†	17	463.7	98	1271	63	20.17
1954/55	Reid J.R.	Wellington	8	279.1	121	496	30	16.53
1955/56	Cave H.B.	Central Districts*	18	673.4	271	1259	50	25.18
1956/57	Cave H.B.	Central Districts	9	358.3	138	685	41	16.70
1957/58	Hayes J.A.	Auckland	6	244.3	49	568	48	11.83
1958/59	Hough K.W.	Auckland	8	411.3	151	701	46	15.23
1959/60	Alabaster J.C.	Otago	9	313	78	824	47	17.53
1960/61	Alabaster J.C.	Otago	10	426.3	125	964	49	19.61
1961/62	Blair R.W.	Wellington	6	252	96	535	44	12,15
1962/63	Blair R.W.	Wellington	7	244.2	77	562	32	17.56
1963/64	Blair R.W.	Wellington	9	408.1	135	856	49	17.46
1964/65	Motz R.C.	Canterbury*	26	890	272	2179	93	23.43
1965/66	Puna N.	Northern Districts	8	338	126	706	38	18.57
1966/67	Pollard V.	Central Districts	11	345.4	141	672	41	16.39
1967/68	Motz R.C.	Canterbury	10	369.2	115	907	47	19.29
1968/69	Motz R.C.	Canterbury	9	265.2	54	880	40	22.00
1969/70	Howarth H.J.	Auckland*	24	991.4	355	2173	100	21.73
1970/71	Collinge R.O.	Wellington	9	230.6	46	677	37	18.29
1971/72	Taylor B.R.	Wellington*	15	560.5	118	1474	69	21.36
1972/73	Collinge R.O.	Wellington*	23	659.2	149	1806	83	21.75
1973/74	Hadlee D.R.	Canterbury*	13	336.3	35	1451	38	38.18
1974/75	Alabaster G.D.	Otago	6	182.2	26	684	34	20.11
1975/76	Collinge R.O.	Northern Districts	9	215.3	39	623	43	14.48
1976/77	Hadlee R.J.	Canterbury	15	418.2	41	1768	49	36.08
1977/78	Hadlee R.J.	Canterbury	10	266.1	56	860	42	20.47
1978/79	Hadlee R.J.	Canterbury	10	299.1	56	909	50	18.18
1979/80	Hadlee R.J.	New Zealand	3	161.3	50	361	19	19.00
1980/81	Hadlee R.J.	New Zealand*	8	349	89	855	37	23.10
1981/82	Hadlee R.J.	Canterbury	10	424.2	135	868	59	14.74
1982/83	Hadlee R.J.	Canterbury*	12	498	147	1132	59	19.18
1983/84	Hadlee R.J.	Canterbury*	10	310.4	111	587	48	12.22
1984/85	Hadlee R.J.	Canterbury*	12	429.5	119	1061	53	20.01
1985/86	Hadlee R.J.	Canterbury*	11	553.1	129	1314	72	18.25
1986/87	Hadlee R.J.	Canterbury*	12	446.1	116	1047	66	15.86

		Team	Matches	O	M	R	W	Ave
1987/88	Chatfield E.J.	Wellington*	9	355.1	114	672	24	28.00
1988/89	Hadlee R.J.	Canterbury*	7	247.5	59	541	34	15.91
1989/90	Hadlee R.J.	New Zealand*	9	349	71	1014	43	23.58
1990/91	Watson W.	New Zealand	8	333.3	92	807	26	31.03
1991/92	Cairns C.L.	Canterbury	8	294	67	872	42	20.76
1992/93	Morrison D.K.	Auckland	8	263.2	66	598	38	15.73
1993/94	Morrison D.K.	Auckland*	9	327.3	59	1021	28	36.46
1994/95	Morrison D.K.	Auckland*	11	368.5	82	1016	40	25.40
1995/96	Cairns C.L.	New Zealand*	8	232.4	62	631	26	24.26
1996/97	Doull S.B.	New Zealand*	8	255.3	67	715	33	21.66
1997/98	Cairns C.L.	Canterbury*	12	399	113	1124	51	22.03
1998/99	Penn A.J.	Central Districts	9	288	76	763	40	19.07
1999/00	Cairns C.L.	New Zealand*	17	508.5	124	1541	67	23.00
2000/01	Tuffey D.R.	Northern Districts*	12	396.5	118	1104	54	20.44
2001/02	Drum C.J.	Auckland	9	317.3	96	827	53	15.60
2002/03	Bond S.E.	Canterbury*	6	183.5	44	600	30	20.00
2003/04	Martin C.S.	Canterbury	12	448	141	1144	53	21.68
2004/05	Vettori D.L.	Northern Districts*	8	395.5	102	1052	40	26.30

† including 16 matches for New Zealand overseas ** includes matches for New Zealand overseas*

TOURING TEAMS IN NEW ZEALAND

		FIRST-CLASS MATCHES				ALL MATCHES			
		P	W	L	D	P	W	L	D
1863/64	G. Parr's England Team	—	—	—	—	4	3	—	1
1876/77	J. Lillywhite's England Team	—	—	—	—	8	6	—	2
1877/78	Australia	—	—	—	—	7	5	1	1
1880/81	Australia	—	—	—	—	10	6	1	3
1881/82	A. Shaw's England Team	—	—	—	—	7	5	—	2
1883/84	Tasmania	4	—	3	1	7	2	3	2
1886/87	Australia	—	—	—	—	5	2	—	3
1887/88	C.A. Smith's England Team	—	—	—	—	3	—	—	3
1888/89	English Footballers	—	—	—	—	1	—	—	1
1889/90	New South Wales	5	4	—	1	7	6	—	1
1893/94	New South Wales	7	4	1	2	8	4	1	3
1894/95	Fiji	6	2	2	2	8	4	2	2
1895/96	New South Wales	5	3	1	1	5	3	1	1
1896/97	Australia	—	—	—	—	5	3	—	2
1896/97	Queensland	5	3	1	1	8	4	1	3
1899/00	Melbourne Cricket Club	—	—	—	—	7	6	—	1
1902/03	Lord Hawke's England Team	7	7	—	—	18	18	—	—
1904/05	Australia	4	3	—	1	6	4	—	2
1905/06	Melbourne Cricket Club	—	—	—	—	10	8	—	2
1906/07	MCC	11	6	2	3	16	10	2	4
1909/10	Australia	6	5	—	1	9	7	—	2
1913/14	A. Sims' Australian Team	8	6	—	2	16	8	—	8
1920/21	Australia	9	6	—	3	15	12	—	3
1922/23	MCC	8	6	—	2	14	11	—	3
1923/24	New South Wales	6	5	—	1	12	8	—	4
1924/25	Victoria	6	1	1	4	12	4	1	7
1926/27	Melbourne Cricket Club	—	—	—	—	13	5	—	8
1927/28	Australia	6	4	—	2	13	6	—	7
1929/30	MCC	8	2	—	6	17	9	—	8
1930/31	West Indies	—	—	—	—	1	—	—	1
1931/32	South Africa	3	3	—	—	3	3	—	—
1932/33	MCC	3	—	—	3	3	—	—	3
1935/36	MCC	8	2	1	5	18	5	1	12
1936/37	MCC	3	1	—	2	3	1	—	2
1938/39	Sir Julien Cahn's XI	1	—	—	1	10	2	—	8
1945/46	Australia	5	5	—	—	5	5	—	—
1946/47	MCC	4	2	—	2	4	2	—	2
1947/48	Fiji	5	2	3	—	17	6	3	8
1949/50	Australia B	5	3	—	2	14	9	—	5
1950/51	MCC	4	3	—	1	4	3	—	1
1951/52	West Indies	4	2	—	2	5	3	—	2
1952/53	South Africa	4	1	—	3	5	1	—	4
1953/54	Fiji	4	1	3	—	17	8	6	3
1954/55	MCC	4	4	—	—	4	4	—	—
1955/56	West Indies	8	6	1	1	15	11	1	3
1956/57	Australia B	7	5	—	2	12	7	—	5
1958/59	MCC	5	3	—	2	5	3	—	2
1959/60	Australia B	6	2	—	4	9	4	—	5

		FIRST-CLASS MATCHES				ALL MATCHES			
		P	W	L	D	P	W	L	D
1960/61	MCC	10	4	1	5	21	11	1	9
1961/62	Fiji	—	—	—	—	22	9	9	4
1961/62	R.A. Roberts' Commonwealth XI	2	2	—	—	3	2	—	1
1962/63	MCC	4	4	—	—	4	4	—	—
1963/64	South Africa	4	1	—	3	7	1	—	6
1964/65	Pakistan	10	2	—	8	12	4	—	8
1965/66	MCC	4	—	—	4	4	—	—	4
1966/67	Australia B	9	1	2	6	10	2	2	6
1967/68	Fiji	—	—	—	—	25	12	7	6
1967/68	India	6	4	1	1	6	4	1	1
1968/69	West Indies	6	1	2	3	7	1	2	4
1969/70	Australia B	8	2	—	6	8	2	—	6
1970/71	MCC	2	1	—	1	5	3	1	1
1972/73	Pakistan	8	5	1	2	11	6	3	2
1973/74	Australia	7	2	1	4	11	6	1	4
1974/75	MCC	3	1	—	2	5	1	—	4
1975/76	India	6	3	1	2	9	3	4	2
1976/77	Australia	6	5	—	1	8	5	2	1
1977/78	Fiji	—	—	—	—	15	5	4	6
1977/78	England	8	3	1	4†	9	4	1	4†
1978/79	Pakistan	8	5	—	3	10	6	1	3
1979/80	West Indies	5	—	2	3	8	2	3	3
1979/80	D.H. Robins' XI	2	—	—	2	8	5	1	2
1980/81	India	5	1	1	3	7	1	3	3
1981/82	Australia	5	1	1	3	11	4	4	3
1982/83	England	—	—	—	—	3	—	3	—
1982/83	Sri Lanka	4	—	3	1	9	1	7	1
1983/84	England	7	1	1	5	11	4	2	5
1984/85	Pakistan	5	1	2	2	9	1	5	3
1985/86	Australia	5	1	1	3	11	5	3	3
1986/87	West Indies	5	1	1	3	9	5	1	3
1987/88	England	7	2	1	4	12	5	3	4
1988/89	Pakistan	5	1	—	4	12	2	5	5
1989/90	India	6	1	1	4	10	2	4	4
1989/90	Australia	1	—	1	—	6	5	1	—
1990/91	Sri Lanka	7	1	—	6	10	1	3	6
1990/91	England	—	—	—	—	3	1	2	—
1991/92	England	7	4	—	3	11	8	—	3
1991/92	Zimbabwe	—	—	—	—	3	1	2	—
1991/92	Australia	—	—	—	—	1	1	—	—
1991/92	Sri Lanka	—	—	—	—	1	1	—	—
1992/93	Pakistan	1	1	—	—	4	2	2	—
1992/93	Australia	4	2	1	1	10	5	4	1
1993/94	Pakistan	5	2	1	2	11	6	2	3†
1993/94	India	3	—	—	3	7	2	2	3
1994/95	West Indies	3	1	—	2	8	6	—	2
1994/95	Australia	—	—	—	—	4	3	1	—
1994/95	South Africa	2	2	—	—	6	3	2	1†
1994/95	India	—	—	—	—	4	2	2	—
1994/95	Sri Lanka	4	2	—	2	9	4	2	3
1994/95	Australian Academy	1	1	—	—	5	5	—	—

		FIRST-CLASS MATCHES				*ALL MATCHES*			
		P	*W*	*L*	*D*	*P*	*W*	*L*	*D*
1995/96	Pakistan	1	1	—	—	5	3	2	—
1995/96	Zimbabwe	4	1	—	3	8	3	2	3
1996/97	England	6	4	1	1	12	6	3	3†
1996/97	Sri Lanka	2	—	2	—	6	2	3	1
1997/98	Bangladesh	4	—	4	—	7	—	6	1
1997/98	Zimbabwe	4	1	3	—	10	3	7	—
1998/99	Pakistan A	5	—	1	4	10	1	4	5
1998/99	India	4	1	2	1	10	3	5	2
1998/99	South Africa	5	1	—	4	13	5	2	6
1999/00	England A	5	3	—	2	10	7	—	3
1999/00	West Indies	4	—	2	2	10	—	8	2
1999/00	Australia	5	4	—	1	11	8	1	2
2000/01	Zimbabwe	2	—	—	2	6	3	1	2
2000/01	Sri Lanka	—	—	—	—	6	4	2	—
2000/01	Pakistan	5	1	2	2	10	3	5	2
2001/02	Bangladesh	3	—	3	—	4	—	3	1
2001/02	England	5	1	1	3	12	4	5	3
2002/03	India	3	—	2	1	11	2	8	1
2003/04	Pakistan	3	1	—	2	9	3	4	2
2003/04	South Africa	4	1	1	2	11	3	6	2
2003/04	Sri Lanka A	4	—	3	1	6	—	5	1
2004/05	Sri Lanka	3	—	1	2	5	—	2	3
2004/05	Australia	3	2	—	1	9	8	—	1

† includes a tie

NB: From 1900 the basis for the inclusion is any of the following:
a) First-class matches were played.
b) The touring side was its country's official team.
c) The touring side played an official New Zealand team.
d) Matches in the 1992 World Cup are not included, although preliminary games played by Zimbabwe, Australia and Sri Lanka are.

NEW ZEALAND TOURING TEAMS

		FIRST-CLASS MATCHES				*ALL MATCHES*			
		P	*W*	*L*	*D*	*P*	*W*	*L*	*D*
1898/99	Australia	2	—	2	—	4	1	2	1
1913/14	Australia	4	1	2	1	9	5	2	2
1925/26	Australia	4	—	1	3	9	3	1	5
1927	Great Britain	26	7	5	14	38	12	5	21
	Ceylon	—	—	—	—	1	—	—	1
1927/28	Australia	1	—	1	—	1	—	1	—
1931	Great Britain	32	6	3	23	36	7	3	26
1937	Great Britain	32	9	9	14	38	14	9	15
	Ceylon	—	—	—	—	1	—	—	1
1937/38	Australia	3	—	3	—	3	—	3	—
1949	Great Britain	32	13	1	18	35	14	1	20
	West Germany	—	—	—	—	1	1	—	—
1953/54	South Africa	16	3	4	9	17	3	4	10
	Australia	3	2	—	1	3	2	—	1
1955/56	Pakistan	6	1	3	2	6	1	3	2
	India	10	2	3	5	10	2	3	5
1958	Great Britain	31	7	6	18 †	35	7	6	22
1961/62	South Africa	18	5	2	11	24	7	2	15
	Australia	3	—	2	1	3	—	2	1
1964/65	India	4	—	1	3	4	—	1	3
	Pakistan	3	—	2	1	3	—	2	1
1965	Great Britain	19	3	6	10	21	4	6	11
	Holland	—	—	—	—	1	—	—	1
	Bermuda	—	—	—	—	2	—	—	2
	USA	—	—	—	—	1	1	—	—
1967/68	Australia	4	—	2	2	7	2	2	3
1969	Great Britain	18	4	3	11	22	5	4	13
1969/70	India	5	1	1	3	5	1	1	3
1969/70	Pakistan	4	1	—	3	4	1	—	3
1969/70	Australia	3	—	—	3	8	3	—	5
1970/71	Australia	1	—	—	1	2	—	1	1
1971/72*	Australia	—	—	—	—	2	1	—	1
1971/72	West Indies	13	1	—	12	16	4	—	12
1972/73	Australia	1	—	—	1	3	2	—	1
1973	Great Britain	19	3	2	14	23	4	3	16
1973/74	Australia	9	2	5	2	13	5	6	2
1974/75	Australia	—	—	—	—	3	3	—	—
1975	England *(Prudential Cup)*	—	—	—	—	4	2	2	—
1976/77	Pakistan	6	1	3	2	7	2	3	2
	India	3	—	2	1	3	—	2	1
1978	Great Britain	16	5	4	7	20	5	8	7
1979	Great Britain *(Prudential Cup)*	—	—	—	—	4	2	2	—
1980/81	Australia	7	1	2	4	29	14	9	6
1982/83	Australia	2	—	—	2 †	4	1	1	2 †
1982/83	Australia	—	—	—	—	18	12	6	—
1983	England	13	7	3	3	21	11	6	4
1983/84	Sri Lanka	5	2	—	3	8	4	1	3
1984/85	Sri Lanka	—	—	—	—	2	1	1	—
	Pakistan	5	—	2	3	9	1	5	3
1984/85	Australia *(WCC)*	—	—	—	—	4	1	2	1
1984/85	West Indies	7	—	2	5	12	—	7	5
1985/86	Australia	6	2	1	3	8	2	1	5

		FIRST-CLASS MATCHES				ALL MATCHES			
		P	W	L	D	P	W	L	D
1985/86	Australia	—	—	—	—	11	3	6	2
1985/86	Sri Lanka	—	—	—	—	2	1	1	—
	Sharjah	—	—	—	—	2	—	2	—
	Hong Kong	—	—	—	—	2	2	—	—
1986	England	15	4	—	11	18	5	1	12
	Holland	—	—	—	—	2	1	1	—
1986/87	Sri Lanka	2	—	—	2	2	—	—	2
1987/88	India *(Reliance World Cup)*	—	—	—	—	6	2	4	—
1987/88	Australia	6	1	2	3	19	8	8	3
1987/88	Sharjah	—	—	—	—	4	2	2	—
1988/89	India	6	1	2	3	10	1	6	3
1988/89	Australia	—	—	—	—	1	—	1	—
1989/90	Australia	3	—	—	3	4	—	1	3
1990	Sharjah	—	—	—	—	3	1	2	—
	England	12	4	2	6	19	8	5	6
1990/91	Pakistan	5	—	3	2	8	—	6	2
1990/91	Australia	—	—	—	—	10	3	7	—
1991/92	Australia	—	—	—	—	6	4	2	—
1992/93	Zimbabwe	3	2	—	1	6	5	—	1
	Sri Lanka	2	—	1	1	7	—	5	2
1993/94	Australia	7	2	3	2	16	5	9	2
1994	Sharjah	—	—	—	—	3	1	2	—
	Great Britain	12	1	3	8	21	8	5	8
1994/95	India	—	—	—	—	4	—	3	1
	South Africa	7	2	3	2	16	3	9	4
1995/96	India	6	—	1	5	11	2	4	5
1995/96	India & Pakistan *(Wills World Cup)*	—	—	—	—	6	3	3	—
1995/96	West Indies	4	1	2	1	13	7	5	1
1996/97	Sharjah	—	—	—	—	5	1	3	1†
1996/97	Pakistan	3	1	1	1	6	2	3	1
1996/97	India *(Independence Cup)*	—	—	—	—	3	1	2	—
1997/98	Kenya	—	—	—	—	3	2	—	1
	Zimbabwe	3	—	—	3	7	2	1	4†
1997/98	Australia	6	—	5	1	21	5	13	3†
1997/98	Sharjah	—	—	—	—	4	1	3	—
1997/98	Sri Lanka	5	1	2	2	11	3	4	4
1998	Malaysia *(Commonwealth Games)*	—	—	—	—	5	4	1	—
1998/99	Bangladesh *(Wills International Cup)*	—	—	—	—	2	1	1	—
1999	England	10	5	2	3	26	14	8	4
1999/00	India	6	—	2	4	11	2	5	4
2000/01	Singapore	—	—	—	—	2	—	2	—
2000/01	Zimbabwe	4	2	—	2	8	4	2	2
2000/01	Kenya	—	—	—	—	3	3	—	—
2000/01	South Africa	6	2	2	2	14	4	7	3
2000/01	Sharjah	—	—	—	—	4	1	3	—
2001/02	Sri Lanka	—	—	—	—	7	3	4	—
2001/02	Australia	5	—	1	4	21	6	8	7
2001/02	Sharjah	—	—	—	—	4	1	3	—
2001/02	Pakistan	1	—	1	—	4	—	4	—
2001/02	West Indies	2	1	—	1	8	3	3	2
2002/03	Australia	—	—	—	—	4	4	—	—
2002/03	Sri Lanka *(ICC Champions Trophy)*	—	—	—	—	4	2	2	—
2002/03	South Africa *(World Cup)*	—	—	—	—	11	7	4	—
2002/03	Sri Lanka	2	—	—	2	9	3	2	4

		FIRST-CLASS MATCHES				ALL MATCHES			
		P	W	L	D	P	W	L	D
2003/04	India	4	—	—	4	10	1	4	5
2003/04	Pakistan	—	—	—	—	5	—	5	—
2003/04	England	7	1	4	2	16	7	5	4
2004	England *(ICC Champions Trophy)*	—	—	—	—	2	1	1	—
2004/05	Bangladesh	3	2	—	1	6	5	—	1
2004/05	Australia	3	—	3	—	6	2	4	—

NB: 1) All tours refer to those undertaken by official New Zealand sides. Unofficial practice matches have not been included in the totals.

2) The first team from New Zealand to tour overseas was Canterbury who visited Victoria and Tasmania in 1878/79. This was the first tour ever undertaken by a domestic association from any country. (None of the games are ranked as first-class.)

3) Where countries are bracketed it indicates this represented a single tour. Where there is more than one entry for the same season but countries are not bracketed, the tours were not connected.

4) The 1974/75, second 1982/83, 1990/91, 1993/94 and 1997/98 tours to Australia included a return trip after the teams had come back to New Zealand. They are all listed as single tours for the purposes of this article.

5) The 1986/87 tour to Sri Lanka was scheduled for 8 matches. The team returned home after 2 matches due to unrest in Sri Lanka.

Eighty-one official New Zealand sides have toured overseas since the first in February, 1899. The teams were as follows:

1) **1898/99 to Australia**
L.T. Cobcroft *(captain)*, F.L. Ashbolt, J.C. Baker, C. Boxshall, A.D. Downes, A.H. Fisher, F.S. Frankish, Hugh B. Lusk, G. Mills, I. Mills, D. Reese, A. Sims, E.F. Upham.

2) **1913/14 to Australia**
D. Reese *(captain)*, J.H. Bennett, C. Boxshall, T.A. Carlton, L.G. Hemus, R.G. Hickmott, W.R. Patrick, C.W. Robinson, D.M. Sandman, R.C. Somervell, A.N.C. Snedden, L.G. Taylor, B.J. Tuckwell, H.J. Tattersall.

3) **1925/26 to Australia**
W.R. Patrick *(captain)*, C.F.W. Allcott, A.W. Alloo, R.C. Blunt, C.G. Crawford, W.H.R. Cunningham, C.C.R. Dacre, H.D. Gillespie, R.W. Hope, K.C. James, T.C. Lowry, D.J. McBeath, C.J. Oliver, R.V. de R. Worker.

4) **1927 to Great Britain, Ceylon and Australia**
T.C. Lowry *(captain)*, C.F.W. Allcott, E.H.L. Bernau, E.D. Blundell*, R.C. Blunt, W.H.R. Cunningham, C.C.R. Dacre, C.S. Dempster, R.H. Fox*, T.D.B. Hay*, M. Henderson, K.C. James, H.M. McGirr, W.E. Merritt, J.E. Mills, C.J. Oliver, M.L. Page.

5) **1931 to Great Britain**
T.C. Lowry *(captain)*, C.F.W. Allcott, R.C. Blunt, I.B. Cromb, C.S. Dempster, K.C. James, J.L. Kerr, A.M. Matheson, W.E. Merritt, J.E. Mills, M.L. Page, R.O. Talbot, H.G. Vivian, G.L. Weir.

6) **1937 to Great Britain, Ceylon and Australia**
M.L. Page *(captain)*, W.N. Carson, J. Cowie, M.P. Donnelly, J.A. Dunning, N. Gallichan, W.A. Hadlee, J.L. Kerr, J.R. Lamason, T.C. Lowry, D.A.R. Moloney, C.K. Parsloe*, A.W. Roberts, E.W.T. Tindill, H.G. Vivian, W.M. Wallace, G.L. Weir.

7) **1949 to Great Britain and West Germany**
W.A. Hadlee *(captain)*, C. Burke, T.B. Burtt, H.B. Cave, J. Cowie, G.F. Cresswell, M.P. Donnelly, J.A. Hayes, F.L.H. Mooney, G.O. Rabone, J.R. Reid, V.J. Scott, F.B. Smith, B. Sutcliffe, W.M. Wallace.

8) **1953/54 to South Africa and Australia**
G.O. Rabone *(captain)*, J.E.F. Beck, W. Bell, R.W. Blair, M.E. Chapple, E.W. Dempster, J.G. Leggat*, I.B. Leggat, A.R. MacGibbon, L.S.M. Miller, F.L.H. Mooney, G.W.F. Overton, M.B. Poore, J.R. Reid, B. Sutcliffe.

9) **1955/1956 to Pakistan and India**
H.B. Cave *(captain)*, J.C. Alabaster, J.W. Guy, J.A. Hayes, N.S. Harford, P.G.Z. Harris, J.G. Leggat, A.R. MacGibbon, S.N. McGregor, T.G. McMahon, A.M. Moir, E.C. Petrie, M.B. Poore, J.R. Reid, B. Sutcliffe.

10) **1958 to Great Britain**
J.R. Reid *(captain)*, J.C. Alabaster, R.W. Blair, H.B. Cave, J.W. D'Arcy, N.S. Harford, J.A. Hayes, T. Meale, A.R. MacGibbon, L.S.M. Miller, A.M. Moir, E.C. Petrie, W.R. Playle, J.T. Sparling, B. Sutcliffe, J.T. Ward.

11) **1961/62 to South Africa and Australia**
J.R. Reid *(captain)*, J.C. Alabaster, G.A. Bartlett, P.T. Barton, F.J. Cameron, M.E. Chapple, A.E. Dick, G.T. Dowling, J.W. Guy, P.G.Z. Harris, S.N. McGregor, R.C. Motz, J.T. Sparling, J.T. Ward, B.W. Yuile.

12) **1964/65 to India, Pakistan, Great Britain, Holland, Bermuda and USA**
J.R. Reid *(captain)*, F.J. Cameron, R.O. Collinge, B.E. Congdon, A.E. Dick*, G.T. Dowling, T.W. Jarvis, R.C. Motz, R.W. Morgan, V. Pollard, B.W. Sinclair, B. Sutcliffe, B.R. Taylor, G.E. Vivian, J.T. Ward, B.W. Yuile.

13) **1967/68 to Australia**
B.W. Sinclair *(captain)*, J.C. Alabaster, M.G. Burgess, R.O. Collinge, B.E. Congdon, R.I. Harford, T.W. Jarvis, R.C. Motz, B.A.G. Murray, V. Pollard, B.R. Taylor, K. Thomson, B.W. Yuile.

14) **1969 to Great Britain, India and Pakistan**
G.T. Dowling *(captain)*, M.G. Burgess, R.O. Collinge, B.E. Congdon, R.S. Cunis, D.R. Hadlee, B.F. Hastings, H.J. Howarth, B.A.G. Murray, B.D. Milburn, V. Pollard, B.R. Taylor, D.G. Trist*, G.M. Turner, K.J. Wadsworth, B.W. Yuile.

15) **1969/70 to Australia**
G.T. Dowling *(captain)*, M.G. Burgess, R.O. Collinge, B.E. Congdon, R.S. Cunis, D.R. Hadlee, B.F. Hastings, H.J. Howarth, R.W. Morgan*, B.W. Sinclair, G.M. Turner, G.E. Vivian, K.J. Wadsworth.

16) **1970/1971 to Australia**
G.T. Dowling *(captain)*, M.G. Burgess, B.E. Congdon, R.O. Collinge, R.S. Cunis, H.J. Howarth, T.W. Jarvis, R.W. Morgan, B.R. Taylor, G.M. Turner, G.E. Vivian, K.J. Wadsworth.

17) **1971/72 to Australia**
R.W. Morgan *(captain)*, B. Andrews, R.W. Anderson, B. Dunning, B.G. Hadlee, R.J. Hadlee, W.A. Greenstreet, G.A. Newdick, R.E. Redmond, M.L. Ryan, M.J.F. Shrimpton, D.G. Trist.

18) **1971/72 to West Indies**
G.T. Dowling *(captain)*, J.C. Alabaster, M.G. Burgess, K.O. Campbell, M.E. Chapple*, R.O. Collinge, B.E. Congdon, R.S. Cunis, B.F. Hastings, H.J. Howarth, T.W. Jarvis, R.W. Morgan*, B.R. Taylor, G.M. Turner, G.E. Vivian, K.J. Wadsworth, M.G. Webb.

19) **1972/73 to Australia**
B.E. Congdon *(captain)*, B. Andrews, R.S. Cunis, B. Dunning, R.J. Hadlee, B.F. Hastings, A.B. Jordan, D.R. O'Sullivan, R.E. Redmond, G.M. Turner, G.E. Vivian, K.J. Wadsworth.

20) **1973 to Great Britain**
B.E. Congdon *(captain)*, R.W. Anderson, M.G. Burgess, R.O. Collinge, E.K. Gillott, D.R. Hadlee, R.J. Hadlee, B.F. Hastings, H.J. Howarth, J.M. Parker, V. Pollard, R.E. Redmond, B.R. Taylor, G.M. Turner, K.J. Wadsworth.

21) **1973/74 to Australia**
B.E. Congdon *(captain)*, G.D. Alabaster, B. Andrews, K.O. Campbell, B.L. Cairns, J.V. Coney*, D.R. Hadlee, R.J. Hadlee, B.F. Hastings, J.F.M. Morrison, D.R. O'Sullivan, J.M. Parker, M.J.F. Shrimpton, G.M. Turner, K.J. Wadsworth.

22) **1974/75 to Australia**
B.E. Congdon *(captain)*, B.L. Cairns, E.J. Chatfield, R.O. Collinge, G.N. Edwards, D.R. Hadlee, B.F. Hastings, G.P. Howarth, H.J. Howarth, J.F.M. Morrison, J.M. Parker, G.M. Turner, K.J. Wadsworth.

23) **1975 to England** *(World Cup)*
G.M. Turner *(captain)*, B.L. Cairns, R.O. Collinge, B.G. Hadlee, D.R. Hadlee, R.J. Hadlee, B.F. Hastings, G.P. Howarth, H.J. Howarth, B.J. McKechnie, J.F.M. Morrison, D.R. O'Sullivan, J.M. Parker, K.J. Wadsworth.

24) **1976/77 to Pakistan and India**
G.M. Turner *(captain)*, R.W. Anderson, M.G. Burgess, B.L. Cairns, R.O. Collinge, R.J. Hadlee, G.P. Howarth, W.K. Lees, J.F.M. Morrison, D.R. O'Sullivan, J.M. Parker, N.M. Parker, P.J. Petherick, A.D.G. Roberts, G.B. Troup.

25) **1978 to Great Britain**
M.G. Burgess *(captain)*, R.W. Anderson, S.L. Boock, B.P. Bracewell, B.L. Cairns, R.O. Collinge*, B.E. Congdon, B.A. Edgar, G.N. Edwards, D.R. Hadlee, R.J. Hadlee, G.P. Howarth, J.M. McIntyre, J.M. Parker, G.B. Thomson, G.B. Troup*, J.G. Wright.

26) **1979 to England** *(World Cup)*
M.G. Burgess *(captain)*, B.L. Cairns, E.J. Chatfield, J.V. Coney, B.A. Edgar, R.J. Hadlee, G.P. Howarth, W.K. Lees, B.J. McKechnie, J.F.M. Morrison, L.W. Stott, G.B. Troup, G.M. Turner, J.G. Wright.

27) **1980/81 to Australia**
G.P. Howarth *(captain)*, B.P. Bracewell*, J.G. Bracewell, S.L. Boock, M.G. Burgess, B.L. Cairns, E.J. Chatfield, J.V. Coney, B.A. Edgar, R.J. Hadlee, W.K. Lees, P.E. McEwan, B.J. McKechnie*, J.M. Parker, I.D.S. Smith, M.C. Snedden, G.B. Troup, J.G. Wright.

28) **1982/83 to Australia**
G.P. Howarth *(captain)*, B.R. Blair, S.M. Carrington, E.J. Chatfield, J.V. Coney, M.D. Crowe, B.A. Edgar, W.K. Lees, J.F.M. Morrison, J.F. Reid, G.K. Robertson, M.C. Snedden, G.B. Troup.

29) **1982/83 to Australia**
G.P. Howarth *(captain)*, B.L. Cairns, E.J. Chatfield, J.V. Coney, J.J. Crowe, M.D. Crowe*, B.A. Edgar, T.J. Franklin*, R.J. Hadlee, W.K. Lees, J.F.M. Morrison, M.C. Snedden, G.B. Troup, G.M. Turner, P.N. Webb, R.J. Webb*, J.G. Wright.

30) **1983 to England**
G.P. Howarth *(captain)*, J.G. Bracewell, B.L. Cairns, E.J. Chatfield, J.V. Coney, J.J. Crowe, M.D. Crowe, B.A. Edgar, T.J. Franklin, E.J. Gray, R.J. Hadlee, W.K. Lees, I.D.S. Smith, M.C. Snedden, S.R. Tracy*, G.M. Turner, J.G. Wright.

31) **1983/84 to Sri Lanka**
G.P. Howarth *(captain)*, S.L. Boock, J.G. Bracewell, B.L. Cairns, E.J. Chatfield, J.V. Coney, J.J. Crowe, M.D. Crowe, B.A. Edgar, R.J. Hadlee, J.F. Reid, I.D.S. Smith, D.A. Stirling, J.G. Wright.

32) **1984/85 to Pakistan and Sri Lanka**
J.V. Coney *(captain)*, S.L. Boock, J.G. Bracewell, B.L. Cairns, E.J. Chatfield, J.J. Crowe, M.D. Crowe, B.A. Edgar, E.J. Gray, P.E. McEwan, J.F. Reid, I.D.S. Smith, M.C. Snedden, D.A. Stirling, J.G. Wright.

33) **1984/85 to Australia** *(World Championship of Cricket)*
G.P. Howarth *(captain)*, B.P. Bracewell, J.G. Bracewell, B.L. Cairns, E.J. Chatfield, J.V. Coney, J.J. Crowe, M.D. Crowe, R.J. Hadlee, P.E. McEwan, J.F. Reid, I.D.S. Smith, M.C. Snedden, J.G. Wright.

34) **1984/85 to West Indies**
G.P. Howarth *(captain)*, S.L. Boock, J.G. Bracewell, B.L. Cairns, E.J. Chatfield, J.V. Coney, J.J. Crowe, M.D. Crowe, R.J. Hadlee, R.T. Hart, K.R. Rutherford, I.D.S. Smith, D.A. Stirling, G.B. Troup, J.G. Wright.

35) **1985/86 to Australia**
J.V. Coney *(captain)*, S.L. Boock, J.G. Bracewell*, V.R. Brown, B.L. Cairns, E.J. Chatfield, J.J. Crowe, M.D. Crowe, B.A. Edgar, T.J. Franklin, R.J. Hadlee, E.B. McSweeney*, J.F. Reid, I.D.S. Smith, M.C. Snedden, J.G. Wright.

36) **1985/86 to Australia**
J.V. Coney *(captain)*, B.R. Blair, S.L. Boock, J.G. Bracewell, E.J. Chatfield, J.J. Crowe, M.D. Crowe, B.A. Edgar, S.R. Gillespie, R.J. Hadlee, E.B. McSweeney, J.F. Reid, M.C. Snedden, J.G. Wright.

37) **1985/86 to Sri Lanka, Sharjah and Hong Kong**
J.G. Wright *(captain)*, T.E. Blain, B.R. Blair, J.G. Bracewell, E.J. Chatfield, J.J. Crowe, M.D. Crowe, E.J. Gray, E.B. McSweeney, G.K. Robertson, K.R. Rutherford, M.C. Snedden, W. Watson.

38) **1986 to England and Holland**
J.V. Coney *(captain)*, B.J. Barrett, T.E. Blain, J.G. Bracewell, E.J. Chatfield, J.J. Crowe, M.D. Crowe, B.A. Edgar, T.J. Franklin, E.J. Gray, R.J. Hadlee, K.R. Rutherford, I.D.S. Smith, D.A. Stirling, W. Watson, J.G. Wright.

39) **1986/87 to Sri Lanka**
J.J. Crowe *(captain)*, J.G. Bracewell, E.J. Chatfield, M.D. Crowe, E.J. Gray, R.J. Hadlee, P.A. Horne, A.H. Jones, E.B. McSweeney, D.K. Morrison, D.N. Patel, K.R. Rutherford, I.D.S. Smith, M.C. Snedden.

40) **1987/88 to India** *(World Cup)*
J.J. Crowe *(captain)*, S.L. Boock, J.G. Bracewell, E.J. Chatfield, M.D. Crowe, P.A. Horne, A.H. Jones, D.K. Morrison, D.N. Patel, K.R. Rutherford, I.D.S. Smith, M.C. Snedden, W. Watson, J.G. Wright.

41) **1987/88 to Australia**
J.J. Crowe *(captain)*, T.E. Blain*, J.G. Bracewell, V.R. Brown*, E.J. Chatfield, M.D. Crowe, S.R. Gillespie*, E.J. Gray, R.J. Hadlee, P.A. Horne, A.H. Jones, D.K. Morrison, D.N. Patel, K.R. Rutherford, I.D.S. Smith, M.C. Snedden, W. Watson, J.G. Wright.

42) **1987/88 to Sharjah**
J.G. Wright *(captain)*, T.E. Blain, E.J. Chatfield, M.J. Greatbatch, R.J. Hadlee, A.H. Jones, C.M. Kuggeleijn, D.K. Morrison, D.N. Patel, K.R. Rutherford, I.D.S. Smith, R.H. Vance, W. Watson.

43) **1988/89 to India**
J.G. Wright *(captain)*, T.E. Blain, J.G. Bracewell, E.J. Chatfield, T.J. Franklin, E.J. Gray, M.J. Greatbatch, R.J. Hadlee, A.H. Jones, C.M. Kuggeleijn, D.K. Morrison, K.R. Rutherford, I.D.S. Smith, M.C. Snedden, R.H. Vance, W. Watson*.

44) **1988/89 to Australia**
J.G. Wright *(captain)*, E.J. Chatfield, J.J. Crowe, M.D. Crowe, M.J. Greatbatch, A.H. Jones, C.M. Kuggeleijn, D.K. Morrison, I.D.S. Smith, M.C. Snedden, R.H. Vance, W. Watson.

45) **1989/90 to Australia**
J.G. Wright *(captain)*, B.P. Bracewell, J.G. Bracewell, C.L. Cairns*, J.J. Crowe, M.D. Crowe, M.J. Greatbatch, A.H. Jones, D.K. Morrison, D.N. Patel*, G.K. Robertson, I.D.S. Smith, M.C. Snedden, R.H. Vance, W. Watson.

46) **1990 to Sharjah and England**
J.G. Wright *(captain)*, J.G. Bracewell, J.J. Crowe, M.D. Crowe, T.J. Franklin, M.J. Greatbatch, Sir R.J. Hadlee, A.H. Jones, J.P. Millmow, D.K. Morrison, A.C. Parore, M.W. Priest, C. Pringle*, K.R. Rutherford, I.D.S. Smith, M.C. Snedden, S.A. Thomson, W. Watson*.

47) **1990/91 to Pakistan**
M.D. Crowe *(captain)*, G.E. Bradburn, T.J. Franklin, M.J. Greatbatch, P.A. Horne, D.K. Morrison, A.C. Parore, D.N. Patel, M.W. Priest, C. Pringle, S.J. Roberts, K.R. Rutherford, I.D.S. Smith, W. Watson, D.J. White.

48) **1990/91 to Australia**
M.D. Crowe *(captain)*, G.E. Bradburn, M.J. Greatbatch, C.Z. Harris, A.H. Jones, G.R. Larsen*, R.T. Latham, D.K. Morrison, R.G. Petrie, C. Pringle, R.B. Reid*, K.R. Rutherford, I.D.S. Smith, W. Watson, J.G. Wright, B.A. Young.

49) **1991/92 to Australia**
M.D. Crowe *(captain)*, G.E. Bradburn, C.L. Cairns, M.J. Greatbatch, C.Z. Harris, T.J. Franklin, A.H. Jones, D.K. Morrison, D.N. Patel, A.C. Parore, C. Pringle, I.D.S. Smith, S.A. Thomson, W. Watson, K.A. Wealleans.

50) **1992/93 to Zimbabwe and Sri Lanka**
M.D. Crowe *(captain)*, G.E. Bradburn*, S.B. Doull, M.J. Greatbatch, M.J. Haslam, C.Z. Harris, B.R. Hartland, A.H. Jones, G.R. Larsen, R.T. Latham, D.J. Nash, M.B. Owens*, D.N. Patel, A.C. Parore, C. Pringle*, K.R. Rutherford, M.L. Su'a, J.T.C. Vaughan*, W. Watson, J.G. Wright*.

51) **1993/94 to Australia**
M.D. Crowe *(captain)*, T.E. Blain, C.L. Cairns, S.B. Doull, R.P. de Groen*, M.J. Greatbatch, C.Z. Harris*, M.J. Haslam, A.H. Jones, R.T. Latham*, G.R. Larsen*, D.K. Morrison, D.N. Patel, B.A. Pocock, C. Pringle*, K.R. Rutherford, M.L. Su'a, S.A. Thomson*, W. Watson, D.J. White*, B.A. Young.

52) **1994 to Sharjah and England**
K.R. Rutherford *(captain)*, M.D. Crowe, H.T. Davis, M.W. Douglas, S.B. Doull, S.P. Fleming, M.J. Greatbatch, M.N. Hart, B.R. Hartland, C.Z. Harris, G.R. Larsen, D.K. Morrison, D.J. Nash, M.B. Owens*, A.C. Parore, B.A. Pocock, C. Pringle, S.A. Thomson, S.J. Roberts*, B.A. Young. (Harris and Douglas were selected only for Sharjah but Douglas re-appeared as an additional player during the England tour. Larsen captained the team in Sharjah as Rutherford was not available for that part of the tour).

53) **1994/95 to India and South Africa**
K.R. Rutherford *(captain)*, M.D. Crowe, R.P. de Groen, S.B. Doull, S.P. Fleming, L.K. Germon, C.Z. Harris, M.N. Hart, B.R. Hartland, D.K. Morrison*, D.J. Murray, D.J. Nash, A.C. Parore, M.W. Priest*, C. Pringle, M.L. Su'a, S.A. Thomson, B.A. Young.

54) **1995/96 to India**
L.K. Germon *(captain)*, N.J. Astle*, C.L. Cairns, M.D. Crowe, S.B. Doull, S.P. Fleming, A.J. Gale, M.J. Greatbatch, M.N. Hart, M.J. Haslam, G.R. Larsen*, D.K. Morrison, D.J. Nash, A.C. Parore, S.A. Thomson, R.G. Twose, B.A. Young.

55) **1995/96 to India and Pakistan** *(World Cup)*
L.K. Germon *(captain)*, N.J. Astle, C.L. Cairns, S.P. Fleming, C.Z. Harris, R.J. Kennedy, G.R. Larsen, D.K. Morrison, D.J. Nash, A.C. Parore, D.N. Patel, C.M. Spearman, S.A. Thomson, R.G. Twose.

56) **1995/96 to West Indies**
L.K. Germon *(captain)*, N.J. Astle, M.D. Bailey*, C.L. Cairns, S.P. Fleming, C.Z. Harris, M.J. Haslam*, R.J. Kennedy, G.R. Larsen, D.K. Morrison, D.J. Nash, A.C. Parore, D.N. Patel, C.M. Spearman, S.A. Thomson, R.G. Twose, J.T.C. Vaughan*.

57) **1996/97 to Sharjah and Pakistan**
L.K. Germon *(captain)*, N.J. Astle, C.L. Cairns, S.B. Doull, S.P. Fleming, M.J. Greatbatch, C.Z. Harris, M.N. Hart*, M.J. Haslam, G.R. Jonas*, R.J. Kennedy*, G.R. Larsen, D.K. Morrison, A.C. Parore, D.N. Patel, C.M. Spearman, J.T.C. Vaughan, P.J. Wiseman*, B.A. Young.

58) **1996/97 to India** *(Independence Cup)*
S.P. Fleming *(captain)*, N.J. Astle, C.L. Cairns, H.T. Davis, C.Z. Harris, M.J. Horne, G.R. Larsen, C.D. McMillan, S.B. O'Connor, A.C. Parore, D.N. Patel, A.J. Penn, D.L. Vettori, B.A. Young.

59) **1997/98 to Kenya & Zimbabwe**
S.P. Fleming *(captain)*, N.J. Astle, C.L. Cairns, H.T. Davis, C.Z. Harris, M.J. Horne, G.R. Larsen, C.D. McMillan, S.B. O'Connor, A.C. Parore, B.A. Pocock, D.G. Sewell, C.M. Spearman, D.L. Vettori, P.J. Wiseman.

60) **1997/98 to Australia**
S.P. Fleming *(captain)*, G.I. Allott, N.J. Astle, C.L. Cairns, H.T. Davis, S.B. Doull, C.J. Drum*, C.Z. Harris*, M.J. Horne, G.R. Larsen*, C.D. McMillan, D.J. Nash*, S.B. O'Connor, A.C. Parore, B.A. Pocock, C.M. Spearman*, R.G. Twose*, D.L. Vettori, B.A. Young.

61) **1997/98 to Sharjah**
S.P. Fleming *(captain)*, N.J. Astle, C.L. Cairns, S.B. Doull, C.Z. Harris, M.J. Horne, L.G. Howell, C.D. McMillan, D.J. Nash, S.B. O'Connor, A.C. Parore, M.W. Priest, P.J. Wiseman.

62) **1997/98 to Sri Lanka**
S.P. Fleming *(captain)*, N.J. Astle, C.L. Cairns, S.B. Doull, C.Z. Harris, M.J. Horne, C.D. McMillan, D.J. Nash, S.B. O'Connor, A.C. Parore, M.W. Priest, C.M. Spearman, A.R. Tait*, D.L. Vettori, P.J. Wiseman, B.A. Young.

63) **1998 to Malaysia** *(Commonwealth Games)*
S.P. Fleming *(captain)*, G.I. Allott, N.J. Astle, M.D. Bailey, M.D. Bell, C.J. Drum, C.Z. Harris, M.J. Horne, C.D. McMillan, S.B. O'Connor, A.C. Parore, A.R. Tait, D.L. Vettori, P.J. Wiseman.

64) **1998/99 to Bangladesh** *(Wills International Cup)*
S.P. Fleming *(captain)*, G.I. Allott, N.J. Astle, M.D. Bailey, M.D. Bell, S.B. Doull, C.Z. Harris, M.J. Horne, C.D. McMillan, S.B. O'Connor, A.C. Parore, A.R. Tait, D.L. Vettori, P.J. Wiseman.

65) **1999 to England**
S.P. Fleming *(captain)*, G.I. Allott, N.J. Astle, M.D. Bell*, C.E. Bulfin, C.L. Cairns, M.G. Croy*, S.B. Doull, C.Z. Harris, M.N. Hart, M.J. Horne, G.R. Larsen, C.D. McMillan, D.J. Nash, S.B. O'Connor*, A.C. Parore, A.J. Penn*, R.G. Twose, D.L. Vettori, B.G.K. Walker*.

66) **1999/00 to India**
S.P. Fleming *(captain)*, N.J. Astle, M.D. Bell, C.L. Cairns, C.J. Drum, C.Z. Harris, M.J. Horne, C.D. McMillan, D.J. Nash, S.B. O'Connor, A.C. Parore, A.J. Penn, C.M. Spearman, G.R. Stead*, S.B. Styris*, A.R. Tait*, R.G. Twose*, D.L. Vettori, P.J. Wiseman.

67) **2000/01 to Singapore, Zimbabwe, Kenya & South Africa**
S.P. Fleming *(captain)*, G.I. Allott, N.J. Astle, C.L. Cairns, C.Z. Harris, M.J. Horne, C.D. McMillan, H.J.H. Marshall, C.S. Martin, D.J. Nash, C.J. Nevin, S.B. O'Connor, A.C. Parore, A.J. Penn, M.H. Richardson, M.S. Sinclair, C.M. Spearman, S.B. Styris, G.P. Sulzberger, D.R. Tuffey, R.G. Twose, D.L. Vettori, B.G.K. Walker, K.P. Walmsley, P.J. Wiseman. (Apart from a number of players being replaced because of injury, this party was reselected and changed several times depending on the nature of the matches being played).

68) 2000/01 to Sharjah
C.D. McMillan *(captain),* A.R. Adams, M.D. Bell, G.E. Bradburn, J.E.C. Franklin, C.Z. Harris, K.D. Mills, C.J. Nevin, J.D.P. Oram, M.S. Sinclair, D.R.Tuffey, L. Vincent, B.G.K. Walker.

69) 2001/02 to Sri Lanka
S.P. Fleming *(captain)*, N.J. Astle, G.E. Bradburn, J.E.C. Franklin, C.Z. Harris, K.D. Mills, C.D. McMillan, D.J. Nash, J.D.P. Oram, A.C. Parore, M.S. Sinclair, D.R.Tuffey, D.L. Vettori, L. Vincent.

70) 2001/02 to Australia
S.P. Fleming *(captain)*, A.R. Adams, N.J. Astle, M.D. Bell, S.E. Bond*, C.L. Cairns, C.J. Drum*, J.E.C. Franklin, C.Z. Harris, B.B. McCullum, C.D. McMillan, C.S. Martin, D.J. Nash, S.B. O'Çonnor, A.C. Parore, M.H. Richardson, M.S. Sinclair, S.B. Styris, G.P. Sulzberger, D.R. Tuffey, D.L. Vettori, L. Vincent, P.J. Wiseman*.

71) 2001/02 to Sharjah & Pakistan
S.P. Fleming *(captain)*, A.R. Adams, N.J. Astle, I.G. Butler, J.E.C. Franklin, C.Z. Harris, R.G. Hart, M.J. Horne, C.D. McMillan, C.S. Martin, C.J. Nevin, J.D.P. Oram, M.H. Richardson, M.S. Sinclair, S.B. Styris, D.R. Tuffey, D.L. Vettori, L. Vincent, B.G.K. Walker.

72) 2001/02 to West Indies
S.P. Fleming *(captain)*, N.J. Astle, S.E. Bond, I.G. Butler, C.Z. Harris, M.N. Hart, R.G. Hart, P.A. Hitchcock, M.J. Horne, C.D. McMillan, C.S. Martin, C.J. Nevin, J.D.P. Oram, M.H. Richardson, S.B. Styris, D.R. Tuffey, D.L. Vettori, L. Vincent.

73) 2002/03 to Australia & Sri Lanka *(ICC Champions Trophy)*
S.P. Fleming *(captain)*, N.J. Astle, S.E. Bond, I.G. Butler*, C.Z. Harris, M.N. Hart*, P.A. Hitchcock, M.J. Horne*, C.D. McMillan*, K.D. Mills, C.J. Nevin, J.D.P. Oram, M.S. Sinclair, S.B. Styris, G.P. Sulzberger, D.R. Tuffey, D.L. Vettori, L. Vincent, B.G.K. Walker*, J.A.F. Yovich*.

74) 2002/03 to South Africa *(World Cup)*
S.P. Fleming *(captain)*, C.L. Cairns, A.R. Adams, N.J. Astle, S.E. Bond, C.Z. Harris, B.B. McCullum, C.D. McMillan, K.D. Mills, J.D.P. Oram, M.S. Sinclair, S.B. Styris, D.R. Tuffey, D.L. Vettori, L. Vincent.

75) 2002/03 to Sri Lanka
S.P. Fleming *(captain)*, A.R. Adams, S.E. Bond, I.G. Butler, C.L. Cairns, C.Z. Harris, R.G. Hart, M.J. Horne, R.A. Jones, B.B. McCullum, K.D. Mills, C.J. Nevin, J.D.P. Oram, M.H. Richardson, M.S. Sinclair, S.B. Styris, D.R. Tuffey, D.L. Vettori, L. Vincent, P.J. Wiseman.

76) 2003/04 to India
S.P. Fleming *(captain)*, N.J. Astle, I.G. Butler, C.L. Cairns*, C.Z. Harris*, R.G. Hart, P.A. Hitchcock*, R.A. Jones, B.B. McCullum*. C.D. McMillan, M.J. Mason, K.D. Mills*, C.J. Nevin*, J.D.P. Oram, M.H. Richardson, S.B. Styris, D.R. Tuffey, D.L. Vettori, L. Vincent, P.J. Wiseman.

77) 2003/04 to Pakistan
C.L. Cairns *(captain)*, D.L. Vettori, T.K. Canning, C.D. Cumming, C.Z. Harris, P.A. Hitchcock, R.A. Jones, B.B. McCullum, H.J.H. Marshall, M.J. Mason, J.D.P. Oram, M.S. Sinclair, D.R. Tuffey, M.D.J. Walker, K.P. Walmsley.

78) 2004 to England
S.P. Fleming *(captain)*, A.R. Adams*, N.J. Astle, S.E. Bond, I.G. Butler*, C.L. Cairns, J.E.C. Franklin*, C.Z. Harris*, G.J. Hopkins*, B.B. McCullum, C.D. McMillan, H.J.H Marshall*, C.S. Martin, K.D. Mills, J.D.P. Oram, M.H.W Papps, M.H. Richardson, S.B. Styris, D.R. Tuffey, D.L. Vettori.

79) **2004 to England** *(Champions Trophy)*
S.P. Fleming *(captain)*, N.J. Astle, I.G. Butler, C.L. Cairns, C.Z. Harris, B.B. McCullum, C.D. McMillan, H.J.H. Marshall, K.D. Mills, J.D.P Oram, M.H.W. Papps, S.B. Styris, D.R. Tuffey, D.L. Vettori.

80) 2004/05 to Bangladesh
S.P. Fleming *(captain)*, A.R. Adams*, N.J. Astle, I.G. Butler, C.L. Cairns*, J.E.C. Franklin, P.G.Fulton*, C.Z. Harris*, B.B. McCullum, C.D. McMillan*, H.J.H. Marshall, C.S. Martin, K.D. Mills, J.D.P. Oram, M.H. Richardson, M.S. Sinclair, S.B. Styris, D.L. Vettori, P.J. Wiseman.

81) 2004/05 to Australia

S.P. Fleming *(captain)*, A.R. Adams*, N.J. Astle, I.G. Butler, C.L. Cairns*, T.K. Canning*, J.E.C. Franklin, C.Z. Harris*, G.J.Hopkins*, B.B. McCullum, C.D. McMillan*, H.J.H. Marshall, C.S. Martin, K.D. Mills, J.D.P.Oram, M.H. Richardson, M.S. Sinclair, S.B. Styris, D.L. Vettori, P.J. Wiseman.

* *replacement or temporary addition to the touring party*

NEW ZEALAND TEST RECORDS

REGISTER OF PLAYERS

	Born	*Died*	*Type*		*Test Career*
Adams Andre Ryan	17/7/1975 Auckland		RHB	RFM	2001/02
Alabaster John Chaloner	11/7/1930 Invercargill		RHB	RLB	1955/56-1971/72
Allcott Cyril Francis Walter	7/10/1896 Lower Moutere	19/11/1973 Auckland	LHB	LM	1929/30-1931/32
Allott Geoffrey Ian	24/12/1971 Christchurch		RHB	LFM	1995/96-1999
Anderson Robert Wickham	2/10/1948 Christchurch		RHB	RLB	1976/77-1978
Anderson William McDougall	8/10/1919 Westport	21/12/1979 Christchurch	LHB	RLBG	1945/46
Andrews Bryan	4/4/1945 Christchurch		RHB	RFM	1973/74
Astle Nathan John	15/9/1971 Christchurch		RHB	RM	1995/96-2004/05
Badcock Frederick Theodore	9/8/1897 Abbottabad, India	19/9/1982 Perth	RHB	RM	1929/30-1932/33
Barber Richard Trevor	3/6/1925 Otaki		RHB	WK	1955/56
Bartlett Gary Alex	3/2/1941 Blenheim		RHB	RF	1961/62-1967/68
Barton Paul Thomas	9/10/1935 Wellington		RHB	SLA	1961/62-1962/63
Beard Donald Derek	14/1/1920 Palmerston North	15/7/1982 Lancaster	RHB	RM	1951/52-1955/56
Beck John Edward Francis	1/8/1934 Wellington	23/4/2000 Waikanae	LHB		1953/54-1955/56
Bell Matthew David	25/2/1977 Dunedin		RHB		1998/99-2001/02
Bell William	5/9/1931 Dunedin	23/7/2002 Auckland	RHB	RLB	1953/54
Bilby Grahame Paul	7/5/1941 Wellington		RHB		1965/66
Blain Tony Elston	17/2/1962 Nelson		RHB	WK	1986-1993/94
Blair Robert William	23/6/1932 Petone		RHB	RFM	1952/53-1963/64
Blunt Roger Charles	3/11/1900 Durham, England	22/6/1966 London	RHB	RLBG	1929/30-1931/32
Bolton Bruce Alfred	31/5/1935 Christchurch		RHB	RLB	1958/59
Bond Shane Edward	7/6/1975 Christchurch		RHB	RF	2001/02-2002/03
Boock Stephen Lewis	20/9/1951 Dunedin		RHB	SLA	1977/78-1988/89
Bracewell Brendon Paul	14/9/1959 Auckland		RHB	RFM	1978-1984/85
Bracewell John Garry	15/4/1958 Auckland		RHB	ROB	1980/81-1990
Bradburn Grant Eric	26/5/1966 Hamilton		RHB	ROB	1990/91-2000/01
Bradburn Wynne Pennell	24/11/1938 Thames		RHB	RSM	1963/64
Brown Vaughan Raymond	3/11/1959 Christchurch		LHB	ROB	1985/86
Burgess Mark Gordon	17/7/1944 Auckland		RHB	ROB	1967/68-1980/81

	Born	Died	Type		Test Career
Burke Cecil	22/3/1914 Auckland	4/8/1997 Auckland	RHB	RLB	1945/46
Burtt Thomas Browning	22/1/1915 Christchurch	24/5/1988 Christchurch	RHB	SLA	1946/47-1952/53
Butler Ian Gareth	24/11/1981 Auckland		RHB	RF	2001/02-2004/05
Butterfield Leonard Arthur	29/8/1913 Christchurch	5/7/1999 Christchurch	RHB	RM	1945/46
Cairns Bernard Lance	10/10/1949 Picton		RHB	RM	1973/74-1985/86
Cairns Christopher Lance	13/6/1970 Picton		RHB	RFM	1989/90-2004
Cameron Francis James	1/6/1932 Dunedin		RHB	RFM	1961/62-1965
Cave Henry Butler	10/10/1922 Wanganui	15/9/1989 Wanganui	RHB	RM	1949-1958
Chapple Murray Ernest	25/7/1930 Christchurch	31/7/1985 Hamilton	RHB	SLA	1952/53-1965/66
Chatfield Ewen John	3/7/1950 Dannevirke		RHB	RM	1974/75-1988/89
Cleverley Donald Charles	23/12/1909 Oamaru	16/2/2004 Southport, Aust.	LHB	RFM	1931/32-1945/46
Collinge Richard Owen	2/4/1946 Wellington		RHB	LFM	1964/65-1978
Colquhoun Ian Alexander	8/6/1924 Wellington	26/2/2005 Paraparaumu Beach	RHB	WK	1954/55
Coney Jeremy Vernon	21/6/1952 Wellington		RHB	RSM	1973/74-1986/87
Congdon Bevan Ernest	11/2/1938 Motueka		RHB	RM	1964/65-1978
Cowie John	30/3/1912 Auckland	3/6/1994 Lower Hutt	RHB	RFM	1937-1949
Cresswell George Fenwick	22/3/1915 Wanganui	10/1/1966 Blenheim	LHB	RM	1949-1950/51
Cromb Ian Burns	25/6/1905 Christchurch	6/3/1984 Christchurch	RHB	RM	1931-1931/32
Crowe Jeffrey John	14/9/1958 Auckland		RHB		1982/83-1989/90
Crowe Martin David	22/9/1962 Auckland		RHB	RM	1981/82-1995/96
Cumming Craig Derek	31/8/1975 Timaru		RHB	RM	2004/05
Cunis Robert Smith	5/1/1941 Whangarei		RHB	RFM	1963/64-1971/72
D'Arcy John William	23/4/1936 Christchurch		RHB		1958
de Groen Richard Paul	5/8/1962 Otorohanga		RHB	RM	1993/94-1994/95
Davis Heath Te-Ihi-O-Te-Rangi	30/11/1971 Lower Hutt		RHB	RF	1994-1997/98
Dempster Charles Stewart	15/11/1903 Wellington	12/2/1974 Wellington	RHB		1929/30-1932/33
Dempster Eric William	25/1/1925 Wellington		LHB	SLA	1952/53-1953/54
Dick Arthur Edward	10/10/1936 Middlemarch		RHB	WK	1961/62-1965
Dickinson George Ritchie	11/3/1903 Dunedin	17/3/1978 Lower Hutt	RHB	RF	1929/30-1931/32
Donnelly Martin Paterson	17/10/1917 Ngaruawahia	22/10/1999 Sydney	LHB	SLA	1937-1949
Doull Simon Blair	6/8/1969 Pukekohe		RHB	RM	1992/93-1999/00
Dowling Graham Thorne	4/3/1937 Christchurch		RHB		1961/62-1971/72
Drum Christopher James	10/7/1974 Auckland		RHB	RFM	2000/01-2001/02

	Born	Died	Type		Test Career
Dunning John Angus	6/2/1903 Omaha	24/6/1971 Adelaide	RHB	RM	1932/33-1937
Edgar Bruce Adrian	23/11/1956 Wellington		LHB	WK	1978-1986
Edwards Graham Neil	27/5/1955 Nelson		RHB	WK	1976/77-1980/81
Emery Raymond William George	28/3/1915 Auckland	18/12/1982 Auckland	RHB	RM	1951/52
Fisher Frederick Eric	28/7/1924 Johnsonville	19/6/1996 Palmerston North	RHB	LM	1952/53
Fleming Stephen Paul	1/4/1973 Christchurch		LHB		1993/94-2004/05
Foley Henry	28/1/1906 Wellington	16/10/1948 Brisbane	LHB		1929/30
Franklin James Edward Charles	7/11/1980 Wellington		LHB	LFM	2000/01-2004/05
Franklin Trevor John	18/3/1962 Auckland		RHB	RM	1983-1990/91
Freeman Douglas Linford	8/9/1914 Sydney	31/5/1994 Sydney	RHB	RLBG	1932/33
Gallichan Norman	3/6/1906 Palmerston North	25/3/1969 Taupo	RHB	SLA	1937
Gedye Sidney Graham	2/5/1929 Otahuhu		RHB		1963/64-1964/65
Germon Lee Kenneth	4/11/1968 Christchurch		RHB	WK	1995/96-1996/97
Gillespie Stuart Ross	2/3/1957 Wanganui		RHB	RFM	1985/86
Gray Evan John	18/11/1954 Wellington		RHB	SLA	1983-1988/89
Greatbatch Mark John	11/12/1963 Auckland		LHB		1987/88-1996/97
Guillen Simpson Clairmonte	24/9/1924 Port of Spain, Trinidad		RHB	WK	1955/56
Guy John William	29/8/1934 Nelson		LHB		1955/56-1961/62
Hadlee Dayle Robert	6/1/1948 Christchurch		RHB	RM	1969-1977/78
Hadlee Richard John	3/7/1951 Christchurch		LHB	RFM	1972/73-1990
Hadlee Walter Arnold	4/6/1915 Lincoln		RHB		1937-1950/51
Harford Noel Sherwin	30/8/1930 Winton	30/3/1981 Auckland	RHB	RM	1955/56-1958
Harford Roy Ivan	30/5/1936 London, England		LHB	WK	1967/68
Harris Chris Zinzan	20/11/1969 Christchurch		LHB	RM	1992/93-2001/02
Harris Parke Gerald Zinzan	18/7/1927 Christchurch	1/12/1991 Christchurch	RHB	ROB	1955/56-1964/65
Harris Roger Meredith	27/7/1933 Otahuhu		RHB	RM	1958/59
Hart Matthew Norman	16/5/1972 Hamilton		LHB	SLA	1993/94-1995/96
Hart Robert Garry	2/12/1974 Hamilton		RHB	WK	2001/02-2003/04
Hartland Blair Robert	22/10/1966 Christchurch		RHB		1991/92-1994
Haslam Mark James	26/9/1972 Bury, England		LHB	SLA	1992/93-1995/96
Hastings Brian Frederick	23/3/1940 Wellington		RHB		1968/69-1975/76
Hayes John Arthur	11/1/1927 Auckland		RHB	RF	1950/51-1958
Henderson Matthew	2/8/1895 Auckland	17/6/1970 Wellington	LHB	LFM	1929/30

	Born	Died	Type			Test Career
Horne	5/12/1970		RHB	RM		1996/97-2002/03
Matthew Jeffery	Auckland					
Horne	21/1/1960		LHB			1986/87-1990/91
Philip Andrew	Upper Hutt					
Hough	24/10/1928		RHB	RM		1958/59
Kenneth William	Sydney					
Howarth	29/3/1951		RHB	ROB		1974/75-1984/85
Geoffrey Philip	Auckland					
Howarth	25/12/1943		LHB	SLA		1969-1976/77
Hedley John	Auckland					
James	12/3/1904	21/8/1976	RHB	WK		1929/30-1932/33
Kenneth Cecil	Wellington	Palmerston North				
Jarvis	29/7/1944		RHB			1964/65-1972/73
Terrence Wayne	Auckland					
Jones	9/5/1959		RHB	ROB		1986/87-1994/95
Andrew Howard	Wellington					
Jones	22/10/1973		RHB			2003/04
Richard Andrew	Auckland					
Kennedy	3/6/1972		RHB	RFM		1995/96
Robert John	Dunedin					
Kerr	28/12/1910		RHB			1931-1937
John Lambert	Dannevirke					
Kuggeleijn	10/5/1956		RHB	ROB		1988/89
Christopher Mary	Auckland					
Larsen	27/9/1962		RHB	RM		1994-1995/96
Gavin Rolf	Wellington					
Latham	12/6/1961		RHB			1991/92-1992/93
Rodney Terry	Christchurch					
Lees	19/3/1952		RHB	WK		1976/77-1983
Warren Kenneth	Dunedin					
Leggat	7/6/1930		RHB	RM		1953/54
Ian Bruce	Invercargill					
Leggat	27/5/1926	9/3/1973	RHB			1951/52-1955/56
John Gordon	Wellington	Christchurch				
Lissette	6/11/1919	24/1/1973	RHB	SLA		1955/56
Allen Fisher	Morrinsville	Hamilton				
Loveridge	15/1/1975		RHB	RLB		1995/96
Greg Riaka	Palmerston North					
Lowry	17/2/1898	20/7/1976	RHB	ROB	WK	1929/30-1931
Thomas Coleman	Fernhill	Hastings				
McCullum	27/9/1981		RHB		WK	2003/04-2004/05
Brendon Barrie	Dunedin					
McEwan	19/12/1953		RHB	RM		1979/80-1984/85
Paul Ernest	Christchurch					
MacGibbon	28/8/1924		RHB	RFM		1950/51-1958
Anthony Roy	Christchurch					
McGirr	5/11/1891	14/4/1964	RHB	RFM		1929/30
Herbert Mendelson	Wellington	Nelson				
McGregor	18/12/1931		RHB			1954/55-1964/65
Spencer Noel	Dunedin					
McLeod	14/10/1900	14/9/1989	LHB	RLB		1929/30
Edwin George	Auckland	Wellington				
McMahon	8/11/1929		RHB	WK		1955/56
Trevor George	Wellington					
McMillan	13/9/1976		RHB	RM		1997/98-2004/05
Craig Douglas	Christchurch					
McRae	25/12/1912	10/8/1986	LHB	LM		1945/46
Donald Alexander Noel	Christchurch	Christchurch				
Marshall	15/2/1979		RHB	RM		2000/01-2004/05
Hamish John Hamilton	Warkworth					
Marshall	15/2/1979		RHB	RM		2004/05
James Andrew Hamilton	Warkworth					
Martin	10/12/1974		RHB	RFM		2000/01-2004/05
Christopher Stewart	Christchurch					

	Born	Died	Type		Test Career
Mason Michael James	27/8/1974 Carterton		RHB	RFM	2003/04
Matheson Alexander Malcolm	27/2/1906 Omaha	31/12/1985 Auckland	RHB	RFM	1929/30-1931
Meale Trevor	11/11/1928 Auckland		LHB		1958
Merritt William Edward	18/8/1908 Sumner	9/6/1977 Christchurch	RHB	RLBG	1929/30-1931
Meuli Edgar Milton	20/2/1926 Hawera		RHB	RLB	1952/53
Milburn Barry Douglas	24/11/1943 Dunedin		RHB	WK	1968/69
Miller Lawrence Somerville Martin	31/3/1923 New Plymouth	17/12/1996 Kapiti	LHB	LSM	1952/53-1958
Mills John Ernest	3/9/1905 Dunedin	11/12/1972 Hamilton	LHB		1929/30-1932/33
Mills Kyle David	15/3/1979 Auckland		RHB	RFM	2004-2004/05
Moir Alexander McKenzie	17/7/1919 Dunedin	17/6/2000 Dunedin	RHB	RLB	1950/51-1958/59
Moloney Denis Andrew Robert	11/8/1910 Dunedin	15/7/1942 El Alamein	RHB	RLB	1937
Mooney Francis Leonard Hugh	26/5/1921 Wellington	8/3/2004 Wellington	RHB	WK	1949-1953/54
Morgan Ross Winston	12/2/1941 Auckland		RHB	ROB	1964/65-1971/72
Morrison Bruce Donald	17/12/1933 Lower Hutt		LHB	RM	1962/63
Morrison Daniel Kyle	3/2/1966 Auckland		RHB	RFM	1987/88-1996/97
Morrison John Francis MacLean	27/8/1947 Wellington		RHB	SLA	1973/74-1981/82
Motz Richard Charles	12/1/1940 Christchurch		RHB	RFM	1961/62-1969
Murray Bruce Alexander Grenfell	18/9/1940 Wellington		RHB	RLB	1967/68-1970/71
Murray Darrin James	4/9/1967 Christchurch		RHB		1994/95
Nash Dion Joseph	20/11/1971 Auckland		RHB	RFM	1992/93-2001/02
Newman Jack	3/7/1902 Brightwater	23/9/1996 Nelson	RHB	LM	1931/32-1932/33
O'Brien Iain Edward	10/7/1976 Lower Hutt		RHB	RM	2004/05
O'Connor Shayne Barry	15/11/1973 Hastings		LHB	LFM	1997/98-2001/02
Oram Jacob David Philip	28/7/1978 Palmerston North		LHB	RM	2002/03-2004/05
O'Sullivan David Robert	16/11/1944 Palmerston North		RHB	SLA	1972/73-1976/77
Overton Guy William Fitzroy	8/6/1919 Dunedin	7/9/1993 Winton	LHB	RFM	1953/54
Owens Michael Barry	11/11/1969 Christchurch		RHB	RFM	1992/93-1994
Page Milford Laurenson	8/5/1902 Lyttelton	13/2/1987 Christchurch	RHB	ROB	1929/30-1937
Papps Michael Hugh William	2/7/1979 Christchurch		RHB		2003/04-2004
Parker John Morton	21/2/1951 Dannevirke		RHB	WK	1972/73-1980/81
Parker Norman Murray	28/8/1948 Dannevirke		RHB	RLB	1976/77
Parore Adam Craig	23/1/1971 Auckland		RHB	WK	1990-2001/02

	Born	Died	Type			Test Career
Patel Dipak Narshibhai	25/10/1958 Nairobi, Kenya		RHB	ROB		1986/87-1996/97
Petherick Peter James	25/9/1942 Ranfurly		RHB	ROB		1976/77
Petrie Eric Charlton	22/5/1927 Ngaruawahia	14/8/2004 Omokoroa	RHB	WK		1955/56-1965/66
Playle William Rodger	1/12/1938 Palmerston North		RHB			1958-1962/63
Pocock Blair Andrew	18/6/1971 Papakura		RHB			1993/94-1997/98
Pollard Victor	7/9/1945 Burnley, England		RHB	ROB		1964/65-1973
Poore Matt Beresford	1/6/1930 Christchurch		RHB	ROB		1952/53-1955/56
Priest Mark Wellings	12/8/1961 Greymouth		LHB	SLA		1990-1997/98
Pringle Christopher	26/1/1968 Auckland		RHB	RFM		1990/91-1994/95
Puna Narotam	28/10/1929 Surat, India	7/6/1996 Hamilton	RHB	ROB		1965/66
Rabone Geoffrey Osbourne	6/11/1921 Gore		RHB	ROB		1949-1954/55
Redmond Rodney Ernest	29/12/1944 Whangarei		LHB	SLA		1972/73
Reid John Fulton	3/3/1956 Auckland		LHB	RLB	WK	1978/79-1985/86
Reid John Richard	3/6/1928 Auckland		RHB	RFM	WK	1949-1965
Richardson Mark Hunter	11/6/1971 Hastings		LHB	SLA		2000/01-2004/05
Roberts Andrew Duncan Glenn	6/5/1947 Te Aroha	26/10/1989 Wellington	RHB	RM		1975/76-1976/77
Roberts Albert William	20/8/1909 Christchurch	13/5/1978 Christchurch	RHB	RM		1929/30-1937
Robertson Gary Keith	15/7/1960 New Plymouth		RHB	RFM		1985/86
Rowe Charles Gordon	30/6/1915 Glasgow, Scotland	9/6/1995 Palmerston North	RHB			1945/46
Rutherford Kenneth Robert	26/10/1965 Dunedin		RHB	RM		1984/85-1994/95
Scott Roy Hamilton	6/3/1917 Clyde		RHB	RM		1946/47
Scott Verdun John	31/7/1916 Devonport	2/8/1980 Devonport	RHB	RM		1945/46-1951/52
Sewell David Graham	20/10/1977 Christchurch		RHB	LFM		1997/98
Shrimpton Michael John Froud	23/6/1940 Feilding		RHB	RLBG		1962/63-1973/74
Sinclair Barry Whitley	23/10/1936 Wellington		RHB			1962/63-1967/68
Sinclair Ian McKay	1/6/1933 Rangiora		LHB	ROB		1955/56
Sinclair Mathew Stuart	9/11/1975 Katherine, Australia		RHB			1999/00-2004/05
Smith Frank Brunton	13/3/1922 Rangiora	6/7/1997 Christchurch		RHB		1946/47-1951/52
Smith Horace Dennis	8/1/1913 Toowoomba, Aust	25/1/1986 Christchurch	RHB	RFM		1932/33
Smith Ian David Stockley	28/2/1957 Nelson		RHB	WK		1980/81-1991/92
Snedden Colin Alexander	7/1/1918 Auckland		RHB	ROB		1946/47
Snedden Martin Colin	23/11/1958 Auckland		LHB	RFM		1980/81-1990
Sparling John Trevor	24/7/1938 Auckland		RHB	ROB		1958-1963/64

	Born	Died	Type		Test Career
Spearman Craig Murray	4/7/1972 Auckland		RHB		1995/96-2000/01
Stead Gary Raymond	9/1/1972 Christchurch		RHB	RLB	1998/99-1999/00
Stirling Derek Alexander	5/10/1961 Upper Hutt		RHB	RFM	1984/85-1986
Styris Scott Bernard	10/7/1975 Brisbane, Aust		RHB	RM	2001/02-2004/05
Su'a Murphy Logo	7/11/1966 Wanganui		LHB	LFM	1991/92-1994/95
Sutcliffe Bert	17/11/1923 Auckland	20/4/2001 Auckland	LHB	SLA	1946/47-1965
Taylor Bruce Richard	12/7/1943 Timaru		LHB	RFM	1964/65-1973
Taylor Donald Dougald	2/3/1923 Auckland	5/12/1980 Auckland	RHB	RLBG	1946/47-1955/56
Thomson Keith	26/2/1941 Methven		RHB		1967/68
Thomson Shane Alexander	27/1/1969 Hamilton		RH1B	ROB	1989/90-1995/96
Tindill Eric William Thomas	18/12/1910 Nelson		LHB	WK	1937-1946/47
Troup Gary Bertram	3/10/1952 Taumarunui		RHB	LFM	1976/77-1985/86
Truscott Peter Bennetts	14/8/1941 Pahiatua		RHB		1964/65
Tuffey Daryl Raymond	11/6/1978 Milton		RHB	RFM	1999/00-2004
Turner Glenn Maitland	26/5/1947 Dunedin		RHB		1968/69-1982/83
Twose Roger Graham	17/4/1968 Torquay, England		LHB	RM	1995/96-1999
Vance Robert Howard	31/3/1955 Wellington		RHB		1987/88-1989/90
Vaughan Justin Thomas Caldwell	30//8/1967 Hereford, England		LHB	RM	1992/93-1996/97
Vettori Daniel Luca	27/1/1979 Auckland		LHB	SLA	1996/97-2004/05
Vincent Lou	11/11/1978 Warkworth		RHB	WK	2001/02-2004/05
Vivian Graham Ellery	28/2/1946 Auckland		LHB	RLB	1964/65-1971/72
Vivian Henry Gifford	4/11/1912 Auckland	12/8/1983 Auckland	LHB	SLA	1931-1937
Wadsworth Kenneth John	30/11/1946 Nelson	19/8/1976 Nelson	RHB	WK	1969-1975/76
Walker Brooke Graeme Keith	25/3/1977 Auckland		RHB	RLB	2000/01-2001/02
Wallace Walter Mervyn	19/12/1916 Auckland		RHB		1936-1952/53
Walmsley Kerry Peter	23/8/1973 Dunedin		RHB	RFM	1994/95-2000/01
Ward John Thomas	11/3/1937 Timaru		RHB	WK	1963/64-1967/68
Watson William	31/8/1965 Auckland		RHB	RFM	1986-1993/94
Watt Leslie	17/9/1924 Waitati	15/11/1996 Dunedin	RHB		1954/55
Webb Murray George	22/6/1947 Invercargill		RHB	RFM	1970/71-1973/74
Webb Peter Neil	14/7/1957 Auckland		RHB	WK	1979/80
Weir Gordon Lindsay	2/6/1908 Auckland	31/10/2003 Auckland	RHB	RM	1929/30-1937

	Born	Died	Type		Test Career
White David John	26/6/1961 Gisborne		RHB	ROB	1990/91
Whitelaw Paul Erskine	10/2/1910 Auckland	28/8/1988 Auckland	RHB		1932/33
Wiseman Paul John	4/5/1970 Auckland		RHB	ROB	1997/98-2004/05
Wright John Geoffrey	5/7/1954 Darfield		LHB	RM	1977/78-1992/93
Young Bryan Andrew	3/11/1964 Whangarei		RHB	WK	1993/94-1998/99
Yuile Bryan William	29/10/1941 Palmerston North		RHB	SLA	1962/63-1969/70

TEST UMPIRES

The following is the complete list of New Zealand test umpires:

Umpire	Tests
Dunne R.S.	39 *
Bowden B.F.	27 *
Aldridge B.L.	26 *
Goodall F.R.	24
Woodward S.J.	24
Cowie D.B.	22 *
Martin W.T.	15
Copps D.E.A.	13
Gardiner W.R.C.	9
Shortt R.W.R.	9
MacKintosh E.C.A.	8
Hastie J.B.R.	7
Cave K.	6
Monteith R.L.	6
Quested D.M.	5
Pengelly M.F.	4
Harris J.C.	4
Morris G.C.	4
Cobcroft L.T.	3
McLellan J.	3
Pearce T.M.	3
Cowie J.	3
Gwynne W.J.C.	3
Kinsella D.A.	3
McHarg R.L.	3
King C.E.	3
Butler W.	2
Forrester J.T.	2
Brown J.M.A.	2
Tonkinson S.B.	2
Currie R.G.	2
Clark L.G.	2
Dumbleton D.P.	2
Watkin E.A.	2
Hill A.L.	2 *
Page W.P.	1
Burgess T.	1
Torrance R.C.	1
Gourlay H.W.	1
Montgomery O.R.	1
Brook E.G.	1
Vine B.	1
Jelley A.E.	1
Tindill E.W.T.	1
Johnston L.C.	1
Burns D.C.	1
Cassie H.B.	1
Bricknell B.A.	1
Higginson I.C.	1

* *includes test matches overseas*

The following overseas umpires have stood in test matches in New Zealand:

Umpire	Tests
Harper D.J. *(Australia)*	6
de Silva E.A.R. *(Sri Lanka)*	6
Hair D.B. *(Australia)*	5
Bucknor S.A. *(West Indies)*	4
Randell S.G. *(Australia)*	3
Orchard D.L. *(South Africa)*	3
Tiffin R.B. *(Zimbabwe)*	3
Shepherd D.R. *(England)*	3
Aleem Dar *(Pakistan)*	3
Koertzen R.E. *(South Africa)*	3
Venkataraghavan S. *(India)*	3
Ramaswamy V.K. *(India)*	2
Cooray B.C. *(Sri Lanka)*	2
Mahboob Shah *(Pakistan)*	2
Davis S.J. *(Australia)*	2
Bird H.D. *(England)*	2
Francis K.T. *(Sri Lanka)*	2
Robinson I.D. *(Zimbabwe)*	1
Nichols E.A. *(West Indies)*	1
Plews N.T. *(England)*	1
Riazuddin *(Pakistan)*	1
Jayaprakash A.V. *(India)*	1
Khizar Hayat *(Pakistan)*	1
Elliott C.S. *(England)*	1
Barker L.H. *(West Indies)*	1
Lloyds J.W. *(England)*	1

The following pairs of umpires have stood together in the most tests:

Pair	Tests
Goodall F.R. & Woodward S.J.	10
Aldridge B.L. & Dunne R.S.	7
Aldridge B.L. & Woodward S.J.	6
Copps D.E.A. & Gardiner W.R.C.	5
Copps D.E.A. & Martin W.T.	4
MacKintosh E.C.A. & Shortt R.W.R.	4
Harris J.C. & Pearce T.M.	3
MacKintosh E.C.A. & Martin W.T.	3
Cobcroft L.T. & Cave K.	3
Dunne R.S. & Woodward S.J.	3

These umpires have stood in every test of a series *(minimum 3 matches):*

Umpire	Opponent	Season
Cave K. (4)	v England	1929/30
Martin W.T. (3)	v England	1965/66
MacKintosh E.C.A. (3)	v West Indies	1968/69
Goodall F.R. (3)	v England	1983/84
Woodward S.J. (3)	v England	1983/84
Aldridge B.L. (3)	v Sri Lanka	1990/91
Aldridge B.L. (3)	v England	1991/92
Dunne R.S. (3)	v England	1991/92
Aldridge B.L. (3)	v Australia	1992/93

TEAM RECORDS

New Zealand's Test Victories

1) v **West Indies** at Auckland 1955/56
NZ 255 & 157-9d WI 145 & 77
NZ won by 190 runs

2) v **South Africa** at Cape Town 1961/62
NZ 385 & 212-9d SA 190 & 335
NZ won by 72 runs

3) v **South Africa** at Port Elizabeth 1961/62
NZ 275 & 228 SA 190 & 273
NZ won by 40 runs

4) v **India** at Christchurch 1967/68
NZ 502 & 88-4 I 288 & 301
NZ won by 6 wickets

5) v **West Indies** at Wellington 1968/69
WI 297 & 148 NZ 282 & 166-4
NZ won by 6 wickets

6) v **India** at Nagpur 1969/70
NZ 319 & 214 I 257 & 109
NZ won by 167 runs

7) v **Pakistan** at Lahore 1969/70
P114 & 208 NZ 241 & 82-5
NZ won by 5 wickets

8) v **Australia** at Christchurch 1973/74
A 223 & 259 NZ 255 & 230-5
NZ won by 5 wickets

9) v **India** at Wellington 1975/76
I 220 & 81 NZ 334
NZ won by an innings and 33 runs

10) v **England** at Wellington 1977/78
NZ 228 & 123 E 215 & 64
NZ won by 72 runs

11) v **West Indies** at Dunedin 1979/80
WI 140 & 212 NZ 249 & 104-9
NZ won by 1 wicket

12) v **India** at Wellington 1980/81
NZ 375 & 100 I 233 & 190
NZ won by 62 runs

13) v **Australia** at Auckland 1981/82
A 210 & 280 NZ 387 & 109-5
NZ won by 5 wickets

14) v **Sri Lanka** at Christchurch 1982/83
NZ 344 SL 144 & 175
NZ won by an innings and 25 runs

15) v **Sri Lanka** at Wellington 1982/83
SL 240 & 93 NZ 201 & 134-4
NZ won by 6 wickets

16) v **England** at Leeds 1983
E 225 & 252 NZ 377 & 103-5
NZ won by 5 wickets

17) v **England** at Christchurch 1983/84
NZ 307 E 82 & 93
NZ won by an innings and 132 runs

18) v **Sri Lanka** at Kandy 1983/84
NZ 276 & 201-8d SL 215 & 97
NZ won by 165 runs

19) v **Sri Lanka** at Colombo 1983/84
SL 225 & 142 NZ 459
NZ won by an innings and 61 runs

20) v **Pakistan** at Auckland 1984/85
P 169 & 183 NZ 451-9d
NZ won by an innings and 99 runs

21) v **Pakistan** at Dunedin 1984/85
P274 & 223 NZ 220 & 278-8
NZ won by 2 wickets

22) v **Australia** at Brisbane 1985/86
A 179 & 333 NZ 553-7d
NZ won by an innings and 41 runs

23) v **Australia** at Perth 1985/86
A 203 & 259 NZ 299 & 164-4
NZ won by 6 wickets

24) v **Australia** at Auckland 1985/86
A 314 & 103 NZ 358 & 160-2
NZ won by 8 wickets

25) v **England** at Nottingham 1986
E 256 & 230 NZ 413 & 77-2
NZ won by 8 wickets

26) v **West Indies** at Christchurch 1986/87
WI 100 & 264 NZ 332-9d & 33-5
NZ won by 5 wickets

27) v **India** at Bombay 1988/89
NZ 236 & 279 I 234 & 145
NZ wonby 136 runs

28) v **India** at Christchurch 1989/90
NZ 459 & 2-0 I 164 & 296
NZ won by 10 wickets

29) v **Australia** at Wellington 1989/90
A 110 & 269 NZ 202 & 181-1
NZ won by 9 wickets

30) v **Zimbabwe** at Harare 1992/93
NZ 335 & 262-5d Z 283-9d & 137
NZ won by 177 runs

31) v **Australia** at Auckland 1992/93
A 139 & 285 NZ 224 & 201-5
NZ won by 5 wickets

32) v **Pakistan** at Christchurch 1993/94
P 344 & 179 NZ 200 & 324-5
NZ won by 5 wickets

33) v **South Africa** at Johannesburg 1994/95
NZ 411 & 194 SA 179 & 289
NZ won by 137 runs

34) v **Pakistan** at Lahore 1996/97
NZ 155 & 311 P 191 & 231
NZ won by 44 runs

35) v **Sri Lanka** at Dunedin 1996/97
NZ 586-7d SL 222 & 328
NZ won by an innings & 36 runs

36) v **Sri Lanka** at Hamilton 1996/97
NZ 222 & 273 SL 170 & 205
NZ won by 120 runs

37) v **Zimbabwe** at Wellington 1997/98
Z 180 & 250 NZ 411 & 20-0
NZ won by 10 wickets

38) v **Zimbabwe** at Auckland 1997/98
Z 170 & 277 NZ 460
NZ won by an innings and 13 runs

39) v **Sri Lanka** at Colombo 1997/98
NZ 305 & 444-6d SL 285 & 297
NZ won by 167 runs

40) v **India** at Wellington 1998/99
I 208 & 356 NZ 352 & 215-6
NZ won by 4 wickets

41) v **England** at Lord's 1999
E 186 & 229 NZ 358 & 60-1
NZ won by 9 wickets

42) v **England** at The Oval 1999
NZ 236 & 162 E 153 & 162
NZ won by 83 runs

43) v **West Indies** at Hamilton 1999/00
WI 365 & 97 NZ 393 & 70-1
NZ won by 9 wickets

44) v **West Indies** at Wellington 1999/00
NZ 518-9d WI 179 & 234
NZ won by an innings and 105 runs

45) v **Zimbabwe** at Bulawayo 2000/01
Z 350 & 119 NZ 338 & 132-3
NZ won by 7 wickets

46) v **Zimbabwe** at Harare 2000/01
NZ 465 & 74-2 Z 166 & 370
NZ won by 8 wickets

47) v **Pakistan** at Hamilton 2000/01
P 104 & 118 NZ 407-4d
NZ won by an innings & 185 runs

48) v **Bangladesh** at Hamilton 2001/02
NZ 365-9d B 205 & 108
NZ won by an innings and 52 runs

49) v **Bangladesh** at Wellington 2001/02
B 132 & 135 NZ 341-6d
NZ won by an innings and 74 runs

50) v **England** at Auckland 2001/02
NZ 202 & 269-9d E 160 & 233
NZ won by 78 runs

51) v **West Indies** at Bridgetown 2001/02
NZ 337 & 243 WI 107 & 269
NZ won by 204 runs

52) v **India** at Wellington 2002/03
I 161 & 121 NZ 247 & 36-0
NZ won by 10 wickets

53) v **India** at Hamilton 2002/03
I 99 & 154 NZ 94 & 160-6
NZ won by 4 wickets

54) v **South Africa** at Auckland 2003/04
SA 296 & 349 NZ 595 & 53-1
NZ won by 9 wickets

55) v **Bangladesh** at Dhaka 2004/05
B 177 & 126 NZ 402
NZ won by an innings and 99 runs

56) v **Bangladesh** at Chittagong 2004/05
NZ 545-6d B 182 & 262
NZ won by an innings and 101 runs

57) v **Sri Lanka** at Wellington 2004/05
SL 211 & 273 NZ 522-9d
NZ won by an innings and 38 runs

Test Record by Series

					Cumulative					
		TOTAL						BY OPPONENT		
Season	Opponent	Won	Lost	Drawn	Won	Lost	Drawn	Won	Lost	Drawn
1929/30	England*	—	1	3	—	1	3	—	1	3
1931	England	—	1	2	—	2	5	—	2	5
1931/32	South Africa*	—	2	—	—	4	5	—	2	—
1932/33	England*	—	—	2	—	4	7	—	2	7
1937	England	—	1	2	—	5	9	—	3	9
1945/46	Australia*	—	1	—	—	6	9	—	1	—
1946/47	England*	—	—	1	—	6	10	—	3	10
1949	England	—	—	4	—	6	14	—	3	14
1950/51	England*	—	1	1	—	7	15	—	4	15
1951/52	West Indies*	—	1	1	—	8	16	—	1	1
1952/53	South Africa*	—	1	1	—	9	17	—	3	1
1953/54	South Africa	—	4	1	—	13	18	—	7	2
1954/55	England*	—	2	—	—	15	18	—	6	15
1955/56	Pakistan	—	2	1	—	17	19	—	2	1
1955/56	India	—	2	3	—	19	22	—	2	3
1955/56	West Indies*	1	3	—	1	22	22	1	4	1
1958	England	—	4	1	1	26	23	—	10	16
1958/59	England*	—	1	1	1	27	24	—	11	17
1961/62	South Africa	2	2	1	3	29	25	2	9	3
1962/63	England*	—	3	—	3	32	25	—	14	17
1963/64	South Africa*	—	—	3	3	32	28	2	9	6
1964/65	Pakistan*	—	—	3	3	32	31	—	2	4
1964/65	India	—	1	3	3	33	34	—	3	6
1964/65	Pakistan	—	2	1	3	35	35	—	4	5
1965	England	—	3	—	3	38	35	—	17	17
1965/66	England*	—	—	3	3	38	38	—	17	20
1967/68	India*	1	3	—	4	41	38	1	6	6
1968/69	West Indies*	1	1	1	5	42	39	2	5	2
1969	England	—	2	1	5	44	40	—	19	21
1969/70	India	1	1	1	6	45	41	2	7	7
1969/70	Pakistan	1	—	2	7	45	43	1	4	7
1970/71	England*	—	1	1	7	46	44	—	20	22
1971/72	West Indies	—	—	5	7	46	49	2	5	7
1972/73	Pakistan*	—	1	2	7	47	51	1	5	9
1973	England	—	2	1	7	49	52	—	22	23
1973/74	Australia	—	2	1	7	51	53	—	3	1
1973/74	Australia*	1	1	1	8	52	54	1	4	2
1974/75	England*	—	1	1	8	53	55	—	23	24
1975/76	India*	1	1	1	9	54	56	3	8	8
1976/77	Pakistan	—	2	1	9	56	57	1	7	10
1976/77	India	—	2	1	9	58	58	3	10	9
1976/77	Australia*	—	1	1	9	59	59	1	5	3
1977/78	England*	1	1	1	10	60	60	1	24	25
1978	England	—	3	—	10	63	60	1	27	25
1978/79	Pakistan*	—	1	2	10	64	62	1	8	12
1979/80	West Indies*	1	—	2	11	64	64	3	5	9
1980/81	Australia	—	2	1	11	66	65	1	7	4
1980/81	India*	1	—	2	12	66	67	4	10	11
1981/82	Australia*	1	1	1	13	67	68	2	8	5
1982/83	Sri Lanka*	2	—	—	15	67	68	2	—	—

		TOTAL			Cumulative			BY OPPONENT		
Season	*Opponent*	*Won*	*Lost*	*Drawn*	*Won*	*Lost*	*Drawn*	*Won*	*Lost*	*Drawn*
1983	England	1	3	—	16	70	68	2	30	25
1983/84	England*	1	—	2	17	70	70	3	30	27
1983/84	Sri Lanka	2	—	1	19	70	71	4	—	1
1984/85	Pakistan	—	2	1	19	72	72	1	10	13
1984/85	Pakistan*	2	—	1	21	72	73	3	10	14
1984/85	West Indies	—	2	2	21	74	75	3	7	11
1985/86	Australia	2	1	—	23	75	75	4	9	5
1985/86	Australia*	1	—	2	24	75	77	5	9	7
1986	England	1	—	2	25	75	79	4	30	29
1986/87	West Indies*	1	1	1	26	76	80	4	8	12
1986/87	Sri Lanka	—	—	1	26	76	81	4	—	2
1987/88	Australia	—	1	2	26	77	83	5	10	9
1987/88	England*	—	—	3	26	77	86	4	30	32
1988/89	India	1	2	—	27	79	86	5	12	11
1988/89	Pakistan*	—	—	2	27	79	88	3	10	16
1989/90	Australia	—	—	1	27	79	89	5	10	10
1989/90	India*	1	—	2	28	79	91	6	12	13
1989/90	Australia*	1	—	—	29	79	91	6	10	10
1990	England	—	1	2	29	80	93	4	41	34
1990/91	Pakistan	—	3	—	29	83	93	3	13	16
1990/91	Sri Lanka*	—	—	3	29	83	96	4	—	5
1991/92	England*	—	2	1	29	85	97	4	33	35
1992/93	Zimbabwe	1	—	1	30	85	98	1	—	1
1992/93	Sri Lanka	—	1	1	30	86	99	4	1	6
1992/93	Pakistan*	—	1	—	30	87	99	3	14	16
1992/93	Australia*	1	1	1	31	88	100	7	11	11
1993/94	Australia	—	2	1	31	90	101	7	13	12
1993/94	Pakistan*	1	2	—	32	92	101	4	16	16
1993/94	India*	—	—	1	32	92	102	6	12	14
1994	England	—	1	2	32	93	104	4	34	37
1994/95	South Africa	1	2	—	33	95	104	3	11	6
1994/95	West Indies*	—	1	1	33	96	105	4	9	13
1994/95	South Africa*	—	1	—	33	97	105	3	12	6
1994/95	Sri Lanka*	—	1	1	33	98	106	4	2	7
1995/96	India	—	1	2	33	99	108	6	13	16
1995/96	Pakistan*	—	1	—	33	100	108	4	17	16
1995/96	Zimbabwe*	—	—	2	33	100	110	1	—	3
1995/96	West Indies	—	1	1	33	101	111	4	10	14
1996/97	Pakistan	1	1	—	34	102	111	5	18	16
1996/97	England*	—	2	1	34	104	112	4	36	38
1996/97	Sri Lanka*	2	—	—	36	104	112	6	2	7
1997/98	Zimbabwe	—	—	2	36	104	114	1	—	5
1997/98	Australia	—	2	1	36	106	115	7	15	13
1997/98	Zimbabwe*	2	—	—	38	106	115	3	—	5
1997/98	Sri Lanka	1	2	—	39	108	115	7	4	7
1998/99	India*	1	—	1	40	108	116	7	13	17
1998/99	South Africa*	—	1	2	40	109	118	3	13	8
1999	England	2	1	1	42	110	119	6	37	39
1999/00	India	—	1	2	42	111	121	7	14	19
1999/00	West Indies*	2	—	—	44	111	121	6	10	14
1999/00	Australia*	—	3	—	44	114	121	7	18	13
2000/01	Zimbabwe	2	—	—	46	114	121	5	—	5

Season	Opponent	TOTAL Won	Lost	Drawn	Cumulative Won	Lost	Drawn	BY OPPONENT Won	Lost	Drawn
2000/01	South Africa	—	2	1	46	116	122	3	15	9
2000/01	Zimbabwe*	—	—	1	46	116	123	5	—	6
2000/01	Pakistan*	1	1	1	47	117	124	6	19	17
2001/02	Australia	—	—	3	47	117	127	7	18	16
2001/02	Bangladesh*	2	—	—	49	117	127	2	—	—
2001/02	England*	1	1	1	50	118	128	7	38	40
2001/02	Pakistan	—	1	—	50	119	128	6	20	17
2001/02	West Indies	1	—	1	51	119	129	7	10	15
2002/03	India*	2	—	—	53	119	129	9	14	19
2002/03	Sri Lanka	—	—	2	53	119	131	7	4	9
2003/04	India	—	—	2	53	119	133	9	14	21
2003/04	Pakistan*	—	1	1	53	120	134	6	21	18
2003/04	South Africa*	1	1	1	54	121	135	4	16	10
2004	England	—	3	—	54	124	135	7	41	40
2004/05	Bangladesh	2	—	—	56	124	135	4	—	—
2004/05	Australia	—	2	—	56	126	135	7	20	16
2004/05	Australia*	—	2	1	56	128	136	7	22	17
2004/05	Sri Lanka*	1	—	1	57	128	137	8	4	10

** home series*

Summary of Results

	Played	Won	Lost	Drawn
v England	88	7	41	40
v Australia	46	7	22	17
v South Africa	30	4	16	10
v West Indies	32	7	10	15
v India	44	9	14	21
v Pakistan	45	6	21	18
v Sri Lanka	22	8	4	10
v Zimbabwe	11	5	—	6
v Bangladesh	4	4	—	—
Total	**322**	**57**	**128**	**137**

Decade by Decade

	Played	Won	Lost	Drawn
1929/30 to 1937	14	—	5	9
1945/46 to 1954/55	19	—	10	9
1955/56 to 1964/65	43	3	23	17
1965/66 to 1974/75	40	5	15	20
1975/76 to 1984/85	54	13	21	20
1985/86 to 1994/95	67	12	24	31
1995/96 to 2004/05	85	24	30	31
Total	**322**	**57**	**128**	**137**

Highest Totals

For

671-4	v Sri Lanka	Wellington	1990/91
630-6d	v India	Mohali	2003/04
595	v South Africa	Auckland	2003/04
586-7d	v Sri Lanka	Dunedin	1996/97
563	v Pakistan	Hamilton	2003/04
561	v Sri Lanka	Napier	2004/05
553-7d	v Australia	Brisbane	1985/86
551-9d	v England	Lord's	1973
545-6d	v Bangladesh	Chittagong	2004/05
543-3d	v West Indies	Georgetown	1971/72
537	v England	Wellington	1983/84
534-9d	v Australia	Perth	2001/02
522-9d	v Sri Lanka	Wellington	2004/05
518-9d	v West Indies	Wellington	1999/00
515-7d	v Sri Lanka	Colombo	2002/03
512-6d	v England	Wellington	1987/88
509	v South Africa	Hamilton	2003/04
505	v South Africa	Cape Town	1953/54
502	v India	Christchurch	1967/68

Against

660-5d	by West Indies	Wellington	1994/95
643	by Pakistan	Lahore	2001/02
621-5d	by South Africa	Auckland	1998/99
616-5d	by Pakistan	Auckland	1988/89
607-6d	by Australia	Brisbane	1993/94
593-6d	by England	Auckland	1974/75
585	by Australia	Brisbane	2004/05
583-7d	by India	Ahmedabad	1999/00
580-9d	by England	Christchurch	1991/92
575-8d	by Australia	Adelaide	2004/05
571-8d	by Pakistan	Christchurch	2000/01
570-8d	by Australia	Wellington	2004/05
567-8d	by England	Nottingham	1994
565-9d	by Pakistan	Karachi	1976/77
564-8	by West Indies	Bridgetown	1971/72
562-7d	by England	Auckland	1962/63
561	by Pakistan	Lahore	1955/56
560-8d	by England	Christchurch	1932/33
558-8d	by Australia	Hobart	2001/02
552	by Australia	Christchurch	1976/77
550	by England	Christchurch	1950/51

Lowest Totals

For

26	v England	Auckland	1954/55
42	v Australia	Wellington	1945/46
47	v England	Lord's	1958
54	v Australia	Wellington	1945/46
65	v England	Christchurch	1970/71

67	v England	Leeds	1958
67	v England	Lord's	1978
70	v Pakistan	Dacca	1955/56
73	v Pakistan	Lahore	2001/02
74	v West Indies	Dunedin	1955/56
74	v England	Lord's	1958
76	v Australia	Brisbane	2004/05
79	v South Africa	Johannesburg	1953/54
79	v Pakistan	Rawalpindi	1964/65
85	v England	Manchester	1958
89	v England	Auckland	1962/63
93	v Pakistan	Hamilton	1992/93
94	v England	Birmingham	1958
94	v West Indies	Bridgetown	1984/85
94	v India	Hamilton	2002/03
97	v England	Nottingham	1973

Against

64	by England	Wellington	1977/78
77	by West Indies	Auckland	1955/56
81	by India	Wellington	1975/76
82	by England	Christchurch	1983/84
83	by India	Mohali	1999/00
88	by India	Bombay	1964/65
89	by India	Hyderabad	1969/70
93	by Sri Lanka	Wellington	1982/83
93	by England	Christchurch	1983/84
97	by Sri Lanka	Kandy	1983/84
97	by West Indies	Hamilton	1999/00
99	by India	Hamilton	2002/03

Longest Innings

Mins	*Runs*			
851	671-4	v Sri Lanka	Wellington	1990/91
815	459	v Sri Lanka	Colombo	1983/84
802	630-6 dec	v India	Mohali	2003/04
790	406-5	v Sri Lanka	Colombo	1986/87
784	512-6 dec	v England	Wellington	1987/88
780	543-3 dec	v West Indies	Georgetown	1971/72
768	551-9 dec	v England	Lord's	1973
760	482-6 dec	v Pakistan	Lahore	1964/65
753	487-7 dec	v Zimbabwe	Wellington	2000/01
738	492	v Pakistan	Wellington	1984/85
732	447	v Pakistan	Wellington	1988/89
724	537	v England	Wellington	1983/84
713	403	v Pakistan	Auckland	1988/89
710	484	v Australia	Wellington	1973/74
709	440	v England	Nottingham	1973

Largest First Innings Leads

*374	v Australia	Brisbane	1985/86
*364	v Sri Lanka	Dunedin	1996/97
*339	v West Indies	Wellington	1999/00
*311	v Sri Lanka	Wellington	2004/05
*303	v Pakistan	Hamilton	2000/01
*299	v Zimbabwe	Harare	2000/01
*299	v South Africa	Auckland	2003/04
298	v England	Lord's	1973
297	v England	Manchester	1999
*295	v India	Christchurch	1989/90
*290	v Zimbabwe	Auckland	1997/98
289	v West Indies	Bridgetown	1971/72
*282	v Pakistan	Auckland	1984/85
*263	v Bangladesh	Chittagong	2004/05
232	v West Indies	Christchurch	1979/80
*232	v West Indies	Christchurch	1986/87
*231	v Zimbabwe	Wellington	1997/98
*225	v England	Christchurch	1983/84
*225	v Bangladesh	Dhaka	2004/05
*214	v India	Christchurch	1967/68
209	v India	Bombay	1964/65
*209	v Bangladesh	Wellington	2001/02
204	v India	Calcutta	1955/56
*203	v Sri Lanka	Colombo	1983/84
*200	v Sri Lanka	Christchurch	1982/83

** New Zealand won the match*

Opposition Following-on

South Africa	Cape Town	1953/54
India	Bombay	1964/65
*India	Christchurch	1967/68
*Sri Lanka	Christchurch	1982/83
*England	Christchurch	1983/84
*India	Christchurch	1989/90
*Sri Lanka	Dunedin	1996/97
*West Indies	Wellington	1999/00
*Zimbabwe	Harare	2000/01
*Bangladesh	Hamilton	2001/02
India	Mohali	2003/04
*Bangladesh	Chittagong	2004/05

** New Zealand won the match*

NB: *New Zealand did not enforce the follow-on v South Africa at Cape Town, 1961/62 and v West Indies at Bridgetown in 2001/02 although they could have done so. They eventually won both games.*

GROUNDS

Results by Grounds

In New Zealand	P	W	L	D
Eden Park, Auckland	46	8	15	23
Jade Stadium, Christchurch	39	7	16	16
Basin Reserve, Wellington	44	12	14	18
Carisbrook, Dunedin	10	3	4	3
McLean Park, Napier	4	—	1	3
Westpac Park, Hamilton	13	5	2	6
Total	**156**	**35**	**52**	**69**

In Australia	P	W	L	D
Melbourne Cricket Ground	3	—	1	2
Sydney Cricket Ground	2	—	1	1
Adelaide Oval	3	—	2	1
WACA Ground, Perth	6	1	2	3
Woolloongabba, Brisbane	7	1	5	1
Bellerive Oval, Hobart	3	—	1	2
Total	**24**	**2**	**12**	**10**

In Sri Lanka	P	W	L	D
Kandy, Asgiriya Stadium	2	1	—	1
Sinhalese Sports Club Ground, Colombo	3	—	2	1
Colombo C.C. Ground, Colombo	2	1	—	1
Tyrone Fernando Stadium, Moratuwa	1	—	—	1
R. Premadasa Stadium, Colombo	1	1	—	—
Galle International Stadium	1	—	1	—
P. Saravanamuttu Stadium	1	—	—	1
Total	**11**	**3**	**3**	**5**

In West Indies	P	W	L	D
Queen's Park Oval, Port of Spain	3	—	—	3
Sabina Park, Kingston	2	—	1	1
Kensington Park, Bridgetown	4	1	2	1
Bourda, Georgetown	2	—	—	2
St Johns Recreation Ground, Antigua	1	—	—	1
Queen's Park, Grenada	1	—	—	1
Total	**13**	**1**	**3**	**9**

In Zimbabwe	P	W	L	D
Bulawayo Athletic Club	1	—	—	1
Harare Sports Club, Harare	3	2	—	1
Queens Sports Club, Bulawayo	2	1	—	1
Total	**6**	**3**	**—**	**3**

In Bangladesh	P	W	L	D
National Stadium, Dhaka	1	1	—	—
Chittagong Stadium	1	1	—	—
Total	**2**	**2**	**—**	**—**

In Pakistan	P	W	L	D
National Stadium, Karachi	6	—	3	3
Bagh-e-Jinnah, Lahore	1	—	1	—
Dacca Stadium, Dacca	2	—	—	2
Niaz Stadium, Hyderabad	2	—	2	—
Rawalpindi Club Ground	1	—	1	—
Lahore (Gaddafi) Stadium	7	2	4	1
Iqbal Stadium, Faisalabad	1	—	1	—
Rawalpindi Cricket Stadium	1	—	1	—
Total	**21**	**2**	**13**	**6**

In South Africa	P	W	L	D
Kingsmead, Durban	3	—	3	—
Ellis Park, Johannesburg	2	—	2	—
New Wanderers, Johannesburg	4	1	1	2
Newlands, Cape Town	3	1	1	1
St George's Park, Port Elizabeth	3	1	2	—
Goodyear Park, Bloemfontein	1	—	1	—
Total	**16**	**3**	**10**	**3**

In England	P	W	L	D
Lord's, London	14	1	6	7
Oval, London	9	1	4	4
Headingley, Leeds	6	1	4	1
Trent Bridge, Nottingham	8	1	5	2
Old Trafford, Manchester	6	—	2	4
Egbaston, Birmingham	4	—	4	—
Total	**47**	**4**	**25**	**18**

In India	P	W	L	D
Brabourne Stadium, Bombay	3	—	2	1
Wankhede Stadium, Bombay	2	1	1	—
Fateh Maidan, (Lal Bahadur Stadium) Hyderbad	3	—	1	2
Feroz Shah Kotla, Delhi	2	—	1	1
Eden Gardens, Calcutta	2	—	—	2
Corporation Stadium, Madras	2	—	1	1
Chepauk, (Chidambaram Stadium) Madras	2	—	1	1
VCA Ground, Nagpur	1	1	—	—
Green Park, Kanpur	2	—	1	1
Chinnaswamy Stadium, Bangalore	2	—	2	—
Barabati Stadium, Cuttack	1	—	—	1
Punjab C.A. Stadium, Mohali	2	—	—	2
Sardar Patel Stadium, Ahmedabad	2	—	—	2
Total	**26**	**2**	**10**	**14**

Record Performances in Tests on Each NZ Ground v All Countries

Venue	*Highest Total* *by NZ* *v NZ*	*Lowest Total* *by NZ* *v NZ*	*Highest Individual Innings* *by NZ* *v NZ*	*Best Bowling* *by NZ* *v NZ*
Auckland 46 Tests	595 2003/04 v South Africa 621-5d 1998/99 by South Africa	26 1954/55 v England 77 1955/56 by West Indies	173 Smith I.D.S. 1989/90 v India 336* Hammond W.R. 1932/33 for England	7-87 Vettori D.L. 1999/00 v Australia 8-76 Prasanna E.A.S. 1975/76 for India
Christchurch 39 Tests	502 1967/68 v India 580-9d 1991/92 by England	65 1970/71 v England 82 1983/84 by England	239 Dowling G.T. 1967/68 v India 258 Nurse S.M. 1968/69 for West Indies	7-116 Hadlee R.J. 1985/86 v Australia 7-47 Tufnell P.C.R. 1991/92 for England
Dunedin 10 Tests	586-7d 1996/97 v Sri Lanka 507-6d 1972/73 by Pakistan	74 1955/56 v West Indies 140 1979/80 by West Indies	267* Young B.A. 1996/97 v Sri Lanka 201 Mushtaq Mohammad 1972/73 for Pakistan	6-51 Hadlee R.J. 1984/85 v Pakistan 7-52 Intikhab Alam 1972/73 for Pakistan
Wellington 44 Tests	671-4 1990/91 v Sri Lanka 660-5d 1994/95 by West Indies	42 1945/46 v Australia 64 1977/78 by England	299 Crowe M.D. 1990/91 v Sri Lanka 267 de Silva P.A. 1990/91 for Sri Lanka	7-23 Hadlee R.J. 1975/76 v India 7-37 Walsh C.A. 1994/95 for West Indies
Napier 4 Tests	561 2004/05 v Sri Lanka 498 2004/05 by Sri Lanka	109 1994/95 v Sri Lanka 183 1994/95 by Sri Lanka	160 Marshall H.J.H. 2004/05 v Sri Lanka 141 Jayawardene D.P.M.D. for Sri Lanka 2004/05	6-54 Martin C.S. 2004/05 v Sri Lanka 5-43 Vaas W.P.J.U.C. 1994/95 for Sri Lanka
Hamilton 13 Tests	563 2003/04 v Pakistan 463 2003/04 by Pakistan	93 1992/93 v Pakistan 97 1999/00 by West Indies	192 Fleming S.P. 2003/04 v Pakistan 190 Dravid R.S. 1998/99 for India	7-27 Cairns C.L. 1999/00 v West Indies 5-22 Waqar Younis 1992/93 for Pakistan
ALL TESTS IN NZ 156 Tests	671-4 1990/91 v Sri Lanka Wellington 660-5d 1994/95 by West Indies Wellington	26 1954/55 v England Auckland 64 1977/78 by England Wellington	299 Crowe M.D. 1990/91 v Sri Lanka Wellington 336* Hammond W.R. 1932/33 for England Auckland	7-23 Hadlee R.J. 1975/76 v India Wellington 8-76 Prasanna E.A.S. 1975/76 for India Auckland

Record Performances in Tests v All Opponents

Opponent	Highest Total by NZ / v NZ	Lowest Total by NZ / v NZ	Highest Individual Innings by NZ / v NZ	Best Bowling by NZ / v NZ
England	551-9d Lord's 1973 593-6 Auckland 1974/75	26 Auckland 1954/55 64 Wellington 1977/78	222 Astle N.J. Christchurch, 2001/02 336* Hammond W.R. Auckland, 1932/33	7-74 Cairns B.L. Leeds, 1983 7-32 Underwood D.L. Lord's, 1969
Australia	553-7d Brisbane 1985/1986 607-6d Brisbane 1993/94	42 Wellington 1945/46 103 Auckland 1985/86	188 Crowe M.D. Brisbane, 1985/86 250 Walters K.D. Christchurch, 1977/78	9-52 Hadlee R.J. Brisbane, 1985/86 6-31 Warne S.K. Hobart 1993/94
South Africa	595 Auckland 2003/04 621-5d Auckland 1998/99	79 Johannesburg 1953/54 148 Johannesburg 1953/54	170 Styris S.B. Auckland, 2003/04 275* Cullinan D.J. Auckland, 1998/99	6-60 Reid J.R. Dunedin, 1963/64 8-53 Lawrence G.B. Johannesburg, 1961/62
West Indies	543-3d Georgetown 1971/72 660-5d Wellington 1994/95	74 Dunedin 1955/56 77 Auckland 1955/56	259 Turner G.M. Georgetown, 1971/72 258 Nurse S.M. Christchurch, 1968/69	7-27 Cairns C.L. Hamilton, 1999/00 7-37 Walsh C.A. Wellington, 1994/95
India	630-6d Mohali 2003/04 583-7d Ahmedabad 1999/00	94 Hamilton 2002/03 81 Wellington 1975/76	239 Dowling G.T. Christchurch, 1967/68 231 Mankad M.H. Madras, 1955/56	7-23 Hadlee R.J. Wellington, 1975/76 8-72 Venkataraghavan S. Delhi, 1964/65
Pakistan	563 Hamilton 2003/04 643 Lahore 2001/02	70 Dacca 1955/56 102 Faisalabad 1990/91	204* Sinclair M.S. Christchurch, 2000/01 329 Inzamam-ul-Haq Lahore, 2001/02	7-52 Pringle C. Faisalabad 1990/91 7-52 Intikhab Alam. Dunedin, 1972/73
Sri Lanka	671-4 Wellington 1990/91 498 Napier 2004/05	102 Colombo 1992/93 93 Wellington 1982/83	299 Crowe M.D. Wellington, 1990/91 267 de Silva P.A. Wellington, 1990/91	6-54 Martin C.S. Napier, 2004/05 6-72 Dharmasena H.D.P.K. Galle, 1997/98
Zimbabwe	487-7d Wellington 2000/01 461 Bulawayo 1997/98	207 Harare 1997/98 119 Bulawayo 2000/01	157 Horne M.J. Auckland, 1997/98 203* Whittall G.J. Bulawayo, 1997/98	6-50 Patel D.N. Harare, 1992/93 8-109 Strang P.A. Bulawayo, 2000/0
Bangladesh	545-6d Chittagong 2004/05 262 Chittagong 2004/05	341-6d Wellington 2001/02 108 Hamilton 2001/02	202 Fleming S.P. Chittagong, 2004/05 67 Mohamad Ashraful Dhaka, 2004/05	7-53 Cairns C.L. Hamilton, 2001/02 6-122 Mohammad Rafique Dhaka, 2004/05

INDIVIDUAL RECORDS

BATTING

Test Centuries

(193 instances)

299	Crowe M.D. v Sri Lanka at Wellington	1990/91
274*	Fleming S.P. v Sri Lanka at Colombo	2002/03
267*	Young B.A. v Sri Lanka at Dunedin	1996/97
259	Turner G.M. v West Indies at Georgetown	1971/72
239	Dowling G.T. v India at Christchurch	1967/68
230*	Sutcliffe B. v India at New Delhi	1955/56
224	Vincent L. v Sri Lanka at Wellington	2004/05
223*	Turner G.M. v West Indies at Kingston	1971/72
222	Astle N.J. v England at Christchurch	2001/02
214	Sinclair M.S. v West Indies at Wellington	1999/00
206	Donnelly M.P. v England at Lord's	1949
204*	Sinclair M.S. v Pakistan at Christchurch	2000/01
202	Fleming S.P. v Bangladesh at Chittagong	2004/05
192	Fleming S.P. v Pakistan at Hamilton	2003/04
188	Crowe M.D. v West Indies at Georgetown	1984/85
188	Crowe M.D. v Australia at Brisbane	1985/86
186	Jones A.H. v Sri Lanka at Wellington	1990/91
185	Wright J.G. v India at Christchurch	1989/90
182	Jarvis T.W. v West Indies at Georgetown	1971/72
180	Reid J.F. v Sri Lanka at Colombo	1983/84
176	Congdon B.E. v England at Nottingham	1973
175	Congdon B.E. v England at Lord's	1973
174*	Coney J.V. v England at Wellington	1983/84
174*	Fleming S.P. v Sri Lanka at Colombo	1997/98
174	Crowe M.D. v Pakistan at Wellington	1988/89
173	Smith I.D.S. v India at Auckland	1989/90
170*	Jones A.H. v India at Auckland	1989/90
170	Styris S.B. v South Africa at Auckland	2003/04
166*	Congdon B.E. v West Indies at Port of Spain	1971/72
161	Edgar B.A. v Australia at Auckland	1981/82
160	Marshall H.J.H. v Sri Lanka at Napier	2004/05
158*	Reid J.F. v Pakistan at Auckland	1984/85
158	Cairns C.L. v South Africa at Auckland	2003/04
157	Horne M.J. v Zimbabwe at Auckland	1997/98
156*	Astle N.J. v Australia at Perth	2001/02
152	Lees W.K. v Pakistan at Karachi	1976/77
151*	Sutcliffe B. v India at Calcutta	1964/65
151*	Hadlee R.J. v Sri Lanka at Colombo	1986/87
150	Jones A.H. v Australia at Adelaide	1987/88
150	Sinclair M.S. v South Africa at Port Elizabeth	2000/01
148	Reid J.F. v Pakistan at Wellington	1984/85
147	Howarth G.P. v West Indies at Christchurch	1979/80
146*	Greatbatch M.J. v Australia at Perth	1989/90
146	Marshall H.J.H. v Australia at Christchurch	2004/05
145	Richardson M.H. v India at Mohali	2003/04
143	Dowling G.T. v India at Dunedin	1967/68
143	Crowe M.D. v England at Wellington	1987/88

143	Jones A.H. v England at Wellington	1991/92
143	Jones A.H. v Australia at Perth	1993/94
143	Richardson M.H. v Bangladesh at Hamilton	2001/02
143	McCullum B.B. v Bangladesh at Dhaka	2004/05
142	Reid J.R. v South Africa at Johannesburg	1961/62
142	Crowe M.D. v England at Lord's	1994
142	McMillan C.D. v Sri Lanka at Colombo	1997/98
142	McMillan C.D. v Zimbabwe at Wellington	2000/01
141	Wright J.G. v Australia at Christchurch	1981/82
141	Astle N.J. v Zimbabwe at Wellington	2000/01
140	Crowe M.D. v Zimbabwe at Harare	1992/93
139	McMillan C.D. v Zimbabwe at Wellington	1997/98
138	Sinclair B.W. v South Africa at Auckland	1963/64
138	Wright J.G. v West Indies at Wellington	1986/87
137*	Sutcliffe B. v India at Hyderabad	1955/56
137*	Howarth G.P. v India at Wellington	1980/81
137*	Vettori D.L. v Pakistan at Hamilton	2003/04
137	Crowe M.D. v Australia at Christchurch	1985/86
137	Crowe M.D. v Australia at Adelaide	1987/88
136	Dempster C.S. v England at Wellington	1929/30
135	Reid J.R. v South Africa at Cape Town	1953/54
133	Greatbatch M.J. v Pakistan at Hamilton	1992/93
133	Horne M.J. v Australia at Hobart	1997/98
132	Congdon B.E. v Australia at Wellington	1973/74
130	Sinclair B.W. v Pakistan at Lahore	1964/65
130	Wright J.G. v England at Auckland	1983/84
130	Fleming S.P. v West Indies at Bridgetown	2001/02
129	Dowling G.T. v India at Bombay	1964/65
129	Edgar B.A. v Pakistan at Christchurch	1978/79
129	Fleming S.P. v England at Auckland	1996/97
128	Reid J.R. v Pakistan at Karachi	1964/65
128	Crowe J.J. v England at Auckland	1983/84
127	Edgar B.A. v West Indies at Auckland	1979/80
126*	Oram J.D.P. v Australia at Brisbane	2004/05
126	Congdon B.E. v West Indies at Bridgetown	1971/72
126	Cairns C.L. v India at Hamilton	1998/99
125	Astle N.J. v West Indies at Bridgetown	1995/96
124	Taylor B.R. v West Indies at Auckland	1967/68
124	Cairns C.L. v Zimbabwe at Harare	2000/01
123*	Reid J.F. v India at Christchurch	1980/81
123	Howarth G.P. v England at Lord's	1978
122	Howarth G.P. v England at Auckland	1977/78
122	Jones A.H. v Sri Lanka at Hamilton	1990/91
121	Parker J.M. v England at Auckland	1974/75
120*	Crowe J.J. v Sri Lanka at Colombo	1986/87
120*	Thomson S.A. v Pakistan at Christchurch	1993/94
120	Dempster C.S. v England at Lord's	1931
120	Reid J.R. v India at Calcutta	1955/56
120	Young B.A. v Pakistan at Christchurch	1993/94
120	Cairns C.L. v Zimbabwe at Auckland	1995/96
119*	Reid J.R. v India at Delhi	1955/56
119*	Burgess M.G. v Pakistan at Dacca	1969/70
119*	Oram J.D.P. v South Africa at Hamilton	2003/04
119	Wright J.G. v England at The Oval	1986
119	Crowe M.D. v West Indies at Wellington	1986/87
119	Latham R.T. v Zimbabwe at Bulawayo	1992/93

119	Styris S.B. v India at Mohali	2003/04
117*	Hastings B.F. v West Indies at Christchurch	1968/69
117*	Wright J.G. v Australia at Wellington	1989/90
117	Mills J.E. v England at Wellington	1929/30
117	Morrison J.F.M. v Australia at Sydney	1973/74
117	Turner G.M. v India at Christchurch	1975/76
117	Fleming S.P. v England at Nottingham	2004
116	Hadlee W.A. v England at Christchurch	1946/47
116	Sutcliffe B. v England at Christchurch	1950/51
116	Pollard V. v England at Nottingham	1973
116	Wright J.G. v England at Wellington	1991/92
115	Crowe M.D. v England at Manchester	1994
114	Sinclair B.W. v England at Auckland	1965/66
114	Howarth G.P. v Pakistan at Napier	1978/79
114	Astle N.J. v Zimbabwe at Auckland	1997/98
114	Astle N.J. v Sri Lanka at Napier	2004/05
113*	Smith I.D.S. v England at Auckland	1983/84
113*	Wright J.G. v India at Napier	1989/90
113	Turner G.M. v India at Kanpur	1976/77
113	Crowe M.D. v India at Auckland	1989/90
112	Crowe J.J. v West Indies at Kingston	1984/85
112	Spearman C.M. v Zimbabwe at Auckland	1995/96
111*	Coney J.V. v Pakistan at Dunedin	1984/85
111	McGregor S.N. v Pakistan at Lahore	1955/56
111	Burgess M.G. v Pakistan at Lahore	1976/77
110*	Turner G.M. v Australia at Christchurch	1973/74
110	Turner G.M. v Pakistan at Dacca	1969/70
110	Hastings B.F. v Pakistan at Auckland	1972/73
110	Wright J.G. v India at Auckland	1980/81
110	Bracewell J.G. v England at Nottingham	1986
110	Horne M.J. v Zimbabwe at Bulawayo	2000/01
110	Parore A.C. v Australia at Perth	2001/02
109	Barton P.T. v South Africa at Port Elizabeth	1961/62
109	Cairns C.L. v Australia at Wellington	1999/00
108*	Crowe M.D. v Pakistan at Lahore	1990/91
108	Parker J.M. v Australia at Sydney	1973/74
108	Reid J.F. v Australia at Brisbane	1985/86
108	Styris S.B. v England at Nottingham	2004
107*	Congdon B.E. v Australia at Christchurch	1976/77
107*	Greatbatch M.J. v England at Auckland	1987/88
107*	Rutherford K.R. v England at Wellington	1987/88
107*	McMillan C.D. v England at Manchester	1999
107	Rabone G.O. v South Africa at Durban	1953/54
107	Redmond R.E. v Pakistan at Auckland	1972/73
107	Wright J.G. v Pakistan at Karachi	1984/85
107	Crowe M.D. v Sri Lanka at Colombo	1992/93
107	Styris S.B. v West Indies at St George's	2001/02
106	Reid J.F. v Pakistan at Hyderabad	1984/85
106	Crowe M.D. v England at Lord's	1986
106	Richardson M.H. v Pakistan at Hamilton	2000/01
106	McMillan C.D. v Bangladesh at Hamilton	2001/02
106	Vincent L. v India at Mohali	2003/04
105*	Pollard V. v England at Lord's	1973
105	Taylor B.R. v India at Calcutta	1964/65
105	Hastings B.F. v West Indies at Bridgetown	1971/72
105	Burgess M.G. v England at Lord's	1973

105	Rutherford K.R. v Sri Lanka at Moratuwa	1992/93
105	Bell M.D. v Pakistan at Hamilton	2000/01
105	Fleming S.P. v Australia at Perth	2001/02
104	Page M.L. v England at Lord's	1931
104	Congdon B.E. v England at Christchurch	1965/66
104	Burgess M.G. v England at Auckland	1970/71
104	Parker J.M. v India at Bombay	1976/77
104	Crowe M.D. v West Indies at Auckland	1986/87
104	Vincent L. v Australia at Perth	2001/02
103	Hadlee R.J. v West Indies at Christchurch	1979/80
103	Wright J.G. v England at Auckland	1987/88
103	Astle N.J. v West Indies at St John's	1995/96
103	Astle N.J. v India at Ahmedabad	2003/04
102*	Astle N.J. v England at Auckland	1996/97
102	Guy J.W. v India at Hyderabad	1955/56
102	Howarth G.P. v England at Auckland	1977/78
102	Rutherford K.R. v Australia at Christchurch	1992/93
101*	Coney J.V. v Australia at Wellington	1985/86
101	Sutcliffe B. v England at Manchester	1949
101	Harris P.G.Z. v South Africa at Cape Town	1961/62
101	Burgess M.G. v West Indies at Kingston	1971/72
101	Hastings B.F. v Australia at Wellington	1973/74
101	Turner G.M. v Australia at Christchurch	1973/74
101	Franklin T.J. v England at Lord's	1990
101	Wright J.G. v Sri Lanka at Hamilton	1990/91
101	Astle N.J. v England at Manchester	1999
101	Richardson M.H. v England at Lord's	2004
100*	Jones A.H. v Sri Lanka at Hamilton	1990/91
100*	Parore A.C. v West Indies at Christchurch	1994/95
100*	McMillan C.D. v India at Mohali	2003/04
100	Vivian H.G. v South Africa at Wellington	1931/32
100	Reid J.R. v England at Christchurch	1962/63
100	Crowe M.D. v England at Wellington	1983/84
100	Horne M.J. v England at Lord's	1999

Century on Test Debut

117 & 7	Mills J.E. v England at Wellington	1929/30
105 & 0*	Taylor B.R. v India at Calcutta	1964/65
107 & 56	Redmond R.E. v Pakistan at Auckland	1972/73
11 & 107*	Greatbatch M.J. v England at Auckland	1987/88
214	Sinclair M.S. v West Indies at Wellington	1999/00
104 & 54	Vincent L. v Australia at Perth	2001/02
107 & 69*	Styris S.B. v West Indies at St George's	2001/02

Centuries in Both Innings of a Test

101 & 110*	Turner G.M. v Australia at Christchurch	1973/74
122 & 102	Howarth G.P. v England at Auckland	1977/78
122 & 100*	Jones A.H. v Sri Lanka at Hamilton	1990/91

NB: *In the same match that Jones achieved this feat A.P. Gurusinha (119 & 102) also scored a century in each innings. This is only the second occasion that a player from each side has scored centuries in each innings of a test (A.R. Morris and D.C.S. Compton, Australia v England, Adelaide, 1946/47).*

200 Runs in a Test

343	Fleming S.P. (274* & 69*) v Sri Lanka at Colombo	2002/03
329	Crowe M.D. (30 & 299) v Sri Lanka at Wellington	1990/91
267	Young B.A. (267*) v Sri Lanka at Dunedin	1996/97
259	Turner G.M. (259) v West Indies at Georgetown	1971/72
254	Sinclair M.S. (204* & 50*) v Pakistan at Christchurch	2000/01
252	Fleming S.P. (78 & 174*) v Sri Lanka at Colombo	1997/98
248	Congdon B.E. (166* & 82) v West Indies at Port of Spain	1971/72
244	Dowling G.T. (239 & 5) v India at Christchurch	1967/68
244	Turner G.M. (223* & 21) v West Indies at Kingston	1971/72
232	Astle N.J. (10 & 222) v England at Christchurch	2001/02
230	Sutcliffe B. (230*) v India at Delhi	1955/56
224	Howarth G.P. (122 & 102) v England at Auckland	1977/78
224	Vincent L. (224) v Sri Lanka at Wellington	2004/05
222	Greatbatch M.J. (76 & 146*) v Australia at Perth	1989/90
222	Jones A.H. (122 & 100*) v Sri Lanka at Hamilton	1990/91
216	Dempster C.S. (136 & 80*) v England at Wellington	1929/30
214	Jones A.H. (150 & 64) v Australia at Adelaide	1987/88
214	Sinclair M.S. (214) v West Indies at Wellington	1999/00
213	Wright J.G. (75 & 138) v West Indies at Wellington	1986/87
211	Turner G.M. (101 & 110*) v Australia at Christchurch	1973/74
206	Donnelly M.P. (206) v England at Lord's	1949
204	Reid J.R. (128 & 76) v Pakistan at Karachi	1964/65
202	Reid J.R. (60 & 142) v South Africa at Johannesburg	1961/62
202	Fleming S.P. (202) v Bangladesh at Chittagong	2004/05
201	Coney J.V. (27 & 174*) v England at Wellington	1983/84
201	Crowe M.D. (140 & 61) v Zimbabwe at Harare	1992/93

A Century and a Fifty in a Test

136 & 80*	Dempster C.S. v England at Wellington	1929/30
52 & 120	Dempster C.S. v England at Lord's	1931
100 & 73	Vivian H.G. v South Africa at Wellington *(aged 19)*	1931/32
107 & 68	Rabone G.O. v South Africa at Durban	1953/54
60 & 142	Reid J.R. v South Africa at Johannesburg	1961/62
74 & 100	Reid J.R. v England at Christchurch	1962/63
128 & 76	Reid J.R. v Pakistan at Karachi	1964/65
59 & 119*	Burgess M.G. v Pakistan at Dacca	1969/70
166* & 82	Congdon B.E. v West Indies at Port of Spain	1971/72
107 & 56	Redmond R.E. v Pakistan at Auckland	1972/73
75 & 138	Wright J.G. v West Indies at Wellington	1986/87
150 & 64	Jones A.H. v Australia at Adelaide	1987/88
76 & 146*	Greatbatch M.J. v Australia at Perth	1989/90
140 & 61	Crowe M.D. v Zimbabwe at Harare	1992/93
105 & 53	Rutherford K.R. v Sri Lanka at Moratuwa	1992/93
57 & 102	Rutherford K.R. v Australia at Christchurch	1992/93
70 & 115	Crowe M.D. v England at Manchester	1994
57 & 120	Cairns C.L. v Zimbabwe at Auckland	1995/96
54 & 125	Astle N.J. v West Indies at Bridgetown	1995/96
78 & 174*	Fleming S.P. v Sri Lanka at Colombo	1997/98
109 & 69	Cairns C.L. v Australia at Wellington	1999/00
141 & 51*	Astle N.J. v Zimbabwe at Wellington	2000/01
204 & 50*	Sinclair M.S. v Pakistan at Christchurch	2000/01
104 & 54	Vincent L. v Australia at Perth	2001/02

107 & 69*	Styris S.B. v West Indies at St George's	2001/02
274* & 69*	Fleming S.P. v Sri Lanka at Colombo	2002/03
103 & 51	Astle N.J. v India at Ahmedabad	2003/04
93 & 101	Richardson M.H. v England at Lord's	2004

NB: *Redmond's feat of scoring a century and a fifty in his only test is unique. Only he and A.G. Ganteaume (112 WI v England, Port of Spain 1947/48) have made a century in their only test.*

Centuries in Three Successive Test Innings

Jones A.H. 186, Wellington, 122 and 100* Hamilton v Sri Lanka 1990/91

Centuries in Two Successive Test Innings

Reid J.R. 119*, Delhi and 120, Calcutta v India 1955/56
Burgess M.G. 119*, Dacca v Pakistan 1969/70 and 104, Auckland v England 1970/71
Congdon B.E. 176, Nottingham and 175, Lord's v England 1973
Pollard V. 116, Nottingham and 105*, Lord's v England 1973
Turner G.M. 101 and 110*, Christchurch v Australia 1973/74
Howarth G.P. 122 and 102, Auckland v England 1977/78 – 94 v England, Oval 1978
Crowe M.D. 143, Wellington v England 1987/88 and 174, Wellington v Pakistan 1988/89
Wright J.G. 185, Christchurch and 113* Napier v India 1989/90
Astle N.J. 125, Bridgetown and 103, St Johns v West Indies 1995/96

NB: *M.G. Burgess scored centuries in three successive tests — all played in different countries! He followed the two centuries above with 15 & 101 v West Indies at Kingston, 1971/72.*

B.E .Congdon scored centuries in successive tests v West Indies 1971/72 — 166 & 82 at Port of Spain and 126 at Bridgetown.*

G.T. Dowling did likewise with 143 & 10 at Dunedin and 239 & 5 at Christchurch v India 1967/68.

In successive tests v Pakistan 1984/85 J.F. Reid scored 106 & 21 at Hyderabad, 97 at Karachi, 148 & 3 at Wellington and 158 at Auckland.*

Fifty on Test Debut

3 & 51	Vivian H.G. v England at The Oval *(aged 18)*	1931
52 & 56	Wallace W.M. v England at Lord's	1937
64 & 0	Moloney D.A.R. v England at Lord's	1937
58	Sutcliffe B. v England at Christchurch	1946/47
50 & 25	Reid J.R. v England at Manchester	1949
93 & 64	Harford N.S. v Pakistan at Lahore	1955/56
54 & 23	Barton P.T. v South Africa at Durban	1961/62
74 & 58	Dowling G.T. v South Africa at Johannesburg	1961/62
64 & 1	Yuile B.W. v England at Auckland	1962/63
10 & 52	Gedye S.G. v South Africa at Wellington	1963/64
66 & 5	Morgan R.W. v Pakistan at Auckland	1964/65
17 & 54	Murray B.A.G. v India at Dunedin	1967/68
50 & 39	Burgess M.G. v India at Dunedin	1967/68
69 & 0*	Thomson K. v India at Christchurch	1967/68
6 & 51*	Howarth G.P. v England at Auckland	1974/75
14 & 92	Anderson R.W. v Pakistan at Lahore	1976/77
55 & 19	Wright J.G. v England at Wellington	1977/78
56 & 0*	Harris C.Z. v Sri Lanka at Moratuwa	1992/93
38 & 53	Young B.A. v Australia at Brisbane	1993/94
16 & 92	Fleming S.P. v India at Hamilton	1993/94
54 & 0	McMillan C.D. v Australia at Brisbane	1997/98
59 & 12	Papps M.H.W. v South Africa at Hamilton	2003/04
57 & 19*	McCullum B.B. v South Africa at Hamilton	2003/04
74 & 7	Cumming C.D. v Australia at Christchurch	2004/05

NB: *H.M. McGirr scored 51 in his first (and only) test innings but it was his second test appearance.*

Two Fifties in a Test

52 & 56	†Wallace W.M. v England at Lord's	1937
58 & 50	Vivian H.G. v England at Old Trafford	1937
96 & 54*	Smith F.B. v England at Headingley	1949
75 & 80	Donnelly M.P. v England at Old Trafford	1949
88 & 54	Sutcliffe B. v England at The Oval	1949
55 & 58	Wallace W.M. v England at The Oval	1949
93 & 64	†Harford N.S. v Pakistan at Lahore	1955/56
74 & 58	†Dowling G.T. v South Africa at Johannesburg	1961/62
55 & 55	Pollard V. v England at Lord's *(aged 19)*	1965
66 & 60	Burgess M.G. v India at Wellington	1967/68
58 & 58	Morrison J.F.M. v England at Auckland	1974/75
54 & 54	Congdon B.E. v India at Auckland	1975/76
55 & 54	Edwards G.N. v England at Auckland	1977/78
62 & 76	Edgar B.A. v England at Nottingham	1983
62 & 60	Howarth G.P. v Sri Lanka at Kandy	1983/84
57 & 84	Crowe M.D. v Pakistan at Dunedin	1984/85
50 & 52	Edgar B.A. v Australia at Sydney	1985/86
56 & 59	Wright J.G. v Australia at Auckland	1985/86
82 & 79	Crowe M.D. v Australia at Melbourne	1987/88
87 & 88	Greatbatch M.J. v Zimbabwe at Bulawayo	1992/93
74 & 89	Rutherford K.R. v Zimbabwe at Harare	1992/93
63 & 59	Rutherford K.R. v India at Hamilton	1993/94
79 & 53	Fleming S.P. v South Africa at Cape Town	1994/95
59 & 51*	Twose R.G. v Pakistan at Christchurch	1995/96
57 & 52	Cairns C.L. v England at Christchurch	1996/97
92 & 84	McMillan C.D. v India at Hamilton	1998/99
93 & 60	Horne M.J. v South Africa at Auckland	1998/99
57 & 99	Fleming S.P. v South Africa at Bloemfontein	2000/01
57 & 71	Vincent L. v England at Wellington	2001/02
95 & 71	Richardson M.H. v West Indies at St George's	2001/02
55 & 55	Richardson M.H. v Sri Lanka at Kandy	2002/03
54 & 83*	McMillan C.D. v India at Ahmedabad	2003/04

† *on debut*

Fifties in Successive Test Innings

The following reached 50 in four successive test innings:

Donnelly M.P. 62, 206, 75 & 80 v England, 1949
Sutcliffe B. 101, 88, 54 v England 1949 and 116 v England 1950/51
Congdon B.E. 166*, 82, 126 and 61* v West Indies 1971/72
54, 54, 58 & 52 v India 1975/76
Coney J.V. 101*, 98, 93 v Australia 1985/86 and 51 v England 1986
Rutherford K.R. 74, 89 v Zimbabwe and 105, 53 v Sri Lanka 1992/93

Highest Score in Each Batting Position

Position in batting order					
1 or 2	267*	Young B.A.	v Sri Lanka	Dunedin	1996/97
3	274*	Fleming S.P.	v Sri Lanka	Colombo	2002/03
4	299	Crowe M.D.	v Sri Lanka	Wellington	1990/91
5	222	Astle N.J.	v England	Christchurch	2001/02
6	174*	Coney J.V.	v England	Wellington	1983/84
7	158	Cairns C.L.	v South Africa	Auckland	2003/04
8	124	Taylor B.R.	v West Indies	Auckland	1968/69
9	173	Smith I.D.S.	v India	Auckland	1989/90
10	83*	Bracewell J.G.	v Australia	Sydney	1985/86
11	68*	Collinge R.O.	v Pakistan	Auckland	1972/73

Century Partnership for The First Wicket

					Final innings total
276	Dempster C.S. Mills J.E.	v England	Wellington	1929/30	440
133	Sutcliffe B. Hadlee W.A.	v England	Christchurch	1946/47	345-9d
112	Sutcliffe B. Scott V.J	v England	Leeds	1949	195-2
121	Sutcliffe B. Scott V.J.	v England	The Oval	1949	345
126	Rabone G.O. Chapple M.E.	v South Africa	Cape Town	1953/54	505
101	McGregor S.N. Leggat J.G.	v India	Delhi	1955/56	112-1
136	Dowling G.T. Jarvis T.W.	v Pakistan	Lahore	1964/65	482-6d
126	Dowling G.T. Murray B.A.G.	v India	Christchurch	1967/68	502
112	Dowling G.T. Turner G.M.	v West Indies	Auckland	1968/69	297-8d
115	Dowling G.T. Turner G.M.	v West Indies	Christchurch	1968/69	367-6
106	Dowling G.T. Murray B.A.G.	v India	Hyderabad	1969/70	181
387	Turner G.M. Jarvis T.W.	v West Indies	Georgetown	1971/72	543-3d
159	Redmond R.E. Turner G.M.	v Pakistan	Auckland	1972/73	402
107	Parker J.M. Turner G.M.	v Australia	Auckland	1973/74	158
100	Wright J.G. Edgar B.A.	v Australia	Sydney	1985/86	193

117	Wright J.G. Franklin T.J.	v England	Auckland	1987/88	350-7d
149	Wright J.G. Franklin T.J.	v India	Napier	1989/90	178-1
185	Wright J.G. Franklin T.J.	v England	Lord's	1990	462-9d
134	Franklin T.J. Wright J.G.	v Sri Lanka	Wellington	1990/91	671-4
161	Franklin T.J. Wright J.G.	v Sri Lanka	Hamilton	1990/91	374-6d
116	Greatbatch M.J. Latham R.T.	v Zimbabwe	Bulawayo	1992/93	325-3d
102	Greatbatch M.J. Latham R.T.	v Zimbabwe	Bulawayo	1992/93	222-5d
110	Hartland B.R. Wright J.G.	v Sri Lanka	Moratuwa	1992/93	195-5
110	Greatbatch M.J. Hartland B.R.	v Pakistan	Hamilton	1992/93	264
111	Greatbatch M.J. Wright J.G.	v Australia	Wellington	1992/93	329
214	Spearman C.M. Twose R.G.	v Zimbabwe	Auckland	1995/96	441-5d
107	Young B.A. Horne M.J.	v South Africa	Christchurch	1998/99	127-1
131	Horne M.J. Stead G.R.	v India	Ahmedabad	1999/00	252-2
102	Richardson M.H. Bell M.D.	v Pakistan	Christchurch	2000/01	476
181	Richardson M.H. Bell M.D.	v Pakistan	Hamilton	2000/01	407-4d
104	Richardson M.H. Horne M.J.	v Bangladesh	Wellington	2001/02	341-6d
117	Richardson M.H. Vincent L.	v West Indies	St George's	2001/02	256-5
231	Richardson M.H. Vincent L.	v India	Mohali	2003/04	630-6d
163	Richardson M.H. Fleming S.P.	v England	Nottingham	2004	384

Pairs in Test Matches Involving New Zealand

By New Zealand *(52)*

*James K.C. v England at Christchurch	1929/30
*Badcock F.T. v England at Christchurch	1929/30
Cowie J. v England at Manchester	1937
*Rowe C.G. v Australia at Wellington	1945/46
*Butterfield L.A. v Australia at Wellington	1945/46
Miller L.S.M. v South Africa at Johannesburg	1953/54
Poore M.B. v England at Auckland	1954/55
Colquhoun I.A. v England at Auckland	1954/55
Hayes J.A. v England at Auckland	1954/55
Blair R.W. v West Indies at Dunedin	1955/56
Cave H.B. v West Indies at Dunedin	1955/56
MacGibbon A.R. v India at Madras	1955/56
Harford N.S. v England at Leeds	1958
Motz R.C. v South Africa at Cape Town	1961/62
Blair R.W. v England at Christchurch	1962/63
Blair R.W. v South Africa at Auckland	1963/64
Shrimpton M.J.F. v South Africa at Auckland	1963/64
Dick A.E. v Pakistan at Rawalpindi	1964/65
Bartlett G.A. v England at Christchurch	1965/66
Jarvis T.W. v Pakistan at Wellington	1972/73
Lees W.K. v England at Christchurch	1977/78
*Bracewell B.P. v England at The Oval	1978
Cairns B.L. v Australia at Brisbane	1980/81
Edgar B.A. v Australia at Perth	1980/81
Troup G.B. v India at Wellington	1980/81
Coney J.V. v Australia at Christchurch	1981/82
Smith I.D.S. v Australia at Christchurch	1981/82
Bracewell J.G. v Pakistan at Hyderabad	1984/85
*Rutherford K.R. v West Indies at Port of Spain	1984/85
Wright J.G. v England at Lord's	1986
Morrison D.K. v Australia at Melbourne	1987/88
*Kuggeleijn C.M. v India at Bangalore	1988/89
Snedden M.C. v India at Hyderabad	1988/89
Morrison D.K. v Sri Lanka at Hamilton	1990/91
Hartland B.R. v England at Auckland	1991/92
Su'a M.L. v Pakistan at Hamilton	1992/93
Morrison D.K. v Australia at Hobart	1993/94
Doull S.B. v West Indies at Wellington	1994/95
Nash D.J. v Sri Lanka at Napier	1994/95
Harris C.Z. v West Indies at Bridgetown	1995/96
Patel D.N. v England at Auckland	1996/97
Doull S.B. v England at Wellington	1996/97
Fleming S.P. v Australia at Hobart	1997/98
Vettori D.L. v Sri Lanka at Galle	1997/98
Wiseman P.J. v India at Wellington	1998/99
Twose R.G. v England at Edgbaston	1999
Wiseman P.J. v India at Kanpur	1999/00
O'Connor S.B. v Australia at Hamilton	1999/00
*Franklin J.E.C. v Pakistan at Auckland	2000/01
Martin C.S. v Pakistan at Auckland	2000/01
Martin C.S. v Pakistan at Lahore	2001/02
Martin C.S. v Australia at Brisbane	2004/05

Against New Zealand *(24)*

Javed Burki for Pakistan at Wellington	1964/65
Jaisimha M.L. for India at Hyderabad	1969/70
Knott A.P.E. for England at Lord's	1973
Stackpole K.R. for Australia at Auckland	1973/74
Chandrasekhar B.S. for India at Wellington	1975/76
Hendrick M. for England at Wellington	1977/78
Kallicharran A.I. for West Indies at Dunedin	1979/80
Wood G.M. for Australia at Perth	1980/81
Holland R.G. for Australia at Brisbane	1985/86
*Patel R.G. for India at Bombay	1988/89
Malcolm D.E. for England at Birmingham	1990
Waqar Younis for Pakistan at Faisalabad	1990/91
Aamer Sohail for Pakistan at Hamilton	1992/93
Langer J.L. for Australia at Auckland	1992/93
Streak H.H. for Zimbabwe at Harare	1997/98
Rennie G.J. for Zimbabwe at Auckland	1997/98
Mbangwa M. for Zimbabwe at Auckland	1997/98
Walsh C.A. for West Indies at Wellington	1999/00
Nkala M.L. for Zimbabwe at Harare	2000/01
Monjurul Islam for Bangladesh at Wellington	2001/02
Laxman V.V.S. for India at Wellington	2002/03
Khan Z. for India at Hamilton	2002/03
Tareq Aziz for Bangladesh at Dhaka	2004/05
Mohammad Ashraful for Bangladesh at Chittagong	2004/05

* *on debut*

BOWLING

Ten Wickets in a Match

(20 instances)

15-123	Hadlee R.J. v Australia at Brisbane	1985/86
12-149	Vettori D.L. v Australia at Auckland	1999/00
12-170	Vettori D.L. v Bangladesh at Chittagong	2004/05
11-58	Hadlee R.J. v India at Wellington	1975/76
11-102	Hadlee R.J. v West Indies at Dunedin	1979/80
11-152	Pringle C. v Pakistan at Faisalabad	1990/91
11-155	Hadlee R.J. v Australia at Perth	1985/86
11-169	Nash D.J. v England at Lord's	1994
11-180	Martin C.S. v South Africa at Auckland	2003/04
10-88	Hadlee R.J. v India at Bombay	1988/89
10-100	Hadlee R.J. v England at Wellington	1977/78
10-100	Cairns C.L. v West Indies at Hamilton	1999/00
10-102	Hadlee R.J. v Sri Lanka at Colombo	1983/84
10-106	Bracewell J.G. v Australia at Auckland	1985/86
10-124	Chatfield E.J. v West Indies at Port of Spain	1984/85
10-140	Cowie J. v England at Manchester	1937
10-140	Hadlee R.J. v England at Nottingham	1986
10-144	Cairns B.L. v England at Leeds	1983
10-166	Troup G.B. v West Indies at Auckland	1979/80
10-176	Hadlee R.J. v Australia at Melbourne	1987/88

Five Wickets in an Innings

(158 instances)

9-52	Hadlee R.J. v Australia at Brisbane	1985/86
7-23	Hadlee R.J. v India at Wellington	1975/76
7-27	Cairns C.L. v West Indies at Hamilton	1999/00
7-52	Pringle C. v Pakistan at Faisalabad	1990/91
7-53	Cairns C.L. v Bangladesh at Hamilton	2001/02
7-65	Doull S.B. v India at Wellington	1998/99
7-74	Taylor B.R. v West Indies at Bridgetown	1971/72
7-74	Cairns B.L. v England at Leeds	1983
7-87	Boock S.L. v Pakistan at Hyderabad	1984/85
7-87	Vettori D.L. v Australia at Auckland	1999/00
7-89	Morrison D.K. v Australia at Wellington	1992/93
7-116	Hadlee R.J. v Australia at Christchurch	1985/86
7-143	Cairns B.L. v England at Wellington	1983/84
6-26	Hadlee R.J. v England at Wellington	1977/78
6-27	Nash D.J. v India at Mohali	1999/00
6-28	Vettori D.L. v Bangladesh at Dhaka	2004/05
6-32	Bracewell J.G. v Australia at Auckland	1985/86
6-37	Morrison D.K. v Australia at Auckland	1992/93
6-38	Bartlett G.A. v India at Christchurch	1967/68
6-40	Cowie J. v Australia at Wellington	1945/46
6-46	Butler I.G. v Pakistan at Wellington	2003/04
6-49	Hadlee R.J. v India at Bombay	1988/89
6-50	Hadlee R.J. v West Indies at Christchurch	1986/87
6-50	Patel D.N. v Zimbabwe at Harare	1992/93
6-51	Hadlee R.J. v Pakistan at Dunedin	1984/85
6-51	Bracewell J.G. v India at Bombay	1988/89
6-52	Cairns C.L. v England at Auckland	1991/92

6-53	Hadlee R.J. v England at The Oval	1983
6-54	Tuffey D.R. v England at Auckland	2001/02
6-54	Martin C.S. v Sri Lanka at Wellington	2004/05
6-57	Hadlee R.J. v Australia at Melbourne	1980/81
6-60	Reid J.R. v South Africa at Dunedin	1963/64
6-63	Motz R.C. v India at Christchurch	1967/68
6-63	Collinge R.O. v India at Christchurch	1975/76
6-64	Vettori D.L. v Sri Lanka at Colombo	1997/98
6-67	Cowie J. v England at Manchester	1937
6-68	Rabone G.O. v South Africa at Cape Town	1953/54
6-68	Hadlee R.J. v West Indies at Dunedin	1979/80
6-69	Motz R.C. v West Indies at Wellington	1968/69
6-69	Morrison D.K. v West Indies at Christchurch	1994/95
6-70	Vettori D.L. v Bangladesh at Chittagong	2004/05
6-71	Hadlee R.J. v Australia at Brisbane	1985/86
6-73	Chatfield E.J. v West Indies at Port of Spain	1984/85
6-76	Cunis R.S. v England at Auckland	1970/71
6-76	Nash D.J. v England at Lord's	1994
6-76	Martin C.S. v South Africa at Auckland	2003/04
6-77	Cairns C.L. v England at Lord's	1999
6-78	Watson W. v Pakistan at Lahore	1990/91
6-80	Hadlee R.J. v England at Lord's	1986
6-80	Hadlee R.J. v England at Nottingham	1986
6-83	Cowie J. v England at Christchurch	1946/47
6-85	Cairns B.L. v West Indies at Christchurch	1979/80
6-85	Bracewell J.G. v Australia at Wellington	1989/90
6-87	Vettori D.L. v Australia at Perth	2001/02
6-90	Hadlee R.J. v Australia at Perth	1985/86
6-95	Troup G.B. v West Indies at Auckland	1979/80
6-100	Hadlee R.J. v Australia at Christchurch	1981/82
6-100	Vettori D.L. v Bangladesh at Chittagong	2004/05
6-105	Hadlee R.J. v West Indies at Auckland	1986/87
6-113	Patel D.N. v Zimbabwe at Bulawayo	1992/93
6-119	Franklin J.E.C v Australia at Auckland	2004/05
6-127	Vettori D.L. v India at Kanpur	1999/00
*6-155	Moir A.M. v England at Christchurch	1950/51
6-162	Burtt T.B. v England at Manchester	1949
*6-168	Cresswell G.F. v England at The Oval	1949
5-26	Taylor B.R. v India at Bombay	1964/65
5-28	Hadlee R.J. v England at Christchurch	1983/84
5-28	Boock S.L. v Sri Lanka at Kandy	1983/84
5-28	Franklin J.E.C v Bangladesh at Dhaka	2004/05
5-29	Hadlee R.J. v Sri Lanka at Colombo	1983/84
5-31	Cairns C.L. v England at The Oval	1999
5-31	Cairns C.L. v Zimbabwe at Bulawayo	2000/01
5-33	Cairns B.L. v India at Wellington	1980/81
5-34	Cameron F.J. v Pakistan at Auckland	1964/65
5-34	Howarth H.J. v India at Nagpur	1969/70
5-34	Hadlee R.J. v West Indies at Dunedin	1979/80
5-39	Hadlee R.J. v Australia at Wellington	1989/90
5-41	Taylor B.R. v West Indies at Port of Spain	1971/72
5-41	Morrison D.K. v Pakistan at Hamilton	1992/93
5-44	Cairns C.L. v West Indies at Wellington	1999/00
5-46	Doull S.B. v Pakistan at Lahore	1996/97
5-47	Hadlee R.J. v India at Christchurch	1980/81

5-48	Cameron F.J. v South Africa at Cape Town	1961/62
5-50	Cairns C.L. v Zimbabwe at Harare	1997/98
5-51	O'Connor S.B. v Australia at Hamilton	1999/00
5-53	Hadlee R.J. v England at Birmingham	1990
5-55	Cairns B.L. v India at Madras	1976/77
5-55	Martin C.S. v South Africa at Wellington	2003/04
5-58	Doull S.B. v Sri Lanka at Dunedin	1996/97
5-61	Morrison D.K. v West Indies at St Johns	1995/96
5-62	Moir A.M. v England at Auckland	1954/55
5-62	Hadlee R.J. v Pakistan at Christchurch	1978/79
5-62	Cairns C.L. v Sri Lanka at Colombo	1997/98
5-62	Vettori D.L. v Australia at Auckland	1999/00
5-63	Hadlee R.J. v Australia at Auckland	1981/82
5-63	Chatfield E.J. v Sri Lanka at Colombo	1983/84
5-63	Davis H.T. v Sri Lanka at Hamilton	1996/97
5-64	MacGibbon A.R. v England at Birmingham	1958
5-65	Congdon B.E. v India at Auckland	1975/76
5-65	Hadlee R.J. v Australia at Sydney	1985/86
5-65	Hadlee R.J. v Australia at Perth	1985/86
5-65	Hadlee R.J. v India at Bangalore	1988/89
5-66	Doull S.B. v Pakistan at Auckland	1993/94
5-67	Boock S.L. v England at Auckland	1977/78
5-67	Hadlee R.J. v Australia at Melbourne	1987/88
5-68	Snedden M.C. v West Indies at Christchurch	1986/87
5-68	Hadlee R.J. v Australia at Adelaide	1987/88
5-69	Burtt T.B. v West Indies at Christchurch	1951/52
5-69	Morrison D.K. v England at Christchurch	1987/88
5-71	Martin C.S. v Zimbabwe at Wellington	2000/01
5-73	Hadlee R.J. v Sri Lanka at Colombo	1983/84
5-73	Su'a M.L. v Pakistan at Hamilton	1992/93
5-73	Doull S.B. v South Africa at Durban	1994/95
5-74	Collinge R.O. v England at Leeds	1973
5-75	Bracewell J.G. v India at Auckland	1980/81
5-75	Morrison D.K. v India at Christchurch	1989/90
5-75	Cairns C.L. v Sri Lanka at Auckland	1990/91
5-75	Doull S.B. v England at Wellington	1996/97
5-77	Hart M.N. v South Africa at Johannesburg	1994/95
5-78	Bond S.E. v West Indies at Bridgetown	2001/02
5-79	Cairns C.L. v England at Nottingham	2004
5-80	Howarth H.J. v Pakistan at Karachi	1969/70
5-82	Collinge R.O. v Australia at Auckland	1973/74
*5-82	Wiseman P.J. v Sri Lanka at Colombo	1997/98
5-83	Cameron F.J. v South Africa at Johannesburg	1961/62
5-84	Hadlee R.J. v England at Lord's	1978
5-84	Vettori D.L. v Sri Lanka at Hamilton	1996/97
5-85	Su'a M.L. v Zimbabwe at Harare	1992/93
*5-86	Taylor B.R. v India at Calcutta	1964/65
5-86	Motz R.C. v India at Dunedin	1967/68
5-87	Cairns B.L. v Australia at Brisbane	1980/81
5-87	Hadlee R.J. v Australia at Perth	1980/81
5-87	Tuffey D.R. v Pakistan at Hamilton	2003/04
5-90	Wiseman P.J. v Zimabwe at Bulawayo	2000/01
5-93	Hadlee R.J. v England at Lord's	1983
5-93	Patel D.N. v Australia at Auckland	1992/93
5-93	Nash D.J. v England at Lord's	1994

5-95	Chatfield E.J. v England at Leeds	1983
5-97	Burtt T.B. v England at Leeds	1949
5-98	Morrison D.K. v India at Napier	1989/90
5-104	Hadlee R.J. v Pakistan at Auckland	1978/79
5-104	Bond S.E. v West Indies at St George's	2001/02
5-104	Martin C.S. v South Africa at Auckland	2003/04
5-106	Vettori D.L. v Australia at Christchurch	2004/05
5-108	Motz R.C. v England at Birmingham	1965
5-109	Hadlee R.J. v Australia at Melbourne	1987/88
5-113	Motz R.C. v West Indies at Christchurch	1968/69
5-117	Boock S.L. v Pakistan at Wellington	1984/85
5-121	Hadlee R.J. v Pakistan at Lahore	1976/77
5-127	Cowie J. v England at Leeds	1949
5-137	Cairns C.L. v Pakistan at Rawalpindi	1996/97
5-138	Vettori D.L. v Australia at Hobart	2001/02
5-145	Morrison D.K. v India at Auckland	1989/90
5-146	Cairns C.L. v Australia at Brisbane	2001/02
5-148	O'Sullivan D.R. v Australia at Adelaide	1973/74
5-152	Martin C.S. v Australia at Brisbane	2004/05
5-152	Vettori D.L. v Australia at Adelaide	2004/05
5-153	Morrison D.K. v Sri Lanka at Wellington	1990/91

** on debut*

Hat-tricks

Petherick P.J. v Pakistan at Lahore	1976/77
Franklin J.E.C. v Bangladesh at Dhaka	2004/05

All Round Cricket

Rabone G.O. 56 and 6-68 & 1-16 v South Africa at Cape Town	1953/54
Taylor B.R. 105 & 0 and 5-86 v India at Calcutta	1964/65
Congdon B.E. 54 & 54 and 5-65 v India at Auckland	1975/76
Hadlee R.J. 54* & 5 and 5-104 & 0-8 v Pakistan at Auckland	1978/79
Hadlee R.J. 51 & 17 and 5-34 & 6-68 v West Indies at Dunedin	1979/80
Hadlee R.J. 84 & 11 and 6-53 & 2-99 v England at The Oval	1983
Cairns B.L. 3 & 64 and 7-143 v England at Wellington	1983/84
Hadlee R.J. 99 and 3-16 & 5-28 v England at Christchurch	1983/84
Hadlee R.J. 54 and 9-52 & 6-71 v Australia at Brisbane	1985/86
Hadlee R.J. 68 and 6-80 & 4-60 v England at Nottingham	1986
Bracewell J.G. 52 & 32 and 2-81 & 6-51 v India at Bombay	1988/89
Patel D.N. 6 & 58* and 2-81 & 6-50 v Zimbabwe at Harare	1992/93
Nash D.J. 56 and 6-76 & 5-93 v England at Lord's	1994
Cairns C.L. 12 & 71* and 5-50 & 0-44 v Zimbabwe at Harare	1997/98
Cairns C.L. 11 & 80 and 5-31 & 1-50 v England at The Oval	1999
Cairns C.L. 72 and 3-73 & 7-27 v West Indies at Hamilton	1999/00
Cairns C.L. 61 & 43 and 5-146 & 1-29 v Australia at Brisbane	2001/02
Vettori D.L. 20 & 59 and 5-152 & 1-35 v Australia at Brisbane	2004/05

** Taylor is the only player from any country to score a century and take five wickets in an innings on debut.*

WICKETKEEPING AND FIELDING

MOST DISMISSALS IN AN INNINGS BY A WICKETKEEPER

7*	Smith I.D.S. v Sri Lanka at Hamilton *(all caught)*	1990/91
5	Harford R.I. v India at Wellington *(all caught)*	1967/68
5	Wadsworth K.J. v Pakistan at Auckland *(all caught)*	1972/73
5	Lees W.K. v Sri Lanka at Wellington *(all caught)*	1982/83
5	Smith I.D.S. v England at Auckland *(4ct 1st)*	1983/84
5	Smith I.D.S. v Sri Lanka at Auckland *(all caught)*	1990/91
5	Parore A.C. v England at Auckland *(all caught)*	1991/92
5	Parore A.C. v Sri Lanka at Colombo *(4ct 1st)*	1992/93
5	Parore A.C. v Zimbabwe at Harare *(all caught)*	2000/01
5	Parore A.C. v Pakistan at Auckland *(all caught)*	2000/01

** equals world test record*

MOST DISMISSALS IN A MATCH

8	Lees W.K. v Sri Lanka at Wellington *(all caught)*	1982/83
8	Smith I.D.S. v Sri Lanka at Hamilton *(all caught)*	1990/91
7	Dick A.E. v South Africa at Durban *(6ct 1st)*	1961/62
7	Harford R.I. v India at Wellington *(all caught)*	1967/68
7	Smith I.D.S. v India at Wellington *(all caught)*	1980/81
7	Smith I.D.S. v England at Leeds *(all caught)*	1983
7	Parore A.C. v Pakistan at Auckland *(all caught)*	2000/01
7	Parore A.C. v Pakistan at Hamilton *(all caught)*	2000/01

MOST STUMPINGS IN AN INNINGS

2	Mooney F.L.H. v England at Leeds	1949
2	Milburn B.D. v West Indies at Christchurch	1968/69
2	Lees W.K. v Pakistan at Hyderabad	1976/77
2	Lees W.K. v Pakistan at Karachi	1976/77
2	Lees W.K. v India at Madras	1976/77

MOST STUMPINGS IN A MATCH

2	5 instances as above plus	
	Smith I.D.S. v Australia at Sydney	1985/86
	Parore A.C. v Australia at Auckland	1999/00

REPLACEMENT WICKETKEEPERS IN TEST MATCHES

Wicketkeeper	*Replacement*	*Dismissal*			
Mooney F.L.H.	Sutcliffe B.	—	v South Africa	Port Elizabeth	1953/54
Petrie E.C.	Reid J.R.	Richardson P.E. *(st)*	v England	Manchester	1958
Petrie E.C.	Reid J.R.	—	v England	Christchurch	1958/59
Ward J.T.	Morgan R.W.	Jaisimha M.L. *(c)*	v India	Calcutta	1964/65
Ward J.T.	Congdon B.E.	Hanumant Singh *(c)*	v India	Delhi	1964/65
Dick A.E.	Reid J.R.	—	v Pakistan	Lahore	1964/65
Dick A.E.	Congdon B.E. (sub)	Pervez Sajjad *(st)*	v Pakistan	Lahore	1964/65
Lees W.K.	Anderson R.W.	—	v Pakistan	Hyderabad	1976/77
Smith I.D.S.	Edgar B.A.	Laird B.M. *(c)*	v Australia	Christchurch	1981/82
Smith I.D.S.	Crowe M.D.	—	v West Indies	Kingston	1984/85
Smith I.D.S.	Horne P.A.	—	v Australia	Melbourne	1987/88
Smith I.D.S.	Blain T.E.	—	v India	Hyderabad	1988/89
Smith I.D.S.	Horne P.A.	—	v Pakistan	Faisalabad	1990/91
Smith I.D.S.	Parore A.C. (sub)	Shoaib Mohammad *(c)* Aaqib Javed *(c)*	v Pakistan	Faisalabad	1990/91

MOST CATCHES IN AN INNINGS

5	Fleming S.P. v Zimbabwe at Harare	1997/98
4	Crowe J.J. v West Indies at Bridgetown	1984/85
4	Crowe M.D. v West Indies at Kingston	1984/85
4	Fleming S.P. v Australia at Brisbane	1997/98

MOST CATCHES IN A MATCH

7	Fleming S.P. v Zimbabwe at Harare	1997/98
6	Young B.A. v Pakistan at Auckland	1993/94
6	Fleming S.P. v Australia at Brisbane	1997/98
5	Harris C.Z. v Zimbabwe at Bulawayo	1997/98
5	Fleming S.P. v India at Wellington	1998/99
5	Sinclair M.S. v Bangladesh at Chittagong	2004/05

RECORD PARTNERSHIPS

NEW ZEALAND v ENGLAND

New Zealand

1st	276	Dempster C.S. & Mills J.E.	Wellington	1929/30
2nd	241	Wright J.G. & Jones A.H.	Wellington	1991/92
3rd	210	Edgar B.A. & Crowe M.D.	Lord's	1986
4th	155	Crowe M.D. & Greatbatch M.J.	Wellington	1987/88
5th	180	Crowe M.D. & Thomson S.A.	Lord's	1994
6th	141	Crowe M.D. & Parore A.C.	Manchester	1994
7th	117	Patel D.N. & Cairns C.L.	Christchurch	1991/92
8th	104	Roberts A.W. & Moloney D.A.R.	Lord's	1937
9th	118	Coney J.V. & Cairns B.L.	Wellington	1983/84
10th	118	Astle N.J. & Cairns C.L.	Christchurch	2001/02

England

1st	223	Fowler G. & Tavare C.J.	The Oval	1983
2nd	369	Edrich J.H. & Barrington K.F.	Leeds	1965
3rd	245	Hammond W.R. & Hardstaff J.	Lord's	1937
4th	266	Denness M.H. & Fletcher K.W.R.	Auckland	1974/75
5th	242	Hammond W.R. & Ames L.E.G.	Christchurch	1932/33
6th	281	Thorpe G.P. & Flintoff A.	Christchurch	2001/02
7th	149	Knott A.P.E. & Lever P.	Auckland	1970/71
8th	246	Ames L.E.G. & Allen G.O.B.	Lord's	1931
9th	163*	Cowdrey M.C. & Smith A.C.	Wellington	1962/63
10th	59	Knott A.P.E. & Gifford N.	Nottingham	1973

NEW ZEALAND v AUSTRALIA

New Zealand

1st	111	Greatbatch M.J. & Wright J.G.	Wellington	1992/93
2nd	132	Horne M.J. & Parore A.C.	Hobart	1997/98
3rd	224	Reid J.F. & Crowe M.D.	Brisbane	1985/86
4th	229	Congdon B.E. & Hastings B.F.	Wellington	1973/74
5th	97	Fleming S.P. & McMillan C.D.	Hobart	2001/02
6th	110	Fleming S.P. & Cairns C.L.	Wellington	1999/00
7th	132*	Coney J.V. & Hadlee R.J.	Wellington	1985/86
8th	253	Astle N.J. & Parore A.C.	Perth	2001/02
9th	73	Howarth H.J. & Hadlee D.R.	Christchurch	1976/77
10th	124	Bracewell J.G. & Boock S.L.	Sydney	1985/86

Australia

1st	224	Langer J.L. & Hayden M.L.	Brisbane	2001/02
2nd	235	Slater M.J. & Boon D.C.	Hobart	1993/94
3rd	264	Chappell I.M. & Chappell G.S.	Wellington	1973/74
4th	184	Langer J.L. & Lehmann D.S.	Adelaide	2004/05
5th	213	Ritchie G.M. & Matthews G.R.J.	Wellington	1985/86
6th	256	Martyn D.R. & Gilchrist A.C.	Wellington	2004/05
7th	217	Walters K.D. & Gilmour G.J.	Christchurch	1976/77
8th	135	Gilchrist A.C. & Lee B.	Brisbane	2001/02
9th	74	Gilchrist A.C. & Kasprowicz M.S.	Auckland	2004/05
10th	114	Gillespie J.N. & McGrath G.D.	Brisbane	2004/05

NEW ZEALAND v SOUTH AFRICA

New Zealand

1st	126	Rabone G.O. & Chapple M.E.	Cape Town	1953/54
2nd	90	Horne M.J. & Astle N.J.	Auckland	1998/99
3rd	125	Richardson M.H. & Styris S.B.	Auckland	2003/04
4th	171	Sinclair B.W. & McGregor S.N.	Auckland	1963/64
5th	176	Reid J.R. & Beck J.E.F.	Cape Town	1953/54
6th	100	Vivian H.G. & Badcock F.T.	Wellington	1931/32
7th	225	Cairns C.L. & Oram J.D.P.	Auckland	2003/04
8th	113	Oram J.D.P. & Vettori D.L.	Hamilton	2003/04
9th	87	Oram J.D.P. & Wiseman P.J.	Hamilton	2003/04
10th	57	Doull S.B. & de Groen R.P.	Johannesburg	1994/95

South Africa

1st	196	Mitchell B. & Christy J.A.H.	Christchurch	1931/32
2nd	315*	Gibbs H.H. & Kallis J.H.	Christchurch	1998/99
3rd	183	Kirsten G. & Cullinan D.J.	Auckland	1998/99
4th	171	Smith G.C. & Kirsten G.	Wellington	2003/04
5th	141	Cullinan D.J. & Rhodes J.N.	Auckland	1998/99
6th	126*	Cullinan D.J. & Pollock S.M.	Auckland	1998/99
7th	246	McGlew D.J. & Murray A.R.A.	Wellington	1952/53
8th	136	McKenzie N.D. & Boje N.	Port Elizabeth	2000/01
9th	60	Pollock P.M. & Adcock N.A.T.	Port Elizabeth	1961/62
10th	47	McGlew D.J. & Bromfield H.D.	Port Elizabeth	1961/62

NEW ZEALAND v WEST INDIES

New Zealand

1st	387	Turner G.M. & Jarvis T.W.	Georgetown	1971/72
2nd	210	Howarth G.P. & Crowe J.J.	Kingston	1984/85
3rd	241	Wright J.G. & Crowe M.D.	Wellington	1986/87
4th	189	Sinclair M.S. & Astle N.J.	Wellington	1999/00
5th	144	Astle N.J. & Vaughan J.T.C.	Bridgetown	1995/96
6th	220	Turner G.M. & Wadsworth K.J.	Kingston	1971/72
7th	143	Crowe M.D. & Smith I.D.S.	Georgetown	1984/85
8th	136	Congdon B.E. & Cunis R.S.	Port of Spain	1971/72
9th	62*	Pollard V. & Cunis R.S.	Auckland	1968/69
10th	45	Morrison D.K. & Kennedy R.J.	Bridgetown	1995/96

West Indies

1st	276	Griffith A.F.G. & Campbell S.L.	Hamilton	1999/00
2nd	269	Fredericks R.C. & Rowe L.G.	Kingston	1971/72
3rd	221	Lara B.C. & Adams J.C.	Wellington	1994/95
4th	162	Weekes E.D. & Smith O.G.	Dunedin	1955/56
	162	Greenidge C.G. & Kallicharan A.I.	Christchurch	1979/80
5th	189	Worrell F.M.M. & Walcott C.L.	Auckland	1951/52
6th	254	Sobers G.S. & Davis C.A.	Bridgetown	1971/72
7th	143	Atkinson D.S. & Goddard J.D.C.	Christchurch	1955/56
8th	83	Richards I.V.A. & Marshall M.D.	Bridgetown	1984/85
9th	70	Marshall M.D. & Garner J.	Bridgetown	1984/85
10th	31	Findlay T.M. & Shillingford G.C.	Bridgetown	1971/72

NEW ZEALAND v INDIA

New Zealand

1st	231	Richardson M.H. & Vincent L.	Mohali	2003/04
2nd	155	Dowling G.T. & Congdon B.E.	Dunedin	1967/68
3rd	222*	Sutcliffe B. & Reid J.R.	New Delhi	1955/56
4th	160	Twose R.G. & McMillan C.D.	Hamilton	1998/99
5th	140	McMillan C.D. & Parore A.C.	Hamilton	1998/99
6th	137	McMillan C.D. & Cairns C.L.	Wellington	1998/99
7th	163	Sutcliffe B. & Taylor B.R.	Calcutta	1964/65
8th	137	Nash D.J. & Vettori D.L.	Wellington	1998/99
9th	136	Smith I.D.S. & Snedden M.C.	Auckland	1989/90
10th	61	Ward J.T. & Collinge R.O.	Madras	1964/65

India

1st	413	Mankad M.H. & Roy P.	Madras	1955/56
2nd	204	Gavaskar S.M. & Amarnath S.	Auckland	1975/76
3rd	238	Umrigar P.R. & Manjrekar V.L.	Hyderabad	1955/56
4th	281	Tendulkar S.R. & Ganguly S.C.	Ahmedabad	1999/00
5th	182	Dravid R.S. & Ganguly S.C.	Ahmedabad	2003/04
6th	193*	Sardesai D.N. & Hanumant Singh	Bombay	1964/65
7th	128	Tendulkar S.R. & More K.S.	Napier	1989/90
8th	144	Dravid R.S. & Srinath J.	Hamilton	1998/99
9th	105	Kirmani S.M.H. & Bedi B.S.	Bombay	1976/77
	105	Kirmani S.M.H. & Yadav N.S.	Auckland	1980/81
10th	57	Desai R.B. & Bedi B.S.	Dunedin	1967/68

NEW ZEALAND v PAKISTAN

New Zealand

1st	181	Richardson M.H. & Bell M.D.	Hamilton	2000/01
2nd	195	Wright J.G. & Howarth G.P.	Napier	1978/79
3rd	178	Sinclair B.W. & Reid J.R.	Lahore	1964/65
4th	147	McMillan C.D. & Fleming S.P.	Hamilton	2000/01
5th	183	Burgess M.G. & Anderson R.W.	Lahore	1976/77
6th	145	Reid J.F. & Hadlee R.J.	Wellington	1984/85
7th	186	Lees W.K. & Hadlee R.J.	Karachi	1976/77
8th	125	Fleming S.P. & Vettori D.L.	Hamilton	2003/04
9th	99	Vettori D.L. & Tuffey D.R.	Hamilton	2003/04
10th	151	Hastings B.F. & Collinge R.O.	Auckland	1972/73

Pakistan

1st	172	Rameez Raja & Shoaib Mohammad	Karachi	1990/91
2nd	262	Saeed Anwar & Ijaz Ahmed	Rawalpindi	1996/97
3rd	248	Shoaib Mohammad & Javed Miandad	Auckland	1988/89
4th	350	Mushtaq Mohammad & Asif Iqbal	Dunedin	1972/73
5th	281	Javed Miandad & Asif Iqbal	Lahore	1976/77
6th	217	Hanif Mohammad & Majid Khan	Lahore	1964/65
7th	308	Waqar Hassan & Imtiaz Ahmed	Lahore	1955/56
8th	89	Anil Dalpat & Iqbal Qasim	Karachi	1984/85
9th	78	Inzamam-ul-Haq & Shoaib Akhtar	Lahore	2001/02
10th	65	Salah-ud-din & Mohammad Farooq	Rawalpindi	1964/65

NEW ZEALAND v SRI LANKA

New Zealand

1st	161	Franklin T.J. & Wright J.G.	Hamilton	1990/91
2nd	172	Richardson M.H. & Fleming S.P.	Colombo	2002/03
3rd	467	Jones A.H. & Crowe M.D.	Wellington	1990/91
4th	240	Fleming S.P. & McMillan C.D.	Colombo	1997/98
5th	151	Rutherford K.R. & Harris C.Z.	Moratuwa	1992/93
6th	246*	Crowe J.J. & Hadlee R.J.	Colombo	1986/87
7th	48	Vincent L. & Franklin J.E.C.	Wellington	2004/05
8th	98	Vincent L. & Mills K.D.	Wellington	2004/05
9th	59	Vincent L. & Wiseman P.J.	Wellington	2004/05
10th	52	Lees W.K. & Chatfield E.J.	Christchurch	1982/83

Sri Lanka

1st	102	Mahanama R.S. & Hathurusinghe U.C.	Colombo	1992/93
2nd	138	Mahanama R.S. & Gurusinha A.P.	Moratuwa	1992/93
3rd	184	Atapattu M.S. & Jayawardene D.P.M.D.	Napier	2004/05
4th	192	Gurusinha A.P. & Tillakaratne H.P.	Dunedin	1994/95
5th	133	Jayawardene D.P.M.D. & Tillakaratne H.P.	Colombo	2002/03
6th	109	Madugalle R.S. & Ranatunga A.	Colombo	1983/84
	109	Kuruppu D.S.B.P. & Madugalle R.S.	Colombo	1986/87
7th	137	Kaluwitharana R.S. & Vaas W.P.J.U.C.	Dunedin	1996/97
8th	89	Samaraweera T.T. & Chandana U.D.U.	Wellington	2004//05
9th	31	Labrooy G.F. & Ratnayake R.J.	Auckland	1990/91
	31	Jayasuriya S.T. & Ratnayake R.J.	Auckland	1990/91
10th	71	Kaluwitharana R.S. & Muralidaran M.	Colombo	1997/98

NEW ZEALAND v ZIMBABWE

New Zealand

1st	214	Spearman C.M. & Twose R.G.	Auckland	1995/96
2nd	127	Latham R.T. & Jones A.H.	Bulawayo	1992/93
3rd	71	Jones A.H. & Crowe M.D.	Bulawayo	1992/93
4th	243	Horne M.J. & Astle N.J.	Auckland	1997/98
5th	222	Astle N.J. & McMillan C.D.	Wellington	2000/01
6th	82*	Parore A.C. & Germon L.K.	Hamilton	1995/96
7th	108	McMillan C.D. & Nash D.J.	Wellington	1997/98
8th	144	Cairns C.L. & Nash D.J.	Harare	2000/01
9th	78	Parore A.C. & Vettori D.L.	Bulawayo	2000/01
10th	27	McMillan C.D. & Doull S.B.	Auckland	1997/98

Zimbabwe

1st	156	Rennie G.J. & Flower G.W.	Harare	1997/98
2nd	107	Arnott K.J. & Campbell A.D.R.	Harare	1992/93
3rd	70	Flower A. & Whittall G.J.	Bulawayo	1997/98
4th	130	Rennie G.J. & Flower A.	Wellington	2000/01
5th	131	Flower A. & Whittall G.J.	Harare	2000/01
6th	151	Whittall G.J. & Streak H.H.	Harare	2000/01
7th	91	Whittall G.J. & Strang P.A.	Hamilton	1995/96
8th	94	Campbell A.D.R. & Streak H.H.	Wellington	1997/98
9th	46	Crocker G.J. & Burmester M.G.	Harare	1992/93
10th	40	Whittall G.J. & Matambanadzo E.	Bulawayo	1997/98

NEW ZEALAND v BANGLADESH

New Zealand

1st	104	Richardson M.H. & Horne M.J.	Wellington	2001/02
2nd	63	Sinclair M.S. & Fleming S.P.	Dhaka	2004/05
3rd	204	Fleming S P & Styris S B	Chittagong	2004/05
4th	130	Fleming S.P. & McMillan C.D.	Wellington	2001/02
5th	190	Richardson M.H. & McMillan C.D.	Hamilton	2001/02
6th	89	McMillan C.D. & Cairns C.L.	Hamilton	2001/02
7th	71	McCullum B.B. & Vettori D.L.	Dhaka	2004/05
8th	57	McCullum B.B. & Franklin J.E.C.	Dhaka	2004/05
9th	20	McCullum B.B. & Wiseman P.J.	Dhaka	2004/05
10th	31	Wiseman P.J. & Butler I.G.	Dhaka	2004/05

Bangladesh

1st	39	Javed Omer & Al Sahariar	Hamilton	2001/02
2nd	32	Javed Omer & Aftab Ahmed	Chittagong	2004/05
3rd	60	Habibul Bashar & Aminul Islam	Hamilton	2001/02
4th	115	Rajin Saleh & Mohammad Ashraful	Dhaka	2004/05
5th	26	Javed Omer & Alok Kapali	Chittagong	2004/05
6th	49	Rajin Saleh & Khalid Masud	Chittagong	2004/05
7th	38	Khalid Masud & Mushfiqur Rahman	Chittagong	2004/05
8th	39	Mushfiqur Rahman & Mohammad Rafique	Chittagong	2004/05
9th	49	Khaled Masud & Masrafe bin Mortaza	Wellington	2001/02
10th	45	Tapash Baisya & Enamul Haque	Chittagong	2004/05

CAREER RECORDS

Averages

	M	I	NO	HS	Runs	Ave	100	50	Ct	St	Wkts	Runs	Ave	Best	5WI	10WM
Adams A.R.	1	2	0	11	18	9.00	—	—	1	—	6	105	17.50	3-44	—	—
Alabaster J.C.	21	34	6	34	272	9.71	—	—	7	—	49	1863	38.02	4-46	—	—
Allcott C.F.W.	6	7	2	33	113	22.60	—	—	3	—	6	541	90.17	2-102	—	—
Allott G.I.	10	15	7	8*	27	3.37	—	—	2	—	19	1111	58.47	4-74	—	—
Anderson R.W.	9	18	0	92	423	23.50	—	3	1	—	—	—	—	—	—	—
Anderson W.M.	1	2	0	4	5	2.50	—	—	1	—	—	—	—	—	—	—
Andrews B.	2	3	2	17	22	22.00	—	—	1	—	2	154	77.00	2-40	—	—
Astle N.J.	71	122	10	222	4235	37.81	10	21	65	—	46	1975	42.93	3-27	—	—
Badcock F.T.	7	9	2	64	137	19.57	—	2	1	—	16	610	38.13	4-80	—	—
Barber R.T.	1	2	0	12	17	8.50	—	—	1	—	—	—	—	—	—	—
Bartlett G.A.	10	18	1	40	263	15.47	—	—	8	—	24	792	33.00	6-38	1	—
Barton P.T.	7	14	0	109	285	20.36	1	1	4	—	—	—	—	—	—	—
Beard D.D.	4	7	2	31	101	20.20	—	—	2	—	9	302	33.56	3-22	—	—
Beck J.E.F.	8	15	0	99	394	26.27	—	3	—	—	—	—	—	—	—	—
Bell M.D.	13	23	1	105	484	22.00	1	2	10	—	—	—	—	—	—	—
Bell W.	2	3	3	21*	21	—	—	—	1	—	2	235	117.50	1-54	—	—
Bilby G.P.	2	4	0	28	55	13.75	—	—	3	—	—	—	—	—	—	—
***Blain** T.E.	11	20	3	78	456	26.82	—	2	19	2	—	—	—	—	—	—
Blair R.W.	19	34	6	64*	189	6.75	—	1	5	—	43	1515	35.23	4-85	—	—
Blunt R.C.	9	13	1	96	330	27.50	—	1	5	—	12	472	39.33	3-17	—	—
Bolton B.A.	2	3	0	33	59	19.67	—	—	1	—	—	—	—	—	—	—
Bond S.E.	10	10	5	17	53	10.60	—	—	4	—	43	1045	24.30	5-78	2	—
Boock S.L.	30	41	8	37	207	6.27	—	—	14	—	74	2564	34.64	7-87	4	—
Bracewell B.P.	6	12	2	8	24	2.40	—	—	1	—	14	585	41.78	3-110	—	—
Bracewell J.G.	41	60	11	110	1001	20.42	1	4	31	—	102	3653	35.81	6-32	4	1
Bradburn G.E.	7	10	2	30*	105	13.12	—	—	6	—	6	460	76.66	3-134	—	—
Bradburn W.P.	2	4	0	32	62	15.50	—	—	2	—	—	—	—	—	—	—
Brown V.R.	2	3	1	36*	51	25.50	—	—	3	—	1	176	176.00	1-17	—	—
Burgess M.G.	50	92	6	119*	2684	31.21	5	14	34	—	6	212	35.33	3-23	—	—
Burke C.	1	2	0	3	4	2.00	—	—	—	—	2	30	15.00	2-30	—	—
Burtt T.B.	10	15	3	42	252	21.00	—	—	2	—	33	1170	35.45	6-162	3	—
Butler I.G.	8	10	2	26	76	9.50	—	—	4	—	24	884	36.83	6-46	1	—
Butterfield L.A.	1	2	0	0	0	0.00	—	—	—	—	0	24	—	—	—	—
Cairns B.L.	43	65	8	64	928	16.28	—	2	30	—	130	4279	32.91	7-74	6	1
Cairns C.L.	62	104	5	158	3320	33.53	5	22	14	—	218	6410	29.40	7-27	13	1
Cameron F.J.	19	30	20	27*	116	11.60	—	—	2	—	62	1849	29.82	5-34	3	—
Cave H.B.	19	31	5	22*	229	8.81	—	—	8	—	34	1467	43.15	4-21	—	—
Chapple M.E.	14	27	1	76	497	19.12	—	3	10	—	1	84	84.00	1-24	—	—
Chatfield E.J.	43	54	33	21*	180	8.57	—	—	7	—	123	3958	32.17	6-73	3	1
Cleverley D.C.	2	4	3	10*	19	19.00	—	—	—	—	0	130	—	—	—	—
Collinge R.O.	35	50	13	68*	533	14.41	—	2	10	—	116	3393	29.25	6-63	3	—
†**Colquhoun** I.A.	2	4	2	1*	1	0.50	—	—	4	—	—	—	—	—	—	—
Coney J.V.	52	85	14	174*	2668	37.57	3	16	64	—	27	966	35.77	3-28	—	—
***Congdon** B.E.	61	114	7	176	3448	32.22	7	19	44*	—	59	2154	36.51	5-65	1	—
Cowie J.	9	13	4	45	90	10.00	—	—	3	—	45	969	21.53	6-40	4	1
Cresswell G.F.	3	5	3	12*	14	7.00	—	—	—	—	13	292	22.46	6-168	1	—
Cromb I.B.	5	8	2	51*	123	20.50	—	1	1	—	8	442	55.25	3-113	—	—
Crowe J.J.	39	65	4	128	1601	26.24	3	6	41	—	0	9	—	—	—	—
Crowe M.D.	77	131	11	299	5444	45.36	17	18	71	—	14	676	48.28	2-25	—	—

	M	I	NO	HS	Runs	Ave	100	50	Ct	St	Wkts	Runs	Ave	Best	5WI	10WM
Cunis R.S.	20	31	8	51	295	12.83	—	1	1	—	51	1887	37.00	6-76	1	—
Cumming C.D.	5	9	1	74	208	26.00	—	1	2	—	—	—	—	—	—	—
D'Arcy J.W.	5	10	0	33	136	13.60	—	—	—	—	—	—	—	—	—	—
de Groen R.P.	5	10	4	26	45	7.50	—	—	—	—	11	505	45.90	3-40	—	—
Davis H.T.	5	7	4	8*	20	6.66	—	—	4	—	17	499	29.35	5-63	1	—
Dempster C.S.	10	15	4	136	723	65.73	2	5	2	—	0	10	—	—	—	—
Dempster E.W.	5	8	2	47	106	17.67	—	—	1	—	2	219	109.50	1-24	—	—
†**Dick** A.E.	17	30	4	50*	370	14.73	—	1	47	4	—	—	—	—	—	—
Dickinson G.R.	3	5	0	11	31	6.20	—	—	3	—	8	245	30.63	3-66	—	—
Donnelly M.P.	7	12	1	206	582	52.91	1	4	7	—	0	20	—	—	—	—
Doull S.B.	32	50	11	46	570	14.61	—	—	16	—	98	2872	29.30	7-65	6	—
Dowling G.T.	39	77	3	239	2306	31.16	3	11	23	—	1	19	19.00	1-19	—	—
Drum C.J.	5	5	2	4	10	3.33	—	—	4	—	16	482	30.12	3-36	—	—
Dunning J.A.	4	6	1	19	38	7.60	—	—	2	—	5	493	98.60	2-35	—	—
***Edgar** B.A.	39	68	4	161	1958	30.59	3	12	14*	—	0	3	—	—	—	—
***Edwards** G.N.	8	15	0	55	377	25.13	—	3	7*	—	—	—	—	—	—	—
Emery R.W.G.	2	4	0	28	46	11.50	—	—	—	—	2	52	26.00	2-52	—	—
Fisher F.E.	1	2	0	14	23	11.50	—	—	—	—	1	78	78.00	1-78	—	—
Fleming S.P.	94	163	10	274*	5912	38.64	8	38	136	—	—	—	—	—	—	—
Foley H.	1	2	0	2	4	2.00	—	—	—	—	—	—	—	—	—	—
Franklin J.E.C.	11	15	2	55	198	15.23	—	1	4	—	41	1177	28.70	6-119	2	—
Franklin T.J.	21	37	1	101	828	23.00	1	4	8	—	—	—	—	—	—	—
Freeman D.L.	2	2	0	1	2	1.00	—	—	—	—	1	169	169.00	1-91	—	—
Gallichan N.	1	2	0	30	32	16.00	—	—	—	—	3	113	37.67	3-99	—	—
Gedye S.G.	4	8	0	55	193	24.13	—	2	—	—	—	—	—	—	—	—
†**Germon** L.K.	12	21	3	55	382	21.22	—	1	27	2	—	—	—	—	—	—
Gillespie S.R.	1	1	0	28	28	28.00	—	—	—	—	1	79	79.00	1-79	—	—
Gray E.J.	10	16	0	50	248	15.50	—	1	6	—	17	886	52.11	3-73	—	—
Greatbatch M.J.	41	71	5	146*	2021	30.62	3	10	27	—	0	0	—	—	—	—
†**Guillen** S.C.	3	6	0	41	98	16.33	—	—	4	1	—	—	—	—	—	—
Guy J.W.	12	23	2	102	440	20.95	1	3	2	—	—	—	—	—	—	—
Hadlee D.R.	26	42	5	56	530	14.32	—	1	8	—	71	2389	33.65	4-30	—	—
Hadlee R.J.	86	134	19	151*	3124	27.16	2	15	39	—	431	9611	22.29	9-52	36	9
Hadlee W.A.	11	19	1	116	543	30.17	1	2	6	—	—	—	—	—	—	—
Harford N.S.	8	15	0	93	229	15.27	—	2	—	—	—	—	—	—	—	—
†**Harford** R.I.	3	5	2	6	7	2.33	—	—	11	—	—	—	—	—	—	—
Harris C.Z.	23	42	4	71	777	20.44	—	5	14	—	16	1170	73.12	2-16	—	—
Harris P.G.Z.	9	18	1	101	378	22.24	1	1	6	—	0	14	—	—	—	—
Harris R.M.	2	3	0	13	31	10.33	—	—	—	—	—	—	—	—	—	—
Hart M.N.	14	24	4	45	353	17.65	—	—	9	—	29	1438	49.58	5-77	1	—
†**Hart** R.G.	11	19	3	57*	260	16.25	—	1	29	1	—	—	—	—	—	—
Hartland B.R.	9	18	0	52	303	16.83	—	1	5	—	—	—	—	—	—	—
Haslam M.J.	4	2	1	3	4	4.00	—	—	2	—	2	245	122.50	1-33	—	—
Hastings B.F.	31	56	6	117*	1510	30.20	4	7	23	—	0	9	—	—	—	—
Hayes J.A.	15	22	7	19	73	4.87	—	—	3	—	30	1217	40.57	4-36	—	—
Henderson M.	1	2	1	6	8	8.00	—	—	1	—	2	64	32.00	2-38	—	—
Horne M.J.	35	65	2	157	1788	28.38	4	5	17	—	0	26	—	—	—	—
Horne P.A.	4	7	0	27	71	10.14	—	—	3	—	—	—	—	—	—	—
Hough K.W.	2	3	2	31*	62	62.00	—	—	1	—	6	175	29.17	3-79	—	—
Howarth G.P.	47	83	5	147	2531	32.44	6	11	29	—	3	271	90.33	1-13	—	—
Howarth H.J.	30	42	18	61	291	12.13	—	1	33	—	86	3178	36.95	5-34	2	—
†**James** K.C.	11	13	2	14	52	4.73	—	—	11	5	—	—	—	—	—	—
Jarvis T.W.	13	22	1	182	625	29.76	1	2	3	—	0	3	—	—	—	—
Jones A.H.	39	74	8	186	2922	44.27	7	11	25	—	1	194	194.00	1-40	—	—

	M	I	NO	HS	Runs	Ave	100	50	Ct	St	Wkts	Runs	Ave	Best	5WI	10WM
Jones R.A.	1	2	0	16	23	11.50	—	—	—	—	—	—	—	—	—	—
Kennedy R.J.	4	5	1	22	28	7.00	—	—	2	—	6	380	63.33	3-28	—	—
Kerr J.L.	7	12	1	59	212	19.27	—	1	4	—	—	—	—	—	—	—
Kuggeleijn C.M.	2	4	0	7	7	1.75	—	—	1	—	1	67	67.00	1-50	—	—
Larsen G.R.	8	13	4	26*	127	14.11	—	—	5	—	24	689	28.70	3-57	—	—
Latham R.T.	4	7	0	119	219	31.28	1	—	5	—	0	6	—	—	—	—
†**Lees** W.K.	21	37	4	152	778	23.57	1	1	52	7	0	4	—	—	—	—
Leggat I.B.	1	1	0	0	0	0.00	—	—	2	—	0	6	—	—	—	—
Leggat J.G.	9	18	2	61	351	21.94	—	2	—	—	—	—	—	—	—	—
Lissette A.F.	2	4	2	1*	2	1.00	—	—	1	—	3	124	41.33	2-73	—	—
Loveridge G.R.	1	1	1	4*	4	—	—	—	—	—	—	—	—	—	—	—
Lowry T.C.	7	8	0	80	223	27.88	—	2	8	—	0	5	—	—	—	—
†**McCullum** B.B.	15	25	2	143	758	32.95	1	5	36	2	—	—	—	—	—	—
McEwan P.E.	4	7	1	40*	96	16.00	—	—	5	—	0	13	—	—	—	—
MacGibbon A.R.	26	46	5	66	814	19.85	—	3	13	—	70	2160	30.86	5-64	1	—
McGirr H.M.	2	1	0	51	51	51.00	—	1	—	—	1	115	115.00	1-65	—	—
McGregor S.N.	25	47	2	111	892	19.82	1	3	9	—	—	—	—	—	—	—
McLeod E.G.	1	2	1	16	18	18.00	—	—	—	—	0	5	—	—	—	—
†**McMahon** T.G.	5	7	4	4*	7	2.33	—	—	7	1	—	—	—	—	—	—
McMillan C.D.	55	91	10	142	3116	38.46	6	19	22	—	28	1257	44.89	3-48	—	—
McRae D.A.N.	1	2	0	8	8	4.00	—	—	—	—	0	44	—	—	—	—
Marshall H.J.H.	7	11	1	160	550	55.00	2	2	—	—	0	4	—	—	—	—
Marshall J.A.H.	3	5	0	52	151	30.20	—	1	1	—	—	—	—	—	—	—
Martin C.S.	23	32	15	7	42	2.47	—	—	6	—	76	2705	35.59	6-54	6	1
Mason M.J.	1	2	0	3	3	1.50	—	—	—	—	0	105	—	—	—	—
Matheson A.M.	2	1	0	7	7	7.00	—	—	2	—	2	136	68.00	2-7	—	—
Meale T.	2	4	0	10	21	5.25	—	—	—	—	—	—	—	—	—	—
Merritt W.E.	6	8	1	19	73	10.43	—	—	2	—	12	617	51.42	4-104	—	—
Meuli E.M.	1	2	0	23	38	19.00	—	—	—	—	—	—	—	—	—	—
†**Milburn** B.D.	3	3	2	4*	8	8.00	—	—	6	2	—	—	—	—	—	—
Miller L.S.M.	13	25	0	47	346	13.84	—	—	1	—	0	1	—	—	—	—
Mills J.E.	7	10	1	117	241	26.78	1	—	1	—	—	—	—	—	—	—
Mills K.D.	4	7	1	31	98	16.33	—	—	1	—	3	273	91.00	2-34	—	—
Moir A.M.	17	30	8	41*	327	14.86	—	—	2	—	28	1418	50.64	6-155	2	—
Moloney D.A.R.	3	6	0	64	156	26.00	—	1	3	—	0	9	—	—	—	—
†**Mooney** F.L.H.	14	22	2	46	343	17.15	—	—	22	8	0	0	—	—	—	—
***Morgan** R.W.	20	34	1	97	734	22.24	—	5	12*	—	5	609	121.80	1-16	—	—
Morrison B.D.	1	2	0	10	10	5.00	—	—	1	—	2	129	64.50	2-129	—	—
Morrison D.K.	48	71	26	42	379	8.42	—	—	14	—	160	5549	34.68	7-89	10	—
Morrison J.F.M.	17	29	0	117	656	22.62	1	3	9	—	2	71	35.50	2-52	—	—
Motz R.C.	32	56	3	60	612	11.55	—	3	9	—	100	3148	31.48	6-63	5	—
Murray B.A.G.	13	26	1	90	598	23.92	—	5	21	—	1	0	0.00	1-0	—	—
Murray D.J.	8	16	1	52	303	20.20	—	1	6	—	—	—	—	—	—	—
Nash D.J.	32	45	14	89*	729	23.51	—	4	13	—	93	2649	28.48	6-27	3	1
Newman J.	3	4	0	19	33	8.25	—	—	—	—	2	254	127.00	2-76	—	—
O'Brien I.E.	2	3	0	5	10	3.33	—	—	1	—	2	197	98.50	1-73	—	—
O'Connor S.B.	19	27	9	20	105	5.83	—	—	6	—	53	1724	32.52	5-51	1	—
O'Sullivan D.R.	11	21	4	23*	158	9.29	—	—	2	—	18	1221	67.83	5-148	1	—
Oram J.D.P.	17	29	6	126*	1002	43.56	2	4	12	—	35	1269	36.25	4-41	—	—
Overton G.W.F.	3	6	1	3*	8	1.60	—	—	1	—	9	258	28.67	3-65	—	—
Owens M.B.	8	12	6	8*	16	2.66	—	—	3	—	17	585	34.44	4-99	—	—
Page M.L.	14	20	0	104	492	24.60	1	2	6	—	5	231	46.20	2-21	—	—
Papps M.H.W.	4	8	1	86	172	24.57	—	2	5	—	—	—	—	—	—	—
Parker J.M.	36	63	2	121	1498	24.56	3	5	30	—	1	24	24.00	1-24	—	—

	M	I	NO	HS	Runs	Ave	100	50	Ct	St	Wkts	Runs	Ave	Best	5WI	10WM
Parker N.M.	3	6	0	40	89	14.83	—	—	2	—	—	—	—	—	—	—
***Parore** A.C.	78	128	19	110	2865	26.28	2	14	197	7	—	—	—	—	—	—
Patel D.N.	37	66	8	99	1200	20.68	—	5	15	—	75	3154	42.05	6-50	3	—
Petherick P.J.	6	11	4	13	34	4.86	—	—	4	—	16	685	42.81	3-90	—	—
†**Petrie** E.C.	14	25	5	55	258	12.90	—	1	25	—	—	—	—	—	—	—
Playle W.R.	8	15	0	65	151	10.07	—	1	4	—	—	—	—	—	—	—
Pocock B.A.	15	29	0	85	665	22.93	—	6	5	—	0	20	—	—	—	—
Pollard V.	32	59	7	116	1266	24.35	2	7	19	—	40	1853	46.33	3-3	—	—
Poore M.B.	14	24	1	45	355	15.43	—	—	1	—	9	367	40.78	2-28	—	—
Priest M.W.	3	4	0	26	56	14.00	—	—	—	—	3	158	52.66	2-42	—	—
Pringle C.	14	21	4	30	175	10.29	—	—	3	—	30	1389	46.30	7-52	1	1
Puna N.	3	5	3	18*	31	15.50	—	—	1	—	4	240	60.00	2-40	—	—
Rabone G.O.	12	20	2	107	562	31.22	1	2	5	—	16	635	36.69	6-68	1	—
Redmond R.E.	1	2	0	107	163	81.50	1	1	—	—	—	—	—	—	—	—
Reid J.F.	19	31	3	180	1296	46.28	6	2	9	—	0	7	—	—	—	—
***Reid** J.R.	58	108	5	142	3428	33.28	6	22	43*	1	85	2835	33.35	6-60	1	—
Richardson M.H.	38	65	3	145	2776	44.77	4	19	26	—	1	21	21.00	1-16	—	—
Roberts A.D.G.	7	12	1	84*	254	23.09	—	1	4	—	4	182	45.50	1-12	—	—
Roberts A.W.	5	10	1	66*	248	27.56	—	3	4	—	7	209	29.86	4-101	—	—
Robertson G.K.	1	1	0	12	12	12.00	—	—	—	—	1	91	91.00	1-91	—	—
Rowe C.G.	1	2	0	0	0	0.00	—	—	1	—	—	—	—	—	—	—
Rutherford K.R.	56	99	8	107*	2465	27.08	3	18	32	—	1	161	161.00	1-38	—	—
Scott R.H.	1	1	0	18	18	18.00	—	—	—	—	1	74	74.00	1-74	—	—
Scott V.J.	10	17	1	84	458	28.63	—	3	7	—	0	14	—	—	—	—
Sewell D.G.	1	1	1	1*	1	—	—	—	—	—	0	90	—	—	—	—
Shrimpton M.J.F.	10	19	0	46	265	13.95	—	—	2	—	5	158	31.60	3-35	—	—
Sinclair B.W.	21	40	1	138	1148	29.44	3	3	8	—	2	32	16.00	2-32	—	—
Sinclair I.M.	2	4	1	18*	25	8.33	—	—	1	—	1	120	120.00	1-79	—	—
Sinclair M.S.	25	42	5	214	1365	36.89	3	4	22	—	0	13	—	—	—	—
Smith F.B.	4	6	1	96	237	47.40	—	2	1	—	—	—	—	—	—	—
Smith H.D.	1	1	0	4	4	4.00	—	—	—	—	1	113	113.00	1-113	—	—
†**Smith** I.D.S.	63	88	17	173	1815	25.56	2	6	168	8	0	5	—	—	—	—
Snedden C.A.	1	—	—	—	—	—	—	—	—	—	0	46	—	—	—	—
Snedden M.C.	25	30	8	33*	327	14.86	—	—	7	—	58	2199	37.91	5-68	1	—
Sparling J.T.	11	20	2	50	229	12.72	—	1	3	—	5	327	65.40	1-9	—	—
Spearman C.M.	19	37	2	112	922	26.34	1	3	20	—	—	—	—	—	—	—
Stead G.R.	5	8	0	78	278	34.75	—	2	2	—	0	1	—	—	—	—
Stirling D.A.	6	9	2	26	108	15.42	—	—	1	—	13	601	46.23	4-88	—	—
Styris S.B.	19	33	2	170	1233	39.77	4	5	16	—	16	833	52.06	3-28	—	—
Su'a M.L.	13	18	5	44	165	12.69	—	—	8	—	36	1377	38.25	5-73	2	—
Sutcliffe B.	42	76	8	230*	2727	40.10	5	15	20	—	4	344	86.00	2-38	—	—
Taylor B.R.	30	50	6	124	898	20.41	2	2	10	—	111	2953	26.60	7-74	4	—
Taylor D.D.	3	5	0	77	159	31.80	—	1	2	—	—	—	—	—	—	—
Thomson K.	2	4	1	69	94	31.33	—	1	—	—	1	9	9.00	1-9	—	—
Thomson S.A.	19	35	4	120*	958	30.90	1	5	7	—	19	953	50.15	3-63	—	—
†**Tindill** E.W.T.	5	9	1	37*	73	9.13	—	—	6	1	—	—	—	—	—	—
Troup G.B.	15	18	6	13*	55	4.58	—	—	2	—	39	1454	37.28	6-95	1	1
Truscott P.B.	1	2	0	26	29	14.50	—	—	1	—	—	—	—	—	—	—
Tuffey D.R.	22	30	7	35	263	11.43	—	—	12	—	66	2057	31.16	6-54	2	—
Turner G.M.	41	73	6	259	2991	44.64	7	14	42	—	0	5	—	—	—	—
Twose R.G.	16	27	2	94	628	25.12	—	6	5	—	3	130	43.33	2-36	—	—
Vance R.H.	4	7	0	68	207	29.57	—	1	—	—	—	—	—	—	—	—
Vaughan J.T.C.	6	12	1	44	201	18.27	—	—	4	—	11	450	40.90	4-27	—	—
Vettori D.L.	62	90	15	137*	1680	22.40	1	9	29	—	196	6989	35.65	7-87	12	2

	M	I	NO	HS	Runs	Ave	100	50	Ct	St	Wkts	Runs	Ave	Best	5WI	10WM
Vincent L.	20	36	1	224	1190	34.00	3	8	19	—	0	2	—	—	—	—
Vivian G.E.	5	6	0	43	110	18.33	—	—	3	—	1	107	107.00	1-14	—	—
Vivian H.G.	7	10	0	100	421	42.10	1	5	4	—	17	633	37.24	4-58	—	—
†**Wadsworth** K.J.	33	51	4	80	1010	21.49	—	5	92	4	—	—	—	—	—	—
Walker B.G.K.	5	8	2	27*	118	19.66	—	—	—	—	5	399	79.80	2-92	—	—
Wallace W.M.	13	21	0	66	439	20.90	—	5	5	—	0	5	—	—	—	—
Walmsley K.P.	3	5	0	5	13	2.60	—	—	—	—	9	391	43.44	3-70	—	—
†**Ward** J.T.	8	12	6	35*	75	12.50	—	—	16	1	—	—	—	—	—	—
Watson W.	15	18	6	11	60	5.00	—	—	4	—	40	1387	34.67	6-78	1	—
Watt L.	1	2	0	2	2	1.00	—	—	—	—	—	—	—	—	—	—
Webb M.G.	3	2	0	12	12	6.00	—	—	—	—	4	471	117.75	2-114	—	—
Webb P.N.	2	3	0	5	11	3.67	—	—	2	—	—	—	—	—	—	—
Weir G.L.	11	16	2	74*	416	29.71	—	3	3	—	7	209	29.86	3-38	—	—
White D.J.	2	4	0	18	31	7.75	—	—	—	—	0	5	—	—	—	—
Whitelaw P.E.	2	4	2	30	64	32.00	—	—	—	—	—	—	—	—	—	—
Wiseman P.J.	25	34	8	36	366	14.07	—	—	11	—	61	2903	47.59	5-82	2	—
Wright J.G.	82	148	7	185	5334	37.82	12	23	38	—	0	5	—	—	—	—
Young B.A.	35	68	4	267*	2034	31.78	2	12	54	—	—	—	—	—	—	—
Yuile B.W.	17	33	6	64	481	17.81	—	1	12	—	34	1213	35.68	4-43	—	—

Note: There were 63 dismissals made by substitutes: M.J. Greatbatch (5), J.G. Bracewell, J.J. Crowe, T.W. Jarvis (4), C.Z. Harris (3), J.A.H. Marshall, D.R. O'Sullivan, A.C. Parore, K.R. Rutherford, G.E. Vivian (2), J.C. Alabaster, R.W. Anderson, S.E. Bond, S.L. Boock, G.E. Bradburn, C. Burke, R.O. Collinge, B.E. Congdon, M.D. Crowe, H.T. Davis, C.J. Drum, E.W. Dempster, G.T. Dowling, B.A. Edgar, G.N. Edwards, S.G. Gedye, M.N. Hart, M.A. Hastings, J.M. How, I.B. Leggat, T.G. McMahon, P.E. McEwan, M.N. McKenzie, H.J.H. Marshall, M.J. Mason, R.C. Motz, S.B. O'Connor, N.M. Parker, M.W. Priest, T.D. Ritchie, L. Vincent, B.G.K. Walker catches and B.E. Congdon a stumping. The latter is one of only two instances in tests of a substitute making a stumping.

† all test appearances were as wicketkeeper.
A.C. Parore had 67 tests as wicketkeeper, T.E. Blain (9), G.N. Edwards (4), B.A. Edgar and J.R. Reid one each.

** record includes catches taken while keeping wicket as follows: A.C. Parore (194), T.E. Blain (18), B.A. Edgar (4), J.R. Reid (2), B.E. Congdon and R.W. Morgan one each. Edwards' catches were all made while keeping wicket.*

SUMMARY OF TEST CAREER RECORDS

Most Matches

Fleming S.P.	94	Burgess M.G.	50	Patel D.N.	37
Hadlee R.J.	86	Morrison D.K.	48	Parker J.M.	36
Wright J.G.	82	Howarth G.P.	47	Collinge R.O.	35
Parore A.C.	78	Cairns B.L.	43	Young B.A.	35
Crowe M.D.	77	Chatfield E.J.	43	Horne M.J.	35
Astle N.J.	71	Sutcliffe B.	42	Wadsworth K.J.	33
Smith I.D.S.	63	Turner G.M.	41	Motz R.C.	32
Cairns C.L.	62	Bracewell J.G.	41	Pollard V.	32
Vettori D.L.	62	Greatbatch M.J.	41	Doull S.B.	32
Congdon B.E.	61	Dowling G.T.	39	Nash D.J.	32
Reid J.R.	58	Edgar B.A.	39	Hastings B.F.	31
Rutherford K.R.	56	Crowe J.J.	39	Howarth H.J.	30
McMillan C.D	55	Jones A.H.	39	Taylor B.R.	30
Coney J.V.	52	Richardson M.H.	38	Boock S.L.	30

Most Runs

Fleming S.P.	5912	Sutcliffe B.	2727	Hastings B.F.	1510
Crowe M.D.	5444	Burgess M.G.	2684	Parker J.M.	1498
Wright J.G.	5334	Coney J.V.	2668	Sinclair M.S.	1365
Astle N.J.	4235	Howarth G.P.	2531	Reid J.F.	1296
Congdon B.E.	3448	Rutherford K.R.	2465	Pollard V.	1266
Reid J.R.	3428	Dowling G.T.	2306	Styris S.B.	1233
Cairns C.L.	3320	Young B.A.	2034	Patel D.N.	1200
Hadlee R.J.	3124	Greatbatch M.J.	2021	Vincent L.	1190
McMillan C.D.	3116	Edgar B.A.	1958	Sinclair B.W.	1148
Turner G.M.	2991	Smith I.D.S.	1815	Wadsworth K.J.	1010
Jones A.H.	2922	Horne M.J.	1788	Oram J.D.P.	1002
Parore A.C.	2865	Vettori D.L.	1680	Bracewell J.G.	1001
Richardson M.H.	2776	Crowe J.J.	1601		

Most Wickets

Hadlee R.J.	431	Motz R.C.	100	MacGibbon A.R.	70
Cairns C.L.	218	Doull S.B.	98	Tuffey D.R.	66
Vettori D.L.	196	Nash D.J.	93	Cameron F.J.	62
Morrison D.K.	160	Howarth H.J.	86	Wiseman P.J.	61
Cairns B.L.	130	Reid J.R.	85	Congdon B.E.	59
Chatfield E.J.	123	Martin C.S.	76	Snedden M.C.	58
Collinge R.O.	116	Patel D.N.	75	O'Connor S.B.	53
Taylor B.R.	111	Boock S.L.	74	Cunis R.S.	51
Bracewell J.G.	102	Hadlee D.R.	71		

Most Catches

Fleming S.P.	136	Reid J.R.	41	Rutherford K.R.	32
Crowe M.D.	71	Crowe J.J.	41	Bracewell J.G.	31
Astle N.J.	65	Hadlee R.J.	39	Parker J.M.	30
Coney J.V.	64	Wright J.G.	38	Cairns B.L.	30
Young B.A.	54	Burgess M.G.	34	Howarth G.P.	29
Congdon B.E.	43	Howarth H.J.	33	Vettori D.L.	29
Turner G.M.	42				

Most Wicketkeeping Dismissals

	Ct	St	Total
Parore A.C.	194	7	201
Smith I.D.S.	168	8	176
Wadsworth K.J.	92	4	96
Lees W.K.	52	7	59
Dick A.E.	47	4	51

Test Captains

			RESULTS			TOSS	
		P	W	L	D	W	L
Fleming S.P.	1996/97 to 2004/05	70	23	24	23	36	34
Reid J.R.	1955/56 to 1965	34	3	18	13	17	17
Howarth G.P.	1979/80 to 1984/85	30	11	7	12	17	13
Dowling G.T.	1967/68 to 1971/72	19	4	7	8	10	9
Rutherford K.R.	1992/93 to 1994/95	18	2	11	5	12	6
Congdon B.E.	1971/72 to 1974/75	17	1	7	9	4	13
Crowe M.D.	1990/91 to 1993/94	16	2	7	7	8	8
Coney J.V.	1984/85 to 1986/87	15	5	4	6	8	7
Wright J.G.	1987/88 to 1990	14	3	3	8	8	6
Germon L.K.	1995/96 to 1996/97	12	1	5	6	6	6
Turner G.M.	1975/76 to 1976/77	10	1	6	3	2	8
Burgess M.G.	1977/78 to 1980/81	10	1	6	3	4	6
Cave H.B.	1955/56	9	0	5	4	5	4
Hadlee W.A.	1945/46 to 1950/51	8	0	2	6	4	4
Lowry T.C.	1929/30 to 1931	7	0	2	5	5	2
Page M.L.	1931/32 to 1937	7	0	3	4	4	3
Crowe J.J.	1986/87 to 1987/88	6	0	1	5	3	3
Rabone G.O.	1953/54 to 1954/55	5	0	4	1	2	3
Sutcliffe B.	1951/52 to 1953/54	4	0	3	1	4	0
Sinclair B.W.	1965/66 to 1967/68	3	0	1	2	3	0
Nash D.J.	1998/99	3	0	1	2	3	0
Wallace W.M.	1952/53	2	0	1	1	0	2
Chapple M.E.	1965/66	1	0	0	1	0	1
Parker J.M.	1976/77	1	0	0	1	0	1
Smith I.D.S.	1990/91	1	0	0	1	1	0
Totals		**322**	**57**	**128**	**137**	**166**	**156**

Test Debuts

New Zealand has now played 322 test matches. In 181 there have been no new test caps. In the other 141 the records are:

11 players making debut 1929/30 v England at Christchurch (NZ's first test match)
6 players making debut 1937 v England at Lord's (NZ's first test since 1932/33)
6 players making debut 1945/46 v Australia at Wellington (NZ's first test after Second World War)
6 players making debut 1946/47 v England at Christchurch (test after one above)
5 players making debut 1961/62 v South Africa at Durban

Of the 12 players who made their debuts in the 1945/46 and 1946/47 tests above, seven did not appear again. In eight successive tests at least one player made his test debut — South Africa 1963/64 (3), Pakistan 1964/65 (3), India 1964/65 (2). In nine successive tests there were no new caps — England 1969 (2), India 1969/70 (3), Pakistan 1969/70 (3), England 1970/71 (1) and South Africa 1998/99 (1), England 1999 (4), India 1999/00 (3), West Indies 1999/00 (1).

Youngest/Oldest Test Players

YOUNGEST PLAYERS			Bat	Bowl
18 years 10 days	Vettori D.L. v England at Wellington	1996/97	3* & 2*	2-98
18 years 197 days	Freeman D.L. v England at Christchurch	1932/33	1	0-78
18 years 267 days	Vivian H.G. v England at The Oval	1931	3 & 51	2-96
18 years 295 days	Collinge R.O. v Pakistan at Wellington	1964/65	0*	2-51 & 3-43
18 years 316 days	Bracewell B.P. v England at The Oval	1978	0 & 0	2-46 & 1-26
19 years 5 days	Vivian G.E. v India at Calcutta	1964/65	1 & 43	0-37 & 1-14
19 years 145 days	Beck J.E.F. v South Africa at Johannesburg	1953/54	16 & 7	
19 years 154 days	Rutherford K.R. v West Indies at Port of Spain	1984/85	0 & 0	
19 years 157 days	Crowe M.D. v Australia at Wellington	1981/82	9	0-14
19 years 163 days	Parore A.C. v England at Birmingham	1990	12* & 20	4ct/1st
19 years 164 days	Cairns C.L. v Australia at Perth	1989/90	1 & 28	0-60
19 years 173 days	Pollard V. India at Madras	1964/65	3	3-90 & 1-32
19 years 186 days	Playle W.R. v England at Birmingham	1958	4 & 8	
19 years 252 days	Donnelly M.P. v England at Lord's	1937	0 & 21	
19 years 340 days	Sewell D.G. v Zimbabwe at Bulawayo	1997/98	1*	0-81 & 0-9
19 years 344 days	Sparling J.T. v England at Leeds	1958	9* & 18	1-78

OLDEST PLAYERS *(age on last day of final test)*

41 years 294 days	Alabaster J.C. v West Indies at Port of Spain	1971/72	18	0-49 & 1-5
41 years 196 days	Sutcliffe B. v England at Birmingham	1965	4* & 53	
40 years 198 days	Congdon B.E. v England at Lord's	1978	2 & 3	0-12

OLDEST PLAYER ON DEBUT

38 years 101 days	McGirr H.M.† v England at Auckland	1929/30		0-46

† he made 51 in his first test innings in his second test

YOUNGEST CENTURY MAKER

19 years 121 days†	Vivian H.G. 100 v South Africa at Wellington	1931/32

† world record at that time

OLDEST CENTURY MAKERS

41 years 109 days	Sutcliffe B. 151* v India at Calcutta	1964/65
39 years 12 days	Congdon B.E. 107* v Australia at Christchurch	1976/77

YOUNGEST CAPTAIN

23 years 319 days	Fleming S.P. v England at Christchurch	1996/97	62 & 11
25 years 252 days	Parker J.M. v Pakistan at Karachi	1976/77	24 & 16

OLDEST CAPTAIN *(age on last day of final test)*

37 years 40 days	Reid J.R. v England at Leeds	1965	54 & 5	
36 years 359 days	Congdon B.E. v England at Christchurch	1974/75	38	0-27
36 years 88 days	Wallace W.M. v South Africa at Auckland	1952/53	23	
36 years 5 days	Wright J.G. v England at Birmingham	1990	24 & 46	

LONGEST INTERVAL BETWEEN TEST APPEARANCES

14 years 28 days Cleverley D.C. — v South Africa at Christchurch 1/3/32
v Australia at Wellington 29/3/46

Only A.J. Traicos (22 years 222 days), G. Gunn (17 years 316 days), Younis Ahmed (17 years 111 days) and J.M.M. Commaille (14 years 95 days) have a longer interval between tests but Cleverley is unique in that the above matches were his only two tests.

NEW ZEALAND LIMITED-OVERS RECORDS

This section of the *Almanack* is devoted to limited-overs matches in New Zealand (other than one-day internationals) and has been compiled from the following games:

1. 644 matches in national competitions (Shell Cup, State Shield etc) from 1971/72 to 2004/05.

2. 50 matches between provincial sides and overseas teams from 1970/71 to 2001/02.

1970/71	Wellington v MCC
	Otago v MCC
	Central Districts v MCC
1972/73	Central Districts v Pakistan
1973/74	Wellington v Australia
	Central Districts v Australia
1975/76	Wellington v India
1977/78	Northern Districts v England XI
1978/79	Auckland v Pakistan
	Canterbury v Pakistan
1979/80	Auckland XI v West Indies
	Central Districts v West Indies
1981/82	Northern Districts v Australia
	Central Districts v Australia
1983/84	Otago v England XI
1984/85	Wellington v New South Wales
1985/86	Auckland v Australia
1986/87	Auckland v West Indies
	Central Districts v South Australia *(4 matches)*
1987/88	Wellington v England
	Auckland v Victoria *(2 matches)*
	Wellington v Queensland
	Canterbury v Queensland
	Otago v Queensland
1988/89	Auckland v Pakistan
1991/92	Auckland v England
	Auckland v Australia
	Northern Districts v Zimbabwe *(2 matches)*
1993/94	Canterbury v New South Wales
1994/95	Auckland v West Indies
	Central Districts v India
	Wellington v South Africa
	Canterbury v Sri Lanka
1996/97	Central Districts v Sri Lanka
1997/98	Canterbury v Bangladesh
1998/99	Northern v Pakistan A
2000/01	Wellington v New South Wales
	Canterbury v Zimbabwe
2001/02	Northern Districts v England *(2 matches)*
2003/04	Wellington v Pakistan
	Northern Districts v South Africa
2004/05	Central Districts v Sri Lanka

3. Three matches in the Data General competition in 1986/87.

4. Six matches in the Shell Shield competition in 1997/98.

5. 30 other matches not involving provincial sides.

1972/73	New Zealand Under 23 XI v Pakistan
1976/77	Australia v Invitation XIs *(2 matches)*
1981/82	North Island v South Island
1982/83	Sri Lanka v NZ Minor Associations *(2 matches)*

1992/93	New Zealand President's XI v Australia
1993/94	North Island v South Island
	Sir Ron Brierley XI v Pakistan
1994/95	North Island v South Island
	Sir Ron Brierley XI v West Indies
	New Zealand Academy XI v Sri Lanka
	New Zealand Academy XI v Australian Academy XI
1996/97	New Zealand Academy XI v England
1997/98	New Zealand Academy XI v Zimbabwe
1998/99	New Zealand A v Pakistan A *(3 matches)*
	New Zealand Academy XI v South Africa
1999/00	New Zealand Academy XI v England A *(2 matches)*
	New Zealand A v England A *(3 matches)*
2000/01	North Island Selection XI v Sri Lanka
2003/04	South Island v North Island
	New Zealand A v Sri Lanka A *(2 matches)*
2004/05	New Zealand v FICA World XI *(3 matches)*
	North Island v South Island

TEAM RECORDS

Highest Totals

376-3	Central Districts v Otago	New Plymouth	1996/97
354-5	Central Districts v Canterbury	Christchurch	2003/04
339-5	Central Districts v Otago	Hastings	1998/99
329-5	Canterbury v Northern Districts	Christchurch	1995/96
328-4	New Zealand A v Sri Lanka A	Lincoln	2003/04
318-5	Auckland v Northern Districts	Auckland	2000/01
313-7	Canterbury v Northern Districts	Timaru	1993/94
309-8	Auckland v Northern Districts	Gisborne	1982/83
309-8	Canterbury v Wellington	Christchurch	2003/04
309-6	Canterbury v Central Districts	Christchurch	1994/95
308-9	Wellington v Canterbury	Christchurch	2003/04
307-3	Canterbury v Wellington	Timaru	2004/05
306-2	Northern Districts v Auckland	Gisborne	1982/83
305-6	Central Districts v Otago	Oamaru	1999/00
300-5	Wellington v Auckland	Wellington	2001/02
300-3	Canterbury v Otago	Timaru	2003/04

Lowest Totals

48	Pakistan v Auckland	Auckland	1988/89
58	Central Districts v Wellington	Wellington	2001/02
64	Otago v Wellington	Alexandra	1984/85
64	Otago v Central Districts	Incercargill	2004/05
66	Wellington v Canterbury	Wellington	1996/97
67	Otago v Central Districts	Invercargill	2000/01
67	Central Districts v Canterbury	Christchurch	2002/03
70	Auckland v Northern Districts	Pukekohe	1977/78
72	New Zealand Academy XI v South Africa	Alexandra	1998/99
73	Auckland v Central Districts	Auckland	2000/01
75	Canterbury v Otago	Christchurch	1973/74
76	Northern Districts v Central Districts	Mt Maunganui	1987/88
76	Otago v Queensland	Dunedin	1987/88
78	Central Districts v Auckland	New Plymouth	1988/89
79	Wellington v Otago	Wellington	1999/00
80	Northern Districts v Wellington	Wellington	1982/83
81	Northern Districts v Zimbabwe	Cambridge	1991/92
81	Central Districts v Northern Districts	Levin	1995/96
81	Wellington v Canterbury	Wellington	1996/97
81	FICA World XI v New Zealand	Hamilton	2004/05
85	Northern Districts v Wellington	Mt Maunganui	1997/98
88	Northern Districts v Canterbury	Christchurch	1994/95
89	Central Districts v Wellington	Wellington	1985/86
91	Otago v Auckland	Auckland	1996/97
92	Auckland v Wellington	Wellington	1971/72
93	Central Districts v Canterbury	Timaru	1995/96
94	Central Districts v Otago	Alexandra	1986/87
95	Wellington v Northern Districts	Tauranga	1989/90
96	Auckland v Canterbury	Christchurch	1995/96
96	Canterbury v Northern Districts	Hamilton	1997/98
97	Central Districts v Auckland	Auckland	1995/96
98	Auckland v Canterbury	Christchurch	1976/77
99	Canterbury v Otago	Dunedin	1983/84

Most Extras in an Innings

55	Northern Districts (271-8)	v Wellington (228)	Hamilton	2002/03
51	NZ Academy XI (183)	v England A (184-4)	Lincoln	1999/00
48	Wellington (211-7)	v Otago (208-8)	Wellington	1996/97
45	Wellington (251-8)	v Otago (250-6)	Alexandra	1997/98
45	England A (219-7)	v New Zealand A (216)	Auckland	1999/00
43	Otago (250-6)	v Wellington (251-8)	Alexandra	1997/98
42	Canterbury (286-8)	v Otago (149)	Christchurch	1996/97
42	Otago (233-9)	v Wellington (200)	Alexandra	1999/00
42	Northern Districts (202-9)	v Auckland (157-6)	Hamilton	2002/03
41	Northern Districts (215)	v Auckland (217-6)	Whangarei	1995/96

Fewest Extras in an Innings

1	Canterbury (205-6)	v Wellington (203)	Timaru	1986/87
2	Pakistan (216-4)	v NZ Under 23 XI	Rotorua	1972/73
2	Otago (114)	v Canterbury (113)	Christchurch	1979/80
2	Auckland (163-4)	v Otago (162)	Oamaru	1981/82
2	Auckland (105)	v Otago (214-9)	Dunedin	1993/94

Tied Match

Wellington v South Africa	Wellington	1994/95

Close Finishes

RUNS *(winning team listed first)*

1	Northern Districts v Canterbury	Hamilton	1982/83
1	Northern Districts v Zimbabwe	Pukekohe	1991/92
1	Auckland v Central Districts	Auckland	1994/95
1	Otago v Auckland	Alexandra	1995/96
1	Central Districts v Wellington	Wellington	1996/97
1	Northern Districts v Wellington *(D/L)*	Taupo	2004/05
2	Central Districts v Northern Districts	Tauranga	1989/90
2	Canterbury v Wellington	Christchurch	1995/96
2	Canterbury v Auckland	Auckland	1999/00
2	Wellington v Otago	Alexandra	2002/03
3	Auckland v Northern Districts	Hamilton	1972/73
3	Auckland v Northern Districts	Auckland	1981/82
3	Canterbury v Wellington	Christchurch	1991/92
3	Northern Districts v Auckland	Mt Maunganui	1993/94
3	Canterbury v Otago	Christchurch	1998/99
3	Wellington v Otago	Queenstown	2001/02
4	Otago v Wellington	Wellington	1987/88
4	Canterbury v Northern Districts	Rotorua	1993/94
4	Wellington v Central Districts	Wellington	1994/95
5	Northern Districts v Otago	Taupo	1995/96
5	Auckland v Otago	Auckland	1999/00
5	Wellington v Auckland	Auckland	2000/01

ONE WICKET *(winning team listed first)*

Wellington v Auckland	Wellington	1973/74
Otago v Canterbury	Christchurch	1979/80
Central Districts v Australia	New Plymouth	1981/82
Canterbury v Central Districts	Christchurch	1986/87
Otago v Northern Districts	Gisborne	1986/87
Auckland v Northern Districts	Hamilton	1989/90

Otago v Auckland	Auckland	1990/91
Wellington v Otago	Alexandra	1992/93
Central Districts v Wellington	Masterton	1993/94
Wellington v Northern Districts	Wellington	1996/97
Central Districts v Canterbury	Napier	1996/97
Wellington v Northern Districts	Whangarei	1999/00
Auckland v Northern Districts	Auckland	1999/00
Otago v Wellington	Dunedin	2000/01
Central Districts v Wellington	Waikanae	2000/01
Canterbury v Auckland	Auckland	2001/02
Otago v Northern Districts	Invercargill	2003/04

SCORES LEVEL *(won by team listed first, having lost fewer wickets)*

Otago (223-5) v Wellington (223-9)	Dunedin	1979/80
Canterbury (182-7) v Auckland (182-9)	Christchurch	1983/84
Canterbury (136-9) v Auckland (136)	Ashburton	1985/86
Queensland (174-8) v Wellington (174)	Wellington	1987/88
Wellington (227-8) v Auckland (227)	Wellington	1995/96
Canterbury (238-6) v Auckland (238-7)	Auckland	1995/96

Large Victories

RUNS *(winning team listed first)*

200	Central Districts v Otago	Hastings	1998/99
200	Central Districts v Otago	Invercargill	2004/05
197	South Africa v New Zealand Academy XI	Alexandra	1998/99
189	New Zealand A v Pakistan A	Mt Maunganui	1998/99
186	Wellington v Auckland	Wellington	1971/72
153	Otago v Wellington	Alexandra	1982/83
152	Canterbury v Central Districts	Napier	1995/96
152	Otago v Auckland	Auckland	2004/05
151	Wellington v Northern Districts	Mt Maunganui	1997/98

TEN WICKETS *(winning team listed first)*

Northern Districts (71-0) v Auckland (70)	Pukekohe	1977/78
West Indies (132-0) v Central Districts (130)	New Plymouth	1979/80
Canterbury (120-0) v Auckland (119)	Christchurch	1987/88
Auckland (81-0) v Central Districts (78)	New Plymouth	1988/89
Wellington (205-0) v Canterbury (202-7)	Wellington	1994/95
Auckland (164-0) v Central Districts (163)	Auckland	1998/99

Most Run Outs

INNINGS

5	Wellington v Auckland	Wellington	1974/75
5	Northern Districts v Wellington	Hamilton	1992/93
5	Central Districts v Northern Districts	Hamilton	2000/01
5	Otago v Canterbury	Alexandra	2004/05

MATCH

7	Wellington v Auckland	Wellington	1974/75
7	Auckland v Canterbury	Auckland	1999/00

INDIVIDUAL RECORDS

Centuries

177	Pyke J.K.	South Australia v Central Districts	Palmerston North	1986/87
161	Hartland B.R.	Canterbury v Northern Districts	Timaru	1993/94
149	Nevin C.J.	Wellington v Central Districts	Wellington	1997/98
147*	Edgar B.A.	Wellington v Northern Districts	Gisborne	1981/82
145	Vincent L.	Auckland v Central Districts	Napier	1999/00
143	Cairns C.L.	Canterbury v Auckland	Christchurch	1994/95
140	Scott D.G.	Auckland v Northern Districts	Hamilton	1986/87
140	Kelly D.P.	Central Districts v Wellington	Waikanae	1999/00
139*	Tendulkar S.R.	India v Central Districts	Napier	1994/95
138	Vettori D.L.	Northern Districts v Canterbury	Auckland	2004/05
134*	Howell L.G.	Canterbury v Otago	Oamaru	1997/98
133*	Vincent L.	Auckland v Northern Districts	Auckland	2000/01
132*	Taylor R.L.	Central Districts v Otago	Dunedin	2003/04
132	Papps M.H.W.	Canterbury v Otago	Alexandra	2003/04
131	Astle N.J.	Canterbury v Wellington	Wellington	1995/96
131	Fleming S.P.	Wellington v Canterbury	Christchurch	2003/04
130*	Crowe J.J.	Auckland v Northern Districts	Auckland	1991/92
129*	Papps M.H.W.	Canterbury v Wellington	Timaru	2004/05
129	Astle N.J.	Canterbury v Northern Districts	Christchurch	1995/96
128*	Edgar B.A.	Wellington v Central Districts	Wanganui	1982/83
128*	Richardson M.H.	Otago v Central Districts	New Plymouth	1996/97
127	Oram J.D.P.	Central Districts v Auckland	Auckland	1997/98
126	Vivian G.E.	Auckland v Wellington	Auckland	1977/78
126	Tavare C.J.	England XI v Otago	Alexandra	1983/84
126	Spearman C.M.	Central Districts v Canterbury	Nelson	1997/98
126	Knight N.V.	England v Northern Districts	Hamilton	2001/02
125	Crowe M.D.	Central Districts v Otago	Alexandra	1988/89
125	McMillan C.D.	Canterbury v Northern Districts	Hamilton	1998/99
125	Oram J.D.P.	Central Districts v Auckland	Auckland	2003/04
124*	Twose R.G.	Wellington v Otago	Wellington	2000/01
124	McMillan C.D.	Canterbury v Northern Districts	Auckland	2004/05
123	Styris S.B.	Northern Districts v Otago	Hamilton	1999/00
123	Astle N.J.	Canterbury v Northern Districts	Gisborne	2004/05
122*	McMillan C.D.	Canterbury v Wellington	Wellington	2002/03
122	Astle N.J.	Canterbury v Wellington	Christchurch	1999/00
122	Parlane M.E.	Northern Districts v Canterbury	Timaru	2002/03
121*	Twose R.G.	Wellington v Northern Districts	Wellington	1996/97
121*	Bell M.D.	Wellington v Central Districts	New Plymouth	1997/98
121	Williams S.C.	West Indies v Sir Ron Brierley XI	Hamilton	1994/95
121	Douglas M.W.	Central Districts v Canterbury	Christchurch	1997/98
121	Astle N.J.	Canterbury v Otago	Christchurch	2000/01
120*	Fleming S.P.	Wellington v Otago	Wellington	2000/01
120*	Fleming S.P.	Wellington v Northern Districts	Wellington	2003/04
118	Reid J.F.	Auckland v Central Districts	Auckland	1985/86
117	Pocock B.A.	Northern Districts v Wellington	Hamilton	1995/96
116	Murray D.J.	Canterbury v Central Districts	Napier	1996/97
116	Barnes A.C.	Auckland v Otago	Alexandra	2003/04
116	Nevin C.J.	Wellington v Auckland	Auckland	2003/04
115*	Rutherford K.R.	Otago v Northern Districts	Alexandra	1991/92
115*	Howell L.G.	Central Districts v Northern Districts	Whangarei	1994/95
115*	Fulton P.G.	Canterbury v Otago	Timaru	2003/04
115	Cairns C.L.	Canterbury v Wellington	Christchurch	1992/93

114	McMillan C.D.	Canterbury v Wellington	Christchurch	1995/96
114	Astle N.J.	Canterbury v Otago	Alexandra	1996/97
113*	Richardson M.H.	Otago v Northern Districts	Mt Maunganui	1996/97
113*	McMillan C D	Canterbury v Otago	Alexandra	2004/05
113	Ingham C.D.	Central Districts v Otago	Napier	1994/95
113	Cairns C.L.	Canterbury v Otago	Christchurch	1996/97
113	Weenink S.W.	Wellington v Central Districts	Wellington	1996/97
111*	Howell L.G.	Central Districts v Otago	New Plymouth	1996/97
111	Parlane M.E.	Northern Districts v Wellington	Whangarei	1999/00
111	Nevin C.J.	Wellington v Auckland	Wellington	2001/02
110	Crowe M.D.	Wellington v Canterbury	Christchurch	1992/93
110	Sinclair M.S.	Central Districts v Otago	Oamaru	1999/00
109*	McMillan C.D.	Canterbury v Central Districts	New Plymouth	2001/02
109	Sleep P.R.	South Australia v Central Districts	New Plymouth	1986/87
109	Crowe M.D.	Wellington v Auckland	Wellington	1990/91
109	Doody B.J.K.	Canterbury v Auckland	Christchurch	1997/98
109	Astle N.J.	Canterbury v Otago	Invercargill	1999/00
109	Astle N.J.	New Zealand v FICA World XI	Wellington	2004/05
109	Vettori D.L.	Northern Districts v Auckland	Auckland	2004/05
108	Blair W.L.	Otago v Auckland	Auckland	1982/83
108	Latham R.T.	Canterbury v Otago	Oamaru	1994/95
108	Campbell S.C.	West Indies v Sir Ron Brierley XI	Hamilton	1994/95
108	Howell L.G.	Central Districts v Wellington	New Plymouth	1995/96
107*	Douglas M.W.	Central Districts v Wellington	New Plymouth	1997/98
107*	Barnes A.C.	Auckland v Northern Districts	Hamilton	1999/00
107	Hick G.A.	Auckland v Otago	Alexandra	1997/98
107	Harris C.Z.	Canterbury v Central Districts	Napier	1998/99
107	Sinclair M.S.	New Zealand A v Sri Lanka A	Lincoln	2003/04
106*	Edgar B.A.	Wellington v Otago	Wellington	1981/82
106*	Lamb A.J.	England XI v Otago	Alexandra	1983/84
106*	de Silva P.A.	Auckland v Canterbury	Auckland	1996/97
106*	Howell L.G.	Auckland v Central Districts	New Plymouth	2001/02
106	Vance R.H.	Wellington v Auckland	Auckland	1981/82
106	McEwan P.E.	Canterbury v Wellington	Wellington	1987/88
106	Chandler P.J.B.	Wellington v Canterbury	Christchurch	1996/97
106	Richardson M.H.	Otago v Central Districts	New Plymouth	1997/98
106	Fleming S.P.	New Zealand v FICA World XI	Christchurch	2004/05
105*	Pamment J.I.	Auckland v Wellington	Wellington	1993/94
105*	Twose R.G.	Wellington v Northern Districts	Wellington	1994/95
105*	Fleming S.P.	Canterbury v Central Districts	Napier	1996/97
105*	Twose R.G.	Central v Bangladesh	Wellington	1997/98
105*	Sinclair M.S.	North Island v South Island	Christchurch	2003/04
105	Inzamam-ul-Haq	Pakistan v Sir Ron Brierley XI	Hamilton	1993/94
105	Twose R.G.	Central v Bangladesh	Wellington	1997/98
104*	Crowe M.D.	Central Districts v Auckland	Auckland	1989/90
104*	Bell M.D.	Wellington v Northern Districts	Mt Maunganui	1997/98
104	Dempsey D.A.	Canterbury v Northern Districts	Hamilton	1980/81
103*	Hartland B.R.	Canterbury v Northern Districts	Christchurch	1991/92
103	McRae G.P.	Central Districts v Auckland	Wanganui	1994/95
103	Twose R.G.	Wellington v Canterbury	Christchurch	1995/96
102*	Burnett G.P.	Wellington v Northern Districts	Hamilton	1992/93
102	Blair W.L.	Otago v Wellington	Dunedin	1979/80
102	Franklin T.J.	Auckland v Northern Districts	Auckland	1981/82
102	Wright J.G.	Canterbury v Wellington	Wellington	1985/86
102	Rutherford K.R.	Otago v Wellington	Alexandra	1993/94

102	Cooper B.G.	Northern Districts v Otago	Alexandra	1994/95
102	Fleming S.P.	Canterbury v Northern Districts	Christchurch	1995/96
102	Twose R.G.	Wellington v Northern Districts	Hamilton	1998/99
102	Hore A.J.	Otago v Wellington	Wellington	2001/02
102	Stewart S.L.	Canterbury v Wellington	Wellington	2003/04
102	Papps M.H.W.	Canterbury v Wellington	Wellington	2004/05
101*	Crowe M.D.	Central Districts v Northern Districts	Whangarei	1983/84
101*	Maynard M.P.	Northern Districts v Auckland	Hamilton	1990/91
101*	Aiken J.M.	Wellington v Canterbury	Wellington	1994/95
101*	Young B.A.	Northern Districts v Central Districts	Mt Maunganui	1995/96
101*	Stead G.R.	Canterbury v Auckland	Auckland	2001/02
101*	Astle N.J.	Canterbury v Central Districts	Christchurch	2001/02
101*	Gaffaney C.B.	Otago v Auckland	Auckland	2004/05
101	White D.J.	Northern Districts v Central Districts	Tauranga	1989/90
101	Burnett G.P.	Northern Districts v Central Districts	Whangarei	1994/95
101	Parlane M.E.	Northern Districts v Canterbury	Taupo	1994/95
101	McMillan C.D.	Canterbury v Central Districts	Christchurch	1994/95
100*	Bell M.D.	Wellington v Canterbury	Wellington	1999/00
100*	Marshall J.A.H.	Northern Districts v Canterbury	Christchurch	2000/01
100	Rutherford I.A.	Otago v Auckland	Auckland	1980/81
100	Hick G.A.	Northern Districts v Canterbury	Rangiora	1987/88
100	Brown S.W.	Auckland v Northern Districts	Hamilton	1990/91
100	Douglas M.W.	Wellington v South Africa	Wellington	1994/95
100	Hart M.N.	Northern Districts v Central Districts	Napier	1996/97
100	Twose R.G.	Wellington v Canterbury	Christchurch	1996/97
100	Wells J.D.	Wellington v Auckland	Wellington	1997/98
100	Stead G.R.	Canterbury v Otago	Oamaru	1997/98
100	Ingram P.J.	Central Districts v Otago	Invercargill	2001/02
100	Nevin C.J.	Wellington v Canterbury	Wellington	2002/03

Fastest Centuries

Balls				
54	Fleming S.P.	New Zealand v FICA World XI	Christchurch	2004/05
65	de Silva P.A.	Auckland v Canterbury	Auckland	1996/97
72	Howell L.G.	Central Districts v Otago	New Plymouth	1996/97
77	McMillan C.D.	Canterbury v Central Districts	New Plymouth	2001/02
78	Astle N.J.	Canterbury v Central Districts	Christchurch	2001/02
79	Hick G.A.	Northern Districts v Canterbury	Rangiora	1987/88
83	Fleming S.P.	Canterbury v Central Districts	Napier	1996/97
83	Nevin C.J.	Wellington v Central Districts	Wellington	1997/98
86	Vettori D.L.	Northern Districts v Canterbury	Auckland	2004/05
87	Marshall J.A.H.	Northern Districts v Canterbury	Christchurch	2000/01
88	Dempsey D.A.	Canterbury v Northern Districts	Hamilton	1980/81
88	Cairns C.L.	Canterbury v Auckland	Christchurch	1994/95
88	Twose R.G.	Wellington v Canterbury	Christchurch	1995/96
89	McMillan C.D.	Canterbury v Wellington	Wellington	2002/03
92	McMillan C.D.	Canterbury v Northern Districts	Hamilton	1998/99
92	McMillan C.D.	Canterbury v Otago	Alexandra	2004/05
94	Fleming S.P.	Canterbury v Northern Districts	Christchurch	1995/96
94	Hore A.J.	Otago v Wellington	Wellington	2001/02
94	McMillan C.D.	Canterbury v Northern Districts	Auckland	2004/05
99	Rutherford K.R.	Otago v Wellington	Alexandra	1993/94
99	Astle N.J.	Canterbury v Northern Districts	Christchurch	1995/96
99	Twose R.G.	Wellington v Canterbury	Christchurch	1996/97

Fastest Fifties

Balls				
20	Cairns C.L.	Canterbury v Northern Districts	Timaru	2002/03
22	Maynard M.P.	Otago v Auckland	Alexandra	1997/98
23	Greatbatch M.J.	Central Districts v Otago	New Plymouth	1996/97
26	Cairns B.L.	Northern Districts v Canterbury	Rangiora	1987/88
26	Bulfin C.E.	Central Districts v Wellington	New Plymouth	1997/98
26	McSkimming W.C.	Otago v Northern Districts	Oamaru	2000/01
27	Loveridge G.R.	Central Districts v Wellington	Wellington	1995/96
27	de Silva P.A.	Auckland v Canterbury	Auckland	1996/97
27	Vettori D.L.	Northern Districts v Auckland	Auckland	1999/00
28	Cooper B.G.	Northern Districts v Otago	Mt Maunganui	1994/95
28	Parlane M.E.	Northern Districts v Wellington	Mt Maunganui	1994/95
28	Spearman C.M.	Central Districts v Otago	New Plymouth	2002/03
29	Fleming S.P.	Wellington v Northern Districts	Taupo	2004/05
30	Spearman C.M.	Auckland v Wellington	Wellington	1995/96
30	Doull S.B.	Northern Districts v England	Hamilton	2001/02
31	Spearman C.M.	Central Districts v Canterbury	Christchurch	2003/04
32	Petrie R.G.	Wellington v Northern Districts	Mt Maunganui	1994/95
32	Howell L.G.	Canterbury v Wellington	Christchurch	1998/99
32	McMillan C.D.	Canterbury v Northern Districts	Hamilton	1998/99
32	Nevin C.J.	Wellington v Canterbury	Wellington	1999/00
32	Horne M.J.	Auckland v Wellington	Wellington	2001/02
32	Hore A.J.	Otago v Wellington	Wellington	2001/02
32	Wilson J.W.	Otago v Auckland	Auckland	2004/05
32	Styris S.B.	Northern Districts v Wellington	Taupo	2004/05
33	Blain T.E.	Central Districts v Wellington	Wellington	1991/92
33	Finch C.W.J.	Otago v Central Districts	New Plymouth	1993/94
33	Brown R.K.	Central Districts v Otago	Hastings	1998/99
33	Horne M.J.	Auckland v Central Districts	Auckland	2001/02
34	Dempsey D.A.	Canterbury v Northern Districts	Hamilton	1980/81
34	Gill S.J.	Central Districts v Wellington	Wanganui	1982/83
34	McEwan P.E.	Canterbury v Central Districts	Ashburton	1988/89
34	Cairns C.L.	Canterbury v Otago	Dunedin	1991/92
34	Howell L.G.	Central Districts v Northern Districts	Taupo	1996/97
34	Hart R.G.	Northern Districts v Wellington	Wellington	1996/97
34	Parlane M.E.	Northern Districts v Central Districts	Hamilton	1997/98
34	Walker M.D.J.	Wellington v Auckland	Wellington	2001/02
34	Vettori D.L.	Northern Districts v Canterbury	Auckland	2004/05

Note: I.D.S. Smith reached fifty from 24 balls for Auckland v Central Districts at Auckland, 1989/90 but the game was abandoned and restarted the following day and none of the performances in the game are included in any records).

Five Wickets in an Innings

7-0-23-7	Watson W.	Auckland v Otago	Auckland	1984/85
8-1-28-7	Penn A.J.	Wellington v Northern Districts	Mt Maunganui	2000/01
7.1-0-49-7	Marshall E.J.	Otago v Auckland	Dunedin	1993/94
10-5-12-6	Barrett B.J.	Northern Districts v Otago	Gisborne	1986/87
5.5-0-12-6	Cairns C.L.	New Zealand v FICA World XI	Hamilton	2004/05
9.3-1-25-6	Mason M.J.	Central Districts v Auckland	Auckland	2003/04
9.5-3-26-6	Vaughan J.T.C.	Auckland v Otago	Auckland	1995/96
10-2-26-6	Su'a M.L.	Auckland v Central Districts	New Plymouth	1995/96
7.7-2-31-6	Intikhab Alam	Pakistan v NZ Under 23 XI	Rotorua	1972/73
10-1-37-6	Cairns C.L.	Canterbury v Wellington	Christchurch	1996/97

9.3-0-43-6	Wisneski W.A.	Canterbury v Auckland	Christchurch	1996/97
10-1-49-6	Penn A.J.	Central Districts v Northern Districts	Napier	1996/97
6-1-7-5	Adams A.R.	Auckland v Northern Districts	Auckland	1999/00
5.3-2-10-5	Hitchcock P.A.	Wellington v Central Districts	Wellington	2001/02
3-0-11-5	Thompson S.	New South Wales v Canterbury	Christchurch	1993/94
8.3-2-12-5	Turner A.D.	Wellington v Otago	Wellington	2002/03
8.1-3-14-5	Shaw H.J.	Canterbury v Central Districts	Christchurch	2002/03
10-4-16-5	Brown C.M.	Auckland v Otago	Auckland	1996/97
8.3-2-17-5	Cederwall G.N.	Wellington v Canterbury	Rangiora	1984/85
8.4-1-19-5	Snedden M.C.	Auckland v Canterbury	Auckland	1982/83
9-2-19-5	Barnes A.C.	Auckland v Central Districts	Auckland	1998/99
10-2-19-5	Penn A.J.	Wellington v Auckland	Auckland	2001/02
10-4-19-5	Hamilton L.J.	Central Districts v Otago	Invercargill	2004/05
10-4-20-5	Visser P.J.	Central Districts v Otago	New Plymouth	1985/86
10-1-20-5	Adams A.R.	Auckland v Central Districts	Auckland	1999/00
10-1-21-5	McNally S.R.	Canterbury v Auckland	Auckland	1984/85
10-4-22-5	Walker M.D.J.	Wellington v Central Districts	New Plymouth	2002/03
5.4-0-22-5	Schwass A.M.	Central Districts v Northern Districts	Taupo	2004/05
7-0-23-5	Collinge R.O.	Wellington v Otago	Wellington	1974/75
10-2-23-5	Brown S.W.	Auckland v Northern Districts	Auckland	1991/92
6.4-0-23-5	Cairns C.L.	Canterbury v Central Districts	Timaru	1995/96
8.5-1-24-5	Wundke S.C.	South Australia v Central Districts	Palmerston North	1986/87
10-4-24-5	Petrie R.G.	Canterbury v Auckland	Christchurch	1989/90
9.3-1-25-5	Maxwell N.D.	Canterbury v Auckland	Christchurch	1997/98
10-2-26-5	Priest M.W.	Canterbury v Auckland	Auckland	1988/89
9-0-27-5	Hunt A.J.	Auckland v Canterbury	Ashburton	1985/86
10-1-28-5	Holland R.G.	NSW v Wellington	Wellington	1984/85
10-2-30-5	Twose R.G.	Wellington v Otago	Alexandra	1995/96
10-3-30-5	Larsen G.R.	Wellington v Auckland	Wellington	1995/96
9.5-0-32-5	Cederwall G.N.	Wellington v Central Districts	Nelson	1984/85
10-2-34-5	Parry D.R.	West Indies v Auckland	Auckland	1979/80
10-1-34-5	Beard D.A.	Northern Districts v Central Districts	New Plymouth	1990/91
10-2-34-5	Anderson C.J.	Canterbury v Wellington	Wellington	2001/02
9-0-34-5	Aldridge G.W.	Northern Districts v Canterbury	Timaru	2004/05
10-1-35-5	Jamieson M.D.	Central Districts v Wellington	Masterton	1980/81
9-0-35-5	O'Brien I.E.	Wellington v Central Districts	Wellington	2004/05
8.5-1-36-5	Robertson G.K.	Central Districts v Northern Districts	Wanganui	1984/85
10-2-38-5	Hellaby A.T.R.	Auckland v Central Districts	Auckland	1987/88
9-0-38-5	McMillan C.D.	Canterbury v Northern Districts	Whangarei	1996/97
9.5-0-39-5	Roberts S.J.	Canterbury v Central Districts	Nelson	1994/95
10-0-39-5	Brown C.M.	Auckland v Northern Districts	Mt Maunganui	1996/97
10-1-41-5	Drum C.J.	Auckland v Canterbury	Christchurch	1998/99
9.5-0-42-5	Su'a M.L.	Auckland v Northern Districts	Auckland	1993/94
10-2-42-5	Blake D.C.	Central Districts v Northern Districts	New Plymouth	1997/98
10-1-43-5	Gale A.J.	Otago v Northern Districts	Alexandra	1991/92
10-0-43-5	Martin C.S.	Canterbury v Northern Districts	Mt Maunganui	1999/00
9.3-3-44-5	Stott L.W.	Auckland v Otago	Oamaru	1981/82
10-0-44-5	Nash D.J.	Northern Districts v Otago	Taupo	1995/96
10-0-45-5	McNally S.R.	Canterbury v Otago	Christchurch	1984/85
10-0-48-5	Leonard D.J.	Central Districts v Canterbury	Levin	1989/90
10-2-58-5	Yardley B.	Australia v Northern Districts	Hamilton	1981/82

(Note: A.J. Alcock had figures of 10-3-31-5 for Central Districts v Canterbury at Christchurch, 1993/94, but the game was abandoned and none of the performances in the game are included in any records).

Most Expensive Bowling

10-0-93-2	Presland C.M.	Northern Districts v Auckland	Gisborne	1982/83
9-0-85-1	Kennedy R.J.	Otago v Canterbury	Christchurch	1996/97
10-1-85-0	Kennedy R.J.	Otago v Central Districts	New Plymouth	1996/97
9-1-84-0	Styris S.B.	Northern Districts v Auckland	Auckland	2000/01
10-0-83-2	Welch G.	Wellington v Central Districts	New Plymouth	1997/98
10-0-80-3	Blair B.R.	Otago v Central Districts	Oamaru	1982/83
9-0-80-0	Rushton N.W.	Otago v Canterbury	Timaru	2003/04
10-0-78-0	Pryor C.R.	Otago v Wellington	Wellington	2000/01
10-2-77-0	Stott L.W.	Auckland v Northern Districts	Gisborne	1982/83
10-0-77-0	Kennedy R.J.	Otago v Canterbury	Oamaru	1997/98
10-0-77-3	Martin B.P.	New Zealand A v Sri Lanka A	lincoln	2003/04
10-0-76-1	Thomson G.B.	Otago v Wellington	Alexandra	1980/81
10-0-76-3	McNally S.R.	Canterbury v Northern Districts	Rangiora	1981/82
10-0-76-2	Findlay C.O.	Central Districts v Canterbury	Christchurch	1998/99
10-0-75-1	Marshall E.J.	Otago v Central Districts	Dannevirke	1992/93
10-0-75-1	Hastings M.A.	Canterbury v Central Districts	New Plymouth	1997/98
10-0-75-1	Martin C.S.	Canterbury v Central Districts	Christchurch	2003/04
ALSO NOTE *(8-ball overs)*				
1-0-18-0	Payton D.H.	Central Districts v Wellington	Wellington	1973/74
1-0-18-1	Redpath I.R.	Australia v Central Districts	New Plymouth	1973/74
2-0-29-0	Child M.J.	Northern Districts v Central Districts	Palmerston North	1975/76
3-0-37-0	Dunning B.	Northern Districts v Canterbury	Christchurch	1977/78
4-0-42-1	Maingay C.T.	Auckland v Wellington	Wellington	1971/72
5-0-48-0	Coles M.J.	Wellington v Canterbury	Christchurch	1975/76
6-0-56-0	Cater S.B.	Wellington v Auckland	Auckland	1977/78
6-0-56-0	Gilmour G.J.	Australia v Invitation XI	Christchurch	1976/77
7-0-68-1	Aldridge C.W.	Northern Districts v Auckland	Auckland	1978/79
ALSO NOTE *(6-ball overs)*				
1-0-22-0	Pryor C.R.	Auckland v Wellington	Wellington	1998/99
2-0-26-0	Roberts S.J.	Canterbury v Wellington	Ohoka	1990/91
3-0-42-1	McMillan C.D.	Canterbury v Central Districts	Napier	1996/97
3.1-0-57-0	Muralitharan M.	FICA World XI v New Zealand	Christchurch	2004/05
4-0-44-0	Roberts S.J.	Canterbury v Auckland	Christchurch	1986/87
5-0-47-0	Kuggeleijn C.M.	Northern Districts v Wellington	Wellington	1990/91
5.3-0-50-0	Abernethy B.	Otago v Auckland	Oamaru	1981/82
6-0-65-0	de Silva D.S.	Sri Lanka v Minor Associations	Wanganui	1982/83
7-0-71-2	Aldridge G.W.	Northern Districts v Wellington	Taupo	2004/05

Most Economical Bowling

10-7-5-2	Boock S.L.	Otago v Central Districts	Alexandra	1986/87
10-5-6-2	Larsen G.R.	Wellington v Otago	Alexandra	1992/93
*8-3-7-2	Williams J.C.	Auckland v Northern Districts	Auckland	1971/72
10-6-8-1	Hills P.W.	Otago v Auckland	Oamaru	1981/82
10-6-8-2	Nuttall A.J.	Canterbury v Wellington	Christchurch	1988/89
10-4-8-0	Duff S.W.	Central Districts v Wellington	New Plymouth	1989/90
10-5-8-3	Vaughan J.T.C.	Auckland v Central Districts	Waikanae	1993/94
10-5-8-1	Harris C.Z.	Canterbury v Auckland	Christchurch	1995/96
*7-0-9-0	Dunning B.	Northern Districts v Canterbury	Christchurch	1976/77
10-6-9-1	Boock S.L.	Otago v Canterbury	Christchurch	1979/80
10-4-9-1	de Mel A.L.F.	Sri Lanka v Minor Associations	Wanganui	1982/83
10-5-9-2	Astle N.J.	Canterbury v Northern Districts	Christchurch	1991/92
10-4-9-2	Astle N.J.	Canterbury v Wellington	Christchurch	1993/94
10-3-9-1	de Groen R.P.	Northern Districts v Central Districts	Levin	1995/96

10-6-9-2	McCullum N.J.	Otago v Auckland	Auckland	2000/01
*7-1-10-2	Kirk C.M.	Canterbury v Otago	Christchurch	1973/74
10-5-10-3	McIntyre J.M.	Auckland v Canterbury	Auckland	1980/81
10-4-10-2	Pigott A.C.S.	Wellington v Northern Districts	Tauranga	1983/84
10-6-10-0	Bracewell J.G.	Auckland v Canterbury	Auckland	1986/87
10-7-10-4	Duers K.G.	Zimbabwe v Northern Districts	Cambridge	1991/92
10-3-10-2	Williams B.R.	Wellington v Northern Districts	Gisborne	1993/94
10-3-10-3	Larsen G.R.	Wellington v Canterbury	Rangiora	1994/95

** 8-ball overs*

(Note: C.M. Brown had figures of 10-5-6-2 for Auckland v Otago at Dunedin, 1993/94 but the game was abandoned and none of the performances in the game are included in any records).

Hat-tricks

7-0-23-7	Watson W.	Auckland v Otago	Auckland	1984/85
10-0-48-4	Briasco P.S.	Central Districts v Auckland	Napier	1989/90
10-1-40-3	Walker M.D.J.	Wellington v Otago	Dunedin	2000/01

Wicketkeeping

DISMISSALS

	(ct/st)				
6	(5/1)	Murray D.A.	West Indies v Central Districts	New Plymouth	1979/80
6	(6/0)	McSweeney E.B.	Wellington v Auckland	Wellington	1982/83
6	(6/0)	McSweeney E.B.	Wellington v Northern Districts	Wellington	1988/89
6	(6/0)	McRae G.P.	Central Districts v Wellington	Masterton	1994/95
5	(5/0)	Dykes R.A.	Auckland v Wellington	Wellington	1973/74
5	(4/1)	Smith I.D.S.	Central Districts v Northern Districts	Hamilton	1981/82
5	(5/0)	Milburn B.D.	Otago v Central Districts	Oamaru	1982/83
5	(5/0)	Wright M.J.E.	Northern Districts v Auckland	Gisborne	1982/83
5	(5/0)	Germon L.K.	Canterbury v Otago	Christchurch	1988/89
5	(3/2)	Blain T.E.	Central Districts v Auckland	New Plymouth	1992/93
5	(4/1)	Adams J.C.	West Indies v Auckland	Auckland	1994/95
5	(4/1)	Nevin C.J.	Wellington v Otago	Wellington	1997/98
5	(4/1)	Nevin C.J.	Wellington v Otago	Wellington	2000/01
5	(5/0)	Griggs B.B.J.	Central Districts v Auckland	Auckland	2000/01
5	(5/0	Vincent L.	Auckland v Otago	Auckland	2002/03
5	(4/1)	Nevin C.J.	North Island v South Island	Christchurch	2003/04
5	(5/0)	McCullum B.B.	New Zealand v FICA World XI	Hamilton	2004/05

THREE STUMPINGS IN AN INNINGS

Rixon S.J.	NSW v Wellington	Wellington	1984/85
Dyer G.C.	NSW v Wellington	Wellington	1986/87

Fielding

CATCHES

5	Wilson J.W.	Otago v Auckland	Dunedin	1993/94
4	Redmond R.E.	Auckland v Otago	Auckland	1972/73
4	Sampson H.C.	Otago v Canterbury	Christchurch	1974/75
4	Howarth G.P.	Invitation XI v Australia	Auckland	1976/77
4	Wiltshire J.R.	Auckland v Northern Districts	Auckland	1978/79
4	Dickeson C.W.	Northern Districts v Canterbury	Hamilton	1980/81
4	Cooper B.G.	Northern Districts v Central Districts	Palmerston North	1982/83
4	Hore A.J.	Otago v Canterbury	Christchurch	1998/99

HISTORY OF THE LIMITED-OVER COMPETITION IN NEW ZEALAND

2004/05 was the 34th season of limited over competition between the six New Zealand first-class sides. In that time there have been several changes both in sponsorship and format.

For the first six seasons a knock-out competition was sponsored by the New Zealand Motor Corporation. Each innings was limited to 40 eight-ball overs during the initial two seasons, reduced to 35 thereafter. In 1977/78 and 1978/79 the sponsors changed and the teams competed for the Gillette Cup. In the first season 30 eight-ball overs were used but the limit reverted to 35 the following year. There was no sponsorship for the competition in 1979/80, known simply as the National Knock-out, where 50 six-ball overs was the limit for each innings.

In 1980/81. the Shell Cup, previously contested for as part of the first-class season, became the limited-over prize and the contest was run on a league basis for the first time with each side playing the other once.

In keeping with the previous limited-over competitions, a final was arranged, this time between the top two teams of the league table, points gained being disregarded at this stage. Fifty six-ball overs was the limit on each innings.

From 1985/86 the competition was held in its entirety, prior to the Shell Trophy series with no final. From 1989/90 the top four teams in the league table went on to semi-final play-offs, previous points being disregarded. The top two teams gained home ground advantage, the venue for the final being decided in a similar manner.

From 1993/94 to 1998/99 the top two sides played each other, with the winner going into the grand final. The loser then played the winner of the game between third and fourth to find the other finalist. From 1999/00, the leading team after the round robin went straight to the final with the second and third-placed sides meeting in a semi-final to find the other finalist. The finals became a best-of-three series.

In 2001/02, with a change of sponsor, the competition was renamed the State Shield. The format remained unaltered except the final reverted to a single game.

Winners of Limited-over Competitions

NEW ZEALAND MOTOR CORPORATION KNOCK-OUT

1971/72	Canterbury
1972/73	Auckland
1973/74	Wellington
1974/75	Wellington
1975/76	Canterbury
1976/77	Canterbury

GILLETTE CUP

1977/78	Canterbury
1978/79	Auckland

NATIONAL KNOCK-OUT

1979/80	Northern Districts

SHELL CUP

1980/81	Auckland
1981/82	Wellington
1982/83	Auckland
1983/84	Auckland
1984/85	Central Districts
1985/86	Canterbury
1986/87	Auckland
1987/88	Otago
1988/89	Wellington
1989/90	Auckland
1990/91	Wellington
1991/92	Canterbury
1992/93	Canterbury
1993/94	Canterbury
1994/95	Northern Districts
1995/96	Canterbury
1996/97	Canterbury
1997/98	Northern Districts
1998/99	Canterbury
1999/00	Canterbury
2000/01	Central Districts

STATE SHIELD

2001/02	Wellington
2002/03	Northern Districts
2003/04	Central Districts
2004/05	Northern Districts

Table of Results

1971/72 — 2004/05

	P	W	L	NR
Auckland	218*	101	101	16
Canterbury	229	133	84	12
Central Districts	211	88	107	16
Northern Districts	221	105	110	6
Otago	204	66	128	10
Wellington	223	125	88	10

** The Auckland and Central Districts totals include a match won by the toss of a coin against Central Districts and Northern Districts respectively.*

Northern Districts v Otago in 1980/81, Auckland v Wellington in 1985/86, Canterbury v Auckland, Auckland v Central Districts and Wellington v Otago in 1991/92, Central Districts v Auckland and Auckland v Wellington in 1996/97, Canterbury v Northern Districts in 1997/98, Central Districts v Canterbury in 1999/00 and Central Districts v Otago, Northern Districts, Canterbury and Auckland and Auckland v Canterbury in 2000/01 were abandoned without a ball being bowled. Wellington v Auckland in 1984/85 and Northern Districts v Canterbury 1988/89 were abandoned after one innings had been completed. The semi-final between Canterbury and Central Districts 1993/94 was due to be replayed after a match had been started and abandoned. However, no play at all was possible in the scheduled replay.

INTER-PROVINCIAL RECORDS

	Highest Score	*Lowest Score*	*Highest Individual Score*	*Best Bowling*
Auckland	318-5 v N.D. 2000/01	70 v N.D. 1977/78	L. Vincent 145 v C.D. 1999/00	W. Watson 7-0-23-7 v Otago 1984/85
Canterbury	329-5 v N.D. 1995/96	75 v Otago 1973/74	B.R. Hartland 161 v N.D. 1993/94	C.L. Cairns 10-1-37-6 v Wellington 1996/97
Central Districts	376-3 v Otago 1996/97	58 v Wellington 2001/02	D.P. Kelly 140 v Wellington 1999/00	M.J. Mason 9.3-1-25-6 v Auckland 2003/04
Northern Districts	306-2 v Auckland 1982/83	76 v C.D. 1987/88	D.L. Vettori 138 v Canterbury 2004/05	B.J. Barrett 10-5-12-6 v Otago 1986/87
Otago	299-9 v CD 2004/05	64 v Wellington/CD 1984/85 2004/05	M.H. Richardson 128* v C.D. 1996/97	E.J. Marshall 7.1-0-49-7 v Auckland 1993/94
Wellington	308-9 v Canterbury 2003/04	66 v Canterbury 1996/97	C.J. Nevin 149 v CD 1997/98	A.J. Penn 8-1-28-7 v ND 2000/01

	Most Economical Bowling	*Most Expensive Bowling*	*Most Catches/ Stumpings in an innings*
Auckland	J.T.C. Vaughan 10-5-8-3 v C.D. 1993/94 J.C. Williams 8-3-7-2 (8 ball overs) v N.D. 1971/72	L.W. Stott 10-2-77-0 v N.D. 1982/83	R.A. Dykes 5c v Wellington 1973/74 L. Vincent 5c v Otago 2002/03
Canterbury	A.J. Nuttall 10-6-8-2 v Wellington 1988/89 C.Z. Harris 10-5-8-1 v Auckland 1995/96	S.R. McNally 10-0-76-3 v N.D. 1981/82	L.K. Germon 5c v Otago 1988/89
Central Districts	S.W. Duff 10-4-8-0 v Wellington 1989/90	C.O. Findlay 10-0-76-2 v Canterbury 1998/99	G.P. McRae 6c v Wellington 1994/95
Northern Districts	R.P. de Groen 10-3-9-1 v C.D. 1995/96	C.M. Presland 10-0-93-2 v Auckland 1982/83	M.J.E. Wright 5c v Auckland 1982/83
Otago	S.L. Boock 10-7-5-2 v C.D. 1986/87	R.J. Kennedy 9-0-85-1 v Canterbury 1996/97 R.J. Kennedy 10-1-85-0 v C.D. 1996/97	B.D. Milburn 5c v C.D. 1982/83 J.W. Wilson 5c v Auckland 1993/94
Wellington	G.R. Larsen 10-5-6-2 v Otago 1992/93	G. Welch 10-0-83-2 v CD 1997/98	E.B. McSweeney 6c v Auckland 1982/83 E.B. McSweeney 6c v N.D. 1988/89

RECORD PARTNERSHIPS

AUCKLAND

1st	166*	Young B.A. & Pocock B.A.	v Central Districts	Auckland	1998/99
2nd	154	Crowe J.J. & Brown S.W.	v Northern Districts	Auckland	1991/92
3rd	129	Crowe J.J. & Vaughan J.T.C.	v Otago	Alexandra	1991/92
4th	157	Nicol R.J. & Barnes A.C.	v Otago	Auckland	2003/04
5th	171	Vivian G.E. & Reid J.F.	v Wellington	Auckland	1977/78
6th	109	Lynch S.M. & Vaughan J.T.C.	v Otago	Auckland	1996/97
7th	87	Mills K.D. & Hitchcock P.A.	v Central Districts	Auckland	2004/05
8th	† 121	Canning T.K. & Morgan R.G.	v Otago	Alexandra	2000/01
9th	59	Mills J.M. & Haslam M.J.	v Wellington	Wellington	1998/99
10th	47	Lyon B.J. & Walmsley K.P.	v Central Districts	Auckland	1997/98
	47*	Parore A.C. & Haslam M.J.	v Canterbury	Auckland	2001/02

CANTERBURY

1st	168	Papps M.H.W. & Astle N.J.	v Wellington	Timaru	2004/05
2nd	† 189	Hartland B.R. & Howell L.G.	v Northern Districts	Timaru	1993/94
3rd	174	McMillan C.D. & Latham R.T.	v Central Districts	Christchurch	1994/95
4th	† 221	Howell L.G. & Stead G.R.	v Otago	Oamaru	1997/98
5th	† 198	Cairns C.L. & Germon L.K.	v Wellington	Christchurch	1992/93
6th	† 142	Cairns C.L. & Fleming S.P.	v Central Districts	Napier	1993/94
7th	74	Redmond A.J. & Wisneski W.A.	v Wellington	Wellington	2001/02
8th	91	Harris C.Z. & Wiseman P.J.	v Central Districts	Christchurch	2003/04
9th	53	Howell L.G. & Petrie R.G.	v Wellington	Wellington	1991/92
10th	34*	Anderson C.J. & Burson R.D.	v Otago	Oamaru	2001/02

CENTRAL DISTRICTS

1st	155	Spearman C.M. & How J.M.	v Canterbury	Christchurch	2003/04
2nd	172	How J.M. & Taylor R.L.	v Northern Districts	Masterton	2004/05
3rd	156	Oram J.D.P. & Douglas M.W.	v Otago	Hastings	1998/99
4th	132	Sinclair M.S. & Oram J.D.P.	v Auckland	Auckland	2003/04
5th	153*	Harden R.J. & Blain T.E.	v Canterbury	Christchurch	1990/91
6th	103	Sandbrook I.P. & Griggs B.B.J.	v Canterbury	Nelson	2002/03
7th	109	Sulzberger G.P. & Furlong C.J.M.	v Otago	Palmerston Nth	1997/98
8th	79	Findlay C.O. & Furlong C.J.M.	v Northern Districts	Nelson	1998/99
9th	92	Loveridge G.R. & Penn A.J.	v Canterbury	Napier	1996/97
10th	50	Garner C.D. & Alcock A.J.	v Otago	Oamaru	1993/94

NORTHERN DISTRICTS

1st	168	Marshall J.A.H. & Vettori D.L.	v Wellington	Hamilton	2002/03
2nd	126*	Parlane M.E. & Parlane N.R.	v Otago	Alexandra	1999/00
3rd	199*	Parker J.M. & Cooper B.G.	v Auckland	Gisborne	1982/83
4th	123	Parore A.C. & Thomson S.A.	v Canterbury	Mt Maunganui	1995/96
5th	137	Nash D.J. & Bradburn G.E.	v Otago	Taupo	1997/98
6th	115	Bell M.D. & Hart M.N.	v Central Districts	Napier	1996/97
7th	96	Styris S.B. & McGlashan P.D.	v Central Districts	Masterton	2004/05
8th	75	Dickeson C.W. & Child M.J.	v Auckland	Pukekohe	1980/81
9th	68*	Hart R.G. & Styris S.B.	v Wellington	Wellington	1996/97
10th	† 62	Aldridge G.W. & Butler I.G.	v Canterbury	Hamilton	2003/04

OTAGO

1st	154	Hore A.J. & Lawson R.A.	v Wellington	Wellington	2001/02
2nd	134*	Richardson M.H. & Lamont M.J.	v Auckland	Auckland	1998/99
3rd	138	Gaffaney C.B. & Lawson R.A.	v Wellington	Dunedin	2003/04
4th	147	Lawson R.A. & Wilson J.W.	v Canterbury	Alexandra	2003/04
5th	130	McKenzie M.N. & McGlashan P.D.	v Northern Districts	Rotorua	2002/03
6th	121	Gaffaney C.B. & Pryor C.R.	v Canterbury	Alexandra	2000/01
7th	103*	Richardson M.H. & Campbell P.A.	v Central Districts	New Plymouth	1996/97
8th	93	McSkimming W.C. & Morland N.D.	v Central Districts	New Plymouth	2002/03
9th	48	Morland N.D. & Rushton N.W.	v Central Districts	Masterton	2003/04
10th	56*	McSkimming W.C. & Sewell D.G.	v Northern Districts	Oamaru	2000/01

WELLINGTON

1st	† 205*	Aiken J.M. & Douglas M.W.	v Canterbury	Wellington	1994/95
2nd	173	Weenink S.W. & Wells J.D.	v Central Districts	Wellington	1996/97
3rd	† 244*	Fleming S.P. & Twose R.G.	v Otago	Wellington	2000/01
4th	143	Jones A.H. & Coney J.V.	v Canterbury	Timaru	1986/87
5th	127	Twose R.G. & Kerr R.J.	v Northern Districts	Wellington	1996/97
6th	102	Bell M.D. & Walker M.D.J.	v Central Districts	Wellington	2003/04
7th	† 130*	Bell M.D. & Mather S.R.	v Northern Districts	Mt Maunganui	1997/98
8th	98*	Taylor B.R. & Collinge R.O.	v Central Districts	Lower Hutt	1971/72
9th	† 98	Doull L.J. & Williams B.R.	v Otago	Alexandra	1993/94
10th	36*	Jefferson M.R. & R.J. Kennedy	v Canterbury	Christchurch	1999/00

† record for all teams

DOMESTIC ONE-DAY CAREER RECORDS

BATTING		*M*	*In*	*NO*	*HS*	*Runs*	*Ave*	*100s*	*50s*
Howell L.G.	*C, CD, A, ND*	105	105	14	134*	3022	33.20	5	22
Astle N.J.	*C*	91	82	12	131	3009	42.98	8	13
Barnes A.C.	*A*	114	112	11	116	2866	28.37	2	20
Harris C.Z.	*C*	103	94	31	107	2852	44.26	1	16
Twose R.G.	*ND, CD, W*	95	93	9	124*	2769	32.96	6	16
Parlane M.E.	*ND, W*	100	100	3	122	2752	28.37	3	16
Nevin C.J.	*W*	95	90	6	149	2429	28.91	4	13
Spearman C.M.	*A, CD*	90	90	1	126	2421	27.20	1	17
Douglas M.W.	*CD, W*	101	98	8	121	2326	25.84	2	10
Fleming S.P.	*C, W*	69	64	10	131	2301	42.61	5	15
Young B.A.	*ND, A*	85	83	8	101*	2284	30.45	1	15
Richardson M.H.	*A, O*	76	74	7	128*	2283	34.07	3	14
Lawson R.A.	*O*	90	87	7	83*	2241	28.01	—	16
Latham R.T.	*C*	84	80	4	108	2206	29.02	1	9
McMillan C.D.	*C*	75	71	10	125	2203	36.11	7	6
Crowe M.D.	*A, CD, W*	57	56	5	125	2171	42.56	5	12
Bailey M.D.	*ND*	103	101	14	76*	2159	24.81	—	11
Cairns C.L.	*ND, C*	85	77	11	143	2145	32.50	3	11
Stead G.R.	*C*	97	86	11	101*	2081	27.74	2	9
Sinclair M.S.	*CD*	79	78	8	110	2073	29.61	1	16
Bell M.D.	*ND, W*	91	87	6	121*	2062	25.45	3	8
Gaffaney C.B.	*O*	86	84	2	101*	2057	25.08	1	10
Bradburn G.E.	*ND*	121	110	15	80*	2048	21.55	—	5

BOWLING		M	O	M	R	W	Ave	R/O	Best
Tait A.R.	*ND*	90	757.4	75	3138	128	24.51	4.14	4-29
Petrie R.G.	*C, W*	100	736	58	3146	119	26.43	4.27	5-24
Harris C.Z.	*C*	103	808.3	58	2873	110	26.11	3.55	4-28
Priest M.W.	*C*	89	724.5	69	2668	106	25.16	3.68	5-26
Astle N.J.	*C*	91	679.1	84	2278	98	23.24	3.35	4-14
Vaughan J.T.C.	*A*	56	500	50	1760	97	18.14	3.52	6-26
Larsen G.R.	*W*	87	765.4	103	2334	94	24.82	3.04	5-30
Gale A.J.	*O*	75	673	69	2583	93	27.77	3.83	5-43
Wisneski W.A.	*CD, C*	70	571.3	40	2538	92	27.58	4.44	6-43
Styris S.B.	*ND*	71	624.5	44	2236	92	24.30	3.57	4-19
Hitchcock P.A.	*A, W*	54	450.5	28	2052	90	22.80	4.55	5-10
Bradburn G.E.	*ND*	121	895.4	59	3264	89	36.67	3.65	4-28
Hart M.N.	*ND*	102	628.1	55	2442	89	27.43	3.88	4-7
Cairns C.L.	*ND, C*	85	538.2	39	2183	88	24.80	4.04	6-37
Twose R.G.	*ND, CD, W*	95	480.3	28	1896	87	21.79	3.94	5-30
Jonas G.R.	*W, O*	56	492	36	2147	86	24.96	4.36	4-18

MOST ECONOMICAL BOWLING *(qualification 100 overs)*

		O	M	R	W	Ave	R/O
Hadlee R.J.	*C*	174.4	33	440	29	15.17	2.51
Boock S.L.	*O*	338.2	74	947	47	20.12	2.79
McIntyre J.M.	*A*	118	25	335	15	22.33	2.83
Webb R.J.	*O*	117.4	16	344	20	17.20	2.92
Mallender N.A.	*O*	458.4	83	1356	72	18.83	2.95
Chatfield E.J.	*W*	305	68	902	50	18.04	2.95

FIELDING		Ct	St	Total
Hart R.G.	*ND*	117	30	147
Nevin C.J.	*W*	132	12	144
McSweeney E.B.	*CD, W*	97	26	123
Germon L.K.	*C, O*	88	18	106
Blain T.E.	*CD, C*	62	15	77
Hopkins G.J.	*ND, C, O*	65	12	77
Croy M.G.	*O*	64	9	73
Young B.A.	*ND, A*	46	12	58
Bradburn G.E.	*ND*	57	—	57
Vincent L.	*A*	53	3	56
Hart M.N.	*ND*	55	—	55
Griggs B.B.J.	*CD*	51	3	54
Harris C.Z.	*C*	53	—	53
Douglas M.W.	*CD, W*	47	5	52

NEW ZEALAND ONE-DAY INTERNATIONAL RECORDS

TEAM RECORDS

Results

1972/73	Pakistan	Christchurch	NZ 187	P 165	*NZ won by 22 runs*
1973	England	Swansea	NZ 158	E 159-3	*England won by 7 wickets*
	England	Manchester	E 167-8		*abandoned*
1973/74	Australia	Dunedin	NZ 194-9	A 195-3	*Australia won by 7 wickets*
	Australia	Christchurch	A 265-5	NZ 234-6	*Australia won by 31 runs*
1974/75	England	Melbourne	NZ 262-8	E 196	*NZ won by 66 runs*
	England	Dunedin	E 136	NZ 15-0	*abandoned*
	England	Wellington	NZ 227	E 35-1	*abandoned*
1975	East Africa	Birmingham	NZ 309-5	EA 128-8	*NZ won by 181 runs*
World Cup	England	Nottingham	E 266-6	NZ 186	*England won by 80 runs*
	India	Manchester	I 230-9	NZ 233-6	*NZ won by 4 wickets*
	West Indies	The Oval	NZ 158	WI 159-5	*West Indies won by 5 wickets*
1975/76	India	Christchurch	I 154	NZ 155-1	*NZ won by 9 wickets*
	India	Auckland	NZ 236-8	I 156	*NZ won by 80 runs*
1976/77	Pakistan	Sialkot	NZ 198-8	P 197-9	*NZ won by 1 run*
1978	England	Scarborough	E 206-8	NZ 187-8	*England won by 19 runs*
	England	Manchester	E 278-5	NZ 152	*England won by 126 runs*
1979	Sri Lanka	Nottingham	SL 189	NZ 190-1	*NZ won by 9 wickets*
World Cup	India	Leeds	I 182	NZ 183-2	*NZ won by 8 wickets*
	West Indies	Nottingham	WI 244-7	NZ 212-9	*West Indies won by 32 runs*
	England	Manchester	E 221-8	NZ 212-9	*England won by 9 runs*
1979/80	West Indies	Christchurch	WI 203-7	NZ 207-9	*NZ won by 1 wicket*
1980/81	Australia	Adelaide	A 217-9	NZ 219-7	*NZ won by 3 wickets*
	Australia	Sydney	A 289-3	NZ 195	*Australia won by 94 runs*
	Australia	Melbourne	NZ 156	A 159-6	*Australia won by 4 wickets*
	India	Perth	I 162	NZ 157	*India won by 5 runs*
	India	Brisbane	I 204	NZ 205-7	*NZ won by 3 wickets*
	India	Adelaide	I 230-7	NZ 224	*India won by 6 runs*
	India	Melbourne	I 112-9	NZ 113-0	*NZ won by 10 wickets*
	Australia	Sydney	NZ 220-8	A 219-7	*NZ won by 1 run*
	India	Brisbane	NZ 242-9	I 220	*NZ won by 22 runs*
	Australia	Sydney	A 180	NZ 23-1	*abandoned*
	Australia	Sydney	NZ 233-6	A 155	*NZ won by 78 runs*
	Australia	Melbourne	NZ 126	A 130-3	*Australia won by 7 wickets*
	Australia	Melbourne	A 235-4	NZ 229-8	*Australia won by 6 runs*
	Australia	Sydney	NZ 215-8	A 218-4	*Australia won by 6 wickets*
1980/81	India	Auckland	NZ 218-6	I 140-9	*NZ won by 78 runs*
	India	Hamilton	NZ 210-8	I 153	*NZ won by 57 runs*

Season	Opponent	Venue	Team 1	Team 2	Result
1981/82	Australia	Auckland	NZ 240-6	A 194	*NZ won by 46 runs*
	Australia	Dunedin	NZ 159-9	A 160-4	*Australia won by 6 wickets*
	Australia	Wellington	NZ 74	A 75-2	*Australia won by 8 wickets*
1982/83	Australia	Melbourne	NZ 181	A 182-2	*Australia won by 8 wickets*
	England	Melbourne	NZ 239-8	E 237-8	*NZ won by 2 runs*
	England	Brisbane	E 267-6	NZ 213	*England won by 54 runs*
	Australia	Sydney	NZ 226-8	A 179	*NZ won by 47 runs*
	England	Sydney	NZ 199	E 200-2	*England won by 8 wickets*
	Australia	Melbourne	NZ 246-6	A 188	*NZ won by 58 runs*
	England	Adelaide	E 296-5	NZ 297-6	*NZ won by 4 wickets*
	Australia	Adelaide	NZ 200-9	A 153	*NZ won by 47 runs*
	England	Perth	E 88-7	NZ 89-3	*NZ won by 7 wickets*
	Australia	Perth	A 191-9	NZ 164	*Australia won by 27 runs*
	Australia	Sydney	NZ 193-7	A 155-4	*Australia won on faster scoring rate*
	Australia	Melbourne	A 302-8	NZ 153	*Australia won by 149 runs*
1982/83	England	Auckland	E 184	NZ 187-4	*NZ won by 6 wickets*
	England	Wellington	NZ 295-6	E 192	*NZ won by 103 runs*
	England	Christchurch	NZ 211-8	E 127	*NZ won by 84 runs*
	Sri Lanka	Dunedin	NZ 183-8	SL 118-9	*NZ won by 65 runs*
	Australia	Sydney	NZ 138-8	A 124	*NZ won by 14 runs*
	Sri Lanka	Napier	SL 167-8	NZ 168-3	*NZ won by 7 wickets*
	Sri Lanka	Auckland	NZ 304-5	SL 188-6	*NZ won by 116 runs*
1983 *World Cup*	England	The Oval	E 322-6	NZ 216	*England won by 106 runs*
	Pakistan	Birmingham	NZ 238-9	P 186	*NZ won by 52 runs*
	Sri Lanka	Bristol	SL 206	NZ 209-5	*NZ won by 5 wickets*
	England	Birmingham	E 234	NZ 238-8	*NZ won by 2 wickets*
	Sri Lanka	Derby	NZ 181	SL 184-7	*Sri Lanka won by 3 wickets*
	Pakistan	Nottingham	P 261-3	NZ 250	*Pakistan won by 11 runs*
1983/84	England	Christchurch	E 188-9	NZ 134	*England won by 54 runs*
	England	Wellington	NZ 135	E 139-4	*England won by 6 wickets*
	England	Auckland	E 209-9	NZ 210-3	*NZ won by 7 wickets*
1983/84	Sri Lanka	Colombo	NZ 234-6	SL 130	*NZ won by 104 runs*
	Sri Lanka	Moratuwa	SL 157-8	NZ 116	*Sri Lanka won by 41 runs*
	Sri Lanka	Colombo	NZ 201-8	SL 115	*NZ won by 86 runs*
1984/85	Sri Lanka	Colombo	NZ 171-6	SL 174-6	*Sri Lanka won by 4 wickets*
	Sri Lanka	Moratuwa	SL 114-9	NZ 118-3	*NZ won by 7 wickets*
	Pakistan	Peshawar	P 191-5	NZ 145	*Pakistan won by 46 runs*
	Pakistan	Faisalabad	P 157-5	NZ 152-7	*Pakistan won by 5 runs*
	Pakistan	Sialkot	NZ 187-9	P 153-8	*NZ won by 34 runs*
	Pakistan	Multan	NZ 213-8	P 214-9	*Pakistan won by 1 wicket*
1984/85	Pakistan	Napier	NZ 277-6	P 167-9	*NZ won by 110 runs*
	Pakistan	Hamilton	P 221-4	NZ 222-6	*NZ won by 4 wickets*
	Pakistan	Christchurch	NZ 264-8	P 251	*NZ won by 13 runs*
	Pakistan	Auckland	P 189		*abandoned*
1984/85 *World Championship of Cricket*	West Indies	Sydney	NZ 57-2		*abandoned*
	Sri Lanka	Melbourne	NZ 223	SL 172	*NZ won by 51 runs*
	India	Sydney	NZ 206	I 207-3	*India won by 7 wickets*
	West Indies	Sydney	NZ 138-9	WI 139-4	*West Indies won by 6 wickets*

1984/85	West Indies	Antigua	WI 231-8	NZ 208-8	*West Indies won by 23 runs*
	West Indies	Port of Spain	NZ 51-3	WI 55-4	*West Indies won by 6 wickets*
	West Indies	Berbice	WI 259-5	NZ 129	*West Indies won by 130 runs*
	West Indies	Port of Spain	NZ 116	WI 117-0	*West Indies won by 10 wickets*
	West Indies	Bridgetown	WI 265-3	NZ 153-8	*West Indies won by 112 runs*
1985/86	Australia	Melbourne	NZ 161-7		*abandoned*
	India	Brisbane	NZ 259-9	I 263-5	*India won by 5 wickets*
	Australia	Sydney	NZ 152	A 153-6	*Australia won by 4 wickets*
	India	Perth	I 113	NZ 115-7	*NZ won by 3 wickets*
	Australia	Perth	NZ 159-6	A 161-6	*Australia won by 4 wickets*
	India	Melbourne	I 238-8	NZ 239-5	*NZ won by 5 wickets*
	India	Adelaide	NZ 172	I 174-5	*India won by 5 wickets*
	Australia	Adelaide	NZ 276-7	A 70	*NZ won by 206 runs*
	Australia	Sydney	A 239-7	NZ 140	*Australia won by 99 runs*
	India	Launceston	I 202-9	NZ 168-9	*India won by 21 runs (target adjusted)*
1985/86	Australia	Dunedin	NZ 186-6	A 156	*NZ won by 30 runs*
	Australia	Christchurch	NZ 258-7	A 205	*NZ won by 53 runs*
	Australia	Wellington	NZ 229-9	A 232-7	*Australia won by 3 wickets*
	Australia	Auckland	A 231	NZ 187-9	*Australia won by 44 runs*
1985/86	Sri Lanka	Colombo	SL 137-9	NZ 140-4	*NZ won by 6 wickets*
	Pakistan	Colombo	NZ 214-8	P 217-6	*Pakistan won by 4 wickets*
	India	Sharjah	NZ 132-8	I 134-7	*India won by 3 wickets*
	Pakistan	Sharjah	NZ 64	P 66-0	*Pakistan won by 10 wickets*
1986	England	Leeds	NZ 217-8	E 170	*NZ won by 47 runs*
	England	Manchester	NZ 284-5	E 286-4	*England won by 6 wickets*
1986/87	West Indies	Dunedin	WI 237-9	NZ 142	*West Indies won by 95 runs*
	West Indies	Auckland	NZ 213	WI 217-4	*West Indies won by 6 wickets*
	West Indies	Wellington	*abandoned without a ball being bowled*		
	West Indies	Christchurch	NZ 191-9	WI 192-0	*West Indies won by 10 wickets*
1987/88	Zimbabwe	Hyderabad	NZ 242-7	Z 239	*NZ won by 3 runs*
World Cup	India	Bangalore	I 252-7	NZ 236-8	*India won by 16 runs*
	Australia	Indore	A 199-4	NZ 196-9	*Australia won by 3 runs*
	Zimbabwe	Calcutta	Z 227-5	NZ 228-6	*NZ won by 4 wickets*
	Australia	Chandigarh	A 251-8	NZ 234	*Australia won by 17 runs*
	India	Nagpur	NZ 221-9	I 224-1	*India won by 9 wickets*
1987/88	Australia	Perth	NZ 232-9	A 231	*NZ won by 1 run*
	Sri Lanka	Sydney	SL 174	NZ 178-4	*NZ won by 6 wickets*
	Australia	Melbourne	A 216	NZ 210-9	*Australia won by 6 runs*
	Sri Lanka	Adelaide	SL 241	NZ 242-6	*NZ won by 4 wickets*
	Sri Lanka	Hobart	NZ 199-7	SL 200-6	*Sri Lanka won by 4 wickets*
	Sri Lanka	Brisbane	SL 164-8	NZ 167-6	*NZ won by 4 wickets*
	Australia	Brisbane	NZ 176-5	A 177-5	*Australia won by 5 wickets*
	Australia	Sydney	A 221-8	NZ 143	*Australia won by 78 runs*
	Australia	Melbourne	NZ 177	A 180-2	*Australia won by 8 wickets*
	Australia	Sydney	NZ 168-5	A 169-4	*Australia won by 6 wickets*

Season	Opponent	Venue	First innings	Second innings	Result
1987/88	England	Dunedin	NZ 204	E 207-5	*England won by 5 wickets*
	England	Christchurch	NZ 186-8	E 188-4	*England won by 6 wickets*
	England	Napier	E 219	NZ 223-3	*NZ won by 7 wickets*
	England	Auckland	E 208	NZ 211-6	*NZ won by 4 wickets*
1987/88	India	Sharjah	I 267-6	NZ 194-8	*India won by 73 runs*
	Sri Lanka	Sharjah	NZ 258-8	SL 159	*NZ won by 99 runs*
	Sri Lanka	Sharjah	NZ 249-7	SL 206-9	*NZ won by 43 runs*
	India	Sharjah	I 250-7	NZ 198	*India won by 52 runs*
1988/89	India	Visakhapatnam	NZ 196-9	I 197-6	*India won by 4 wickets*
	India	Cuttack	NZ 160-7	I 161-5	*India won by 5 wickets*
	India	Indore	I 222-6	NZ 169-9	*India won by 53 runs*
	India	Baroda	NZ 278-3	I 282-8	*India won by 2 wickets*
	India	Jammu	*abandoned without a ball being bowled*		
1988/89	Pakistan	Dunedin	P 170-9	NZ 174-2	*NZ won by 8 wickets*
	Pakistan	Christchurch	P 170-7	NZ 171-3	*NZ won by 7 wickets*
	Pakistan	Wellington	P 253-6	NZ 254-4	*NZ won by 6 wickets*
	Pakistan	Auckland	NZ 249	P 251-3	*Pakistan won by 7 wickets*
	Pakistan	Hamilton	P 138-9	NZ 139-3	*NZ won by 7 wickets*
1989/90	India	Dunedin	NZ 246-6	I 138	*NZ won by 108 runs*
	Australia	Christchurch	A 244-8	NZ 94	*Australia won by 150 runs*
	India	Wellington	I 221	NZ 220	*India won by 1 run*
	Australia	Auckland	A 239-6	NZ 167-2	*Australia won on faster scoring rate*
	Australia	Auckland	NZ 162	A 164-2	*Australia won by 8 wickets*
1989/90	Australia	Sharjah	A 258-5	NZ 195-7	*Australia won by 63 runs*
	Bangladesh	Sharjah	NZ 338-4	B 177-5	*NZ won by 161 runs*
	Pakistan	Sharjah	NZ 74	P 75-2	*Pakistan won by 8 wickets*
1990	England	Leeds	E 295-6	NZ 298-6	*NZ won by 4 wickets*
	England	The Oval	NZ 212-6	E 213-4	*England won by 6 wickets*
1990/91	Pakistan	Lahore	P 196-8	NZ 177	*Pakistan won by 19 runs*
	Pakistan	Peshawar	NZ 127	P 128-2	*Pakistan won by 8 wickets*
	Pakistan	Sialkot	P 223-2	NZ 118	*Pakistan won by 105 runs*
1990/91	Australia	Sydney	A 236-9	NZ 174-7	*Australia won by 61 runs target reduced*
	England	Adelaide	NZ 199-6	E 192-9	*NZ won by 7 runs*
	Australia	Adelaide	NZ 208-7	A 210-4	*Australia won by 6 wickets*
	England	Perth	NZ 158	E 161-6	*England won by 4 wickets*
	Australia	Melbourne	A 263-7	NZ 224-8	*Australia won by 39 runs*
	England	Sydney	E 194	NZ 161	*England won by 33 runs*
	England	Brisbane	E 203-6	NZ 204-2	*NZ won by 8 wickets*
	Australia	Hobart	NZ 194-6	A 193	*NZ won by 1 run*
	Australia	Sydney	NZ 199-7	A 202-4	*Australia won by 6 wickets*
	Australia	Melbourne	NZ 208-6	A 209-3	*Australia won by 7 wickets*
1990/91	Sri Lanka	Napier	SL 177-8	NZ 178-5	*NZ won by 5 wickets*
	Sri Lanka	Auckland	NZ 242-5	SL 201	*NZ won by 41 runs*
	Sri Lanka	Dunedin	NZ 272-6	SL 165	*NZ won by 107 runs*
	England	Christchurch	E 230-7	NZ 216-8	*England won by 14 runs*
	England	Wellington	NZ 196-8	E 187	*NZ won by 9 runs*
	England	Auckland	NZ 224-7	E 217	*NZ won by 7 runs*

Season	Opponent	Venue	First innings	Second innings	Result
1991/92	England	Auckland	NZ 178-7	E 179-3	*England won by 7 wickets*
	England	Dunedin	NZ 186-7	E 188-7	*England won by 3 wickets*
	England	Christchurch	E 255-7	NZ 184-8	*England won by 71 runs*
1991/92	Australia	Auckland	NZ 248-6	A 211	*NZ won by 37 runs*
World Cup	Sri Lanka	Hamilton	SL 206-9	NZ 210-4	*NZ won by 6 wickets*
	South Africa	Auckland	SA 190-7	NZ 191-3	*NZ won by 7 wickets*
	Zimbabwe	Napier	NZ 163-3	Z 105-7	*NZ won by 49 runs target reduced*
	West Indies	Auckland	WI 203-7	NZ 206-5	*NZ won by 5 wickets*
	India	Dunedin	I 230-6	NZ 231-6	*NZ won by 4 wickets*
	England	Wellington	E 200-8	NZ 201-3	*NZ won by 7 wickets*
	Pakistan	Christchurch	NZ 166	P 167-3	*Pakistan won by 7 wickets*
	Pakistan	Auckland	NZ 262-7	P 264-6	*Pakistan won by 4 wickets*
1992/93	Zimbabwe	Bulawayo	NZ 244-7	Z 222-9	*NZ won by 22 runs*
	Zimbabwe	Harare	Z 271-6	NZ 272-6	*NZ won by 4 wickets*
1992/93	Sri Lanka	Colombo	NZ 166-9	SL 41-2	*abandoned*
	Sri Lanka	Colombo	NZ 190-7	SL 192-2	*SL won by 8 wickets*
	Sri Lanka	Colombo	SL 262-6	NZ 231	*SL won by 31 runs*
1992/93	Pakistan	Wellington	P 158-8	NZ 108	*Pakistan won by 50 runs*
	Pakistan	Napier	P 136-8	NZ 137-4	*NZ won by 6 wickets*
	Pakistan	Auckland	P 139	NZ 140-4	*NZ won by 6 wickets*
1992/93	Australia	Dunedin	A 258-4	NZ 129	*Australia won by 129 runs*
	Australia	Christchurch	NZ 196-8	A 197-9	*Australia won by 1 wicket*
	Australia	Wellington	NZ 214	A 126	*NZ won by 88 runs*
	Australia	Hamilton	A 247-7	NZ 250-7	*NZ won by 3 wickets*
	Australia	Auckland	A 232-8	NZ 229-8	*Australia won by 3 runs*
1993/94	South Africa	Adelaide	*abandoned without a ball being bowled*		
	Australia	Adelaide	NZ 135	A 136-2	*Australia won by 8 wickets*
	Australia	Melbourne	A 202-5	NZ 199-9	*Australia won by 3 runs*
	South Africa	Hobart	SA 147-7	NZ 148-6	*NZ won by 4 wickets*
	South Africa	Brisbane	NZ 256-7	SA 219-8	*NZ won by 9 runs target reduced*
	Australia	Sydney	NZ 198-9	A 185	*NZ won by 13 runs*
	South Africa	Perth	NZ 150	SA 151-5	*SA won by 5 wickets*
	Australia	Melbourne	A 217-3	NZ 166	*Australia won by 51 runs*
1993/94	Pakistan	Dunedin	NZ 122-9	P 123-5	*Pakistan won by 5 wickets*
	Pakistan	Auckland	P 146	NZ 110	*Pakistan won by 36 runs*
	Pakistan	Wellington	P 213-6	NZ 202-8	*Pakistan won by 11 runs*
	Pakistan	Auckland	P 161-9	NZ 161	*Tie*
	Pakistan	Christchurch	P 145-9	NZ 146-3	*NZ won by 7 wickets*
	India	Napier	NZ 240-5	I 212-9	*NZ won by 28 runs*
	India	Auckland	NZ 142	I 143-3	*India won by 7 wickets*
	India	Wellington	I 255-5	NZ 243-9	*India won by 12 runs*
	India	Christchurch	I 222-6	NZ 223-4	*NZ won by 6 wickets*
1993/94	Australia	Sharjah	NZ 207-9	A 208-3	*Australia won by 7 wickets*
	Sri Lanka	Sharjah	NZ 217-8	SL 215-9	*NZ won by 2 runs*
	Pakistan	Sharjah	P 328-2	NZ 266-7	*Pakistan won by 62 runs*
1994	England	Birmingham	E 224-8	NZ 182	*England won by 42 runs*
	England	Lord's	*abandoned without a ball being bowled*		

1994/95	West Indies	Goa	WI 123	NZ 25-1	*abandoned*
	India	Baroda	NZ 269-4	I 271-3	*India won by 7 wickets*
	West Indies	Guwahati	WI 306-6	NZ 171-9	*West Indies won by 135 runs*
	India	Delhi	I 289-3	NZ 182	*India won by 107 runs*
1994/95	South Africa	Cape Town	SA 203-8	NZ 134	*South Africa won by 69 runs*
	Sri Lanka	Bloemfontein	SL 288-4	NZ 66-1	*abandoned*
	South Africa	Verwoerdburg	SA 314-7	NZ 233	*South Africa won by 81 runs*
	Pakistan	Port Elizabeth	NZ 201	P 206-5	*Pakistan won by 5 wickets*
	Sri Lanka	East London	NZ 255-4	SL 257-5	*Sri Lanka won by 5 wickets*
	Pakistan	East London	NZ 172	P 175-5	*Pakistan won by 5 wickets*
1994/95	West Indies	Auckland	NZ 167-6	WI 149-1	*West Indies won by 9 wickets target reduced*
	West Indies	Wellington	WI 246-7	NZ 205	*West Indies won by 41 runs*
	West Indies	Christchurch	NZ 146	WI 149-1	*West Indies won by 9 wickets*
1994/95	India	Napier	I 160	NZ 162-6	*NZ won by 4 wickets*
	Australia	Auckland	A 254-5	NZ 227-9	*Australia won by 27 runs*
	South Africa	Christchurch	NZ 249-7	SA 203	*NZ won by 46 runs*
	Australia	Auckland	NZ 137-9	A 138-4	*Australia won by 6 wickets*
1994/95	Sri Lanka	Christchurch	NZ 271-6	SL 238	*NZ won by 33 runs*
	Sri Lanka	Hamilton	NZ 280-6	SL 117-6	*NZ won by 57 runs target reduced*
	Sri Lanka	Auckland	SL 250-6	NZ 199	*Sri Lanka won by 51 runs*
1995/96	India	Jamshedpur	I 236	NZ 237-2	*NZ won by 8 wickets*
	India	Amritsar	NZ 145	I 146-4	*India won by 6 wickets*
	India	Goa	*abandoned without a ball being bowled*		
	India	Pune	NZ 235-6	I 236-5	*India won by 5 wickets*
	India	Nagpur	NZ 348-8	I 249	*NZ won by 99 runs*
	India	Bombay	NZ 126	I 128-4	*India won by 6 wickets*
1995/96	Pakistan	Dunedin	P 189-9	NZ 169	*Pakistan won by 20 runs*
	Pakistan	Christchurch	P 232-9	NZ 236-9	*NZ won by 1 wicket*
	Pakistan	Wellington	P 261-4	NZ 207	*Pakistan won by 54 runs*
	Pakistan	Auckland	NZ 244-8	P 212	*NZ won by 32 runs*
1995/96	Zimbabwe	Auckland	NZ 278-5	Z 204	*NZ won by 74 runs*
	Zimbabwe	Wellington	Z 181-9	NZ 184-4	*NZ won by 6 wickets*
	Zimbabwe	Napier	Z 267-7	NZ 246	*Zimbabwe won by 21 runs*
1995/96	England	Ahmedabad	NZ 239-6	E 228-9	*NZ won by 11 runs*
World Cup	Holland	Baroda	NZ 307-8	H 188-7	*NZ won by 119 runs*
	South Africa	Faisalabad	NZ 177-9	SA 178-5	*Sth Africa won by 5 wickets*
	UAE	Faisalabad	NZ 276-8	UAE 167-9	*NZ won by 109 runs*
	Pakistan	Lahore	P 281-5	NZ 235	*Pakistan won by 46 runs*
	Australia	Madras	NZ 286-9	A 289-4	*Australia won by 6 wickets*
1995/96	West Indies	Kingston	NZ 243	WI 247-9	*West Indies won by 1 wicket*
	West Indies	Port of Spain	WI 238-7	NZ 239-6	*NZ won by 4 wickets*
	West Indies	Port of Spain	NZ 219-8	WI 225-3	*West Indies won by 7 wickets*
	West Indies	Georgetown	NZ 158	WI 154	*NZ won by 4 runs*
	West Indies	Arnos Vale	NZ 241-8	WI 242-3	*West Indies won by 7 wickets*

1996/97	Sri Lanka	Sharjah	NZ 206-8	SL 177	*NZ won by 29 runs*
	Pakistan	Sharjah	NZ 197	P 198-6	*Pakistan won by 4 wickets*
	Sri Lanka	Sharjah	NZ 169-8	SL 169	*Tie*
	Pakistan	Sharjah	NZ 192	P 196-6	*Pakistan won by 4 wickets*
	Pakistan	Sharjah	P 160	NZ 119	*Pakistan won by 41 runs*
1996/97	Pakistan	Gujranwala	P 228-8	NZ 217	*Pakistan won by 11 runs*
	Pakistan	Sialkot	P 277-9	NZ 231	*Pakistan won by 46 runs*
	Pakistan	Karachi	P 234-4	NZ 235-3	*NZ won by 7 wickets*
1996/97	England	Christchurch	NZ 222-6	E 226-6	*England won by 4 wickets*
	England	Auckland	NZ 253-8	E 134-4	*England won by 6 wickets target reduced*
	England	Napier	NZ 237	E 237-8	*Tie*
	England	Auckland	NZ 153	E 144	*NZ won by 9 runs*
	England	Wellington	NZ 228-8	E 200	*NZ won by 28 runs*
1996/97	Sri Lanka	Auckland	*abandoned without a ball being bowled*		
	Sri Lanka	Christchurch	NZ 201-9	SL 202-4	*Sri Lanka won by 6 wickets*
	Sri Lanka	Wellington	NZ 201	SL 132	*NZ won by 69 runs*
1996/97	Pakistan	Mohali	NZ 285-7	P 263-9	*NZ won by 22 runs*
	India	Bangalore	NZ 220-9	I 221-2	*India won by 8 wickets*
	Sri Lanka	Hyderabad	SL 214	NZ 162	*Sri Lanka won by 52 runs*
1997/98	Zimbabwe	Bulawayo	Z 233-8	NZ 233-9	*Tie*
	Zimbabwe	Harare	NZ 185-7	Z 188-7	*Zimbabwe won by 3 wickets*
	Zimbabwe	Harare	NZ 294-7	Z 211	*NZ won by 83 runs*
1997/98	South Africa	Adelaide	NZ 224-6	SA 177	*NZ won by 47 runs*
	Australia	Adelaide	NZ 260-7	A 263-7	*Australia won by 3 wickets*
	South Africa	Hobart	SA 174-9	NZ 173-7	*South Africa won by 1 run*
	Australia	Melbourne	NZ 141	A 142-4	*Australia won by 6 wickets*
	South Africa	Brisbane	SA 300-6	NZ 298-9	*South Africa won by 2 runs*
	Australia	Sydney	A 250	NZ 119	*Australia won by 131 runs*
	South Africa	Perth	SA 233-7	NZ 166	*South Africa won by 67 runs*
	Australia	Melbourne	A 251-4	NZ 253-6	*NZ won by 4 wickets*
1997/98	Zimbabwe	Hamilton	NZ 248-7	Z 208	*NZ won by 40 runs*
	Zimbabwe	Wellington	Z 138	NZ 139-2	*NZ won by 8 wickets*
	Australia	Christchurch	NZ 212-7	A 215-3	*Australia won by 7 wickets*
	Australia	Wellington	A 297-6	NZ 231	*Australia won by 66 runs*
	Australia	Napier	A 236	NZ 240-3	*NZ won by 7 wickets*
	Australia	Auckland	NZ 223-7	A 193	*NZ won by 30 runs*
	Zimbabwe	Christchurch	Z 228-7	NZ 227-9	*Zimbabwe won by 1 run*
	Zimbabwe	Napier	Z 207-8	NZ 211-1	*NZ won by 9 wickets*
	Zimbabwe	Auckland	NZ 231-9	Z 229-9	*NZ won by 2 runs*
1997/98	India	Sharjah	I 220-9	NZ 205	*India won by 15 runs*
	Australia	Sharjah	NZ 159	A 160-4	*Australia won by 6 wickets*
	India	Sharjah	I 181	NZ 183-6	*NZ won by 4 wickets*
	Australia	Sharjah	NZ 259-5	A 261-5	*Australia won by 5 wickets*
1997/98	Sri Lanka	Colombo	NZ 200-9	SL 201-3	*Sri Lanka won by 7 wickets*
	India	Colombo	NZ 219-8	I 131-3	*abandoned*
	Sri Lanka	Galle	*abandoned without a ball being bowled*		
	India	Galle	*abandoned without a ball being bowled*		
	India	Colombo	NZ 128-5		*abandoned*
	Sri Lanka	Colombo	SL 293-4	NZ 206	*Sri Lanka won by 87 runs*

1998/99	Zimbabwe	Dhaka	Z 258-7	NZ 260-5	*NZ won by 5 wickets*
ICC Knockout	Sri Lanka	Dhaka	NZ 188	SL 191-5	*Sri Lanka won by 5 wickets*
1998/99	India	Taupo	I 257-5	NZ 200-5	*NZ won by 5 wickets (D/L)*
	India	Napier	NZ 213	I 214-8	*India won by 2 wickets*
	India	Wellington	I 208-4	NZ 89-2	*abandoned*
	India	Auckland	NZ 207-7	I 208-5	*India won by 5 wickets*
	India	Christchurch	NZ 300-8	I 230	*NZ won by 70 runs*
1998/99	South Africa	Dunedin	SA 211	NZ 215-7	*NZ won by 3 wickets*
	South Africa	Christchurch	NZ 220-9	SA 224-3	*SA won by 7 wickets*
	South Africa	Auckland	SA 212-7	NZ 215-3	*NZ won by 7 wickets*
	South Africa	Napier	NZ 257-8	SA 10-0	*abandoned*
	South Africa	Napier	NZ 191	SA 194-8	*SA won by 2 wickets*
	South Africa	Auckland	SA 290-5	NZ 147	*SA won by 143 runs*
	South Africa	Wellington	SA 249-4		*abandoned*
1999	Bangladesh	Chelmsford	B 116	NZ 117-4	*NZ won by 6 wickets*
World Cup	Australia	Cardiff	A 213-8	NZ 214-5	*NZ won by 5 wickets*
	West Indies	Southampton	NZ 156	WI 158-3	*WI won by 7 wickets*
	Pakistan	Derby	P 269-8	NZ 207-8	*Pakistan won by 62 runs*
	Scotland	Edinburgh	S 121	NZ 123-4	*NZ won by 6 wickets*
	Zimbabwe	Leeds	Z 175	NZ 70-3	*abandoned*
	South Africa	Birmingham	SA 287-5	NZ 213-8	*SA won by 74 runs*
	India	Nottingham	I 251-6	NZ 253-5	*NZ won by 5 wickets*
	Pakistan	Manchester	NZ 241-7	P 242-1	*Pakistan won by 9 wickets*
1999/00	India	Rajkot	NZ 349-9	I 306	*NZ won by 43 runs*
	India	Hyderabad	I 376-2	NZ 202	*India won by 174 runs*
	India	Gwalior	I 261-5	NZ 247-8	*India won by 14 runs*
	India	Guwahati	NZ 236-9	I 188	*NZ won by 48 runs*
	India	Delhi	NZ 179-9	I 181-3	*India won by 7 wickets*
1999/00	West Indies	Auckland	WI 268-7	NZ 250-7	*NZ won by 3 wickets (D/L)*
	West Indies	Taupo	WI 192	NZ 194-3	*NZ won by 7 wickets*
	West Indies	Napier	WI 159	NZ 160-6	*NZ won by 4 wickets*
	West Indies	Wellington	WI 171-9	NZ 172-2	*NZ won by 8 wickets*
	West Indies	Christchurch	NZ 302-6	WI 282	*NZ won by 20 runs*
1999/00	Australia	Wellington	A 119-1	NZ	*Abandoned*
	Australia	Auckland	NZ 122	A 123-5	*Australia won by 5 wickets*
	Australia	Dunedin	A 310-4	NZ 260	*Australia won by 50 runs*
	Australia	Christchurch	A 349-6	NZ 301-9	*Australia won by 48 runs*
	Australia	Napier	NZ 243-9	A 245-5	*Australia won by 5 wickets*
	Australia	Auckland	A 191	NZ 194-3	*NZ won by 7 wickets*
2000/01	Pakistan	Singapore	P 191-6	NZ 179	*Pakistan won by 12 runs*
	South Africa	Singapore	NZ 158	SA 159-2	*SA won by 8 wickets*
2000/01	Zimbabwe	Harare	Z 183-8	NZ 184-3	*NZ won by 7 wickets*
	Zimbabwe	Bulawayo	Z 273-5	NZ 252	*Zimbabwe won by 21 runs*
	Zimbabwe	Bulawayo	NZ 264-8	Z 268-4	*Zimbabwe won by 6 wkts*
2000/01	Zimbabwe	Nairobi	NZ 265-7	Z 201	*NZ won by 64 runs*
ICC Knockout	Pakistan	Nairobi	P 252	NZ 255-6	*NZ won by 4 wickets*
	India	Nairobi	I 264-6	NZ 265-6	*NZ won by 4 wickets*

2000/01	South Africa	Potchefstroom	SA 191-2	NZ	*abandoned*
	South Africa	Benoni	NZ 194-8	SA 197-4	*SA won by 6 wkts*
	South Africa	Centurion	SA 324-4	NZ 189	*SA won by 115 runs (D/L)*
	South Africa	Kimberley	NZ 287-6	SA 289-5	*SA won by 5 wickets*
	South Africa	Durban	NZ 114-5	SA 158-4	*SA won by 6 wickets(D/L)*
	South Africa	Cape Town	NZ 256-9	SA 258-7	*SA won by 3 wickets*
2000/01	Zimbabwe	Taupo	Z 300-7	NZ 210	*Zimbabwe won by 70 runs (D/L)*
	Zimbabwe	Wellington	Z 236-7	NZ 237-2	*NZ won by 8 wickets*
	Zimbabwe	Auckland	NZ 273-9	Z 274-9	*Zimbabwe won by 1 wicket*
2000/01	Sri Lanka	Napier	SL 213-8	NZ 152	*Sri Lanka won by 61 runs*
	Sri Lanka	Wellington	NZ 205-8	SL 209-7	*Sri Lanka won by 3 wickets*
	Sri Lanka	Auckland	NZ 181	SL 182-1	*Sri Lanka won by 9 wickets*
	Sri Lanka	Hamilton	NZ 182-9	SL 155-5	*Sri Lanka won by 3 runs (D/L)*
	Sri Lanka	Christchurch	NZ 282-6	SL 269	*NZ won by 13 runs*
2000/01	Pakistan	Auckland	NZ 149	P 150-4	*Pakistan won by 6 wickets*
	Pakistan	Napier	P 135	NZ 136-4	*NZ won by 6 wickets*
	Pakistan	Wellington	P 243-9	NZ 215	*Pakistan won by 28 runs*
	Pakistan	Christchurch	NZ 284-5	P 146	*NZ won by 138 runs*
	Pakistan	Dunedin	P 285	NZ 290-6	*NZ won by 4 wickets*
2000/01	Sri Lanka	Sharjah	SL 269-9	NZ 163	*Sri Lanka won by 106 runs*
	Pakistan	Sharjah	NZ 266-7	P 270-2	*Pakistan won by 8 wickets*
	Pakistan	Sharjah	NZ 127	P 131-3	*Pakistan won by 7 wickets*
	Sri Lanka	Sharjah	NZ 248-6	SL 169-8	*NZ won by 79 runs*
2001/02	Sri Lanka	Colombo	SL 220	NZ 204-9	*Sri Lanka won by 16 runs*
	India	Colombo	NZ 211-8	I 127	*NZ won by 84 runs*
	Sri Lanka	Colombo	NZ 236-8	SL 240-5	*Sri Lanka won by 5 wickets*
	India	Colombo	NZ 200	I 133	*NZ won by 67 runs*
	Sri Lanka	Colombo	SL 221-6	NZ 115-9	*Sri Lanka won by 106 runs*
	India	Colombo	NZ 264-7	I 267-3	*India won by 7 wickets*
2001/02	Australia	Melbourne	NZ 199-8	A 176	*NZ won by 23 runs*
	South Africa	Hobart	SA 257-7	NZ 231-9	*SA won by 26 runs*
	Australia	Sydney	NZ 235-9	A 212	*NZ won by 23 runs*
	South Africa	Brisbane	SA 241	NZ 244-6	*NZ won by 4 wickets*
	Australia	Adelaide	NZ 242-5	A 165	*NZ won by 77 runs*
	South Africa	Adelaide	SA 253-5	NZ 160	*SA won by 93 runs*
	Australia	Melbourne	NZ 245-8	A 248-8	*Australia won by 2 wickets*
	South Africa	Perth	SA 270-5	NZ 203-8	*SA won by 67 runs*
	South Africa	Melbourne	NZ 190	SA 191-2	*SA won by 8 wickets*
	South Africa	Sydney	NZ 175	SA 173-4	*SA won by 6 wickets (D/L)*
2001/02	England	Christchurch	E 196	NZ 198-6	*NZ won by 4 wickets*
	England	Wellington	NZ 244-8	E 89	*NZ won by 155 runs*
	England	Napier	E 244-5	NZ 201	*England won by 43 runs*
	England	Auckland	E 193-6	NZ 189	*England won by 33 runs (D/L)*
	England	Dunedin	E 218-8	NZ 223-5	*NZ won by 5 wickets*
2001/02	Sri Lanka	Sharjah	NZ 218-8	SL 207	*NZ won by 11 runs*
	Pakistan	Sharjah	P 288-6	NZ 237-8	*Pakistan won by 51 runs*
	Sri Lanka	Sharjah	SL 243-9	NZ 197-9	*Sri Lanka won by 46 runs*
	Pakistan	Sharjah	NZ 213-9	P 217-2	*Pakistan won by 8 wickets*
2001/02	Pakistan	Karachi	P 275-6	NZ 122	*Pakistan won by 153 runs*
	Pakistan	Rawalpindi	NZ 277-5	P 278-7	*Pakistan won by 3 wickets*
	Pakistan	Lahore	P 278-5	NZ 212	*Pakistan won by 66 runs*

2001/02	West Indies	Kingston	NZ 176	WI	*abandoned*
	West Indies	Gros Islet	NZ 248-7	WI 250-4	*West Indies won by 6 wickets*
	West Indies	Gros Islet	NZ 210-7	WI 211-3	*West Indies won by 7 wickets*
	West Indies	Port of Spain	NZ 212-5	WI 202-9	*NZ won by 9 runs (D/L)*
	West Indies	Arnos Vale	NZ 291-8	WI 292-6	*West Indies won by 4 wickets*
2002/03	Australia	Colombo	A 296-7	NZ 132	*Australia won by 164 runs*
Champions Trophy	Bangladesh	Colombo	NZ 244-9	B 77	*NZ won by 167 runs*
2002/03	India	Auckland	I 108	NZ 109-7	*NZ won by 3 wickets*
	India	Napier	NZ 254-9	I 219	*NZ won by 35 runs*
	India	Christchurch	I 108	NZ 109-5	*NZ won by 5 wickets*
	India	Queenstown	I 122	NZ 123-3	*NZ won by 7 wickets*
	India	Wellington	NZ 168	I 169-8	*India won by 2 wickets*
	India	Auckland	NZ 199-9	I 200-9	*India won by 1 wicket*
	India	Hamilton	I 122	NZ 125-4	*NZ won by 6 wickets*
2002/03	Sri Lanka	Bloemfontein	SL 272-7	NZ 225	*Sri Lanka won by 47 runs*
World	West Indies	Port Elizabeth	NZ 241-7	WI 221	*NZ won by 20 runs*
Cup	South Africa	Johannesburg	SL 306-6	NZ 229-1	*NZ won by 9 wickets (D/L)*
	Kenya	Nairobi			*NZ forfeited the match*
	Bangladesh	Kimberley	B 198-7	NZ 199-3	*NZ won by 7 wickets*
	Canada	Benoni	C 196	NZ 197-5	*NZ won by 5 wickets*
	Zimbabwe	Bloemfontein	Z 252-7	NZ 253-4	*NZ won by 6 wickets*
	Australia	Port Elizabeth	A 208-9	NZ 112	*Australia won by 96 runs*
	India	Centurion	NZ 146	I 150-3	*India won by 7 wickets*
2002/03	Pakistan	Dambulla	P 116	NZ 117-3	*NZ won by 7 wickets*
	Sri Lanka	Dambulla	NZ 139	SL 143-5	*Sri Lanka won by 5 wickets*
	Sri Lanka	Dambulla	NZ 156-8	SL 147	*NZ won by 9 runs*
	Pakistan	Dambulla	P 203-9	NZ 181	*Pakistan won by 22 runs*
	Pakistan	Dambulla	P 198	NZ 200-6	*NZ won by 4 wickets*
2003/04	India	Chennai	I 141-3	NZ	*abandoned*
	Australia	Faridabad	NZ 97	A 101-2	*Australia won by 8 wickets*
	Australia	Pune	NZ 258-9	A 259-8	*Australia won by 2 wickets*
	India	Cuttack	I 246-6	NZ 249-9	*NZ won by 4 wickets*
	Australia	Guwahati	A 225-7	NZ 181	*Australia won by 44 runs*
	India	Hyderabad	I 353-5	NZ 208	*India won by 145 runs*
2003/04	Pakistan	Lahore	NZ 291-5	P 292-7	*Pakistan won by 3 wickets*
	Pakistan	Lahore	P 281-6	NZ 157	*Pakistan won by 124 runs*
	Pakistan	Faisalabad	P 314-7	NZ 263-7	*Pakistan won by 51 runs*
	Pakistan	Rawalpindi	NZ 183	P 184-3	*Pakistan won by 7 wickets*
	Pakistan	Rawalpindi	P 277-4	NZ 228-6	*Pakistan won by 49 runs*
2003/04	Pakistan	Auckland	P 229-7	NZ 230-6	*NZ won by 4 wickets*
	Pakistan	Queenstown	NZ 235-8	P 236-4	*Pakistan won by 6 wickets*
	Pakistan	Christchurch	P 255-9	NZ 259-3	*NZ won by 7 wickets*
	Pakistan	Napier	P 126	NZ 127-2	*NZ won by 8 wickets*
	Pakistan	Wellington	NZ 307-8	P 303	*NZ won by 4 runs*
2003/04	South Africa	Auckland	NZ 225-8	SA 226-5	*SA won by 5 wickets*
	South Africa	Christchurch	SA 253-8	NZ 255-5	*NZ won by 5 wickets*
	South Africa	Wellington	NZ 254-5	SA 249-7	*NZ won by 5 runs*
	South Africa	Dunedin	SA 259-7	NZ 264-4	*NZ won by 6 wickets*
	South Africa	Auckland	NZ 193-8	SA 175-5	*NZ won by 2 runs (D/L)*
	South Africa	Napier	SA 186-9	NZ 190-5	*NZ won by 5 wickets*

2004	England	Manchester	*abandoned without a ball being bowled*		
	West Indies	Birmingham	WI 122-4	NZ 97-2	*abandoned*
	England	Chester-le-Street	E 101	NZ 103-3	*NZ won by 7 wickets*
	West Indies	Cardiff	WI 216	NZ 220-5	*NZ won by 5 wickets*
	England	Bristol	E 237-7	NZ 241-4	*NZ won by 6 wickets*
	West Indies	Southampton	*abandoned without a ball being bowled*		
	West Indies	Lord's	NZ 266	WI 159	*NZ won by 107 runs*
2004	USA	The Oval	NZ 347-4	USA 137	*NZ won by 210 runs*
Champions Trophy	Australia	The Oval	NZ 198	A 199-3	*Australia won by 7 wickets*
2004/05	Bangladesh	Chittagong	NZ 224	B 86	*NZ won by 138 runs*
	Bangladesh	Dhaka	B 146	NZ 148-7	*NZ won by 3 wickets*
	Bangladesh	Dhaka	NZ 250-7	B 167-7	*NZ won by 83 runs*
2004/05	Australia	Melbourne	A 246-9	NZ 247-6	*NZ won by 4 wickets*
	Australia	Sydney	A 261-7	NZ 244	*Australia won by 17 runs*
	Australia	Brisbane	*abandoned without a ball being bowled*		
2004/05	Sri Lanka	Auckland	SL 141	NZ 144-3	*NZ won by 7 wickets*
2004/05	Australia	Wellington	A 236-7	NZ 226	*Australia won by 10 runs*
	Australia	Christchurch	A 314-6	NZ 208	*Australia won by 106 runs*
	Australia	Auckland	A 264-5	NZ 178	*Australia won by 86 runs*
	Australia	Welllington	NZ 233	A 236-3	*Australia won by 7 wickets*
	Australia	Napier	A 347-5	NZ 225-8	*Australia won by 122 runs*

Summary of Results

	Played	Won	Lost	Tie	Abandoned
v Australia	97	26	68	—	3
v England	55	26	25	1	3
v India	72	33	35	—	4
v Pakistan	77	28	47	1	1
v Sri Lanka	56	29	24	1	2
v West Indies	40	13	22	—	5
v South Africa	40	14	23	—	3
v East Africa	1	1	—	—	—
v Zimbabwe	26	17	7	1	1
v Bangladesh	7	7	—	—	—
v Holland	1	1	—	—	—
v UAE	1	1	—	—	—
v Scotland	1	1	—	—	—
v Canada	1	1	—	—	—
v USA	1	1	—	—	—
TOTALS	**476**	**199**	**251**	**4**	**22**

In addition, New Zealand forfeited their match against Kenya, at Nairobi, 2002/03

One-day International Captains

		Results					Toss	
		P	W	L	Tie	NR	W	L
Fleming S.P.	1996/97 to 2004/04	174	75	87	1	11	81	93
Howarth G.P.	1979/80 to 1984/85	60	31	26	—	3	23	37
Crowe M.D.	1989/90 to 1992/93	44	21	22	—	1	26	18
Rutherford K.R.	1993/94 to 1994/95	37	10	24	1	2	19	18
Germon L.K.	1995/96 to 1996/97	36	15	19	2	—	19	17
Wright J.G.	1982/83 to 1990	31	16	15	—	—	20	11
Coney J.V.	1984/85 to 1986/87	25	8	16	—	1	12	13
Crowe J.J.	1985/86 to 1987/88	16	4	12	—	—	7	9
Turner G.M.	1974/75 to 1976/77	8	5	2	—	1	5	3
Burgess M.G.	1978 to 1980/81	8	2	6	—	—	6	2
McMillan C.D.	2000/01 to 2001/02	8	2	6	—	—	3	5
Congdon B.E.	1972/73 to 1974/75	7	2	3	—	2	4	3
Nash D.J.	1998/99	7	3	3	—	1	4	3
Cairns C.L.	2001/02-2003/04	7	1	6	—	—	4	3
Larsen G.R.	1993/94	3	1	2	—	—	2	1
Vettori D.L.	2004/05	3	3	—	—	—	2	1
Jones A.H.	1992/93	2	—	2	—	—	1	1
TOTALS		**476**	**199**	**251**	**4**	**22**	**238**	**238**

Other One-day Internationals Played in New Zealand

1989/90	Christchurch	A	187-9	I	169	*Australia won by 18 runs*
	Hamilton	I	211-8	A	212-3	*Australia won by 7 wickets*
1991/92	New Plymouth	Z	312-4	SL	313-7	*Sri Lanka won by 3 wickets*
World Cup	Wellington	SA	195	SL	198-7	*Sri Lanka won by 3 wickets*
	Christchurch	SA	200-8	WI	136	*South Africa won by 64 runs*
	Hamilton	I	203-7	Z	104-1	*India won by 55 runs**
	Wellington	I	197	WI	195-5	*West Indies won by 5 wickets**
1994/95	Wellington	SA	123	A	124-7	*Australia won by 3 wickets*
	Hamilton	SA	223-6	I	209-9	*South Africa won by 14 runs*
	Dunedin	A	250-6	I	252-5	*India won by 5 wickets*

* *target reduced*

Highest Totals

376-2	India v New Zealand	Hyderabad	1999/00
353-5	India v New Zealand	Hyderabad	2003/04
349-9	New Zealand v India	Rajkot	1999/00
349-6	Australia v New Zealand	Christchurch	1999/00
348-8	New Zealand v India	Nagpur	1995/96
347-4	New Zealand v USA	The Oval	2004
347-5	Australia v New Zealand	Napier	2004/05
338-4	New Zealand v Bangladesh	Sharjah	1989/90
328-2	Pakistan v New Zealand	Sharjah	1993/94
324-4	South Africa v New Zealand	Centurion	2000/01
322-6	England v New Zealand	The Oval	1983
314-7	South Africa v New Zealand	Verwoerdburg	1994/95
314-7	Pakistan v New Zealand	Faisalabad	2003/04
314-6	Australia v New Zealand	Christchurch	2004/05
313-7	Sri Lanka v Zimbabwe	New Plymouth	1991/92
312-4	Zimbabwe v Sri Lanka	New Plymouth	1991/92
310-4	Australia v New Zealand	Dunedin	1999/00
309-5	New Zealand v East Africa	Birmingham	1975
307-5	New Zealand v Holland	Baroda	1995/96
307-8	New Zealand v Pakistan	Wellington	2003/04
306-6	West Indies v New Zealand	Guwahati	1994/85
306-6	South Africa v New Zealand	Johannesburg	2002/03
306	India v New Zealand	Rajkot	1999/00
304-5	New Zealand v Sri Lanka	Auckland	1982/83
303	Pakistan v New Zealand	Wellington	2003/04
302-8	Australia v New Zealand	Melbourne	1982/83
302-6	New Zealand v West Indies	Christchurch	1999/00
301-9	New Zealand v Australia	Christchurch	1999/00
300-6	South Africa v New Zealand	Brisbane	1997/98
300-8	New Zealand v India	Christchurch	1998/99
300-7	Zimbabwe v New Zealand	Taupo	2000/01

Lowest Totals

64	New Zealand v Pakistan	Sharjah	1985/86
70	Australia v New Zealand	Adelaide	1985/86
74	New Zealand v Australia	Wellington	1981/82
74	New Zealand v Pakistan	Sharjah	1989/90
77	Bangladesh v New Zealand	Kimberley	2002/03
89	England v New Zealand	Wellington	2001/02
94	New Zealand v Australia	Christchurch	1989/90
97	New Zealand v Ausytralia	Faridabad	2003/04

Highest Match Aggregates

655	India v New Zealand	Rajkot	1999/00
650	New Zealand v Australia	Christchurch	1999/00
625	Zimbabwe v Sri Lanka	New Plymouth	1991/92
610	New Zealand v Pakistan	Wellington	2003/04

Lowest Match Aggregates

130	New Zealand v Pakistan	Sharjah	1985/86
149	New Zealand v Australia	Wellington	1981/82
149	New Zealand v Pakistan	Sharjah	1989/90
198	New Zealand v Australia	Faridabad	2003/04

INDIVIDUAL RECORDS

Centuries

171*	Turner G.M.	v East Africa	Birmingham	1975
145*	Astle N.J.	v USA	The Oval	2004
141	Styris S.B.	v Sri Lanka	Bloemfontein	2002/03
140	Turner G.M.	v Sri Lanka	Auckland	1982/83
134*	Fleming S.P.	v South Africa	Johannesburg	2002/03
130	Harris C.Z.	v Australia	Madras	1995/96
122*	Astle N.J.	v England	Dunedin	2001/02
120	Astle N.J.	v Zimbabwe	Auckland	1995/96
120	Astle N.J.	v India	Rajkot	1999/00
119	Astle N.J.	v Pakistan	Dunedin	2000/01
118*	Sinclair M.S.	v Sri Lanka	Sharjah	2000/01
117	Astle N.J.	v Pakistan	Mohali	1996/97
117	Sinclair M.S.	v Pakistan	Sharjah	2000/01
117	Astle N.J.	v India	Colombo	2001/02
116*	Fleming S.P.	v Australia	Melbourne	1997/98
115*	Fleming S.P.	v Pakistan	Christchurch	2003/04
115	Cairns C.L.	v India	Christchurch	1998/99
114*	Turner G.M.	v India	Manchester	1975
114	Astle N.J.	v India	Nagpur	1995/96
111*	Fleming S.P.	v Australia	Napier	1997/98
111	Greatbatch M.J.	v England	The Oval	1990
108	Rutherford K.R.	v India	Baroda	1994/95
108	Parore A.C.	v South Africa	Verwoerdburg	1994/95
108	Astle N.J.	v India	Colombo	2001/02
108	Fleming S.P.	v South Africa	Christchurch	2003/04
107*	Crowe M.D.	v India	Jamshedpur	1995/96
106*	Fleming S.P.	v West Indies	PortofSpain	1995/96
105*	Crowe M.D.	v England	Auckland	1983/84
105	McMillan C.D.	v Pakistan	Rawalpindi	2001/02
104*	Astle N.J.	v Zimbabwe	Napier	1997/98
104*	McMillan C.D.	v Pakistan	Christchurch	2000/01
104	Wadsworth K.J.	v Australia	Christchurch	1973/74
104	Crowe M.D.	v India	Dunedin	1989/90
104	Astle N.J.	v Australia	Napier	1999/00
103	Cairns C.L.	v India	Pune	1995/96
103	Twose R.G.	v South Africa	Cape Town	2000/01
102*	Edgar B.A.	v Australia	Melbourne	1980/81
102*	Greatbatch M.J.	v England	Leeds	1990
102*	Rutherford K.R.	v Sri Lanka	East London	1994/95
102*	Cairns C.L.	v India	Nairobi	2000/01
102*	Cairns C.L.	v South Africa	Brisbane	2001/02
102*	Astle N.J.	v Zimbabwe	Bloemfontein	2002/03
101*	Marshall H.J.H.	v Pakistan	Faisalabad	2003/04
101*	Styris S.B.	v Pakistan	Auckland	2003/04
101	Congdon B.E.	v England	Wellington	1974/75
101	Wright J.G.	v England	Napier	1987/88
101	Astle N.J.	v England	Ahmedabad	1995/96
100*	Crowe M.D.	v Australia	Auckland	1991/92
100*	Astle N.J.	v South Africa	Auckland	1998/99

Successive Centuries

Greatbatch M.J. (2) 102* and 111 v England 1990

Most Successive Fifties

Jones A.H. (6) 57 v India and 55*, 62*, 67, 82, 63* v Pakistan 1988/89

Five Wickets in an Innings

10-2-23-6	Bond S.E.	v Australia	Port Elizabeth	2002/03
7-0-25-6	Styris S.B.	v West Indies	Port of Spain	2001/02
10-2-22-5	Hart M.N.	v West Indies	Goa	1994/95
8.4-1-22-5	Adams A.R.	v India	Queenstown	2002/03
7-1-23-5	Collinge R.O.	v India	Christchurch	1975/76
10.1-4-25-5	Hadlee R.J.	v Sri Lanka	Bristol	1983
9.2-2-25-5	Bond S.E.	v Australia	Adelaide	2001/02
8.3-4-26-5	Hadlee R.J.	v Australia	Sydney	1980/81
10-3-26-5	Oram J.D.P.	v India	Auckland	2002/03
11-3-28-5	Cairns B.L.	v England	Scarborough	1978
9.2-1-30-5	Vettori D.L.	v West Indies	Lord's	2004
9-1-32-5	Hadlee R.J.	v India	Perth	1980/81
10-2-32-5	Hadlee R.J.	v England	Christchurch	1983/84
10-1-32-5	Latham R.T.	v Australia	Auckland	1992/93
10-1-34-5	Chatfield E.J.	v Australia	Adelaide	1980/81
10-0-34-5	Morrison D.K.	v Sri Lanka	Sharjah	1996/97
9.4-1-36-5	Oram J.D.P.	v USA	The Oval	2004
10-0-38-5	Hadlee R.J.	v Pakistan	Dunedin	1988/89
10-0-39-5	O'Connor S.B.	v Zimbabwe	Wellington	1997/98
10-0-42-5	Harris C.Z.	v Pakistan	Sialkot	1996/97
7.4-0-4-25	Cairns C.L.	v Australia	Napier	1997/98
10-1-42-5	Franklin J.E.C.	v England	ChesterleStreet	2004
11-1-45-5	Pringle C.	v England	Birmingham	1994
10-0-46-5	Morrison D.K.	v Pakistan	Christchurch	1995/96
9.2-0-46-5	O'Connor S.B.	v Pakistan	Nairobi	2000/01

Most Economical Bowling

10-4-8-1	Chatfield E.J.	v Sri Lanka	Dunedin	1982/83
12-6-10-0	Hadlee R.J.	v East Africa	Birmingham	1975
10-6-10-0	Cairns B.L.	v Sri Lanka	Dunedin	1982/83
10-2-11-2	Tuffey D.R.	v India	Christchurch	2002/03
10-5-12-2	Larsen G.R.	v South Africa	Hobart	1993/94
10-2-12-1	Harris C.Z.	v Pakistan	Napier	2000/01
10-5-13-0	Chatfield E.J.	v India	Adelaide	1985/86
10-3-14-2	Snedden M.C.	v Pakistan	Hamilton	1988/89
10-5-14-1	Larsen G.R.	v Zimbabwe	Wellington	1995/96
10-4-14-4	Vettori D.L.	v Sri Lanka	Dambulla	2002/03
10-3-14-3	Vettori D.L.	v USA	The Oval	2004
10-2-15-2	Chatfield E.J.	v England	Dunedin	1987/88
10-2-15-1	Watson W.	v England	Christchurch	1990/91
10-3-15-3	Allott G.I.	v Scotland	Edinburgh	1999
10-3-15-1	Harris C.Z.	v West Indies	Wellington	1999/00

Most Expensive Bowling

12-1-105-2	Snedden M.C.	v England	The Oval	1983
9-0-85-0	Drum C.J.	v India	Hyderabad	1999/00
11-0-84-0	Cairns B.L.	v England	Manchester	1978
10-0-80-1	Canning T.K.	v Australia	Napier	2004/05
†7-0-77-1	Congdon B.E.	v Australia	Christchurch	1973/74
10-0-77-0	Oram J.D.P.	v Australia	Sydney	2004/05
10-0-76-1	Snedden M.C.	v England	Brisbane	1982/83
10-0-76-1	Troup G.B.	v England	Adelaide	1982/83
10-0-76-0	Cairns C.L.	v Australia	Christchurch	1999/00
10-0-76-1	Hamilton L.J.	v Australia	Napier	2004/05
10-0-75-1	Chatfield E.J.	v Pakistan	Christchurch	1984/85
10-0-75-0	de Groen R.P.	v Sri Lanka	Bloemfontein	1994/95

† 8-ball overs

Most Dismissals in an Innings

*5	Parore A.C.	v West Indies	Goa	1994/95
†5	McCullum B.B.	v India	Napier	2002/03
5	McCullum B.B	v India	Christchurch	2002/03
5	McCullum B.B.	v South Africa	Napier	2003/04
4	Lees W.K.	v India	Leeds	1979
4	Bracewell J.G. *(sub)*	v Australia	Adelaide	1980/81
4	Lees W.K.	v Australia	Sydney	1982/83
4	Parore A.C.	v Pakistan	Napier	1992/93
4	Blain T.E.	v South Africa	Hobart	1993/94
4	Rutherford K.R.	v India	Napier	1994/95
4	Germon L.K.	v Sri Lanka	Sharjah	1996/97
*4	Germon L.K.	v England	Wellington	1996/97
†4	Parore A.C.	v West Indies	Wellington	1999/00
4	Harris C.Z.	v Sri Lanka	Colombo	2001/02
4	McCullum B.B.	v Sri Lanka	Dambulla	2002/03
4	McCullum B.B.	v Pakistan	Dambulla	2002/03

† includes one stumping
** includes two stumpings*

WALTER HADLEE TROPHIES

Awarded for the most meritorious batting and bowling performances by a New Zealand player in one-day internationals under the board's jurisdiction and other one-day matches as designated from time to time by the Board of Control.

BATTING		BOWLING	
1988/89	Jones A.H.	1988/89	Snedden M.C.
1989/90	Crowe M.D.	1989/90	Snedden M.C.
1990/91	Crowe M.D.	1990/91	Pringle C.
1991/92	Crowe M.D.	1991/92	Patel D.N.
1992/93	Crowe M.D.	1992/93	Larsen G.R.
1993/94	Thomson S.A.	1993/94	Pringle C.
1994/95	Parore A.C.	1994/95	Pringle C.
1995/96	Astle N.J.	1995/96	Larsen G.R.
1996/97	Fleming S.P.	1996/97	Harris C.Z.
1997/98	Harris C.Z.	1997/98	Cairns C.L.
1998/99	Astle N.J.	1998/99	Allott G.I.
1999/00	Astle N.J.	1999/00	Allott G.I.
2000/01	Twose R.G.	2000/01	Tuffey D.R.
2001/02	Astle N.J.	2001/02	Bond S.E.
2002/03	Fleming S.P.	2002/03	Bond S.E.
2003/04	Fleming S.P.	2003/04	Tuffey D.R.
2004/05	Marshall H.J.H.	2004/05	Vettori D.L.

RECORD PARTNERSHIPS

New Zealand v England

New Zealand				
1st	152	Turner G.M. & Edgar B.A.	Wellington	1982/83
2nd	104	Fleming S.P. & Marshall H.J.H.	Bristol	2004
3rd	160	Howarth G.P. & Crowe M.D.	Auckland	1983/84
4th	100	Astle N.J. & McMillan C.D.	Dunedin	2001/02
5th	113	Crowe M.D. & Crowe J.J.	Manchester	1986
6th	122	Rutherford K.R. & Harris C.Z.	Christchurch	1990/91
7th	70	Coney J.V. & Hadlee R.J.	Birmingham	1983
8th	68	Congdon B.E. & Cairns B.L.	Scarborough	1978
9th	63	Hadlee R.J. & Troup G.B.	Brisbane	1982/83
10th	30	Hart M.N. & Morrison D.K.	Birmingham	1994
England				
1st	193	Gooch G.A. & Athey C.W.J.	Manchester	1986
2nd	113	Gooch G.A. & Smith R.A.	Leeds	1990
3rd	190*	Tavare C.J. & Lamb A.J.	Sydney	1982/83
4th	122	Strauss A.J. & Flintoff A.	Bristol	2004
5th	113	Gower D.I. & Randall D.W.	Brisbane	1982/83
6th	68	Randall D.W. & Marks V.J.	Christchurch	1983/84
7th	58	White C. & Cork D.G.	Napier	1996/97
8th	53	Gower D.I. & Marks V.J.	Auckland	1982/83
9th	15	Thorpe G.P. & Gough D.	Wellington	1996/97
10th	27	Gough D. & Caddick A.R.	Wellington	1996/97

New Zealand v Australia

New Zealand

1st	125	Rutherford K.R. & Edgar B.A.	Christchurch	1985/86
2nd	128	Astle N.J. & Vincent L.	Adelaide	2001/02
	128	Astle N.J. & Sinclair M.S.	Melbourne	2004/05
3rd	121	Astle N.J. & Twose R.G.	Dunedin	1999/00
4th	168	Germon L.K. & Harris C.Z.	Madras	1995/96
5th	148	Twose R.G. & Cairns C.L.	Cardiff	1999
6th	130	Wadsworth K.J. & Congdon B.E.	Christchurch	1973/74
7th	89	Harris C.Z. & Nash D.J.	Auckland	1997/98
8th	72	Harris C.Z. & Vettori D.L.	Melbourne	2001/02
9th	70	Vettori D.L. & Mills K.D.	Sydney	2004/05
10th	50	Mills K.D. & Bond S.E.	Colombo	2002/03

Australia

1st	189	Waugh M.E. & Gilchrist A.C.	Christchurch	1999/00
2nd	151	Dyson J. & Chappell G.S.	Sydney	1980/81
3rd	133	Hayden M.L. & Martyn D.R.	Christchurch	2004/05
4th	132	Ponting R.T. & Lehmann D.S.	Sydney	1997/98
5th	115*	Laird B.M. & Border A.R.	Dunedin	1981/82
6th	136*	Clarke M.J. & Hussey M.E.K.	Auckland	2004/05
7th	74	Lehmann D.S. & Hogg G.B.	Sydney	2004/05
8th	97	Bevan M.G. & Bichel A.J.	Port Elizabeth	2002/03
9th	46	Marsh R.W. & Lawson G.F.	Adelaide	1980/81
10th	31	Martyn D.R. & McGrath G.D.	Auckland	1999/00

New Zealand v India

New Zealand

1st	140	Wright J.G. & Jones A.H.	Baroda	1988/89
2nd	138	Astle N.J. & Fleming S.P.	Colombo	2001/02
3rd	180	Parore A.C. & Rutherford K.R.	Baroda	1994/95
4th	152	Crowe M.D. & Rutherford K.R.	Dunedin	1989/90
5th	147	Twose R.G. & Cairns C.L.	Pune	1995/96
6th	122	Cairns C.L. & Harris C.Z.	Nairobi	2000/01
7th	79	Burgess M.G. & Cairns B.L.	Adelaide	1980/81
8th	43	Nash D.J. & Vettori D.L.	Colombo	2001/02
9th	39	Snedden M.C. & Watson W.	Nagpur	1987/88
10th	52*	Tuffey D.R. & Bond S.E.	Auckland	2002/03

India

1st	182	Sehwag V. & Tendulkar S.R.	Hyderabad	2003/04
2nd	331	Tendulkar S.R. & Dravid R.S.	Hyderabad	1999/00
3rd	158	Sidhu N.S. & Amarnath M.	Sharjah	1987/88
4th	129*	Kaif M. & Dravid R.S.	Centurion	2002/03
5th	92	Vengsarkar D.B. & Patil S.M.	Brisbane	1980/81
6th	127	Azharuddin M. & Sharma A.K.	Baroda	1988/89
7th	55	Abid Ali S. & Madan Lal S.	Manchester	1975
8th	82*	Kapil Dev & More K.S.	Bangalore	1987/88
9th	60	Abid Ali S. & Venkataraghavan S.	Manchester	1975
10th	24	Kumble A.R. & Prasad B.K.V.	Rajkot	1999/00

New Zealand v Pakistan

New Zealand				
1st	193	Fleming S.P. & Astle N.J.	Dunedin	2000/01
2nd	148	Fleming S.P. & Marshall H.J.H.	Christchurch	2003/04
3rd	135	Astle N.J. & Twose R.G.	Nairobi	2000/01
4th	157	Marshall H.J.H. & McMillan C.D.	Wellington	2003/04
5th	108*	Crowe M.D. & Smith I.D.S.	Wellington	1988/89
6th	112*	McMillan C.D. & Harris C.Z.	Christchurch	2000/01
7th	115	Parore A.C. & Germon L.K.	Sharjah	1996/97
8th	48*	Harris C.Z. & Larsen G.R.	Sharjah	1993/94
9th	59	Lees W.K. & Bracewell J.G.	Nottingham	1983
10th	33	Germon L.K. & Morrison D.K.	Wellington	1995/96
Pakistan				
1st	199	Yasir Hameed & Imran Farhat	Rawalpindi	2003/04
2nd	263	Aamer Sohail & InzamamulHaq	Sharjah	1993/94
3rd	157*	Saeed Anwar & InzamamulHaq	Sharjah	2000/01
4th	161	Yousuf Youhana & Younis Khan	Karachi	2001/02
5th	108*	Ijaz Ahmed & Wasim Akram	Karachi	1996/97
6th	94	InzamamulHaq & Abdul Razzaq	Wellington	2003/04
7th	108	Rameez Raja & Anil Dalpat	Christchurch	1984/85
8th	65*	Abdul Razzaq & Mohammad Sami	Lahore	2003/04
9th	31*	Salim Malik & Mushtaq Ahmed	Gujranwala	1996/97
10th	39	Shoaib Akhtar & Mohammad Sami	Napier	2003/04

New Zealand v West Indies

New Zealand				
1st	120	Fleming S.P. & Astle N.J.	Lord's	2004
2nd	105	Wright J.G. & Crowe M.D.	Auckland	1986/87
	105	Astle N.J. & Fleming S.P.	Napier	1999/00
3rd	170	Astle N.J. & Twose R.G.	Christchurch	1999/00
4th	139	McMillan C.D. & Vincent L.	Arnos Vale	2001/02
5th	92	Fleming S.P. & Cairns C.L.	Port of Spain	1995/96
6th	122*	Astle N.J. & Styris S.B.	Port of Spain	2001/02
7th	111	Parore A.C. & Patel D.N.	Kingston	1995/96
8th	60	Coney J.V. & Hadlee R.J.	Christchurch	1979/80
9th	44*	Harris C.Z. & Vaughan J.T.C.	Arnos Vale	1995/96
10th	48*	Nash D.J. & Pringle C.	Guwahati	1994/95
West Indies				
1st	192*	Greenidge C.G. & Haynes D.L.	Christchurch	1986/87
2nd	184	Haynes D.L. & Gomes H.A.	Bridgetown	1984/85
3rd	186	Lara B.C. & Simmons P.V.	Arnos Vale	1995/96
4th	120	Hooper C.L. & Richards I.V.A.	Dunedin	1986/87
5th	91	Adams J.C. & Holder R.I.C.	Port of Spain	1995/96
6th	38	Chanderpaul S. & Powell R.L.	Lord's	2004
7th	98	Sarwan R.R. & Jacobs R.D.	Port Elizabeth	2002/03
8th	48	Perry N.O. & Dillon M.	Napier	1999/00
9th	32	Holder R.I.C. & Ambrose C.E.L.	Georgetown	1995/96
10th	26*	Harper R.A. & Walsh C.A.	Kingston	1995/96

New Zealand v Sri Lanka

New Zealand				
1st	132	Turner G.M. & Edgar B.A.	Auckland	1982/83
2nd	141	Sinclair M.S. & Bell M.D.	Sharjah	2000/01
3rd	136	Parore A.C. & Rutherford K.R.	East London	1994/95
4th	97	Reid J.F. & Crowe J.J.	Colombo	1983/84
5th	75	Astle N.J. & Greatbatch M.J.	Sharjah	1996/97
6th	95	Blain T.E. & Hadlee R.J.	Hobart	1987/88
7th	85*	Harris C.Z. & Vincent L.	Christchurch	2000/01
8th	43	Smith I.D.S. & Cairns B.L.	Melbourne	1984/85
	43	Larsen G.R. & Doull S.B.	Wellington	1996/97
9th	47*	Cairns B.L. & Boock S.L.	Colombo	1983/84
10th	65	Snedden M.C. & Chatfield E.J.	Derby	1983
Sri Lanka				
1st	158	Jayasuriya S.T. & Atapattu M.S.	Auckland	2000/01
2nd	170	Jayasuriya S.T. & Tillakaratne H.P.	Bloemfontein	2002/03
3rd	184	Jayasuriya S.T. & Jayawardene D.P.M.D.	Sharjah	2000/01
4th	127	Kaluwitharana R.S. & Ranatunga A.	Dhaka	1998/99
5th	110	Atapattu M.S. & Arnold R.P.	Colombo	2001/02
6th	103*	Arnold R.P. & Perera A.S.A.	Colombo	2001/02
7th	52	de Alwis R.G. & Ratnayeke J.R.	Sydney	1987/88
8th	56	de Silva D.S. & Ratnayeke J.R.	Napier	1982/83
9th	45*	Ranatunga A. & de Silva D.S.	Moratuwa	1983/84
10th	29	de Silva D.S. & John V.	Melbourne	1984/85

New Zealand v Zimbabwe

New Zealand				
1st	153	Sinclair M.S. & Astle N.J.	Wellington	2000/01
2nd	103	Astle N.J. & Parore A.C.	Wellington	1997/98
3rd	152	Spearman C.M. & Twose R.G.	Harare	2000/01
4th	130	Crowe M.D. & Rutherford K.R.	Harare	1992/93
5th	95	Twose R.G. & McMillan C.D.	Nairobi	2000/01
6th	75	Cairns C.L. & Harris C.Z.	Hamilton	1997/98
7th	50	Harris C.Z. & Parore A.C.	Christchurch	1997/98
8th	58	McMillan C.D. & Styris S.B.	Auckland	2000/01
9th	55	Harris C.Z. & Larsen G.R.	Bulawayo	1997/98
10th	28	Franklin J.E.C. & Martin C.S.	Taupo	2000/01
Zimbabwe				
1st	124	Flower A. & Flower G.W.	Harare	1992/93
2nd	91	Campbell A.D.R. & Carlisle S.V.	Wellington	2000/01
3rd	154	Carlisle S.V. & Flower A.	Taupo	2000/01
4th	123	Rennie G.J. & Campbell A.D.R.	Harare	1997/98
5th	70	Flower A. & Whittall G.J.	Christchurch	1997/98
6th	82	Flower A. & Viljoen D.P.	Auckland	2000/01
7th	68	Taibu T. & Streak H.H.	Bloemfontein	2002/03
8th	117	Houghton D.L. & Butchart I.P.	Hyderabad	1987/88
9th	54*	Strang P.A. & Rennie J.A.	Napier	1997/98
10th	23	Strang B.C. & Whittall A.R.	Harare	1997/98

New Zealand v South Africa

New Zealand

1st	114	Greatbatch M.J. & Latham R.T.	Auckland	1991/92
2nd	140*	Fleming S.P. & Astle N.J.	Johannesburg	2002/03
3rd	126	Marshall H.J.H. & Styris S.B.	Dunedin	2003/04
4th	150	Twose R.G. & Cairns C.L.	Cape Town	2000/01
5th	106	Parore A.C. & Thomson S.A.	Centurion	1994/95
6th	124	McMillan C.D. & Harris C.Z.	Adelaide	1997/98
7th	84*	Cairns C.L. & Parore A.C.	Brisbane	2001/02
8th	69	Parore A.C. & Nash D.J.	Brisbane	1997/98
9th	47*	Parore A.C. & Vettori D.L.	Perth	2001/02
10th	29*	Parore A.C. & Bond S.E.	Hobart	2001/02

South Africa

1st	176	Kirsten G. & Gibbs H.H.	Birmingham	1999
2nd	172	Kirsten G. & Kallis J.H.	Kimberley	2000/01
3rd	139*	Kallis J.H. & Dippenaar H.H.	Melbourne	2001/02
4th	145	Kallis J.H. & Cullinan D.J.	Auckland	1998/99
5th	138	Rhodes J.N. & Boucher M.V.	Perth	2001/02
6th	97*	Rhodes J.N. & Pollock S.M.	Perth	2001/02
7th	63	Prince A.G. & Klusener L.	Napier	2003/04
8th	69*	Klusener L. & Abrahams S.	Cape Town	2000/01
9th	22*	Pollock S.M. & Ntini M.	Christchurch	2003/04
10th	67*	Morkel J.A. & Ntini M.	Napier	2003/04

New Zealand v Bangladesh

New Zealand

1st	158	Crowe M.D. & Wright J.G.	Sharjah	1989/90
2nd	66	Fleming S.P. & Sinclair M.S.	Colombo	2002/03
3rd	91	Jones A.H. & Greatbatch M.J.	Sharjah	1989/90
4th	61*	Styris S.B. & Cairns C.L.	Kimberley	2002/03
5th	86	Styris S.B. & McMillan C.D.	Dhaka	2004/05
6th	49	Styris S.B. & Cairns C.L.	Chittagong	2004/05
7th	43	Cairns C.L. & Vettori D.L.	Dhaka	2004/05
8th	23	Cairns C.L. & Vettori D.L.	Chittagong	2004/05
9th	33	Cairns C.L. & Adams A.R.	Chittagong	2004/05
10th	2*	Mills K.D. & Hitchcock P.A.	Colombo	2002/03

Bangladesh

1st	19	Hannan Sarkar & Mohammad Ashraful	Kimberley	2002/03
2nd	27	Mohammad Rafique & Nafees Iqbal	Dhaka	2004/05
3rd	42	Azhar Hussain & Akram Khan	Sharjah	1989/90
4th	38	Nafees Iqbal & Mohammad Ashraful	Dhaka	2004/05
5th	34	Mohammad Ashraful & Akram Khan	Kimberley	2002/03
6th	56	Rajin Saleh & Khalid Masud	Dhaka	2004/05
7th	29	Khalid Masud & Alok Kapali	Dhaka	2004/05
8th	70*	Khalid Masud & Mohammad Rafique	Kimberley	2002/03
9th	14	Mohammad Rafique & Monjurul Islam	Colombo	2002/03
10th	20	Hasibul Hussain & Monjurul Islam	Chelmsford	1999

CAREER RECORDS

Averages

	M	In	NO	HS	Runs	Ave	100	50	Ct	St	Balls	Runs	Wkts	Ave	5WI	Best	R/100B	B/W
Adams A.R.	32	25	7	45	342	19.00	—	—	4	—	1474	1261	44	28.65	1	5-22	86	34
Allott G.I.	31	11	6	7*	17	3.40	—	—	5	—	1528	1207	52	23.21	—	4-35	78	29
Anderson R.W.	2	2	1	12	16	16.00	—	—	1	—	—	—	—	—	—	—	—	—
Astle N.J.	192	188	11	145*	6162	34.81	14	36	73	—	4521	3497	95	36.81	—	4-43	77	48
Bailey M.D.	1	—	—	—	—	—	—	—	—	—	—	—	—	—	—	—	—	—
Bell M.D.	7	7	0	66	133	19.00	—	1	1	—	—	—	—	—	—	—	—	—
Blain T.E.	38	38	11	49*	442	16.37	—	—	37	1	—	—	—	—	—	—	—	—
Blair B.R.	14	14	2	29*	174	12.50	—	—	4	—	30	34	1	34.00	—	1-7	113	30
Bond S.E.	27	13	6	31*	122	17.42	—	—	8	—	1370	969	51	19.00	2	6-23	70	26
Boock S.L.	14	7	4	12	30	10.00	—	—	5	—	700	513	15	34.20	—	3-28	73	46
Bracewell B.P.	1	1	1	0*	0	—	—	—	—	—	66	41	1	41.00	—	1-41	62	66
Bracewell J.G.	53	43	12	43	512	16.51	—	—	19	—	2447	1884	33	57.09	—	2-3	76	74
Bradburn G.E.	11	10	3	30	60	8.57	—	—	2	—	385	318	6	53.00	—	2-18	82	64
Brown V.R.	3	3	0	32	44	14.66	—	—	2	—	66	75	1	75.00	—	1-24	113	66
Bulfin C.E.	4	2	1	7*	9	9.00	—	—	1	—	102	109	0	—	—	—	106	—
Burgess M.G.	26	20	0	47	336	16.80	—	—	8	—	74	69	1	69.00	—	1-10	93	74
Butler I.G.	15	6	4	3	6	3.00	—	—	6	—	593	558	14	39.85	—	3-41	94	42
Cairns B.L.	78	65	6	60	987	16.73	—	2	19	—	4015	2717	89	30.47	1	5-28	67	45
Cairns C.L.	*204	184	22	115	4767	29.42	4	25	64	—	7766	6150	193	31.86	1	5-42	79	40
Canning T.K.	4	4	1	23*	52	17.33	—	—	1	—	204	203	5	40.60		2-30	100	41
Chatfield E.J.	115	48	37	19*	118	10.72	—	—	19	—	6129	3666	142	25.81	1	5-34	59	43
Collinge R.O.	16	10	4	19	53	8.83	—	—	1	—	915	517	19	27.21	1	5-23	56	48
Coman P.G.	3	3	0	38	62	20.66	—	—	2	—	—	—	—	—	—	—	—	—
Coney J.V.	88	80	19	66*	1874	30.72	—	8	40	—	2931	2039	54	37.75	—	4-46	69	54
Congdon B.E.	12	10	3	101	373	54.71	1	2	1	—	501	322	8	40.25	—	2-17	64	62
Crowe J.J.	75	71	12	88*	1518	25.72	—	7	28	—	6	1	0	—	—	—	16	—
Crowe M.D.	143	140	18	107*	4704	38.55	4	34	66	—	1296	954	29	32.89	—	2-9	73	44
Cumming C.D.	12	12	1	45*	161	14.63	—	—	6	—	18	17	0	—	—	—	94	—
Davis H.T.	11	6	4	7*	13	6.50	—	—	2	—	432	436	11	39.63	—	4-35	100	39
de Groen R.P.	12	8	3	7*	12	2.40	—	—	2	—	549	478	8	59.75	—	2-34	87	68
Douglas M.W.	6	6	0	30	55	9.16	—	—	2	—	—	—	—	—	—	—	—	—
Doull S.B.	42	27	13	22	172	12.28	—	—	10	—	1745	1459	36	40.52	—	4-25	83	48
Drum C.J.	5	2	2	7*	9	—	—	—	1	—	216	261	4	65.25	—	2-31	120	54
Edgar B.A.	64	64	5	102*	1814	30.74	1	10	12	—	12	5	0	—	—	—	41	—
Edwards G.N.	7	7	0	41	164	23.42	—	—	7	—	6	5	1	5.00	—	1-5	83	6
Fleming S.P.	*235	226	19	134*	6648	32.11	6	38	112	—	29	28	1	28.00	—	1-8	97	29
Franklin J.E.C.	30	16	3	25*	116	8.92	—	—	9	—	1302	1127	29	38.86	1	5-42	87	45
Franklin T.J.	3	3	0	21	27	9.00	—	—	—	—	—	—	—	—	—	—	—	—
Fulton P.G.	1	1	0	9	9	9.00	—	—	1	—	—	—	—	—	—	—	—	—
Germon L.K.	37	31	5	89	519	19.96	—	3	21	9	—	—	—	—	—	—	—	—
Gillespie S.R.	19	11	5	18*	70	11.66	—	—	7	—	963	736	23	32.00	—	4-30	76	41
Gray E.J.	10	7	1	38	98	16.33	—	—	3	—	386	286	8	35.75	—	2-26	74	48
Greatbatch M.J.	84	83	5	111	2206	28.28	2	13	35	—	6	5	0	—	—	—	83	—
Hadlee B.G.	2	2	1	19	26	26.00	—	—	—	—	—	—	—	—	—	—	—	—
Hadlee D.R.	12	8	2	20	56	9.33	—	—	3	—	683	410	23	17.82	—	4-34	60	29
Hadlee R.J.	115	98	17	79	1751	21.61	—	4	27	—	6182	3407	158	21.56	5	5-25	55	39
Hamilton L.J.	2	2	2	2*	3	—	—	—	—	—	108	143	1	143.00	—	1-76	132	108
Harris C.Z.	250	213	62	130	4379	29.00	1	16	96		10667	7613	203	37.50	1	5-42	71	53
Hart M.N.	13	8	0	16	61	7.62	—	—	7	—	572	373	13	28.69	1	5-22	65	44
Hart R.G.	2	1	0	0	0	0.00	—	—	1	—	—	—	—	—	—	—	—	—
Hart R.T.	1	1	0	3	3	3.00	—	—	—	—	—	—	—	—	—	—	—	—
Hartland B.R.	16	16	1	68*	311	20.73	—	2	5	—	—	—	—	—	—	—	—	—
Haslam M.J.	1	1	0	9	9	—	—	—	—	—	30	28	1	28.00	—	1-28	93	30
Hastings B.F.	12	10	1	37	176	19.55	—	—	4	—	—	—	—	—	—	—	—	—
Hayes R.L.	1	1	0	13	13	13.00	—	—	—	—	42	31	0	—	—	—	73	—
Hitchcock P.A.	13	6	2	10	30	7.50	—	—	4	—	516	412	12	34.33	—	3-30	79	43
Hopkins G.J.	5	1	0	0	0	0.00	—	—	8	—	—	—	—	—	—	—	—	—
Horne M.J.	50	48	0	74	980	20.41	—	5	12	—	—	—	—	—	—	—	—	—
Horne P.A.	4	4	0	18	50	12.50	—	—	—	—	—	—	—	—	—	—	—	—
Howarth G.P.	71	66	5	76	1384	22.72	—	6	16	—	90	68	3	22.67	—	1-4	75	30

	M	In	NO	HS	Runs	Ave	100	50	Ct	St	Balls	Runs	Wkts	Ave	5WI	Best	R/100B	B/W
Howarth H.J.	10	6	3	11	21	7.00	—	—	3	—	556	304	14	27.71	—	3-24	54	39
Howell L.G.	12	12	0	68	287	23.92	—	4	2	—	—	—	—	—	—	—	—	—
Jones A.H.	87	87	9	93	2784	35.69	—	25	23	—	306	216	4	54.00	—	2-42	70	76
Jones R.A.	5	5	0	63	168	33.60	—	1	—	—	—	—	—	—	—	—	—	—
Kennedy R.J.	7	4	3	8*	17	17.00	—	—	1	—	312	283	5	56.60	—	2-36	90	62
Kuggeleijn C.M.	16	11	2	40	142	15.77	—	—	9	—	817	604	12	50.33	—	2-31	74	68
Larsen G.R.	121	70	27	37	629	14.62	—	—	23	—	6368	4000	113	35.39	—	4-24	62	56
Latham R.T.	33	33	4	60	583	20.10	—	1	11	—	450	386	11	35.09	1	5-32	85	40
Lees W.K.	31	24	5	26	215	11.31	—	—	28	2	—	—	—	—	—	—	—	—
McCullum B.B.	62	47	12	56*	721	20.60	—	2	80	3	—	—	—	—	—	—	—	—
McEwan P.E.	17	15	0	41	204	13.60	—	—	1	—	420	353	6	58.83	—	2-29	84	70
McKechnie B.J.	14	8	4	27	54	13.50	—	—	2	—	818	495	19	26.05	—	3-23	60	43
McMillan C.D.	162	152	13	105	3872	27.85	2	23	40	—	1541	1399	39	35.87	—	3-20	91	40
McSweeney E.B.	16	14	5	18*	73	8.11	—	—	14	3	—	—	—	—	—	—	—	—
Marshall H.J.H.	35	33	6	101*	1031	38.18	1	10	9	—	—	—	—	—	—	—	—	—
Marshall J.A.H.	3	3	0	14	23	7.66	—	—	—	—	—	—	—	—	—	—	—	—
Mason M.J.	5	1	1	13*	13	—	—	—	—	—	294	260	4	65.00	—	2-35	88	73
Martin C.S.	7	5	1	3	6	1.50	—	—	2	—	324	270	5	54.00	—	2-56	83	64
Millmow J.P.	5	1	1	0*	0	—	—	—	1	—	270	232	4	58.00	—	2-22	85	67
Mills K.D.	44	26	11	44*	197	13.13	—	—	10	—	2105	1662	52	31.96	—	4-14	79	40
Morrison D.K.	96	43	24	20*	171	9.00	—	—	19	—	4586	3470	126	27.53	2	5-34	75	36
Morrison J.F.M.	19	16	3	55	301	23.15	—	1	6	—	283	199	8	24.87	—	3-24	70	35
Murray D.J.	1	1	0	3	3	3.00	—	—	—	—	—	—	—	—	—	—	—	—
Nash D.J.	81	53	13	42	624	15.60	—	—	25	—	3416	2622	64	40.96	—	4-38	76	53
Nevin C.J.	37	36	0	74	732	20.33	—	4	16	3	—	—	—	—	—	—	—	—
O'Connor S.B.	38	13	6	8	24	3.42	—	—	11	—	1487	1397	46	30.36	2	5-39	93	32
O'Sullivan D.R.	3	2	1	1*	2	2.00	—	—	—	—	168	123	2	61.50	—	1-38	73	84
Oram J.D.P.	70	53	6	81	827	17.59	—	3	16	—	3215	2372	83	28.57	2	5-26	74	39
Owens M.B.	1	1	0	0	0	0.00	—	—	—	—	48	37	0	—	—	—	77	—
Papps M.H.W.	6	6	2	92*	207	51.75	—	2	1	—	—	—	—	—	—	—	—	—
Parker J.M.	25	21	0	66	280	13.33	—	1	11	1	16	10	1	10.00	—	1-10	62	16
Parker N.M.	1	1	0	0	0	0.00	—	—	1	—	—	—	—	—	—	—	—	—
Parore A.C.	179	161	32	108	3314	25.68	1	14	116	25	—	—	—	—	—	—	—	—
Patel D.N.	75	63	10	71	623	11.75	—	1	23	—	3251	2260	45	50.22	—	3-22	69	72
Penn A.J.	5	3	1	15	23	11.50	—	—	1	—	159	201	1	201.00	—	1-50	126	159
Petrie R.G.	12	8	3	21	65	13.00	—	—	2	—	660	449	12	37.41	—	2-25	68	55
Pollard V.	3	2	0	55	67	33.50	—	1	1	—	—	—	—	—	—	—	—	—
Priest M.W.	18	14	4	24	103	10.30	—	—	2	—	752	590	8	73.75	—	2-27	78	94
Pringle C.	64	41	19	34*	193	8.77	—	—	7	—	3314	2459	103	23.87	1	5-45	74	32
Redmond R.E.	2	1	0	3	3	3.00	—	—	—	—	—	—	—	—	—	—	—	—
Reid J.F.	25	24	1	88	633	27.16	—	4	5	—	—	—	—	—	—	—	—	—
Reid R.B.	9	9	0	64	248	27.55	—	2	3	—	7	13	1	13.00	—	1-13	185	7
Richardson M.H.	4	4	0	26	42	10.50	—	—	1	—	—	—	—	—	—	—	—	—
Roberts A.D.G.	1	1	0	16	16	16.00	—	—	1	—	56	30	1	30.00	—	1-30	53	56
Roberts S.J.	2	1	1	1*	1	—	—	—	—	—	42	47	0	—	—	—	111	—
Robertson G.K.	10	6	0	17	49	8.16	—	—	2	—	498	321	6	53.50	—	2-29	64	83
Rutherford K.R.	121	115	9	108	3143	29.65	2	18	41	—	389	323	10	32.30	—	2-39	83	38
Sinclair M.S.	45	44	2	118*	1180	28.09	2	7	15		—	—	—	—	—	—	—	—
Smith I.D.S.	98	77	16	62*	1055	17.29	—	3	81	5	—	—	—	—	—	—	—	—
Snedden M.C.	93	54	19	64	535	15.28	—	1	19	—	4525	3237	114	28.39	—	4-34	71	39
Spearman C.M.	51	50	0	86	936	18.72	—	5	15	—	3	6	0	—	—	—	—	—
Stirling D.A.	6	5	2	13*	21	7.00	—	—	3	—	246	207	6	34.33	—	2-29	84	41
Stott L.W.	1	—	—	—	—	—	—	—	1	—	72	48	3	16.00	—	3-48	66	24
Styris S.B.	96	82	12	141	1902	27.17	2	10	38		3591	2816	95	29.64	1	6-25	78	38
Su'a M.L.	12	7	2	12*	24	4.80	—	—	1	—	463	367	9	40.77	—	4-59	79	51
Sulzberger G.P.	3	2	1	6*	9	9.00	—	—	—	—	132	102	3	34.00	—	1-28	77	44
Tait A.R.	5	5	2	13*	35	11.66	—	—	—	—	120	88	3	29.33	—	2-37	73	40
Taylor B.R.	2	1	0	22	22	22.00	—	—	1	—	114	62	4	15.50	—	3-25	54	28
Thomson S.A.	56	52	10	83	964	22.95	—	5	18	—	2121	1602	42	38.14	—	3-14	75	50
Troup G.B.	22	12	8	39	101	25.25	—	—	2	—	1180	791	32	23.97	—	4-19	67	36
Turner G.M.	41	40	6	171*	1598	47.00	3	9	13	—	6	0	0	—	—	—	—	—
Tuffey D.R.	76	40	20	20*	144	7.20	—	—	19	—	3470	2693	90	29.92	—	4-24	78	39
Twose R.G.	87	81	11	103	2717	38.81	1	20	37	—	272	237	4	59.25	—	2-31	87	68
Vance R.H.	8	8	0	96	248	31.00	—	1	4	—	—	—	—	—	—	—	—	—

	M	*In*	*NO*	*HS*	*Runs*	*Ave*	*100*	*50*	*Ct*	*St*	*Balls*	*Runs*	*Wkts*	*Ave*	*5WI*	*Best*	*R/100B*	*B/W*
Vaughan J.T.C.	18	16	7	33	162	18.00	—	—	4	—	696	524	15	34.93	—	4-33	75	46
Vettori D.L.	*150	92	30	83	851	13.72	—	1	33	—	6725	4795	139	34.82	1	5-30	71	48
Vincent L.	62	60	8	60*	1134	21.80	—	4	23	—	2	3	0	—	—	—	—	—
Vivian G.E.	1	1	0	14	14	14.00	—	—	—	—	—	—	—	—	—	—	—	—
Wadsworth K.J.	14	11	1	104	302	30.20	1	—	15	3	—	—	—	—	—	—	—	—
Walker B.G.K.	11	7	4	16*	47	15.66	—	—	5	—	438	417	8	52.12	—	2-43	95	54
Walker M.D.J.	3	1	0	10	10	10.00	—	—	2	—	132	119	4	29.75	—	4-49	90	33
Walmsley K.P.	2	—	—	—	—	—	—	—	—	—	120	117	2	58.60	—	1-53	97	60
Watson W.	61	24	13	21	86	7.81	—	—	9	—	3251	2247	74	30.36	—	4-27	69	43
Webb P.N.	5	5	1	10*	38	9.50	—	—	3	—	—	—	—	—	—	—	—	—
Webb R.J.	3	1	1	6*	6	—	—	—	—	—	161	105	4	26.25	—	2-28	65	40
White D.J.	3	3	0	15	37	12.33	—	—	1	—	—	—	—	—	—	—	—	—
Wilson J.W.	6	6	1	44*	103	20.60	—	—	4	—	242	260	4	65.00	—	2-21	107	61
Wiseman P.J.	15	7	5	16	45	22.50	—	—	2	—	450	368	12	30.66	—	4-45	81	37
Wisneski W.A.	3	2	1	6	10	10.00	—	—	1	—	114	123	0	—	—	—	107	—
Wright J.G.	149	148	1	101	3891	26.46	1	24	51	—	24	8	0	—	—	—	33	—
Young B.A.	74	73	5	74	1668	24.52	—	9	28	—	—	—	—	—	—	—	—	—

** includes one match for ICC World XI*

AMENDMENTS

To previous editions

2004
Page 30
Vettori's 137 was against Pakistan

Page 34
C.L. Cairns hit seven sixes against South Africa

Pages 149 and 176
Wiseman's partner in the sixth wicket partnership was Chris Harris

Page 182
Robinson and Rushton were not making their debuts

SUMMARY OF ONE-DAY INTERNATIONAL CAREER RECORDS

Most Matches

Harris C.Z.	250	Wright J.G.	149	Morrison D.K.	96
Fleming S.P.	235	Crowe M.D.	143	Styris S.B.	96
Cairns C.L.	204	Rutherford K.R.	121	Snedden M.C.	93
Astle N.J.	192	Larsen G.R.	121	Coney J.V.	88
Parore A.C.	179	Chatfield E.J.	115	Jones A.H.	87
McMillan C.D.	162	Hadlee R.J.	115	Twose R.G.	87
Vettori D.L.	150	Smith I.D.S.	98	Greatbatch M.J.	84

Most Runs

		Ave			Ave
Fleming S.P.	6648	32.11	Styris S.B.	1902	27.17
Astle N.J.	6162	34.81	Coney J.V.	1874	30.72
Cairns C.L.	4767	29.42	Edgar B.A.	1814	30.74
Crowe M.D.	4704	38.55	Hadlee R.J.	1751	21.61
Harris C.Z.	4379	29.00	Young B.A.	1668	24.52
Wright J.G.	3891	26.46	Turner G.M.	1598	47.00
McMillan C.D.	3872	27.85	Crowe J.J.	1518	25.72
Parore A.C.	3314	25.68	Howarth G.P.	1384	22.72
Rutherford K.R.	3143	29.65	Sinclair M.S.	1180	28.09
Jones A.H.	2784	35.69	Vincent L.	1134	21.80
Twose R.G.	2717	38.81	Smith I.D.S.	1055	17.29
Greatbatch M.J.	2206	28.28	Marshall H.J.H.	1031	38.18

Most Wickets

		Ave			Ave
Harris C.Z.	203	37.50	Morrison D.K.	126	27.53
Cairns C.L.	193	31.86	Snedden M.C.	114	28.39
Hadlee R.J.	158	21.56	Larsen G.R.	113	35.39
Chatfield E.J.	142	25.81	Pringle C.	103	23.87
Vettori D.L.	139	34.49			

Most Economical Bowling

(qualification 600 balls)

	Balls bowled	Runs conceded	Runs conceded per 100 balls		Balls bowled	Runs conceded	Runs conceded per 100 balls
Hadlee R.J.	6182	3407	55.11	Larsen G.R.	6368	4000	62.81
Collinge R.O.	915	517	56.50	Troup G.B.	1180	791	67.03
Chatfield E.J.	6129	3666	59.81	Cairns B.L.	4015	2717	67.67
Hadlee D.R.	683	410	60.02	Petrie R.G.	660	449	68.03
McKechnie B.J.	818	495	60.51	Watson W.	3251	2247	69.11

Best Strike Rates

(qualification 600 balls)

	Balls bowled	Wickets	Balls per wicket		Balls bowled	Wickets	Balls per wicket
Bond S.E.	1370	51	26.86	Adams A.R.	1474	44	32.75
Allott G.I.	1528	52	29.38	Morrison D.K.	4586	126	36.39
Hadlee D.R.	683	23	29.69	Troup G.B.	1180	32	36.87
Pringle C.	3314	103	32.17	Tuffey D.R.	3470	90	38.55
O'Connor S.B.	1487	46	32.33	Oram J.D.P.	3215	83	38.73

Register of New Zealand One-day Cricketers Who Have Not Played Test Cricket

	Born	Type	
Bailey	26/11/1970	RHB	RM
Mark David	Hamilton		
Blair	27/12/1957	LHB	RM
Bruce Robert	Dunedin		
Bulfin	19/8/1973	RHB	RFM
Carl Edwin	Blenheim		
Canning	7/4/1977	RHB	RFM
Tamahau Karangatukituki	Adelaide, Australia		
Coman	13/4/1943	RHB	
Peter George	Christchurch		
Douglas	20/10/1968	LHB	
Mark William	Nelson		
Fulton	1/2/1979	RHB	RM
Peter Gordon	Christchurch		
Hadlee	14/12/1941	RHB	
Barry George	Christchurch		
Hamilton	5/4/1973	RHB	LFM
Lance John	Papakura		
Hart	7/11/1961	RHB	
Ronald Terence	Lower Hutt		
Hayes	9/5/1971	RHB	RFM
Roydon Leslie	Paeroa		
Hitchcock	23/1/1975	RHB	RM
Paul Anthony	Whangarei		
Hopkins	24/11/1976	RHB	WK
Gareth James	Lower Hutt		
Howell	8/7/1972	RHB	
Llorne Gregory	Napier		
McKechnie	6/11/1953	RHB	RM
Brian John	Gore		
McSweeney	8/3/1957	RHB	WK
Ervin Bruce	Wellington		
Millmow	22/9/1967	RHB	RFM
Jonathan Paul	Wellington		
Nevin	3/8/1975	RHB	WK
Christopher John	Dunedin		
Penn	27/7/1974	RHB	RFM
Andrew Jonathan	Wanganui		
Petrie	23/8/1967	RHB	RFM
Richard George	Christchurch		
Reid	3/12/1958	RHB	
Richard Bruce	Lower Hutt		
Roberts	22/3/1965	RHB	RFM
Stuart James	Christchurch		
Stott	8/12/1946	RHB	RM
Leslie Warren	Rochdale, England		
Sulzberger	14/3/1973	LHB	ROB
Glen Paul	Kaponga		
Tait	13/6/1972	RHB	RM
Alex Ross	Paparoa		
Webb	15/9/1952	RHB	RFM
Richard John	Invercargill		
Walker	17/1/1977	RHB	RM
Matthew David John	Opunake		
Wilson	24/10/1973	RHB	RFM
Jeffrey William	Invercargill		
Wisneski	19/2/1969	RHB	RM
Warren Anthony	New Plymouth		

MINOR CRICKET

HIGHEST TEAM TOTALS

922-9	Australians v South Canterbury	Temuka	1913/14
741	Murphy's Pipe Works v Petone	Wellington	1919/20
709	Australians v Southland	Invercargill	1913/14
701-6 dec	Murphy's Pipe Works v Seatoun	Wellington	1919/20
686	Nelson City v Buller	Nelson	1954/55
681	New Zealand v Northern Districts (NSW)	West Maitland	1925/26
653-9 dec	Hawkes Bay v Wairarapa	Napier	1946/47
† 650-9 dec	Manawatu v South Canterbury	Palmerston North	1993/94
† 649	Nelson v Wairarapa	Nelson	1984/85
† 643	Nelson v North Canterbury	Nelson	1984/85
† 641-7	Nelson v Taranaki	Nelson	1983/84
633-7 dec	North v Returned Soldiers	Wellington	1917/18
† 633-9	Wellington City v Bay of Plenty	Mt Maunganui	1997/98
† 632	Nelson v Waikato	Nelson	1963/64
629-7 dec	Midland II v Railways	Wellington	1921/22
623	North Canterbury v South Canterbury	Christchurch	1907/08
619-3	Cornwall U19 v Sri Lanka CC U19	Auckland	1997/98
611	Australian Academy XI v NZ Academy XI	Lincoln	1999/00
609	Napier United A v Napier United B	Napier	1898/99
603-7 dec	Tinwald v Ashburton A	Ashburton	1927/28
603-7 dec	Australians v Wairarapa	Masteron	1949/50
603-8 dec	New South Wales v South Canterbury	Timaru	1923/24
602-9 dec	New Zealand v Melbourne CC	Christchurch	1926/27
† 602	Nelson v Hawkes Bay	Nelson	1959/60

† *denotes Hawke Cup/U-Bix Cup/Fuji Xerox Cup Challenge match*

HIGHEST INDIVIDUAL SCORES

400	C.D. Knight	Cornwall U19 v Sri Lanka CC U19	Auckland	1997/98
354	J.N. Crawford	Australians v South Canterbury	Temuka	1913/14
343*	J. Gray	Sydenham v Christ's College	Christchurch	1917/18
335	W.W. Armstrong	Melbourne CC v Southland	Invercargill	1905/06
334*	Harold B. Lusk	West Christchurch v St Albans	Christchurch	1915/16
324*	D.N. Hakaraia	Waitakere U17 v Howick Pakuranga U17	Auckland	1999/00
311	H.M. Butterworth	School B v Wanganui	Wanganui	1914/15
303*	M.D. Bell	ND U20 v Wellington U20	Wanganui	1994/95
300*	W. Hendy	Auckland Suburban Association v Christchurch HSOB	Christchurch	1925/26

HIGHEST PARTNERSHIPS

	Wkt				
518	2nd	A. Young & F.L. McMahon	Wanderers v Taruheru	Gisborne	1910/11
441	1st	J.E. Mills & H.D. Gillespie	Eden v University	Auckland	1924/25
437*	2nd	R. Eden & M.R. Eden	Wanderers v Wakefield	Nelson	1922/23
394	1st	R.S. Scragg & J.V. Hill	Central Districts A v Otago A	P. North	2001/02
393	1st	M.E.L. Lane & J. Lane	Marlborough v Buller	Blenheim	1992/93
391	4th	T.P.L. Reaney & H. Hawthorne	Hawkes Bay v Wairarapa	Napier	1946/47
375	2nd	A.C. Barnes & S.M. Lynch	Cornwall v Waitakere	Auckland	1996/97
374*	1st	T.D. Astle & K.R. Ambler	Canterbury U19 v Auckland U19	Lincoln	2004/05
360	1st	G. Marshall & H.C. Wilson	Napier United A v Napier United B	Napier	1898/99
360	1st	B. Sutcliffe & F.J. Craig	Takapuna Grammar v Mt Albert Grammar	Devonport	1942/43